The Bankers' Handbook

THE BANKERS' HANDBOOK

Edited by

WILLIAM H. BAUGHN
Dean, Graduate School of Business Administration
University of Colorado
Boulder, Colorado

and

CHARLS E. WALKER
President, Charls E. Walker Associates, Inc.
Washington, D.C.

Revised Edition

DOW JONES-IRWIN
Homewood, Illinois 60430

© RICHARD D. IRWIN, INC., 1966 and 1978

ISBN 0-87094-154-2
Library of Congress Catalog Card No. 77–089797

Printed in the United States of America

1 2 3 4 5 6 7 8 9 0 K 5 4 3 2 1 0 9 8

Preface

In the decade since the publication of *The Bankers' Handbook*, the banking system of the nation has undergone substantial changes in size, structure, and functions. The complex American economy that the system serves has itself expanded rapidly during that period and has had to adjust to the usual stresses brought on by growth and cyclical changes. In terms of assets, commercial banking is approximately twice as large as ten years ago. That growth has been shared by all sizes of banks. Many small banks have become medium-sized, departmentalized institutions; regional banks have expanded rapidly; and money-center banks have become much larger and more complex financial institutions.

During the period the bank holding company movement has changed the nature of the banking systems in many states. Both the one bank holding company and the multibank form of organization received much attention in the early 1970s. Bank holding companies not only created statewide banking systems in states where branching was prohibited, but also provided a vehicle by which banks could diversify into a wider range of financial services and could cross state lines in providing some of those services. In addition, laws relating to branch banking have been modified in a number of states, with a resulting sharp impact upon the banking system of those states.

Diversity still characterizes the banking system of the United States. As part of the private enterprise system, and within the regulatory constraints affecting each bank, management selects its form of organization, competitive strategy, and services to offer. Faced with the continuing expansion of other financial institutions that provide competitive financial services and with the erosion of the barriers that have, in the past, given commercial banks their unique identity, banks today must find new ways to improve efficiency and remain competitive within broad financial markets.

Providing the services included in a typical bank requires a cluster of professional talents that vary widely in educational demands. Personnel in banking continue to enter the industry with wide variations in experience and educational backgrounds. The industry must provide the kind of education and experience necessary to enable that diverse group to become bankers. Thus, banking continues to be, as it has been for well over 75 years, a leader in adult education.

This revised edition of *The Bankers' Handbook* is designed as a basic reference on the subject matter that will be most important to performance in banking in the years ahead. It has been written by 104 contributing authors, each selected for his or her expertise in the specific subject area. The group includes many of the influential leaders in American banking today; they are among those who will shape the future of our banking system.

Since banking is more of an art than a science, it is inevitable that there will be some difference of opinion on specific aspects of some of the subject matter included in this *Handbook*. Those differences are related to the backgrounds and experiences of the authors and to the banking institutions they represent. But such differences are a source of strength to the total banking system—they help insure innovation and experimentation in banking practices. The points of view expressed in each chapter are those held by the contributing authors.

We are grateful to all of the authors for their contributions to the *Handbook*.

February 1978   WILLIAM H. BAUGHN
                                                         CHARLS E. WALKER

Contributing Authors

Conrad Acosta   Vice President, Barnett Bank of Jacksonville, N.A., Jacksonville, Florida

Willard Alexander   General Vice President, The Citizens and Southern National Bank, Atlanta, Georgia

Dwight L. Allen   Vice President, City National Bank and Trust Company, Columbus, Ohio

Ralph W. Berrey   Vice President, Valley National Bank, Phoenix, Arizona

Alexander B. Berry III   Senior Vice President, Bank of Virginia, Richmond, Virginia

Claude H. Booker, Jr.   President, First National Bank and Trust Company, Augusta, Georgia

John R. Boyd, CFA,   Vice President, Seattle-First National Bank, Seattle, Washington

D. Dale Browning   Senior Vice President, Colorado National Bank, Denver, Colorado

James A. Cassin   Senior Vice President, First National Bank, Chicago, Illinois

Samuel B. Chase, Jr.   Golembe Associates, Inc., Washington, D.C.

A. H. Cloud   Partner, Peat, Marwick, Mitchell and Company, Dallas, Texas

Philip E. Coldwell   Member, Board of Governors, Federal Reserve System, Washington, D.C.

James J. DeCantillon   Vice President, Continental Illinois National Bank and Trust Company of Chicago, Chicago, Illinois

Lawrence N. DeLeers, Jr.   First Vice President, First Wisconsin National Bank of Milwaukee, Milwaukee, Wisconsin

Kenneth R. Dew   Senior Vice President, Bankers Trust Company, Des Moines, Iowa

Robert R. Dince   Associate Deputy Comptroller of the Currency for Economic Research and Operational Analysis, Washington, D.C.

Arlin Disselkoen   Senior Vice President, Greeley National Bank, Greeley, Colorado

Michael Doman   Regional Administrator of National Banks, Eleventh National Bank Region, Dallas, Texas

Richard E. Dooley   President, Colonial Penn Group Data Corp, Philadelphia, Pennsylvania (formerly Stuart School of Management and Finance, Illinois Institute of Technology, Chicago, Illinois; Vice President, First National Bank, Chicago, Illinois)

David P. Eastburn   President, Federal Reserve Bank, Philadelphia, Pennsylvania

David E. Ellison   Senior Vice President, Seattle-First National Bank, Seattle, Washington

Robert M. Freeman   Senior Executive Vice President, Bank of Virginia, Richmond, Virginia

Tilford C. Gaines   Senior Vice President and Economist, Manufacturers Hanover Trust Company, New York, New York

John R. Gallaudet   Vice President, The National State Bank, Elizabeth, New Jersey

Edward J. Gannon   Executive Vice President, Charls E. Walker Associates, Inc., Washington, D.C.

Richard C. Georgia   Vice President, First National Bank of New Jersey, Totowa, New Jersey

Carter H. Golembe   Chairman, Golembe Associates Inc., Washington, D.C.

Allen Good   Vice President, First Tennessee Bank, N.A., Memphis, Tennessee

Mary M. Graye   Vice President and Personnel Director, First Wisconsin National Bank, Madison, Wisconsin

John W. H. Gushée   Senior Vice President, The Arizona Bank, Phoenix, Arizona

David B. Harper   President, Gateway National Bank, St. Louis, Missouri

Milton M. Harris   President, Maryland National Leasing Corporation, Baltimore, Maryland

James L. Hayes   President, American Management Associations, New York, New York

Richard O. Hawkins   Extension Economist, Farm Management, University of Minnesota, St. Paul, Minnesota

Sherman Hazeltine Chairman, First National Bank of Arizona, Phoenix, Arizona

W. C. Henry Group Vice President, Trust Company Bank, Atlanta, Georgia

Milan G. Hiben Vice President, Bank for Savings and Loan Associations, Chicago, Illinois

Robert M. Horton General Manager, Trusco Data Systems, Atlanta, Georgia

W. Lee Hoskins Vice President and Director of Research, Federal Reserve Bank, Philadelphia, Pennsylvania

Donald S. Howard Senior Vice President—Finance, Citibank, N.A., New York, New York

William Hurst Vice President, Bank of America, San Francisco, California

Paul D. Hutchins Assistant Vice President, Valley National Bank, Phoenix, Arizona

Edward A. Jesser, Jr. Chairman, United Jersey Bank, Hackensack, New Jersey

Herbert E. Johnson Senior Vice President, Continental Illinois National Bank, Chicago, Illinois

Willis Johnson, Jr. Vice President, Trust Company Bank, Atlanta, Georgia

Robert M. Klingler Vice President, The Central Trust Company, N.A., Cincinnati, Ohio

H. Felix Kloman President, Risk Planning Group, Darien, Connecticut

Lawrence E. Kreider Executive Vice President, Conference of State Bank Supervisors, Washington, D.C.

Eugene J. Laka Vice President, Citibank, N.A., New York, New York

Rufus F. Land Senior Vice President, North Carolina National Bank, Charlotte, North Carolina

G. Timothy Lane Senior Vice President, Barnett Banks of Florida, Inc., Jacksonville, Florida

C. Eugene Looper Vice President and Corporate Director of Personnel, Southeast Banking Corporation, Miami, Florida

William D. Loring Chairman and President, Mesa United Bank of Grand Junction, Grand Junction, Colorado

Ken L. Lott President, Merchants National Bank of Mobile, Mobile, Alabama

William H. Low, CBA Auditor, Society National Bank, Cleveland, Ohio

Louis B. Lundborg   Chairman (retired), Bank of America, San Francisco, California

H. B. McDonald   Assistant Vice President, The First National Bank of Atlanta, Atlanta, Georgia

Harold F. McHugh   Senior Vice President, National Bank of North America, New York, New York

George W. McKinney, Jr.   Senior Vice President, Irving Trust Company, New York, New York

William B. McNeill   Senior Vice President, Branch Banking and Trust Company, Wilson, North Carolina

William T. Maher, Jr.   Vice President, Citibank, N.A., New York, New York

Donald R. Mandich   President, Detroit Bank & Trust Company, Detroit, Michigan

Irving Margol   Senior Vice President, Security Pacific National Bank, Los Angeles, California

Edward L. Mercaldo   Vice President, Bank of Montreal, London, England (formerly Executive Vice President, Funds Management Group, Equibank N.A., Pittsburgh, Pennsylvania)

Z. Christopher Mercer   Assistant Treasurer; First Tennessee National Corporation, Memphis, Tennessee

Martin F. Mertz   Partner in Charge of Banking Practice, Peat, Marwick, Mitchell & Co., New York, New York

Hubert C. Mott   Senior Vice President, United Jersey Bank, Hackensack, New Jersey

Robert G. Myers   Vice President, Merchants National Bank of Mobile, Mobile, Alabama

Paul S. Nadler   Professor of Business Administration, Rutgers University, Newark, New Jersey

Craig G. Nelson   President, Associated Computer Services, Inc., Portland, Oregon

Thomas F. O'Connell   Program Manager Corporate Investment Portfolio, International Business Machines Corporation, Armonk, New York (formerly Senior Vice President and Treasurer, Fidelcor, Inc., Philadelphia, Pennsylvania)

A. Gordon Oliver   Executive Vice President, The Citizens and Southern National Bank, Augusta, Georgia

A. B. Padgett   Vice President, Trust Company Bank, Atlanta, Georgia

Leslie W. Peterson   President, Farmers State Bank, Trimont, Minnesota

Frank A. Plummer Chairman, First Alabama Bancshares, Inc., Montgomery, Alabama

Robert Proctor Vice President, Security Pacific National Bank, Los Angeles, California

Kenneth A. Randall President, The Conference Board, New York, New York; formerly, Chairman, United Virginia Bankshares, Incorporated, Richmond, Virginia

Robert R. Robertson Senior Vice President, First City National Bank, Houston, Texas

Jack Robison Assistant Treasurer, Cook Industries, Inc., Memphis, Tennessee (formerly Vice President, First Tennessee Bank, N.A., Memphis, Tennessee)

Edward M. Roob Senior Vice President, First National Bank of Chicago, Chicago, Illinois

Richard M. Rosenberg Executive Vice President, Wells Fargo Bank, San Francisco, California

William H. Sayre Executive Vice President, The Fidelity Bank, Philadelphia, Pennsylvania

Philip F. Searle Chairman and Chief Executive Officer, Flagship Banks Inc., Miami, Florida

Robert B. Shanahan Executive Vice President, Liberty National Bank and Trust Company, Buffalo, New York

Karl M. Shelton Senior Vice President, Seattle-First National Bank, Seattle, Washington

Lawrence M. Small Senior Vice President, Citibank, N.A., New York, New York

James E. Smith Executive Vice President, First Chicago Corporation, Chicago, Illinois; formerly, 23d Comptroller of the Currency

James L. Smith Senior Vice President, Security Pacific National Bank, Los Angeles, California

M. Carl Sneeden Vice President, Third National Bank, Nashville, Tennessee

David T. Snowdon Vice President (retired), Mellon Bank, N. A., Pittsburgh, Pennsylvania

John W. Spiegel Treasurer, Trust Company of Georgia, Atlanta, Georgia

Thomas I. Storrs Chairman, NCNB Corporation, Charlotte, North Carolina

Gordon P. Sweeney Senior Vice President, Warren Management Consultants, Charlotte, North Carolina

Eugene M. Tangney Senior Vice President, The First National Bank of Boston, Boston, Massachusetts

Contents

List of Illustrations   xxxi

SECTION I
ORGANIZING AND MANAGING THE BANKING CORPORATION

1.   Bank Investor Relations—A New World *by Frank A. Plummer*   3

The New Environment for Financial Information. Traditional and New Regulatory Authorities. The Security Analyst. Fiduciaries and Institutional Holders. Bank Clients. The Small Investor. Recognition of the Stockholder. Investor Relations Program. Investor Contacts. Annual Stockholders' Meeting. Correspondence. Annual Report. Continuity of Stockholder Contacts. Press Relations. Current Developments.

2.   The Bank's Board of Directors—Functions and Responsibilities *by Sherman Hazeltine*   15

Qualification and Election. The Directors' Oath. Directors' Duties: *Powers. Liabilities. Indemnification. Responsibilities.* Personal Attributes. Relations with Management. Composition of Board of Directors. Directors' Standing Committees: *The Executive Committee. The Examining Committee. Trust Committees. Salary Committee. Other Committees.* Retirement Policy for Directors. Conclusion.

3.   Alternative Organizational Structures *by Philip F. Searle*   26

Forms of Banking: *Unit Banking. Branch Banking. Holding Company (Group) Banking. Chain Banking. Satellite and Affiliate Banking. Correspondent Banking.* Basic Organizational Structure: *Grouping of Functions. Line and Staff Functions.* Centralization Versus Decentralization: *Different Degrees of Decentralization. Regionalization.* Unit Banking. Branch Banking: *Benefits of Branch Banking. Branch Administration. Future of Branch Banking.* Holding Company Banking: *Advantages of the Holding Company Form of Banking Structure. Disadvantages of* the Holding Company Form of Banking Structure. Structural Alternatives in Holding Company Management Organizations. Future of Bank Holding Companies. Other Forms of Banking.

4. The Environment of Bank Management
   by Kenneth A. Randall   48

   The Modern Environment. Professionalization of Banking. Dimensions of the Job: *Delegation of Authority. The Board of Directors. Other Relationships.* Organizational Response.

5. Evolving Corporate Policy *by Thomas I. Storrs*   56

   What Is a Policy? Policies Do Evolve. Policies Form a Hierarchy. Consistency Versus Adaptability. Who Are the Policy Makers? Continuity Versus Change.

6. Formulating Social Policy as an Integral Part of Bank Policy
   by Louis B. Lundborg   64

   Historical Precedent. New Elements. Relevance to Banks. Banks, The Community—And Beyond the Community. What Is Expected. General Principles and Tailored Applications. One Bank's Social Policy Structure. Practices Examined. Precepts.

7. The Process of Bank Management *by James L. Hayes*   74

   Planning. Organization. Coordination. Motivation. Control.

8. Effective Communication of Corporate Policies and
   Objectives *by B. Finley Vinson*   86

   The Ever-Changing Communications Environment. The Willingness to Communicate the Plan and Plan the Communications. The "Communications Audit." The Pattern for Planning. The Flair and Flexibility of Communicating. The Lip Service Syndrome.

SECTION II
MANAGING HUMAN RESOURCES

9. Manpower Planning and Management
   by Lawrence M. Small and Eugene J. Laka   101

   A New Attitude. Rising to the Challenge. Tools of Manpower Planning and Management. Executive Planning. Official Placement and Transfer Service. Career Development Program.

10. Employee Selection *by Irving Margol and Robert Proctor*   110

Introduction. Estimation of Personnel Needs. Determining the Job. Recruitment: *The Concept of Job Relatedness. Defining the Recruitment Market: Traditional and Nontraditional Sources. A Fresh Look at Old Sources.* Application Selection: A Systems Approach: *The Employment Application. Testing. The Interview. Reference Checks. Medical Examinations.* The Selection Decision.

11. Management of the Training Function
    by Gordon P. Sweeney   132

Senior Management's Role. Organization Considerations. Staffing the Training Function. Special Facilities. Source of Training Programs. Summary and Conclusions.

12. Supervision for Effective Manpower Utilization
    by Dwight L. Allen   143

Responsibility of Supervisors. Dual Responsibilities. Position of Front-Line Supervisors. Improving Supervisory Performance: *Training. The Selection Process. Use of Past Performance Record.* Adjustment of the Supervisory Role. Styles of Supervision. Summary.

13. Performance-Oriented Personnel Development Programs
    by Richard C. Georgia   154

Measuring Performance. Management by Objectives: *Objectives and Goals. Listing of Duties. Setting Goals. Types of Goals. Discussion/ Acceptance of Goals. Timetables. Evaluation.* Individually Tailored Development: *Analysis of Employee. Matchup—Skills to Needs.* On-the-Job Training. Conclusion.

14. Salary Administration—Improving Your Return on
    Investment *by John Turney*   164

Pay Structure Based on Competitive Salary Levels. Individual Pay Decisions Based on Performance. Performance Standards and Improvement Goals. Establishing a Salary Administration Program: *Use of Job Descriptions and Questionnaires. Defining Your Labor Market. Determining an Appropriate Position in the Market. Bench Mark Jobs. Salary Surveys. Salary Ranges. Amount and Frequency of Increases. Job Evaluation Techniques. Keeping the Program Up-to-Date. What to Tell Employees about the Program.* Planning for Improved Productivity: *Setting Objectives. Reviewing Objectives.* Performance Evaluation: *Performance Appraisal. Separating Salary Increases from Performance Evaluations.* Pay Planning. Equal Employment Opportunity Compliance. Evaluating the Salary Program.

15. Employee Incentives and Benefit Programs
    by C. Eugene Looper   177

Growth of the Fringe Benefits. The Need for Evaluation. Analyzing Effectiveness and Cost. Defining Benefits. Salary and Wages for Time Not
Worked. Payments for Employee Security: *Legally Required Employee
Benefit Payments. Voluntary Employee Benefit Payments. Supplemental
Retirement Plans. Life, Accident, and Dismemberment Insurance. Noninsured Sick Pay. Hospitalization and Major Medical Insurance.* Payments
for General Employee Welfare. Payments for Company Assets Given
to Employees. Conclusion.

16. Equal Employment Opportunity and Affirmative
    Action Programs in Banks *by Mary M. Graye*   188

Introduction. Equal Employment Opportunity: *The Federal Level. State
and Local Level.* The Discrimination Complaint: *Complaint Resolution.*
Reporting Requirements under the 1964 Civil Rights Act. Contract Compliance: *Federal Government Contract Compliance Programs. State and
Local Government Contract Compliance Programs.* Developing an Affirmative Action Program for the Bank: *Importance. Preliminary Research. Program Components.* Compliance Review: *Desk Audit. On-Site
Review. Exit Conference. Termination of the Compliance Review.* Conclusion.

17. Other Federal Regulations Applicable to Bank Employees
    by Edwin C. Wallace, Jr.   201

Fair Labor Standards Act (Wage-Hour Law): *Minimum Wage and Overtime Requirements. Fluctuating Workweek. Exempt Employees. Equal
Pay. Child Labor.* Age Discrimination in Employment Act: *Enforcement
and Record Retention.* National Labor Relations Act: *Rights of Employ-
ees. Unfair Labor Practices. Collective Bargaining. Enforcement.* Social
Security Act. The Occupational Safety and Health Act (OSHA). Federal
Wage Garnishment Law. Universal Military Training and Service Act.
Executive Order 11701. Other Federal Banking Regulations: *Regulations
of the Comptroller of the Currency. Rules and Regulations, Board of
Governors of the Federal Reserve System. United States Code, Title 12.*
Conclusion.

SECTION III
SYSTEMS

18. Systems for Producing Bank Services—Concepts
    and Needs *by John W. Spiegel and Robert M. Horton*   221

Identifying the Market. Delivering Services. Processing Data. The Future.

19. Managing the Data Processing System for Banks
    by Craig G. Nelson 230

Managing the Service Bureau or Correspondent Bank. Managing In-House Data Processing: *Computer Operations. Project Development. Technical Support.* Managing the Cooperative. Conclusion.

20. Electronic Funds Transfer (EFTS) in Depository
    Institutions *by Eugene M. Tangney* 241

Introduction. Automated Clearing House Service. Automated Teller Machines. Point of Sale. Telephone Bill-Paying System. EFTS and the Consumer.

21. Information Systems for Banks *by Richard E. Dooley* 255

Philosophical Background. The Relationship Between Data and Information. Definitional Implications for Data Processing and Information Systems. How Humans Fit In—Communicating, Cooperating, Efficiently and Effectively. Evolution and Merger of Three Separate Disciplines in the Current Body of Professional Knowledge; A New Awareness. Harnessing This New Awareness in Accepted Management Perspectives. The Contribution of Data Processing and Computer Technology. Putting It All Together Like an Orange. A Graphic Framework.

SECTION IV
PLANNING AND CONTROL

22. Comprehensive Corporate Planning for Banks
    by Herbert E. Johnson 273

Introduction. What Is Planning? *Evolution of Planning. Expectations of Accomplishment.* The Planning Process: *Plan to Plan. Environmental Analysis and Situation Appraisal. Objectives and Strategies. Programs, Budgets, and Controls. Annual Planning Cycle.* Organization for Planning. Conclusion.

23. Profit Planning and Budgeting *by Leonard Weil* 288

Budgeting. Profit Planning: *Influence of Product Mix. Range of Business Decisions. Control of Profit Plan.*

24. Profitability Analysis, Cost Systems, and Pricing Policies
    by John Zimmermann and H. B. McDonald 295

Nature of Costs: *Classification by Volume Sensitivity. Interest Costs.* Cost Allocation. Organizational, Product, and Customer Profitability: *Organi-*

zational Profitability. Customer Profitability. Product Profitability. Pricing Policies.

25. Control and Measurement of Financial Performance
    by Donald S. Howard and William T. Maher, Jr.   313

    Need for Senior Management Sponsorship and Involvement. Need for
    a Common Language. Recognition of Performance. Understanding and
    Participation by Those Being Measured. Educational Process. Tailoring
    the System. Timely and Accurate Reporting. Report Responsibility. Goal
    Congruence. Establishment of Appropriate Indicators of Performance.
    Establishment of Reporting System. Valuation of Funds between Profit
    Centers. The Review Process. Conclusion.

26. The General Accounting System *by Arlin Disselkoen*   326

    The General Ledger. Statement of Condition: *Cash and Due from Banks.*
    Investments. Federal Funds Sold. Loans. Reserve for Loan Losses. Bank
    Premises and Equipment. Accrued Interest Receivable. Other Assets.
    Liabilities: *Demand Deposits. Savings Deposits. Time Deposits. Federal*
    Funds Purchased. Liabilities for Borrowed Money. Other Liabilities. Sub-
    ordinated Notes and Debentures. Equity Capital: *Common Stock. Surplus.*
    Undivided Profits. Reserves for Contingencies and Other Capital Re-
    serves. The Income Statement. Accounting as a Management Tool.

27. Audit and Internal Control *by William H. Low, C.B.A.*   338

    Director's Responsibility. Auditor and Staff. Auditor Qualifications. Audit
    Responsibilities. Audit Program. Audit Procedures. Audit Work Papers.
    Audit Findings. Audit Report. Audit Follow-Up. EDP Auditing. EDP
    Audit Program. Audit Software. Internal Control and Safeguards. Person-
    nel Policy Covering Internal Audits. Fraud. Conclusion.

28. External Audits for Banks *by A. H. Cloud and*
    Martin F. Mertz   348

    Internal and External Audits and the Responsibilities of Bank Manage-
    ment: *Moral Responsibility of Bank Directors. Legal Responsibility of*
    Bank Directors. Obligation of Banks to Interested Parties. Relationship
    of External Audit Function to Internal Audit and Control. Selection of
    a Qualified Auditor: *Examinations by Supervisory Authorities. Examina-*
    tions by Directors. Examinations by Internal Auditor. Audit by Qualified
    Independent Public Accountants. Scope of Bank Audits: *Evaluation of*
    Internal Audit and Control. Accountability and Proof. Confirmation
    with Third Parties. Evaluation of Assets. Problems of Bank Audits:
    Exposure and Control. Surprise Element. Staffing. Timing. Planning.
    Audit Reports: *Short- and Long-Form Report. Deviations from Standard*
    Form Reports. Audit Reports without Accompanying Financial State-
    ments. Internal Control and System Comments. Conclusion.

29. Tax Planning for Banks *by Milan G. Hiben* 364

General Statement. Evaluation of Tax Considerations: *Tax-Exempt Securities. Amortization of Bond Premium and Accretion of Discount. Investment Tax Credit. Foreign Taxes. Impact of State Income and Franchise Taxes. Minimum Implications Regarding Tax Preference Items. Reserve for Losses on Loans. Minimum Tax. Net Operating Loss Carry-back.* Development of a Tax Planning Philosophy: *Future Tax Legislation.* Implementation of a Tax Plan.

30. Risk Management *by H. Felix Kloman* 373

Introduction. Exposure Identification. Risk Evaluation. Risk Control. Risk Financing and Insurance. Risk Management Administration.

SECTION V
FINANCIAL MANAGEMENT

31. Resource Allocation to Attain Corporate Goals
by Edward L. Mercaldo 389

Introduction. Personnel Resources. Technological Capacity. Capital Structure. Asset/Liability Relationships. Utilization of Resources. Summary.

32. Legal and Regulatory Constraints on Financial Management
by Samuel B. Chase, Jr. 401

Introduction. Constraints on Raising Funds: *Deposits. Nondeposit Sources of Funds.* Constraints on Uses of Funds: *Restraints on Ownership of Tangible Property and Equity Investments. Restraints on Loans. Restraints on Investments. Restraints on Foreign Activities. Additional Discretionary Restraints. Restraints Related to Trust Activities.* Bank Holding Companies.

33. Planning to Meet Liquidity Requirements—Concepts and
Tools *by George W. McKinney, Jr.* 411

Shifts in Liquidity Planning: *Asset Allocation. Asset Management. Liability Management. Funds Management.* Discipline and Informed Judgment: *Decisions not Precise. A Framework for Analysis. Supplemental Factors to Consider. Investments a Residual.* How Much Liquidity? *Each Bank Is Unique. Use Charts Constructively. Analyzing Loans and Deposits. Estimating Liquidity Needs. Exceptions to Bear in Mind.* In Which Assets? *The Liquidity Account. Compare Liquidity with Needs. Liability Management.* When? *The Cyclical Low. The Expansion. The Peak. The Contraction.* Summary.

34. Evolution and Overview of Asset/Liability Management
    by Rufus F. Land   433

Introduction. Asset Creation and Funding Activities: *Trading. Portfolio Management. Asset/Liability Management.* Evolution of Asset/Liability Management: *Asset Management. Liability Management. Asset/Liability Management.* Principles of Asset/Liability Management: *Differentiation of Risk. Focus on Overall Position. Explicit Consideration of Uncertainty.* Conclusion.

35. Managing the Bank's Money Position
    by James J. DeCantillon   445

The Bank's Money Position. Reserve Requirements—The Accounting Mechanism. Operational Aspects of the Money Position. The Money Position Manager. Analyzing and Forecasting Banking System Reserve Availability. Conclusion.

36. Capital Planning and Capital Adequacy
    by Ronald Terry and Z. Christopher Mercer   454

Bank Capital. Bank Holding Company Capital. Purposes of Bank Capital. Relativity of Capital Adequacy. Implications for Capital Planning. Small Versus Large Banks. Sources of Capital. Other Considerations in Planning for Capital Adequacy. Greater Emphasis on Capital Planning. Balanced Growth. Summary.

SECTION VI
INVESTMENTS AND SECURITIES MARKETS

37. The Short–Term Money Market—Functions and Instruments
    by Thomas F. O'Connell   469

Federal Funds. Certificates of Deposit. Repurchase Agreements. Eurodollar Market. Foreign Short-Term Investments. Commercial Paper: *Prime Finance Commercial Paper. Prime Industrial Commercial Paper. Bank Commercial Paper.* Bankers Acceptances. Arbitrage Markets. Hedging in Interest-Rate Future Contracts. Investment Objectives: *Quality Considerations. Liquidity.*

38. The Instruments and Markets for Government Securities
    by G. Timothy Lane and Conrad Acosta   480

Recent History of the Federal Debt. The Public Debt: *Treasury Bills. Treasury Notes and Bonds.* The Markets for Treasury Securities. The Dealer Community and the Federal Reserve System. The Risk/Reward Consideration of Treasury Securities.

39. Instruments and Markets for Government Agency
Securities *by Ralph W. Berrey and Paul D. Hutchins* 495

Agency Debt Expansion, Acceptance and Marketability. Farm Credit System: *Banks for Cooperatives. Federal Intermediate Credit Banks. Federal Land Banks. Farm Credit Discount Notes.* Federal National Mortgage Association. Federal Home Loan Banks. Federal Home Loan Mortgage Corporation. United States Postal Service. Tennessee Valley Authority. Government National Mortgage Association. Export-Import Bank of the United States. Farmers Home Administration. District of Columbia Armory Board.

40. Municipal Bonds: Underwriting, Trading, and Investment
Portfolio Usage in Commercial Banks *by Karl M. Shelton* 511

Categories of Municipal Bonds. The Markets. Use in Bank Portfolios: *Maturities.* Ratings of Municipal Securities. Diversification. Market Structure.Portfolio Management. Quality. Taxable Municipal Bonds. Conclusion.

41. Portfolio Management—Guidelines for a Commercial Bank
by Edward M. Roob and Thomas A. Vaughn 522

Investment Objectives and the Constraints: *Assess the Bank's Over-all Risk Position. Study Liquidity Requirements versus Income Needs. Analyze the Pledging Requirements to Secure Public Funds. Evaluate the Bank's Overall Tax Position, Both Current and Future.* Portfolio Strategies: *"Three-Part" Portfolio Strategy. Type of Investment, Diversification, and Quality. Portfolio Maturity Structure.* Swapping: *Yield Pick-Up Swap. The Substitution Swap or Replacement Swap. The Intermarket Swap. The Yield Anticipation Swap. Tax-Loss Trading. Gain Trading. Open-Ending.* Improving Returns on Government Securities Portfolios: *Repurchase Agreements ("Repos"). Resale Agreements ("Resales"). Lending of Government Securities. Liability Management.* Authority and Control Procedures: *Reasons for Having a Written Policy. The Elements of an Investment Policy.* Conclusion.

SECTION VII
CREDIT POLICY AND ADMINISTRATION

42. Establishing Credit Policy—Criteria and Concepts
by Edward A. Jesser, Jr. and Hubert C. Mott 541

Written Credit Policy. Rationale for Credit Policy. Distribution of Types of Loans. Loan Authority. Pricing Policy. Standards for Lending. Standards for Special Lending Areas. Conclusion.

43. Credit and Loan Administration *by Harold F. McHugh*   556

Credit Department. Training. Loan Review. Commercial Loan Accounting. Conclusion.

44. Credit Administration—Systems and Procedures
    by William D. Loring   568

Portfolio Control and Planning. Integrating Systems and Procedures. Loan Work Flow. Loan Administration Procedures. Portfolio Organization. Loan Reports. Conclusion.

45. Financial Analysis for Credit Decisions *by David T. Snowdon* 579

Financial Statements. Comparison Method of Analysis. Trend Percentage Method of Analysis. Ratio Method of Analysis. Common-Size Industry Comparison Method of Analysis. Statement of Financial Position. Pro Forma Statements. Forecasting. Evaluation of Financial Information. Economic Evaluation. Evaluation of Management. Making the Decision. Conclusion.

46. Handling Problem Loans *by Willard Alexander*   602

Events to Watch For. Early Warning Signs. Fact Finding and Reevaluation. Continuation of the Business. Liquidation of the Business: *Election of Bankruptcy.* Summary.

SECTION VIII
SPECIAL CREDIT AREAS

47. Seasonal and Revolving Credit Arrangements
    by William H. Sayre   613

The Working Capital Cycle. Seasonal Lines of Credit. Revolving Credit Arrangements. Pricing.

48. Secured Lending *by Ken L. Lott and Robert G. Myers*   622

General Considerations: *Four Phases in Secured Lending.* Inventory Loans: *Establishing Value. Systems of Control. Alternative Control Methods. Use of Warehouse Receipts. Perfecting Security Interest.* Loans Secured by Accounts Receivable: *Establishing Value. Methods Used. Perfecting the Security Interest.* Loans Secured by Stocks and Bonds: *Control and Evaluation.* Loans Secured by Cash Value of Life Insurance Policies. Loans Secured by Petroleum Production, Ship Mortgages, and Aircraft. Conclusion.

49. Commodity and In-Transit Loans *by Allen Good and Jack Robison* 650

General. Secured Commodity Loans—Warehouse Receipts: *Warehouses. Negotiability. Insurance. Storage Charges. Uniform Commercial Code. Demand Loans. Discount Loans. Bankers' Acceptances. Margins. Marketability. Influence of the Government.* Secured Commodity Loans—In-Transit Documents: *Trust Receipts. Bills of Lading. Freight Forwarders.* Commodity Loans to Grain Companies: *Unsecured Commodity Loans.* Hedging and the Futures Market. Conclusion.

50. Longer Term Lending to Business *by Claude H. Booker, Jr. and W. C. Henry* 665

Introduction. History and Evolution of Term Lending. Bank Policy Considerations. Various Forms of Term Loans. Analyzing the Risk. Term Loan Agreements. After the Loan Is Made. Conclusion.

51. Equipment Leasing *by Milton M. Harris* 673

Definition. Types of Equipment Leases. Attractions to Lessors and Lessees. Alternatives Open to a Bank Which Wishes to Participate in the Equipment Leasing. Credit Evaluation. Yield Evaluation. Book Earnings, Cash Earnings, and Taxable Earnings. Obtaining Business. Competition. Summary.

52. Agricultural Loans *by Leslie W. Peterson and Richard O. Hawkins* 691

Introduction. The Agricultural Credit Request. Analysis of the Credit: *Analyzing Financial Soundness. Analyzing Profitability. Analyzing Repayment Capacity. Adding up the Score.* Loan Administration. Conclusion.

53. Construction Mortgage and Real Estate Warehousing Loans *by John R. Gallaudet* 703

Marketing. Underwriting the Loan. Advances. Takeouts (Long-Term Loans). Documentation. Mortgage Loan Warehousing.

54. Residential Mortgage Loans *by James M. Walsh* 719

Forms of Home Ownership. Financing for Individual Ownership: *Appraisal Methods.* Types of Loans: *Conventional Loans. FHA Insured Loans. VA Loans.* Competitive Forces: *Determining Size of Payment. Value of Single Family Mortgage Lending.* Secondary Mortgage Market. Other Ownership Forms. Conclusion.

55. Mortgage Lending: Income-Producing Properties
by *James M. Walsh*   729

Limiting Risk—Loans on Residential Property: *Techniques of Appraisal. Further Underwriting Considerations. Debt Service Coverage. Other Residential Producing Properties.* The Shopping Center: *Escalation. Vacancy. The Developer. Construction of the Legal Entity.* Office Buildings. General Considerations. Limiting the Amount of the Loan. Limitation of Term. The Purchase and Sale Agreement. Conclusion.

56. Consumer Credit—Role and Concepts *by James L. Smith*   741

Trends in Consumer Credit: *Types of Installment Credit by Commercial Banks.* The Changing Legal Environment. Consumerism. Competition. Conclusions.

57. Primary Areas of Consumer Credit *by William B. McNeill*   750

Introduction. Direct Lending: *The Credit Statement. The Credit Interview. The Credit Investigation. Credit Evaluation. Amount of Credit. Frequency of Disclosure Statements and Credit Investigations. Loan Closing. Loan Classifications and Terms. Profitability. Benefits to Customer and Bank. Marketing Direct Consumer Loan Services. Direct Lending to Small Business. Source of Appraisals. General Precautions in Direct Lending. Lien Perfection.* Unsecured Open-End Revolving Credit. Indirect Dealer Originated Financing: *Classes of Dealer Originated Business. Bank Plans of Retail Financing. No Liability. Dealer Reserve Accounts. Dealer Services Provided by Bank Plan. Wholesale Floor Planning. Other Loan Services. Pricing Indirect Dealer Services. Precautions in Indirect Dealer Financing. Benefits to Bank. Marketing the Indirect Dealer Plan. Dealer Service Company Plan. Future Trends in Dealer Financing.* Summary.

SECTION IX
INTERNATIONAL BANKING

58. International Relationships of U.S. Banks
by *Constant M. Van Vlierden and William Hurst*   771

The Historical Development of International Banking in the United States: *Background. The Geographical Spread of U.S. Banks. Organizational and Functional Expansion.* The Expansion of U.S. International Banking Since World War II: *The Global Economy. The International Banking Market. Policies of the U.S. Government. Policies of Foreign Governments.* New International Relationships of U.S. Banks: *Banks and Governments. Interbank Relationships.* Conclusions.

59. Meeting the Banking Needs of Multinational Companies
by *John A. Waage* 789

What Is a Multinational Company? The Rapid Growth of Multinational Companies and International Banks. What Are the Banking Needs of the Multinationals? *Bankers' Views. Multinational Views. A Catalog of Services and Needs.* Needs and Responses Are Dynamic. External Factors Affect the Financing Needs of Multinationals. Bank Pricing and Unbundling: *Bank Costing and Pricing. Multinational Desires for "Unbundling."* Outlook.

60. Commercial Banks in the Eurocurrency Markets
by *Lawrence N. DeLeers, Jr.* 800

Origin and Growth. Nature of the Market: *Definition of the Term "Eurocurrency." The Supply of Funds. Market Uses and Users. Relationship to Foreign Exchange Market.* Bank Management of a Eurocurrency Book: *Risks Involved. Controls Employed. Conditions Precedent.* The Eurocurrency Loan. Summary.

61. Special Aspects of International Credits
by *Donald R. Mandich* 817

Types of International Loans. Translation and Analysis of Foreign Statements. Country Risk: *Economic Risk. International Liquidity. Political Risk.* Legal Problems. Foreign Currency Loans. Syndicated Loans and Broker Paper. Maturities of Loans. Funding. Interest Rates. Country Limits. Conclusion.

SECTION X
RETAIL BANKING

62. The Function of Retail Banking *by A. Gordon Oliver* 837

The Environment. Organizational Considerations. Planning for Profitability. Knowing What It Costs. Knowing the Market. What Retail Services Should Be Offered. Marketing Activities. Personnel Function. Monitoring Efforts. The Legal Environment. Concepts in Retail Management. Interaction with the Bank as a Whole. Conclusion.

63. Development, Pricing, and Merchandising—Retail Banking Services *by Robert M. Freeman and Alexander B. Berry III* 848

Introduction. The Customer and Ideas: Where It All Starts. Product Evaluation. Product Implementation: *Marketing and Advertising. Operations and Systems. Retail Service. Staff Training and Education. Legal. The Monitoring Mechanism.* Pricing. Conclusion.

64. The Organization and Operation of a Consumer Loan
Department *by Robert B. Shanahan*   862

The Organization: *Integral Part of the Total Bank. Choosing a Depart-
ment Head. Chain of Command. Functional or Service Offering. Choosing Personnel. Where to Locate.* Policy Considerations: *Service Offerings.
Direct or Indirect. Closed End or Open-End. Degree of Centralization.*
The Importance of Specific Policies: *Loan Policy. Lending Authorities.
Credit Policy. Rate Policies.* Legal Consideration: *Organize for Control.
Methods for Monitoring. Communicating.* The Operation of the Department: *Variables to Consider. Checks and Balances.* Collections, Adjustments, Recoveries: *Organization of Collection Department. Collection
Procedures, Notices, and Calls.* The Branch Function: *Manager's Participation. Branch Dealer Relations. Collections in Branches.* Cost Control
and Auditing: *Problems of Cost Control. Auditing.* Miscellaneous Considerations: *Insurance.* Management Reporting: *Sufficiency of Reports.*

65. Bank Cards *by D. Dale Browning*   879

Bank Card Operations: *Organizational Structure. Administration. Credit
and Collections. Operations. Service Departments. Service to Merchants.
Customer Service. Agent Bank Service. Fraud Control.* Evolution of Bank
Card Associations: *BankAmericard (now VISA). Master Charge.* Or-
ganization of Bank Card Associations: *VISA U.S.A., Inc. VISA Interna-
tional Service Association. Interbank Card Association (ICA).* Interbank
Associations: *Advantages. Disadvantages.* Comparison of ICA and VISA.
Duality. Debit Cards: *Entree. Signet.* EFTS Development. Summary.

66. Safekeeping Services *by James A. Cassin*   895

Introduction. Safe Deposit Services. Operational Procedures: *The Contract.* Types of Rentals: *Individual Rentals. Co-Renters. Corporations.
Unincorporated Organizations. Partnerships. Fiduciaries. Government
Agencies. Minors.* Deputies. Access Procedures. Audit Procedures. Vault
Equipment. Customer Relations. Legal Counsel. Pricing. Security. Custody Services: *Operational Considerations. Liability. Current Developments.* Summary.

67. Electronic Delivery Systems for Retail Services
by Robert M. Klingler   909

The Need for New Retail Delivery Systems. Establishing Objectives and
Justifications. Automated Teller Machines. Point of Sale Terminals. *Check
Authorization Systems. Deposit Taking. Evaluation of EFTS.* Direct Deposit and Preauthorized Payments. Automatic Telephone Payments. Balance Inquiry. Summary.

SECTION XI
MANAGING NONDEPOSIT ASSETS FOR THE PUBLIC

68. The Function and Organization of Fiduciary Services
    by David E. Ellison   923

    Characteristics of Fiduciary Services. Organizational Form. Profitability.
    Competition.

69. Fiduciary Services by Business Line *by David E. Ellison*   929

    The Bank As Trustee. The Bank as Agent. Business Line I, Personal
    Trust Services: *Accounts for the Trustor. Accounts Established for Benefit
    of Other than the Trustor.* Business Line II, Services for Corporations:
    *Employee Benefit Accounts. Investment Management for Charitable
    Foundations. Business Advisory Accounts. Trustee for Bond Issues. Pay-
    ing Agent for Bond Issues. Transfer Agent.*

70. Investment Management of Securities as Fiduciary Assets
    by David E. Ellison and John R. Boyd   936

    Investment Committees. Investment Research and Forecasting: *Eco-
    nomic Data and Forecasts. Industry/Company Data and Forecasts.
    Securities Market Data and Forecasts.* Portfolio Management. Establish-
    ment of Investment Objectives: *Variability in the Rate of Return. Liquid-
    ity. Time Horizon.* Securities Trading. Performance Measurement.
    Employee Retirement Income Security Act of 1974. Trends and Develop-
    ments. Summary.

SECTION XII
MARKETING THE BANK'S SERVICES

71. Developing the Marketing Plan and Strategies
    by Richard M. Rosenberg   949

    Market Analysis and Correct Market Positions: *Banking Market Penetra-
    tion or Share of Market. Competitive Factors.* External Environment Fac-
    tors Affecting the Marketing Plan. Establishment of Strategic Marketing
    Objectives. Establishment of Tactical Marketing Objectives. Marketing
    Implementation Plan: *Marketing Research Plan. Product Development
    Plan. Communications Plan. Sales Plan.* Marketing Evaluation Process:
    Market Response. Competitive Response. Conclusion.

72. Developing Corporate Services *by Robert R. Robertson*   961

    Definition of Corporate Services. Examples of Corporate Services. The
    Need for Corporate Services: *Survival. Competition.* Creation of Innova-
    tive Corporate Services. Conception of Innovative Corporate Service

Ideas: *On-going Consideration. Specific Assignment of Authority, Responsibility, and Accountability.* Tentative Approval of a Particular Corporate Service Conceptual Idea. Development of the Corporate Service Conceptual Idea. Final Approval of the New Corporate Service. Implementation of the New Corporate Service. Planning, Organizing, Leading, and Controlling New Corporate Services. Hypothetical New Corporate Service Case: *Conception of Innovative Corporate Service Ideas. Tentative Approval of a Particular Idea. Development of the Corporate Service Conceptual Idea. Final Approval of the New Corporate Service. Implementation of the New Corporate Service.*

73. Correspondent Bank Services *by John W. H. Gushée*   973

History and Scope. Interbank Services. General Banking: *Check Clearing. Funds Transfer. Coin and Currency. Collections.* Credit Services: *Loan Participations. Direct Lending. Credit Information. Other Credit Services.* Portfolio and Investment Services: *Securities Trading. Safekeeping Services. Investment Advice.* International Services: *Operating Services. Financial Services. Marketing Services.* Trust Services: *Investment Counseling. Custodial Services.* Management Assistance and Special Services: *Management Consulting. Automated Data Processing. Business Development. Credit Card. Other Management Services.* Correspondent Banking's Changing Environment: *Compensation. Credit Exposure. Future Challenges.* Conclusion.

74. Bank Advertising—Principles and Guidelines
by M. Carl Sneeden   990

Planning. How to Create Media Plans. Research: Pretesting and Posttesting. Advertising Agencies. Conclusion.

75. Bank Advertising—The Budgeting Process
by M. Carl Sneeden   1001

Budgeting Methods: *Percentage of Sales. Competitive Analysis. Available Funds. Need Determination.* Marginal Analysis. Framework for Budgeting Decisions and Research. Methods of Setting Forth the Allocation of Budgeted Funds: *Services. Corporate Advertising. Processes.*

76. Community Relations Programs *by Willis Johnson, Jr. and A. B. Padgett*   1016

The Role of Community Leadership. A Corporate Responsibility. Terminology. Two Basic Ingredients. Responsibility. Organization. The Community Relations Officer. A Typical Job Description. Matters of Style. Statement of Policy. Direct versus Indirect. A Bank Foundation? Budgeting Community Relations. Defining Specific Areas. Public versus Private. Other Areas of Service. Minority Loan Programs. Bank People-Power. Measuring Effectiveness. Developing Leadership. Some Public Relations Aspects. Summary.

77. Marketing Research in Banking *by Kenneth R. Dew*   1032

Management Support. Economic Justification. Avoiding the Pitfalls. Developing the Research Program: *Internal Information Base. External Research Efforts. The Quick 'n Dirty Venture. Professional Participation.* Executing the Marketing Research Project: *Budgeting. Questionnaire Design. Interviewing Techniques. Tabulation. Interpretation. Implementation.* Role of Marketing Research in the Future: *Greater Sophistication. Computer Utilization. Managing Change and Product Development.*

SECTION XIII
BANK REGULATION AND SUPERVISION

78. The Office of the Comptroller of the Currency and the Structure of American Banking *by James E. Smith and Robert R. Dince*   1049

The Background. Banking and Regulation. Chartering Policy at the OCC: *Banking Factors. Market Factors.* Impact of the McFadden Act on National Banks. Customer Access to Banking. Retail Electronic Banking. OCC Position. The Future. Conclusion.

79. Regulations on Bank Soundness, Competition, and Structure—State Banking Departments *by Lawrence E. Kreider*   1060

Purpose and Goals of State Banking Departments. Goals of State Bank Commissioners as a United Body. Composition of State System. Place in Regulatory Structure. State Leadership in New Techniques and Procedures. Inherent Strengths of State Banking Departments. Inherent Weaknesses of State System. State and National Systems Complement One Another. Evolving Patterns of State Banking Departments.

80. Regulations on Competition and Structure— Federal Reserve System *by Philip E. Coldwell*   1067

Bank Structure Legislation. Bank Mergers. Bank Holding Company Acquisions of Banks. Holding Company Nonbanking Activities. Branch Banking. Maximum Rates on Deposits. Monetary Policy Effects. Conclusion.

81. The FDIC, Deposit Insurance, and Systemwide Risk *by Frank Wille*   1078

Jurisdiction Changes Since the Mid-60s. The Building Blocks of Public Confidence. The Measurement of Systemwide Risk. Bank Examinations and the Development of "Problem Bank" Lists. FDIC's Options for Containing Systemwide Risk. Financial Resources of the FDIC. Conclusion.

82. The Nature and Purpose of Supervisory Examinations
    by Michael Doman   1090
    Structure of Bank Supervision. Objectives of Bank Supervision: *Statutory.*
    Concepts. Purpose of Supervision. Functions of Bank Regulation. The
    Examination Process: *Follow-up Procedures. Early Warning Systems.* The
    Regulation Process. The Charter Process. Other Examination Responsi-
    bilities: *Trust. Consumer. EDP. International.*

SECTION XIV
THE U.S. BANKING SYSTEM

83. The Evolving Banking Structure *by Carter H. Golembe*   1105
    The American Banking Structure in the Middle 1970s. The Changing
    Banking Structure. Concluding Observations.

84. Influence of Monetary Policy on Commercial Banking
    by David P. Eastburn and W. Lee Hoskins   1116
    Monetary Policy: What, Why, and How? Monetary Action and Banker
    Reaction. Impact of Monetary Policy on Commercial Banking: The Rec-
    ord. Policymaker and Banker: Cross Purposes? The Future.

85. Fiscal Policy, Debt Management, and Commercial Banking
    by Tilford C. Gaines   1136
    Fiscal Policy. Debt Management: *Type of Securities Used. Interest Ceil-*
    ings. Public Finance and the Commercial Banking System.

86. The Rise of Minority Banking *by Edward J. Gannon*
    and David B. Harper   1145
    Impetus for Growth. Problems Crop Up Early: *Problems of Raising Capi-*
    tal. Lending Problems. Other Problem Areas. Positive Factors at Work:
    Convenience Factor. Opportunities for Minority Students. Programs of
    Assistance. Prospects for Future.

SECTION XV
THE YEARS AHEAD

87. The Next Ten Years in U.S. Banking *by Paul S. Nadler*   1156
    The Competitive Environment. Regulatory Environment Changes.
    Structure. Bank Service. People. Profit. Conclusion.

Index   1169

List of Illustrations

Exhibit
1-1. Relative Performance of Bank Stocks. 4
1-2. Stockholder Questionnaire 7–8
1-3. Agenda 11
10-1. Some Components of a Human Resource Staffing System. 111
10-2. The Selection Process 119
10-3. Sample Application Form 121–22
10-4. Interpretative Guidelines for Interviewers 125–29
10-5. The Selection Decision 131
14-1. Guideline for Clerical Employees. 169
17-1. Record Requirements 208–09
20-1. Payment System Transactions 242
20-2. Present Check System 242
20-3. Present Check System 243
20-4. EFTS Today 247
20-5. Developing EFTS 248
22-1. Annual Planning Cycle 284
24-1. Profit Contribution for National Accounts Profit Center . . 303
24-2. ABC Corporation—Source and Use Statement 304
24-3. ABC Corporation—Profit Contribution Statement 305
24-4. Product Profitability Analysis—Year Ending 12/31—
       Funds Providing Functions 307
24-5. Product Profitability Analysis—Year Ending 12/31—
       Funds Using Functions 308
24-6. Product Profitability Analysis—Year Ending December 31,
       19— Nonfund Functions 309
24-7. Product Profitability Analysis Demand Deposits—
       Commercial—Year Ending December 31, 19— 310
24-8. Product Profitability Analysis Commercial Loan—
       Business, Commercial and Industrial—Year Ending
       December 31, 19— 311
25-1. The Management Profit Report ($ in Thousands) 322–23
26-1. Community Bank Statement of Condition 328
26-2. Hometown Bank Sources and Disposition of Income 336

29–1. Yields and Yield Spreads, Five-Year Prime Municipals versus Five-Year U.S. Treasury Securities 365

29–2. Net Operating Loss Carry-Back 370

29–3. Preplanned Tax Liability 371

31–1. Illustration of Core Line Deposits 394

31–2. Effect of Three Strategies on Earnings per Share 398

33–1. Percentage Distribution of Assets and Liabilities for All Commercial Banks, December 31, 1976 416

33–2. Comparative Measures of Growth 419

33–3. State National Bank Demand Deposits of Individuals, Partnerships, and Corporations 420

33–4. State National Bank Total Net Deposits in Five Recoveries 421

33–5. Net Deposits (excluding negotiable CDs) 422

33–6. Net Deposits and Estimated Minimum Deposit Levels (excluding negotiable CDs) 424

33–7. Nonmoney Market Loans and Estimated Maximum Loan Levels 425

33–8. Liquidity Needs for Loans and Deposits 427

33–9. Money Market Assets and Liquidity Needs for Loans and Deposits 429

33–10. The Interest Rate Cycle 430

34–1. Distribution of Assets, All Commercial Banks (year-end) . . 435

34–2. Distribution of Liabilities, All Commercial Banks (year-end) 436

34–3. Effect of the Components of Interest-Rate Risk upon Net Interest Margin 438–39

34–4. Total Bank Risk 441

34–5. Substitution of Risk 442

34–6. Impact of Various Strategies 443

35–1. Treasury Deposits at Federal Reserve Banks (billions of dollars) 451

36–1. Balance Sheet and Income Statement Interrelationships . . 456

38–1. Summary of Federal Debt and Resulting Surplus or Deficit (in millions of dollars) 481

38–2. Marketable Interest-Bearing Public Debt (in millions of dollars) 481

38–3. Average Length of Marketable Interest-Bearing Public Debt Held by Private Investors (in millions of dollars) . . . 483

39–1. Consolidated Bonds and Discount Notes of Banks for Cooperatives, Federal Intermediate Credit Banks, and Federal Land Banks 499

39–2. Securities Issued by Government and Government-Sponsored Agencies 509

40–1. Number of State and Local Governmental Units by Type 516

40–2. Total State and Local Debt Outstanding 517

41–1. Example of Typical Yield Pickup Swap 529

41–2. Example of Typical Substitution Swap 530

41–3. Example of Municipal Bond Tax-Loss Trade 532–33

45–1. Spread Sheet for Balance Sheet Data 584

45–2. Spread Sheet—Operating Data 585
45–3. Projection of Financial Statements.................. 596–97
48–1. Establishing Value of Collateral and Margin........... 629
51–1. Leverage Lease...................................... 677–78
51–2. Yield Evaluation of Leverage Lease.................. 685
51–3. Use of 10–Year Debt............................... 688
53–1. Construction Checklist—Four Advance Schedule 709
53–2. Tripartite Buy and Sell Agreement 712–13
53–3. Construction Rider 714–15
55–1. Income Stream Pyramid 733
56–1. Percentage Holdings of Installment Credit by Financial Institutions and Retail Outlets: 1940–1976 744
56–2. Types of Installment Credit Held by Commercial Banks Expressed as Percentages: 1940–1976................. 745
58–1. Geographical Distribution of Assets and Liabilities of Major Foreign Branches of U.S. Banks, December 31, 1976 (in $ billion) 773
58–2. U.S. Bank Holding Company Organization............. 776
58–3. Claims of U.S. Banks on Selected Less Developed Countries, March 31, 1977............................ 786
65–1. Comparison of Interbank and VISA Domestic Statistics .. 891
75–1. The Marketing Response Curve: Revenue as a Function of Advertising (thousands of dollars)................. 1003
75–2. Average Marketing Expenditures by Service Type and Deposit Size: All Reporting Banks—1976 1006
75–3. Percentage of Reporting Bank Budgets Spent on Each Service in 1976 by Deposit Size.................... 1007
75–4. Schedule of Expenditure Levels, with Associated Sales Revenues and Profits.............................. 1010–11
75–4A. Schedule of Expenditure Levels. 1011
75–4B. Total Revenue and Total Profit as Functions of Advertising Expenditures ($ thousands)....................... 1011
75–5. Flowchart for Planning and Evaluating the Advertising Budget 1013
76–1. Example of a Bank's Statement of Policy Concerning Involvement in Community Affairs.................... 1022
76–2. Fact Sheet for Grant Consideration 1024
76–3. Record of Community Activities 1028–29
78–1. Commuting Flows in the 50 Largest SMSAs (1970). 1054
83–1. Number and Deposits of Commercial Banks, December 31, 1976 1108
84–1. Gross National Product and Money Supply, 1915–1976. .. 1118
84–2. Money Stock (M_1) as of August 31, 1977 (billions of dollars) 1120
84–3. Selected Liabilities of Commercial Banks, 1961–1977.... 1125
84–4. Net Increase in Liabilities of Commercial Banks and Their Affiliates 1127
84–5. Total Deposits of All Banks with Less than $100 Million in Deposits 1128

84–6. Holdings of Loans and Securities as Share of Total Assets, Commercial Banks, 1961–1977.................... 1130
84–7. Average Rate of Return to Capital, 1946–1977 (net profit per $100 of total capital accounts)................. 1132

SECTION I

ORGANIZING AND MANAGING THE BANKING CORPORATION

Chapter 1 _____

Bank Investor Relations—
A New World

Frank A. Plummer*

What is new? In the realm of stockholder relations, "Everything is new." In the early 1970s the explosion of the multibank holding company created a need. That need was access to capital markets. Rapid internal growth, bank acquisitions, nonbank acquisitions—all of these developments created a seemingly insatiable requirement for capital.

Simultaneously, the independent banker found that the stockholders had a new awareness of the changing scene and an increased desire for information concerning the value of their equity holdings.

During the late 1960s and early 1970s, bank equity values were soaring to new heights. There was growing interest in new banking terms: book value, price-earnings ratios, return on equity. Except in a few money market institutions, this was new terminology in the traditional banking world.

Before the stockholder could absorb the changes, the environment had changed. In rapid succession a number of adverse impacts confronted the banking scene: a recession appeared on the horizon; the financial world was shocked by the failure of some large banks; the real estate investment trust debacle developed; credit losses rose and earnings dropped; municipal bonds lost their popularity.

This changing scenario resulted in plunging equity values. Bank stocks suffered more severely than the Dow Jones Average, and when equity markets improved, bank stocks fell behind. Some banks escaped

_____
* Chairman, First Alabama Bancshares, Inc., Montgomery, Alabama.

3

Exhibit 1–1
Relative Performance of Bank Stocks

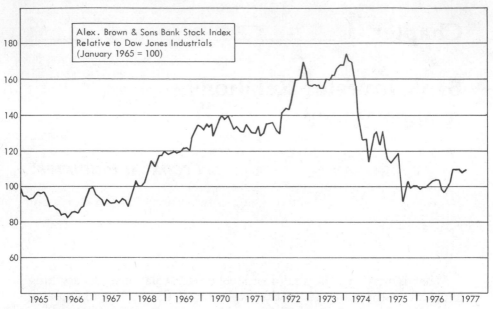

Source: Alex. Brown & Sons, Baltimore, Maryland.

the extreme traumata of real estate markets and deteriorating credits that impaired earnings, but even these were "tarred with the brush." Banks suffering unusual losses were forced to reduce or eliminate dividends. All of these developments adversely affected the popularity of bank stocks and increased the need for better investor relations.

THE NEW ENVIRONMENT FOR FINANCIAL INFORMATION

Due to the rapidly shifting banking scene, new voices suddenly demanded more detailed knowledge of bank and bank holding company data. All of these recipients of information play an important role in the eventual market value of bank equities. It is necessary to understand the roles played by these new "actors" on the scene, and the motivating forces behind their demands. Any successful stockholder relations program must satisfy the requirements of the following groups and individuals.

TRADITIONAL AND NEW REGULATORY AUTHORITIES

For many years the banker has been familiar with the requirements of the Comptroller of Currency, the Federal Reserve, the Federal Deposit Insurance Corporation, and supervisor of state banks. However, in recent years, primarily due to weaknesses revealed in the banking system and legislative pressures, all of these agencies have accelerated their demands for financial data.

Following the Bank Holding Company Act of 1970, the Federal Reserve found it necessary to require far more penetrating financial studies as a protective measure for the capital structure of the banking system. The most exacting demands and pressures for detailed information have been promulgated by the Securities Exchange Commission as the banking industry has issued registered securities.

At the moment a new, powerful force is making its power known to bankers. The Financial Accounting Standards Board is rapidly revising traditional accounting procedures for industry and the financial world. These new developments cannot be ignored by the banking industry, and may have far-reaching effects on capital structures and bank equities.

THE SECURITY ANALYST

The security analyst is a sales representative of "your ideas." One should not expect much analysis unless one is operating a major successful bank. Banks outside of this limited category should expect the analyst to repackage information and data from the bank. If this assumption is accepted, it stresses the importance of clear, accurate data. Normally, the analyst is concerned with earnings per share outlook together with current "hot" items such as loan losses, nonaccruals, international posture, and experience.

FIDUCIARIES AND INSTITUTIONAL HOLDERS

These groups are in a position of public trust. They may require different information from the security analysts and place more emphasis on market strategies and policies. It is essential that large institutions maintain a dialogue with these public representatives as the large banks are considered a bellwether in particular areas such as disclosure.

BANK CLIENTS

One of the most interesting developments of the last few years has been the acceleration of demands for financial information by the large corporate customer or correspondent bank. Formerly, only a few sophisticated corporations demanded a minimal amount of information. During the climate of large bank failures in recent years, new demands have developed. Today large depositors, large borrowers, debenture holders, traders in money market instruments—all segments of the financial community—require timely, accurate information.

THE SMALL INVESTOR

The requirements of the many recipients of this financial data often obscure the real target of a communications program, the small- and average-sized investor. This group, historically, has been the source of original capital funds. Under certain market conditions, they may be the only source of capital funds. As the bank becomes successful and grows, this group is frequently overlooked. The small investor is normally a faithful follower if he or she believes the bank is well operated and a force for good in the community, primarily helping people help themselves. Basically, for the average-sized bank the investor relations program is directed to the individual investor.

RECOGNITION OF THE STOCKHOLDER

This prologue merely sets the theme of the chapter and the importance of the stockholder in today's marketplace for both small and large banks. On recognizing this importance, possibly for the first time in several decades, how does management communicate with the stockholder? Before launching into what might be an ill-advised, misdirected plan of action, it is well to identify the marketplace. Who owns the bank? What does one want in terms of information? With only a small number of stockholders, it may be possible for the local banker to possess this knowledge, but a list of stockholders numbering hundreds or even thousands does not lend itself to easy mental classification techniques. A stockholder profile can easily be developed; however, the following minimal aspects should be classified: size of holdings, geographical location, type (male or female), joint tenancy, institutional (trust or corporate).

Once a profile has been established, meaningful surveys based on using well-planned questionnaires can develop a wealth of data. Questions can be asked to determine the motivation for owning stock, reaction to dividend policies, and satisfaction or dissatisfaction with present bank publications, and so on. The computer age has a simplified the accruing of these data and updating them on a timely schedule. These data provide a sound basis for an intelligent, productive program of stockholder relations.

In recent years the science of conducting productive surveys has been highly developed. Many banks find it helpful to employ an outside consultant who does not conduct the survey but does suggest methods to be used and points out the pros and cons of each technique. The type of information desired, or the accessibility of the stockholder, may dictate a choice between personal calls, letters, telephone calls, and the number of stockholders to be contacted. Assuming that the letter questionnaire technique is employed, Exhibit 1–2 outlines a typical questionnaire. Certain financial institutions may wish to present different inquiries to develop a particular theme or to solve a special problem such as dividend policy.

Exhibit 1–2
Stockholder Questionnaire

At First United Bancshares your 1,000 employees are sensitive to the fact that we have 5,000 bosses. Your directors and management believe it would be helpful to know more about the desires and thinking of our stockholders as we continue to develop policies for your bank. It is also helpful to understand your relationship to the bank as both a stockholder and a client.

May we thank you in advance for the data and direction you may give us.

1. Do you own First United Bancshares stock as:
   An Individual ___ Joint Tenancy ___
   Custodian ___ Corporation ___
   Institutional Investor ___ Other ___
2. Please check your age grouping.
   Under 30 ___ 30–50 ___ Over 50 ___
3. What is your marital status?
   Single ___ Married ___ Widowed ___
4. Please indicate your sex.
   Male ___ Female ___
5. Where is your place of residence?
   Alabama ___ Southeast ___ Other ___
6. Do you have an account at one of First United Bancshares' affiliate banks? Yes ___ No ___
   If so, indicate type of accounts:
   Checking ___ Savings ___
   Certificates of Deposit ___
   Loans ___ Trust ___ Other _____
7. Is First United Bancshares your principal bank? Yes ___ No ___
8. Do you personally know a member of our staff?
	Yes	No
Director	___	___
Officer	___	___
Employee	___	___
9. How many shares of First United Bancshares stock do you own?
   1–99 ___ 100–999 ___ 1,000 or over ___
10. Do you own other bank stocks? Yes ___ No ___

Exhibit 1–2 (*Continued*)

---

11. Did you purchase your First United Bancshares stock? Yes ＿＿
    No ＿＿
    If so, did you do so because:
    A stock broker recommended it   ＿＿
    Your Financial adviser recommended it   ＿＿
    You were impressed with the services received at our banks ＿＿
    Other ＿＿＿＿＿＿＿＿＿＿＿＿＿＿＿＿＿＿＿＿＿＿＿＿＿＿＿＿＿

12. Do you consider your holdings in our stock a long-term investment?
    Yes ＿＿ No ＿＿

13. Are you primarily interested in income or appreciation?
    Income ＿＿ Appreciation ＿＿

14. When dividend rates are increased do you prefer:
    All dividends paid in cash   ＿＿
    More stock dividends   ＿＿
    Combination of cash and stock dividends   ＿＿

15. Would you like an opportunity to reinvest your cash dividends at
    market prices? Yes ＿＿ No ＿＿

16. Do you think the financial condition and review of activities of
    First United Bancshares are well presented in annual and quarterly
    reports? Yes ＿＿ No ＿＿
    If no, would you like:
    More financial information supplied   ＿＿
    Less expensive reports   ＿＿
    More simplified financial information   ＿＿
    Other ＿＿＿＿＿＿＿＿＿＿＿＿＿＿＿＿＿＿＿＿＿＿＿＿＿＿＿＿＿

17. Please add your comments on management policies or service areas
    that can be improved: ＿＿＿＿＿＿＿＿＿＿＿＿＿＿＿＿＿＿＿＿
    ＿＿＿＿＿＿＿＿＿＿＿＿＿＿＿＿＿＿＿＿＿＿＿＿＿＿＿＿＿＿＿
    ＿＿＿＿＿＿＿＿＿＿＿＿＿＿＿＿＿＿＿＿＿＿＿＿＿＿＿＿＿＿＿

    Stockholder signature* ＿＿＿＿＿＿＿＿＿＿＿＿＿＿＿＿＿＿＿
    *You need not sign if you prefer to remain anonymous.

It is most important to gain the perspective of the stockholder in
order to have a sound basis for formulating an investor relations program. Exhibit 1–2 is primarily attempting to develop stockholder reaction to dividend policy while simultaneously exploring minor areas
of stockholder interest.

INVESTOR RELATIONS PROGRAM

At this point a valuable background of data has been accumulated.
The need for a program has been established, and the stockholder
and marketplace identified. Contact with the stockholder has estab-

lished, to a degree, what information is desired in the area of communications, financial returns, and depth of concern with management policies. Now, a program can be initiated tailored to the institution.

The first priority for such a program should be to set objectives. The program must encompass the following minimal ingredients: compliance with the law and regulatory directives; establishment of credibility; outline of information disseminated; timely schedule for release; and methods of news release. Objectives should be outlined and endorsed at the directors' table. Without this understanding and endorsement, any program will be severely handicapped. Obviously, a particular bank will have objectives tailored to its own needs.

It is essential to establish responsibility and control for the program and create the organization for execution. A program of this importance must be under the control of the chief executive officer, but in medium- and large-sized institutions the day-to-day responsibility may be delegated to a public affairs officer, the marketing officer, or possibly the comptroller. Although the officer directly charged with the task will vary from bank to bank, there must always be well-coordinated staff work. The financial data must be timely and accurate. All officers concerned must be contacted in assembling the data, writing the script, reviewing the news release, and coordinating the details of distribution. There are other requirements relating to the face-to-face confrontation with stockholders.

Early in the program, it is important to relate the objectives of the program to costs. What part of the budget should be allocated to stockholder relations? How should the money be spent? In this day of escalating costs, unless this part of the program is carefully reviewed, considerable money may be wasted on an ineffectual program or a program can fail because of the lack of sufficient dollars.

At this stage, we have determined the need for a program, identified the market, established objectives, assigned responsibility, and determined the approximate allocation of funds; we are now ready for the implementation of the plan. There are many facets of the program to explore in the area of communications.

INVESTOR CONTACTS

In many institutions a personal call program may be the first and most important step. Certainly, this is true where large holdings are concentrated in a few hands. A personal call establishes the prestige of the stockholder, affords the opportunity for one-on-one constructive criticism, and, when possible, establishes the best of all forums. This type of program can often be merged with "account responsibility calls," when the program is compatible and qualified officers are se-

lected for this important task. The board of directors can plan an important role in a well-coordinated "call program." In the small bank and
community, they are particularly significant. Their views are important
to stockholders and good assignments for directors will produce excellent results.

ANNUAL STOCKHOLDERS' MEETING

Historically, the typical annual stockholders' meeting was attended
by the "immediate family": directors, bank counsel, possibly a few
large stockholders. Today it is not unusual for holding companies and
large- and medium-sized banks to have several hundred stockholders
in attendance. A large attendance does not automatically happen unless
there are unusual developments that are of public knowledge and
interest. A well-planned effort is necessary to ensure attendance.

The stockholder must be notified well in advance. Prior to the meeting, the stockholder is often contacted by a personal visit or telephone
call. Normally, a social period with light refreshments precedes the
meeting. This social hour is a critical period. Stockholders require,
deserve, and enjoy attention. Senior management should be omnipres-
ent and for this one day, at least, assume the cloak of a politician. A
successful prelude may ward off many potentially awkward situations
during the official meeting.

The meeting itself should be well organized with a meaningful
agenda. It presents an opportunity for management to explain the
previous year's performance and review plans for the current year.
Considerable skill can be developed in this area by drawing the line
between too much or too little information. Use of charts, slides, and
more sophisticated audio and video equipment can break the monot-
ony of routine reports. If these techniques are used, they should be
well handled; a sloppy performance reflects on the institution.

In order to produce an even flow of business, it is important to
have the motions typewritten in advance and assigned to a director
or stockholder. The seconding motion is also assigned to another individual. A duplicate copy is in the possession of the chairman.

A well-trained secretarial staff should have tabulated the proxies
in advance, and this staff should thoroughly understand the technique
of adjusting last minute proxies and the shares voting in person for
the benefit of the Proxy Committee and Judges of Election.

When special programs are developed for the meeting, most chair-
men prefer to present their personal reports immediately prior to
the report of the Proxy Committee, near the conclusion of the meeting,
in order to prevent an "anticlimax."

The important segments of an agenda for the typical meeting are outlined in Exhibit 1–3.

Legal requirements may vary with the laws of incorporation. The bank's attorney should check the agenda in advance to determine compliance.

The individual bank must adapt the program to the audience and the facilities available. The use of slides or handouts are options which may be considered. It is an opportunity to demonstrate depth in management, and can be an opportunity for sales before an affluent market.

Exhibit 1–3
Agenda

1. Call to order.
2. Announcement that shareholder list is present.
3. Appointment and preliminary report of Proxy Committee.
4. Nomination of chairman and secretary of the meeting.
5. Election of chairman and secretary of the meeting.
6. Motion to dispense with reading of the minutes of the previous meeting.
7. Appointment of Judges of Election.
8. Appointment of Resolutions Committee.
9. Introduction and statement of auditors.
10. Nomination of directors.
11. Election of directors.
12. Chairman's report.
13. Question and answer period.
14. Report of Proxy Committee.
15. Report of Judges of Election.
16. Report of Resolutions Committee.
17. Adjournment.

If a sales pitch is part of the program, it should be handled subtly and not detract from the primary purpose of the meeting.

Large institutions with stockholdings over a wide geographical area are now supplementing official stockholder meetings with report meetings at strategic locations. Obviously, the format of a report meeting will differ from that of an official stockholders' meeting because there will be no technical requirements. In this technological era, closed circuit TV may be the next development.

A question and answer period can be handled with confidence if management anticipates the questions and prepares the responses accordingly. Answers should be short and factual in order to establish credibility.

CORRESPONDENCE

A new stockholder should be acknowledged by letter the day his or her name appears on the stockholder list. The mechanics for a welcome letter should be established, but the letter should be personalized, when appropriate, and in all cases reviewed frequently to avoid the appearance of a sterotyped, meaningless mailing.

Letters from stockholders will be received from time to time, and these letters should be directed to the chief executive officer and answered with 24 hours. Stockholders can be a source of constructive ideas, and their suggestions should be carefully reviewed.

There are a number of mass mailing to stockholders during the year. These mailings should be related and carefully programmed and disciplined. Stockholders, understandably, become annoyed when they receive mishandled, ill-directed mail. They conclude that the bank is wasting their money, and a poor image of efficient operations is established.

Several other opportunities are available for contact with stockholders, such as the annual report, quarterly reports, dividend mailings, and special events. Early in the year, management should decide on an overall theme and particular developments that should be emphasized. Continuity can be developed so that over the 12 month period programmed information can be presented without redundancy.

ANNUAL REPORT

It must be recognized that of all communications the annual report ranks first in importance. Superior staff work is required as the time schedule is developed, and there must be coordination between departments as they prepare their respective contributions to this report. Fundamental management decisions are required to determine the theme of the report, physical size, clarity of presentation, and so on.

It is imperative that the report explain to the stockholder how the bank should be evaluated and assist the stockholder in this evaluation. The stockholder should understand the successes or failures encountered during the year, and if failures are outlined, a corrective program of measures for improvement should be presented. The stockholder will understand management's objectives and the rate of progress in reaching these objectives.

CONTINUITY OF STOCKHOLDER CONTACTS

For the small institution with unlisted securities, contacts with the financial world are not of earthshaking importance. In many communities the bank president is the sole market maker. However, even in the small bank, contact should probably be maintained with a security dealer interested in your area. You can periodically test the waters and develop a feel for the popularity, or lack thereof, of your security. Special situations may make the role of the investment adviser important.

A method of acknowledging that stockholders have sold their stock is important. Occasionally, you learn why stockholders are disgruntled, and often you make a friend who repurchases your equity the next time he or she buys bank equities. Some authorities believe that termination letters may be a source of embarrassment, yet they can be quite useful.

In today's volatile economic and equity markets, overnight developments can make stockholder contact imperative. A standby operating procedure for contacting stockholders by calls, telephone, wire, and so on, is a timely aid. Financial institutions with listed securities are now exposed to the entire banking fraternity and the financial world. This glass-walled house is a new experience.

It would be reassuring if one could present a foolproof formula for working with the security market makers. Many institutions have a highly sophisticated program of presenting their data to security analysts. Frequent visits to money market centers, visits to the home office by the analyst, participation on panels and seminars, en masse presentation to investor groups—all are part of this scenario. The intensity of the relationship must obviously be a decision by individual bank management. Whatever the degree of cultivation, certain ingredients of the program are necessary. The brokerage firm is the intermediary between the bank and the investor. The broker's reputation is at stake. You must determine the information he or she requires and then furnish it in an accurate, timely, understandable manner. Above all, credibility must be established and maintained. Problems cannot be sugarcoated to return and haunt you.

Once a program has been established, continuity must be maintained through both good and bad times. Lack of continuity will destroy your relationship with the financial community.

PRESS RELATIONS

A difficult and sensitive area is press relations. It is no deep, dark secret that, normally, the news media do not possess an in-depth knowledge of financial matters. All press relations should be carefully edited, delivered, and explained. Any verbal release will probably be highly garbled and misleading to stockholders. A continuing effort should be made to cultivate and educate media representatives.

CURRENT DEVELOPMENTS

The banking industry's problems previously enumerated have elevated investor relations to a top-priority position. The subject cannot be treated lightly when we are aware that there is litigation in our courts accusing bank management and directors of negligence and wrongdoing. No banking subject has received more attention in recent months than "disclosures." All branches of government are engaged in debate, and many voices from the private sector have joined the chorus. The current wave of consumerism has heightened its intensity.

No extreme position appears prudent until the problem has been calmly and rationally reviewed, although some large institutions are apparently rushing to "let it all hang out." Certain guidelines are clearly indicated:

1. Disclosure must comply with legal and regulatory requirements.
2. Banking's traditional posture of "client confidentiality" must be maintained.
3. Disclosure should provide basic, understandable data that will assist the investor in determining present and future values of the investment.
4. Everday operations must be under constant scrutiny of highly skilled legal, accounting, and public relations counsel.
5. Directors must be fully informed on policy and this policy continually updated.

Students of banking requiring an in-depth knowledge of investor relations as related to bank stock analysts should gain the benefit of excellent material written by David C. Cates and Robert M. Baylis.[1] These two authors are recognized authorities in this field.

The "gut" key to investor relations will be performance. There is no defense for ethical or moral wrongdoing in the banking profession. Skills must be developed to a level that fosters pride, not embarrassment. When banks are sound, liquid, and profitable, stockholder relations is a rewarding phase of banking.

---

[1] David C. Cates, *Bank Investor Relations,* Bank Marketing Association, Chicago, Illinois and Robert M. Baylis, "Stockholder Communications for Banks," *The Bankers Magazine,* Spring, 1974.

Chapter 2

The Bank's Board of Directors— Functions and Responsibilities

*Sherman Hazeltine**

Thorough discussion of banks' boards of directors runs the gamut in size from the smallest community-centered bank to the largest internationally oriented metropolitan institution. Structurally, this includes the independent unit bank, the branch banking system, and the member of a "chain" group or bank holding company. Accordingly, this chapter is general in nature. To avoid the necessity for numerous exceptions to stated rules, it is anticipated that the reader will easily sense those specific areas where reference must be made to current state or federal statute, or to regulations promulgated by the Comptroller of the Currency or the Federal Reserve Board.

QUALIFICATION AND ELECTION

In a bank, as in any corporation, the board of directors represents the top echelon of authority, for it is the voice of the shareholders. The required Notice to Shareholders telling the time, date, and place of the annual meeting also presents a list of proposed directors for the coming year. National banks are required to set forth only the nominees' occupation and, if an officer of the bank, any remuneration over $30,000 annually. To this may be added pertinent data relative to qualifications, amount of the bank's stock owned, and details as to pension or other direct benefits accruing to each from the bank. Proxy solicitations by banks with more than 500 shareholders are much more

---

* Chairman, First National Bank of Arizona, Phoenix, Arizona.

complex. To ensure compliance with SEC disclosure requirements, the services of an attorney are recommended.

It is the privilege of the shareholders to accept or reject, in whole or in part, the suggested list of candidates. Each year the total number of directors to be elected is determined at the annual meeting. If the Articles of Incorporation are so drawn, a national bank may properly increase the number of its directors within limits (not more than 2 if the number of directors last elected by the shareholders was 15 or less, and not more than 4 if the number last elected was 16 or more) and appoint persons to fill the resulting vacancies between meetings of shareholders. This authority granted by the shareholders to the directors affords flexibility and the opportunity to acquire other qualified members as they may become available.

The number of members of the board varies according to the size of the bank and the decision of its shareholders. National banks and other banks which are members of the Federal Reserve System are required by law to have a minimum of 5 directors and a maximum of 25. A study made a few years ago among national banks indicated that banks with assets up to $15 million had a range of 5 to 19 directors, 11 being the median number. Banks with assets from $15 to $25 million had from 10 to 25, the median being 15; banks whose assets exceed $50 million had from 17 to 25, with 21 being the median number. State statutes which specify the number of directors for state-chartered banks vary considerably. Some specify a minimum number (usually five but as low as three), some set both a minimum and a maximum, while in other states the limits on the size of the board are set according to the size of the bank. Within the limits set by law, the size of the board may be changed by amendment to the articles of association approved by the stockholders. The articles of association may provide for a flexible number of directors (say seven to nine); in this case the stockholders decide at the annual meeting the number to be elected for that year.

National bank directors serve for one year and cannot be removed during that term either by their fellow directors or by the stockholders. However, one or more directors may be removed by the Board of Governors of the Federal Reserve System for continued unsound banking practices.

At its organization meeting, normally held immediately following the annual meeting of shareholders, the new board elects officers for the ensuing year, fixes their salaries, and adopts such routine resolutions as may be appropriate to clear the agenda of subsequent board meetings. The directors' standing committees are appointed at this time.

In order to qualify, each director must own capital stock in the bank, free and clear of hypothecation, although the amount of stock ownership may vary with circumstances. Section 72 of the National Banking Law (Title 12 of the United States Code) provides in part that all directors of a national bank must own in their own right shares of the capital stock of the association of which they are a director, the aggregate par value of which shall not be less than $1,000 except in the case of the very small bank when $500 or par value is sufficient. Needless to say, state-chartered banks must adhere to the appropriate statute.

THE DIRECTORS' OATH

The "Oath of Director," to which all directors in a national banking association must subscribe annually, sets forth succinctly the legal responsibilities inherent in a directorate and is equally applicable to directors of state-chartered institutions.

I, the undersigned, Director of the [bank] located at [address] being a citizen of the United States, and a resident of the State of [insert], do solemnly swear [affirm] that I will, so far as the duty devolves on me, diligently and honestly administer the affairs of said Association, that I will not knowingly violate, or willingly permit to be violated, any of the Statutes of the United States under which this Association has been organized; and that I am the owner, in good faith and in my own right, of the number of shares of stock of the aggregate par value required by said Statutes, subscribed by me as standing in my name on the books of the said Association; and that the same is not hypothecated or in any way pledged as security for any loan or debt.

The foregoing oath is not mere ritual, and in times of stress can rise to haunt the careless individual who has accepted the honor (or possible social prestige) of being a bank director without a sense of responsibility for the incumbent obligation. The Comptroller of the Currency has issued a concise booklet entitled *Duties and Liabilities of Directors of National Banks* for the benefit of directors, new and old, in the discharge of their legal responsibilities. Although the publication is specifically applicable to national banks, directors of state-chartered banking institutions may well find guidance from the text in question. For a national bank no exception is permitted with respect to the requirement for United States citizenship.

DIRECTORS' DUTIES

The powers, duties, responsibilities, and liabilities of the board of directors are determined by a combination of statutory law, common law, articles of association, bylaws, and custom. Some of these responsibilities and liabilities are spelled out in statutes designed to give the bank director, because of the quasi-public nature of banking, a special position among corporate directors. The directors' responsibilities are geared to the protection of both the depositor and shareholder. Where the interests of both are at risk, court decisions tend to favor the depositor as against the shareholder; the directors may be held liable in their individual capacities for attributable damages sustained.

Powers

The extent to which the board takes an active part in operating decisions will vary with the size of the bank and other circumstances. In small banks it is normal for the board to review in detail, or approve in advance, all lending and investment activity. In larger banks the board characteristically delegates this authority to committees and officers. This right to delegate authority can be applied to matters requiring the highest judgment. However, delegation does not relieve the board of its responsibility for supervision. Powers reserved to the board in the bylaws, charter, or statute cannot be delegated. When a board is dissolved the powers that it has delegated terminate.

Liabilities

An individual who takes the oath as a director of a national bank assumes substantial liabilities. As long as the bank operates without trouble (failure, embezzlement, stockholder suits, and so on), these assumed liabilities go almost unnoticed by the individual director. If a new board takes over after a fight for control, or if the supervisory authorities uncover practices which result in losses to depositors or to the Federal Deposit Insurance Corporation, the director may face legal action.

Directors must exercise honest and diligent supervision of the bank's activities and are responsible for proper management. These obligations are so general in scope that only by reviewing court decisions can one discover certain guidelines which indicate their extent; even then, courts are prone to modify their decisions with slightly different circumstances. It has been established that the director is liable not only for wrongs, but also for negligence.

Specific liabilities given national bank directors include:

1. Personal liability to the bank, stockholders, or any other person for knowingly permitting an officer or agent to violate any provision of the National Banking Act (such as filing false reports and making excessive loans).
2. Liability for violating or knowingly permitting agents to violate regulations of the Federal Reserve Act or Federal Reserve Board.

The nebulous nature of director liability may be exemplified in the instance of litigation arising from a contested corporate takeover. Conflict of interest or insider knowledge asserted by the plaintiff against the bank's management may well extend to its directors.

Indemnification

Where the articles of association are not previously so drawn, it has become common practice for the board of directors to recommend to the shareholders an amendment to the articles to provide for the indemnification for reasonable expenses incurred by directors, officers, and employees of the bank which may arise out of their defense in a legal proceeding brought against them as a result of their duties with the bank. Indemnification or reimbursement would not apply where such person had been adjudged guilty of or found liable for gross negligence, willful misconduct, or criminal acts.

Responsibilities

Total and absolute confidentiality of business that transpires or is discussed in the bank is the first and paramount responsibility of every director. This is not only an ethical but a legal responsibility. Nothing short of default can so damage the reputation of a bank as to have the confidential nature of its transactions impugned. Inviolable confidence must originate in the board of directors if it is to be expected of management and staff.

So that they may carry out their responsibilities with the proper care and diligence, it has been established that the directors have certain duties. The listing of these duties does not imply that these are the only things directors must do to fulfill their responsibilities.

1. Regularity of attendance at all meetings of the board is noted by the several supervisory authorities and a record is kept. Failure to be present at a meeting does not relieve a director from liability for improper management. It is the responsibility of the directors to inform themselves of what transpired at any meeting missed.
2. Participation at board meetings is expected, with special reference to areas of particular knowledge or expertise. Whereas the usual directors are not deemed to be or become experts in bank operations, it is both to their and the bank's advantage for them to become reasonably informed on the practices and policies of the institution of which they are directors.
3. Directors must satisfy themselves that the internal audit procedures are adequate and in force even though this is the particular

responsibility of the Examining Committee. All personal transactions of directors with their own bank must be at arm's length and of such quality as to exceed routine standards.

4. A basic responsibility of the board of directors is to evaluate management and to be assured at all times that planning for management succession is satisfactory.

PERSONAL ATTRIBUTES

In many corporations, the director's responsibility is focused almost exclusively on the particular affairs of the corporation. Since banks by their very nature are quasi-public institutions, the director not only is responsible to the shareholders, safeguarding their investment and establishing practices presumed to be conducive to profitability over both the near and long term, but the director must also be concerned with the public interest. It is for this reason that bank directors historically have enjoyed a certain distinction in the financial community. To be sustained, this distinction must be earned. Outlining the qualifications for a director is not a simple matter, for there is much that is subjective and much that depends upon the existing membership of the board, as well as the size and type of bank involved. However, the one fundamental in every instance is complete personal integrity. A director's well-earned reputation for honesty and fair dealing accrues to his bank.

Additional attributes desirable in the director include:

1. The candidate is forward looking and has demonstrated progressiveness in his or her own business or profession. It is well for the candidate to be either a recognized leader, or a "comer" in his or her particular field, be it agriculture, business, industry, the law, or some branch of science.
2. The candidate is well known and a respected citizen.
3. The candidate knows the community and its people.
4. The candidate is in a position to direct additional banking business to the bank.
5. The candidate has knowledge and appreciation of public reaction.
6. The candidate is familiar with not only local economic activity but is attuned to the national and international economy as it affects the bank.

RELATIONS WITH MANAGEMENT

In banks as in all corporate structures there is a significant distinction between the functions of the board of directors and those of management. Whereas the board is ultimately responsible to the shareholders for the success of the institution, the proximate responsibility for its successful operation is that of management. Policy is made by the board, but it must be implemented by management. Only rarely should the board intervene directly in operational matter. In the unhappy event that management appears unable to produce the desired results it becomes the responsibility of the board to institute such changes in management as seem required.

The board has no greater responsibility than to maintain a constant appraisal of management. A paradox sometimes arises in that frequently the nomination of candidates for the bank's board is from management. When that is the case the moment of truth can be grim.

COMPOSITION OF BOARD OF DIRECTORS

There is a difference of opinion as to the composition of bank boards of directors with respect to "inside" and "outside" members. By "inside" is meant those connected with the active management of the bank, whereas "outside" refers to all others. The basic argument is that a board comprised wholly of insiders tends to become at best myopic, at worst self-serving. Conversely, since few outside directors are aware of the mechanics of bank management, this lack of knowledge may result in the promulgation of impractical policies. The trend of recent years is toward the limitation of inside directors to a few holding top-management positions.

Perennial discussion arises concerning statutory prohibition of interlocking directorates among financial institutions. Whereas the proponents of such legislation concern themselves primarily with restraint of trade and collusive practices, a corollary argument in support of the complete separation of the directorates of financial institutions is that "no man can serve two masters."

Because the contribution made by a competent board of directors is of such value, adequate fees should be paid outside directors. Such fees are usually geared to attendance of all regular and special sessions of the board. Where committee meetings are held on days other than the regular meeting date for the board, a fee should be paid to compensate the directors for interruption of their personal affairs. Both punctuality and regularity of attendance on the part of directors are of great importance if they are to discharge their duties properly. The organization of the material presented to the board should be such as to minimize the amount of time taken for its consideration.

In addition to meeting fees, which are fixed by the board at its organizational meeting following the annual meeting of shareholders, it is becoming popular to establish an annual retainer for directors.

A retainer suggests that directors have responsibilities to refer business to the bank and otherwise to support it throughout the year, apart from attending meetings. In addition, directors are entitled to reimbursement for expenses incurred on behalf of the bank. Accident and liability insurance coverage, where provided for officers, should be applicable to directors when acting on behalf of the bank.

DIRECTORS' STANDING COMMITTEES

Standing committees for the discharge of certain statutory functions enable the chairman of the board to select those persons best fitted by talent and availability for specific areas of service. Typical standing committees are the executive, examining, trust, and salary committees.

The Executive Committee

This committee is generally composed of senior members who can meet with sufficient regularity between regularly scheduled meetings of the full board to dispose promptly of routine problems requiring board action and also handle such emergency matters as may arise. The Executive Committee, by proper provision contained in the by-laws, typically is empowered to decide all questions of policy and personnel, have general management of the affairs of the association, and must file copies of all minutes of all meetings with the board of directors. The board of directors is authorized to delegate to the Executive Committee any powers and authority of the board in the management of the business and affairs of the association, except the power to fill vacancies, declare dividends, and adopt, amend, or repeal bylaws. The Executive Committee frequently reviews loans and discounts passed upon by the Finance Committee of the bank's management.

In smaller institutions the Executive Committee may also serve as its Finance Committee. Board members who are closely in touch with the local financial situation bring additional perspective to credit reviews. Although it is not necessary for the actions of the Executive Committee to be ratified by the board at its next subsequent meeting, the minutes of the Executive Committee should be recorded in sufficient detail that all other board members may be kept fully informed. Restricting the use of the Executive Committee to practical limits and emergency matters can help maintain its proper relation with the full board.

The Examining Committee

Historically, the board of directors has been charged with conducting an independent examination of the affairs of the bank annually, and, in fact, national bank directors are so charged by law. In smaller institutions the directors often conduct the examination themselves and in so doing learn far more concerning the conduct of the bank's affairs than they would ever know otherwise. However, in larger institutions it is impractical for the directors to conduct examinations. Reliance must be placed either on outside auditors (a not inexpensive undertaking) or on the maintenance of close supervision over the bank's own auditing and examining department. This last arrangement works very well if carried out faithfully and with a clear view of the extreme importance of the function.

It is essential that the directors' Examining Committee be comprised of members whose talents fit them for this type of work, since it serves as the principal means by which all other directors are kept informed not only as to the character of the bank's assets and liabilities, but as to the competence of the bank's auditing and examining department as well. The Examining Committee should also give close scrutiny to all reports of examination by the supervisory authorities, reporting to the full board any matters disclosed by an examination which are serious or which seem to need action by the board.

Trust Committees

Legal requirements call for a Trust Investment Committee which may also act as a Trust Committee. Many banks have two committees, each with a different function, investment, or administration. The Trust Committees play a vital role. Services of an attorney must always be available to the Trust Committee. Directors with competence in the field of investments, or the supervision of real estate, can serve admirably in discharging this important committee function. Life underwriters, as well as those engaged in investment counseling, may well be considered for a place on the directors' Trust Investment Committee. Because of the growing importance of the trust function as a competitive tool supporting the commercial side of modern banks, the Trust Committees are a potent factor in the realm of bank business development.

Salary Committee

The Salary Committee is usually confined to outside directors. Although it generally addresses itself specifically to the salaries of top management, in so doing it must be informed as to the basic philosophy and structure of the bank's total salary program. This, in turn, is interrelated with the personnel function which, while a management responsibility, can benefit from the perspective of mature and experienced directors from other lines of business.

Other Committees

At least two more committees can be mentioned which afford great strength of an aggressive bank. One is a Business Development Committee which, by utilizing the talents of those directors gifted in the fields of advertising, public relations, and market research, can both focus and magnify management's efforts along these specialized lines. On the record, bankers tend to be somewhat unsophisticated in these areas and can well do with all the outside help they can muster. By the establishment of a standing committee directed toward business development, the entire staff of the bank is kept aware of the importance placed by the board on this phase of operations. The committee's monthly report should maintain the emphasis.

One other committee might be devoted to management evaluation. This committee should be comprised of board members well versed in business administration. It is not at all necessary that they be experienced bankers. The committees should serve as would an outside management consulting firm in studying the operations of the bank. The typical bank director has little knowledge of the actual methods employed—either in the mechanics of the investment function, the handling of personnel, property maintenance, or any of the vast variety of day-to-day operations which in total represent the workings of the bank. Because of the tendency of bankers to do things the same way simply because of precedent—to maintain records for the sake of records, and so on—the scrutiny of outside, experienced eyes can be most helpful.

This committee activity must never be undertaken as a witch hunt or as an usurpation of management. There must be a clear understanding as to the frame of reference within which any discussion between directors and middle management is conducted. The bank's staff must never be afforded grounds for wondering whether suddenly it has acquired a new set of superiors, nor confused by tactless comments which could undermine the established chain of command. Under a properly drawn job description, and with a definite plan of procedure prescribed, a management evaluation committee affords a splendid line of communication between the working management of the bank and its board of directors. In addition, by being able at all times to answer why and how, the self-esteem of management itself is fostered. It should be noted that appointment of this committee is not common practice in American banks, and it cannot be recommended in the absence of directors whose qualifications would suit them for the duties contemplated.

Rotation of directors among the several committees may prove worthwhile. While all directors acquire a general knowledge of what is going on by virtue of the reports delivered regularly at the board meetings, only by participating at the working level can broad experience be gained.

RETIREMENT POLICY FOR DIRECTORS

To afford proper representation from business, industry, and finance a bank should have a board comprised of a balanced mixture of leaders in these areas. It is also advisable to seek a good cross section by age. A board comprised solely of young men, though demonstrably competent in their particular fields, will not have been tested by the years, nor will it have had the opportunity to gain the respect of the community on a basis of performance. Conversely, a board comprised solely of those who have attained the pinnacle of their effectiveness, but are of an average age which could disrupt the continuity of the board simply by the inexorable workings of time, can place the bank in a difficult position.

To avoid this, an increasing number of well-managed banks have adopted retirement programs for their boards, thus facing up to the necessity of maintaining the vitality and continuity so essential to this crucial function. Opinions differ as to the proper age for retirement just as they differ with respect to disqualification for further board membership when the individual in question is no longer actively engaged in his or her earlier occupation. Although circumstances alter cases, by and large that rule leads to the best results which avoids the subsequent necessity for making embarrassing exceptions for particular cases.

CONCLUSION

The operation of a bank's board of directors should never be routine. Banking is a flexible and highly competitive business. It is the duty of the board to establish clearly defined policies consonant with changing times, and to demand of management both reasonable adherence to policy and creditable standards of performance thereunder.

This is a cooperative endeavor, the results of which are only partially judged by daily achievements. In the final analysis, the real success of a board of directors and management alike is measured by the success of the bank.

Chapter 3

Alternative Organizational Structures

*Philip F. Searle**

The particular organizational structure which a commercial banking organization adopts depends upon a number of factors. Among these are the financial aspects of the decision, opportunities in the marketplace, competitive considerations, and legal constraints related to the structure of the commercial banking system as they apply to that particular banking organization. The latter is of particular importance, for the structure of commercial banking in the United States is very complex. The United States is the only nation which contemporarily attempts to meet its basic needs for financial services and accommodation with a system which is comprised of thousands of separate banking corporations supervised by 50 state authorities, three federal agencies on a direct basis, and several other federal agencies assuming varying degrees of less-direct regulatory involvement.

FORMS OF BANKING

It is not the purpose of this chapter to go into the history of the evolution of the commercial banking structure of the United States. Suffice it to say that it is that structure which in large part governs the form of banking selected by banking organizations, although in a number of states there are alternative forms of structure available to banks. Subject to regulatory approval, a bank may elect to remain independent, or join a holding company, or merge with another bank,

---

* Chairman and Chief Executive Officer, Flagship Banks Inc., Miami, Florida.

or be part of an informal chain, and so on. Basically, however, although the banking system of the nation retains important small unit characteristics, there have been growing pressures for banking organizations which are sufficiently large to finance expanding businesses and industries. These structures have resulted in a development of various types of multioffice banking.

Unit Banking

A unit bank is one which conducts all of its business at one location. This definition should be expanded to mean not only a bank operating at a single location, but also one which is independently owned and managed. It is difficult to count the number of such banks with precision, but it is estimated that approximately one half of the nation's banks come under that expanded definition.

Branch Banking

Branch banking refers to a system whereby a single legal entity operates more than one office. The basic characteristic of a branch banking system is that the various operations are controlled from a main office, though obviously the degree of managerial independence delegated to branch managers varies considerably among various banking organizations.

Holding Company (Group) Banking

Holding company banking, which was in the past frequently described as "group banking," takes two forms. A bank holding company, under federal law, is a corporation that controls one or more banks in the United States. Under the law, a bank holding company is closely regulated by the Federal Reserve Board and is permitted to engage only in banking and in activities closely related to banking.

One form of holding company banking is thus the multibank holding company; i.e., the bank holding company which controls two or more banks (and may also control one or more nonbank subsidiaries engaged in activities closely related to banking). The other type of bank holding company is a corporation that controls just one bank and also may control one or more nonbank subsidiaries engaged in activities closely related to banking.

Chain Banking

Chain banking commonly refers to the ownership or control of two or more banks by one or more individuals. Information on the number of banks included in chains is sketchy at best, but it is certain that chain banking is far less extensive than holding company banking or branch banking. In January 1963, a report on chain banking was submitted by Chairman Wright Patman to the Select Committee on Small Business of the House of Representatives. That report utilized a much broader definition of a chain, attempting to redefine "control," and to include a number of other forms of ownership, including bank nominees, insurance companies, brokerage firms, and so on, in addition to individuals. Further, the new definition suggests that bank loans secured by stock in other banks might provide a chain relationship among banks.

Satellite and Affiliate Banking

Satellite and affiliate banking resemble chain banking; there is usually common ownership of the affiliated banks, although that is not necessarily a factor. In a number of instances partial common ownership exists. Essentially, an affiliate bank is one which is organized by the directors of another bank, which may provide assistance in organizing the bank, in its original financing, and in its staffing. A satellite bank is one which also has an affiliate relationship, but this description is usually applied in instances where the new bank is located some distance from the larger "parent" bank and makes extensive use of the various facilities provided by that bank. Understandably, satellite and affiliate banking relationships exist primarily in states which prohibit or inhibit branching.

Correspondent Banking

Correspondent banking was developed originally in response to a need for a system of collecting checks drawn on banks located in other parts of the country, as well as a necessary supplement to the unit banking system with respect to other services. Decades ago, when payment of interest was permitted on demand accounts, country banks maintained deposit accounts with city correspondents, which competed for the deposits by paying interest on them and providing various free services. Even though payment of interest on demand accounts is no longer permitted, a wide variety of services is still provided by correspondent banks for their bank depositors.

Correspondent banking can be described as a business relationship between two banks, and it, therefore, would not necessarily be a form of multioffice banking. Nonetheless, there are certain relationships between country banks and their city correspondents which are so intimate as to suggest that the result is a form of multioffice banking.

Where a country bank relies upon its city correspondent for management, investment, and operational advice, such a bank may actually be less independent than a satellite bank, or even less independent than a large and predominant branch in a branching system.

BASIC ORGANIZATIONAL STRUCTURE[1]

It is not the intent of this chapter to discuss the actual internal organizational structure of the banking entity, nor the process of managing such entity. However, the determination as to which organizational structure is to be utilized (i.e., unit, branch, holding company, or group banking), where there is sufficient flexibility to allow a choice between two or more such options, inevitably involves consideration of certain basic elements of organization structure.

The various functions of the banking organization must be grouped logically. This grouping may be achieved by specialization, by desired results, or, in the case of branch banks or multibank holding companies, by geographical areas. Specialization refers to the nature of the function, such as the credit function, the business development function, the operational function, or the trust function. By such grouping, the maximum of specialized knowledge and skill is utilized.

Grouping of Functions

Grouping by specialization is the grouping of staff and service activities that are to be provided for the benefit of many functions; i.e., the personnel staff gives counsel and guidance to all divisions of the organization, including top management. Activities related to the provision of stationery, office supplies, and equipment are for the benefit of all. Centralization of these specialized services is usually economical.

Although there is not universal agreement as to the effectiveness of grouping of duties by the desired end result, this form of organization clearly has a place in banking. Many managers believe that the person who makes a loan should be responsible for its collection, inasmuch as the granting of a credit is not an end in itself. This responsibility does not imply that the lending officer must also do the clerical processing and engage in all phases of collection, but it does mean that the officer granting the credit is responsible for seeing that all proper steps are taken to assure repayment of the obligation. Otherwise, that officer could escape the responsibility for a poor credit decision.

Other examples of this philosophy are embodied in the "profit cen-

---

[1] See Frank M. Dana, "Organizational Structure and the Process of Bank Management," in William H. Baughn and Charls E. Walker, eds., *Bankers' Handbook* (Homewood, Ill.: Dow Jones-Irwin, Inc., 1966), pp. 38–44.

ter" approach to management. Such centers include branches, departments, subsidiary banks (in the case of multibank holding companies) wherein the branch manager, department head, or subsidiary chief executive officer (CEO) as appropriate, are responsible for the results of the operations of each such grouping.

Line and Staff Functions

Irrespective of the basic organization structure adopted by the banking entity, another important principle which must be observed in designing that structure is to segregate clearly the line functions from the staff functions. Line functions are those which are directly involved in accomplishing the objectives of the bank, such as processing deposit accounts and lending money. Only those persons with line responsibility and authority initiate and carry through the primary activities necessary to reach the objectives of the institution. These individuals could well be termed the "chain of command" which is formed by successive delegation of authority and responsibility from the top of the organization to the bottom. These relationships of one level to the next are "line" relationships.

As an example, a lending officer is a line officer. By acting upon loan applications, he or she directly performs the duty that is essential to accomplishing one of the objectives of the bank. On the other hand, a personnel officer is a staff officer. This officer helps the line officers perform their duties more effectively by counsel, guidance, and assistance, but has no authority over them. "Staff" thus refers to the supporting elements, to the people who give specialized advice, assistance, and service in such disciplines as planning, organizing, accounting, control, methods, and personnel administration.

CENTRALIZATION VERSUS DECENTRALIZATION

Except in unit banking structures, a key question is how much authority is to be placed at the branch or the subsidiary bank level, as distinguished from the regional or group headquarters or the institutional or head office or parent corporation level. The degree of authority delegated to the branch managers or the subsidiary bank chief executive officers, and through them, to their subordinates may range from practically none to almost complete autonomy. The branch or the subsidiary bank may be, in fact, the local bank rendering all needed services and making virtually all decisions. At the other extreme is the subsidiary bank and/or the branch that is little more than a teller's window, receiving deposits, cashing checks, and handling the most routine transactions.

Most branch organizations delegate authorities somewhere in-between these extremes. Most multibank holding companies tend to delegate even more authority to their subsidiary banks, although there is a discernible trend toward less local autonomy in multibank holding company organizations. Determination of the degree of delegation or local autonomy is frequently influenced by the competition. Perhaps an ever greater influence is the availability of competent personnel at the local level to properly discharge responsibility.

In all except unit banking organizations another significant question is how much centralization of processing is contemplated. While there may be considerable decentralization of decision making, centralization of routine processing may produce significant savings. Furthermore, certain processes may be centralized while others are decentralized to branches, to larger subsidiary banks, or to regional service centers. Deposit accounting, for example, might be handled in the branch, in a larger subsidiary bank, or a regional headquarters, whereas processing of consumer installment loans and real estate loans might be more centralized. Clearings and transit might receive different treatment than collateral loans. The ultimate solution to these problems must be pragmatic, taking into account distances, the availability of effective transportation and/or communication, and the period of time within which the processing must be accomplished. Other pertinent factors have to do with the economics of the choices and the quality and the accuracy of the results achieved.

Management's attitude toward business development is another important factor that must be considered before the basic organizational structure is finalized. Inevitably there will be different plans for various types of business customers. Major corporations, such as those of a regional or national character, may call for attention beyong the capability of branch officers or the chief executive officer of a smaller, multibank holding company subsidiary. At the other extreme are such personal services as Christmas clubs and school savings, which can be readily promoted at the branch or the subsidiary bank level. Complicated and more sophisticated specialties, such as trust and international banking, may call for centralized attention. More complicated types of credits, such as large construction loans, leasing, municipal financing, and dealer plans may require a sophistication that is not present in typical branch or smaller subsidiary bank.

The basic question is whether a specialist located in the central or regional office should promote these specialized services. Also a factor is the degree of potential for these various services in the branch or subsidiary bank service areas, and the expenses that can be afforded to pursue such prospects.

Different Degrees of Decentralization

A.   Little authority and decision making at the branch or subsidiary
     bank level (this is the situation when most of the authority is re-
     tained and exercised at the head office or at the holding company
     headquarters).

Pros

   Functional Expertise. Obviously, it is less costly overall to have a
   few experts in the head office or the holding company headquarters for functions such as loans, operations, and marketing than
   to have such expertise in every branch or subsidiary bank.

   Minimum Training of Personnel. The less expertise that is required
   at the branch or subsidiary bank level, the less training of such
   personnel will be necessary.

   Maximum Control. Since most decisions are made centrally, there
   is little difficulty in controlling the decision makers.

   Little or No Reporting, Reviewing, and Discussions. Conversely,
   to the extent that decisions are made in the branches or the subsidiary banks, maintenance of some control over application of policy
   is necessary. This can result in time-consuming preparation, review of reports, and ensuing discussions or correspondence.

   Centralized Processing. There is a natural tendency toward centralization of processing when decisions are made in the head office
   or in the headquarters of the multibank holding company.

Cons

   *Fewer Services in Branches or Banking Subsidiaries and Perhaps
   in the Banking Organization as a Whole.* Many services cannot
   be rendered, at least acceptably, unless those in the branches or
   the subsidiary banks having contact with the customer are able
   to perform them. Some services have a time factor or a person-
   to-person relationship that will not permit referral to headquarters
   for decision or action.

   Slower Service. Akin to the foregoing are the services that can be
   performed by referral to the head office or the holding company
   headquarters but which are delayed because of the time of communication, the multiple handling, or the reference to off-premise
   records.

   Impersonal Service and Customer Dissatisfaction. Lack of opportunity for the customers to state their cases face-to-face with the
   decision maker can be disturbing and frustrating for them. Coupled with this is the decision maker's lack of personal knowledge,
   and to some degree, interest in customers and their problems.

Less Interest in Local Welfare and Local Activities. Unless the decision makers participate actively in local affairs, it is difficult for the banking organization, whatever its structure, to demonstrate its good citizenship. In competition with unit bankers or branch managers, and subsidiary bank CEOs who possess a relatively high degree of autonomy, it is unlikely that a branch manager with little authority can become "the local banker."

Imbalances of Functional Impacts. When each head office or headquarters of a multibank holding company exercises substantial functional authority over the branch manager or the subsidiary bank manager, it is inescapable that there will be "pushing and pulling." The impact of the activities of various functional heads in the home office can hardly be a balanced mix that represents top management's intentions. The head office or headquarters operational function may strive for efficiency and economy at the same time that the business development function is pressing for promotion, good public relations, and the ultimate in customer service and satisfaction. While these are not necessarily incompatible, the degree of emphasis that each branch manager or subsidiary bank CEO will give to the respective functions is likely to be influenced by the impact upon him of the representative of each function rather than by the best overall interests in the bank. This violates one of the cardinal principles of organization; i.e., no person should have more than one "boss."

B. Maximum authority in decision making at the branch or the subsidiary bank level (this is in contrast to the foregoing centralization in the organizational structure which occurs when the head office or the headquarters of the multibank holding company functions only in advising, assisting, observing, and reporting).

Pros

Widest Variety of Services Conveniently Rendered. When possessed with sufficient expertise and authority, branch or subsidiary bank personnel can render almost any service without reference to administrative specialists. This is to the advantage of the customer in obtaining desired services conveniently and promptly. It is to the advantage of the bank because it can sell services which it could not otherwise sell.

Most Personal Service. Not only can the services be rendered more conveniently and promptly, but there is the likelihood of greater personal interest on the part of the staff member. Also, the staff member can adapt the service to the needs and preferences of the customer.

Greatest Knowledge of and Interest in Local Conditions. This is
the basis for good corporate citizenship. Active participation in
community affairs by the bank staff not only discharges a civic
obligation, but reflects credit upon the institution.

Maximize Job Satisfaction. This is an advantage particularly applicable to branch managers and subsidiary bank CEOs. Instead of
being the proverbial "cog in a wheel," the manager or subsidiary
CEO is the "wheel." Managers have the challenge of the authority,
responsibility, and accountability for a full service banking operation and are measured and rewarded on the basis of the growth,
soundness, and profitableness of the banking unit. Their contribution to the welfare of the overall banking organization is that
which not only their superiors can measure, but which they can
also measure for themselves. Further, there exists the prestige
of being the local banker and not merely the paid functionary
of a distant head office or multibank holding company headquarters.

Maximum Motivation to Develop Branch or Subsidiary Bank. When
a person is operating on his or her own, pride and self-interest
stimulate the individual to greater ingenuity and effort.

Minimum Problems of Communication. When the authority to
make most decisions is vested in the branch or in the subsidiary
bank, the necessity for communication with the head office or
with the holding company headquarters is lessened substantially.

Broadest Development of Personnel. It is incumbent upon the local
banking unit to work with its staff to develop in it the competencies
necessary to make the right decisions and otherwise to discharge
responsibilities of a nearly autonomous banking entity. This development is in the best interests of each employee, the local banking
entity and the community. It provides opportunities for advancement to the individual and a needed pool of talent for the banking
organization overall.

Cons

Problem of Achieving Uniformity. A high degree of decentralized
decision making may result in undesirable differences in the interpretation and implementation of institutional policies. Effective
communication of top management's desires is more difficult.

Problems of Control. Not only must policies be communicated, but
there must be adequate means of detecting noncompliance or
misinterpretation without in effect removing the authority of the
branch manager or subsidiary CEO. It is therefore essential that
there exist within the organization methods of measurement and

control by which the superior can measure achievement, performance, and status.

Problems of Training and Development. The more numerous the
technical services rendered in the branches or the subsidiary
banks, and the wider the dispersion of such banking facilities,
the greater the problem of providing training and assistance in
self-development. Carefully tailored programs for training and
development, capably executed, are an absolute necessity.

Regionalization

In other than unit banks, another major aspect of organizational
structuring to be considered is that of regionalization. This approach
places the most decision making neither in the branches or subsidiary
banks, nor in the head office or holding company headquarters, but
rather in a regional headquarters. There are several variations of regionalization, but they all have the following characteristics:

1. They do not offer all of the advantages of maximum authority at
   the branch or the subsidiary bank level.
2. They do not have all of the disadvantages of highly centralized
   authority.
3. They do not require the breadth of personnel competence in the
   branch or subsidiary.

One type of regionalization provides what is essentially a duplication
of head office administration in each regional headquarters. This structure has a regional chief executive officer and frequently one or more
general assistants, depending upon the overall size of the region both
in terms of assets and geography. There would be certain functional
specialists and their staffs in the regional office. This approach adds
two levels to the organizational structure over the plan in which maximum authority and autonomy is delegated to the branches or the subsidiary banks.

The more levels through which top management must communicate
with those in the branches or the subsidiary banks and, conversely,
communication by the branches or the subsidary banks to top management, the more likelihood exists of potential misunderstanding and
loss of impact. These additional levels also tend to be costly and to
slow down action and reaction.

In spite of the foregoing disadvantages, regionalization may be justified. Until the appropriate competency can be created in branch or
the subsidiary bank staffs, regional administrative personnel may be
the best way of providing needed support. There is the danger, however, that instead of promoting the development of competency at

the branch or subsidiary bank level, regional staffs might become permanent "crutches." Another plus factor to the regional organization is that these headquarters may help to preserve the image of a bank as a local institution after it has been acquired either to be merged into a bank system or to be operated as a subsidiary of a holding company.

Another type of regional organization is at first glance similar to the foregoing type, but differs substantially in that regional personnel have no authority over the branches or the subsidiary banks. The regional office serves as liaison between the respective administrative functions in the head officer or the holding company headquarters, and the branches or the subsidiary banks.

They provide the banking units counsel and advice related to their respective specializations, and observe and report to their functional superiors in the head office those situations which they believe need correcting, and which they have been unable to normalize by their usual methods. Where the levels of competencies in the branches or the subsidiary banks permit, this organizational plan is clearly superior to the authoritative regional plan because it permits reasonable autonomy in the branches or the affiliate banks.

Some banking organizations attempt to reduce the expense of this additional organization layer by having the regional functions, whichever of the foregoing philosophies is followed, vested in a large branch or large subsidiary bank. The branch manager or the subsidiary bank chief executive officer serves as the regional head, and utilizes certain of his or her own staff personnel to provide support, monitoring, and guidance to the smaller banking entities to be a part of that region. Although such responsibilities and duties inevitably reduce the ability of those managers to perform full-time duties for the organization to which they are basically assigned, this concept of regional organization can result in less overall cost and shorter lines of communication between top management and the banking units. It is, however, essential that the larger branches or banking subsidiaries serving as regional headquarters (in addition to their roles as banking organizations) be well staffed and possess the capacities and authorities to provide the desired services and direction.

Just as there are different plans for regionalization, there are differences in relationships between regions and the head office of a branch system or the headquarters of a multibank holding company. In one version, the head of each region reports to top management. Specialists in the region report to the regional manager and have only a staff relationship with their respective head office staff on a line basis, and are under only the broad supervision of the head of the region. Each approach has some potentially vexing relationship problems inherent in it, especially in terms of communications and responsibility relationships. Of a special concern is the situation where the regional specialists are responsible to more than one superior.

The foregoing discussions, have covered various approaches to organizing larger banking organizations. It is axiomatic that in the larger banking organization, special care must be devoted to effective management controls. Good communications, clear definition of authorities and responsibilities, the setting of goals, the monitoring of results, the initiation and carrying out of corrective actions—all of these are important in any banking organization. All become more critical in the multi-unit banking structure frequently operating in widely dispersed or significantly dissimilar markets.

UNIT BANKING[2]

As was noted earlier, a unit bank is one which conducts all of its business at one location. Less than a dozen states permit only unit banking, although in certain of those states unit banks are permitted to belong to multibank holding companies. Because of the large number of unit banks, the fact that they operate in different types of markets, their coexistence in certain states with branch banks and/or subsidiaries of multibank holding companies, and differences between the economies of various states, it is difficult to generalize as to the characteristics of unit banks. Nonetheless, there are some generalities which can be applied to unit banks as a whole, although there are, of course, many exceptions either absolute or by degrees, to these observations.

Unit banks tend to be smaller in total assets and to operate in smaller communities. They tend to have less management and employee turnover, and are assumed to have a reputation of being friendlier and closer to their customers than are branch banks or subsidiary banks in multibank holding company systems. They frequently have, and capitalize upon, the "country banker" or "community banker" image, which includes financial counseling (not necessarily sophisticated, but often very effective) and a quick reaction time to credit requests.

The range of services which they offer is usually smaller than that provided by multiple office banking systems, but this fact must be viewed in the perspective that the ability to provide additional services is, at least in part, a function of size. Unit banks generally lack the level of in-house technical competency in a variety of banking disciplines which may be available, at least upon call, to branch banks or subsidiary banks in multibank holding company systems. They are gen-

---

[2] See Bernard Shull and Paul Horvitz, "The Impact of Branch Banking on Bank Performance," *The National Banking Review,* vol. 2 (December 1964), pp. 141–86.

erally less sophisticated in lending techniques and loan administration, usually relying more upon their personal knowledge of the borrower in making credit decisions.

The ownership of unit banks often is in the hands of a few shareholders, and the management group frequently has a significant ownership interest in the institution. This usually results in a built-in informal incentive program for the stockholder/management.

In terms of general financial characteristics, unit banks have lower loan-to-deposit ratios, higher ratios of time and savings deposits to total deposits, and lower salary and fringe benefit expenses as a percentage of total revenues, all as compared to multiunit banking systems.

Unit banks perform somewhat differently in branch states than they do in unit bank states. Unit banks in branch banking states experience a different type of competition, whether through direct competition or the possibility of market entry by branch banks, than in unit banking states. Loan-to-asset ratios are also considerably higher at unit banks in branch banking states.

In recent years there have been rather frequent references to the fact that there were too many small banks; that the small bank was doomed to extinction; that the small unit bank could not and did not deserve to survive. A variety of reasons was given for such observations, among them being the lack of the technical and financial capacities to serve larger customers, the relative inflexibility of such banks in terms of interest rate sensitivity both on loans and on deposits, the difficulty such banks encounter in attracting talented successor management, and the difficulties in disposing of large blocks of bank stock in small unit banks upon the death of the major shareholder/chief executive officer.

There is doubtless some merit to the foregoing reasons why some unit banks will have difficulty in the future. Nonetheless, there are also persuasive reasons why many unit banks survive and will continue to be a constructive force in their own community and an important element within the banking industry of the United States. There will be available to unit banks technical services from correspondents and from service centers which will enable those banks to provide sophisticated modern banking services, especially those of an electronic nature, to their customers. There are already informal groupings of banks which provide technical and financial services on a group basis which the individual banks themselves could not furnish. There are growing indications that the quality of life in many of the communities served by unit banks is more attractive to a number of talented young bankers than the more lucrative compensatory packages offered by banking organizations in metropolitan areas, given the comparative quality of life in those environments, and that attracting competent management to promising unit banks may not be as difficult as was perceived earlier.

Undoubtedly the growth of "pure" unit banking has been slowed, and many of these banks will by merger or affiliation join multiunit banking systems. Nonetheless, there are markets, many of them in smaller communities, where such banks can flourish and can be an integral part of the economic fabric of that market. Thus the report of the impending demise of the "pure" unit bank is indeed premature.

BRANCH BANKING

As was noted earlier, branch banking refers to a system whereby a single legal entity operates more than one office. Another view of many banks is that branches are distribution points for bank services. In most instances these are in a very real sense "retail" facilities, although in certain large banking organizations branches can function more as "wholesale" facilities, offering banking services tailored for the specialized needs of certain types of larger corporate customers operating in that branch's market.

There is a natural desire on the part of many commercial bankers to expand the services offered by their banks into promising new markets and to implement such expansion on as efficient a basis as possible. Expansion into such areas by establishing a new branch of an existing bank is often the best method by which such expansion of services can be achieved.

Benefits of Branch Banking[3]

1. Better Service to the Public. Branching tends to reduce the population per banking office, making more banking facilities available to the public and thereby making banking more convenient.

2. Better Bank Management. Banks tend to have better training programs when they realize the necessity for providing branch managers. More qualified personnel may be attracted when there are visible needs for branch managers.

3. Better Use of Bank Resources. Facilities for branch offices are usually less expensive and less pretentious than those of a unit bank of comparable size. Further, there are savings with respect to branch office operations as compared to unit bank operations in such areas as a separate board of directors, advertising, purchasing, and administrative costs. Certain of these savings will result from the elimination of the necessity of maintaining separate accounting and reporting for

---

[3] See John W. Budina and Virgil Brewer, "Branch Banking: What It All Means," *Florida Banker,* January 1976, pp. 18–20.

each location. The financial, operational, and human resources of banks are more effectively utilized when entering new markets with a branch than in entering new markets with a new unit bank.

4. Broader Diversification of Assets and Deposits. Branch banking systems tend to have a better mix of loans and deposits in terms of types of customers and geographical diversification. While the head office of a branch bank located in a downtown area will have a heavier concentration of commercial business, it can operate branches in suburban areas and compete for individual deposits and consumer loans to augment the commercial activities of the main office. Conversely, banks with headquarters in suburban areas may be able to branch in commercial-type downtown areas and compete for commercial loans and business deposits to reduce dependence on consumer loans and individual deposits. Penetration of such downtown markets by suburban banks, however, tends to be more difficult and costly than penetration of suburban markets by banks headquartered in downtown areas.

5. Better Mobility of Funds. Certain market areas generate more deposits than can be loaned, while others generate loan demand which cannot be met by deposits available locally. A branch system can more readily shift funds to the markets where they are needed. Informal arrangements by unit banks for loan participations cannot move funds from a capital-surplus to a capital-deficient area as effectively or with such certainty as can a branch system or a multibank holding company.

6. Better Service to Existing Customers. A bank may be able to continue to serve existing customers when these customers move from one area to another or to a neighboring community where that bank happens to operate a branch. In these situations, the cost of establishing new relationships and opening new accounts is reduced very substantially. Given the mobility of the nation's population, this advantage can be a meaningful one for branch banks.

7. Broader Variety of Services. Services provided by multiple office banks can include more sophisticated forms of commercial and installment lending, international banking, automated customer services, a variety of personal and corporate trust services, and the like. Because branch systems tend to be larger banks, they are in a better position to afford the personnel and the facilities to offer such services, both through their head office and through their branches.

8. More Competitive. Partly because of the broader base of services described above, and also because of the ability to penetrate various geographic markets with banking units other than the head office, branch systems can be more competitive than unit banks. They are in a position to take advantage of market potentials in shopping malls, dense residential areas, and other areas with high consumer traffic, and to better compete with unit banks as well as with other financial institutions which increasingly offer a range of services similar to those provided by commercial banks.

9. Flexibility When a Location Becomes Unprofitable. When market conditions change such that a banking location no longer possesses long-term potentials, it is much less expensive and traumatic to close the branch (or to move it elsewhere) than to dissolve a bank.

Branch Administration[4]

The subject of branch administration is broad, for there are varying needs of markets which can dictate the administrative and managerial philosophies applicable to the branch system. These can vary widely among banks. The pros and cons of centralization versus decentralization were discussed earlier; the relative degree of decentralization will inevitably impact the branch administration system utilized by a bank.

Irrespective of the administrative concepts employed by the bank, it must be recognized that the branch manager is a major determinent of success. In virtually all branching systems, it is necessary that the branch manager possess a relatively broad range of banking skills, although not necessarily as broad as those considered essential for the chief executive officer of a unit bank of comparable size.

The branch manager is responsible for maintaining adequate safeguards over assets, including loans, physical assets, and work force assets. The branch manager normally operates in a retail environment, and must also be a marketing and business development manager.

For the branch managers to function effectively, it is necessary that they be provided specific objectives and plans for achieving those objectives. Bank management must ensure that lines of communication are open and clear. Branch managers must know what is expected of them, and be able to secure support in those areas which they need to achieve those goals. Adequate, timely, and accurate reporting of actual performance must be provided to all levels of management, so the branch managers will be able to react to deviations from their own plans, and top management also will be able to monitor performance and institute corrective action where necessary.

Because there must be procedural consistency in each branch of the system, it is the responsibility of the branch manager to insist upon consistent and accurate adherence to the established procedures. Uniformity is necessary because of the centralization of the bookkeeping and check processing functions.

---

[4] See Hugh Spinozzi, "Administering a Branch System," *Florida Banker,* March 1976, pp. 67–72.

Branch systems typically have procedural manuals which aid the branch managers and their subordinates in adhering to standardized procedures. Many branch systems also utilize control documents which provide in a single source a reference file for the evaluation of the performance of the branch.

Future of Branch Banking

There are certain trends now apparent with respect to branch banking:

1. State branching statutes will continue to be liberalized, both by states and perhaps by federal legislation.
2. A significant number of unit banks will become branches by merger, especially as state branching laws are liberalized.
3. There will be an increasing emphasis on electronic service delivery vis-à-vis the traditional "brick and mortar" branch.
4. There will be less reliance upon the traditional "brick and mortar" branches than in the past, and a number of such installations will be discontinued because of high operating costs and/or declining market potentials.
5. New "brick and mortar" branches will tend to be less elaborate and less expensive, and will utilize more electronic service delivery capabilities.
6. Branch systems will be supplemented by off-premise automatic teller machines of a free-standing nature, located in company facilities where employees can utilize such installations, and as point-of-sale terminals in business establishments.
7. Banks will be allowed to branch across state lines, the initial changes being where major markets are located in two or more states; it is likely state lines will first be crossed by automatic teller machine branches than by "brick and mortar" branches.
8. There will be greater competition facing commercial bank branches, especially from nonbank competitors with ever increasing numbers of bank-like powers. The home access to financial services by telephone will represent an additional future competitive threat to bank branches.
9. Relative to other forms of banking structure, branch banking will continue to become more and more important as a type of banking structure.

HOLDING COMPANY BANKING

The growth of the bank holding company form of organizational structure has been very significant in recent years. An overriding reason for the formation of bank holding companies in earlier years was the fact that such companies could assume many of the characteristics of branching systems. Later growth of the bank holding companies has also involved the desire of banking organizations to broaden their service base by offering financially related services.

Advantages of the Holding Company Form of Banking Structure

In the case of the larger bank holding companies there are advantages to be realized in corporate financing. These include a wider range of choices and opportunities in financing, the advantage of leveraging, a larger borrowing limit, broader access to capital and money markets, the existence of the corporation as a stronger credit eligible for more attractive terms, improved marketability for its stock, and the use of excess capital of banking subsidiaries for holding company expansion.

The bank holding company has the advantage of offering a potentially expanded base of financial services. A particular advantage in connection with these services is that they may be offered without geographical limitations; about 40 percent of such applications approved in recent years has involved companies operating in states other than the holding company's primary state of activity.

This form of structure offers advantages to the community or local market served. Local bank identity is maintained with the banking subsidiary having its own official staff and its own board of directors. There may remain within the bank a high degree of local autonomy in such areas as loans, community activities, and use of local services and/or suppliers where they can be provided the bank on a cost-effective basis. Bank subsidiaries have greater lending capacity, for the combined resources of the bank holding company's subsidiaries can be aggregated to meet large local demands for credit. Loan demand in capital-shortage markets can be met by participatory assistance from other banking subsidiaries in capital-surplus markets. There is the availability, especially in the case of smaller banking subsidiaries, of a number of specialized skills and expanded services that bank might not otherwise be able to provide its customers. These include assistance and counseling in the more complicated types of credits, investment advice, data processing services, trust services, international banking, and the like. The local subsidiary bank, through being able to provide such additional services and capacities, can be a more effective competitor in its own market.

When a bank is acquired by a holding company, there are advantages to the acquiree bank's shareholders. Assuming that the affiliation is effected on a stock-for-stock basis, the shareholder receives a more marketable and widely traded stock. There is a better diversification of earning assets, rather than having loans entirely dependent upon only a local economy. There exists greater ease and flexibility in meeting the bank's own capital requirements. Finally, competent, continuing management of the bank is assured, which cannot always be a certainty when the bank operates independently.

There are advantages to the officers and employees of banks affiliated with bank holding companies. More career opportunities will arise in a larger banking organization. Promising employees have more opportunities for advancement, and the existence of a systemwide fringe benefit program gives candidates for transfer or promotion greater mobility. Senior officers of subsidiary banks may spend more of their time on the financial and economic needs of their communities and their customers, for many time-consuming routine duties are performed for them and their staff by the parent corporation staff.

Disadvantages of the Holding Company Form of Banking Structure

The management of a bank holding company must coordinate the efforts of several separate and distinct management teams for optimum long-range return to shareholders of the parent corporation. In dealing with the boards of directors of the subsidiary banks, therefore, the parent corporation must provide logical, well-conceived, and convincingly presented policies and programs in order to receive the maximum of cooperation from such boards.

Advice from the parent corporation is normally expected in a number of important areas, including annual budget, the election and/or promotion of senior officers, the choice of new directors, officer salaries and/or bonuses, dividend policy, capital expenditures, and a number of other policy and operational subjects.

The accounting and reporting of financial data of subsidiary banks tend to be more complicated and is somewhat more burdensome than for a single bank. The separate identity of the subsidiary banks results in multiplying budget and profit-planning problems by as many banks as there are in the group.

Minority shareholders can present various problems. They may question the amount or the propriety of parent corporation management or service fees charged the subsidiaries. They may react unfavorably to the elimination of dividends in order to increase retained earnings in a subsidiary where such was done for the purposes of increasing its capital position, irrespective of the propriety of such an action.

Where a bank has excess capital, the existence of minority shareholders may discourage paying exceptionally large upstream dividends, even though such a dividend would otherwise be justified.

Although there may be little effect upon the individual subsidiary, bank holding companies are subject to an additional layer of supervision: the Securities and Exchange Commission. There is also supervision of the parent corporation by the Federal Reserve System, as well as normal bank regulatory supervision of the banking subsidiaries.

The operating expenses of the parent corporation come between the shareholders and earnings of the subsidiaries, although this disadvantage is reduced as the holding company becomes more effective and achieves the benefits of economies of scale. Nonetheless, these expenses, if not properly controlled, can become a source of concern to bank regulators and to minority shareholders, especially if the banking subsidiary absorbing these charges is not especially profitable.

Depending upon the particular state, there can be differing tax treatments of bank stocks as compared with the tax treatment of dividends of bank holding companies. In addition, Federal Reserve regulations make the movement of excess funds between banking subsidiaries more cumbersome than would be the case for a branch system.

If management of the parent corporation does not have the proper abilities and experience, excessive involvement in activities of nonbank subsidiaries can produce disadvantageous results to the holding company by poor earnings and stock price, even if the company's banking affiliates are consistently performing well. Further, too great an emphasis on "growth for growth's sake" on the part of management may result in excessive prices being paid to acquire new subsidiaries, diluting per share earnings.

Structural Alternatives in Holding Company Management Organizations

The majority of holding companies today attempt to achieve a workable, and yet an inevitably delicate balance between local autonomy for the banking subsidiary, and at the same time achieve sufficient centralization of functions to gain group efficiencies.

In the production of banking services for subsidiaries, the relationship between the holding company and the subsidiaries can take several forms. The holding company can create service subsidiaries or service staff groups. It can use the staff and the production facilities of the "lead" bank or it may serve simply as an arrangement through which groups of banks secure needed services from larger banks or from service centers outside of the holding company. In some cases, the subsidiary banks (in what is obviously a very loosely knit kind of holding company relationship) can produce their own services or obtain them from banks or other sources of their own choice.

Although there is a discernible trend toward more centralization of service functions and policy making by holding companies, the majority of such companies currently operate with rather moderate policies. Wherever possible, there is an avoidance of duplication of staff specialization in the parent corporation and the major subsidiaries. Those functions are centralized if economies of scale can be realized. Meaningful local autonomy is usually most evident in the providing of customer services by the banking subsidiaries especially in meeting the credit needs of the bank's market. The holding company's expertise and capacity are frequently brought to bear in this regard as needed. Finally, while individual banks are motivated to be effective, imaginative, and resourceful in their local efforts, strong controls are maintained by the parent corporation in basic areas to ensure that the profit plan produces optimum results.

Future of Bank Holding Companies

1. The bank holding company movement has matured partly because of the problems it has endured in recent years, and in part because it had already achieved much of its potential growth prior to the 1974–76 recession.

2. The pace of acquiring banks will not reach earlier proportions; there will be fewer candidates, and bank holding companies will not be willing and/or able to pay prices comparable to those paid in the past.

3. The centralization of bank holding company functions, service delivery, and control will proceed rapidly. Companies will operate more economically and will report better performance.

4. The trend toward the acquisition of a broad array of nonbank financial affiliates will be slower than in the past.

5. There will be a continuing concern on the part of the regulatory agencies with respect to capital adequacy, liquidity, servicing of debt, the managerial and financial condition of bank holding companies and their subsidiaries, potential competition, leveraging, and upstreamed management charges.

6. There will be only an occasional addition to the "laundry list" of permitted nonbank activities for bank holding companies. These will be in very limited areas. Approval of bank holding company entry into any of these activities will be subjected to more demanding requirements of demonstrating public benefits, needs, and convenience.

7. Continuing efforts will be made to insulate the activities and

the risks of nonbank subsidiaries so that they cannot jeopardize the solvency and the safety of the banking subsidiaries.

8. The bank holding company segment of the banking industry consists in part of many young, relatively inexperienced companies. That segment has learned many valuable lessons in the 1970s and will benefit from them.

9. The bank holding company form of structure is a viable type of organization and is especially well suited to take advantage of technological changes which are now appearing in banking and which will occur in the future. The performance of such companies will improve as bank holding companies mature, consolidate, and grow less rapidly but more soundly.

OTHER FORMS OF BANKING

Any discussion of other forms of banking structure pales when viewed in the overall context of the relentless trend toward expanded branching powers, the maturation of the bank holding company structure, and the demonstrated ability of the well-managed, independent unit banks in promising markets to survive and to prosper, even when faced with branch or holding company subsidiary competition. Chain, satellite, and affiliate banking all seem destined to assume less and less importance as the other major trends continue. Appropos of this is a (June 1976) order of the Federal Reserve Board which reiterates that it will apply to chain banking situations the standards as to financial and managerial resources that it applies to multibank holding company applications. These other forms of organization, already representing only a very minor segment of the banking industry, will play a decreasing role and will be confined to relatively special instances where some unusual advantage can be gained.

Correspondent banking, however, while likely to be less important should continue to be a major influence in the nation's banking structure. Correspondent banking would be affected significantly by the payment of interest on demand deposits (either by correspondent banks or by the Federal Reserve Banks, or by both). Thus, it seems clear that the services of correspondent banks will continue to be used by unit banks. Smaller banks will continue to need assistance with overloans and overlines and will be increasingly dependent upon larger banking organizations in their efforts to bring the benefits of advancing banking technology to their customers. If there is a promising future for independent banks, there is also a promising future for correspondent banking.

Chapter 4

The Environment of Bank Management

Kenneth A. Randall*

"Winds of Change" is a cliché often applied to our economic and banking system. But the new challenges that confront the banking system are more like gales than mere gusts. And they portend changes in bank organization—particularly organization of top management.

Organization, as we know it, is a management means of structuring people and work to achieve an end or an objective—whether that be a product or service. Top-management organization is designed to specify the mission that gives meaning to the objective and its means of attainment. If the organization survives and prospers, presumably top management has done something right in the way it has organized itself and its operations.

Banking has clearly survived. Its 150-year history of living through all kinds of problems—wildcat banking, money panics, bank failures of the 1930s, reconstruction of the Western world—would indicate an ability to organize to meet changing needs and objectives. But there's reason to believe that banks have survived in spite of their organization rather than because of it.

THE MODERN ENVIRONMENT

Today's changing economy calls for a restructuring of banking so that it can more effectively do its basic work as a converter of funds. In that respect, banking is not substantially different from any other

* President, The Conference Board, New York, New York. (Formerly, Chairman, United Virginia Bankshares Incorporated, Richmond, Virginia.)

industry that constantly examines and reorganizes to fulfill business objectives more effectively.

But the basic work of banking endows it with a special institutional role. In the United States, it is the basic catalyst, the lubricant, that makes the total economy function, produce, and grow. In this respect, banking is different; it has a distinct role. And in today's world, events and pressures force special emphasis on organization of top management so that it can devote time, skill, and emphasis to that mission. The focus in one word is leadership.

The events and pressures that force a new focus on leadership for banking need little elaboration—especially for the banking community. Since World War II, the world has redefined itself into new economic and philosophic power units. The part defined as the "Free World" is made up of those countries that are basically the non-Communist, market-oriented societies of Western Europe, North America, and the Pacific Basin. From time to time, the more developed countries in Latin America also participate in this bloc of "Free World" nations. In juxtaposition to this group of nations are the two groups espousing Communist ideologies—one, the Soviet Union and the Comecon (Council for Mutual Economic Assistance) countries that make up the European interface; the second, that group that has aligned itself around the People's Republic of China and the Communistic philosophies that have developed in the Orient. A fourth group, still lacking leadership, is an unstable mix of underdeveloped or nondeveloped nations with important supplies of raw materials and energy components necessary for the preservation of the more developed, industrially based northern neighbors.

Of these major groups, that portion we may call the "Free World," or at least the non-Communist market group, finds itself in the least disciplined and perhaps the most difficult position to compete with the monolithic Communist structures that border them on the east and on the west.

Among the nations involved in this bloc of market-oriented economies is a growing sense of interdependence. There is recognition that no one economy can go it alone; that they must interrelate their development programs and activities. There is a heightened awareness that the maintenance of vitality of the Free World relies most heavily on the economic leadership that can be provided by the United States. Business and banking leaders through the Free World are asking: "Does the United States have the economic vitality, the economic will, the economic commitment to be the strong leader? Can it provide an economy strong enough to bring the other participating nations up to a standard of well-being for their people?"

Compounding this concern for the vitality of the Free World has been the growth since World War II of the one person/one vote philosophy. This very powerful tool has enabled the populace of each nation to vest with government the responsibility for maintenance of employment, stability of price levels, and rising standards of living. And when government exhortations or decrees fail, there occur further incursions into the workings of the economy through nationalized industries, incomes policies, or what might generally be called managed economies.

Thus, between competitive pressures of the Communist blocs and the internal national pressures for more managed economies, the plea of the Free World bloc is a clarion. That plea places new burdens, new opportunities, domestically and internationally, on top management of the banking community.

PROFESSIONALIZATION OF BANKING

Indeed, in the world of today, it may even be appropriate to paraphrase an old saw, that "banking is too important to be left to the bankers." At least that may be the case if, by bankers, we mean the stereotype of the 30s, 40s, and even the 50s, when the banker was largely the product of long-term employment; when a new bank president could proudly announce that his election to high office was the result of perseverance from his early days when hired as a runner of 15-plus or minus a few years. During those long ago days, banking was an "art" to be learned by time spent in the office and practiced by men in blue pin-striped suits with gold chains across the vest—a posture not totally removed from even today's banking scene.

That particular stereotype gave way in the 50s and 60s to a different image. The professional—the credit man and his co-technician, the investment man—came into their own as the supertrained few who moved into top positions. Banks were major recruiters at the graduate schools of business. They offered a story of and a reputation for career development that was outstanding.

This new breed and the post-World War II demands upon credit created an environment that promoted expansion. We saw the rise of credit leverage become a major factor in corporate growth with the U.S. banks and banks abroad ready, willing, and able to exploit this new market for their services.

The worldwide expansion of banking was expressed in the traditional measure of footings in domestic operations, in the creation of a London office, and overseas branches. The domestic image of the aggressive virile bank was found in new architectural monuments—the new head office in the center of every city of size in America and the expansion of branches where possible. Banking was size, posture, image, and art. Banking had confidence in its role, its power, its full knowledge of its tomorrows. The full proof of banking's position would be visible in the harvest of the future. The conventional indexes all supported the knowledge of the harvest in earnings per share and price-earnings ratios.

New services, new markets, capital expansion with debt instruments, and the flexibility of the holding company were the elements of this new banking. But then came the 70s to demonstrate the frailty of straight-line progressions. The problems that started with Penn Central, currency exchange losses and frauds, construction loans, real estate insurance trusts (REITs), condominiums, W. T. Grant, and poor loans were then exacerbated by a major business downturn. Lessons were learned: Buildings can become a drag on earnings; the "best loans" in national and international credits are not riskless; tax equivalent earnings are only real when you have taxable earnings; capital does not come just from debentures; Wall Street can be fickle; boards of directors are not just to tie business to the bank and expand loans; the SEC can act as a bank regulator; not all loan loss reserves can be used to absorb loan losses; and Congress is not impressed by banking's role.

From this cauldron of experience emerged new bankers—many with patched and scarred skins—more fully aware of the traditionally important role of banking. Once again, banking recognized that it is a converter of funds, and that the fractional reserve system limits the ability of banks to locate and buy deposits.

A second fundamental relearned is that banking was, is, and shall be the spread of risk over large numbers. Concentration of credit or investments only to maximize return is courting again future disaster.

The fundamentals then are the locating and purchasing of deposits, the placing of these deposits out in earning assets of quality, and the spread of risk through investments and through lending capacity, and putting it all together in an efficient operation. And, at the risk of offending "friends" at some banks, "bankers" at others, the total experience suggests that it is "managers" and management who are truly fundamental to both the functions and mission of banking.

DIMENSIONS OF THE JOB

Against this backdrop of new and vital pressures, old and spotty history, and varied personalities, what are the salient points of organization that merit attention? Most significantly, how does top management organize itself to carry out its essential work?

"Essential work," pragmatically speaking, derives its definition from what the chief executive finds important in providing leadership. Prescriptions for leadership are difficult to come by. But experience and portents point to four distinct areas that constitute the essential work of the chief executive officer (CEO)—and by derivation of top management—in fulfilling that leadership role.

Delegation of Authority

A most significant body of work grows out of the fact that the CEO manages a diverse group of resources—capital, time, and people—that have to be organized. Relative to organization, the more obvious questions management must answer are relatively simple—and basic to any organization. They relate to the essential architecture of the functional elements of the business, to the structure of delegated authority that makes it possible to convert a complex of varied functions into groups of coordinated activities that are capable of achieving mutually supportive goals. On the architecture—i.e., the grouping of activities and attendant delegation of authority—banking can, and has, learned much from other types of industry, principally manufacturing. The advantages of divisionalization and decentralization cannot be overstressed. A careful analysis of banking operations can produce internal regrouping of functions that provide emphasis for specialized services, discrete markets, and regional needs. When such regroupings are accompanied by greater delegation of authority, top management finds it possible to hold lower levels accountable for specific results.

Of course, widespread delegation of authority implies planning and control or evaluation mechanisms that the chief executive can rely on. It implies that the determination of the parameters of reserved authority, and conversely the limits of delegated authority, is most crucial to the chief executive. It's his or her job to determine what decisions are so high risk or have such great impact on the short- and long-run viability of the bank that they must be reserved to the top. Objectives, plans, policies, budgets clearly are of this nature. So are decisions relating to managerial succession and the development of rewards systems that provide incentives rather than disincentives. Thus, the chief executive has to give a substantial organizational emphasis to staff units that can act as an intelligence agency—in the best sense of the term. The use of staff to provide certain essential services is commonplace. What warrants stress is the more effective use of corporate staff units, especially highly developed finance, personnel, and planning units that can operate as agencies of corporate planning and control. Essentially, that's another way of saying that staff is the organizational mechanism whose critical role is to assure the CEO that all organizational elements are working toward mutually supportive goals.

The Board of Directors

Relationships with the board of directors constitute a second major body of work that preoccupies the chief executive. For all that the board is his superior, is the body to whom he is legally accountable, is the one force that can fire him, it is the chief executive who supplies leadership for the board. The extent of board members' commitment and involvement in the company's affairs arises from the stimulus provided by the chief executive. He plays a primary role in recruiting members, he is the primary source of information, he can optimize the skills and knowledge the board members bring to the corporation.

Granted that recent events are shifting some of the initiatives, the effectiveness of the board in fulfilling its stewardship role is still largely determined by the chief executive. The tasks involved in developing and maintaining good relationships with the board are too many to enumerate. But, summarily, this considerable work serves to:

1. Help the board to carry out that which it is accountable for.
2. Allow the board to constantly assess whether it can continue to have trust and confidence in the chief executive.

Other Relationships

Time and effort involved in relations with key customers, banking associations, counterpart contacts or peer group meetings, conferences, and so on constitute a third important body of work. Here clearly, in many instances, the time required is greater than the importance attached. But it is recognized that there is only one chief executive in any company. For banking chief executives, the risks involved in not pursuing these necessary contacts—where substitutes for the CEO personally are unacceptable—are too great to hazard. The opportunities they may and often do represent are too great to miss.

The fourth body of work—which emerges as the fastest growing and potentially most crucial—is inadequately summarized in such terms as external relations or public affairs. Relations with the external community, with external pressure groups, and with government at all levels are a burgeoning part of the CEO's job. Banking, because of its catalytic role in economic development, has been and continues to be the target of constituencies that seek legislative reforms and regulatory restraint. And governments at all levels are not hesitant to pile regulation upon regulation that tend to inhibit the effectiveness of the banking industry.

In short, the total external socio-legal environment—with government as a principal factor in creating that environment—is the domain the CEO grapples with. To understand, to react to, to operate as a voice in shaping that environment, commands his or her attention.

Obviously, these four bodies of work are not discrete. They operate synergistically to create the whirlpool of activity that constitutes the work of the CEO—and top management. Conceptually, the CEO can be looked at as the executive on the spot—with the spot being at the vortex of vectors the CEO must respond to:

The organization he or she heads.

The board of directors to whom he or she is legally accountable.

The peer groups with which he or she must associate.

The community at large, principally government, that increasingly redefines both the mission and accountability of the CEO.

ORGANIZATIONAL RESPONSE

Today, organization of top management in banking has meaning and is effective only to the extent that it provides adequate emphasis to this total body of work. Proliferation of lofty titles, at which banking is quite accomplished, is not the answer.

What is increasingly apparent is that even the most competent chief executive lacks the time, skills, and omniscience to adequately contend with all these vectors. In certain respects, this is not a novel situation. Traditionally, it's brushed off by setting up what has been called a Mr. Outside and Mr. Inside. Unfortunately, this suggests an old refrain: "And don't mess with Mr. In-Between." These days it's Mr. In-Between who has the action.

What this suggests—indeed urges—as an approach to organization structure is an analysis of the time, effort, and skills required to adequately provide the coordinated action and decision making that spells leadership. For some companies, a two-person team at the top may be adequate; one, probably the chief executive, concentrates his or her time and attention on the board and external factors; the other, probably labeled a chief administrative officer, concentrates on internal organization elements. But to avoid being considered merely Mr. Outside, the chief executive must retain significant areas of decision making, significant involvement and communication links that will allow him to say with comfort, "The buck stops here."

Beyond the more evident two-person team at the summit is the collegial chief executive office. Such a top-management organization recommends itself for larger banking institutions, whose operations are more far-flung and complex, whose turnaround time is necessarily longer and, most importantly, whose functions enjoy high visibility and play a critical catalytic role in national and international economic development.

In creating a "chief executive office," the CEO does not abandon his ultimate accountability. Rather, the CEO assembles a small group of individuals of varied skills and backgrounds whose primary responsibility as a group is to concentrate their time an attention on what has already been referred to as the work of top management. Special areas of attention may be assigned and/or discrete areas of decision making may be delegated within the group—with the CEO, of course, retaining those relationships that require such personal involvement as contacts with government agencies.

The effectiveness of the chief executive office depends, to a large extent, on shared vision and compatible personal chemistry among its members. But the key is clearly the chief executive and his or her capacity to use the office as an enlarged linchpin between the internal working of the organization and the larger world of which it is a part. Thus, in a final sense, the chief executive organizes top management to develop and carry out a mission that is congruent with the changing world.

Reflecting on the duties and responsibilities of American banking, it is in this matter of congruency that I find most crucial to be the problem of leadership in the Western world. Because of banking's reach into all facets of our economic life, the mantle of leadership falls upon the banker's shoulders. Indeed, the preservation of the Western society may only be accomplished if the banking community takes a broad view of its responsibility and, with full commitment, prepares itself to fill the role of leader.

Chapter 5

Evolving Corporate Policy

Thomas I. Storrs*

WHAT IS A POLICY?

Policy is a series of decisions made in advance.

There is a core of truth in this statement which is heard in varying forms from corporate philosophers and planners. Most corporate decisions must be made within the framework of established policies, procedures, and usage. Few companies could afford the luxury of dealing with each transaction from Square One, researching the effects of alternative actions, evaluating them for costs and benefits, and selecting the optimum course.

There is a parallel in individual behavior. Imagine a day in which you made every decision without looking to your experience and your acquired reference points. The choice of a necktie would require evaluation of each tie on the rack as to its compatibility with the suit you proposed to wear, and so on through the day. Instead of this laborious procedure, you do in fact draw on the lessons of experience, both your own and others, to guide your decisions. We generally describe these guiding rules as principles, ethics, habits, or other terms that indicate a continuing force in our behavior.

The corporation is a creature of the state, and its basic guiding rules are the laws which apply to it. A corporate officer ignores this fact at his or her own peril, and most corporations spend substantial sums of money to assure their compliance with the statutes that apply to them.

* Chairman, NCNB Corporation, Charlotte, North Carolina.

I am very much obliged to my associates, Frank Gentry and John Jamison, for their substantial contribution to this chapter.

Next in importance after the laws of the state come the corporation's self-imposed laws, the policies it has adopted in pursuit of its corporate goals. Some of these policies are merely reiterations of applicable laws:

Example: "There shall be no discrimination in employment practices because of race, sex, religion, or national origin.

Others simply recognize moral principles which are so widely held as to have the force of unwritten law:

Example: "No employee shall deal with a customer or supplier in which he or she has an ownership interest."

Unique to the corporation are the policies which have as their purpose the achievement of the corporation's specific goals. That statement opens an attractive door for semanticists to debate goals versus policy. As a working hypothesis, consider goals as susceptible to definition and measurement, while policies generally are not.

Goal: "This bank will be the leading international bank in the Texas Panhandle."

Policy: "This bank will provide resources to meet all the international needs of its domestic customers."

Policies can become so specific as to constitute descriptions of procedures.

Example: "This bank will finance only new cars, except that used cars may be financed when they are:
1. Less than two years old.
2. Domestic makes.
3. Undamaged in wrecks, etc."

There is nothing to prevent such specificity except the judgment of the policy makers.

Since the dawning of the age of the computer, it has been popular to devise systems in which routine decision making is delegated to the computer in order to optimize the use of our scarcest resource, the competent human decision maker. One can readily visualize a policy framework superimposed upon a procedural structure to comprise a program which would guide the disposition of each proposed and actual transaction. As a transaction reached such a program, it would be screened for conformity to broad policies, then, if approved, tested more specifically against detailed criteria, and having passed this stage, turned over to procedural instructions for accomplishment.

Example: Proposed automobile loan.
1. New: To item 2.
    Used: To item 3.

2. Downpayment > 20 percent: to item 4.
    Downpayment < 20 percent: reject
3. Age < 2 years: to item 4.
    Age > 2 years: reject.
4. Borrower's unencumbered income > payments: approve.
    Borrower's unencumbered income < payments: reject.

    And so on.

Such an approach has proved very useful in the application of *procedures* to decisions affecting a flow of transactions. Credit scoring of consumer loan applications, for instance, is adaptable to this type of application.

It is a less suitable system for the translation of *policy* into action, primarily because this translation must provide for a two-way flow of data. A meaningful body of policy which provides guidance for the handling of current transactions changes shape in response to changes in its environment and changes in the transactions which are explicitly or implicitly offered to the firm. Thus policy makers—and more about *them* later—require continuing input about transactions which do not take place as well as those that do.

Examples: "What are the other characteristics of consumer credit applicants who are rejected because of a policy against loans to part-time workers?"

"Are policies governing the employment of tellers unduly restricting the future availability of managers?"

Needs for such data can rarely be adequately foreseen. In other words, it would be very difficult to design a computer system that would not only implement policy at the routine level but *also* provide appropriate feedback for the modification of policy. These modifications, by their nature, are dependent upon changes in factors which managers and planners regard as given—or at least subject only to forces for change which are difficult to predict.

POLICIES DO EVOLVE

Despite being the reference lines for current operations and future planning, policies are not immutable. A good set of policies cannot, like blue chip stocks of a simpler age, be acquired and locked in a safe deposit box. Indeed, the structure for change may be the most important feature of a body of policy.

There is general agreement that the best operating decisions are made at that level of management closest to the facts which also has an undestanding of the policy issues involved (as well as competent decision makers!). A similar rule may hold for the evolution of corporate policy: The best policy *originates* at the level closest to the facts where there is a competent executive who has authority over the activities affected and who has the necessary understanding of the immediate effects of a policy change on the company's progress toward its goals.

Example: The chief commercial loan officers may be ideally situated to *propose* modifications in lending policy to adapt to changes in loan markets, competition, interest rates, etc.

Note two key words in the above: *originates* and *propose.* Facts flow upward in an organization like salmon swimming upstream to spawn. There is competition, the current is fierce, and some obstructions can be bypassed only by special arrangements. It is essential that these facts be captured as early as possible in policy proposals before they succumb to the opposition. It is equally essential that these proposals be subject to review and final approval at a point in the organization where corporate goals are fully understood. What is good for commercial lenders may not be best for the total bank, even though many of the best ideas for changing commercial loan policies will come from commercial lenders.

This fact provides an interesting challenge to top management. It can be adequately met only by paying careful attention to the environment for the easy flow of facts and ideas that might suggest modification of policy (keep those salmon ladders working!) and the adoption of well-understood goals for the corporation.

POLICIES FORM A HIERARCHY

Some policies are subordinate to others even though all are called corporate policy. We touched on this when we noted that obedience to the law must come before everything else and that, if pursuing the dictates of some company policy in a particular instance could lead to a violation of the law, then clearly we must obey the law. However, there is a hierarchy of policy of another sort which is manifest when all elements of a policy in a given area do not prove equally adaptable and sensitive to changes in the operations environment. For example, the goal of being "the leading international bank in the Texas Panhandle" may or may not require a policy of "taking position in the foreign exchange markets to accommodate customer needs." It is clear, however, that to be the leader the bank may occasionally need to modify its foreign exchange policy in response to a competitor's move.

To clarify this point and illustrate the process of policy setting, we can follow the evolution of a hierarchy of policies at an actual banking company. The example is from the general field of balance sheet management, although it could be drawn from almost any major policy area of the bank. (The discussion that follows is not a substitute for other sections of this handbook dealing with management problems in asset and liability management.)

Many banks have a policy of "managing the balance sheet to minimize the impact on earnings of uncontrollable movement in market rates of interest." At the bank with which the author is most familiar, this has been a policy for many years. This policy has not changed, but pursuing it has caused many changes in corporate policy with respect to acceptable pricing and terms of loans, criteria for proposed acquisitions, and several other areas.

In the 1960s, this bank had a surplus of fixed-rate liabilities in the form of demand deposits and, to a lesser extent, consumer savings deposits. As a result, earnings went up and down with the prime interest rate. To correct this imbalance of interest-sensitive assets and liabilities, two new policies were adopted: First, the bank's holding company sought to acquire firms that were countercyclical to the bank in their market sensitivities. The most obvious step was the acquisition of a consumer finance company, which makes fixed-rate consumer loans, financed in part with commercial paper or bank lines, and, therefore, has higher earnings when market rates are low. Second, the bank itself adopted a policy of "aggressively seeking consumer loans, including indirect loans made through dealers," to bolster the countercyclical side of its own portfolio.

As might be expected, these two policies were successful, and the fundamental imbalance between interest-sensitive assets and liabilities was corrected. In fact, had the policies not been adjusted later, the imbalance would have been overcorrected and a new problem created. By the early 1970s, the acquisitions policy had to be changed completely and the indirect consumer loan policy had to be modified in order to limit the growth of fixed-rate assets to a level that could be funded with fixed-rate liabilities. Interestingly, the policy adjustment with respect to fixed-rate assets proved to be more difficult to communicate and implement than was the original policy. As long as the interest-sensitivity gap existed, a fairly simple and aggressive policy of asset creation was appropriate. However, once balance was achieved, fine tuning was necessary. The process of fine tuning by top management can very easily be viewed as indecision by those whose entire job is dedicated to the creation of one type of asset. This illustrates that, while policy must be made at the top, its successful implementation requires that it be understood at all levels of the organization.

In this balance sheet management case, policy had to adapt and evolve because of its own success. Policy changes or adjustments can also be forced by changes in the external environment. That also happened in the example under discussion. Before 1974, the prime rate had never exceeded 10 percent. In addition, changes in both the prime and money market rates had been rather gradual in those earlier years as the Federal Reserve focused more on interest rates than on money market aggregates. The prime rate and money market rates now change very rapidly, and no one knows how high, or low, rates may go in the future.

These external events did not affect the fundamental policy of "managing the balance sheet to minimize the impact on earnings of uncontrollable movement in market rates of interest." However, these external factors made implementation of the basic policy more difficult and complex and forced changes in several subordinate policies and the creation of some new policies.

Before external factors forced changes in underlying assumptions, the policy statements had not been concerned with the commercial loan portfolio. However, statutory interest rate ceilings, which had not previously been a problem, came into play and converted some floating-rate assets into fixed-rate assets. Finally, with rapidly changing rates, the tendency for spreads to narrow in a rising market and to widen in a falling market became an important factor.

In order to cope with these changes, the firm reorganized certain staff functions, and a small balance sheet management unit was specifically charged with recommending subordinate policies *and* procedures to implement the basic policy, which remains the same in spite of drastic changes in both the environment and the bank's position.

It is now policy "to the extent possible to write commercial loans on a floating-rate basis tied to daily changes in the prime." It is also policy to require line groups to provide information on the level and nature of their assets and liabilities so that tactical decisions can be made by senior management to keep the net interest margin on a steady growth path.

Reflecting on the evolution of policy in this case, the most striking fact is that the basic corporate policy has not changed. However, subordinate policies and organizational relationships have changed. Evolution of policies is not a neat, textbook process, but it is necessary if policy is to be alive and useful rather than a collection of platitudes.

CONSISTENCY VERSUS ADAPTABILITY

While basic policy can be consistent and relatively stable over time, the subordinate policies in the hierarchy are subject to frequent change. In a large, diversified firm with a decentralized profit center structure, a key responsibility of policy makers is to allow enough variation to meet the special needs of various units, without allowing this variety to undermine the discipline of the basic policy.

Suppose that the company in our case had adopted a policy that "all commercial loans should float with the prime on the day the prime changes." Its commercial finance and factoring subsidiary competes in an industry which has for a long time floated all rates on a monthly basis. A branch of the bank in a small town faces only one competitor, a local bank which makes all loans on a fixed-rate basis. The branch manager feels that he must meet his competition or lose profitable business. The leasing subsidiary operates in another state which forbids variable payment leases. How should policy adapt in each of these cases? What is the trade-off between consistency and adaptability?

The leasing company case is the simplest. It will obey the law. The question becomes one of how much emphasis to place on leases in that state. The small-town branch is more interesting. It seems likely that there is a demand for floating-rate loans in the town if they are properly marketed. And a capable manager will find ways to float as much of the branch portfolio as possible. Certainly, this manager can be expected to request more exceptions than other branch managers, but the policy continues to apply. The commercial finance subsidiary is somewhere between these, facing an ingrained industry practice but not a legal requirement; here the combined judgment of the subsidiary manager and the executive management must be brought to bear to determine whether to treat the situation as an exception of policy or to treat it as a permanent adaptation of policy to a particular line of business.

WHO ARE THE POLICY MAKERS?

Ask a chief executive officer to list the function of the board of directors, and the first entry will be: "Sets the policies of the corporation." Ask an outside director his or her role relative to policy and he or she will say, "I object when I learn of policies with which I am not in agreement." Ask a candid chief executive officer what his role is relative to policy, and he will likely say:

One of my most important duties is to give final approval to policy proposals. I sometimes originate some proposals, but more typically they come to me through my senior associates who evaluate their probable results and give me their views as to whether they should be adopted. I must concern myself with the contribution of the changes toward achieving the company's goals and the possible risks and adverse effects which they entail. I take this responsibility seriously, for I am the final checkpoint among the officers on the allocation of corporate resources.

Now, ask this paragon of candor about the role of the board of directors in setting policy, and he will be less precise in his answer:

First, I try to make sure that my directors are familiar with our more important policies, for they are ultimately responsible for them and sometimes must take formal actions to implement them. The process of presenting a policy change to the board forces me to do my job well, for I don't like director questions I can't answer, and that aversion of mine forces my subordinates to do a particularly good job of preparation before they come to me. My board has diverse backgrounds and the give-and-take between us sometimes brings up ideas which the officers have missed. I can't remember formal action in a board meeting to modify one of our policy proposals, but I know I have made changes based on the reactions of board members, some of which were very subtle.

Don't misunderstand me. My outside board members do not have my knowledge of the facts of our business, and there's no practical way that they can. They look to me for directional leadership of the firm, for we've agreed that it is my job to fill that role. But they do oversee my performance, and that includes frequent review of goals and evaluation of policies for their contribution to the attainment of those goals. I find that evaluation vital to corporate health.

CONTINUITY VERSUS CHANGE

So, policies provide the cement between the building blocks of experience and the corporate structures of today. But it has to be a plastic cement, never hardening out unduly against the forces of change.

Corporate leadership—both management and directors—face no more challenging task than managing this change. Organizational strength thus lies in ability to adapt wisely to changes rather than in a Maginot Line of fortresslike policies firmly implanted in the facts of another age.

Chapter 6

Formulating Social Policy as an Integral Part of Bank Policy

Louis B. Lundborg*

Corporate policy today must contain an ingredient that has become increasingly crucial to all lines of business, but is even more relevant to banking. It is the element of social policy—the definition of the bank's concept of its corporate role and responsibilities in relation to the community it serves and to society as a whole. In today's world—and tomorrow's—that ingredient is so basic that it could appropriately be taken as the starting point for all policy formulation; but as a minimum it should be used as a gauge against which to test all other segments of the bank's corporate policy.

HISTORICAL PRECEDENT

The examination and questioning of the social responsibilities and social performance of business is not a new phenomenon.

St. Thomas Aquinas, considered by many to have been the greatest mind of the Middle Ages, once wrote that business could be justified only so long as it was used for one definite purpose; namely, "the good estate of the household." The good businessman, Aquinas said, would sell at a just price to provide a living wage in order to promote the common good.

All of society's institutions—businesses, governments, educational systems, professions, and churches—have been questioned from time to time as to their contribution to the common good. When these

* Chairman (retired), Bank of America, San Francisco, California.

institutions have listened to the questions openly and reformed themselves so as to be in more general harmony with the values of the society in which they exist, they have usually survived the questioning and, indeed, prospered by it. But when they have neither listened to the questioning nor instituted reform, several things have happened. In the least dramatic circumstance their influence has declined. More often, and in addition, they have been "legislated" and the legislation has often been punitive as well as remedial. In the most dramatic circumstances, the institutions being questioned have been abolished. This concept of questioning, followed by change, is an historical fact that we all need to bear constantly in mind as we look to the future.

But while it is not new, this questioning is more profound, more consistent, and more sophisticated than at any time in the past.

NEW ELEMENTS

What are the new factors that bring the issue so sharply into focus now? In other words "why corporate responsibility—now?"

There are four major reasons.

First, our society is faced with some enormous problems. The corporation does not exist in a vacuum. The society is our environment— the soil from which we draw our nourishment. If we fail to take active steps to assist in alleviating the society's problem, we, in effect, are befouling our own nest.

Second, the dramatic rise in consumer sentiment in the United States demands a new searching look at business ethic and attitude.

Third, we are in the midst of a far-reaching change in value systems. The corporation that fails to perceive this and does not amend its own value systems to conform more generally to those held by the society at large is going to find itself in deep and serious trouble.

Public Franchise.   Fourth, and related to all of the three previous points, is the question of corporate legitimacy. Corporations in the final analysis exist by public consent—public franchise if you will. Institutions, be they corporate or public, derive their right to exist on the basis that the majority of people feel they are serving important societal needs.

The corporation has to earn its right to exist and to function—and it has to earn that right all over again every single day of its life. That is what we mean when we refer to franchise: it is not a fixed, vested property; it is not a guaranteed right. It is a privilege that can be given—has been given—and can be taken away.

Therefore, the corporation has no choice but to consider public needs and values and to formulate its policies accordingly. It must do so as a matter of earning its franchise, as a matter of self-preservation, and as a matter of obligation to do its share of the world's necessary work.

RELEVANCE TO BANKS

What is true for corporations is especially true for banks, basically because banks are more central to business and to society than any other field of business. The history of American banking is intertwined with the growing understanding that banking is so basic to society's needs it cannot be left unregulated. More than having "gone public" one could say that banking *is* public.

Since commercial banking is so extensively regulated, the question arises, "Doesn't this ensure responsibility?" At the risk of telling a weary traveler that the crest of the next hill isn't the last on the journey, the answer is definitely "no."

The fact is regulation cannot cover all elements of policy. And policy options which were once agreed to be the sole purview of the corporate executive have now moved into the public arena. Public expectations about the role and performance of large corporations have undergone a remarkable change over the past ten years and this change in expectations will continue to evolve.

For as long as we can see into the future this transfiguration of expectations will be one of the most important, if not *the* most important facing American management. The corporation that fails to perceive this and does not amend its own value systems to conform more generally to those held by the society at large is going to find itself in deep and serious trouble.

If we believe that—and we should—then it is up to us to make our contributions to society so significant that there will be no vacuum for government to walk in and fill. The encroachments of government into private life have always been, to some degree, in response to default.

This means that we must take the initiative in seeking out the places where we can make our greatest contributions.

BANKS, THE COMMUNITY—AND BEYOND THE COMMUNITY

Banks already are, and have historically been, closely tied into community life. A banker knows the community's people, its businesses, its strengths and weaknesses, its beauties and its ugly spots. Opportunities for community service grow so naturally out of the bank's daily activities that bankers are constantly found in key positions in the community fund and in other charitable and civic organizations. He or she may be a member of the school board, the local chamber of commerce, or the municipal finance committee. Whatever is happening in the community, a banker is likely to be involved in it somewhere.

But problems and interface today go far beyond historical dimensions, and far beyond community. The era of the "open society" is upon us. The times ahead are so dynamic that no company, least of all banks, can safely follow past patterns or drift along without a plan or policy, merely reacting to situations.

The problems of our time—the rise in consumerism, the emerging new value system reflected in the public and our employees, and the questioning of the legitimacy of some or of all business practice—directly affect the banking industry. No corporation, no industry, and certainly, no bank can remain healthy in a hostile environment. These forces that now impact upon business in general and banks in particular will have a profound effect upon the future of your bank and mine. Therefore, a bank's approach to social policy must be as basic and integral a part of its business plan and policy as is its loan or trust functions.

WHAT IS EXPECTED

To earn our franchise, we are expected to do the right things on at least three levels:

At the first and most basic level, produce and deliver our product or our service at a quality and at a price that the market will find acceptable.

Then, to carry on our own operations in a way that is fair to our employees, to our customers, and to our suppliers, and that minimizes damage to the environment in which we operate.

And finally, to be aware of the problems of the total community and of the total society, and to do our share toward solving them.

The evolution of public attitudes toward these responsibilities and the gradual progression from the lowest level toward the highest has been steady and accelerating.

At the basic level, the public's expectations for business are already pretty well undergirded by laws—laws that we can expect to see updated wherever performance falls short of promise.

At the middle level, most of us have lived through the full cycle as public attitudes have translated themselves into laws and regulations in labor relations, in consumer practices, and in environmental conditions.

In the consumer area I can remember when the doctrine of caveat emptor still ruled. In essence, what today's consumerist movement means is that caveat emptor is not only dead but buried miles beneath the earth, and in its place has arisen the doctrine of let the seller beware. The consumer has demanded the right to be informed, the right to safety, the right to choice, and the right to be heard. The rights of consumerism have already had, and will continue to have, a profound effect on the marketplace.

The consumerist movement is not a fact that will pass. It will not pass because it has been institutionalized. The storefront lawyers, the class action suit, the governmentally organized consumer affairs specialist, and the host of consumer protection legislation have served to build the consumer movement into the fabric of our society.

At the higher level, the past few years have seen public expectations change in a volatile fashion. If nothing else, this has hammered home the need to deal with these problems in a rational way.

The formulation of social policy as an integral part of basic policy making is, therefore, simply the creation of a management system to be responsive to the changing needs and expectations of all public sectors.

GENERAL PRINCIPLES AND TAILORED APPLICATIONS

I would not be so presumptuous as to advocate a specific course of social responsibility for every individual bank. Each bank's serving area differs. The problems of one community are not the same as another's. The policies, problems, resources, skills, and size of each bank will also differ. But I am also certain that each of our banks in its own way must begin, or accelerate, a long-range program of social responsibility. And the most important things my own bank has done have had nothing to do with size, and only incidentally to do with the fact that we were a bank. So, although I can offer no universal blueprint, there are certain principles and methodologies that we have followed at Bank of America that may be of help to other banks.

Transcending any principle about the implementation of social policy is one critical factor. It sounds simple, but it is difficult: we must train ourselves to hear the question being asked.

Unfortunately, for all too human reasons, it is sometimes difficult to hear the question. One of the more common reasons is that we don't like the questioner. But I suggest that the operative issue is not the legitimacy of the questioner, but the legitimacy of the question. So, my transcendent advice is to try to hear the question.

Within this framework of a reasonable openness to question, I think there are several fundamentals to an effective social policy orientation for any bank.

The first is a clear, unambiguous, definitive statement in writing by the senior management concerning the general principles of corporate conduct in relation to social issues.

Depending on how the particular bank records its basic policies, this statement can be contained either in a separate formal policy document, or as a section in an annual report, or in a standard practice manual for employees, or in a major address by the chief executive officer. What is important is not its typographical form but the fact that it make crystal clear to all officers and employees just what the company expects of them in this area.

Second is a continuous series of unambiguous statements by corporate management on specific issues. Let me give an example of the second.

General Motors' chief executive officer, addressing himself to the question of equal opportunity and his company's policy in this regard, wrote as follows:

> We are not in a position to change our people's personal biases or prejudices. However, it must be made abundantly clear that it is the policy of this corporation to carry out a viable affirmative action program for our minority employees. Every supervisor, middle management officer, or senior executive at General Motors is entitled to personal beliefs, but those beliefs must not interfere with company policy. Therefore, anyone who is not able to conform with company policy in equal opportunity employment and affirmative action has no place at General Motors.

I find that message quite clear. And, I suspect, so did everyone else.

Top-management pronouncements, however important, will not do the entire job. We don't allow the auditing of our banks' books to rest on the hope that men of goodwill will make everything balance out right. I think the same applies to the social policy function. We must bring to it the same methodology as we bring to other areas of our business. That, in effect, means setting priorities, establishing goals, assigning responsibilities, establishing accountability, and measuring results. The method for accomplishing this at Bank of America may not be directly applicable or appropriate to your banks. However, I think the methodology we have evolved over the past few years is sound. Therefore, let me describe our mechanism in the hope that it may have some adaptive value to you.

ONE BANK'S SOCIAL POLICY STRUCTURE

We have two operating committees mandated to monitor all matters relating to the bank's social performance. The first is the Public Policy Committee of the board of directors. This group is composed of six outside directors who meet monthly to review the bank's performance in social, political, and environmental areas. They monitor existing programs and, when necessary, recommend policy changes.

The board committee walks a very careful chalk line to be sure that it deals only with policy, and does not try to make operating decisions that are the proper prerogative of management. But it pulls no punches and takes its job very seriously.

Within the bank management itself, we have a senior committee, called the Social Policy Committee. This group is responsible for identifying problems and issues and changing bank policy and practice where appropriate. It also designs positive programs to fill the needs of the bank's different publics. The nine-member committee is made up of executive officers of the bank who are charged with operating many of the bank's major divisions. It is configured this way since the members' functional responsibilities have a major impact on the bank's social performance. To give you an idea of the level of this committee, it is composed of the executive vice president in charge of the California Division (our branch system throughout California), the executive vice president and general counsel, the executive vice presidents for loans, personnel administration, international banking planning and strategy, the controller of the bank, and the vice president in charge of internal communication.

To support these two committees, we have a social policy department which has overall responsibility for identifying issues and needs, making recommendations for change, and coordinating, administering and/or monitoring socially oriented research programs and activities throughout the bank. The staff includes an environmental and land-use consultant and the urban affairs department with offices in Northern and Southern California. The urban affairs department is the program management arm of social policy and is responsible for the bank's special housing, small business, urban development, minority purchasing, executive loan, and volunteer efforts.

One member of the social policy department is specifically responsible for tracking committee-approved recommendations from their inception to completion and makes periodic status reports to the group.

If no progress is reported by the end of a specified period (usually a quarter), the staff member moves into action. First he or she talks with the person directly responsible for the implementation; if nothing happens there, the next stop is with the member of the committee who oversees that function; if there is still foot-dragging at that level, it is reported to the full committee. If it were necessary, the next step would be to the president of the bank.

The fundamental methodology we use to bring issues to the committee works as follows: We subscribe to various surveys that measure the public pulse on socially oriented issues. We then, either through research by staff or by task force groups formed from people throughout the bank, analyze these issues in terms of bank policy and practice. Finally, as a result of this analysis, recommendations for change in policy or practice are directed to the two implementing committees.

When we got into this business, a task force of ten teams, consisting of 24 officers, was organized just to examine consumer-related practices. They identified nearly 100 practices that might confront the bank with consumer issues, and reported back to the Social Policy Committee with a broad range of recommended changes in policies and practices. Not all of these recommendations were approved, of course; in some cases, there were valid reasons why other factors should outweigh the possible consumer complaints. But a large percentage were approved and have been implemented; and in no case was a questionable practice allowed to be continued by default, just because no one wanted—or dared—to look at it.

PRACTICES EXAMINED

The practices dealt with range across the board: Corporate disclosure; Arab boycott; redlining; housing; environmental issues; pollution control financing; default and collection practices; a booklet that explains in simple language the terms and conditions of all savings and checking account programs including not only the standard situations but the many potential booby traps; relationships with credit agencies in terms of fairness to the consumer; the method and effectiveness of handling complaints throughout the bank system; forms in simple English; forms in Spanish; privacy of customer and employee records; the revising of credit and loan applications and procedures to eliminate any obvious or subtle points of racial or sexual discrimination; on through to basic employment and promotion practices—the whole area of Affirmative Action and equal employment opportunity, including support of memberships in discriminatory service and social clubs.

One issue that became a matter of policy consideration clear up to the board-level committee was one of those innocent-sounding things—the question of whether loan interest should be calculated on a 360-day or a 365-day year—but it amounted to several million dollars difference in cost. This was typical of the issues that arise in every company: a practice that was originally quite clearly justified and proper, but was brought into question by the passage of time. When interest had to be calculated by hand, the only feasible method was to figure on the basis of 12, 30–day months—360 days. But with the computer, no such problem. Yet the change is painful, in more ways than money cost alone.

Not all efforts to be responsive need be limited to the bank's in-house expertise and resources. There is a largely untapped resource also in establishing cooperative relationships with educational institutions, public agencies, other banks, and businesses.

PRECEPTS

A few precepts are worth reviewing in structuring to deal with social policy:

First, it is important to make a top-to-bottom commitment to a permanent, continuing program. There is no use going into this exercise at all, if you are approaching it only as cosmetics. The cosmetic approach reminds me of the *New Yorker* cartoon of the big business tycoon sitting behind his polished mahogany desk—he is on the telephone obviously talking to one of his underlings, and he says "Get hold of one of those public relations fellers and tell him we want him to give our corporation a soul."

Second, and corollary, if there is no commitment to the principle that your interest and society's interests are parallel and compatible, stay out of the game. If you engage in socially oriented activities without real commitment to this principle, sooner or later your credibility is going to be challenged.

The third principle is that credibility is the real name of the game: if your credibility can be successfully challenged, nothing else you do in the societal field will stand up anyway. You can visibly give away great sums of money in the community and wake up one morning to see your good public image go down the drain because of discrimination or redlining charges in the local press. So you are better off to do nothing—say nothing—than to be caught talking out of both sides of your mouth.

Unfortunately, the fourth principle is that you can't really *do* nothing. You can *say* nothing; but you literally can't do nothing in the field of corporate social responsibility and hope to survive.

Fifth, even if you *could* do nothing, you should not want to, because the things you might reasonably, rationally think of doing in this field are as good for you as they are for your different publics.

Sixth, to make social responsibility effectively operational you must delineate clearly all the areas of responsibility, from top to bottom. You must assign responsibility and commensurate authority for the implementation of this activity to an executive who reports to the chief executive officer, and who is senior enough to command the respect and attention of all other senior people. It should be a major, if not a full-time, responsibility for that executive (depending upon the size of the bank).

Finally, make follow-up and monitoring an integral part of the program.

The SEC and the New York Stock Exchange have been pressing all public companies to establish audit committees. I have been chairman of a couple of those committees, and we have set as our objective—the objective of the whole audit process, including the audit committee, outside auditors, and internal audit staff—to make sure there never are any surprises. The social policy formulation process we have been reviewing is a direct parallel.

Perhaps I can make the job a little easier, in confronting this area, by removing a large element of uncertainty—the question of "do I or don't I?" In my judgment, the rising expectations of others will leave none of us any choice.

And, in the end, it is nonsense to debate whether business has such a thing as a corporate social responsibility—of course it has. It has an obligation to act responsibly, in every sense of that word: to be aware of the consequences of its acts—the social consequences, the economic, moral and political consequences—to be aware and then so govern those acts that they will be beneficial, not harmful, to the community and to the broader society.

Chapter 7

The Process of Bank Management

*James L. Hayes**

The successful banker in time finds that he or she is a manager. Suddenly, trying to make the decision as to what it is that happens when one manages as against what happens when someone is doing the banking business is a very important part of any manager's life. It is a most important first decision. It takes a little while to learn that as we enter the management field at the first levels of supervision we still will be expected to do a great deal of the banking function but we must find out what those first tasks are as supervisors. As we progress through the banking organization, we eventually may come to the top of a very large organization in which most of the banker's time is given to management. In effect this individual is no longer really a banker in the sense of the functions which he or she performs. Making this distinction is critical in performing as a competent manager.

Of course there are a good many managers who feel that management techniques are merely elaborations of what good administrators do instinctively, and who extoll seat of the pants management. Though most of us can cite cases where an inspired hunch saved the day in a critical situation, it would be foolish to suggest that good management techniques inhibit good judgment or impede cool decision making. After all, these techniques were designed to make management more effective. Like all tools they are only as good as the person who uses them—but in good hands they can do much to enhance creativity and effectiveness.

On the other hand, techniques can become so institutionalized and

* President, American Management Associations, New York, New York.

inflexible that they become stumbling blocks instead of stepping stones to achievement; but these dangers are readily avoided when management procedures are kept flexible and adaptable to differing needs and situations. It is important to remember that *while* the decision is being made. The neat separate elements of the management process must always be examined within the complex interrelationships in which they take place in reality. And, like all realities, they are prone to the wide variations produced by the behavior of the people involved in management. It is the people in the process that constitute the dynamics of management—and that determine its success or failure.

The successful bank manager must be far more than a prudent custodian of the public's money, financial adviser and source of capital, wise investor, and keen analyst. This is the technical side of the business. But in addition to the technical side, the banker must take into account the social milieu in which he functions and the people he or she serves. The banker must be sensitive to the trends of the economy (local, national, and international) and also be aware of many other aspects of the environment—ecological, sociological, and political. Some or all of these are what we may achieve when we become the successful "banker."

In addition to those whose activities are purely banking, there exists the large group of individuals, from first-line supervisors to the chief executive officer, who are involved in both banking and management. The most important career decision any individual makes is the decision to be a manager—to engage in activities that are different from being just a banker.

Whether in banking or any other field, all managers engage in the same process. First-line supervisors may find that the management function occupies only a small part of available time and technical banking uses up most of the time. But as we progress up the ladder, more and more time must be devoted to the management process. The chief executive officer—the president or chairman—spends very little time in pure banking decisions and a very large portion of his or her time in managing. Of course, the proportions at any level vary with the size of the bank.

So it follows that while the process of management can be described in the same terms, the decisions involved in the process will have two major variables—the magnitude of the decisions and the span of time involved. For instance, the president's decisions may involve millions of dollars and the first-line supervisor may be talking in hundreds. The president is talking 5 years in the future; the supervisor, the next 30 days.

This variation in magnitude of decisions and time spans plus our natural abilities, education, and training dictate which tools and techniques we use in decision making. Tools and techniques are quite different from the concepts of management. The concepts are more or less unchanging. Tools and techniques, however, are myriad and change frequently. The value of any tool or technique is its impact on human performance.

What, then, is this process in which all managers engage? One standard classification is a process characterized by planning, organizing, coordinating, motivating, and controlling. Some managers would add communicating, negotiating, decision making, directing, and others. Since these labels are used to separate an integral process into compartments for purpose of study and discussion, differences are more in definition than reality. No element stands alone when applied to the decision-making process. For instance, a manager cannot plan without involving control, organization, and everything else to some degree. Motivation depends on organization, control, and planning. Our description of the process of management is a sequence of topics which helps our understanding; but these topics never exist in isolation. The management process can start almost at any point in the cycle, but good management will always reflect the entire cycle.

PLANNING

We usually start the process with planning. Planning is deciding where we would like to be in the future and what and who may be involved in our getting there. Rudyard Kipling described it well in *The Elephant's Child:*

> I keep six honest serving-men
>   (They taught me all I knew);
> Their names are What and Why and
>   When
> And How and Where and Who.

Basic to planning is answering some questions about our bank, our branch, or our department in the bank. Why does this bank (branch or department) exist? How does this department contribute to the efforts of other departments? What business or businesses are we really in? Obviously, these questions could be extended as we are trying to find our mission. Is there an unusual service we provide? Is our branch dedicated to a specific geographic section of our city?

No one person arrives at this decision; it is, rather, the team—the president and vice presidents, the vice president of investments and members of his/her section, the vice president of marketing and those in the department, a branch manager and staff.

Next, planning involves setting long- and short-range objectives, sometimes called goals. It is important to note that we do not have long- *and* short-range plans. We have one plan with long- and short-range objectives. The long-range objectives tend to show a few points we would like to reach in the future—what size bank do we wish to be? What new markets do we want to serve? What kind of loan portfolio would we like to have—fewer construction loans, more automobile loans, a credit card line? At department level we may think about size some years from now, devices we may need to take care of increased volume, physical space requirements, new types of personnel, and so on.

Short-term planning tends to be much more detailed with many measurable goals. Usually short-term plans are accompanied by a budget. Many managers can reach objectives but far fewer can do it within the confines of a budget. It is important to recognize that a budget alone is not a plan. It is a part of a plan—a very necessary part.

Planning is far more complex than getting from here to there. It is the basis for cost control, budgetary administration, morale and productivity. In effect, any deficiency in these areas points to a defect in planning. The amateur manager often treats these manifestations of poor planning as problems in themselves and literally wastes money be avoiding the more basic necessity—a good plan.

Many techniques and tools help in planning. The technique known as management by objectives (MBO) is a useful one. By itself MBO may not do very much for any organization, but in the hands of an accomplished manager it is a basic tool. Good managers have always used MBO. Not everyone who used MBO, however, is a manager. It can be just a "gimmick." Likewise, forecasting of all kinds, statistical analysis, the computer, sampling, and many other tools and techniques can either be very useful or again just "gimmicks."

The plan—the book, the budget, and support documents—is the tangible evidence of planning by someone. Unless managers themselves do planning in every department of a bank, the plan may be more of a threat than the essential document it should be. Planning is a concept, an attitude, a very basic posture of the manager. If a bank should have no formal planning document, the manager is not absolved from planning. To the contrary, the large bank with a planning department may find its efforts dissipated by line managers who do not accept this basic responsibility of leadership.

ORGANIZATION

Organization follows and supports plan. When the goals have been set and the policy determined, we organize to fulfill the objectives.

This involves determining how to allocate resources in relation to the objectives, setting priorities, and assuring their fulfillment by making available the necessary people, plant, and materials. If you don't know what you're doing, after all, you can't possibly know how many people it takes to do it.

When managers organize, they should organize to reach objectives. Organizing is bring people together in a way that most effectively and efficiently will achieve the objectives. Let us suppose that you have A, B, and C working with you. You are the leader, the manager. What are we saying? We are indicating that if everyone does his or her job, the sum total of all efforts ideally will result in the objective you have all participated in setting. It follows that if there are no objectives, you cannot be organized. You simply have an organization— something that is different from the people in it. It also follows that if each individual does not know his or her job, the sum total of effort can be the objective only by coincidence.

Organization may be by function or similarity of work—investments, commercial banking, internal auditing, loans, and so on. It may be by geography—the West Side Branch, the Main Branch, Suburban Branch—or, in the holding company, by banks or divisions—the First National Bank, the Commercial Finance Co., the Exchange Bank. It may be all of these in the very large banking institution.

Organizing involves definition of jobs in writing. The chart is the picture of the organization. We draw the chart to help definition and to communicate relationships of different units. Far more importantly, however, organizing is bringing people into relationships where each individual can find satisfaction in the job and yet all are united in a common accomplishment of the objectives.

Organizing stresses team accomplishment. The objective is the responsibility of the team. To bring this about, participation is required. The manager, being the accountable individual, uses participation as the technique that will result in the common ownership or responsibility for the objectives. Distinguishing between responsibility and accountability is basic to understanding what managers do when they organize.

Delineating jobs is done with techniques called job descriptions and standards of performance. A job description is a statement of what the individual managers will be held accountable for. In no way does the job description describe what the manager does. As a member of a team, the manager will do everything he or she can to help the team reach its objectives.

Job descriptions tend to be general, or sometimes too complex. The manager therefore uses standards of performance to describe the results that will exist when the statements in a job description are satisfactorily performed. This written understanding allows the members of the team to measure their performance regularly while awaiting formal evaluation. The primary purpose of standards and evaluation is development and rewards—both very important to the management process.

Since the entire concept of organization is built on the principle of division of labor, the organized manager masters the art of delegation. Those to whom a task is given must have the authority to effect all those things for which he or she is accountable by reason of the job description and the standards of performance. This giving of power in the form of authority is called delegation.

Since the recipient of delegated authority already shares in the responsibility for the team objectives, the acceptance of accountability for a particular activity in reaching the objective—the job—creates a new responsibility. In effect the manager delegates authority and creates a new responsibility without losing his or her responsibility for managing the total team. The manager of a loan department may give authority to a loan officer. This loan officer is responsible for his or her actions but the manager of the loan department has not lost any responsibility and is still accountable for the entire department's results. Thus, delegation leads to a form of decentralization, and this operates most efficiently when the manager clearly understands that all members of the team must have decisions circumscribed by an awareness of legal restrictions, policies and procedures, statements of moral and ethical beliefs, and budgets.

Finally, organization is about people. It is an interrelationship of people, held together by shared objectives, and every aspect of being human enters into it. Therefore, the principles and technology of human resource development—recruiting, training, career planning, organizational development—offer each manager an array of approaches through which individual talents can be blended and orchestrated within the specific details or framework of organization.

COORDINATION

For many years, little was said about the managerial process involving coordination. More and more this aspect becomes important as we deal with various business functions and many human personalities.

When organizations are divided into manageable units and authority is delegated, each unit tends to become a bit autonomous in its activities. While effective planning will establish objectives that unite groups in an organization, as we get into complex organizations, the relationship of group to group is not as strongly unified by objectives. For instance, the vice presidents of a bank will work together because they share the responsibility for the objectives of the bank. But it may not be as easy for the trust department with its objectives to cooperate with the loan department and its objectives. Indeed legal implications might breed great autonomy in this instance. Yet they are both in the same bank, both can market the others services, and both are developing personnel who may be future managers in the bank.

Every manager is a coordinator, playing an active directing role, and a cooperator, displaying an attitudinal role within the total organization. As a coordinator, the manager coordinates the team he or she leads, coordinates the team with other teams, coordinates the team in external relationships.

While the element of coordination would seem to provide the context for keeping individuals working together, the unlimited potential of any person will sometimes manifest itself in actions that move away from the consonance of the team. How can we ask individuals to be creative, or give them freedom to act without expecting ideas that are unworkable, beyond budget, or in the province of another department? Thus, coordination demands a sense of timing—diplomatically holding back one activity while pushing another; filling in when a job is vacant; consoling and encouraging; reexplaining objectives and redefining jobs. All of these are informed by a sensitivity to the human dimensions which impact on getting a job done.

When the manager is in the middle or lower part of the organization, it is more difficult.to understand what another and unrelated activity seeks to accomplish. Yet the manager will lend every effort to be sure that the team cooperates with other teams in unrelated areas. The people in investments might want some information on marketing. The marketing manager might not perceive any need for the information, but as a coordinator would seek to understand why Investments want it and direct others to cooperate. Sometimes we get so busy with our own activities that requests from other departments are extra burdens. It is the manager who constantly senses *one* bank and constantly directs cooperation and joint relationships.

It is not easy for the public to think of a bank as using some people's money to serve other people. The wise use of bank funds pays for interest on deposits, for capital expansion in part, and for overhead expenses. To see the local citizenry as an important relationship is easier for public relations and marketing than it is for accounting or bookkeeping. Yet the external relationships of all bank departments to the community is a major concern of the manager. He or she constantly coordinates internal bank teams with external publics if required or desired.

There are various tools and techniques available for coordination.

In that coordination deals with many different people, and seeks to wed all functions or elements of the management process into a unified concept, communication is the most important of these tools.

At the heart of good communication is personal integrity. To be not only heard, but attended to, our words must convey a sense of truth, so those who listen, know they can trust what they hear. Truth and experience are the critical touchstones. The experienced managers have a wealth of useful know-how at their disposal. They can teach the art of a job on the job, at any level, if there is honest sharing of experience and feelings with subordinates, clarifying their own thinking in the process of giving it to others; if the managers learn and use the well-developed techniques that will best transmit their messages; and if there is willingness to listen and encourage honest feedback—and use it.

The manager cannot communicate an idea any clearer than the idea is in his or her own mind. On a staircase in one of the IBM schools five treads bear these legends in ascending order: Read—Listen—Observe—Discuss—Think. This list sums up magnificently the process of learning. It is basic to clarifying ideas before communicating.

Conferences and meetings are other coordinating devices. Being a good conference leader is an asset to the manager. The wise composition of committees, defining their functions, designating dates for completion of their tasks and possible dissolution—this is an area of great importance. Good committees are growth opportunities for all involved. All can learn about how others think, what they do, the limits of their jobs, the aspirations of a department. These are coordinating concepts.

As the education level of all people rises, the need to negotiate decisions seems to increase. Negotiation is a coordinating tool, and demands an open mind, a willingness to be persuaded by logic, an ability to listen. The manager tries to understand both or several sides of a problem. Tries to get one to give a bit and another to take. And, insofar as decision-making time will allow, keep all motivated to live with the resolution of the situation. Negotiation is a great skill.

Coordination of workers and of jobs is an increasingly important skill area, and will be a prime factor in the success of the managers of the future. Like a good traffic cop, the effective manager must coordinate the individuals participating in the effort to produce, taking into account their personal goals and the broad objectives of the enterprise, and giving them wise direction. Coordination is a carefully timed blending technique for directing a complex aggregate to function cooperatively and smoothly. A sense of timing is essential for the coordinator; and patience is absolutely vital. He or she must also be able to see the overall pattern to be achieved. The coordinator must create a climate of confidence and trust for those he or she directs, so they will not resist strictures that are imposed.

MOTIVATION

There is probably no area of management which has undergone more genuine research and about which more has been written than motivation. The real key to employee performance, of course, is motivation—as every good supervisor is aware. Unfortunately, most of what we do is more manipulative than motivating. Since motivation has much to do with objectives—how we fit in with the team, the extent to which group goals are our goals—job satisfaction and team accomplishment are closely related to motivation.

Basically people motivate themselves. The manager provides the stimuli for these individuals. These stimuli may range from the pervasive environment in which we work—physical and human—to simple manipulative devices that seem to inspire some people. Why do some wish to work in *this* bank rather than *that* one? And do you think anyone is motivated to better performance by a television set or a trip to Mexico? We know a great deal about the effectiveness of certain motivational elements and the temporary utility of others.

The manager is constantly aware of the aspirations of the individual. Job satisfaction is linked to success on the job. Every good manager provides a system by which the individual can measure his or her own success. This should be confirmed from time to time by the manager. There are various techniques to accomplish this—evaluation, appraisal, performance review, merit rating. While the labels may vary, there are two different processes which are essential: review for development and review for compensation. These two processes are very different and the well-managed organization has both. The individual should be able to measure himself or herself with reasonable accuracy at any time. Obviously this involves other elements we have discussed, particularly standards of performance.

The manager must learn to use evaluation techniques to measure the performance of people, of organizations, and of programs. Having developed the yardstick or norm against which to measure, we must overcome our own reluctance to judge and realize that creative evaluation can be one of our most useful management tools. If we use it to stress strengths and seek constructive ideas for improvement of weaknesses—rather than find faults and belittle subordinates—we will find that it stimulates motivation and performance, promotes understanding, and encourages closer working relationships.

Rewards and incentives are tools that help. Properly they are not motivational but are necessary to recognize when the self-motivated manager has done a good job. This requires the bank to provide an intelligent compensation system as an aid to the individual manager.

Most people want opportunity to grow in their jobs and in the institution. Good managers open career paths to those on the team, realizing that good people who perform well will eventually leave the team. The manager, in this case, is constantly helping others to grow, particularly if management development is involved as well as skill training.

There are many other activities that signal interest on the part of the manager—recognition of outstanding performance, symbols of status (the parking place, the name on the door, the title, the office location) but none of these are as important as being a genuine team member, in effect sharing with the leader. This allows for absorbing disappointments as well as sharing success, and praise is far more important than criticism.

CONTROL

The manager uses controls to control. As Peter Drucker points out, we must not think of controls as the plural of control. Control is what the manager does. He or she controls to do it. Basically, a manager's control is self-control. Having set up the plan, the manager now wants to direct other managerial activities to achieve the plan. Every other function of the management process is therefore involved, and in turn how well the other functions are being carried out will influence the control system. How we plan, the effectiveness of our organization, motivational processes that we use, and our coordinating activities—all have an influence on control. When we speak of controls we are seeking feedback mechanisms that will tell us how we should exercise our personal control in modifying the way in which we are carrying out other management functions.

Control depends very much upon a good tracking or monitoring system. These systems should be more like thermostats than thermometers. What we get by way of information should cause something to happen, automatically if possible. Information in itself may be nothing more than a cost. If a bank has planned to increase its loans for construction, the manager will want to know month by month whether the objective is being achieved. Controls will indicate this. If progress is on plan, the information which evidences this results from the controls we have introduced, in this case a reporting system. Control is then exercised by transmitting this information to those individuals, departments, and so on, who are the "people" of the plan, and who must understand the meaning of such progress. If we are off plan, we need to know what direction we are off plan, plus or minus. Now the managerial control may be exercised in the area of motivating someone who is lagging or inspiring cooperation from another department or communicating some financial aspect that would result in a change of policy. When the manager controls there is a deliberate attempt to identify the problem or situation involved and institute corrective steps to get back on plan. In some cases we may find that our plan is too conservative and motivating a team to exceed plan may be in order.

There are certain norms that the manager observes in exercising the controlling function. The first one is to place controls at the highly sensitive points so that major deficiencies or deviations can be detected early. The manager, for instance, would want to know that the total expenses for a month are 25 percent in excess of what was budgeted *before* knowing precisely which expenses are involved in the overage. Contrast this situation with one in which expenses for the month are exactly on budget but we discover that the expense involving travel is 100 percent over budget whereas the expense involving advertising is completely under budget. As you can see these two situations require a different approach by the manager.

Controls and the control process should always bear some relationship to cost. Banks discovered this long ago in looking at their over and shorts. The popular idea that banks balance to the penny every night exists in many people's minds but would be totally impractical from the standpoint of the amount of money spent to achieve it. In effect, controls must be economical.

The manager wants controls that are comprehensive, and constantly guards against receiving bits and pieces of information that will cause action without getting all the bits and pieces into a relationship. This is why we will ask our accounting department to give us a complete statement of where we stand at a particular point.

Finally, controls should be balanced. This is always most apparent when we try to control both quantity and quality. In many situations if we put a strong control point on quantity, we are likely to lower the quality of the activity. To the contrary, if we make great effort to get quality, we may find that quantity is lacking. Balancing these two is very important. In no place is this more apparent than in the loan function. To believe that we must put a certain amount of money to work in loans can create a pressure for lowering the quality of the loans made and thus increasing the long-term risks. At some subsequent point we are likely to get very concerned about the quality of our loans only to find that those who are responding cannot place the money that we have available. Finding the balance is important.

As we look at the control function we must remember a great deal about human relations. Creative and brilliant people do not like an overt control system. But they do want to participate in the planning process and by this method can usually be involved in setting objectives so that they control themselves. To the contrary, any organization will have certain types of people who must be checked on continuously so that day-by-day correctional processes may be introduced if required. It is also important to note that in the banking world the high fiduciary responsibility that is involved in the entire banking process tends to provide more control mechanisms than may be either efficient or effective. But to fulfill legal responsibilities with a great number of people involves, it is sometimes necessary to increase feedback mechanisms. All bankers are familiar with the few sad cases of embezzlement where better control would have helped.

When we "close the loop" through control, we must think of the audit function. Auditing is a process which provides information on both financial and management activities. In the case of internal auditing, auditors should provide their services without any prior announcement. Auditors do not in most cases have the authority to say what should be done but simply to evaluate what is happening. Ideally the information is then fed back to the manager whose department is audited, to that manager's manager and to someone at the top of the organization. An ideal audit system would then provide for a short period for the manager who has been audited to correct any deviation. Part of the "correction" might be a recommendation for a change in policy, the prevalence of a dangerous situation, and so on. This is the way in which management becomes alerted to the need for a change in the organization. Auditors, therefore, should be looked upon as providing assistance to good management rather than as solely monitoring.

The manager who has control is always sensitive to the fact that a situation is never as good as it might be. This means that when things are going well and are on target it may be an indication that we ought to set our goals a little higher, render a service a little better. In effect, we come back to the planning process and, therefore, have completed what many refer to as the management cycle.

Management can be a very exciting and challenging career in itself. Once we distinguish that managing is different from just banking and involves the opportunity to develop other bankers, the chance to see plans work, and particularly the opportunity to help people grow, we will achieve a unique kind of reward and personal satisfaction that can never come from the banking function alone.

Chapter 8

Effective Communication of Corporate Policies and Objectives

B. Finley Vinson*

There is no question that business and banking are experiencing diminishing public confidence. A. W. Clausen, president of the Bank of America, describes this problem concisely:

There's been a massive erosion of public confidence. As of this moment, the public is rightly skeptical of our practices and preachings. Integrity is not some impractical notion dreamed up by naïve do-gooders. Our integrity is the foundation for, the very basis of our ability to do business. If the market ever goes under, our favorite villains—socialist economies and government regulators—won't be to blame. We will. If we're not concerned, then we're just not sensitive to the reality of the problem or today's world.[1]

This reading on the pulse of the national conscience was borne out by "The Study of American Opinion, 1976" conducted among 5,448 consumers by *U.S. News & World Report.*

Here are the eight areas in which business was ranked strongest: developing new products; providing products and services to meet people's needs; hiring members of minority groups; communicating with stockholders; paying good wages; improving the standard of living; providing fair return to investors; and providing steady work.

Now study our weakest points: communicating with the general public; being interested in customers; communicating with employees; providing value for the money; dealing with shortages; controlling pol-

---

* Chairman, First National Bank, Little Rock, Arkansas.
[1] "The Embattled Businessman," *Newsweek,* February 16, 1976.

lution; conserving natural resources; and being honest in what is said about products.

While business can be satisfied to some degree about the strong points, the weak ones are reasons to cringe—and to act. No one in banking today can sit back on his laurels, assuming that his skirts are clean and that it's too bad that "the other guys" are messing up "our image." The challenge is clear. At every level of bank management, we have a responsibility to establish sound corporate policies and objectives and then to effectively communicate them both in word and deed.

The threats to our credibility are real and to expect them to be silenced by time is to shirk one of our primary management tasks. The consequences of not dealing with this situation will further erode our position in the marketplace and eventually can lead to a fight for our very survival on the American scene.

THE EVER-CHANGING COMMUNICATIONS ENVIRONMENT

The atmosphere for public communication has evolved through a complex process that can be traced to three key socioeconomic factors.

First, the influence of public opinion has grown at an accelerated rate over the past 50 years due to improved communications technology. What happens in any part of the world can virtually overnight affect the way people perceive who we are and what we do on the local level. This interconnection makes it imperative that managers remain well-informed and responsive.

The second factor relates to what sociologists term "The Great Change." Evolving over the past 150 years, this "Change" reflects the fact that society was rural oriented, now is urban oriented; was independent in nature, now is greatly interdependent; was agrarian, now is commercial and industrial; and had simple mores, now has very complex standards with much element of choice. This process continues. Banking must recognize the changes and make adaptations too.

Third, the bigness of elements has created the potentiality for a lack of sensitivity by the major institutions in our nation today. "Big Business," "Big Government," "Big Labor," and "Big Banking" all sound "Big Ugly." The obvious advantages of this growth can quickly be lost if customers are not treated like people and the tail starts wagging the dog.

As bankers, we can identify with all of these factors because we play such a front-line role within the communities we serve. However, recognition and anticipation of these changes within this shifting communications environment becomes more and more difficult the further up the management ladder you go.

It is hard for us to remember "the good old days" in banking the way that they really were, but they did have one key communications advantage even if they did not have computers. With small staffs and single locations, top management had almost a face-to-face rapport with every public upon which the bank's success depended. Policies and objectives were communicated on a personal level. Complaints could be heard and corrections made right on the spot. The give-and-take of business life was a public opinion poll every minute of the banking day.

The complexities of managing banking operations today and the convenience that we have sought to provide through multibranching has disarmed top bank management of that communications advantage. However, those policies and objectives still need to be communicated. Those complaints still need to be heard. Those corrections still need to be made. That pulse-taking still is essential to customer satisfaction and business development.

Getting that job done effectively requires attention, sensitivity, and planning. In addition, at the chief executive officer level, it calls for a new brand of manager.

Management study after management study shows that chief executives list their own institution's credibility as one of the top issues facing them. One recent report showed that 40 percent of the chief executives of major American corporations spend up to half of their time with such nontraditional concerns as consumer affairs, relations with the media, local communities, and government at all levels.

This trend toward selection of top management that can deal effectively in anticipating and responding to the many public issues affecting banking is not temporary. The nature of the banking business and the society in which it operates will absolutely demand managers who are creative, sensitive, and communicative.

THE WILLINGNESS TO COMMUNICATE THE PLAN AND PLAN THE COMMUNICATIONS

A chief characteristic of business and finance in the 1800s and the early part of this century was the very secretive manner in which affairs were conducted, especially the making of policy and the planning of its implementation. This "closed door" attitude by bankers and businessmen led to the attacks of the muckrakers and regulatory authorities with resultant governmental safeguards.

Fortunately, the image of the "robber barons" has passed, but the instinct of secrecy in too many quarters may still remain to the detriment of banking and society. This secrecy may not be intentional, but it may be perceived as such if bank management does not come to grips with tackling the communications problem at the very highest level.

It is absolutely essential that senior management involve itself in planning, implementing, and evaluating the effectiveness of its communications programs. This willingness to plan communications and to communicate that plan is a task that has become too important for simple relegation to some distant departmental shelf. Banks—no matter how small or how big—are a reflection and extension of the attitudes of management as expressed through corporate policies, objectives, and actions.

Once that management concept is grasped and understood, any bank is then on the road to establishing a healthy internal and external relationship. This committment to communications may seem obvious to many and agreeable to all. However, the proof is in the doing and, as the ageless axiom goes, "good public relations is 90 percent doing good and only 10 percent talking about it."

With that introduction of the term "public relations," it is important to have an appropriate definition of the term. Public relations is a planned effort approved at the management level to influence opinion by acceptable performance using two-way communications.

From a practical standpoint, too many bank managers have a very distorted view about this particular communications task. These misunderstandings have centered on notions that "marketing and public relations people are only interested in spending the bank's money while the rest of us are trying to make it" or that this area is an organizational catchall where projects that don't fit any other slot can be routed. Some of these views may reflect the way things have been in too many banks. However, they do not mirror the way things should be in a forward-looking, concerned banking operation.

Just like any other corporate arm, the bank's communications staff should receive top-level attention and leadership, the necessary financial and labor force resources to meet its goals and realistic parameters in which to achieve them.

By the same token, bank management should expect its communications staff to operate from a planned program consistent with organizational objectives that is approved by senior management; to be flexible in meeting the unexpected corporate requirements; to supply systematic self-criticism and examination of the attitudes of the bank's publics; to act as policy adviser in the problem-solving process; and to serve as producers of communications materials.

In addition to senior management and the internal staff, many banks should employ one other resource on the communications team—outside professional public relations/marketing counsel. The value of such practitioners primarily lies in the objectivity that they can bring to the situation, the broad range of experience that they've had in solving business communications problems, the flexibility of staff that can add depth to the internal staff and the broad range of skills that can be contributed on an as-needed basis.

Armed with a willingness to become deeply involved in this process and surrounded by this staff nucleus, management is then professionally prepared to more effectively utilize the communications tools, techniques and horsepower to support its objectives.

THE "COMMUNICATIONS AUDIT"

An important first step in developing or reorienting any organization's communications program—even before goal setting—is to establish a bench mark for planning. The most professional method of approaching this task within the bank structure is to conduct a "communications audit."

This audit should be broken into three specific segments:

1. Objective Evaluation of Current Bank Programs. Prepared by an external marketing/public relations counseling firm, this effort should focus on the bank's present goals, organizational structure, marketing program, internal communications, publicity, advertising, investor reporting procedures, and other related areas.

2. Opinion Research. Conducted either by personal interview, mail or telephone, this formalized study should be contracted through an independent opinion research firm. The format for this program will differ from situation to situation. However, it most definitely should measure customer and noncustomer attitudes toward the bank with regard to policies, services, personnel, perceived image, community involvement, and market position. This study should serve as a bench mark with a continuing program so that correlation with future reports can be easily accomplished to identify attitude shifts.

3. Market Study. In order to gain a better perspective of the marketplace in which the bank operates, a market study should be prepared to provide demographic, media and competition information. The demographic section should supply a profile of the bank's market with breakouts in such groupings as age, income, occupational categories, and similar data. Media information should be supplied on coverage (circulation, viewers, listeners, etc.) with demographic profiles on each along with news policies and opportunities for use in publicity planning. Information on competitive institutions should give data on other banks, savings and loan associations, credit unions, and any other key financial services within the market. The profile on each institution should be compiled to provide an analysis of management, marketing efforts, publicity, community involvement, internal/external problem areas, and any anticipated changes within those organizations that may create attitude changes.

Once these three documents have been prepared, then the bank's communications team can launch discussion and formulation of goals and plans based on an objective common ground. The commonality of approach and effort is one of the key benefits that the total group can gain through the audit method.

Analysis of the data usually points out some very clear patterns within the bank's and competition's activities while also quantifying—possibly for the first time—market positions that you'll never find on a financial statement. (One word of warning: Your confidence in your decision-making ability may be shaken. It is amazing that when you work within an organization how quickly the trees in the forest fade from view. Your own perceptions of public reaction to bank operations may be completely off-base and your ideas and the public's ideas about what is effective communication may be two different ball games.)

A side benefit of the audit will be a growing management awareness of the importance of opinion and marketing research. During the past ten years, great strides have been made in improving the accuracy and scope of attitudinal and motivational techniques. To a large degree, these advances make it unnecessary for the manager to just "play his hunches" on important marketing and public relations planning decisions. Such studies never provide definitive answers. However, they do provide important guideposts for decision making, and alert management to problems that may be festering. Therefore, the type of information gained in the communications audit phase becomes invaluable during the planning period since it allows management to deal with the current situation with an eye to anticipating trends and problems that may be just over the horizon.

THE PATTERN FOR PLANNING

Reduced to its most elementary steps, bank communications programming can be divided into four phases: (1) research; (2) planning; (3) implementation; and (4) evaluation.

While none of these periods necessarily outweigh another in importance, the involvement of senior management does require a greater commitment during the planning phase. The two key activities within this stage involve the establishment of communications goals and the formulation of projects that will most effectively interpret and convey organizational objectives. In essence, all of this effort is directed to reinforcing favorable attitudes, changing unfavorable ones, or creating new favorable attitudes.

Using the research compiled during the management audit and long-term objectives as a guide, the first step is to formalize practical goals. They must be flexible to accommodate the rapid changes that typify the nature and scope of operations in a growth organization. In addition, they should be attainable since the setting of overly ambitious or inappropriate goals may result in desperate efforts to assure achievement through unprofessional activities.

In written form, these goals should be spelled out as role and scope statements. In other words, say that the goal is "to increase earnings by 5 percent," certainly a noble pursuit. However, the goal in this form only gives a role statement. To restate the goal as being "to increase earnings by 5 percent by the third quarter of the fiscal year," then both the role and scope are covered, thus, setting the mission and supplying a target date. Too many communications plans are loaded with "blue sky" goals. They are commendable in their thought, but their use as a management document for action leaves much to be desired.

Fixed on specific and attainable goals, the communications team can then proceed to the discussion and planning of how its many "publics" will be affected by the action plan.

The "public" in public relations is not a faceless crowd. By definition, a public is a group of people who are affected by the same affairs. In other words, they all have a mutuality of interests. For bank management, there are eight basic publics for communications consideration: (1) customers, (2) employees, (3) shareholders, (4) the local community, (5) the news media, (6) government, (7) the financial community, and (8) education.

Each one of these publics play a significant role in the success of any banking operation with their importance weighted by management's objectives and goals. Through the communications audit, the prevailing attitudes within each one of these groups toward the bank will have been measured. These measurements correlated with established goals will now provide the basis upon which action planning can actually begin—first, by setting objectives for each public and, second, by establishing plans for information or educational programs. Of course, both of these steps will be influenced greatly by timing, resources, and budget.

In practice, much of this planning activity is centered around continuing bank communications programs along with consideration of special near-term projects. Examples of continuing programs include employee meetings and newsletters, quarterly and annual reports to shareholders, publicity releases to the media, and advertising campaigns to influence customers and the community. Special projects include such activities as open houses, brochure series, briefings for governmental officials, assembly programs within schools, presentations for financial analysts, and sponsorship of communitywide events.

Approached in another way, the bank's messages in the marketplace are essentially transmitted in two different forms: the tools that the bank can control and the ones that it cannot. A very basic list of the tools that the bank can manage includes house publications, handbooks, manuals, books, letters, bulletin boards, posters, enclosures, advertising, meetings, speeches, audio-visual presentations, exhibits, tours, and stage events. The key to communicating effectively in these and many other forms (including the uncontrolled ones, such as news coverage) is to do everything possible to assure that the sender's words must mean the same thing to the receiver that they do to the sender.

The variety of tools available for communicating the bank's messages grows virtually every day. Their employment will depend, to a large degree, on budgetary considerations, their appropriateness to the mission that they are to accomplish and the imagination and judgment of the communications team.

Because of space limitations, an extensive discussion of those tools is not possible within this handbook. However, any bank manager who will become intimately involved in this planning process will wish to study some of the vast amount of professional literature available on these subjects.

While few valid generalizations can be made about message content, timing and tools because of the diversity of situations to be faced by each communications team, certain criteria for bank programming learned from experience can be presented as a guide:

1. Do not fall into the trap of always "doing it the way we did it last year." Even if you consider last year's program a success, eventually success will beget boredom—much to the pleasure of your competitors.
2. Stymie your urge to plan advertising programs rather than communications programs. Like it or not, the credibility of paid advertising is continuing to slump while the cost of creating and placing it still is on the upswing. No one tool in your communications inventory is a panacea. Simply consider advertising to be one of your tools and, when you use it—make it count.
3. Do not try to be all things to all people. You as an individual can't be. Why expect the bank's communications to appeal to everyone effectively? It is a mission impossible. With today's marketing and public relations expertise, it is much smarter to decide

which market segments you want and can go after—then develop specialized plans to make it happen.

4. Be aware of the specialized needs of your employees and shareholders. They are the most powerful and most believeable communications forces on your team. Keep them informed about the good news and the bad. Show them that you appreciate their confidence and support—publicly.

5. Stay abreast of current communications techniques and bring the best of them to your market through your own bank's program. Adapt successful practices being used in businesses outside of banking. It keeps your competitors on their toes—and off balance.

Communications planning is an imaginative process in a systematized format with each step logically following the other. Once goals, publics, messages, tools, and timing have been determined, then budgeting must be accomplished with as sharp a pencil as possible.

The budgeting process requires copious attention to detail since the dollars and cents will naturally influence the plan's ultimate survival. With budgeting completed, then the total plan should be committed to paper for presentation to senior management, for final approval.

Once approved, the strategy and major elements of the plan should be presented to the board of directors and to all employees for their information. Too often, this step is dropped because of lack of time or interest when, in reality, it is foolhardy to expect directors and staff to be able to support communications programs that they don't know about.

During the implementation phase, senior management should be given regular status reports and be included in any major plan changes should the necessity arise.

The final step—evaluation—completes the cycle and serves as a basis for future planning. While it is frequently difficult to quantify results, to point to specific achievements and to objectively review the outcome, even a subjective attempt should be made. Where specific goals have been reached, documentation and analysis should be forwarded to senior management for review. When goals have not been reached or when measurement toward the target is iffy, a report should be made to at least identify problem areas and apparent strengths and weaknesses.

THE FLAIR AND FLEXIBILITY OF COMMUNICATING

Style and stereotype have an important influence upon communications, for communication is not a rational process. How we think and develop attitudes is composed of several parts emotion for every one part reason. The facts do not always persuade. To a large degree, we make judgments based on the stereotypes that we've fixed in our minds over the years. These mental collection points once established influence how we view events, people, places, and institutions.

The "image" of banking, for instance, has much to do with how each one of our publics deals with us. By the same token, our own "image" of banking as bankers has a powerful influence on the way we approach our conduct of the business. Too many bankers take themselves too seriously instead of giving that same status to their responsibility to communicate effectively with their customers, communities, and other publics.

It's a matter of management style and personal leadership. If we believe that banking is a traditional, somewhat stuffy-type of business then we'll tend to communicate just that. If, on the other hand, we believe that banking can be a modern vital force within the communities we serve and a business that is not locked in to its own conservative stereotype, then we can blaze new pathways for service, communication, and profitability.

Perhaps no other business is so uniquely capable of innovation in the area of public affairs as banking. We are highly exposed within our communities, attract to our staffs some of the best minds available, serve the total spectrum of the society in a business relationship, possess an economic force of major importance and are looked to for community leadership. We have an opportunity to help our communities and our businesses that is virtually unparalleled by any other segment within the private sector.

The secret to taking advantage of this opportunity lies purely within the imaginative leadership of management in planning, financing, and becoming involved in meaningful public affairs programs.

Norborne Berkeley, Jr., president and chief administrative officer of Chemical New York Corporation and Chemical Bank, has been an active spokesman within our industry on the importance of making banking a significant social force. His views and the lessons that his bank has learned within the area of social involvement are sound. Here is what he told the 1974 Bank Marketing Association/American Bankers Association Public Affairs Conference:

First, money in terms of hard cash contributions is not the answer to anything if not accompanied by personal involvement on the part of our own personnel. I am not saying that there is not a proper place for contributions. What I am saying is that contributions are not a public affairs program.

Second, we found that they were most effective when we applied the tools of banking to the community as opposed to seeing our role as that of social workers.

Third, the scattergun approach—a little help here and another program there—leaves you with a handful of smoke. We've learned that it was necessary to select targets, develop an approach and see it through—just as we would any business venture.

Fourth, if the program involves a specific community—and many of them do—self-determination for the people of that community is essential. Imposed solutions from the outside, even when accompanied by financial resources, are unwelcome and rarely effective.

Fifth, the impetus of the public affairs function should come from top management, who must be directly involved. Unless those who operate the program on a day-to-day basis have easy access to decisionmaking members of management, an effective public affairs program is an impossibility—and probably a waste of money.

And, finally, if we've learned nothing else over the past few years, we have most certainly learned that we do not have to rationalize nor apologize to our stockholders for supporting an active program for public affairs. There are certain realities about our particular business that demand banking take a leadership role in these matters and we would, in fact, do our stockholders a great disservice by failing to recognize this.

Aside from broadly based public affairs programs, bank management also must have the flexibility to take advantage of communications targets of opportunity. This balance of long-term social responsibility and short-term community responsiveness will pay dividends in immeasurable public favor.

When community crises or problems arise, do not be hesitant to step forward and lend a hand. Too many bankers do not, fearing that they will be expected to give too much or be spread too thin. However, there is a lot of truth in "a friend in need is a friend indeed" and also—in many cases—a lot of favorable news coverage and customer reaction to be found there, too.

For instance, what if a tornado or some other natural disaster strikes your community? Act quickly. Volunteer to commit bank staff members to the emergency effort, offer bank facilities to aid in collecting supplies, and so on, and make short-term loans available to help victims with payment of medical care, rebuilding, and other expenses.

However, it should not take such a drastic emergency to pull you up from your chair and get you out in your community. The point is that circumstances will arise giving you a natural opportunity to put your words of community concern into action and, when they do, stop talking and put your bank where your mouth is.

THE LIP SERVICE SYNDROME

Management's growing awareness of the importance of bank communications doesn't necessarily mean that this area will automatically receive the top-level attention that it requires and deserves. In fact, the so-called bottom-line bankers may not even fully accept the premise that communications expertise has developed into a management characteristic to be cultivated and maximized.

However, this "lip service syndrome" is a shortsighted approach to modern bank management which will lead to a continuing erosion of public confidence in our business. Carried to its extremes, this lack of faith could eventually result in greater government intervention and regulation—something that even a "bottom-line" guy can understand.

In summary, effective communication of bank objectives and policies is rooted in common sense and sensitivity. This willingness to communicate, and to translate corporate thought into corporate deed establishes the dialogue and environment for progressive banking operations. In effect, the successful achievement of that objective will always separate the great banks from the good ones.

MANAGING HUMAN RESOURCES

Chapter 9

Manpower Planning and Management

Lawrence M. Small*

Eugene J. Laka†

The recent past has been marked by rapid technological change. In our generation we have developed antibiotics and heart pacemakers, productive uses of nuclear energy, large-scale computers, and, in the banking industry, the replacement of paper processing with electronic transaction services.

The ability to achieve such vast and rapid change has been influenced to a large degree by the evolution of systematic, meticulous planning techniques. Virtually every major industry has incorporated in its management style the use of detailed planning procedures before it undertakes any new effort. We are only beginning, however, to bring this same planning discipline to bear on the most important resource in any activity: the human being.

How do people work together in such a manner to get the peak potential and enthusiasm out of a team and each of its members? Business has a new and keener appreciation of this question today. As a result, "personnel" has already largely given way to more sophisticated "manpower planning and management," and the decade ahead will doubtless witness marked progress in this field.

---
* Senior Vice President, Citibank, N.A., New York, New York.

† Vice President, Citibank, N.A., New York, New York.

A NEW ATTITUDE

There are several reasons for this new attitude toward people.

Although every generation has demanded new and higher skills of its workers, this generation seems to have intensified the demand far more than any before it. Manual laborers have become operators of heavy machinery, bookkeepers have become computer programmers, and first-level supervisors have become experts on a body of equal opportunity and affirmative action laws, codes, regulations, and reports that would do justice to a lawyer of an earlier age.

Consequently, one reason for the increasing corporate concern with "personnel" is the increasing demand for technology and regulation, and the corresponding growth in the difficulty of finding or preparing people to meet such demand.

A second reason is the magnitude of the modern "ripple effect." The Industrial Age has seen the shift of business from cottage industry to multinational. Today a good idea or wise decision in one place can bring benefits around the world. A mistake in London can have repercussions in Singapore. This makes business much more sensitive about people in decision-making positions, and influences a company's attitude toward its manpower planning and management. Moreover, as the world marketplace has become more competitive, the productivity of people—as well as machines—becomes crucially important.

A third factor applies directly to banks. As business grows geographically and in technical sophistication, it demands banking capabilities to match these growing needs. Consequently, today a major bank has to recruit not just tellers and loan officers, but experts in petroleum exploration, agribusiness, transportation, and other fields, and in the business practices and needs of many countries. This adds a new dimension to the bank's traditional "personnel" function.

RISING TO THE CHALLENGE

Companies generally and banks particularly are rising to this challenge at different speeds and in differing degrees. Some hew to the narrow personnel sense of replacement hiring, training, promotion, and determining wages. But most business has already adopted the broader view: manpower planning and management must not only have the right kinds of people in the right jobs today, but also provide today for the needs of the future.

This modern, broad approach is the direction of the future, and although experience will shape the way it evolves, the discipline breaks down into four functions.

1. Management must determine how many and what kinds of people will be needed to achieve future goals.

2. Management must have a reasonably accurate picture of the skills and human resources the bank now possesses.
3. Management must measure accurately the difference between needs and resources for meeting goals.
4. Management must develop and maintain programs that will have the necessary human resources developed by the time needed.

No bank will ever eliminate the gap between what is needed and what is on hand. Needs will change from day to day with business conditions, opening opportunities, and new ideas. Human resources will change with the normal turnover of people and with the growth and maturation of their skills. The process is a continuing one. The final of the four functions is not a conclusion, but a target—a moving target. Let's examine those functions in more detail.

Step 1, forecasting, implies that manpower planning and management must be part of the executive process of setting future corporate goals and deciding how to pursue them. Its contribution is to give other executives a complete picture of the present staff's potential, and an estimate of the amount of new talent or training of existing staff which is needed to achieve corporate objectives.

In addition to assuring that top management appreciates from the outset the manpower implications of any course it adopts, participating in long-range planning also ensures that those responsible for personnel know from the outset what the future will demand of them.

Step 2 is the evaluation of existing resources. The natural expectation that a company will be aware of all the talents and skills it possesses doesn't always hold true. Most employees work at jobs that utilize only part of their talents. Often management comes to think of the talents people use in their work from day to day as their full range of talents, and forgets those held in reserve. Even in small companies with relatively few employees, it's possible for management to lose sight of skills that exist beneath the surface. The skills which management is looking for in order to pursue some new course may exist in its present staff. The larger the bank, the larger the probable pool of unmined talent. But even in a small bank it is important to have fairly complete records on all employees, and a bank that employs tens of thousands cannot for practical purposes deal with manpower planning issues without a good records system. A personnel data system that compiles complete information on education, work history, and performance can provide corporate planners with an invaluable tool with which to assess the bank's ability to move into new business areas.

Step 3 might be called anticipating future problems. It is the measurement between the human resources expected to be needed and those already available. This comparison not only shows the planner what talent needs to be acquired, but also suggests a timetable to accomplish this and allows the time needed to study alternatives between hiring new talent and training existing staff.

Step 4 is planning manpower programs: eliminating the gap between present resources and future needs. It involves setting long-range policies on recruitment, internal transfer, training and development, and costs.

TOOLS OF MANPOWER PLANNING AND MANAGEMENT

The methods banks may use to integrate their manpower and business planning range from simple judgment to highly complex computer simulation models.

The most fundamental tool is the supervisor's firsthand knowledge of people. It can be used effectively by a president of a small bank judging an entire staff, the chairman of a bank holding company evaluating top executives, or a manager of any unit of any size between the two. The supervisor's judgment has the advantage of firsthand observation of people at work from day to day. This approach relies, however, on supervisors whose skill in assessing others may test the Peter Principle at one end of the scale, and Weil's law at the other.[1] Nonetheless, although supervisor estimates are not always consistent, and although they become less useful the further projections are made into the future, they are useful for quick short-range planning.

Another planning technique is the "prime indicator" method, which relates manpower needs to volume of business. A chemical company, for example, might determine that it needs one new worker for every projected 1,000-ton increase in production of a particular chemical. This method could be elaborated to determine that of every five new workers hired, one would be a foreman, three would be laborers, and one a mechanic.

The prime indicator method is of limited value in banking because of the variety of functions within a bank and among banks. One bank might usefully figure it would need another teller for every X new depositors, or a given number of new employees for so many more dollars in assets. But different groups or divisions within a large bank might have many different prime indicators, depending on their products or services. Improvements in technology would, of couse, necessitate periodic revision of the prime indicators, as an output per employee rose.

---

[1] The Peter Principle states that in any hierarchy people who perform well keep getting promoted to more difficult jobs, until they reach a level at which they do not do well—where they remain. It is often summarized: "Every manager rises to the level of his own incompetence." Weil's Law states: "The first-class manager surrounds himself with subordinates as good as or better than himself. The second-class manager surrounds himself with third-class people."

Another simple method of personnel planning is the replacement chart or succession plan. This graphic device ensures that all the important positions in an organization have enough backup personnel. Ordinarily, a chart shows the key positions in a company and their incumbents, with qualified successors listed for each. A glance at the chart may show where weaknesses lie, and action can be taken to correct them. In addition, as successors are identified, individual development plans can be designed to prepare them to take over the more important positions.

Supervisor estimates, prime indicators, and replacement charts are all fairly useful methods of personnel planning that rely fundamentally on subjective judgment.

In recent years the development of technology has led to experiments in using this new capability to improve the personnel-planning process. These innovations are still in their early stages.

A variety of planning models have evolved spanning a broad range of complexity and sophistication. Some attempt to forecast personnel needs by analyzing past trends in hiring, promotion, transfer, attrition, and the like. Others require computer programs and attempt to do complete skills inventories of entire corporations as a means of classifying personnel policies and practices.

The effectiveness of computer simulation is a function of the completeness of the data put into it, and the number of variables accounted for in the programming. At this point in its evolution, the technique is still in its experimental stages, and the results computers have turned out are often of little use and often misleading. This should not invalidate the whole idea of the computer's value in planning. What it means is that the process has not been sufficiently refined to the point where we can completely rely on it. Nor can we blithely assume that computers will eventually be able to take over the whole job of planning human resources. It is unlikely that computers will ever be able to account for all the variances in human behavior. Still, given the experience of the recent past, it is inevitable that some of the more sophisticated analyses made possible by computer technology will play an increasingly important role in manpower planning.

EXECUTIVE PLANNING

It is not possible to lay down rules for an ideal personnel planning and management process. The best method is the one that best fits the needs, goals, size, and personality of the particular bank. It is interesting to observe, however, that the principles used by Citicorp, a bank holding company with more than 46,000 employees, are almost identical with principles appropriate for the smallest bank in the remotest crossroads in the country. The principles rely basically on supervisor judgment.

Several of the company's characteristics have shaped the way Citicorp has set up its personnel-management planning.

One, obviously, is sheer size. Another is that an unusually large proportion is made up of professionals—about one fifth of the total worldwide work force. With such large numbers, it's impossible to rely on the collective memories of top management to identify and keep track of the talent within the organization and to provide for its most effective utilization. Therefore, the human resources management and planning function must not be isolated on the executive level, but must reach deep down through the entire organization.

Another characteristic, related to the first, is Citicorp's decentralized organization. The company is composed of more than a thousand separate profit centers. Each center is responsible for its own budgeting and marketing strategy and for its own manpower planning and management. The organization is such that decisions relating to the delivery of products and services are made by people closest to the market. They know best the needs and opportunities surrounding them. The personnel-planning process reaches down to this level for the same reason. Manpower planning is done in all geographical locations and at every level of management. This bottoms-up approach works from the grass roots all the way to the top of the corporation.

The importance of manpower planning at Citicorp is underscored by the fact that the chairman and president personally, twice a year, spend a full week with the heads of the seven major groups in the bank, formally reviewing their present staffing and provisions for the future. After individual meetings with each of the group heads, they meet with all of them together to discuss steps to achieve improved distribution of the most able corporate officers among the groups.

These reviews with the heads of each of the seven groups, of course, are a culmination of thorough manpower reviews within each group. Each January and June, the head of every division within each group prepares a presentation showing present organization and any planned organizational changes, ranking the best officers by performance and potential, naming backups for key positions, and identifying any staffing needs he cannot fill from within his own organization. In the larger units of the bank, formal reviews are held at levels below the division.

The group head consolidates all the divisions' presentations to prepare for his meeting with the chairman, and in so doing reevaluates all the top positions and their incumbents, determines where critical openings may arise, and identifies personnel that might be available for transfer during the next six months.

When the group head meets with the chairman and president, he is not accompanied by the group's personnel officer, but goes alone. This policy ensures that each group head is personally and thoroughly familiar with his most important resource—people. The chairman and president consider manpower planning of such importance that they assume rather than delegate responsibility for it, and they require that each group head also make it a personal concern of the highest priority.

The meeting with the chairman and president follows a standard agenda that covers the organization, key positions, high-potential officers, and affirmative action. The group head brings to the meeting a book with material on these topics in a standard format.

Under the first agenda item, *organization,* the group head reviews whether its existing structure is best suited for achieving present and future goals, and discusses organizational changes that might improve the group's future capability. Since the organizational structure is closely related to business strategies, this provides another opportunity to coordinate business and personnel planning.

Next on the agenda is a discussion of *key positions*—those considered of enough importance to warrant top management's concern with current staffing and backup candidates. One hundred general management positions and about 50 specialist positions are identified as key. The importance of the position, not the incumbent, is considered. The list of key positions changes as changing goals and opportunities shift priorities. For example, the development of a new technology or expansion into new markets might cause some leadership positions to be regarded as key, but they might cease to be so after the change is complete and the operation is running routinely. All of this data is displayed graphically in a central location for reference purposes.

In discussing which positions are most important, the group head will discuss the performance of the officers who now occupy these positions, highlighting their strengths and weaknesses. He will discuss the depth of backup talent, and the ability of immediate successors to step into them. In choosing backups, the group head is not confined to talent within his area. The group head may and often does use the total institution as a source. If necessary, the need for outside recruiting will be discussed. This phase will also deal with openings that result from transfers or organizational changes.

The next agenda item is discussion of *high-potential individuals* below the group head level who, because of demonstrated competence, are considered capable of holding one of the top 100 positions. They are considered corporate resources whose development is crucial and whose assignments require the approval of the chairman or president. Each group head not only identifies *high-potential* officers, but ranks them to show top management how they compare with one another.

Any proposed transfer of a *high-potential* officer is discussed at this review.

Also discussed under this agenda item are officers who, relatively early in their careers, show promise of becoming *high-potential* individuals within five years. The executives discuss their on-the-job performance, who should be added or dropped from the list, and what assignments the officers should be given to expand their experience and develop their capabilities.

The final agenda item is *affirmative action.* Group heads review the progress of women and minorities within their organizations to ensure they are meeting not only legal requirements but also corporate objectives. The agenda focuses particularly on identifying those capable of promotion to senior positions.

After the meetings with group heads individually, the chairman and president and all group heads convene in a general meeting to discuss the distribution of talent in the institution as a whole.

Here group heads discuss the senior positions they wish to fill, and the senior officers available for transfer. Group heads have developed a cooperative attitude toward exchanging talent, because experience has proved that in these interchanges as much talent flows into a business group as flows out, and the result is a reservoir of officers with a much broader and deeper range of experience and capability.

OFFICIAL PLACEMENT AND TRANSFER SERVICE

To provide junior officers the same kind of opportunity and mobility that this system affords, an official placement and transfer service has been developed. A committee of representatives of all major business groups meets twice a month to match people and job openings. Staff members who would like to enlarge their experience by transferring discuss this possibility with their supervisors, then give a resume to their group's representative to the committee. In the same way, each group keeps its representative to the committee informed of all positions that are open or that are expected to become open. The committee, of course, cannot actually make the transfers, but it refers appropriate candidates to the groups that have openings.

CAREER DEVELOPMENT PROGRAM

Citicorp has also set up the Career Development Program. It offers staff members who are not officers but who have earned college degrees an opportunity to be considered for management-trainee or professional jobs. This program has stimulated a high degree of response and enthusiasm within the staff; it has extended planning and development to the grass-roots level; and it has helped identify talent at every level.

Although the systems described here involve an organization with more than 46,000 people scattered all over the world, the principles are remarkably similar to those that might apply to the smallest bank in a local community.

The first principle is the commitment of top management to assume personal responsibility and devote time and effort to the development and utilization of talent. By extension, this principle applies all the way down the organization, where line officers, not personnel staff, implement and manage the process.

Another principle large banks may have in common with small ones is that of simplicity. Citicorp's approach uses, but is not dependent upon computer systems or advanced technology. It is flexible and simple, and it relies on judgment.

The third principle is the integration of personnel planning and the overall strategic planning of the business. It is essential for efficient and economic management to match the right person with the right job, and never to let the two types of planning become separated.

As time passes, the methods we use will improve, and the equipment at our disposal will help, but for large banks or small, simple or complex, these principles are likely to remain unchanged.

Chapter 10

Employee Selection

Irving Margol*

Robert Proctor†

INTRODUCTION

The human resources of a business are an integral part of all of its activities. Although this chapter is primarily concerned with the selection and recruitment of human resources, it should be recognized that development of those resources is dependent upon other organizational resources; selection cannot be studied in isolation. Rather, selection, development, and utilization of human resources must be considered as one integrated process, designed to incorporate both present and future needs of the company. Therefore, the company's goals should be clearly defined and established so that selection can be based upon finding personnel capable of realizing those goals.

ESTIMATION OF PERSONNEL NEEDS

Regardless of the method used to forecast needs and regularize recruitment to satisfy those needs, requirements must be estimated, and people must be hired with future demands in mind. This, in addition to normal replacement due to attrition. In many organizations, advance preparations are not made to ascertain how much manpower of various kinds are needed. Only after vacancies occur are steps taken to find replacements or additions to the staff. Without getting into a

* Senior Vice President, Security Pacific National Bank, Los Angeles, California.

† Vice President, Security Pacific National Bank, Los Angeles, California.

Exhibit 10–1
Some Components of a Human Resource Staffing System

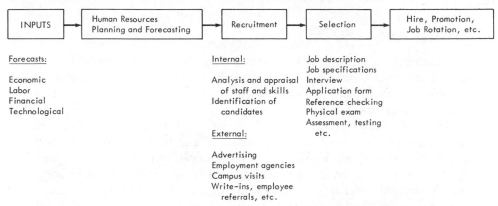

| INPUTS | Human Resources Planning and Forecasting | Recruitment | Selection | Hire, Promotion, Job Rotation, etc. |

Forecasts:

Economic
Labor
Financial
Technological

Internal:

Analysis and appraisal
  of staff and skills
Identification of
  candidates

External:

Advertising
Employment agencies
Campus visits
Write-ins, employee
  referrals, etc.

Job description
Job specifications
Interview
Application form
Reference checking
Physical exam
Assessment, testing
  etc.

complete study of human resources planning, Exhibit 10–1 shows the major components of a staffing system.

DETERMINING THE JOB

An individual is hired to perform a job. Therefore, the description of the job, its requirements, physical and mental characteristics, as well as any stated criteria for its successful handling should be known before seeking candidates. In determining a job, three processes are involved:

Job analysis is a process through which a determination can be made relative to the tangible and intangible aspects of a position. The job analysis activity looks at subjective and objective characteristics including criteria such as accountabilities, responsibilities, knowledge, aptitude, and capacity that are expected of the job and required of the incumbent. The analysis is usually conducted by both observation and study, and as a result a job description describing the position and not the person is developed, as well as a job specification.

Job descriptions are simple, concisely written statements delineating the accountabilities and objective requirements of a job and are used in communicating what is expected of the incumbent in the performance of his or her job. The contents are a summary of the duties to be performed and a statement of the end results expected of job performance.

Job specifications include statements of mental, physical, and other personal demands made of the job incumbent. They serve as the personal criterion to assist in selection and training of individuals. In effect,

they translate the job requirement from duties to those human characteristics necessary to perform the job.

RECRUITMENT

Recruitment in today's labor market is dynamic and complex for
all organizations, public or private, profit and nonprofit, and requires
a constant monitoring of methods and results to be cost effective. The
banking industry is no exception.

Today we contend with a steady diet of technological advance and
its impact on jobs. Socioeconomic change and technological progress
are visible in the marketplace where we compete for talent as well
as business and innovative recruiting techniques are required. In addition, state and federal regulatory bodies carrying potent enforcement
powers are developing precedent daily for monitoring the recruitment
and selection activities of all employers. Banks, like other sectors of
industry, have historically drawn from more or less traditional labor
sources not always reflective of the whole community.

We can no longer afford to rely upon our traditional assumptions
about jobs and what it takes to do them. Recruitment strategy should
be examined with some very key questions in mind.

1. What are the real and current staffing needs of the bank? Do tradi-
    tional standards lead us to seek overqualified individuals for some
    positions?
2. What are our sources of applicants? Have traditional standards
    caused us to overlook viable sources of talent?
3. How does the whole community view the bank? Is our image and/
    or hiring reputation helping or hindering recruitment results?

Recruitment volume may vary with the company's needs. But regardless of the number of jobs to be filled, recruitment practices
strongly influence the effectiveness of selection and can represent a
sizable portion of the cost involved.

The Concept of Job Relatedness

Job requirements or specifications should be regularly analyzed for
their accuracy and performance relatedness. It is difficult to develop
and focus a cost effective recruitment program if it is based on outdated
assumptions. We may be wasting time and money attempting to attract
applicants that are over- (or under-) qualified for our job needs. Continued reliance on degrees, diplomas, and fixed years of experience for
certain jobs may be irrelevant and wasteful.

For example, we may find on analysis the high school diploma useless as a performance predictor for clerical jobs, the baccalaureate degree no longer useful in predicting performance for management trainees. Perhaps we could hire individuals or promote individuals with lesser qualifications and train them to the desired level of performance. When the minimum qualifications for a job are needlessly high, very real problems result. Although we may intend to upgrade our work force, it is not likely to be the final result. We restrict our range of recruiting options by not giving persons who may actually perform well on the job a chance. We waste recruiting effort accessing sources which may not warrant the costs.

Defining the Recruitment Market: Traditional and Nontraditional Sources

In the interest of developing a work force which reflects the makeup of the community from which we recruit, a key requirement in Equal Employment and Affirmative Action statutes today, it is critical to do a complete and thorough analysis of all community sources. Many of these will be new and untried. Many of the local skills agencies developed from state and federal grants which have employment referral services may be capable of referring applicants well matched to your bank's job needs. Many times that capability takes time to develop. An ongoing supportive relationship in the community is critical if some of these nontraditional recruitment sources are to be established as viable and competitive referral sources. This is rather a new slant on the role of the recruiter. It requires a broader, more community-minded perspective on the bank's recruitment needs. Directories are available for accessing such agencies as the National Urban League, the GI Forum, the National Organization of Women, SER—to name a few.

Another key variable in assessing recruitment strategy is the condition of the labor market. Significant changes (besides the usual ups and downs of the economy) have occurred in the work force over the last decade. A change of great importance to banks is the growing population of white-collar workers (those involved in clerical, office, and sales work) compared to blue-collar workers. Banks are obliged to recruit in labor markets far more competitive than the past, and the trend continues. It is apparent we can't overlook any available source of qualified applicants. Present sources should be evaluated and fresh ones identified.

Ideally, in evaluating sources of applicants, the personnel manager should attempt to differentiate successful from unsuccessful employees. This information can hopefully be obtained from performance records, turnover records, and similar sources. If records also contain the recruitment source of the employee it should be determinable with some accuracy which sources have been most (and least) productive over the years. Once the productive sources are identified, recruiting effectiveness (and costs) are subject to greater control. This sort of examination may also reveal startling information about particular selection standards. For example, trainees traditionally recruited from a certain graduate school may prove to be less successful on the job than employees with lesser academic backgrounds. In this example the advanced degree requirement may not be justified.

A Fresh Look at Old Sources

Many of our traditional sources must be regarded from an analytical point of view. *Employee referrals,* historically a very valuable source of employees, can create problems if relied upon too heavily. This is particularly the case when the existing staff does not fully reflect the minority makeup of the community. Referrals may be predominately nonminority which would cause the bank's recruiting practices to have a disparate effect upon the minority sectors. Used exclusively under these conditions, a nonminority work force could be perpetuated indefinitely. The Equal Employment Opportunity Commission is very explicit about such conditions.

We've already noted that conditions of the labor market may influence availability of applicants. This is especially true with *walk-in applicants.* Similar to the employee referral, walk-in applicants may also not reflect the diversity of the community for a number of reasons. The location of the bank may make it difficult for certain groups to contact the employment office or indeed be aware of job openings. The past hiring practices of the bank may lead potential employees to believe they won't be hired anyway and choose not to visit the employment office.

A better representation of candidates is more likely when the employment office is well marked and handy to walk-in traffic, and when the environment inside is cheery and congenial.

It is particularly difficult for residents of urban or central city areas to apply when the employment office is situated in areas remote to them. This condition is frequently restrictive for minority groups who comprise a large percentage of the urban population and have limited transportation facilities.

Advertising, long a popular and effective method for acquainting the community with our job openings, offers a highly visible opportunity for the employer to publicize job requirements, the organization, and to depict the organization as an equal opportunity employer. At the same time, he or she may run sizable risks by using potentially discriminatory phrasing in the ads. For example, a typical general phrase we've all seen in one form or another that is overly restrictive is "the opening for an aggressive, ambitious, young executive who knows where he's going." Implied here are several overly restrictive conditions for employment; the applicant must be male and young, potentially discouraging women as well as older workers. Both groups are protected specifically by federal and many state statutes. In addition, some individuals may be unlikely to relate to the terms "ambitious," "dynamic," "executive," especially if they feel the employer has not actively utilized minorities at the management level. They may feel the ad is simply not intended for them. Moreover, advertising, unlike the walk-in and employee referral sources, is expensive. Therefore, it behooves us all as employers to vigorously analyze and evaluate our advertising practices to be certain potentially qualified candidates are not needlessly overlooked.

Ads should always contain a statement affirming that the employer is an equal opportunity employer. If qualifications are mentioned they should be demonstrably related to performance requirements since they are conspicuously published for the world to see.

Probably the most potentially productive recruitment source available to most employers today is *the campus* at all levels. Even though it becomes for many employers more difficult to demonstrate the job relatedness of a specific degree, the fact remains the campuses house large groups of potential job applicants. They are there in one place, serviced by the placement office and are readily accessible to employers. As college campuses become more and more aware of employers changing technological needs in terms of course content and of employers' needs to develop work forces which provide equal opportunity for all community groups, the campuses should remain a viable source of employees.

However, some campuses are far more responsive to employer and community needs and trends than others, and we as employers must continually evaluate each of our campus sources to determine which have provided us with the most successive employees. This is an ongoing, record-keeping, analysis type of activity that can have significant dollars and cents payoff to the employer.

The community college in particular offers a potentially fruitful source of employees. Because of their accessibility to the whole community in terms of location, lower entry requirements, and lower tuition they are far more promising in terms of their minority mix than the four-year institutions. As organizations realize that a four-year degree may indeed be unrealistic for certain jobs, the recruitment and placement activity on the two-year campus has begun to accelerate. In addition, many employers offer educational aid programs whereby the two-year graduates can, on their own time and with the bank's help, complete a four-year degree program if indeed it is mutually desirable and job related.

An additional recruitment source on campus with enormous potential is in the form of an old idea updated, *cooperative education.* Cooperative education has been around for a long time. However, only recently, with the advent of federal grants through HEW and increasing participation by both four- and two-year colleges, has the employer's awareness of this tremendous resource surfaced. Basically, cooperative education offers the employer the opportunity to develop a relationship with the cooperative education offices on local campuses whereby students are hired on a rotating basis for actual employment. While employed, the student is not only earning a salary on a real productive job but is usually, depending upon the particular arrangement with the institution, earning unit credit for the work experience. There is no one best format for cooperative education. The beauty of this source is that almost every case can be tailor-made to meet the needs of not only the student but of the employer and the institution. All parties may benefit. The campuses, of course, are anxious to attract more students—readily done when students are seeking career development through actual employment. The students are able to earn money while remaining in school augmenting their income and lightening the financial burden of an education. The employer is able to attract and acquaint over a prolonged period preferred applicants for existing jobs and ultimately offers employment based on a great deal more information—an actual employment track record—than through traditional means where selection is based merely on an interview and an application; both of limited value as information sources.

To be sure, campus recruiting, even at the high school level, can be expensive to maintain and you should be readily able to determine if results warrant such expense. Some companies have elaborate budgets for campus visits and maintain constant liaison with placement offices, coordinating among other things, summer and part-time employment programs. Other organizations are less dependent on the campus in meeting staffing needs. In any case, turnover and performance records should provide one useful evaluating measure and help to safeguard against overhiring in terms of qualifications really essential to job performance.

Employment agencies, both public and private, are also good sources of applicants in some situations depending upon the organization's needs, the level of vacancies, and the scarcity of the specific skill(s) involved. Employment agencies can be an integral part of the overall recruitment picture. However, it should be noted that employment agencies, like college recruiting and like advertising, are expensive, perhaps the most expensive. In addition, they are also subject to legislation governing employment (e.g., EEOC Guidelines, the Office of Federal Contract Compliance [OFCC], etc.). The bank should disregard such things as test scores reported by agencies when recommending their candidates, unless the agency can demonstrate that these tests have been validated as required by the federal guidelines. If it cannot demonstrate that the tests meet guideline standards, their use is unlawful (EEOC Guidelines, Section 1607.10, on employment agencies) and the bank may be liable.

Again, many public agencies offer placement recruitment services at no charge to the employer or the applicant and are usually reflective of particular groups within the community. You should survey your community for these and maintain regular contact with them to ensure your recruitment practices do not exclude any community groups. By all means, the local state employment office should not be overlooked. OFCC's Order Number 4 should be consulted when searching out such sources in that it contains a comprehensive listing.

It is always desirable to affirm in writing to all agencies being utilized that your bank is an equal opportunity employer and require from them a reciprocal affirmation in writing.

Perhaps the most helpful ongoing tool a recruiter can have is the *prospect file*. We rarely find individuals applying who are perfectly matched to jobs that happen to be open. However, if a list of qualified candidates is kept as individuals apply in a prospect file, it can be an economical as well as compliant tool for recruitment.

As a final comment on recruitment we must note that cost effective recruitment is a much easier proposition when the bank is favorably regarded throughout the community. Bankers, in the normal course of their jobs, tend to develop in-depth community relationships and actively participate in community activities. The effects of these activities should readily reflect in recruitment efforts. On the other hand, we must be continually alert for effects of possible reputation or community image the organization may have for such things as low pay, lack of advancement, discrimination, whether or not these perceptions are accurate. Even though we may know those conditions no longer exist in the organization, it is critical that the reputation for such conditions does not exist in the community. The effects of such a reputation can be, among other things, crippling to your recruitment efforts.

APPLICATION SELECTION: A SYSTEMS APPROACH

The actual selection of applicants requires close attention to two key factors. First, job relevant specifications not only facilitate better and more cost effective recruitment but are also critical to the economy and regulatory compliance of the selection system. It is difficult to imagine a selection system to be truly cost-beneficial as well as compliant unless close attention has been paid to job specifications.

Second, the selection process must be standardized. It is critical that each individual has equal opportunity to demonstrate his or her qualifications for the job. Both the EEOC and OFCC Guidelines specify conditions for validating selection procedures. While technical questions are still being argued in the public arena, two things are clear: (1) employers are now and will continue to be required to demonstrate the job relatedness of their selection procedures (validation), and (2) validation is dependent upon accurate selection records at each step of the process, and uniform application of the process. Selection should comprise a step by step process which systematically gathers all job relevant information about a candidate.

The selection system should provide for the process to be terminated properly at any step if it becomes apparent that the candidate is no longer a suitable match for the job. Exhibit 10–2 depicts a typical step-by-step selection process. The first contact with the applicant sets the mood for what is to come. It is very important for the receptionist to create a good first impression treating applicants in such a way as to put them at ease. This is true even if there is no opening. The job seeker may well come back as a customer.

If a receptionist normally greets applicants and refers them to someone else for a preliminary interview, the routine must be uniform and consistent. If he or she has the responsibility of screening applicants, the receptionist should be (1) thoroughly familiar with the selection system, (2) trained and qualified to conduct a preliminary interview, (3) able to describe qualifications for any open positions, and (4) able to state specific job related reasons for rejecting or screening out an applicant.

The preliminary interview is basically a screening process and should identify any obvious mismatches between applicant and job opening. For example, a comparison of the types of jobs open with the applicant's salary requirements, general experience, and job preferences can indicate the advisability of further consideration.

The Employment Application

At some point in the selection process you will want a formal application for each person applying for a position. The application and the kinds of information it contains have come under increasing regulatory scrutiny in recent years. Many companies have revised their application form because of some of the traditional kinds of questions contained were felt to be potentially discriminatory. In many cases, appli-

Exhibit 10–2
The Selection Process

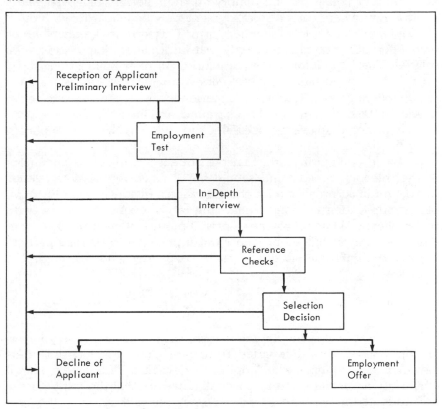

cations have required information that is directly discriminatory; i.e., questions regarding age, marriage, and race. These questions can be easily spotted and removed. More difficult are those questions which may be construed as discriminatory and there is considerable discussion as to what is included in this category. At this point there appear to be no universally right answers. However, the principal guideline for evaluating and redesigning, if necessary, an application form is again the concept of job relatedness. Questions which might be helpful in analyzing the application are (1) Is all the information required truly related to performance of the job in question? (2) Is information required which might better be gathered once the applicant is on board (information necessary for company benefits, and payroll information)?

The application should be as clean and direct as possible. It should contain a statement that the company is an equal opportunity employer and it should, in the event that references and background will be checked, inform the applicant the conditions under which this will be done and that it will be done with their permission, particularly in situations where current employment may be jeopardized. Exhibit 10–3 contains a sample application form. This form is like many which have been designed to gather only that information demonstrably job related. The basic information categories on most applications today include the applicant's complete work history, his or her educational experience, any other training or experience which may serve to better delineate the applicant's total background, and finally references, preferably former employers (especially supervisors), that the applicant can provide.

It should be kept in mind that the application itself is a document of the selection process and should be retained for possible agency inspection in accordance with the guidelines. In addition, a fully completed application becomes a planning tool for a full interview with the applicant. While it provides a partial picture of what the applicant has done, to make judgments about the applicant's fitness for a particular job the information ought to be expanded fully through the interview.

Testing

Properly validated employment tests can greatly improve your selection system. A well-designed testing program can aid the interviewer in determining what applicants demonstrate the best overall qualifications for the job. It is essential, however, that the test be properly validated in accordance with the guidelines if you intend to use scores in the selection decision. Validity in this sense means a definite relationship can be shown between test performance and job performance; that is to say people who do well on the test will generally do well on the job. If a test which has not been validated for employee selection is currently being used, you should first determine if it rejects disproportionate numbers of protected class groups. If not, the guidelines do not require any adjustment. However, the test may not be serving your company's best interests. If it is not validated for the job(s) it is selecting for, it is probably a waste of time and money at the very least. At the worst, it may lead you to select candidates highly unlikely to succeed on the job.

On the one hand, a test may simply not be helping you. Applicants who do poorly are just as likely to succeed on the job as those who do well. On the other hand, a validation study might reveal that those who score highest on your test are the most likely to fail on the job. Allowing either condition to continue is bad business.

If investigation reveals a test to be rejecting minorities at a higher

Exhibit 10–3
Sample Application Form

ANSWER ALL QUESTIONS COMPLETELY — THE INFORMATION YOU SUPPLY WILL BE FULLY VERIFIED, AND YOU SHOULD AVOID ANY

MISSTATEMENTS WHICH WOULD JEOPARDIZE YOUR CONSIDERATION FOR EMPLOYMENT.

PLEASE PRINT

SOCIAL SECURITY NUMBER	DATE OF APPLICATION MO. DAY YR.

APPLICATION FOR POSITION
WITH

_____

AN EQUAL OPPORTUNITY EMPLOYER

LAST NAME (Same as Social Security Card)	FIRST NAME	MIDDLE INITIAL	TYPE OF WORK OR POSITION DESIRED	MONTHLY SALARY DESIRED (DOLLARS ONLY)	SHIFT DESIRED DAY	NIGHT	MIDNT.

TYPE OF EMPLOYMENT FULL TIME	PART TIME	TEM-PORARY	TOTAL NUMBER OF HOURS PER WEEK DESIRED	HOW DID YOU HEAR ABOUT THE COMPANY? FILL IN RECRUIT-ING SOURCE CODE	RECRUITING SOURCE CODES
					0 = Newspaper Ad 6 = Walk-In 1 = Employee Referral 7 = Government Agency 2 = Agency Referral 8 = Campus Referral 3 = Rehire 9 = OCI (on campus 4 = High School/Jr. College interview) Recruitment 11 = Other 5 = Company/Customer Referral

PERSONAL

PLEASE INDICATE OTHER NAMES UNDER WHICH YOU HAVE WORKED OR OBTAINED EDUCATION, FOR REFERENCE CHECKING PURPOSES.

HOME ADDRESS (Number, Street, City, Zip)   TELEPHONE NUMBER ( )

HAVE YOU EVER WORKED FOR   ☐ YES   ☐ NO   IF YOU ARE UNDER 18 YEARS OF AGE, DO YOU HAVE A WORK PERMIT? ☐ YES ☐ NO   (If yes, show your work permit to your interviewer.)

IF YOU ARE NOT A CITIZEN OF THE UNITED STATES, ARE YOU LEGALLY ALLOWED TO WORK IN THE U.S.? ☐ YES ☐ NO   (If yes, enter your alien registration number, and show your alien registration card to your interviewer.) # _____

HEALTH

DO YOU HAVE ANY DISABILITIES WHICH WOULD PREVENT YOU FROM PERFORMING THE JOB(S) FOR WHICH YOU ARE APPLYING?   ☐ YES   ☐ NO   IF YES, EXPLAIN

EDUCATION

	NAME OF HIGH SCHOOL LAST ATTENDED AND ALL COLLEGES ATTENDED	LOCATION (ADDRESS - CITY, STATE)	FROM MO YR	TO MO YR	DEGREES CONFERRED
HIGH SCHOOL					
COLLEGE					
COLLEGE					
GRADUATE WORK					
BUSINESS SCHOOL					

MAJOR STUDIES   MINOR STUDIES

WHAT OTHER STUDIES HAVE YOU PURSUED, INCLUDING EXTENSION COURSES?

DO YOU HAVE ANY SPECIAL QUALIFICATIONS OR SKILLS?

FOR CLERICAL APPLICANTS ONLY: DO YOU TYPE? ☐ YES ☐ NO	DO YOU TAKE SHORTHAND? ☐ YES ☐ NO	WHAT OFFICE MACHINES DO YOU OPERATE?

08514-2 3-76 RRS   DO NOT SEPARATE PAGES — TURN TO BACK PAGE

Exhibit 10–3 (*continued*)

EMPLOYMENT DATA

List all employment for the past 5 years, or since leaving school, starting with your most recent position. Also list all volunteer experience at any time which relates to the job for which you are applying. All time must be accounted for including U.S. military service. If you were unemployed for any period state the nature of your activities. As your work experience is an important factor in finding a position for which you are best suited, complete carefully.

FROM		TO		EMPLOYER'S NAME AND COMPLETE ADDRESS (NO., STREET, CITY)	YOUR POSITION AND DUTIES	REASON FOR LEAVING
MO	YR	MO	YR			
START WITH MOST RECENT EMPLOYMENT						

HAVE YOU EVER BEEN CONVICTED OF A FELONY OR A MISDEMEANOR?   (OMIT TRAFFIC CITATIONS)

    ☐ YES   ☐ NO

IF YES, PLEASE GIVE FULL DETAILS

HAVE YOU EVER HAD A BOND REFUSED OR CANCELLED?
    ☐ YES   ☐ NO

IF YES, EXPLAIN

I UNDERSTAND PROOF OF AGE WILL BE REQUIRED UPON EMPLOYMENT AND I HEREBY AFFIRM THAT MY ANSWERS TO THE FOREGOING QUESTIONS ARE TRUE AND CORRECT AND THAT I HAVE NOT KNOWINGLY WITHHELD ANY FACT OR CIRCUMSTANCE THAT WOULD, IF DIS— CLOSED, AFFECT MY APPLICATION UNFAVORABLY. I UNDERSTAND THAT MISSTATEMENTS HEREON MAY BE CAUSE FOR DISMISSAL.

I ALSO UNDERSTAND THAT IF AN APPROPRIATE POSITION EXISTS FOR WHICH I AM QUALIFIED, I WILL BE CONTACTED WITHIN TEN (10) DAYS FROM THE DATE OF THIS APPLICATION.

_____
        (APPLICANT'S SIGNATURE)

TO BE COMPLETED BY EMPLOYING UNIT IF APPLICANT IS HIRED

ORG. CODE   INTERVIEWER'S NAME (PRINT)   APPLICANT'S ENTRY DATE

TO BE COMPLETED BY PERSONNEL RECORDS IF APPLICANT IS HIRED

08514-2 3-76 RRS

rate than nonminorities, you should: (1) continue to test and accumulate the data but do not use scores in selection; (2) discontinue testing immediately; or (3) seek qualified assistance in designing research to either follow-up on alternative 1 or develop and validate a new test program from scratch. The message here is that validation of selection procedure is the most prudent course.

How tests are administered can have a profound effect on their validity and usefulness. Standardization of testing practices is absolutely essential. Fundamentals of proper test administration should be strictly observed. Testing conditions to be observed and controlled include:

1. All materials (pencils, scratch paper, typing paper) ready.
2. Clocks or timing devices accurate and in good working order.
3. Any machines involved (typewriters, etc.) ready.
4. A quiet and spacious room, well lighted, at 72° F.
5. Uniform testing procedures and well-trained test administrators.
6. Relaxed atmosphere.

Points (5) and (6) cannot be overemphasized. The handling of people in a testing situation can significantly influence test performance. The role of the test administrator is critical to a useful testing program. The test administrator must be skillful in (1) putting individuals at ease; (2) explaining test instructions; (3) answering fully all questions pertaining to the test and instructions; (4) recognizing and handling individual anxieties; (5) recognizing and handling special communications problems, such as language deficiencies, sight, hearing, or other disabilities; (6) controlling prescribed test times accurately; and (7) scoring test accurately.

The interviewer's job is made easier when he or she has the application and test data around which to plan an interview. When tests have been properly validated, results are most helpful in assessing applicants, job aptitude, job knowledge and/or job skills.

However, like the application, test performances are just one source of information. They tell us little about an individual's communicative skills or depth of experience. They give us the best indication of whether an applicant can perform on a given job but not necessarily whether he or she will. This judgment must be based on information from all sources.

The Interview

The interview is one of the most widely used selection tools today. We have for years relied upon the interview as a central means of developing information about candidates. We are becoming increasingly aware, however, that the interview for most jobs has limitations.

It is not our purpose here to discuss techniques of interviewing but rather the uses of the interview and how it should be integrated into a systematic selection process. When information from the application and test performance (if available) is complete and interest in the applicant continues, qualifications should be discussed in-depth. The interview is the most flexible of all our selection tools in that it enables us to clarify and expand on information previously gathered by the application.

A well-conducted interview can provide a great deal of information about the applicant. However, keep in mind that only information which can be shown to be related to success on the particular job(s) under consideration can be used in the selection decision. Also, there are certain questions which cannot be asked during the interview in that they tend to be discriminatory in nature. These questions are primarily those dealing with religious affiliation, ethnic background, and national origin. Exhibit 10–4 contains an interpretative guideline to assist interviewers in phrasing questions properly. You should, however, consult local and state merchant groups or, if you have one, your State Fair Employment Practices Commission. They may also publish this type of material. The interview is best suited for providing answers to four primary questions:

1. Does the applicant appear to have adequate communicative skills for success on the job in question? For example, some jobs require extensive public contact and/or heavy staff interface. Other jobs do not. The interviewer must make a judgment as to the relative fit of the applicant's communicative skills to the job requirements in question. The decision involves matching demonstrated skills and aptitudes of an individual to a specific set of job behaviors. The interviewer must, of course, be thoroughly familiar with the behaviors necessary for success on the job being filled.
2. What does the applicant want to do? An individual will probably not be happy nor remain long on a job for which he or she has no particular interest. Hearing the applicant's aspirations helps to determine if a mutually beneficial job match-up exists.
3. What is the applicant's track record? What has he done? The applicant's work experience and job history has a specific bearing on the kind of job he is likely to do. Once the type and level of experience essential to do the job is determined, the interviewer can use the application to develop a plan for exploring the applicant's past achievements and how they relate to the job under considerations.
4. What is the applicant like personally? The individual's appearance, general manner, neatness and personality traits can be factors in

Exhibit 10-4
Interpretative Guidelines for Interviewers

Subject	Acceptable Preemployment Inquiries	Unacceptable Preemployment Inquiries
Name	Have you ever worked for this company under a different name?	Former name of applicant whose name has been changed by court order or otherwise.
	Have you ever been convicted of a crime under another name?	Maiden name of a married woman applicant.
	Other names under which the applicant has worked in order to check educational or employment records or references, if it is standard practice to check such references.	Inquiries concerning specific questions about the name which would indicate applicant's lineage, ancestry, national origin or descent.
Address and Duration of Residence	Inquiry into place and length of current and previous addresses	Specific inquiry into foreign addresses which would indicate national origin.
		Length of residency in the United States?
Sex and marital status		Sex of applicant.
		Marital status of applicant.
		Dependents of applicant.
		Maiden name of applicant.
Birthplace	Can you, after employment, submit a birth certificate or other proof of U.S. citizenship?	Birthplace of applicant.
		Birthplace of applicant's parents, spouse, or other relatives.
		Requirements that applicant submit birth certificate, naturalization, or baptismal record.
		Any other inquiry into national origin.

Exhibit 10-4 (*continued*)

Subject	Acceptable Preemployment Inquiries	Unacceptable Preemployment Inquiries
Age	If under 18 years of age, does applicant have work permit?	Requirement that applicant produce proof of age in the form of a birth certificate or baptismal record.
	Statement that hire is subject to verification of age at time of going on payroll.	Requirement that applicant state age or date of birth.
Religion creed	An applicant may be told "This is a six-day job. We work Monday through Saturday."	Whether an applicant for employment regularly attends a house of worship.
	An applicant may be advised concerning normal hours and days of work required by the job to avoid possible conflict with religious or other personal convictions	Applicants may not be told that employees are required to work on religious holidays which are observed as days of complete prayer by members of their specific faith.
Race or color		Complexion, color of skin, eyes, hair, or other questions directly or indirectly indicating race or color.
Photograph	May be required *after* hiring for identification purposes.	Requirement that applicant affix photograph to application form.
		Request applicant, at applicant's option, to submit photograph.
		Requirement of photograph after interview but before hiring.
Citizenship	If you are not a U.S. citizen, are you in the country on a visa which would permit you to work here?	Of what country are you a citizen?
		Whether applicant, parents or spouse are naturalized or native born U.S. citizens.

Height		Any inquiry into height of applicant, except where it is a bona fide occupational requirement.
		Date when applicant or parents or spouse acquired U.S. citizenship.
		Requirement that applicant produce naturalization papers or first papers.
		Whether applicant's parents or spouse are citizens of the United States.
National origin or ancestry and languages	Languages applicant reads, speaks or writes fluently.	Language commonly used by applicant in applicant's home.
		Applicant's nationality, lineage, ancestry, national origin, descent or parentage.
		Date of arrival in United States or port of entry; how long a resident of United States.
		Nationality of applicant's parents or spouse; maiden name of applicant's wife or mother.
		Language commonly used by applicant. Mother tongue.
		How applicant acquired ability to read, write or speak a foreign language.
		An inquiry into place of birth of applicant, parents, grandparents, spouse.
Workdays and shifts	Statement by employer of regular days, hours, or shift to be worked.	Any inquiry into willingness to work any particular religious holiday.

Exhibit 10-4 (*concluded*)

Subject	Acceptable Preemployment Inquiries	Unacceptable Preemployment Inquiries
Education	Inquiry into the academic vocational or professional education of an applicant and the schools attended.	Any inquiry asking specifically the nationality, racial or religious affiliation of a school.
Experience	Inquiry into work experience.	Inquiry into general military service.
Character, arrests and convictions	Have you ever been convicted of any crime? If so, when, where and disposition of case?	The number and kinds of arrests of an applicant.
Relatives	Names and addresses of parents or guardians of minor applicants.	For other than minor applicant, name and/or address of any relative.
		The maiden name of the wife of a male applicant or the maiden name of the mother of a male or female applicant for employment
		What dependents have you?
		Names of applicant's relatives already employed by this company or by any competitor.
Military experience	Military experience of applicant in the Armed Forces of the United States.	Inquiry into an applicant's general military experience.
	Whether applicant has received any notice to report for duty in the Armed Forces.	National Guard or Reserve units of applicant.

Inquiry into willingness to work required schedule.

	Rank attained.	Draft classification or other eligibility for military service.
	Which branch of service.	Applicant's whereabouts in 1914–18, 1941–45, or 1950–53.
	Require military discharge papers after being hired.	Dates and condition of discharge.
Notice in case of emergency		Name and address of relative or person to be notified in case of accident or emergency.
Organizations	What offices are held, if any.	List all clubs, social fraternities, societies, lodges or organizations to which the applicant belongs, other than professional, trade, or service organizations.
References	Names of persons willing to provide professional and/or character references for applicant.	Request of name of applicant's bishop, pastor or religious leader.
Miscellaneous	Notice to applicant that any misstatements or omissions of material facts in the application may be cause for dismissal.	

the selection and placement decision depending upon the job. This is a delicate area, however, especially in the light of constantly changing patterns of thought concerning fashions and dress styles. Judgments as to what constitutes proper appearance or personality for a given job become highly subjective and it is difficult to demonstrate the relationship of these factors to job behaviors. While this information can be useful to the interviewer, it should be weighed very cautiously in light of all the other information gathered.

One of the most useful functions of the interview is selling your candidate on the job and the company once it is determined to make an offer. This function should not be overlooked. It does little good to develop a modern, effective selection system to identify qualified candidates, if, in the end, we are unable to convert them to employees. Of course, the importance of selling an applicant may vary with the type of job and labor market fluctuations. By the same token, the interview can also be helpful in declining an applicant. Many times a personal touch is appreciated. Any selection system that sends applicants away with a bitter taste is surely inviting trouble in some form.

Reference Checks

Reference checks can be helpful in verifying and clarifying information already gathered about an applicant. They should be made only when there is a strong interest in the applicant and always with permission. When new information is developed through reference checking, it should be utilized with caution. It is usually opinion and must be evaluated in light of all other available information about the applicant. Generally, it is most helpful to get the reference from prior supervisors who have had close contact with the individual and are qualified to provide useful information if indeed they are willing to do so. An applicant should not be declined because of negative information unless it is clearly reliable and strongly indicates that the applicant will not be likely to perform the job in question satisfactorily.

Medical Examinations

An additional piece of information sometimes required is a pre-employment physical examination. Physicals as a selection standard should fall under the same standard of job relatedness as test interviews. Since medical examinations tend to be expensive, they should probably come as the last formal step in the process when they are used.

The Selection Decision

When applied in a uniform manner, the selection system will produce profiles on each candidate which can then be assessed and

Exhibit 10–5
The Selection Decision

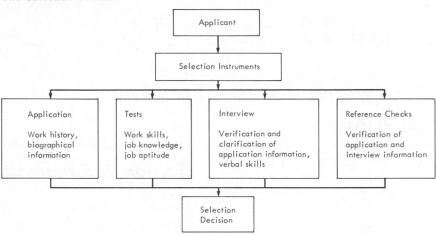

compared against the job specifications in question. Even though a final choice may be difficult, the qualifications of each candidate can be systematically compared using the information gathered with each of the standardized selection instruments (Exhibit 10–5). Each applicant will have had an equal opportunity to demonstrate his or her qualifications. The bank's selection requirements (specifications) at each step in the system and from time to time should be reevaluated to be sure the applicants with the highest likelihood to succeed in the job are being consistently identified and selected.

Chapter 11

Management of the Training Function

Gordon P. Sweeney*

Often considered an expense of doing business, formal bank training is rapidly developing into a viable human resource profession. As with several other organization technologies, training has its special vocabulary and jargon. It might be worthwhile to define certain special training terms as we use them in this section.

Training. Any developmental activity which increases knowledge and skill related to banking functions and services.

Programs. Any internal or external materials, format or other teaching aids which are used to instruct in a training process.

Feedback. A process of informal and formal evaluation, concerned here with training effectiveness.

Organizational Development. A process of determining overall bank goals and strategies and unifying various bank departments to achieve maximum results.

Management Development. As referred to in this chapter, the same issues as outlined under training.

Training as a profession has existed for many years. In banking it is relatively new as a corporate, full-time function if we dismiss on-the-job types of activities which we have all encountered. The assumption in this chapter is that a bank or holding company has a formal training function which is responsible for increasing the knowledge and/or skill of bank employees.

* Senior Vice President, Warren Management Consultants, Charlotte, North Carolina.

SENIOR MANAGEMENT'S ROLE

The commitment of top management to training success cannot be overemphasized. Too often senior executives allow their role in this function to be passive, reflecting the view if other banks train, so we should also. However, there are positive approaches open to management, some which will help ensure better training results.

1. Top management must identify performance objectives satisfactory to its board of directors, and its stockholders. These objectives should be clearly stated, well understood, and subject to accurate measurement. Normally such criteria will be stated in financial terms such as increases in loans, deposits, and per share earnings, or decrease in interest and noninterest costs. The point is to have targets against which individual performances can be assigned and then measured. As individuals demonstrate success or failure in achieving such targets, criteria for training programs can be established.

2. Several of management goals will be of short-run duration. Others will have a longer term priority. Ability to distinguish these timetables is essential to training planning. Management needs to know how long a period is available to build up knowledge and skills to accomplish bank operating goals.

3. Another important senior management responsibility is to help its organization discover which customer base is best for the bank. A marketing plan should indicate which kinds of special employee skills may be required to penetrate various customer groups. Training programs can then be developed that supply the appropriate skills.

4. If senior management sees the training function as an investment in the growth of the organization to help meet its objectives, then budgeting for training staff, funds for training materials, time off regular working hours to attend programs, and all such related expenses will be allocated properly. That is not to suggest blind faith, but to stress training can and does have a return only when the function relates specifically in aiding management achieve its objectives. Management review of training results can then be tied back to the operating plan.

5. Senior management must also ensure that each and every employee has access to training and development, even though some employees may not want to take advantage of the opportunity.

ORGANIZATION CONSIDERATIONS

Where best does the training function belong? Under personnel, operations, banking? Traditionally, the function has been assigned to "operations" because that is where the personnel function is usually located. As banks grew and holding companies emerged, and as they became subject to more external influences, there evolved a separate personnel or "human resource" activity. It then became the norm to assign "corporate training" to the personnel office. A good argument can be made to support this location. The responsibility of the personnel department is to attract, develop, motivate, and retain qualified staff. It supports the other banking functions as they use people to perform the essential functions. In a holding company the integration of corporate training and planning is especially appropriate. The relationship between planning and training cannot be stressed too strongly.

When does a bank justify a full-time training specialist? There is no precise answer. Surveys suggest that when a bank reaches $100 million in assets, the opportunity for the function begins to emerge as a full-time, day-to-day activity. Much depends upon the banking climate—does the bank have branch privileges? Does a holding company extend across county lines? Certainly by the time a bank reaches $250 million in assets it has the number of people, the needs for many special skills, and the operating diversity to require formal full-time training.

Who is accountable for training? Where is it accomplished? Should line managers and supervisors carry out the training function? Whether a bank has a full-time person as training manager or not, it is imperative to include as many line managers as feasible in the training process. The effectiveness of the training program depends upon:

a. The needs analysis which discovered the weaknesses or operating deficiencies.
b. The communication by line supervisors as to why the training is needed and who needs the help.
c. The follow-up after training to see whether improved performance is apparent.
d. The flexibility of programs to meet specific group needs when further training needs are apparent.

Contributions from line and senior management on what is "expected on the job" is the most critical training ingredient to make the investment in training return its costs. As a bank grows (i.e. adds branches or new banks), "satellite" training functions may become economical and effective. This dispersion puts pressure on overall quality of training design, classroom expertise, and follow-up. However, it may be better to "decentralize" to insure prompt response to "local" needs. This is particularly true with respect to large metropolitan branch banks, statewide branching, and bank holding companies.

The training manager is primarily responsible for determining program requirements as they relate to training. Specifically, he must decide whether to purchase or build a program to meet the training needs (economic as well as staff considerations). Then he must:

Construct the program.

Deliver the program.

Follow up the results.

Discover ways to improve, if repeated.

Decide when it no longer serves original need.

Report to management what financial results were obtained.

Assist others (line managers) to instruct more effectively.

Obtain from line managers constant feedback about current programs and present and future needs.

Advise on the acquisition of external training when appropriate.

Most, if not all, training programs suffer because the financial cost/benefit relationships are not presented effectively to management. The cost side, except for allocation of indirect expenses (such as salaries of participants, instructors, heat, and light) is identifiable. The difficult but important task is to show why, in financial terms, a training program is worthwhile. How will the program increase income? Or decrease expenses? If neither of these is apparent, then the program is a waste of time and money. Training must be included as a regular part of all formal financial planning and budgeting efforts. In budget meetings to discuss future operations, the need for improved personnel performance, the role of training, and the cost/benefit relationships involved should be an important part of the agenda.

As the training manager gains experience with the training function, the bank may want to establish a formal income/cost center administration of training to be associated with units of the bank. This will provide several management controls:

a. Line managers will only "pay" for training which effectively enhances their results.

b. Training staff must "produce" worthwhile programs.

c. Organizational goals of each unit will be measured in common, financial terms.

STAFFING THE TRAINING FUNCTION

What type of individual makes the best professional trainer? Where are candidates recruited? Should they have banking knowledge and experience? There are no simple answers to these questions for all situations. There are, however, some characteristics which distinguish effective training managers for banks:

1. They should be financially oriented and not just behavioral theorists.
2. They should be capable of providing a catalytic influence.
3. They should have a profound sense of what it means to exert change on organizations and individuals.
4. They should be less concerned with programs than with helping line managers identify and remedy performance problems.
5. They must seek recognition through the evaluation of better or improved results reported by line managers.
6. They must persist when training process sputters.
7. They must be skilled in oral and written presentation.
8. They should continually investigate "how to" support the organization to achieve higher goals.

The following are some of the more important subject matter areas essential to the trainer:

Money and banking	Management styles
Federal Reserve System	Needs analysis
Economics	Performance measurement
Finance, investments, operations, etc.	Managing subordinates
How adults learn	Environmental issues
Reinforcement of behavior	Presentation/Delivery techniques
Organizational behavior	Bank policies
Organizational development	

The list, though incomplete, is still overwhelming. What the profile demonstrates is the blend of skills and knowledge which have to do with understanding and shaping organizations and their people. To do the trainer's role professionally demands continuing preparation, and a willingness to examine all possible alternatives and only then, in tandem with the functional area, to suggest training programs to correct deficiencies.

Is college necessary? Not universally. It can provide a background head start, especially with respect to knowledge in certain areas. It does or should assist research or investigative skill. It may lend self-assurance. All of these are important. However, the "right" person must have the ability to assist in behavior change.

How many trainers does a bank require? A "true" professional may be all that is necessary with additional help coming from prepared line managers. Furthermore, the size of the full-time training staff is a function of the department's ability to economically "produce" the programs to solve training needs. It may be more beneficial to purchase outside than to design in-house. It may be more effective to hire, as needed, select professionals to conduct sessions. The determinants depend upon costs/benefit relationships. What is to be accomplished? What is the actual problem? What is the time for implementation?

Where are the candidates for the job? There may already be someone with the educational experience, potential, and inclination working in the bank. If not, an intermediary should probably be used to help locate, screen, and select the right candidate. This offers several advantages:

1. It helps avoid "unpleasant" reactions from another bank or company.
2. It avoids wasted interviewing of people who are clearly unqualified.
3. It helps avoid "turning down" unqualified candidates.
4. It allows a hiring criteria against which possible candidates can be measured from a wide labor market.
5. It is probably less expensive in the long run.

What future does a professional trainer have in banking? Possible career paths include:

A *Human Resources Function*	*B* *Line Management*	*C* *Corporate Planning*
Training	Banking	Operations
Recruiting	Lending	Holding company staff
Compensation	Investments	

This wide range exists because the trainers are involved in all functions of banking; because they need broad and thorough preparation to be effective; because they have had to acquire "on-the-job" knowledge in order to be effective with training programs; and because they have negotiated with most line and staff managers.

Some banks use staff assignments in personnel and training as interim steps in an overall career program. Other banks see the need to develop in-house expertise in personnel and training and insist on longer term tenure to build up the professional role. Whatever the style, the nature of trainers' experience should make them unusually qualified for a variety of career assignments.

SPECIAL FACILITIES

Training requires varying degrees of on- and off-site accommodations. Some banks use board rooms to conduct classes; others employ lunchrooms; others use much more elaborate facilities, equipped with audio/visual assists.

Classroom facilities, at a minimum, should provide versatile presentation capacity. Possible formats and multiple uses of such facilities include:

1. *Theater Style.*   Maximum seating for lecture-panel discussion.
2. *Seminar Style.*   Discussion oriented—less seating capacity.
3. *Workshop Style.*   Maximum audience participation—smallest seating arrangement.
4. *Staff/Employee Meeting.*
5. *Community Groups.*   (If security is not a problem.)
6. *Stockholder Meetings.*

(While the last two do not relate to training, they are included to illustrate how to justify space for full-time training and related uses.)

Training quarters should emphasize:

1. *Visual Reinforcement.*   Use of flip charts, overhead projectors, blackboards.
2. *Audience Contact.*   Use of encounter seating—people face each other.
3. *Audio Support.*   Sound reinforcement through use of sound/slide and movie devices.

Some kinds of training demand isolation where employees can practice without interruption. Typical of these needs are:

1. Teller Training.   Many believe this is too expensive. There are ways to "pool" teller training needs with other banks to reduce costs, thus justifying a formal school. To be sure, some internal procedures are different, as are teller machines. However, many basics are generic to this function and can produce excellent training results.

2. Other examples of this type of practice training are:

A.   Proof/transit
B.   Bookkeeping
C.   Data processing
D.   Accounting

There are many typical classroom training opportunities which best accommodate to seminar, panels, workshop approaches. Some examples are:

1.   Supervisory skills training.
2.   Management development.
3.   Organizational development.
4.   Credit and loan training.
5.   Trust new business classes.

6. Trust investment seminars.
7. Communication seminars.

Finally, there are some training programs which are best accomplished completely off-site. Examples include:

1. Executive (senior level) policy meetings.
2. Planning sessions.
3. Executive development and the emphasis on leadership skills.

There are, therefore, excellent alternatives to conducting training "in-house." Some programs can best be served from a "training center" approach. Other programs, such as supervisory skills, can be conducted in both internal and off-site facilities.

SOURCE OF TRAINING PROGRAMS

To build or to buy?—that is a major question. Obviously, definite variables enter into such a decision.

To Build Own Program

Cons	*Pros*
1. Time consuming.	1. Tailored to bank.
2. May not have in-house talent.	2. Needs known.
3. May not carry enough prestige.	3. Know how employees react.
4. No history of program working.	4. Provides worthwhile experience for future programs.
5. Wasted effort in design.	5. Should be less expensive than out-of-pocket purchase.
6. Takes on "trial and error" style.	6. It is the bank's product—no false promises.

The purchase side should be analyzed in the same manner.

To Purchase a Training Program

Cons	*Pros*
1. Not always related to banking.	1. Available now.
2. If not, people don't easily transfer learning from nonbank material.	2. Tested and used by others.
3. Usually seen as high expense item.	3. Eliminates waste.
4. Once purchased, no assurance on making program work.	4. May be "prestigious."
5. Almost always needs expensive adaptation to own bank.	5. Can learn how to build future programs.

No one can tell in advance whether one way is better than the other. A great deal depends upon analysis:

1. Does a bank have the talent to build a training program?
2. Are the needs properly assessed?
3. Is the time available to build, experiment, change, modify, edit, experiment again, and so on?
4. Is the need for a program transient? Will the program be repeated or is it one-time only?

These and other questions have to be considered. Since it is human nature to make your own wheel, one danger to guard against is the vested interest of the trainer. It may not be economically feasible to reinvent each new training program required by a bank.

Assume existence of a program, whether homemade or purchased. It is usually best to "pilot" the program with an operating unit before broadening its application. Pilot programs offer several advantages in starting new training efforts:

1. They give the program a chance to work with a real audience before it is used bankwide.
2. They allow an opportunity to make corrections prior to final adoption.
3. They permit an evaluation of assumptions and determination of whether program will meet objectives.
4. They permit a "failure" without an entire organization participating in the debacle.
5. They provide a "live" feedback, which is essential to an effective training endeavor.

The most effective method for presenting training programs for management approval—and for obtaining financing—is to portray:

1. The cost of the design and/or purchase.
2. The cost of operating *without* improved performance.
3. The cost of training time necessary to increase knowledge and skill.
4. Income improvement from better operating performance.
5. Income to be gained from more effective personnel performance.
6. Income benefit from reduced errors, higher productivity, better cross selling; in short, whatever the operating need is perceived to be.
7. Income benefit from higher personnel morale, including lower turnover, absenteeism, and customer dissatisfaction.

Training programs are justifiable only if they integrate with overall bank or holding company operating goals. They cannot and should not be a "personnel" activity. They can accomplish desired results only when fully in harmony with line management's operating objectives. Training is a staff service which follows the lead of management. The total training program includes:

A. A full briefing of the expectations for each participant.
B. Full disclosure of what specific performance activity is desirable.
C. Establishment of priorities:
    1. How will the bank be able to measure performance improvement?
    2. What kind of changes will be required by line management and senior management?
    3. What corrective action is necessary to sustain improved performance? Who is responsible for the follow-up? (Training managers and line managers have a dual accountability.)
    4. A constant evaluation by the training manager to determine whether programs:
        a. Continue to meet original needs and objectives.
        b. Apply to changing audiences.
        c. Need to be revised in context, style, frequency.
        d. Should be discontinued.

There is no substitute for "tracking" results of all training efforts. Dynamic presentations can indeed help employees learn. The skilled speaker can hold attention. Training efforts should be rewarding experiences. All this is true. The "bottom line" test is whether the bank realizes the program's intent and objectives. Too frequently, training is seen and experienced as a form of entertainment. Although it may be pleasant to have enjoyment as employees learn new content or new behaviors, the professional trainer is more concerned with:

1. Does the program meet the operating need?
2. Does the feedback from employees exhibit their understanding and need for change?
3. Does the program telegraph strengths and weaknesses in employees' ability to learn and/or change?
4. Will the trainer be able to summarize for line management what the employees have learned from the training exercise?
5. Will the trainer be able to measure, with the line manager, how employees are performing differently than before?

SUMMARY AND CONCLUSIONS

What can go wrong with training programs? When training professionals share experiences, inevitably they discuss symptoms of failure which more appropriately should be defined as high frustration. There are common obstacles to the success of training programs.

1. Senior management may not comprehend how training benefits the bank. This may be a communications breakdown, or the trainer ignoring senior management's need to understand in financial (as opposed to behavioral) terms what advantages accrue with effective training packages.

2. The trainer and line manager may improperly define the operating problems which lead to misunderstanding. Obviously, unless the proper "needs analysis" is conducted, permitting valid and reliable discovery, it is difficult if not impossible to produce a training program which will help the bank.

3. Too frequently employees recommended by line managers for training are poorly prepared for their participation. Managers and employees should be given full particulars about the program's objectives—how those objectives were established and especially how trainees could personally benefit from the experience.

4. Another major area of concern is the follow-up process. More often than not, training programs falter when these programs do not take into account how well the line areas are performing. When "graduates" return from formal training to their jobs, they should be "debriefed" by their supervisors about their training experience, as well as counseled how the line function will evaluate future operating results. It is the trainer's reponsibility to coordinate this follow-up.

5. Senior management should periodically reinforce training efforts. Endorsement of a program when it commences is to be expected. But, continued, obvious support of the program as it matures will help ensure optimum cooperation and participation at all levels.

6. Finally, there is a constant need to keep training material up to date. It can be ineffective to continue the same training program year after year. Bank objectives change. So do its people and so should the training.

Training in a bank is everyone's job, some more formally than others. The training manager is the catalyst. Through professional training methods which the manager can provide, the bank has an opportunity to harmonize short- and long-range objectives with employees who can develop ever increasing knowledge and skill.

Only with clearly defined and measurable goals will banks achieve the results that stockholders, boards of directors, customers, and participants expect and deserve.

Chapter 12

Supervision for Effective Manpower Utilization

Dwight L. Allen *

The effective use of manpower becomes increasingly important as its cost continues to rise. In banking, where payroll cost is usually exceeded only by interest expense, optimum use of staff is a necessity if maximum profits are to be realized.

RESPONSIBILITY OF SUPERVISORS

Proper use of the bank's manpower is the responsibility of supervisors. This duty is discharged by converting the policies of management into action by the employees. As the buffer between the two worlds of management and employee, the first-line supervisor must reconcile the logic of management's policies with the emotions of employees as these policies are applied in actual work. Policies and directions which are logical in the board room are not always seen as reasonable when applied to individual situations.

Supervisors must interpret management attitudes for the employee and the employee attitudes to management. Thus, management's impact on the employees occurs mainly through the supervisors. This is, and should be, the primary and frequently sole point of contact between these two groups.

Supervisors are a part of management. At the same time, they spend their working time in the employees' world, which has a different orientation from that of management. Consequently, it is difficult for

---

* Vice President, City National Bank and Trust Company, Columbus, Ohio.

supervisors to gain acceptance from both parties of interest. Management often views the supervisors as being too employee-oriented and lacking management perspective. Employees frequently see them as representing only the interests of management.

Only the supervisory position straddles the two worlds of management and employees. All other levels of management are flanked by other layers of the same type, albeit of different rank, but still management. The front-line supervisory position is at the end of the management chain, flanked by management on one side and employees on the other. Therefore, until the supervisor translates management's policies into actions by the employees, nothing will happen.

DUAL RESPONSIBILITIES

Supervisors in commercial banks have an added difficulty in performing well, because many of them are part-time. There are some large employee units in banks which require all of a person's time to supervise. But, there are also usually smaller units which require some supervisory direction, but not the full time of one person.

In these instances, the person with supervisory responsibility usually has additional responsibilities of a technical nature. In a small branch, for example, the supervisory teller has other assignments, and the loan officer will have the added duties of supervising other loan personnel.

When a person has dual responsibilities, the one which is most visible to management usually receives first attention. In almost all cases, technical responsibilities are represented by paperwork. Loan applications, commerical or installment notes, credit reports, teller sheets, budgets, and other reports, by piling up on a desk or in an in-basket, demand attention. Supervisory responsibilities, on the other hand, are not so frequently represented by paper flow. The need to provide more training, help solve personal problems at home, grant salary increases, provide discipline, or resolve personality clashes among subordinates are seldom represented by pieces of paper, but they are crucial to effective supervision.

Consequently, technical responsibility tends to pile up in a visible fashion when not handled promptly; supervisory responsibilities do not. The supervisor naturally tends to spend the most time on those duties which are visible.

One way to solve this problem and enhance supervisory performance in the process is to represent supervisory responsibilities with "paper" whenever possible. If supervisory duties are represented by paperwork which piles up visibly if not done then these responsibilities will demand more attention.

POSITION OF FRONT-LINE SUPERVISORS

In spite of its problems and ambiguities, the position of front-line supervisors are essential to good management. If a bank is to function effectively, supervisors must be given authority. If they are not properly trained, this authority can be dangerous because the front-line supervisor can bind the bank just as surely as high-level officers. Many banks are in court every day defending themselves against decisions or actions of low-level supervisors.

There is a distressing tendency to overlook the importance of supervisors. They are seldom included in management meetings and, all too often, there is no formal communication plan to assure that supervisors are informed about decisions and new policies affecting their work.

Supervisory meetings are seldom held on a periodic basis. While officers frequently attend management courses, it is rare that a supervisor is permitted to do so. This reflects the regrettable tendency to view supervisors as employees rather than management.

To the contrary, supervisors, even at the lowest level, are part of management, simply because their decisions and actions are usually and properly construed as being those of management. They need, therefore, to be aware of their authority and to be able to use it appropriately. This requires training so the supervisor can use authority effectively and without placing the organization in jeopardy.

IMPROVING SUPERVISORY PERFORMANCE

There are only two ways to improve supervisory performance. One is to better train those persons who are already supervisors, and the other is to improve the selection process for future supervisors.

There are some innate traits which enhance supervisory performance. In the main, however, supervisory skills are acquired rather than inherited—supervisors are made, not born. One reason is that on many occasions the supervisor is required to perform and think in ways which are diametrically opposed to human nature. Unselfishness, objectivity, equal feeling for all, not having favorites—these are some of the traits necessary in a supervisor which do not come naturally but must be learned.

Training

Training can be divided into four segments—short- or long-range and off-premise or in-bank.

Short-range training usually consists of attendance at a concentrated training course. This is more effective if the attendees are young and have not yet reached the age where a classroom represents a "threat." The acceptance of the competition of a group-learning experience, such as a classroom, tends to fade the longer one is removed from the time of formal learning.

Short-range training usually attempts to reconstruct the workplace and telescope its experience into a much briefer time span.

Training in the long-range consists of planned job placement to give varied experiences in different supervisory environments, since supervisory style is not a constant but should vary with the type of work and persons supervised. When time permits, the slower, evolutionary process can produce solid supervisors whose skills are sharpened by actual experience.

Short-range training may take place away from the bank, unless the bank is a large one with its own training staff. Such supervisory schools impart through lecture, role playing, and other group participation experiences the essence of supervision. Like any practical aspect of education or training, it must be quickly applied if maximum value is to be received. Perhaps the major problem with supervisory school is the delay in the opportunity to apply the theory until the students are back in a real work situation.

In smaller banks, the most effective training can be an assignment to work with a competent supervisor. We learn much from watching what people do and why they do it. Working with a successful boss can be one of the best methods of acquiring supervisory skills.

The training of supervisors is slow, expensive, and often inefficient in the short range. Only in the long term does training make sense. Therefore, it takes farsighted management to recognize that the training investment pays great dividends.

The Selection Process

The best way to improve supervision is also the quickest—selecting the right persons for future supervisory vacancies. One method of selection, the Assessment Center, is slowly gaining acceptance in banks. Large industrial organizations have been using this method for many years.

The hesitancy in using this method results primarily from the fact that it requires a commitment of time on the part of some members of middle management. These time commitments are short—usually three to five days—but complete during the time the program is functioning.

The Assessment Center evaluates, for supervisory potential, four to eight persons at each session. It does this by placing the participants in situations which simulate the life of a supervisor.

Prior to starting an Assessment Center, agreement must be reached as to what qualilties the organization desires in its supervisory staff. These are grouped according to importance. Exercises are then constructed to give the participants an opportunity to demonstrate the degree to which they possess, and can use, the various qualities.

For example, some important qualities necessary for effective supervision may be leadership, judgment, oral communication, orientation toward people, and tolerance of stress. Situations are designed to include these factors and the participants are observed by evaluators who note how they perform.

A typical evaluation session consists of two days of exercises under the observation of evaluators. Usually there is one evaluator per participant, although one evaluator may be used for two participants.

During these two days, the evaluator makes no decisions but records as objectively as possible the performance of the trainees. On the third day, the participants return to work, evaluators exchange views and then the group reaches a consensus on the degree to which each trainee possesses the various qualities. The observations and the opinions should be recorded and discussed later with the participants, if they so desire.

In a properly conducted assessment session, there should be opportunity to make approximately the same number of observations as would normally occur in two years of actual work. This is possible by the construction of specific situations which are constantly placing the participant in a supervisory role. Under normal working conditions, such situations would occur only every week or even less frequently.

The accuracy of evaluations through the Assessment Centers has been verified by several studies. If a person does not perform well during the session, the odds are heavily against his or her developing into a satisfactory supervisor.

The advantages of this method of selecting supervisors are the short time required, validity, and objectivity. The disadvantages are the necessity of key members of management devoting full-time for several days, the expertise needed by the training department in constructing useful exercises, and the reactions of those supervisory candidates who are rejected.

The evaluators should be at least two levels above the position for which the assessment session is being held. For example, if potential for the first level of officer is being judged, then the evaluators should be third-level officers. If the exercise is to select first-level supervisors, then the evaluators would perhaps be first-level officers. Proponents of this selection method believe that the selection of good management potential is an important function that is worth the time. One misjudgment in the selection of management personnel can be costly in terms of both time and earnings.

Perhaps the greatest concern involves those candidates who do not acquit themselves well during the exercise. They may react negatively and even resign from the bank. In practice, however, these employees usually recognize that their performance was subpar and accept their limitations in the area of supervision. Since this is a realization that will eventually come anyway, it is better for all parties if it is recognized after an assessment exercise rather than after months of poor performance as a supervisor.

Use of Past Performance Record

One of the most common methods of selecting supervisors is on the basis of past performance. To be valid, judgments on supervisory potential should be made by a number of supervisors who, over a period of time, have had the opportunity to view the candidate as he or she performs each day.

If this method of long-range examination is to be used, job rotation should not be left to happenstance, but should be planned and executed in a formal manner so there will be a good cross section of supervisors in a position to make valid judgments.

The judgments and observations of the supervisor should be shared periodically with the trainee so there might be encouragement for satisfactory growth and performance and correction in those areas where improvement is needed.

The periodic observations should be recorded and filed because over a period of time the accumulative evidence from different sources will merge into a pattern for the individual trainee.

Persons who want positions of leadership usually seek them out. This desire for control, for the satisfaction of decision making, for the prestige that accompanies responsibility will be satisifed outside the office if not permitted there. Public service projects, churches, fraternal clubs, community groups all require leadership too.

An indication of leadership ability may be gleaned from activities, and results, in such nonwork situations. Performance of employees who are consistently involved as leaders in such groups should be reviewed carefully to see if that skill and experience might not be transferable to the bank.

In this respect, it is a good practice to ask employees to record their outside organizational activities and positions held for inclusion

with other personnel records. The more evidence available for evaluation, the better the decision.

It is difficult to predict how an individual will perform in a supervisory position. It is a position of power, and power can have peculiar
effects on people and personalities. Consequently, before making the
official designation, there is merit in having a project assigned to the
candidate as a final test.

Such a test can range from such things as being in charge of a
social function to leadership in opening a new branch. These assignments all contain the necessity for coordination, planning, control, follow-up, and personal interaction with others, the same qualities required of a supervisor.

The assigned project should be of sufficient duration and importance
as to be a true test of management ability. Since the assignment is
temporary, it is much easier to defer a decision as to promotion without
impairing the employee's morale.

ADJUSTMENT OF THE SUPERVISORY ROLE

Promotion to a supervisory position is an extremely important milestone in an individual's career. The organizational structure of most
banks limits this promotion to about one out of ten employees. All
management jobs are basically alike regardless of level; the job of the
first-line supervisor and of the president are more similar than different.
Elevation to this new world of management causes many adjustments
and almost always is accompanied by some degree of trauma.

Some individuals cannot make the adjustment from employee to
supervisor. In spite of this fact, few organizations seem to explain the
consequences of failure when offering the supervisory promotion. This
omission is particularly serious in those banks that follow the policy
of "up or out."

This "up or out" policy is based on the valid premise that once
having been in a position of leadership an individual should not return
to the ranks. In many cases this is the attitude of the employee concerned because of personal pride and the shame of failure. The question
quickly arises as to what disposition is to be made of a person who is
removed from a supervisory position. One obvious alternative is dismissal from the bank; another is transfer to a different part of the
bank. The least desirable alternative is demotion to the job formerly
held.

The consequences of failure should be carefully explained at the
time the promotion to supervisor is tendered. Too often the discussion
centers around the new salary, the new location, the new challenges,
and little mention is made of the new risks.

One matter for discussion with the prospective supervisor is the requirement to "play God." The very nature of the management process requires the supervisor, at all levels, to make decisions affecting peoples lives. "Playing God" is abhorrent to most people because they recognize their fallibility and shrink from decision making involving their fellow man.

The necessity of making such a decision should be explored with the prospective supervisor. Unless there is acceptance of this facet of the management process, supervision cannot be effective. In the glow of the promotion process this fact can escape the new supervisor.

To be effective in manpower utilization, a supervisor must have some insight into supervisory styles in general, and his or her own individual style in particular.

STYLES OF SUPERVISION

There are basically three supervisory types or styles: autocratic, free-reign, and democratic. Any of these styles may be proper and effective depending upon the leader, the followers, and the situation. None is intrinsically bad and none should be automatically eliminated as undesirable.

In the autocratic style of supervision, communication is almost completely one-way. The supervisor functions very much like a dictator. He or she determines what should be done and issues instructions accordingly. There are few group meetings as the supervisor generally is not accustomed to receiving input because it is seen as interfering with his or her prerogative as leader. All the autocratic supervisor wants is obedience.

The autocratic style is useful, almost necessary, when the subordinates are untrained or undisciplined. It is also useful when subordinates are very aggressive or insecure.

In a bank the autocratic supervisory style fits best in the proof and transit departments where employees are usually young, tenure is limited, and deadlines are numerous. The autocratic style produces quick decisions and is efficient in that there is little discussion—only direction.

The autocratic supervisor seldom creates great motivation because the employee quickly realizes obedience and quick response are all that is expected. Therefore, there is less interest in the job.

The principal disadvantage with this type of supervision is the reaction of the work group when the leader is not present. Without the prime motivator, the supervisor, there is little reason to be diligent and the efforts of the work group go slack.

At the opposite end of the spectrum from the autocratic supervisor is the free-reign leader. This style of leadership produces very little communication. The leader plays the role of an information source for subordinates and is not expected to provide leadership as much as technical expertise.

For free-reign supervision to be effective, the subordinates must be experienced and highly trained. They must tend toward individualism and be of a temperament that does not require a boss to reinforce them. Since there is a minimum of control, the goals must be clear.

Free-reign supervision can be especially effective in a bank marketing department. Marketing personnel are often creative persons who need the high satisfactions and the individual freedom permitted by the laissez-faire leadership approach.

The democratic style of supervision creates more cooperation than the other two approaches. It also requires more time because of the vast amount of communication necessary if the democratic supervisor is to be effective. Many meetings are required for the exchange of information, and there is a great deal of communication among subordinates and between them and the supervisor.

The democratic supervisor is primarily a moderator. He or she encourages the group to participate and make suggestions. Accordingly, the group must be stable and one that works well together.

One disadvantage of democratic leadership is the loss of too much time communicating. It is easy for group discussions to get out of control with expressions of discontent replacing beneficial suggestions. The democratic supervisor must be skilled in personal interactions and must be in control of the group without appearing to be dictating to it.

Each style of supervision—autocratic, free-reign, democratic—has its time and place. There are circumstances in which each is useful and effective and the good supervisor will use each from time to time. However, most leaders have a predominant style of supervision and each leader should be aware of his or her tendency.

SUMMARY

As indicated previously, the supervisory job, while part of the management chain, tends to fall between management and employees. Management may view the supervisor as too oriented toward employees. Comments are made about the lack of "management view."

The employees, on the other hand, often feel that the supervisor is always defending management and has interests other than theirs.

Fraternizing with employees by supervisors is a dangerous activity. Employees are very sensitive to favoritism and such activity is interpreted as favoring certain employees. As a consequence, supervisors soon find it good policy to isolate themselves against nonwork contact. In fact, this posture is usually encouraged by the employees who view such contact with the supervisor as an attempt to gain favor.

At the same time, supervisors must be careful about their relationships with their superiors because it, too, can be easily viewed as currying favor.

This tends to leave the supervisor with only the camaraderie of fellow supervisors, and they are separated from him or her by space and responsibility. Management can fill this void, and perform a real service to its supervisory staff by having periodic meetings of the group.

These meetings fill an important psychological need in that they signal to the supervisor that he or she is truly a member of management. Also, they further communications among layers of management, an important factor that is all too easy to neglect. But the principal advantage of supervisory meetings is the opportunity afforded for supervisors to fraternize, share experiences, and to realize that others in the bank also live in the twilight zone between employees and management.

To perform effectively as a supervisor, the incumbent must have real authority. It is easy to delegate responsibility, but the delegation of authority is much more difficult. In many instances, the supervisor is not permitted to participate in the employment, pay, separation, or promotion process. Without the authority to make genuine decisions about the personnel supervised, the supervisor is merely a messenger—often at a high salary. Many banks could reduce costs by paying less for "supervisor-messengers" in recognition of the little authority they actually have. The other alternative is to see that authority is given to supervisors so the higher pay will be justified.

The management group of a bank is a very small percentage of the total staff. The organizational structure demanded by the banking functions dictates that relatively few will be leaders. This necessity for a small leadership group increases their importance. Their attitudes, work habits, and style permeate the entire organization. The leaders, in short, are emulated by their subordinates.

An effective organization starts with effective leadership, and the leadership closest to the employees reposes in the supervisory staff. By selecting and training this cadre well, a bank will discover a multiplying effect which will tend to upgrade the entire staff.

More than ever before the effective utilization of manpower is critical to profitability. The cost of manpower has risen far beyond prior predictions and it appears that the increases will continue. The payroll is now one of the prime factors dealt with by the top echelon of the bank. No longer is it something of concern primarily to the personnel department.

The effective "use" of the payroll depends on the supervisor. Incumbents in this position can assure that the bank receives what it is paying for or, if supervision is not handled properly, preside at the greatest expense leak in the bank. Unused manpower is an expensive waste.

Standby time, stockpiled talent, made-work, and sporadic time off are the habits and practices of the past when low interest costs and attractive government bond yields made banking easy. Today a bank cannot succeed with a lackadaisical approach to its manpower asset.

The job of the supervisor is a most difficult one. However, in spite of the difficulties it is one which must be performed adequately for the institution to be successful.

Supervisors do not arrive in full bloom. They must be selected with care and then trained carefully. Their development cannot be left to chance.

Chapter 13

Performance-Oriented Personnel Development Programs

Richard C. Georgia*

The goal of personnel management and development today is to use talents and abilities in jobs which have meaning, and in which real contributions can be made. Call it a desire to motivate, a recognition of the worker, a realization of the views of society; call it what you will, but in actuality it is understanding the need to match job and person, so that both better productivity and worker satisfaction result.

The attitude and philosophy of today's workers regarding what they believe they can contribute to and desire from employers are considerably different from a few generations ago. The approach by management, of necessity if for no other reason, is more accommodating to the worker's viewpoint. The purpose of the organization has no great meaning for an individual unless there is an acceptance of his or her skills and talents, and a true effort is made to put these to work in the right job—the job where the individual can see his or her goals fulfilled, and where management sees a need fulfilled which contributes to the bank in serving its customers. Policies which recognize knowledge, individual ability, and performance should be paramount in bank management.

MEASURING PERFORMANCE

Performance must be measured. The quality of work, how much is produced, cooperation of the worker, initiative to help wherever

---

* Vice President, First National Bank of New Jersey, Totowa, New Jersey.

needed, knowledge of the job, and dependability as measured by good attendance and attitude, all are criteria upon which a worker is evaluated. Such appraisals are of value particularly in the clerical and entry-level jobs. But, performance on more complex and "development jobs" usually requires a more comprehensive appraisal. Often the more involved review of abilities and performance must accommodate to a considerable degree the individualism so evident in the labor force today. The person coming to the employer for initial hiring brings not only certain skills, experience, and knowledge; that person also brings attitude, outlook, and philosophy, plus, in most instances, a desire to obtain a job in which his or her particular skills can be utilized and personal aspirations fulfilled.

Difficult as it may be for both the applicant and interviewer to match talents to job, the more demanding problem will be to continue this matchup in future years of service. Employees (and this includes everyone who draws a paycheck—file clerk to president) demand more satisfaction from the jobs as their careers develop. In addition, they want to be measured on objective rather than subjective criteria.

"Individualism" has been accompanied by the growth of participative programs. Members of an organization want to be included in the decisions which affect them. There is probably no greater participation desired than that of the evaluation or appraisal of their performance—for from the review process comes such meaningful results as salary increases, increased benefits, promotion, and additional training. These, again, apply to every employee, but, perhaps, even more so to the upper level employee than to the newer worker. Many banks have refined the appraisal process to include a "give and take" discussion between supervisor and employee. It has become almost universal for comments of the employee to be noted on the rating sheet, along with comments of the supervisor. Many banks have the employee initial the review form. Participative appraisal of performance is now more the rule than the exception.

Where such an environment exists, you are more likely to find what some call the sophisticated "performance-oriented development" programs—namely, management by objectives (MBO), individually tailored development, and related measurement programs.

MANAGEMENT BY OBJECTIVES

"Management by objectives" has a dual interpretation. It is "managing" as an aspect of leadership and executive skill, using various objectives and goals as measurement tools. It is also recognition of the objectives and goals themselves as contributing to the process of "managing." Reaching goals and attaining objectives may well be a part of "managing." Certainly the two connotations do have a common thread. They both recognize the need to establish overall objectives.

There is nothing new and modern about MBO. A successful performance-oriented plan has objectives and goals built into its procedural form. Such techniques have been used for years, even though not labeled as "MBO." Often MBO has often been viewed as applicable only in judging the performance of management personnel. In addition, MBO can and should be used at all levels of the work force; the degree of involvement and flexibility will depend upon the degree of skill or creativity needed. Thus, beginning and elementary jobs have limited allowance for an MBO-type of performance appraisal because there are so few opportunities for deviation from already established goals and measurements. For example, if it has been determined from experience that an encoder in a proof and transit department should do an average of 5,000 items in seven hours, then it will be rather foolish for an employee and a supervisor to mutually set a different goal.

Objectives and Goals

MBO concerns itself with *objectives, goals,* and *measurements.* For this purpose, "objectives" are those accomplishments which are to be ultimately reached and are within the overall plan of the organization. "Goals" are the short-term targets and lead toward the objectives; they satisfy the "how, when, and where" aspect. "Measurements" ask "were the goals attained and were the objectives reached?" Another way of expressing the relationships is that objectives are what you set your sights on, meeting goals to help you get there, and measurements are an indication of success or failure and whether you got there and how well. MBO also concerns itself with the bigger picture, thus helping stimulate both employee and supervisor to think. This results from goal setting, striving to attain these goals, and then analyzing performance. The resulting development of thinking processes can be of priceless benefit to employees and the organization.

Basic steps in MBO are:

Listing of primary and secondary duties.

Developing initial goals.

Discussion and acceptance (supervisor and employee).

Timetable and steps toward achieving goals.

Measurement and checkback.

Results—success, failure, or degrees thereof.

Reward.

Listing of Duties

The employee reviews the present job and recognized duties which are primary, usually present each day. Some of these duties are quite ordinary; some may be complex and difficult. Other duties are periodic, such as weekly or quarterly. Using this analysis, the employee lists on a work sheet the primary duties. Having completed this, secondary duties are listed next. There is an immediate advantage to this procedure. In reviewing the duties of the job, the employee acquires more of a complete picture of responsibilities. Quite naturally, this may lead to suggestions as to how some duties might be altered, and perhaps some new responsibilities added. This is precisely the next step in MBO.

Setting Goals

People tend to set goals at levels higher than their previous performance—a rather natural instinct. This, of course, is a plus factor in MBO. However, the employee should be cautious in not setting goals beyond real capability. Many employees believe they must create high goals to win acceptance by superiors, but often more intermediate and attainable goals would be better. To achieve a less ambitious goal is better than to fail in reaching an artificially higher set goal. Moreover, achievement in meeting goals has led to employees suggesting higher, more involved goals. Success is a great motivator.

The very process of creating goals has often had more of an effect on the employee's performance than has the discovery of actual performance. A parallel thought is that when the work involved has been more difficult, or even setting goals has been difficult, urging the participant to "go the extra mile" has improved performance.

Types of Goals

Goals usually fall into three categories: an extension of already regularly performed tasks, the attempt to perform them better, or innovative solutions to problems. MBO authorities have seldom classified one type of goal setting as preferential. However, the more imaginative and demanding the goal, the more challenge to the worker and, as a result, the greater the rewards of success.

The employee develops some goals which he or she believes can be accomplished. These may be deleting some functions which are found to be not related or can be more efficiently done in another job, adding some new tasks which seem relevant, or a new way in which better to do a task. Measurable goals often are a stumbling block to employees. The priority duties are listed rather routinely, but the degree to which these established duties might be changed for greater efficiency is difficult to foresee. Early analysis often fails to broaden the measurement. Some employees and supervisors find that setting target dates and degrees of progress are measurable goals in actuality. Some employees let the standardized objectives of the department be their goals. Since analyzing one's job and trying to pick out areas for improvement, to say nothing of suggesting new ideas, is not a normally demanded skill of an employee, goal setting takes considerable time and patience. The necessary time is essential. Job duties which can be itemized or counted, or which have volume factors, require special training, or are recognizably complex make the setting of goals a bit easier.

Discussion/Acceptance of Goals

The employee's ideas must be discussed with the supervisor and agreement reached whereby the supervisor approves progress to date. An open discussion between employee and supervisor and mutually reached accord are essential. The discussion with the supervisor is not only crucial, but enlightening. Some supervisors believe they must so direct staff that little, if any, tolerance is permitted to ideas coming from below. Such supervisors usually determine departmental goals and also individual employee goals; the employee has little to do with it. There may be some units in which such an authoritative form of management is needed, but the need for this approach should be thoroughly analyzed and challenged, for it will usually stifle the MBO process. Yet, structured, controlled production units are by their very nature directive-type units. However, even in such departments there should exist some possibilities for input from employees.

A good environment for MBO is one in which the supervisor sets general objectives and the employee is allowed to develop goals within the plan. Some units, because of type of work or personalities, are conducive to employees generating plans, ideas, and goals. The supervisor then encompasses these ideas within the departmental objectives. This is a crucial point in MBO; if not done effectively, nothing can succeed beyond it. Plans which have had trouble in becoming successful usually stumble at this stage—where the dictatorial mood is obvious or where employee-developed goals are seldom reviewed, or worse, left in limbo.

Timetables

Following the supervisor-employee discussion, the ideas and suggestions should result in a "blueprint." This initial effort should be refined, and that refinement consists of specific target dates, intermediate goals, and periodic reviews to ensure the program is progressing satisfactorily.

Target dates will not be difficult. What will be challenging at this stage will be the composition and frequency of the review. Success stories in MBO offer some clues. The time available and the needs of both the supervisor and employee should be recognized. Some of the goals will require different timetables. The structure will seldom be satisfied by one approach, but rather by realizing that the individual parts must be treated. Work flow, conditions and commitments within the department will necessitate different reviews. The production and progress of the employee, along with his or her knowledge, experience, and motivation will create a pace. Although reviews follow no definite prescription, it is acknowledged they seem to fall into monthly or quarterly periods. It is also generally agreed that an annual review is too long to wait.

There are some distinct advantages to the review—a "stitch in time" may be needed and timely correction can prevent future problems. The review indicates organization and direction, and it shows that necessary time will be permitted for the mechanics of MBO.

Now comes a real test. The preparatory work has been done. The need now is to start action to achieve goals and to measure progress by frequently checking back and determining how the timetables, the desired results, and the accomplishments are falling into place.

Goals have been agreed upon and both the supervisor and employee have committed toward these goals. The employee, having had such an important and creative part in the development stages, must now produce results. Both supervisor and employee will have to be aware of conditions, both positive and negative, which will affect success. These conditions are numerous, but to cite a few: absenteeism, severe and sudden volume of work in unit; unusual customer demands; a change in priorities in the unit; emergencies; and lack of departmental support because of conditions beyond the unit's control. Any and all of these problems can be corrected if they are recognized and a desire is there to correct the situation. The program does not have to be scuttled: calmness, diplomacy, and reasonableness will work wonders. Flexibility is an essential ingredient. New target goals, new timetables, new discussions, frequent review, and much added effort will be necessary because of changing conditions.

Evaluation

A concluding step in MBO is to evaluate how the goals and objectives were reached. The employee's skill and ability will be recognizable as the degree of success is determined. Some objectives may be fully met, and the reasons for success well understood. Some objectives may be only partially met, and an analysis should uncover the various reasons for these incomplete results. The contribution of the employee, and of the supervisor will be obvious. This is one of the strengths of MBO.

The results of a good MBO program are efficient production and adequate reward to those who have contributed to the accomplishment. Recognition should be given in the accepted manner of salary adjustment, promotion, and advancement.

The positive aspects of MBO are many:

Departments plan and project.

Communication process is strengthened.

Employee participation aids morale.

Employee participation brings out skills and talents.

Greater efficiency and improved performance are possible.

Employee knows what is expected in way of performance.

Develops management and leadership potential.

There are some negatives:

Difficulty in pinpointing and writing objectives.

Must have top-management support and participation.

Measurement of objectives can be difficult.

Reviews may be inadequate and infrequent.

Lack of real planning and real commitment.

Demands on time.

Lack of continuity and emphasis and priority.

However, the problems can be overcome primarily by one major decision—management should realize that production and efficiency will be greater with an MBO program. The necessary commitment and time should be made available.

INDIVIDUALLY TAILORED DEVELOPMENT

Another program within performance-oriented personnel development is the individually tailored program. The concept is sound and noble. However this type of a program demands a great deal of time and a real commitment to democratic participation on the part of the employee.

It may seem as if an astute management ordinarily recognizes individual development and the matching of employee talents to the needs of the employer. Unfortunately this is the exception rather than the rule. Two proofs are offered: too many banks are without planned successor management; and the complaint from exiting employees that their skills were not used and they had not achieved job satisfaction. When a program is developed which utilizes the skills of the staff, and those skills are matched to those areas in the bank which need them, job turnover and job dissatisfaction will be greatly reduced. This builds future management—to say nothing of enhancing profits.

Analysis of Employee

A program of individually tailored development requires considerable skill from those in the personnel, planning, and development units administering such a program. First of all, a thorough analysis of the employee must be made. This means not only gathering information from personnel records, but in-depth discussion with the employee, acceptable and allowable testing, and guidance from trained staff members.

After information is gathered on the individual, the needs of the bank must be thoroughly searched. Current needs are not too difficult to pinpoint. Future needs often avoid discovery and description, or more unfortunately, are incorrectly presented or incorrectly evaluated. A good planning staff is essential—or at least a staff member knowledgeable and versatile in this responsibility. The project needs the support of such areas as comptroller and budgetary functions, steering committee, upper level executives—even board members in some cases.

Matchup—Skills to Needs

A determination of the needs of the bank should show where certain positions are or will be vacant, the type of job responsibilities, and suggestions on future performance requirements for the positions.

A matchup of individuals to needs would be the normal sequence. However, that is rarely the case except in most immediate situations where skills are available and the staffing need is present. More often, a timetable of training and a format of development must be prepared.

The timetable for the employee may require service in various units to broaden experience; specific academic courses at local schools or in-house classes such as those conducted by the American Institute of Banking; attendance at seminars or banking schools; writing reports; and completion of assigned projects.

What results from this program is the opportunity to appraise the performance of the individual at various steps in the development program. Fortunately, subjective evaluation is less necessary in well-developed, individually tailored programs, mainly because the individual's performance is so observable and the degree of attainment of determined objectives is so apparent. Objective evaluation increases the probability that the right individual will be placed in the right position.

ON-THE-JOB TRAINING

The long-tested and productive system of on-the-job training (OJT) is a third facet of performance oriented development.

Long on the scene, OJT has a success story not easily matched. Perhaps the unsophisticated reason is the best—it works. The training an individual receives is the training long known to be required for the job duties to be adequately performed. The skills needed by the individual also have been well established, and the only unknown is the level of skill he or she possesses.

Organizations find need, at times, to tailor certain aspects of OJT to the individual, and likewise to help the individual adjust to certain aspects of OJT. The strength of OJT is that it has a simplicity which produces results and is perhaps the most practical of all of the performance-oriented development programs. Banks have found OJT to be the answer to a large percentage of training needs, but have more often than not confined this program to clerical and less complicated jobs. But in recent years, OJT has been found to be readily adaptable to more complex, training-for-management type of jobs. Again, the performance of the individual against established and predetermined objectives is measureable in objective terms.

CONCLUSION

Banks have used scores of development programs which seemed to be well structured and should have resulted in success. In many cases, the expertise of consultants has been used, formalized and rather sophisticated procedures have been developed, specific training plans created, and considerable expense has been involved. All too often, the results have not measured up to expectations. Perhaps a crucial factor is that the steps of the program draw greater attention than the performance of the participants. Programs should not be justified because of their own structure, but rather for what that structure produces. Elementary as that sounds, it is often overlooked.

The value of a performance-oriented development program is that the product is the *performance*. From that performance, objective measurement can be made of both the participant's progress and the contribution the program makes to the bank.

The typical subjective review of performance has obvious shortcomings. Supervisors and employees realize that such reviews zero in on weaknesses and the degree to which an employee fails to be "average." All too often, the review of an employee's performance is of a negative nature, rather than positive and optimistic. Many raters stress the failure of the worker to measure up to what is generally regarded as the accepted norm. Performances which have been unusually good in certain aspects may be overlooked because of a generalized attitude on the rater's part that the employee "isn't up to par."

In contrast, performance-oriented development programs offer appraisals which avoid such subjective rating and instead evaluate the actuality of performance. They measure progress toward achievement of goals which are known and have been set by both supervisor and employee. These programs give the boss and the worker insight and the emphasis shifts to an analysis of how well performance matches such insight and all that is related to it.

A positive comment heard many times from those involved in performance-oriented programs is that the element of "judging" changes to an element of "guidance and working together." This should increase productivity, lower costs, result in greater efficiency, sharpen management skills, and boost morale. In the final analysis, the justification for performance-oriented development programs is in the bottom line.

Chapter 14

Salary Administration— Improving Your Return on Investment

*John Turney**

Salaries are generally the second largest operating expense in retail banking, exceeded only by interest on savings and time deposits. The effectiveness with which these dollars are spent will have a major impact on bank profitability. This chapter is intended as an overview of the keys to improving your return on this investment.

The fundamental objectives of a salary administration program are to attract, retain, and motivate qualified employees at a reasonable cost to the employer. A further objective—and one which has received far too little emphasis—is to foster improved employee productivity.

Judged by these objectives, the keys to an effective salary administration program are:

1. An overall pay structure based on, and appropriately related to, competitive pay levels.
2. Individual pay decisions based on performance.
3. Realistic performance standards and improvement goals set with employees.

It should be recognized, of course, that these cornerstones will not always be practicable. They might be less applicable, for example, if a union were involved or if for some reason evaluation of individual performance was impracticable. However, each plays an essential role if your bank is to get the maximum return on its salary dollars.

* Vice President, Bank of America, San Francisco, California.

Pay Structure Based on Competitive Salary Levels

Overall pay levels may be influenced by a number of considerations, including union negotiations, profitability, changes in living costs, and prevailing wage levels. To the extent that the prerogative of setting pay levels is retained by management, it is suggested that of these considerations, primary emphasis be given to competitive levels. These levels are the best indicator of the supply of, and demand for, employee services, and therefore represent the value of these services in the marketplace. Paying employees on this basis will provide reasonable assurance that your salary structure will be sufficient to attract and retain qualified employees, and will keep your salary costs in line with those of your competitors.

Changes in the cost of living do not necessarily parallel changes in prevailing wage levels and are, therefore, not a sound measure of the value of employees' services. Thus, they are not recommended as a basis for changes in salary structure or for individual pay decisions.

Individual Pay Decisions Based on Performance

Presumably, the first objective of a sound salary program—attracting qualified employees—could be met simply by maintaining salaries at competitive levels. However, individual pay must be directly related to performance in order to realize the full potential from your salary dollars. Obviously, if the rewards for outstanding performance are not clearly distinguishable from those for average performance, there is little incentive to improve productivity. Paying on a merit basis is also useful in "managing" turnover in that it encourages the less productive employees to leave the company and the more productive to stay.

Performance Standards and Improvement Goals

Although paying on the basis of performance will have a positive impact on employee motivation, you need to do more in order to get the maximum impact from your salary program. Employees need to have a clear understanding of what is expected of them and of how their performance can be improved. This requires periodic discussion of performance standards and the setting of realistic improvment goals.

It should be emphasized that the relationship between pay and performance in itself is not enough—what employees perceive is what counts. Therefore, salary actions should be timed, to the extent possible, to recognize significant achievements, and the reasons for actions, or the lack thereof, should be clearly communicated.

ESTABLISHING A SALARY ADMINISTRATION PROGRAM

The size of the bank should be considered before designing a salary administration program. If it is small and one or two senior officers know all the jobs and the performance of each employee, there is probably little need for a highly structured program. If, on the other hand, the bank is too large for one or two officers to keep track of all jobs and employees, there is probably a need for a more formalized program. However, it should be kept as simple and flexible as possible. Unnecessary rules tend to become a substitute for good judgment, restrict management's prerogatives, and lead to actions which don't always make good sense.

A certain amount of structure is inevitable in larger banks, but it should be confined to those levels where consistency is considered necessary. More structure is usually needed at the clerical level because of the number of supervisors making salary decisions and because of equal pay and related concerns. However, it need not extend to the higher officer levels, even in the larger banks.

Needless to say, having a rule or guideline for every situation also inhibits the development of managerial skills since supervisors are not required to make and stand by their own judgments to the same extent as would otherwise be necessary.

Use of Job Descriptions and Questionnaires

Most organizations find that it is not practical to maintain formal descriptions on all jobs. They are not necessary for salary administration purposes and are costly to write and keep up to date.

Formal job descriptions, however, do fill a need in two cases. When conducting a salary survey, it is necessary to have formal descriptions of the jobs included in the survey. Also, so-called generic job descriptions are typically written for jobs with a large number of incumbents.

Although a formal description may not be needed, some sort of written document covering each job is considered necessary in a formal salary administration program. A job questionnaire completed by the incumbent or supervisor is usually the most practical approach. If the questionnaire is prepared by the incumbent, it should be signed by the supervisor. The questionnaire then becomes the basis for evaluation of the position. The evaluation should, of course, also be documented.

Defining Your Labor Market

Although it sounds simple enough, defining the companies you want to compete with in the labor market may require a great deal of thought. This is particularly true in a large bank which may compete in different markets for different types of employees. For those jobs which are clearly bank related, such as tellers, for example, relating your rates to those paid by other banks and financial institutions is believed most appropriate. Job comparability will usually be easier to establish; benefits, job security, and other noncash considerations will be generally comparable; and the chances of your labor costs getting out of line with your competitors will be minimized. Comparisons with companies in other industries may be appropriate, on the other hand, for specialized jobs, such as investment analysts or attorneys. Job comparability should be analyzed carefully in such instances, however, before drawing conclusions as to the appropriateness of pay levels.

Size of organization is another factor which should be taken into consideration in identifying companies with which to relate your pay levels. Whenever possible, it is suggested that comparisons be made with companies of similar size since they are more likely to have jobs of similar scope and responsibility.

The geographical scope of your labor market should also be considered when identifying your competitors. For instance, if you are located in a suburban area, you may be able to compete in the local area for your clerical staff, but you may have to compete with the urban area for your officers. You may even choose to compete on a national level for some of your senior officers.

Determining an Appropriate Position in the Market

Another important issue which needs to be resolved is the question of where your bank's salary structure should be relative to the other employers with whom you have decided to compete in the labor market. It is suggested that policies be kept rather general in this area in order to retain as much flexibility as possible. A statement to the effect that the bank's policy is "to be competitive with other banks of similar size" is considered preferable, for example, to one stating a policy of paying rates "above the average" paid by your competitors. This point may be expanded upon by stating that a competitive salary is one which attracts qualified applicants to the bank. It is probably neither the highest nor the lowest in the industry, but more likely somewhere in the middle. This will give management maximum flexibility in determining appropriate pay levels. In all probability there will be good reasons for paying a little below the market for some jobs and a little above on others.

Bench Mark Jobs

Bench mark jobs are typically the highly populated positions which have direct comparisons in the external market. To the extent possible, bench marks should be chosen from all job families, skill levels, and departments within the bank. Bench mark jobs are priced in the outside job market by means of salary surveys.

Salary Surveys

Generally, in a very small bank, an informal salary survey is adequate to determine the appropriateness of the bank's salary levels. This may involve nothing more than a few phone calls or visits to colleagues in other banks and companies to discuss pay levels for a few key jobs. Also, surveys on clerical jobs are often available from employer associations and other sources at a relatively small cost.

Larger banks generally find it worth their while to participate in more formal studies, ranging from those they conduct themselves to extensive surveys conducted by outside consultants. The latter may cover hundreds of individual jobs in banks all over the United States. The results of such surveys are typically published by bank-size groupings in order to make the data more useful.

Salary Ranges

The amount of research and planning that goes into developing salary ranges is likely to be a function of the size of the bank. However, even the smallest banks will probably find them helpful in administering salaries. Basically, a range is simply a span, from minimum to maximum, representing the value of a particular job. In addition to range minimums and maximums, it is common to specify points within ranges, such as midpoints and quartiles. The latter are frequently used to determine the frequency and amount of salary increases for which an employee may be eligible.

Salary ranges may be established very informally, with no more than a general "feel" for the market, or on the basis of extensive surveys. They also vary in that some follow a precise arithmetic pattern, with specific percentage steps between midpoints and percentage spreads between minimums and maximums, while others are constructed much less methodically. The important thing, of course, is the appropriateness of the pay levels which the ranges represent, rather than the degree of precision with which they are constructed.

Amount and Frequency of Increases

Generally, the amount and frequency of salary increases will vary with the employee's performance, position in his or her salary range, competitive conditions and, to a lesser extent, the level of the position.

Intervals between increases typically range from 3 to 6 months for newly hired clerical employees to 18 months or so for employees whose pay is believed to be well in line for their performance and level of responsibility. Guidelines for increase amounts are typically stated as percentages of salary and should, of course, be related to the merit budget. Even if the amount of money available is limited, it is vital that any increases given distinguish between different levels of individual performance.

Exhibit 14–1
Guidelines for Clerical Employees

Salary range	Far exceeded standards	Exceeded standards	Met standards	Interval
Upper third	4%–5%	No increase	No increase	13–18 months
Middle third	5%–6½%	4%–5%	No increase	8–12 months
Lower third	6½%–7½%	5%–6½%	4%–5%	4–7 months

An illustration of a guideline for clerical employees is shown in Exhibit 14–1.

Job Evaluation Techniques

Up to this point, the impression may have been given that all that needs to be done to establish salary ranges is to determine the competitive pay level for each job in the external market. In actual practice, however, many jobs can't be matched readily with jobs in other companies, and even if they could, it might be impracticable to do so from the standpoint of time and expense. As a result, the generally accepted approach is to determine the market for a relatively small number of bench mark jobs, set salary ranges accordingly, and then to evaluate the remaining jobs through some form of job evaluation. In its simplest form, this might involve simply ranking the jobs by comparing them with one another and then slotting them into the salary ranges. Although more elaborate systems are usually used in large companies, the job slotting approach is probably quite adequate for smaller banks.

Most of the more formal job evaluation systems differ from simple ranking primarily in that they call for analysis of each of the basic elements of a job rather than analyzing the job as a whole. For example, one of the leading systems assesses jobs on the basis of accountability, know-how, and problem solving. The elements, or factors as they are typically called, may be rated against other jobs within the bank or against degree definitions. In either case, each element of the job is given a certain number of points which are then summed up and converted to a job grade or dollar value.

The results produced by the more elaborate systems of job evaluation usually do not differ materially from the results achieved through simple ranking, particularly if the analyses are done by an experienced analyst. However, they require the individual doing the analysis to follow a more disciplined approach. The latter is likely to produce more consistent results if analyses are made by a number of different individuals since the system leads each analyst through essentially the same thought process. This, of course, becomes more important in a larger bank. Other things being equal, a more formal evaluation system is also likely to be more defensible against charges of discrimination.

Elaborate job evaluation systems also have some potential disadvantages. Perhaps the major problem is that people in the organization often seem to lose sight of the purpose and limitations of the system and come to believe that the results which it produces somehow transcend market and other practical considerations. A job evaluation system is nothing more than a disciplined approach to assist in reaching practical business decisions. To the extent that it is available, market data should also be taken into consideration. Finally, both job evaluation and market data need to be weighed in light of your organization's basic objectives of attracting and retaining qualified employees at a fair cost.

For those banks which perceive a need for a formal job evaluation plan, it is suggested that consideration be given to employing the services of an experienced consultant. *Salary Administration for Community Banks,* published by the American Bankers Association, is also an excellent source of more detailed information on conducting salary surveys, establishing salary ranges, and job evaluation techniques.

Keeping the Program Up-to-Date

Keeping a salary administration program up to date requires a periodic review of job classifications and of the salary structure.

While job classifications may be reviewed by the personnel department, it is believed that this responsibility is more appropriately placed with line supervisors. Whether all classifications are reviewed at one time—perhaps annually—or on an individual basis throughout the year is largely a matter of convenience.

The review of the salary structure, on the other hand, can more appropriately be done by a staff employee or group. In the larger banks, the function is usually performed in the personnel department, based on an analysis of salary survey data. An annual review is recommended, followed by an explanation to the staff of the results of the study and any action to be taken.

What to Tell Employees about the Program

If a salary administration program is to be fully effective, employees need to understand the organization's pay philosophy and practices. They should be informed of the objectives of the program, how pay levels are determined and the considerations involved in making individual pay decisions. If the organization has formal guidelines for salary ranges and increases, each employee should know his or her range and the salary treatment which can be expected for various levels of performance.

Market data is perhaps the most sensitive subject in communicating a salary program. Employees are understandably curious about surveys which may have an influence on their salaries, but disclosure of this information presents a number of problems. First, employers normally provide this type of data in strict confidence, and release of the information to employees would be considered a breach of this confidence. Questions of job comparability and market position would also be difficult to deal with. For these reasons, disclosure of salary survey data is not recommended.

PLANNING FOR IMPROVED PRODUCTIVITY

As pointed out earlier, employees must understand what is expected of them, including how their performance can be improved, in order to perform up to their potential. Performance planning is simply a term used to describe the mutual planning and objective setting which must take place in order to develop that understanding. If it is done right, employees will know what the bank is trying to accomplish, what their specific contribution ought to be, and how they can do a better job. In addition, they will have become more deeply committed to their work because they will have participated in defining it and in establishing their own objectives. The end result will be to make jobs more satisfying and the bank more productive.

Performance planning starts with a mutual understanding on the part of supervisor and employee as to what the employee is expected to accomplish. After this understanding has been reached, it is suggested that the employee's accountabilities be listed on a work sheet.

Setting Objectives

In order to gain the maximum impact from performance planning, subordinates should be encouraged to plan their own objectives, at least tentatively, prior to meeting with their supervisors. Objectives should be realistic, challenging, and tailored to the individual's performance. Therefore, the objectives set for the best employee must be different from those set for the poorest performer if they are to represent improvement for both and, at the same time, be realistic for each of them. After they have been mutually agreed upon, the objectives should be listed on the work sheet following the listing of accountabilities.

Reviewing Objectives

Generally speaking, progress toward meeting objectives can be reviewed most effectively through day-to-day, informal conversations between supervisor and employee. Supervisors may, however, wish to schedule more formal sessions periodically to be sure the review is given proper emphasis.

Objectives must be flexible and should be viewed as moving targets. If changing circumstances impact on the chances of achieving an objective, the supervisor and subordinate should discuss the matter and adjust the performance plan accordingly.

When significant progress toward improvement is made or an objective is achieved, it should be noted on the work sheet. At some point, new objectives should be added or the process should be started over with a new performance plan. Completed work sheets should be kept for use in performance evaluations.

Performance planning is effective only when the communication lines between supervisor and employee are kept open at all times. The supervisor should supply continuous feedback on his or her perception of the subordinate's performance, and the subordinate should point out any problems or obstacles not evident to the supervisor.

The process of improving productivity through performance planning is no mystery. It requires good planning and continual communication between supervisor and subordinate.

PERFORMANCE EVALUATION

If you do a good job of performance planning, performance evaluation will take place on an ongoing basis. Most larger companies go a step further, however, and require supervisors to "sum up" the performance of each employee periodically in a written report. The report usually includes an overall rating, categorizing the employee's performance in one of several defined performance groupings.

The reasons given for requiring formal performance evaluations typically include helping employees to improve their performance, identifying strong and weak performers, and assisting management in making and defending salary actions.

In weighing the results of the typical formal performance evaluation in a banking environment, it is important to distinguish between the process of evaluation—including the analysis of the employee's strengths and weaknesses—and the categorization of that performance into a defined grouping. The evaluation itself is necessary for each of the reasons stated and, if properly done, should be essentially salutary from the standpoint of both employee and supervisor. Categorizing the employee's performance, on the other hand, frequently turns out to be a traumatic experience for the employee and certainly a stressful (if not traumatic) one for the supervisor.

Although these problems can be minimized with good performance planning and open, ongoing communications between supervisor and employee, the categorization almost invariably comes down to a subjective judgment on the part of the supervisor. Most supervisors are understandably uncomfortable in this type of situation, and their concern over defending their judgments typically leads to overrating.

In spite of the unsalutary aspects of performance categorization, it is probably more or less necessary—up to a certain level—in large organizations. Basically, this is because a large number of individuals—including relatively inexperienced supervisors—are usually involved in salary actions, and a more structured approach requires each individual to go through somewhat the same mental process is a little easier, the decisions are a little easier to defend, and the salary treatment accorded employees is probably a little more consistent. At higher levels in the organization, these problems do not exist to the same degree, however, and the disadvantages of performance categorization may outweigh the advantages.

Performance Appraisal

Basically, performance evaluation should focus on the results achieved by the employee in all areas of his or her job. In weighing the areas covered in the performance plan, it should be kept in mind that the objectives were tailored individually to the employee's level of experience and competence. Thus, accomplishment of all objectives by one employee might represent only average performance while another employee might have performed at a higher level even though he or she had fallen short in some areas of the plan.

Finally, and perhaps most importantly, the employee's performance should be ranked relative to others in the unit before categorizing the employee's performance at a particular level. In the absence of some sort of absolute standard—which doesn't exist for the vast majority of bank jobs—this is frequently the soundest measure by which to assess the value of an employee's contribution. If relative differences are not recognized—if, for example, all employees were rated at the same level—the potential positive impact of a merit salary program on productivity would be substantially diminished.

Supervisors should strive to raise their standards as a means of increasing employee productivity. This is one of the reasons why it is generally counterproductive to attempt to tell employees precisely what the standard for a given level of performance will be several months or a year in the future. Employees should be told the areas in which they should improve in order to raise their performance level, but it should be acknowledged that the standards themselves are to some degree relative and that the supervisor is not, therefore, in a position to say precisely what they will be in the future. For example, if standards are defined in advance and turn out to be too low, the supervisor may be committed to rating too many employees at a given level, thus losing much of the motivational value of the merit system.

Separating Salary Increases from Performance Evaluations

Although an employee's pay should obviously be related to his or her performance, it is recommended that pay actions be separated in point of time from the formal evaluation. This will usually reduce the anxiety associated with the appraisal and help to keep the discussion on a more objective basis.

PAY PLANNING

Most organizations which administer salaries on a performance basis use merit increase budgets to assist in budgeting and controlling salary expense. Such budgets are typically prepared annually based on an analysis of the organization's competitive pay position, anticipated changes in competitive pay levels and projected earnings. Budgets for different units within the organization may vary, based on the relative position of pay levels within the unit. For example, a department with a preponderance of employees low in their respective ranges would receive an above-average budget.

Effective merit salary administration requires careful planning in order to distribute the budgeted increase dollars in the most effective manner. This may be accomplished informally in very small banks, but a more formal program is recommended for larger organizations. It is suggested that supervisors begin the process by ranking all employees in their unit vertically on a work sheet according to their individual contribution. The projected salary actions can then be scheduled horizontally on the work sheet by the month in which the action is planned. The ranking can then be compared with projected year-end salaries. If the actions have been well planned, the relationship between employees' projected salaries at the end of the planning period and their contributions will usually be in better alignment than it was at the beginning of the period. Normally, of course, employees' salaries must be kept within the range for their positions (assuming ranges have been established) and the total increases granted must be within the supervisor's approved budget. Needless to say, the pay plan should be reviewed periodically in order to keep it up to date.

EQUAL EMPLOYMENT OPPORTUNITY COMPLIANCE

Salary administration is becoming increasingly complex as a result of federal and state legislation designed to protect employees from discrimination based on race, color, religion, sex, national origin, age, or handicap. Compliance with the requirements of this legislation should be audited at least annually.

A suggested approach is to segregate the employees in each protected group by time on the job and performance, if performance ratings are available, and compare the average salary for each subgroup with the average for the comparable subgroups in the rest of the population. For minorities, each protected grouping should also be compared with the comparable grouping of nonminorities.

If performance ratings are available, the same type of analysis should be made to determine whether the distribution of performance ratings for the protected group is essentially the same as it is for the remaining population (and, in the case of minorities, for nonminorities). Job evaluations should also be reviewed for inequities, particularly those which have commonly been filled by women or other groups which may have been discriminated against in the past.

If these analyses do not indicate any significant disparities, the bank's pay policies are probably in compliance with the law. It is wise, however, to remain on the lookout for individual pay problems in individual units.

If any disparities are found, further analyses should be made in order to identify the units involved, the reasons for the disparities and any action which should be taken to redress them.

EVALUATING THE SALARY PROGRAM

A salary program should be evaluated continuously to determine the effectiveness with which its basic objectives are being accomplished. Although there are some fairly objective indicators which should be weighed in the evaluation process, it also requires a number of subjective judgments.

In a fairly large organization, monthly employment, and turnover trends are excellent indicators of the organization's success in attracting and retaining qualified employees. These may include the number of job applicants; the number, type, and location of job vacancies; the length of time job requisitions have been open, the number of job offers accepted and rejected, the reasons for rejection and the extent and reasons for turnover. Turnover analyses should, of course, include performance levels of terminees, since one objective of an effective merit salary program is to encourage the weaker performers to leave and the stronger ones to remain with the organization.

Another area which needs to be studied carefully is the competitiveness of the bank's salary levels. Obviously, this is vital in determining the reasonableness of the organization's salary costs.

Although the impact of a salary program on motivation and productivity is almost impossible to assess directly, there are some objective indicators which should be reviewed in this area, also. If the organization has performance ratings, their distribution should be analyzed at least quarterly. Unless they are controlled by executive fiat (an approach which may not be entirely without merit), most companies find that keeping the ratings from drifting inexorably upward is a continual challenge. Apart from performance ratings, the size of, and intervals between, salary increases should also be analyzed regularly by job level to make certain that differences in performance are being properly recogized. It may also be appropriate to review the quality and extent of performance planning periodically, if such a program has been established.

Chapter 15

Employee Incentives and Benefit Programs

C. Eugene Looper*

Employee incentives and benefit programs, commonly called "fringe benefits," have become an important fact of life for the American banking industry. In order to get good workers and to keep them, financial institutions cannot offer simply high pay, short hours, and moderate tasks. In addition, they must offer a lengthening list of inducements over and beyond actual salary. Employee benefits now range in worth from $1 coffee breaks to billion dollar trust funds.

The benefits area of compensation is a complex field for business and government interaction. The past decade has witnessed the enactment of far-reaching legislation by Congress. Aside from the Civil Rights Acts of the mid-1960s, the more important legislative acts relating to employee benefits were the massive reorganization of the social security system in 1972; the Health Maintenance Organization Act of 1973; and the Employee Retirement Income Security Act of 1974 (ERISA). These may well be followed by National Health Insurance.

The impact of this legislation on the employer-employee relationship and upon the "compensation package" is overwhelming. The social security change affects the level of retirement income, survivor's benefits and disability benefits. The Employee Retirement Income Security Act affects every pension, profit sharing, and welfare plan. The Health Maintenance Organization Act sets the stage for National Health Insurance.

---

* Vice President and Corporate Director of Personnel, Southeast Banking Corporation, Miami, Florida.

177

GROWTH OF THE FRINGE BENEFITS

Prior to the 1930s, so-called fringe benefits were fringes because they were within the practical discretion of the employer to give or not to give. Today, the employer has in fact little discretion as to whether or not a fringe benefit program will be extended. The government, through social security, unemployment compensation, and worker's compensation, has made mandatory the employer's payment of a significant percentage of payroll. In 1963, these legally required payments amounted to approximately 11.6 cents per payroll hour. Expressed as a percent of payroll legally required payments amounted to some 4.8 percent. The fringe benefit study by the U.S. Chamber of Commerce for the year 1963 reported that pensions and other agreed upon payments amounted to 11.4 percent of payroll; paid rest, lunch hours, and so on, equaled 2.8 percent of payroll; payment for time not worked reached 8.5 percent; profit sharing and bonus payments were 5.4 percent. The total "fringe package" for the banking industry in 1963 amounted to 32.9 percent of payroll.

Ten years later, the U.S. Chamber of Commerce analysis of the fringe benefit program in 1973 showed an increase in legally required payments to 6.3 percent of payroll. Pensions and other agreed upon payments amounted to 11.4 percent of payroll; paid rest periods represented 4.1 percent of payroll; payment for time not worked equaled 10 percent of payroll; and other items including profit sharing, contributions to employee education, and so on, equaled 5.4 percent of payroll. Thus, the total fringe package for the banking industry in 1973 amounted to 37.2 percent of payroll. Note that the significant increases were in government required expenditures for social security, unemployment compensation, and worker's compensation, and in the dramatic increase in pay for time not worked. The 1973 U.S. Chamber of Commerce survey reported that the average benefits cost was $3,230 per employee or 154.1 cents per hour. The 1975 survey by the U.S. Chamber of Commerce disclosed for the banking industry the cost of employee benefits as "cents per payroll hour" of 186.6, an increase of 31.5 cents per hour in a two-year span of time!

THE NEED FOR EVALUATION

Obviously, the benefit package is a major labor-cost factor and must, therefore, be evaluated and controlled by management, as permitted by the legal framework of regulation. Employee benefits are part and parcel of the company's total compensation program. The cost of such benefits is obviously substantial in relation to the total cost of doing business and cannot be obscured under meaningless titles. It is important therefore that the banking industry make careful analysis not only of salary costs but of related personnel costs. The chart of accounts should clearly and accurately disclose true personnel costs. Executive perquisites should not be coded under "promotional activities" nor should the cost of food service be obscured under "occupancy."

ANALYZING EFFECTIVENESS AND COST

It is equally important that management of the banking industry evaluate the effectiveness of the benefit program. Strictly viewed from the standpoint of motivation, any employment compensation package will reach a point of diminishing return. It would appear that now banks in general have achieved so universal a level of employee benefit contribution that it no longer serves as a significant motivation factor. However, if the benefit program is deficient, then it becomes a *dis-satisfier*; whereas if it is sufficient, it simply becomes one of the maintainers of employee motivation. In other words, if the employee benefit package is deficient, it can reduce employee motivation, make the hiring process difficult, and contribute to a high turnover. On the other hand, if the employee benefit package is sufficient, then regardless of how much it may be improved, it would not appear to improve job performance beyond the neutral point.

The continued addition of new expenditures for benefits will obviously have a decreasing profitability. The problem here, of course, is the development of new benefits. As a new benefit is added to the fringe benefit package of a leading bank, it becomes in due course of time mandatory that other corporations adopt the program. More benefits and more costly benefits appear inevitable. Government required benefit costs will continue to rise. It is also evident that the coming decade will witness an increase in company-paid benefits such as more time off with pay; more liberal vesting in retirement; portable pensions; extended medical indemnity benefits; an expansion of group legal insurance; and the emergence of group automobile, group homeowner's insurance and group travel programs. The latter will assist the employee in utilization of expanded leisure time!

With the satisfaction of the benefit area through group insurance programs, pension plans, social security, unemployment compensation, wage continuation plans, vacation, and sick leave programs, *cash compensation* becomes more important in the total compensation package than heretofore. In short, fringe benefits, although they benefit the employee, are more and more construed as neither pay for work performed nor a spendable payment. Instead, they are regarded as conditions of employment under which employees work—a part of the total corporate-government social security system.

With increased competition and a decreasing profit margin, greater emphasis must be placed on work performance. This will enhance the need for vastly improved techniques for judging how well individuals do their work and the relation of achievement to specific salary dollars. More and more in the future, incentive compensation will be regarded as a primary motivator. "Incentive compensation" in this context goes beyond the typical "merit" pay plan. This type of pay is for outstanding work performance and is paid as an extra lump-sum payment over and beyond regular salary. To enhance productivity, new innovative *incentive* compensation concepts and plans will be needed to maintain a reasonable profit margin in the banking industry. The key to bank profitability in this decade is employee productivity.

DEFINING BENEFITS

What are benefits? No standard definition exists which meets every company's concept of benefits. In general, however, they fall into four major categories:

1. Payments for time not worked.
2. Payments for employee security.
3. Payments for employee recreation, education, and health.
4. Payments for company assets given to employees.

In general, those items have characteristics in common:

1. They all cost the employer money.
2. Their cost goes up or down as the size and age of the work force changes.
3. They either add to the employee's pay or are of some current or future benefit.
4. They are available to all or a great majority of the employees.

SALARY AND WAGES FOR TIME NOT WORKED

According to the 1976 Survey of Bank Personnel Policies and Procedures conducted by the Bank Administration Institute (BAI), 90 percent of banks required two consecutive weeks' vacation when eligible. Over 65 percent give one week's vacation for six months' service; 85 percent give two weeks for one year of service, and 58 percent of the banks extend three weeks with ten years of service. The granting of four weeks' vacation after 15 years is becoming common. Some few banks have now extended four weeks' vacation after eight years of service. The BAI survey quoted compared with the survey made by the predecessor NABAC in 1964 indicates a dramatic shift in the emphasis on more vacations, holidays, and the recognition of two rest periods per day instead of the historical morning coffee break.

Financial institutions are moving more and more into defining in writing time off with pay policies. The majority of the banks participating in the 1976 BAI survey (3,963) have set forth definitive policies relative to time off with pay for death or illness in the immediate family, marriage, personal business, medical and dental appointments.

PAYMENTS FOR EMPLOYEE SECURITY

Legally Required Employee Benefit Payments

Banks are required by law to pay all or part of the costs of federal and state sponsored old age and survivors insurance, unemployment compensation insurance, worker's compensation insurance. The most important of the legally required payments is of course social security. In 1975, the average wage was $628 per month. The social security average benefit was $206 (33 percent). In 1955, the average wage was $208 per month; social security produced $70 per month (33.6 percent). It is also important to note from the standpoint of coordinated benefit planning, the sizable death benefit available in the social security program. A covered worker age 29 with maximum social security wages, with a wife age 29, and children ages 2 and 4, has a current death benefit or survivor's income of $786 per month while both children are eligible. A benefit resumes for the widow when she reaches age 65. If commutable to a lump sum, the value of this benefit is $110,104 to the worker or about eight times his salary of $13,200 per year.

Also increasing in significance is unemployment compensation. The movement in the United States toward guaranteed income will bring more and more emphasis on unemployment compensation taxes, hence, greater cost to the banking industry. A common unemployment compensation benefit in 1976 was $80 a week for 52 weeks. Frequently the cost of severance pay not only included the normal two weeks, but additional 52 weeks under unemployment compensation.

Worker's compensation is also increasing in costs due to increased medical expense charges. Significant increases in medical charges occurred in 1975, 1976, and also were anticipated in 1977. It is, therefore, imperative that workers' compensation benefits be fully integrated into group medical and group disability insurance plans.

Voluntary Employee Benefit Payments

Retirement Payment Contribution. Pension plans were in effect in 72 percent of the banks surveyed by the Bank Administration Institute in 1976. Some 92 percent pay the entire cost; 63 percent maintain a compulsory retirement at age 65; age 55 is still the primary age for early retirement eligibility. Probably the most significant event in the history of pensions was the passage of the Employee Retirement Income Security Act of 1974 (ERISA). Changes mandated by ERISA affect most pension plans to the extent that virtually every existing plan will have to be redesigned in order to comply with ERISA's provisions. Some of the major provisions of the act that affect the benefits structure of existing plans are as follows:

Participation. Generally an individual who has accrued one year of service (1,000 hours) and has attained age 25 must be granted eligibility for retirement plan participation.

Accrued Benefit. Accrued benefit is the benefit the employee has earned for service with the company and is payable at the normal retirement age. The definition of the accrued benefit formula is set forth in ERISA. The Act did not go as far as making pensions portable, but the next logical step for pension legislation may well be to provide for true portable pensions.

Funding. From the standpoint of the bank's profit planning the impact of pension funding requirements of ERISA is profound. Under the Act a bank's minimum annual contribution to a defined benefit plan must be paid each year in full. Past service benefits must be funded according to a fixed formula. Management discretion has for all practical purposes been eliminated.

The full financial impact of ERISA is only beginning to be felt in the banking industry. Further, the increased reporting responsibilities add significantly to the clerical and statistical tasks of the personnel department and to the cost of operation of the benefit program.

Supplemental Retirement Plans

The impact of ERISA on supplemental retirement plans such as profit sharing and savings plan has so far resulted in a reduction in such plans due to the increased costs of funding pensions under the new legislation.

The major areas of supplemental retirement plans affected by the new legislation is limited to eligibility, vesting (including reemployment), investments in employer securities and fiduciary responsibilities. Virtually every such plan will require minor surgery to comply with the laws. However, there will be little practical effect on the operation of many such plans because they now operate within the new restrictions.

There are two basic types of plans which are commonly used by financial institutions to supplement or substitute for pension plans:

Profit Sharing. This is a plan whereby benefits are derived from a profit sharing formula rather than being primarily or entirely related to employer contributions. In current practice the profit sharing contribution is a percentage of total base salary payroll with considerable variation, ranging from 3 percent to more than 15 percent among financial institutions.

Thrift/Savings. These plans are technically profit sharing plans but whose benefits are primarily or entirely related to a matching formula in which the company matches a stated percentage of employee contributions. Normally the maximum match employee contribution is in the order of 6 percent–8 percent of pay and company contributions are generally less than 50 percent of employee contributions.

Many responsible personnel managers are reevaluating the real value of a defined pension benefit plan in light of the uncertainties surrounding the funding requirements, the contingent employer liability for nonforfeitable benefits, and reporting and disclosure requirements. Prudent business management for financial institutions may indicate the movement away from defined benefit plans to a more flexible participative type of retirement income as provided in the thrift/savings type program.

Life, Accident, and Dismemberment Insurance

Almost all financial institutions offer group life insurance plans. The majority of the banks reporting under the Bank Administration Institute survey pay the entire premium. Generally financial institutions use a multiple of salary to determine group life insurance amounts. The general rule appears to be two times salary; however, in light of inflation a number of institutions have moved to the four times salary range. At the same time group accidental death and dismemberment insurance usually written in conjunction with group life has become a widespread death benefit. An increasing number of companies are providing an arrangement whereby an employee may buy group life insurance for a spouse or dependent children. The cost is moderate and the impact on employee goodwill is significant.

Long-term disability insurance has gained in popularity in the last decade and is now a normal part of the benefit program. Generally the cost is shared with employees.

Noninsured Sick Pay

The noninsured sick pay program provides for salary continuation for an employee who cannot work because of sickness or accident. Noninsured sick pay is common among financial institutions. In many cases, the sick leave plan is informal (i.e., the amount of sick pay is determined on a case-by-case basis); however, there is a strong trend among financial institutions to make a more finite definition of sick pay and other time off with pay. In the BAI survey of 1976, 60.7 percent of the some 4,000 banks responding had written sick leave policies. With the further refinement of affirmative action programs, written policies will be necessary to ensure equality of treatment. With this development it will be necessary to determine what constitutes a reasonable number of days absent during the calendar year for such purposes. In the BAI survey of 1976, 15.6 percent of the banks reported 4 to 6 days to be reasonable; 38 percent reported 7 to 9 days; and 30 percent reported 10 to 12 days.

Hospitalization and Major Medical Insurance

Medical expense plans for employees protect against expenses arising from illness and accident not associated with employment. Dependents of employees are generally covered. Child coverage begins two weeks after birth and ends after a specified age, typically 19. Under most plans, coverage of mature children may be extended if the child is a full-time student or is disabled.

Two distinct types of medical plans are in usage: basic medical and hospital plans providing specified reimbursement for each kind of service. The other is the Major Medical Plan which defines a broad range of covered expenses encompassing essentially all services that may be required for diagnosis and treatment of an ailment. The thrust of major medical is to consider the whole bill for such illnesses for a covered employee or dependent. The typical major medical plan has a cash deductible and a co-insurance of, generally, 80 percent. In the BAI survey, 41 percent of the responding banks shared the cost with the employee and 57 percent paid the entire premium. In the remaining banks the individual staff member paid the entire premium. Of the 3,900 banks reporting, only 111 banks did not have a major medical insurance plan in 1976. Dental expenses are included in approximately 21 percent of the plans.

It is generally conceded by most personnel managers that the health insurance benefit is the most important to the employee and is the plan that needs constant monitoring to maintain current effectiveness.

The increasing cost of medical insurance has given rise to a widespread interest in self-administered plans and/or the use of administrative services contract whereby the insurance carrier is simply employed to administer the plan. "Reserves" are not carried by the insurance company. The employer pays on a current basis. For a large group of covered employees the benefits manager should explore cost effectiveness of a number of approaches to funding the health insurance program. A detailed cash flow analysis of premium payments vis-à-vis disbursement per claim period should be made for all covered groups.

The rising cost trend in overall medical care can be expected to continue. Although higher prices usually result in lessened demand in the marketplace, this has not been the case of health care where lives are at stake. Thus the employer in planning the benefit budget for the future years must allocate an increasing share to health care.

PAYMENTS FOR GENERAL EMPLOYEE WELFARE

These include:

1. Cost of operating employee recreational facilities.
2. Cost of employee athletic, recreational, and social activities.
3. Company parties.
4. Employee publications.
5. Employment physicals.
6. Expenditures for employee training and education.

There is no particular pattern among banks in the area of payment for services given to employees except in the area of expenditures for employee training and education. It has been a common practice in the banking industry for many decades to support educational endeavors. The tuition refund for the American Institute of Banking courses is the common and almost universal practice. Further, many banks have gone into additional tuition refund for college and graduate level courses which enhance job performance and provide opportunity for career advancement. Cost considerations, however, are forcing financial institutions to take another look at the provision of adult education. Provision of general adult education is represented by a portion of the AIB curriculum. Financial institutions must look to the public educational resources to supply training in English, mathematics, and the basic arts and sciences. Company dollar expenditures for education will more and more be related to functional job training to maximize productivity.

PAYMENTS FOR COMPANY ASSETS GIVEN TO EMPLOYEES

Stock Purchase Plans. These are plans that focus primarily on the purchase of company common stock, without the tax shelter benefits of the qualified stock option approach. A price discount is usually offered and most regular, full-time employees are included in the plan. In recent years, several leading financial institutions have abandoned profit sharing plans and substituted stock purchase plans. Such plans are more cost effective from the standpoint of the corporation and perhaps induce the employee to more productivity since an ownership position in the company is assumed.

Free Company Services.   Examples of such services are free checking accounts, reduced loan rates, use of company vehicles without charge, free parking privileges, and so on. Such free services appear to be a constantly expanding array and are considered more and more to be a normal part of the employment privilege.

Net Loss on Company-Operated Food Service Facilities.   This type of benefit varies greatly among financial institutions, primarily according to size. The larger financial institutions tend to provide cafeteria or dining facilities for all staff members. Frequently, private dining areas are offered the executive group. A major consultant in the field of benefits estimates a salary equivalent of $300 per year for company-paid meals and $200 a year for company-subsidized cafeterias. The salary equivalent rate for an executive dining room is $600 per year for company-paid meals and $400 a year for subsidized meals. The objective in food service extended to employees should be to recover cost of food and labor; however, this appears to be seldom achieved.

CONCLUSION

Bank management must be concerned with a strict tabulation and realistic cost analysis of all employee benefits. These benefits, together with salary and overtime payments, are personnel costs and must be utilized in assessing productivity.

Bank management is constantly bombarded with countless suggestions concerning extension of various and sundry benefits and services to employees. These are all in the name of increasing employee morale and, hence, productivity. It is not infrequent, when someone or some group makes recommendations for adding a fringe benefit or practice, that notation is made that X bank does this. Banks need to "count noses" less. Rather, they must look to their profit pattern and recognize a saturation in the fringes or extras that they can afford to extend.

The break-even point in employee incentives can be reached, and beyond this point money is wasted. Increasingly, bank management must follow and analyze both federal and local governmental security programs. These programs increase taxes and employee contributions and must, therefore, be carefully evaluated in the total personnel cost figure.

Fundamentally, banks as well as other employers must provide a benefit program of economically justified proportions. American business, generally, has achieved such a program. The emphasis must be now, and in the future, on *cash compensation* determined by objective standards of merit. While some employees consider fringes to be of increasing importance, the real employee incentive is, and will be, an equitable salary structure flowing from objectively established criteria for job performance, augmented by "performance awards" given for outstanding individual work achievement.

Chapter 16

Equal Employment Opportunity and Affirmative Action Programs in Banks

*Mary M. Graye**

INTRODUCTION

Why does the banking industry always seem to receive publicity for its success (or lack of success) in providing meaningful jobs for women and minorities?

There are several reasons why banks are looked to, and even expected, to take the role of leadership in equal employment opportunity.

First, banks in their unique role as financial intermediaries have broad contact with business firms in all industries.

Second, because of the stature and influence of the banking industry, many equal employment opportunity advocates feel that, if banking takes a leadership role, other industries and businesses will follow.

Third, banks have excellent training resources available, their work forces have high percentages of women and many larger banks are in the cities where high concentrations of ethnic minorities are located. We should expect the pressure on the banking industry to continue, if not intensify, through the early 1980s.

This means that for all banks affirmative action planning will have to be a major component of a good human resource management system.

This chapter will examine the legal basis for equal employment

* Vice President and Personnel Director, First Wisconsin National Bank, Madison, Wisconsin.

opportunity and affirmative action, trace their evolution, describe how they apply to banking, and provide some of the information necessary to develop an Affirmative Action Program.

EQUAL EMPLOYMENT OPPORTUNITY

The Federal Level

While the patriots who drafted the Bill of Rights of the U.S. Constitution intended to make all Americans equal under the law, it was not until the enactment of the 1964 Civil Rights Act that the framework for enforcing equal employment opportunity in employment was established. Title VII of the 1964 Civil Rights Act prohibits employers from discriminating against an individual seeking employment, or a current employee, on the basis of his or her race, color, religion, sex, or national origin. As amended, in 1972, it covers all employers involved in interstate commerce with 15 or more employees. All banks with 15 or more employees, therefore, are subject to this law. It empowers the Equal Employment Opportunity Commission (EEOC) to institute suits directly in a federal district court in cases of alleged violation of the antidiscriminations prohibitions of the law. The law also provides guidelines to process claims, elaborates on unlawful employment practices, and requires certain employers to display informational posters informing their employees of claim filing procedures, as well as reporting information on work force composition.

The act, as adopted, was extremely broad and general. In attempts to clarify the act's application, over the years the EEOC has issued a series of guidelines, opinion letters, commission interpretations and decisions. Included in these are the "EEOC Guidelines on Discrimination because of Sex," "EEO Guidelines on Discrimination because of National Origin," "Guidelines on Employee Selection Procedures," and others.

Many of the EEOC interpretations have been tested in court. Others have not yet been tested or in the process of working their way through the court system and final decisions as to whether or not they will become enforceable remain in doubt. As a result, despite the fact that over a decade has elapsed since the original passage of the 1964 Civil Rights Act, it remains one of the most rapidly changing areas of the law.

State and Local Level

Because the 1964 Civil Rights Act does not cover the very small (fewer than 15 employees) employers, including small banks, and those firms not involved in interstate commerce, many states and municipalities have enacted equal opportunity laws. Banks under the jurisdiction of federal law should not make the mistake of assuming that they are not covered by state and local rules and regulations. Many banks may find that they are under the jurisdiction of as many as three or four different levels of government in the equal employment area, each with its own sets of statutes, its own enforcement and complaint handling apparatus, and its own set of actions for offenders. Many state and local rules and regulations are stronger than the federal act or extend coverage to groups not affected by the 1964 Civil Rights Act.

THE DISCRIMINATION COMPLAINT

Complaint Resolution

Federal Level. If an employee or applicant for employment feels he or she has been discriminated against in violation of federal law, it is likely he or she will file a complaint with a district office of the Equal Employment Opportunity Commission. The Commission serves the affected bank a written notice of the charge (including the date, place, and circumstances of the alleged violation) and investigates the charge. If the Commission determines after the investigation that there is not reasonable cause to believe the violation occurred, it notifies the business and the complainant and dismisses the charge (subject to appeal by the complainant). If the Commission finds in its investigation that there is reasonable cause to believe the violation occurred, it will first attempt to resolve the complaint through informal conferences, conciliation, and persuasion. If conciliation fails to result in an agreement acceptable to the Commission, the Commission, or the complainant, may bring civil action against the bank. The case is then resolved in the court system. If the court finds the bank has intentionally engaged or is intentionally engaging in an unlawful employment practice, it may enjoin the organization from engaging in that practice, and order any action the court determines is appropriate, including but not limited to reinstatement or hiring of employees, back pay, or other relief.

State and Local Level. Usually state and municipal regulations prescribe complaint resolution processes similar to the federal process. However, if a bank receives notification from a state or local agency that an employment discrimination claim has been filed with one of those agencies, it would be wise to obtain information on how they operate.

In many cases, due to overlapping jurisdiction, a potential complainant has the option of filing charges with more than one agency. The EEOC usually will delay taking action on cases while they are in the process of being handled by state or local authorities pursuant to their statutes. In its investigation of the case under federal statutes, the EEOC may place considerable emphasis on the findings of state and local investigatory agencies.

What to Do If You Are Charged with Discrimination. A charge of discrimination in employment is a serious matter. An adverse decision can set a precedent that may result in successful claims by other employees or applicants, result in negative publicity for the bank, cost a considerable amount of money, and result in a disruption of bank operations. A complaint should be placed in the hands of an attorney with experience in this area of the law as soon as received. Great care should be taken to prevent any action by any employee of the bank that might be construed as harassment of the person filing the complaint. Harassment is specifically forbidden in the 1964 Civil Rights Act and can result in turning a complaint that would have been resolved in your favor into one that results in an adverse decision for the bank.

REPORTING REQUIREMENTS UNDER THE 1964 CIVIL RIGHTS ACT

Employers covered by the act with 100 or more employees should annually file an "Employer Information Report EEO-1." Deadline date for filing is May 31 of each year but is occasionally extended. Forms and information can be obtained from and are filed with the Joint Reporting Committee, Washington, D.C. The form collects information indicating the sex and minority identification of employees in nine standard occupational categories and provides the EEOC with detailed information about employment of minorities and women regionally, by industry, and nationally.

While banks with 50–99 employees are not required to file form EEO-1 with the Joint Reporting Committee, they *are* required to file these forms with the director of the Equal Opportunity Program, U.S. Treasury Department, which administers Bank Federal Contract Compliance (see next section). It is each bank's responsibility to determine whether or not it must file the report and initiate action to ensure that the report is filed.

CONTRACT COMPLIANCE

The 1964 Civil Rights Act provides a mechanism for eliminating discrimination by employers by defining what is unlawful and prosecuting those employers acting unlawfully. However, many equal employment opportunity advocates felt that this legislation alone was not sufficient to overcome the effects of past discriminatory practices. In response to their advocacy for additional government involvement in the equal employment opportunity areas, Contract Compliance Programs were initiated at the federal, state, and local levels.

Federal Government Contract Compliance Programs

With Executive Order No. 11246 dated September 24, 1965, the president extended the 1964 Civil Rights Act to federal government contractors and, in addition, required covered contractors to develop Affirmative Action Programs. The main responsibility for administering the order was given to the Office of Federal Contract Compliance (OFCC), an agency separate from the EEOC.

While the OFCC has the primary responsibility for managing the federal government's Contract Compliance Program, responsibility for monitoring compliance of firms within an industry is the responsibility of the federal regulatory agency overseeing that industry. Thus, in the banking industry, contract compliance is the responsibility of the U.S. Treasury Department. However, actions taken by the Treasury Department's Office of Equal Opportunity Programs are subject to review by the OFCC.

Questions by banks as to whether they were federal government contractors were clarified in 1966 in a presidential announcement and in actions taken by the OFCC and the Treasury Department in 1967 and 1968. Currently any bank accepting federal deposits or acting as a paying agent for U.S. savings bonds and notes is considered to be a federal contractor regardless of the number of employees.

While the president's Executive Order No. 11246 (and No. 11375 which extended EEOC programs to include sex discrimination) in many ways paralleled the 1964 Civil Rights Act, it differs in one very important way. By requiring a contractor to develop an Affirmative Action Program, it initiates a form of self-monitoring of compliance with equal employment opportunity laws. Instead of placing the burden on an employee to identify an employer's violation, and having the courts require an employer to modify that *individual* illegal practice identified by the employee, the burden is placed on the employer to monitor *all* of its employment practices, identify those that are illegal and take corrective action. In addition, the employer must examine the work force composition, identify areas where women or minorities are underutilized in relation to their availability and develop programs, goals, and timetables to adjust the representation of women and minorities to their availability.

State and Local Government Contract Compliance Programs

As part of their Affirmative Action Programs, state and local government units (they are also federal government contractors) are required to develop Contract Compliance Programs for their subcontractors. Thus, a bank which accepts deposits or conducts other business with state and local government units may find that it is asked to provide them with a copy of its Affirmative Action program.

DEVELOPING AN AFFIRMATIVE ACTION PROGRAM FOR THE BANK

Importance

If the bank is a federal depository or a paying agent for U.S. savings bonds and notes, you are required to have an Affirmative Action Program. If you have 50 or more employees the program must be in writing. An Affirmative Action Program should be updated annually and should include a policy statement, policy dissemination, responsibility for the program, work force analysis, audit of personnel practices, goal setting and program development, and implementation and follow through, as described below.

The training of managers and supervisors in EEO and Affirmative Action also should be an important part of your Affirmative Action Program. It makes sense for two reasons: First, training of supervisors and managers decreases the likelihood of an employee or applicant filing a discrimination charge against the bank. And second, even if a charge is filed, it certainly does not hurt the chances for a settlement in the bank's favor if it appears that the bank is trying to implement an effective Affirmative Action Program and supervisory and management training programs are an important part of a sound Affirmative Action Program.

In addition to complying with legal requirements, the development of an Affirmative Action Program may also improve personnel decisions for the bank. Although banks are not required to submit Affirmative Action Programs in writing, it is important that a program be prepared annually, so that the plan will be available in case of an on-site contract compliance review and for other reasons described later.

Preliminary Research

Before attempting to develop an Affirmative Action Program it is important to have up-to-date information available regarding the required content and format of an Affirmative Action Program. Each year the laws change and require that supplemental material be obtained on a regular basis. It is also important to secure current information because the approved format for the presentation of data can vary from one compliance agency to another.

As the U.S. Treasury Department is the government agency most likely to be reviewing the Affirmative Action Program of any large bank, it is wise to contact the U.S. Treasury Department Regional Office for any information it has available. For the First Wisconsin National Bank, the pamphlet produced by the Chicago Regional Office, titled "Revised Order No. 4 and No. 14, Financial Institution Orientation Session," was very helpful in that it contained suggested forms and formats to use in developing the program. In addition, a copy of the most recent "Treasury Department Guidelines on Affirmative Action Programs for Banks, Savings and Loan Associations and Saving Banks" and copies of Revised Orders No. 4 and No. 14 (OFCC Regulations) should be secured.

Two pamphlets produced by the American Banker's Association, the "Affirmative Action Guidebook" and the "Annotated Employment Application," were also extremely helpful. These can be obtained by writing to the American Banker's Association, Washington, D.C.

An excellent way of obtaining copies of the 1964 Civil Rights Act, EEOC opinions, interpretations, and guidelines and keeping up to date on these matters is by subscribing to a good personnel reporting service.

It is also recommended that the bank obtain copies of its state and local equal employment opportunity or affirmative action statutes.

Program Components

Policy Statement. The bank's Policy Statement on Equal Employment Opportunity and Affirmative Action expresses commitment on the part of the chief executive officer to the principles of equal employment opportunity and affirmative action, assigns responsibility for administration and supervision of the Affirmative Action Program and establishes reporting and monitoring procedures. However, beyond meeting the requirements of an Affirmative Action Policy Statement, it may be used to publicize the results of past affirmative action efforts, and encourage the participation of women and minorities in all activities.

A bank's Policy Statement on Equal Employment Opportunity and Affirmative Action services as an important communicative device both within and outside the bank as it affects how the bank is evaluated by employees and the community.

Policy Dissemination. A policy, once established, is of little use unless it is efficiently and effectively communicated. The bank's Policy Statement must be communicated both inside and outside the organization. Including the Policy Statement in the bank's policy manual; publicizing the bank's program in the bank newsletter, annual report, and other internal media; holding meetings with executive management, managers, and supervisors to explain the intent of the policy and their responsibilities in its implementation; conducting orientation and staff training; and distributing the policy and posting it on bulletin boards are all excellent techniques for internal policy dissemination. A great deal of attention should be paid to the quality of the communications as there is a substantial difference between communications that meet the technical requirements and those that illustrate a strong active commitment on the part of the bank.

External communication techniques include notifying recruiting sources of the bank's policy and encouraging them to refer minorities and women for all available positions; sending letters describing the bank's commitment to minority and women's organizations, community leaders, schools, and churches; communicating to prospective employees of the existence of the bank's policy; and including women and minorities in consumer or help wanted advertising.

It is important to keep records of all internal and external policy communication so that evidence can be given to a compliance officer that the bank's Policy Statement has been disseminated.

Responsibility for Program Implementation. The responsibility for directing a bank's Affirmative Action Program should be assigned to an employee who has the necessary top management support and staffing to execute the assignment and has the authority and freedom to make decisions. Included in the affirmative action officer's responsibilities are such things as developing policy statements and programs, assisting in the identification of problem areas, assisting line management in arriving at solutions to problems, designing and implementing audit and reporting systems, serving as liaison between the bank and groups serving women and minorities, and keeping management informed of developments in the equal opportunity field.

It is also important that managers and supervisors be aware that they carry a major responsibility for the achievement of goals in their area. Their responsibilities include such things as assisting in the identification of problem areas and development of goals and timetables, active community involvement with organizations serving women and minorities, audit of hiring and training programs in their area, career counseling and review of qualifications of all employees to ensure that women and minorities are being provided full advancement opportunities, and periodic audit to ensure program compliance.

Work Force Analysis of the Bank.   Work force analysis is one component of an Affirmative Action Program where the actual analysis technique and format may vary substantially from one compliance agency to another.

In most cases, the Regional Office of the U.S. Treasury Department is the agency to be contacted for information on the format of the work force analysis, as this is the agency most likely to review the bank's program. In general the work force analysis consists of information compiled by job groups, salary classification, and an organizational unit on all employees indicating their race and sex. This information, once compiled, is compared with the availability of trained or trainable women and minorities by category to determine whether underutilization of either women or minorities exists. Once underutilization has been identified, reasonable goals and timetables must be established to eliminate the underutilization.

Information on availability of women and minorities may be obtained from a variety of different sources. The statistics unit of the State Job Service can provide you with statistical information on representation of women and minorities in the local population, work force, and unemployment force. Information on the availability of women and minorities with the training required for your jobs is available from local high schools, business and technical schools, and universities. The 1970 census provides national and regional information in selected occupations. If the bank recruits nationally for management jobs, information available from the EEOC on work force composition within the banking industry may be helpful. This information may be obtained by writing the Equal Employment Opportunity Commission, Washington, D.C. Consideration must be given to the minority and female composition of promotable and trainable employees in the bank's own work force.

The work force analysis should be revised annually so that it accurately reflects the composition of bank employees.

Audit of Personnel Practices.   The personnel practices audit is another area where obtaining current information is extremely important. In 1977, a great deal of controversy existed between the EEOC and other federal government compliance agencies as to the extent of validating employee selection procedures. Validation is a statistical study that shows whether or not a selection technique such as testing and interviewing is a valid predictor of performance on the job. The EEOC wanted all selection procedures validated that eliminated a disproportionally large percentage of minorities and women. The other government agencies felt that there were procedures for which validation techniques were not feasible or appropriate.

In any event, for the audit of personnel practices section, it is necessary to collect information on applicant flow, referrals, placements, transfers, promotions, and terminations. By comparing statistics in these areas to information on availability of women and minorities, one can pinpoint areas where a policy or technique is resulting in a disproportionate number of minorities or women being eliminated. Once these areas of adverse impact have been identified, an examination of the technique or procedure in question will determine whether it is a valid predictor of job performance or should be modified in some way to eliminate the adverse impact. For example, the bank may find that it is hiring a disproportionately low percentage of minorities in relation to their availability. Examination of the process might reveal that the applicant flow rate is well below availability and by adding recruiting sources that traditionally refer high percentages of minorities, the bank might be able to increase its applicant flow to availability, thereby increasing the selection rate of minorities.

In addition to monitoring recruitment, referrals, placements, transfers, promotions, and terminations, compensation program should be examined, including both salaries and benefits, to determine whether there are inequities between men and women or minorities and nonminorities. This area is very crucial because allowing inequities to continue can later result in sizable pay settlements, adverse publicity, and internal disruption.

Goal Setting and Program Development. As discussed in previous sections, setting goals to rectify problems discovered by the work force analysis and audit of personnel practices is a vital part of the Affirmative Action Program. Short-term (one year) and long-term goals should be set and discussed and revised annually in the Affirmative Action Program. Obviously, program development is one way to help achieve goals. For example, sound recruitment programs will provide the necessary applicants to achieve the hiring goals. Recruitment programs might include such approaches as listing jobs with specialized sources designed to meet the needs of minorities and women, inclusion of women and minorities on the recruiting staff, participation in job fairs and career days, work study and summer employment programs, good policy dissemination, and job requirements that are truly reflective of the skill requirements of the job.

Implementation of training programs is another important component of program development. Training might include programs to make supervisors and managers aware of their Affirmative Action Program responsibilities and programs to make employees aware of the existence of an Affirmative Action Program and encouraging them to take advantage of training available through it. Such programs as those of the American Institute of Banking (AIB), resident banking schools, seminars in specialized areas, and in-bank skill training programs might be specifically oriented toward preparing minorities and women for advancement.

Technical requirements, such as display of posters, desegregation and equality in facilities, and harassment prevention are important elements of program development.

Community action by the bank and its employees will assist in attracting qualified women and minorities. Financial support and participation in such organizations as the National Alliance of Businessmen, Urban League, secondary schools, or colleges offering special programs for women and minorities, merit employment counsels, and community relations boards are suggested.

Implementation and Follow-through.   While the previously discussed components are important elements of an Affirmative Action Program, plans for implementation and follow-through are vital to the success of the program. Making managers aware of their specific responsibilities during the planning period is an initial step. Review of results during and at the end of the reporting period is a second step. These results should be communicated to both senior management and supervisors and managers. Planning for the next program period should place particular emphasis on determining why goals and timetables were not met in previous periods and developing ways of meeting those goals in future planning periods. Finally, the development of the new goals and timetables should be communicated to senior management, as well as managers and supervisors.

COMPLIANCE REVIEW

It is not necessary to submit a bank's Affirmative Action Program to the U.S. Treasury Department on a regular basis. Instead, the Treasury Department utilizes a technique called a Compliance Review to evaluate an Affirmative Action Program's compliance with the regulations and the extent to which the program is being carried out. As bank size and compliance status vary, it is impossible to predict how frequently each bank will be reviewed.

Desk Audit

The initial phase of a U.S. Treasury Department Compliance Review is the desk audit. In a certified letter the Treasury Department will ask for data to conduct the desk audit and establish a 30-day deadline for its submission. Generally the data requested will be a copy of the bank's Affirmative Action Program and other related support data. The purpose of the desk audit is to identify areas of possible deficiency, matters on which additional information is required, and data which will require on-site verification. Upon completing the desk audit, the U.S. Treasury Department equal opportunity specialist assigned to the review will contact the bank to establish a mutually agreeable date for the on-site review. A letter will be sent confirming the date of the review and requesting any additional data necessary to evaluate the contractor's compliance status.

On-Site Review

The on-site review begins with the equal opportunity specialist discussing what the review will cover, the approximate length of time the review will take, how the review will be conducted and asking that the records, policies, and procedures requested in the confirmation letter be available. He or she also will make arrangements for an exit conference with the chief executive officer. The review will proceed with analysis of deficiencies, review of files, charting of data, sampling of information, and interviews with employees. The equal opportunity specialist will attempt to confirm that such program elements as the involvement of managers and supervisors in goal setting and the communication of policy actually took place. The equal opportunity specialist may also contact community leaders or organizations sensitive to the needs of women and minorities to determine to what extent they are aware of the bank's Affirmative Action Program.

Exit Conference

In an exit conference with the bank's chief executive officer, the equal opportunity specialist will present an evaluation of the overall EEOC posture of the facility, identify all Affirmative Action Program deficiencies that must be resolved before the Affirmative Action Program can be accepted by the U.S. Treasury Department, and discuss the adequacy or inadequacy of the goals and timetables.

Termination of the Compliance Review

Within 60 days of the time the Affirmative Action Program was initially received by the field office of the Treasury Department, the regional manager must find the bank in compliance or take action to have a show cause notice be issued. The purpose of a show cause notice would be to provide the bank with a detailed listing of deficiencies, inform the bank that failure to correct deficiencies will result in court action, and offer an opportunity for the bank to respond.

CONCLUSION

The issues of equal employment opportunity and affirmative action are extremely complex. It is tempting to delay dealing with those two related issues until circumstances dictate that one must.

However the type of circumstances that require a bank to take action, a discrimination complaint or a compliance review, are both best dealt with by a bank that has invested the time and effort to develop an effective Affirmative Action Program. An effective program decreases the likelihood of an adverse discrimination decision and increases the probability of a positive compliance review.

Chapter 17

Other Federal Regulations Applicable to Bank Employees

Edwin C. Wallace, Jr. *

A number of laws and regulations governing the employment relationship between banks and bank employees were discussed in the preceding chapters of this section. This chapter highlights additional government requirements which must be observed in managing human resources.

Neither the list of laws, nor the treatment of many of the individual laws covered here can be exhaustive. Consequently, one caveat is in order before proceeding. Just as any provision of law may be subject to different interpretations, so may any generalized statement regarding such a provision be subject to different interpretations or be contradicted by citing an exception or a special qualification to the rule. This is true of much that follows. The intent is to provide a broad overview of the laws and regulations, not a detailed guide to legal compliance.

FAIR LABOR STANDARDS ACT (WAGE-HOUR LAW)

The Fair Labor Standards Act, commonly known as the Wage-Hour Law, was enacted in 1938 to establish fair pay standards for covered employees. Specifically, the law sets requirements for the payment of minimum wages and overtime pay, establishes special restrictions on the employment of children, and prohibits discrimination in pay rates on the basis of sex.

Bank employees are covered under the act because banks regularly utilize the channels of interstate commerce in the course of operations.

* Corporate Staff Officer, Personnel, Virginia National Bank, Norfolk, Virginia.

Such interstate activity includes the preparation of documents which cross state lines, the handling, receiving, or transmitting of money or documents across state lines and the interstate use of communications channels such as telephones, telegraph, and the mails. Employees may be covered, even though they do not directly participate in these interstate activities.

Minimum Wage and Overtime Requirements

Simply stated, employers are required to pay each covered employee at least the minimum wage for each *hour worked* and one and one half times the employee's *regular rate of pay* for each *hour worked* over 40 hours in each *work week*. This statement becomes a little more complicated upon closer examination of the italicized phrases which are defined as follows:

1. *Hours worked* is all time during which an employee is required or permitted to work at the bank, at home, or any other place. Questions frequently arise about the following areas:
    a. Short breaks or rest periods count as work time.
    b. Meal periods of approximately 30 minutes or longer during which an employee is completely relieved from all work duties do not count as work time.
    c. Required attendance at lectures, meetings, and training programs is work time.
    d. Normal commuting to and from work does not count as work time.
    e. Travel time involved in answering an "emergency" call to work and travel time between work sites that is all in a day's work count as work time.
    f. Travel time involved in out of town travel that does not keep the employee away from home overnight counts as work time. Normal home to office commuting time and normal meal periods may be deducted from total out of town travel time.
    g. Travel as a passenger that keeps an employee away from home overnight is generally counted as work time only to the extent that the travel time coincides with the employee's normally scheduled work hours (or on corresponding hours on Saturdays or Sundays). If the employee is *required* to drive on such trips because public transportation is unavailable, all driving time counts as work time.
    h. Work for charitable or civic organizations counts as work time only if it is performed (1) at the request or under the direction or control of the employer, or (2) while the employee is required to be on the employer's premises.

2. *Regular rate of pay* is defined to include all remuneration for employment paid to, or on behalf of, the employee. There are several specific types of payments that are excluded from this definition:
   a. Gifts which are not given on the basis of hours worked, production, or efficiency.
   b. Payments made for holidays, vacation, illness, and so on, and payments made to reimburse an employee for expenses incurred on behalf of the employer (such as travel expenses).
   c. Discretionary bonuses and payments under a bona fide profit sharing, thrift, or savings plan.
   d. Payments made to a trustee or a third party to provide benefits under a bona fide employee benefit plan.
   e. Certain overtime premiums.
3. A *work week* is defined as a regularly recurring period of 168 consecutive hours (seven days). It may begin and end on any day of the week and any hour of the day.

Fluctuating Workweek

An alternative method of calculating overtime is allowed under certain conditions. This method is referred to as the "fluctuating workweek" method. Under permissible circumstances, an employer and employee may enter into an agreement the effect of which is that the employee's weekly salary is straight-time compensation for all hours worked—including those beyond 40—and one-half time for the hours in excess of 40.

The following example illustrates the regular method of overtime calculation versus the fluctuating work week method:

Example: An employee paid a salary of $120 per week works 48 hours in a given work week.

Regular Method
Regular pay $120.00
Overtime pay
$120 (regular pay) ÷ 40 (hours per week) = $3.00 (hourly rate)
$3.00 (hourly rate) × 1½ = $4.50 (overtime rate)
$4.50 × 8 (overtime hours) .... $ 36.00

Total pay for week $156.00

Fluctuating Workweek Method
Regular pay $120.00
Overtime pay
$120 (regular pay) ÷ 48 (hours worked) = $2.50 (hourly rate)
$2.50 (hourly rate) × ½ = $1.25 (overtime rate)
$1.25 × 8 (overtime hours) .... $ 10.00

Total pay for week $130.00

Although significant savings may be derived using this method, it may also have a negative impact on the morale of employees. This potential negative impact is reflected in the slang term that is frequently used for the fluctuating workweek method—"Chinese overtime."

Exempt Employees

Exemption from the minimum wage and overtime provisions of the act is provided for certain "white-collar" employees. Whether an employee is exempt depends upon duties, responsibilities, and salary level. Title is not a determining factor. Listed below are various categories of exempt employees and the criteria used to determine whether an employee falls into each category:

1. Executives
   a. Primary duty must be management of the establishment or a recognized department.
   b. Must regularly direct the work of at least two full-time employees.
   c. Must have the authority to hire and fire, or so recommend.
   d. Must regularly exercise discretionary powers.
   e. Must devote no more than 20 percent of the workweek to nonexempt work.
   f. Must earn a salary of at least $155 per week.
      Note. The 20 percent test need not be met if (1) the employee is in sole charge of the establishment where employed, or (2) owns at least 20 percent of the establishment. Also, an employee who earns at least $250 per week need only meet the first two tests to be exempt.
2. Administrative Employees. There are three types of administrative employees: (1) Executive and administrative assistants, such as executive secretaries, assistants to the general manager, and confidential assistants; (2) staff employees who are advisory specialists for management; and (3) those who perform special assignments, often away from their employer's workplace.
   a. Primary duty must be responsible, office or nonmanual work of substantial importance to management or operation of the business.
   b. Must customarily and regularly exercise discretion and independent judgment, as distinguished from using skills and following established procedures, including power to make important decisions.
   c. Must spend no more than 20 percent of workweek on nonexempt work—that is, work not closely related to administrative duties.

    d. Must be paid at least $155 per week.

      Note. Only the first two tests must be met by employees earning at least $250 per week.

3. Professional Employees
   a. Work must require advanced knowledge in a field of science or learning, usually obtained by a long course of specialized intellectual instruction at a college or university, or work must be original and creative, and results must depend mainly on invention, imagination and talent.
   b. Must consistently exercise discretion and judgment.
   c. Must do work that is mainly intellectual and varied, as distinguished from routine or mechanical duties.
   d. Must spend no more than 20 percent of the workweek on activities not closely related to professional duties.
   e. Must be paid at least $170 per week.
       Note. Only the first test must be met if the employee earns at least $250 per week.

4. Outside Salesmen
   a. Must normally work away from the employer's place of business in making sales or obtaining orders or contracts for services.
   b. Time spent on nonexempt work may not exceed 20 percent of the workweek of nonexempt employees of the same employer.

Equal Pay

The Fair Labor Standards Act was amended in 1963 by the Equal Pay Act. This amendment prohibits discrimination in pay between covered employees on the basis of sex. It applies to employees of the same establishment who perform work which requires equal skill, effort, and responsibility, and which is performed under similar working conditions. The act does not prohibit discrimination on the basis of bona fide seniority systems, merit systems, or systems which measure earnings by quality or quantity of production, or any other factor other than sex. An employer may not reduce the wages of any employee in order to comply.

Any wage difference approved under the Equal Pay Act is valid under the subsequently enacted Civil Rights Act of 1964.

Child Labor

The child labor provisions of the Fair Labor Standards Act were designed to protect minor employees between the ages of 14 and 18 from "oppressive child labor" practices. Special provisions are provided for the employment of individuals in certain age brackets:

A. Over age 18:
    1. No restrictions.
B. Ages 16 to 18.
    1. Employees between ages 16 and 18 may be employed in any occupation except those declared hazardous.
C. Ages 14 to 16:
    1. Employment of individuals between the ages of 14 and 16 is allowed only under the following conditions:
        a. The employer must obtain and maintain on file an unexpired certificate of age issued by appropriate federal or state authorities.
        b. Employment must be confined to the following periods:
            (1) When school is in session.
                i. Outside school hours.
                ii. Not more than three hours in any one day.
                iii. Between 7 A.M. and 7 P.M.
            (2) When school is not in session.
                i. Not more than 40 hours in any one week.
                ii. Between 7 A.M. and 9 P.M.
        c. The work must be in nonhazardous occupations.

In states where state law establishes stricter restrictions, state law prevails.

AGE DISCRIMINATION IN EMPLOYMENT ACT

The Age Discrimination in Employment Act of 1967 imposes requirements on employers, labor organizations, and employment agencies in order to protect individuals between the ages of 40 and 65. Employers with 20 or more employees and who are engaged in commerce are covered.

Under the act it is illegal for an employer:

1. To fail or refuse to hire or to discharge any individual or otherwise discriminate against any individual with respect to compensation, terms, conditions, or privileges of employment, because of such individual's age.
2. To limit, segregate, or classify employees in any way which would deprive or tend to deprive any individual of employment opportunities or otherwise adversely affect their status as an employee because of the individual's age.
3. To reduce the wage rate of any employee in order to comply with the act.

4. To retaliate against any employee or applicant for asserting his or her rights under the act.
5. To indicate any preference, limitation, specification, or discrimination based on age in its employment advertising.

It is *not* illegal under the act for an employer:

1. To discriminate where age is a bona fide occupational qualification or where differentiation is made on some basis other than age.
2. To observe the terms of bona fide seniority system or benefit plan which is not a subterfuge to the act.
3. To discharge or otherwise discipline an individual for a good cause.

Enforcement and Record Retention

The Fair Labor Standards Act, Equal Pay Act, and Age Discrimination Act are administered and enforced by the Wage and Hour Division of the U.S. Department of Labor. The administrator of the Wage and Hour Division, through his compliance officers, may make necessary inspections and investigations to determine compliance with the law.

Exhibit 17–1 indicates the required records under these acts and the period of time over which these records must be retained.[1]

NATIONAL LABOR RELATIONS ACT

The purpose of the act is to define and protect the rights of employees and employers, to encourage collective bargaining, and to eliminate certain practices on the part of labor and management that are harmful to the general welfare. Primarily, the act governs labor and management actions in unionized organizations.

Although attempts to organize banks have increased in recent years, there are currently relatively few unionized banks. Because of this and because of the complexity of the law, the following is a very "broadbrush" description. Perhaps of equal value to the layman's knowledge of the law that may be gleaned from this section is the advice to seek competent legal advice from a labor relations specialist at the first sign of any union organizing activity.

Rights of Employees

Under the provisions of the National Labor Relations Act, employees are guaranteed the right:

---

[1] *Federal Wage Hour Handbook for Banks* (American Bankers Association—Bank Personnel Division, 1975), p. 31.

Exhibit 17–1
Record Requirements

Authority (Federal)	Records to Be Retained	Time Period Required
Fair Labor Standards Act 1938 **Nonexempt requirements**	**A.** Employee's name, address, birthdate (if under age 19), sex, occupation, hour, and day when employee's workweek begins, hours worked each day and each workweek. Basis on which wages are paid, regular hourly rate for any overtime, weekly amount and nature of payment excluded from the regular rate, total daily or weekly straight-time earnings, total overtime earnings for workweek, all wage additions or deductions and total wages paid each pay period, dates of payment and of pay period.	**A. For three years:** Basic payroll records, relevant union or individual employment contracts, applicable certificates and notices of wage-hour administrator, sales and purchase records. **For two years:** Basic time and earnings cards, wage rate tables, worktime schedules, shipping and billing records, records of additions to or deductions from wages.
Exempt requirements (executive, administrative, professional and outside salesman)	**B.** Employee's name, address, birthdate (if under 19), sex, occupation, time of day, and day of week on which the employee's workweek begins, total wages paid each pay period, date of payment and the pay period, date of payment and the pay period covered by payment.	
Equal Pay Law (Section 11C of Wage-Hour Law of 1962)	**A.** Employee's name in full, home address, date of birth (if under 19), sex and occupation in which employed; time of day and day of week in which workweek begins; regular rate of pay for any week when overtime pay is due; hours worked each workday and total hours worked each week, total daily or weekly straight-time earnings; total overtime pay in excess of straight-time; total additions or deductions	**A.** Not specified.

from wages for each pay period; total wages paid each pay period; date of payment and pay period covered.

B. Additionally, employers must keep any records they normally retain of: wage payments, wage rates, job evaluations, job descriptions, merit systems, seniority systems, collective bargaining agreements, descriptions of pay practices or other matters explaining whether they are based on a factor other than sex.

B. Two years.

Age Discrimination Act 1967

A. Payroll records containing each employee's name, address, date of birth, occupation, rate of pay, and compensation earned each week.

A. Three years.

B. Personnel records relating to (1) job applications, resumes, or other replies to job advertisements, including records pertaining to failure to hire; (2) promotion, demotion, transfer, selection for training, layoff, recall or discharge; (3) job orders submitted to employment agency or union; (4) test papers in connection with employment—administered aptitude or other employment tests; (5) physical examination results; (6) job advertisements or notices to employers regarding openings, promotions, training programs or opportunities for overtime work.

B. One year from date of personnel action to which record relates, except 90 days for application forms and other pre-employment records for temporary jobs.

C. Employee benefit plans, written seniority or merit rating systems.

C. Period plan or system is in effect plus one year.

To self-organization.

To form, join, or assist labor organizations.

To bargain collectively through representatives of their own choosing.

To engage in other concerted activities for the purpose of collective bargaining or other mutual aid or protection.

To refrain from any or all of such activities except to the extent that such right may be affected by an agreement requiring membership in a labor organization as a condition of employment.

It should be noted that these rights are guaranteed to employees whether or not they are unionized. Consequently, nonunionized employees also enjoy the protection of the law when undertaking a "concerted action"—an action taken by two or more employees for their mutual aid or protection.

Unfair Labor Practices

The law enumerates unfair labor practices on the part of both employers and labor organizations.

1. *Employers* may not:
    a. Interfere with, restrain, or coerce employees exercising their rights under the act.
    b. Dominate or support a labor organization.
    c. Encourage or discourage membership in a labor organization by discriminating in hiring or in tenure, terms or conditions of employment.
    d. Discriminate against employees for filing charges or testifying with the National Labor Relations Board.
    e. Refuse to bargain in good faith about wages, hours, and other conditions of employment with a duly selected bargaining representative.
2. *Labor organizations* may not:
    a. Restrain or coerce employees in the exercise of their rights under the act.
    b. Cause an employer to discriminate against an employee in regard to wages, hours, and other conditions of employment for the purpose of encouraging or discouraging membership in a labor organization.
    c. Refuse to bargain in good faith with an employer about wages, hours, and other conditions of employment.
    d. Engage in strikes and boycotts or take other specified actions to accomplish illegal purposes.

    e. Charge excessive or discriminatory membership fees where union membership is required as a condition of employment.

    f. Featherbed.

    g. Use picketing as a device to organize employees or gain recognition as an employee representative.

Collective Bargaining

Employers are required to bargain with duly designated or selected employee representatives of employees in an appropriate bargaining unit. An "appropriate bargaining unit" is a group of two or more employees who share common employment interests and conditions and may reasonably be grouped together for purposes of collective bargaining.

The National Labor Relations Board determines whether or not an employee group constitutes an appropriate bargaining unit by examining the circumstances of each situation. Consequently, there is no clear-cut guideline as to what group may or may not be determined to be an appropriate bargaining unit. However, in determining an appropriate bargaining unit, the NLRB considers such criteria as geographic proximity, commonality of personnel policies and pay practices, and transfers into and out of the unit.

·Enforcement

Responsibility for enforcing the act has been delegated by Congress to the National Labor Relations Board (NLRB). To assist in administering the law, the NLRB has established regional and field offices throughout the states.

The three main functions of the NLRB are: (1) to interpret the act, (2) to conduct representative elections and certify results, and (3) to prevent employers and unions from engaging in unfair labor practices. The NLRB acts only upon requests in the form of "petitions" requesting elections and "charges" of unfair labor practices.

SOCIAL SECURITY ACT

The Social Security Act is one of the most far-reaching pieces of social welfare legislation in the United States. The act covers every private employer and nine out of ten workers. Social security was originally established on the principle of employers and employees sharing the cost of providing old age and unemployment benefits. The original concept of shared cost has been maintained—but the level of benefits, the types of benefits, and the number of people covered have increased dramatically over the years. Amendments to the Social Security Act tying increases in benefit levels to the Consumer Price Index practically ensure increases in future benefit levels and taxes. These future increases must be considered in projecting employee salary costs and planning employee benefits.

The social security system is financed through taxes paid by employers, employees, and self-employed individuals under the Federal Insurance Contributions Act (FICA) and the Self-Employed Contributions Act. The taxes must be paid by both the employer and the employee on all taxable wages up to the annual maximum. Determination of an employer's liability for taxes depends largely on whether or not employees meet the definition of "employee" under the act and the amount of taxable "wages." As a practical matter, almost every employee is covered. The basic test for determining whether an employee is covered is whether or not the employee is subject to the will and control of an employer with regard to *what* and *how* the work is to be done. Whether or not the employer exercises this right does not matter. Exceptions exist for certain classes of employees.

The wages subject to FICA taxes include cash wages, tips, bonuses, commissions, and the value of any remuneration paid in other than cash. Payments generally not subject to taxes include sick pay and retirement payments. The amount of tax is determined by applying a FICA tax rate to the taxable wages which are less than the current maximum social security wage base in any calendar year. Both the tax rate and the maximum wage base are subject to annual increases. The Internal Revenue Service collects the taxes from employers, who are required to withhold the employee portion. Every employer liable for FICA taxes must submit a quarterly return reporting income tax withheld from wages, the employer FICA tax and employee FICA taxes withheld from wages. The frequency of payment is at least quarterly, with more frequent payments required for higher tax liabilities.

Benefits provided to participants by the amended Social Security Act cover a wide variety of social, welfare, and public assistance programs. The social security system covers 11 major programs in three major categories:

1. Social Insurance
    a. Old age, survivors, and disability income.
    b. Unemployment insurance.
    c. Health insurance for aged (Medicare).
2. Public Assistance and Welfare Assistance
    a. Supplemental security income for the aged, blind, and disabled.

     b. Medicaid.
     c. Aid to families with dependent children.
     d. Grants to states for services to aged, blind, and disabled.
3. Children's Services
     a. Maternal and child health services.
     b. Services for crippled children.
     c. Child welfare services.
     d. Mental retardation services.

Some of these programs are administered in conjunction with state governments with federal subsidies from the social security system. Consideration should be given to such benefits as retirement income, disability income, Medicare and Medicaid in developing benefit programs to ensure that benefits already provided under these programs are not duplicated.

THE OCCUPATIONAL SAFETY AND HEALTH ACT (OSHA)

OSHA covers virtually every employer in the United States. Basically the law requires employers to maintain workplaces free from recognized hazards and to meet certain minimum safety standards for specific hazards. The law sets standards, provides for inspections, imposes severe penalties for repeated serious violations, and requires mandatory reporting and disclosure to both the Department of Labor and employees.

While the law is addressed principally to manufacturing and construction industries, many of the safety standards and requirements, such as those related to electricity and provisions of toilet facilities, apply to all industries. Banks which have warehouses, print shops, courier services, etc., should insure that the work areas meet specific OSHA requirements and that workers follow prescribed OSHA rules.

Enforcement of OSHA is through the Department of Labor. Violations of safety regulations may be found through on-site inspections or through employee complaints to the Department of Labor.

If a violation is found, the Department of Labor issues a citation. The employer has 15 working days to contest. If the citation is not contested, it becomes final and binding. Contested violations are heard by the OSHA Review Commission. Findings may be appealed through the U.S. Court of Appeals. In the case of repeated violations, penalties may be up to $10,000 or six months in prison or both.

Detailed records must be kept of all occupational injuries and any serious accidents or deaths must be reported to the area OSHA director within 48 hours. An annual summary of all occupational injuries must be posted in each work location. Forms for maintaining the records are available from local area offices.

FEDERAL WAGE GARNISHMENT LAW

Title III of the Consumer Credit Protection Act contains provisions governing the garnishment of employee wages. A garnishment is any legal or equitable procedure through which earnings of any individual are required to be withheld for payment of any debt.

Only a portion of an employee's disposable earnings are subject to garnishment. Disposable earnings are earnings remaining after legally required withholdings. The maximum amount of an employee's disposable earnings which is subject to garnishment in any workweek may not exceed the lesser of:

a. 25 percent of disposable earnings for that week.
b. The amount by which disposable earnings for that week exceeds 30 times the federal minimum hourly wage in effect at the time that earnings are payable.

Discharging of an employee because his or her earnings have been subject to garnishment for any one indebtedness is prohibited. "One indebtedness" refers to a single debt, regardless of the number of levies made or number of proceedings brought for its collection.

UNIVERSAL MILITARY TRAINING AND SERVICE ACT

This act protects the reemployment rights of veterans returning from the satisfactory performance of military service. Basically, the law provides that if a veteran applies for reemployment within a certain period after discharge, he or she *must* be reemployed in the same position or one of the same seniority, status, and pay.

Veterans must apply within 90 days after release from active duty and must still be qualified to perform their previous job. Seniority must be adjusted to reflect military service and the employer cannot discharge the employee for one year without sufficient cause.

The reemployment rights apply to both inductees and voluntary enlistees. The rights apply for employees who voluntarily extend their period of service provided the total period is not more than four years.

Special provisions are made for Ready Reserve Trainees. Ready Reservists who undergo three to six months' training must reapply within 31 days of separation.

Employees who receive discharges under "undesirable," "bad conduct," "dishonorable," or "conditions other than honorable" are not entitled to reemployment rights.

EXECUTIVE ORDER 11701

Executive Order 11701 directed the Secretary of Labor to issue regulations requiring federal contractors to list job openings with appropriate government employment agencies in order to aid the employment of Vietnam veterans. The regulations themselves require each contractor to list all appropriate job openings with the state employment system. Each contractor must file quarterly reports providing (1) the number of people hired, (2) the number of disabled veterans hired, and (3) the number of Vietnam veterans hired.

OTHER FEDERAL BANKING REGULATIONS

Regulations of the Comptroller of the Currency

The regulations contained in this section apply to employees of national banks.

Sec. 4.18 (c)   Prohibits disclosure of information contained in a report of examination to any person or organization not officially connected with the bank.

Sec. 7.4020   Prohibits officers, clerks, tellers, and bookkeepers from being designated to act as proxy.

Sec. 7.4205   Prohibits, without the written consent of the FDIC, persons who have been convicted of any criminal offense involving dishonesty or breach of trust from serving as a director, officer, or employee.

Sec. 7.4415   Prohibits an officer from administering the oath to be taken by directors.

Sec. 7.5000   Permits a bank to adopt reasonable bonus or profit sharing plans.

Sec. 7.5010   Encourages banks to adopt qualified pension plans.

Sec. 7.5015   Permits the provision of employee stock purchase and stock option plans.

Sec. 7.5215   Requires adequate fidelity coverage for officers and employees.

Sec. 7.5217   Permits banks to provide indemnification coverage for directors, officers, and other employees.

Sec. 7.5220   Permits a board of directors to enter into reasonable employment contracts with officers and employees.

Sec. 7.5225   Establishes reporting requirements for known or suspected defalcations involving bank personnel and any mysterious disappearances of $1,000 or more.

Sec. 7.5230   Permits banks to purchase homes of transferred employees. Requires early divestment of title to such property.

Sec. 7.7115   Permits banks to purchase keyman insurance.

Sec. 9.7   Permits the board of directors to delegate fiduciary powers to officers, employees, and committees. Requires bonding of trust department employees.

Sec. 9.12   Limits self-dealing transactions involving fiduciary accounts.

Sec. 9.15   Requires board of director approval to permit any officer or employee to retain any compensation for acting as co-fiduciary with the bank in the administration of a fiduciary account.

Sec. 21.2   Requires the board of directors to designate an officer or other employee to be responsible for meeting prescribed security standards.

Sec. 23   Requires each director and principal officer to file a Statement of Interest, Form CC-9030-29, which is to be kept at the bank's main office and revised as significant changes occur.

Rules and Regulations, Board of Governors of the Federal Reserve System

These rules and regulations apply to employees of Federal Reserve System member banks:

Sec. 212   Regulation L provides that only under certain exceptions may directors, officers and employees of member banks serve simultaneously as a director, officer or employee of any other bank, banking association, savings bank, or trust company organized under the National Bank Act or the laws of any state or the District of Columbia.

Sec. 215   Regulation 0 limits loans which may be made to executive officers of member banks.

Sec. 216   Regulation P requires the board of directors of Federal Reserve Banks and state member banks to designate an officer or other employee to be responsible for meeting prescribed security standards.

Sec. 218   Regulation R prohibits directors, officers and employees of member banks from serving as an employee, officer, or director of certain organizations that deal with securities.

United States Code, Title 12

Sec. 375(a)   Limits loans which may be made to executive officers of member banks.

Sec. 376   Limits interest rates which may be paid by member banks on deposits of directors, officers, attorneys and employees to the interest rates paid to other depositors.

Sec. 503   Imposes personal liability upon directors and officers of member banks who knowingly violate or permit others to violate certain sections of Title 12 and Title 18 of the U.S. Code.

CONCLUSION

Government regulation of the conditions of employment is here to stay. The changes imposed by new laws and government regulatory agencies will undoubtedly continue to increase. As regulation restricts management choices in the human resource management field, banks and other employers will have to ensure both legal compliance and imaginative use of the options available. The banking industry itself is one of the most regulated industries—and the burden of complying with multiple and sometimes conflicting government agencies, laws, and regulations can be a difficult one. The record keeping and reporting requirements, the continual threat of lawsuit, and the constantly changing regulations, all contribute to the complexity of personnel administration.

SECTION III

SYSTEMS

Chapter 18

Systems for Producing Bank Services—Concepts and Needs

John W. Spiegel[*]

Robert M. Horton[†]

The U.S. banking industry has seldom faced more significant changes to its franchise or to the services rendered by individual banks. Regulations are proposed which would quickly and materially change the heretofore government-provided and protected franchise to provide demand deposit accounts. The benefits associated with the unique right to offer checking accounts have been eroded as other industries developed near demand deposit services. Others now accept deposits against future charges, accept savings deposits to be transferred to another upon oral or written request, and accept deposits to be paid against "drafts." Current legislative proposals would broaden the activities of competitive industries. Savings and loan associations, savings banks, and commercial banks have tested NOW (negotiable orders of withdrawal) accounts throughout the northeastern United States. Within a short time, such accounts probably will be allowed throughout the United States.

Payment of interest on accounts has led bankers to analyze the profitability of their services. Many have found that they are subsidizing certain activities such as checking accounts provided individuals from the return on others. This has led further to the recognition that competition has exploited the rich pricing of certain services, the ones subsidizing the loss services.

[*] Treasurer, Trust Company of Georgia, Atlanta, Georgia.

[†] General Manager, Trusco Data Systems, Atlanta, Georgia.

221

In addition to the competitive and regulatory climate, recent economic conditions have led bankers to reexamine with some concern the future earning power of their institutions. Earnings do not seem assured as once thought. Recessions have materially influenced the short-term earnings of many. And, inflation, which increases bank operating expenses and making alternative nondeposit account employment of corporate funds more attractive, foretells continuing pressures on profits.

Much attention is now being focused on how to divide the market and how to process and deliver services more efficiently. The following material discusses the use of computer technology as a tool for bank management in addressing these questions. This discussion centers around specific/developing usages in a rapidly changing environment.

IDENTIFYING THE MARKET

In order to identify profitable markets for bank services or profitable services to provide in a particular market, one must tap sources of market information. Such sources are, in the data processing vernacular, identified as data bases. Data base is defined here as customer and demographic information which may be stored in a machine readable form. Many banks pull together such valuable, already available information in their computer files by utilizing central information, management information, and market analysis computer systems. These systems allow for the creation and maintenance of the data bases. Such data bases contain names, addresses, account balances, credit information, and type of services used by the bank's customers. Due to the reluctance of individuals to give personal information to any corporate organization, most bank data bases have been limited to the above-described information. Some banks have obtained personal information when customers were applying for loans.

The organization of the data bases may allow for random or sequential information accessing. Accessing material in a random fashion means that a detail may be obtained from the data base without reviewing the complete data base. This is accomplished by using indexing systems to identify the location of relevant information. The random access method is used to locate information about an individual customer. The sequential method provides access from the first file record of information to the last. This requires reviewing every file in a filing cabinet from front to back. The sequential access method utilized in marketplace identification systems selects certain information from files based on preestablished criteria.

The information accessed based on preestablished criteria can be about current or potential customers. Such information can tell something about a customer or prospect or identify an unknown. For example, finding that a customer has a substantial checking account but no savings account may identify a prospect for a new savings account. And knowing that a noncustomer is in a neighborhood where the bank has a branch can lead to capturing new business.

In providing corporate services, loan and investment decisions will be made utilizing information in data bases. A prospecting aid may result from analyzing information in the data base by trend analysis, customer profitability reviews, and potential investment comparisons. Systems for identifying corporate marketing opportunities are complex and expensive but potential benefits may also be great.

DELIVERING SERVICES

From 1960 to the mid-1970s, computer systems for processing information related to bank services were oriented primarily toward batch processing. Computer operations departments would run major updating programs in the evening and early morning hours and deliver reports to the using departments by 8:00 or 9:00 A.M. As branches became a primary vehicle for delivering retail services, audio response units became a common device for providing balance information to tellers. During this period the check became more accepted as a substitute for cash. The number of checks being handled by banks grew at an alarming rate. In the early 70s the SCOPE, Special Committee on Paperless Entries, study in California and the COPE, Committee on Paperless Entries, study in Georgia described the problems associated with processing the growing volume of checks and suggested approaches to electronic funds transfers, including point of sale systems. As the interest in these systems grew, a number of areas within banks began to use on-line terminal systems. The most common beginning was in charge card departments where on-line terminals were used to obtain direct computer access for data entry and credit authorization. Also, banks began to supplement their branches and banking hours with automatic teller machines. Remote job entry was another type of communication system found in states which allowed for some form of statewide banking or in heavy correspondent service bureau environments. Remote job entry systems commonly had a small computer hooked via telephone lines to a large computer. The small computer was used to collect data and send it to a larger computer, and later receive updated data and print reports. All of these communication systems have proven successful in meeting specific needs and the number of such systems has grown rapidly.

Little has yet been done to develop efficient communications networks. In 1974, several hardware vendors announced new teller terminal equipment and new communication approaches. The large hardware and software investment required to install a teller system led many bankers to review their current communications systems and to assess in what ways services should be provided. The review disclosed, in many cases, uncoordinated communication systems. Services had been provided to users primarily on a direct line basis. The teller systems required complex communications networks with associated expensive telephone costs. The concept of planned, integrated networks became an objective. On-line systems are now beginning to share the communications networks that permeated a bank's branch system. The communications network has been and will continue to be a facilitator for providing traditional and new services. The network will be the spokes of the service wheel that will reach back to the hub or the data base. The rim of the wheel will be the terminals or other connecting equipment used by bank staff or by customers.

The network provides bank management flexibility in using on-line computer capabilities more broadly. This typically is accomplished by attaching terminals to the network and establishing unique authorization codes, limiting the terminals' capabilities. A profile of such a network of terminals might include:

Telephones for audio response.

Teller terminals.

Automated teller machines.

CIF terminals.

Inquiry and data entry terminals.

Telephones are used to contact audio response systems for inquiring on balances and placing holds against accounts. More sophisticated systems include loan payoffs and procedural information. In some banks, audio response systems are being used in verifying or guaranteeing checks for merchants.

Teller terminals are internal to the bank and are installed to reduce check cashing losses, increase productivity, and provide uniformity in operating procedures and versatility in service offerings. A full function teller system may include electronic journaling, paper truncation, full cash drawer control, and teller scheduling and modeling.

Automated teller machines are the 24-hours-a-day, computer-operated cash dispenser, funds transferer, and deposit receiver. Until recently, such machines were not tied directly to the banks' computer records. To limit risk, bankers were selective in distributing cards to activate the machines. As banks have put the machines on-line to the main computers, the availability of balance information has allowed the system to make decisions on individual transactions, and thus significantly reduced the risks associated with issuing cards to all customers.

Terminals with access to central information files allow for rapid identification of customers as well as decentralized data entry from the branches. These terminals will be used in the future to access information on the profitability of a customer's relationship with the bank.

The general utility terminals or inquiry/data entry terminals are being found throughout banks. These terminals are used for a myriad of purposes ranging from simple data input to complex credit analysis.

The foregoing dealt with internal uses of the network and delivery of retail services. The network also has implications for broadening services to a bank's corporate customers. For example, terminals can be located in the corporate treasurer's office, providing for balance inquiry, or in the corporate secretary's office, providing direct access to shareholder information. This approach to distribution of information is a natural extension to the network.

Data processing has faced a major challenge in adapting quickly to new technology and the need for more controlled operating procedures in order to serve adequately the requirements of on-line systems. The word "availability" has a new meaning today. "Availability" in the "batch environment" meant having reports ready at the opening of business each morning. "Availability" for on-line systems means three-to-five-second response time on a terminal every time a person requests information or enters data. Visibility for data processing occurs when there is poor availability.

To lower "visibility" and raise "availability," most data processing centers have installed new internal procedures. Such new operating and control procedures are being broadly discussed under the label of "complex systems management." Complex systems management is often divided into four segments:

1. Failure planning.
2. Change control.
3. Incident reporting.
4. Measurement reporting.

Failure planning is the process of developing a plan of action to be followed in case of component failure. A component is any part of the data processing facility, including people, equipment, and physical facilities. Failure planning includes a range of plans for recovery from a complete disaster or total destruction to failure of a single terminal in the network. Such plans include arrangements for out-of-geographic-area processing, off-premise file retention, redundant equipment, redundant networking, standards, security procedures, cross training, and management succession.

Change control refers to the management control of any change which has potential impact on the production system. Such changes include additions, removal or rearrangement of any piece or pieces of equipment, modifications to systems, and conversions of data to operating systems. The purpose of change control is to manage positively and to limit any adverse impact on the user.

Incident reporting is concerned with documenting problems and tracking problem resolution. Three basic problem areas are addressed. The first relates to discrepancies in various reports from normal ongoing production. These are usually discovered by a user. Another involves situations in which an incident occurs or is encountered in the operations area which interrupts normal production. And the third is associated with interruptions in the teleprocessing network lines and related hardware. As incidents are reported, incident reporting procedures should ensure proper management notice and assignment of responsibility for follow-up.

Measurement reporting is a tool used in analyzing the success of the complex system management concepts. Measurement reporting is an organized approach to measuring on-line availability, batch schedules made and missed, equipment downtime, application downtime, incidents reported and resolved, system development and maintenance measurements. Personnel evaluations may be included, noting absenteeism, turnover, and specific achievements. Measurement reporting has tiers of frequency of reporting from instantaneous to annual reporting, and also tiers of management to whom reports are made.

PROCESSING DATA

As data processing has evolved, the systems that have been used to process bank services have become more sophisticated and flexible. This is particularly true in the more complicated systems such as trust and commercial loan systems. Once such systems are installed, daily processing is often more easily managed, requiring only moderate attention. Also, the number of people involved is often reduced, thus lowering the level of management involvement. The major daily processing challenge is in clearing and posting checks. This process begins at a teller's window or clearinghouse and flows through the proof department, the MICR sorter/readers, bookkeeping, and the Federal Reserve System.

In recent years, the item processing environment has been influenced by critical time schedules, unprecedented and unpredictable volumes, increased operating expense, and high costs associated with delays in fund availability. With the added problems of rising number of human errors, lack of adequately trained personnel, and complications of overtaxed transportation and communication facilities, the task of controlling this increasingly critical process has grown significantly.

New equipment and software systems, aimed at building efficiencies in item processing, were introduced during the mid-70s. These have led to increased personnel productivity, funds availability, and machine productivity. A major enhancement that allowed for many new capabilities was image matching.

Image matching is the process by which, during the first pass of documents through a reader/sorter, all machine readable data is captured and maintained in direct access storage. Nonmachine readable information is entered into its proper place in the data base by means of an on-line terminal. On subsequent passes, each document is matched with its image as recorded on the prior pass. Image matching enables the system to detect and compensate for unreadable characters as well as to assist in the isolation of missing items or missorts from previous passes. This facilitates pass-to-pass reconciliation. Image matching also permits an incoming sequence number to be carried from pass to pass, thus providing the bank's adjustment department with auditing and tracing information.

New software has led to improved handling of rejected items. High speed reentry of rejected checks has decreased the number of items that had to be reencoded by as much as 50 percent. High-speed reject reentry is the ability to enter rejects back into the sorter for a second try. This procedure necessitates matching the item with its partial image in the data base that was created on the initial pass of the item. Approaches to supplement high-speed reject reentry are slower than sorter/reader handling, but faster and less costly than reencoding the item. They include machines which optically read the material which MICR reader/sorters missed and on-line terminals for manual entry of any part or all of the data on an item. Most on-line re-entry systems allow for correcting just the bad character or characters not read by the sorter/reader.

New software has also incorporated the ability to handle new features contained in the newer reader/sorter equipment. These are primarily in utilizing unique item numbering, microfilming on the reader/sorter, and exploiting expanded pocket distribution capabilities.

The new reader/sorter hardware announced by vendors in the mid-70s was the first significant upgrade of such equipment since the initial introduction of MICR. Most of the new offerings have increased document speeds by 20 percent to 30 percent and reduced reject rates by more sophisticated reading mechanisms. As previously mentioned, the sorter/readers have had cameras added for microfilming items in an automated environment. Also, sorter/readers have self-contained logic which allows for off-line maintenance and diagnostics, operator prompting, and time independence.

Deposit and loan account items are captured for the purpose of posting accounts and later rendering statements to customers. As computer systems have been updated, new approaches to posting and statement rendering have been installed. These innovations purport to improve customer service, reduce postage expense, conform reporting to Fair Credit Billing Act of 1975 guidelines, and reduce personnel expense.

Improvements in customer service have come in the areas of automatic funds transfers, automatic overdraft coverage, combined statements and descriptive statements. With the growing acceptance of automated clearinghouses as a means of transferring funds, customers have become more willing to accept automatic payment of certain level payment bills and loans, as well as transfers between checking and savings accounts. Such transfers of funds can be clearly described on statements. No transaction tickets are required. The descriptive statement can be easier for some customers to understand and less expensive for the bank to handle and mail. The customer acceptance of this approach encourages efforts to eliminate returning other items to the customer. Many banks have successfully added loan balances, charge card balances and savings balances to monthly demand deposit account statements. Customer acceptance of this type of statement has been generally favorable. Charge card systems with descriptive billings are another strong indication of customers' willingness to accept truncation of some items from statements. A necessary step in eliminating the major item, checks, is the inclusion of the check sequence number on the statement. A large number of banks have made this move and are in a position to examine the previously unthinkable alternative of eliminating checks from statements.

THE FUTURE

Major future developments can be expected in communications networks, data base utilization, and production systems refinements. The communications network will be instrumental in providing management information from the data bases. The much touted management information system of the early 1970s should become a reality in the late 1970s. Also, the communications networks will be the foundation for electronic funds transfer systems/point of sale systems. As this subject is dealt with in another chapter, the only point made here is that soon the question of switching messages will be addressed by the banking industry. As EFTS/POS is made available to consumers by multiple banks and card services, switching will become mandatory to allow banks and card services to verify balance information and transfer funds. The major problem in the development of the switching system will be to install controls that limit and detect fraud and to build compatibility of communications protocols.

Refinement of the production systems provides profitable opportunities. Banks must continue building efficiencies into current systems and, as in the case of management information systems, bank management must participate in identifying need and potential return. Some of the areas to be addressed are automating credit decisions, reducing the rate of growth of report printing, increasing the use of microfilm or microfiche, and increasing the use of terminals in operating departments.

New systems that will have an impact on streamlining bank services are found in the areas of word processing, archival retrieval systems, on-line interactive training, and modeling of all types.

A primary challenge for banking and data processing managers will be to broaden knowledge of each other's needs. Stronger participation by bankers is required in establishing data processing direction and priorities.

Chapter 19

Managing the Data Processing System for Banks

*Craig G. Nelson**

The importance of data processing within the banking industry has been increasing rapidly over the past several years. At one time, it was relatively easy to install simple basic accounting systems used primarily to reduce manual effort and related expense. Systems such as demand deposit, savings and others were readily available and inexpensive to implement. Top management could limit its involvement in the data processing function to merely ensuring that reporting was satisfactory and provided on a timely basis. Today's complex and expensive systems, coupled with the evolution of electronic banking, place greater emphasis on the data processing activity. This emphasis in turn places additional responsibility on top-level management to plan and control the activity.

This chapter will concern itself with executive management of the data processing function. Lower level management is the responsibility of the data-processing manager and requires a high degree of technical understanding. The established techniques available for control by lower level managers are extensive and complex and will be discussed only when necessary to adequately define the environment which must be managed by the executive.

The amount and type of top-level management depends on the approach used for data processing services. Smaller banks that must obtain services from an outside source are limited in the amount of management influence they can exert. There are several alternatives

* President, Associated Computer Services, Inc., Portland, Oregon.

to outside services for smaller banks and the amount of management involvement depends on the approach selected. Both service bureaus and correspondent banks are basically treated the same from a management standpoint since neither offers ownership and only limited control is possible. Banks with their own in-house facilities demand greater executive involvement and the majority of this chapter will be devoted to discussing this alternative. Another outside source for data processing services is the cooperative. This approach affords the bank ownership, provides a high degree of management influence, and is therefore aligned closely to in-house.

The management approach for the service bureau or correspondent bank will be explored first.

MANAGING THE SERVICE BUREAU OR CORRESPONDENT BANK

Since there is no ownership with a service bureau or correspondent bank, direct management is not possible. Actual management is the servicer's responsibility and other means must be used to ensure satisfactory performance. The most important of these is initial servicer selection. Three major areas which should be considered in the selection process are: type of services available, cost of services relative to quality, and servicer's long-range plans.

Before beginning the selection process, it is necessary for each bank to determine its own individual data processing requirements. Once determined, available servicers should be investigated in depth to ensure their systems are comprehensive enough to meet these requirements. Both quality and flexibility must be considered when analyzing type of services offered. During the selection process the quality of data processing systems must be established by a thorough analysis of each application and then servicer performance examined closely. The best source of information in determining performance is user banks—not the servicer. Interviews with several users can provide confirmation of servicer's claims regarding systems and performance.

Another consideration is expense. Pricing should be in relation to quality of service and caliber of systems. Banks wishing only to reduce paperwork through use of basic accounting systems should find them available at a relatively low cost. Banks located in more competitive areas require more competitive systems which are expensive not only to process but to develop, and service fees will be higher. A consideration for the more progressive banks is cooperation on special requests, which may be necessary to enable the bank to retain its individuality and expand its service base. Most servicers will develop special systems or programs at an additional expense. This should be verified prior to making a commitment.

Long-range planning on the part of the servicer is especially important as banks become increasingly dependent upon more advanced data processing systems such as on-line central information file (CIF) an electronic funds transfer. Services may be acceptable at the time of investigation, but if provisions are not made for future banking developments, serviced banks may soon lose their competitive position.

After the servicer is selected, controlling is the prime concern. Audits of system quality, accuracy, and timeliness are simple to perform and will pinpoint any unfavorable trends. In addition, a review of other servicers should be conducted periodically to provide a measurement in evaluating present performance and to ensure alternatives are readily available should a change in servicer become necessary. If performance falls below an acceptable level and the servicer is unable to effect improvement within a reasonable period of time, withdrawal should be considered. Although expensive, once withdrawal becomes inevitable, the sooner it is accomplished, the better. Prolonged unacceptable performance affects customer satisfaction, employee morale, and the competitive position of the bank.

Using these indirect management techniques allows limited control over a service bureau or correspondent bank.

MANAGING IN-HOUSE DATA PROCESSING

The in-house approach to data processing naturally provides the greatest opportunity for top-management involvement. In fact, executive involvement is mandatory if services are to be of a high caliber and utilized effectively.

The objective of the data processing activity must support the overall objective of the bank and will determine the type of systems, organization of the data processing section, capacity of equipment, and size of staff. If the prime objective is only to reduce paperwork and expense, the data processing activity will be limited. The systems research and development section will be small and will primarily provide maintenance of previously installed accounting systems. With the advent of electronic banking, few banks will be interested in this alternative. The banks that are will be located in remote and less competitive areas. Banks that must compete through a high level of service will require comprehensive systems and a large research and development staff.

In order to properly plan over the long term, executive management must be aware of trends, be concerned for the future, understand the impact of data processing on its bank's growth and be able to utilize its data processing facilities to their fullest advantage. Without this understanding and involvement, it is probable that bank services will experience limited growth and become increasingly inefficient and expensive.

Executive management does not require technical competence to effectively manage the data-processing activity. Nontechnical controls are available such as audit reports, the profit plan, and many others which will be incorporated throughout the chapter. The merits of auditing are obvious, as in any accounting function. Audit reports will be one of the prime indicators of inefficiencies for the bank executive. The profit plan provides a measurement of expense in relation to income and each bank must establish its own acceptable expense budget for both research and development of new systems and daily production processing.

Data-processing management must possess technical competence as well as upper level management skills and the ability to control. Because of the technical orientation of data processing personnel, additional responsibility is placed on management to ensure effective communications with other bank areas. The data processing manager or manager's primary experience should be in data processing, not in banking. The importance of capable data processing management must not be underestimated since it will be the principal influence on the entire department's productivity.

One of the prerequisites to an effective data processing section is a strong organizational structure. There are many organizational alternatives and selection will depend on need. Regardless of structure used, management functions within the areas themselves are basically the same. A standard structure is to have the data processing manager reporting to the executive responsible for bank operations, either directly or indirectly. The computer operations and project development sections then report to the data processing manager. This alternative, although acceptable for smaller banks, is not recommended for larger or more enterprising banks. For these, there is a better alternative.

The structure which promotes the greatest use of expertise and simultaneously strengthens the data processing function is separate reporting of operations and project development. The computer operations area is responsible for production processing and should report to bank operations. The project development area is research oriented and should report to the executive responsible for planning. These departments can then function independently in much the same way as production and engineering in a manufacturing environment.

This type of reporting structure provides greater security as development and operations personnel are completely separate. The priorities of the two departments are not in conflict as often happens in a single reporting structure and there is less likelihood of unfavorable influence between them. Separate cost control is possible which is desirable since the department functions are different. Each area can establish its own objectives and optimize performance. It should be emphasized that separate reporting is not feasible without a strong policy and procedure system to interface the two departments.

A third area, technical support, primarily provides assistance to the production department and should also report to the bank operations area.

These management considerations apply to all data processing. In addition, there are unique requirements within the three specific areas—computer operations, project development, and technical support—which will be discussed individually. Prior to exploring the controls necessary to effect proper management, the function and organization of each area must be clearly understood.

Computer Operations

The computer operations area's primary function is processing daily production systems on an accurate and timely basis. This area is not concerned with systems development with the exception of merging completed systems into the production work flow and running system tests. Since testing is extremely important to project development personnel if they are to meet established schedules, it must be given a high priority. Adequate machine and personnel time must be included in computer operations planning to accommodate this function. In processing daily jobs, little intervention from project development personnel is required if adequate documentation is available, primarily comprehensive operating instructions. Program problems that occur during production processing are referred back to project development with detailed information for correction.

Management will be most effective if the computer operations department is separated into functionally oriented subsections. A logical division for the larger installation is data preparation, computer processing, data control, and distribution. Each of these subsections is headed by either a supervisor or lead person with the responsibility of assigning work, establishing schedules, and otherwise directing the activities for which they are responsible. Additionally, depending on size of the department, various levels of supervision can be incorporated to provide better control. The manager or supervisor responsible for the entire department must have a total overview in order to manage personnel, establish procedures, resolve problems and make major decisions affecting processing. These various levels of supervision provide natural promotional opportunity and employee incentive for advancement.

Controls within the computer operations area fall basically into three categories: procedures, schedules, and performance reports. Of the three, the one with the greatest impact is procedures. These must conform to the standards set by management. If they are well designed, they will allow exceptional control and ensure a smooth running operation provided they are enforced.

Scheduling for efficiency is required for a well-controlled environment. Program and system run times, interface requirements, and job priorities must be considered in setting computer-processing schedules. The scheduling of personnel and work flow must be done in conjunction with optimizing computer throughput. Streamlining the work flow in this manner can save substantial expense through elimination of idle personnel and machine time.

The final area of control is performance reports, which are indicators of unfavorable trends and inefficiencies. One type is a manually prepared daily report which indicates production problems and schedule variances. Another type is a computer-generated control report automatically prepared on a less frequent basis such as monthly. Well-designed automated reports provide useful information including cost to process each system; amount of time and expense for data preparation, computer processing, data control, and distribution; and computer utilization indicating time and expense for testing, compiling, and rerunning programs. These reports can be categorized by individual program, system, and operator. Although expensive to develop, the cost can easily be recovered if the reports are used to analyze and correct inefficiencies that might normally be overlooked without them.

Another critical area within computer operations is security. Due to the sensitive type of processing, strict security measures must be adhered to. Access to the computer center must be restricted to authorized personnel only. Evacuation and file retention and recovery procedures should be established and reviewed on a periodic basis to ensure they remain satisfactory. Backup facilities should be located or other emergency plans developed in the event of physical damage to the computer center. Computer operators, keypunch operators, and other key personnel with the opportunity to alter records should be rotated periodically to minimize chances of fraud. These are very general security measures and there are many excellent publications available on the subject of security safeguards.

Project Development

Systems and programming or project development is the area with responsibility for investigating and developing new systems and for maintaining systems after implementation. In developing systems, there are two methods commonly used in the banking industry. They may be totally developed in-house or software may be purchased and modified to meet bank requirements. The major drawback to developing in-house is the length of time required from initial system design to final implementation. This method requires a larger development staff and increases the demand on other facilities such as computer time. The primary advantage to in-house development is that systems can be custom designed to the bank's own specifications.

The second method, software purchase, is a better alternative in most instances. There are many excellent systems available, although at considerable expense. Purchasing software requires extensive investigation to ensure the final selection best meets the bank's requirements. System performance, documentation, vendor support, and contract terms must all be evaluated thoroughly. Implementation of purchased software is faster as the primary development has already been completed and although in-house modifications are still necessary, the project development staff can be smaller than required for total in-house development.

Establishing and motivating a staff of data processing professionals requires an approach different than those used for other areas in the banking organization. As with data processing management, technical competence is more important than banking experience. Although data processing people do relate to their employer, like in other specialized fields, they usually relate more to their own profession. Salaries must therefore be competitive to those of comparable positions within the data processing field, rather than within the organization. They are frequently more interested in advancement within their profession and promotional opportunity must be provided accordingly.

The working environment is also important. Adequate facilities must be available to allow timely completion of assigned projects. Professional development personnel become discouraged if their projects are delayed because of inadequate test time over which they have no control. Serious morale problems and high turnover may result.

Project development personnel primarily consist of computer programmers, programmer analysts, and systems analysts. As implied by the term "systems and programming," often personnel are separated by function. A better alternative is a team approach. In the team environment, groups are established according to project needs and the combination of personnel assigned to each team depends on complexity of the project and required completion date. One systems analyst may be designated project or team leader. This organization approach provides better training and backup, and in conjunction, employee progression opportunity.

Controls for the project development section are similar to the computer operations area. Strong, well-designed procedures which conform to established standards are required for developing and implementing new systems. These standards must be set by management and developed by technical personnel. Procedures and documentation, if they adhere to standards, will provide effective control, reduce errors, and increase productivity.

As in computer operations, scheduling is a prime concern. Target dates must be set for each phase of development and frequent reports submitted indicating project status. Because of the impact on other department plans, problems that may affect the completion of a system must be reported immediately. Establishing realistic schedules requires experience and must take into consideration unexpected setbacks and continuing maintenance. In researching new systems, each team should establish its own schedules and after management approval, should be held responsible for meeting them.

Performance reports are also an integral part of project development control. Effective use of the reports is necessary for management to pinpoint unfavorable trends and ensure efficiency. A well-designed project control system will provide needed information such as cost to develop each program and each system; and time spent in the various functions such as systems design, programming, and testing. Analyzing this information will indicate where action must be taken to optimize performance. These reports should be designed to measure performance not only of each project development person but of each team as well. In addition to an automated control system, a project development status report prepared manually on a more frequent basis can also be a valuable tool. These reports should include information such as project status, schedule changes, system problems encountered, and steps taken to resolve them. As is true with any performance report, their value will be limited unless they result in action being taken when indicated.

Security is as important in the project development area as it is in the computer operations section. Since program documentation is highly confidential, adequate security procedures should be maintained to ensure it is inaccessible to unauthorized personnel. Duplicate sets of documentation should be stored off premises in the event originals are destroyed. Entry to the project development area should be restricted.

Although controls for project development and computer operations are similar—management techniques are not. Because of the nature of the project development activity, management by objectives work very well. Project or tasks may require many months or even years to complete and objectives and schedules are necessary to measure progress. Major projects are often broken down into subsystems which also have established completion dates. Thus unfavorable trends in performance can be determined well in advance of overall system completion. Controlling complex projects through establishment of subsystems enables much easier management of the project development activity.

Since the banking data processing field is changing rapidly and becoming extremely competitive, another very important management consideration is the caliber of the project development area. Involvement of this area in planning for the bank's future is becoming a necessity. The expertise of project development professionals is a valuable resource which should be utilized to its fullest potential.

Technical Support

Technical support, as its name implies, provides technical assistance to project development and computer operations. Many specific responsibilities are in fact too technical to discuss in this chapter and do not directly involve top-level management. Other more general functions which require executive involvement may be assigned this area. One of these, which will influence the entire data processing effort, is development of standards.

Policy, established by top-level management, must be translated and documented in the form of policy standards and procedures. The actual translation will often be done by the department most affected by a particular standard, with the assistance of technical support. Project development may develop systems and programming documentation requirements while computer operations may design a computer run book. Once developed, overall responsibility for publishing, maintaining, and enforcing these standards and procedures should preferably be assigned to technical support. If not, other priorities such as production processing and systems design may take precedence to the detriment of standards and procedures. Because they are essential to proper management and control, they must not be neglected. This can be avoided by assigning them to another area where they have top priority.

Another function often delegated to technical support is facilities planning which can include software, hardware, floor space, and even personnel. Long-range planning is a prerequisite to proper data processing facilities planning and ultimate approval must be the responsibility of top-level management.

Technical support should also develop and maintain the automated systems used in controlling project development and computer operations. These may be costly, however, data processing represents a sizable expense and part of that expense must be incurred to control the total.

This description of the computer operations, project development, and technical support areas was included to aid top management in better understanding the data processing function and is not intended to encourage excessive involvement in day-to-day activity.

MANAGING THE COOPERATIVE

Banks wishing to maintain control over the data-processing function without incurring the high cost of installing their own computer center have another alternative—the cooperative. With the pooled resources of the cooperative it is economically feasible to develop sophisticated systems without adversely affecting the finances of any one bank. This is becoming especially important with the advent of electronic banking.

Selecting a cooperative is similar to selecting any other outside servicer. Type of services offered, cost of services relative to quality, and long-range plans are areas that must be investigated. Since top-level management is a reality with the cooperative, the effectiveness of existing management must be considered as well as the amount of influence a new bank will have on that management.

Executive management of the cooperative is basically the same as in-house with one exception—due to joint ownership, the management approach must be participative. This is a recognized successful approach and is often used even when not required. Participative management often results in better decision making as it is based on the opinions of several qualified people. To successfully apply this approach to the cooperative, every bank should be represented on the participative management team, normally the board of directors. To prevent top-level management from becoming excessively involved in day-to-day activities, the cooperative board should consist of the chief executive officer of each member bank. Decision making on the part of the board should be at the top level and should include establishing policy, service fees, and approving major expenditures. If the addition of banks to the cooperative results in the board of directors becoming too large and, therefore, ineffective, a management committee can be elected to direct the cooperative activity.

Since this group is responsible for establishing the objectives of the cooperative as well as the objectives of their own individual banks, the cooperative will take on the character of the banks themselves. Once the objectives have been established, it is up to the cooperative management to ensure those objectives are met following the same course as outlined in the in-house alternative. The board of directors or management committee can oversee and control the cooperative activities through use of audits, profit plan performance, and a continual review of the timeliness and accuracy of services. With proper top-level management, the cooperative can perform better than either a service bureau or correspondent, and for the smaller bank it is a better alternative than in-house.

CONCLUSION

With the evolution of data processing in banking, its relative importance is increasing dramatically. It is no longer limited to simple accounting systems. Terms such as electronic funds transfer, automated clearinghouse, and point of sale are becoming commonplace in their usage. Markets once considered the sole property of the commercial banks are starting to erode as competition provides new consumer services through use of sophisticated data processing systems. Competition is extremely important within the banking industry now, and it will probably become even more acute as more of these services enter the market. No bank can afford to let itself get too far behind the competition, and from all indications, the competition is forging ahead. If data processing in commercial banking is to succeed in providing competitive consumer services, top-level management must take an active and decisive role in its direction.

Chapter 20

Electronic Funds Transfer (EFTS) in Depository Institutions

*Eugene M. Tangney**

INTRODUCTION

Although electronic funds transfer (EFTS) has been, in some areas, in development for the past six to eight years, it is still in its infancy. Federal and state banking laws and regulations severely limit the expansion of this new delivery system. The ultimate user, the consumer, has not shown positive signs that it is a system which he or she will use or desires, although the principal benefits of the system are to provide better services at lower costs to the depository institutions. The configuration that will eventually be constructed is still in a state of change and innovations will continue to come upon the scene in the next few years.

Funds transfer systems were once thought of as being primarily the use of coin, currency, and checks. This transfer system was considered to be one of the principal functions of commercial banks, since banks were the record keepers and the safekeepers of the money supply. The money supply being in today's world (called M_1) is in coin and currency and in demand deposits of commercial banks.

The check accounts for 94/96 cents of every dollar spent. (See Exhibit 20–1.) The check became popular in 1870 and 1880 due to the severe restrictions placed on the issuance of currency under the National Banking Acts of 1863 and 1865, and it has become the most popular method of payment in the United States today. In the year 1976, some 28 billion checks were written in the United States and

* Senior Vice President, The First National Bank of Boston, Boston, Massachusetts.

Exhibit 20-1
Payment System Transactions

	Number	Value
Cash....................	87%	3%
Check	11%	96%
Credit card	2%	1%
	100%	100%
Total................ 249 billion	$7,251 billion

Source: "The Consequences of Electronic Funds Transfer," National Science Foundation, June 1975. Estimates for mid-1970s. Excludes Bank Wire and Fed Wire Transactions, and checks over $10,000.

by 1980, if this growth rate continues, will grow to 42–44 billion. This number is up from 5 billion in 1945, 9 billion in 1955, and 17 billion in 1965, which represents in more practical terms 104 million checks each business day, and on a 24-hour basis, 4 million checks per hour. This 7 percent compounded growth rate has continued for the past 15 years.

Each check costs the banking system approximately 25 to 27 cents from the time the payer issues the check until it arrives back in his or her statement, for a cost to the commercial banking industry of some $5 billion a year. Total costs to society are shown in Exhibit 20–3. These checks can be drawn on any one of 14,000 commercial banks located in the 50 states. Now they can also be drawn on many of the thrift institutions located in New England who are empowered

Exhibit 20-2
Present Check System

	Growth of Checks (billions of checks)
1945.............................	5.0
1965.............................	17.0
1970.............................	22.0
1971.............................	23.0
1972.............................	24.6
1973.............................	22.5
1974.............................	24.3
1975.............................	26.0

Annual compound growth rate of 7 percent.
Each check handled seven times within the banking system.
Source: *Monetary and Systems Planning Report of the American Bankers Association*, April 1971, and FDIC Surveys.

Exhibit 20–3
Present Check System

	Cost of Check Processing	
	(*$ billions*)	(*percents check*)
FED...................................	$ 0.15	½
Commercial banks......................	6.73	27
Households............................	3.40	13½
Business and government.................	1.20	5
Total	$11.48	46
Excluding households		32½

Source: "The Cost of the U.S. Payments System," *Journal of Bank Research*, Winter 1975, p. 242; and "The Consequence of Electronic Funds Transfer," National Science Foundation, June 1975.

to have negotiable orders of withdrawal (NOW) accounts. The credit union draft system is adding additional volume. All indications (studies, the commission reports, etc.) indicate that the thrift institutions are going to play an important part in the future payments system.

The check clearing system is a unique combination of large communications, transportation and computer networks. It is probably the most efficient paper-oriented communications system in the United States. The larger commercial correspondent banks and the Federal Reserve System have worked on a partnership basis, whereby the Federal Reserve System maintains the main arteries in the flow of checks between and within districts, and the large commercial banks, acting as correspondent banks, prepare and presort the checks for the system. It has been an outstanding cooperative effort between the public and private sectors, and has provided and is providing a safe, secure and speedy payments system. A check drawn or deposited on an East Coast bank, even in late afternoon will generally be processed and delivered to the West Coast bank within a 12-hour period.

A brief description of the present check processing system is important since this, along with consumer convenience, will be one of the principal reasons for the forward thrust into electronic funds transfer. Each of the 28 billion checks written in the United States must be handled an average of seven times and can be drawn against any one of the 14,000 commercial banks, or any one of the hundreds of savings banks and savings and loan associations located in the New England area. To handle this amount of paper, the commercial banking industry has become the largest single user of computers in the United States, except for the U.S. government. These computers perform many activities in the banking industry, but one of their principal functions is the processing of checks through magnetic ink character recognition

(MICR) sorter/readers. These computers are able to process these checks at the rate of 100,000 per hour, and handle the related payments and the bookkeeping necessary for the funds transfer system to function in the United States.

The money supply, in fact all banking records in their physical form, are represented by electronic characters on magnetic tapes and connected to these computers. One of the principal functions of the entire computer network of all depository institutions is to move these electronic characters from one account to another, whether it be in the same bank and located only inches away, or in one of the commercial banks, savings and loans, credit unions, or savings banks in any of the 50 states. This is the basic function of the payments system. Today, all financial information is transcribed from pieces of paper, the check being the most obvious one. Once transcribed, the information is automatically handled, except under our present system, because of legal technicalities and banking custom, the paper must also move with the information. Therefore, even though the banking system is highly automated, the payments system is still basically labor intensive because of these paper handling requirements. Sixty percent of the cost of processing this information is personnel cost and 40 percent is equipment, overhead, occupancy, and transportation costs.

Productivity gains, although substantial in the past few years, are basically restricted to something less than 2 percent per year. In the same vein the communications industry over the past 20 years has maintained a productivity gain of from 6 percent to 7 percent. One of the principal benefits of incorporating electronic funds transfer into the payments system is to allow financial depository institutions to expand productivity much faster than is possible under a paper system.

A second important factor in the development and implementation of EFTS into our payments system is the high cost of delivering banking services through the banking networks. The 14,000 commercial banks have some 26,000 branches; the 481 mutual savings banks have 1,500 branches; 5,170 savings and loans have 7,000 branches; and there are 12,700 credit unions. This adds to 67,000 different physical locations which deliver banking services to the consuming public. The consumer services received from the financial depository institutions are generally of low-dollar size, but recurring type services. For example, 85 percent of the consumer check transactions are for under $100. Today most large dollar business and industrial financial transfers do not take place by utilizing the check system. These types of transactions are already present users of EFTS in the banking system.

The objective of electronic funds transfer projects is to bring together the banking industry, the retail industry, and the communications industry in an effort to provide a far more convenient, efficient and lower cost system to the American consumer. The basic problems preventing the banking industry today from installing a major EFT system are legal, governmental, and regulatory in nature.

The commercial banking system today is supervised by three separate federal governmental organizations—Comptroller of the Currency, Federal Deposit Insurance Corporation, and the Federal Reserve System—plus 50 supervisory authorities of the states. To change the delivery system of depository institutions, it is necessary to conform to the rules, sometimes conflicting, of these federal and state regulatory agencies. In addition, there are separate federal and sometimes state regulatory agencies for each type of financial institution.

This problem led to the creation in 1975 of the National Commission on Electronic Funds Transfer. For 18 months this Commission reviewed the problems involved and made recommendations to solve the problems. It suggested to both federal and state governments legislation that will allow an electronic funds transfer system to be implemented into the American banking system.

One of the basic components necessary to understand how EFTS will affect not only the funds transfer system of the United States, but also how it will interface with the consumer, is to realize that money in its physical form today is represented by magnetic characters on our computer network. To move funds from one account to another, in effect, only moves those magnetic characters. That principle is used today in EFTS and banking and has been used for the past 20 years.

EFTS already exists in the payments system of America today, but it is used primarily for large-dollar transactions involving payments between larger corporate accounts, the government and the banking system. The largest system in existence today is the Federal Reserve Wire System. This is a computer network which ties in 213 of the largest banks on-line to the 37 Federal Reserve Bank offices, and allows funds to be transferred to and from 5,782 member banks and, through the correspondent bank system, to the 14,000 commercial banks and 18,000 thrift institutions. It processes $23 trillion per year, handling 10 million transactions, the average transaction being over $2 million. This system also interfaces with the telephone and telegraphic systems. It has been operational for the past 50 years, has worked well, and serves an extremely important segment of our banking system. There is no paper required in the system and all funds are transferred electronically.

Large correspondent banks have maintained the Bank Wire System, a system leased from Western Union connecting 14 of the largest banks of New York and Chicago with 240 subscribers. It maintains communications through switches in New York and Chicago. Funds are transferred through correspondent balances and this allows informational messages to be sent as well as funds transferred. This system is being completely redesigned as Bank Wire System II, the ownership of which will be assumed by all of the subscribers and is being put into operation in 1977.

Another example of existing electronic funds transfer in our banking system is CHIPS (Clearing House Interbank Payments System)—a system designed and operated by the New York Clearing House for interbank payments. This is a purely electronic funds transfer system that handles the clearing and settlement of primarily Eurodollar transactions of large regional banks, and branches of foreign banks located in New York City. The transactions are processed through a system consisting of small electronic terminals tied through the telephone network to computers located in the New York Clearing House. It allows for not only processing of daily payments, but for the warehousing of messages, and in 1975 had some $60 billion per day processed through the system. The settlement mechanism of this system, as well as settlements with the Federal Reserve Wire System, is done through the Federal Reserve System.

Another large EFT system that will be coming on-line and will handle primarily international banking transactions is Society of Worldwide Interbank Financial Telecommunications, better known by the acronym SWIFT. This system which will connect large foreign, as well as domestic banks, in an EFT mode will have some 300 banks in 15 countries including 36 American banks in the system. It will have switches in Brussels and Amsterdam that will connect with the larger U.S. European, and Canadian banks.

The two major credit card systems of the United States have developed national EFT system through their authorization networks. The Interbank Network Authorization System (INAS) is a credit card system located in St. Louis which connects 156 processing centers operated 24 hours a day and handles credit authorizations for 35 million cardholders. The transmission of interchange items and statement billing allows for the tape to tape transmission of dollar draft settlement of large creditcard transactions. BankAmericard System (now VISA) operates full interconnecting switches, handles some 150 processing centers for 29 million cardholders. This system allows for credit authorization interchange in transmission of sales items and settlement through the Federal Reserve System.

Therefore, in the banking system are included some very sophisticated electronic funds transfer systems, but these relate to only large-dollar items or credit card transactions.

Exhibit 20–4
EFTS Today

Federal Reserve Wire System

Bank Wire System
Bank Wire System II

CHIPS (Clearing House Interbank Payments System)
SWIFT (Society for Worldwide Interbank Financial Telecommunication)
Credit Card Systems

These are examples of systems that allow monies and information to be transferred on a completely automated basis without the use of a piece of paper. Although these EFT systems are growing, they are not designed for the large number of small-dollar amount checks or debits to an individual account that flow to and from the consumer.

There are several other pressures on individual financial institutions, as well as the industry as a whole, to increase the efficiency and lower the cost of the present payments system. The future of retail banking will bring even greater pressures in years to come because of these low-dollar transactions and the high cost of service. The principal costs are our large branch networks and the paper and related costs of personnel and transportation. EFTS is designed to reduce these costs. But to do so habits of consumers must be influenced. Banking and branching laws must be redesigned and a marriage brought about between retail industries and banking.

The principal advantages of EFTS will be the improved services to the consumer—the user of these payment systems. It will give to the consumer a far better product, far more conveniences, and hopefully a lower cost. Some of the potential consumer benefits that can be obtained through the EFT system are: (1) create more competitive markets for the services offered by the various financial institutions; (2) expand the consumers' choice among payment alternatives (i.e., coin, currency, checks, EFT services, and the particular types of financial institutions); (3) offer greater consumer convenience by providing easier, more efficient and expanded access to financial deposits and loan accounts; (4) increase the security of financial transactions; and (5) reduce the cost of the financial transaction, not only to the consumer, but to society as a whole.

With that background, the remainder of this chapter will be devoted to the principal methods by which electronic funds transfer will be incorporated into the American payments system. Below are listed the four basic systems that are being developed by depository institutions, singularly or collectively:

1. Automated clearing houses
2. Automated teller machines
3. Point-of-sale terminals
4. Telephone bill paying

Exhibit 20–5
Developing EFTS

Automated clearing houses (ACH)
Retail (POS) systems
   Check verification.
   Credit authorization/data capture.
   Debit transactions.
   Deposit and withdrawal.
   Loan advances.
ATMs
Telephone banking

AUTOMATED CLEARING HOUSE SERVICE

This system has been in the design stage for the past seven years. It offers through automated batch-type processing the direct deposit and direct payment of small recurring consumer-type payments. It allows for the direct deposit of payroll, dividends, government transfer payments, and so on, into individuals' checking and savings accounts electronically on a *preauthorized* scheduled basis. The system also allows for the preauthorized recurring type of bill payment, such as life insurance policies, mortgage payments, utility bills, and other types of fixed payments. These payments can be deposited or withdrawn automatically from an individual's checking or savings account. The automated clearing house (ACH) is probably the one area where the greatest amount of organizational planning, computer software development and implementation of an EFT system has been accomplished to date in the American financial system.

The foundation of the ACH goes back to 1968 when the Monetary and Payments System Planning (MAPS) Committee of the American Bankers Association was formed. After a three-year study, it was recommended that a comprehensive nationwide clearing and settlement system for electronic payments be developed, the development of which was not solely dependent on or controlled by the Federal Reserve. It further recommended that such a system be eventually capable of handling bank, corporate, government, and consumer payments. As part of the report, it was suggested that the clearinghouse associations throughout the United States form separate groups to study the payments system in their locations and to function as the principal coordinating committee for each area of the country.

During April and May 1970, the American Bankers Association MAPS Committee, jointly with Arthur D. Little Company, developed a check payment system study to assess the characteristics of the present system, to review the capabilities of the system, and to determine how long the present system could be sustained. Among the major recommendations of this report was the establishment of an electronic payments distribution system to facilitate paperless entries. Several other studies were made such as that by Atlanta Committee on Paperless Entries (COPE) committee. The goal of that organization was to implement an ACH in the Atlanta area.

The first automated clearing house to begin operation was the California ACH (CACHA). In April 1973, the Georgia Automated Clearing House Association was formed and operations began in May 1973. The automated task force commissioned by the ABA was to develop by mid-1973 automated clearinghouse standards. The task force's goal was to develop necessary conditions for the interregional exchange of ACH transactions. The task force provided the framework for a National Automated Clearing House Association and the report is considered by many to be the major milestone in ACH development.

The National Automated Clearing House Association (NACHA) was formed in July 1974. The charter membership numbered 18 ACHs, although only 4 were then operational—California, Georgia, New England, and the upper Midwest. Between mid-1974 and early 1976, 15 automated clearing houses became operational subsequent to formation of NACHA. By December 1976, there were 32 ACH members of NACHA. Monthly volume soon rose from 75,000 to about 5,250,000 items. In the spring of 1975 the first federal recurring payment program began, which involved the U.S. Treasury Department's direct deposit of social security checks. The program was a pilot project involving Florida and Georgia and subsequently has spread throughout the United States. By December 1976 there were 4,687,000 government credits processed monthly through the ACH system.

Automated clearing house transactions have several basic parts. The transaction is initiated by the *consumer* or his (her) *employer* who preauthorizes a payment to be made from the consumer's account or into the consumer's account. The information is contained on computer magnetic tapes which are sent from the employer or the consumers' bill paying institution to an *originating bank*. Here the computer tape is processed by the originating bank's computer system and entries to and from the account from that bank are stripped off. The tape is then sent to the automated clearing house, which receives tapes from all originating banks within its area of operation. The ACH sorts the entries by receiving institution and transmits, either by physically transporting the tapes or by data communication, the information to the *receiving institution* which then debits or credits the individual consumer's account or the individual corporate account that is to receive the financial deposits.

The function of the automated clearing house is basically very simple and performs the same basic function as a clearinghouse that handles checks, except that it processes both debits and credits and involves the passing of information from one computer to another indicating a debit and a credit, the customer's name, account number, and net amount due. Because of high-speed sort patterns, the computers are capable of handling hundreds of millions of these transactions in a short period of time. The computer and communication technology here in the United States has been perfected to the point where it is obvious that the utilization of this technology is essential if the banking system is to increase its productivity.

The automated clearing houses have many of the same functional requirements as any organization. A structural organization, directors, sets of rules, budgets, staff and a business plan—prerequisites for putting together an active program. The most important factor in the development of the ACH movement is cooperation among competing institutions. In addition to these functional necessities, an ACH has three basic operational requirements:

1. A delivery system capable of delivering items to multiple destinations.
2. Data processing capability, both hardware and software.
3. Settlement capabilities.

Of the three, the delivery system commands by far the greatest portion of the budget. While the ACHs that are presently operating have their own organizational components, budgets, business plans, rules, and so on—they all use the Federal Reserve to some degree for their operational needs. But in all cases, settlement for transactions are made on the books of the Federal Reserve System.

Consumer interest has always been in the forefront of the planners' thoughts. For instance, all transactions must have the written permission of the consumer before any activity can take place. The consumer's right to charge back items against his or her account have been extended to 15 days from the time he or she is notified of such charges, or a total of 45 days. The system is designed to give the customer maximum freedom over his accounts and funds. It is designed to: (1) process the routine low-decision type of payment whether it be payment to an individual or charges against the individual; (2) provide a safe and fast method for a large volume of bill issuers to collect their funds in a reasonably low-labor intensive method, and also, for large distributors of funds, a means to disburse funds in a similar manner; (3) allow all those economic units that issue or receive a large volume of payments to disburse funds in a way that will protect not only the recipient but also the issuers of these payments. Today 32 automated clearing houses make up the membership of the National Automated Clearing House Association. There are some basic problems that the ACHs must face in the next few years if they are to become a viable part of the EFT system, the most important being consumer acceptance of this type of payment mechanism. The banking system has produced, over the past 50 years, a payments system (checks) which has generally satisfied their needs both in service and price. The consumer has enjoyed the phenomenon of the banking system called "float" whereby it is possible to obtain funds one, two, or possibly three days before a check is charged against an account. This benefit will be eliminated.

The consumer also wishes to have full control of financial transactions. The preauthorized, predetermined bill paying service has not yet been conceived by the consumer to be a better service than the present check system. Successful marketing of this service will be necessary for its full acceptance by the consumer. The federal government's social security and payroll direct payment system is successful, and is the one encouraging area in the acceptance of the automated clearing house into the payments system.

The second major issue facing the automated clearing house is the access to the clearinghouses by thrift institutions. Approximately 13 ACHs have now accepted, on a fully equitable basis, all types of thrift institutions, both as originating and receiving banks. This has not been a uniform acceptance by all ACHs and is a problem that must be solved within the next few years if the clearinghouses are to become an integral part of the payments system. It does appear that thrift institutions and deposits in thrift institutions will become part of the payments system in this country.

AUTOMATED TELLER MACHINES

The next area of EFTS as it relates to financial institutions is the automated teller machine (ATM). This machine can operate in an off-line mode in which information is collected and stored in the terminal itself, and subsequently updated in a batch mode (generally on a daily basis). ATMs can also operate in an on-line mode whereby the terminal is tied directly into a computer system and, through the means of real-time systems, update depository and loan accounts at the time the transaction is taking place. These machines have been used in banking for the past ten years and vary from a relatively small, inexpensive, unsophisticated cash disbursement machine to a fully automated banking terminal by which many of the routine consumer-type transactions can take place through the terminal without the interfacing of a bank employee.

The system involves the use of a plastic card with a magnetic stripe attached thereon. The terminal has a reading head which reads the information on the magnetic stripe. It generally requires that the customer have a personal identification number (PIN) which, in connection with the account number that is inscribed magnetically on the back of the card, is the key to allow the consumer to activate the terminal. This type of equipment allows the consumer access to his or her account on a 24-hour, seven days-a-week basis. Results thus far have ranged from outstanding to poor, depending upon the marketing, and the approach which the financial institution has used in introducing this type of banking to its customers. Use of ATMs is generally expensive for the financial institution because of the security necessary to maintain currency within the machine. The cost of maintenance of the equipment and downtime have been high in many instances, but the operational experiences have proven to be fair to good, and the security has been excellent.

When ATMs were first used there were several regulatory policy positions by the Comptroller of the Currency and the Federal Home Loan Bank Board which allowed these instruments to be installed without the necessity of their being considered to be a branch bank or in conflict with the branch banking laws. Court decisions, seven in number, including an appeals court in Washington, D.C., have decreed that these instruments are branches for national banks. The progress of this service in the banking system is now in limbo awaiting either court action or legislative changes so that ATMs can function without being considered a branch. The cost of going through the branch application route would make these terminals economically unfeasible. Problems concerning the sharing of these instruments between institutions constitute another major obstacle in their progress. Thus far the cost per transaction (because of low volume and high costs) has been such that their future, without some technological changes or reduction in the maintenance cost, is doubtful.

POINT OF SALE

The third area of EFTS is the point-of-sale (POS) services. These services utilize a small on-line electronic terminal that is located in a retail establishment and tied to the bank's computer. These instruments are operated with the use of a plastic card with a magnetic stripe. Generally the information contained on the stripe consists of the customer's account number bank number and types of account. It activates the computer network when a personal identification number (PIN) is separately used to input into the system, and allows the customer to perform routine banking services. These include deposit, withdrawal, overdraft banking, funds transfer, loan payment, and bill payments.

This system, still in its infancy, probably will prove to be the most economically viable system to be developed. It is a volume-sensitive operation which requires huge amounts of capital, and must cover a large geographic area if it is to be successful. Potentially, this system could be tied to a merchant's automated system for checkout inventory control and numerous other applications, giving it the possibility of becoming an extremely acceptable and effective system that ties the retail and financial institutions together. A great amount of marketing and changes in consumer banking habits will be necessary to make the system successful. There are many problems facing the POS system legislatively and legally. The problems of privacy, security of the consumer's financial assets, state's rights, the dual banking system and branch laws, are all involved in the future of POS.

TELEPHONE BILL-PAYING SYSTEM

The fourth type of system is telephone bill-paying system for the automatic payment of bills by the use of the home phone. This involves the dialing of a bank computer number, a merchant's number, customer account number, and the amount of the bill to be paid. This system records on a magnetic tape at the financial institution, and the accounts are updated in a batch mode similar to checks. It allows for a customer to remain at home and, with the use of the telephone, pay bills and distribute payments without the use of paper or the necessity of postage charges.

EFTS AND THE CONSUMER

There is little question that electronic funds transfer can become a positive movement in the financial depository institutions delivery of services to its consumer customers. EFTS can offer 24-hour access to funds; it can expand the number and kinds of locations from which financial transactions can be effected; it will permit the consumer to deal with the depository institutions more efficiently over greater geographic distance; it will make it easier for the consumer to transfer funds among accounts in different financial institutions. The total system could be very advantageous to both the consumer and financial institutions that serve them. There are certain issues which are being addressed by financial institutions that will impede or hasten this development, depending upon the outcome.

One issue is the protection from unauthorized access and the dissemination of personal financial information. The legal rights and duties of the consumer under EFTS must be spelled out to his or her advantage. The security from errors or fraudulent use must be well delineated by the financial institutions. Lastly, the consumer's right to privacy must be protected.

All of these consumer issues should be included in a review of the present operations of our payment system and the relation of the financial institution to the consumer. Financial institutions must function in a practical manner so that high losses will not be sustained because of the problems of remote locations. The check has functioned well in giving both the consumer, as well as the financial institutions, protection in their day-to-day dealings. If the basic rules that pertain to the check can be transferred into the EFT system, then many of these problems should disappear.

For instance, in the check system there are responsibilities laid upon both the consumer and the financial institution. If consumers are careless about check writing, if they are careless about their signatures, if they are careless about the way they prepare the check—they are responsible. Likewise, depository institutions should not perform any act concerning a customer's deposit account unless it is specifically warranted to do so. These types of mutual responsibilities should be incorporated in future rules and regulations concerning electronic funds transfer. Many of these problems have not been solved. Many of these solutions will be determined by the experience of both the consumer and the financial institutions as they move into the EFTS world.

Many of these subjects have been given attention by the president's EFTS Commission. Recommendations based on the report of that commission will be considered by the Congress, state legislatures, as well as the regulatory agencies of the United States. These are not insurmountable problems, they are problems that can be solved by using our present payments system as a guide. If this is done, then the concerns of the consumer should be reduced to a minimum, and the benefits of the system should be enjoyed by all.

Chapter 21

Information Systems for Banks

Richard E. Dooley*

PHILOSOPHICAL BACKGROUND

The idea of an information system in a bank has been and still is a topic of broad confusion and skepticism in bank management circles. Some of this confusion is a result of the connection between information systems and the management process. The latter is an art and therefore likely will always be somewhat elusive and personalized in its practice. More uncertainty or misunderstanding is brought about by seeing information systems as a "high form" of data processing. The latter is a science (new, and not yet certified perhaps, but it qualifies today) with physical, visual attributes like computers, or printed output, and an endless mosaic of jargon, products, and applications that seem far removed from many bank managers' more urgent interests.

Futhermore, the problem of "computerese" and the deep ambiguity of the English language often obstruct one's ability to deal with these concepts. This problem of words is very prevalent in any technology. Unfortunately, the topic of this chapter is further burdened by "content-free expressions," or "40-mile words." That is, the phrases or labels used can mean almost anything, and one needs to know the exact context, or specific speaker involved. Plus, some of these phrases are too general to carry much meaning for the uninitiated. He or she gets swamped in "alphabet soup."

However, not only is it important to get some basic concepts down clearly in order to understand information systems in banking, but

---

* President, Colonial Penn Group Data Corp, Philadelphia, Pennsylvania. (Formerly, Stuart School of Management and Finance, Illinois Institute of Technology, Chicago, Illinois; Vice President, First National Bank, Chicago, Illinois.)

to ultimately implement information systems in banking. It is an absolute must (not just ideally) to have this philosophical base in place.

Let's strike right to the heart of this matter with a basic definition and differentiation of the words "data" and "information."

THE RELATIONSHIP BETWEEN DATA AND INFORMATION

In the use of the words "data" and "information" we have widespread lack of clarity that is a source of deep trouble. The words surely do overlap in meaning, but they are in fact used interchangeably by many technicians and managers alike.

If you were thoughtfully to review your use of each word, describing with various other words or phrases what comes to mind when each term is used, a list like the following might be constructed.

Data	Information
Raw facts or statistics	Formated or analyzed
Digital or alphanumeric	Analog or graphic
Unrelated	Related or comparative
Too much	Incomplete
Creates confusion	Reduces uncertainty*
Neutral or objective	Often subjective
Yet to be processed	In a useful or relevant state
Hard	Soft
Oriented to the past	Oriented to the future*
Used by machines	Used by humans
Is Known or available	Contains a "surprise" or new insight
(no "data" related	Connected to decision making*
concept comes to	Helps control change*
mind for these	Need to reach objectives*
"information" concepts)	Need to solve problems
	Connected to risk taking*

And so on, via each person's
 own experience!

 * Identified as a managerial activity.

By pursuing such a study or survey, one may generate some "ground rules" about the use of the two terms:

1. Data and information do partially overlap in practical day-to-day business use. Very often, one element can be both; e.g., customer balances. The balance might be simply stored in a file (as data) or used (as information) to help a lending officer make a decision about a rate charged.
2. One person's data is sometimes another person's information and

vice versa. For instance, a marketing executive may find certain statistics useful in considering establishing new market objectives. That's information. The auditor might consider these very same "certain statistics" unrelated, valueless, or simply raw data.

3. The crucial test in determining what is information is simply: Is it *useful* in some managerial activity like those indicated above?

4. Information is not all data originated. Though there is a process of transformation that often moves or changes data to information, all information is not "data based." Some information comes as rumors, dreams, hunches, gossip, corridor conversation, and so on. In fact, many executives rely more on this kind of information, or at least feel more comfortable with it, than with information derived from data records.

   Interestingly enough, many data processing professionals have been reluctant to admit this. They have pushed the idea that better or more computers equals better or more data, and that better or more data equals better or more information, and that better or more information equals better or more management. Of course, we know now that the value transferred through each of these (i.e., computers-data-information-management) is not direct nor simple, and often is below expectations, or to be truthful, less than was promised.

5. Primarily because of the phenomena mentioned in (2) above, data and information change back and forth as they move vertically or horizontally in a business enterprise (i.e., up or down through responsibility levels or across functional organization lines). This is a very difficult design constraint for the developers of information systems. Imagine saying to the engineers of a new production assembly line: "Look, first, we'll be building and moving cars, but then as we get over that, our product must change into a boat and around the corner it shifts into airplanes." That would be as equally difficult an engineering design request as some information systems designs have, in fact, been, albeit unknowingly, by either bank management or the computer technicians involved.

DEFINITIONAL IMPLICATIONS FOR DATA PROCESSING AND INFORMATION SYSTEMS

This exercise can now be expanded to define and differentiate between data processing and information systems. After some consideration, as above, of our actual use of these two phrases as labels for organizational units, a list like the following might be generated.

Data Processing	Information Systems
Tools/techniques	Problems/objectives
Technicians/specialists	Users/managers
Production/operations	Management/marketplace
Provide stability	Bring about change
Transactions	Models
Routine or known calculations	New equations which lack precedence
Structured problems	Unstructured problems
Machine/computer	Human
Efficiency	Effectiveness

Ironically, in most banks it is the same set of workers or specialists who are charged with accomplishing both.

We have learned slowly that we cannot obtain the list in the right-hand column by promulgating a name change in the official list of departments. In fact, doing so is extremely misleading and results in unrealistic expectations if we change the formal label to "information systems" when what is really going on is data processing work.

There is, of course, an inherent relationship between these two pairs, data versus information, and data processing versus information systems.

An attempt has been made to differentiate these two pairs, but the connection in each set is very strong. They are really more like opposite ends or different directions in a continuum. The continuum being, simply a conceptual one to help our understanding.

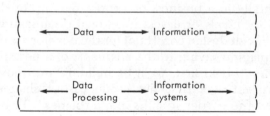

Please keep this graphic arrangement in mind while the topic is approached from another angle.

HOW HUMANS FIT IN—COMMUNICATING, COOPERATING, EFFICIENTLY AND EFFECTIVELY

One of the things we are trying to do in data processing is to communicate. Regardless of how large the temptation may be to smirk at that statement, let it stand for the moment. It is a fact that the professionals in the field of data processing do not universally perceive this nor do they practice it successfully. It is also true that other groups (e.g., bank managers) do not perceive or practice it to any greater extent in their areas.

We want to communicate to facilitate getting something done in the work process. This always involves people, an insultingly fundamental concept, but again not clearly perceived nor successfully practiced by either group. This communication among people is usually needed so they can act as "teams" or task forces or organizational units in the process of carrying through the production or work function.

It is that simple. We want to communicate in data processing so people can work more efficiently, or as Peter Drucker says *"do things right."*

If we move from data processing to information systems, the same conceptual framework holds. We have simply shifted to a different set of people, this time managers. As was true above with the "workers," we want to communicate and we want as managers to work together. In addition, we have added another goal. We want to be effective; i.e., *do right things.* Thus, information systems conceptually are aimed at helping managers be efficient and effective in the management process and hopefully this results in the "worker" being more efficient in the work process; i.e., where data processing takes place.

The shift is signified by the change in focus from data to information. Once we are in the topical arena of information, we have moved (conceptually) from the production function to the management function, information being one of a manager's main tools, at least potentially. In practice, we all know how many managers successfully utilize other tools or techniques like luck, or inaction, or other people's decisions, or the economy.

Thus as we move to the right in the continuum graphically represented above, we require more communication and we begin to establish the need for "linking" of people in teams or units.

EVOLUTION AND MERGER OF THREE SEPARATE DISCIPLINES IN THE CURRENT BODY OF PROFESSIONAL KNOWLEDGE; A NEW AWARENESS

As further background to understanding information systems in banking, please refer to the following graphic representation of what are generally thought of as three separate academic disciplines.

A	B	C
Industrial management	Computer sciences	Decision support systems

Let the first column *(A)* represent the production function or the classic assembly line. In banking we usually call this operations.

Let the second column *(B)* represent the use of computer technology in a business. In banking this is often referred to as EDP (electronic data processing) or to just data processing.

Let the third column *(C)* represent the various skills, techniques, or often just theories that high-level technicians or mathematicians (they think of themselves in different categories) try to apply in business. In banking this is usually the operations research or management sciences or information systems department. There are some trends or relationships here which ae worth studying:

1. Column *A* is perhaps 75 years old, well thought out in theory and applied in practical business situations. The manufacturing, processing, engineering industries practice its principles by second nature. Schools are expected to turn out well-prepared graduates for entry into these fields. The service industries, such as banking or insurance, have only lately begun to accept the fact that production management or industrial engineering is relevant to their work processes also. Some bankers in recent years have accepted the idea, if not the words, that their operations department is a "factory." So though the field is old, its appreciation in banking is still new.
2. Column *B* is perhaps 30 years old; probably 20, at the most, in banking.
3. Column *C*'s age is more arbitrary. In its mature form, information systems are only one to five years old and for some firms or industries is yet unborn.
4. Increasingly, all three are becoming connected or merging. There are many common techniques or ideas. Theories from one can be applied in another. For example, floor layout, which is a basic topic or body of knowledge in classical industrial management has been recently applied to the computer rooms of most large organizations. An illustration is work flow in relation to machine placement and human work stations like input/output windows.
5. Service industries often emphasized column *B* or *C* more in their hiring of "technically trained" people. Now they are consciously including graduates with industrial engineering backgrounds. Some banks, for instance, have recognized that their check clearing system or deposit handling activities are basically horizontal work flows like an assembly line. They just are moving paper (or data really) instead of physical products. However, since most of this work is done in data processing, this assembly line is often invisible because it is moving at the speed of light.

    The media is the electronic process. So banks do not see it as a production line. And for years, banks did not intensely apply lessons, ideas, and rules from basic industrial management. For instance, many banks organize their check clearing production function in many horizontal pieces to fit their departmental structure which is vertical for other reasons. How many factories have you seen where the planning, controlling, and operating of the assembly line was not one unit, matching the whole horizontal flow? In the author's opinion, there is an accelerating movement toward recognizing the applicability of column *A* ideas/people in service business and in banking in particular.

6. Increasingly, all three columns are being grouped in a loose confederation of departments, at the top called something such as "the administration department." Of course, senior management involved is often not experienced in *B* or even *C* of these related bodies of knowledge.

7. As the production function or assembly line was both automated and computerized over the last 25 years, much of column *A* was "taken over" by column *B* people. And, these computer specialists often know little or nothing about classical production management. Banking to a considerable extent moved right into column *B*, without evolving through column *A*. Our systems often reflect this abortive growth path.

8. As column *B* "took over," many productionlike work processes, some traditional management controls or information flows were lost. They no longer worked at the speed of light. Or, they just were not programmed into the computer system at all.

9. In the near future, all three columns will have merged and any manager responsible for them will have to have or must quickly acquire strong conceptual foundations or practical understanding of what is involved in each. As they merge, it becomes more difficult (confusing) for an executive whose viewpoint by education and/or experience is, let's say, only marketing or only finance to relate at all to the new larger (merged) body of knowledge.

10. Unfortunately, this new larger or merged body of knowledge, organizationally is now often represented by a large centralized staff of technically oriented personnel. They are surrounded by communication barriers and unsympathetic users of the services. There is inefficient or ineffective ultimate use by management of the skills, ideas, and theories for the "nonprofessional" who might be, let's say, a loan officer or bank manager. It may not be just painful; it is maddening. In some firms, the "heat" generated between the two sides is "incandescent."

11. Education would help; so would cross-training or personnel transfers, relaxing of the emotional "heat," or team management, which spans organizational barriers or combines appropriate skills

in new working groups. Finally, simply, a basic conceptual grasp of what has happened these last few years would help immensely.

HARNESSING THIS NEW AWARENESS IN ACCEPTED MANAGEMENT PERSPECTIVES

Some managers, particularly in banking, are not fully aware of the inherent connection between their management process and the disciplines or columns covered above. Below is another graphic representation of the idea.

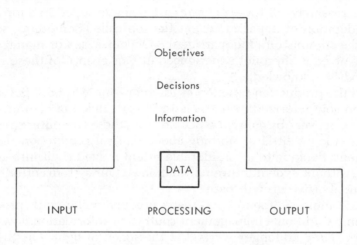

Let the bottom bar of this "inverted T" represent the production function or assembly line in its simplest form. Using the "black box" analysis model of input, output, and some magical processing in between, we can relate to most of banking's normal work flows, such as check clearing, deposit handling, and loan payments. As pointed out in the previous section, these are banking's "assembly lines," done at electronic speeds, usually in the "data processing department." In banking, that is what we "process," alphanumeric digits.

Now going back to our examination of the difference between data and information, we can state that the only reason managers need data is because they have information requirements. And the only reason managers have information requirements is because they have decisions to make or alternatives to choose among. And, again, the only reason that managers make decisions is to reach certain goals or objectives. That is the management process. Oversimplified to an extent that unnerves some managers it is that noncomplex when we examine the fundamental elements involved.

Management simulation games follow this conceptual model rather well. Student input sets of decisions which are processed by some data processing shop and results in "output" being returned to each team. This output is data. The team's job is, of course, to use that data (useful data = information) as information in chosen areas of activity (decisions) to bring about certain changes or levels in their balance sheet or income statement (objectives). Obviously, the whole process of defining and agreeing on objectives, choosing decisions or actions to reach those objectives, and finding the information required to time the decision, using a team approach, is a very provocative, relevant exercise in teaching banking management.

A serious problem is that in many organizations, the two functions are not so well integrated as the symbolic representation implies. In fact, they are often uncoupled completely, looking more like this:

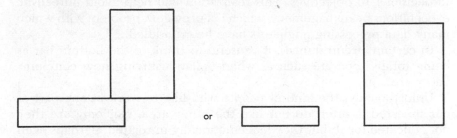

When we think about this partial connection or complete lack of it, between the management process and the production process, the limiting or negative impact is primarily in the management process, because a great deal of the data that is needed to help satisfy managers' information requirements is, in fact, in the production function. So any poor connection in these processes lessens the effectiveness of the remainder of the management in other functions or at other levels. Management being largely an information business, and information being largely data originated, this poor connection gets much more burdensome when we focus only on data processing systems, or certain functional areas that are highly computerized.

To overcome this situation, many firms have tried to build into, or link up with their production systems, a "management information system" usually after the production system was in place. Symbolically, they try to jam the top part of the inverted T down into the bottom bar. It does not work well. And what makes the situation worse is the fact that most production systems (all the early ones) were designed and implemented with the objective of moving the work and little attention given to the need to support the attached management process. For example, demand deposit systems (DDA usually is the acronym) were first built just to post the checks and deposits, print the statements, list some work exceptions like overdrafts, and not much more. That was okay then. It was a big accomplishment just to do that. And we were not yet skilled at understanding either the philosophy or the engineering implied by the full connection.

But in 1977 there is no defense for building any system just to do production work. All systems should be built with both objectives (production efficiency and management effectiveness) as design goals.

The schematic used here to help construct these ideas implies that all management information comes from the production system. But, as we reviewed earlier, all information is not "data" based. It can be and often is derived from other sources such as the rumor mill. So even the best designed, perfectly implemented system, taking advantage of improved perspective of this connection will only partially satisfy the needed flow through production, to data, to information, to decisions, to objectives. This realization will help avoid unrealistic expectations by management, which is a prevalent problem with which many data processing engineers have been saddled.

In certain circumstances, it is useful to think of the bottom bar as being totally separate such as when dollar justifying new computer hardware.

Unfortunately, the kind of people who like to work in one part of our inverted T often do not like the other area. Not only are they not educated for it, but they feel emotionally unrelated, perhaps even alienated completely. Universities have not helped much because their usual curricula produces people tending one way or the other. People are needed who can walk well along either bar, and are comfortable with the ambiguity and multidimensional aspects involved in management, but also at peace with the logic, sequence, and detail which are so predominant in production. Most especially, those people who are in charge of building systems (project leaders, user representatives, systems managers, whatever they are called) should understand each bar and the need for, but limited potential, of the connection. They should be able to identify and communicate the ever-present trade-offs implicit in the modern twin goals of production efficiency and management effectiveness such as the need for precision in complete accounting records, versus the need for quick trend information in marketing plans.

Acquiring this "bridged vision" is crucial for optimizing the interrelationship between data processing and information systems described above.

THE CONTRIBUTION OF DATA PROCESSING AND
COMPUTER TECHNOLOGY

Technology in general has advanced much faster than most firms were capable of absorbing it. In fact, to be more realistic, the advancement has been much faster than they needed to or wanted to absorb it from a pure business standpoint. Without trying to summarize completely the current state-of-the-art, let us simply review a few key conditions:

1. Our ability to store, manipulate, and access data in computer hardware of various kinds has multiplied at a high rate.
2. The sophistication of available vendor software and hireable programming skills has improved significantly.
3. Our experience in planning, organizing, controlling, and leading efforts to link the accomplishments described in (1) and (2) above in business production systems is considerably better than even a few years ago.

The area which requires our most focused attention today is the "bridging," or supporting of the management process. Progress here will come less from the data processing world and more from the line or executive manager who has the new awareness this chapter is intended to highlight. The data processing industry has done about all it can. In its own way, it is as ready to begin supplying real support to the management process as it ever will be. Little more can be done to data, say store it, or transport it, and so on, in order to help process it into information. What can be done much better is to supply a design perspective that provides a continuous communication link to the management process. This work is almost completely removed from computers or systems and really is a function of how well we hire, train, transfer, listen, talk, and provide feedback. It is behavioral in nature. In a very real way, the baton for leadership has passed to the personnel or management development function, because the obstacles to progress are today in this arena not in the technology itself.

PUTTING IT ALL TOGETHER LIKE AN ORANGE

Many, and probably most, people both inside the information systems profession and outside it have a very narrow and parochial view of what information systems are all about. There are people who think information systems relate only to machines. In their view, neither vacuum tube machines, card-oriented machines, nor transistor machines or tape devices can support an information system. They believe that only the large-scale monolithic circuit, large main storage, and huge external storage machines can support an information system. Another position is the notion that small hardware (minis, or distributive computing) will provide the real base for an information system.

At another level is a person concerned with the data base. This person reasons that if information is not stored, it cannot be accessed.

This little tautology leads in no time to the conclusion that the more that is stored, the better. An information system is, thus, a huge data base.

"Nonsense!" says another person. "What good is information if you cannot get at it? What is important is how information is indexed and stored and how it is provided." (The "librarian" viewpoint.)

"Right!" says the fourth person. "But your emphasis is wrong. It is not indexing and storage that is important; it is how it is delivered. If you have a sophisticated terminal network, you have a true information system for then people can interact with the data."

"But," says the fifth person, "Most of your data is badly arranged. What is information but basic data that is set up and presented in a way that makes it clear and concise. The important emphasis is graphic arts."

"That is right, but we all seem to be skirting the basic issue, the environment, the medium. How can you have a true information system outside of a management communication center?"

At this point, the seventh person chimes in, "But you are all missing the point—missing it completely. Management, after all, is decision making. A management information system requires a formal approach to decision analysis; it requires management scientists."

"You are close to the truth," says the eighth. "The trouble is that all of you are concerned with today, and decisions are made for tomorrow. Planning is the crucial skill."

Two problems are present. First, each of these sets of people considers that only their skill is critical, but secondly that theirs is virtually the only skill.

We have to take all these pieces and put them together. Piece by piece, slice by slice, each section, each special interest has to be balanced one against the other. Once they are put together and appear to the outside world as one orange, as a coherent information system, then comes the difficult management job.

That job is to squeeze the orange, to get the juices flowing, to get the people communicating and to get them to recognizing the contribution of other people, without rupturing any of the delicate membranes that give each particular skill its sense of professionalism.

If we add programming, analysis, machine operations (maxi, mini and micro), small group dynamics or industrial psychology, marketing, cost accounting, and economic forecasting, we have many competing skills or professions, each of which carries its own definition of information systems and believes its approach is best. By their own lights this may be a legitimate view.

Of course, many firms do not have or need all these information systems skills. The set needed, and the relative influence of each (the

size of the orange slices and their number, so to speak) is different
for different banks. So the orange or composite of professionals needed
to contribute to real information systems technology is reflective of
the bank's size, marketplace, business maturity, chosen objectives, and
other variables. Again, this often requires a hiring, training, and communicating effort.

Further, since most of the named professions are populated with
"prima donna" types with their own internal professional bias, getting
them to understand teamwork across professional lines is, indeed, a
difficult job. This "tower of Babel" condition has produced much conflicting literature and conference panel comment.

Balance and placement are contributions senior management must
make. The skills need orchestration by the executives who do in fact
see/control the whole of the enterprise.

Generalizations Covering Information Systems

1. Information and data are corporate resources. They must be managed as such. Organizational or personality barriers which may
   have existed between the storage and use of data need to be dissolved. But systems should not be designed with the naïve assumption that this will be the case. People tend to personalize ownership
   of data. Security and privacy are two major issues which highlight
   the corporate perspective required.
2. Information systems are an investment, not an expense. The investment mentality (longer term, multiple pieces) is necessary to optimize the utilization of information. The classical 12-month budget
   cycle and its inherent expansions and contractions, is a troublesome
   tool to manage information systems. Such systems take longer and
   require consistent funding over that time frame. Actually, a good
   information systems shop is much like a "portfolio." There are
   some risky systems, some routine ones, some small ones, and some
   very large ones. It takes the same management mentality to run
   such a system.
3. Sharing is always required. There is never enough test time, or
   good project leaders, or core, or terminals, or programmers. Data
   processing/information systems managers do not have enough authority, time, resources, just as any line manager is limited here
   also. So both groups need to be realistic when requiring the other.
   Classic resource allocation in two dimensions is a process yet to
   be practiced well in the banking information systems business.
4. Technological change is more difficult in the user area. The effect
   of technological change can often be handled more easily in a
   data processing shop than in the line or user area. Thus, a technician
   often underestimates the amount of "total" change required by

a shift in some piece of the hardware or software. The "ripple effect" goes much further out and lasts longer than the description of the "stone dropped" into the water.

5. No leapfrogging. Catching up by skipping a phase or some steps in the usual evolutionary process is extremely risky, usually disastrous. That is, we should have an existing manual system before automating anything. Or, moving to distributed processing directly from decentralized batch processing without evolving through a centralized on-line environment is a highly risky leap to make. As some banks are learning both currently.

6. Systems work is management work. The very process of designing and implementing systems requires a very high degree of planning, organizing, leading, controlling, communicating, and closing. Yet we seldom train systems people extensively in these arts. They then concentrate on the code or the hardware architecture, to the detriment of the final outcome.

7. Computer systems are inflexible; humans are elastic. Employees often make up for inadequacies in a work flow, say, when someone is absent, or a chart of accounts is out of date. But a computer system in its programs must be completely up to date and run the same way every day. Thus, in the shift from one environment (human) to the other (iron) we give up certain useful capacities.

8. Computerizing poor management will make it worse. Our aim, of course, in information systems is to support good management. We may or may not succeed. That is the whole risk. But, if management talent is absent or poor, there is no probability of success. A system will make it worse.

A GRAPHIC FRAMEWORK

If no corporate philosophy on information systems exists, the data processing function tends to evolve in a fragmented, nonstandardized or nonintegrated way, as diagramed here.

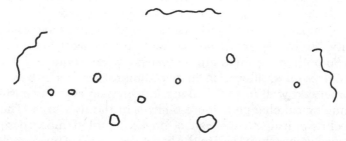

Note: each circle represents a system in a set with no unified or integrated plan (as shown by the disconnected umbrella).

If we just believe in the theory or the ultimate promises, our schematic for information systems might look like this.

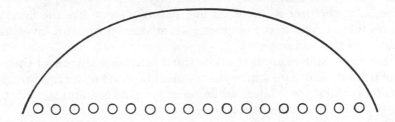

Where the "umbrella" represents a unifying plan or management direction and the neat row of small circles represents multiple properly designed and implemented systems, this is the textbook approach. No one has a set of systems, or a M.I.S., which looks like this and likely never will.

But by aiming at that ideal, by understanding it as an "ever-receding possibility," we can achieve a data processing/information systems status which approximates this figure.

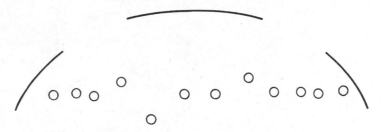

Note: This plan has some gaps in philosophy and some systems that represent "overkill" or "underkill."

There are realistically speaking some gaps in the philosophy of a long-range plan. There are some systems out of standard or not connected to the data base, but in general we have moved ahead considerably from the first of these three illustrations by getting the third situation while aiming at the second one. There are firms, even banks, which have achieved this "compromise state," or level of imperfect plan. It is quite possible in 1977 to do so.

Some bank managers shy away from management information systems because they say they have never seen one, or that they are just theory, or that to get there will take too long and cost too much money.

The truth is there is no such thing as a perfect management information system. It is just an idea, or dream. But it is an idea or dream to shoot for and in the process of trying to reach this goal, the general efficiency of our production systems and the connective support for more effective management will both be better.

Actually, the process involved in creating a scene like the first illustration takes longer and costs more when viewed from an investment position of five to ten years.

The compromises implicit in the third figure simply reflect the reality of business life; e.g., some systems must be done on a crash program basis (and will show it later) while some systems can and should stand alone outside of the main computer complex.

The reason that a management information system concept has been so difficult to define, justify, or see is that it does not exist in any other way than in the form of an idea or concept. What do exist are models, computers, programs, terminals, networks, and so on, which may or may not reflect the philosophy. Once management and the technically based staff agree on philosophy, one can improve slowly the pieces of, and connections between, our production systems and our management process, providing over time an always evolving information system that moves toward the ultimate idea or textbook approach.

 SECTION IV

PLANNING AND CONTROL

Chapter 22

Comprehensive Corporate Planning for Banks

*Herbert E. Johnson**

INTRODUCTION

The purpose of this chapter is to provide a broad view into the nature of comprehensive corporate planning for commercial banks. *Comprehensive* is used in the sense that many kinds of planning over several time horizons are needed to guide the modern bank toward its future, *corporate* in the sense that all levels, units, individuals, and specialists must participate in planning to weld the organization into a functioning whole. The intent of the chapter is not only to describe the structure and the requirements of planning, but to instill a sense of the necessity for planning to manage the organization properly.

Much of the literature on planning is addressed to the practices and problems of industrial firms, governments, and the military in a way that is not directly applicable to commercial banks. Banking has not yet developed a literature of planning, nor has a unique planning style emerged. Because planning is not yet a science or even an organized set of practices, there is not a commercial bank planning model that can be lifted from the shelf (even of a very successful bank) and implemented as a planning system in another bank. Each organization is a unique blend of past practices, present management, markets, customers, and social setting that requires individual treatment. Therefore, each bank must adopt its own philosophy of management and planning and assemble the set of planning skills and techniques that best match the needs of the organization. These needs will change

* Senior Vice President, Continental Illinois National Bank, Chicago, Illinois.

significantly over time as the skills and style of managements change through experience and changes in the environment surrounding the bank. This chapter is addressed to developing an understanding of the concepts, structure, and process of comprehensive corporate planning for commercial banks.

WHAT IS PLANNING?

Simply stated, planning is a systematic approach to problem solving and decision making. The major purposes of planning are to improve the quality of performance in order to establish the future direction to be taken by the organization and to increase the profitability. It should pull all of the separate pieces of the organization together into a functioning whole to achieve the best possible earnings position. It is anticipatory and always deals with the future of the organization. It is the means of identifying the set of future conditions desired by management and of devising the means of achieving the realization of those ambitions.

Perhaps it is as important to determine what planning is not as to state what it is. Planning is not forecasting. Although forecasting is an important ingredient in almost all planning activity, it is the future condition desired that forms the basis of plans, and this outcome may be quite different from the conclusion of a forecast. Also, planning is neither making future decisions nor a blueprint for the future that is made at one time and then worked until completion. Decisions are made each day on the basis of the best information available that day. New information and intervening events will make every plan obsolete over a relatively short period of time.

Frequently, an outcome of the activities of planning will be the construction of a plan, although a plan is not a necessary outcome. A plan, or even an aggregation of plans, is not clear evidence that effective planning has taken place. The real benefits that flow to the organization from planning will be the result of learning and development that flow from the discipline of the process. So, it is the planning process that will make the most important contribution to the bank.

Evolution of Planning

As recently as the mid-1960s, only a few commercial banks had a detailed budgeting system, and a comprehensive planning program as a formal managerial process was almost unknown. The planning practices that did exist were related to operational problems and practices, particularly the planning requirements of computerization, and the balance sheet planning necessary to maintain liquidity, permit tax planning, and to meet the requirements of bank regulation.

Between then and now, banks have discovered liability management, have expanded into nationwide and international conglomerate sellers of financial services through bank holding companies, and have become conscious of the way investors evaluate the growth potential of all investments, including banks. These are heady events that call for an aggressive managerial style uncommon in banking of the past. Planning has become a necessary part of the growth-oriented managerial style.

At the same time, other banks have experienced the pain of a competitive thrust into the markets that are critical for their survival, or suffered from the sudden discovery of an unexpected decline in margins or gross profit. While quite different in character, defensive reactions are as stimulating to a planning style of management as is aggressive expansion.

Over the past decade, planning has emerged as a powerful management technique to address the kinds of problems enumerated above. Three conceptually different phases of planning can be identified:

1. Many banks have developed an effective *budgeting or annual planning program* to organize action plans and the schedules needed to allocate resources among the specific units of the organization.
2. Some banks have added an *intermediate or operational planning program* with a two- to five-year horizon concentrating on implementing the strategies of the major functions and activities.
3. A few banks have instituted a longer term *strategic planning process* to determine what they should be doing in terms of the direction of the organization, identifying opportunities to be undertaken, and determining the allocation of the resources to these ends.

Budgeting, intermediate and strategic planning are characterized as phases of planning because they tend to be developed sequentially by most organizations in the order stated. As each phase is developed it is added to the existing planning system and the process becomes continuous. Even though the ultimate planning structure may be known, the learning process required probably dictates that the implementation of the more advanced stages of planning must wait on the development of management planning skills and the development of a substantial knowledge base of the industry, markets, and the individual organization.

Expectations of Accomplishment

Before any formal efforts at planning are undertaken, a thorough examination of the expectations of results should be agreed upon by management. Unless the expectations are reasonable, and noted as a part of the orientation to planning, the results will almost always be disappointing to some members of management and the process will be under constant attack even though important results are being achieved. A planning system usually requires three to five years of persistent effort to achieve a smoothly working operation. Therefore, expectations for planning should be stated in terms of both short- and long-term anticipated outcomes.

To meet the expectations of management, the planning process agreed upon should identify the ends sought by the organization and the means of achieving those ends. Four basic steps are involved:

1. A plan to plan that introduces each planning cycle with a statement of the specific tasks to be completed, the responsibilities assigned, time frames, and the results expected.
2. Studies to provide the *situation appraisal* of the firm and the assumptions about the future environments in which the bank will operate.
3. A means of producing the objectives, strategies, programs, and budgets, particularly the financial and other resource allocations.
4. A means to monitor and control the organization toward achievement of objectives.

Results are, in part, a function of the style of planning. For example, the planning effort can proceed upward from the basic profit/cost centers of the organization being aggregated into a corporate plan of objectives and strategies as a summation of the parts—a bottom-up communication to the executive level. Or, planning can begin with a leadership document of long-term objectives and basic strategies from the executive office that guides the planning efforts of the profit centers and establishes the basic thrust of the organization—a top-down communication to the organization of the ambitions of the leaders. A combination of top-down/bottom-up planning will permit each level to comment on and modify the documents received from above and below in a participative give and take between the levels of management: a negotiated planning agreement. The latter procedure seems to be the direction that many planning styles settle on after several cycles of one or both of the directional systems of planning.

THE PLANNING PROCESS

The planning process presented here is a simple model that is an elaboration of the four steps to identify ends and means mentioned earlier. Because many banks operate in a decentralized manner through specialized functions and subsidiaries, the process is described in terms of organizational steps and sequence. Each level in the bank can use this outline to work through a planning cycle and produce a plan. However, the emphasis will be on the procedures at the corporate level that are strategic in nature. Other chapters in this book are addressed to the planning problems below the corporate level.

Plan to Plan

The planning cycle begins with an agreement between the levels of management on a *plan to plan*. This is a descriptive document that lays out the tasks to be completed with an assignment of the roles and the responsibilities necessary to complete the cycle.

The first time through a planning process requires an elaborate plan to plan. A thorough presentation of why a plan is needed and the results expected as well as the relationship of the planning staff to management and the organization of the planning effort should be explained in that initial document. Each of these subjects will be discussed later in this chapter. For each succeeding planning cycle, the plan to plan should establish the objectives of the new planning cycle and any changes in procedures and emphasis.

The conclusions from the plan to plan study should be formalized into a *planning manual* that describes the process and indicates the assignments and procedures. The planning manual usually includes some samples of the more difficult steps and the forms needed to guide the development of the plan. For example, objectives, strategies, programs, and budgets need to be described in detail and examples from prior cycles provided. Properly constructed, the planning manual can become an important teaching tool for the new manager who is planning for the first time and it will reinforce planning as a management style for the entire organization.

The plan to plan and the planning manual provide a structure for the planning organization which may differ from the formal organization of the bank. While there is a strong tendency to follow the organization chart, a good case can be made for organizing the planning effort around markets or business units with common interests. Finally, the plan to plan and the planning manual establish the time frames and the important check points of progress that will guide the specific cycle of planning.

Environmental Analysis and Situation Appraisal

An *environmental analysis* establishes the *opportunities and threats* that lie outside the organization. Environmental, in this sense, encompasses all of the external aspects of an envelope surrounding the activities of the bank. The *situation appraisal*, on the other hand, is concerned with the ability of the organization to perform the essential tasks of the businesses in which it wishes to specialize.

The environmental analysis establishes a consistent set of assumptions within which planning can proceed. Within each organization there are usually individuals who can state these assumptions in a form that is appropriate for planning. Also, there are many consulting groups, bank-related research organizations, and bank associations that are prepared to provide guidance on some aspects of environmental analysis. However, these groups are unable to supply the analysis that is required to fit the local environment to the specific organization. That fit can only be supplied by someone who is intimately familiar with the organization, its management, and its ambitions.

After the individual or the consulting firm has arrived at the macro-conclusions for each area of the environmental analysis, the statements of assumptions and the guidelines to be used for planning purposes are then formulated by executive management. The conclusions are formulated on the basis of an examination of the economic climate, the anticipated social and political changes, the technological developments, the legislative and regulatory changes, and a summation of competitive pressures likely to be experienced.

The intensity with which each of these areas is examined changes with an estimate of the current importance of developments that are occurring in the specific category. For example, during 1974–75 a discussion of the recession and the prospects for recovery may have dominated the environmental appraisal. This year, the prospects for electronic banking or a new trust investment service may receive a heavy emphasis. The purpose of the environmental analysis is to establish the opportunities and threats to the future operation of the bank that occur in the environment.

The situation appraisal begins with a look inside the firm to identify the *strengths and weaknesses* of the organization. Some of the major areas of the firm to be examined include: management, organization, lines of service, geographic presence, pricing strategy, human resources, and the systems support. Each of these areas can be examined for each major category of the organization in terms of efficiency, effectiveness, the integration within the organization, and the image created. The purpose of this examination is to determine the ability of the organization to respond to the opportunities and threats previously identified. When completed, the strengths and weaknesses can be laid against the opportunities and threats found in the environment to address the formation of objectives and strategies that must be undertaken in succeeding stages of the planning process.

A second aspect of the situation appraisal is concerned with the examination of where the bank stands today in terms of financial performance. Each department and division of the bank must determine where it is today and how the current position was achieved. The research is first directed toward developing the data on major categories of assets and liabilities such as loans, deposits, total assets, earning assets, and equity. The collection of data begins in terms of aggregates to provide the history, and then proceeds to simple analytical measures such as rate of growth and a measure of stability. The next step is to develop comparisons with the total area of competition so that a measure of market share can be developed.

A useful tool to determine relative position is to build a comparative data base from a panel of banks considered to be competitive in various markets and products. The position of the bank in each of the major areas in which financial objectives have been stated is compared in terms of compound growth rates over the past five years with each bank in the panel. An important contribution of these measures is to see whether others in similar circumstances have been able to achieve the objectives stated as ambitions for your bank and thus to judge whether the objective is appropriate or impossible to attain.

The final step in the environmental analysis and situation appraisal is to assemble the results of the investigation of the environmental analysis and the situation appraisal into a set of statements that describe the current position of the bank. The environment that lies outside the organization has been examined providing the external conditions and constraints under which the bank must operate. The existing organization and management have been evaluated to determine the ability of the firm to respond to these external challenges. Finally, a data base on the financial characteristics and the banking aspects of the business has been constructed. We are now ready to study the objectives and strategies that guide the firm today as a major step in the process of stating the objectives and strategies that will guide the future of the bank.

Objectives and Strategies

The most critical, and at the same time, the most difficult of the tasks in planning is to establish the objectives and strategies of the bank for the future. Strategic management—the managing of the bank toward and by the objectives and strategies of the organization—is a new and dramatic development in management and planning.

The search for objectives begins with an examination of the organization as it exists today with a statement that identifies each of the major businesses and major markets served. When these have been identified, the current objectives and strategies of each unit are stated. There is a natural tendency to follow organizational lines when working on this part of the task. But that is not the only way to look at the bank. Many times an entirely different and revealing view of the organization results when we attempt to step back and ask: How does the user of our services view us?

The basic values of management ultimately will determine the character of each organization. How management views their customers, competition, government regulation, employees, suppliers, and all others who have a stake in the success or failure of the firm will determine the character and the image projected. To the extent possible, the philosophy of the management ought to be stated explicitly and incorporated into the literature of the firm at this point in the planning process.

A capsule statement of the current strategies at the corporate level and for each of the major businesses should be prepared for the guidance of the executive management. While this is not a document that will receive wide dissemination, it is critical that the members of the executive management agree on the major thrusts of the firm. For example, if the members of executive management are not agreed on a locational strategy, then every proposal for a new location becomes a new decision with the entire network to be examined and evaluated de novo.

The examination of strengths/weaknesses and opportunities/threats probably uncovered a number of core problems that need to be attacked as part of the planning process. For example, the need to establish a consistent pricing policy relative to all customers, or the means of payment for services rendered, are important policies to be established in every bank. The identification of these core problems and the assignment of responsibility for this resolution and implementation are important aspects of the planning at this point in the process.

The second step in establishing objectives is to formulate the existing objectives into a concise and consistent set of statements. The categories of objectives should include at least the following: financial, market position, management and organizational development, innovation, personnel, and public responsibility. Many more categories of objectives could be identified, but the communication problems multiply as the number of statements increase and the organization may fail to achieve attachment to a large number of objectives. It is the recognition of the relationship of daily activities to the achievement of specific objectives that turns these statements into powerful guiding forces for the bank.

The financial and market position objectives tend to be quantitative, while the remaining objectives are usually stated in more qualitative terms. A bank probably will state financial objectives at least in terms of net income, return on equity, asset leverage, return on earning assets, and retained earnings. Market position objectives will be stated in terms of market share, locations, investments, and divestments of products and subsidiaries. Management objectives will be stated in terms of developing professional managers, internal promotion, and the management style of the bank. Public responsibility objectives will be stated in terms of ethical standards of conduct, participation in public life, and contributions to the resolution of social problems.

We are now ready to assemble the existing parts of the planning process into a *statement of objectives for the future*. The essential studies supporting these statements include the environmental analysis, situation appraisal, the *statement of current objectives and strategies*, and the categories of corporate objectives.

The statement of objectives for the future begins with a *statement of purpose*, or the fundamental thrust of the firm. For many firms, the purpose statement has provided a most important guidance mechanism, clearly delineating the fundamental business of the firm. A purpose statement is particularly important for a firm in the financial services business as a means of staking out the particular specialties or market segments in which the firm wishes to specialize. For banks, the purpose identifies the segment of the lending market to be emphasized.

Each time that the planning process is undertaken, the important businesses, principal markets, and management philosophy should be examined in detail and restated. While it is true that these conditions change very gradually, a restatement provides an opportunity for management to reevaluate its position and to achieve a new commitment to the principles stated. In addition, new members of management will want to place their stamp of approval on these statements and may suggest important modifications in emphasis.

The new statement of objectives is intended to identify the destination of the bank, embodying the grand design and the great ambitions of the executive management. As such, the statement serves to notify everyone of the expectations of corporate performance.

Programs, Budgets, and Controls

The final step is to convert the strategies into specific assignments and responsibilities, a group of activities designated as *action plans*. Action plans are undertaken by the line organization to implement the objectives and strategies of the executive office identified in the earlier planning steps. They are communicated to the organization through specific assignments that identify specific projects, short-term goals, resource requirements, and establish the times for accomplishment.

The action plans result in very specific resource allocation that can be quantified through a *budget.* A budget is a detailed schedule of income and expense statement and the financial and profitability goals expressed in the first year of an action plan. Budgets are prepared by the profit and cost centers, the lowest organizational level in planning.

In a bank, the principal resources to be allocated are manpower and funds. Implicit in the manpower allocation are space, facilities, and materials. Implicit in the funds allocation are commitments and usage of loans and investments.

The budgets that flow from the action plans provide the interface between the long-term, strategic, managerial type of planning described thus far in this book and the specific quantitative budgeting or profit planning for the year ahead.

Another way of looking at the distinction is to characterize budgeting as the response of the organization in terms of what can be done with the specific, current resources to achieve the ambitions expressed in the leadership documents flowing from the objective/strategy setting sessions. Frequently, the distinction is identified as the bottoms-up response through budgets to the top-down leadership expressed in *corporate and line/staff unit* objectives and strategies.

In addition to management direction, the establishment of action plans and budgets provides specific numbers for activities undertaken that can be used to monitor performance. The measurement of variance from budget provides the basis for a periodic review of progress toward goals, and ultimately the objectives.

The essence of *control* is the ability to establish the standards of performance anticipated from each organizational unit. Standards are forthcoming from the sequential steps stated as a part of the action plan and from the quarterly and annual targets in budgets and strategies. Performance can be measured against the standards established and corrective action undertaken.

Tracking performance is difficult because the assumed conditions underlying the action plan and budget have changed and the manager has adjusted to match the current set of conditions. Sometimes organization changes can cause difficulty with the new manager being assigned the problems or reaping benefits not of his or her planning. To track performance accurately, a sophisticated, flexible accounting system is needed to keep up with all of the changes in plans. But, some tracking system is needed to provide the base for a periodic review of progress. The control phase that is a part of the review is based on setting standards for the sequence of steps in action plans and budgets, measuring performance against those standards and taking corrective action to regain the planned position.

What we have described in the sequence of steps of the planning process is an information gathering system and the objective-plan-control sequence of planning.

We have now returned to the place at which we can start a new planning cycle—plan to plan. The monitoring and review information that flows from the controls step provides a modification of the previous plan to plan and a natural input to the beginning of the next planning cycle.

Annual Planning Cycle

The planning process should proceed through an annual cycle that permits ample time to reconsider or reorient the thrust of each level of the organization, yet forces a deadline that activates the next stage of planning. Each stage of planning requires the leadership and guidance from the previous stage. The planning style depicted here is a combination of the top-down management style at the corporate level strategic plan, combined with a bottom-up response from the profit/cost center level in the annual budget.

The planning process begins with a plan to plan and planning manuals to guide the planning programs at each level. Of course, after the first cycle, there is a growing body of information and past studies to provide the base from which the new planning cycle is launched. The first quarter of the year will be devoted to the production of the *corporate plan* which sets out the long-term objectives of the total organization as visualized by the chairman, president, and other members of the executive office. The planning horizon for these discussions is a minimum of five years and the issues studied are essentially strategic in nature.

The Corporate Plan is presented to the heads of the line and staff units for discussion and modification. Each unit head is expected to respond to the corporate plan in each of the categories presented. The head of each unit, along with his or her senior officers, participates in a review and critique of the units, objectives, strategies, and programs. A consolidation of the results of these discussions and preparation is called the *business or operational plan.*

It is interesting to note the interrelationships between the plans as we descend through the organization. The executive officers and the corporation as a whole have objectives and strategies they will strive to achieve as a result of the corporate plan. These strategies in turn become the objectives for the next lower level of management to achieve, which, in turn develop its own set of strategies and programs. The strategies at the second level become the objectives to be achieved at the third level and so on down through the organization.

Exhibit 22–1
Annual Planning Cycle

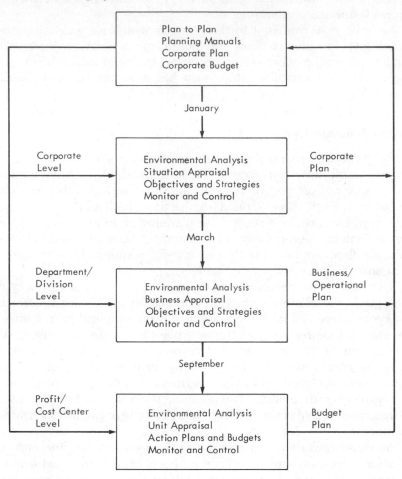

In this manner, a congruence of objectives can flow down through the organization from the broadest objectives of the corporation to the action plan at the lowest level management.

By September, the completion of objectives and strategies for line/ staff units and any independent business areas provides the leadership documents for the guidance of the *budget plan.* The budget plan is the basic budgeting document that is strictly tactical in nature with a planning horizon of one year. Up to this point, the direction of the planning effort has essentially been top-down, although there has been a substantial amount of negotiation and participation as the direction comes down to each level of management.

The preparation of the budget plan provides the opportunity to prepare detailed schedules of resource requirements to carry out the objectives and strategies established by higher levels of the organization. The consolidation of these schedules pyramids up through each of the organizational levels to the consolidation for the total corporation. This system provides a response from the basic organizational unit to the corporation as to their collective ability to achieve the corporate objectives given the resource and market constraints. The existence of a gap between the ambitions of the Corporate leadership and the realities of the response from the responsibility centers identifies the opportunities for change in the organization. It is also a measure of the ambitions for growth of the leadership of the organization.

The annual planning cycle is concluded in December when the consolidated corporate budget plan for the year ahead is discussed with the corporate office and compared to the corporate plan which began the process. The cycle is now complete and the materials have been generated that will provide the starting point for the next annual cycle.

ORGANIZATION FOR PLANNING

The chief executive officer (CEO) is the key individual in introducing the planning process. Without this support, a top-down, leadership type of planning process is not possible and any planning efforts are in jeopardy. It is possible to have a bottoms-up budgeting type of planning system that pyramids to the corporate level and may be called a *corporate plan*. However, this type of planning will result only in the sum of departmental plans, not truly corporate strategies. A strict bottom-up planning style is educational and informational in character, but the planning will not result in a significant change in direction for the bank.

The chief executive should educate and communicate the essential elements of the planning philosophy to all levels of management so that everyone understands and engages in planning. Willingness of the CEO to accept responsibility and help manage the formal planning process does not guarantee success, but it is a necessary condition for progress. The principal role of the CEO is not to make all of the key decisions, but to develop an organization and a process by which decisions can be made. He is seeking a means of unleashing the decision-making power of the organization.

The effective CEO will delegate some planning tasks and establish a system of decision making. He will be involved in establishing the reasons for planning, identify roles of planning coordinators and line personnel, and indoctrinate the organization through memos and speeches on the achievements expected.

The managers of the organization are unlikely to become involved themselves until they see clear evidence that the CEO intends to use planning as his style of management. Before planning begins, all managers should be able to identify their responsibilities, know the resources under their control, and have standards of performance that measure their contributions.

Each level of management should be made ready for planning through a period of training that includes the leadership of the CEO. After their training, the managers should have time remaining in their schedules to perform the planning tasks expected of them in the plan to plan.

In support of the CEO, the planning coordinator visualizes the planning system that is most appropriate for the organization. While there are many planning systems, tools, and techniques in existence, the final product is individual to the firm and must fit the CEO, line executives, the remainder of the organization, the specific markets, and the industry.

The planning coordinator works through management, helping it develop plans rather than producing the plans as a staff project. He or she develops the schedules, coordinates and monitors the planning process, suggests alternative approaches, looks at the outside environment and its impact on the bank, and sees that plans are properly documented. After acceptance, the planning coordinator helps monitor and control performance to assure performance according to plan.

The CEO, management, and the planning coordinators need the support of a broad spectrum of staff services. In particular, the information generating capability of the controller, market research, and computer-related specialties are important to the planning process.

CONCLUSION

A number of concepts fundamental to a successful application of planning in a commercial bank have emerged in this chapter. The theme throughout has been that planning will produce results if the process is oriented toward the identification and achievement of objectives, clearly identifies roles and responsibilities, involves all levels of management, assigns specific tasks and times for completion, and provides for review and control. It is the discipline, education, and cooperative effort of the planning process that provide the real benefit to be received by the organization from planning. The resulting plan is an interim report from an ongoing process.

In a small bank, planning can proceed in a very informal manner with a simple planning structure and the result will be as effective in directing management efforts as occurs in a very large organization with a sophisticated planning system. As size and complexity increase however, the need for a system of planning becomes more apparent and the process becomes more formal. Much of the formality of planning systems such as manuals, report forms, and timetables is to direct the user and to assure a consistent style that will communicate to everyone within a complex organization. For every organization, therefore, some process of planning should exist. For most banks the planning process should be on an annual basis with specific results expected, and steps designated to achieve completion and individual assignments.

The planning for each unit of the organization is the responsibility of the manager. The manager starts the process with his thoughts on the objectives, strategies, goals, and programs, and he should maintain close control over the development of planning throughout the process. Planning, to be successful, needs the commitment, guidance, and leadership of the chief executive and the senior officers. That leadership should be expressed through an explicit statement of the values and philosophy of management. Therefore, while planning frequently is a team effort, it is not a staff function to be completed outside the unit and submitted to the manager for his approval. Planning is an important and necessary management function.

Chapter 23

Profit Planning and Budgeting

*Leonard Weil**

Banks have been engaged in a budgeting process for many years. Only in more recent years have banks become involved in a process now identified as profit planning. It is our purpose to encourage banks to engage in both. Budgeting is a process which has been used for a much longer period of time and which is far more familiar. A budget is a management tool which consists of a detailed plan of the projected income and expense for a finite period of time. It involves a forecast of sales or income, a projection of expense and arrives at a net profit figure for the company.

One of the newer variables in the approach to budgeting that has been made popular because of its use by President Carter is called "zero-based budgeting." In this approach to budgeting all department expenses and cost figures related to the past are eliminated and each department or division must justify all of its expenses for the future period as though it were starting from the very beginning. The advantage of this approach to budgeting is that it does not permit past abuses of overstaffing or overspending to be built into future budgets. In every division or department each person must be justified in the zero-budgeting approach. The same is true for each and every expenditure.

Until the period of the middle 1960s, banks faced a relatively stable environment and, therefore, the use of budgets was considered adequate for the planning process which banks followed. After that time rapid changes took place in the environment, and a few banks felt that the planning process would have to become broader, more thorough and more all-encompassing. From this need arose the process

---

* President, Manufacturers Bank, Los Angeles, California.

now called profit planning. Almost all literature on the subject of profit planning describes it as a strategy, and in the more recent years it is a strategy which involves both asset management and liability management, as well as manpower and facilities management. Profit planning is far more comprehensive than budgeting, although many bankers have for years used elements of profit planning as they have prepared their budgets. Profit planning examines future opportunities, whereas budgeting does not. Profit planning should attempt to identify risks and opportunities, while budgeting does not. Profit planning should start with the establishment of a desired corporate profit goal. Profit planning forces management to establish objectives and goals for the total company activity. Profit planning must involve every unit of the business entity and, in so doing, can serve as a tool for motivation so long as it involves the participation of department supervisors and managers and permits them to have responsibility and authority for helping to achieve the corporate profit goal.

BUDGETING

It is appropriate to review the budgeting process before getting into the details of profit planning. Budgeting is a process which, in order to be successful, must involve not only senior management but also department heads and supervisors. Each of these levels must participate to make any budgeting program a success. Generally, the budget starts with projections of the various sources of income. In budgeting, greater reliance is placed on extrapolating trend lines from the past in arriving at estimates of income, than would be the case in profit planning. This does not mean that budgeting of income or any other part of the budgeting process is purely mechanical. However, to the extent that broader alternatives are brought into play in the budgeting process of income, the closer the budget becomes to a profit plan. It is not possible to overstress that all division heads, department heads, and supervisors must be involved in budget preparation, if the budget is to be a success. These several groups must provide inputs in developing the income projections for the budget. It is not possible to develop income projections without taking into consideration the external environmental factors which will affect the bank's ability to market its products for the period under consideration. General business conditions, local business conditions, and the level of interest rates are only a few of the external factors to be considered when projecting income levels for the bank.

The next step in the budgeting process is to project the level of expense. Here, too, it is necessary that each level of management be involved and participate in providing projections of expenses for the period. This is the step in this process of participation that projections of additions to staff should be made, salary increases should be projected and, on the other hand, evaluation should be made to determine if existing expenses and existing staff will be necessary for this projected future period. Non-income producing departments or functions, such as advertising, must also provide their estimates. Rare is the budgeting process that is completed with only one set of projections. Ordinarily, the process will require several sets of projections which must be reviewed, corrected, and reconciled before final budget decisions are made. Hopefully, the final budget will be reached with the concurrence of all of the participants, so that all levels of management and employees can feel responsible for the end product and for achieving the figures which are established in the budget.

In order to maximize the benefits from the budgeting process, a bank should have a system that compares its monthly results with the budget. In many cases this is done by arranging to have the budget computerized so that the computer develops monthly comparisons with the budget. These comparisons provide management with a valuable tool for judging performance. Comparisons of actual performance with the budget should be made available to each department head so that he or she may see how the department is performing. In some banks this comparison of actual with budget is provided manually, but it is extremely important that such comparisons be made on a regular basis or much of the value of the budgeting process will be lost.

A budget cannot be treated as a static element in the management process. As changes take place within the bank, it may be necessary to alter the budget from time to time so that it will reflect actual changes that are taking place either in the bank or in the external environment.

If management finds that individual divisions or departments are not meeting their budget projections, it is important that a review be conducted immediately to determine the reasons therefor. This is the control element provided in the budgeting process which enables management to determine where weaknesses exist and to provide for pinpointing the problem areas so that curative measures can be taken rapidly.

PROFIT PLANNING

Profit planning is a more complex process than budgeting and starts with an attempt to establish a corporate profit goal. This goal can be considered in terms of a return on equity, return on assets, or profit for each dollar of revenue. Return on equity may be the profit goal which receives higher priority. On the other hand, to some banks an equal or greater priority may be assigned to the corporate profit goal of obtaining the highest possible return on assets. In other cases either equal, greater or lesser priority can be directed for the ratio of net income as a percentage of gross income.

In establishing these corporate profit goals, there should be some comparison with banks in the area, with banks of a particular size and possibly with all banks, so that it is possible for management to make adequate comparisons and arrive at its goals. Trends in past profit performance by the bank should be analyzed to determine the extent to which improvement should be expected.

The profit planning process must give careful attention to the probable chances in the environmental conditions that will affect prosperity of the bank for the period under consideration. Among these environmental conditions are the general business picture and the stage of the business cycle, as well as major local developments that will influence population growth and income levels in the community. Further, the outlook for investment markets and the level of interest rates will have a profound influence upon the profit plan for the period, as will the expected competitive position of other banks and other types of financial institutions.

In a real sense, conceptual profit planning involves the proper assessment and realistic evaluation of these external factors, since these conditions determine the availability of earning assets, the rate of return on assets, the cost of funds secured, and the expense patterns for the things that the bank must buy.

Influence of Product Mix

The profit plan must determine what the expected product mix among earning assets will be for the period ahead. If the conditions indicate that customers will not be borrowing for commercial loan purposes, it may be appropriate to include in the profit plan an expansion in installment lending and/or real estate lending. Or, the situation may indicate an increase in the proportion of earning assets which will be invested in securities. Further, product mix includes not only asset structure, but also the prospects of expanding fee income and other revenue producing activities. Arriving at a concensus on the appropriate product mix that is compatible with expected conditions and having these conclusions accepted by division heads, department heads and supervisors may be a most important step in profit planning.

Appropriate consideration must be given to the question as to whether it is possible to attempt to change the product mix by increased advertising expenditures, improved marketing programs, changes in marketing focus, or by expanded cross selling efforts. The cost/benefit relationships of such expenditures in relationship to expected results must be carefully considered in establishing goals for the year. The bank's competitive position in relationship to its market segments must be reassessed each time the profit plan is made. If a bank is becoming too dependent on one or a few industries or upon one or a few customers, consideration should be given to expenditures directed to desirable changes in customer patterns.

Range of Business Decisions

In effect, the profit planning process includes a whole range of business judgments on alternative courses of action for the coming year. Consideration has to be given to whether or not existing facilities will be adequate for the future and when plans should be made for new facilities or new locations. In a sense, decisions on new branches or new bank quarters are longer term decisions and affect more than the current profit planning period. Yet, the impact on the current period of these decisions becomes an important part of the profit plan. Decisions on computer facilities, what type, and how obtained have assumed a major role in profit planning in recent years. The question to "rent or buy" has loomed large in the decision-making process.

Also, in the last few years one of the most critical factors in attempting to develop bank profit planning is what should be done about bank capital. The relative capital position of each bank influences that bank's growth policies. In some cases, banks have had to adopt either slow growth or no growth policies because of capital shortages, with a direct effect on the profit plan. In other cases, banks have been able to develop plans for debt financing, a method of financing which must receive a different kind of emphasis in profit planning than does the acquisition of equity capital.

Although it may sound strange, probably the most important component in profit planning is the people factor. How many employees are required to perform the activities that are planned for the coming year, and at what levels will this personnel be needed? What replacements must be provided for people who are retiring? What new activities must be staffed? What productivity levels can be expected during the coming year in the several parts of the bank? What salary adjustments will be needed to keep the bank competitive in its personnel markets? Are additional expenditures for retirement programs or health and medical programs going to be needed during the year? Would a profit sharing plan benefit the bank's continuing levels of profitability? All of these are important factors to be considered in assessing the impact of the bank personnel requirements on the profit plan.

It should be emphasized that the objective of profit planning is not just to arrive at a "plan." The process of profit planning can serve as a very important means of communication within the bank to focus the attention of the entire organization on the need for effectiveness and efficiency. In addition, it is an excellent means of communicating expectations to all levels of bank personnel. Thus, the full benefits of profit planning depends upon participation by many people, so that each participant feels that he or she is contributing to the success of the bank. There is no better educational tool in banking than successful profit planning.

Control of Profit Plan

It is important that the profit plan be monitored and controlled throughout the year as the program unfolds. To do this it is essential that the bank establish responsibility center units with appropriate budgets. These budgets will provide information on revenue and expense so that a comparison can be made of the achievement of each of the responsibility centers. This budget control system provides managers with data on their controllable revenues and expenses. One of the basic premises of any such plan is to have each manager responsible for control of items on the basis of his or her greatest degree of influence over these items. Reports for each responsibility center should be prepared at least monthly to give the level of performance on a current basis, as well as on an accumulated year to date basis. Through this reporting, inefficient operations or unattainable goals can be pinpointed by budget variances. Such variances can be acted upon quickly. The more significant the variance, the more rapid should be the action to correct the situation.

Under most profit planning systems, there are established profit centers, normally all revenue-producing functions in the bank. Each of these profit centers is monitored throughout the year in line with expected profit generation with both revenue and expense levels measured against budgets. In addition to the profit centers, there are administrative and staff functions whose expenses are charged to the profit centers on some predetermined basis and in relationship to the contribution made to each profit center by each of these administrative services.

The wide range of activities involved in a profit plan and the need to have the plan monitored and updated throughout the year make it important to use a computerized system to implement the plan.

Most banks now have their profit plans installed on a computer to facilitate the monthly reports and to provide the opportunity for control and measurement. Without the assist of a computer system, the implementation of comprehensive profit planning in a complex organization is most difficult.

Profit planning in a bank, if properly implemented, can be among the most valuable tools of bank management. It is an excellent training tool for young managers, for such a system requires an orderly analysis of alternatives and requires that specific numbers be assigned to expected results. This process involves division heads, department heads, and supervisors in a team effort to plan the level of profitability and to encourage each group to perform more efficiently to attain goals that they have established. Further, the planning process helps focus attention on the areas of greatest profit potential and assists management in allocating the bank's resources in the most profitable manner. In our complex business society, profit planning is almost a necessity. Each bank's management must give serious attention to the extent and type of profit planning and budgeting system that can be used most effectively in the bank because management can be almost certain that its most aggressive competitors are using these management tools.

Chapter 24

Profitability Analysis, Cost Systems, and Pricing Policies

*John Zimmermann**

H. B. McDonald†

Recent trends in banking have forced the banker to make pricing decisions with a greater degree of accuracy and frequency than ever before. Greater availability of short-term money market investments is inducing corporate treasurers to put idle checking account balances to work. Consequently, corporate excess demand deposits continue to decrease at a significant rate, with the result that traditional sources of "free funds" are drying up at the time that costs of banking are increasing. In today's banking environment, a well-founded knowledge of costs must be the basis of pricing decisions. This knowledge affords bank management a dynamic and powerful competitive tool.

Cost and profitability analyses are applicable to a variety of banking objectives. While used primarily to determine comparative profitability among organizational units, customers, and products (or services), these analyses also provide quantitative guidelines for performance evaluations, policy decisions, market analyses, and resource allocations.

In the past, bank accounting has been oriented principally toward the requirements of regulatory agencies. The prescribed accounting classifications of various federal and state regulators and other external bodies limited the usefulness of conventional bank accounting statement formats as a basis for costing and pricing decisions. By contrast,

---
* Senior Vice President and Controller, The First National Bank of Atlanta, Atlanta, Georgia.

† Assistant Vice President, The First National Bank of Atlanta, Atlanta, Georgia.

the current trend in bank accounting is in the direction of comprehensive management accounting systems that not only meet external requirements, but also address the internal reporting, cost, and analysis requirements of today's bankers.

The subject of profitability analyses, cost systems, and pricing policies is vast, with many theories and articles written on the subject. This chapter portrays only some of the many acceptable philosophies and concepts relating to these subjects. It should be understood that what is proper for one organization may not work in another. To be utilized, the management accounting systems must be understood and must complement the style of the organization.

The material in this chapter has been organized to cover: (1) the nature of costs; (2) cost allocation; (3) organizational, product, and customer profitability; and (4) pricing policies.

NATURE OF COSTS

The operating costs (exclusive of interest cost and provision for possible credit losses) of the organization can be broken down into:

1. Direct production costs.
2. Selling costs.
3. Overhead costs.
   a. Direct support.
   b. Indirect support.
   c. General and administrative.

The above operating costs can be further segregated based on volume sensitivity into:

1. Variable costs.
2. Fixed costs.

An explanation of the above terms follows and is essential to understanding the subject.

Direct Production Costs. These are costs of production that can be directly attributed to a function or unit of output. Included in direct production costs are personnel costs, occupancy costs, supplies, and so on. It should be understood that direct production costs can have both fixed and variable components depending upon capacity constraints. When considered over a sufficient range of volume, direct production costs are usually variable. For example, a department may have one supervisor and ten employees. If volume increases sufficiently to require 20 employees, it may be necessary to add a second supervisor and acquire additional space.

Selling Costs. These include costs of account representatives, product advertising, travel, transportation and entertainment, and so on. It should be pointed out that because most of these costs are classified as account administration or customer service expenses, they are often omitted from any product cost analysis.

Overhead Costs. These are costs not directly assignable to a given activity or function. Overhead can be grouped into the following categories:

Direct support includes all production management above that of the direct supervisory position, with any costs incurred in service support departments or other expenses directly associated with supporting a production area (for example, department managers, their secretaries and other support personnel).

Indirect support consists of expenses further removed from the actual production, but necessary for the organization to function (for example, personnel department, security, purchasing, and the like).

General and administrative costs are generally bankwide in nature which cannot be distributed on any direct basis since they are directly related either to organizational units or products (for example—institutional advertising, executive salaries, etc.).

Classification by Volume Sensitivity

Variable Costs. These are costs that change in direct proportion to changes in volume. There are degrees of variability in all costs; however, the factor that determines variable costs is the relevant range of volume or time being considered.

Fixed Costs. These are costs that do not change in direct proportion to volume changes. For example, the number of employees in the purchasing department does not increase in direct proportion to the units produced in the production areas.

Interest Costs

Not covered in the above definitions but nevertheless of significant consideration in bank cost accounting is the allocation of interest cost to specific organizational units, products and customers. A bank's interest expense can be equated to a manufacturing company's cost of raw materials, except a bank has more difficulty in identifying the specific uses of its major raw materials. The source of funds for a particular loan, and consequently the interest cost for that loan, is difficult to identify. There is no one proven method for allocating interest cost. Three concepts often used are the pool rate, the marginal rate, and the multiple pool rate. It is highly important that interest costs be allocated, but it should be accepted that there is no single correct method. The method selected must depend on the objectives of bank management and different methods may be chosen over a number of years by the same organization.

COST ALLOCATION

Cost allocation can be defined as the process of transferring cost data from one responsibility center to another, based upon benefits received by the second center, in order to provide management with a more precise presentation of profitability analyses.

To simplify the cost allocation process and make it more meaningful, responsibility centers should be assigned on the basis of functional areas. For example, the assignment of responsibility centers in the bookkeeping area might be as follows:

> Department: *Bookkeeping*
> Responsibility centers
> Bookkeeping administration
> Personal account processing
> Company account processing
> Return item processing
> Customer service

After the responsibility centers have been established, costs can be assigned to each center on a specific basis.

The next step is the determination of the transfer basis or unit that will reflect the best measure of service provided to other responsibility centers. The effort applied to this determination depends upon the accuracy desired and the cost of developing and maintaining the data. Some easier items to allocate are as follows:

Function	*Allocation Basis*
Printing	Number of forms provided
Bookkeeping	Number of items posted
Proof encoding	Number of items encoded

The following procedures may be used to allocate costs to responsibility centers receiving the benefits of another responsibility center:

Standards are predetermined target costs requiring development of cost standards for each transfer unit. This method enables actual costs incurred to be compared to standard costs.

Fixed dollars are used where it is unlikely that the degree of effort will change from period to period, and is often based upon a budgeted amount.

Percentage of activity is used where activities are collected. The dollars allocated are a function of the recipient responsibility center's percentage of total activities. This method is an alternate to the use of standards.

Fixed percentage is used where statistical data cannot be collected economically by the service providing responsibility center, or where sampling has been used to approximate the level of service. It may be appropriate to simply use percentages developed by management estimates in lieu of engineered allocations.

Transfer price is used where there is a desire for a responsibility center to be evaluated on its financial performance. The transfer price should be market or cost related, and can be negotiated between service rendering and receiving units. The use of standards in determining the transfer price is a logical extension of this procedure.

Once a basis for allocating costs has been established, it is necessary to decide upon a procedure for handling the allocations. Three common methods used are the direct, step, and reciprocal methods.

Direct Method.   Under this method all allocations are made directly to the responsibility centers that are the ultimate users. Responsibility centers that do not provide a service to the ultimate user are treated as overhead, and may be allocated on the basis of direct labor hours, salary dollars, total direct costs, etc.

Step Method.   The step method allows the recognition of services rendered from one service department to another. This recognition is accomplished through levels or sequences of allocations in which a responsibility center or group of responsibility centers are allocated to other centers. These responsibility centers are then closed, if appropriate. After a cost center is allocated (closed) no subsequent allocations can be made to it. The inaccuracies caused by this limitation can be minimized if those responsibility centers affecting the greatest number of other centers or those allocating the largest dollars are placed early in the sequence.

Reciprocal Method.   This is a complex modification of the step method in that service departments can be closed into each other. This is done using a series of simultaneous equations, continuous allocation until the error factor is insignificant, matrix algebra, or trial and error.

ORGANIZATIONAL, PRODUCT, AND CUSTOMER PROFITABILITY

The growth of many banking institutions has necessitated extensive delegation of authority and responsibility, creating a commitment to internal management accounting systems and organizational profitability reporting. There are three distinct types of bank profitability presentations—organizational, customer, and product. Although these presentations differ in output, they are actually only different perspectives or arrangements of the same underlying accounting and operating data.

Organizational Profitability

Management accounting is basically the coordination and distribution of accounting information into individual organizational units. The objective of the management accounting system is not only to provide management with accurate and timely information but also to provide control at the supervisory level. The role played by individual organizational units in management accounting is vital because the organizational unit is the most effective point at which costs can be controlled.

Before designing a system of organizational profitability, management must thoroughly appraise the organizational structure. To be effective, the structure of the organization should reflect a hierarchy of reporting with well-defined spheres of responsibility and authority. The profitability system must then operate in conformity with the organizational structure.

The reporting system must be designed so that information pyramids upward to each consecutive managerial level. An example of this structure is illustrated below:

President
Summary of
division reports
↑
Division Head
Summary of
department reports
↑
Department Head
Summary of detailed
responsibility center
reports
↑
Responsibility Unit
Detailed reports

The direct accumulation of income and expense by responsibility center and their pyramiding in the organization is the simplest type of profitability system. Expanding this concept into a refined measure of organizational profitability requires development of a sophisticated intrabank cost allocation system.

The initial phase of determining organizational profitability is to examine the responsibility centers and to classify them as either a direct profit center, a direct production center, or an overhead center. Generally, the classification is made according to the nature of costs to be assigned (see definitions provided earlier in this chapter). For example, direct sales expense should be accumulated in units designated as direct profit centers; direct production expense should be accumulated in direct production centers; costs not directly related to production processes, marketing, or sales should be accumulated in overhead centers. Unfortunately, units may fit into more than one of the three categories. A branch is a case in point, since it has characteristics of both a direct profit center and a direct production center. However, predetermined and consistent classification of responsibility centers is necessary to determine which expenses should be directly charged to a particular center, and which allocation methods to use for production and overhead centers. Additional characteristics of the three major types of responsibility centers are as follows:

Direct Profit Centers. Direct profit centers are the sales areas of the organization which are primarily responsible for the generation of income. Direct sales expense, as well as income, should be assigned to these centers. Unlike other types of responsibility centers, direct profit centers are assigned balance sheet items such as deposits, loans, float and required reserves in order to properly reflect the assets and liabilities controlled by the center's manager. Direct profit centers are given credit for funds provided or charged for funds used based upon a predetermined transfer rate. In addition, credit loss provisions are charged to these centers. In a refined cost allocation system, direct profit centers are also charged with allocated production and overhead expense.

Direct Production Centers. These centers are the units used to accumulate expenses directly associated with a production process. A production center is generally responsible for providing processing steps for a limited number of products (such as, central proof encoding). Production centers are also identifiable with one or more statistics related to each product (for example, number of deposited items on corporate demand deposits). An effective cost system must provide the means for collecting appropriate statistics. The product/statistic relationships facilitates allocation of the costs of production centers to direct profit centers.

Overhead Centers. Overhead centers are areas that are charged with the costs that can not be directly associated with either the production or marketing of a product. Generally, allocation of these costs is less specific and more arbitrary than the allocation of direct production costs. There are three types of overhead centers which are distinguished by their degree of direct relationship to a product. These centers can be defined as direct support and indirect support and general and administrative.

Direct and indirect support centers are areas that provide centralized operations for the total organization. Organizational areas such as a printing department, a word processing center, or a division manager's cost center are good examples of direct support centers. Because these centers support a limited and definable segment of the business, cost allocation can usually be performed with high precision. Organizational units such as personnel and building services are indirect support centers and their cost should be distributed to other areas on a systematic basis (for example, by allocating cost based upon the number of employees and square footage, respectively).

General and administrative centers are used to collect costs of staff services provided to the overall organization (for example, the controller and executive functions). Costs assigned to these centers are not directly associated with any particular product nor are they readily allocable. These costs must be absorbed at the total organization level, or may be allocated to direct profit centers on an arbitary basis.

Once the various types of responsibility units are identified and appropriate allocations are established for the production and overhead centers, organizational profit contribution can be measured. There are several levels of profit contribution that can be defined for a responsibility unit.

Exhibit 24–1 illustrates a profit center report produced by the system described above. The four levels measuring profit contribution are described below:

Profit Level I contribution—revenue after operating expenses. This level represents the most basic reporting of profit contribution. It provides a comparison of direct income and expense recorded in that unit prior to any allocation of production and overhead costs. Direct revenues and expenses are usually those for which the unit manager has a direct decision-making responsibility.

Profit Level II contribution—Level I after allocation of direct production expenses. This level includes all the direct processing costs of the products being managed in the profit center.

Profit Level III contribution—Level II after direct and indirect support expenses. This level additionally reflects the costs of internal bank services.

Profit Level IV—Level III after general and administrative overhead. This level of profitability reflects full absorption of all bank costs. The sum of Level IV profitability for all responsibility centers must equal the total bank pretax income.

Exhibit 24–1
Profit Contribution for National Accounts Profit Center

		Actual	Budget Variance	Prior Period Variance
Revenue from funds		$8,482	$371—	$814
Charge for net funds used.		(325)	31—	79—
Provision for credit losses		(300)	0	42
Net margin		7,857	340—	851
Other income		362	35	17
Direct sales expense				
Staff.	$ 525			
Occupancy.	64			
Equipment.	23			
Advertising.	89			
Other.	278	(979)	133—	72—
Profit Level I.		7,240	172—	940
Direct production expense				
Data processing	343			
Bookkeeping	190			
Proof and transit	901			
Reconcilement	83			
Loan processing	31			
Other production centers	1,189	(2,737)	22—	15
Profit Level II.		4,503	150—	925
Direct and indirect support expense				
Personnel	33			
Building services	5			
Other service center	197	(235)	11—	7
Profit Level III		4,268	139—	918
General and administrative overhead expense				
Executive.	121			
Controller.	95			
Other overhead centers	186	(402)	24	1
Profit Level IV		$3,866	$163—	$917

Note: — indicates down from budget or prior period.

Customer Profitability

Customer profitability is a natural extension of the concepts employed to derive organizational profitability and addresses the analysis of individual customer relationships as opposed to organizational areas. To review the profitability of every customer relationship is unjustifiable from a cost point of view. For this reason, the value of this system is best realized in the review and evaluation of large corporate and correspondent bank customers. The profitability of individual consumers and small companies is best reflected through a product profitability system.

Identifying the total relationship of a given customer can be a difficult task as some organizations include such items as trust fees, interest-bearing deposits, international banking services, data processing services, and money market transactions in their analyses while other organizations may feel that some or all of these items should be treated on a stand-alone basis.

For each customer relationship under review, a source and use of funds statement (example presented as Exhibit 24–2) should be pro-

Exhibit 24–2
ABC Corporation—Source and Use Statement

Uses
Demand loans $127,212
Term loans—Net of unearned 2,966

Earning assets 130,178

Float 143,146
Reserves 20,927

Nonearning assets 164,073

Total funds used 294,251

Sources
Demand deposits 298,612
Noninterest bearing CDs 15,380

Total fund sources 313,992

Net funds used (provided)............................ $(19,741)

duced. The information contained in this exhibit is normally available from various accounting systems, with the possible exception of float, which may require a sampling of the activities in the customer's accounts.

The summation of direct income and expense for the corporate customer relationship corresponds to the accumulation of income and expense in an organizational profit center. Direct production costs are allocated to the customer center in the same manner used to transfer costs to the direct profit center (via standard costs and statistics). There should also be a charge for funds used and/or a credit for funds provided in accordance with the bank's transfer rate policy.

Since a single account officer normally services many accounts, the assignment of selling expense to individual customers can become complex, but can be accomplished using percentage allocations.

Overhead cost can be allocated; however, the marginal profitability (defined as Profit Level II contribution) of the customer relationship often is sufficient to make appropriate management decisions.

As with organizational profit centers, a profit goal should be established for the customer relationship which is consistent with the profit goal of the organization. If the organization's goal is a 1 percent return on assets after income tax, the customer's marginal profit goal must exceed a 2 percent return on total funds used so that the pricing structure will cover overhead and carrying costs of unallocated nonearning assets on a pretax basis.

Exhibit 24–3 illustrates a profit contribution statement for a corporate customer which meets the above criteria. After allowing 30 per-

Exhibit 24–3
ABC Corporation—Profit Contribution Statement

Interest on demand loans................	$10,042	
Interest on term loans...................	360	
Fees on loans...........................	378	
Revenue from funds...................		$10,780
Net funds credit (cost)...................		(1,184)
Provision for credit losses................		(752)
Net margin...........................		8,844
Service charges.........................		1,074
Selling costs		(1,165)
Checking account services...............	379	
Teleconcentration.......................	190	
Lockbox................................	651	
Accounts reconcilement	81	
Loan processing	61	
Direct production costs................		(1,362)
Profit Level II contribution		7,391
Profit Level II return on assets............ 2.51%		
Overhead (30% of selling and direct production costs)........................		(706)
Profit Level IV contribution		$ 6,685
Profit Level IV return on assets........... 2.27%		

cent of direct and production costs to cover overhead and carrying costs of nonearning assets, the return on total funds used exceeds a 2 percent goal.

Product Profitability

Product profitability is a method of accumulating financial data relating to the bank's products and structuring this data in a format consistent with the management decision process. This information enables management to assess each product according to overall profitability goals. The knowledge that a particular product is unprofitable does not necessarily allow a bank to discontinue the product; however, it does provide a basis for an informed decision as to the degree to which a product is offered. The knowledge of which products are most profitable enables the bank to optimize its product mix.

The bank's general ledger is already classified by product with the exception of operating and interest expenses, and in presenting product profitability analyses these expenses must be assigned to specific products. As with organizational profitability, the operating expenses must first be accumulated in responsibility centers and then these centers must be classified as direct profit, direct production, and overhead centers.

The costs of direct and indirect overhead support centers should be allocated to responsibility centers for which internal service is provided, using the same methods and techniques as applied in developing organizational profitability. After this is accomplished, all operating costs will be in either a direct profit or a production center, with the exception of general and administrative. Each profit and production center can then be examined to determine the proper assignment of costs to specific products. In some profit and production centers costs can be easily identified with a very limited number of products (for example, a credit card operation). In contrast, a full service branch approximates a total bank with costs being assigned to many products.

Costs of general and administrative centers are accumulated and assigned on an arbitrary basis across all product lines. After all components have been classified in each center, they can be aggregated into fixed and variable operating costs by product. In addition, interest expense must also be assigned by product.

Exhibits 24–4 through 24–6 provide examples of profitability analyses of the various products of a bank. Exhibits 24–7 and 24–8 provide a more detailed example of the elements which must be considered in determining the profitability of a particular product.

For illustrated purposes these examples use the "pool of funds" approach, with a pool rate of 6 percent.

Exhibit 24-4
Product Profitability Analysis—Year Ending 12/31/— Funds Providing Functions

Function:	Gross Balance	Deductions	Investable Balance	Percent of Investment Balance	Interest Expense	Variable Handling Expense	Income	Credit for funds Provided	Marginal Profitability	Fixed Expenses	Net Contribution
Demand deposits											
Commercial	$ 32,863	$ 9,817	$ 23,046	10.13%	$ —	$ 521	$ 71	$ 1,382	$ 932	$ 299	$ 633
Personal	29,516	7,201	22,315	9.81	—	626	165	1,338	877	306	571
Special	5,168	851	4,317	1.90	—	278	209	259	190	124	66
Public	8,246	9,167	(921)	(0.41)	—	64	507	(55)	388	25	363
Trust	1,600	1,779	(179)	(0.08)	—		108	(10)	98	—	98
Total demand deposits	77,393	28,815	48,578	21.36%	—	1,489	1,060	2,914	2,485	754	1,731
Time deposits											
Certificates of deposit											
Consumer	12,318	579	11,739	5.16%	851	16	—	704	(163)	18	(181)
Corporate trust	89,876	92,571	(2,695)	(1.19)	5,198	4	5,547	(161)	184	1	183
Money market	17,267	845	16,422	7.22	1,069	19	—	985	(103)	17	(120)
Long term	40,927	1,228	39,699	17.46	2,974	50	—	2,381	(643)	43	(686)
Public funds	11,328	11,621	(293)	(0.13)	567	16	687	(17)	87	13	74
Total certificates of deposit	171,716	106,844	64,872	28.53%	10,659	105	6,234	3,892	(638)	92	(730)
Regular savings	65,067	1,789	63,278	27.83%	2,851	269	—	3,796	676	183	493
First choice	31,539	1,535	30,004	13.19	1,609	72	—	1,800	119	46	73
Christmas Club	1,273	55	1,218	0.54	45	27	—	73	1	12	(11)
Trust (interest bearing)	900	939	(39)	(0.02)	55	2	60	(2)	1	—	1
Trust (Noninterest bearing)	1,500	1,571	(71)	(0.03)	—	2	101	(4)	95	—	95
Total other time deposits	100,279	5,889	94,390	41.51%	4,560	372	$ 161	5,663	892	241	651
Total time deposits	271,995	112,733	159,262	70.03%	15,219	477	6,395	9,555	254	333	(79)
Equity capital and unassigned	19,567	—	19,567	8.61%	622	938	1,406	1,167	1,013	2,896	(1,883)
Total funds providing functions	$368,955	$141,548	$227,407	100.00%	$15,841	$2,904	$8,861	$13,636	$3,752	$3,983	$ (231)

Exhibit 24-5
Product Profitability Analysis—Year Ending 12/31/— Funds Using Functions

Function	Gross Balance	Deductions	Invested Balance	Percent of Total Gross Balances	Interest Income	Other Income	Cost of Funds Used	Variable Handling Cost	Risk Cost	Marginal Profitability	Fixed Cost	Net Contribution
Commercial loans												
Business, commercial and industrial	$ 45,708	$ 9,943	$ 35,765	18.92%	$ 4,004	$ 22	$ 2,146	$125	$ 421	$1,334	$ 248	$1,086
Individual	11,276	1,185	10,091	4.67	971	—	605	58	36	272	162	110
Agricultural	876	88	788	0.36	78	—	47	3	—	28	5	23
Financial institutions	1,736	347	1,389	0.72	135	—	83	4	—	48	6	42
Tax exempt	6,496	—	6,496	2.69	365	—	389	14	—	(38)	24	(62)
Other	2,157	216	1,941	0.89	170	—	116	5	—	49	7	42
Total commercial loans	68,249	11,779	56,470	28.25%	5,723	22	3,386	209	457	1,693	452	1,241
Direct lease financing	5,808	228	5,580	2.40%	706	35	335	288	141	(23)	101	(124)
Installment loans												
Direct												
Automobile	4,017	57	3,960	1.66%	453	8	237	98	35	91	112	(21)
Personal	8,275	285	7,990	3.43	972	16	479	224	178	107	174	(67)
Home improvement	712	6	706	0.29	82	9	42	21	4	24	40	(16)
Other	2,720	57	2,663	1.13	276	5	159	40	37	45	37	8
Total direct	15,724	405	15,319	6.51%	1,783	38	917	383	254	267	363	(96)
Indirect												
Automobile	15,115	628	14,487	6.26%	1,565	27	869	209	289	225	98	127
Home improvement	2,787	70	2,717	1.15	257	20	163	40	20	54	16	38
Other	851	7	844	0.35	100	2	50	36	5	11	12	(1)
Mobile home	4,926	67	4,859	2.04	395	7	291	16	4	91	12	79
Total indirect	23,679	772	22,907	9.80%	2,317	56	1,373	301	318	381	138	243
Total installment loans	39,403	1,177	38,226	16.31%	4,100	94	2,290	684	572	648	501	147
Floor plan												
Direct	6,225	772	5,453	2.58%	549	20	327	26	—	216	35	181
Lease	2,078	208	1,870	0.86	182	—	112	5	—	65	10	55
Total floor plan	8,303	980	7,323	3.44%	731	20	439	31	—	281	45	236
Mortgage loans												
Commercial	20,536	—	20,536	8.50%	1,594	10	1,232	20	—	352	41	311
Residential	38,389	—	38,389	15.89	2,813	24	2,303	76	—	458	86	372
Agricultural	1,138	—	1,138	0.47	94	—	68	2	—	24	3	21
Tax exempt	6,288	—	6,288	2.61	352	—	377	4	—	(29)	7	(36)
Other	535	—	535	0.22	45	—	32	1	—	12	2	10
Total mortgage loans	66,886	—	66,886	27.69%	4,898	34	4,012	103	—	817	139	678
Investments												
Taxable	40,728	—	40,728	16.86%	2,764	—	2,443	3	—	318	5	313
Nontaxable	9,657	—	9,657	4.00	398	—	579	1	—	(182)	2	(184)
Trading	2,537	—	2,537	1.05	867	—	152	17	—	698	30	668
Total investments	52,922	—	52,922	21.91%	4,029	—	3,174	21	—	834	37	797
Total fund using functions	$241,571	$14,164	$227,407	100.00%	$20,187	$205	$13,636	$1,336	$1,170	$4,250	$1,275	$2,975

Exhibit 24-6
Product Profitability Analysis—Year Ending December 31, 19— Nonfund Functions

Function	Fee Income	Credit (charge) for Funds Provided or Used	Variable Handling Cost	Marginal Profitability	Fixed Cost	Net Contribution
Trust services						
Estates	$244	—	$ 75	$169	$128	$ 41
Personal	377	—	142	235	164	71
Employee benefits	44	—	52	(8)	74	(82)
Total trust services	665	—	269	396	366	30
Municipal and corporate services	84	—	99	(15)	73	(88)
Money market—customer	11	—	17	(6)	21	(27)
EDP services	183	—	80	103	78	25
Credit card—merchant	24	—	8	16	6	10
Safe deposit	85	—	41	44	33	11
Utility payment	21	—	44	(23)	17	(40)
Special customer service	120	—	149	(29)	67	(96)
One account	20	—	104	(84)	20	(104)
Total nonfund functions	$548	—	$542	$ 6	$315	($309)

Exhibit 24–7
Product Profitability Analysis Demand Deposits—Commercial—Year Ending December 31, 19—

	Amount	Percent of Gross Balance
Balances:		
General ledger	$32,863	100.00%
Deductions:		
Float/pledge	5,429	16.52
Reserves	3,063	9.32
Overdrafts/cash items	1,249	3.80
Due from banks	76	0.23
Total deductions	9,817	29.87%
Investable	$23,046	70.13%
Net credit for funds provided at 6%:		
Credit for funds provided	$ 1,971	6.00%
Value of funds used	(589)	(1.79)
Net credit for funds provided	1,382	4.21%
Variable handling costs:		
Interest	0	0.00
Processing	521	1.59
Total variable costs	521	1.59%
Other income:		
Service charges and fees	71	0.22
Total other income	71	0.22%
Marginal profitability	932	2.84%
Fixed costs	299	0.91
Net contribution	$ 633	1.93%

PRICING POLICIES

Until recently, price adjustments have not been a significant alternative for improving a bank's profitability. The great majority of revenue has been provided from loans and investments, and the price on these products is largely uncontrollable. Rates are determined by national money markets, or are limited by competition or local usury laws. The only true pricing flexibility allowed by the marketplace generally has been a function of credit risk. Historically, banks have directed their profit improvement efforts at expanding the deposit base, controlling costs, and reducing credit losses. Pricing considerations have normally dealt with temporary price reduction promotions to improve market share.

Exhibit 24–8
Product Profitability Analysis Commercial Loan—Business, Commercial and Industrial—Year Ending December 31, 19—

	Amount	Percent of Gross Balance
Balances:		
General ledger	$45,708	100.00%
Deductions:		
Compensating balances	9,258	20.25
Reserve for loan losses	685	1.50
Total deductions	9,943	21.75%
Invested	$35,765	78.25%
Interest and other income		
Interest	$ 4,004	8.76%
Other	22	0.05
Total interest and other income	4,026	8.81%
Net charges for funds used at 6%		
Charge for funds used	2,742	6.00
Value of funds provided	(596)	(1.31)
Net charge for funds used	2,146	4.69%
Variable handling costs	125	0.28
Risk costs	421	0.92
Marginal profitability	1,334	2.92%
Fixed costs	248	0.54
Net contribution	$ 1,086	2.38%

In recent years, bank pricing policy has become a critical issue, but only because the growing competition for funds has required development of fee income alternatives, and because a wide variety of innovative services has been introduced to attract corporate and consumer deposits. In these areas, a formal pricing policy which is based on sound cost accounting knowledge is essential.

As in all other industries, the price of bank services is a function of cost, sales volume, and required profit margin. As discussed throughout this chapter, costs must be classified as production costs, selling costs, and overhead (plus interest and credit loss expense). After performing the basic cost identification, the next step is to segregate costs into fixed and variable components. The need for this step is obvious. Pricing policy should maximize revenue increases (marginal revenue) with respect to cost increases (marginal cost). Simply illustrated, basic cost identification may show a product to be currently generating inadequate profits. In this case, there are two available pricing decisions; raise prices and risk lower sales volume, or lower prices in anticipation of stimulating sales to the point of increasing total revenues. Even with an accurate prediction of customer reaction to new prices, the decision can be made only with knowledge of what volume changes will do to overall expense levels.

Chapter 25

Control and Measurement of Financial Performance

Donald S. Howard*

William T. Maher, Jr.†

Every successful business enterprise has important and significant objectives which it is attempting to achieve. In today's increasingly competitive world, the careful monitoring of these objectives over time is essential. Quite clearly, the achievement of specific financial objectives is an essential part of the success of any business. The purpose of a financial control and measurement system is to closely monitor the actual financial results against agreed upon objectives.

Control and measurement is the process by which management assures itself, insofar as is feasible, that actions taken by the members of an organization conform to management's plans and policies. Accounting and financial information is useful in control as a means of communication, of motivation, and of appraisal. As a means of communication, the financial reporting structure can assist in informing the organization about management's plans and programs and, in general, the types of action that management wishes the organization to take.

It is axiomatic that no business can survive unless it operates at a profit. In addition, history has taught us that businesses which are most successful are those which are able to optimize their profits within the competitive environment in which they are required to operate. The banking industry is no exception to this rule. Consequently, suc-

---
* Senior Vice President—Finance, Citibank, N.A., New York, New York.
† Vice President, Citibank, N.A., New York, New York.

cessful banks have devoted considerable time and effort over the last decade toward the establishment of effective financial control and measurement systems. Such systems within the banking industry have permitted managers at all levels to follow their performance and the performance of the total organization opposite the agreed upon financial objectives.

NEED FOR SENIOR MANAGEMENT SPONSORSHIP AND INVOLVEMENT

Perhaps it is redundant but at the same time necessary to state at the outset that a system for controlling and measuring financial performance cannot be successful unless it receives senior management's sponsorship as well as senior management involvement. Many systems have been developed by the very best expert technicians operating in a staff capacity but have been unsuccessful because they lacked the required senior management involvement. The business organization must be convinced that management considers the system to be important. Unless the system is part of the day-to-day management process at the most senior levels, it could become a paper shuffling operation which provides employment for many accounting clerks and staff people but does nothing in terms of improving the management of the organization and the achievement of its principal objectives. In the final analysis, the success of a system for controlling and measuring financial performance is directly tied to the degree of senior management involvement.

Those who have had experience in the establishment of financial control and measurement systems are convinced that managers at all levels will respond to those things that senior management has indicated will be the basis for reviewing and evaluating their performance. Involvement and utilization is a sure signal, probably the only effective signal, that management is interested in the control and measurement system.

NEED FOR A COMMON LANGUAGE

Basically, this involvement and utilization imply the development of a common language within the organization which utilizes the terminology associated with the key financial objectives. For instance, a banking organization which has established specific objectives for risk asset growth and average returns on risk assets should continually use such terminology in its discussions with various levels of management. It should not be uncommon for the various managers to talk about their RORA (return on risk asset) for the last month or the last quarter, and so on. What the organization should be striving for is a new language which becomes the vehicle for common understanding of the major financial objectives of the business. It is necessary for the common language to be based on narrow, tight, and well-understood definitions.

RECOGNITION OF PERFORMANCE

In addition, management utilization of the system involves praise or other reward for good performance, criticism of or removal of the causes for a poor performance, or specific questions leading to the praise or criticism. If, in contrast, reports on performance are prepared and disappear into executive offices and are never heard from again, the managers within the organization will quickly assume that senior management is not paying attention to the control and measurement system. They will further conclude that if management doesn't pay attention why should they?

UNDERSTANDING AND PARTICIPATION BY THOSE BEING MEASURED

Control and measurement is exercised in part by setting up standards of expected performance and comparing actual performance with these standards. The established standard should be very hard and easily measurable. For instance, "we will improve the net spread on our risk assets by ten basis points," is a hard measurable standard. An example of a loose and difficult measurable standard would be "we will attempt to improve the profit margin on our risk assets business."

The standard is likely to be effective as a means of control only if the person being judged agrees that it is an equitable standard and at the same time understands the basic concepts which form the foundation for the system as well as the key measurements of performance. Unless these conditions are met, the individual will most likely pay no attention to comparisons between his or her performance and the standard and will tend to resist the system's use at every opportunity. The best way to assure this agreement and understanding is to ask the person whose performance is to be measured to participate in the process of setting the standard. In order to participate intelligently, the managers need to understand clearly what the control system is, what they are expected to do, what basis they are going to be judged on, and so on. Such an understanding probably cannot be achieved by written communication. Frequent meetings of managers and subordinates at all levels of the organization are required for discussion and explanation.

EDUCATIONAL PROCESS

Considerable time and effort should be devoted to an educational process at the outset as well as on a continuing basis to ensure that managers at all levels understand the fundamental concepts. Such an educational process is a two-way communication. In the first instance, there is a detailed explanation of the inner workings of the system and the key measurements as well as an opportunity for the managers to question and perhaps identify potential fallacies which may not be known to the staff people who have developed the system but well known to the line managers. In other words, the intellectual underpinnings must be consistent with the real world.

TAILORING THE SYSTEM

In establishing a financial control and measurement system, it is also important to tailor the system to meet the particular organizational structure of the business as well as the management style of the organization. In some organizations, a high degree of centralized control may be necessary. In another organization which has a decentralized management structure, an entirely different system may be appropriate to meet the difference in style and structure. In other words, a manager at a given level will tend to resist detailed questions about certain income and expense items if the organization is largely decentralized and managers are generally measured on their bottom line results and not on the basis of individual actions which lead to those bottom line results. Again, it is important for the educational process to focus on the organizational structure, management style, and specific criteria for measuring performance.

TIMELY AND ACCURATE REPORTING

Many financial control and measurement systems have failed or fallen into decay as a result of untimely and/or inaccurate reporting. To be truly effective, reports should be received within a matter of days after the close of an accounting period and they should be accurate. A manager should be able to quickly review and relate to his or her performance for the prior period. As a matter of fact, if a system is really doing its job, managers should anxiously await the reports which show their performance. In many ways, the managers should see themselves as players participating in a game of achieving the overall financial objectives of the enterprise. Consequently, the believability of the numbers is critical.

REPORT RESPONSIBILITY

In some organizations it has been necessary and appropriate to decentralize the reporting function rather than having all reports generated from a centralized point. The management of such organizations have felt that a (bottoms-up) generation of the numbers by individual managers tended to make the numbers more reliable and at the same time the reporting process took on a higher degree of credibility. Prior experience seemed to indicate that a (tops-down) approach to the generation of the numbers gave individual managers the opportunity to point to inaccuracies in numbers which led to a lack of credibility for the overall system.

GOAL CONGRUENCE

The financial control and measurement system should be designed so that actions that it leads people to take, in accordance with their perceived self-interest, are actions that are also in the best interest of the enterprise. The goals of the people in the organization should be consistent with the goals of the total business enterprise.

It should be recognized however that *perfect* congruence of goals may be difficult to achieve. Nevertheless, at a minimum, the system should not encourage individuals to act against the best interest of the company. For example, if the system rewards individuals on the basis of gross income generated without regard to the level of expenses incurred, it could lead to incremental business which is unprofitable on a bottom line basis. Over time, this could be very detrimental to the total organization. It is therefore important to ask two separate questions about a control technique: (1) What will it motivate people to do in their own self-interest? and (2) Are these actions in the best interest of the company over the long term?

ESTABLISHMENT OF APPROPRIATE INDICATORS OF PERFORMANCE

For a banking organization as for any organization, it is important to carefully focus on key indicators of financial performance which are necessary to follow in order to achieve success. For most banks, it is probably necessary to establish indicators on at least two different levels. In the first instance, specific corporate levels indicators should be established and then followed very closely by the senior management of the organization. For instance, it would probably be appropriate for a banking organization to consider the following indicators of performance:

Growth in:
  Earnings
  Earnings per share
  Risk assets
Return on:
  Stockholders' equity
  Risk assets (RORA)
  Total assets
Capital ratios:
  Capital to risk assets
  Capital to total assets
Competitive standing

It is important that the corporate level indicators be established on the basis of the factors which are of major concern, attention, and action of senior management. Top-management responsibility is to the stockholders and therefore the indicators at this level must relate to the fulfillment of this responsibility. Growth in earnings and earnings per share, as well as RORA and return on stockholders' equity are central measures of profitability and growth. Capital ratios and risk asset growth are parameters closely watched by regulators and management to make sure earning streams are not at the expense of security. Finally, a look at performance versus key competitors provides a background against which to gauge and plan future performance.

Once the appropriate corporate level indicators have been established, it is then important to focus on the proper indicators at lower levels of the organization. To the greatest extent possible, there should be a consistency of the indicators at the two difference levels.

A possible list of indicators at lower levels of the organization would be as follows:

Risk assets.
Profit center earnings (PCE).
Return on risk assets (RORA).
Interest differential revenue.
Commissions.
Staff payments (salary expense and fringe benefit cost).
Number of employees.

Direct other operating expense.

Credit write-offs.

Just looking at PCE does not tell the story in terms of the corporate objectives. RORA shows to what extent the earnings of a profit center are adequate for the level of capital required to support the assets it employs to generate those earnings.

On the expense side, many firms have found that employee totals and salaries must be carefully monitored and continually reviewed in terms of the cost benefit trade-offs. Along these lines, it is appropriate to mention that at least once each year each major staff area should probably be reviewed on the basis of a zero budget. In other words, the total budget by major program or activity should be justified and not just the incremental cost from the prior year.

In addition to the common indicators at the lower levels, each area should be encouraged to develop specialized indicators of performance for review at all levels of management such as:

Retail	Operating	Corporate
Transaction volumes	Cost	Spreads
Collections	Timeliness	Loan commitments
Market share	Quality	Rate sensitivity of portfolio

Market share and transaction volumes are important to a retail business, while loan spreads are more characteristic of the corporate business. Cost and quality are paramount to an operating cost center.

Once indicators have been agreed upon, they become the basis for reviewing, controlling, and measuring performance. Specific objectives for these indicators are established as part of the budget process and actual results are measured against the budgeted objectives.

In summary, it is important that the indicators at all levels, but especially at the lower level, be simple, easily trackable and consistent with indicators at other levels.

ESTABLISHMENT OF REPORTING SYSTEM

Within a banking organization, a system for controlling and measuring financial performance must include the assignment of responsibility for all assets and liabilities as well as all items of income and expense. Ideally, the general ledger and the subsidiary ledger should be supported by subsystems which identify appropriate portions of assets and liabilities and income and expense to individual managers who exercise authority over such items. It should be recognized that this can be a difficult task but at the same time if the system is to have credibility and be effective, it must be done. Without such identifying subsystems, it is extremely difficult to enforce accountability. This can be accomplished by assigning to each management unit a numerical designator which is attached to all loans, deposits, commissions, salary, expenses, and so on. Once the identification process has taken place, the capabilities of today's computers are extremely helpful in keeping track of such items as they pass through the banking organization. At the end of the month or specific accounting period, reports can be generated from the computer data base to meet the needs of the individual managers as well as the senior management of the organization.

The report should be generated in a format which matches the previously identified key indicators for each area. A sample management profit report is shown in Exhibit 25–1, (pp. 322–23).

VALUATION OF FUNDS BETWEEN PROFIT CENTERS

The system for controlling and measuring financial performance within a banking organization must carefully focus on the proper valuation of funds which are generated by one profit center and used by another profit center. Generally, a banking organization is structured along marketing and/or customer grouping lines. Consequently, a group of banking customers within one market segment may have more loans than deposits while another may have more deposits than loans.

The rate (or price) at which these funds are transferred obviously will affect a manager's profit performance. Therefore, it should be a rate that best motivates profit center managers with respect to the generation and use of funds. It must also be a rate that will be viewed by managers as realistic and equitable. To do this, the valuation rate, which is generally referred to as a "pool rate," must reflect the proper value of funds being transferred.

Varying methods have been used by banks for establishing a pool rate. Two of the more common methods used by banks have been: (1) a pool rate based on the average earning rate of the bank's investment portfolio; (2) an average cost of funds rate representing the average interest rate paid for various types of funds.

Within the last decade, a new and different approach for establishing the pool rate for transferring funds between profit centers has evolved. The approach represents a marginal costing concept. Essentially, it is based on the concept that money and/or funds have a value in the open market. To acquire incremental funds, it would be necessary to pay the interest rate dictated by this free market. Consequently, decisions to expand or reduce assets or liabilities in a banking organization should be based on this value for the funds.

A pool rate approach, which is tied to the average earning rate of the bank's investment portfolio, has been rejected in recent years for two major reasons: (1) the rate earned on the investment portfolio reflects in part the effectiveness or ineffectiveness of the portfolio manager in making past investment decisions. To this extent, the average rate earned does not reflect the current economic value of funds; (2) the rate will probably not motivate the deposit generating officer nor the lending officer to make decisions in light of current money market conditions, since the rate is the result of investment decisions made over a period of years and in no way a reflection of the current market environment and rate levels.

The second method, which is based upon an average cost of funds, has also been rejected by many banking institutions in recent years. It has been rejected on the basis that it is not representative of the real world. For instance, a banking organization has a mixture of funds from demand deposits, savings deposits, federal funds, negotiable CDs, other time deposits, and so on. If that same banking organization wanted to acquire an additional $50 million for purposes of making a new loan, it would be most unlikely that the funds mix (and therefore average rate) of the additional $50 million would be the same as the average mix prior to the incremental addition.

Most major banks have now moved toward a marginal valuation of funds concept. They concluded that they needed a pool rate which would motivate their managers to make decisions which were consistent with the overall objectives of the total banking organization. They felt that the pool rate should evaluate the economics of decisions for the profit center manager in the same manner that the individual decisions affect the shareholders.

In thinking about the pool rate, they asked the following questions:

a. If an opportunity arises to attract new deposits in the market area, how much should we be willing to pay? Obviously, any rate less than what is currently being paid for the bank's highest cost funds would result in less expense to the bank once the higher cost funds are replaced with the new funds.
b. How should the individual bank determine the rate or the price to the borrower for a new loan? The rate obviously should consider the cost to attract deposits to fund the new loan.

With these two points in mind, how does an individual bank determine its transfer pool rate? Quite clearly, it should be determined by the cost of acquiring marginal funds in the free marketplace. A

Exhibit 25-1
The Management Profit Report ($ in thousands)

Management Profit Report Banking Group A	Actual			Budget			Variance From Budget		
	Average Amount ($)	Rate (%)	Revenue/ Expense ($)	Average Amount ($)	Rate (%)	Revenue/ Expense ($)	Average Amount ($)	Rate (%)	Revenue/ Expense ($)
Revenue from funds used:									
1. Loans									
2. Other earning assets									
3. Transfer pool									
4. Total Revenue from funds used									
Interest cost on funds									
5. Demand									
6. Negotiable CDs									
7. Other time									
8. Transfer pool									
9. Total interest cost									
10. Interest differential revenue									
11. Fees from services									
12. Net revenue before operating expenses									
Operating expenses									
13. Staff payments									
14. Other operating expenses									

15. Total operating expenses							
16. Net write-offs							
17. Controllable contribution							
18. Fixed costs							
19. Group and Institutional services							
20. Total fixed costs							
21. Earnings before income taxes							
22. Income taxes							
23. Profit center earnings							
24. Return on risk assets							
25. Number of employees							

free market is defined as a funds market in which the bank can readily attract new funds or withdraw funds if they mature. The reason is very straightforward; if a cheaper source of funds were expandable, the individual bank should increase its use of such funds to the maximum extent possible (after due attention to its liquidity requirement) and thereby reduce the use of more expensive funds. This would leave only the most expensive source of funds, in an available market, to be expanded, if the need should arise.

Many banks which have adopted a marginal funds concept for the establishment of their pool rate have used the cost of the negotiable certificate of deposit as the money market instrument which best reflects their marginal cost of funds. Normally, in both high- and low-rate environments (in the absence of restrictive regulations), the negotiable certificate of deposit is the most reasonable money market instrument for determining the marginal value of funds. It meets the criteria of being highly competitive, being readily available in the money market, and being sensitive to pricing for either expansion or contraction of a bank's funding needs. Furthermore, no cheaper source of funds would be readily available since they would have been expanded to their fullest before acquiring higher costing CDs.

In summary, the establishment of a proper rate for transferring funds between profit centers is critical to the viability and creditability of a system for controlling and measuring financial performance in a banking organization.

THE REVIEW PROCESS

An integral part of a system for measuring and controlling financial performance is a structured and disciplined review process. Each banking organization should carefully analyze its own management structure and management style and then develop a review process which is consistent with that structure and style. Some organizations may conclude that a "one-on-one" review process is appropriate whereby a manager reviews with his supervisor on a monthly or quarterly basis the progress in his area versus the committed objective. In other organizations, a larger review meeting, conducted by the supervising officer and many managers at the same level, may be more appropriate. Regardless of the method chosen, it is important that all of the managers in the organization clearly understand the process and know exactly what is expected of them at the review meetings. The requirements and approach to the reviews should be communicated far enough in advance so that managers can adequately prepare themselves for the meetings.

The reviews should be conducted in an open atmosphere on the basis of a team approach to the resolution of key issues. At all times, an adversary approach should be avoided.

Within the organization, staff people can be very helpful in identifying issues which appear to surface from a review of the numbers at their level. However, the staff people should not in any way invade the management province of the individual managers.

It is important to avoid a mass of numbers and paperwork. The reviews will be much more effective if the emphasis is placed on substantive issues which lie behind the actual numbers. Without this kind of a structured and disciplined review process, the system for controlling and measuring financial performance will fall far short of its intended purpose.

CONCLUSION

Over the past decade, most successful banking organizations have concluded that an effective system for controlling and measuring financial performance is an important part of their management process. They have learned from experience that the major objectives of the corporation can be better achieved if key indicators of performance are established at all management levels. Further, experience has taught them that the indicators of performance should be few in number and at the same time they should be easily understood and readibly trackable. However, the key to the success of any system which controls and measures financial performance is directly related to the continued active involvement of management at the most senior levels.

Chapter 26

The General Accounting System

Arlin Disselkoen*

The accounting system of a bank must be organized so that accurate and dependable information is readily available for a variety of users—management, governmental regulatory agencies, investors, and other users of bank services (depositors and borrowers). The accounting systems provide the means to measure past performance so that management can make sound decisions for the future. Bank management should expect to obtain from the accounting records basic data that can be analyzed and used for planning and control. Governmental regulatory agencies specify the components of the bank's accounting system so that information will be available to them in a standardized format for comparison with other banks. Investors expect the bank's accounting records to reflect accurately the status of its assets and liabilities and provide an understandable record by which profitability can be determined. Depositors and borrowers are interested in a bank's soundness and liquidity.

It follows that the general accounting system must conform to "generally accepted accounting principles." While these general principles do, in some cases, provide alternative ways of handling certain accounting transactions with a differential effect on profitability and asset structure, bank accounting has been moving toward greater and greater uniformity. The influence of the regulatory authorities has been significant in that movement. There still exists a difference of opinion on the treatment of some items, such as the recognition and treatment of questionable loans. Bank security analysts, bank accountants, and public accountants have had much discussion on some of these issues.

---

* Senior Vice President, Greeley National Bank, Greeley, Colorado.

The bank may keep its accounting system either on a cash basis or on an accrual basis. There are numerous modifications which amount to a "semiaccrual" accounting system under which some major items are accrued and others handled on a cash basis. In recent years, most banks have moved to an accrual accounting system, since this system produces a much more accurate picture of the bank profitability on a period to period basis. Through the accrual system, the income and expenses are brought into the accounting system at the time they are earned or incurred, and not when the cash transaction takes place.

THE GENERAL LEDGER

The basic record of the accounting system is the general ledger. Summary entries into the general ledger are made each day and include all transactions which have affected the bank's assets, liabilities, capital accounts, and income or expense accounts. The general ledger records cover only the accounts of the bank itself, and do not include any assets held by the bank in a fiduciary capacity. The entries in the general ledger normally come from subsidiary records, such as journals, registers, transaction tickets, and similar records. In effect, the general ledger is a set of control accounts for subsidiary records for the various departments and activities of the bank. The accounts in the ledger are so arranged that an orderly and meaningful presentation of the information can be readily taken from this chart of accounts.

STATEMENT OF CONDITION

Management receives a daily report on the assets and liabilities of the bank through a "statement of condition." This report is normally in the same format as the report of condition, or "call report," that is prepared quarterly to be presented to the regulatory agencies. The daily statement of condition is prepared from the balance in the general ledger accounts following daily entries into those accounts. A condensed version of a statement of condition, including all of the major categories of assets and liabilities, is shown in Exhibit 26–1. This is a condensed version of the call report prescribed by regulatory agencies.

The main accounts in the statement of condition are described as follows.

Cash and Due from Banks

This account shows the total of all coin and currency in the bank vault, plus all funds held in deposit accounts with other commercial banks. Included also are the checks on other banks that are in the

Exhibit 26–1

COMMERCIAL BANK
Statement of Condition
December 31, 19—

Cash and due from banks...............................		$11,100,000
U.S. Treasury securities................................		1,600,000
U.S. government agencies and corporations.....................................		13,400,000
Obligations of states and political subdivisions................................		16,350,000
Other securities.......................................		50,000
Federal funds sold		300,000
Loans..	$54,000,000	
Reserve for loan loss..................................	550,000	
Loans (net of reserves)................................		53,450,000
Bank premises and equipment		2,100,000
Accrued interest receivable		700,000
Other assets		600,000
Total assets		$99,650,000
Demand deposits......................................		29,400,000
Savings deposits......................................		24,500,000
Time deposits..		34,300,000
Total deposits...................................		$88,200,000
Federal funds purchased...............................		1,000,000
Liabilities for borrowed money.......................................		2,200,000
Other liabilities		350,000
Total liabilities..................................		$91,750,000
Subordinated notes and debentures		1,000,000
Equity capital:		
Common stock..		2,000,000
Surplus..		3,200,000
Undivided profits.....................................		1,600,000
Reserve for contingencies..............................		100,000
Total Capital....................................		6,900,000
Total Liabilities and Capital......................		$99,650,000

process of collection (generally called float). For member banks, the required reserve balance that is kept with the Federal Reserve Bank is part of this account.

Investments

Securities purchased and held for the bank's own portfolio are shown in this account. These investments are carried on the books of the bank at book value, which is the net of purchase price (cost) less any amortization of premium on bonds purchased at an amount above par value, plus any discount that has been accrued on securities that were purchased at an amount below par value. Securities held are divided into several major categories:

U.S. Treasury Securities. This account includes direct obligation of the U.S. government, such as Treasury bills, notes, and bonds.

U.S. Government Agency Corporations. Included are bonds, notes and debentures of U.S. government corporations and agencies such as the Federal Intermediate Credit Bank, the Federal Land Bank, Federal Home Loan Banks, and Banks for Cooperatives.

Obligations of States and Political Subdivisions. This account contains the value of obligations, including warrants and tax anticipation notes, that have been issued by municipalities or by school, irrigation, drainage and reclaimation districts. Included also are obligations of local housing authorities.

Other Securities. This is normally not a major account, but does include Federal Reserve Bank stock (required to be held by member banks), and miscellaneous securities that are acquired by the bank.

Federal Funds Sold

Banks with collected funds in excess of the required allowances in the Federal Reserve account may sell (loan) these funds to other commercial banks on a one business day basis. The funds are loaned to banks that need the added balances in their reserve account. This category also includes repurchase agreements, a situation where a bank with excess funds purchases securities from another bank and simultaneously executes an agreement to resell the identical or similar securities at a predetermined future date and price.

Loans

This account is normally the largest asset account. It includes all obligations to the bank made in the form of loans to individuals, partnerships, corporations, financial institutions, banks (both domestic and foreign), brokers, dealers in securities and governmental units and agencies, either on a secured or unsecured basis. It also includes unauthorized loans, such as overdrafts on demand deposit checking accounts.

Some types of installment loans where repayment is scheduled on a monthly basis include interest that is calculated at the beginning of the loan and added to the face value of the loan. When these loans are included on the balance sheet, the interest that has been collected but not yet earned is deducted from the loan total.

Reserve for Loan Losses

Sound accounting procedures require that banks set aside from operating earnings sufficient reserves to cover possible losses on loans. The amount required will vary with individual banks, depending on the quality of their loan portfolio and their actual loan loss experience. Amounts determined by bank management (with the concurrence of supervisory authorities) determined to be loan losses are deducted from this account. Conversely, any recoveries on loans previously charged off are added to the balance in the reserve account. The balance in this account is shown on the asset side of the balance as a direct deduction from the total loan account.

Bank Premises and Equipment

Included in this account is the book value of all fixed assets, such as land, buildings, leasehold improvements and furniture and equipment. The book value is cost less depreciation charged and the account is shown on a net basis.

Accrued Interest Receivable

As mentioned earlier, modern accounting practice requires that all major items of income be included in the books as the income is earned, rather than when it is collected. This account, therefore, contains all interest income, on loans as well as securities, that has been earned, but as of the date of the statement, has not yet been collected.

Other Assets

Included here would be a variety of items, depending on the individual bank. Illustrative items would be prepaid expenses, direct lease financing, real estate owned other than bank premises, and investments in consolidated subsidiaries.

LIABILITIES

The double entry system of accounting requires that assets be offset by the total of liabilities and equity capital. The major liability accounts are the several types of deposits which comprise the primary source of funds for a bank.

Demand Deposits

Demand deposits are normally checking accounts deposited by individuals, partnerships, corporations, governmental bodies, or associations or groups of individuals. These funds are withdrawn primarily by check, although the funds can be transferred by bank wire and through the various systems currently available in the form of electronic funds transfer systems. As the name indicates, the funds are payable on demand. Also included in this category are official checks, such as cashier checks and certified checks, until these items clear.

Savings Deposits

Savings deposits are received from sources similar to demand deposits, although there is a dollar limit on the amount that can be deposited in a savings account by a corporation. These savings deposits earn interest on the balance maintained (the rate varies among banks).

Time Deposits

Time deposits are also from the same source as the two categories mentioned above, but these deposits have a specified maturity or renewal dates. In certain cases, there are special withdrawal conditions. Deposits can be evidenced by certificates (either negotiable or nonnegotiable) and other instruments. The interest rate paid varies with the amount with the stated maturity date.

Federal Funds Purchased

This account is the exact opposite of the asset account "Federal Funds Sold." In this instance, the bank has borrowed federal reserve balances from other banks on a one business day basis. Included also in this account are liabilities based upon the situation where the bank sells securities with an agreement to repurchase the identical or similar securities at a later date. In cases where banks make a market in federal funds, the bank may, on any one day, find itself in the position of being both a purchaser and a seller of federal funds.

Liabilities for Borrowed Money

This account represents borrowing by the bank from commercial banks (either secured or unsecured) or from the Federal Reserve Bank where the bank is a member of the Federal Reserve System.

Other Liabilities

This account would normally include major categories of expenses that have been accrued but not yet paid, such as income or real estate taxes due, interest accrued on time and savings deposits, and dividends declared but not paid.

Subordinated Notes and Debentures

The liability is carried between "total liabilities" (all of the items shown above are liabilities) and the equity capital section on the balance sheet. In this account are capital notes or debentures that have been issued by the bank. Capital notes and debentures have a specified interest rate and a definite maturity date. Holders of these investments are subordinated to depositors but do not share in the earnings of the bank as do the holders of common stock.

EQUITY CAPITAL

Equity capital is represented by common stock outstanding, surplus, undivided profits, and equity reserves. If the bank has issued preferred stock, that stock will also be included as part of equity capital.

Common Stock

This account shows the total par value of common stock that has been authorized and is outstanding at the time of the statement.

Surplus

Surplus account is the total of all amounts transferred from undivided profits, plus any amount that was paid for capital stock over its par value, or "paid in surplus."

Undivided Profits

Although some part of undivided profits may have been placed on the books at the time stock was sold, the major portion is net operating earnings that have been recorded and not been paid out in the form of dividends, nor transferred to other capital accounts.

Reserves for Contingencies and Other Capital Reserves

This account represents any amount that has been transferred from undivided profits into this account for either specific capital reserve purposes, or for unforeseen declines or shrinkages in the book value of assets. In 1976, regulations were issued that required banks to place in the reserve for contingencies account amounts for reserves for loan losses that arose from a transfer from the undivided profits account.

This account should not include any elements of known loss or losses, the amount of which can be estimated with reasonable accuracy.

The above list describes the principal accounts included in the statement of condition or balance sheet. Banks may maintain numerous divisions of those accounts to provide detailed information on the categories of assets and liabilities in which management has a special interest. Division of the accounts must be such so that they can be aggregated into the form required for the call reports (consolidated statement of condition) required by the supervisory authorities. For that reporting, the accounts must fit exactly into the categories specified, no modifications being allowed in the description of the individual accounts.

THE INCOME STATEMENT

The objective of bank management, guided by the directors and for the ultimate benefit of stockholders, is to operate the bank in such a way as to make a profit. The business of banking involves using deposits, borrowed funds, and capital funds to acquire earning assets and to do so in a way to cover expenses and produce a profit. This process must be tempered by prudent management that safeguards the assets and adheres to regulations while responding to the credit needs of the community.

The income produced from assets is recorded in a series of income accounts and the cost of acquiring deposits and managing the assets and liabilities is recorded in expense accounts, both group of accounts being a part of the general ledger. Income and expense accounts become the basis for the preparation of the income, or operating statement which measures net income (according to recognized accounting principles) for a given accounting period.

Since most operating statements are prepared on a monthly basis, the income and expense accounts are closed each month. Accruals are made for income and expense accounts to reflect the actual expenses that have been incurred that month and the income that has been earned that month, regardless of whether the cash transactions have taken place. Income and expense items that are too small to justify the special effort of an accrual calculation normally are booked as income or expense as received or paid.

The primary income (or revenue) accounts are stated below.

Interest and Fees on Loans

This source of income includes all revenue collected on loans, including interest and discount earned plus fees and other charges levied against loans.

Income on Federal Funds Sold

Income that is received on federal funds is normally recorded daily, since the interest is usually received when the funds are paid for these one business day transactions. Included also is interest earned from transactions covering securities sold under repurchase agreements.

Interest on Securities

Included in this account is interest collected, plus the accrual of discount, minus the amortization of premiums on U.S. treasury securities, the obligations of U.S. government agencies, the obligations of states and political subdivisions, and on any other securities.

Income from Fiduciary Activity

If a bank conducts trust activities, the income or other charges for services performed by the trust department would be included here.

Service Charges on Deposit Accounts

Banks levy charges on checking accounts, based either on activity levels (such as checks paid, deposits made, and checks deposited) or related to minimum deposit balance, or both. Such charges are usually collected monthly and arc a part of the bank's income stream.

Other Service Charges, Commissions and Fees

This revenue account would include a variety of miscellaneous revenue sources such as check cashing fees, loan participation fees, fees from servicing mortgage loans, direct lease finance income, insurance income, or fees for issuing official checks.

Other Income

This account would include all other sources of revenue. Normal items in this account would be income from the rental of safe deposit boxes, tellers' overages, and capital gains or losses on the sale of furniture, fixtures, and equipment.

Expenses are classified into logical categories to provide the basis for analysis and management control. The expense categories specified by regulatory authorities encourage uniform treatment of expenses and make it feasible to compare expense levels among banks in a meaningful way. The primary expense categories are noted below.

Salaries and Employee Benefits

This expense category is often a major expense item for the bank. It includes direct compensation of all officers and employees, plus benefits such as bonuses, contributions to pension or retirement plans, profit sharing contributions, insurance premiums paid by the bank for hospitalization or life insurance, and any other fringe benefits. Also included would be overtime wages.

Interest on Deposits

Any interest paid on time or savings deposits is included in this account. Expense is booked when the funds are on deposit at the bank and while the benefit is received from the funds, rather than when the interest is actually paid or credited to the depositor's accounts. In recent years, the higher rates paid on such deposits and the increasing proportion of time and savings deposits to total deposits, make interest expense items a major outlay by the bank.

Expense of Federal Funds Purchased

Interest expense is booked and paid daily as the funds are borrowed and when the benefit is received. Normally interest is not accrued since the payment of interest occurs when the funds are borrowed. Also included in this account would be interest paid on transactions under which securities are sold under repurchase agreements.

Interest on Borrowed Money

This expense is interest paid on subordinated notes and debentures, along with any interest paid on current borrowings or bills payable.

Net Occupancy Expense

This account represents the total expense connected with the owning, renting, and maintaining the bank premises. Expense items would include utilities, insurance, janitorial services, interest on mortgages, real estate taxes, and depreciation charges. This category is net of rental income on bank premises.

Furniture and Equipment Expense

This account covers repairs and maintenance of furniture and equipment, any taxes on this equipment, rental costs of equipment, and depreciation charges.

Provision for Possible Loan Losses

The amount estimated by bank management to be sufficient to bring the balance in the Reserve for Loan Losses Account to an adequate level to absorb expected loan losses is charged to this account. The charge is based upon management's knowledge of its loan portfolio.

Other Expenses

This expense group includes a variety of outlays such as advertising expenses, insurance costs, stationery and supplies, postage, telephone expense, directors' fees, and contributions.

Exhibit 26–2 is a summary of the typical operating statement (sources and disposition of income). The sum of the several categories of operat-

Exhibit 26–2

HOMETOWN BANK
Sources and Disposition of Income
January 1–December 31, 19—

Operating Income:

Interest and fees on loans	$433,795
Income on federal funds sold	22,946
Interest on U.S. Treasury securities	44,406
Interest on U.S. government agencies and corporations	23,489
Interest on obligations of states and political subdivisions	49,185
Interest on other bonds and securities	5,332
Income from trust department	16,019
Service charges on deposit accounts	15,553
Other service charges, commissions, and fees	16,535
Other income	38,321
Total operating income	$665,581

Operating Expense:

Salaries and employee benefits	$126,866
Interest on deposits	262,459
Expense of federal funds purchased	33,229
Interest on borrowed money	3,771
Interest on subordinated notes and debentures	2.940
Net occupancy expense of bank premises	23,246
Furniture and equipment expense	15,327
Provision for possible loan losses	36,124
Other expenses	71,850
Total operating expenses	$575,812

Income before income taxes and securities gain (loss)		$ 89,769
Applicable income taxes on operating earnings		17,926
Income before securities gains (losses)		$ 71,843
Securities gain	$3,437	
Applicable income taxes	1,269	2,168
Net Income		$ 74,011

ing expenses produces total operating expenses, which, when deducted from total operating income, produces "income before income taxes and securities gains and losses." Estimated income tax applied to that level of income is deducted to produce the figure "income before security gains and losses." Any security gains or losses are called "below the line" items, because they are not considered a part of normal operating income of a bank. Any such gain or loss, after adjustment for the applicable income taxes effect, is added to or subtracted from the above figure to produce stated net income.

ACCOUNTING AS A MANAGEMENT TOOL

Financial statements are prepared for many reasons, one of which is that internal management depends on accurate financial data being produced by the accounting system. It is in the area of internal reporting that the accountant can probably make his or her greatest contribution to the bank. There is unlimited opportunity for imagination and creativity in providing timely and accurate information to all levels of management. Such information is the basis for judging the liquidity status of the bank and the major factors which affect profitability. The accounting system becomes the basis for budgeting and profit planning. Cost accounting systems augment the general accounting system and help set standards and levels of expectations, as well as to establish prices for various bank services. Further, the accounting system must be in such form and maintained in such a way as to facilitate the auditing function in the bank.

While the methods of accounting have progressed over the years from journal entries and posting by hand to complicated computer accounting systems, the basic structure of the general accounts does not change significantly. New expense and income categories may be added. Refinements are made in asset, liability, and capital accounts, and much more elaborate uses are made of accounting data for management and supervisory purposes. Yet double-entry system of accounting requires a certain basic structure. The many different users of financial information on a bank's activities depend upon that system for their basic information.

Chapter 27

Audit and Internal Control

William H. Low, CBA*

The importance of an internal control and audit system in every bank is a long established axiom for safeguarding the assets of the bank for depositors and stockholders. The scope of the audit program and the complexity of the system for internal control will necessarily vary with the size and structure of the bank's organization.

The status of the auditor and the audit program have raised considerably in recent years as a result of the expanding professional expertise among auditors. An auditor who utilizes the most effective methods and techniques can provide meaningful information to management on the status of the bank's accounting system and its operations and, thus, earn the continued support of the management. To do so, the auditor must not only stay current in changes in bank accounting systems and operations but must also constantly upgrade audit techniques and procedures to cope with changes, especially in the field of computerization.

DIRECTOR'S RESPONSIBILITY

The board of directors has the prime responsibility of seeing that the bank has an effective audit and internal control program. The broad responsibilities of bank directors are discussed in an earlier chapter, but few of these responsibilities are as important as the board's responsibility for an effective auditing program.

The board of directors through the use of its Audit Committee must provide for an effective review of the internal and external audit pro-

---

* Auditor, Society National Bank, Cleveland, Ohio.

gram on a continuous basis. The scope of the audit committee activities should include: the selection of the auditors, approval of the overall scope of the audit, review of results of the audit, approval of the system for internal controls, and a periodic review of that system. An audit committee, properly staffed, can provide for independent review of the internal and external audit program and can give increased assurance to the board of directors, stockholders, and to the public as to the soundness of the bank.

AUDITOR AND STAFF

An important element of a successful audit program is independence. In order to be effective the auditors must serve in a staff relationship, without authority or direct control over those people and departments whose work they review. Moreover, this review and appraisal of the work of others does not relieve them of their own assigned responsibilities.

The auditor must have complete authority in carrying out the audit program and in reporting his or her findings. The auditor may be administratively responsible to a senior officer at the policy-making level, and should normally send copies of the reports to the bank's chief executive officer and to others, as required. However, the auditor's ultimate reporting responsibility is directly to the board or its audit committee.

In the selection of the auditor and the audit staff, it is essential to attract and develop a professional group of personnel with adequate technical competence. Further, a program of continued education should be maintained and include periodic attendance at seminars, as well as in-house training sessions led by capable and experienced personnel.

AUDITOR QUALIFICATIONS

An effective audit program requires an auditor not only with excellent professional competence, but a staff composed of well-rounded individuals with many attributes. A statement on internal auditing and the auditor by the Bank Administration Institute describes the qualifications of the auditor as follows:

Qualifications of the auditor have a direct bearing on the adequacy of an internal audit and control program. Selecting a person of proper capabilities for the job is of utmost importance.

The job specifications for a good auditor call for an unusual combination of personal qualities: sound judgement, integrity, imagination, initiative, courage, a high degree of objectivity, and skill in personal relationships. An educational background that includes accounting theory and practice and commercial law is recommended. The auditor must know audit standards, objectives, and procedures. He needs to have general knowledge of all aspects of bank operating procedures and practices.

Flexibility in adjusting to changing conditions is essential if the audit and control program is to keep pace with new systems, procedures, and services, as well as changes in laws and regulations.[1]

At least two professional associations have aided in raising the bank auditor to professional status through their continuing educational programs and professional designations. The Bank Administration Institute and the Institute of Internal Auditors offer professional designations to candidates who qualify and pass the eligibility requirements. These two programs have been very successful in furthering the professional status of internal bank auditing.

AUDIT RESPONSIBILITIES

As stated earlier, the board of directors has the responsibility for assuring that management has established and is maintaining an adequate system of audit and internal control. Therefore, the board should require that management formulate and implement policies providing for and supporting an internal auditing organization within the bank. These policies should authorize the auditor to issue audit reports and make recommendations, and should require appropriate response and necessary corrective action to such recommendations.

The general responsibilities of the internal auditor are summarized best by the Institute of Internal Auditors in their "Statement of Responsibilities of the Internal Auditor" as follows:[2]

> Internal auditing is an independent appraisal activity within an organization for the review of operations as a service to management. It is a managerial control which functions by measuring and evaluating the effectiveness of other controls.
>
> This objective can be attained by the following activities:
>
> Reviewing and appraising the soundness, adequacy, and application of accounting, financial, and other operating controls, and promoting effective control at reasonable cost.
>
> Ascertaining the extent of compliance with established policies, plans, and procedures.
>
> Ascertaining the extent to which company assets are accounted for and safeguarded from losses of all kinds.

---

[1] From "A Statement of Principle on Internal Auditing and the Auditor," adopted by the Bank Administration Institute in 1966.

[2] Originally issued in 1947 and revised in 1957 and 1971.

Ascertaining the reliability of management data developed within the organization.

Appraising the quality of performance in carrying out assigned responsibilities.

Recommending operating improvements.

AUDIT PROGRAM

As the first step in scope of establishing a complete auditing system, the auditor should establish and document the scope of the program. A list of principal objectives should include the following:

1. *Assets.* To determine that assets are in existence at the audit date, that they are fairly stated in accordance with generally accepted accounting principles, and that they are adequately safeguarded.
2. *Liabilities.* To determine that all liabilities are disclosed and accounted for, and transactions are promptly and properly recorded in accounts.
3. *Income.* To determine that all income which should accrue from invested assets or services has been recorded properly.
4. *Expenses.* To determine that all costs and expenses are recorded properly and supported as charges against the bank.
5. *Internal Control.* To ascertain that the system of internal control and accounting are functioning properly.
6. *Errors and Recommendations.* To prevent and detect material errors or defalcations. To recognize areas in the bank's operations where increased efficiencies, cost reductions or improvements can be made.

In order to accomplish these program objectives, the audit work should be properly planned, supervised, and evaluated.

A formal written audit program should provide for individual comprehensive audits of each department and function of the bank. Further, in order to accomplish the desired frequency of audits and to complete the annual program, an annual timetable should be prepared. An audit date and man-hours budget should be established. The schedule should be given to the audit staff to anticipate deadlines, but the schedule must remain confidential so as to retain the element of surprise audits.

AUDIT PROCEDURES

An important element in modern auditing is to coordinate the account balance verification procedures with a review and evaluation of internal control. The extent of detailed audit procedures to be undertaken is dependent on the evaluation of the adequacy of internal con-trols. For instance, if the internal control is satisfactory, the staff is justified in performing only basic audit procedures and confirmation of accounts. If internal control is deemed unsatisfactory, it is essential to extend the auditing procedures for further validity tests.

The practical way to illustrate this approach is to begin by interview-ing the head of the division or department being audited to determine the procedures and controls established in a given bank function. The auditor accumulates the related data and can either prepare a flowchart or document the procedures in narrative style. The next step would be for the auditor to observe and test to determine the extent to which the established controls and procedures are actually functioning. An evaluation can then be made which would further determine the ex-tent of further testing of transactions. Finally, after additional tests are made, the auditor can then make a judgment as to the adequacy of internal control.

AUDIT WORK PAPERS

The audit work papers are the tools of an auditor. Good work papers contain step-by-step audit instructions and, in the completed form, reflect the documentation of the audit tests completed and the audit findings. During an audit the work papers can be a valuable aid in documenting what audit work has been completed and what further work is to be done. After the audit has been completed, the work papers facilitate oral discussions of the audit findings and preparation of the audit report.

Since the work papers are valuable evidence of the audit work, they should be well organized, neat, accurate, and maintained for their useful life even after the audit.

AUDIT FINDINGS

Upon completion of the field work of each audit, the audit supervisor reviews the work completed to determine that sufficient evidence has been acquired during the audit to provide for the conclusions in the audit report. The results of the auditor's inquiries, observations, tests, and confirmations represent the sources of his or her opinions and recommendations and can be summarily called the "audit findings." All of the supporting materials acquired in the audit should be well documented in such a way to facilitate easy reference at a later date. Further, the findings should be presented clearly to support the conclu-sions found in the audit report.

At the conclusion of the audit the audit findings should be discussed thoroughly with the person responsible for the unit audited. Such a discussion is important to ensure a clear understanding of the findings and an opportunity to encourage support for corrective action or recommended changes.

AUDIT REPORT

The audit report is probably the most important phase of the audit since the quality of the audit performed is often judged primarily by the contents of the written audit report. Therefore, it is essential that the audit report be written with great care and prepared promptly after each audit. The report should be written in a manner to be helpful to the person responsible for the unit audited, and in clear, concise language. This idea was exposed effectively by Leonard E. Berry when he said, "The tone should convey the idea that improvement is needed, not that you are only reporting deficiencies."[3]

The audit report should contain a summary of the audit findings and include the auditor's overall opinion of the unit audited. The auditor should not only include comments and recommendations on problem areas, but also suggest workable solutions. The auditor should consider the optimum cost-benefit relationship prior to recommending stronger internal controls. The report should be constructive in nature but, when warranted, praise should also be included.

As Lawrence B. Sawyer said, "Reports are the auditor's opportunity to get management's undivided attention. That is how he should regard reporting—as an opportunity. He should not see it as dreary drudgery, but rather as a prized opportunity to show management what he has to offer toward business betterment."[4]

AUDIT FOLLOW-UP

To finalize the audit report process, the audit department should request a prompt reply as to the corrective action taken on audit exceptions and recommendations. The auditor should make a final check to determine that the corrective action is satisfactory.

EDP AUDITING

Due to the rapid changes and increased complexity of computer-based accounting systems, the modern auditor has been challenged to stay abreast and adapt his audit responsibilities and capabilities.

---

[3] Leonard E. Berry, "Are You a Thick-Skinned Auditor?" *The Internal Auditor,* January/February 1976, p. 46.

[4] Lawrence B. Sawyer, "The Practice of Modern Internal Auditing," (The Institute of Internal Auditors, Inc., 1973), p. 356.

Without an adequate knowledge of electronic data processing (EDP), the auditor is not capable of evaluating the accounting controls as effected from the point of computer input, through the computer processes, and resulting as output on computer reports. Therefore, a portion of the regular training given to each member of the audit staff must be devoted to a familiarization of computers, programming, and system design.

In the larger banks and on larger audit staffs, one or more EDP audit specialists will be required to perform the detailed EDP audit assignments.

EDP AUDIT PROGRAM

In all audits it is essential to review internal controls. Whenever a computer system is involved, it is also necessary to review the computer-processing system and the controls involved in that environment.

An EDP audit program is not complete without conducting independent audits of the computer operations department, as well as the systems and programming department. An additional type of EDP audit that should be considered is a post-implementation audit. This audit is an independent review of a new system conducted shortly after installation to determine that a new operating system is performing as originally defined and intended. Such an audit can be beneficial to management, as well as the user to assess the effectiveness of project control.

The internal auditor also has the responsibility to be involved in new systems development and can be of assistance in the system design. It is important that adequate controls be built into the system and it is of importance that these controls be determined in the initial design phase. Another way in which the auditor's experience can be utilized is in the development of adequate test data to ensure complete testing of the new system.

AUDIT SOFTWARE

Audit software programs are rapidly becoming a valuable tool for the auditor. It is feasible to write computer audit programs for many audit purposes such as trial listings, testing or sampling of accounts, confirmation notices, calculations, comparing records, and creating exception reports of audit significance. The imagination of the auditor is the only limitation in using the computer for audit purposes. Audit time and costs can be saved and the validity of the audit findings can be improved. The use of audit software can be a valuable aid in coping with the growth of accounts and transactions processed by the computer in increasing complex systems.

The total area of EDP auditing is such a challenging field of endeavor that the internal auditor, to be effective, must maintain a high level of competence in all fields of electronic data processing, but especially in the development of computer software. Charles A. Pauley made a statement in the same vein when he said: "So whether we think in terms of service to management or simply in terms of self-preservation, the conclusion is the same. We auditors have a responsibility to insure that our organizations are protected from the consequences of faulty systems design. And, we take whatever action is necessary to meet the challenges that this responsibility presents."[5]

INTERNAL CONTROL AND SAFEGUARDS

Internal control is an essential tool of management of every bank. A system of internal control includes a plan of organization, directors' policies, management directives, adequate personnel, and a system of checks and balances throughout the operations to safeguard the assets and provide accurate accounting data. An added function of internal control is to encourage adherence to prescribed management policies and promote operational efficiency.

It is very important that the system of internal control be reviewed periodically by someone independent of the operations and controls and to evaluate the system objectively. For this reason the auditor is the best candidate to evaluate internal controls and report to management on compliance and/or deviations.

One of the most important internal controls to maintain is a separation of duties in each function of the bank. No one person should dominate a transaction from start to finish. If more than one person is involved in each transaction an automatic check is provided. An example of this concept is that a loan officer should never be allowed to disburse note proceeds, take note payments, or post loan accounting records.

Another effective internal control policy is to require all personnel to take an uninterrupted vacation of at least two weeks each year. A similar policy to enforce absence from the same duties is to periodically rotate the duties of personnel. With these two properly administered policies any exceptions to procedures can be brought to the attention of a second party for investigation.

An additional important internal control is often referred to as either

---

[5] Charles A. Pauley, "Audit Responsibilities in the Design of Computerized Systems," *The Internal Auditor*, July/August 1969, p. 32.

joint custody, dual custody, or dual control. Joint custody is safeguarding of bank assets, records, or other valuables by means of requiring two or more persons to complete transactions, or to access vaults or locked storage.

The usual example of dual custody is to provide dual locks or combinations to vaults and make it necessary for two employees to access such locked storage. It is important that each employee be carefully selected for this responsibility as each should be conscientious in carrying out his or her duties.

PERSONNEL POLICY COVERING INTERNAL AUDITS

The foundation of internal control is very dependent on well-qualified and motivated personnel. Personnel policies should be documented for proper selection, training, adequate compensation and fringe benefits, and effective supervision of all bank personnel.

There has been a recent trend among banks to establish a "conflict of interest policy" and require bank personnel to make an annual written statement on compliance with such policy.

FRAUD

It is of utmost importance for banks to maintain public confidence in financial institutions. The bank auditor can contribute immensely to a bank's image by determining that internal controls and operating procedures are functioning in a way to protect the bank from losses due to inefficiencies, inaccuracies, irregularities, and willful manipulations.

Prevention and detection of internal and external fraud in banks have always been major functions of bank auditors. There is no part of the auditor's duties more important that than to provide systems and procedures to reduce fraud. The audit program should be designed to provide a review of internal controls to detect opportunity for fraud. Where weaknesses are found, or if any suspicious acts or employees are reported, the auditor should implement adequate audit procedures.

External frauds generally cost banks more than internal fraud losses. Prevention of external frauds is aided by appropriate security devices, on-line teller systems, and adequate training and supervision of tellers.

CONCLUSION

The internal auditor must reflect a management viewpoint and be concerned with cost reduction and profitability, as well as safeguarding the assets and ensuring the effective utilization of the bank's resources.

This enlarged viewpoint and scope of auditing is termed "operational auditing" and is accomplished simultaneously with the financial audit. This expanded and more important role mentioned can be severed by the auditor who sheds the daily operating functions of internal control and places them in the hands of operating management. Such an arrangement also enables the auditor to exercise independence when evaluating the internal controls.

Substantial challenges and opportunities are available for the innovative auditor. The auditor who stays abreast of the continuous changes in banking and auditing and maintains high professional standards can be a valuable member of the management team.

Chapter 28

External Audits for Banks

*A. H. Cloud**

Martin F. Mertz†

One of the important questions bank managements and boards of directors must answer in considering external audits for banks is, "Do we need an external audit?" There are many answers which could be given to this question. However, most of these can be summarized in bank directors' moral and legal responsibilities for bank operations; the obligation of banks to disclose and report accurate, reliable data to interested parties; and the relationship of external audits to internal audit and internal control in all industries including banks.

Each of these factors and the manner in which it justifies the need for bank audits is discussed in the following paragraphs.

INTERNAL AND EXTERNAL AUDITS AND THE RESPONSIBILITIES OF BANK MANAGEMENT

Moral Responsibility of Bank Directors

The directors of U.S. banks occupy a place of responsibility and power in the national economy, in that the policy direction of the banks of the nation is ultimately charged to the board of directors. In electing directors, bank stockholders normally try to elect individuals in the community who are successful, reputable, and on whom

---

* Partner, Peat, Marwick, Mitchell & Co., Dallas, Texas.

† Partner in Charge of Banking Practice, Peat, Marwick, Mitchell & Co., New York, New York.

they and the general public can rely with confidence to exercise sound judgment in directing the affairs of the bank. It is to these individuals that bank stockholders and depositors look to obtain the maximum return on invested capital while at the same time provide the necessary safeguards over community funds. These responsibilities, which include broad responsibility for determining that the condition of the bank is sound, that its transactions are properly recorded, and that its condition and results of operations are factually reported and disclosed to those who are relying on them, should not be lightly accepted or casually fulfilled.

Legal Responsibility of Bank Directors

The legal responsibility of bank directors to cause audits of banks to be made is not clearly defined.

At the state level, banking statutes are inconsistent in requirements for outside audits of banks. Some state banking statutes have no outside examination requirements. Others have statutes which are couched in general, ambiguous language, and hence offer no guidance to the directors. Still other statutes call for outside examination but waive the requirements under certain conditions.

At the national level, there are more specific stipulations for outside examinations of banks. Regulation F of the Federal Reserve Board of Governors, issued pursuant to the Securities Acts Amendments of 1964, and the similar regulations issued by the Federal Deposit Insurance Corporation and the Comptroller of the Currency, pursuant to the same act, require banks under the supervision of these authorities, and having in excess of 500 stockholders, to report annually on an accrual accounting basis. This report must be certified by the principal accounting officer of the bank and its auditor, or by an independent public accountant.

In addition, Regulation 9 of the Comptroller of the Currency includes the following requirement with respect to audits of bank trust departments:

A committee of directors, exclusive of any active officers of the bank, shall at least once during each calendar year and within 15 months of the last such audit, make suitable audits of the trust department or cause suitable audits to be made by auditors responsible only to the board of directors, and at such time shall ascertain whether the department has been administered in accordance with law, Regulation 9, and sound fiduciary principles. The board of directors may elect, in lieu of such periodic audits, to adopt an adequate continuous audit system. A report of the audits and examination required under this section, together with the action taken thereon, shall be noted in the minutes of the board of directors.

At the individual bank level, the bylaws of many banks require bank directors to make, or cause to be made, periodic examinations of a bank on their own behalf. However, in far too many banks this legal requirement goes unheeded. Further, directors are liable for common-law negligence (failure to use reasonable or ordinary care) in directing the affairs of the bank, as evidenced by many court decisions to that effect.

Obligation of Banks to Interested Parties

Banks invest billions of dollars each year—by lending, by investing in securities, and by investing trust funds in their fiduciary capacity. In doing so, they obtain and depend upon accurate, reliable, certified financial information. They can act intelligently and competently because of the disclosure requirements and certification of financial statements practices applied to other businesses.

In order to obtain funds for such investments, banks compete with other financial institutions for available funds from many sources. Each of these available sources—individual depositors, commercial depositors, corporate treasurers, investors, and stockholders—is an interested group desiring and deserving accurate, reliable financial information with which to appraise the financial condition and results of operation of a bank before entrusting funds to the bank as a depositor or investing funds in it.

In order to compete successfully in the marketplace for capital funds, which are necessary to sustain continued growth, both in the individual bank and in the banking industry as a whole, banks must instill confidence in the financial information they report. Such confidence can be earned by a historic record of growth, by evidence of a competent investment policy based on soundly invested assets embodying adequate liquidity, and by periodic disclosure of these and other pertinent facts through financial reports certified by a reliable independent public accountant.

Relationship of External Audit Function to Internal Audit and Control

The preceding chapter discussed internal audit and fraud control in banks. It is important that the reader understand the triangular relationship of internal control, internal audit, and external audit, and the manner in which each complements the other.

The American Institute of Certified Public Accountants defines internal control in the following manner:

Internal control comprises a plan of organization and all of the coordinated methods and measures adopted within a business to:

(1) Safeguard its assets.
(2) Check the accuracy and reliability of its accounting data.
(3) Promote operational efficiency.
(4) Encourage adherence to prescribed managerial policies.

As discussed later in the "Audit Reports" section of this chapter, an audit is of necessity of a test nature. Accordingly, the auditor's examination, based on the concept of selective testing of the data being examined, is subject to the inherent risk that material errors or irregularities, if they exist, will not be detected. Instead, an effective internal control system represents the principal, although not infallible, safeguard against potential errors or irregularities. The establishment of an internal control system is the responsibility of bank management. It is the responsibility of the internal audit function to review the system and to make sufficient tests of the records and procedures of the bank to determine whether the internal control procedures are being adhered to in actual practice. Thus, the internal audit function provides internal assurance to bank management and to bank boards of directors that the internal control system is operating effectively.

The external auditor uses the internal audit and control functions in conducting an examination of a bank. The primary objective of an examination of bank financial statements by an independent public accountant is the expression of an opinion on the fairness with which those statements present the financial position of the bank, the results of its operations, and the changes in its financial position in accordance with generally accepted accounting principles consistently applied. To accomplish this objective, the independent accountant reviews and test checks the internal audit and internal control efforts of the bank and adjusts the scope of his work accordingly, in order to perform only sufficient audit work to enable him to express an opinion on the financial statements. It follows that a sound internal control system, under continuous review and test by a competent internal auditor, can decrease materially the nature and extent of auditing procedures required by an independent public accountant to express an opinion on the financial statements of a bank. Thus, the work of the independent public accountant gives bank management and the board of directors of the bank an objective professional appraisal of the effectiveness of the internal audit and internal control program of the bank with constructive recommendations for improvement, and provides an independent opinion on the financial statements of the bank.

In summary, a continuous system of effective internal controls, a competent, modern internal audit program and annual audits by qualified independent public accountants are considered essential to the fulfillment of the responsibilities of bank managements and boards of directors.

SELECTION OF A QUALIFIED AUDITOR

The preceding paragraphs outlined the need for external audits for banks. The question naturally arises, "Who is qualified to conduct them?"

Examinations by Supervisory Authorities

Many bankers, and bank directors, rely on the assumption that examinations conducted by supervisory authorities constitute bank audits, and that such examinations relieve directors and bank management of the audit responsibility. This is a false assumption. The purpose of supervisory examinations, as expressed generally by the agencies involved, is to determine whether or not the bank is solvent, is complying with the applicable statutes, and is being directed by competent management employing sound management policies. In comparing external bank audits with supervisory examinations, a former chairman of the Federal Deposit Insurance Corporation stated: "An examination does utilize some audit techniques—but it is not an audit."

Bank directors, who are vested with the responsibility for periodic bank audits, have no control over the scope of the supervisory examination or its timing. The procedures carried out by the supervisory authorities vary from bank to bank, depending upon their opinion of the quality of management and the time available for examination. Many supervisory authorities have had a continuing shortage of personnel and have been unable to conduct all of the bank examinations planned during a specified period.

With respect to the obligation of banks to disclose independent, accurate, reliable data to interested parties, it is important to note that the examination standards and procedures of supervisory agencies vary from state to state, as do the education, training, and experience qualifications required of examiners. Such inconsistencies offer little assurance to interested parties that reliable procedures are being observed in supervisory authority examinations. It is generally recognized that supervisory examinations and related actions are directed primarily toward protection of the depositor, rather than the stockholder.

In addition, reports issued by supervisory authorities, which include comments and recommendations resulting from examinations, are considered to be the property of the supervisory authorities and are issued to the bank and its board of directors for confidential use. Inasmuch as such examination reports are not a matter of public record, they are not available to bank stockholders and depositors, or to potential bank depositors, creditors, investors, or investment analysts.

Examinations by Directors

The directors of many banks have attempted to fulfill their examination responsibilities by conducting periodic examinations themselves. Although these efforts are commendable, they rarely constitute effective audits. Experience, education, training, technical knowledge, and banking know-how are required to make effective bank audits, and members of the examining committee of a board of directors normally do not possess such technical qualifications. In addition, bank directors, with their own business interests to pursue, do not have the time to devote to the proper planning, entry, performance, and follow-up necessary to an effective bank audit. In attempting to direct the examination themselves, directors quite often rely heavily on bank officers and employees to carry out the audit program. Advance notice to bank personnel is obviously a contradiction of one of the most important elements involved in a bank audit—the surprise element. In essence, directors are not qualified or in a position to audit a bank effectively.

Examinations by Internal Auditor

In other banks, principally larger banks, the directors' examining committee often relies upon the internal auditor to fulfill the directors' examination responsibilities. Assuming that the internal auditor of the bank is qualified by education, training, experience, and technical knowledge, the internal auditor of a bank can never be completely independent. Almost without exception, bank internal auditors report administratively to some member of bank management. Even though internal auditors report functionally directly to the board of directors, from a practical aspect they cannot criticize bank management policies, practices, procedures, or reports without considering the possibility of endangering their own professional careers within the bank. Further, the internal audit activities of many banks need considerable improvement in organization, personnel, programs, techniques, work papers, and reports. The effectiveness of an internal auditor examination on behalf of the directors is also hindered by an inability to preserve the important surprise element of a bank examination.

Audit by Qualified Independent Public Accountants

Independent public accountants are licensed to practice by their individual states. The issuance of these licenses indicate that the accountants have the professional qualifications, education, and experience to practice as such. If they are certified public accountants, it is evidence that they also have passed a uniform certified public accountant examination offered by all states. In conducting the audit of any concern, an independent public accountant must comply with generally accepted auditing standards adopted by fellow practitioners. It is because of these standards that bank managements, bank directors, stockholders, and other interested parties who read independent public accountants' reports on bank financial statements are able to rely on those reports and the independent opinion expressed therein.

For all of the reasons described, it seems reasonable to conclude that qualified independent public accountants should be engaged to conduct bank audits and to fulfill the audit responsibility of bank managements and boards of directors.

An independent public accountant should spend sufficient time and effort to become familiar with the operating practices and accounting principles applicable to the concern being audited. Accordingly, in selecting the independent public accountant to conduct the bank examination, the examining committee of the board of directors should ascertain that he or she has not only the proper professional qualifications but also sufficient familiarity with the banking industry and with internal bank operations.

SCOPE OF BANK AUDITS

Except for the selection of a qualified firm of independent public accountants to conduct the bank audit, perhaps the most important decision the board of directors must make, in consultation with the accountants, concerns the scope of the audit.

Basically, the scope of a bank audit is not too different from that of any commercial enterprise. However, it is important that the board of directors understand the major scope requirements leading to the expression of an unqualified opinion on bank financial statements. These major scope requirements, and the approach to satisfying those requirements in audits of small- to medium-sized banks, are discussed in the following paragraphs.

Evaluation of Internal Audit and Control

One of the auditing standards complied with by independent public accountants is that there is to be a proper study and evaluation of existing internal control as a basis for reliance thereon and for determination of the resulting auditing procedures to be applied. This evaluation is aided tremendously if an internal auditor has been continuously evaluating such internal control and reporting internally thereon. It is preferable for the independent accountant to visit the bank and evaluate internal control prior to commencement of the examination. However, in order to protect the surprise element considered necessary to an effective examination, it is not always possible for the accountant to make such a preliminary evaluation. Accordingly, on bank audits, it is generally necessary for the independent accountant to review and evaluate internal control as soon as possible following actual commencement of the audit and to adjust the extent of his or her auditing procedures at that time.

If the bank is large enough to maintain its own internal auditing function, the examination will include a review and evaluation of the internal auditing program. This review will cover the existing procedures, frequency schedules, working papers, and other data evidencing the work carried out by the internal audit function, as well as a review of the reports rendered, in order to determine the adequacy of the internal control and internal audit activities in providing reasonable internal protection to the bank and to evaluate the extent to which the external auditor can rely on the internal audit work.

Accountability and Proof

The accountability and proof phase of the examination includes a simultaneous accounting for and balance of all assets and liabilities of the bank. To effect such a simultaneous accounting, the independent accountant must in his preliminary investigation locate all accounting records and negotiable assets within the bank, and, later, plan for effective control over these items immediately upon entry into the bank on the date of the examination. In auditing large banks which have effective internal controls and internal audit functions, the auditor may decide that simultaneous accounting is unnecessary and, instead, may audit separate departments, functions or accounts at various times during the year.

This phase also includes testing selected transactions and entries affecting all of the bank accounts; inspecting and examining notes, collateral, and other documents in support of loans; and counting and inspecting currency, coin, securities, and other negotiable items located on bank premises. It also includes a review of the specialized departments or activities whose transactions ordinarily are not reflected in the general ledger accounts, such as the collection department, mortgage servicing activities, safekeeping of securities for customers, and the trust department. With respect to the trust department, it is customary for the board of directors to engage the accountant to audit the trust department of the bank simultaneously with the audit of other banking functions.

Confirmation with Third Parties

The confirmation phase of the examination involves loans and deposit balances recorded on the books of the bank. This direct confirmation is normally on a test basis, with the size of the test sample being determined by the independent public accountant after his review of the internal control and internal auditing procedures in effect in the institution, and by his observations of and conclusions relating to the nature of the accounts concerned and the condition of the pertinent bank records. Also included in the scope of the accountant's examination is direct confirmation of due from and due to bank accounts, clearings, items in process of collection, loans and/or securities held by others for safekeeping or for other purposes, and miscellaneous assets and liabilities located outside the bank.

Evaluation of Assets

The evaluation phase of the examination consists of a determination of the fair value and collectibility of loans, investments, and other assets, and a judgment with respect to the adequacy of related valuation reserves. In making this evaluation, independent accountants review the classification of loans and investments resulting from the most recent supervisory examination and use this evaluation to assist them in determining the extent to which they must evaluate individual loans and investments. The evaluation of loans involves valuing collateral in support of selected secured loans and analyzing financial statements held by the bank in support of selected unsecured loans.

The evaluation of loans and investments appears to represent a duplication of the efforts of the supervisory examiners, and to some extent it does. However, such an evaluation is considered necessary in order for the accountant to express an unqualified opinion with respect to the financial statements. In addition, many bankers and bank directors consider this phase of the accountant's audit as the most useful and helpful, as they are able to receive the benefit of the accountant's strong financial background and wide experience with the financial statements and operations of various industries. Such a qualified, independent appraisal affords bank directors a reliable basis for measuring the adequacy of the allowances for loan losses provided by the bank and the competency of bank management in developing and administering the loans of the bank.

The preceding comments relating to the scope of an independent public accountant's examination are a general summary of a scope of sufficient breadth to enable an accountant to express an opinion on the normal financial statements of a bank. This scope summary represents innumerable detailed auditing procedures, involving counting, inspecting, trial balancing, confirming, and reconciling the records, ledgers, entries, source documents, and other data supporting the various assets, liability, income, and expense accounts of the bank. Because of the importance of an unrestricted scope to the expression of an unqualified opinion, it is again emphasized that a directors' examining committee discuss the scope of the proposed audit in detail with the accountant at the time he or she is engaged. This preliminary determination of the scope of the examination to be undertaken will result in a board of directors' obtaining the type of audit and audit report it desires.

PROBLEMS OF BANK AUDITS

The negotiability of many bank assets, and the numerous records and documents required to account to its borrowers and depositors in a satisfactory and timely manner, require that the independent public accountant consider in advance of the audit many special problems peculiar to banking. It is important for bank management and boards of directors to be aware of the more significant of these problems in order to discuss them intelligently with the accountant prior to commencement of the audit. Advance consideration and planned solution of these problem areas will result in a more effective, smoother bank audit.

Exposure and Control

The independent accountant should expect to find relatively large amounts of cash and negotiable items on hand at the time of entry. Such items will include currency and coin, investment securities held for its own account, securities held as collateral on loans, securities held in safekeeping and custody, unissued savings bonds and travelers checks, unissued money orders, securities held for trust accounts, and similar items.

Consequently, the independent accountant must give consideration to this exposure by obtaining complete, tight control over such items at the inception of the audit without interfering with the routine operations of the bank. This immediate control must embrace not only the physical cash and negotiable items but also the related records. Effective control also must be exercised over all asset and liability records which are to be confirmed, including clearing, due from and due to bank, loan and deposit accounts. Audit control must not be released until the accountant is completely satisfied that significant exceptions or differences have been cleared, or until sufficient data have been extracted from the records to assure the accountant that he or she can identify or reconstruct pertinent data at a later date.

Surprise Element

For the same reasons which require immediate control over negotiable items upon commencement of the audit, and to assist in effecting such control, bank audits should be made on a surprise basis, without prior notification to any director, officer, or employee. To enable the accountant to do this, it is customary to provide him with a letter from the chairman of the examining committee of the board of directors at the time the accountant is engaged, authorizing the accountant and his staff accountants to enter the bank for the purpose of conducting an audit.

In order to preserve the element of surprise, the audit date should be left to the discretion of the accountant. In selecting the date, the accountant should recognize several pertinent factors. Audits should be spaced reasonably from year to year, and patterns must not be established. The planned audit date should be confirmed by the accountant confidentially with the pertinent supervisory authorities in order to prevent a conflict with supervisory examination dates.

Prior to issuance of supervisory authority regulations pursuant to the Securities Acts Amendments of 1964, essentially all bank audits were made at a surprise date during any month of the year, rather than at year-end. However, the year-end disclosure requirements and standardized accounting principles established by certain of those regulations for banks having in excess of 500 stockholders are being recognized by many state and national banks not subject to the regulations. Consequently, many banks have adopted the procedure, which is customary for other significant commercial enterprises, of having their year-end financial statements audited by independent public accountants.

Even in the case of year-end certifications it is important that the certified public accountant maintain the audit surprise element. This is accomplished by performing a material portion of the audit procedures at an interim surprise visit (or visits) during the year and by completing the audit and issuing the audit report shortly after December 31. Where state laws so require, or where directors consider it desirable, the scope of the interim surprise visit can be designed to serve as a directors' examination. In such instances, the accountant can issue a suitable report on the directors' examination and, upon completion of supplementary auditing procedures at year-end, can issue a report certifying the year-end financial statements of the bank.

Staffing

Bank audits require a considerable number of accountants the first few days for control inspections, counts, confirmations, and trial balances of loan and deposit accounts. Thereafter, the number of required accountants decreases significantly. Many of the audit tasks performed during the first few days are of short duration, which requires that the accountants be reasonably familiar with the work they are assigned, that they be effectively supervised, and that the movement of audit personnel be well planned. Failure to observe these principles results in lost motion and time and increases the cost of the audit.

In this respect, the independent public accountant should attempt to minimize the cost of the audit by using bank personnel to assist the accountant whenever possible. In doing so, however, he or she must constantly be aware of the generally accepted auditing standards requiring that the examination be performed by persons having adequate technical training and proficiency as auditors, and that assistants be properly supervised. Even so, there are many opportunities for the accountant to reduce audit time significantly by using bank personnel discreetly under his control to supplement the work of the accountant, and bank directors should explore this possibility with the accountant at the time he is engaged.

Timing

The time of the month, the day of the week, and the exact time of entrance into the bank are audit subjects deserving full consideration.

The most effective and efficient time of the month and day of the week depend upon the economic conditions of the community and the operating practices of the individual bank. It is undesirable to commence bank audits on a day immediately preceding the normal payday of an unusually large commercial customer, as banks normally accumulate an unusual amount of cash at that time. Likewise, audits should not begin on the day following a late opening of a bank, because many banks "close out" in the early afternoon of the late opening day and consider transactions consummated thereafter as business of the next day. Such "after-hours" business can pose a significant reconcilement problem, particularly to the uninitiated auditor.

The exact time of entrance—that is, in the morning or in the afternoon—also is important. Beginning the audit in the afternoon is generally considered the easier way; however, this does not provide optimum control conditions, and therefore is not considered the better way.

Tellers are proving their work, bookkeepers are either sorting or posting items of the current day or are posting items of the previous day, transit letters are in an interim state of preparation, all of which make it difficult to establish and maintain control. There is always a possibility that changes can be made after the audit has commenced.

In contrast, the morning entrance before cash and "book" vaults are opened provides maximum control. Theoretically, all cash, negotiable items, and accountability records are locked and not susceptible to change after the accountant enters the premises. The morning entrance requires more skill in assuring that tellers' windows and customer service facilities are opened at the usual time, and in conducting certain audit procedures and controlling records while customers are transacting their business.

Planning

The relatively high degree of exposure and control, the importance of maintaining the surprise element, and the need for efficient assignment and utilization of audit personnel demand that all phases of the audit be planned thoroughly in advance. Because of the rapid movement of accountable items within an individual bank and throughout the banking system of the nation, once control is lost or never established over a significant document or group of documents, it is too late to attempt to correct it. A major procedural mistake can invalidate the effectiveness of the entire audit, or materially increase the cost of the audit through efforts to extend auditing procedures to compensate for the oversight.

Specifically, the independent public accountant must have an understanding—not intended to be all-inclusive—of the overall organization of the bank, the activities conducted by each of its departments, the volume of such activities, and the general operating and accounting procedures and systems being used. He should be familiar with the physical layout of the bank, and with the number, location and contents of all vaults. He should determine the type of internal control over vaults and the times they are opened or closed. The accountant should determine the number, type, location and approximate cash balances of each teller. He should obtain or prepare a summary of the flow of routine work in the various departments, particularly the teller, proof and transit, and bookkeeping functions, in order to plan appropriate cutoffs for control purposes.

AUDIT REPORTS

As previously stated, the principal objective of an independent public accountant in a bank audit is to obtain sufficient evidential matter to enable him to express an opinion with respect to the financial statements of the bank. The type of report he issues is governed by the desires of the client and by the scope and findings of the audit.

Short- and Long-Form Report

The typical short-form report prepared by independent public accountants consists of a one-page accountant's report accompanied by the financial statements being reported upon and by notes to those financial statements. The one-page report normally consists of a scope paragraph and an opinion paragraph. The scope paragraph makes reference to the fact that the audit was made in accordance with generally accepted auditing standards and included such tests of the accounting records and such other auditing procedures as the accountant considered necessary in the circumstances. The opinion paragraph expresses the opinion of the accountant with respect to whether the accompanying financial statements present fairly the financial position, results of operations and changes in financial position of the institution, in conformity with generally accepted accounting principles applied on a basis consistent with that of the preceding period.

The long-form report is essentially the same as the short form, except that the one-page accountant's report makes reference to supplementary data and comments which are submitted for the information of the reader immediately following the financial statements and the notes thereto. This reference to supplementary data and comments, and a statement of the responsibility assumed by the accountant for the fairness of presentation of such supplementary data, normally is included in the opinion paragraph of the accountant's report or in a separate paragraph immediately thereafter. The long-form report is more costly, is unnecessary and, therefore, is becoming less common.

Deviations from Standard Form Reports

A report in which an independent public accountant expresses an unqualified opinion on the financial statements of a bank is desirable. Restrictions in the scope of an audit, departures from generally accepted accounting principles, and other circumstances, however, require an accountant to deviate from the standard form of report to comply with generally accepted auditing standards and the code of ethics of the American Institute of Certified Public Accountants. In such instances, the certified public accountant may issue a qualified opinion report or an adverse opinion report (in which he or she expresses an opinion that the financial statements do not present fairly the financial position and results of operation of the institution). Where the scope of the audit has been restricted to a sufficient extent, the accountant may have been prevented from obtaining sufficient evidential matter to enable him to express any opinion, in which event he is required to deny an opinion on the financial statements.

With respect to bank audits, the principal reasons requiring deviations from the standard form of accountants reports are scope restrictions imposed by banks or lack of conformity with generally accepted accounting principles. Typical scope restrictions are those involving confirmation of loan or deposit accounts, or evaluation of investment securities and loans. Because of the significant size of these assets and liabilities in relation to the overall statement of condition of a bank, prohibiting the accountant from following these audit procedures normally results in at least a qualification of his opinion and perhaps in a denial of an opinion, depending upon the judgment of the independent public accountant in the circumstances.

Audit Reports without Accompanying Financial Statements

Where the audit scope is so restricted, or where persons without the required professional auditing qualifications are used to such an extent, that the independent public accountants are never in a position to consider expressing an opinion on the financial statements of the bank, they may issue another type of report. This report generally describes the circumstances sorrounding the audit, states that it was not undertaken for the purpose of expressing an opinion on the financial statements, and includes explanatory scope comments and audit findings relating to work performed in specific areas of the bank. In issuing reports of this type, the certified public accountant is prohibited, by generally accepted auditing standards and by the code of ethics of the American Institute of Certified Public Accountants, from including financial statements purporting to show financial condition or results of operations along with the report, except under circumstances which severely limit the value of and reliance on such statements. This type of report obviously is not the most desirable; nevertheless, it is the only alternative under the circumstances.

Internal Control and System Comments

Among the greatest values which accrue to bank management or boards of directors in employing an external auditor are the constructive recommendations for improving on the bank's system of internal control and its internal auditing activities. As previously stated, in order to conduct a competent bank audit, the independent public accountant reviews, and evaluates the existing system of internal control. Weaknesses which the accountant observes, and the recommendations for correcting those weaknesses, should be directed to the attention of bank management and the board of directors in a separate letter addressed to bank management.

CONCLUSION

The need for bank audits is apparent, after considering the moral and legal responsibility of directors, the obligation of banks to disclose accurate, reliable data to interested parties, and the manner in which external audits complement the work of the internal audit and internal control functions of a bank. Directors generally cannot rely on supervisory authority examinations or on the competence of examinations performed by them or by internal auditors on their behalf. The best qualified person to conduct such audits is a knowledgeable firm of independent public accountants. Bank audits should be of sufficient scope to enable the independent public accountant to express an unqualified opinion on the financial statements of the bank. In conducting the audit, the independent public accountant must be aware of, and make preparations for significant audit problems peculiar to bank audits. The accountant issues an audit report which delineates the degree of responsibility the accountant is assuming for the fairness of presentation of the financial statements and any accompanying supplementary data. In a separate letter, the independent accountant should apprise bank management of significant weaknesses in internal control and internal audit activities and should make appropriate recommendations for correcting those weaknesses.

Chapter 29

Tax Planning for Banks

Milan G. Hiben*

Tax planning as an integral part of corporate and profit planning presupposes the advance preparation of a budget which coordinates the financial plans and projections in advance, thereby predetermining the results for a series of future periods.

If one presumes that the ultimate measurement of effective management is the maximization of net income over a period of time, then preplanning the impact of taxes on income is a prerequisite of effective management. With a nonparticipating partner sharing in practically one half of one's taxable income above $50,000, good tax administration dictates the use of all tax considerations that reduce the tax burden and increase net income. The use of certain tax considerations may have an impact on more than the current year, again necessitating forward planning.

Usually the comptroller or cashier, or whoever acts in the capacity of the financial officer of a bank, prepares or is responsible for the preparation of budgets which should include tax planning.

GENERAL STATEMENT

As a generalization in characterizing income tax liability, all income is taxable and all related expense is deductible. The purpose of applying various tax considerations (with the exception of tax-exempt interest earned and the investment tax credit) is to defer tax liability, possibly into perpetuity—but not eliminate it—thus to preserve deductions against taxable income.

---

* Vice President, Bank for Savings and Loan Associations, Chicago, Illinois.

364

All tax references in this chapter are of necessity generalizations for ease of understanding. The Tax Code should be consulted for specific reference and application.

EVALUATION OF TAX CONSIDERATIONS

Tax-Exempt Securities

Municipal securities, described in detail in Chapter 40, offer the greatest opportunity for small- and medium-sized institutions to reduce tax liability. The inclusion of municipal securities in the investment portfolio presupposes that sufficient taxable income will be earned to offset maximized allowable deductions by a margin sufficient to take advantage of the low normal tax rate, which is currently 22 percent on the first $25,000 of taxable net income and 20 percent on the next $25,000.

Tax-exempt income should be budgeted to offset net taxable income at the 48 percent rate since market yields (taxable vis-à-vis nontaxable yields) generally begin to attribute an advantage to tax-exempt income when the rate on taxable income exceeds 35 percent. As Exhibit 29–1 indicates the taxable equivalent is based on a corporate tax rate of 48 percent. To calculate the tax equivalent rate divide the tax exempt yield by the reciprocal of 48 percent or 52 percent. Thus 3.65% ÷ 52% results in a taxable equivalent yield of 7.02%. There would be a loss in offsetting income that is taxed at 22 percent with tax-exempt income. The reciprocal of a surtax rate of 22 percent, or 78 percent divided into 3.65 percent would result in a taxable equivalent yield of 4.68 percent. Obviously, the taxable rate of 5.96 percent is significantly higher.

Exhibit 29–1
Yields and Yield Spreads, Five-Year Prime Municipals versus Five-Year U.S. Treasury Securities

	Prime Municipals		*U.S. Treasury Securities*	*Yield Spread*
	Tax-Exempt Yield	*Taxable Equivalent**	*Taxable Yield*	
1971.	3.65%	7.02%	5.96%	+1.06%
1972.	3.60	6.92	5.90	+1.02
1973.	4.25	8.17	6.76	+1.41
1974.	4.90	9.42	7.73	+1.69
1975.	4.83	9.29	7.61	+1.68
1976.	4.15	7.98	7.20	+ .78

* Corporate tax rate 48 percent.

Amortization of Bond Premium and Accretion of Discount

The amortization of bond premium (the amount that is paid above the par amount) is required for tax-exempt securities but all other securities involving a premium need not be amortized. However, once an election has been made in the first tax return following the purchase of a security at a premium, the bank must follow the same practice in succeeding years.

The effect of amortizing the premium on tax-exempt bonds is to reduce the tax basis of the security to par at maturity. The purpose is to reduce the taxable loss or increase the taxable profit on the sale if the securities are sold prior to maturity at a loss or a profit. Thus, the tax consequences are calculated using the adjusted book value (original cost less amortization of premium). No tax deduction is allowable for the amortization of premium paid on tax-exempt bonds. Amortization of premium on taxable bonds is fully deductible in computing taxable income. If premium is not amortized, no deduction from gross income is made until the securities either mature or are sold at which time the premium is deductible as a loss.

The accretion of discount of investment securities is not required; however, it is recommended in order to reflect more realistically the timely earnings of securities purchased at a discount. The tax liability resulting from accretion of discount should be reserved so that it will be available for payment in the year in which the security matures. Having lost the advantage of long-term capital gains on the sale or exchange of bonds, debentures, notes, and other evidences of indebtedness, original issue discount is no longer a consideration and can now be ignored. Original issue discount occurs when securities are sold at a discount at the time they are originally issued in the primary market as differentiated from purchasing a security at a discount in the secondary market from a previous owner. The selection of a year as a gain year or loss year is no longer a critical choice since all gains, long or short term, are taxed as ordinary income just as losses both short or long term are fully deductible. The subsequent section on operating loss carry-back describes the remaining advantage in choosing a loss or gain year.

Investment Tax Credit

The Internal Revenue Code permits a credit against federal income taxes of a percentage of qualified investment in certain depreciable assets. Examples of property that qualify for the credit are alterations and additions such as elevators and escalators, vaults, walk-up and drive-in teller windows, and night depositories. Other qualifiable property includes furniture, fixtures, equipment, movable partitions, carpeting and automobiles. Full credit is allowable only for property additions that have a useful life of seven years or longer. On properties with a tangible useful life of five to seven years, only two thirds of the cost can be used to calculate the investment credit. For assets with a useful life of three to five years, one third of the cost qualifies. The total investment credit with respect to new and used property is limited to $25,000 plus 50 percent of the tax liability in excess of $25,000. If investment credit property is prematurely disposed of before the end of its useful life, some portion of the credit might have to be added to the tax liability of the bank in the year of disposition.

The Internal Revenue Code also permits the carry-back and carry-over of unused investment tax credits. According to the tax code, the use of an investment tax credit in no way impairs or alters the ordinary depreciation of those properties.

Foreign Taxes

Except for the money center banks and a few large regional banks, the tax consequences of international banking for the smaller bank are most likely inconsequential and is only mentioned here to recognize that they do exist. For those banks participating in international banking activities, suffice it to say that their tax departments should be well versed in the longer term ramifications of foreign taxes.

Restating interest and other income at its gross value rather than at net of foreign taxes may result in some advantage. Recognition of tax treaties, foreign exchange gains and losses, and changing withholding tax rates at the source could affect tax liability here and abroad.

Impact of State Income and Franchise Taxes

State and other local taxing entities may have different procedural rules in determining taxable income from that of federal taxable income. There may be variances in the accounting methods and rules may exclude certain credits, deductions, and exceptions that are normally considered when calculating the tax impact on prospective investments. Familiarization with specific state renewal codes, therefore, is essential to effective tax planning.

Minimum Implications Regarding Tax Preference Items

Since the Tax Reform Act of 1969, a special tax has been assessed against tax preference items. A preference arises when income is taxed at a lower than the normal rate as in the case of capital gains, or

when an expense (deduction) is increased such as accelerated depreciation. The Tax Reform Act of 1976 increased the minimum tax rate
on preference items from 10 percent to 15 percent and reduced the
annual exclusion from $30,000 to $10,000. The act did, however, retain
as an alternative to the reduced annual exclusion the choice of excluding the full amount of regular taxes paid if it were greater than the
reduced and annual exclusion. The increase in the tax rate became
effective for taxable years beginning after year-end 1977. These items
include capital gains, accelerated depreciation, and the excess of the
addition to the reserve for loan losses over the allowable addition to
the reserve, had the reserve been maintained for all taxable years
on the basis of actual loss experience.

Reserve for Losses on Loans

Additions to the reserve for losses on loans, under the percentage
of loans outstanding formula, continues to be drastically reduced. Under the percentage method of additions to the loan loss reserve, the
amount added for a taxable year shall be the amount necessary to
increase the balance of the reserve at the end of the taxable year to
the allowable percentage of eligible loans outstanding at the end of
the year. For years after 1975, but before 1982, the percentage factor
is reduced from 1.8 percent to 1.2 percent of such loans outstanding.
For taxable years beginning after 1981, the rate will be reduced from
1.2 percent to 0.6 percent. For taxable years beginning after 1987, a
bank will be required to use its own experience in determining the
amount of the bad debt deduction, since the use of the percentage
method of calculating additions to the loan loss reserve will have
expired.

A bank has the option of using the experience method before 1987.
This method also permits it to add to its bad debt reserve the amount
called for on the basis of its actual experience as shown by losses for
the current year and the five preceding taxable years.

The amount determined under the experience method for a taxable
year is the greater of the amount necessary to increase the balance
of the reserve at the end of the taxable year to the amount which
bears the same ratio to loans outstanding at the close of the taxable
year as (1) the total bad debts sustained during such year and the
five preceding taxable years, with adjustments for recoveries of bad
debts during the period, bears to (2) the sum of the loans outstanding
at the close of such six taxable years. An alternative method is to take
the lower of the balance of the reserve as of the close of the base
year (the last taxable year before adopting the experience method),
or the amount which bears the same ratio to loans outstanding at the

close of the taxable year as the balance of the reserve at the close of the base year bears to the amount of loans outstanding at the close of that year, if the amount of loans outstanding at the close of the taxable year is less than the amount of such loans outstanding at the close of the base year.

Minimum Tax

While the effect of the minimum tax on tax preference items has reduced the benefits of those specific tax reductions and deductions, the impact of the changes in the minimum tax in the Tax Reform Act of 1976 should not materially alter the use of tax preference items in tax-planning strategy.

For banks and other financial institutions, the minimum tax rate for taxable years beginning after December 31, 1977 will be 15 percent and the excludable portion of preference income will be the greater of $10,000 or the federal income tax decreased by the amount of certain credits mentioned above. The effective minimum tax rate for a 48 percent taxpayer is 22.2 percent. Example:

Deductions due to accelerated depreciation or amount of the addition to loan loss in excess of actual loss experience	$10,000
Decrease in tax liability as a result of larger deduction.	4,800
Total of net preference income subject to minimum tax	$14,800
Minimum tax rate	15%
Increase in minimum tax resulting from additional deduction of $10,000	$ 2,220
Effective minimum tax rate	22.2%

For taxable years beginning after December 31, 1977, no carry-over of unused tax may be used to offset preference income subject to the minimum tax.

Net Operating Loss Carry-back

The Tax Reform Act of 1976 significantly improved the net operating loss carry-back for banks. Generally, the new provision in the tax law enables banks to carry back for ten years any net operating loss. This has important tax implications for banks that have large tax credits from leasing operations, tax losses on bonds, and tax-exempt income. A bank may experience a sizable current net operating loss for tax

Exhibit 29–2
Net Operating Loss Carry-Back

	Typical Operating Result	Effect of Net Operating Loss	Difference
Income	$1,400,000	$1,400,000	$ 0
Less: Tax-exempt income	200,000	200,000	0
Adjusted income........................	$1,200,000	$1,200,000	0
Less: Total expenses	1,150,000	1,350,000*	$(200,000)
Net taxable income	$ 50,000	$ (150,000)	$(200,000)
Less: Taxes (recoverable)	10,500	(65,500)†	76,000
After tax income........................	$ 39,500	$ (84,500)	$(124,000)
Add: Tax-exempt income	200,000	200,000	0
Net income	$ 239,500	$ 115,500	$(124,000)

* Due to large loan losses, bond losses, operating losses, and so on.
† Recovery dependent on the amount of taxable income excludable from surtax in the year to which losses are carried back. Example $150,000 loss; $25,000 × normal tax rate of 22 percent, $125,000 at the surtax rate of 48 percent. In other years the tax rates in effect may have been 20 percent on the first $25,000 of income, 22 percent on the next $25,000, and 48 percent on the income in excess of $50,000.

purposes and thus recover previously paid taxes, which when added to income that is excludable from taxable income, may produce a favorable net after tax income result.

Exhibit 29–2 illustrates the effect of a net operating loss carry-back that results in the recovery of previously paid income taxes.

DEVELOPMENT OF A TAX PLANNING PHILOSOPHY

Since the tax laws are very specific as to the intent of Congress, there should be no hesitancy in using whatever provisions result in the largest net after tax income. Every taxpayer should presume there is purpose and reason to provisions that permit an increase in deductions or a reduction in tax liability. There should be no presumption of inequity in the law. If there appears to be, it is Congress' responsibility to rectify those inequities—not the individual's or corporate taxpayer's responsibility. Tax planning presumes no moral obligation to pay more than the law demands.

Qualifying capitalized expenditures for a faster recovery may impose on current profits, and inhibit capital formation. There appears to be a tendency to write off all capitalized expenditures as quickly as possible and irrespective of the impact on net worth.

An evaluation of the appropriate decision does not necessarily lend itself exclusively to quantitative analysis. The impact on customers,

Exhibit 29–3
Preplanned Tax Liability

	No Tax-Exempt Income	Too Much Tax-Exempt Income	Appropriate Amount of Tax-Exempt Income
Gross income	$700,000	$ 644,000	$ 665,000
Less: Tax-exempt income	0	96,000	60,000
Adjusted gross income	$700,000	$ 548,000	$ 605,000
Expense	550,000	550,000	550,000
Taxable income	$150,000	$ (2,000)	$ 55,000
Income taxes	58,500	(440)	12,900
Net after tax income	$ 91,500	$ (1,560)	$ 42,100
Add: Tax-exempt income	0	96,000	60,000
Net income	$ 91,500	$ 94,440	$ 102,100
Par amount of tax exempts	0	$2,000,000	$1,250,000
Yield on government securities		7.60%	7.60%
Yield on tax-exempt securities		4.80%	4.80%
Taxable income		$—152,000	$ —95,000
Nontaxable income		+ 96,000	+60,000
Decrease in gross income above		$ —56,000	$ —35,000

the community, and the stockholder is a qualitative judgment that should be reflected in the decision. Short-term advantages may be detrimental in the long term.

The example in Exhibit 29–3 above illustrates the advantage of preplanning tax liability.

Future Tax Legislation

Each succeeding "tax reform act" may well result in more stringent qualifications in deferring tax payments. Any provision which permits tax payment deferral would appear to be a prime subject for successive tax reform. In tax planning, the value of a tax deferral provision should be realized within the first five years after its enactment in anticipation of its being materially altered.

IMPLEMENTATION OF A TAX PLAN

A series of alternative long-range financial projections should precede detail fiscal budgeting. The effect of different tax considerations on bottom line projections should indicate the most advantageous choices to be exercised.

A five-year forecast would be the minimal length of time to judge the impact of tax credits from lease operations and tax-exempt state and municipal bond income. The objective of tax planning is to maximize net after tax income over a period of time and not merely minimize taxes to be paid in the next fiscal year.

Tax planning should be an integral part of every bank's overall planning in order to ensure the most profitable results.

Chapter 30

Risk Management

H. Felix Kloman*

INTRODUCTION

A major objective in the operation of any successful banking institution is the conservation of its resources from accidental loss. These accidental loss exposures, affecting human, financial, physical and natural resources, are diverse and ever-changing. They include not only loss of money, securities, and other valuable property from a bank's custody, but also loss or physical damage to property which it owns or over which it exercises some degree of fiduciary control. Most importantly, they include the many and varied types of third-party liabilities which seem to be growing in frequency and severity: Workers' compensation, auto, directors' and officers', fiduciary, professional liability, and so on.

In a sense, the risk management process is as important to a bank's continuity and its operating health as personnel, loan, trust, and other activities. Without a coordinated and continuous effort to uncover significant loss exposures, to apply reasonable and effective risk controls and to ensure that the financial integrity of the banking institution will not be impaired after a loss, a bank may find that public confidence will be eroded, stockholders disenchanted, and directors less than friendly.

The risk management process is an outgrowth of insurance, which for many years was considered the major means of protecting against accidental losses. While risk management has its roots in insurance management, insurance is, in reality, only a portion of the risk financing segment of the risk management process. Risk management has ex-

---

* President, Risk Planning Group, Darien, Connecticut.

panded to become an orderly process for treating all aspects of uncertainty of accidental loss.

While certain types of risk are essentially managerial in nature (political, innovative, loan and currency fluctuation, for example), most types of accidental loss exposures can and should be treated in a risk management program. These include: physical damage to assets or resources; nonavailability of the use of assets or resources which causes a reduction in earnings or earning power; adverse judgments at law; fraud and criminal violence; and the death and disability of key employees.

The elements of risk management include:

1. *Exposure Identification.* The creation of a continuous discovery process to identify those resources for which a bank is responsible, and the accidental loss exposures that could materially affect them.
2. *Risk Evaluation.* The measurement of financial risk by analyzing past loss frequency and severity and by estimating future probabilities.
3. *Risk Control.* The reduction or elimination of risk or loss, within proper and economic restraints, through careful procedures and practices in security, personnel safety, property conservation, automotive-fleet safety, and emergency planning.
4. *Risk Finance.* The provision of sufficient funds to meet loss situations *if* they occur by use of both internal and external financial resources, including insurance.
5. *Risk Management Administration.* The development of administrative techniques to carry out the risk management process most effectively, using skills available inside and outside the bank.

The objective of bank risk management, then, is the conservation of the institution's resources, earnings and services from the effects of accidental loss or destruction at the minimum reasonable expense.

EXPOSURE IDENTIFICATION

The first step in the bank risk management process is to identify bank resources. They include:

1. *Physical Resources.* The real and personal property which the bank owns or for which it may be legally responsible, including trust, foreclosed or repossessed property under certain circumstances. Office buildings, branches, automated tellers, boilers, furniture and fixtures, fine arts, data-processing equipment and vehicles all fall into this category.
2. *Human Resources.* Quite obviously, "people" are essential to the continuation of banking services, and a bank risk management

officer should identify those who may be considered key to the fulfillment of ongoing responsibilities. This identification should extend beyond critical executives to, for example, data-processing employees, important personnel within outside service organizations, certain directors and, in some circumstances, key customers and depositors.

3. *Natural Resources.* The availability of certain natural resources, such as water, clean air, or the various forms of energy upon which we rely, are too often taken for granted. They are indeed important to the continuity of banking operations.

4. *Financial Resources.* The capital, deposits, and collateral upon which the American banking industry rests are derived from stockholders, depositors, customers, *and* the government. These resources need to be carefully inventoried.

5. *Intangible Resources.* While these are difficult, if not impossible, to value in traditional terms, any bank relies upon intangible resources such as communications media (mail or telephone), adequate transportation facilities for its employees and customers, or the availability of critical skills from various specialties such as legal and accounting.

In addition, the operation of a holding company often involves resources not common to a normal bank—resources which require careful identification in the risk management process.

Identification of resources only begins the risk management process. There are many accidental loss exposures which can seriously affect one or more of these resources:

1. *Natural Exposures.* Most frequently termed "acts of God," these exposures include earthquake, flood, windstorm and tornado, and other perils over which a banking institution and its personnel may have little or no direct control.

2. *Direct Exposures.* Many accidental losses are within human control and these include crime in its various forms (internal and external), fire, explosion, collision, transportation risks, vandalism, and malicious mischief.

3. *Indirect Exposures.* Many direct exposures may also have indirect consequences, generally related to extra expenses incurred in order to maintain operations, or to potential loss of income. These types of exposures are often overlooked by banks and many times represent greater risks of loss than those associated with direct physical damage.

4. *Human Exposures.* Death, disability, accidental injury, sickness, or old age can quite obviously affect all of the human resources within any bank. In particular, smoking, drug addiction, alcoholism,

and obesity have been cited as four of the most serious health problems in the United States, all of which create untold costs for banks and their employees.

5. *Third-Party Liabilities.* The potential financial losses arising out of unintentional or intentional torts, statutory liabilities and contractual liabilities are probably the most serious loss exposures facing any bank. While the frequency and severity of liability losses have not been as severe as, for example, crime losses, the growing litigiousness of a highly affluent society, inflation, and changing social values indicate a steadily worsening situation. The types of liabilities for which a bank can be held responsible are many and diverse, including advertising, automobile, aircraft (owned, nonowned, repossessed or trust), bailee (night depository, safe deposit boxes, etc.), contractual, directors' and officers', employer's (under workers' compensation statutes), liquor law, product, professional, personal injury (libel, slander, and defamation of character), and the liability of an owner for his premises.

There are two or more recent forms of liability which threaten to create new difficulties for banks. The Employee Retirement Income Security Act of 1974 creates a statutory fiduciary liability. While many bankers believe that ERISA imposes no real liability beyond that already accepted under the "prudent man" rule, the publicity attendant to the new law is certainly going to spawn increased litigation.

A second, and perhaps more worrisome, area is that of professional liability. A number of recent cases have created precedents for the imposition of liability against bankers who fail to discharge their obligations in a "professional" manner, through either error or omission.

Methods of identifying bank resources and the exposures which can affect them remain largely subjective. There is nothing that will replace an effective cycle of interviews with department heads and physical inspections of all bank properties. Beyond this, the American Bankers Association has suggested the use of a "Bank Exposure Analysis Flowchart" and Bank Resource and Exposure Checklists.[1] In addition, the alert bank officer will periodically review additional important documents, such as:

Annual financial reports.

Historical loss records for an individual bank and for banks as a whole (see FBI, FDIC, and other agencies for information).

Budgets, both operating and capital.

---

[1] See Exhibits 1, 2 and 3 in *The Risk and Insurance Management Guide for Financial Institutions* (Washington, D.C.: American Bankers Association, 1976).

Minutes of the board of directors meetings.

Accounting ledgers.

Appropriation requests.

Key leases, contracts and agreements.

In addition to these largely internal sources of information, the bank officer charged with risk management responsibilities will also wish to obtain assistance from the Insurance and Protection Division of the American Bankers Association, the Risk and Insurance Management Society, and from the many publications that are now available in the risk and insurance management area.

In summary, loss exposures are elusive and changing. The bank risk management officer must apply all of these risk discovery techniques in an alert and intelligent manner to identify every exposure to loss, not once or periodically, but continually. The goals should be a complete knowledge of all bank operations and a continuous questioning of the ways in which a bank may be exposed to accidental loss.

RISK EVALUATION

Quite obviously, there are some exposures to accidental loss which are inconsequential in nature, while others have a potentially catastrophic impact. Risk evaluation is the measurement of financial risk in terms of frequency and severity probabilities so that the bank's risk management officer can devote maximum attention to those exposures which have the greatest potential impact on the bank.

Risk evaluation begins with the designation of some form of financial value to all bank resources and earnings. The evaluation process can be reasonably sophisticated in the case of real or personal property, using such methods as fair market value, book value, replacement cost, reproduction cost or actual cash value, or for financial resources including securities and cash. Evaluation of human or intangible resources, however, can be a far more difficult and subjective task.

The value of any resource also includes the income, earnings, or cash flow that it generates and which may be affected following a direct loss, or extra expenses needed to continue a particular operation, such as a branch or a data-processing facility, until the damaged property is repaired or replaced. An indirect exposure usually refers to the economic loss resulting from the inability to use or possess a piece of property. Some other examples of indirect loss are:

The cost of debris removal.

Expenses occasioned by the enforcement of municipal ordinances governing demolition or reconstruction to new codes not in effect when the structure was originally built.

Loss of rental value of bank-owned and -occupied property.

Reproduction cost of data-processing media or valuable papers.

Extra expenses to use other computer facilities or to return to manual services.

After a tentative value has been attached to each resource, the bank risk management officer should estimate the potential *frequency* and *severity* of each exposure situation or occurrence. While the past history of an individual bank can be a guide, most banks are too small to rely on this history alone. Even overall industry loss histories, compiled by insurance companies, the banking industry or the Federal Bureau of Investigation, can be statistically incomplete and misleading. Any historical study should be weighed carefully for credibility in making forecasts. Many banks are beginning to use sophisticated quantitative skills in preparing simulation models and actuarial forecasts upon which better decisions can be made with regard to risk control and risk funding.

Judgment also dictates that consideration be given not only to the worst *possible* but the more *probable* size of loss that might occur. Many banks are beginning to use "maximum possible loss" and "maximum probable loss" estimates for the total losses that can arise from a single occurrence:

Maximum possible loss is the greatest total loss that might be suffered assuming the "worst" condition—safety and protection devices fail to operate.

Maximum probable loss would be the worst loss to be expected under "average" conditions, assuming that most, if not all, control mechanisms and procedures are operating effectively.

Risk evaluation, like exposure identification, is a continuing process. While in some areas it may be subject to precise measurement, as in property values and cash exposures, more often than not the bank officer will find that subjective judgment will prevail.

As a basic minimum, every bank should maintain at least a five-year history of financial, property, and third-party liability accidental losses, both insured and uninsured, showing both the number of occurrences in each year as well as the amount which has actually been paid or which may be still held in an internal or insurance company reserve.

A successful risk evaluation effort will depend heavily upon the accuracy of these loss records and on the ability of a bank officer to use subjective judgment in evaluating those losses which have the highest frequency and severity potentials.

RISK CONTROL

After identifying exposures and evaluating financial risk, the bank risk management officer must then move to the most important step in the risk management process—risk control. The objective is the elimination and/or reduction of not only loss but risk itself. One of the major problems, however, found in many banking institutions is that risk control may be fragmented, administratively controlled by different areas of management. More and more banks are recognizing that social, economic and legal pressures demand a more coordinated approach to:

1. Define risk control areas and develop bank "policy" for the approval of the board.
2. Develop procedures for each control policy.
3. Provide constructive assistance so that each department can follow procedures realistically.
4. Monitor actual compliance on a periodic basis.

The elements of a risk control program for a bank will include:

1. *Protection and Security.*   Governed in large part by the Bank Protection Act of 1968 and Regulation P of the Federal Reserve System. Effective guidance can be found in the American Bankers Association *Bank Protection Manual.*
2. *Personnel Safety.*   Meeting the requirements of the Federal Occupational Safety and Health Act of 1970 (OSHA) and state statutes, setting standards for work safety, the work environment and record keeping. The American Bankers Association booklet, *Occupational Safety and Health of Bank Employees,* is an effective guide for action in this area.
3. *Property Conservation.*   The physical assets of a banking institution should be properly protected from fire and other perils. Effective guidance can be found through the many specialized publications of the National Fire Protection Association, and other organizations.
4. *Emergency Preparedness.*   Every bank should establish and pretest a plan of action to handle emergencies such as a bomb threat, natural disaster, or fire and assure that such plans are brought up to date periodically. Section 3.7 of the ABA's *Bank Protection Manual* and the *Disaster Planning Guide* of the Defense Civil Preparedness Agency provide concrete guidelines for creating such a plan.

Other risk control responsibilities include the development of policies and procedures for the safe operation of bank-owned or -leased automotive vehicles, for the distribution of products that are indeed fit for human use or consumption, and for the development of procedures to assure that the bank is not involved in any environmental pollution.

RISK FINANCING AND INSURANCE

Despite even the most complete exposure identification and risk control programs designed to reduce risk and/or loss to a minimum for any banking institution, new exposures still manage to appear, controls fail to achieve their intended purpose and banks will face the prospect of significant financial loss. The well-managed bank will, therefore, set as its risk finance and insurance objective the availability of sufficient funds after any conceivable loss so that the bank can continue to serve its depositors and customers, and maintain a reasonable return to its stockholders. This objective can be further defined to include:

Making the best use of *total* financial resources available to the bank.

Providing sufficient funds to meet the worst possible loss events.

Providing the maximum stability of risk funding costs over time.

Taking maximum cash flow advantages in the operation of the risk funding plan.

Obtaining the lowest reasonable direct cost, commensurate with the funds that are made available, and the services that are offered by certain funding media.

In the past, the greatest weakness of a bank risk financing program has been an over-reliance on insurance alone as a funding tool. A bank risk management officer, in reviewing funding alternatives, should consider not only insurance but current and retained earnings, reserves (funded or unfunded), credit with shareholders, the public, other financial institutions and various governmental agencies, sharing or "pooling" possibilities with similar financial institutions and, of course, a bank's intangible "goodwill" with society at large. While insurance remains one of the most frequently used methods of handling risk of accidental loss, it is by no means the only method or the least expensive.

Before considering insurance as a funding mechanism, a bank risk management officer should define the bank's capacity for retaining risk. Perhaps no area is more important or more generally overlooked by most banks. Simply because of its financial size, a bank has a certain ability to retain the smaller or the more recurring claims which can be predicted with some degree of assurance. Furthermore, the funneling of smaller claims through the insurance mechanism is distinctly uneconomical over time since insurance companies will attempt to collect from $1.50 to $2 in premiums for each dollar spent in claims, to cover overhead, commissions, and profit.

Self-insurance, in whole or part, is growing significantly as a bank risk funding technique, especially as difficulties are experienced with the conventional insurance market. Factors which should be considered in any decision relating to risk retention include:

1. *Managerial.* There should be a specific written guideline from the board concerning the maximum amount of accidental loss that the bank would be willing to self-assume in a single fiscal period. One guideline for this limit is $100 of risk retention per occurrence for every $1 million of deposits.
2. *Financial.* The economic value of a risk assumption decision should be measured in terms of premium costs, the amount and timing of possible losses, and service considerations.
3. *Psychological.* The risk-acceptance or risk-aversion characteristics of management and the board should be carefully considered.
4. *Spread-of-Risk.* Following the "law of large numbers," a full or partial self-insurance decision is improved by having a larger number of similar type risks, none of which might be subject to a single catastrophe.
5. *Loss Records.* Risk assumption or self-insurance requires a thorough data base of past losses, both insured and uninsured, with reasonable estimates or forecasts made for the future.
6. *Risk Control.* No risk retention program can be successful without a coordinated, internal risk control program.

Risk retention can be carried out by the full self-insurance of certain types of exposures, such as damage to plate glass, collision damage to owned or leased vehicles, or teller shorts. These losses can be charged directly to the offending department or branch, or to a preestablished reserve.

Partial self-insurance can be practiced through the use of deductibles under either property and liability insurance contracts, or bonds, or through the use of sophisticated retrospective rating plans. In any decision regarding risk retention, however, due consideration should be given not only to the premium credits available from insurance companies but to administrative savings, services that may be provided by insurance carriers, and the long-term preservation of the insurance market.

The purchase of insurance itself requires a careful approach to the marketplace. Few bank officers will have the time to become insurance specialists. While the *Digest of Bank Insurance,* available from the Insurance and Protection Division of the ABA, and fellow officers at correspondent banks can provide valuable counsel, most banks officers will depend on the advice of insurance agents and brokers. It is therefore extremely important that these advisers be carefully selected and that the bank avoid some of the traditional pitfalls of insurance purchasing, such as using too many agents or selecting agents solely through considerations of reciprocity.

In most cases, a bank needs but *one* qualified insurance agent or broker. If more agents are used, each should be assigned a specific area of responsibility. An agent or broker can be selected in a number of ways:

1. *Open Bidding.* Specifications for one or more forms of insurance can be distributed to any or all agents and brokers, with the selection being based on the agent with the lowest insurance company bid.
2. *Selective Bidding.* Several agents and brokers can be selected based on their respective qualifications to serve the bank and can be assigned specific insurance markets, to which specifications are given. Again the final selection of an agent or broker depends on the low bid.
3. *Presentation.* Agents and brokers can be asked to make a presentation to a bank committee which then selects the single agent or broker on the strength of this presentation and references.

Of these three methods, the third is strongly recommended. Furthermore, if specifications are drawn up for bids for various insurance carriers, it is generally agreed that such a process should not take place more frequently than once every six years (generally two policy renewal cycles). Bidding more frequently can be distinctly counterproductive, as insurance underwriters may be either reluctant to quote or may inflate their bids.

For simplicity, the insurance generally purchased by banks can be divided into five categories, full information on which can be found in the *Digest of Bank Insurance:*

1. *Financial Coverages.* These include the Bankers Blanket Bond— the single most important coverage for a financial institution and such related insurance as excess bonds, transit coverages, safe deposit liability insurance, registered mail, first-class mail, and excess securities bonds.
2. *Bank Property Coverages.* These include both fire and "all risk" contracts on buildings, contents, and property in transit. "All risk" protection may include collapse, water damage, earthquake, and flood, in addition to the more common fire, extended coverage, vandalism, and malicious mischief coverages. Other coverages include boiler and machinery, business interruption, extra expense

and coverage on electronic data-processing equipment and media, plus other valuable papers.

3. *Bank Liability Coverages.* These include all forms of public liability insurance, automobile insurance, and workers' compensation. Umbrella or excess liability protection is essential, generally with minimum limits of $1 million. For even the smallest bank, a limit of $1 million is recommended. Directors' and officers' liability insurance, when purchased, should include the personal liability of a bank officer who serves at the request of the bank as a director of one of the bank's customers, if that customer does not carry its own directors' and officers' coverage. Also included in the liability category is insurance for other legal liabilities, such as fiduciary liability for the bank's own benefit plan and professional liability arising out of errors and omissions involved in data processing or other work performed for outsiders.

4. *Departmental Coverages.* These coverages include all insurances related primarily to a specific bank operation. The trust department, for example, acting in a fiduciary capacity may purchase property and liability insurance for the benefit of its accounts. It may also consider trust department errors and omissions insurance (surcharge liability) for its clients and for its management of the employee benefit programs of customers. Installment loan, travel, mortgage loan and insurance agency departments all have specialized forms of insurance available, including mortgage guaranty insurance and credit life and disability insurance.

5. *Employee Benefits Coverages.* Generally these coverages will be coordinated with the Personnel Department, which prescribes the scope of benefits. However, the bank risk management officer should have the authority to finance the benefits and purchase insurance when necessary. In some instances, insurance may be less preferred than self-administered or trusteed plans.

For all types of insurance, consideration should be given to some general standards that apply to all contracts:

Named Insured. The actual named insured should be consistent on all bank insurance policies and, in the case of liability policies, should be broad enough to include all officers, directors, employees of the bank, and others who may be acting on behalf of the bank. Under the bond temporary employees and employees of an electronic data-processing firm should also be included.

Limits. For property insurance coverages, the limits should be related to either the "actual cash value" or "replacement value" of the property involved, taking care that co-insurance requirements are met. For bonds, the American Bankers Association sets periodically certain recommended minimums, based on bank size, and these can be found in the *Digest of Bank Insurance.* Liability insurance limits are quite subjective but, as mentioned above, even the smallest bank is well advised to have a minimum limit of $1 million.

Notice of Cancellation. *All* insurance contracts should include provision for a minimum of 60 days' written notice by the insurance company before cancellation, nonrenewal, or material reduction in coverage can become effective.

Participation in Risk. The bank risk management officer should give continuous consideration to the participation in insurable risk by the use of deductibles, franchises, or retrospective rating plans, where available.

Loss Adjustment. All losses should be settled with and payable to the bank, and the requirement for proper notification of loss to the insurance company should begin only after the bank's risk manager or similar officer is made aware of a loss.

Expiration Dates. A bank will generally find it advantageous to have as many of its contracts as possible expire on a common date, preferably coincidental with the bank's fiscal year.

Premium Payment. Cash flow is an important consideration in any risk financing program. While insurance policies may be issued for terms of from one to three years, it is possible to pay premiums on annual, quarterly, or monthly bases so as to generate significant cash flow savings to the bank.

In summary, a risk financing program will reflect all of the financial resources available to a bank, using insurance as only one of these financial resources.

RISK MANAGEMENT ADMINISTRATION

The administration of a risk management program requires continuous direction, generally by a bank operations officer specifically assigned this task. In the larger banks, this officer will be on a full-time basis, perhaps assisted by a staff. In small institutions, risk management will be a duty in addition to many others. Because the actual administrative techniques will vary from bank to bank, the following general requirements should be considered:

Written Policy. The preparation and approval by the board of directors of a written statement or policy on risk and insurance management is essential to any program. The following is suggested for consideration:

_____ is to be protected against accidental loss or losses which, in the aggregate during any financial period, would significantly affect personnel, property, the budget, or the ability of the Bank to continue to fulfill its responsibilities to its depositors, shareholders, and the public. In no event shall any loss of life or major personal injury to employees or members of the public be acceptable.

The Bank will apply to risks of accidental loss the risk management process, which includes a systematic and continuous identification of loss exposures, the analysis of these exposures in terms of frequency and severity probabilities, the application of sound risk control procedures, and the financing of risk consistent with the Bank's financial resources.

In recognition of its financial resources and the spread of its physical assets, the Bank will accept retention of uninsured losses up to the following limits:

Not more than $___ arising out of a single event or occurrence;

Not more than $___ aggregate during any fiscal year

The administration of the Bank's Risk Management Program is assigned to _____, reporting to _____.

Organization.   Many banks have found that, in addition to the designation of a single officer to accept responsibility for the program, the creation of a risk management committee can be useful. In large institutions, "unit" risk managers have been designated at branches and within departments to enhance communications with the risk management officer. The security function can and probably should be included within risk management.

Responsibilities.   Possible responsibilities for a bank risk management officer will include the normal steps of exposure identification, risk evaluation, risk control, and risk funding, as well as more specific duties such as review of all major leases and contracts, review of major loans and lease financing; coordination with internal audit, liaison with data processing, coordination with personnel on the design and funding of benefit programs and maintenance of essential records.

Communications.   Effective communication lines to and from the risk management officer are essential and will include, for most banks, a brief annual report, a "risk management manual" which might include an insurance policy schedule (a sample schedule is available from the Insurance and Protection Division of the ABA), use of training and films, the conduct of departmental seminars and periodic interviews and inspections.

Outside Assistance.   In addition to the full range of specific services available from the Insurance and Protection Division of the ABA, and from risk and insurance management officers in neighboring and corresponding banks, a bank will also have available to it assistance from accounting firms, risk and insurance management consulting organizations, insurance agents and brokers, and insurance companies. All should be used to develop an effective program. Another source is the Risk and Insurance Management Society, a professional organization of risk and insurance managers of American industry, headquartered in New York City.

The success of any bank risk management program will be measured by the degree to which its resources, human, physical, natural and financial, have been effectively conserved from risks of accidental loss.

_____ SECTION V

FINANCIAL MANAGEMENT

Chapter 31

Resource Allocation to Attain Corporate Goals

Edward L. Mercaldo*

INTRODUCTION

The process of allocation of bank or holding company resources to ensure the attainment of corporate goals is a long-term and continuous discipline. The need to make conscious realignment of the institution's resources is highlighted by a review of some of the factors which are currently attacking bank profit margins, including:

1. Shrinking "free" deposits.
2. Increased costs of doing business; i.e., personnel, occupancy, and regulatory compliance costs.
3. Increased competition from fellow bankers, thrifts and nonbanks.
4. Consumer awareness and willingness to shop for the best deal available.
5. Inflation and narrower interest margins.
6. Increased levels of loan losses and nonearning assets.

Obviously, many of the tools used in asset and liability management are valuable inputs into the process, but it is more than a simple exercise in rearranging numbers. There is no panacea. It is rather achieving awareness of the institution's basic resources, testing the adequacy of those resources against the stated goals and objectives of the organization and, finally, developing plans to augment the resources based upon the planning process.

---
* Vice President, Bank of Montreal, London, England (formerly Executive Vice President, Funds Management Group, Equibank N.A., Pittsburgh, Pennsylvania).

Perhaps the most important step in the process of allocating bank or holding company resources to attain corporate goals is that of defining the available resources of the institution with a view toward identifying existing strengths and weaknesses of the organization.

A broad definition of a bank's or bank holding company's[1] "resources" is appropriate in this discussion. These would include the following: capital, market share, personnel, image, plant, technical capability, and balance sheet structure. This chapter will concentrate upon personnel, technical capability, capital resources, and key asset/liability relationships.

Management and deployment of these resources revolve around many factors, including economic conditions, growth trends, market activity, management style and capability and regulatory requirements or constraints.

PERSONNEL RESOURCES

The quality of the personnel resource is vital to the ongoing success of a bank. We, as an industry, are becoming increasingly aware that a key variant in bank performance and one of the prime factors of consistent profit performance lies in the overall quality of the bank's staff and management. There are several indicators of personnel quality that bankers should monitor:

A. Rate of turnover of management personnel.
B. Number of key managers developed in the bank's own management training program.
C. Number of officers recruited annually by other institutions.

While all institutions have management needs from time to time which require outside hires, those banks with the strongest track records are staffed mainly of management teams which are largely homegrown.

The first requirement is a survey of the current management team and potential replacements. Inability to name replacements indicates organizational weakness. Next, growth projections over the next five years should be compared with a list of potential candidates for anticipated positions. Obviously, a shortage of qualified candidates compared to projected positions indicates corrective action is in order.

In addition to ascertaining that adequate numbers of qualified people are being recruited, trained and retained by the bank for its growing requirements, management must determine that career paths are

---

[1] Subsequently "bank" will be used to refer to both individual banks and bank holding companies.

being channeled into those areas most important to the goals and objectives of the bank. For example, a bank with heavy emphasis on large corporate or correspondent banking would have different requirements for educational backgrounds and a different approach to in-house training than a bank whose main thrust is developing a broad retail base.

Both the speed and extent to which the bank or bank holding company can commit its overall resources depends to a large extent on the quality, depth, and variety of human resources at its command. Just as it would be foolhardy for a bank to embark on an ambitious program to expand its construction loan volume without having a competent staff of construction loan officers, it is imprudent for a bank holding company to expand into some of the more sophisticated fields of the financial services industry, such as leasing or factoring, without an appropriate degree of expertise.

TECHNOLOGICAL CAPACITY

Closely related to personnel is the factor of technological capacity. Obviously, the bank needs well-trained, qualified personnel in order to make the technical side of the business function. This resource becomes crucial because the banking industry is becoming more and more technologically oriented, and needs more than ever to begin to develop technology as a resource. Look at several key questions facing banking today:

1. How can banks reduce the "paper handling" costs?
2. Are there methods available to halt or stabilize employment expense?
3. Since most consumers choose a financial institution based upon convenience, can services be made more convenient?
4. What do banks need to offer corporate customers to improve domestic and international cash flows?
5. How can banks monitor corporate profitability by account or group of accounts?
6. How can current market penetration and market share be measured?

The answers to many of these questions reside in the technology that is available or will be available within the next few years. Bankers should look closely at this resource. The byword today is flexibility. Changes in technology can provide solutions to many of these questions, and bankers must be able to adapt computers, communications devices, data bases, and related technology quickly and efficiently to meet their needs.

CAPITAL STRUCTURE

The next major resource to be analyzed in a review process is the bank's capital structure. Increasing emphasis has been placed on bank capital adequacy by bank regulatory authorities, the SEC, and the capital market itself. These factors make the acquisition, retention, and overall management of the bank's capital a key issue for bankers.

One of the first steps to be taken in capital management is a systematic review of the bank's current capital composition in comparison with industry averages for similar sized banks. Such a review will point out whether the institution is better than, worse than, or on a par with similar sized institutions in the industry. Currently there are services available which rank banks, by size categories, as to various capital adequacy ratios. Obviously, this type of review will help to determine if immediate steps or adjustments are necessary or, conversely, if no action is warranted.

Assuming that the bank's capital structure is in line with industry averages and requirements, an attempt should be made to project the institution's capital generation possibilities over the next five years, or the actual planning horizon used by the organization. Many may refer to such a projection as an art, not a science; but certainly it should not be guesswork as it is in many companies today. The institution's recent earnings pattern and history, its current capital adequacy, and dividend payout ratio should all be important data in developing a reasonable projection of internal capital generation.

Next the banker should study projected levels of asset and liabilities over a similar time frame. In addition to projected levels of core deposits and liabilities based on historical trends, the effects of planned changes in the normal growth pattern, anticipated changes in state, local, or national banking laws, changing market conditions, and economic projections should all be taken into consideration.

A comparison of the two projections of internal capital generation and projected capital needs may show the potential need for additional capital from outside sources. On the other hand, it may show that this particular resource will be in adequate, but not excessive, supply and should be channeled into only the higher yielding areas of return for the particular bank.

ASSET/LIABILITY RELATIONSHIPS

A major resource that a bank has to work with in its efforts to attain corporate goals is its core liability structure, often called the deposit base. This resource results from a market position and is unique to each banking institution. Oftentimes it is the resource that takes the longest lead time to develop and is the most difficult to change in a significant way.

Intelligent planning for the use of this major resource requires a thorough understanding of the bank's core deposits. Most banks exclude negotiable CDs, federal funds purchased, and other money market liabilities when computing the core deposit base. A cursory look at the liability side of the bank's balance sheet normally does not tell the whole story. For example, the classification of passbook savings deposits as short-term funds can be very misleading for most banks. Actually, retail savings deposits are assuming greater importance to most banks because of the decreasing trend of commercial demand deposits. For savings deposits, a core base can be established by plotting the figures in this category over a long period of time. This type of analysis will show that despite fluctuations from one fiscal period to another, there is a base to this particular deposit category which can be safely employed in longer term and higher yielding assets than normally might be considered prudent without such understanding. The following example can be used for purposes of illustration:

Passbook Savings Deposits	*(millions)*	*Passbook Savings Deposits*	*(millions)*
June 1966	$220	December 1966	$226
June 1967	232	December 1967	228
June 1968	235	December 1968	240
June 1969	245	December 1969	250
June 1970	262	December 1970	258
June 1971	271	December 1971	280
June 1972	285	December 1972	305
June 1973	310	December 1973	322
June 1974	320	December 1974	310
June 1975	328	December 1975	335
June 1976	333	December 1976	347

These figures presented in this fashion shed little light on the subject. However, plotted on a time chart they become more significant.

Despite fluctuations from period to period, a clear trend or "core" for this deposit category can be established for both demand deposits and savings deposits. In addition to being a helpful tool for current decision making, definition of the bank's core deposit base also enables management to project the deposit structure of the bank into the future and to determine if special steps or plans are necessary to alter or improve the projected position of the bank. This may be done by utilizing statistical techniques to determine what factors might influence this growth.

EXHIBIT 31–1
Illustration of Core Line Deposits

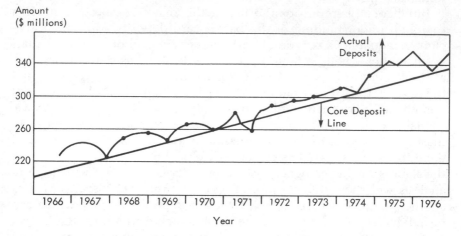

Amount
($ millions)

A useful approach in analyzing the bank's current status in asset/liability mix would involve the following elements:

A. Analysis of asset structure to determine:
   1. Interest rate sensitivity.[2]
   2. Maturity and cash flow.
   3. Special relationships or tie-ins to liabilities.
   4. Core loan demand.
B. Analysis of liabilities to determine:
   1. Interest rate sensitivity.
   2. Core deposit structure.
   3. Dependence of liabilities on particular assets.
C. Comparison of assets and liabilities to establish relationships between:
   1. Interest rate sensitivity.
   2. Core deposits/core loans.
   3. Balance in overall structure of the bank.

The purpose of this analysis is to get a general picture of the bank's overall balance in the composition of the asset/liability index. Banks which have consistent earnings patterns in all types of interest rate environments can be assumed to have a fair degree of equilibrium between interest sensitive assets and interest sensitive liabilities.

---

[2] Rate sensitivity can be defined in many ways. Most bankers pick an arbitrary time period, for example, 180 days, and consider all assets or liabilities which may change interest rates within that period (either because of maturity or terms of the instrument) to be "rate sensitive." The important point is to be consistent.

A bank which has higher than normal earnings in periods of high, short-term interest rates and, conversely, lower than normal earnings in periods of low, short-term rates can be assumed to have an imbalance of interest sensitive assets over interest sensitive liabilities. This may result in an underutilization of the core deposit base. Although the use of the core deposit base to properly align tends to eliminate windfall profits, doing so provides earnings consistency which allows bank management to spend more of its valuable time on longer range utilization of the institution's resources.

UTILIZATION OF RESOURCES

A study of the organization's resources will reveal the bank to be in one of three basic situations:

A. Underutilization of resources.
B. Adequate utilization of resources.
C. Overutilization or straining of resources.

Underutilization of resources will usually result in earnings consistently below industry averages, and probably a slow growth record. In addition to disappointing shareholders, such institutions are not contributing significantly to the economic development of the areas in which they operate.

Overutilization of resources may provide temporary benefits to the organization in the form of high return on equity, rapid growth, and increased market share. Such overutilization or straining of resources is oftentimes not penalized during periods of general economic wellbeing. However, economic downturns often affect institutions guilty of such excesses with a variety of problems, including lack of liquidity, rising loan losses, declining earnings, loss of market share, and operational problems. Many problems fall in the category of lack of sufficient or depth of management expertise.

Generally speaking, a full, but well-planned, use of the organization's resources will result in more consistent growth and development of the bank. While the level of utilization of the human and technical resources of the organization is to a large degree judgmental, the questions of capital and core liability utilization are more easily measured.

Once the overall analysis of the bank's resources, personnel, capital, and core deposits has been completed, intelligent utilization of the resources can be planned, taking into consideration bank objectives and the current level of utilization of resources.

The first step in the process of resource allocation is to determine the nature and amount of resources that can be allocated immediately. Several brief examples may be used for illustrative purposes.

Example 1.   Assume that the bank has an especially strong mortgage activity and a great deal of technical expertise and depth of personnel. A logical use of the resource would be acquisition or de novo formation of a mortgage servicing company at the holding company level.

Example 2.   Assume that the bank has an excess of interest sensitive assets over interest sensitive liabilities (underutilization of core deposit base). The bank could consider several alternatives including increased consumer lending, fixed-rate (medium-term) loans, or acquisition of longer maturity governments and municipals, all of which should provide greater returns than yields on short-term assets.

Example 3.   Assume that the bank has better than average expertise in data processing and bank operations, including competent staff and unused equipment capacity. A decision might be made to offer operations services to correspondent banks, aggressively package cash management services for corporate clients, offer special electronic funds transfer services to retail firms and consumers, or other related activities which would utilize these resources properly.

A definite distinction should be made between developing a long-range plan of resource allocation and shorter term tactical requirements which may call for temporary moves in a different direction. To illustrate, assume that the bank has as a stated objective the increase in its retail market share and in its current position has higher levels of interest sensitive assets than liabilities. Although the long-range goal may be to increase consumer lending volumes by 50 percent, it must be recognized that this type of an increase in consumer lending might take several years to accomplish. It may well mean that the bank will have to employ a portion of the available funds in more readily available fixed-rate assets, such as fixed-rate term loans, medium-term governments and reinvest the cash flow into consumer loans as the base of this business grows. The long-term objective can be maintained, but attention must be given to the interim effects on the profit and loss statement of simply waiting for the desired levels to be reached while utilizing resources at less than their fullest potential.

In today's environment, increasing attention is being paid by bankers to *both* sides of the balance sheet. Care must be exercised in developing the asset mix to look beyond the stated rates of various categories of assets to determine the true net yield to the bank. Because of generally increasing operating costs, banks are giving special consideration to use of the investment portfolio as the most flexible tool available for making adjustments in the basic structure of the institution.

There are several reasons for this flexibility:

1.   Changes in investment assets can be made immediately—no need for a marketing program or personnel training.

2. Changes can be made in substantial dollar amounts—size of the markets.
3. The stated yield is virtually the net yield received—low overhead.
4. Incorrect decisions or changing conditions are mitigated because of the nature of the assets themselves. Investment assets can be sold or used to support liabilities at favorable cost—public deposits or short public deposits and repurchase agreements.

The nature of the bank's objectives (i.e., whether they are aggressive or conservative) dictates the posture followed in allocating the bank's resources. Banks generally follow either a conservative posture of defensive allocation or aggressive allocation of resources.

A defensive allocation of resources is designed to protect the core deposit base, to maintain market share, and to stabilize earnings. An aggressive allocation attempts to increase the growth rate, maximize earnings potential and take advantage of unusual or unique resources of the institution. The decision to pursue an aggressive or defensive posture in the allocation of resources should be tempered by the status of such resources, as well as the objectives of the bank and the current and projected economic environment.

There are many tools available to the bank executive in the task of resource allocation. Most helpful, many feel, is the use of a computer model in analyzing the bank's structure and determining potential beneficial changes in the structure. Aside from the benefit of providing an enormous volume of calculations in a brief time frame, models have the rather significant advantage of allowing management to test numerous alternative strategies to secure profitable results. The successful utilization of a bank model encourages discipline in categorizing assets and liabilities and requires management to look at the bank in a logical and consistent manner.

There are three basic types of models:

1. Mechanical models which are offered by many of the accounting firms. These models simply do a large number of mechanical calculations. They can serve a useful purpose for banks just beginning the activity.
2. Linear programming models, or optimization models, were developed by several large banks a few years back. These models are quite complex and expensive to run. They generate a great deal of information and are very dependent on extremely accurate input in order to produce meaningful output.
3. Econometric models are basically mechanical models with the added input of an economic forecast or series of forecasts. The advantage of such models is that they project operating results based on a variety of asset and liability strategies and economic situations.

An example of the output from such a model is shown in the matrix in Exhibit 31–2 under three sets of strategies: (1) momentum (the bank continues with its same basic asset and liability mix), (2) commercial (the bank alters its asset mix and places a much greater emphasis on commercial loans), and (3) consumer (the bank alters its asset mix and places more emphasis upon consumer, or fixed-rate loans). The effect of each strategy upon earning per share is shown under three sets of economic conditions: (1) a stable economy, (2) an inflationary economy, (3) a downturn in the economy. The purpose of this technique is to provide management with probable results from various strategies under alternative economic conditions.

Exhibit 31–2
Effect of Three Strategies on Earnings Per Share

| | *Economy* | | |
Strategy	*Stable*	*Inflation*	*Downturn*
Momentum	$2.35	$2.37	$2.29
Commercial	2.30	2.40	2.28
Consumer	2.37	2.38	2.34

In this example bank management can see that the most profitable strategy to follow would be the consumer strategy, if economic conditions are stable; the commercial strategy if the economy turns inflationary; and the consumer alternative if there is an economic downturn. Management can also see that certain strategies have wider variances than others based on varying economic conditions.

A word of caution is in order. Although models can make the alternatives clear, they cannot make decisions. They simply show what is likely to happen under a combination of different asset and liability mixes and varying economic conditions. The decision about which way to allocate the bank's resources is still up to the banker.

A second major assist that can be used in the process of allocation of the resources is the bank's committee structure and board of directors. Properly used, the committee structure is helpful both in the continuing process of information gathering and, equally important, in the implementation of resource allocation decisions.

Both the loan committee and investment committee can provide insight to activity in the marketplace. The policy or executive committee of most banks considers and passes on most major resource allocation decisions.

More and more banks are utilizing the collective talents of the board of directors in resource allocation decisions, and, perhaps more importantly, in choosing between two or more attractive possibilities for deployment of resources. The well-informed bank director has not only pertinent business experience to call upon, but also the advantage of looking at proposals in an independent and objective manner.

A third tool used in the process is the organization's planning system, both annual and long range. Both the yearly profit plan and the long-range planning effort of the institution have important roles in the resource allocation process. The submission of plans by operating units in the planning process provide middle management's suggestions for allocation of the organization's resources. The final plan accepted and agreed upon by top management and operating divisions of the bank represents a myriad of choices between various courses of action in the deployment of resources.

It is accepted practice to monitor closely operating results against the profit plan projections. Most banks not only follow this procedure, but also make provisions for contingency planning or altering the profit plan if conditions change significantly. Unfortunately, such careful monitoring is not always true in the long-range planning effort. Two types of checks should be performed on longer range planning activities. First of all, specific projects should have a payout or cost/benefit schedule so that bank management can be alerted to any problems or difficulties as early as possible before wasting of the bank's resources can occur. The second type of monitoring is a periodic review and updating of the long-range plan tested against current assumptions and the bank's progress toward reaching its objectives.

SUMMARY

The allocation of the bank's resources to attain corporate goals is the essence of bank management. Intelligent choices are vital because there are definite limits to the resources and many outside factors affect bank profits. Among these factors are increased competition, changing deposit patterns, increased costs, inflation, and asset deterioration caused in part by economic conditions.

While there are many technical factors to be considered in the process of resource allocation, the process itself is an art as well as a scientific exercise. Sound business and banking judgment must supplement raw statistical data and projections. The first step in the exercise is an analysis of the current status of the bank's principal resources, including capital, technical capacity, personnel and core liabilities structure. The current level of utilization of these resources and the current position of the bank vis-à-vis its corporate objectives are important points of departure in planning resource use.

Once the study has been completed, two types of plans should be developed. These are short-term tactical plans and long-term strategic plans. Also, a decision should be made whether to follow a program of defensive or aggressive allocation of resources. This decision is influenced by the state of the available resources, as well as the objectives of the organization and the current and projected economic developments.

Numerous tools are available to bank management, including models, comparative studies, and management talents. Use should be made of the bank's committee structure as both a base for information gathering and policy dissemination. The board of directors should be used as a sounding board and source of independent judgment. Finally, a system for careful monitoring of resource allocation decisions should be established and those decisions altered if so warranted by changing conditions.

Chapter 32

Legal and Regulatory Constraints on Financial Management

Samuel B. Chase, Jr.*

INTRODUCTION

Although the array of financial services performed by commercial banks is very broad, their most vital function, at least aside from the central role they play in the payments mechanism, is serving as "financial intermediaries." They do this by raising money—mainly through deposits—and lending the funds they raise to myriad borrowers.

Commercial banks hold a substantial part of all debt of U.S. individuals, nonfinancial businesses, and governmental units. In addition, banks extend considerable amounts of credit to financial institutions, including other banks. Most of this lending was financed by domestic deposits, both demand deposits and time and savings deposits.

In addition, of course, the largest U.S. banks play a leading role in the system of international financial intermediation. Although this chapter gives only cursory treatment to the international aspects of legal and regulatory restraints on banks, it is to be expected that this aspect of regulation will become increasingly important in future years.

Both in raising funds and in placing them, commercial banks must live within a body of laws, regulations, and supervisory standards that would require thousands of pages to describe completely. Although most laws, regulations, and supervisory standards that constrain the financial operations of banks are intended to promote the soundness of the banking system (which is not to say that they always have that effect), they are sometimes used to serve other social purposes as well.

---

* Golembe Associates, Inc., Washington, D.C.

Often a constraint that is originally imposed for one purpose comes to be used for another.

A clear example of change in the purpose served by a governmental restraint is provided by reserve requirements imposed by the Federal Reserve System. Member banks must hold reserves, either in currency or in noninterest-bearing deposit balances at Federal Reserve Banks, equal to specified percentages of deposits that are set by the Federal Reserve Board within ranges allowed by statute. In 1977, reserve requirement percentages varied, by type of deposit and by size of bank, from 3 percent on passbook savings deposits, up to 16¼ percent for demand deposits over $400 million.

These requirements were part of the Federal Reserve Act of 1913, whose major purpose was to bring to an end the liquidity crises that had afflicted the nation. Requiring cash reserves was considered an important way to assure that banks would maintain adequate liquidity.

As the role of the central bank has become better understood, however, and as its responsibility for the general health of the economy has broadened, reserve requirements have come to be considered mainly as an instrument of monetary policy. Having reserve requirements enables the central bank to exert a more precise influence on the total amount of commercial bank deposits, credit, and thereby, it is believed, the level of GNP. Moreover, discretionary changes in reserve requirements provide a powerful method of creating excess reserves, or reserve shortages, on an overnight basis, should the Federal Reserve wish to do so. Thus, the function of reserves as a source of liquidity now receives little emphasis.

In addition to the fact that governmentally imposed restrictions have changing or sometimes conflicting purposes, the dual nature of the U.S. commercial bank chartering and regulation further complicates matters. Again, reserve requirements may be used for illustrative purposes. For state-chartered commercial banks that do not belong to the Federal Reserve System (national banks must be members), state-mandated reserve requirements apply. These differ markedly, both from the reserve requirements for members of the Federal Reserve System and from one state to another. Not only are percentage requirements not uniform, but it is not uncommon for nonmember banks to be able to satisfy at least part of them with earning assets, or with cash items in the process of collection. The generally less costly systems of reserve requirements for state nonmember banks have helped cause an erosion of Federal Reserve membership that boiled up into a major banking policy issue in the mid-1970s.

Despite the diversity of state laws and regulations under which commercial banks must operate, the presence of the federal government in chartering and supervising banks, in operating the central bank, and in providing deposit insurance, have imposed important measures of uniformity. The critical pieces of federal legislation in this respect are the National Bank Act, which was originally passed in 1863, the Federal Reserve Act, passed in 1913, the Banking Acts of 1933 and 1935, and the Bank Holding Company Act of 1956. (All of these laws have been amended numerous times since their original enactment.)

For example, the Federal Reserve Act has helped set the tone for state reserve requirements though it has certainly not brought uniformity. The 1930s legislation created, among other things, federal deposit insurance. Since many statutory and regulatory restrictions apply to all federally insured banks, and nearly all commercial banks are insured, deposit insurance has provided a centralized "handle" on state nonmembers. In addition, the 1933 act severely circumscribed underwriting of securities other than certain government obligations by any commercial bank—whether or not insured.

The Bank Holding Company Act, originally aimed at controlling the growth of multibank holding companies, was amended in 1970 to bring under federal regulation one-bank holding companies which were being used increasingly to avoid restrictions on the financial activities of banks per se. The 1970 amendments have thus added a new and formidable dimension to the federal presence in banking regulation, centralized in the Federal Reserve Board, which administers the act.

Thus, the system of restraints under which banks raise and place funds is enormously complex, not only because both the federal government and all 50 states are involved, but also because, at the federal level, several separate bodies of statutes govern federal intervention, and three separate federal bank regulatory agencies—the Federal Deposit Insurance Corporation, the comptroller of the currency, and the Federal Reserve Board—administer these statutes.

The following three sections deal, in turn, with constraints on the ways banks raise funds, the ways they place funds, and the operation of bank holding companies, which are overseen by the Federal Reserve Board.

CONSTRAINTS ON RAISING FUNDS

Deposits

Most of the significant restraints on ways banks raise funds are related to competition for deposits. Some insight into the complexity of the regulation of deposit competition may be grasped by consulting the monthly *Federal Reserve Bulletin,* which reports the vast array of ceiling rates on various types and maturities of time and savings deposits offered by banks.

The very definition of deposits (as opposed to, say federal funds or bank debt) and the distinction between time and demand deposits, are largely creatures of government regulation. Not only does the Federal Reserve Act set different ranges of reserve requirements for different types of deposits, but the Banking Act of 1933, by providing for time deposit rate ceilings and a flat statutory prohibition of interest on demand deposits, has made necessary a detailed and tortuous system of regulations and rulings as to what constitutes a deposit of each type.

Interested readers are referred to Federal Reserve Regulation D, which specifies reserve requirements for domestic deposits of member banks, Regulation M, which governs reserve requirements applicable to foreign branches (including those operating in the Eurodollar market), and Regulation Q, which sets interest rate ceilings for time and savings deposits and defines different clauses of such deposits.

In 1933, when federal deposit interest rate controls were first enacted, it was believed by their sponsors that they would serve the public interest by: (1) preventing New York City banks from pulling funds into the nation's financial center in the form of interbank deposits for use in making unproductive or even downright dangerous call loans to stock market speculators; and (2) preventing banks from bidding too aggressively for deposits simply in order to grow. The latter instinct was viewed as destructive because banks would thereby incur high-interest costs which could then be covered only by "reaching" for risky assets that weakened their solvency. The basic idea was that bankers were not very smart.

Subsequent investigations of experience leading up to the 1930s legislation have not tended to bear out either of the foregoing theories about the evils of uncontrolled rates of interest on deposits. Over time, however, the banking system has tended to adjust to such controls, and the purposes of "Regulation Q" ceilings on time deposit interest rates have changed.

In 1966, federally insured mutual savings banks and savings and loan associations were brought under federal rate ceilings (set by the FDIC and the FSLIC) for the first time. Since then, time and savings deposit rate ceilings have been aimed largely at assuring an adequate flow of funds to thrift institutions (and thereby the mortgage market) at rates the thrift institutions are judged capable of paying. Certificates of deposit in denominations of $100,000 or more have been exempt from ceiling interest rates since the summer of 1970. These so-called large CDs are the principal tool of large-bank liability management. They are used primarily to raise funds in the open market and are expanded and contracted along with loan demand.

Practically no disinterested party believes that the present complex system of differential ceiling rates, with higher rates allowed to thrift institutions than commercial banks, either serves to assure an adequate flow of funds to the mortgage market or, for that matter, any other social purpose. But removal of the ceilings would cause problems of adjustment, and in mid-1977 it appears that the ceilings will remain.

Congress has permitted all commercial banks and thrift institutions in the six New England states to effectively circumvent the statutory prohibition of interest on demand deposits by issuing special NOW (negotiable orders of withdrawal) savings accounts against which checks may be drawn. Under federal and state regulations, ownerships of these accounts is restricted to households and not-for-profit institutions. It is generally expected that NOW accounts will spread nationwide before the end of the decade.

Nondeposit Sources of Funds

Aside from deposits, commercial banks raise most of their funds from federal funds loans, sales of capital stock and subordinated debt, and retained earnings.

Federal funds borrowing involves mainly overnight loans of balances at Federal Reserve Banks. Such short-term borrowing, along with the use of short-term, large denomination CDs is subject to scrutiny by bank supervisory authorities who see excessive use of "managed liabilities" as a potentially harmful source of illiquidity.

The sale of bank capital instruments is subject to both federal and state regulation, including registration of public issues. Much supervisory effort is expended in attempting to assure that banks maintain "adequate capital." Just what is adequate has never been successfully defined, however, and except in the case of new banks, no formal statutory or regulatory capital requirements are imposed. Still, supervisors can and do exert pressures on thinly capitalized banks, and at times use their "cease-and-desist" authority to bring about compliance with their wishes. Therefore, banks must underwrite the growth of deposits with growing capital, and one of the most important constraints on the long-run growth of the U.S. banking system is its ability to generate retained earnings and to sell new issues of equity and subordinated debt.

CONSTRAINTS ON USES OF FUNDS

Statutory limitations prohibit banks from holding certain assets, or exceeding certain specified limits in the allocation of their funds among particular uses. Regulations promulgated by the banking agencies further delineate and confine the permissible boundaries of funds allocations. Finally, numerous supervisory standards are applied by supervisors on a discretionary basis in individual cases.

Most restrictions on the uses of bank funds find their origins in a legislative or regulatory agency concern with the closely allied goals of protecting depositors and the soundness of the banking system. As was pointed out earlier, intervention designed for one purpose sometimes takes on other purposes as well. Moreover, a given restraint may have more than one objective. One purpose of restraints on the banking system that is hard to pin down objectively is the prevention of "undue concentration of power." This concern underlies many of the restrictions on the ways banks use their resources.

Restraints on Ownership of Tangible Property and Equity Investments

Banks are chartered primarily for the purpose of taking deposits and extending credit, and severe limits are imposed on direct ownership of property and equity investments. Bank acquisitions of assets other than loans and investments are for the most part restricted to the following four categories:

1. Investments in bank premises, which, for member banks, are limited by federal law to the amount of paid-in capital, with the exception that permission may be obtained from the Comptroller of the Currency or the Federal Reserve Board to exceed these limits.
2. Property acquired as a result of defaults on collateralized loans, which is not subject to explicit statutory or regulatory limits. However, bank supervisory authorities encourage early disposal.
3. Property leased to customers which for national banks may include personal property and public buildings and facilities. The amount of such property acquired by national banks is not subject to limits comparable to those on loans to individual customers (discussed below). The major requirement is that the lessee become owner of the property at the expiration of the lease, which makes the lease similar in many ways to an extension of credit. Of the 46 states that permit the commercial banks they charter to engage in leasing, 9 have no restrictions on such activities, while the other 37 impose various requirements including restrictions on the types and amounts of property that may be leased.
4. Investments in equity securities, which are generally prohibited. Some states do not impose this prohibition, however, and there are important exceptions to the general rule. Commercial banks generally can own stock in subsidiary corporations that engage in activities that are permitted to the banks themselves, usually within limits tied to the bank's capital accounts. Equity ownership is permitted—again within specific limits—in certain specified

types of corporations, such as Edge Act corporations (which engage in foreign banking activities), service corporations, Small Business Investment Companies, and the Federal National Mortgage Association. Finally, banks can, of course, acquire securities posted as collateral for defaulted loans.

Restraints on Loans

The most important uses of bank funds are, of course, loans. Statutory loan limits, conventionally expressed as percentages of capital accounts, govern the maximum amount a bank can lend to any one borrower. The limit in the case of national banks is 10 percent of capital accounts; for state-chartered banks, the limits are typically less restrictive. Numerous exceptions to the general rules, both for national and state banks, provide for more liberal limits in the case of specified types of secured loans or to loans to certain public agencies.

Special restrictions apply to mortgage loans. Both the National Bank Act and the statutes of 24 states set limits on aggregate real estate loans of any given bank. In the case of national banks, total real estate loans (excluding those insured by FHA or VA) are limited to the total amount of time and savings deposits. Various restrictions also govern maturities of mortgage loans and ratios of loans to the appraised values of the underlying properties. However, 19 states do not impose either statutory restrictions of this sort nor aggregate limits on real estate lending.

Loans by Federal Reserve member banks to their affiliates are also restricted. With some exceptions, loans to any one affiliate may not exceed 10 percent of capital accounts and to all affiliates combined, 20 percent of capital accounts. In addition, any such loans must be collateralized by securities having market values equal to or, for some kinds of collateral, more than the amounts loaned.

Both federal and state statutes severely limit the types and amounts of loans banks can make to their own officers. Such loans generally must be for personal use, with the least restrictive limits applied to loans secured by personal residences. In the case of loans to directors, statutes normally specify procedures for approving such loans, usually including the consent of other directors. Federal law requires all member banks to keep on file reports of "significant" transactions with their directors.

Important restrictions are placed on stock market loans—i.e., loans secured by stocks, warrants, and convertible bonds. The Federal Reserve Act requires the Board of Governors to specify, for all lenders, the maximum ratios of such loans to the values of the securities used as collateral. The primary purpose of these "margin requirements" is to restrain stock market speculation, though they also limit risk-taking by banks.

Restraints on Investments

Statutory limits on securities investments tend to be similar to those applied to loans to single borrowers. Except for U.S. Treasury and federal agency debt and general obligations of state and local governments, holdings of securities of any one issuer are typically limited to a specified percentage of total capital accounts. Under federal statute, banks are, with certain exceptions, allowed to underwrite only those types of securities that are exempt from these limits.

Restraints on Foreign Activities

Federal banking statutes impose certain specific constraints on foreign activities, although these limitations are not, for the most part, very severe. Many state banking statutes do not address the matter of foreign activities at all.

There are no statutory restrictions on banks acting as dealers in foreign exchange. Member banks, as well as many state nonmembers, are subject to statutory limitations on their investments in foreign branches. Limits are also applied to direct equity investments by U.S. banks in foreign banks and Edge Act subsidiaries.

Additional Discretionary Restraints

Important additional constraints are applied on a discretionary basis as part of the bank supervisory function. For example, supervisors concern themselves with the overall liquidity of individual banks and with the qualities of loan and investment portfolios. Although the supervisory standards of the regulatory agencies vary somewhat, and are not codified, they are quite similar. All three federal supervisory agencies have the power to issue "cease-and-desist" orders and to institute officer removal proceedings to prevent or correct unsound banking practices, but some state agencies have no such authority.

Restraints Related to Trust Activities

A final set of important constraints related to asset acquisitions arises in connection with trust activities. Trust departments are prohibited from engaging in broker-dealer functions otherwise not permitted to commercial banking. This means that they cannot commingle their agency accounts for investment purposes. The theory is that such commingling effectively constitutes the creation and issuance of new securities similar to mutual fund shares. In practice, the result is that trust departments are severely hampered in serving smaller customers.

Various statutes pertaining to fiduciary responsibility and conflicts of interest limit trust activities. Investment of trust and agency accounts in mutual fund shares is prohibited by statute. Particular problems are raised by the need to limit exchanges of information between the banking and trust departments of a bank—giving rise to what has come to be called the "Chinese Wall"—and the extent to which trust departments can keep funds in trust accounts on deposit in their own banks. This relationship between the commercial banking departments and the trust department may be the subject of more explicit regulations in the future.

BANK HOLDING COMPANIES

Bank holding companies have somewhat greater flexibility in financial management than do banks per se. In addition to owning banks, holding companies may engage in activities determined by the Federal Reserve Board to be "so closely related to banking or managing or controlling banks as to be a proper incident thereto." Among the activities that have been permitted by the Board are making loans, factoring, mortgage banking, operating industrial banks or industrial loan companies, leasing real or personal property (providing the leasing transaction is the functional equivalent of an extension of credit), and issuing travelers checks and money orders. A complete list of permissible activities may be found in Federal Reserve Regulation Y.

For the most part, banks can engage in the same activities. The flexibility provided by using the holding company and its nonbank subsidiaries arises largely from two facts: (1) these institutions are not confined to operating in a single state, as are banks, and (2) certain restraints on raising funds that apply to banks do not apply to holding companies. For example, travelers checks issued by member banks are subject to reserve requirements, while those issued by nonbank subsidiaries of holding companies are not. Similarly, bank holding companies can raise funds to finance nonbank activities in the commercial paper market and thereby escape both reserve requirements and Regulation Q ceiling rates of interest. (Reserve requirements are applied, however, to any proceeds of commercial paper issued that are channeled to member banks.)

In addition to specifying the activities that are permissible for bank holding companies, the Federal Reserve Board must pass on applications to engage in such activities, either de novo or through acquisitions of a going concern. Through its power to deny applications, the Board derives considerable influence on the financial management of bank holding companies and their subsidiaries. This power has been used with particular force to bring about improved capitalization of subsidiaries, especially banks. It is also used to control leveraging of equity investments by the parent company. The Federal Reserve can impose specific restrictions on the ways parent companies and nonbank subsidiaries raise funds. For example, it does not permit subsidiaries such as sales finance companies to issue "thrift notes," which might be confused with deposits, from the premises of affiliated banks.

Chapter 33

Planning to Meet Liquidity Requirements—Concepts and Tools

George W. McKinney, Jr.*

From time to time, a new generation of bank managements becomes convinced that banking is an entirely new ballgame, that the precautions of the past are no longer appropriate, and that modern banking requires aggressive approaches that supersede the disciplines of an earlier era. They have a point. The forms, the approaches, even the customers of banking change. Certainly the mechanical procedures associated with banking today are markedly different from those of another era. With respect to the basics, though, they're wrong. The fundamental principles of banking are the same today as they were a hundred years ago.

SHIFTS IN LIQUIDITY PLANNING

Asset Allocation

Over the past half century, approaches to liquidity planning have seen several important shifts. In the late 1930s and the 1940s, when banks generally had plenty of liquidity and the big worry was primarily what to do with it, the basic approach was "asset allocation." In earlier years, bankers conceptually lumped together all of the funds at their disposal, regardless of where they came from; these funds were then

---

* Senior Vice President, Irving Trust Company, New York, New York.

411

parceled out in different kinds of assets according to rules of thumb or arbitrary percentage allocations. Later this procedure was refined into hypothetically breaking up the bank into a series of "minibanks." Thus there was conceptually a "demand deposit bank," a "time deposit bank," and so on. Based on the presumed stability of each of the different sources of funds, the resources of each "minibank" were deployed differently. Thus savings deposits, which supposedly were more stable, were invested more heavily in longer term assets such as mortgages. Demand deposits were allocated relatively more heavily in commercial loans. Important vestiges of asset allocation thinking can still be found in various approaches to liquidity management today, even in and perhaps especially in some of the more esoteric econometric models.

Asset Management

In the immediate postwar years, thought about liquidity management moved toward the broader concept of overall asset management. Essentially, this new development recognized the dimension of time as relevant to banking. Attempts were made to estimate the swings in liquidity needs over the course of the business cycle, and to vary the maturity of assets, particularly the maturity of marketable investments, to meet those needs in ways that would be most profitable for the bank. Much of the thought that went into asset management is relevant in today's environment, and asset management is still an integral part of liquidity planning by banks today.

Liability Management

Starting in the early 1960s and growing rapidly for more than a decade, liability management became the new, glamorous approach to liquidity management. Unfortunately, the approach was so new that inevitably some banks overplayed the game and got in over their heads. By the mid 1970s, some of the banking heroes who had played the leverage game to the hilt in the early 1970s were again making headlines as participants in the rather significant increase in bank failures at that time. The experience of those years, though, demonstrated that there is an appropriate and important place for liability management in banking, if used with discretion and discipline. It has also become clear that, since liability management depends heavily on the use of market instruments which are more readily available to larger banks, the ability to use liability management effectively varies directly with the size of the bank.

The latest step in the evolution of the theory of liquidity management follows logically from the earlier phases. Asset allocation approaches recognized that banks should try to have some control over their balance sheets and some provision for liquidity. Asset management techniques were developed in recognition of the fact that needed liquidity can be provided more efficiently and at considerably greater profit to the bank by varying the maturity structure of its assets at different phases of the business cycle. Liability management grew up largely because commercial bank access to funds they could lend out became progressively more difficult in those years, and thus managed liabilities came to supply a permanent source of funds. Liability management also brought a recognition that the maturity structure of liabilities could be varied in the reverse way from that of assets, further improving the efficiency with which banks meet their liquidity needs and adding to their profitability.

Funds Management

Today's approaches to liquidity management recognize that the basic problem is management of the entire balance sheet in such a way as to optimize net return on the bank's capital over time, while simultaneously providing safety for depositors' funds and liquidity as needed. Modern management techniques, including sophisticated computer programs, are used to manage interest rate spreads and to plan profits most effectively. Liquidity management is only a facet of the overall management of the bank's funds—but it is an exceedingly important facet.

DISCIPLINE AND INFORMED JUDGMENT

The basic issue in the management of bank funds is the use of discipline and informed judgment to achieve a delicate balance between assuming risk as a means of increasing income, on the one hand, and keeping the bank's resources both safe and liquid, on the other. Discipline is necessary because the element of time is so important. The balance sheet cannot be structured with only today's relationships in mind; the banker must be constantly aware of cyclical and other trends which will influence the bank's position in the months and years to come, and he must plan to meet them. The banker has to have in the back of his mind all the time the fact that every business cycle is different, but that there is always a business cycle. This requires alertness, patience, and restraint.

Information is necessary because liquidity management, as is the broader concept of total funds management, is a highly individualized problem. No two banks do the same kind of business even in the same kind of community, and no two banks have the same liquidity needs.

Therefore it is not possible to put down any formula which provides the answer to the liquidity needs of all banks. Instead, each bank must go through the tedious process of reviewing its asset and liability composition and trends and of carefully analyzing them to determine what its liquidity needs will most likely be.

The most important factor in liquidity planning is judgment. Judgment is needed to arrive at a balanced decision that considers rationally the several competing objectives the banker must keep in mind, and to assure optimal consideration of profits, safety, and liquidity over the entire business cycle. Perhaps this factor, more than any other, may separate the thinking banker from the more shortsighted competitor.

Decisions not Precise

Decisions in the area of liquidity planning are necessarily inexact. Because most of them depend on the application of informed judgment, they can be argued by reasonable people. For example, how much liquidity does a bank need? How can it best meet its liquidity needs? How much capital is enough? How many bad loans does a bank have? How bad are they? How safe are its investments? How dependable are its deposits? How much purchased money can the bank buy—CDs, federal funds, whatever—if the going really gets rough?

In the final analysis, none of these questions can be answered definitively. None can come out of the computer without qualitative supplemental evaluation. And every single answer could be argued different ways by reasonable people.

In fact, the answers all depend on a myriad of factors most of which will come into play in the future: the economy, the fortunes of the bank's customers, the strength and particular skills of management, and so on. The banker can think about them, argue about them, but at best he or she will only come up with well-informed guesses. If not careful, the banker can spend a lot of time and money working up detailed mathematical calculations on a computer that, with a great deal of precision, will provide answers that have very little to do with the basic broad problem the bank is dealing with. Actually, mathematics is very helpful with "which" form of liquidity the bank needs to use, and modern theoretical analysis in many cases concentrates on "which." Unfortunately, though, mathematics isn't too good at telling "how much" or "when." And recent bank failures have basically presented problems of "how much" (in that banks have on occasion failed to provide adequate liquidity) or "when" (in that assets or liabilities were lengthened, or shortened, too much at the wrong time).

This chapter will be largely concerned with "how much" and "when." Other chapters concentrate on other aspects of funds management: resource allocation, liability management, money position management, and capital management.

A Framework for Analysis

Since funds management is so heavily dependent on informed judgment, it must be built about an outline or framework for thought. It is necessarily an attempt to organize a vast amount of information so the banker can think about it effectively and can have the best possible framework on which to reach decisions about the subject.

Basically, this starts with the balance sheet. It is not possible to devise an effective funds management program without reference to the balance sheet. In fact, it can be argued that the balance sheet by itself is adequate to serve as the basis for an effective funds management program—certainly one for a smaller bank. One such approach is outlined below.

The balance sheet shown in Exhibit 33-1 gives a breakdown of assets and liabilities not customarily used in bank accounting. Rather, it's a functional breakdown intended to highlight those components of the balance sheet most useful in planning for liquidity management. Every bank has a certain amount of cash assets, consisting of cash in vault, reserves at the Federal Reserve if it's a member bank, and balances with correspondents. It also holds certain liquid assets which, at least for purposes of liquidity planning, should be segregated in records maintained for that purpose. This liquidity account, comprised of short-term, high-grade, readily marketable securities and possibly certain types of loans, is of crucial importance in the management of bank funds. Longer term portfolio investments are a necessary part of the balance sheet, and of course loans and discounts generally take the lion's share. For simplicity, we will ignore the category of other assets.

It is similarly useful to classify the other side of the balance sheet into broad conceptual groupings of demand deposits, time deposits, money market deposits and liabilities, and capital accounts. Other liabilities will be ignored, as are other assets.

A key factor to bear in mind is that not one of these asset or liability items can change without a concurrent change in at least one other category. For example, the bank cannot increase its loans without either decreasing investments, liquid assets or cash assets, or increasing one of the items on the liabilities side of the balance sheet. All the categories are continually changing, of course. The management of bank funds involves adjusting to changes in these interdependent fac-

Exhibit 33–1

Percentage Distribution of Assets and Liabilities for All Commercial Banks, December 31, 1976

All Other Assets	5%		8%	Capital Accounts
			3%	Other Liabilities
			14%	Money Market Deposits and Liabilities (including negotiable certificates of deposit)
Loans and Discounts	52%		42%	Time Deposits
Investments	16%			
Liquid Assets	14%		33%	Demand Deposits
Cash Assets (including reserves)	13%			
	Assets		Liabilities	

Source: Board of Governors of the Federal Reserve System. Partly estimated by Irving Trust Company.

tors as they occur and planning ahead so that appropriate consideration is given to the element of time. This is done primarily by managing the composition of the assets, working largely through the liquidity account, and by influencing both the size and composition of the bank's liabilities and capital accounts. The bank's funds can only come from the capital it accumulates from the sale of securities and by retention of earnings, from deposits competitively attracted and retained, and from borrowing. The use to which those funds are put should reflect such factors as the cost and availability of those funds, the amount and nature of the deposits, and the adequacy of the bank's capital.

Supplemental Factors to Consider

In putting its funds to work in various assets, the bank should also have some intangibles in mind. Overall risk may be evaluated by giving thought to the strength of the assets and to the volatility and dependability of the liabilities on the bank's books. The strength of the bank's capital, too, is a factor. So are the predilections of the bank's management concerning risk; banking institutions do differ in this respect. Bank managements also differ significantly with respect to their ability to handle risk. One management team may be strongest in consumer loans, or in commercial loans, or it may have particular strengths in investment management.

Finally, it should be recognized that a commercial bank has a major obligation to its customers and community to meet their legitimate credit demands to the limit of its capacity to do so. In recent years the functional distinctions between commercial banks and other financial institutions have become more and more blurred, a trend that is likely to continue in the future. Until such time as boundaries between institutions disappear, though, commercial banking will continue to be a specialized business that benefits from sticking to its area of activities. Further, banks are a politically vulnerable group, and a failure to meet community credit needs would ultimately lead to legislative changes that would be damaging to them.

Investments a Residual

If we grant that banks should give loans preference over other types of business, then we appropriately view the employment of other funds in longer term investments as a residual function where funds may be placed for profit to the extent that profitable loan opportunities are not available. After the needs for cash reserves, liquidity, and loan demand have been met, the bank should logically invest any residual in its investment account as a means of increasing income. Of course, there are certain minimum needs for investments that must be satisfied. Consideration should be given to the amount that will be needed for pledging as collateral to public funds or for other purposes, and the investment community is likely to look with disfavor on the stock of a bank that doesn't carry at least some undefined minimum amount of government securities on its books. Also, banks with heavy exposure in other areas of the balance sheet (e.g., a relatively large amount of high-risk loans) may want some volume of governments to balance off the bank's total risk exposure. Beyond such minima, though, it would be good to view the bond account as a residual use of funds after legitimate and profitable loan demands have been met.

The primary function of the investment account is the earning of income, though it can also be used as an emergency backstop to the liquidity account. The longer term securities in the investment account can be sold and the proceeds used to make loans or meet deposit declines. However, liquidity pressures are likely to be greatest at precisely those times when bond prices are lowest, so the use of the investment account to provide liquidity is likely to involve some loss on the sale of the assets. Since using the investment account in this way is rather expensive, it should be done only to cover miscalculations in the liquidity account.

Conversely, the primary function of the liquidity account is to provide liquidity, although it can have an auxiliary income-producing function. To reach too far to increase earnings on the liquidity account, however, may result in acquiring overly risky assets which, even though their maturity is short, may produce a loss when sold in a depressed market.

Again, planning to meet the bank's liquidity needs involves adjusting to changes in the various interdependent factors in the balance sheet and planning ahead in those adjustments in such a way as to provide adequate liquidity and safety and yet at the same time to optimize the flow of profits over time.

There are at least three dimensions of liquidity management: (1) How much? (2) In which? (3) When?

HOW MUCH LIQUIDITY?

Why does a bank need liquidity? To the extent that assets and liabilities (deposits or purchased funds) are deliberately or coincidentally matched with respect to maturities, liquidity is not a problem. The maturing asset can usually be counted on to provide the funds to pay off the maturing liability. The Eurodollar market is typically handled on a matched-maturity basis; many banks are trying to match their assets and liabilities so that more of both long- and short-term maturities fall due on the same schedule. Matching maturities tends to help keep rate spreads constant and stabilize earnings. However, a commercial bank is limited in the extent to which it can match maturities, and there is always some (large) unmatched segment of the balance sheet.

The bank would not need any liquidity if its deposits grew at a steady rate, and if loan growth were predictable and could be met from that deposit growth. However, both deposits and loans are subject to cyclical, seasonal, random, and long-term variations. For most banks, long-term trends are comparatively stable; the bank will grow at perhaps x percent a year over time. But that growth rate may be changed drastically by the addition (or loss) of a new business in the community. Or such things as changes in the nationwide rate of inflation can influence the bank's rate of growth.

Each Bank Is Unique

Cyclical fluctuations influence each bank in a different way. But the bank with loans and deposits which are not subject to some systematic variance over the course of the business cycle is a rarity. Also, most banks have clearly identifiable seasonal patterns in loans and deposits, in that they will vary up or down by about the same percentage magnitude at the same time each year. Cyclical trends are generally more important for larger banks, and seasonal trends more of a problem for small banks. Finally, all banks are subject to day-to-day random variations in deposits and loans which can be rather sizable. It is essential to know and understand how these trends affect a bank's loans and deposits before management can plan adequately to meet the bank's liquidity needs.

Use Charts Constructively

Perhaps the best way to find out how these trends affect a bank is to use charts. Some people prefer tables. However, the problems and results of liquidity planning must be shared with other persons, and charts seem to be grasped more readily than tabular data. Ready access to a computer, of course, offers canned programs that can be used to estimate seasonal patterns. But charts are still useful to help explain results.

Semilogarithmic charts (designed to show rate of changes) are often useful. Exhibit 33–2 shows why. The lines in both panels of this chart

Exhibit 33–2
Comparative Measures of Growth

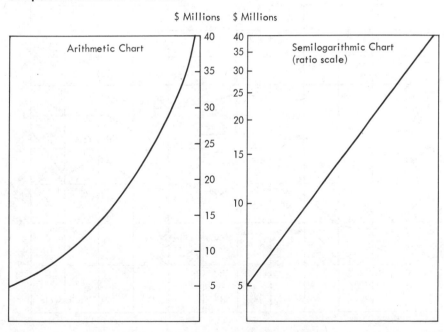

show the same growth: from $5 to $40 million over the same period of time. However, the chart in the left panel (on arithmetic paper which records equal dollar changes as equal vertical distances on the chart) visually emphasizes the growing *number* of dollars of deposits added each year, and gives the incorrect impression that the bank's growth rate has increased over time. The same data on the semilog chart in the right panel, which records equal percentage changes as equal vertical distances on the chart, give the correct impression that the bank has grown at an equal *percentage* rate year after year. Since the world we live in is basically one in which geometric progressions prevail, semilog (ratio) charts give a much more realistic picture of that world.

A layered chart, in which the months of several years in sequence are plotted one above the other, is quite useful in showing the size and timing of seasonal patterns. From Exhibit 33–3, for example, it is easy to identify the typical percentage increase in deposits (or loans) from one month or season to another by seeing how much change occurred each year over the past several years.

Exhibit 33–3

STATE NATIONAL BANK
Demand Deposits of Individuals, Partnerships
and Corporations

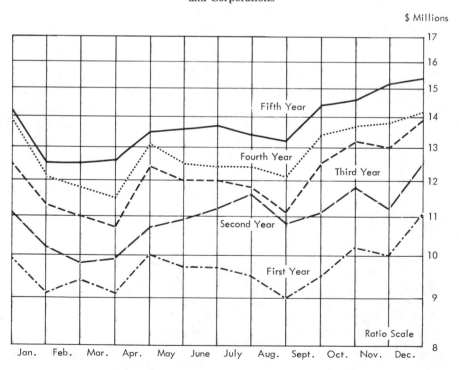

A similar technique can be used in estimating the size of cyclical variations in loans and deposits (Exhibit 33–4). In this case, the low point in the business cycle can be plotted at the same point on the horizontal axis of the chart, and the amount of change in various cycles can then be traced with ease. A parallel approach can be used to analyze behavior around business cycle peaks.

Other charts should be prepared to cover a period of several years (see, e.g., Exhibit 33–5) to define clearly what the growth trends are and to show the loan and deposit experience during recessions and recoveries. To do this adequately, at least two full business cycles should be covered.

Monthly data are probably adequate for most purposes and certainly for most small banks. Most larger banks would want to plot the data more frequently, perhaps as of reserve computation dates. Averages of daily figures should be used since any one day's results may be erratic and therefore misleading.

How many items should be charted? The answer depends, of course, on the size of the bank and the complexity of its business. However,

Exhibit 33–4

STATE NATIONAL BANK
Total Net Deposits in Five Recoveries

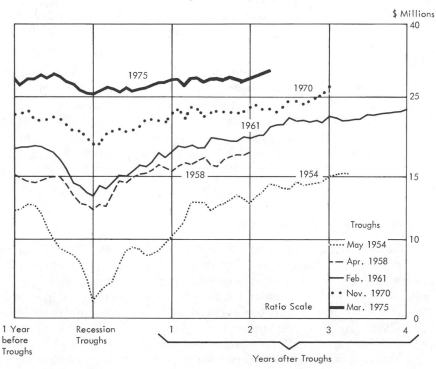

Exhibit 33–5
Net Deposits (excluding negotiable CDs)

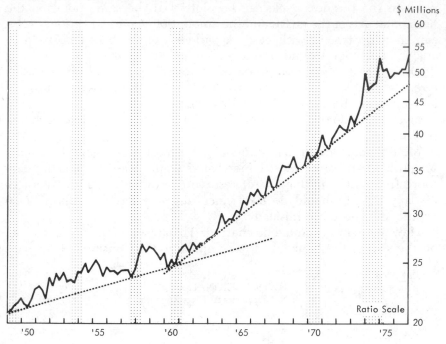

management is interested in finding out about the behavior of deposits, loans, investments, and liquid assets. Thus those four categories provide a minimum that should be charted; major components of each category are also good candidates for analysis. Most bankers will probably want to chart more items so they can understand more of the details of operations. But it is important to avoid undertaking an overly ambitious program which is more likely to wind up on the scrap heap than a more modest one.

Analyzing Loans and Deposits

Whatever the technique, the objective is to evaluate the importance of various factors bearing on deposit and loan trends. For example, seasonal patterns of deposits are usually much more important in agricultural areas and at smaller banks. Deposits can vary 10 percent, 20 percent, or more from the average, at about the same time each year. Particular attention should be paid to large accounts or to those that are felt to be particularly active and volatile. For example, public deposits require a study of the type of deposit and the probable duration of the deposited funds with the bank. Various types of public deposits behave in quite different ways. If they are important to a bank, it may be worthwhile to analyze them closely.

Time and savings deposits, too, differ in character depending on the type of deposit. For example, seasonal patterns in savings deposits are usually quite clearly pronounced. There is a tendency for them to decline on certain dates, such as tax dates, and management should know what these tendencies are. Special problems should be treated with special care. For example, if a bank has a large concentration of negotiable CDs, particular attention should be given to them.

Seasonal and cyclical patterns of loans, although varying widely among banks, can be important. Keeping track of commitments and unused lines of credit may provide some help in estimating future loan expansion. Management should know the extent to which lines are used by customers under various conditions.

Estimating Liquidity Needs

Once the charts and other background information provide the best possible basis for understanding how loans and deposits behave under different sets of circumstances, a fairly simple procedure offers a means of estimating the likely volume of liquidity that may be needed and that should be provided to meet fluctuations in deposits and loans. One such procedure, described by the Federal Reserve Bank of New York as the "baseline" procedure and by the New York State Bankers Association as "hard-core" deposits, is to draw a line through low points on the deposit chart (Exhibit 33–5). This provides a visual picture of the secular growth of the bank's deposits and, on the assumption that this growth will continue into the future, indicates how much deposits fluctuate above that basic trend. Further, it shows how far above that trend deposits are at any particular moment in time. By looking at the chart, a banker can read off the distance between the baseline and the current level of deposits. A bank should be reasonably prepared to provide for liquidity to meet future movements in deposits if at all times if it holds an amount equal to that difference.

Of course, there's a great deal of conjecture and judgment in such an approach. For example, the growth rate of the bank in the illustration increased significantly after 1960 largely due to the rising rate of inflation. Certainly over the succeeding decade the bank could have appropriately counted on a faster growth rate than in the years before the mid-60s. If inflation slows, though, the bank's growth rate will likely slow, too. Changes of this sort will inevitably influence the bank's future, and they can't be picked up instantaneously from a chart. That's why judgment is so important in analyzing banks' liquidity needs.

Another approach to the same problem is shown in Exhibit 33–6. Instead of extrapolating a line as in Exhibit 33–5, the banker considers all the facts available and arrives at a judgment as to the lowest level (the "floor") to which he or she thinks deposits may possibly decline at any point within some specific period—for example, within the next 12 months. This is not as easy as the preceding approach, but it has the advantage of forcing one to think about the issues—probably the most important part of the exercise. If management constantly reviews and updates projections, it will find that from month to month estimates of what the next 12 months hold in store will inevitably be revised. Over time projections of the minimum level likely during the upcoming 12 months will be revised up or down, and will appear as "stair steps" on the chart. Again, as in Exhibit 33–5, the estimate of liquidity needed for possible deposit withdrawals can be derived by reading

Exhibit 33–6
Net Deposits and Estimated Minimum Deposit Levels (excluding negotiable CDs)

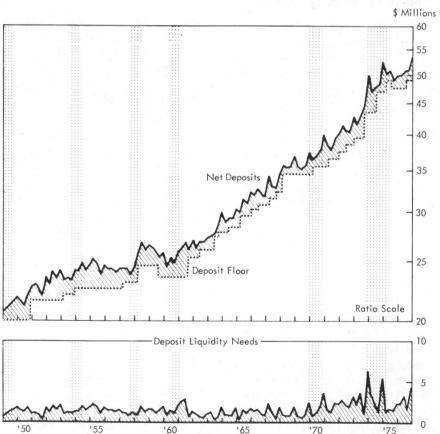

off the distance between the "floor" and the current level of deposits. Note that the amount will vary from day to day as the current level of deposits moves up and down.

Either technique can be used to estimate a loan "ceiling." If the stair-step judgmental approach is used, the banker will, as in Exhibit 33–7, estimate the highest level to which he expects loans may rise within the next 12 months. This forms a set of stair steps above the level of loans on the chart, similar to the "floor" under deposits in Exhibit 33–6. Since loans may reach the estimated loan "ceiling" at

Exhibit 33–7
Nonmoney Market Loans and Estimated Maximum Loan Levels

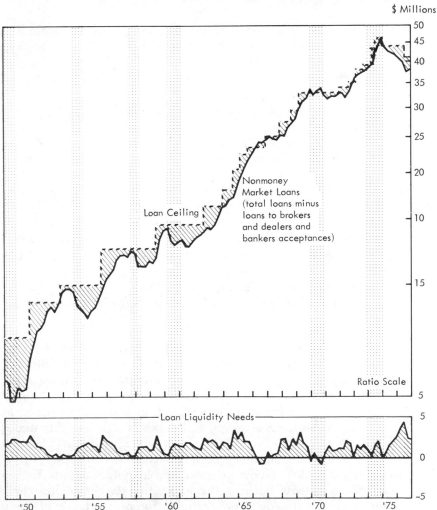

some time within the next 12 months, the bank should be prepared to meet that level of loan demand by making sure that it has an amount of liquidity equal to the difference between the "ceiling" and the current level of loans.

Exceptions to Bear in Mind

Adding together the estimated deposit liquidity needs plus estimated loan liquidity needs gives a good first approximation of the total needs for liquidity for most banks. These estimates are combined in Exhibit 33–8. However, several caveats should be borne in mind in estimating loan and deposit liquidity needs.

1. Allow for the reserves that will be released if deposits decline to the floor. If, for example, the bank loses $10 million of deposits and has an average of 10 percent reserve requirements against them, it must provide only $9 million in liquidity, since the decline in deposits would release $1 million of reserves.
2. If reserve requirement changes are likely, allowance may be made for them.
3. The prudent banker might want to add a little extra liquidity to provide funds for a good investment opportunity at some time in the future.
4. If a bank has a strong seasonal pattern, and if the seasonal peak in loans does not come at the same time as the seasonal low in deposits, there will be a certain overlap and deposit and loan changes will in some degree provide liquidity for each other. Liquidity needs may be adjusted downward by the amount of this overlap.
5. The supervisory authorities have some firm ideas about liquidity needs, generally based on formulas. These must be taken into account in planning.

Note that the amount of liquidity needed varies with the current levels of loans and deposits. Liquidity needs are at their greatest at cyclical and seasonal troughs when loans are low and deposits are high, since liquidity will have to be used up in meeting any subsequent decline in deposits and the expected growth in loans. Conversely, at a cyclical peak, when loans are high and deposits soft, liquidity needs are at a minimum.

Perfection in insuring adequate liquidity would involve always having just enough liquidity to cover deposit and loan fluctuations. Excess liquidity reduces income because the idle funds do not realize their full earnings potential. Too little liquidity forces costly emergency

Exhibit 33–8
Liquidity Needs for Loans and Deposits

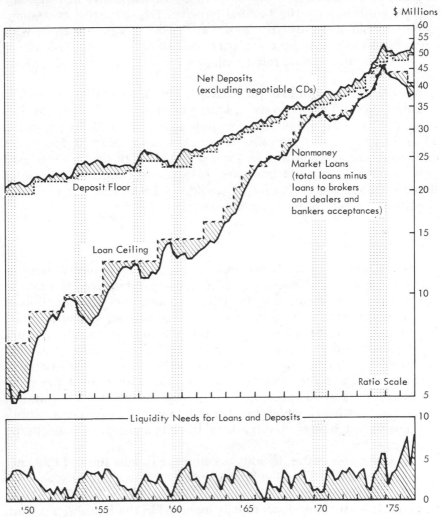

measures to be undertaken at unfavorable times. But, of course, perfection is impossible in practice.

IN WHICH ASSETS?

The most obvious resource to meet liquidity needs is cash assets. But that's the wrong answer. A bank usually has every reason to keep cash assets at a minimum at all times. Currency and coin represent

merely a security problem and earn nothing. Excess reserve deposits
at the Federal Reserve Bank do nothing for the bank; in fact, they
complicate things for the Federal Reserve. Deposits with correspondents should logically be kept at levels commensurate with
services rendered by the correspondents. Basically, then, cash assets,
if held to the appropriate minimum, provide little in meeting liquidity
needs.

Many analysts count loan runoff as a source of liquidity. It is a source
of cash flow, and in one sense a source of liquidity. The paydown of
loans can be used either to make new loans or for other purposes.
Thus loan runoff can logically be counted as liquidity, if gross loan
extensions are also counted as a use of liquidity. In the analysis used
here, however, only net increases in loans are counted as a use of
liquidity. Thus, for symmetry, it would not be logical to count loan
runoffs as a means of meeting *net* loan growth.

The Liquidity Account

The liquidity account is the real source of asset liquidity. Accordingly, it should be carefully identified and separated from the investment account in accounting for liquidity purposes. The function of
the liquidity account is to provide funds quickly and at little or no
loss to meet deposit declines or increases in loan demand. The account
is composed of short-term, readily marketable, high-grade assets held
and used for liquidity purposes. Some banks include nonmarketable
securities that are very close to maturity. Loans that meet the functional criteria for the account may also be included. For example,
money market loans, which involve only minimal customer relations
and are in fact treated like marketable obligations, may logically be
included.

The maturities in the liquidity account are usually limited to a one-
or two-year range. The dividing line between the liquidity account
and the investment account is, of course, an arbitrary one. The longer
the maturities that are conceptually included in the liquidity account,
the more susceptible they are to market fluctuations and the greater
the risk of loss in their possible sale to provide liquidity.

Compare Liquidity with Needs

The liquidity needs, identified by charting loans and deposits and
estimating the loan ceiling and deposit floor, should be compared
against current holdings of assets in the liquidity account (see Exhibit
33–9). The objective, of course, is to hold just that amount of short-
term assets in the liquidity account which is adequate to meet the

Exhibit 33–9
Money Market Assets and Liquidity Needs for Loans and Deposits

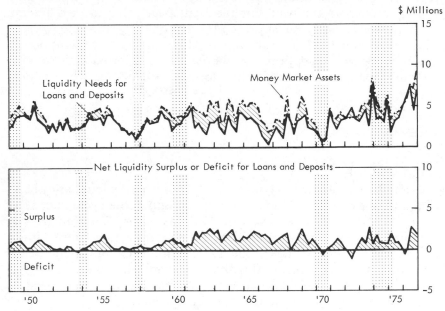

estimated liquidity needs. If, after careful analysis, the conclusion is that the bank has more liquid assets than are needed, the solution is to purchase more longer term investments for the normally greater yield. Conversely, if the volume of liquid assets held does not equal estimated needs, either the bank should acquire additional liquid assets by disposing of longer term securities, or it should make specific plans to use purchased funds (liability management) to meet liquidity needs when they arise.

Liability Management

If the bank relies on liability management to any great extent, and most large banks do, a technique similar to that described for asset management can be used. Various aspects of liability management will be treated in a later chapter. Essentially, though, the principles are the same. Management needs to evaluate access to the money market, and how much of that access has already been used. One technique, parallel to that described for asset liquidity management, is to make an estimate of current total borrowing capacity, in a manner similar to the loan ceiling and deposit floor. That borrowing capacity can be plotted alongside the current level of liabilities, and the two compared. If liabilities are below the best estimate of the borrowing capacity (bearing in mind that borrowing capacity may be reduced if bad news about the bank hits the front page), that unused amount of borrowing capacity can appropriately count as liquidity. Conversely, if the bank is currently borrowing more than the market might permit if conditions worsened, provision should be made for enough liquidity in some other form to meet that decline in liabilities when it does occur.

WHEN?

The Cyclical Low

Exhibit 33–10 illustrates typical rate trends over the four basic phases of the business cycle. At the low point (trough) in the cycle, monetary policy is at maximum ease as the Federal Reserve System tries to stimulate the economy by expanding the nation's money supply. Interest rates may be at or near their low for the cycle and bond prices near their cyclical high. At this time the bank should keep its asset liquidity at high levels and maturities short. Purchased funds will be at low levels and should remain low for a while.

Exhibit 33–10
The Interest Rate Cycle

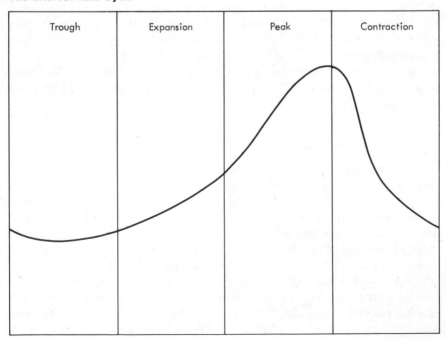

Trough	Expansion	Peak	Contraction

The Expansion

In the expansion phase of the cycle, after the trough in economic activity is clearly passed, monetary policy will begin to tighten. As loan demand picks up modestly, some liquidity will be used to meet that loan growth. In this phase of the cycle the bank should begin to build total footings to levels that are believed appropriate for the next boom period, and liability maturities should be lengthened. This allows the bank to purchase money at today's rates to lend out at tomorrow's higher rates. The question of when to start lengthening maturities is difficult, and the time varies with each expansion. The ideal time is six months to a year before short-term rates start to move up steeply— i.e., late in the expansion when the economy is approaching capacity output. If the bank moves too early, the usual premium paid for long CD money eats up too much of the profit. If it waits too long, others get the same idea and the CD rate moves up quickly. On average, since 1960 the best time to lengthen has been one to two years after the trough in the business cycle.

The Peak

The decision to lengthen liabilities should be implemented gradually, on a planned and deliberately paced schedule that will build up long-term liabilities to some previously determined total. Then this level of long-term liabilities should be maintained until the peak of the business cycle appears close. But a bank should not wait too long. The ideal time to begin shortening is more than six months and perhaps a full year before the business cycle peaks. This is the most vulnerable phase of the cycle for liability management, for the decline in interest rates typically proceeds much more rapidly than did the preceding upswing in rates. It's much better to move too quickly and to have to carry assets with high-interest rate, short-term liabilities during the boom than it is to wait too long to shorten liabilities and to be encumbered with long-term CDs outstanding while interest rates on loans are declining sharply.

It is important to recognize monetary policy is at its tightest and individual bank liquidity should therefore be largely depleted. At this time, asset maturities should be kept quite long to lock in good yields. Liability maturities should already have been shortened and remain short.

The Contraction

The contraction phase of the cycle seldom lasts as long as expected. In this phase, monetary policy eases and interest rates drop much faster than they rose during the expansion. The bank should now begin rebuilding liquidity, but deliberately rather than on a crash basis. Asset maturities should be shortened on a schedule that will "round the horn" at the trough of the cycle. This does not have to be done all at once, and it is extremely difficult to hit the low point in the interest rate cycle. One of the most common mistakes in managing funds is to try to do it all "at the right time." It is usually far better to make a number of small mistakes than to make one big one. The better part of wisdom is to wait a while to start lengthening liabilities.

In short, it is a mistake to try to fine tune interest rate planning too closely. No one is capable of forecasting interest rates with great precision. However, the *trend* of business and the *direction* of rates can be predicted with sufficient accuracy to be quite helpful in improving the bank's profitability with minimal exposure to risk. And it is important to note that the trend of business is all that is needed for the type of liquidity planning outlined in this chapter. The business trend largely determines movements in interest rates, and liquidity needs and interest rates move in tandem. Thus if a bank plans for the appropriate *volume* of liquidity needs, the acquisition and use of that liquidity will automatically be most propitiously timed for the best profit performance.

SUMMARY

In summary, there are at least three aspects of planning to meet liquidity needs: How much? In which? and When? Computer models and modern mathematical techniques help in selecting which assets and liabilities should be used under various sets of circumstances, but they are not very useful with respect to "how much" and "when." One way or another, the banker must specifically think about "how much"—the amount of liquidity the bank should have. The use of deposit floors and loan ceilings (or of baseline trends) provides a good mechanical framework for that thought. Such techniques force the banker to at least look at the fundamentals. Consideration of time— "when"—requires that the bank manage its assets and liabilities and coordinate the two over the course of the business cycle. Since interest rates tend to move in such a way as to automatically be most advantageous for the banker who appropriately plans for meeting his or her liquidity needs, specific interest rate forecasts are not necessary in analyzing the needs for and provision of liquidity. All that is needed is a good estimate of the quantity of liquidity needed.

Chapter 34

Evolution and Overview of Asset/Liability Management

Rufus F. Land*

INTRODUCTION

Asset/liability management is a term which designates a funds management philosophy that is steadily gaining acceptance in today's banking circles. The term implies that it involves managing a bank's assets and liabilities—an implication that might lead one to question the newness of such an approach. Recently, however, an increasing number of banks have adopted an explicit and coordinated approach to the management of both sides of the balance sheet. Thus, asset/liability management, as an integrated funds management philosophy, plays a role of much greater magnitude than the simplistic definition "managing assets and liabilities" denotes.

The principles involved in the practice of such a philosophy are more easily understood if one first considers where asset/liability management stands in relation to asset creation and funding activities and how the philosophy has evolved over the past four decades.

ASSET CREATION AND FUNDING ACTIVITIES

Asset creation and funding activities in a bank fall under two basic categories: trading and portfolio management. It is important that one understand the role of each in asset creation and funding and the distinction between them. It should be noted that for a majority of banks, portfolio management is the only asset creation and funding

---

* Senior Vice President, North Carolina National Bank, Charlotte, North Carolina.

activity, with trading generally limited to larger banks with the resources necessary to support such an activity.

Trading

Trading can be defined as responding to day-to-day risks while operating within established limits. Dealers in the foreign exchange and bond departments of banks are but two examples of those employed in the trading function.

Portfolio Management

The second category, portfolio management, involves selecting the most efficient mix of assets and liabilities for a given portfolio. This selection is subject to overall constraints as to market and customer considerations, levels of interest rates, maturity structure, and types of instrument. Portfolio management also entails adjusting to new constraints.

In the past, portfolio management has been thought of in terms of managing an investment portfolio. However, in present-day banking there are several managed portfolios that are made up of assets or liabilities that are traded in the open market. Price and condition of sale are set by market conditions and not by direct negotiation with the lender or borrower. In addition, there are also portfolios composed of assets or liabilities under terms worked out directly with the customers. The activities involved in managing the customer-negotiated portfolios are significantly different from the activities in managing assets or liabilities acquired in the open market.

Asset/Liability Management

Asset/liability management, while not specifically an asset creation and funding activity, is closely entwined with both trading and portfolio management. Asset/liability management is the managerial process of developing and evaluating overall objectives, policies and strategies based upon a number of factors. These factors include the environmental conditions and outlook, opportunities in the marketplace, risk preferences, and risk-reward characteristics. The implementation of asset/liability management policies is carried out through asset creation and funding activities.

EVOLUTION OF ASSET/LIABILITY MANAGEMENT

An examination of the distribution of assets and liabilities of commercial banks over the past four decades clearly reveals the major shifts that have occurred in bank management philosophy. Exhibits 34–1 and 34–2 show the wide differences that have existed in the asset/ liability mix since 1941.

Asset Management

Asset management was the primary bank management philosophy of the 1940s and 1950s. In the early 1940s, a large proportion of commercial banks' assets were cash items and U.S. Treasury securities. Banks added substantially to their holdings of U.S. Treasury securities as part of the war financing effort. By 1947, cash items and U.S. Treasury securities accounted for approximately 70 percent of the total assets of commercial banks. (See Exhibit 34–1.)

Exhibit 34–1
Distribution of Assets, All Commercial Banks (year-end)

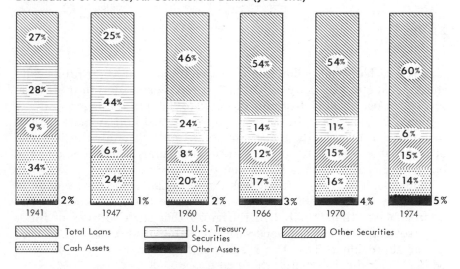

The postwar years featured a strengthening economy and an acceleration in loan demand, making loans an attractive earning asset. As a result, loan growth during this period was funded largely by reducing holdings of cash and U.S. Treasury securities. The dramatic increase in loan volume was not accompanied by a corresponding growth in deposits.

Liability Management

The shortage of funds to support loan growth was intensified in the 60s when corporate treasures began to withdraw their idle demand deposits and invest these funds in open-market assets, such as commer-

Exhibit 34–2
Distribution of Liabilities, All Commercial Banks (year-end)

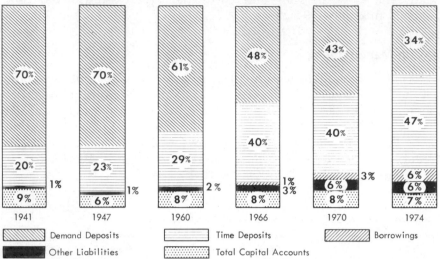

cial paper, that would allow them to earn interest on their funds. Substantial loan growth, coupled with a less rapid expansion in traditional sources of bank funds, fostered the shift to liability management.

Banks began raising funds in the open market and at market rates to finance asset growth. Banks obtained funds through the issuance of negotiable certificates of deposit, federal funds purchases, and the borrowing of Eurodollars from their overseas branches.

Thus, liability management was the dominant funds management philosophy of the 1960s and early 1970s. The basic weakness of this approach was that it failed to recognize that such sources of funds for asset expansion is not necessarily available at all times, or at least not at affordable prices. The result was high-cost financing of assets whose yields did not match these costs.

Asset/Liability Management

The third major shift in funds management philosophy occurred about the mid-70s. This new philosophy, consisting of an approach which simultaneously considers both sides of the balance sheet, has been labeled asset/liability management or balance sheet management.

PRINCIPLES OF ASSET/LIABILITY MANAGEMENT

As practiced by banks today, the typical approach to asset/liability management consists of three major components. They are: differentiation of risk, focus on overall position, and explicit consideration of uncertainty.

Differentiation of Risk

Asset/liability management differentiates between the three types of risk associated with the asset creation and funding activities: credit risk, liquidity risk and interest-rate risk.

Credit Risk. Credit risk is the risk that the full value of the asset may not be realized at maturity. Customer selectivity can serve to reduce this type of risk. It is for the purpose of trying to measure this risk that banks perform credit analyses of prospective customers.

Liquidity Risk. The second type of risk that asset/liability management recognizes is liquidity risk. This can be defined as the risk that a shortage of funds will require some assets to be funded through the liquidation of other assets under unfavorable conditions, or the acquisition of additional funds on an unfavorable basis.

Interest-Rate Risk. Interest-rate risk is the risk that earnings will be influenced by changes in the level of interest rates. Changes in a bank's net interest margin due to interest-rate risk can be traced to one or more of three factors: (1) balance sheet structure; (2) changes in internal spreads; or (3) changes in external (market) spreads.

1. *Balance Sheet Structure.* That portion of the change in a bank's net interest margin due solely to the interest-rate and maturity characteristics of the bank's assets and liabilities is said to be due to balance sheet structure. Thus, the balance sheet structure component of interest-rate risk is commonly thought of as the degree of rate sensitivity of assets and liabilities and the balance between rate-sensitive assets and liabilities.

2. *Changes in Internal Spreads.* The second component of interest-rate risk is internal spreads or net interest margin changes due to changes in the spread between market rates and realized rates on the bank's assets or liabilities. Examples of this type or spread are the spreads between the national prime rate and the bank's commercial loan yield or that between the national 90-day CD rate and the actual cost of funds raised by the bank in the form of CDs.

    The impact of internal spreads can be subdivided into two parts: the realized and the residual effect. The realized effect of a change in internal spreads is the impact of interest-rate changes on the net interest margin which occurs while the change in rates is taking place. Thus, the realized CD cost in 180 days will differ from the rates at which CDs are issued during that 180 days. Residual effect represents the lag effects of the outstanding CD's adjusting to current market rates; that is to say, the net interest margin will continue to change after interest rates have stabilized.

3. *Changes in External or Market Spreads.* Changes in a bank's net interest margin due to interest-rate risk can also be caused by changes in external (market) spreads. Examples of external spreads are the spreads between national prime and the national federal funds rate or between national prime and the national 90-day CD rate.

Exhibit 34–3 illustrates the effect on net interest margin of changes due to each of the three components of interest rate risk.

EXHIBIT 34–3
Effect of the Components of Interest-Rate Risk upon Net Interest Margin

The following example demonstrates net interest margin changes due to each of the three components of interest-rate risk. Base Case, Case No. 1, Case No. 2, and Case No. 3 represent simplified versions of a bank's balance sheet for four successive years, along with the corresponding internal and external rate structures.

It should be noted that net interest margin changes can rarely be attributed to a single component. More often, they are due to a combination of the components. The following example, however, has been constructed so that net interest margin changes from one balance sheet to the next can be attributed to a single component. The steps necessary to determine the cause of the change are outlined below:

1. Assume the following levels and rates:

	Base Case	Case No. 1	Case No. 2	Case No. 3
Levels ($000)				
Commercial loans	$1,000	$1,000	$1,000	$1,000
Investments	600	600	600	600
Available demand deposits...	500	500	500	500
Savings deposits............	300	300	300	300
Certificates of deposit........	500	500	500	500
Federal funds purchased.....	300	300	300	300
Internal rates (percent):				
Commercial loan yield.....	8.00%	8.75%	9.00%	9.25%
Investments	7.50	7.50	7.50	7.50
Savings deposits............	5.50	5.50	5.50	5.50
Certificates of deposit........	6.25	7.00	7.00	7.00
Federal funds..............	5.50	6.25	6.25	6.25
External rates (percent):				
Prime....................	7.00%	7.75%	7.75%	8.00%
90-day CDs..............	6.00	6.75	6.75	6.75
Federal funds.............	5.50	6.25	6.25	6.25

EXHIBIT 34–3 *(continued)*

2.   What is the net increase margin in each case?

Base case ($000)	$80.0	($1,000 × 8.00%)
These figures are added because there is income interest associated with an asset	+45.0	(600 × 7.50%)
These figures are sub-tracted because there is interest expense associated with a liability	−16.5 −31.25 −16.5 $60.75	(300 × 5.50%) (500 × 6.25%) (300 × 5.50%)
Case No. 1 ($000)	$87.5 +45.0 −16.5 −35.0 −18.75 $62.25	($1,000 × 8.75%) (600 × 7.50%) (300 × 5.50%) (500 × 7.00%) (300 × 6.25%)
Case No. 2 ($000)	$90.0 +45.0 −16.5 −35.0 −18.75 $64.75	($1,000 × 9.00%) (600 × 7.50%) (300 × 5.50%) (500 × 7.00%) (300 × 6.25%)
Case No. 3 ($000)	$92.5 +45.0 −16.5 −35.0 −18.75 $67.25	($1,000 × 9.25%) (600 × 7.50%) (300 × 5.50%) (500 × 7.00%) (300 × 6.25%)

3.   Therefore, from the Base Case to Case No. 1, the net interest margin increased $1,500, from Case No. 1 to Case No. 2 it increased $2,500, and from Case No. 2 to Case No. 3 it increased another $2,500.

4.   Since balance sheet levels for the Base Case, Case No. 1, Case No. 2, and Case No. 3 are identical, it is interest-rate changes that are responsible for the changes in the net interest margin. To determine what component of interest-rate risk is responsible for the net interest margin change, it is necessary to examine three factors (rates, internal spreads and external spreads) to see what changed in each case.

Base Case to Case No. 1.

   Rates—Commercial loan yield, CDs, federal funds, and prime all went up by 75 basis points.

EXHIBIT 34–3 *(concluded)*

Internal spreads—Unchanged.

External spreads—Unchanged.

Therefore, balance sheet structure was responsible for the net interest margin change. Since there was an excess of rate sensitive assets, the rise in rates (with spreads unchanged) had a favorable effect on the net interest margin (+$1,500).

Case No. 1 to Case No. 2

Rates—Commercial loan yield increased 25 basis points; other rates remained constant.

Internal Spreads—Commercial loan yield versus prime increased 25 basis points.

External Spreads—Unchanged.

In Case No. 1 to Case No. 2, the change in net interest margin was due to the change in internal spreads. The amount of the impact was the change in the internal spread (.25) times the asset it affected (commercial loans of $1,000), or $2,500.

Case No. 2 to Case No. 3

Rates—Prime and commercial loan yield both went up 25 basis points.

Internal Spreads—Unchanged.

External Spreads—Prime versus federal funds went up 25 basis points, prime versus 90-day CDs increased 25 basic points.

External spreads, therefore, were responsible for the change (+$2,500) in the net interest margin.

Focus on Overall Position

The second principle of asset/liability management is focus on overall position. This means that the bank's total position is considered rather than viewing situations in isolation.

A distinction must also be made between actual and perceived risks. Since objective evaluation of risk is difficult at best, it is easy to understand why a bank's actual risks (as measured after the fact) may be different from the way the risk is perceived by bank management in arriving at its decisions. In addition, persons assessing these risks from outside the bank (externally) may judge the extent and nature of the risks to be different from either the actual risk or the risks as perceived by bank management. Exhibit 34–4 is an illustration of risk differences. Note that the difference between actual and perceived risks (from either the management or external view) may be in relation to the amount of total risk as well as the proportion of each type of risk assumed.

It is possible, in certain situations, to substitute one type of risk for another. It is not, however, always desirable to do so. It has already been pointed out that credit risk may be reduced by customer selectivity. In different ways, interest-rate and liquidity risk may also be altered. For instance, the pricing of a loan can affect the interest-rate risk of loan, while the method of funding may alter the liquidity risk.

Exhibit 34–4
Total Bank Risk

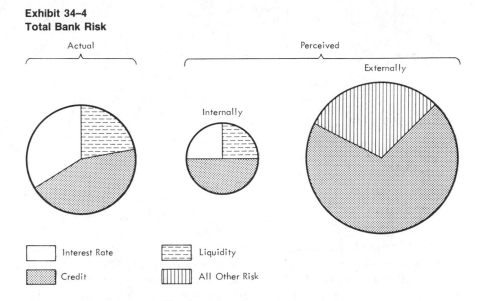

Exhibit 34–5 demonstrates the process of substituting one type of risk for another. In a situation ("before" in the exhibit) the environment may have changed in loan demand and loan quality so that the credit risk may be deemed excessive. Adjusting to that change might require a reduction in lending activity to reduce the degree of credit risk ("interim" status). But that adjustment could reduce overall earning assets and leave unused capacity. The bank, in examining opportunity for added earning assets, could conclude that attractive investments in municipal securities offered the best alternative. Expanded investments would take care of unused capacity and maintain credit risks at an acceptable level under current conditions, but would increase interest rate and liquidity risks.

Exhibit 34–5
Substitution of Risk

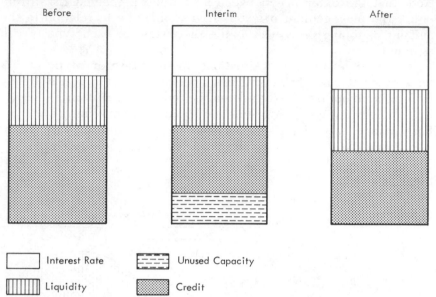

Before   Interim   After

☐ Interest Rate   ⊟ Unused Capacity

▥ Liquidity   ▦ Credit

Explicit Consideration of Uncertainty

The third major principle of asset/liability management is explicit consideration of uncertainty. The first step in adherence to this principle is forecasting the economic and financial environment. With a forecast in hand, the evaluation of alternative strategies is possible. But there is uncertainty associated with any forecast. For that reason, in testing a proposed strategy, it is necessary to consider not only the "most likely" economic outlook, but also possible variations. The goal is not necessarily to develop an asset/liability management strategy which will maximize the bank's net interest margin. What should be aimed for is the highest potential net interest margin under expected economic conditions while providing protection on the downside in the event the "most likely" scenario does not come into being.

There are many different ways to look at the impact that variations from the "most likely" scenario would have on the net interest margin. By assigning probabilities to various economic scenarios, it is possible to use the "expected value" concept to evaluate different strategies. Exhibit 34–6 shows how this could be done.

Certain economic scenarios would be spelled out with an estimated probability for each to occur. Several different asset/liability management strategies would be evaluated (in terms of profitability) for each

Exhibit 34–6
Impact of Various Strategies

	I (50%)	*II (30%)*	*III (15%)*	*IV (5%)*	*Expected Value*
		Likelihood of Economic Scenarios (*probable profits in $000*)			
Strategy A.........	$117	$120	$110	$ 95	$115.8
Strategy B........	107	102	112	122	107.0
Strategy C	112	115	112	117	113.6

economic scenario. The "maximum expected value" is a weighted statistical value for each strategy influenced by the probability of each scenario taking place. The bank may not wish to select the strategy that will maximize that value. It might be wiser to select a strategy that was not overexposed to any one economic scenario. For example, Strategy A maximizes the "expected value"; but under Scenario IV (though a small probability of taking place) that strategy would produce very unfavorable results. On the other hand, Strategy C would provide stable profits under all economic scenarios.

CONCLUSION

Over the past 30 years, major changes have occurred in the composition of banks' balance sheets. There has been a relative buildup of loans and time deposits and a decline in relative proportion of cash, investments, and demand deposits. This changing composition has become more pronounced in recent years.

The environment that appears to be unfolding for the future is characterized by a further shift toward interest-bearing liabilities, use of increasing proportions of debt by all sectors of the economy, and intensified competition from other financial institutions.

There are, however, some positive countervailing forces to those developments. On a long-term basis, the demands for credit are expected to outpace the rate of savings accumulation. This scarcity of funds will enable banks to price their products more realistically. Recent behavior of the prime rate compared to federal funds and other money market rates shows that bankers are already becoming more aggressive in pricing their services.

Small- to medium-sized banks will have a more stable deposit base than money center and regional banks. This is because they rely primarily on local sources of funds.

Perhaps the most important positive factor for the future is that banks have always been successful in adapting to change. The recent shift in funds management philosophy to asset/liability management is a prime example of banks' ability to adapt to changes in the economic and financial environment.

Banks are becoming increasingly aware that it is not necessary to be a large bank to apply an integrated approach to asset/liability management. The basic concept is much more important than the refinement or specific tools. With a minimum of effort, it is possible to a good understanding of the bank's overall position. And such an understanding is the edge banks need to thrive in an ever-changing environment.

Chapter 35 _____

Managing the Bank's Money Position

James J. DeCantillon*

THE BANK'S MONEY POSITION

The level of complexity and sophistication of almost all aspects of commercial banking has increased markedly in the past 10 years. No single operation reflects this growing complexity more than the management of the bank's money position. The tremendous growth of the American banking system in these ten years has resulted in a rapid increase in the quantity of interbank money transfers. It is the responsibility of the bank's money position manager to monitor these money transfers and ensure that the institution's money needs are effectively met.

The complexity of bank cash management varies, of course, with the size of the institution. Large money center clearing banks transact several billions of dollars in money transfers daily whereas some smaller regional banks experience quite minimal money flows. Regardless of the volume of money transfers, efficient cash management can produce significant benefits to any bank.

The challenge of efficient utilization of bank funds is not new to bank management. Generations of bankers have been confronted with the problem of meeting current cash requirements while minimizing holdings of nonearning assets. Efficient money management is applicable whether a bank manages its cash through adjustments in income-earning assets or purchased liabilities. In either case, direct benefits

_____
* Vice President, Continental Illinois National Bank and Trust Company of Chicago, Chicago, Illinois.

445

through increased asset yields or reduced interest expense can be derived through the minimization of cash balances.

Although every bank must practice money management, this article will concern itself only with money management in the context of Federal Reserve member bank reserve account management. The member bank's money need can be defined as that quantity of reserves held necessary to meet its statutory reserve requirement. Efficiency is measured by the bank's ability to meet this requirement without holding excess reserve account balances. Through study of this rather specific money management analysis along with the chapters on bank liquidity and liability management, one can derive a general impression of banking industry money needs and management.

RESERVE REQUIREMENTS—THE ACCOUNTING MECHANISM

The member bank's daily reserve requirement is computed as a fraction of its total deposit structure. Federal Reserve Regulation D reserve requirements are applied to the bank's weekly average totals of demand, time, savings, and Eurodollar deposits, determining a single reserve account balance to be held two weeks hence. Prior to September 1968, reserves were maintained on a concurrent basis with deposits. At that time Regulation D was altered to provide for lagged reserve maintenance. This alteration stipulated that reserve requirements would be computed from daily average deposit aggregates through one settlement week (the reserve computation period). This reserve requirement level would then become effective for the settlement week beginning two weeks later (the reserve maintenance period). With this alteration, the Federal Reserve is now provided with the commercial banking system's aggregate reserve requirement the week it becomes effective. This knowledge facilitates the federal open-market desk's ability to manipulate banking system reserve availability to a position consistent with its short-term monetary policy directives.

During the seven-day reserve settlement period beginning Thursday, a member bank must carry an average daily balance in its reserve account approximating its required reserve level. This daily averaging process implies that the bank can, on any particular day, carry a very minimal or very high balance. All that is required for a proper "settlement" is that the bank's daily average reserve account balance fall within a 2 percent per day (14 percent for the seven-day period) interval of its reserve requirement. To the extent that daily average balances fall beneath the allowable interval, an unallowable deficiency in settlement will have occurred and the bank will be penalized by its district Federal Reserve Bank at the rate of 2 percent above the going discount rate on the amount of the unallowable deficiency. If daily average

reserve holdings exceed the 2 percent allowable, an unallowable excess will have occurred and the bank will suffer a loss of earnings due to the idle use of funds.

That portion of the bank's daily average reserve account balance falling within the 2 percent interval is an "allowable settlement carry-over" and applied by the Federal Reserve toward the bank's next settlement period reserve requirement. If the bank is allowably deficient, for example, that daily average deficiency will be added to the next period's reserve requirement—effectively forcing it to maintain a greater quantity of reserves in the next period to compensate for the deficiency of the past period. Thus, reserve account maintenance is a simple averaging process on a daily and weekly basis.

The Federal Reserve scrutinizes very closely the settlement performance of its member banks. Those with frequent unallowable settlements or frequent exercise of their discount window borrowing privilege (especially in periods of central bank credit restraint) stand in jeopardy of having their senior management formally contacted and criticized by officials of their district Federal Reserve Bank.

OPERATIONAL ASPECTS OF THE MONEY POSITION

Reserve account management ultimately encompasses all practical aspects of bank money management. Traditional concepts of bank money management include vault cash, correspondent bank demand account balance, cash items in the process of collection (checks being remitted to the Federal Reserve for collection), as well as reserve account management. An examination of these aspects of money management follows.

A bank must carry enough vault cash to meet the public's demand for currency. Vault cash holdings in a reserve computation period are a direct offset to a bank's statutory reserve requirement two weeks hence. These characteristics of vault cash should induce the bank to hold a very prudent currency cushion to satisfy its normal seasonal as well as any unanticipated currency demands. Fluctuations in the bank's vault cash needs can be met through an exchange of currency for reserve account balances with its Federal Reserve Bank. Therefore, reserve account management involves directly the management of vault cash.

The Federal Reserve System provides a clearinghouse mechanism for checks drawn on member banks. Money management implies the monitoring of cash items in the process of collection. To precisely monitor each clearing check would be a time-consuming and basically unwarranted exercise as the aggregate money flows they entail tend to be quite constant and predictable. When the checks are finally

cleared, payment is made to the remitting bank through a Federal Reserve credit to its reserve account. Checks drawn against the bank are "paid" through a Federal Reserve debit of its reserve account. Check clearing activity, then, impacts directly upon reserve account management.

Demand balances held at correspondent banks compensate the correspondent for services provided. These balances must be held at a minimum tolerable level if money management is to be efficiently performed. Fluctuations in "due from bank" balances result in corresponding, but opposite, fluctuations in the bank's reserve account balance.

Similar to the impact of due from bank balance fluctuations on the reserve account are the effects of any deposit and funds borrowed or sold fluctuations. Any increase in the bank's deposit or funds borrowed (primarily federal funds purchased and securities sold under agreement to repurchase) liability structure will have a corresponding impact on the reserve account. An increase in the bank's funds sold (generally federal funds sold and securities purchased under agreement to resell) or decrease in its deposit structure will result in a corresponding, but opposite, fluctuation in reserve account balances.

THE MONEY POSITION MANAGER

The money position manager operates at one of the important nerve centers of the bank. The manager is ultimately responsible for accurate daily forecasting of the bank's money need. Armed with this forecast he must monitor closely the various deposit and money transfers that affect his bank's reserve account if a proper daily average balance is to be maintained.

Numerous areas of a large money center bank execute the deposit, due from bank account, funds borrowed or sold, check clearing, security, and loan transactions that affect reserve account balances. As mentioned at the onset, the quantity and dollar volume of these transactions can be very large and quite volatile on a daily basis. It is extremely important, therefore, that the money position manager be in the center of a communications network that accurately and punctually reports all such transactions if efficient management of cash balances is to be accomplished. For a smaller bank experiencing few transactions affecting reserve balances, the money manager may well be the officer responsible for their execution and accordingly have first-hand knowledge of the immediate status of the reserve account. As such, money management can be a routine and secondary, albeit very important, bank operation.

Reserve account management is more often, however, a minute-to-minute proposition requiring constant concentration on bank money transfers and an instinct for detecting and reacting to a continuously changing reserve account position. This is especially true of the Wednesday settlement day if the bank is to close the day with a reserve account balance that will average its daily reserve holdings within the 2 percent allowable settlement interval. The federal funds market (the market for banking system reserves) must also be monitored especially closely on Wednesday. If a developing cumulative banking system reserve excess or deficiency is not detected, the funds market may trade at an extreme interest-rate level and make the bank's settlement process a very costly, if not impossible, operation.

As a member of the bank's asset and liability management team, the money position manager's responsibilities often include dealings in the negotiable certificate of deposit, repurchase agreement, Eurodollar, dealer and broker loan, federal and municipal government securities, and, of course, federal funds market. The bank's size and its bias toward asset or liability management in meeting its money need will determine the money manager's relative involvement in one or several of these markets. His intimate knowledge of these markets will help guide his daily activity in the investment of excess reserves and/or generation of needed marginal funds.

The money position manager, in his role as reserve account custodian, is an important liaison between the bank and its district Federal Reserve Bank. In assisting with the contracting of any discount window loans or the resolution of reserve accounting errors, the money manager's ability to deal personally with Federal Reserve discount and operations officers is a valuable asset to the bank.

ANALYZING AND FORECASTING BANKING SYSTEM RESERVE AVAILABILITY

As the most efficient market for managing a bank's money position, the technical nature of the federal funds market should be understood by every banker. This section will analyze those operating factors that are most important in the determination of the demand for and supply of banking system reserves.

The banking system's total demand for federal funds is basically determined by its aggregate reserve requirement. This reserve requirement aggregate may fluctuate weekly by as much as $1 billion but normally varies within $250 million. Primarily a function of the deposit structure of the banking system, required reserves fluctuate in sympathy with the stage of the business cycle in the economy—

increasing as deposits are created through credit extension in an expansion and declining as deposits decrease in periods of credit and general economic contraction.

The aggregate of member bank vault cash holdings is an offset to this reserve requirement level. As mentioned earlier, the Federal Reserve reduces a bank's reserve requirement by the daily average quantity of its vault cash holdings during the reserve computation period. Therefore, the banking system's aggregate demand for federal funds is reduced by its total vault cash level. Vault cash holdings fluctuate seasonally to high points near holiday periods and decline cyclically during the first week of the month as cash is demanded by the public to make cash monthly billing payments.

The level of working balances held by the U.S. Treasury in its accounts at Federal Reserve Banks is easily the most important operating factor determining the supply of reserves in the banking system. An increase in these Treasury account balances reduces directly banking system reserves while a reduction increases reserve availability. The Treasury operationally employs its Tax and Loan Accounts with commercial banks to smooth the reserve availability impact of its tax receipts. Tax payments are deposited in Tax and Loan Accounts and systematically "called" into Treasury accounts at the Federal Reserve absorbing reserves directly from member banks. As the Treasury spends general funds, the checks representing these payments clear against their Federal Reserve accounts and are deposited in commercial bank accounts, subsequently supplying reserves directly to the banking system.

As shown on Exhibit 35–1, Treasury balances held in Federal Reserve Banks have become much more volatile in recent years. This increased volatility is basically the result of two factors. First, the Treasury has recently instituted a policy of making more rapid and larger calls on its Tax and Loan Account balances at commercial banks, (giving less regard than previously to the reserve-absorbing impact) in an effort to maintain minimum non-earning working balances in the commercial banking system. Second, the large federal government fiscal expenditures and budgetary deficits of recent years have led to a greater quantity of deposit clearings through these Treasury accounts.

The quantity of currency in circulation in the economy directly affects reserve availability. As mentioned previously, currency is required by the public to meet seasonal transactory demand. A commercial bank satisfies this fluctuating currency demand through the exchange with its Federal Reserve Bank of reserve account balances for currency. Thus, as currency in circulation increases, commercial bank reserves decline, and vice versa.

Federal Reserve float is a measure of check clearing inefficiency

Exhibit 35–1
Treasury Deposits at Federal Reserve Banks* (billions of dollars)

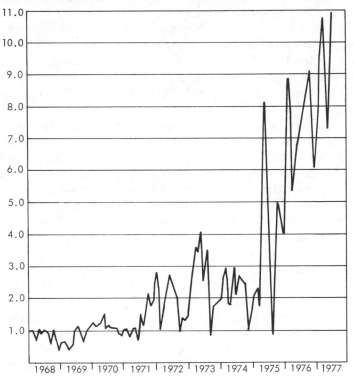

* Monthly averages of daily figures.
Source: Federal Reserve Bank of St. Louis.

in the Federal Reserve clearinghouse system. Its level represents a supply of reserves to the banking system. When a check is presented to a member bank for deposit and remitted to the Federal Reserve for collection, the bank is guaranteed a reserve account credit within two days. It is the responsibility of the Federal Reserve to present the check for payment to the bank upon which it was drawn. If this collection is not made within two days, the receiving bank is credited without a coincidental debit to the paying bank and float is subsequently created. The level of float is most directly a function of the quantity of checks clearing nationwide and therefore displays the seasonal patterns of currency in circulation fluctuations. Inclement weather and transportation worker strikes are other factors often leading to unusually high levels of float.

Other factors, namely fluctuations in Federal Reserve foreign exchange holdings and foreign official institution deposits held at Federal

Reserve Banks have the potential to affect reserve availability. These factors do not fluctuate widely from week to week, however, and therefore are of secondary importance.

One of the Federal Reserve System's most important daily responsibilities is the maintenance of orderly trading in the federal funds market. This implies that the Federal Reserve is responsible for counteracting the reserve availability impacts of cyclical and seasonal fluctuations in the aforementioned operating factors. Primarily through the open-market purchase and sale of U.S. government securities, the Federal Reserve is able to manipulate reserve availability in the banking system directly and influence the interest rate level of federal funds. This federal funds rate, as an important marginal cost of bank funds, is a major determinant of the cost and availability of credit in the economy.

It is very important that the money position manager understand these technical operating factors and the Federal Reserve's subsequent operational strategy in affecting reserve availability through government securities market intervention. To the extent that the money position manager utilizes the federal funds market as the most efficient market for equilibrating bank cash flows, he should be familiar with the technical and institutional forces that determine the federal funds rate. Knowledge of these forces may well provide him the ability to forecast short-run fluctuations in the market's trading level and, therefore, maximize the bank's return on investment of its excess reserves and/or minimize the cost of its marginal reserve account funding.

As discussed in a previous section, reserve account management is an averaging process that allows for the development of a cumulative deficient or excess reserve maintenance position early in the settlement week. If the money manager determines that the banking system operating factors on balance will absorb sufficient reserves to provide technical demand pressure and higher trading levels in the federal funds market before the Federal Reserve can or will intervene to increase availability, a strategy of maintaining an early week average reserve account excess should be employed. This excess position will, then, force the money manager to carry fewer daily average reserves later in the week if he is to "average down" reserve balances by Wednesday for a proper settlement. Carrying fewer reserves late in the week implies that the bank will be selling a greater daily average quantity of its excess reserve balances at a higher federal funds market yield or purchasing a lesser daily average quantity of needed reserves at this higher federal funds market cost. A strategy of maintaining an early week cumulative reserve account deficiency similarly would be dictated if the operating factors are forecast to produce supply pressure on balance through the settlement period.

The process by which these technical operating factors are estimated need not be complex and time consuming. In order to forecast with a good degree of accuracy, a simple charting of the weekly averages is all that is required. Over several years of data accumulation, these graphs will provide distinct cyclical and seasonal trends that can be extrapolated for estimation. Imputing into these estimates any extraneous factors impacting abnormally upon the operating factors (such as a snowstorm producing increased float or less aggressive Treasury calls of their Tax and Loan Account balances producing a lesser reserve-absorbing increase in Treasury balances held at Federal Reserve Banks) should result in surprisingly accurate forecasts.

For the large money center bank, this reserve availability forecasting and reserve account funding strategy implementation can result in several thousands of dollars in interest expense saved or incremental investment interest earned each settlement week. The economic justification of such timely analysis should also prove beneficial to even the smallest of commercial banks.

CONCLUSION

Future growth of the American banking system will result in a continually increasing volume of banking transactions affecting member bank reserve account balances. Growth in the economy accompanying this banking system expansion should result in increasingly volatile technical banking system operating factors determining reserve availability. In light of these eventualities, bank money management should continue its development as a specialized and sophisticated aspect of commercial banking. One need only recall the double digit short-term interest rates of 1974 to realize what an extremely important facet of daily commercial bank operation efficient money management represents.

Chapter 36

Capital Planning and Capital Adequacy

*Ronald Terry**

Z. Christopher Mercer†

The purpose of this chapter is to discuss the general topic, "Capital Planning and Capital Adequacy." Since the word "capital" appears twice in the chapter title, an appropriate beginning for this discussion requires an understanding of what capital is.

Capital is an economic good in that it is a scarce resource. Economists often use the term capital to refer to the physical means of production, but a generalized definition of capital is "anything (other than a free human being) which yields valuable services over an appreciable period of time."[1] In finance, however, the term capital usually refers to the capital structure of a firm, by which is meant the permanent financing of the firm. Generally, capital consists of long-term debt, preferred stock, if any, and common equity, and excludes all short-term liabilities such as bank notes or trade credits.

BANK CAPITAL

Bank capital is more difficult to define because of the regulated nature of the banking industry. Some observers would include only shareholders' equity in bank capital. Others would add in capital notes.

---

* Chairman, First Tennessee National Corporation, Memphis, Tennessee.

† Assistant Treasurer, First Tennessee National Corporation, Memphis, Tennessee.

[1] George J. Stigler, *The Theory of Price*, 3d. ed. (New York: The Macmillan Company, 1966), p. 275.

Some would include all long-term debt, still others would indicate all or a portion of the reserve for loan losses. There is, in short, no concensus definition of bank capital. Rather than dwelling upon definitional problems, this chapter will define bank capital as including common equity, capital notes, and any other long-term debt which is subordinated to the claims of depositors.[2,3]

The central importance of capital in the life cycle of a bank can be seen in Exhibit 36–1. Initially, capital, as shown on the balance sheet, allows a properly chartered bank to open an office and to begin accepting deposit liabilities. The acquired funds are then converted into loans and other earning assets, which generate income. The resulting flow of income is shown on the statement of income. Net income is available either for distribution in the form of dividends to shareholders or for earnings retention. Retained earnings serve to replenish the stock of capital, and the process continues. Capital, then, is the basic resource of a bank. It is the resource which allows a bank to acquire assets and to operate over time.

BANK HOLDING COMPANY CAPITAL

Bank holding company capital can be defined the same as bank capital. But distinctions are made between the capital of banks and of bank holding companies, and these distinctions can lead to curious results.

One of the major functions of bank holding companies is to provide capital for rapidly growing affiliate banks. Holding companies have therefore obtained long-term debt in recent years. Although this debt is long term, it is not generally subordinated, and therefore, according to the definition above, is not capital. This debt has been invested in affiliate banks, either as equity or as subordinated debt (usually capital notes). As a result of such transactions, bank capital is created, but there is no addition to net bank holding company capital. It is therefore possible, given a standard of capital adequacy, for a bank holding company to be undercapitalized, while all of its subsidiary banks are well capitalized.

---

[2] Long-term debt in this usage should have, at time of issue, a maturity of seven years or longer for bullet (single-payment) notes, or in the case of serial notes with scheduled periodic payments, a weighted average maturity of seven years or longer, with no note having a maturity of less than five years (See Board of Governors of the Federal Reserve System, *Amendments to Regulation D*, effective July 26, 1976).

[3] Although the regulatory definition of bank capital differs from agency to agency, and from publication to publication, this definition is consistent with that used in a recent Federal Reserve digest. See Harvey Rosenblum, "Bank Capital Adequacy," *Business Conditions* (published by the Federal Reserve Bank of Chicago, September 1976), p. 3.

Exhibit 36–1
Balance Sheet and Income Statement Interrelationships

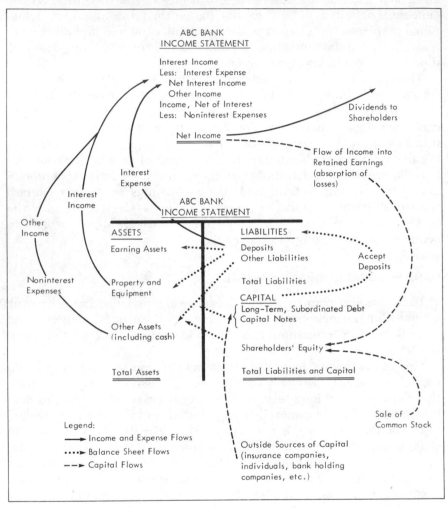

The chapter will draw further distinctions between banks and bank holding companies when appropriate. However, this chapter will not include a detailed discussion of specific capital instruments. Further, specific capital ratios will not be presented for analysis.

PURPOSES OF BANK CAPITAL

Bank capital, according to the traditional point of view, serves two basic functions. First, according to this view, capital serves as a cushion to absorb unexpected and perhaps calamitous losses, allowing a bank to continue operating until its problems can be overcome. But the historical record shows little evidence that less well-capitalized banks are more likely to fail than better capitalized banks. Generally, no researcher has been able to find any strong correlation between bank failure and the level of capital. The experience of banking system insolvency indicates that the most significant causes of solvency are competence and integrity of management. The most significant causes of insolvency have been managerial incompetence and bad faith.[4]

The traditional function of capital is to provide protection for uninsured depositors. Since the viability of the banking system (and of any individual bank) is highly dependent upon public confidence, capital also serves to maintain that public confidence. But the existence of the Federal Deposit Insurance Corporation effectively serves to protect the financial interests of most of the nation's depositors. As of December 31, 1976, the FDIC insured deposits in about 98 percent of the nation's almost 15 thousand commercial banks.[5] Also, for the period January 1, 1934 through December 31, 1975, some 521 failures or near-bank failures occurred. Nearly 3 million depositors were affected. By the end of 1975, over 99 percent of these depositors had received or were assured of full payment of their deposits by the FDIC. Further, over 99 percent of the total deposits in the 521 banks had been paid to or made available to the depositors.[6] The existence of the FDIC, then, has diminished the importance of capital in providing depositor protection for insured depositors.

The traditional view of bank capital adequacy, which is the regulatory view, defines capital adequacy relative to total assets which are at risk and to total liabilities subject to withdrawal. But as has already been noted, this traditional view does not pass the test of history with respect to predicting either bank performance or bank failures. And federal deposit insurance reduces the importance of capital as a means of depositor protection. In either case, the traditional approach presumes that calamity will occur and that strong capital is the means of insuring that banks survive.

If the two traditional functions of bank capital are in question, and bank regulators set relative standards of capital adequacy, it is reasonable to ask what the standards are. That this question is being asked

---

[4] For a more detailed review of research into the causes of bank failure, see George J. Vojta, *Bank Capital Adequacy* (New York: First National City Bank [now Citibank], 1973), pp. 8–10.

[5] *FDIC Highlights of Operations—1975* (Washington, D.C.: Federal Deposit Insurance Corporation, March 15, 1976) p. 5.

[6] *Ibid.*, p. 15.

within the banking industry is evidenced by the constant debate over capital adequacy during recent years.

An important study by Wesley Lindow provides the perspective of history.[7] Banking system capital ratios (measured by relating capital to total assets, deposits, or risk assets) have been basically declining since the early 1800s.

Early in the 1800s the ratio of capital to total assets ranged around 60% and drifted down steadily thereafter. By the early 1900s this ratio had fallen to about 20% and the rapid expansion of bank assets during World War I and the 1920s pulled it down below 13%. This downward trend was temporarily reversed by the cataclysmic events of the Depression years, but subsequent expansion of bank assets in the late 1930s and the war years brought the capital-to-total assets ratio down to a low of 6% in 1945. Some improvement has occurred since then, but the ratio has stayed below 10% for the last 20 years.[8]

The trend which Lindow traced through the early 1960s has continued to the present. Federal Reserve figures show that capital ratios continued to decline through 1974, rising slightly only in the years 1969 and 1975.[9]

The implication of these studies is that there has not been a consistent, normative standard of bank capital adequacy in this country. By one interpretation, banking system capital ratios are now too thin relative to history. But another interpretation of the longer term trend described by Lindow is that the banking system and the regulators have learned to live with (relatively) less capital. At any rate, it is evident that regulatory standards of capital adequacy have been lowered over the years, because aggregate capital ratios have fallen over time.

Regardless of the standard at a given point in time, regulatory agencies use capital as a control device. By stating (or not stating) minimum standards in terms of specific capital ratios, regulators can use capital as a lever to encourage or discourage bank and bank holding company expansion. And recent evidence suggests that bank regulators can and do influence incremental capital decisions by banks.[10] Regulatory standards of capital adequacy, then, are an outgrowth of the regulatory mission of maintaining a stable banking system and safeguarding the

---

[7] Wesley Lindow, "Bank Capital and Risk Assets," *The National Banking Review*, vol. 1, no. 1 (September, 1963).

[8] *Ibid.*, p. 30.

[9] Rosenblum, "Bank Capital Adequacy," p. 3.

[10] See John J. Mingo, "Regulatory Influence on Bank Capital Investment," *Journal of Finance*, September 1975.

interest of banking system depositors. However, the standards are basically static in nature, and fail to consider adequately the importance of current earnings in the determination of capital adequacy.

Exhibit 36–1 helps illustrate the importance of earnings in the determination of capital adequacy. Examination of the figure indicates three basic sources of capital for a bank: Capital notes and other long-term, subordinated debt, the sale of common stock, and the flow of income into retained earnings. The acquisition of long-term debt and the sale of equity are infrequent events for a bank. The flow of current earnings into retained earnings is the only regular source of net additions to bank capital.

Concentration upon the dynamic flow of bank earnings, is leading to an alternate view of bank capital.[11] Capital, according to this view, allows a bank or bank holding company to acquire the assets it needs to compete in the marketplace. Additionally, it serves as a source of financial strength, allowing a particular company to absorb losses of an unexpected and catastrophic nature; i.e., losses not covered by current period earnings. But the newer view does not presume a worst case need for capital. Most losses are not calamitous in nature. Capital, therefore, does not serve as a cushion against normal loan losses, which can be anticipated. These losses must be provided for through charges to current operating income. To the extent that current earnings exceed the normal losses incurred incident to being in the banking business, protection is provided for unusual losses.

The level of earnings, according to the newer view of bank capital (which is the usual financial view of capital outside the banking industry), is an extremely important determinant of an institution's capital adequacy. The higher are current earnings, the greater is a bank's capital strength. This statement should however, be tempered. Higher earnings do enable a bank to sustain current loses. But higher earnings resulting primarily from excessive leverage can expose a bank to higher potential, if not actual, losses. Highly leveraged earnings, then, should be discounted somewhat as a source of capital strength. Additionally, higher earnings imply potentially higher retained earnings, which are a primary source of net additions to a bank's capital stock.

Management competence was mentioned earlier as a primary determinant of bank solvency. One of the best indicators of good management is earnings performance over time. Management competence and earnings, then, become primary factors in measuring capital adequacy. This new view of bank capital adequacy relates earnings strength to the required level of capital. A recent study by a research firm illustrates this view of capital adequacy very well. In summarizing

---

[11] Vojta, *Bank Capital Adequacy*. See also footnote 13.

a discussion of the absorption by merger of Security National Bank of Hempstead, Long Island, by Chemical Bank, the report states that:

. . . a bank's capital adequacy is only as strong as its *earnings.* At the same time that Security's capital ranked 6th in is deposit "peer" group, its earned asset ratio ranked 51st (for 1973). In other words, its ability to cover its operating losses without impacting its capital accounts and build capital for future asset growth through *future earnings* retention was slipping rapidly, thereby making the capital position suspect. This static/dynamic aspect of capital analysis—the notion that a bank's capital position at any point in time can be adequately defined only in terms of its ability to earn over time—has become a fact of life in this day and age of banking revolution.[12]

The analyst's quotation above defines capital adequacy in terms of a bank's ability to earn over time. Implicit in this definition is the importance of earnings quality and earnings substainability, both of which lead back to balance sheet considerations. The importance of this newer approach, as opposed to the more static, traditional approach to examining bank capital adequacy, is in its emphasis upon the dynamic flow of earnings in a banking organization.

RELATIVITY OF CAPITAL ADEQUACY

Capital adequacy is an illusory term. There exists in the banking literature an obvious lack of consensus as to its meaning. Bank regulators take one basic approach to the subject based upon the regulatory objective of depositor protection.

Another view is taken by the shareholders of bank stock, who, through purchase decisions in the marketplace, influence capital adequacy. In this regard, the price of a bank's stock (or its price-earnings multiple) reflects investor confidence in that the stock price measures the ability to compete for incremental capital. Favorable acceptance of a new stock issue is interpreted by some to reflect the adequacy of a bank's capital.

Bankers are, therefore, forced to take an eclectic view of capital adequacy. Inasmuch as banking is a regulated industry, the regulatory agencies must be satisfied that bank capital is "adequate." In that banks compete for investment dollars in the marketplace, bankers must further satisfy bank stock analysts, whose reports have a strong bearing on the acceptability of their stock by existing and potential investors. Bankers must also satisfy the rating agencies, whose evaluations deter-

---

[12] *Bank Capital and Earnings: "Adequacy" Redefined* (New York: Keefe, Bruyette & Woods, Inc., June 1, 1975), p. 2.

mine credit ratings, and therefore the cost and availability of funds in the long-term debt and commercial paper markets.

At this stage it is important to note that, although this chapter has attempted to document the relativity of standards of capital adequacy for banks, and by inference, for bank holding companies, it has not attempted to define capital adequacy in any explicit fashion. The omission of a suggested definition is intentional, for capital adequacy is relative, not only to point of view (i.e., regulatory, investor, and so on) but also to individual banks given a particular point of view. It is further relative, as has been shown, historically.

The implicit assumption behind most attempts to measure capital adequacy is *ceteris paribus,* that all other things remain the same. In the real world, when comparing banks, other things are seldom the same. Many things, including management ability, geographical location, risk asset mix, exposure to rate sensitive liabilities, stage of historical development, and others will influence the "adequacy" of one bank's capital relative to another. Any judgment about the adequacy of bank capital necessarily involves value judgments with respect to which role of capital is considered most important, and, given a standard, what represents adequate performance when judged by that standard.

IMPLICATIONS FOR CAPITAL PLANNING

Capital planning is the process of determining the most appropriate level and mix of capital, however defined, given the relevant internal and external constraints, the assumptions being made about the future, and the context of a corporation's objectives. The primary purpose of capital planning is to develop a capital structure which supports overall corporate objectives, and which is consistent with the risks involved in the corporation's activities. Capital planning is, therefore, very important in the context of overall balance sheet management, and involves balancing the cost of alternate capital structures to maximize returns to shareholders, subject to acceptable risk constraints.

The fact that there are no simple determinants of capital adequacy for banks reinforces the importance of capital planning as an integral part of the management process. A given bank's capital position today is the result of past management decisions. Its capital position in the future will be influenced greatly by current management decisions. The bank's capital position, and hence its capital adequacy, is a management decision variable.

Bank managements must bear in mind the divergent interests of the regulatory authorities and the marketplace. Regulators are concerned with the best interests of depositors, while the marketplace is also concerned with the interests of investors and creditors. Neither the regulators nor the marketplace can be ignored, nor can both be completely satisfied.

In addition to external constraints placed on the capital planning process by regulatory concerns, marketplace comparisons, and the general competitive environment, the capital planning process must consider internal constraints. One group of internal constraints is structure related. Overall asset size and composition are important among this group. Others include asset quality, risk factors attached to concentrations of loans, and historical loan loss experience.

A second set of internal constriants relate to the overall financial philosophy of management, particularly for bank holding companies. Some holding companies (usually the largest ones) concern themselves with capitalization on a consolidated basis rather than at the subsidiary level. Others espouse another approach to subsidiary capitalization, called the "building block" approach. Under this concept, each operating entity is capitalized in accordance with its respective industry norm, and thereby maintains its relative financial independence, although actual financing may be centralized at the holding company level. Still other philosophical constraints are imposed by a management's philosophy with respect to financial leverage and financial risk.

All the constraints, both internal and external, should be recognized early in the capital planning process. Otherwise, capital planning can be saddled with unrealistic and conflicting objectives. Given the constraints, the important trade-offs have to be resolved.

SMALL VERSUS LARGE BANKS

Capital planning is a necessary function for both large and small banking institutions. Both have similar purposes. Each must attempt to define and achieve an appropriate level and mix of capital. Also, each is concerned with the same basic questions: How much additional capital is required? When is it needed? What form of capital is appropriate? How and where will it be raised? What will it cost? Further, both small and large institutions must resolve the inherent trade-offs between the interests of depositors, shareholders, and creditors.

Despite the similarities, there are numerous differences in planning in large and small banks. The capital planning process is more involved and complex for larger banks, and particularly for bank holding companies. Holding companies must identify the needs of various subsidiaries after considering different capital ratio targets for banking and nonbanking subsidiaries. Holding companies must determine appropriate forms of capital as well as borrowing vehicles. Debt, e.g., may be placed more advantageously at the holding company level, or it may be advantageous to place it directly in a subsidiary. Adding to the complexities of the capital planning process for bank holding companies is the requirement of registering new capital issues with the Securities and Exchange Commission.

The complexity of capital planning for large banks, though, is somewhat mitigated by the fact that they have more alternative sources of capital. Small banks encounter severe problems in raising capital, and often cannot look beyond their own communities for sources of supply. Larger institutions, on the other hand, have access to wider capital markets because of better name recognition, less risk (due to geographic dispersion of assets), and the larger amounts involved. Money center institutions also have access to foreign sources of capital.

SOURCES OF CAPITAL

There are three basic sources of capital for most banks: retained earnings, the sale of equity, and the sale or placement of various debt instruments. The working defintion of bank capital stated earlier indicates two sources of capital, shareholder's equity and long-term debt. The definition does not place sufficient emphasis upon the most important source of net additions to bank capital, the flow of retained earnings, which can be seen most clearly by reexamining Exhibit 36–1.

Retained earnings, or net income less dividends paid to shareholders, is the most regular source of increase in bank equity, and therefore capital. This flow relationship between the income statement and the balance sheet reinforces the newer view of capital adequacy, which examines the adequacy of a bank's capital primarily in relation to its current earnings. To the extent that retained earnings grow as fast or faster than a bank can add profitable business, there will be no need to seek additional capital (assuming an adequate beginning capitalization). Given that a bank must finance additional growth with capital from outside, faster growth in retained earnings decreases the amount of capital that must be obtained.

Stock prices and debt ratings are based largely upon projected earnings growth. Since projections are based in large measure on current earnings and the historical earnings trend, relatively good earnings provide for future additions to capital in a less obvious fashion. Lower costs on a debt issue resulting from a higher rating in effect decrease interest expense on the acquired long-term debt. Lower interest costs, other things remaining the same, raise net income, which in turn adds to the capital stock through retained earnings. Finally, if it is necessary to raise additional equity capital to finance growth, a higher stock price resulting from a better earnings trend will decrease the cost of the new equity. To the extent that fewer new shares are issued to raise a given amount of equity, the lower future dividend payout will again increase retained earnings, in turn providing increases in bank equity capital.

OTHER CONSIDERATIONS IN PLANNING FOR CAPITAL ADEQUACY

The preceding discussion of the importance of earnings as a source of capital, though perhaps obvious, points out some of the complex issues that enter into the capital planning process. The external constraints placed on banks by the regulators and the marketplace, and the internal constraints effected by a given bank's total environment and by its management's philosophy, are joined by several other important considerations to establish the overall context within which that bank will conduct its own capital planning.

A corporation's earnings objectives will enter into the capital planning process and influence decisions regarding capitalization. If return on equity is the primary objective, emphasis will be placed on the use of debt capital. A higher return on equity goal might imply the need for a relatively high dividend payout ratio. Emphasis upon the use of financial leverage available through debt will increase the fixed charges resulting from interest expense and therefore increase financial risk.

Emphasis on return on assets will lead to different results in capital planning. A return on assets approach emphasizes the markup, or rate differential spread received on assets. This approach discourages ballooning of the balance sheet for the sake of size. The approach also encourages off-balance sheet financing and noninterest income. Again, as with other objectives, a return on assets focus has important implications for capital planning.

Growth in earnings per share is another earnings-related objective. If this goal is paramount, the use of financial leverage will be encouraged. It can lead to short-run profit maximization rather than longer run wealth maximization. Emphasis on per share earnings also discourages high dividend payout ratios.

These three earnings objectives, return on equity, return on assets, and growth in earnings per share, again point out the interrelationships between the capital planning process and overall balance sheet and profit management for banks. They further illustrate the significant trade-offs that must enter into a given institution's overall capitalization policy.

GREATER EMPHASIS ON CAPITAL PLANNING

Capital planning is a multidimensional process. It must be responsive to both external and internal constraints. The ideal result of the capital planning process for a bank should be a capitalization policy that is, to the extent possible, regarded as satisfactory by the bank's regulators, investors, and creditors. It should also provide for the maintenance of that state of capital adequacy over time, as well as for the achievement of related balance sheet and profit objectives. And finally, since standards of capital adequacy change over time, the process should be sufficiently flexible to incorporate these changes.

Recent trends (e.g., 1969–77) in the banking industry indicate that for many banks and bank holding companies the capital planning process has not worked in ideal fashion. Many banks lost sight of capital planning by setting earnings per share goals, which in turn were allowed to determine balance sheet positions. Further evidence suggests that the secular decline in capital ratios described by Lindow has continued and been accentuated during the recent period.[13] In addition, the financing of growth with short-term purchased funds served to reduce liquidity for many banks. In 1975 these purchased funds represented 33 percent of total funds used, compared with only 4 percent in 1960.[14]

BALANCED GROWTH

In the future, assuming that the regulatory authorities stand firm in what is seen as a renewed resolve to prevent further deterioration of banking capital ratios, total asset growth will have to be tied more closely to capital growth than in the recent past. Loan growth will become more a function of capital growth. Given that a bank's balance sheet is adequately capitalized, its earnings must be optimized subject to the constraint of maintaining the balance sheet "in balance."

This prescription for balanced growth calls for the maintenance of several basic balance sheet interrelationships. The growth in earning assets, e.g., must equal or exceed total asset growth. Otherwise, the efficiency of utilization of acquired funds, including demand deposits and consumer savings, will deteriorate. Operating spreads will decline as a result. The growth of rate sensitive, or purchased funds, should be controlled relative to the growth of earning assets in the context of the (current) rate environment. Otherwise, in high rate environ-

---

[13] Donald P. Jacobs, H. Prescott Berghley, and John H. Boyd, *The Financial Structure of Bank Holding Companies* (Chicago: Association of Reserve City Bankers, 1975), pp. 16–17.

[14] Justin T. Watson, "A Regulatory View of Capital Adequacy," *Journal of Bank Research*, Autumn 1975, p. 170.

ments, spreads will be reduced. In any rate environment, liquidity will be reduced if there is excessive dependence upon rate sensitive liabilities. The growth of net interest income should equal or exceed earning asset growth; otherwise, spreads will be adversely impacted.

In addition, capital growth should parallel the growth in earning assets. To the extent that this is not possible because of rapid growth in the market, the gap between the growth of capital and the greater growth of earning assets should be minimized through earnings retention. In a rapid growth environment, it may be necessary to go to the debt or equity markets to obtain additional capital in anticipation of growth to keep the balance sheet in balance. A bank going to market under the assumptions outlined here would more likely be favorably received and be able to obtain new capital at relatively lower costs than less well-balanced organizations.

SUMMARY

Capital adequacy is a relative term. There is no precise level or composition of capital that is "adequate" for all banks. The problem of defining an adequate capitalization policy for a given bank is compounded by the external demands placed upon bank capital. Bank managements must resolve the inherent conflict between the differing views of capital adequacy held by regulatory agencies, bank shareholders and bank creditors. To be good in the eyes of ones public does not necessarily imply similar standing with other publics. Bank managements must satisfy the external demands placed upon bank capital, and define capital adequacy in terms that will allow the achievement of internal, corporate goals.

A capitalization policy that is "adequate" from all external and internal viewpoints, will seldom be the result of chance. The capital position for a bank or bank holding company is the result of past management decisions, and its future position is a management decision variable. The vehicle for achieving corporate goals with respect to capital is the capital planning process, and this process is closely related to the achievement of many other, conflicting goals. Capital planning must be carefully coordinated with the overall management of the balance sheet, and must help lay the foundation for the setting of corporate goals and priorities.

Capital planning is a dynamic process which, over time, should bring a particular bank or bank holding company closer to its own definition of capital adequacy. If the term "in balance" is applied to this capital position, it is clear that the capital planning process must continue if a bank is to remain in balance over time.

_____ **SECTION VI**

INVESTMENTS AND SECURITIES MARKETS

Chapter 37

The Short-Term Money Market— Functions and Instruments

*Thomas F. O'Connell**

The money market functions as a buffer between investors with surplus funds and qualified borrowers deficient in funds. The market serves the short-term needs of investors seeking a current market return for monies, while seeking to avoid undue credit risk.

This chapter will discuss prime money market instruments that provide funds on or near a future target date or alternately within 24 hours of an unexpected need. The emphasis will be on liquidity, quality, and current market return.

The instruments discussed will have common characteristics such as a fixed rate of return for the time to maturity, marketability from a credit standpoint, and marketability from a breadth of market standpoint.

The money market can be described as a clearing place for money and money substitutes, where individuals and corporations, particularly financial corporations, provide for the liquidity needed in the course of normal business. It includes that part of outstanding credit instruments which investors believe will provide for their liquidity needs.

Inherent in the money market is the concept of liquidity. However, at a point in time, a 30-year U.S. government security could be considered highly liquid, while at other times, a U.S. Treasury bill will not produce sale proceeds that approximate cost. Liquidity is an absolute concept—convertible into money at or near cost. Liquidity in the

* Program Manager Corporate Investment Portfolio, International Business Machines Corporation, Armonk, New York. (Formerly Senior Vice President and Treasurer, Fidelcor, Inc., Philadelphia, Pennsylvania.)

money market is a relative concept—usually present, but not always.

The money market has existed for many years. Over 100 years ago, there was an active short-term investment market in London's financial district. Much has been written of the power of financial institutions then centered about Lombard Street in the city.

As the American economy turned from basically agricultural to more commercial, the role of regional money centers took on importance. Early American economic history—and money panics—resulted from the seasonal and structural imbalances of our payments system. Many panics were caused by a liquidity imbalance. The Federal Reserve System was created to provide solutions to these periodic liquidity crises.

The money market we know today had its origins in the postdepression era. As the country emerged from the depression and World War II, the need for liquidity became evident. Money assets in the 30s, 40s and early 50s had minimal value. As world trade expanded and corporations expanded across the globe, cash management techniques developed. Money had value—even for a very short period of time!

As an alternative to holding precautionary balances in a demand account which yields no return other than to offset service charges, most corporations invest in marketable securities. These funds can be designated as secondary reserves or "near money." Savings accounts are used, but they are less flexible and usually yield less than marketable securities. Smaller firms may find savings accounts a satisfactory reservoir for surplus funds but larger firms usually place excess cash in marketable securities.

The prime requisite for these reserves is that they can be depended upon for quick cash. The investment must be marketable. An acceptable market requires large issues with a large number of potential buyers and sellers. To assure little or no loss in value while the securities are held, the instruments must involve little investment risk (low credit, market, or country risk). This implies that the securities will be high-quality (low-risk) debt securities of short maturity.

FEDERAL FUNDS

The Federal Reserve, in its execution of open-market policy, affects the federal funds market. The cost and availability of federal funds is indicative of current monetary policy. If the trend of the funds rate is stable to declining, an investor can deduce that monetary policy is accommodative. What are federal funds?

Federal funds represent member bank deposits at a Federal Reserve Bank. Trading federal funds refers to the sale or the purchase of these deposit balances at rates of interest set by the parties to the trade.

Most banks participate in the "funds" market as either buyers or sellers to maintain their legal reserves at required levels. A few banks trade, both buying and selling funds to achieve a minimum cost.

Reserves held with the Federal Reserve Bank are nonearning assets, so banks strive to keep such balances to a minimum. The rising trend of interest rates since the end of 1961 has encouraged banks to fully utilize their excess funds. The growth of the market for federal funds has been a contributing factor in the fuller utilization of bank funds and the reduction of excess reserves. Additionally, federal fund trading serves to redistribute reserves among banks which cushions the effects of regional and temporary pressures within the banking system.

A cyclical change in the level of bank reserves quickly affects the yields on other short-term paper. Transactions in federal funds are ideally suited to meeting the changing day-to-day needs of bank money position management. By buying or selling federal funds, a bank can make adjustments for either a deficit or surplus condition in its position. Through the mechanism of the funds market, corporate and financial liquidity can be marshaled to the most efficient peak.

CERTIFICATES OF DEPOSIT

In the mid-50s, the banking system was faced with a new challenge. Corporate treasurers realized that idle demand balances were valuable only to their bankers. Rather than permit these idle funds to remain undisturbed, they began to invest a portion of these funds in U.S. Treasury bills or other income-producing, short-term investments. By early 1961, a large New York City bank began marketing a time certificate of deposit, later to be commonly known as a CD. Certificates of deposit were not new. What made the idea work was the added characteristic of negotiability. The development of an organized, reliable secondary market for CDs expanded the use of this new liquidity instrument. Changes in Federal Reserve regulations regarding the payment of interest on various types of time deposits fostered the rapid growth of CDs.

Most large banks are active in the issuance of CDs and most large money market dealers make active markets for the better known bank names. The secondary market, which provides liquidity to the institutional investor, has proven to be the catalyst for the growth of this market. Many large banks derive a sizable portion of their deposit base from the issuance of negotiable CDs.

The rates paid on primary issue CDs reflect both the level of loan demand and bank liquidity, as well as the rates available on secondary market certificates. The changing influence of monetary policy affects the interest rate levels available from CDs. And, as in other areas of the money market, expectations on the direction of interest rates affect both the basic rate and the maturity.

A fairly recent change in Federal Reserve regulations permits the deposit of corporate funds into a savings account. Currently the maximum deposit is $150,000. Through telephoned instructions, a corporate investor can transfer funds from a demand account into a savings account, and later complete the cycle, all by way of telephoned instructions. The corporate depositor earns a competitive rate of return and enjoys added liquidity.

REPURCHASE AGREEMENTS

The repurchase agreement is a money market instrument which represents the sale of short-term securities and their subsequent repurchase after a specified period of time. Normally, the sale consists of the transfer of U.S. government securities, but some "Repos" or "RP" have Federal Agency securities or certificates of deposit as the underlying collateral. The contract supporting the transaction usually specifies the par value of securities, the unit price of the trade, the maturity date, and the percentage yield to the investor on the amount so invested.

The market developed as a method of financing a government dealer's inventory, particularly during periods of tight money. This broader based source of financing permits a dealer to carry a larger position. In recent years, the Federal Reserve, in execution of open-market policy, has extended RP to both recognized government dealers and also to customers of dealers. Although the Federal Reserve deals only with the dealers, who in turn act as principal for their customers, the recent expansion of the RP process permits more efficient execution of monetary policy.

Many short-term investors make use of the RP market. The investor selects his or her date of resale (usually ranging from one day to several months), and a rate is established. This procedure permits the full employment of funds from date of availability to date of need. The investor is relieved of market risk—receiving his original investment plus interest at the contracted rate. The rate at any given point in time reflects the rate on federal funds, both overnight and term, the rate posted by commercial banks for dealer loans, and the rate available in the Treasury bill market itself. There are occasional repurchase agreements that extend to the maturity of the underlying security.

EURODOLLAR MARKET

A Eurocurrency deposit is created when a bank or branch in one country accepts a deposit denominated in the currency of another.

This deposit then forms the basis for asset expansion by the receiving bank (often a foreign branch of an American bank). The market for Eurodollars had its origin in the post-World War II era as American economic and military aid provided billions of dollars to offshore— mainly European—recipients. The part of the Eurocurrency market dominated in dollars is referred to as the Eurodollar market.

The major instrument of the Eurocurrency market is the interbank deposit. Other instruments include negotiable certificates of deposit, bankers' acceptances, commercial paper, and loans. A deposit is created when an investor, holding a foreign currency balance places these funds with a bank. The funds are usually handled by a major bank. The deposit is evidenced by a written agreement detailing the terms of the deposit. The terms of the deposit usually limit its payment until the maturity date specified in the agreement. A lender needing funds prior to the maturity of his or her interbank deposit normally borrows funds from another lender until the original deposit matures.

The rate established for Eurocurrency deposits among the largest and most creditworthy banks is called the London Interbank Rate (LIBO). Typically, a deposit is made for a 6-month period, although 1-, 2-, 3-, and 12-months deposits can be arranged.

There is no central exchange for Eurocurrency trading. The marketplace consists of worldwide participants who transact their business by telephone, telex, and cable. Settlement on a trade normally takes place on the second business day following the trade.

Funds are exchanged through a correspondent bank in the country of the currency in which the loan is made, or the currency can be converted into another country's currency by way of the foreign exchange markets. Generally all of the terms of the trade are worked out at the time the trade is executed—amount, maturity, rate, currency, and commission.

A growing portion of Eurocurrency funds are now being placed with a bank under a Eurodollar negotiable certificate of deposit. Usually there is a slight reduction in the rate paid on such a deposit, but the negotiability provides an attraction to a wider group of investors.

Many offshore branches of American banks compete for Eurodollar funds through the issuance of Eurodollar certificates of deposit. These funds can be loaned offshore or redeposited offshore. In addition, when there is a rate advantage, the Eurodollar market provides an excellent source of domestic bank funds.

FOREIGN SHORT-TERM INVESTMENTS

Many investors in recent years have turned to foreign money market securities as a source of diversification and added return. Inherent in such considerations are marketability, quality, country risks, and most importantly, the foreign exchange risk.

Such a short-term investment in a foreign money market instrument usually involves the conversion of domestic dollars into the appropriate foreign currency. This results in the exposure to the exchange risk at maturity. To guard against the risk, a prudent investor hedges the investment by fixing the dollar value of foreign currency proceeds of the investment at the time the investment is made. Often the difference between the spot and forward conversion costs determines the overall attractiveness of the investment. The presence of a foreign exchange hedge complicates the liquidation of such an investment prior to the scheduled maturity.

Nevertheless, the net yield available in such foreign investments in countries such as England, Canada, and Japan offers attractive alternate investments to the U.S. Treasury bill and commercial paper markets.

COMMERCIAL PAPER

There is a highly organized market for the unsecured promissory notes of major industrial, utility, and finance companies. The market provides an attractive source of short-term funds to creditworthy issuers. This market has existed for well over 100 years, yet its growth has greatly expanded in the last 30 or 40 years—primarily since the mid-50s. While some companies continue to use the traditional commercial paper market as a supplemental source of funds, many companies raise the bulk of their funds through the direct sale of their short-term paper.

At one time, country banks supplemented their earning asset base with brokers' loans and commercial paper. An occasional institutional investor placed excess short-term funds in the paper market. Today, many corporate investors both issue paper and invest in the paper market. Nonfinancial corporations provide the major support to this market.

Prime Finance Commercial Paper

Prime finance paper is issued directly by leading sales finance companies. The paper is sold directly to investors or through the investor's bank as agent. Directly placed paper today makes up the bulk of the market. Paper is issued from 1 to 270 days and is usually sold on a discount basis, although interest-bearing paper can be purchased. The investor selects the issue and maturity date that meets investment needs.

Most issuers of commercial paper will arrange to repurchase or prepay the note should an unexpected need arise. However, many issuers will pay only the effective rate for this shorter period of time held if there were a rate differential at issue date. Other companies will pay the full rate regardless of the shorter period. Many companies provide their investors with rate protection for up to three days. If, in this period, rates are increased, the rate on the original note will reflect this higher rate. Some companies will permit a maturity extension of up to 15 days at the rate in effect on outstanding paper.

Prime Industrial Commercial Paper

The term "prime industrial paper" refers to the unsecured promissory notes of major industrial firms that have an excellent credit rating. The notes are usually sold through commercial paper dealers who position the paper on an inventory basis. Maturities are selected by the dealer, but the dealer can provide for the investor's earlier need for funds through a repurchase arrangement. At any given point in time, a particular issuer may not be borrowing through this market, but usually an acceptable alternate name will be available.

Bank Commercial Paper

The late-60s and early-70s saw the rapid growth of one bank holding companies. Many of the nonbank subsidiaries of these companies, such as small loan companies are financed through the proceeds of bank holding company commercial paper.

Even before the rapid growth of one bank holding companies, some banks were active issuers of commercial paper to ease a money position adversely affected by Federal Reserve Regulation Q. Proceeds from paper sold were used by the commercial paper issuing subsidiary to buy loans from the bank. This operation provided funds so that the bank could continue lending activity.

Currently bank issued paper requires a reserve against the proceeds; and, therefore, increases the cost of funds so generated.

Bank holding company paper trades at a higher discount rate than similarly rated industrial and utility issued paper. Perhaps the market discriminates against bank paper because of the ultimate use of such proceeds.

BANKERS ACCEPTANCES

Bankers acceptance is a draft that a bank has promised to pay at maturity. It represents an irrevocable obligation of the drawee bank. The corporation that draws the draft, all who endorse the draft without qualification, and the accepting bank all remain liable for payment to the holder at maturity.

An American importer, say a department store, buys clocks from a German exporter. The store might have its bank issue a letter of credit in favor of the exporter. The letter of credit states the details of the shipment and the value for which the exporter may draw a draft on the bank. The store agrees to pay the bank at the maturity of the draft (when shipment has been received and the condition verified). The bank looks to the store for payment; and, the exporter, the drawer of the draft, remains liable until the shipment is received. The German exporter discounts the draft at the local bank which is aware of the American bank letter of credit. The shipping documents and draft are sent to the American bank, where the draft is stamped "accepted" by the American bank. The draft, now an acceptance, is an obligation of the "accepting" bank. Usually the German bank will discount the acceptance with the American bank. The American bank might elect to hold the acceptance as an earning asset, or it might sell the "bill" to an acceptance dealer or another investor.

Another variation of the origin of an acceptance could result when the exporter sends the clocks directly to the store. The clocks are released only when the value of the shipment is paid by the accepting bank to the exporter. To secure the funds for payment, the store would draw a time draft on the American bank. When the American bank accepts the draft, payment is made to the exporter and the goods are released to the store.

The following transactions are also frequently financed by way of acceptance financing: shipment of goods between countries, domestic intracountry shipments, domestic or foreign storage of marketable commodities which are held by an independent warehouse, and dollar exchange with banks of approved foreign countries.

There has never been a default on a legitimately created acceptance. Even when banks are declared insolvent, the proceeds of the self-liquidating transaction are paid to the holder of the acceptance.

The acceptance is drawn for a specific period of time and normally is not subject to renewal. A market for acceptance is made by most major money market firms. These dealers negotiate a bid and offered price, rather than post a set rate. In recent years, accepting banks generally retain the acceptances which they have created; and, the Federal Reserve can be a factor in the market through its open-market activity in acceptances.

Many banks have created an instrument called an "ineligible" acceptance. This instrument has all the market characteristics of the traditional "bankers bill" yet the purpose for which the acceptance was created fails to meet the requirements necessary for orthodox acceptance financing. Rather, it is in fact a marketable domestic loan. "Ineligibles" trade at some discount from true acceptance rates, yet they comprise a sizable portion of the market.

ARBITRAGE MARKETS

Webster defines arbitrage as "simultaneous purchase and sale of the same or equivalent security in order to profit from price discrepancies."

Arbitrage has existed in many markets for a long time. There have been regional and country differences in the prices of commodities. Prices of the same security on different regional stock exchanges can vary for short periods of time. An arbitrageur is engaged in the business of spotting these differences and capitalizing on the price differences, buying a security in one market and selling it in another.

This basic concept has been expanded into two distinct trading areas:

1. In the fixed income market—say the U.S. governments market—one can draw a yield curve of the current yield level of the marketplace. Changing expectations on fiscal and monetary policy will influence the slope of the yield curve at any given point in time. One can develop, over a period of time—say, six months' normal spreads between a two-year government maturity and a four-year maturity. However, for various reasons, the spread at a point in time could be greater or lesser than usual. An investor can examine the market—via the yield curve—and determine that the spread is at variance with normal relationships. The investor could determine that one security is overpriced and the other underpriced. The sale of the former and the purchase of the latter should produce a profit as the yields return to more traditional relationships.

2. The other variation to this activity would involve the construction of a yield curve and the determination that a particular security is undervalued or overvalued. The short sale of the overpriced security or the purchase of the undervalued security would likely result in a future profit.

Many investors apply this market dynamics concept to various instruments in the money market. An investor can borrow funds for six months in the domestic market—term funds or issue a six-month CD—and invest the proceeds in a high-quality offshore instrument such as a six-month Eurodollar certificate. There are credit considerations, but the object is to "lock-in" a favorable spread and profit.

HEDGING IN INTEREST-RATE FUTURE CONTRACTS

In early 1976, the Chicago Board of Trade instituted trading in two different types of interest-rate future contracts. An investor can buy or sell three-month U.S. Treasury bills for future delivery. A Government National Mortgage Association Pass-through Certificate contract can also be traded.

Future trading has occurred for over a century, principally in agricultural goods. It was designed to allow a dealer in commodities to shift the price risks of fluctuating agricultural goods to another person willing to accept that risk. Prices fluctuate because of such things as weather, time of the year, availability of competing goods, the state of the domestic and worldwide economy, and other factors. The essence of a futures contract trade is the ability to offset one's position by making an opposite trade. The clearinghouse functions as a broker, buying from a seller, and selling to a buyer. Speculators are an essential part of the futures market for they take risks and provide liquidity to the market.

A financial institution should not speculate; it wishes to minimize risk. A short hedge occurs when an investor negotiates a future contract sale rather than a sale in the cash market. At some point, the contract is bought back when the investor is ready to make a sale in the cash market.

An investor would consider a short hedge if it were felt that interest rates were likely to firm. If rates rise, the investor would face a loss on the investment portfolio. Using the futures market, the investor could sell in the futures market to protect against the price depreciation associated with an increase in rates. As rates rise, the value of the futures contract would decline and the investor can buy back the futures contract at a gain, which would tend to offset the loss in the portfolio. The effectiveness of the hedge is a product of how closely price movements in one instrument are reflected by movements in the other instrument.

A long hedge occurs by buying a futures contract rather than buying in the cash market. The long contract will be sold when the hedger is ready to buy in the cash market. As an example of the long hedge, an institutional investor may be able to forecast cash flow several months into the future. The inflow could result from scheduled maturities or anticipated growth of fund sources. The investor might find that today's yields are quite attractive and may wish to lock in the yield. To do this, the investor would take a long position by buying in the futures market. Then, if the forecast is correct and interest rates fall with a corresponding rise in security prices, the additional cost of the security in the cash market will approximate the gain enjoyed in the futures market.

INVESTMENT OBJECTIVES

Quality Considerations

Direct obligations of the U.S. government are free of credit risk. The government can simply create money to fund its maturing debt. However, there does exist the risk of interest-rate fluctuation—the market risk.

Obligations whose principal and interest is backed by a pledge of the full faith and credit of the United States follow closely the quality of direct government obligations. Next to these in quality are the credit instruments of federal agency issues. Here there is no direct obligation for the federal government to meet principal and interest when due, yet the agencies represent an obligation of an instrumentality of the federal government.

The remaining vast array of money market instruments possess credit qualities that are difficult to assess from a credit-ranking standpoint. The major credit-rating agencies rate municipal credits and commercial paper issues based on quality standards. These standards are consistent, yet the marketplace tends to rank a prime rated bank name in a slightly less favorable light than a similiar prime rated industrial credit. Even bank obligations, while similarly rated, tend to be regarded in a descending scale based on size and location.

Liquidity

As previously mentioned, liquidity, or marketability is a sometimes thing. In a rising market, longer, weaker credits enjoy a high degree of marketability. An investment can often be liquidated at or above the purchase price. However, in a declining market, even a very short-term prime credit might be marketable, yet at a considerable concession to the purchase price or expected maturity value.

Such factors as breadth of the market, quality of the issuer, and market penetration all influence liquidity considerations. For instance, the spread between bid and ask price on Treasury bills is an indication of the size of both the number of investors and market makers as well as the sheer volume of Treasury bills outstanding. This situation would not exist in the case of a local issuer of a limited amount of say, commercial paper.

Many money market instruments enjoy a ready market in most phases of the interest-rate cycle. There is more than a casual relation between the size and frequency of issue of the various instruments and the existence of a good secondary market for such instruments.

The yield curve existent at a given point in time is a good indication of the liqudity of a given maturity. In periods where the yield curve rises sharply over a short period of months, one should expect a lower level of liquidity than when a yield curve is more gradually sloped.

Finally, the task of an investment manager is complicated by such things as changing interest-rate expectations, the cost and availability of credit, and political considerations. The major task is to assemble a portfolio of assets that meet the test of quality, marketability, and maturity that produces an optimum return. The ultimate use of the funds dictates the proper degree of risk as contrasted to return.

Chapter 38

The Instruments and Markets for Government Securities

G. Timothy Lane*
Conrad Acosta†

The securities of the U.S. government enjoy a higher degree of acceptance and distribution among virtually all classes of investors than any other type of domestic debt security currently available.

There are several factors contributing to this widespread acceptance of Treasury securities. First, and most importantly, direct obligations of the U.S. Treasury are secured by the unlimited ability of the federal government to levy and collect taxes sufficient to cover debt service on this huge floating debt. This is the source of the classification of Treasury securities as "riskless" assets and qualify the securities as eligible investments for a wide range of investors, who, through legal restrictions or personal preference, require securities with a minimum of credit risk. Second, the maturity distribution of these instruments, ranging in maturity at any point in time from a few days to a maximum of 30 years, meets the liquidity and maturity requirements of the great majority of investors. Finally, the huge amounts of relatively few issues outstanding, coupled with a finely developed dealer network, provide investors with the ability to buy or sell large amounts of securities quickly and easily without undue risk of appreciably affecting market prices. All of these characteristics mentioned are desirable attributes for at least a portion of the assets of commercial banks and account

* Senior Vice President, Barnett Banks of Florida, Inc., Jacksonville, Florida.
† Vice President, Barnett Bank of Jacksonville, N.A., Jacksonville, Florida.

for banks as being one of the prime investors in Treasury securities. As of December 1976, it was estimated that, of a total of $409.5 billion in total privately held debt, commercial banks held $102.5 billion, or 25.0 percent of the total. While on June 30, 1976, commercial banks in the United States held $90.1 billion in U.S. Treasury securities. This figure represented 9.4 percent of their total assets of $963.5 billion and 38.4 percent of the total investment and trading account securities of $234.7 billion.

Exhibit 38–1
Summary of Federal Debt and Resulting Surplus or Deficit (in millions of dollars)

End of Fiscal Year	Total Public Debt Securities	Public Debt Securities Held by Government	Public Debt Securities Held by Public	Surplus or Deficit (−)
1966	316,097	64,316	251,782	− 3,796
1967	322,893	71,809	251,084	− 8,702
1968	345,369	76,138	269,231	−25,161
1969	352,895	84,815	268,080	3,236
1970	370,094	95,170	274,924	− 2,845
1971	397,305	102,888	294,417	−23,033
1972	426,435	111,460	314,976	−23,227
1973	457,317	123,385	333,932	−14,301
1974	474,235	138,206	336,029	− 3,460
1975	533,188	145,283	387,905	−43,604
1976	620,432	149,611	470,821	−65,605

Note: Components may not equal total due to rounding.
Source: *Treasury Bulletin*, April, 1977, pp. 1, 21.

Exhibit 38–2
Marketable Interest-Bearing Public Debt (in millions of dollars)

End of Fiscal Year	Total	Treasury Bills	Treasury Notes	Treasury Bonds
1966	207,475	54,929	50,649	101,897
1967	205,061	58,535	49,108	97,418
1968	226,592	64,440	71,073	91,079
1969	226,107	68,356	78,946	78,805
1970	232,599	76,154	93,489	62,956
1971	245,473	86,677	104,807	53,989
1972	257,202	94,648	113,419	49,135
1973	262,972	100,061	117,840	45,071
1974	266,575	105,019	128,419	33,137
1975	315,605	128,569	150,257	36,779
1976	392,281	161,198	191,758	39,626
1977 (end of March)	435,379	164,264	229,625	41,490

Note: Components may not equal total due to rounding.
Source: *Treasury Bulletin*, April, 1977, p. 22.

The importance of various investors following the level and techniques of Treasury financing, as well as the reasons for engaging in open-market financing, should not be underestimated because of the impact that the level of financing and the resulting budget surplus or deficit has on all interest rates and the economy overall. The U.S. Treasury is the largest single issuer of debt and there are more investors actively participating in investments in Treasury securities than any other type of instrument. For this reason, the impact of U.S. financing is felt quickly, not only in the government securities markets, but in all markets dealing with fixed-income securities. As mentioned previously, Treasury securities are recognized as "riskless" from a credit standpoint and, as such, there is no premium attached to these rates as a credit risk premium. All other rates are scaled upward from Treasury securities, the level depending upon the risk factor.

RECENT HISTORY OF THE FEDERAL DEBT

The federal debt was approximately $16 billion at the end of the 1920s. However, during the severe economic depression of the 1930s the debt increased significantly. This was due partly to the borrowing which was necessary to offset declining revenues which had been previously budgeted, but significantly, the debt grew as a result of the widespread acceptance on the part of many prominent economists of the economic theories of English economist John Maynard Keynes. This theory proposed that, basically, the economy needed a strong financial stimulus and the government was the only power with the ability to "prime the pump" of the stagnant economy and the funds necessary for this priming should come through borrowing. As a result of this, the total privately held debt reached $33.4 billion in December of 1939. While the level of the debt at this time represented a truly significant increase over the debt just ten years earlier, the greatest increase was to come as a result of the massive mobilization of the country during World War II, not only to finance the training and equipping of American soldiers, but also to provide military and economic assistance to Allies engaged in conducting this massive world war. In February 1946, the total privately held debt stood at $231.6 billion. By June 1952, the private debt had been paid down to $194.8 billion and remained close to this level through the 1950s. Significant reductions, however, could not be made, mainly due to the Korean War and sizable expenses incurred to maintain adequate defenses worldwide and to provide economic assistance to many countries as a result of World War II and the Korean War.

The decade of the 1960s began with a lackluster economy, but with new political leadership anxious to experiment with new economic theories. One consequence of this new leadership was the longest sustained peacetime economic advance the United States had ever experienced. However, seeds were planted in the middle of the decade which not only thwarted this advance, but which also proved to be the catalyst which would lead the country through the most severe economic crisis since the 1930s.

In 1965, the United States became increasingly engaged in an expensive, unpopular, and ultimately futile war in Vietnam. At this point, despite a robust domestic economy and virtual full employment, there was no significant attempt made for tax increases to finance the war and cool the economy. Moreover, massive federally funded social programs, collectively known as the War on Poverty, were simultaneously introduced and implemented, further stimulating an already overheated economy.

Exhibit 38–3
Average Length of Marketable
Interest-Bearing Public Debt Held
by Private Investors (in millions of dollars)

End of Fiscal Year	*Average Length*
1966	4 yrs. 11 mos.
1967	4 yrs. 7 mos.
1968	4 yrs. 5 mos.
1969	4 yrs. 2 mos.
1970	3 yrs. 8 mos.
1971	3 yrs. 6 mos.
1972	3 yrs. 3 mos.
1973	3 yrs. 1 mo.
1974	2 yrs. 11 mos.
1975	2 yrs. 8 mos.
1976	2 yrs. 7 mos.
1977 (end of February)	2 yrs. 9 mos.

Source: *Treasury Bulletin.*

Mushrooming inflationary pressures coupled with increasing unemployment served to underscore the frustration which was compounded by the further war effort in Southeast Asia in the early 1970s. As the decade reached its midpoint, it was evident that a substantial economic downturn was to be accompanied with record high-interest rates.

The resulting economic recession proved to be the most severe and pervasive since the Great Depression of the 1930s and was a result of the economic boom of the 1960s and early 1970s, aggravated by severe inflationary psychology, industrial shortages, and crop failures worldwide. In 1975, a record volume $83 billion in U.S. government securities were sold and dominated the securities markets, while fiscal 1976 closed with a record budget deficit of over $65 billion.

THE PUBLIC DEBT

U.S. government securities are issued by authority of the Second Liberty Bond Act which was enacted in September 1917. This act limits the amount of obligations which may be outstanding at any time. Subsequent legislation gives the Treasury discretion as to the method of sale, the types of securities issued, and the prices at which they may be sold, subject to interest rate ceilings.

Direct obligations of the U.S. Treasury may be broken down into marketable and nonmarketable issues. Marketable issues, which comprise the bulk of the debt, include Treasury bills, notes, and bonds (Treasury certificates have not been issued since 1967). Nonmarketable issues include U.S. Savings Bonds which may not be purchased by commercial banks except in a trust capacity; Retirement Plan Bonds which are eligible for purchase by self-employed individuals as part of a retirement program; Depository Bonds that are issued to depositories and financial agents of the Treasury as a means of providing these agents some income for services provided to the government; Treasury Bonds, Investment Series B 2¾ percent due April 1, 1980, bonds issued in exchange for marketable 2.5 percent bonds due June and December 1972, and may in turn be exchanged for 1.5 percent five-year, marketable Treasury notes at the option of the owner; Special Issues that are sold directly by the Treasury to various U.S. agencies and trust funds; *REA Series 2% Treasury Bonds—REA* that were issued in connection with financing the Rural Electrification Administration; *State and Local Government Series* which may be issued to states and local municipalities as a temporary investment medium for the proceeds of funds received from local bond issues which were sold to "advance refund" their own debt; Foreign Series that are special issues available to foreign governments or monetary authorities as an investment medium for U.S. dollars obtained as a result of supporting the foreign exchange rate of the dollar.

Treasury Bills

U.S. Treasury bills are short-term, discounted obligations issued on a regular basis by the Treasury. Normally, the Treasury will announce the routine sale through auction of a 13-week (91 day) and 26-week (182 day) bill approximately 4 days prior to the sale each Monday for payment and delivery the following Thursday. (If Monday is a holiday, the subscription will be entered the preceding Friday. If Thursday is a holiday, the new bill will be issued for delivery the following Friday.) Investors desirous of subscribing to (ordering) these issues must enter subscription forms to the Federal Reserve Bank for their district by the 1:30 P.M. eastern time deadline.

Every fourth Wednesday, the Treasury auctions a 52-week (one year) bill for delivery and payment the following Tuesday.

The minimum denomination of Treasury bills is $10,000, issued in bearer form only and is paid at maturity at face (par) value with no accrued interest.

Due to the short-term nature of bills (maximum maturity of one year), a wide variety of maturities, and the ease with which they may be bought or sold in large or small blocks, Treasury bills appeal to a wide range of investors. In addition, the Treasury has incorporated the use of several different variations which increase their appeal even more. One of these is the *Tax Anticipation Bill* (TAB). In an effort to raise additional temporary funds needed before the receipt of taxes due quarterly and to provide corporations with an investment vehicle for funds to be used for tax payments, the Treasury has issued these special issues ranging in maturity from one to nine months. The issues are sold through auction on a discount basis with the final maturity five–seven days after a quarterly tax date. Holders of these instruments may use the bills at par value for payment of federal income taxes due quarterly. The effect is that the taxpaying investor will receive five to seven days "free" interest. Commercial banks which enter subscriptions for themselves or for their customers may usually pay for TABs through a partial credit to their Treasury Tax and Loan Account (TT&L). This means simply that the cash to complete the payment to the Treasury is not needed by the bank until a call is made against the TT&L Account. This period will usually range from one day to as much as two weeks and represents the period of time the bank will, in effect, earn interest before funds are needed to pay for the securities. A recent development which the Treasury has also used periodically is the use of *Cash Management Bills.* These issues normally have a very short maturity of under 30 days and are sold to coincide with the maturity of an existing issue. In the issues sold to date, there has been a large (usually $10 million) minimum order that may be entered. The bills give the Treasury excellent flexibility in raising additional funds for short periods of time and provide large investors with an attractive outlet for temporary funds.

Treasury bills are sold on a discount basis through competitive bids entered at a dollar price representing the price at which the bidding investors will pay for the issue. The price must be expressed in no more than three decimal places; i.e., 98.328.

Competitive subscriptions will be accepted and accumulated by Federal Reserve Banks in their capacity as the fiscal agent for the Treasury. Subscriptions with the highest prices (lowest discount) will be accepted first and each succeeding lower price will be accepted until the entire issue has been filled. Investors desiring to buy a portion of the issue, but choosing not to bid on a competitive basis may enter a *noncompetitive* subscription for up to $500,000 of the issue and will be assured of receiving this amount at the average price of all accepted tenders.

Treasury bills are traded on a bank discount basis and computed on a 360-day year, using the actual number of days in the period. Due to the fact that bills are traded at a discount, the true yield is greater than the nominal discount basis, and the longer the bill has to run to maturity, the greater the difference. It should be kept in mind, for comparative purposes, however, that there is no income realized until the bill is sold or matured. For bills with a maturity or holding period longer than six months, there is no opportunity to invest interest as there would be with coupon issues.

The following formula is used to compute the discount:

$$A = \frac{B}{360} \times D$$
$$P = \$100 - A$$

where

D = Number of days to maturity.
B = Discount basis.
A = Amount of discount.
P = Dollar price.

Find the price of a Treasury bill due in 91 days on a 5.62 percent discount basis:

$$
\begin{aligned}
A &= \frac{B}{360} \times D \\
&= \frac{5.62}{360} \times 91 \\
&= 1.4206111\% \text{ full discount} \\
&= \$98.57939 \text{ per \$100 maturity value} \\
P &= 100 - A \\
&= 100 - \$1.4206111 \\
&= \$98.58 \text{ dollar price for } 5.62\% \text{ discount basis} \\
&\quad \text{for 91-day maturity}
\end{aligned}
$$

The following formulas may be used to compute special figures desired when Treasury bills are sold prior to maturity:

I. Effective yield for the time a bill is held:

$$\text{Gain or loss in yield} = \frac{\substack{\text{Days to maturity}\\\text{at date of sale}}}{\text{Days held}} \times (\text{Purchase yield} - \text{Sale yield})$$

Assume that a 91-day bill purchased at 5.62 percent is held for 30 days and sold at 5.74 percent. What is the yield for the time held?

$$\text{Gain or loss in yield} = \frac{61 \times (5.62 - 5.74)}{30}$$

$$= \frac{61 \times (-0.12)}{30}$$

$$= -0.24$$

Purchase yield. 5.62%
Gain or loss in yield. . . . . −0.24

Rate of return for time held 5.38%

II. To find the number of days a bill must be held to break even in yield:

$$\substack{\text{Days to maturity}\\\text{at date of sale}} = \frac{\substack{\text{Days to maturity}\\\text{at date of purchase}}}{\text{Sale yield}} \times \text{Purchase yield}$$

Assume that a 91-day bill is bought at 5.62 percent. How long must it be held to avoid a loss if it is sold at 5.74 percent?

$$\substack{\text{Days to maturity}\\\text{at date of sale}} = \frac{91 \times 5.62}{5.74} = 89$$

Days to maturity at purchase. 91
Days to maturity at sale 89

Break-even period. . . . . 2 days

III. To determine the yield at which a bill may be sold to avoid a loss after holding for a specified period of time:

$$\text{Sale yield} = \frac{\substack{\text{Days to maturity}\\\text{at purchase}}}{\text{Days to maturity at sale}} \times \text{Purchase yield}$$

Assume that a 91-day bill is bought at 5.62 percent and held for 30 days. At what yield can it be sold to break even?

$$\text{Sale yield} = \frac{91 \times 5.62}{61} = 8.38$$

Sale yield required to break even is 8.38%.

Treasury Notes and Bonds

Treasury notes are interest-bearing securities with a maturity of one to ten years (prior to March 1976, notes were limited to a maximum of seven years) with no limit on the interest rate which may be paid.

Treasury bonds are interest-bearing issues with no limitation on maturity. It is expected, however, that Treasury issues through ten years maturity will generally be notes and issues longer than ten years will be bonds. Treasury bonds have a maximum coupon rate of 4.25 percent; however, in March 1971, this restriction was modified by legislation permitting the issuance of up to $10 billion in bonds without regard to coupon rate. The exception was further modified and increased to $12 billion in March 1976, and was increased to $17 billion in June 1976.

As of May 1976, there were nine issues of Treasury bonds eligible to be used in payment of federal estate taxes at par values. These issues have coupons ranging from 3 percent–4.25 percent with maturities from June 15, 1983 to November 15, 1998, and consequently, trade at a substantial discount. Due to their value as being eligible for payment of estate taxes, the yields are not as attractive as alternative investments and the bonds are usually not purchased except in anticipation of federal estate taxes.

The Treasury has used a variety of techniques in issuing coupon securities. A common method is the "rights offering," in which a new, longer issue is offered by the Treasury in exchange for a maturing or relatively short-term issue. In order to insure that investors will make the swap and extend maturity, the new issue is offered at an attractive rate in relation to alternative investments. Due to the desirability of the new issue, coupled with the fact that it may be purchased at original offering price only by exchanging the old issue, the latter develops a value in excess of its value as a pure investment, this additional value is known as "rights value." Investors should recognize that this "rights value" will disappear when the issue is no longer eligible for exchange into the new issue. The options available to the investors who hold these "rights" are, first, swap the old issue for the new issue as a permanent investment. Second, swap the old issue for the new issue and sell the new issue if the maturity or other characteristics are not desirable. Third, sell the old issue and take advantage of the temporarily inflated price. It should be clear that the investor who chooses to do nothing during the period of time in which the issue has the "rights value" will lose the benefit of this temporary value.

Another common technique is the *cash auction* of an issue in which the coupon is set, but the price and resulting yield are determined by competitive bids on a dollar price basis. A variation of this is the auction of an issue in which there is no coupon set prior to auction. Investors bid for the issue on a yield basis to two decimal places (i.e., 7.28 percent) and the coupon rate is determined after the results are tabulated to provide an average yield up to 0.125 percent more than the coupon rate. In the first example in which the coupon rate is predetermined, investors bid on a dollar basis out to two decimal places; i.e., 99.52. The subscriptions are tabulated and awarded first to the highest price, then each succeeding higher price until the entire issue has been awarded. In a cash auction on a yield basis, subscriptions are awarded first to the subscribers with the lowest yield (resulting in highest price), and continues with each succeeding lowest yield until the entire issue has been awarded.

In most instances, the Treasury permits investors to subscribe to a certain maximum amount of notes or bonds at the average price of all accepted tenders. This permits small investors or others who would not bid for an issue and compete with professional traders to participate in the financing and buy a portion of the issue at a reasonable price. Recently, the maximum available at the average price at original offering for notes and bonds has been $500,000. Several recent bond auctions have provided that awards for the bonds will be made by the *uniform-price* or *Dutch-auction* technique in which all accepted tenders are awarded bonds at the lowest accepted price.

In February 1976, the Treasury experimented with the *yield-spread* subscription technique. At that time, the Treasury offered a seven-year 8 percent note to investors at a price of 100. Similar securities were available at that time to yield approximately 7⅝ percent and the 8 percent notes, worth approximately 101½ on the open market, quite naturally, received an overwhelming response from investors and speculators alike. In an attempt to limit speculation, the Treasury increased the normal 5 percent deposit required of all investors, except banks and securities firms, to 20 percent. Despite this, the subscriptions totaled more than $29 billion and the Treasury increased the size of the issue from $3.5 billion to $6 billion, but nevertheless, reduced the announced $500,000 limit to $200,000. In May 1976, a 10-year 7⅞ percent note was sold on similar terms. In this offering, however, the Treasury required a 20 percent deposit from each subscriber, including banks and securities firms, and assured those entering tenders and a 20 percent deposit of receiving up to $500,000. This offering, while not as spectacular as the sale of the 7-year 8 percent notes was, nevertheless, a success and the Treasury also increased the size of the issue to partially meet the demand for the note.

It should be pointed out that each official circular which offers Treasury financing terms includes a comment emphasizing that the amounts of the issue and individual allotments may be amended at the discretion of the Secretary of the Treasury. Investors should be aware of this discretionary authority. There have been cases where investors entered subscriptions for securities, and, in anticipation of buying a certain amount, immediately sold their expected allotment and discovered later that the award was substantially less than expected. They were then in a position of having to buy, in the open market at what may be significantly higher prices, sufficient securities to complete their delivery.

THE MARKETS FOR TREASURY SECURITIES

The primary market for Treasury securities may be characterized as a relatively small number of highly specialized dealers who maintain the ability and willingness to buy or sell large amounts of Treasury securities to banks, other dealers, and large corporations at any point in time and under virtually all market conditions.

Specifically, government bond trading is conducted in the over-the-counter market, although bonds are listed on the New York Stock Exchange. There are 30 dealers comprising the Association of Primary Dealers in Government Securities. These dealers report their position daily to the Federal Reserve Bank of New York and are the dealers through whom the New York Federal Reserve conducts open-market operations.

Normal trading hours are from 10 A.M. to 3:30 P.M. eastern time each business day, although there have been instances when trading extends beyond this time.

Most trades are "regular;" that is, delivery and payment are to be made the next business day. If mutually agreed upon by the dealer and customer, a trade may be for "cash," i.e., delivery the same day as the trade; or, delivery on some specified date in the future.

The delivery of Treasuries is normally made to the Federal Reserve Bank or other safekeeping bank specified by the buyer "versus payment" and this safekeeping bank will pay the selling dealer upon receipt of the securities. This payment is made in federal funds.

The prices of Treasuries are determined in a highly competitive environment and reflect not only the dealers cost and desired profit margin, but also the expectations of the trend of interest rates and resulting market value of the securities. Characteristically, the government bond dealer is ready to buy securities at the "bid" side of the market and sell securities at the "offered" or "asked" side of the market. As a practical matter, many bond dealers tend to emphasize and be more competitive in a particular area of the market and may not be as competitive in other areas. For this reason it may be advisable for a market participant to have an idea of the prices of several dealers before he or she consummates a trade.

Normally, there is no commission involved in Treasury security transactions, the profit margin being the spread between the bid and asked price of the dealer. This spread is usually very small and reflects government bond trading as being a low-markup–high-volume business, as it usually is.

Treasury bills are quoted in basis points, or 1/100 of a percentage point. The difference between bid and ask will normally range from 2 to 6 basis points, with 4 basis points being a common spread. For example, a dealer may bid 5.42 percent for the 91-day bill and simultaneously offer it at 5.38 percent. This spread reflects a difference in money of only $100 per $1 million and represents the profit for making a market as well as risking capital in the event yields increase and the market value of the holdings decline.

Treasury notes and bonds are quoted in dollar prices in fractions of 1/32. For example, a price of 99 12/ means 99 12/32, or 99.375. As was the case illustrated in bills, notes, and bonds are also quoted in relatively small increments in price, but because notes and bonds are generally of a longer maturity, thus having greater market risk, and are not traded as actively or in the amounts that bills are, the spread between bid and asked usually represents a greater amount of dollars. As an example, a recent two-year note was quoted 99 26/32 bid and 99 30/32 asked, a difference of 4/32 or $1,250 per $1 million. At the same time a 25-year bond issue was bid 102 4/32, asked 102 20/32, a difference of 16/32 or $5,000 per $1 million. It should be noted that the longer the maturity of an issue, the greater the spread will usually be. This increased margin will usually be required to offset the greater risk of loss inherent in the longer issues. This may be illustrated by referring to the change in price necessary to effect a given change in yield on a short-term issue as opposed to one of longer maturity. For each 1/32 change in price of the 2-year note the yield will change 0.017 percent. Whereas, a 1/32 change in price on the 25-year bond will result in a yield change of only 0.003 percent. Consequently, a much greater price change will be necessary on the longer issue as opposed to the shorter issue to effect a given yield change. In addition to this, individual dealers will increase this spread in order to reduce their risk if they feel the market may decline. Conversely, if they feel the market will improve in price, the spread will normally narrow.

The Federal Reserve wire systems enables Treasuries and some federal agencies to be delivered between Federal Reserve Banks almost instantaneously by telegraphic transfer after the trade has been made and the delivering (selling) party communicates the transaction to the Federal Reserve Bank. The seller will either deliver the securities to his Federal Reserve Bank for transfer or instruct the Federal Reserve Bank to withdraw the securities from safekeeping and make the delivery. The wire system is not a physical transfer of securities, but simply a message between Federal Reserve Banks instructing the receiving Federal Reserve Bank to issue a specific security to a customer in its district.

In recent years, the Federal Reserve System has developed a "book-entry" safekeeping system in which bearer Treasury securities are converted and held in custody at the Federal Reserve Banks in book-entry form. This system has developed in response to the risks and costs associated with physically transferring large amounts of bearer instruments between safekeeping agents. The system permits Treasuries and agencies belonging to a member bank, as well as those belonging to a fiduciary account or a customer of a member bank, to be held free of charge at the Federal Reserve Bank or branch which services that member bank.

THE DEALER COMMUNITY AND THE FEDERAL RESERVE SYSTEM

It should be made clear at the onset of any discussion relating to federal open-market operations that the commercial banking system is the conduit through which the Federal Reserve System conducts monetary policy. This is true whether the operation in question is a change in reserve requirement, a change in the discount rate or through open-market operations in the government securities market. The impact is felt on the banking system first, filters down through other segments of the business community, and ultimately affects the economy.

The principal method by which monetary authorities alter the supply of reserve in the banking system is through open-market operations. The federal open-market trading desk of the New York Federal Reserve Bank, acting under general policy directives of the Federal Open-Market Committee, periodically buys or sells government securities as a means of influencing the level of reserves in the system and, consequently, the cost of marginal sources of funds. These transactions are handled on a competitive basis through the 30 reporting dealers previously mentioned. The payment of securities purchased by the trading desk is through a credit to the Federal Reserve account if the dealer is a bank or through a credit to the reserve account of the dealer's clearing bank if the purchase is through a nonbank dealer. In both instances, the result is the same—reserves in the banking system have been increased through this infusion of cash credits. The opposite occurs when the trading desk sells securities. The payment of securities is made by a charge to the reserve account of the dealer bank or from the reserve account of the dealer's clearing bank. Reserves in the system are thus reduced.

In addition to outright purchases of securities, the trading desk may temporarily increase or reduce the level of reserves through repurchase agreements known as "Repos" or reverse repurchase agreements known as "matched sales." A Repo is a purchase and a matched sale is the sale of securities by the trading desk on a short-term basis with a simultaneous agreement to reverse the transaction at a specified later date. Most transactions are reversed within 7 days, but may run as long as 15 days. These transactions provide a means of influencing the level of reserves in the banking system when it is expected that only a temporary increase or reduction in reserves is necessary. Repos and matched sales are handled on a yield basis and dealers bid or offer the securities in competition with other dealers.

The government bond dealer plays a very important role in addition to those already mentioned, in being willing and able to buy or sell large amounts of short-term government securities to provide or absorb reserves to or from individual banks as their need arises. The dealer, then, is a middleman through which banks needing reserves sell securities and banks having excess reserves buy securities and, in the process, excess reserves of one area are transferred to other areas which are deficit in reserves. In this manner, reserves of the banking system are distributed among geographical areas.

THE RISK/REWARD CONSIDERATION OF TREASURY SECURITIES

Some mention and comment should be made of the common classification of Treasuries as "riskless" assets. It is true, from a credit standpoint that government securities stand at the top of the list and enjoy a superior status as quality instruments. Treasuries are, however, fixed-income securities and are subject to the same variations and swings in market values in response to changing interest rates as are other fixed-income obligations. The investor who is desirous of buying Treasuries should be aware of the relationship between income promised by the coupon and yield of an issue versus the potential market loss of an issue upon sale which is inherent in all fixed-income obligations.

This awareness is especially vital when one considers that treasuries are primarily utilized as secondary reserve assets by most banks and are not usually purchased with the intent of their being exposed to a high degree of market risk.

During the past several years, we have experienced extremely volatile swings in interest rates which in turn have produced extreme variations in market values of fixed-income securities.

A few examples should be sufficient to illustrate this point:

Date	6½% Treasury 8/15/76		7% Treasury 11/15/79		7% Treasury 5/15/98	
Feb. 1, 1974........	99.125	(6.88%)	100.3125	(6.93%)	95.00	(7.44%)
July 9, 1974	95.625	(8.83%)	93.125	(8.63%)	87.500	(8.19%)
Feb. 25, 1975.......	100.5625	(6.09%)	100.1875	(6.95%)	93.500	(7.60%)
Sept. 12, 1975	99.03125	(7.61%)	95.4375	(8.31%)	86.00	(8.38%)

In the example above, the purchase on February 1, 1974, of the 7 percent Treasury note due November 15, 1979, at a yield of 6.93 percent, would have produced only a nominal 0.05 percent increase in yield over the 6½ percent due August 15, 1976, for an issue 39 months longer in maturity. By July 9, 1974, the 7s would have declined in market value more than 7 full points in price, while the 6½ percent would have declined only 3½ points. This greater decline in market value was only fractionally offset by the small improvement in yield. Similar comparisons may be made of the other examples.

The investors primary concern in choosing one issue over another of different maturity is in determining whether the improvement in income, which normally comes from extending maturity, is sufficient to compensate for the greater risk of depreciation loss which is inherent in an issue of longer maturity. It should be noted also that, characteristically, a bank usually needs to liquidate secondary reserve assets at a point in time that interest rates are rising and market values are declining. It is probable then, that the greatest need to liquidate securities coincide with these securities being at or near their low point in price.

Chapter 39

Instruments and Markets for Government Agency Securities

*Ralph W. Berrey**

Paul D. Hutchins†

"Agency" securities, as the term is generally used in the market-place, include debt of both government and government-sponsored agencies which in either case may or may not include an expressed liability assumed by the United States. Exhibit 39–2 at the end of this chapter lists the government and government-sponsored agencies, their outstanding securities at December 31, 1976, and indicates those securities for which no expressed liability is assumed. The chapter itself covers first those securities for which no expressed liability is assumed, principally because of the dominance in the markets of the "Big-Five" issuers—Federal Home Loan Banks, Federal National Mortgage Association, the Farm Credit System's Banks for Cooperatives, Federal Intermediate Credit Banks, and Federal Land Banks.

AGENCY DEBT EXPANSION, ACCEPTANCE AND MARKETABILITY

Over the years agency securities have become increasingly important in the marketplace and increasingly well accepted by a wide variety of investors. While interest-bearing U.S. public debt increased by a substantial $328 billion plus, or 200 percent, over the ten years ending December 31, 1976, the $69 billion increase in agency debt repre-

* Vice President, Valley National Bank, Phoenix, Arizona.
† Assistant Vice President, Valley National Bank, Phoenix, Arizona.

sented 480 percent. And the commercial banking system's holdings of agency securities relative to U.S. governments at December 31, 1976 was a substantial 25 percent. This is up from just 6 percent ten years earlier. The lion's share of the increased agency debt is represented by the discount notes, bonds, and debentures of the "Big-Five," although participation certificates have tended to become increasingly important.

The increased use by banks of agency securities reflects their acceptance as having quality and pledging characteristics approaching governments, generally an attractively higher yield than governments of similar maturity, and in the case of the "Big Five," at least, a high degree of marketability.

Bonds and debentures of the Federal Home Loan Banks, Federal National Mortgage Association, the Banks for Cooperatives, the Federal Intermediate Credit Banks, and the Federal Land Banks are offered periodically by their fiscal agents through dealers, including banks. Dealers maintain very active secondary markets for these issues, and holders should experience no difficulty in disposing of even large blocks near the bid side of the market. However, since individual issues are comparatively small, offerings by individual holders can become limited as time progresses. Consequently, in arranging purchases it is generally wiser to consider more recently offered issues unless dealers can offer older issues at yields comparable to those for the newer issues.

Since a secondary market is maintained by both government dealers and dealer banks for federal agency issues and the issues maintain a high degree of creditworthiness, comparable in many ways to direct U.S. government debt, the federal agency issues are deemed suitable for most portfolio investments, including banks as evidenced by their substantial and increasing use of these securities. Indeed, federal agency issues can play a major role in portfolio management when one considers the opportunities that exist from alternating from direct government issues to federal securities and back again.

Typically, during periods of tight credit and high-interest rates, a wider rate spread exists between like maturities of direct governments and federal agency issues than during a period of low-interest rates and easier credit. As a result, when spreads between government and agency issues are close, the portfolio manager may wish to reverse from an agency issue into a government issue. Then, when the cycle reverses and the spreads widen, an opposite reversal from government bonds into agency bonds would be necessary. Typically, a portfolio manager would minimize potential losses as rates increased in the first instance and maximize income and potential profits with agencies acquired during a higher rate period. While the widening and contraction of spreads is usually associated with longer term fluctuations in demand for credit, occasionally, technical factors can cause the same effect over a shorter time frame. Therefore, it is wise for the portfolio manager to consistently be aware of these spread relationships.

Methods for handling original offerings of other agency issues vary considerably from direct auction by the issuer to public underwritings. Further, their availability in the secondary market and the ease with which they can be sold also reflect the variety of issues, size, market acceptance, and the like. For these reasons, when investors are considering using agency securities other than the "Big Five," where subsequent sale is a possibility, thorough investigation of marketability should be made.

A measure of how viable the secondary market is can be determined by examining the spread relationship between the bid and asked price of several different agencies within the same maturity range. As a general observation, those agencies with a narrower spread between the bid and asked price can be expected to have a better acceptance in the secondary market than those agencies with a wider spread.

When the Banks for Cooperatives, Federal Intermediate Credit Bank, Federal Land Bank, Federal National Mortgage Association, or the Federal Home Loan Bank offer bonds and debentures, they do it through an underwriting group. Each agency has its own underwriting group which receives an allotment of bonds from the agency at a discount. The underwriting members then offer the bonds at par to the public. The purpose of the underwriting group is not only to distribute the bonds but also to distribute them in a broad geographical area to as many investment groups as possible. During this bond-issuing process, four important dates are met. On the *announcement date,* the issuing agency announces the kind of financing package it is going to bring to market. This announcement includes which maturities will be offered and the dollar amount of the bonds which will be offered for each maturity. Since each of the "Big-Five" agencies has a regular place on the calendar for issuing new debt, the announcement dates are either announced in advance or can be anticipated with a fair degree of accuracy. The *pricing date* is usually the day after the announcement date and on this day the agency announces the coupon rate on the issues. The *offering date* is the day the agency officially offers the entire package to the market. Some agencies will not allow the new bonds to be traded in the market until the day after the offering date. However, other agencies do allow their bonds to start trading at noon on the offering date. The final date is the *dated date.* On this date bonds are issued, payment collected, and the owners begin accruing interest. There is usually about a two-week interval between the offering date and the dated date. Since there is approximately a two-week delay between the offering date and the dated date, new securities of the "Big Five" are quite often popular trading account items in view of the fact they can be traded for two weeks before payment is made. Because of their continual presence on a regular basis, the "Big Five" can underwrite their own securities. Other agencies choose other methods. For instance, the Government National Mortgage Association (GNMA) holds a public auction of its mortgage-backed securities allowing the marketplace to determine what an acceptable offering level should be. Still other agencies offer their securities through negotiated syndicates. The issues offered by some agencies trade more like corporate bonds than federal agency securities. Tennessee Valley Authority bonds are an example of bonds which have this characteristic.

FARM CREDIT SYSTEM

The marketable securities of the system represent outstanding debt of the 37 Banks for Cooperatives, Federal Intermediate Credit Banks and Federal Land Banks. There are 12 of each of the three groups of banks located in the same city of the 12 Farm Credit districts plus a Central Bank for Cooperatives in Denver. Debt is issued through the fiscal agent in New York City.

These banks plus Federal Land Bank Associations and Production Credit Associations are a vehicle in 50 states and Puerto Rico for providing credit and related services to farmers, ranchers, producers, or harvesters of aquatic products, rural homeowners, and farm-related businesses, as well as to cooperatives and associations of cooperatives. Each bank and association is audited and examined at least annually by the Farm Credit Administration, an independent agency of the U.S. Government. Current authority for the agency, the banks, and the association comes from the Farm Credit Act of 1971. Thus, while the banks' marketable obligations do not represent government debt, direct or guaranteed, they are obligations of federally chartered institutions operating under government supervision, and they are secured.

Banks for Cooperatives

These banks, organized under the Farm Credit Act of 1933, make loans to eligible associations, participate in loans with other Banks for Cooperatives and make loans to each other for short periods. The principal activity of the Central Bank for Cooperatives is participation in larger district bank loans as well as loans for short periods to district banks. The banks operate on a patronage refund basis in the form of cash and stock, and have been owned by cooperative associations since 1968. The amount of $148 million from retired stock is held by the

Exhibit 39–1
Consolidated Bonds and Discount Notes of Banks for Cooperatives, Federal Intermediate Credit Banks, and Federal Land Banks

Denominations:	Bonds: $5,000, $10,000, $50,000, $100,000, $500,000. Notes: $50,000, $100,000, $1,000,000.
Form:	Bearer, except some older Federal Land Bank bonds may be registered.
Call Provisions:	Only Federal Land Bank bonds may be callable.
Eligibility:	Eligible as investments by national banks, state member banks of the Federal Reserve System, Federal Credit Unions, and Federal Savings and Loan Associations. Under the laws of various states, also legal investments for savings banks, trust companies and trust funds.
Taxation:	Income is exempt from state and local income taxes but subject to federal income tax.
Collateral:	Secured by collateral at least equal to bonds and notes outstanding in form of obligations of borrowers, obligations of the United States or its agencies, other readily marketable securities approved by Farm Credit Administration, or cash.

United States in a revolving fund and is available for purchase of stock if necessary. The banks' net worth at December 31, 1976 was $52 billion.

Consolidated bonds are usually issued on the first of each month with a six-month maturity date. Occasionally, a maturity date of up to ten years can also be offered. The bonds are the joint and several obligations of the 13 banks, and the total outstanding may not exceed 20 times capital and surplus of the 13 banks. There is an established market for these bonds since there is a regular program for issuance and a recurring supply each month. When a new issue is brought to market and is traded on a "when issue" basis, a very close spread between the bid and asked price can be expected. Bonds for the Banks for Cooperatives are issued in minimum denominations of $5,000. Further information regarding collateral, eligibility, legality, form, denominations, and taxation is available in Exhibit 39–1.

Federal Intermediate Credit Banks

These banks, authorized by the Agricultural Credit Act of 1923, operate primarily as banks of discount. They make loans to, and discount agricultural and livestock paper for Production Credit Associations, banks, agricultural credit corporations, and livestock loan companies. They also can make loans to, and borrow from, Federal Land Banks and Banks for Cooperatives. Their capital stock has been owned by Production Credit Associations since 1968. The amount of $112 million is held by the United States in a revolving fund and is available for the purchase of stock if necessary. The banks' net worth at December 31, 1976 was $755 million.

Consolidated bonds are also issued the first of each month with a maturity date of nine months. Longer maturities of up to ten years may be issued when needed. These bonds are the joint and several obligations of the 12 banks, and the total outstanding may not exceed 20 times capital and surplus of the 12 banks. As mentioned previously, the regular monthly program of issuing new debt helps to insure an active market for these FICB issues. The bonds are issued in minimum denominations of $5,000 and additional information concerning the characteristics of the bonds can be found in Exhibit 39–1.

Federal Land Banks

These banks, authorized by the Federal Farm Loan Act of 1916, make long-term, first-mortgage loans through Federal Land Bank Associations. Borrowers subscribe to an association's stock in an amount equal to 5 percent of the loan, and the stock is pledged to the association as collateral to the loan. The association in turn subscribes to Federal Land Bank stock equal to 5 percent of the loan which is also pledged as collateral. Stock is retired at repayment of the loan. Federal Land Bank stock is owned by Federal Land Bank Associations with no government investment in the banks since 1947. The banks' net worth at December 31, 1976, was $1,861 million.

Consolidated bonds are issued on a quarterly basis with maturities ranging from a few months to 20 years. Usually bonds are issued in maturities of a year or longer. These bonds are the joint and several obligations of the 12 banks, and the total outstanding may not exceed 20 times capital and surplus. The bonds are issued in minimum denominations of $1,000 and all FLB bonds are available in bearer form only. As mentioned before, the regular availability of these bonds make them highly marketable and an active secondary market for these issues is maintained. Additional information on the characteristics of these bonds is available in Exhibit 39–1.

Farm Credit Bank Discount Notes

The purpose of these notes, a systemwide debt instrument of the 37 banks, is to complement commercial bank borrowings, to provide necessary interim funds between conventional bond sales and to increase flexibility in making adjustments to seasonal changes in loan volume. The first discount notes were offered January 13, 1975. Maturities range from 5 to 150 days. The notes are offered by a limited number of dealers on a discount basis using a 360-day year. The same dealers who act as a primary issuer also maintain a secondary market for these notes. If a purchaser wishes to sell a note prior to maturity, it can be sold in the secondary market. Further information concerning the characteristics of these notes can also be found in Exhibit 39–1.

FEDERAL NATIONAL MORTGAGE ASSOCIATION

Federal National Mortgage Association (FNMA), originally chartered in 1938, was partitioned in 1968 into the present Federal National Mortgage Association and the new Government National Mortgage Association (see section below).

FNMA's functions revolve around secondary market and lending operations for residential mortgages. Originally these operations involved Federal Housing Administration insured mortgages, Administrator of Veterans' Affairs guaranteed mortgages and Farmers Home Administration insured loans. In 1972, open-market operations were expanded to include conventional, uninsured, and nonguaranteed mortgages. Essentially FNMA makes purchases, commitments, and secured loans when available mortgage funds are in short supply and sales when funds are more readily available. FNMA works with an approved list including mortgage companies, savings and loan associations and life insurance companies, and with federal agencies authorized to sell mortgages or loans and to acquire FNMA stock.

FNMA became privately owned in 1968 when Treasury held preferred stock was retired. Sellers of mortgages to, and borrowers from, FNMA are required to subscribe to FNMA stock. In addition, there was a rights offering of its common in 1970, and some shares have been issued in connection with Convertible Debentures. FNMA has also issued nonconvertible Capital Debentures.

FNMA is subject to federal supervision involving the Secretary of Housing and Urban Development and Secretary of the Treasury.

Federal National Mortgage Association Debentures, Series SM. May be sold to private investors, or under certain conditions up to $2,250 million to the Secretary of the Treasury, in an amount no greater than the lesser of 25 times capital and surplus or its aggregate holdings of cash, mortgages or other securities (including U.S. Treasury), and obligations, participations or other instruments which are lawful investments for fiduciary, trust, or public funds. And for this purpose, Capital Debentures are considered part of capital.

These bonds are issued on a quarterly basis through the New York fiscal agent. Various maturities usually extend from 18 months to 25 years. The debentures are issued in bearer form only in denominations of $10,000, $25,000, $50,000, $100,000, and $500,000. They are not callable nor is there any specific exemption from state or local taxing authorites. There is a very active market for FNMA obligations and generally all outstanding obligations can be bought and sold in the secondary market. FNMA debentures are lawful investments and may be accepted as security for all fiduciary, trust, and public funds under the authority and control of the United States or its officers. While the debentures do not represent government debt, direct or guaranteed, they are obligations of a federally chartered institution operating under government supervision.

Short-Term Discount Notes.   These notes, which were first offered in April 1960, are sold by a select number of dealers in a maturity range from 30 to 270 days. A minimum initial order of $50,000 is required with multiples of $5,000 available above this minimum. Those dealers who act as primary issuers also maintain a secondary market for the notes which can be sold prior to maturity if needed. The amount which may be issued in relation to capital and certain assets is included in the amount applicable to SM Debentures above. The tax features are also the same.

FNMA Mortgage-Backed Bonds are issued with GNMA guarantee (see details under "Government National Mortgage Association").

FEDERAL HOME LOAN BANKS

The 12 banks are part of the Federal Home Loan Bank System, established in 1932. The system provides reserve credit for private financial institutions to enable them to make ample credit available to homeowners and buyers and to meet unusual withdrawal needs.

The banks are under the direction of the Federal Home Loan Bank Board, Washington, D.C., an independent agency of the government, which also directs the activities of the Federal Savings and Loan Insurance Corporation and supervises the system of Federal Savings and Loan Associations. Any savings and loan association, cooperative bank, homestead association, insurance company, or savings bank may become a member of the bank system under certain conditions, and all Federal Savings and Loan Associations are required to be members. Members at December 31, 1976 numbered 4,236, including 4,157 savings and loan associations, 77 savings banks, and 2 insurance companies.

Member institutions subscribe to bank stock in an amount equal to the greater of 1 percent of home mortgage loans or $500. The banks completed retirement of all government held stock in 1951.

Secured and unsecured advances are made to members with their stock serving as additional collateral.

Consolidated bonds of varying maturity, sold periodically by the banks through their fiscal agent in Washington, D.C., are joint and several obligations of the 12 banks. The total outstanding may not exceed 12 times capital stock and reserves. Further, the banks must maintain at all times secured advances, guaranteed mortgages, U.S. government securities, direct or guaranteed, or cash equal to bonds outstanding.

In addition, the Secretary of the Treasury is authorized to buy up to $4 billion of the banks' obligations. While the banks' marketable obligations do not represent government debt, direct or guaranteed, they are obligations of federally chartered institutions operating under government supervision.

Consolidated bonds are lawful investments and may be accepted as security for all fiduciary, trust, and public funds under the authority and control of the United States or its officers. Income is exempt from state and local income taxes but subject to federal income taxes. Bonds are available in bearer form in denominations of $10,000, $50,000, and $100,000, and they are noncallable. Because of a regular quarterly issuing schedule followed by the FHLB, new bonds are issued as old ones mature. This establishes a wide range of maturity options to the investor and helps to maintain an active secondary market for the securities.

Consolidated Discount Notes. Initially offered in May 1974, by a select number of dealers, these obligations are available in maturities of 30 to 270 days in denominations of $100,000 and $1 million. They are subject to the same restrictions and collateral as consolidated bonds and are identical as to legality, acceptability, and tax status. The same dealers who act as primary issuers also maintain a secondary market for both the purchase and sale of outstanding notes.

FEDERAL HOME LOAN MORTGAGE CORPORATION

Federal Home Loan Mortgage Corporation (FHLMC) was created in 1970 to expand the availability of mortgage credit by establishing a viable secondary market for conventional residential mortgages and improving the existing secondary market for FHA and VA insured and guaranteed mortgages. It is authorized to purchase residential mortgages from members of the Federal Home Loan Bank system or other approved financial institutions whose deposits are insured by U.S. government agencies. Funds from the sale of mortgages or bonds are used to purchase secondary market residential mortgages.

FHLMC's capital stock consists entirely of nonvoting common, issuable only to the 12 Federal Home Loan Banks. Its board consists of the three members of the Federal Home Loan Bank Board, and the chairman of each is the same. FHLMC raises funds through the sale of *mortgage backed bonds* guaranteed by GNMA (for details, see "Government National Mortgage Association"), *participation certificates,* and *guaranteed mortgage certificates.*

Participation certificates represent undivided interests in groups of mortgages acquired by FHLMC from eligible seller/servicers. They are offered for sale by FHLMC on a continuing basis with principal and interest remitted monthly as received. Denominations range from $100,000 to $1 million. FHLMC guarantees interest at the certificate rate and the principal. FHLMC maintains a register of holders of participation certificates which are transferable.

As of December 31, 1976, there was in excess of $1 billion in participation certificates outstanding. These certificates are offered by an eight-member primary dealer group comprised of major dealer underwriters and one large bank. These dealers maintain a secondary market for the securities and will provide a market quote upon request.

Guaranteed mortgage certificates represent an undivided interest in specified conventional mortgage participations guaranteed and held in trust by FHLMC. The latter guarantees return of the certificate rate and annual payment of principal in minimum scheduled amounts. The certificates are noncallable and issued in denominations of $100,000, $500,000, and $1 million. Interest is paid semiannually and principal annually as opposed to participation certificates, and a buyer may sell back to FHLMC the certificates at par after 15 years. The first GMCs were 8.20s issued February 25, 1975 to mature February 25, 2005.

UNITED STATES POSTAL SERVICE

The United States Postal Service was created as an independent establishment of the Executive Branch of the U.S. Government, succeeding to the business of the Post Office Department. As such it has the authority to issue debt obligations to finance capital expenditures and current operations. At present there are outstanding $250 million 6⅞ percent U.S. Postal Service Bonds, Series A, due February 1, 1997. They are callable after February 1, 1982 and earlier, starting July 1, 1978, $10 million per year, for Sinking and Improvement Fund. They are available in coupon and registered form, denominations of $10,000, $25,000, $100,000, and $500,000. They are not guaranteed by the United States, but there are restrictive covenants. Girard Trust Bank, Philadelphia, is Trustee. The bonds are lawful investments and may be accepted as security for all fiduciary, trust, and public funds under the control and authority of the U.S. government. These bonds are exempt from state and local income taxes.

TENNESSEE VALLEY AUTHORITY

Tennessee Valley Authority is a wholly owned corporate entity of the United States created by the Tennessee Valley Authority Act of 1933. Its activities include navigation, flood control, production and sale of electric power, fertilizer and munitions research, and conservation of natural resources. It is managed by three directors appointed by the president.

TVA is authorized to issue bonds, notes, and other indebtedness up to $5 billion to assist in its power program, which is segregated from nonpower activities. Debt service, payable solely from power proceeds, has precedence over payments to the U.S. Treasury. It issues both bonds and notes which are secured by a first charge on net power proceeds; i.e., net income before interest and depreciation.

Discount notes are sold at auction periodically on a competitive basis. Long-term bonds are sold periodically at competitive bidding. Notes are issued in bearer form in denominations of $5,000, $10,000, $100,000, and $1 million. Coupon bonds are issued in denominations of $1,000 and $5,000, and registered bonds are issued in denominations of $1,000, and any multiple.

While interest is subject to federal income taxes, it is exempt from state and local income taxes. TVA obligations are legal investments for fiduciary, trust, and public funds under control of the U.S. government and are approved by the Treasury as collateral security for the deposit of public funds.

GOVERNMENT NATIONAL MORTGAGE ASSOCIATION

Government National Mortgage Association (GNMA) is a corporation, without capital stock, within the Department of Housing and Urban Development. It was created in 1968, when FNMA was partitioned, to assume its *special assistance* and *management and liquidation functions.*

In the area of special assistance, GNMA is authorized: (1) to provide assistance for financing residential mortgages by making commitments and purchasing mortgages determined by the president to be in the national interest or originated under programs specifically authorized by Congress; (2) to guarantee payment of principal and interest of securities issued by nonfederal entities backed by pools of mortgage loans issued or guaranteed by the Federal Housing Administration,

Veterans' Administration, or Farmers Home Administration. This function includes the so-called Tandem Plan in which GNMA commits to buy, or buys, mortgages at rates more favorable than the going market rate. GNMA then works in tandem with FNMA or other investors selling at prevailing market rates and absorbing the difference as a subsidy.

The management and liquidation functions have the objective of facilitating the financing of GNMA's own mortgages and obligations and those in which certain departments or agencies of the federal government have a financial interest. This is accomplished through the sale of participation certificates, mortgage-backed bonds, and pass-through securities.

Participation Certificates.   This program provides for a pooling of mortgages or obligations of GNMA and various departments or agencies. GNMA, as trustee, sells to private investors participations in the interest and income payments from the pooled mortgages or obligations. GNMA is trustee of three trusts with outstanding participation certificates.

1. *The Government Mortgages Liquidation Trust*
    (Also trustee, Administrator of Veterans Affairs)
2. *The Federal Assets Liquidation Trust*
    (Also trustees, heads of Farmers Home Administration, Department of Agriculture, Department of Health, Education, and Welfare, Department of Housing and Urban Development, Veterans' Administration, and Small Business Administration)
3. *The Federal Assets Financing Trust*
    (Other trustees, see above)

GNMA Participation Certificates are, in effect, guaranteed under the terms of the Sales Participation Act of 1966. The law authorizes the selling agency to make "indefinite and unlimited" drawings on the Treasury, if needed, to service the certificates. Because of this provision, the attorney general of the United States has designated all participation certificates as direct obligations of the United States. Income is not exempt from federal, state, or local income taxes.

Certificates of the three trusts are available in denominations ranging from $5,000 to $1 million in both bearer or registered form. Most registered dealers maintain a secondary market for these securities and quotes can be obtained from them.

The Government Mortgage Liquidation Trust has four issues outstanding, one offered June 16, 1965, due $35 million each July 1 through 1980; another offered November 17, 1965, due $25 million each December 1 through 1980; a third offered April 4, 1966, due $42 million each April 1 through 1981; the fourth offered June 23, 1966 due $60 million each June 23 through 1981.

The Federal Assets Liquidation Trust and the Federal Assets Financing Trust have six issues outstanding. Three were issued in January, April, and December 1967, and are due January 19, 1982, April 6, 1987, and December 11, 1987. Three were issued in 1968 and are due February 1, 1988, April 8, 1988, August 14, 1978 and August 12, 1988.

Mortgage-Backed Securities Program. GNMA is authorized to guarantee timely payment of principal and interest of securities issued by other entities based upon pools of FHA and VA insured or guaranteed mortgages. This guaranty pledges the full faith and credit of the United States to timely payment of amounts due to holders of such securities, which include pass-through securities and mortgage-backed bonds.

Pass-Through Securities. In this program, principal and interest payments on mortgage pools are passed through to holders of certificates after deduction of servicing and guaranty fees. The mortgages in the pools include single-family, project, and mobile home loans. Certificates have stated maturities equal to those on the underlying mortgages with actual, or expected, maturities less because of prepayments. Yields on pools of single-family mortgages are also quoted on a 12-year life based upon FHA's actuarial experience. Prepayments are distributed proportionately to all certificate holders in the pool. As of June 30, 1976, more than $4 billion GNMA pass-throughs had been issued. These securities enjoy a very broad market and all major security dealers make a market in them. Most quote sheets prepared by these dealers have GNMA pass-throughs on them and they are also listed in *The Wall Street Journal.*

Government National Mortgage Association—FNMA, Mortgage-Backed Bonds are a general obligation of Federal National Mortgage Association secured by mortgages held in trust at least equal to bonds outstanding. Timely payment of principal and interest is guaranteed by GNMA, and the guarantee is backed by the "full faith and credit" of the United States. They are not exempt from federal, state, or local income taxes. Denominations available are $25,000, $100,000, $500,000 and $1 million.

Government National Mortgage Association—FHLMC, Mortgage-Backed Bonds are mortgage-backed obligations of Federal Home Loan Mortgage Corporation. Timely payment of principal and interest is guaranteed by GNMA, and the guarantee is backed by the "full faith and credit" of the United States. They are not exempt from federal, state, or local income taxes. Denominations available are $25,000, $100,000, $500,000, and $1 million.

EXPORT-IMPORT BANK OF THE UNITED STATES

The Export-Import Bank, originally established in 1934, has as its purpose to aid in financing and to facilitate exports and imports between the United States and other nations, agencies, or nationals. This is accomplished by extending loans, guarantees, and credit insurance. Its five-man board of directors is appointed by the president of the United States. Its $1 billion of outstanding capital stock is all owned by the U.S. Treasury. Outstanding debt is in the form of participation certificates and debentures. The attorney general stated in a 1966 opinion that the Export-Import Bank's contractual liabilities constitute general obligations of the United States backed by its full faith and credit.

Participation certificates outstanding at present include only the $250 million 5.10s issued February 20, 1967 to mature February 20, 1982. They are not callable; they are available in coupon and registered form, denominations of $5,000, $10,000, $25,000, $100,000, $500,000, and $1 million. Income is not exempt from federal, state, or local taxes.

Debentures outstanding at present include seven issues, totaling $1,500 million, with maturities ranging in 1978 and 1979. They are not callable; they are available in coupon and registered form, denominations from $5,000 to $1 million. Income is not exempt from federal, state, or local taxes.

FARMERS HOME ADMINISTRATION

The Farmers Home Administration, an agency in the U.S. Department of Agriculture, provides credit, and management advice, to farm and other rural families. The agency makes loans from revolving funds, from annual appropriations, and from funds provided by private investors. Repayment of principal and interest to private investors is fully guaranteed by the U.S. government.

While investors may acquire insured individual and block notes directly, period offerings of *Farmers Home Insured Notes, Insurance Contracts* and *Certificates of Beneficial Interest* have been made. The insurance contracts are transferable and provide purchasers of denominations of varied amounts, annual payment of interest, and repurchase at fixed maturity date.

The more recently offered certificates of beneficial interest are available in denominations of $25,000, $50,000, $100,000, $500,000, and $1 million. Interest is not exempt from federal, state, or local income taxes. They are acceptable security for deposits of public monies such as Treasury Tax and Loan Account.

DISTRICT OF COLUMBIA ARMORY BOARD

The District of Columbia Armory Board was created by an act of Congress in 1948 to construct, maintain, and operate the District of

Exhibit 39–2

	Outstanding December 31, 1976 (Par Values— millions of dollars)
Securities Issued by Government Agencies	
Export-Import Bank:	
Debentures	$ 1,900
Participation certificates	250
Issues to state and local governments	143
Total	2,293
Government National Mortgage Association:	
Participation certificates	4,120
Postal Service:	
*Bonds	250
Tennessee Valley Authority:	
*Bonds	1,825
Federal Housing Administration:	
Debentures	575
Total	$ 9,063
Securities Issued by Government-Sponsored Agencies and District of Columbia	
Farm Credit Banks:	
*Discount Notes	$ 728
Banks for Cooperatives:	
*Debentures	4,330
Federal Intermediate Credit Banks:	
*Debentures	10,494
Federal Land Banks:	
*Bonds	17,127
Total	$32,679
Federal Home Loan Banks:	
*Discount notes	322
*Bonds	16,489
Total	$16,811
Farmers Home Administration:	
Insured Notes	5,408
FHLMC:	
*Mortgage-backed bonds and certificates	1,690
*Issued to state and local governments	360
Total	$ 2,050
Federal National Mortgage Association:	
*Discount notes	1,607
*Debentures	27,148
*Capital debentures	1,064
Mortgage-backed bonds	200
Issued to state and local governments	547
Total	$30,566
District of Columbia:	
Bonds	20
Total	$87,534

* Agency issues for which no expressed liability is assumed by the United States.
Source: *Treasury Bulletin.*

Columbia Stadium project. The $19,800,000 of 4.20% sinking-fund bonds issued June 1, 1960, mature December 1, 1979. While debt service is payable solely from revenues, the bonds are unconditionally guaranteed as to principal and interest by the United States of America. Interest, payable semiannually, is subject to federal income taxes.

Chapter 40 _____

Municipal Bonds: Underwriting, Trading, and Investment Portfolio Usage in Commercial Banks

Karl M. Shelton*

Municipal bonds represent evidence of debt of state and local governments in the United States. The term, "municipal," is used rather broadly to describe a wide range of bonds of states, counties, cities, and various other political subdivisions of government. The main distinguishing feature of municipal bonds is that the income derived therefrom is exempt from all federal income taxes.

CATEGORIES OF MUNICIPAL BONDS

There are basically two broad categories of municipal bonds, general obligation and revenue. General obligation bonds are backed by the full faith and credit of the issuer. They can be described as being backed by unlimited ad valorem taxes on all taxable property of the issuing entity without limitation as to rate or amount. In the case of political subdivisions, in effect, this constitutes a first lien on all taxable property. States which rely on retail sales and/or excise taxes (i.e., on gasoline) pledge their general state revenues.

The second broad category is that of revenue bonds. They are often used to finance a revenue-producing facility such as a toll road or bridge, athletic stadium, airport facility, or various types of municipal utilities. Revenue bonds are payable solely from the earnings of a spe-

_____
* Senior Vice President, Seattle-First National Bank, Seattle, Washington.

cific project or undertaking. This classification of bonds includes obligations not payable from or guaranteed by the general taxing power of the state or local government unit. The revenue securing these bonds may appear in the form of special taxes such as those on cigarettes, gasoline, liquor and beer; as user charges for toll roads and bridges or for airport or marine facilities; as metered billings for water, gas, or electricity; or as rental revenues for housing or office space.

A municipal bond is "a promise to pay a specified amount of money at a specified date and to pay periodically the specified rate of interest." Most general obligation bonds are issued with serial maturities. In other words, there are bonds maturing each year over the life of the issue. On the other hand many revenue issues are issued as "term" bonds with all bonds coming due on the same stated date, similar to a corporate issue. Quite frequently there is use of a combination of serial and term bonds with respect to revenue bond financing. In the case of both revenue and general obligation bonds, maturities are designed to coincide with the useful life of the facility being financed with the bond proceeds.

Unlike their corporate counterparts, municipals are still generally issued in "bearer" form. In recent years the $5,000 denomination has become the common unit on newly issued bonds opposed to the $1,000 denomination which was prevalent for many years. Interest is received by detaching a coupon from the bond and presenting the coupon for payment to the paying agent, this usually being done through the banking system. While the coupon type is the most common, most municipalities also offer the privilege of registration, if desired. This registration may be as to principal only, interest only, or both.

THE MARKETS

There are basically two separate and distinct markets for municipal bonds. These are the primary or new issuance market and the secondary or outstanding issue market. Primary markets are involved with the underwriting process for initial issuance of debt, in which several steps are involved. First is the authorization which may come by vote of the people or through statutory authority, such as that of a council or authority which is allowed to issue limited amounts of debt without voter approval. The next step is the setting of details of the issues such as dollar amount, maturity, date and time of sale, and other pertinent details. This is usually spelled out in a prospectus which provides financial data as well as economic and demographic information. The next step is advertisement for bids which may be local but is usually in a national financial publication such as *The Bond Buyer*. This notice of sale also provides the basic details of the issue and puts potential bidders on notice of the upcoming sale. Simultaneously with these steps the municipality has usually requested a rating from one or both of the established rating agencies, (i.e., Moody's Investors Service and Standard & Poors, Inc.). From information supplied by the issuing municipality the rating agencies analyze the issue and usually establish their rating shortly prior to the sale date.

There are basically two types of primary markets: negotiated and competitive. In the case of negotiated issues the municipality works with one dealer or syndicate in order to arrive at an agreed-upon price for marketing the issue. The greatest portion of municipal debt is marketed through competitive bidding by various underwriters. This process works as follows: except for very small issues, underwriters (usually commercial banks or investment bankers) will form syndicates composed of a group of dealers, in order to submit a bid for the issue. At the appointed time and date the various bids are opened and the syndicate offering to purchase the bonds at the lowest possible net interest cost to the municipality will be awarded the bonds. At that point the syndicate owns the bonds and the municipality is assured of receiving their money, if all conditions for a valid delivery at the time of settlement are met. From this point any variation in price will produce a profit or loss for the syndicate and will not affect the proceeds to be received by the issuing municipality. The underwriting syndicate members will now proceed to sell the bonds to the various types of investors at yields they feel represent market rates for the various maturities they are offering.

All transactions in municipal debt, after the original underwriting, are said to be traded in the secondary market. This is the buying and selling by various dealers in an over-the-counter marketplace, since there is no formal exchange for trading municipal securities.

Prior to the passage of the Securities Act Amendment of 1975 the municipal market had been a virtually unregulated market. This act established the Municipal Rulemaking Board which was charged with promulgating rules and regulations under which municipal bond dealers would function. This board recommends such rules to the Securities and Exchange Commission which serves as the controlling authority for publishing such regulations. In 1977 many regulations have been published and others are in the preparation, all designed to provide a more efficient, disciplined market for municipal debt.

USE IN BANK PORTFOLIOS

The after-tax yields on municipal bonds have historically been attractive to high-tax bracket investors versus other fixed-income investments. Commercial banks have held large amounts of these securities because of their high marginal tax rates (i.e., the rate at which the next dollar of income will be taxed, usually 48 percent). In recent years, however, the percentage of municipal bonds relative to total assets has been declining for most major banks. This has resulted in part because the rate of total taxes on earnings has declined as banks have expanded abroad and also increased their leasing activity. Income from municipals has, therefore, become relatively less attractive. Holdings were also impacted in recent years by the decline in earnings associated with nonaccrual of loan income in conjunction with real estate loans and the transfer of additional amounts into loan loss reserves.

Maturities

As a general rule, municipal bonds represent the largest portion of the residual or permanent investment portfolio. Various banks use different maturity schedules. Probably the most commonly used are the "laddered" or spaced maturity concept and the "dumbbell" or "barbell" approach. For a bank using the "laddered" approach the prime goal is to have basically the same amount of bonds maturing each year over a specified range of years; for example, 1 to 15 years. This means the current year's maturities will be reinvested into the longest maturity being used in their portfolio. This produces an average maturity of exactly one-half the longest maturity.

Under the "dumbbell" philosophy only very short and long maturities are used leaving the intermediate range open. This method requires constant reinvestment of short maturities into short maturities which serve as a portion of the "stored" liquidity of a bank, while the longer maturities must be sold as they move into the intermediate range. This concept basically is designed for use with an ascending yield curve in order to maximize earnings by investing in the longest maturities which normally would provide the highest yields. As they move into the intermediate range the prices of the bonds should rise and therefore produce profits. However, yield curves are not always ascending and as economic conditions change the yield structure also changes which means that sales may take place at losses. Few major banks and even fewer community banks are now using this maturity concept.

As in the management of any asset, it is extremely important that maturity management be undertaken in the context of what is best suited for the individual bank's loan and deposit structure. Each bank should decide the maturity structure best suited for it, and the investment portfolio policy should take this into consideration. Rather than following an established pattern of either "laddered" or "dumbbell," most banks find their needs better served by purchasing municipals based on the yield available on a particular maturity rather than a set pattern. There seems to be no magic to having exactly the same amount of bonds coming due each year or having only the longest maturities. There are always opportunities to fill in a given year at favorable yields.

RATINGS OF MUNICIPAL SECURITIES

The rating of a municipal security is very important to a bank. The two prime rating agencies for municipal securities are Moody's Investors Service, which rates debt of $600,000 or more, and Standard & Poors, which rates debt over $1 million. Their criteria for rating an issue are very similar and an investor should consult their rating manuals for this criteria and the definitions of each rating category. Moody's ratings range from "Aaa" down through "Caa" while Standard & Poors' range from "AAA" through "D." The various supervisory authorities for all banks have agreed that issues rated Aaa through Baa by the former and AAA through BBB by the latter will be considered as investment grade securities and, therefore, as eligible for commercial bank portfolios. However, virtually every bank will have securities in its portfolio which are nonrated. In many cases bonds are nonrated due to an insufficient amount of debt outstanding, or some other compelling reason. If the bank holding these securities is doing so for some public purpose (the municipality may be located in the bank's marketing area), the examiners will usually not comment on the security. If, however, the bank owns securities which have deteriorated in quality to a rating below Baa or BBB, the issues will be classified as doubtful or speculative and reserves or charge-off may be required by the examining authority.

Since mid-1975 there has been much controversy as to the validity of ratings, largely centered around the withdrawal and lowering of New York City's rating, and the rating placed on securities of the Municipal Assistance Corporation of New York, an agency which was created by the state of New York to assist in working out the municipal debt problems of New York City. These controversies have raised doubt as to the meaningfulness and validity of other ratings and several lawsuits are pending in relation to ratings.

A collateral problem to the rating question has been the question of disclosure. At several points in 1975 no bids were received for municipal issues which were being auctioned because the underwriters believed that there was inadequate disclosure of financial data about the issuing municipality. This will be a continuing question until definitive rules are established for the municipal market by the Municipal

Rulemaking Board and published by the SEC. This will be an ongoing process as the Rulemaking Board continues to define a code of operation for the municipal bond industry.

While ratings of the primary rating agencies serve as a focal point, large banks go beyond the rating and make their own evaluation. Most money center banks and many regional banks have specialists who prepare their own analyses as a supplement to the ratings. In many instances the bank feels it can develop better "on the spot" information through direct contact with the issuing municipality than through reliance on the rating agency. Additionally there are several rating services in operation in various states which concentrate on debt in their area. These include North Carolina, South Carolina, Texas, and Ohio. Ratings are also offered by Fitch & Whites Investors Services.

DIVERSIFICATION

Probably more than any other type of asset, tax-exempt securities offer the bank opportunities to diversify. Because there is municipal debt issued by so many various types of units of government, totaling approximately 78,000 individual units, the investor has a myriad of choices. (See Exhibit 40–1.)

Diversification is primarily classified along economic or geographic lines, although there can be other measures such as political or demographic. The bond account serves as the prime vehicle for diversification. As an example if a bank is located in a market heavily dominated by a single industry, which would probably mean that a large portion of its loan portfolio is directly tied to that industry, it would probably want to purchase bonds of municipalities that are dominated by a completely different type of industry or one which has a diversified industrial base. The concept is one of "not having all your eggs in one basket" and a spreading of risks. If a significant portion of the

Exhibit 40–1
Number of State and Local Governmental Units by Type

Type of Unit	1952*	1957*	1962	1967	1972
State.	50	50	50	50	50
County	3,052	3,050	3,043	3,049	3,044
Municipality.	16,807	17,215	18,000	18,048	18,517
Township	17,202	17,198	17,142	17,105	16,991
School district	67,355	50,454	34,678	21,782	15,781
Special district.	12,340	14,424	18,323	21,264	23,885
Total	116,806	102,391	91,236	81,298	78,268

* Adjusted to include Alaska and Hawaii.
Source: *Moody's Municipal and Government Manual, 1975.*

total portfolio is composed of small, usually unmarketable, local issues which are tied to a loan portfolio which represents a heavy concentration of risk in the local economy, the bank should make a special effort to diversify through its purchases for the bond account.

MARKET STRUCTURE

In recent years the issuance of debt by state and local government has helped to create a capital market which is second in size only to the market for U.S. government securities (see Exhibit 40–2). Annual volume has been increasing each year in line with the growth of communities and the expanded need for municipal services. The municipal market is composed of approximately 750 investment dealers, 150

Exhibit 40–2
Total State and Local Debt Outstanding

	Total		State		Local	
Year	*Billions of Dollars*	*Percent of Total*	*Billions of Dollars*	*Percent of Total*	*Billions of Dollars*	*Percent of Total*
1952............	$ 30.1	100%	$ 6.9	23%	$ 23.2	77%
1957............	52.7	100	13.7	26	39.0	74
1962............	81.3	100	22.0	27	59.3	73
1967............	114.6	100	32.5	28	82.1	72
1968............	121.2	100	35.7	29	85.5	71
1969............	133.5	100	39.6	30	93.9	70
1970............	143.6	100	42.0	29	101.6	71
1971............	158.8	100	47.8	30	111.0	70
1972............	174.6	100	54.5	31	120.1	69
1973............	188.4	100	59.4	32	129.0	68
1974............	206.6	100	65.3	32	141.3	68
1975............	221.2	100	72.1	33	149.1	67

Source: Adapted from *Municipal Finance Statistics*, p. 8, and Bureau of the Census, *Governmental Finances* (Washington, D.C.: U.S. Government Printing Office).

dealer banks, and a few brokers. While it operates in an over-the-counter market environment, the size of the market may be gauged by the volume of offerings appearing in the *Blue List*, which is a daily publication of dealer offerings. During 1976, total offerings ranged from a low of $533 million to a high of $1.05 billion.

A broad gauge of levels and attractiveness of municipal bonds is the *Bond Buyer Index* which is published each Thursday by *The Daily Bond Buyer*. This is a grouping of 20 bonds maturing in 20 years and includes issues from each of the top four rating groups. By following this index an investor can determine the general movements in interest rates which have occurred over a broad span of years. There is also an index maintained of 11 high-grade (Aa or better) issues, reported on a weekly basis. By tracking the performance of the high-grade 11-bond index versus the overall 20-bond index, an investor can determine the sector of the market which is reflecting the greatest area of change.

PORTFOLIO MANAGEMENT

The primary function in managing any bank portfolio is the merging of three factors: safety, liquidity, and income. For most banks the function of providing for adequate liquidity tends to take precedence over the other two but each must be considered. While most banks have moved more toward "bought" liquidity or purchase of liabilities, it is still important to retain a degree of liquidity in the "stored" area by holding securities which can be readily converted into cash in the event of deposit losses or loan build-up. While U.S. government and federal agency securities provide the largest portion of most "stored" liquidity, the use of short-term, tax-exempt issues such as government-guaranteed project notes provide banks with a source of liquidity *and* tax-exempt income. Money center banks and larger regional banks tend to make more use of short-term tax exempts as a part of their portfolio than do smaller community banks.

The permanent or residual portion of the portfolio is looked to more for income purposes, since it represents the commitment of funds, over and above loan demand, to longer term assets which are expected to provide generally higher returns. In this respect safety is a definite consideration and is measured primarily by the rating on the particular issuer.

In viewing any investment portfolio the entire account must be looked at in the same context. It is difficult to isolate on a particular portion and manage it in a vacuum. All portions need to be considered and defined in the overall basic portfolio management philosophy. The portfolio policy should spell out the types of eligible investments, recommended maturity range and average maturity, quality considerations, liquidity considerations, and the tie-in that the investment portfolio must make with the overall asset/liability management philosophy. The portfolio must be viewed as an integral part of the bank and to assure coordination, the person charged with investment portfolio management should be a member of the policy-making group of the bank. In many smaller banks, management of the municipal portion does not receive the proper attention since the person charged with responsibility may have several other duties. Any bank with over $250 million in total assets should assign a full-time officer to portfolio management.

QUALITY

As mentioned before, the degree of risk is measured primarily by the agencies in establishing ratings. A review of the definitions of each rating would indicate that the quality of a bond is being measured by its freedom from risk. In other words, "Aaa" indicates relative freedom from risk while "Baa" indicates more risk. The two broad categories of risk to be measured are (1) risks related to ability and willingness to pay, and (2) risks related to the possibilities of revised capitalization. Ability to pay for general obligation bonds is related to the economic environment of the community, taxing power, the industrial base and diversity, stability of government, and the willingness of that local government to meet its committed obligations. The principal focus of a revenue bond issue is ability to pay, reflecting the capacity of the activity financed to generate income in excess of its debt service requirements (plus other considerations which have been included in the covenants tied to the issue such as toll or rate setting, potential competition, and adequate insurance coverage).

The second broad category of risk related to capitalization relates to whether the present debt load will be changed materially by additional borrowings. Most revenue bond projects carefully spell out the provisions under which any additional bonds might be issued and this is included in the trust indenture covering the issue. It is always advisable to look beyond the bond resolution itself in order to assure adequate protection of the income stream for retiring the debt. The general obligation bondholder is not assured that no additional bonds will be issued. It has become more and more prevalent in recent years to revise debt limits and to issue additional bonds based on a growing tax base. The holder of a general obligation bond has no legal recourse when a municipality decides to increase its debt by any means authorized by state law. The quality of revenue bonds tends to be assured by contract while that of general obligation bonds is not. From this aspect alone, revenue bonds could be considered a preferred investment over general obligation bonds. The problems of "moral" obligation bonds and the New York City situation have tended to cloud the whole question of risk and quality in recent months and entirely new views may arise out of these situations which could dramatically alter the municipal bond marketplace.

TAXABLE MUNICIPAL BONDS

Legislation has been proposed which would establish a system which would provide for issuance of optional taxable municipal bonds. A municipality could elect to issue tax-exempt bonds, or to issue taxable securities and receive a federal subsidy of between 33.33 percent–50 percent of the interest cost. This subsidy would cover the additional interest over and above what would have been paid if the municipality had issued tax-exempt bonds.

These proposals have been associated with tax reform measures in Congress and while committee hearings have been conducted on the subject no action has been taken in the full Congress on such a proposal. This is a development which should be watched closely in upcoming sessions of Congress as it seems to be gathering more support, and opposition has slackened. There has been no discussion of any changes with respect to outstanding municipal issues. They would retain their tax-exempt status.

Proponents of the taxable bond option argue that it will broaden the market for state and local securities by attracting pension funds, life insurance companies, and more individuals that are presently participating in the tax-exempt market. The pressure for such legislation seems to run parallel with the difficulties of issuance of municipal bonds.

CONCLUSION

Municipal bonds are issued by states and local government units for capital purposes. The most distinct feature of municipal debt versus other forms of debt is that interest income on municipal bonds is exempt from federal income taxation. They are secured by general taxing powers (general obligations bonds) or by revenues from a project financed with bond proceeds (revenue bonds). Commercial banks invest in municipal bonds, as well as underwriting and trading these securities within certain limitations prescribed by regulatory authorities.

Bank investment portfolios serve as a source of liquidity and earnings. Municipal bonds primarily serve the latter purpose due to their longer maturities and the attraction of tax-exempt income to high, marginal tax bracket investors. Internal bank investment portfolio policy should address questions of diversification, rating, and maturity mix of the municipal portfolio. Specific rating limits are identified by bank regulators. Ratings should be supplemented by internal credit review.

Banks with separate departments which underwrite new issues in the primary market or trade outstanding municipal securities in the secondary market are referred to as "dealer" banks. There are limits on the types of municipal securities in which banks may deal, as opposed to those in which they may invest. Dealer banks must register with the SEC and the staff must meet certain qualifications. While municipals are held in portfolios for interest income, banks profit from underwriting and trading these securities by selling them to other dealers or portfolios.

The Municipal Securities Rulemaking Board is promulgating rules related to disclosure and trade practices which will bring municipal securities industry regulation closer in line to that which exists for corporations under the SEC. Finally, and in the future, legislative and regulatory pressures may lead to federally subsidized, taxable municipal securities.

Chapter 41

Portfolio Management— Guidelines for a Commercial Bank

Edward M. Roob*

Thomas A. Vaughn†

Investment policies vary widely among commercial banks, due to differences in size, location, and loan and deposit history. Policies also can and do differ even among banks that are quite similar in these areas because portfolio management is an art and not an exact science.

Thus, the purpose of this chapter is not to espouse or promote any particular investment policy as being the "best possible" one. Rather, it simply is an attempt to point out certain basic factors which should be considered by any bank that is attempting to develop a sound investment program.

Some of the factors mentioned below may appear almost too elementary and obvious to warrant much thought or discussion. However, it is precisely because these factors seem so rudimentary that they are overlooked and neglected by many bank managements. Successful portfolio management starts with a step-by-step analysis along the lines suggested below.

INVESTMENT OBJECTIVES AND THE CONSTRAINTS

The first step is to establish and/or recognize your investment objectives and the constraints under which you operate. Portfolio policy obviously must be made in the context of a bank's total needs and

* Senior Vice President, First National Bank of Chicago, Chicago, Illinois.

† Vice President, First National Bank of Chicago, Chicago, Illinois.

requirements; it cannot operate in isolation. Thus, a careful inventory should be made in each of the areas discussed below.

Assess the Bank's Overall Risk Position

Guidelines, Ratios, Measurement Methods. Unfortunately, there are no nice, neat empirical formulas and measuring devices for determining the proper loan/deposit ratio, correct level of capital, and so on for any given bank. Take the matter of capital adequacy as an illustration. Recently, one of the leading bank stock analysts (Harry Keefe of Keefe, Bruyette & Woods, Inc.) stated, "I personally don't know what is the proper capital/asset ratio for a bank and from what I have read, nobody else does either." Therefore, we recommend that each bank management be guided by the following two factors in analyzing the characteristics and conditions of its own bank.

1. Compare your bank's overall makeup with other banks similar in size, structure, location, and so on. Comparisons with industry averages or with banks greatly different in size and/or general composition can be greatly misleading. An obvious example would be a small country bank located in a one-crop locality attempting to "copy" a large city bank in is asset/liability mix, investment strategy, and so forth.
2. Each bank management also needs to decide the asset/liability structure and ratio levels it is "comfortable" with. Variations in ratios among banks that are quite alike in size, location, type of customer, and so on are permissible and should not become a matter of concern, provided that these variations are kept within reasonable limits. For instance, a particular bank may determine to maintain a capital/asset ratio of 7 percent, even though the average for other highly similar banks is 8 percent.

Loan Portfolios and Deposits. Analyze the loan portfolios and the deposits in terms of compositing past history and future trends:

1. The composition of these accounts; i.e., the kinds and amounts of loans and deposits, the types of customers served.
2. Past history (paying particular attention to the volatility of these accounts); both with respect to cyclical as well as seasonal variations.
3. Developing estimates of the type and magnitude of probable future trends.

Capital Position. Review your bank's capital position in relation to its current capital structure and its ability to support future growth and/or a changing asset mix.

1. Evaluate the adequacy of the bank's current capital structure.
2. Try to determine the ability of the current capital account to support your bank's projected future growth and/or a changing asset mix. (As an example, a bank with a 7 percent capital/asset ratio earning 10 percent on its capital, and having a 50 percent dividend payout and an annual asset growth of 12 percent will find that its 7 percent capital ratio will drop to 5.1 percent at the end of five years.)

Investment Personnel and Effort. Evaluate both the amount of "in house" investment expertise available and the effort applied to the bank's investment account. Lack of investment personnel and effort can be partially (but not fully) overcome through using the investment services of large correspondents and various other advisory sources.

Study Liquidity Requirements versus Income Needs

Every portfolio manager faces the mutually exclusive choice between yield and liquidity. This is the classic "trade-off" problem in bank portfolio management.

In analyzing this problem, it is best to begin by trying to make a careful distinction between the liquidity portion of the investment account and the earnings portion. Then, attempt to determine how much emphasis the bank desires to place on each portion.

Estimate the probable impact of future bank growth and other developments on liquidity and earnings requirements.

Analyze the Pledging Requirements to Secure Public Funds

Assess the bank's past and present pledging needs in terms of types and amounts of securities required.

Determine the amount of "safety margin" desired (i.e., the amount over and above both the required average monthly or yearly balance and the peaks for each pledge account). Again, it will be necessary to estimate the probable future requirements.

Evaluate the Bank's Overall Tax Position, Both Current and Future

Develop a suitable forecast of your bank's asset/liability mix and earnings. Study the possible tax impact of leasing operations, foreign tax credits, transfers to loan-loss reserves, tax-loss trading in the investment accounts, and so on.

Consider possible future legislation and its effect on the tax position.

For example, states and municipalities are trending toward the imposition of local income taxes, and in-state or local municipal issues may or may not be exempted from such taxes.

Failure to adequately assess future tax requirements may mean having to sell or swap large amounts of bonds in a depressed market.

PORTFOLIO STRATEGIES

Once the bank's investment needs and constraints have been clearly established and agreed upon, the next step is to begin developing appropriate and specific portfolio policies and strategies. Unless the proper foundation has been laid, bank investment policy becomes a haphazard, "fly by the seat of your pants" process. Correct investment decisions then come about as a matter of pure luck rather than from studied judgment.

"Three-Part" Portfolio Strategy

Divide the portfolio into a liquidity account, an income account, and a "swing" account.

1. Under this technique, it becomes much easier to readily identify those securities held specifically for long-term investment and those held primarily for liquidity purposes.
2. The traditional portfolio subdivision of a government account, municipal account, and a corporate or other securities account fails to provide an accurate picture of this liquidity/income distinction. Likewise, length of maturity can be misleading because under certain circumstances (as for example in anticipation of rising interest rates) a large portion of the earnings or income account might be held temporarily in short-term issues. The real distinction should be the purpose for which the securities are held, and the liquidity-*income*-"swing" segmentation brings this out most clearly.
3. The "swing" portion of the portfolio is the cushioning factor between the liquidity portion and the earnings portion. Funds are shifted into and out of this portion depending upon market conditions and outlook.

This type of portfolio strategy requires a clear understanding of the difference between liquidity, marketability, and safety.

1. *Liquidity.* Measures the ability to quickly convert a security into cash at a price reasonably close to its current book value.
2. *Marketability.* Measures the relative ease of buying or selling large amounts of a particular security without unduly affecting its market price.

3. *Safety.* Measures the relative degree of creditworthiness of a security; i.e., the ability and willingness of a borrower to meet principal and interest payments when due.

The distinction among these terms is quite important from a portfolio management viewpoint. As a practical illustration, a security such as an intermediate term Treasury note has the highest level of safety and marketability, but it still may not provide very much true liquidity if the current market price is well below book value.

Type of Investment, Diversification, and Quality

The higher a bank's overall risk position (as determined under the section discussing overall risk position), the lower should be the risk exposure in the investment account. For example, a bank in a town heavily dominated by one company should attempt to offset the high relative risk in its loan and deposit accounts by reducing risk as much as possible in its bond investment account through means of greater diversification—emphasizing higher rated issues, and increasing the holdings of governments and short-term municipals.

Diversification. Proper diversification is a very necessary component of sound bank investment policy. However, diversification often is carried too far. Generally speaking, banks' portfolios tend to be overdiversified rather than underdiversified.

Most people generally think of overdiversification in terms of having too many different credits in the portfolio (i.e., holding a large number of widely dispersed state and municipal issues). However, over diversification also can result from holding too many maturities of a given issuer; for instance, holding a dozen different Treasury bill issues when two or three would be just as suitable.

Quality. The investor should recognize that both credit quality and ratings are relative. A bond with an Aaa rating should not be considered as being an issue which has no credit risk associated with it, but merely that it has greater basic strength and creditworthiness than lesser rated bonds in the opinion of the rating agency. Remember, bond analysis and rating leans heavily upon subjective matters; only a part of the analytical process can be based upon objective measures.

Undue emphasis should not be placed upon quality. Certainly, nothing destroys the performance of a portfolio like a default in principal, but there are many gradations in quality between the highest grade municipals and those relatively few that represent a serious risk of default. Remember, quality entails a cost (namely, an income give-up).

The rating services are not infallible. A local bank may be just as qualified to rate the credits in its region as is a national rating agency.

Portfolio Maturity Structure

The "Ladder" Portfolio

1. This technique derives its name from the fact that approximately the same number of bonds mature at regularly spaced intervals. A simple illustration would be a portfolio with maturities ranging from one to ten years with about 10 percent of the bonds coming due each year.
2. Under this type of system, the proceeds from maturities are reinvested at the longest end of the maturity schedule. (In the previous illustration, this would call for reinvestment in ten-year issues.)
3. The ladder portfolio does offer several advantages:
   a. It requires less investment expertise and management than other types of maturity schedules.
   b. It has a certain degree of "built-in" liquidity because a relatively constant number of bonds mature each year.
   c. It avoids "gambling" on changes in interest rates since maturity proceeds always are simply reinvested at the long end of the ladder.
4. The disadvantages of the ladder concept are:
   a. It will lead to poor investment decisions in certain kinds of markets (such as maintaining the ladder structure when the market seems to be calling for a general shortening, lengthening, and so on).
   b. It tends to operate against yield maximization; over the course of an interest rate cycle, it merely will match the average yields available.
   c. Like many "formula" techniques, a major drawback is that it is overly rigid and restrictive.

The "Dumbbell" or "Hourglass" Portfolio

1. In this type of portfolio system, funds are invested mainly in short and long maturities; there are few, if any, intermediates. Obviously, the short-term segment is the liquidity portion and little emphasis is placed upon income in this part of the portfolio. However, maximization of income is the major objective in the long-term portion.
2. The long and short portions are not held at fixed amounts as is the case under the "ladder" system. Rather, the percentages invested in either short-term or long-term securities will vary, depending upon management's assessment of the market.
3. The advantages of this system are:
   a. A potentially high return since the portfolio manager is able to take advantage of market swings.
   b. A substantial degree of liquidity since a significant portion of the account may be invested in short-term issues.

4. The "dumbbell" technique is not without its disadvantages. The major ones are:
   a. It calls for a great degree of investment expertise and "guts" due to the higher risk nature of this type of maturity structure and the difficulty of correctly calling market movements.
   b. It requires a continual willingness to trade and take losses when necessary.
   c. It may be difficult to trade large amounts of the investments as quickly as the anticipated market movements demand.

The "Cyclical" Portfolio

1. This type of portfolio concept calls for shortening the maturities when interest rates are likely to rise and for lengthening maturities whenever yields are expected to decline.
2. This concept is ideal in theory but is hard to implement because of the following two factors:
   a. First, there is the difficulty of being able to accurately forecast interest rate movements (and then to be able to trade a large enough portion of the account within the required time frame).
   b. Second, despite the introduction of liability management techniques, bank portfolios still are confronted to some extent by the "classic yield trap." Loan demand and interest rate cycles tend to coincide, thereby creating a dual problem. When loan demand is high, the portfolio has no money to invest in the high yielding bonds. When demand it slack, the portfolio is under pressure to increase profits by extending maturities at the wrong time.

Combinations and "Modified Ladders." In view of the disadvantages listed for each of the above-mentioned portfolio maturity structures, most banks tend to use a combination of these techniques. Perhaps the system most widely used is one which could be termed a "modified ladder" portfolio. Under this system, a bank maintains a reasonable level maturity schedule but allows itself enough flexibility to take some advantage of market swings or other possible future developments. In other words, this even ladder can be "bent out of shape" in order to maximize earnings, improve liquidity, or meet other needs and requirements.

SWAPPING

Swapping is a technique whereby one or more issues are sold and the proceeds are used to purchase other investments in order to take advantage of varying yield spread relationships between quality grades, maturities, and types of investments.

Prior to the late 1960s, most bank portfolios engaged in relatively little swapping. Bond management activity consisted primarily of "buying and holding to maturity." The elimination of bank portfolio capital gains benefits in 1969 removed former trading restrictions so that considerable progress has been made in the direction of active portfolio management through techniques such as swapping.

Yield Pick-Up Swap

This type of swap involves the replacement of one security by another offering a higher yield but similar in all other aspects such as

Exhibit 41–1
Example of Typical Yield Pickup Swap

Sell: $1,000,000 (par value) U.S. Treasury 5⅞% due 8/31/76 at 98.375 to yield 7.70%

Buy: $1,060,000 (par value) Treasury bills due 8/24/76 at 7.32% (discount yield) to yield 7.82% (coupon equivalent)
Assumption: settlement date of trade is 9/16/75

1. If the 5⅞% Treasury notes are held to maturity, then the holder would receive $1,000,000 in principal plus $58,750 in interest for a total on 8/31/76 of $1,058,750.

2. If the 5⅞% Treasury notes are sold and the proceeds are reinvested in $1,060,000 par value of Treasury bills due 8/24/76, then the results would be as follows:

Sale price of 5⅞% notes (98⅜)..	$983,750
Accrued interest	2,582
Total proceeds of sale	$986,332
Purchase price of bills	986,072
Remaining funds..................................	$ 260
Maturity proceeds of bills to be received on 8/24/76..............................	$1,060,000

3. The two advantages of making this swap are as follows:

First advantage:

Maturity proceeds of bills................................	$1,060,000
Maturity proceeds of notes..............................	1,058,750
Advantage of swap	$ 1,250

Second advantage:

Maturity date of bills..	8/24/76
Maturity date of notes	8/31/76
Advantage of swap	7 days*

* That is, we are able to obtain our proceeds seven days earlier and thereby can reinvest these proceeds for this period of time and thereby obtain an added advantage.

quality and maturity. As the name implies, the objective is to increase the total return over the life of the security. An example is shown in Exhibit 41–1.

The Substitution Swap or Replacement Swap

In a substitution or replacement swap, the portfolio manager continuously analyzes the spread relationships among groups of similar types of securities. A swap is made whenever the yield spread between two highly similar bonds reaches some extreme limit (as a result of temporary market imbalances). The portfolio manager hopes to obtain a profitable "reversal" of this swap at a later date when the spread returns to a more normal historical level. This technique usually is referred to as an *arbitrage*.

The major obstacle to the substitution swap is the absolute necessity

Exhibit 41–2
Example of Typical Substitution Swap*

Sell: U.S. Treasury 6 3/4% due 5/31/77 at 98.03125 to yield 7.97%
Buy: U.S. Treasury 6 7/8% due 5/15/77 at 98.3125 to yield 7.95%

1. Above trade results in a small yield give-up.
2. However, this trade is made on the basis of past yield spread relationships between these two issues.
3. Past records indicate that the widest spread between these two issues occurred when the 6 3/4s yielded 15-basis points more than the 6 7/8s while the narrowest spread resulted in the 6 7/8s yielding 3-basis points more than the 6 3/4s.
4. Thus, on the basis of past history, a portfolio manager should sell the 6 3/4s and buy the 6 7/8s whenever the spread relationship narrows with the intention of reversing the swap when the hoped-for spread widening occurs at some later date.
5. In our example, this is precisely what occurs. In 30 days, the following swap was made:

Sell: U.S. Treasury 6 7/8% due 5/15/77 at 98.28125 to yield 7.97%
Buy: U.S. Treasury 6 3/4% due 5/31/77 at 97.84375 to yield 8.10%
Result: Although a 1/32nd loss (0.03125) was sustained on the 6 7/8s, the 6 3/4s were purchased at a price 6/32s lower (0.1875) than they were originally sold at, thereby resulting in a net profit of 5/32s (0.15625) or $1,562.50 per million par value.

---

* This swap was based upon actual market prices which existed during August and September 1975.

to give up yield to maturity when required. However, this yield give-up is only temporary. A substitution swap may require giving up nominal yield for a short while with the intention of eventually being able to increase the total real return. An example is shown in Exhibit 41–2.

The Intermarket Swap

This type of swap attempts to take advantage of changing yield spread relationships between various segments of the bond market. These segments can be differentiated by: (1) type of issue (example—Treasuries versus Agencies); (2) quality (example—Aaa versus A rated general obligation municipals); or (3) coupon rate, and so on.

The changing spread between these segments may represent either a temporary market aberration (which will revert to more normal levels in the near future) or the beginning of a new trend or market structure.

As an illustration of a changing market structure, consider what might be expected to occur during a period of high interest rates. First, the supply of government agency securities will tend to increase sharply because, among other things, disintermediation in the savings and loan industry will require indreased borrowings by the Federal Home Loan Banks; also, FNMA will see the need to supply funds to the housing market. At the same time, the supply of U.S. Treasury issues will diminish since high interest rates normally are associated with a good economy and increased government tax receipts (and therefore less direct Treasury borrowing). Finally, banks will have less money for investment due to strong loan demand. All of these factors will tend to cause the spreads between Treasuries and Agencies to widen significantly. This widened spread relationship can be expected to reverse when interest rates decline because: (i) issuance of new agency financings will lessen; (ii) direct Treasury borrowings will increase as the economy moves into a recession; (iii) banks are able to obtain more money for investments due to a decline in loan demand and also by increasing their issuance of CDs.

An unusually clear intermarket swap opportunity arose in late 1973. At that time, the yields on GNMA (Ginnie Mae) "pass-throughs" rose to very high levels relative to government Agency issues, because the primary buyers of the pass-throughs (savings and loans institutions) were experiencing a deposit drain. Many bank portfolio managers bought these securities since they believed that major pension funds soon would pick up the purchasing slack left by savings and loan associations and the unusually large spread between the pass-throughs and the Agencies would narrow sharply. This is precisely what occurred and those portfolios which had swapped into pass-throughs at the correct time realized a 50 to 70 basis point spread reversal.

The Yield Anticipation Swap

In a yield anticipation swap, the portfolio manager attempts to predict bond yields for some future period of time and then makes swaps based upon this prediction. For example, if yields are expected to

Exhibit 41–3
Example of Municipal Bond Tax-Loss Trade

Sell: $100,000 par value ABC City 4% due 10/1/85 at 7.00% (78.68)
Buy: $100,000 par value XYZ County 4% due 10/1/85 at 7.00% (78.68)

Original cost of ABC bonds	$100,000
Proceeds of sale	78,680
Gross loss	$ 21,320
Tax savings (50%)	10,660
Net loss	$ 10,660
Maturity value of XYZ bonds	$100,000
Original cost	78,680
Gross gain	$ 21,320
Tax on gain (50%)	10,660
Net gain	$ 10,660

Value of Trade: Depends upon rate at which the $10,660 tax saving can be reinvested until 10/1/85. If the tax savings are used to purchase additional XYZ County bonds (the most common type of trade), then the advantage of this trade amounts to $6,590 as shown below.

Issue	Amount	Coupon	Maturity	Yield	Original Cost	Price
Sell:						
ABC City	100,000	4.00%	10/ 1/85	4.00%	$100,000	$78.68
Buy:						
XYZ County	113,000	4,000%	10/ 1/85	6.09%	$88,908	$78.68

Comparative Statistics	Sell	Buy	Change
Average coupon	4.00%	4.00%	0.00%
Average yield	4.00%	6.09%	2.09%
Average maturity	10.00 yr.	10.00 yr.	0.00 yr.
Annual coupon income	4,000	4,520	520
Annual amortization	0	0	0
	4,000	4,000	4,000
Annual accretion	0	1,205	1,205
Annual return	4,000	5,725	1,725

Loss on Sale:
Book value of present holdings............................... $100,000
Sale proceeds.. 78,680

Gross loss .... $ 21,320
Tax savings... 10,660

Net loss.. $ 10,660
Funds Available For Reinvestment:
Sale proceeds.. 78,680
Tax savings... 10,660

Funds available for reinvestment............................. $ 89,340
Cost of bonds purchased............................... 88,908

Remaining funds .... $ 432
Break-Even Calculations:
Annual return on present holdings 4,000
Net loss on sales (annualized)................................ 1,066

Amount to be recovered annually........................ $ 5,066
Funds available for reinvestment............................. 89,340
Break-even yield....................................... 5.67%

Supplemental Information

Time Needed to Recover Loss.
Increased annual return of $1,725 recovers net loss of $10,660 in 6.18 years.
This is 3.92 years prior to the average maturity of the present holdings.

Additional Return on Swap:
Increased annual return....................................... $ 1,725
Average maturity of present holdings.......................... 10.00 yr.
Gross increased return $17,250
Less: net loss 10,660

Net increased return....................................... $ 6,590

decline sharply (and bond prices to rise) in the near future, the portfolio manager would be inclined to swap short maturities for longer maturities because he would want to "lock in" the current high level of yields for as long as possible (and also to seek some capital appreciation).

Needless to say, predicting future rates with any degree of accuracy and consistency is an endeavor fraught with danger. Therefore, yield anticipation swaps have a high degree of risk.

Tax-Loss Trading

A tax-loss trade is simply a swap in which the bonds that are sold are disposed of at a loss. Thus, any of the various types of swaps listed above would fall into the tax-loss category if the sale side of the swap resulted in a loss.

Exhibit 41–3 presents a simplified tax-loss trade involving two municipal bonds. For ease of explanation, we have ignored transaction costs and made the assumption that the coupon rate, maturity, and quality of the bonds sold and bought are exactly the same. The tax rate is assumed to be 50 percent.

At first glance, there seems to be no advantage to making this swap, merely an exchange of comparable securities. Coupon income stays the same. The future gain is exactly equal to the current loss and the tax consequences offset each other. However, there is an advantage. Today's tax liability has been reduced and the offsetting tax increase will not be incurred until a later date. In effect, we have the use of the cash saved through decreasing the tax liability, at no cost.

In high-rate periods, investment policy should aim for tax loss trades to eliminate low-yield, high-cost holdings and replace them with higher yield current issues, particularly since taxable earnings would tend to be relatively high at these times.

Every portfolio manager should be fully familiar with the federal tax implications of selling and buying like bonds when a loss is incurred on the sale and the sale and repurchase dates are on the same day within a short period of time. Reference should be made to Section 1091 of the Internal Revenue Code which lists the "wash sale" rules and regulations.

Gain Trading

In taxable securities, a profit is the same whether taken now or over time by holding to maturity. In low-rate periods, investment policy should aim for profit taking and shortening of maturities.

Gain trading municipals, however, converts tax-exempt income into a taxable capital gain. There can be reasons for profit taking in municipals (as, for example, at times when the portfolio manager believes bond prices are due to fall and it will be possible to buy the same bonds back more cheaply at a later date). But we should recognize that the tax mechanics work against gain trading in municipal securities.

Open-Ending

This term *open-ending* can refer to one of two investment techniques.

1. Advance refunding of maturities or executing the buy side of a swap considerably before executing the sale side. (This is done when interest rates are expected to decline and bond prices to rise).

2. Temporarily keeping maturity proceeds in very short-term highly liquid assets (or cash) or executing the sale side of a swap before completing the buy side. (This procedure is used when rates are expected to rise and prices to fall).

IMPROVING RETURNS ON GOVERNMENT SECURITIES PORTFOLIOS

Repurchase Agreements ("Repos")

A sale under an agreement to repurchase is comparable to a collateralized borrowing. In a repurchase agreement, a portfolio manager will sell certain of his holdings and agree to buy back these same securities on a specified date. The portfolio must pay interest at the agreed Repo rate, but the coupon interest continues to accrue to the portfolio.

The advantage of a repurchase agreement is that the portfolio manager receives cash (i.e., is able to borrow) often at a rate lower than other costs of funds. As an example, let us assume the 30-day term funds rate is 7 percent while the 30-day Repo rate is 6.5 percent. Under these circumstances, the portfolio manager could capture the 50-basis point spread by doing a Repo at 6.5 percent and then selling the money he raised at a rate of 7 percent.

Resale Agreements ("Resales")

A purchase under an agreement to resell is comparable to a collateralized loan. This technique may be used as an interim investment of excess funds for the portfolio.

Lending of Government Securities

Lending government securities is another avenue for increasing a bank's investment income with very little risk. A portfolio manager simply lends a security to a government securities dealer and, in return, receives similar collateral with a market value of 102 percent of the loaned security. The bank earns a 0.50 percent fee for such a loan.

The portfolio does not give up any pledging ability while lending securities since the securities it receives as collateral are of like pledgeability. In addition, a bank may wish to lend securities rather than do a Repo if it is unable to reinvest the cash obtained in a repurchase agreement at a significant yield spread. The lending process currently allows 50-basis points in additional portfolio earnings.

Liability Management

As previously mentioned, bank portfolio management in the past called for selling portfolio securities to meet liquidity needs resulting from deposit drains and strong loan demand. This usually occurred at times when investment opportunities were the most rewarding. On the other hand, a large amount of excess funds generally was available for investment when yields were least attractive and income was needed. Time after time, banks found themselves caught in this "yield trap."

The purpose of liability management is to meet demands for funds by purchasing liabilities (Federal Reserve funds, certificates of deposit, and so on) rather than by selling assets (i.e., portfolio securities). This relatively new technique doesn't simplify the total asset/liability management problem but it does change bank liquidity concepts and frees the portfolio to some extent from its predestined cyclical fate of prior years.

These factors have liberalized investment policy and brought about a new recognition and awareness that a bank is a money processor or dealer. A bank's raw material is money in its marketable form.

AUTHORITY AND CONTROL PROCEDURES

The establishment of a clear, concise authority and control procedures is a highly essential part of portfolio policy. Without sound authority and control procedures, it becomes difficult both to chart future courses of action and to properly assess past performance. By all means, adopt a written investment policy.

Reasons for Having a Written Policy

There are two principal reasons for having a written investment policy:

1. Portfolio constraints, goals, and objectives become clear only when the persons involved in their development and implementation have agreed in their precise wording.
2. A written policy also provides a continuing understanding of these constraints, goals and objectives.

The Elements of an Investment Policy

The following elements should be incorporated in every investment policy:

1. In order to effectively react to changing economic and market conditions as well as new bank constraints and goals, every policy must have a sufficient amount of built-in flexibility and should be reviewed periodically. This factor should help to allay fears that a written policy will become too restrictive.

2. To provide for delegation of authority while maintaining control. In our opinion, this can best be accomplished through establishing a senior investment committee and appointing one bank officer to act as investment portfolio manager. Ideally, the duties and responsibilities of each should be as follows:

   a. Senior Investment Committee
      (1) Should be composed of members of senior management and/or the board of directors.
      (2) Should be ultimately responsible for establishing policy and the basic investment parameters and guidelines.

   b. Portfolio Manager
      (1) His role should involve the active day-to-day management of the investment accounts.
      (2) Should be able to recommend specific investment programs and major courses of portfolio action to the senior investment committee.
      (3) Must have sufficient freedom of action to operate effectively. The senior committee must not "tie his hands" with an unrealistically tight, rigid policy.
      (4) Even if the person responsible for the daily management of the portfolio has other nonportfolio related duties, his first and primary responsibility must be the investment account.

3. To develop suitable methods of investment performance measurement and establish the type and frequency of reviews, the report formats, and so on.

4. Do not confuse the investment account with a trading position. Recognize the basic difference in the outlook of these two areas.

   a. The trader must concentrate on the very short-term aspects of the market. He needs a "feel" for what the market is likely to do during the next two to three days.

   b. The portfolio manager should be looking to the longer term and must avoid the temptation to be caught up in the momentary trading sentiment.

5. For these reasons, strong consideration should be given to completely separating the portfolio account from the trading function because:

   a. Both must be allowed the necessary freedom to operate most effectively. Otherwise, one's gain may well be the other's loss;

$b.$ It avoids the temptation to bury trading mistakes in the portfolio.

CONCLUSION

In recent years, bank portfolio management has been confronted with new and greater problems. Bond prices and interest rates have become much more volatile, banks have expanded their activities into new areas of operation, and attention has been focused on managing liabilities as well as assets. These changes have begun to raise many searching questions about portfolio management in general and various investment techniques and strategies in particular.

We do not claim that the guidelines discussed in this chapter will provide all the answers to bank portfolio-related questions. Neither do we feel that following these guidelines and principles will guarantee a superior investment performance. We do believe, however, they will provide a solid framework within which a bank may more surely and easily achieve improved investment results.

SECTION VII

CREDIT POLICY AND ADMINISTRATION

Chapter 42

Establishing Credit Policy—
Criteria and Concepts

Edward A. Jesser, Jr.*

Hubert C. Mott†

The obvious question that arises first in any discussion of credit policy is, why have a credit policy at all? Not all banks do, even today, although a far greater percentage have established such a policy in recent years—particularly since the supervisory authorities have placed great emphasis lately on banks having a written policy almost to the point of requiring it. One answer may be found in the following statement:

The restrictions placed by law, administrative agencies, and bank examiners do not provide answers to many questions regarding safe, sound, and profitable bank lending. Questions regarding the size of the loan portfolio, the maturity of all loans, and the type of loans to be made are left unanswered. Loans may be criticized by the bank examiners it is true, and some loans are prohibited and others limited, but such criticisms and restrictions do not establish a lending policy for a bank. These questions and many others about lending must be answered by each individual bank.[1]

WRITTEN CREDIT POLICY

A primary purpose of a written credit policy is to provide a framework of standards and points of reference within which individual

---

* Chairman, United Jersey Bank, Hackensack, New Jersey.

† Senior Vice President, United Jersey Bank, Hackensack, New Jersey.

[1] Edward W. Reed, *Commercial Bank Management* (New York and London: Harper & Row, 1963), p. 193.

lending personnel can operate with confidence, relative uniformity and flexibility, while making their own decisions within delegated authority, without the necessity for constant referral to higher management. Without it, there is a tendency to either concentrate all decision making in one or two people at or near the top. This is likely to result in slower decisions and inability of loan officers to develop their full potential, or a dangerous diversity of lending practices and philosophies within the organization, probably leading ultimately to an inordinate number of problem loans. Stated another way, a function of loan policy is to create attitudes which lending personnel can use as a decision-making aid.

In addition to establishing uniform guidelines for loan officers and satisfying the regulatory agencies, a written loan policy can aid management in defining objectives of the bank. Like any other business, a commercial bank establishes particular objectives to be met.

[A loan] policy establishes the direction and use of the funds of a bank that have derived from stockholders and depositors, . . . and influences the decision on whether or not to lend.

A loan policy is also a necessity for a bank if it is to attain its objectives and also serve the public. . . . Its lending must be conducted in an orderly . . . manner.[2]

The second question that should occur to one in a discussion of loan or credit policy (the words loan policy and credit policy will be used interchangeably here, as we fail to discern any substantive differences in meaning or common usage) is who should establish such policy. The importance of the matter mandates that the ultimate responsibility ascend to the highest level; i.e., the board of directors. While we do not suggest that the statement of loan policy should actually be written by the board, it should be approved by it, and not in a cursory or perfunctory manner, but rather after careful explanation, consideration and discussion. The actual drafting will probably be done by the senior lending officer in consultation with the chief executive officer, with help from associates and subordinates. Obviously, the level of origin will vary with the size and structure of the organization.

What should loan policy include? There can be some variations based on needs of a particular organization, but at least the following areas should be covered in any comprehensive statement of loan policy:

1. *Legal Considerations.* The bank's legal lending limit and other constraints should be set forth, in order to avoid inadvertent violation of banking regulations.
2. *Delegation of Authority.* Each individual authorized to extend credit should know precisely how much and under what conditions

---

[2] Ibid., p. 193.

he or she may commit the bank's funds. These authorities should be approved by written resolution of the board of directors at least annually and kept current at all times.

3. *Types of Credit Extension.* One of the most substantive parts of a loan policy is a delineation of which types of loans are acceptable and which are not.

4. *Pricing.* The price to be charged for the goods or services rendered is very important. Relative uniformity within the same market is necessary. Without it, individuals have few guidelines for quoting rates or fees, and the variations resulting from human nature will be a source of customer dissatisfaction.

5. *Market Area.* Each bank should establish its proper market area, based upon among other things, the size and sophistication of its organization, its ability to service its customers, and its ability to absorb risks. Given the bank's capital, defining market area is probably more important in the lending function than in any other aspect of banking.

6. *Loan Standards.* This is a definition of the types of credit to be extended, wherein qualitative standards for acceptable loans are set forth.

7. *Credit Granting Procedures.* This subject may be covered in a separate manual, and in larger banks usually is, but should not be overlooked, as it is very much a factor in the achievement of sound loan standards. Without proper procedures, policy and standards are not likely to be achieved.

RATIONALE FOR CREDIT POLICY

The next step after establishing the rationale for and definition of credit policy is to get into the specifics of one's own institution and delineate the policy that best fits its peculiar needs. A word should be given about individual variations. Some areas of credit policy should differ from bank to bank, reflecting the bank's size, asset composition, liability composition, earnings, capital, loan loss reserve, and the ability of lending officers and support personnel. The type of market and clientele should also be considered in determining the degree of risk the bank is willing to assume. Although credit policy may vary from bank to bank, sound loan standards and credit-granting procedures should not vary appreciably at any given time.

Definition of the bank's asset management objectives is an excellent prelude to the writing of a specific loan policy. Maximum and optimum loan to deposit ratios should be considered, as this has a direct bearing on the size of the loan portfolio. The bank's capital and risk asset ratios should be carefully considered, as well as the size of the loan loss reserve, in establishing the maximum risk that can be assumed. Earnings history and prospects are important as well, since a bank with strong earnings can better stand loan losses. The degree of risk in other assets, essentially the investment portfolio, is an important consideration. Recent events highlight this fact, as it is obvious that a portfolio heavy in municipals selling at large discounts, and with real risk of default, adds to the overall loss potential rather than providing the cushion of a sound investment portfolio.

If it is to be less than the bank's legal limit, the maximum commitment to any one borrower should be established. Many banks have so-called house limits. There is usually some flexibility, but exceptions should require a very high level of authority and should be carefully controlled. Exact definition of a borrower's total liability to the bank is a necessity in controlling loans within either legal or house limits. In general, all related liabilities, direct, indirect, and contingent, of borrower, guarantors, or endorsers, and related entities should be considered and carefully defined. An example of such language is:

In extending credit, a borrower is considered as including any subsidiary, affiliate or related business, corporation, partnership, proprietorship, etc., as well as officers of the business, their wives or related persons, etc. An officer not having a substantial interest in the corporation may, for lending authority purposes, be considered not related if he does not guarantee or endorse. It is imperative that we do not exceed our lending authority by grouping loans in this manner, so that the failure of the overall operation could cause numerous problems.

The bank's market area should be established and defined, whether it be the town or city, county or region, state, nation, or the world. The economic characteristics of the market a bank serves will influence the composition of its portfolio by type, maturity, and repayment plan of loans. Most important in establishing market area for loans is the ability of the lending staff to safely and adequately service the portfolio. The greater the distance from the account officer, the less the likelihood of frequent, close contact with the borrower and, therefore, the greater the risk. Certainly it should be a policy that only the strongest credits should be accepted in the outer limits of one's geographic area.

DISTRIBUTION OF TYPES OF LOANS

The distribution of the various types of loans within the overall portfolio is another basic management decision. There are a number of factors which bear directly on the decision as to the desired levels of commercial and industrial loans, real estate loans, and consumer credit. Among these are the nature and stability of deposits, the percentage of time versus demand, and deposit trends. A relatively high level of stable time deposits in contrast with a preponderance of volatile demand deposits, obviously points a bank toward mortgage and other longer term, higher yielding loans. Of course, the needs of the area served and the availability of various types of suitable loans has an impact.

A decision should also be made as to whether it is necessary or desirable to establish dollar or percentage limits for subcategories of loans. For instance, it could be important to establish a limit as to the amount of *nonresidential* real estate mortgage loans the bank is willing to make. Another example might be to establish some relationship between direct and indirect retail installment paper, or a limitation on dealer floor plan lines, or home improvement paper.

It is usually easier in writing a credit policy to state categorically those types of loans which are *not* acceptable than it is to list every nuance of acceptable credit extensions. The statement on acceptable loans can be broader and less specific, and should emphasize the recognized obligation of the bank to meet the legitimate credit needs of its trade area, and its commitment to do so to the best of its ability. The major reason banks are chartered is to serve the legitimate credit needs of the area in which they are located. Examples of desirable loans would include:

1. Short-term working capital loans that are self-liquidating in nature.
2. Loans to experienced farmers where source of repayment is clear, such as crop loans.
3. Loans to finance the carrying of commodities where the collateral is negotiable warehouse receipts.
4. Nonspeculative construction loans with firm takeout commitments from reliable long-term lenders.
5. Floor plan lending (if it appeals to you).
6. Various kinds of consumer loans.
7. Construction loans on housing.
8. Term and revolving credits.[3]

Other desirable types of loans might be first mortgages on single-family homes with adequate equity, loans secured by accounts receivable, and loans secured by good quality marketable securities, properly margined.

Unacceptable types of loans could vary somewhat from one institution to another but should always include illegal loans and loans solely for speculative purpose.

---

[3] Robert B. Maloane, *The Journal of Commercial Bank Lending* (Robert Morris Associates, June 1976).

Other types of unacceptable loans might include:

1. Loans to finance change in business ownership.
2. Construction loans without a firm takeout.
3. Loans secured by second mortgages on real estate.
4. Construction loans on condominiums unless they are presold.
5. Loans to new businesses, unless well collateralized.
6. So-called bullet loans or nonamortizing term loans.
7. Unsecured loans for real estate purposes.
8. Loans where the source of payment is solely public or private financing, not firmly committed.
9. Loans based on unmarketable securities.

This list is far from complete, including only some types more or less generally regarded as undesirable for commercial banks. Depending on the type and location and size of the bank, others which might be included are: term loans of more than a certain maturity; nonresidential, long-term real estate loans; revolving credits; floor plan lines; loans to second-mortgage companies; construction loans; unsecured loans to individuals; and "ship" loans. The list could be broadened, but it should be understood that some or all of these types may be highly acceptable to some banks, although inappropriate for others.

LOAN AUTHORITY

Aside from all of the previously mentioned possible constraints (such as deposit mix, capital, loan loss reserve, and earnings), one essential condition should be met as to any type of lending—that there are sufficient qualified people to evaluate the risks and follow and collect the loans in a timely manner. Many forms of lending today require personnel with special knowledge and training. It is most imprudent for a bank to embark on a program of making accounts receivable loans, construction loans, or aircraft loans without having sufficient well-trained and qualified individuals to handle this financing.

The delegation of lending authority is an integral part of loan policy and usually exists in some form or other even though the bank may have no other written loan policy. Even the smallest bank usually has to delegate some lending authority to one or more of its officers, since the directors normally do not meet frequently enough to serve the credit needs of the bank's borrowing customers. The degree and extent of delegation of loan authority by bank boards of directors, as well as forms of lending organization within banks, run the whole gamut from near zero to almost 100 percent.

This is an entire subject in itself, but suffice it to say the various systems seem to fall into three broad categories: (1) individual authorities, (2) groups or combinations of two or more individuals, and (3) formal committees. While some banks function with only one of these methods of approving loans, most banks employ a combination of two or more.

A typical description of the loan approval function in a medium-sized bank might be as follows:[4]

1. A definition as to what constitutes "secured" and "unsecured" lending for loan approval purposes.
2. A definition of "borrower's total liability" to protect the bank against maximum extensions of credit to various affiliates, subsidiaries, principals, and related entities, all dependent on one basic enterprise, which could be undertaken by an officer or combination of officers. This is known as the "one ball of wax" principle, and it continues to be sound.
3. The establishment of officers' loan committee(s), naming the members, the chairman and secretary, quorum and voting procedures, and the maximum amount of each type of loan the committee may approve. Possible variations include separate commercial, mortgage, installment, and international loan committees, senior and junior committees and regional loan committees in the case of extensive branch operations.
4. The establishment of combination authorities, whereby certain individuals jointly or with others may approve loans up to specified amounts. An example might be that while no one individual could lend more than $250,000, certain combinations of two could approve loans up to $500,000 and three of a designated list could go up to $750,000.
5. The listing of individual loan limits, by name and amount, secured and unsecured, and by type where appropriate (mortgage officers limited to mortgage loans, for example). The maximum authority would range from very modest amounts for inexperienced individuals and those in junior positions to large sums for senior lending officers and executive officers.

There are distinctly different philosophies among equally qualified bankers as to how much individual lending authority should be granted.

Basically, variation arises from different philosophies as to whether individual or collective action should dominate loan decisions. One view is that in order to render prompt decisions and command mutual respect, the individual loan officer should be granted considerable latitude. . . . The other view is that since the capacities of lending officers vary widely, loan authority limits must fit the weakest officer in each bank.[4]

---

[4] Douglas A. Hayes, *Bank Lending Policies, Issues and Practices,* Michigan Business Studies, Vol. XVI, no. 3 (Ann Arbor, Mich.: Bureau of Business Research, Graduate School of Business Administration, The University of Michigan, 1964), p. 44.

Some banks grant authority up to the bank's legal limit to all lending officers, a very lenient approach. Others are very strict, requiring practically all loans to be approved by the board of directors. Surely the optimum arrangement lies somewhere between the two extremes. Individuals are not equally qualified to extend the bank's legal limit without undue risk. By the same token, a bank that cannot delegate any authority to its officers must be staffed with inferior personnel—which is an indictment of the board of directors.

PRICING POLICY

No written loan policy would be complete without guidelines for the pricing of various types of credit. Without such a policy in writing, confusion and uncertainty, inconsistency, and—in all probability, unprofitability—would result.

Interest rate policies can range from general statements to very specific schedules. The general type would list broad ranges for certain categories of loans, with the goal of guiding the loan officer in pricing his loan, but allowing sufficient latitude to enable him to take into account the inherent differences between borrowers, particularly in the commercial field.

Pricing should be based upon total yield, taking into account proper credit for average collected demand balances and related business, as well as the relative credit risk, and the term and liquidity of the loan. In mortgage lending the quality of the real estate and the percentage of loan to value often justify gradations in the rate schedules.

The cost of money of the individual bank should, of course, be taken into consideration in the pricing of credit. Banks with high average cost of funds should attempt to achieve higher loan yields—with one all-important caveat. If the bank's capital structure and earnings are weak and more than usual loan losses would cause an earnings or capital adequacy problem, a high-risk loan portfolio is an invitation to disaster. It is essential to remember that in pricing a loan, consideration must be given not only to the cost of funds and the cost to administer the loan, but the important factor of risk.

The deterrent to maximum loan pricing is competition. Price competition among banks can at times reach serious proportions, although in recent years such periods have not been extensive or frequent. At times, however, loan practices that have been detrimental to the banking industry as a whole, as well as to individual banks, have occurred. Perhaps the correct axiom here is that it is proper to meet competition selectively as long as it doesn't have an overall major harmful effect on the bank's balance sheet or income statement, but "don't let the competition make your loans for you." That old adage is everlastingly true!

The disadvantages of a detailed schedule of interest rates are that opportunities or customers may be lost over a quarter of a percent, or delays may occur while a line officer attempts to contact a superior for advice or approval of an exception. If too many exceptions are granted, the schedule becomes meaningless and uniformity is lost. A further disadvantage is that a rigid schedule permits no exercise of individual judgment and may stifle personal growth, as does a too restrictive lending authority. Schedules also get out of date rapidly in changing economic times and are useless and even misleading if not frequently updated, which can be costly in a large organization. Reasonably broad but explicit guidelines should be favored over very detailed and rigid price schedules. As stated by the American Bankers Association:

A primary defect of schedules is that maximum rates often become minimums, or vice versa. Loan managers must constantly remind personnel that rate differentials exist, and that differentials are determined by such factors as risk, deposit balances, liquidity of collateral, and type of repayment program, while continuing to maintain fair standards for all customers.[5]

STANDARDS FOR LENDING

To discuss specific principles and standards is to get into the "nitty-gritty" of lending, which is beyond the purpose of this chapter. Yet one cannot fully discuss a loan policy without properly becoming involved in this subject to some extent. It is true that the line between policy and administration is often a fine one, but certainly a broad outline of what constitutes an acceptable loan is an integral part of loan policy. It is proper and beneficial in discussing this subject to separate it into the three major types of loans—commercial, real estate mortgage, and consumer installment. There are overlaps, but essentially the industry recognizes these three categories, and most banks segregate and departmentalize them.

In considering principles for commercial loans, some or all of the following criteria or information should be used.

A. Annual financial statements of firm (and its principals, when closely held).
B. Additional financial information when setting up a line of credit, arranging a seasonal loan, when the loan is not being repaid as agreed, or when a borrower's financial condition takes an unfavorable turn during the course of the loan.
C. Guarantees by the principals in case of small or closely held businesses.

---

[5] The American Bankers Association, Commercial Lending Division, *A Guide to Developing Commercial Lending Policy* (Washington, D.C., 1973), p. 11.

D. Lines of credit considerations such as compensating balances, periods of payout, and separate loan agreements.

E. Criteria to support unsecured loans.

F. Note renewal considerations.

G. When business loans are on a secured basis, there are considerations concerning the security held that may influence the loan amount as a percentage of the collateral held and the maturity of the loan.

    1. Securities.
        a. Government and other high-grade issues.
        b. Listed stocks and those unlisted but publicly traded.
        c. Stocks of closely held corporations.

    2. Equipment.
        a. Specialized equipment.
        b. Readily marketable equipment.

    3. Receivables.
        a. Types of receivables acceptable for assignment.
        b. Margin requirements on those acceptable.
        c. Notification procedures.
        d. Time period for which loans will be made.

    4. Inventories.
        a. Floating liens on all inventories.
        b. Field warehousing loans.
        c. Commodity loans against bills of lading or warehouse receipts.

H. Loan commitments.
    1. Time limitations.
    2. Amount committed.

I. Considerations in term loans to businesses.
    1. Maximum term of loans.
    2. Repayment schedules (monthly, quarterly, semiannually, or annually) related to the nature of collateral and capacity of borrower.
    3. Purposes for which term loans will be made.
        a. Purchase of equipment.
        b. Refund long-term debt.
        c. Increase working capital.
        d. Construct plant or plant addition.
        e. Purchase other companies.
    4. Loan agreement restrictions.

Some banks have attempted to set up loan guidelines which supplement the statement of loan policy. These guidelines may be further broken down into general and specific principles—in effect, a move by stages from the general to the specific. The specific principles might be considered to be operational instructions and therefore more properly the subject of a loan operating manual. If no such written manual or instructions exists it is far better to include this material as an adjunct to the loan policy statement than to relegate it to the "pass-on-by-word-of-mouth" category. An example of this type of loan policy-guidelines statement of a medium-large regional bank follows:

General Principles

1. The bank should not have an undue concentration of loans in any one industry.
2. All *commercial* borrowing customers of the bank should maintain account relationships and others should be encouraged to do so. If a customer moves out of the bank's trade area, loans should, within a reasonable period of time, be paid or transferred to the bank where the borrower has his or her account. Commercial borrowers should maintain compensating balances.
3. A credit file should be maintained on each borrowing account with memoranda for each loan showing the basis for the loan, purpose, conditions, rate and terms of repayment, as well as any other pertinent information, including the authority for granting the loan.
4. All loans other than those secured by Class A collateral should be supported by financial statements signed by the borrower or prepared by a certified public accountant. Statements are considered current if not more than one year old. Occasionally a statement may be waived if the borrower is known to be of such financial strength or there is other evidence of his or her unquestioned ability to handle the obligation. A memorandum outlining this evidence should be on file.
5. Loans to closely held companies should carry the endorsement of the principals.
6. All loans except those secured by passbooks should have a plan of liquidation at the time they are made, and the liquidating program should be documented in the file.
7. Quarterly financial statements, or at a minimum quarterly sales and earnings figures, should be required on all major lines and loans.
8. Periods of tight money have been frequent occurrences in recent years. When such periods occur, the bank will give priority to the legitimate credit requirements of its existing customers while at the same time discouraging credit for speculative ventures and for those ventures which would contribute to inflation.
9. Each lending officer is responsible for following his loans, maintaining contact with his customers, and protecting the bank where

necessary. In addition, a loan review section will review loans on a periodic basis, taking into account factors bearing on the risk, such as the financial condition of the borrower, the value of collateral, agreements concerning repayment and the borrower's past record.

Specific Principles

1. Short-term loans to business concerns should normally be on notes drawn for a term of not more than 90 days.
2. Loan commitments except for lines of credit and revolving credits, will run for a period of 90 days unles there is a stated expiration date.
3. On secured loans the following suggested maximum loan to collateral percentages apply:
    a. 97 percent against the bank's own savings passbooks.
    b. 90 percent against U.S. government bonds.
    c. 80 percent against new vehicles and equipment.
    d. 70 percent–85 percent against municipal bonds (depending on their rating).
    e. 70 percent against convertible debentures.
    f. 70 percent against stock traded on NYSE.[6]
    g. 60 percent against stock traded on ASE.[6]
    h. 50 percent against stock traded OTC.[6]
4. Lines of credit normally run for a period of one year unless otherwise stated. All lines are subject to annual review.
5. Confirmation of lines of credit, when in writing should contain a clause conditioning the continued approval upon a maintenance of a satisfactory financial condition as evidenced by financial statements and other information submitted to or coming to the attention of the bank.
6. "Guidance lines" are approved for the internal guidance of the account officer and should not be confirmed either verbally or in writing to the customer.
7. Lines of credit other than revolving lines should normally be cleaned up for 30 days during each 12-month period.
8. Lines to depositor status savings and loan associations should be limited to approximately one fourth of the free reserves and undivided profit of the association and should be on a guidance basis only. Borrowing should be on a short-term basis (90 days) to cover temporary fluctuations of deposits or investments. Additional bor-

---

[6] Provided the stock is selling for more than $10 per share and the number of shares involved does not represent an undue concentration of the total number shares outstanding of the company.

rowings for longer terms should be secured by blocks of mortgage or acceptable securities.

9. Term loans should be protected by written loan agreement.
10. Loans to directors or businesses in which directors have major interests must be approved by the board of directors of the bank.
11. By regulation, all loans to officers must be approved by the board of directors and loans to their spouses must be reported to the board. The maximum amounts are set by Federal Reserve.
    a. $5,000—unsecured, secured, or installment.
    b. $10,000—education of children.
    c. $30,000—mortgage.
    Officers are required to report to the board any loan they have at another bank within ten days of completion.
12. Before a customer note is accepted for discount, a satisfactory check should be obtained on the maker from his or her bank of account.
13. The bank should not accept as collateral securities registered in the name of a brokerage house.

STANDARDS FOR SPECIAL LENDING AREAS

The establishment of standards for mortgage lending break down naturally into two areas, residential one-to-four family lending and multifamily residential and commercial and industrial loans. The problem is simpler for those banks that only engage in residential mortgage lending. In that case the most important questions are the geographic area acceptable, maximum ratio of loan to value, minimum credit criteria, appraisal requirements, and prepayment penalties. The setting of standards for multifamily and commercial and industrial loans is a subject unto itself and one which apparently requires further and continuous study as conditions change, as witnessed by the continuing real estate lending debacle of 1974. Construction lending entails a different set of problems. Some general principles of broad applicability to mortgage lending can be established, most of which have been noted before, but specifics should be in operating manuals, administered by qualified specialists. Banks should resolutely oppose financing of builder-developers to the extent of 100 percent or more of value, and the idea of capitalizing all interest expense into a construction loan.

Principles for the extension of consumer loans should be established, and are of equal importance. Some considerations which might be included in a statement of loan principles are the following:

A. Requirement of signature of spouse in addition to borrower on loan, if legally obtainable.

B. Requirement of current financial statements on loans in excess of a specific amount when on an unsecured and or on a secured basis.
C. Current credit reports from credit investigating agency and a statement of obligations by borrower.
D. Types of collateral as they influence loan value and maturity guidelines.
   1. New automobiles.
   2. Used automobiles.
   3. Household furniture and appliances.
   4. Sporting equipment (such as boats, campers, or trailers).
   5. Real estate.
   6. Marketable securities.
   7. Maturity limits when loans are secured by cash surrender value of life insurance or savings accounts.
E. Required depository relationship.
F. Dealer-generated loans.
   1. Required financial information from dealer.
   2. Deposit relationship.
   3. Guaranty considerations.
      a. Full recourse.
      b. Limited recourse.
      c. Without recourse.
      d. Reserve allocation.
   4. Repossession arrangements.
   5. Income participation.

CONCLUSION

A natural adjunct to the establishment of a written loan policy is the implementation of policy through institution and execution of effective loan and credit procedures. This is a separate subject which will be covered elsewhere, but it is so closely related to loan policy that at least a brief mention of it is imperative. A bare outline of some of the important aspects follows:

1. Written loan memoranda.
2. Financial statement analysis.
3. Credit investigation.
4. Maintenance of credit files.
5. Loan reports and controls.
6. Loan review and workout.

One final but extremely important aspect of credit policy is its administration. Well-written statements of sound lending policy and principles are not worth the paper they are printed on unless they are adhered to. There can be no question that the ultimate responsibility for compliance rests with the board of directors. The policy statement was approved by the directors; the board should monitor compliance. The most direct tool in this regard is the auditor, who should report directly to the board. The audits should be geared to detect major violations, which should be reported to the board. In addition, the independent auditors should include the checking of compliance with policy in their audit program and report violations to directors.

Executive officers of the bank also have primary responsibility, of course. By direction of their subordinates and by personal example they should constantly emphasize to all the staff the importance of operating within the framework of policy guidelines.

The actual day-to-day administration of loan policy rests with the senior lending officer and his or her staff. It is the senior lending officer who must set the example and make the difficult decisions. It is important that when the occasional deviation or exception is permitted, he or she explain to all involved the reasons behind the decision, emphasizing that while all rules should be flexible to a degree, exceptions should be rare and not frivolously granted. If the bank is large enough to have a loan review officer or department, this is the natural arm for the senior lending officer to employ for the purpose of detecting and reporting policy violation. The most knowledgeable and skilled management will not be successful in maintaining a sound loan portfolio unless there is strict, consistent accountability at all levels of management.

Chapter 43

Credit and Loan Administration

Harold F. McHugh*

   The preceding chapter has dealt with the need for and formulation of a definite loan policy. Loan policies generally differ from bank to bank in order to meet specific needs of the individual institution and the community it serves. Its purpose, however, is uniform and three-fold: to guide and assist the loan officer in making sound loans, to minimize risk to depositors' funds, and to produce loans which will generate a satisfactory return on the stockholder's investment. In this chapter we will deal with the various systems of organization and credit administration of commercial loans which enable the bank to maximize earnings through a consistent application of basic credit principles and sound management of the loan portfolio.

   Among the duties of the line loan officer is the servicing of existing borrowing relationships and the development of attractive new loan business. Credit administration, on the other hand, is a staff supervisory function which, if properly organized, will be separate from the loan granting process. Its responsibility is to formulate policy, define credit standards, and establish systems and controls which will result in adherence to loan policy, and, in turn, ensure a continuing high quality of loan portfolio with minimum losses. Additionally, credit administration provides management with current information on the bank's major earning asset. Close cooperation between the line and staff functions is required to achieve the desired results.

   A loan policy, as previously stated, is formulated to guide and assist loan personnel in making sound loans. The first step toward accomplishing this objective is a full understanding of the written loan policy

---

* Senior Vice President, National Bank of North America, New York, New York.

by the line officers and the reasoning behind it. Close communication between the credit policy-making level and the line is essential to good administration. Unless properly disseminated and understood, the goals of a sound loan policy will be difficult to attain.

Policy alone, however, is not the sole solution to achieving a desirable portfolio. It is important that the loan officer have the necessary knowledge and experience to apply basic credit principles in order to arrive at a sound decision. Management must, therefore, see to it that excessive authority is not delegated to the inexperienced and unqualified lender. Authority should be granted to the individual loan officer as it is earned. Starting with a limited amount of loan authority, an officer should be given increased responsibility as his or her performance indicates the ability to analyze financial information and use sound credit judgment in reaching loan decisions. Credit administration through its various functions can play an important role in determining those qualified for increased loan authority and should be involved in decisions concerning such increases.

Depending on the size, organizational structure, and experience level of the bank's lending staff, a single approval on loans within an individual's authority may be sufficient. When loan requests are in excess of an individual's authority, approval by an officer with greater responsibility should be obtained. In this manner, the large dollar risks are handled by the more capable senior lenders. The individual loan approval method, when properly administered, builds confidence in loan officers and usually results in better service for the customer. It may also be desirable, where practical, to require a second approving signature of a higher authority on all loans, thus providing an additional opinion as to the viability of the credit. A comprehensive loan policy will usually include those details covering the manner in which the officer can exercise this authority. Should it not, separate rules governing the extension of credit, which specify exactly how such authority may be used, are advisable.

Where large loans (in relation to the bank's legal limit) are under consideration, a formal loan committee often proves beneficial. The committee may consist of either members of the board of directors or the senior and more experienced officers of the bank. In large banks, where volume is heavy, individual committees may be formed on a regional or geographic basis. Similarly, they may be formed for approval of loans in such specialized areas as accounts receivable, financing, commercial, international, leasing, and real estate loans. In those instances where one committee considers for approval various types of loans, representation among the membership by officers who have knowledge and expertise in the areas of special lending adds additional support to the approval of loan requests. Legal counsel can also prove extremely helpful if it is either represented by membership on the committee or is present at all loan committee meetings.

Each system, or combination of systems, has its advantages and disadvantages and should be adopted with the following considerations in mind: size of the bank, its loan policy, the competency of the lending staff, and other related factors. In any event, the approval system must be structured so that it encourages decision making and loan granting at the customer contact level as much as possible. In no way should it be considered a deterrent to loan making or to discourage a loan officer's initiative in negotiating terms. On the contrary, it should be a means of encouraging the loan officer to seek and make sound loans which add to the growth of the bank's portfolio and assist in the economic development of the community and region.

CREDIT DEPARTMENT

Certain basic credit functions must be performed in even the simplest form of lending—thus, the need for experienced credit officers and staff and where warranted, a separate credit department. This department provides services for both management and the line loan officer which are vital to the maintenance of a sound loan portfolio. Depending on the size of the department, it may also provide services for customers and correspondent banks, generate reports for management, directors and the various regulatory agencies, as well as service the loan officer's needs. It also is an excellent training area for future loan officers. Basic to every credit department, however, are the functions and responsibility of record keeping and credit analysis. These latter functions, while separate and distinct, are closely related and provide the loan officer with the necessary information on which to base a sound credit decision.

The record-keeping function, which might be considered more operational in nature, involves the maintenance of a complete credit file of historical information for each individual borrower. This file should contain such data as opening date of the account, prior loan experience, and a record of the balances maintained. Also included should be current financial information such as balance sheets, income statements, cash flow projections, schedules, and other accounting information deemed appropriate. Memoranda covering interviews with the borrower, and details provided by outside credit reporting agencies, as well as information developed by the credit department (from such sources as other banks, suppliers, competitors, and industry surveys) are also an integral part of the credit file. In addition, current correspondence and other pertinent information should be included. The file, however, should not be a catchall for miscellaneous nonessential data. It is the duty of the department to see that the credit file is periodically purged of extraneous material by the loan officer or other qualified personnel. In short, the file should contain sufficient information about the borrower so that a loan officer unfamiliar with the relationship can read it and arrive at a reasonably intelligent credit decision.

Although the maintenance of files cannot be overstressed, the key function of the credit department is the evaluation of the information developed for the credit file. This evaluation or analysis is usually performed by a member of the credit department and is a substantial time-saver for the loan officer, whose time can thereby be put to more productive use. More importantly, it provides an independent objective analysis of the customer's financial stability and ability to generate sufficient cash flow to service the bank debt. Needless to say, the review and analysis of the financial and other information accumulated in the credit file must be accomplished by highly qualified credit personnel who have a thorough knowledge of accounting principles and have developed the techniques of credit evaluation. Their expertise and judgment, when recognized and respected by the account officer, will prove instrumental in the final loan decision.

The credit department's analytical servicing of the account does not end with the initial evaluation as to creditworthiness and the subsequent granting of the loan. It is necessary for a continual involvement in the review of additional information developed from time to time in order to be certain that the borrower is in compliance with loan agreement covenants, is meeting cash flow projections, and does not experience adverse conditions which might impair his or her ability to repay bank debt as agreed. This follow-up must be on a regular basis because, as statistics show, most losses occur on loans which were acceptable bank risks when originally granted and which subsequently deteriorated because of circumstances which were not initially anticipated by the borrower or the bank.

TRAINING

An equally important aspect of credit administration is the continual improvement in the level of expertise of the lending staff. The obvious means of achieving this goal is to provide programs which will introduce new employees to the techniques of credit analysis and lending and will provide existing lenders with the opportunity to expand their credit skills. Most banks have a satisfactory number of competent experienced lenders. Maintaining a steady flow of young people to replace these individuals as they move on to higher responsibility or toward retirement presents a continuing challenge. Rapid growth also places an undue burden on the existing lending staff if competent additions are not made. Without a reliable source of capable people to replace or supplement existing personnel, growth can be hampered and portfolio quality may deteriorate.

Before establishing a training program for any bank, there must be a firm commitment by management for full support. Management must be in complete agreement with the need for such a program and recognize that the initial expense involved will be justified in future years through a continuing supply of high caliber loan officers and fewer loans of substandard quality. Without such support, the efforts and good intentions of those involved can prove futile. Once approved, the task of providing a training program should be a joint effort of the personnel department and credit administration, because the day-to-day activities of credit and loan administration provide the most logical place for training and exposure to the basics of good lending.

When considering the establishment of any training program, the specific needs of the bank must first be determined. Smaller banks may have need for only a limited number of junior personnel at the entry level each year. A formal classroom and seminar-type program on the basic principles of credit granting and financial statement analysis would therefore not be feasible. New employees whose career paths are directed toward the credit and loan areas of these banks can be provided with individual training under the guidance of more senior officers. Supplementary training for existing loan officers should be considered in order to provide a means of expanding existing knowledge and increasing the level of professional proficiency.

Medium-sized and larger banks are usually better equipped to provide a more formal training program for entry level employees. The bank which has a separate credit department, loan review program and workout section, offers an excellent opportunity for developing the uninitiated. An on-the-job program supplemented by regular classroom or lecture sessions proves most effective. A program of this type should consist of a series of well-planned classroom periods, so timed as to coincide with the actual work that the individuals are assigned to at the time. Thus, while being assigned to the investigation, statement spreading, analysis, and other areas of credit administration, the trainee will be introduced to the technical aspects of the position through classroom exposure. As a result, the use of various skills is developed as the learning process is going on. It further provides a means of accomplishing much of the everyday work which is required to service the line. The formal training program so designed also permits the personnel department to select job applicants who have the academic background which is a prerequisite to the form of training to which they will be exposed. Regular monitoring of each individual's progress under such a system provides supervisors with the opportunity of weeding out those who do not evidence good aptitude for lending assignments. These trainees can then be directed to other careers within the bank.

Real estate construction and mortgage loans, accounts receivable and lease financing, as well as the financing of international transactions, require special skills which may not be required of branch loan officers. Because of the complexities of these types of loans, programs to provide exposure to the techniques of lending in these areas should also be incorporated in any comprehensive training program. This supplemental education, when given to the individuals who have completed the basic credit training program, will produce officers capable of dealing with the special nature of these types of financing.

Vital to any system of training and development are the qualifications of the teacher. Not only is technical competence important, the ability to communicate is essential. Many of the finest lenders in banks lack the patience, inclination, or ability to pass their knowledge on to others. Careful selection must then be made of those persons who will be charged with the development of future loan officers, whether it be on a one-to-one basis or in a more formal program.

LOAN REVIEW

Very few members of senior management will question the need to be regularly apprised of the status of the bank's major earning asset—loans. In smaller banks, which have a limited portfolio, it is possible for one or more senior officers to have close familiarity with the larger and more complex credits. Intimate knowledge of the professional competency of a limited number of loan personnel is also likely. At larger banks, however, it is difficult, if not impossible, for senior management to be so closely involved. Besides constraints applied by increased volume, the wide area of responsibility, including multibranch aspects, precludes this prospect. In addition, the highly sophisticated and ever changing methods of structuring loans to meet the financing needs of commercial and industrial borrowers have made it increasingly difficult for a limited number of members of top management to be properly informed as to the overall quality of loans at any given time. This problem is further complicated by the diverse nature of the specialized financing in certain types of lending (e.g., accounts receivable, agriculture, commercial and industrial, international, leasing, real estate).

At some point in the growth of the bank, it becomes not only desirable, but necessary to establish some system for developing this information. Management must have some internal independent means of determining the quality of the loan portfolio. This can be accomplished with an independent review procedure which will examine the loan portfolio on a continuing basis to determine the creditworthiness of the loans. The responsibility of developing such information on an ongoing basis is charged to "loan review."

Timing of the examination of loans may vary from bank to bank. This will depend on the desires of management, the technical competency of the loan officers and the size of the loan review staff. The review system may be used as a condition prior to the granting of the loan. Before approval the proposal is investigated and analyzed to determine that it meets established policy and credit standards. A review at this point of the loan-making process becomes in effect a second signature approval system and is most effective where the lending staff requires initial support. The sacrifice here is that no independent policing is performed after the loan is booked.

Review of credits after the loan has been made is generally a more effective control. Sufficient investigation and credit analysis is normally performed at the inception of the loan. Deterioration and weakness, if any, tend to develop after the loan is made. Changes in the economy, industry, management or other unanticipated circumstances may subsequently adversely affect the ability of the borrower to repay the bank debt. Thus, continued vigilance on the part of the loan officer is required so that detection of these conditions can be made at an early stage. If the relationship is not being properly policed by the account officer, serious problems may result. A review at some subsequent date after the loan has been made will tend to bring these weaknesses to light. Likewise, deficiencies in documentation and collateral may more readily be uncovered if the loan is again objectively analyzed by an independent group at some predetermined time after it has been booked.

While periodic review on a regular basis is desirable, the department must have reasonable flexibility. A preplanned schedule of examination of the various loans or loan areas of the bank is necessary in order to achieve full coverage. The department must, however, be able to deviate from schedule in the event that its services are required elsewhere on special assignments. Should the senior loan officer, credit administrator, or other members of management feel a concern for a particular loan, area of lending, or industry, loan review should be able to move immediately to evaluate that situation. Information obtained from various reports and other sources such as past due lists, overdraft reports, delinquent statement schedules, loan agreement violations, audit reports, trade reports, and newspaper articles can also serve as a trigger to alert the department to the necessity of a special review.

A predetermined rating system will provide a means of classifying loans as to liquidity and risk. Classifications consistent with those of the national or state examiners should be used. Where signs of weakness or deterioration are detected, corrective action must be recommended. The classification which results from these periodic reviews should then be conveyed to the loan officer so that the appropriate action may be taken. Without such recommendations and resultant action, only limited benefit is derived by the bank. Periodic follow-up is then advisable to ascertain if the prescribed steps have been taken to improve the quality of the loan and lessen the bank's exposure.

Classification or grading of loans, however, is only a part of the review process. In addition, the review should include steps which insure that established loan policies are being adhered to, that proper credit files are being maintained, and that collateral and documentation meet prescribed standards. The physical verification of collateral and documentation need not be a function of the loan review department. This can more efficiently be accomplished by the auditing department in the normal course of their audit.

To realize maximum benefit from the work performed by loan review, the reporting responsibility of this department must be to other than those involved in making the loans which are being reviewed. In most instances, it is advisable to have an internal organization plan which calls for direct reporting to the chief executive officer of the bank and/or the board of directors. This can be accomplished by making the loan review a part of the credit administration group or, in smaller banks where no such group exists, part of the auditing department. When loan review is used as a condition prior to approval, the reporting line should be to the senior loan officer. Reports on loans with high-risk classifications should be forwarded to the workout specialist who in turn can offer guidance to the account officer or recommend transfer of the loan for special handling.

Ideally, the loan review staff should be fully acquainted with loan policy, possess strong analytical abilities, and be able to write clearly and concisely. Additionally, a good cross section of experience, including successful line loan background, is helpful to the department. Previous lending experience enables the review officer to better understand the loan officer's position relative to the customer and should improve his or her ability to communicate criticism more effectively. The staff members of the department must be capable of performing their duties efficiently without antagonizing the lending officer. A greater extent of effectiveness will be obtained if the review and loan officers cooperate to achieve the same goals. Where substantial portions of the portfolio are being employed to finance highly specialized industries, expertise is not only required of the lending staff but also of the review personnel. With these qualifications, the review officer should be able to arrive at an objective and sound evaluation of the creditworthiness of the borrower. Too much emphasis cannot be placed on the fact that the review process should be viewed as a means of constructively assisting the loan officer and not as a management spy system.

COMMERCIAL LOAN ACCOUNTING

Traditionally, the operations aspect of commercial lending has been considered to be merely a bookkeeping function. The customer's indebtedness is recorded and loan operations personnel disburse the loan proceeds to the customer in accordance with instructions received from lending officers at the time. At the time the initial loan is being booked or renewals are being recorded, the loan administration area of the bank has yet another opportunity to supervise the lending function of the bank.

The loan operations department, if used as more than a mere bookkeeping operation, can examine loans for specific requirements before the funds are credited to the customer's account. Quality control and policy compliance activities can be performed at this point. Loans granted in excess of individual loan authority can be referred back to the account officer for proper approval. Examination for sufficient documentation or improper completion of documents can be an effective second line of support for the loan officer and prevent possible future difficulty in the event that the bank must eventually rely on liquidation of the collateral for repayment of the loan. Inadequate collateral or other exceptions which may be in violation of loan policy can be checked at this time and corrected before the bank has committed the funds. The centralization of record keeping which has come about with the installation of computerized loan accounting substantially facilitates the use of such an entry control system.

In order to provide this support to the loan officer, the loan operations department requires supervisors and employees who have special qualifications. A thorough knowledge of the loan policy of the bank and the various loan authorities and approval systems is necessary. Equally important is a complete understanding of various documentations required for each type of loan and how each form is to be completed. Above all, the supervisor must have the responsibility and the authority to bring any deficiency or deviation from policy to the attention of the loan officer. These duties must be performed with tact and conviction. The benefits that can be derived from this approach to the utilization of loan operations employees are numerous. Foremost of these benefits is the independent nature of their function. Loan administration, instead of having to rely on infrequent audits and reviews, can monitor compliances with the policies and procedures of the bank on a daily basis before funds are disbursed.

Adequate information must be available to senior management at all times concerning the overall condition of the bank. The loan operational units, as custodian of the loan records, have control over much of the desired information required to make an accurate appraisal of the direction in which the bank is progressing. With the advent of automation of loan accounting systems, an ever increasing amount of information is quickly available for monitoring the performance of the borrower, the account officer, and the bank itself.

Information regarding the size, profitability, and liquidity of the portfolio are readily available and should be regularly reported. A considerable number of additional reports can be generated which will be of immeasurable value toward the goal of maintaining a sound and profitable portfolio. To avoid undue exposure to any one borrower, industry, or geographic area, specific reports concerning various types of concentration are easily produced. Maturity reports prepared by the loan operations department can provide sufficient time to update credit information on the borrower so that an informed decision can be made with respect to the treatment of the maturing debt. Profitability can also be judged at this time and rate adjustments made if warranted. Past-due interest and principal reports provide valuable information to the loan review department. One of the early internal signs of possible weakness in the financial condition of a borrower is the failure to meet principal and interest payments promptly. Such delinquency may serve as an alert signal which would cause the loan review officer to inquire into the possible financial problems of the borrower which might result in difficulty in collecting the outstanding loan.

Depending on the size of the bank and the nature of the loan accounting system, it is possible to determine the standard of performance in profitability, and quality and loss experience of loans administered by a given loan officer. Armed with these reports, management can follow the progress of loan officers and determine whether or not additional credit training is required. Results obtained from this report can also serve to guide management in increasing individual authority or promoting individuals to positions of more responsibility.

Most of the activities of credit and loan administration are directed toward identifying individual situations which may represent unacceptable credit risks. Reports produced by the commercial loan operations department reflect the cumulative effect of these risks on the total loans outstanding. Unfavorable trends, delinquencies, classified loans, or concentration resulting in an unbalanced portfolio are readily discernable. Prompt corrective action can then be taken to amend loan policy or credit criteria to reverse possible unfavorable trends.

The lending of money, no matter what precautions may be taken by the lender, entails some measure of risk taking. Through the employment of capable lending officers, prescribed credit procedures, and established policy, an attempt is made to approve only "money-good" loans and to reduce this exposure to a minimum acceptable to the bank. The various activities of credit and loan administration are designed to keep these loans from becoming more than prudent business risks. Nevertheless, circumstances beyond the control of the borrower, the lender, and credit administration frequently cause well-conceived loans to become workout situations. When this occurs, the bank must use its best efforts to collect the outstanding loan and reduce the potential charge-off as much as possible. Problem loans and workouts are discussed in detail in a later chapter.

CONCLUSION

The aforementioned credit and loan supervisory activities are recommended in some form for all commercial lending institutions. Equally as important as the various means of controlling the quality of loans are the performance requirements of those involved. No compromise can be made with the high standards which must be maintained. Those individuals entrusted with duties of credit and loan administration must be knowledgeable and experienced in the field of commercial bank lending and must be able to work harmoniously with others. They must be of good character, resolute of mind, have sound judgment, and not hesitant in voicing their opinion of matters which are contrary to good lending practices.

Achieving and maintaining a sound and a profitable loan portfolio involves the constant vigilance and continuous efforts of those assigned to the duties of credit and loan administration. Proper organizational structure and discipline as outlined below is instrumental in providing the means to obtain maximum results.

1. A well-defined written loan policy.
2. A properly conceived approval system.
3. Development through continuous training of highly competent lending officers.
4. Thorough investigation and objective analysis of the borrower's management, ability, and financial capacity.
5. Quality control and policy compliance verification at the time the loan is booked.

6. Regular independent review of all loans for possible deficiencies or deteriorating financial condition.

7. Established procedures for effective collection of problem loans.

These safeguards should enable the bank to make good loans, maintain the integrity of the existing portfolio, and minimize loss through charge-off of uncollectable loans. Loan policy implementation and risk assessment, however, must have a positive thrust and not an inhibiting force so that the loan officer can treat each request for extension of credit as an opportunity to perform one of the basic functions for which the bank was established.

Chapter 44

Credit Administration—Systems and Procedures

William D. Loring*

Credit administration—systems and procedures—deals with the various ways in which a bank is operationally and procedurally organized to conduct its lending activities. Because other chapters cover consumer loan practices in considerable detail, this chapter is restricted primarily to a review of commercial lending systems and procedures.

Though the activities of credit administration, or loan administration as it is sometimes called, are accomplished through people, the term is more directly associated with the work product and functions provided by the bank's lending staff and not with their direct supervision. Some bankers view credit administration as having to do with the supervision of systems and procedures for managing the portfolio after its acquisition. A broader view would hold that totally, well-integrated loan systems must begin with the development of loan policy, which is provided primarily for preconditioning the final product; that is, the quality, safety, and profitability of the bank's loan portfolio, one of the principal goals of sound credit administration.

For purposes of clarity, a loan procedure is defined herein simply as the way in which loan work is uniformly accomplished. Some loan procedures deal with such routine activities as the manner in which credit inquiries are processed, how loans are approved, or how loan proceeds are advanced to the borrower. Other loan procedures, such as the pricing of loans or the classification of loans, are not as routine but like all loan procedures are equally repetitive. The term, "loan

---

* Chairman and President, Mesa United Bank of Grand Junction, Grand Junction, Colorado.

system," is used somewhat interchangeably with "loan procedure," except that a system is better described by its general purpose or policy content than by how it is procedurally accomplished. Thus, a "system" has a more generic or larger meaning than is conveyed by the word "procedure."

PORTFOLIO CONTROL AND PLANNING

Effective credit administration is essentially a management exercise wherein loan administrative goals or policies, staff and portfolio organization, and operating procedures are sufficiently interrelated so as to produce a controllable result. It is not enough, for instance, for bank management to decide to establish loan limits for borrowers. The restriction must be communicated to all line officers. Control points must be established, and most importantly, accurate and continuous monitoring must occur. Thus, while the principal goal of credit administration is a sound and profitable portfolio, management's principal strategy for gaining such balance is control and forward planning.

Control in a loan administration sense is a process wherein the loan manager is able to relate portfolio results to preestablished acquisition and investment criteria consciously selected by the manager, followed by an evaluation of those results and a similarly conscious effort to plan for and effect future changes to the portfolio. Though the process is neither as abstruse nor as malleable as the foregoing statement would seem to infer, it is clearly a manageable process and the degree to which it is so depends significantly upon the receipt of accurate and timely portfolio information arranged in ways that will validate or test a portfolio objective. This point is very important and is therefore restated; namely, that for a loan system to be effective its purpose or purposes must be patently clear. Control involves a day-by-day reaction and adjustment process. Planning, on the other hand, is concerned with the forward thinking process of resetting portfolio goals; i.e., credit quality, liquidity, maturity, industry concentration, profitability, growth, and restriction policies.

Loan auditing, a specific kind of control process, is also derived from well-thought out and executed loan systems and procedures, and, to the degree that bank management is inclined to evaluate the lending staff through the results of work performed, loan information systems can be an important source of performance measurements.

INTEGRATING SYSTEMS AND PROCEDURES

Loan procedures should be designed to work comfortably with a bank's established organization and work flow patterns, which do, of course, vary considerably from bank to bank. It is, therefore, possible that a particular loan procedure which works very well in one bank will not work at all in another bank. The relationship between organization, procedures, and the particular or unique management style of a bank is so close that a change effected in one of these areas will probably create a need for change elsewhere in a bank's loan system.

For instance, management may wish to eliminate or restrict the practice of routinely renewing customer notes by changing the authority for renewing notes from a procedure that permits individual loan officer's renewal discretion to an approval process that "approves" the renewal in the same manner in which a new loan is approved. The example here assumes a more rigorous approval procedure prevails with regard to new loans, and thus, by changing the renewal authority, a more rigorous renewal procedure is established. The example illustrates how a modest loan approval procedural change, made for the purpose of effecting a qualitative change to the loan portfolio, also impacts on work flow, probably on work forms, and in this instance probably even on customer relations. Organization, loan systems, and loan procedures must be coordinated and mutually supportive, and it is the nature of their integration that changing an organizational, systems, or procedural factor will usually create a need for change elsewhere in the lending activity.

LOAN WORK FLOW

The typical flow of loan work of a bank begins with an accumulation of borrower financial statements, credit reports, and bank prepared analyses. This material, together with correspondence, is gathered into a customer credit file and, in itself, represents an important source for evaluating the bank's loan portfolio. An affirmative decision to commit the bank to a loan is typically documented by a Commitment Sheet or Line Sheet. This is an internal (noncustomer) bank form on which a great deal of systems initiating information and reporting codes are assigned. The Commitment Sheet also specifically informs staff personnel how the loan is to be administered; it operates as a work sheet and finally is the specific control document which auditing or loan review personnel examine for verifying the sufficiency of the lending authority.

Loan closing instruments (i.e., promissory notes, security agreements, loan agreements, mortgages, guarantees and hypothecations to name a few) are prepared by the bank and executed by the borrower. The filing, recording, and safekeeping of documents is provided for. Debit and credit entries are prepared and bookkeeping and collateral records established. After-the-fact loan reports are generated providing industry, yield, maturity, concentration and other management, lender, and regulatory information. Loan review systems are usually triggered by either a first advance to the borrower or by receipt of a copy of the Commitment Sheet. Payment notices, overdue notices and other tickler reports are produced as required.

Full repayment usually concludes this veritable flow of paper work; however, in most commercial banks where the customer relationship is ongoing, close communications with the account continues as does some form of record keeping. It should also be pointed out that the foregoing chronological review of loan work flow is brief and there do exist a great number of other special system "loops" or operations for performing specialized loan work.

LOAN ADMINISTRATION PROCEDURES

This and the next several paragraphs will review some of the more important considerations for implementing the procedural needs of a well-managed lending department with regard to loan approval, loan pricing, loan closing, collection, and loan review. The conceptual nature of these activities will be presumed to be generally understood, however, if they are not, reference elsewhere in this handbook will provide adequate description.

Loan approval procedures more clearly reflect management loan philosophy than perhaps any other activity in the bank with the possible exception of commercial marketing practices. The role of the board of directors, the directors' Executive Committee or Loan Committee, and the bank's chief executive officer and/or president as loan approvers and loan reviewers are clearly reflected in the bank's loan approval procedures. Individual officer-lending limits, joint or cumulative officer-lending authority, loan committee authority and various postcommitment review functions are prescribed in the approval procedures. Any given bank will have consciously or intuitively designed a set of approval procedures which best fit its needs; e.g., the skill and experience of its lending staff, its turnover, the complexities and risks inherent in the various types of loans to be made, the size and even the location of the bank. Implementation of approval procedures generally flows very directly from the design of the system and from the style of management of a particular bank. Lending authority is clearly and specifically communicated to the lending staff as well as the auditing and loan review staff. Approval forms reflecting specific approval requirements are produced. Supervisory persons and loan officers are held accountable for implementing approval procedures, and auditors and examiners review loans after they are committed or advanced to determine if loans were approved in accordance with approval policies.

A common operating problem that occurs in the area of loan approval is the need to advance or approve a commitment out of policy or in nonconformance with approved procedures. This need is often anticipated through improved customer management and planning; however, the need for an emergency approval occurs regardless and is, therefore, provided for in the authorized loan approval procedures as an "exception" procedure.

Loan pricing procedures vary considerably in their complexity. Some banks depend upon the use of promulgated interest rate schedules by loan types very much like a retailer prices merchandise. Most banks, however, place the responsibility for negotiating loan pricing with the loan officer who is provided a guideline or formula for establishing appropriate interest rates. This process has in recent years come more and more to be accomplished in the form of a computation, wherein the borrower's investable free balances are subtracted from the cost to the bank of the resources used to fund the loan. Handling costs, risk considerations, and the bank's profit goals are factored in and together produce a desired or target interest rate for that particular loan.

Implementing a complex loan pricing system obviously places great pressure on the loan officer to understand factors involved in loan pricing. Careful training therefore is usually conducted. Some banks "approve" loan pricing very much in the same manner that a loan is approved. Other banks separate the two functions and permit the loan officer considerable discretion for setting pricing based upon a formula which he or she reconciles to the conditions of the marketplace.

In determining the role of the loan officer, management will have already thought through various assumptions which, in effect, have been turned over to the loan officer for execution. If a loan pricing formula is used, management will have chosen from among several methods for determining the cost of resource funds, which incidentally will usually have differing effects on loan pricing during periods of rising interest rates than will occur during periods of falling interest rates. Management will have chosen a profit goal, and finally, will have established bank cost factors to be used in measuring customer deposit profitability, with float being probably the most critical determinant.

Implementing loan pricing procedures thus requires considerable assistance from cost accounting, a very clear determination of the loan officer's role in negotiating interest rates, and an ability to monitor continuously cost factors and pricing results.

Loan closing procedures are usually accomplished by staff personnel especially trained in loan documentation and bank bookkeeping techniques. Loan officer involvement may or may not include supervising the preparation and execution of loan documents by the borrower.

He or she is almost always, however, required to review or sign off on loan documents after they have been completed and executed. Principal procedural considerations usually will have to do with the kind and number of forms to be used and their subsequent handling. These practices will be significantly dictated by bank counsel and the bank's internal operating and reporting needs. Their implementation, therefore, becomes primarily an internal operational matter. However, some loan closings are anything but routine and, because of their effect on the quality of a loan, are usually turned over to bank counsel for processing or review. For instance, an incorrectly recorded real estate description will often render the bank's lien position valueless.

One of the more problematic procedures which banks have difficulty fully implementing is that of obtaining all financial statements and all fully executed loan documents prior to advancing loan proceeds to the borrower. There occur many situations when to do so will work a severe difficulty on the borrower and, in some instances, will contravene established business practices. Banks have therefore instituted a series of exception procedures for handling these kinds of problems, with the most common practice being to grant the loan officer of account clearly defined discretionary authority for advancing loan funds prior to receipt of all loan documents. A well-managed bank maintains careful records to such exceptions, regularly reviewing their status, and the "follow-through" record of each loan officer.

Clearly, the implementation of loan closing procedures require considerable staff training, constant access to well-informed legal advice, and a careful understanding of the risks inherent in "exception" processing. Most loan audit trails begin in the loan closing area and, thus, require close coordination with auditing practices.

Loan collection procedures are more often approached from a technique or "how to" point of view. This is appropriate because the point at issue is what is the most expeditious way in which to recover bank capital. There are, however, a few procedural or policy matters which will be reviewed.

The point in time when the bank ceases to accrue interest on a problem loan is established automatically by some banks upon passage of a predetermined period of delinquency. This practice is fairly common with respect to installment loans, though considerably less so with respect to business loans, where a system of individual evaluation is conducted prior to placing the loan on a nonaccrual status. Both procedures require careful and continuous attention. Nonimplementation of a satisfactory system will lead to a misstatement of earnings.

Primary responsibility for collecting problem commercial loans is, in most banks, charged to the officer of account; however, larger banks more often turn this responsibility over to a commercial loan collection specialist on the theory that the originating loan officer's interest in the account may be such that something less than a totally objective and vigorous collection will occur. And second, that the collection specialist, trained in creditor's rights and bankruptcy law, is more skillful in collecting problem loans and the marketing and customer handling talents of the line loan officer are being wasted on a long and difficult collection. The difference in these two philosophies (i.e., every loan officer must collect his or her own loans, or it is better to turn the collection over to a specialist) will create two distinctly different sets of procedural arrangements. Assignment procedures, the timing and use of legal counsel, expense accounting, and even authority for pursuing legal avenues for collection will differ.

A particularly difficult problem for bankers in the area of loan collections has to do with compromising full repayment. This problem manifests itself in a variety of ways: whether or not to recover collection costs or to forgive interest, or principal, whether or not to pursue guarantors. These are issues which tend to be handled on the merits of each individual case, even though bank policy is reasonably uniform in suggesting there is no room for compromising a borrower's debt. Because of the diverse ways of dealing with these kinds of problems and because of the dollars and liability at jeopardy, banks procedurally document these decisions in senior committee formal actions.

Finally, collection procedures will always provide for some form of special reporting, primarily to senior management and to the bank's board of directors. Implementing problem loan reporting is a reasonable straightforward endeavor, except that unlike regular loan reports considerable additional information such as interest receivable, unpaid collection costs, collateral type and value, and estimated ultimate loss is also reported.

Loan review procedures involve two distinct operations, a review of all loan documents to determine their adequacy and completeness, and a review of the financial characteristics of the borrower to determine the feasibility of repayment. These reviews are always conducted after the loan has been committed or advanced on the premise that problems do not begin to show themselves until after the loan is closed and, second, that independently reviewed loans will be better managed than nonreviewed loans. How these processes are conducted is covered more thoroughly in Chapter 43.

There arise, however, special implementation considerations in the establishment of a loan review activity and most of these go straight to the heart of credit administration strategy. Loan review provides bank management with one of its best tools for monitoring loan quality and quantifying specific weaknesses in the portfolio and in loan procedures. A first consideration is the development of loan quality classifications or grades, which may or may not conform with a particular regulator's examination classifications. The bank's internal loan grading system will differ to the extent to which management wishes greater or lessor supervisory leverage on the portfolio. For instance, a bank's definition of a substandard loan may include loans with speculative repayment factors which, in themselves, would not always result in classification by a national bank examiner.

Related to loan grading definitions is the matter of dealing with differences of opinion regarding the classification of specific loans. At issue is the judgment of the loan reviewer and the loan officer, as well as the independent nature of the loan review function itself. Procedures for resolving these differences are typically provided by referring the dispute to either senior management or to a senior review committee.

Another procedural consideration will have to do with how management chooses to deal with loans graded anything less than satisfactory. For instance, some banks restrict much of a loan officer's discretionary authority for renewing or advancing under a line commitment or for paying overdrafts, or for amending loan terms and instead require that authority for such actions be placed with a supervisor or special loan committee. In effect, the entire administration of a substandard loan will be shared or regularly reviewed with management.

A final consideration is the extent to which fallout loan statistics and experiences will be used to feed back into loan policy, loan acquisition practices, and loan procedures. This feedback occurs through special reports forwarded by loan review to management, or it occurs as a result of the organizational location of loan review with respect to senior management and to the lending activity, or a combination of the two. The regular use of this imporant source of loan data and procedural effectiveness is important to all banks.

PORTFOLIO ORGANIZATION

The organizational structure of the lending activities of the bank basically reflects the marketing strategies and operating requirements necessitated by the particular types of loans which the bank carries on its ledgers. The loan portfolio itself often reflects a similar organization, though not always necessarily so, and due to the development of computer technology, the portfolio of most banks today is, in fact, simultaneously organized in various ways so as to provide different information to different people.

Every loan will have a loan officer assignment and a basic market or loan administrative group assignment, such as national accounts, agribusiness, real estate, or consumer installment. Other organizational assignments include geographic codes, industry codes, liquidity and risk classifications, forward commitment classifications, regulatory industry, and call codes to name some of the more important, though not all the ways in which a bank's portfolio may be programmed.

LOAN REPORTS

In addition to the multiple coding of loans, the principal key to all loan reporting systems is provided by a basic bookkeeping system which daily updates principal, interest receivable, the per diem accrual, loan maturity and in the case of add-on interest loans, earned and unearned interest. The system also tracks total outstanding commitments to each borrower and reports both the used and unused portion of the commitment. Specific reports are prepared in accordance with individual bank's needs; however, the three most common reports, prepared by most banks, include a loan status report which provides total portfolio accounting information. This is usually prepared weekly and is supplemented with a daily transaction journal which details all debit and credit entries for each business day. The third report is the daily loan activity report which is a simplified schedule of loan advances and payments made during the day of report.

Reference to the first two reports or a combination of the two is made regularly by loan officers and loan operations personnel to determine payoff amounts, current aggregate borrowing, and to some extent the history of a borrower's use of bank credit. For banks which utilize an on-line loan system instantaneous access to such information is provided on a cathode ray tube video presentation.

Other reports which are regularly used by loan officers and their supervisors for managing their assigned accounts include a loan maturing report which lists all loans maturing within a two- to three-week period. These will be listed in order of maturity. Delinquency reports used by banks are usually organized by the period of delinquency. At monthly or quarterly intervals, loan officers are usually provided a separate list of all assigned loans, together with aggregate balances, gross income, average yield, and, in some cases, income after allocated lending costs.

Routine reports to management, again derived from the same basic accounting information (principal, interest rate, income, maturity), typically are organized by loan groups or types of loans, though are as easily set forth by loan officer assignment, industry codes, or other industry arrangements. Again, these reports include loans outstanding, total commitments, unused commitments, average yields, and income for the month, quarter, or year to date. Income performance reports have become possible in recent years wherein customer profitability, as determined by the bank's deposit bookkeeping system, is collated with loan accounting systems so as to provide total customer activity and a relative profitability index. Again, the profitability report may be organized in a number of different ways, i.e., by loan officer, loan group, market, industry, or by bank totals. Other regular reports to management include delinquency reports, substandard loan reports, and the daily loan activity lists.

A number of special reports are prepared for bank management with the content and organization of such reports based upon the specific needs of the bank. Three of these deserve comment. The first is a portfolio liquidity report which sets forth loan payment runoff and, separately, a monthly summary of loan maturities. Information from this report is used to help guide liability or funds management planning. A second report is a forward commitment report which classifies all the bank's forward line commitments, undisbursed project and operating loans, and, in some instances, commercial letters of credit and banker acceptance exposures. Information from this report is used to measure the potential impact of borrower call on the bank's resources. The third report, or in some cases, combination of reports is a risk concentration report which organizes used and unused commitments by different kinds of risk, such as unsecured loans, real estate construction loans, feeder livestock loans, and REIT loans. It is interesting to note that some loans may be classified in two or more categories of risk and whether or not this is done will depend upon how a particular bank wishes to manage portfolio concentrations. Information from these reports is used to assess the concentration of portfolio risk in any one industry, geographic area, or loan type.

There is a third group of reports exclusively prepared for reporting loan information to bank regulatory agencies. These include call reports, Federal Reserve Bank industry reports, and special reports for federal, state and comptroller of the currency examiners. Again, the basic information is identical to that used by the bank, except that in these reports it is arranged to conform to the regulator's format.

CONCLUSION

The work which is performed in all banks essentially accomplishes a similar result, particularly as it relates to lending. Banks move credit into areas of the economy which are growing or in other ways require the use of capital. Loans are advanced and repaid. As we have seen, however, very considerable management of this straightforward task is required. In the next chapter, many of the risk and loan structuring considerations which go into lending are discussed. In this and the two preceding chapters, much of the policy and internal management of lending is covered.

As has been pointed out, there exists a multiplicity of challenges and opportunities for banks in choosing the manner in which they administer their loan systems and procedures. These differences occur for many, many reasons. Loan systems and procedures are designed to fit existing management patterns and eventually become a part of and reflect the style of that management.

The ultimate goal of sound credit administration, however, regardless of style, is a soundly managed loan portfolio. Whether a bank is large or small, this calls for systems and procedures which are workable, dependable, and responsive to changing loan market conditions.

Loan approval, loan closing, and loan collection together with many other loan procedures assure the daily operating continuity of the bank's loan departments. However, as business life has speeded up and grown in complexity, much faster response times are required of bank managers. To help accomplish this, much innovation has taken place in banking in the last decade. Today loan review systems and sophisticated loan accounting and information systems provide in-depth continuous reports to management, assuring as never before that loan managers are able to remain close to the bank's principal earning asset, the loan portfolio. Controlling loan quality and planning for its growth and improvement are key management tasks and responsibilities.

Chapter 45

Financial Analysis
for Credit Decisions

*David T. Snowdon**

The making of a credit decision involves essentially five major elements. First is the determination of the prospective borrower's real problem as opposed to his or her evaluation of the problem. This will involve an in-depth interview with the management to discover whether or not a bank loan is a possible solution to the problem or whether advice or better collection of receivables, an elimination of obsolete inventory, or liquidation of other assets might be a better solution.

The second step in the decision-making process is the gathering of essential factual data. This involves approaching a number of sources, including the prospective borrower; a visit to the plant, store, or other business location; checking with other banks and trade suppliers; examining court records; purchasing credit agency reports; reviewing manuals and newspapers; and, very importantly, examining the bank's records for its own experience. The details of how this process is carried out are described elsewhere in this volume and will not be dealt with further other than to recognize these steps as necessary for credit decision making.

The third step involves the financial analysis of the data collected so as to put it in better form for evaluation and understanding. After the data has been analyzed, the fourth step is the evaluation of the information. The fifth and final step is the making of the decision.

This chapter will deal primarily with the financial analysis of the

---

* Vice President (retired), Mellon Bank, N.A., Pittsburgh, Pennsylvania.

data followed by brief discussions of the evaluation of the data and the decision-making process.

FINANCIAL STATEMENTS

In dealing with financial analysis, it is highly important that the analyst or the lender begins with reliable financial statements. It is generally agreed that the most reliable data consists of financial statements audited by independent, competent certified public accountants. While it is recognized that there are other public accountants who for various reasons have not qualified as certified public accountants, it is generally believed that the certified public accountant certificate evidences a degree of expertise and independence that carries considerable weight in the acceptance of these financial statements.

The American Institute of Certified Public Accountants operates under a set of generally accepted auditing standards which are rules governing the auditing of financial statements as well as the issuing of the letter of opinion which the accountant writes in conveying the financial statement information to the board of directors or the principal owners of the company or firm whose affairs have been audited.

The opinions accompanying audited statements or statements with which a CPA has been involved generally fall into the following categories.

Unqualified Opinion.   An unqualified opinion is issued in connection with financial statements where the accountant has been given complete freedom as to the scope of the audit examination and is able to state that the books and records have been kept in accordance with generally accepted accounting principles applied on a basis consistent with previous years and that the statements present the financial data fairly. The accounting firm, however, does not guarantee the absolute accuracy of the statements which are the basic responsibility of the company whose figures have been audited.

An example of an unqualified opinion, made available through the courtesy of Coopers & Lybrand, CPAs, is as follows:

To the Board of Directors
Sample Manufacturing Company
(City and state or country)
    We have examined the balance sheet of Sample Manufacturing Company as of December 31, 19___ and the related statements of income, changes in shareholders' equity and changes in financial position for the year then ended. Our examination was made in accordance with generally accepted auditing standards, and accordingly included such tests of the accounting records and such other auditing procedures as we considered necessary in the circumstances. We previously examined

and reported on the financial statements of the company for the year
19___ (prior year).

In our opinion, the aforementioned financial statements present fairly
the financial position of Sample Manufacturing Company at December
31, 19___ and 19___, and the results of its operations and the changes in
its financial position for the years then ended, in conformity with generally accepted accounting principles applied on a consistent basis.

Qualified Opinion.　An accountant's opinion may be qualified because it is "subject to" certain occurrences or limitations or the opinion
may be qualified "except for" certain occurrences or limitations. Some
of the reasons given why an opinion may be qualified "subject to"
are because of the financial position of the company, its historical losses,
or the existence of a loan default. A qualification of "except for" can
come about because generally accepted accounting principles have
not been followed and that income has been included in the financial
statement for which no tax provision has been made. Other types of
variations of generally accepted accounting principles may also occur
which would still permit the issuance of a qualified opinion.

An example of a qualified opinion, also from Coopers & Lybrand,
is as follows:

To the Board of Directors
Sample Manufacturing Company
(City and state or country)

We have examined the balance sheet of Sample Manufacturing Company
as of December 31, 19___ and the related statements of income, changes
in shareholders' equity and changes in financial position for the year
then ended. Our examination was made in accordance with generally
accepted auditing standards, and accordingly included such tests of the
accounting records and such other auditing procedures as we considered
necessary in the circumstances.

The company has provided for depreciation of plant and equipment
on the straight-line basis in the aforementioned financial statements;
however, for income tax purposes the company has used the double
declining balance method of computing its depreciation. In computing
the provision for income taxes for the year ended December 31, 19___,
the computation was based upon the higher depreciation used for tax
return purposes. In our opinion, generally accepted accounting principles
require that deferred income taxes, applicable to the difference between
depreciation for financial statement purposes and income tax purposes,
should be provided for in the financial statements. No such provision
is included in the aforementioned financial statements; therefore, the
provision for income taxes and deferred income taxes are understated
by _____, net income and retained earnings are overstated by
a like amount and net income per share is overstated by $_____.

In our opinion, except that provision has not been made for the de-

ferred income taxes as described in the foregoing paragraph, the aforementioned financial statements present fairly the financial position of
Sample Manufacturing Company at December 31, 19__ and the results
of its operations and the changes in its financial position for the year
then ended, in conformity with generally accepted accounting principles
applied on a basis consistent with that of the preceding year.

Disclaimer or Denial of Opinion. This type of opinion comes about
where the accountant finds that the financial statements, for example,
have been prepared under procedures which were at variance with
generally accepted accounting principles and the amount involved is
so significant that the financial statements, in the opinion of the accountant, do not fairly present the financial position, results of operations, or changes in financial position in conformity with generally
accepted accounting principles.

An example from Coopers & Lybrand of a disclaimed or denied
opinion follows:

To the Board of Directors
Sample Finance Company
(City and state or country)

We have examined the balance sheet of Sample Finance Company
as of December 31, 19__ and the related statements of income, changes
in shareholders' equity and chances in financial position for the year
then ended. Our examination was made in accordance with generally
accepted auditing standards, and accordingly, included such tests of the
accounting records and such other auditing procedures as we considered
necessary in the circumstances.

The company has heretofore followed the practice of recording interest income over the term of each contract on the sum-of-the-months-
digits method. For the year ended December 31, 19__ the company
adopted the practice of recording total interest to be earned on the
outstanding receivable as income at the date the loan is made. As a
result of this change, reported net income and funds provided from
operations for the year ended December 31, 19__ and retained earnings
as of that date are each _____ greater than they otherwise would
have been. Also loans receivable (as reduced by unearned income) are
_____ greater than they otherwise would have been at December
31, 19__.

In view of the material effect on the financial statements of the above-
noted change to a practice which we believe is at variance with generally
accepted accounting principles, we are of the opinion that the aforementioned financial statements do not present fairly the financial position
of Sample Finance Company at December 31, 19__, or the results of
its operations or the changes in its financial position for the year then
ended, in conformity with generally accepted accounting principles.

Unaudited Statements. A final type of opinion letter presented by independent certified public accountants is in situations where the books of the company have been reviewed without audit. In this event, the accountant, if a letter is included with the financial statements (and some accountants refuse to include any letter in such circumstances) should point out that the books have not been audited and that no opinion is being expressed. Each page of the accompanying financial statements should also be marked "unaudited."

An example of this type of opinion letter which Coopers & Lybrand made available follows:

> Mr. John D. Smith, President
> Sample Manufacturing Company
> (City and state or country)
>
> The accompanying balance sheet of Sample Manufacturing Company as of December 31, 19__ and the related statements of income, changes in shareholders' equity and changes in financial position for the year then ended were not audited by us and accordingly we do not express an opinion on them.

Instead of statements prepared by independent certified public accountants or other outside professional accountants, banks also receive from some prospective borrowers financial statements prepared by the staff of the company which staff may have varying degrees of accounting skills. Where very small businesses are involved income tax returns may sometimes be used and, in the case of interim statements, trial balance data may be relied upon occasionally. Bankers have found it necessary sometimes to accept estimated statements but this latter type of data is generally not very reliable and the lender must look primarily beyond the financial statements to the integrity of the customer and to any specific collateral which might be pledged.

COMPARISON METHOD OF ANALYSIS

There are various financial analysis techniques which have been used by bank lenders and other credit grantors for years. One of the earliest methods is known as the comparison method of analysis. In conducting this type of analysis, financial statements for periods ranging from two to as many years as are available are placed on a comparison form or spread sheet, an example of which is shown in Exhibits 45–1 and 45–2.

The basic concept of this method of analysis is to place on the comparison form statements as of the end of the company's fiscal year. The assets are generally listed in the order of their liquidity with current assets such as cash, trade accounts receivable, and inventories

Exhibit 45–1
Spread Sheet for Balance Sheet Data

NAME   BUSINESS

		ASSETS	Type Date			%			%			%			%			%
	1	Cash																
	2	Marketable Securities																
	3	Receivables—Trade																
	4	Less: Bad Debt Allowance																
	5																	
	6	Inventories																
	7																	
	8																	
	9	All Other Current																
	10	TOTAL CURRENT ASSETS																
	11	Fixed Assets—Net																
	12																	
	13																	
	14	Investments																
	15																	
	16	All Other Noncurrent																
	17	TOTAL NONCURRENT ASSETS																
	18	TOTAL ASSETS																
		LIABILITIES																
	19	Notes Payable—Banks																
	20																	
	21																	
	22	Accounts Payable—Trade																
	23	Taxes																
	24	Current Maturities of L. T. Debt																
	25																	
	26	All Other Current																
	27	TOTAL CURRENT DEBT																
	28	Long Term Debt																
	29																	
	30	All Other Noncurrent																
	31	TOTAL NONCURRENT DEBT																
	32	TOTAL UNSUBORDINATED DEBT																
	33																	
	34																	
	35	Subordinated Debt																
	36	TOTAL LIABILITIES																
	37																	
	38	Capital—Preferred Stock																
	39	Capital—Common Stock																
	40	Paid-in Surplus																
	41	Retained Earnings																
	42	NET WORTH																
	43	TOTAL LIABILITIES & NET WORTH																
	44																	
	45	NET WORKING CAPITAL (10 — 27)																
	46	CAPITAL FUNDS (35 + 42)																
	47	Ratios: Quick																
	48	Current																
	49	Fixed Assets to Net Worth																
	50	Total Debt to Net Worth																
	51	Total Unsub. to Cap. Funds																
	52	Sales to Receivables (Days)																
	53	Cost of Sales to Inv. (Days)																
	54	Sales to Net Work. Cap.																
	55	Sales to Net Worth																
	56	Contingent Liabilities																
	57																	
	58																	

Source: Robert Morris Associates.

Exhibit 45–2
Spread Sheet—Operating Data

	OPERATIONS		%		%		%		%		%
101	NET SALES										
102	Materials Used										
103	Labor										
104	Manufacturing Expenses										
105											
106	COST OF GOODS SOLD										
107	GROSS PROFIT										
108	Selling Expenses										
109	General & Adm. Expenses										
110											
111	TOTAL OPERATING EXPENSES										
112	OPERATING PROFIT										
113	Other Income										
114											
115	Other Expense										
116											
117	PROFIT BEFORE TAX										
118	Income Taxes										
119											
120	NET PROFIT AFTER TAX										
	RATIOS:										
121	% Profit to Net Worth										
122	% Profit to Total Assets										
123											
	RECONCILIATION of RETAINED EARN										
124	Retained Earnings—Beginning										
125	Add: Net Profit										
126											
127											
128	Less: Net Loss										
129	Dividends										
130											
131											
132	Retained Earnings—Ending										
	SOURCE & APPLICATION OF FUNDS:										
	Source of Funds:										
133	Net Profit										
134	Depr., Amort., Depletion										
135											
136											
137	Increase—Noncurrent Debt										
138											
139											
140											
141	Other Accounts—Net										
142	Decrease Net Working Capital										
143	TOTAL SOURCES										
	Application of Funds:										
144	Dividends Paid										
145											
146											
147	Purchase of Fixed Assets										
148	Decrease—Noncurrent Debt										
149											
150											
151											
152	Other Accounts—Net										
153	Increase Net Working Capital										
154	TOTAL APPLICATIONS										

Source: Robert Morris Associates.

listed first. Current assets are defined as those assets which in the normal course of business will be liquidated within one year from statement date, or in some industries such as installment selling or contracting, within the normal operating cycle. These are followed by the noncurrent assets which are generally listed in accordance with their value to the company or their active use in the productive process.

The liability segment of the balance sheet carries first the current liabilities described as those which by their terms will fall due within one year from statement date or within the normal operating cycle. Noncurrent liabilities, in addition to debts maturing beyond one year from statement date, include various provisions for possible contingencies as well as subordinated debt, whether completely subordinated to all creditors or to selected creditors.

The equity or net worth segment of the balance sheet then follows with common stock usually listed first followed by preferred stock, then retained earnings, capital surplus, or other equity.

On the reverse side of the comparison form may be listed the operating figures starting with net sales and carrying through to net profits after all charges. This is generally followed by a reconcilement of net worth or equity accounts and in many bank comparison forms in more recent years, an analysis of the changes in financial position or working capital is provided.

Interim statements are generally placed on separate comparison forms. Interims covering the months or quarters for the same fiscal year are carried on the same page of the comparison form. When year-to-year interim information is regularly available, it is sometimes desirable to place all semiannual interims for example on the same page of the form.

In using this method of analysis the proper classification of the statement items on the comparison form has analytic value. Before placing an item on the form, the analyst should evaluate the item as to its real value and whether it is being properly classified under the circumstances. Any doubt about where the item should be placed should be resolved by a thorough review of the original financial statement, together with explanatory footnotes, or if necessary through consultation with the borrower or the accountant who prepared the statement. This activity in itself will enhance the knowledge and understanding of the analyst regarding the company.

After the statements have been spread appropriately on the comparison form, the analyst should note changes in the trends of the dollar value of key statement items such as current assets, including cash, receivables, and inventories; current liabilities, including bank loans, current maturities of long-term debt, accounts payable, income tax accruals, and other accruals. Long-term items should be examined to note the changes in key obligations such as secured and unsecured debt both publicly and privately held. Changes in net worth or equity, including capital stock, retained earnings, and net worth reserves or provisions are also very important. Finally, changes should be noted in key operating items such as net sales, gross profit, significant income and expense items, and net profits, before and after taxes.

It is important to note changes in unusually large amounts particularly if the items are traditionally rather stable as these changes often indicate either improper spreading; switches in management philosophy or policy; or the occurrence of situations beyond the control of management. Special attention should be paid to withdrawals by the owners; reduction in debt to owners or other key management persons; unusual salary or bonus increases; or the advancing of money to officers, employees, or persons outside of the business. The channeling of an excessive amount of earnings into fixed assets, slow-moving inventory, or uncollectible receivables also is a sign of potential financial trouble ahead.

TREND PERCENTAGE METHOD OF ANALYSIS

This method of analysis is based on the premise that if the trend of key statement items can be set forth on a percentage basis from one year to the next, it will give the analyst a much clearer picture of the changing condition of the customer. There are two ways in which the trend percentage is calculated: (1) Each item whose trend is to be traced is considered to be at 100 percent in the first year of the series. Subsequent years are calculated by dividing the dollar value of each item in the subsequent years by the first year's dollar value of that item to determine the percentage change. (2) The other approach is to divide the dollar value of each item in subsequent years by the dollar value of the immediately preceding year to develop a trend percentage. Either method if used consistently will produce essentially the same results.

Some analysts calculate the trend percentage for every item in the financial statement, but many analysts select key items only. For example, under the selective approach an analyst might calculate the trend percentage of net sales, gross profits, net profits, receivables, inventories, fixed assets, short- and long-term bank debt, trade payables, other long-term debt, and certain net worth items. The concept underlying this method is that when the percentages are calculated as shown above, they provide a clearer picture of the changes than would the dollar changes alone. Many analysts combine both methods to obtain more effective results.

RATIO METHOD OF ANALYSIS

This is a widely used method of analysis. Since a ratio is the expression of a relationship between two statement items, it is important to keep the following points in mind when using ratios: (1) To be effective ratios should be calculated by using items that are in fact closely related to one another. For example, net sales and accounts receivable bear a close relationship to each other as do net sales and net worth or fixed assets and net worth. (2) It should be kept in mind that both elements making up a ratio are equally important and both should be examined closely when a ratio shows an unfavorable relationship. In using the ratio of net sales to net working capital, it should be kept in mind that it may often look good because the net sales have increased or it may look good because the net working capital has decreased. In this latter instance the ratio change would not be considered a favorable one while in the former instance it would. (3) Ratios do not stand alone but should be evaluated in the light of other ratios and other changes in financial position as evidenced by other analytical techniques. (4) The trend of a ratio is as important as the value of the ratio at any given point in time.

Various ratios are used by different analysts. The ratios selected by each analyst might depend on the types of loans a lender might make or might depend on the lender's attitude toward ratios as a technique of analysis. It is not necessary to use all of the ratios all of the time and many lenders use certain so-called basic ratios most of the time but supplement them with additional ratios as the analysis involved requires.

Following is a suggested list of ratios grouped according to the function they perform in analysis and what each ratio purports to show:

1. *Liquidity Ratios.* These ratios primarily measure the ability of the company to pay its short-term obligations.
   a. Current Ratio. This is a quantitative ratio that measures the quantity of current assets available to pay the current liabilities. Another way of evaluating the current ratio is to consider it as the degree to which the current assets can decline before the company is unable to pay its current liabilities. Net working capital, which is the difference between the current assets and current liabilities, is often compared with the current ratio to show the extent in dollars by which the current assets can decline before the company will be unable to pay its current liabilities.
   b. Quick Ratio or Acid Test Ratio. This ratio is designed to refine the current ratio and is a qualitative ratio in that it shows the ability of the cash plus the receivables to pay the current

liabilities. On the supposition that there is no question about the cash, the value of the ratio depends a great deal on the quality of the accounts receivable.

 c. Net Sales to Net Receivables. This ratio is often converted into days' receivables outstanding by dividing 360 by the ratio to obtain days' receivables outstanding. Some analysts divide 365 or 366 by the ratio. This is a qualitative ratio which attempts to measure the collectibility or quality of the accounts receivable. The theory is that the higher the ratio the more frequent the turnover of receivables, although a true turnover ratio is based on average net receivables as opposed to the net receivables on a specific date. When converted to days, the amount of days' receivables outstanding is compared with the selling terms to determine whether or not the ratio is satisfactory. For example, a company selling on net 30-day terms should have days' outstandings of between 30–45 days for the ratio to be considered satisfactory.

 d. Cost of Sales to Inventory. This ratio, which is also a qualitative ratio, is an attempt to measure the quality of the inventory and is calculated by using a cost of sales inasmuch as inventory is carried on a cost basis. However, some analysts historically have used net sales to inventory and as long as the ratio selected is used consistently it does not make too much difference which calculation is chosen. Like the net sales to net receivables ratio, this ratio can be converted into days' inventory outstanding by dividing it into 360, 365, or 366. Its quality can be measured by comparing it with the production period or the amount of time necessary to convert raw materials into finished goods ready for sale.

 e. Net Sales to Net Working Capital. This relationship is an effort to measure the turnover of the net working capital or the effectiveness with which the net working capital is being utilized. The higher it is the better it is considered to be unless it increases rather swiftly from year to year when a question can readily be raised as to whether the company is growing too fast and is developing too much in the way of sales as compared to the net working capital available. This conclusion would be reinforced if there was a slowdown in the turnover of receivables or inventory or if the current ratio were declining at the same time.

2. *Capital Strength Ratios.* These ratios attempt to measure the overall capital strength of the company, principally by measuring the net worth, the total debt, and the amount of fixed assets. Two ratios are generally used to measure capital strength which are:

a. Tangible Net Worth to Total Debt.   This ratio is also often
calculated as total debt to tangible net worth and either approach is appropriate. It should be kept in mind, however,
that the first calculation shows the ratio as improving as it
becomes larger while the second indicates the ratio is improving as it becomes smaller. This is a quantitative ratio much
like the current ratio. It measures the quantity of net worth
in relation to the total debt of the company and, used in connection with the net worth, which is the difference between the
total assets and the total liabilities, measures the degree to
which the total assets of the business can shrink and the company still be able to pay its total liabilities.

b. Tangible Net Worth to Net Fixed Assets.   This ratio is often
calculated as net fixed assets to tangible net worth. As in the
preceding ratio, the first calculation results in the ratio being
considered good as it increases while the second calculation
results in the ratio being considered good as it decreases. This
is a qualitative ratio inasmuch as it attempts to measure the
quality of the net worth by showing the degree to which net
worth is involved in supporting the company's fixed assets.
The theory is that fixed assets cannot be liquidated to pay debts
in the normal course of business. Their major function is to
generate earnings. An excessive amount of fixed assets would
add to fixed costs and limit the company's ability to show satisfactory earnings. It would also tie up assets in nonliquid form
thus hampering prompt debt repayment.

3. *Efficiency Ratios.*   These ratios represent an effort to measure the
effectiveness with which the management is operating the business.
It will be noted that they are all related to net sales and are based
on the theory that, in general, the greater volume of net sales
generated the more effective the management is in operating the
assets at its disposal.

a. Net Sales to Tangible Net Worth.   This ratio shows the effectiveness with which the net worth is utilized, although like
the net sales to net working capital, it can indicate potential
problems if it grows too fast, particularly if the tangible net
worth to total debt and the current ratio are decreasing at
the same time. This condition is known as overtrading. If the
ratio is not high enough, or is not growing at a reasonable
rate, the company would be said to be undertrading.

b. Net Sales to Net Fixed Assets.   This ratio, too, is a measure
of efficiency and shows how effectively the net fixed assets
are being used in producing sales. In general, the higher the

net sales to fixed assets the more effectively the fixed assets, including the plant and equipment, are being operated.

c. Net Sales to Total Assets. This is a qualitative ratio showing the effectiveness with which the management is using the total assets available to produce sales volume. It indicates how efficient the management is in operating the business as a whole, especially when the ratio is evaluated in combination with the profitability ratios.

4. *Coverage Ratios.* These ratios indicate the degree to which net profits plus noncash charges, such as depreciation or amortiziation, for example, cover interest or interest and principal payments on debt. These ratios are primarily used to determine whether the company can pay its long-term debt obligations on schedule on the assumption that the higher the degree of coverage the more certain will be the ability of the company to handle these obligations satisfactorily.

a. Net Profit before Noncash Charges to Interest on Long-Term Debt. This ratio as stated includes the coverage of interest in determining net profit and the ratio, therefore, indicates the excess coverage existing after the interest has been paid. It indicates the degree to which net profit can decline before the company will be unable to pay its interest in full. The inability to pay interest would trigger action by debtholders and could ultimately result in the bankruptcy of the company. A steadily declining ratio is a reliable sign of approaching financial difficulty.

b. Net Profit before Noncash Charges to Current Long-Term Debt Payments. This ratio, which indicates that interest has been paid before net profit has been determined, has the additional value of indicating the degree to which the current payments on long-term debt can be made. The inability to make these debt payments, as in the case of the inability to pay interest, could result in unfavorable action by debtholders, including bankruptcy of the company. A steadily declining ratio is a reliable sign of approaching danger.

5. *Profitability Ratios.* These ratios have as their principal purpose the determination of the profitability of the company and in that sense they also help to measure management's effectiveness.

a. Gross Profit to Net Sales. This ratio measures the cost of preparing a product or service for sale and the margin between such preparation cost and the selling price. In many companies the ratio tends to remain stable or, if the company is doing well, to grow slowly. If it changes substantially from one period to another, there is an indication that there may have been a write-up or a write-down of inventory. This possibility should be investigated by the analyst. On the other hand, such a change may be the result of an improvement in purchasing raw materials or may be due to greater efficiency in the manufacturing process. In any event, it is important to look behind the ratio, as is true of all ratios, to ascertain the reason for the change.

b.   Key Expense Items to Net Sales.   These are measured by various ratios showing the degree to which important expense items are affecting net profit. Expenses that are often related to net sales for this purpose are: management salaries; total salaries; bonus or pension payments; selling expense, including delivery expense; and similar major expenses. When key expenses are ascertained to be out of line, management should be urged to take steps to reduce or control them.

c.   Net Profit (before and after Taxes) to Net Sales.   Many analysts will calculate this ratio on a before-tax basis on the theory that the company generally has little control over the amount of income taxes it must pay and that the true measure of management's ability to earn is net profit before taxes. This concept could be applied to the following two ratios as well. On the other hand, many analysts use net profit after taxes is determining this and the two subsequent ratios because they believe that net profit after all charges is the net profit with which the management has to work and, therefore, is the most meaningful. Many analysts use both approaches.

d.   Net Profit to Net Worth.   This ratio measures the degree to which management is able to employ the investors' capital profitably. If the ratio is satisfactory or unusually good, it makes it easier for management to attract new investors to the business. A satisfactory and improving ratio also makes the business much more attractive as an investment to the present owners and provides an incentive to keep it as a viable and continuing profitable organization.

e.   Net Profit to Total Assets.   This ratio measures the effectiveness with which management employs the total assets at its disposal. In the eyes of many analysts this is the most effective measure of management's ability.

The ratios that are most frequently used by many analysts are: current ratio; net sales to net receivables; cost of sales to inventory; net worth to total debt or the reverse calculation; net profit to net sales; and net profit to net worth. However, a number of analysts emphasize other ratios so there is no absolute rule of thumb as to which ratios are most effective. The ratios chosen will often vary with the credit or company being analyzed and the purpose for which the analysis is being prepared.

COMMON-SIZE INDUSTRY COMPARISON METHOD OF ANALYSIS

Another widely used technique of analysis is to compare a prospective borrower's financial statement with the financial statement of the industry in which the company operates. This is known as an industry or a trade comparison. A method developed by the Robert Morris Associates requires obtaining the statements of a number of companies in a given industry. The items in the statements are added together into one industry financial statement. Each item in the balance sheet is divided by total assets and each item in the operating statement is divided by net sales. Total assets thus equal 100 percent and every item in the industry balance sheet is expressed as a percentage of total assets. Similarly each item in the industry operating statement is expressed as a percentage of net sales. By using this method the individual company figures being analyzed are also reduced to a percentage or common-size basis in the same manner. The percentages of the company under analysis are compared with the percentages for the industry to indicate the degree to which the subject company might be out of line with its industry. The Robert Morris Associates also computes a selected group of ratios for each industry, developing the median, the upper quartile, and the lower quartile ratio for each industry. The company's ratios when compared with these provide an additional means of evaluating the company's financial condition and progress.

The theory behind this method is that when the company's figures vary markedly from the industry figures, the analyst should examine them more closely to determine the reason. The fact that there is a variation does not necessarily mean that the company is doing either poorly or well as there may be special reasons why its figures are different from those of the industry. On the other hand, such investigation may well turn up either a serious problem or a benefit which the prospective borrower may have.

Dun & Bradstreet, Inc. calculates a group of ratios for a number of lines of business. These ratios are listed from the best to the worst and the median, the upper quartile, and the lower quartile are determined. A number of trade associations publish studies and some may use other methods for making comparisons between the selected company and its industry.

This technique has value mainly to ascertain the degree to which a company varies from its industry standards. It should always be kept in mind by the analyst that these are either average figures or median figures and the ratios shown are not necessarily models of the ideal company in the industry. Industry statements are affected by all of the differences that exist among companies in the same industry. These, for example, include: multiple product lines; accounting differences; differences in geographic location; variations in customer mix; and variations in selling terms. The method is valuable, however, when used with appropriate reservations and it is attaining increasing acceptance among analysts as a supplement to other analysis techniques.

STATEMENT OF FINANCIAL POSITION

An increasingly used method of analysis is the statement of financial position, sometimes known as the analysis of net working capital changes, the source and application of funds statement, or the cash flow statement, although this latter designation is somewhat of a misnomer. In carrying out this method of analysis, the various items on the company's balance sheet are compared from one period to another and the changes in dollar amount recorded. These changes are usually grouped into two segments showing those changes which increase net working capital or which generate funds and in the other segment those changes which decrease net working capital or which use or apply funds. In any event, the method analyzes the flow of funds through the business as opposed to the flow of cash alone.

To visualize the operation of this method more effectively, the following schedule of financial changes which affect net working capital can be helpful:

Changes Which Increase Net Working Capital (sources of funds)

Decreases in noncurrent assets.

Increases in noncurrent liabilities.

Increases in net worth or equity.

Changes Which Decrease Net Working Capital (uses or applications of funds)

Increases in noncurrent assets.

Decreases in noncurrent liabilities.

Decreases in net worth or equity.

Along with the changes in the noncurrent segment of the balance sheet, the analyst should set up a schedule noting the changes in the current section. This schedule shows the distribution of the current assets and the current liabilities and is a summary of the composition of net working capital.

PRO FORMA STATEMENTS

The preparation of pro forma statements is a device used by many lending officers and analysts to ascertain whether or not a given financial transaction is financially feasible. The essentials of the process are to place opposite each item in the balance sheet the amount by which that item will be changed by virtue of the proposed transaction. These changes are then projected into a new balance sheet which will give a picture of how the company will appear if the transaction is carried out as proposed. The lender may try other proposals to make the transaction more viable if the prospective borrower's proposal is not otherwise acceptable. Pro forma statements are also developed as a by-product of forecasting.

FORECASTING

A technique that is being used more frequently is the forecasting of financial statement data. Using this device the prospective borrower, with the assistance of an accountant or banker, projects the company's financial statements over a period of time such as one year, five years, or ten years. These projections are based upon assumptions made by the prospective borrower or the banker or both and can be prepared in varying degrees of detail. As part of the forecasting process a cash forecast can also be prepared as can pro forma balance sheet and operating statements.

The Robert Morris Associates makes available an effective forecasting form shown in Exhibit 45–3. This form is especially good for the use of smaller to medium-sized companies.

Forecasting provides the following advantages:

1. The prospective borrower is forced to put into actual figures its plans for the period forecast. The process can be even more valuable to the company if all the members of the staff who have a part in the company's living up to its forecast are involved in its preparation. It will help the banker to ascertain when the company will need funds; how much it will need; and how and when the obligation will be repaid.
2. The company will be able to check its progress from month to month as the actual data for each month can be measured against the monthly forecast and necessary changes made quickly.
3. Forecasts, although subject to error and future unpredictable

Exhibit 45–3
Projection of Financial Statements

PROJECTION OF
FINANCIAL STATEMENTS

SUBMITTED BY_____

			ACTUAL	PROJECTIONS					
SPREAD IN HUNDREDS ☐	DATE								
SPREAD IN THOUSANDS ☐	PERIOD								

P	1	NET SALES									
R	2	Less: Materials Used									
O	3	Direct Labor									
F	4	Other Manufacturing Expense									
I	5										
T	6	COST OF GOODS SOLD									
	7	GROSS PROFIT									
and	8	Less: Sales Expense									
	9	General and Administrative Expense									
L	10										
O	11	OPERATING PROFIT									
S	12	Less: Other Expense or *Income* (Net)									
S	13	Income Tax Provision									
	14										
	15	NET PROFIT									
C	16	CASH BALANCE (Opening)									
A	17	Plus RECEIPTS: Receivable Collections									
S	18										
H	19										
	20	Bank Loan Proceeds									
	21	Total									
P	22	Less: DISBURSEMENTS: Trade Payables									
R	23	Direct Labor									
O	24	Other M'fg Expense									
J	25	Sales, Gen'l and Adm. Exp.									
E	26	Fixed Asset Additions									
C	27	Income Taxes									
T	28										
I	29	Dividends or Withdrawals									
O	30										
N	31	Bank Loan Repayment									
	32	Total									
	33	CASH BALANCE (Closing)									
	34	ASSETS: Cash									
	35	Marketable Securities									
	36	Receivables (Net)									
	37	Inventory (Net)									
	38										
	39	CURRENT ASSETS									
B	40	Fixed Assets (Net)									
A	41										
L	42										
A	43										
N	44	Deferred Charges									
C	45	TOTAL ASSETS									
E	46	LIABILITIES: Notes Payable—Banks									
	47	Trade Payables									
S	48	Income Tax									
H	49										
E	50										
E	51	Accruals									
T	52	CURRENT LIABILITIES									
	53										
	54										
	55										
	56	CAPITAL STOCK ∣ Net Worth for									
	57	SURPLUS ∫ Partnership or Individual									
	58	TOTAL LIABILITIES AND NET WORTH									
	59	WORKING CAPITAL									

Exhibit 45–3 *(continued)*

SALES FORECAST

Consider (1) Previous years business; (2) estimates of (a) Sales Department (b) Purchasing Department (c) Production Department; and (3) Allowances for (a) Economic Outlook (b) Government regulations (c) Market (d) Styles (e) Peak periods. Space for comments at right. ☞

INDICATE FACTORS USED IN PREPARING PROJECTION

1. Average receivable collection period in days   ———
2. Inventory Turnover in Days   ———
3. Trade Payable Turnover in Days   ———
4. % Federal Tax to Profits before Tax   %———
5. Depreciation per Year $———
6. Total Officers' or Partners' Compensation per month $———

SUGGESTIONS FOR PREPARATION OF PROJECTION

Other Estimates needed for each period of the Projection are underlined below.

Blank lines in Projection are to accommodate unusual items of significance.

References to the Divisions of the Projection are abbreviated as follows:

Profit and Loss Statement	is PL
Cash Projection Receipts	is CR
Cash Projection Disbursements	is CD
Balance Sheet Assets	is BA
Balance Sheet Liabilities	is BL

In the first column, record the actual PROFIT AND LOSS STATEMENT and BALANCE SHEET of date immediately prior to projection period.

In each subsequent column covering a projection period (month, quarter, etc.):

1. Enter on date line, projection period covered and ending date thereof.

2. Complete PL, recording NET SALES, less all discounts and allowances; showing costs and expenses as indicated. *Compute NET PROFIT OR LOSS.

3. Record in CD on lines indicated, PL entries for DIRECT LABOR, OTHER MF'G EXPENSE, SALES, GENERAL and ADMINISTRATIVE EXPENSE and OTHER EXPENSE, less depreciation expense included therein. Record in CR, OTHER INCOME (PL).

4. Combine FIXED ASSETS (per prior column BA) and fixed asset additions, subtract depreciation expense and enter result in FIXED ASSETS (BA). Record cost of fixed asset additions in CD.

5. Combine INCOME TAX PROVISION (PL) with INCOME TAXES (per prior column BL), subtract payment of income tax and record result as INCOME TAXES (BL). Record income tax payment in CD.

6. Combine NET PROFIT or LOSS (PL) with SURPLUS or NET WORTH (per prior column BL), subtract DIVIDENDS OR WITHDRAWALS, record result as SURPLUS or NET WORTH (BL). Record DIVIDENDS or WITHDRAWALS in CD.

7. Record CASH (per prior column BA) as CASH BALANCE (opening) (CR).

8. Combine RECEIVABLES (per prior column BA) with NET SALES (PL), allocate resulting total between RECEIVABLE COLLECTIONS (CR) and RECEIVABLES (BA) per average collection period (Factor 1 above).

9. Combine TRADE PAYABLES (per prior column BL), with cost of material purchased (less discounts), allocate resulting total between TRADE PAYABLES (CD) and TRADE PAYABLES (BL) per turnover of payables (Factor 3 above),

10. Combine INVENTORY (per prior column BA), cost of materials purchased (less discounts) and DIRECT LABOR and OTHER M'FG EXPENSE (PL), subtract COST OF GOODS SOLD (PL), record result in INVENTORY (BA).

11. Review all items in prior column Balance Sheet (except CASH and NOTES PAYABLE—BANKS) for which no entries have been made in present period BALANCE SHEET. If there is no change in these items, transfer to present period BALANCE SHEET. If items are changed, reflect changes through CR or CD. Carry deferred charges (BA) and accruals (BL) without change.

12. Foot CASH PROJECTION: If cash deficiency indicated, enter amount to adjust in BANK LOAN PROCEEDS (CR); Combine this adjustment with NOTES PAYABLE—BANKS (per prior column BL) and enter as NOTES PAYABLE—BANKS (BL); if excessive cash is indicated, and NOTES PAYABLE—BANKS (per prior column BL) appears, provide BANK LOAN REPAYMENT (CD); reduce NOTES PAYABLE—BANKS (per prior column BL) by this provision, entering result as NOTES PAYABLE—BANKS (BL). Refoot CASH PROJECTION and enter resulting CASH BALANCE (closing) as CASH (BA).

13. Foot and balance BALANCE SHEET.

COMMENTS

For Manufacturer projecting substantial increases or decreases in inventory during projection period.
Enter as title on Line No. 5(PL).
"INCREASE OR DECREASE IN WORK IN PROCESS AND FINISHED INVENTORIES" — record increase in red, decrease in black.

Note: This form has a total of 15 horizontal columns. Ten columns have been eliminated for brevity.
Source: Robert Morris Associates.

events, do give the management which uses them a sense of direction. When it becomes necessary to consider changing direction, the management has a basis upon which to make such decisions.

EVALUATION OF FINANCIAL INFORMATION

In evaluating financial and other information two basic concepts are employed: (1) the going concern concept, and (2) the liquidation concept.

Using the going concern concept the analyst or lender should keep in mind the following points:

1. Ability to pay obligations as they mature.
2. Ability to earn profits consistently.
3. Ability to channel profits into appropriate assets for the long-range benefit of the company.
4. Ability to maintain quality of product or service.
5. Ability to borrow funds as needed.

On the other hand, when the liquidation concept is employed, the lender is trying to ascertain how the loan will be repaid in the event of unexpected difficulty. This concept gives high priority to:

1. Ability to convert assets into cash to pay obligations if the borrower gets into financial difficulty.
2. Ability to cover liabilities by sufficient assets after allowance for asset shrinkage should a forced sale of assets be required.

Analysis of a prospective borrower involves both concepts so that the lender may have confidence that the loan can be repaid even if the company encounters financial difficulties. In general, unless a bank loan is being made to carry out a planned liquidation, the loan ought not to be made unless the lender can feel satisfied that the company will continue to exist as a viable operating entity.

The methods of analysis discussed in this chapter should be used as tools to aid the lender in arriving at a sound decision. No method is infallible nor should any be used alone to the exclusion of other means of aiding in the decision process. Conversely, not all techniques are used in any single analysis. Good judgment in evaluating the total situation is the most essential ingredient in making sound credit decisions.

ECONOMIC EVALUATION

Since business is not done in a vacuum, a lender must always take into account the various economic influences that may affect a prospective borrower, such as:

1. Economic value of the product or service.
2. Business cycle fluctuations.
3. Evolution of the industry.
4. Laws and regulations covering taxes; environmental considerations; health and safety; and concerns of consumers.
5. Labor union requirements.

EVALUATION OF MANAGEMENT

Most important of all in evaluating a prospective credit risk is the character and the ability of management. It is well understood that character is the most difficult of all elements to evaluate and strong reliance obviously must be placed on the management's reputation as a reflection of its character. Reputation involves both business reputation and personal reputation. Business reputation is measured by management's relations with its employees, its customers, suppliers and the public in general. Personal reputation involves such matters as the personal habits of the members of the management group and encompasses such items as willingness to pay personal obligations; family relationships; personal participation in civic, religious, and other community activities; and general attitude of neighbors, friends, and business associates toward the individuals making up the management group.

The other major aspect in evaluating management is its ability. This is reflected by the depth and breadth of its numbers, skills, and personal abilities. It also involves the technical ability and experience of the management group as evidenced by product and service quality. Another important consideration in measuring management's ability is the ability and experience of the individual members of the management group to manage an organization as opposed to technical skills. This is evidenced by the financial progress of the company; ability and willingness to innovate in new product lines or services; willingness and ability to meet changing competitive conditions; surmounting unfavorable economic conditions; adjusting to new styles of management as needs arise; and operating in such a manner that the company becomes one of the leaders in its industry or area rather than a follower.

MAKING THE DECISION

The final step in making a loan is the decision and its implementation. This involves listing and weighing the favorable and unfavorable factors affecting the company's creditworthiness. It involves arriving at as many feasible solutions to the company's problem as possible and listing and weighing the favorable and unfavorable elements of each feasible solution. In weighing the factors affecting either the company's creditworthiness or bearing upon the respective solutions, the decision maker should recognize the relative values of each factor; should recognize the intangible as well as the tangible factors; and should allow for a reasonable margin of error so as to take into account factors not possible to consider at the time the decision is being made.

The next step is to select the best solution from the standpoint of both the lender and the prospective borrower. Then the next one or more acceptable solutions should be selected in the event that the first solution is unacceptable to the company and the lender is willing to consider alternative approaches. These should be arranged in the order of their attractiveness to the lender with awareness of the degrees of risk to the bank in each solution considered. It is important that all solutions considered are feasible and productive for the prospective borrower as well as for the bank.

The lender should determine alternative sources of collecting the proposed loan in the event the primary source proves inadequate. Some major sources of repayment are:

1. Earnings.
2. Liquidation of assets in normal course of business.
3. Transfer of the loan to another lender.
4. New capital brought into the business.
5. Liquidation of collateral pledged on the loan.
6. Realization of funds from guarantors of the loan.
7. Liquidation of assets outside of the normal course of business such as sale of subsidiaries, entire plants, franchises, and patent rights.
8. Sale or merger of entire business.

There are many social and ethical considerations which in prior years were not considered of major significance. They are playing an increasingly important part in a lender's decision. For example, how should minority owned businesses be financed? Some of the considerations are whether or not lower interest rates should be set for this type of business; whether specific loan funds should be set aside; and whether greater than ordinary risks should be assumed, and if so, to what degree. Allied with the financing of minority owned businesses is the financing of low-income housing. Many of the same considerations affecting business loans would be applicable for this type of lending.

Other areas of social and ethical significance are the financing of projects for business and industry to improve the quality of the environment. Also the community in which a lender operates is placing increasing pressure on bankers to avoid making loans which are considered to be of negative social value. Such types of loans would include:

1. Loans to manufacturers whose processes or products pollute the air and water.

2. Loans to companies which operate in countries with unacceptable racial policies.

Because of the increasing number of lawsuits against industries whose products cause damage and pollution or which may violate some of the many consumer and safety laws and regulations, these possibilities must also be taken into account by lenders from a risk standpoint. Such lawsuits may even affect a borrower's financial position far beyond the time the loans are made.

Finally, there are ethical considerations which are receiving increasing publicity in today's cultural climate. These involve the person making the loan and include such matters as:

1. Maintaining the confidentiality of banking relationships.
2. Personal investments in the borrowing company.
3. Acceptance of excessive gifts or favors from borrowers.
4. Buying at special advantageous prices from borrowers.

CONCLUSION

Loans made successfully should be repaid according to their terms. This involves establishing procedures, discussed elsewhere in this volume, for follow-up, review, and in some instances where plans have not worked out properly, for handling workout situations. In all of these functions, continuing financial analysis is a necessary ingredient. The steps described in this chapter are essential if follow-up is to be successful. Kept in proper perspective financial analysis is a valid and important tool for lenders.

Chapter 46

Handling Problem Loans

Willard Alexander*

Lending provides a major source of income for commercial banks. It is inevitable, however, that even with the soundest of loan policies, some loan losses will occur if community needs are to be served. Inasmuch as loans to businesses expose a bank to substantially higher losses than any other type of credit, it is important to keep losses on these credits within relatively small margins in order to realize a profit.

It has been said that a bank "never" makes a bad loan—a loan goes bad only after it has been made. This may be true in part, but surveillance of the borrower's operations after a loan has been made is a necessary part of lending. A banker with a watchful eye can often help a business customer steer clear of financial difficulty *before* it begins, thus holding problem loans to a minimum.

A bank has a problem loan on its hands when one of its commercial credits is at or close to insolvency. To be classified as a true problem loan, the credit must be significantly large relative to the size of the bank; this excludes installment or charge card debt to an individual.

Problem loans are costly for a bank; there are costs that go far beyond the loan charge-off and which directly affect the bottom line. Because of time spent in a workout situation, profit opportunities are missed and less time is available to call on good clients or to seek out potential customers. Many dollars are spent for the legal and professional fees necessary to handle the credit properly. And, the demoralizing effect that handling a loan of this type has on the officers involved can take its toll in terms of self-confidence or willingness to take reasonable risks on future credits.

---

* General Vice President, The Citizens and Southern National Bank, Atlanta, Georgia.

EVENTS TO WATCH FOR

How do problem loans come into being? Many things cause a problem loan to develop but there are several events which frequently trigger a problem situation. The alert loan officer will watch for these events and can often anticipate a problem before it occurs or gets out of hand.

1. Major problems can develop in a business when a change in management occurs. The account officer should be on the lookout for difficulty when there is loss of the top executive, keyman, or head sales representative. The company's operations will most likely change somewhat, reflecting the new personality that has entered, and often the change can be for the worse.

2. The lender should also be aware of significant changes in the personal habits of current management. Although unrelated to the business at first, health problems, divorce, death of a close friend or relative, and so on can cause top executives to change habits rapidly in a short period of time. Close and early surveillance of the credit can help an officer gain insight into senior management's normal patterns so that later changes can be more easily detected.

3. Changes in industry trends may directly affect a thriving business so that it can no longer compete profitably. For example, a carpet manufacturer producing woven carpeting may not be prepared for the entrance and gradual acceptance of tufted carpeting on the market. When the consumer-buying trend moves almost exclusively to tufting, demand for the woven variety plunges, causing the company's sales to do likewise. Therefore, the lender should keep informed about the environment of each industry in which his customers operate.

4. Deterioration in the overall economy can turn a good loan into a weak one. During unusual inflation or depression, many companies experience difficulties. During such times the lending officer will usually need to pay extra attention to marginal credits.

5. Rapid expansion in a business often leads to problems. When sales are booming, management often becomes overly ambitious, eager to increase the size of the plant. However, in trying to do too much too fast, management may be unable to cope with the added staff and equipment, and problems set in. It is a responsibility of the account officer to understand what the borrower is doing and help him set a prudent plan for expansion which will allow the company to control growth.

As much as possible, a lender needs to keep an arm's length from the borrower's management so that he may realistically appraise the company and identify potential problems. This is usually harder to do in a small town since the borrower and lender probably know each other on a social basis. However, once an account officer becomes involved with management on a personal basis, there may be a tendency for the officer to see what he thinks he knows rather than the facts as they really are.

EARLY WARNING SIGNS

Several early warning signs can alert an account officer to problems already in existence.

1. The first of these may be a company's delay in furnishing financial information. When statements do not arrive promptly, and the borrower gives repeated excuses and the statements still are not available, problems are probably on their way. Any change from earlier patterns in furnishing financial information should be viewed with a wary eye.

2. From the beginning of the banking relationship, the account officer should know who the company's major trade suppliers are. Should the officer discover that a major supplier is contemplating reducing credit to the customer, or cutting it off entirely, this could be a sign that the borrowing company is facing serious financial difficulties. In medium to larger banks, the credit department may handle credit inquiries from trade suppliers, so that the account officer is unaware that such inquiries had been made. Therefore, close contact with the credit department so as to be kept informed is important.

3. Real value can come from making regular visits to the customer's place of business rather than holding all meetings in the bank. It usually takes an experienced observer to determine precisely how things are going, and the lender will have to work at determining if conditions are slipping. He should observe the general state of repair and maintenance of the plant and equipment, morale of the junior officers and employees, and, of course, the inventory. Since overstated inventory is one way of inflating financial statements, the lender should study the statements to be familiar with the inventory's dollar value and the main categories (either raw material or finished goods). While visiting, it is also a good idea to inspect the larger inventory items as well.

4. Any significant change in the level of balances a company is keeping should alert the lender to a potential problem. While it is not necessary to pry unduly into a company's activities, it is the lender's right and responsibility to keep posted on the borrower's finances by inspecting the deposit account. There may be a satisfactory reason why the account is not being maintained as called for in the loan agreement, but, if so, the account officer should be aware of it.

5. A lender should obtain annual credit reports on each commercial customer. Suits or judgments on file against borrowers may be discov-

ered through such reports. Also, the lending officer needs to be aware of all court proceedings involving the customers, as well as how they pay the trade, and so on. The credit department should send such information to the lending officer as a matter of routine.

FACT FINDING AND RE-EVALUATION

If a credit shows any one or a combination of these warning signals, the account officer should quickly begin an in-bank investigation to determine whether or not a substantial problem exists. In gathering this information, the officer should be extremely careful not to alert the borrower, outside creditors, suppliers, other banks, and so on, to his or her suspicions, but collect all the data possible from internal sources.

The lender may have reviewed the company's financial data many times before, but he should now do so again in light of whatever information led him to suspect a problem. Any internal action which might in some way reveal new data about the company's position should be taken at this point.

If the investigation shows that a company indeed has a serious problem, the next step should be to contact the bank's attorney. It is possible for the lender to reduce legal fees involved by making certain he has conducted a thorough internal investigation and has a good grasp of the situation. The lender can then present the lawyer with a concise, comprehensive written summary of the existing situation, along with a list of the questions to be answered. In addition, all loan documentation should be reviewed with the attorney for accuracy and completeness. The lender's first priority is to protect the bank's interest, and if the loan documentation appears faulty, it should be corrected at once if possible. This is essential if the loan is collateralized. Courthouse records should be also checked to make certain liens are properly recorded.

Having completed the background preparation, the account officer should reevaluate the credit in light of the new information, and prepare a written report assessing the present situation. At this point, another lending officer, usually senior to the one handling the account, should be called upon to review the facts and discuss the different strategies of action for developing a game plan. If the bank proceeds one way, how will the borrower react? In what position will the bank be? If another route is taken, what will the company management's reaction be?

All the foregoing should be done and the bank's plan of action set before the borrower is approached with the problem. Unpleasant as it may be, the situation must be faced squarely and as objectively as possible so that the best course of action can be taken for the good of both the bank and the business.

It may be prudent to move the account from the originating loan officer to another who is not as close to the borrower, or to a "problem loan unit" which may be less reluctant to take any unpleasant steps necessary to protect the bank. Since the originating loan officer should have better insight into the company and its management's capabilities and attitude, this is a difficult decision. Also, the originator will emerge as a better loan officer if he is able to work through the problem himself. Here the old saying applies: "good judgment comes from experience— usually an experience that was a result of bad judgment." Therefore, if the loan officer has not identified too strongly with the borrower, and has been able to prepare a fresh review of the situation as it truly exists, it may be a good idea to let him remain with the account. In any event, a problem loan should have close supervision by a senior officer through the workout period.

CONTINUATION OF THE BUSINESS

At the appropriate time the decision must be made whether to try to keep the company in business or to permit it to liquidate. Based on what the bank knows of the existing management, product and competition, it may be that the situation is temporary and can be overcome in time with the bank's assistance. Perhaps restructuring of debt could ease the strain over the long term. There are, however, certain external factors which may be beyond control of management—for instance, the economy—which must certainly be taken into consideration when deciding whether to continue or liquidate the business.

Even if the problems appear too far gone to remedy, the decision might be to continue the business on an interim basis in order to get the bank's position better established. If there are documentation gaps, and a need to refile in court, it might be wise to keep the company going for at least 120 days in an attempt to avoid actions against the bank for securing unfair preference.

It should be noted that if the bank decided to advance funds to keep the company in operation temporarily, legal advice will be needed before doing so. If a bank advances funds for payroll purposes without advancing sufficient funds to pay the accompanying withholding taxes, the bank may assume the liability of paying the taxes at a later date if the company has not done so. This liability could also be created for the bank if it handles payroll checks by creating an overdraft on the company's account, and the company does not subsequently pay the withholding taxes. Obviously, for protection of the bank, sound legal counsel is advisable.

Liquidation may be inevitable. However, if it would be possible to delay complete liquidation and scale the business down in order to reduce assets, the debt would be lowered, and both the bank and the company could well be in better positions.

Whether from being too highly leveraged or unable to show a profit, a business that has been experiencing difficulty may have already begun a course of action which will deplete some of its assets. If it hasn't, and the decision has been made to keep the business going, temporarily or otherwise, several steps can be taken in an attempt to improve the picture.

The first measure should be to eliminate or reduce every expense possible. Begin at the top. The lender, company president, and advisers should examine the company's expenses line by line to determine those which are absolutely essential. The principals should decide how much they are willing to cut their salaries and personal expenses charged to the company. It should then be made clear to the rest of the staff that all expenses must be kept to the minimum. Naturally, any dividends payments should be stopped at once.

Next, inventory should be reduced and accounts receivable should be analyzed carefully. Methods of handling customer claims for returned and damaged merchandise should be studied. Although receivables generally shrink in liquidation, if credits and claims have not been handled properly, it may be that the receivables were substantially overstated to begin with.

Also, problems may occur if accounts receivable have concentrations. Even if these customers are financially strong, they will frequently claim rather large credits due them. For this reason, no more than 20–25 percent of a company sales volume should be to a single customer, and even this is a high percentage.

Next, any idle equipment or plants not essential to current operations should be disposed of. The lender should look at production techniques to see if he can offer objective suggestions which might improve the product or the profit margins.

To improve the cash flow, the company's payments should be analyzed to determine which are not required by contract and could be deferred. Perhaps some of the accounts payable can be postponed. If debt of current maturity can be extended and/or subordinated to bank debt, this also could be helpful.

Finally, the lending officer should discuss with management the possibility of obtaining new equity capital from officers or other sources.

Keeping a financially fragile company in business requires not only diligent effort on the part of lending officers, but often creativity and ingenuity as well. Although generally tried and true guidelines can be applied in most situations, each credit is different and the workout plan must be tailor-made to obtain the best results possible for all parties involved.

In most situations, lenders prefer to keep borrowers out of bankruptcy. Notwithstanding the emotional distress of the proceedings, they involve actions in federal courts and are expensive for everyone. Therefore, if the borrower and his or her creditors can cooperate in solving the problem, all parties will benefit. However, any time the lender feels that the borrower is trying to defraud the bank, conceal assets, or carry assets away, it would be wise to take legal action regardless of the debt outstanding that might otherwise be salvaged.

LIQUIDATION OF THE BUSINESS

If liquidation appears to be the only course open to the bank, there are several alternative ways to proceed. Before the lender can act in this regard, however, the borrower must be in default on some part of the bank debt instrument, or the note would have to be due.

If liquidation is decided upon, the bank should immediately bring in those professional resources, such as attorneys and accountants, needed to help protect its position.

Next, the lender should be certain he has all the collateral on the business he can possibly obtain. Remember, however, that although banks can take any security available for debt previously contracted, the effect that taking it can have on other creditors must be considered. For example, obtaining an inventory lien may scare trade suppliers into cutting off the source of supplies the company must have to continue functioning.

If debt is owed to officers, affiliates, or subsidiaries of the company, it may be possible to subordinate it to bank debt. Not only should the lender attempt to get the debt subordinated, but he should try to induce officers, affiliates, or subsidiaries to guarantee the bank debt, obtaining a pledge of the note to secure the guarantee. It is best to show the subordination on the face of the note, keeping the note in the bank to make certain it does not get transferred to an innocent party who might become a holder in due course.

It may be worth additional dollars to the bank to purchase senior liens from other creditors. The lender should also keep in mind that the right of offset may be applicable in liquidation; however, advice should be sought from the bank's attorney before applying it.

In some circumstances, the lender may agree to compromise the bank's debt. For example, a company may owe the bank $100,000. Complete liquidation of the assets may yield $75,000. If the officers are willing to sell personal assets yielding another $10,000, the bank may decide to accept the $85,000 as sufficient payment of the obligation, and dismiss the remaining $15,000 owed.

A borrower who is financially embarrassed may decide to call a meeting of creditors to inform them of the existing situation. Often, these meetings are hastily arranged and not carefully thought out, and little is accomplished. If a lender learns that the borrower is close to calling a meeting of creditors, he should immediately attempt to meet with the borrower, along with the attorneys from each side. Assuming the borrower will cooperate, the banker can then assist in planning a concrete, viable plan of action to present to creditors.

It may be that liquidation will take the form of an informal settlement between the company and its creditors. The assets will be sold and the proceeds distributed among the creditors based on an agreement approved by all parties involved. Liquidation can also be accomplished through a formal assignment of assets to a third party responsible for liquidating them and distributing the proceeds. The advantages to these methods, formal or informal, are speed, efficiency, and lower cost.

Election of Bankruptcy

The borrower, however, may not wish to follow any of these paths, and may elect instead to file for voluntary bankruptcy or reorganization. If either of these paths is chosen, the situation should be followed closely by the bank's legal counsel.

In many problem loan situations, the company is not willing to voluntarily declare bankruptcy, therefore the creditors may wish to petition the court to force the business to take this step. To do this requires three or more creditors with claims aggregating a minimum of $500 to join together and allege insolvency on the part of their debtor. Or one creditor may prove that an "act of bankruptcy" has been committed by the company.

Acts of bankruptcy involve certain steps taken by a business which give rights to legal action on the part of creditors. Any meeting of creditors that is called by the debtor, for instance, is considered to be an act of bankruptcy.

When creditors attempt to force involuntary bankruptcy, the company in debt has a right to contest the petition and to receive a trial before a jury.

Whatever path is chosen to work out the company's debt problem, the lender must be careful to carry all steps to a logical conclusion. Loose ends can generate further losses or the possibility of legal action against the bank.

SUMMARY

Clearly, bankruptcy in any form is not a pleasant experience for the debtor or the lender. Many bankruptcies could be avoided, or their impact reduced, however, if bank lending officers followed a few guidelines in dealing with their commercial customers.

By knowing and frequently servicing the borrower, potential problems can be recognized early. Regular plant visits keep the account officer in touch with the company so that he or she can observe how it is actually operating. Complete and careful analysis of the business and its principals can help him learn the facts about all aspects of the business and its management. Diligence in obtaining and perfecting security agreements is important when the loan is made, as well as later if inadequacies in documentation are discovered. Proper use of attorneys and accountants can minimize legal problems throughout the entire relationship. And, if a problem develops and persists regardless of the lender's close attention, the courage to take unpopular actions with the debtor may reduce the ultimate damage to all parties involved.

SECTION VIII

SPECIAL CREDIT AREAS

Chapter 47

Seasonal and Revolving Credit Arrangements

William H. Sayre*

A business concern has two major financing needs, working capital, those funds necessary to finance the seasonal needs of a business' working capital cycle; and capital expansion or replacement which requires funds over a longer period of time. Lines of credit are best used for the seasonal needs of a business due to their generally informal nature while revolving credit arrangements which sometimes fund into term loans, are used to support capital expansion or in certain cases to fund past expenditures which have depleted cash and therefore, decreased working capital.

The use of the line of credit or revolving credit is not mutually exclusive of the many other factors used in determining whether to extend under either form when granting credit. In fact, often, banks will extend both to the same borrower. Under the revolving credit, obviously due to the term characteristic, there may be greater financial risk. The banking industry has undergone considerable change in the last 20 years. In the past, lines of credit were usually made available to concerns which had shown a historical ability to be totally out of bank debt yearly and whose growth pattern was stable. Inflation and technical obsolescence were minor factors. Therefore, one could look for liquidation of assets or call on a secondary financial lender to take over the financing. Today, one must look at a concern's ability to earn a *cash* profit over a period of time. One has read of numerous examples in recent times of businesses which have collapsed or are workout

---

* Executive Vice President, The Fidelity Bank, Philadelphia, Pennsylvania.

situations because while a book profit or modest loss was recorded, there was a substantial cash drain. Certain REITS, Grants, and Equity Funding appear to be extreme examples where earnings were shown but cash profit was not.

THE WORKING CAPITAL CYCLE

Each company has a definite working capital cycle which parallels the concern's manufacturing, stocking, and selling cycle. Some companies have more than one cycle a year usually dependent on the number of selling seasons. Some cycles may be so short that the need for financing is continuous because of an overlap. For example, a textbook or religious book publisher begins his printing process in the late winter continuing through early summer for delivering to wholesalers and schools in the late summer. It then collects the receivables in the fall, collecting orders in the fall and winter, and begins a new printing cycle in the spring. The firm might also have a smaller printing run in the fall for the spring semester. A clothing or shoe manufacturer has two definite working capital cycles. The first is to manufacture winter clothing or shoes in the spring for sale over the summer to enable retailers to have new winter stock. In late summer and fall the same manufacturer will be manufacturing goods to be sold in late winter to the same retailer for its spring selling season. An example of the selling cycle being so short that there is an overlap in the working capital cycle causing almost a constant need for funds is in certain sectors of the agricultural industry. In both the produce and fowl sectors where the selling cycle may occur three, four, or more times a year, the need for working capital financing is almost constant because the seller is collecting receivables at the same time he or she is beginning the new planting or growing season.

What is important to keep in mind is that each company and each industry does have a manufacturing-selling cycle, and hence, a working capital cycle.

SEASONAL LINES OF CREDIT

A significant portion of a bank's commercial loan portfolio is in the form of lines of credit granted to business concerns to enable the concern to finance the expanded part of their seasonal selling and manufacturing cycle. A line of credit is a commitment by a bank to a business concern for a certain sum of money whereby the borrower may borrow, repay, reborrow any sum under the commitment for a given period of time. Lines of credit are generally granted by the financial institution for a period of one year. In addition to the amount, there is an understanding as to the rate of interest charged, which usually varies with the bank's best lending rate and compensating balances to be maintained. Compensating balances will be further discussed under "Pricing."

Funds borrowed under a line of credit are generally used to pay labor, suppliers, and other incidental costs while the concern goes through its manufacturing and selling cycle which necessitates the carrying of higher inventories and receivables until the goods are sold, receivables collected and converted into cash. The company's peak borrowing needs therefore should coincide with its production-selling cycle peak. When the cycle is at its low point, there should be more than sufficient cash funds to rest the line of credit (repay all borrowings) and provide cash to maintain plant and production at the lower cyclical level.

Earlier, a line of credit was described as being a commitment between the bank and the borrower. Many people refer to a line of credit as an informal arrangement. However, over the years some courts have taken the view that the arrangement is not informal, but formal, even though the arrangement may be only an oral understanding or simple letter with no formal acceptance by the borrower. In certain cases, the courts have held that a business concern has been injured when it committed to purchase inventory on the basis of a line of credit only to find the line was no longer available. Therefore, when extending a line of credit to a customer or prospect, one must be sure of the concern's financial stability.

The use of lines of credit has been expanded to act also as an insurance facility to business concerns which have access to the commercial paper market. This market, as previously explained in Chapter 37, is where large, financially strong corporations have access to a pool of investors who are willing to invest in specific short-term notes issued by certain financially strong corporations for a period of less than nine months. These investors usually require that there be lines of credit from banking institutions in an amount sufficient to refinance the commercial paper issued if there are not enough investors in the marketplace to refinance the commercial paper coming due. These lines of credit issued by the banks are known as backup lines or secondary and tertiary lines. The bank receives either a compensating balance or a fee for providing this commitment. A recent development is to provide the issuing corporation with a two-year line of credit commitment. This permits the corporation to carry its commercial paper borrowings, which are always issued for periods less than nine months on the issuing corporation's balance sheet, as long-term indebtedness since there is a definite commitment from banks to underwrite the financing for a period greater than a year. Even though this is a firm two-year commitment, it is discussed under lines of credit because there is seldom more than a simple letter agreement (often without typical loan agreement covenants) between the borrower and bank and the purpose of the commercial paper is generally to finance working capital requirements. The combination of the commercial paper rate plus cost of carrying compensating balances is almost always less than borrowing at the bank's rate (commonly known as prime) plus required balances.

Over the last decade the financial markets have become far more sophisticated. Both the corporate investor, such as companies with excess cash, pension funds, and mutual funds, and the corporate borrower have found ways to do business directly without using the banks as an intermediary. This is generally done through the issuance of commercial paper which is nothing more than an IOU from a corporation sold by a broker in the marketplace. The dramatic growth of this market has substantially changed the mix of the loan portfolio in a commercial bank. The portfolio mix of line of credit commitments fall into two categories: first, a line of credit to a creditworthy borrower who will maintain deposit balances with the bank or pay a fee in support of the line but who will only borrow when *(a)* the commercial paper market investors disappear or *(b)* when the interest cost of commercial paper exceeds the cost of borrowing at the bank. The second category of line of credit users is the customer who does not have access to any other borrowing source but banks. The bank must be prepared to serve both types of borrowers but usually serves the former only in times of difficult market conditions. The bank must be sure to have its own availability of funds in order to meet its commitments particularly to those companies which do not have access to public markets in times of financial stress.

REVOLVING CREDIT ARRANGEMENTS

A revolving credit arrangement is a formal binding agreement between a business concern and a financial institution whereby the financial institution agrees to hold available a certain sum of money which may be borrowed, repaid, and reborrowed usually over a period of several years. Two- and three-year terms are most common; longer terms are not unknown. In return, the concern pays a commitment fee for this privilege (usually one half of 1 percent) and further agrees to certain terms and conditions pertaining to its method of operation and financial condition. Often a revolving credit will fund into a pre-approved term loan at the termination date of the revolver. Revolving credits came into being when corporations desired to have a guaranteed source of funds during a capital expansion program where the total cost of the project is uncertain. The corporation found this advantageous despite having to pay a commitment fee and not knowing the actual interest cost because unlike a bond issue where one would have to borrow the funds now and, then, use the funds as they were needed, therefore being forced to invest the excess funds at a lower return, the concern could borrow the funds as needed and when the project was complete, go to the long-term market for an amount equivalent to the final cost of the project. The company at that time also has a better feel for how well the new or expanded project is operating and whether additional long-term funds ought to be raised because it took longer to get operating in such a manner as to contribute to the profitability or cash flow of the company. The use of the revolving credit arrangement by business concerns has greatly expanded, accelerated by the recent money crunch. In addition to being used for capital expansion, revolvers are now being used to finance longer term working capital needs, acquisitions, and backup facilities for the issuance of letters of credit to support commercial paper borrowings. One, however, still finds the major users of revolving credits to be the capital intensive industries, such as the airlines, utilities, trucking, and extractive mining and coal, where there is a constant revolving need to finance long-term assets which individually would logically be financed by term loans.

A revolving credit arrangement therefore should be viewed by the loan officer as if he or she were extending a term credit. The analysis required is much more complex and requires among other things, a thorough look into the long-term future prospects of the company itself, its relationship within its industry, whether the company or the industry could be forced into a competitive disadvantage due to style, technological, or environmental factors. Earnings and cash flow capabilities of the concern become very important in determining the ability to repay since repayment in most cases is not from the liquidation of assets. A company requesting a revolver is particularly difficult to analyze because there is no known repayment schedule except at maturity or when it eventually funds into a pre-arranged term loan. The sum of the borrowings is uncertain and many times, less than the committed amount is borrowed. This forces one to look at the worst case scenarios in evaluating the risk.

When a bank extends a revolving credit accommodation, it is granting a credit accommodation available over a period of time. Therefore, for both the benefit of the bank and the customer, a formal loan agreement should be prepared. In addition to the amount, term, interest rate, and purpose, the agreement should have various covenants outlining certain standards the company will meet during the lifetime of the accommodation. Below are listed a sampling of what might be included. It by no means is all-inclusive and one should include others depending on the borrower or circumstances.

Working capital.	Maintain a certain level of current assets over current liabilities.
Dividends.	A restriction on the amount of dividends paid.
Capital expenditures.	Limitation on monies used to purchase plant and equipment.
Insurance.	Company agrees to maintain certain levels and types of insurance—including fire, casualty, work interruption, liability, directors' insurance, etc.
Lines of business.	Limitations placed on borrower as it regards mergers, acquisitions, disposing of assets or materially changing its method of operation.
Indebtedness.	Limitation on the amount of funds borrowed from other sources.

PRICING

The post-World War II period has witnessed major changes in the commercial banking system that have permanently altered the profitability structure of commercial bank lending. In responding to these changes bankers have, especially during the last five to ten years, devised a variety of new pricing techniques. In all probability, the pricing of bank loans and commitments will continue to evolve. The hallmark of this evolution will be variety and flexibility for the borrower. Competition and a changing regulatory climate will continue as major influences. An understanding of the changes during the last 30 years will help us understand the current state of the art and the essential elements of future pricing systems.

Interest, deposit balances, and fees have always constituted the income side of any lending relationship. It is only in more recent years, however, that fees have received their due attention. The reason for the increased attention is easily understood. For many years, corporate customers maintained their deposit balances at their major bank or banks. The level of balances was dictated more by existing funds than by any plans to restrict the balances to a level commensurate with services rendered by the depository bank. Interest rates were too low to compensate for the effort necesary to "manage" cash. When a customer wished to borrow (and it was usually short term) the rate was set based on market rates that were relatively stable. There was no real need to measure the depositor's balances since, first, they were usually substantial and, second, they were often all the cash the customer maintained anywhere. Even with low-interest rates the banks had a sure formula for success. Loans and investments were funded primarily with demand deposits, which paid no interest, and to a lesser extent with low-rate savings accounts. Two events disturbed the banker's comfortable life and foreshadowed the highly sophisticated and competitive pricing arrangements prevalent today: higher interest rates and formalized cash management services. Higher rates made it worthwhile for the corporate treasurer to invest the "excess" balances previously maintained in bank accounts and a growing commercial paper market provided a ready vehicle for short-term investment. At the same time, bankers were busy educating treasurers in how to reduce the excess balances at the "other banks" in order to concentrate them at their own banks. A little knowledge proved to be a dangerous thing with the inevitable result that "excess" deposit balances were reduced at all banks. For the first time bankers had to question whether their borrowers were maintaining "appropriate" balances (which somehow came to be 20 percent of borrowings).

The banks certainly appreciated the value of idle money since they had become substantial purchasers of the very investment funds which had previously been interest-free bank deposits. With these funds, banks could expand loan volume more rapidly. It is true banks were borrowing short and increasingly lending long but by having the loan rate float this risk was eliminated. The banks were now in a spread business, and a very attractive business it was since a seemingly limitless quantity of funds could be purchased and then loaned out at a spread. The only limit on profits was the speed with which the business development officer (nee loan officer) could lend funds to borrowers. Liability management was the new formula for success, the alchemy that would turn leaden money into golden profits.

In the 1970s, very high-interest rates and tight money conspired to present a new problem; namely, availability of funds. Banks were forced to ration credit and in many cases did so on the basis of deposit balances maintained by corporate customers. Corporate treasurers and bankers finally realized that banks' unique service was not money but its guaranteed availability. Bankers began formalizing their charges for commitments and the old rubric of 20 percent balances on borrowings was changed to 10 percent on commitment plus 10 percent on borrowings. With the principle of charging for a commitment formalized (with help from the SEC disclosure requirements regarding compensating balances), the competitive market proceeded to devise a variety of ways for companies to pay for credit services. The common thread running through all new pricing schemes was the total yield concept. It is in terms of this total yield that most pricing is today measured.

The yield concept recognized two important facts. First, the pricing arrangement for credit includes a charge for availability and a charge for usage. Second, the yield to the bank (and cost to the customer) is a function of both the amount of usage and the three elements of compensation (rate, balances, and fees). If a customer borrows $1,000 at 8 percent interest with a 20 percent compensation balance, that customer is in effect paying $80 interest for the use of $800 or 10 percent. The real cost (and the real yield to the bank if one ignores, for simplicity, reserve requirements and if one assumes a loan is funded in part with the borrower's compensating balances) is, therefore, 125 percent of the stated or nominal interest rate. By pricing on a yield basis the lender could finally agree to relinquish the compensating balance requirement and still protect his earnings by charging a straight rate. A 125 percent of prime would always produce a yield equivalent to prime with 20 percent compensating balances. Similarly, 10 percent compensating balances and a rate of 114 percent of prime would always equate to 125 percent of prime. By knowing the total yield derived from rate and balances (and fees as well), the lender or borrower could compute the increase needed in one element of the price in order to offset a decrease in another. The amount of usage of a commitment became important in measuring the yield on funds actually borrowed because payment was being made for unused availability. If a commitment priced at any rate (fixed or floating) plus compensating balances equal to 10 percent of the commitment plus 10 percent of borrowings is used only 50 percent, actual compensating balances will equal 30 percent of borrowings. The actual yield will be equal to 142.8 percent of the stated rate rather than the 125 percent of the stated rate which results if the commitment is fully borrowed. Likewise, the yield on funds borrowed increases if there is a commitment fee on the unused portion of the commitment. The generalized rule is that where a customer is charged (fees or balances) for the unused portion of a commitment, the yield on funds actually borrowed increases as the usage under the commitment decreases. Banks have now realized that they can reduce the pricing structure (e.g., from a balance requirement of 10 percent on commitment plus 10 percent on borrowings to 5 percent on commitment plus 15 percent on borrowings) and still maintain an adequate yield on borrowings by contractually limiting the average usage (e.g., to 50 percent of the commitment).

Probably the major change in pricing is the practice of charging borrowers a fee in lieu of balances or deficient balance fee. The fee (which is charged retrospectively) is computed by multiplying the amount by which balances are short of the requirement under the agreed-upon pricing times an interest rate. In order to maintain the total yield indicated by the pricing of the commitment, the rate used for such computations should be the yield rate at the actual usage level. In many cases, however, banks have computed these fees at lower rates (e.g., Federal funds rate, prime rate, stated loan rate). The knowledgeable lender will also address the questions of how frequently to bill these fees and how long the excess balances in one period will be allowed to be carried forward to offset deficiencies in another period.

This discussion would not be complete without a brief mention of "double counting" of deposit balances—a malevolent practice banks are finally abandoning. It goes without saying that the whole thrust of pricing commitments and loans today is to charge for all services rendered. Therefore, compensating balances used to support credit facilities should be the collected balances remaining after deducting sufficient collected balances to service deposit activity charges.

Pricing of bank loans has been and will continue to be a function of risk, term, and competition. The most significant changes that have taken place are in two areas. The first is the recognition that banks should charge for both the availability of credit (commitment) and the usage (borrowings). Second, bankers have realized that overall profitability or yield is a function of rate, balances and fees and that these three elements are interchangeable, even retrospectively, as long as the lender is wise enough to quote *and to enforce* pricing as a total yield.

Chapter 48 _____

Secured Lending

Ken L. Lott*

Robert G. Myers†

The purpose of this chapter is twofold. First, an attempt will be made to reduce the broad and diverse subject matter of secured lending into some of its simplest common denominators and from these, to develop some practical guidelines which can be applied to most secured transactions. Second, an attempt will be made to review some of the more important areas in secured lending not covered elsewhere in the handbook. The following topics will be discussed at some length: loans secured by inventory, accounts receivable, stocks and bonds, and similar collateral. In addition, the subjects to be discussed more briefly are: loans secured by cash value of life insurance, petroleum, ship mortgages, and aircraft.

Before we discuss secured lending, perhaps it is appropriate to examine Webster's definition of collateral: "related to but not strictly a part of the main thing or matter under consideration." In terms of banking it is obvious from looking at the definition that the main thing or matter under consideration is the loan and the collateral is that which is related to it. Even though good lending policy and strict adherence to the fundamentals of credit foster sound loans, collateral is an inept substitute for either. While space permits only a cursory examination of lending policy and the basics of credit, any discussion of lending that fails to consider these essentials would be fruitless.

_____
* President, Merchants National Bank of Mobile, Mobile, Alabama.

† Vice President, Merchants National Bank of Mobile, Mobile, Alabama.

GENERAL CONSIDERATIONS

Prudence in lending requires critical self-examination. A wise lender knows his or her own limitations, seeks advice when necessary, and seldom makes the same mistake twice. Lending policy should evolve only after careful consideration has been given to the bank's management, organization, trade area, objectives, history, markets, lending personnel, loan portfolio, experience in various fields, areas of expertise and problem areas. The product of this consideration and its subsequent follow-up should be guidelines which promote sound loans and eliminate many unnecessary risks. Some key elements relating to secured lending which should be covered by loan policy are:

1. Types of collateral considered desirable and undesirable.
2. Margin requirements for different types of collateral.
3. Term of loans for each type of collateral.
4. Interest rate.
5. Method of determining and documenting the value of collateral.
6. Documentation standards.
7. Procedures for handling each type of loan.

We have all been exposed to this old axiom in one form or another, "Collateral cannot make a bad loan good but it can make a good loan better." On the other hand, adherence to the basics of credit is the best way to ensure that the lender starts first with a good loan. A few moments to analyze the following questions will often reveal an unsound loan:

1. Are the borrower's character, reputation, and ability satisfactory?
2. What is the purpose of the loan?
3. Will the loan benefit both the borrower and the lender?
4. How, when, and from what source will the loan be repaid?
5. Is the capital of the borrower adequate?
6. Is the loan practical considering the above questions and all of the other factors which must be considered?

Admittedly, secured lending came about partly in recognition of the fact that some borrowers fail to meet all of the criteria necessary for unsecured financing. The tool of secured lending can be effectively used to compensate to a certain extent for some deficiencies, such as temporary shortages of working capital or of inadequate capital. It can never serve as a substitute for character and ability. A secured loan should never be made to permit a borrower to acquire collateral if selling the collateral is the only source of repayment.

Risk is inherent in lending, and a banker's ability to recognize and deal effectively with it gets right to the essence of lending. Secured lending then should serve as a vehicle to enable one to reduce risks to an acceptable level so that banks can better fulfill their responsibilities to their customers, communities, shareholders, and employees. The reduction of risks to an acceptable level is the principal function of collateral. When a secured loan is properly handled, collateral values should always exceed loan balances so that the lender never loses the option of liquidating collateral if necessary. In theory, this seems quite simple but experience soon proves that it is easier said than done. A logical and systematic approach to each secured transaction can however, assist the lender in minimizing the risks associated with secured lending. One approach is to divide each secured transaction into four phases. First, the value of the collateral should be established and the proper margin determined. The second step is to control and evaluate the collateral throughout the life of the credit. Third, the lender must perfect a security interest in the collateral, and last, but most important, he or she must review the overall credit on a regular basis.

Four Phases in Secured Lending

Let us take a moment to further discuss these four areas. Establishing the value of certain types of collateral can in itself be a very difficult process; in fact, it is impossible in some cases. For instance, what is the value of a specialized electronic component, an inventory represented by a new product not yet marketed, or a disputed account receivable? The term *value,* for purposes of this discussion, means the dollar amount the *lender* would receive upon liquidating the collateral within a reasonable period of time. There is a definite distinction between the lender's selling collateral under a distressed situation and the borrower's selling collateral under ordinary circumstances. One should also bear in mind that, while some items have value, their marketability is limited and it may take years to dispose of some forms of collateral. If the value of the collateral cannot be established, the safest course is to decline the extension of credit or look for an alternate method of handling the loan. If collateral values can be established with a reasonable degree of accuracy, the question of a proper margin must be addressed. A proper margin should protect the lender from possible fluctuations in collateral values, the lower price that will normally prevail in a liquidation situation, carrying costs, selling expenses, attorney's fees, and other contingencies.

The process of controlling and evaluating collateral over a period of time depends upon the type of collateral involved. Each presents its own peculiar and often interesting problems to be dealt with by the lender. The objective is to know at all times how much collateral exists, its location, and its value. Since each type of collateral requires its own consideration, this subject will be discussed in connection with each specific form.

The Uniform Commercial Code which is now in effect in all states except Louisiana has gone a long way toward simplifying the legal aspects of most secured transactions. It should be pointed out however, that the Codes enacted by the various states differ in some respects and as of July 1976, 16 states had the 1972 Revised Code. Most of the topics discussed in subsequent paragraphs are subject to the Code, so a discussion of some of the basic provisions and terminology might be appropriate. Basically, what the lender looks for is a perfected security interest. This means in simple terms that the lender has rights in collateral that will be valid against the borrower, his or her creditors, and third parties. Actually, there are several steps in obtaining a perfected security interest.

In most transactions, it is necesary to begin by obtaining a security agreement. This is the contract between the borrower and the lender in which the debtor assigns his specific property to the creditor as collateral for the loan, and in which the lender agrees that he does not own the property and that the collateral is taken only to secure the repayment of a loan. The creditor's security interest attaches to the specified collateral only upon meeting three conditions as specified in Article 9 in the Uniform Commercial Code: "a security interest cannot attach until there is agreement that it attach and value is given and the debtor has rights in the collateral. It attaches as soon as all of the events in the preceding sentence have taken place unless explicit agreement postpones the time of attaching." Of course, the key elements in this definition are:

1. The creditor must give value.
2. The debtor must have rights in the collateral.
3. Both parties must agree that the creditor is to have a security interest in the collateral. Section 9–203 in part provides that a security interest is not enforceable against the debtor or third parties unless: The collateral is in the possession of the secured party or the debtor has signed a security agreement.

Once these conditions have been complied with, the creditor will have obtained a security interest in or lien against the borrower's collateral. The other essential aspect is that the creditor also wants his position perfected against the borrower's other creditors and third parties. To perfect a security interest, the lender normally files a financing statement with the secretary of state, probate officer, or other office of appropriate jurisdiction or perfects his security interest by maintaining possession of the collateral. The Code's general rule of priority is of utmost importance since it provides, with certain exceptions mention in Section 9–312, that the creditor with the earliest perfected security interest has priority over the other creditors. A lender should always ascertain the existence of prior perfected security interests and if there are none, perfect his security interest promptly. A basic working knowledge of the Code is essential in the field of security lending. However, many difficult questions are best left to the legal profession. When a lender is unsure of his position, it is always advisable to consult an attorney.

The fourth and final step is to review the overall credit on a regular basis. This step is extremely important and can prevent many problems by detecting adverse trends early enough so that remedial action can be taken. Every banker has an obligation to be as knowledgeable as possible about the customer's business and to give a borrower the benefit of his advice. Often a little counseling at an early stage is all that is needed. This is certainly a better solution than liquidation. If the review process is regular, thorough, objective, and if the results of the review are considered by the lending officer and followed up, it will serve its purpose. Some of the questions which need to be asked are:

1. Has there been any significant change in management?
2. Are audited financial statements received on a regular and timely basis?
3. Have the statements been carefully analyzed and compared internally, with industry averages, and with consideration for any adverse trends either in the balance sheet or operating statements?
4. What has been the trend in depository balances in the bank?
5. How are trade obligations being handled?
6. Has the plant site been visited and an inspection of collateral made?
7. Is the borrower adhering to the repayment schedule?
8. Is the interest rate fair and adequate?
9. What are current economic, industrial, and competitive situations?
10. Do margins need revision?

INVENTORY LOANS

Article 9–109(4) of the Uniform Commercial Code defines goods as inventory "if they are held by a person who holds them for sale or lease or to be furnished under contracts of service or if he has so furnished them, or if they are raw materials, work in process or materials used or consumed in a business. Inventory of a person is not to be classified as his equipment." It is obvious in looking at this definition that we are talking about a broad subject area ranging from the financing of manufacturing inventories to wholesaling and retailing inventories as well as the infinite variety of different goods which could constitute inventory.

Inventory financing is one of the most difficult and troublesome areas for many lenders. Experience, special staff, and a great deal of expertise are necessary in many applications. Why is inventory lending so difficult? First, as has been already mentioned, no lender can be familiar with all of the various types of inventory he might consider financing. Inventory, being a trading asset, can constantly change from raw materials to finished products to receivables to cash. Most inventory loans result in term loans even if evidenced by short-term or demand notes. If it is a term loan, it is subjected additionally to the uncertainties which time always creates. Banks for many years have successfully engaged in the classic type of inventory lending, a short-term loan against a high level of inventory which is due primarily to seasonal factors with repayment coming from the cash generated by a reduction of inventory to normal levels.

It is in other areas as well that difficulty has been experienced, principally when loans against inventory have been made to growth companies, to companies with inadequate capital and/or working capital, or to companies in conjunction with an accounts receivable loan. In addition, inventory is often taken as additional collateral to shore up an already deteriorated credit situation. Except in the case of an inventory loan in which repayment comes from the reduction of an asset, the lender is looking to the profits and depreciation of the business for repayment. As in most inventory financing situations, it is unrealistic to place much confidence in the other two sources of repayment: the injection of new capital, or transfer of the debt to another lender. This is a basic point every lender recognizes but at some time has overlooked. Repayment plans should be based on accurate cash flow projections and should take into consideration the relationship that must exist between sales or cost of sales and inventory in a going concern.

Establishing Value

Perhaps the process of establishing the value and determining the proper margin for an inventory loan can best be illustrated with a simple and somewhat hypothetical example. The process involves establishing what quantity of inventory is on hand, its composition, whether it is and will continue to be marketable and at what price, and how much liquidation expense is involved. Let us use as an example a small food processor. The company is relatively new, undercapitalized and has a working capital shortage. However, the prospects for this company seem to be exceptionally bright. We have first considered the bank's lending policy and all of the basic credit fundamentals and believe that the loan will be sound if properly secured. The analysis in Exhibit 48–1 is used to arrive at the value of the collateral and a proper margin.

In this particular example, a loan of $95,000 could be justified. This would be an advance of roughly 67 percent of the borrower's cost of $142,750 or 84 percent of estimated value. A review of the major factors considered in arriving at these figures is necessary.

1. *Quantity.* The quantities of raw materials, work-in-process and finished product are determined by a physical inventory conducted by the lender. It is always advisable for the lender to perform the inventory rather than relying on the borrower.
2. *Composition, Mix, and Quality.* The physical inventory revealed that the major items of inventory were raw materials and finished products. Lump crabmeat and mixed crabmeat made up the bulk of raw materials. Work-in-process in this particular example is a minor item. As a general rule, raw materials and finished products have better marketability and liquidating values than work-in-process. In this example, no value is assigned to the smaller items of raw materials as well as work-in-process, since it is usually desirable to base an inventory loan only on the major items of inventory.
3. *Present Marketability.* Raw crabmeat is readily marketable through wholesale channels and its price can be established through brokers and various publications. Since it can be sold on a wholesale market, liquidation could be accomplished rapidly. The packing cartons are assigned no value since they are for a special application and probably cannot be sold. Raw crabmeat can be sold at the prevailing wholesale price, the price used as the unit value. The finished product is assigned a value of 50 percent of the current selling price. The product is compared with competitive products in terms of price and quality. Food brokers and retailers are consulted and their opinions considered in arriving at the estimated liquidation price. Consideration was given to the fact that selling price represents cost and profit in a going concern and when a liquidation occurs that the borrower is usually not covering cost. It is estimated that 45 day's sales are on hand and liquidation can be accomplished in 90 days.
4. *Seasonal Characteristics.* Raw crabmeat is purchased on a seasonal basis but is sold frozen throughout the year. Its sale should present no problems. The finished product has slightly seasonal characteristics but not enough to delay a sale within 90 days. Cau-

Exhibit 48–1
Establishing Value of Collateral and Margin

Item	Quantity	Unit Cost or Price	Borrower's Cost	Estimated Value	Liquidation Expense	Estimated Value Less Liquidation Expense
Raw Materials:						
Lump crabmeat.....	10,000 lbs.	Retail: $4.25 per lb. Wholesale: 3.25 per lb. Cost: 3.20 per lb.	$ 32,000	$ 32,500	$ 1,500 (brokerage fee)	$31,000
Mixed crabmeat.....	10,000 lbs.	Retail: $3.80 per lb. Wholesale: 3.00 per lb. Cost: 2.95 per lb.	29,500	30,000	$ 1,500 (brokerage fee)	28,500
Celery, onions bell peppers, etc....	50 cases	$100 per case	5,000	0	0	0
Spices.............	10 cases	$75 per case	750	0	0	0
Cartons...........	20 cases	$125 per case	2,500	0	0	0
Work-in-Process:						
A mixture of the above	Miscellaneous	$3,000 (cost)	3,000	0	0	0
Finished Product:	10,000 cases	$100 per case (selling price) $70 per case (borrower's cost) $50 per case (estimated liquidating price)	70,000	50,000	$ 5,000 (brokerage fee) 300 (insurance) 500 (storage) $ 8,000 (contingency for price fluctuation) 700 (attorney's fees)	44,200
Totals........			$142,750	$112,500	$17,500	(8,700) $95,000

tion was exercised to determine that no held-over seasonal inventory was on hand.

5. *Price Stability.*   Reliable information indicates that the wholesale price of raw crabmeat fluctuates within a range of 80 cents per pound. An allowance of 40 cents per pound has been made for price fluctuation.

6. *Perishability and Obsolescence.*   All of the major items of the inventory are perishable. The premises are well suited for storage and the inventory is well insured with the lender named as loss payee. The inventory will not be subject to physical deterioration unless stored for one year or more.

7. *Cost to Liquidate.*   Selling, storage, and insurance costs, as well as attorney's fees have been provided for. Note that the estimated liquidating cost of raw crabmeat is very low since it can be sold on an established market whereas the finished product cannot, and additional selling expense is involved.

Even though this example is an oversimplification, it nevertheless demonstrates that, with a little analysis, the lender can determine with a reasonable degree of accuracy the value of many types of inventories.

If initially we are satisfied that we can adequately establish the value of the inventory and have determined a proper margin then we move on to the question of how to properly control the inventory.

Systems of Control

The systems of control in banking today range from a blanket assignment of inventory to financing under warehouse receipt. Every banker who has handled an inventory loan simply relying on a blanket assignment of inventory has probably found himself in the same position as the author: going out to a failing borrower's premises with hopes of collecting a loan through the sale of the inventory, finding no inventory there, and subsequently writing off the loan. Perhaps the only place that a blanket assignment of inventory and proceeds is appropriate is in connection with an accounts receivable loan which otherwise stands on its own, or is being taken as additional collateral to an already weak loan. One step removed from the blanket assignment is an inventory loan where the lender relies on the borrower to furnish a report of inventory on hand on some regular basis. The lender then makes advances based on a given percentage of the borrower's reported inventory. This method, although not recommended, can work satisfactorily if the borrower remains honest and the accounting procedures are adequate. Good financial statements and at least a yearly audit add some support to this method of handling inventory loans. The major disadvantages are that the lender must rely on the borrower for the inventory reports, and usually these reports do not contain sufficient details for an accurate monitoring of inventory composition or of quality and mix and the true character of a borrower is not really tested until he is faced with adverse circumstances.

If an inventory loan is properly supervised, much of the risk can be eliminated. Let us first look at the usual steps involved in properly supervising an inventory loan without warehousing and, second, one with warehousing. As previously mentioned, many inventory loans without warehousing require a good deal of experience and a specialized staff. Probably out of the more than 14,000 commercial banks, only the largest 150–200 banks could justify the expense of maintaining a separate department and staff for handling this type of loan. This is not to say that smaller banks cannot successfully master this type of financing, but it requires diligence, some experience, and a lot of extra work for the job to be properly done.

The first step is a complete and systematic review of the borrower's accounting system and procedures. If any deficiencies are found, the borrower will be required to correct them and then a reporting system set up. The borrower then submits regular reports to the lender based on an agreed-upon system. A thorough initial physical inventory is conducted by the lender and any additional corrections called for on the borrower's books are made. After this has been done, the next major task is a periodic physical audit by the lender. Normally the lender will audit at least every 60 days. These audits should establish any weakness in the reporting system, determine the quantity, quality, mix, and composition of the inventory, detect fraud and in general allow the lender to be fully informed of the overall status of the collateral. A relationship based on the meeting of minds between the borrower and the lender is always beneficial to both parties, and this is especially desirable when financing inventory. There is no better way to accomplish this than by written agreement. In addition to the points already covered, therefore, it is desirable to have a loan agreement spelling out in detail the rights and duties of both parties. Some of the more important items to be considered with an inventory loan are:

1. Defining what inventory is eligible for loan purposes with consideration for the lender's desire to limit advances on certain types of inventory such as work-in-process, slow moving items, small items, or any one particular item.
2. Establishing the percentage of advance or margin on eligible inventory.
3. Setting overall loan limits.

4. Establishing a rate.
5. Requiring prior approval for advances on certain types of inventory.
6. Establishing repayment agreement or term of line.
7. Establishing a detailed procedure to be followed under the loan from beginning to end.

Alternative Control Methods

Assuming that the bank does not have the staff, expertise and time to properly evaluate and control a given inventory financing situation, what are the alternatives? One method of solving the problem, is of course, to ask for assistance from a correspondent bank or one of its subsidiaries specializing in this type of lending and to let the correspondent set up the collateral control system on a participation basis. There are a number of fine commercial finance companies specializing in secured lending, and they are often quite willing to work with lenders in a participation arrangement. At the present time, participants will normally charge 4 percent to 6 percent above prime on their portion of the credit. One drawback under this arrangement is that normally, in the case of smaller borrowers, a participant's preference for a loan in excess of $150,000 often precludes it.

A second alternative is to use a collateral control service. A number of old-line warehouse companies and other companies are now providing collateral control services which differ from the above in that they do not enter into the loan but rather guarantee to the lender the validity of accounts receivable and the availability of physical inventory. The fees charged for this type of service vary widely depending on the value of the guaranteed or controlled collateral and other considerations. Fees ranging from 1 percent to 3 percent are not uncommon. Space does not permit a full discussion of the various services of this type. However, they can be utilized with satisfactory results. The advantage to the lender of a participation or collateral control service is the benefit of the wide experience possessed by most of these companies. In addition, they provide excellent reporting systems, keeping the lender informed of the status of the collateral, and, by the same token, assume all the responsibilities of setting up systems, procedures, and so on to properly control the inventory. In some loan situations, the lender can reduce his exposure considerably by obtaining the guarantee of an appropriate government agency such as the Small Business Administration or the Farmers Home Administration. This is particularly desirable when the lender has questions about his ability to ascertain the true value of the collateral, control of the inventory, or consideration of the unusual risk involved in the credit. Government guaranties are a subject in themselves and are thoroughly covered in a number of publications.

Use of Warehouse Receipts

Warehouse receipt financing has the important element of third-party control not common to the types of inventory financing already discussed. In this type of financing, the borrower's inventory is placed in a warehouse under third-party control and the warehouseman issues to the lender warehouse receipts, the documents of title covering those goods stored with the warehouseman. In this way the lender, of course, can control the movement of the inventory from the warehouse and therefore knows exactly how much inventory secures the loan. Warehouse receipt financing is particularly applicable to slow-moving goods or bulk quantities of one item, and can also be adapted more easily to loans of smaller amounts than can some of the other methods of financing inventory. Article 7 of the Uniform Commercial Code covers warehouse receipts, bills of lading, and other documents of title. The Code's definition of a warehouseman is "a person engaged in the business of storing goods for hire." Furthermore, the Code states that any warehouseman may issue a warehouse receipt. Article 7–202 outlines the essential terms and optional terms of a warehouse receipt which should be read and compared against any receipt before lending against the receipts. The essential items to be contained in a warehouse receipt are:

1. Location of the warehouse.
2. Date receipt was issued.
3. Consecutive numbering of receipts.
4. Whether the goods are to be delivered to the bearer, to a specified person, or to order of a specified person.
5. Storage charges except where goods are stored in a field warehouse.
6. A description of the goods or packages.
7. Signature of the warehouseman or authorized agent.
8. Whether the warehouseman solely or jointly owns any of the goods for which a receipt has been issued.
9. A statement by the warehouseman of any lien or security interest claimed by him.

Additionally, as optional information, the warehouse receipt may contain any other items which are not contrary to the provisions of the Code. The terminology used to describe different types of warehouses is sometimes confusing and loosely used. Therefore, some brief definitions are necessary:

1. *Terminal Warehouse.* Refers to the location of the warehouse as being separate and distinct from the firm or firms owning the goods stored in the warehouse and being operated by a public warehouseman.
2. *Field Warehouse.* A warehouse on or near the premises of the firm depositing goods in the warehouse.
3. *Bonded Warehouse.* Represents a warehouse filing a bond with an agency of the federal government against nonpayment of customs or taxes.
4. *Licensed Warehouse.* Should refer to licensing, either by federal or state governments.
5. *Public Warehouse.* Warehouseman has no ownership interest in the goods stored.
6. *Private Warehouse.* Warehouse operated or controlled by a firm owning a part of the goods stored.

Caution should be exercised if the lender is not familiar with a warehouseman. In many instances a warehouseman will put the terms bonded, licensed, etc. in the wording of the receipt when this is contrary to fact.

Regardless of the terminology or the type of warehouse, the important elements in a warehouse receipt loan are third-party control by a public warehouseman, and his reputation, financial position, and character. The warehouseman should be investigated as thoroughly as one would his own borrower since the collateral is stored in his warehouse and subject to his control and disposition. There are many reliable, well-established and well-known warehouse companies with whom lenders can deal confidently. However, if one does not know his warehouseman, some of the questions that should be answered in addition to his general reputation and financial condition are:

1. Does the receipt conform to the Code requirements?
2. Does he maintain adequate insurance and fidelity bonding? The insurance coverage of many warehouses omits certain hazards and perils. If this is the case, the borrower's insurance policy should be checked to make sure his coverage is adequate and that the lender is named as the loss payee.
3. Is the warehouse suited for the borrower's inventory?

Bankers in some instances might want to take advantage of the provisions of 12 U.S.C. 84(6). It permits certain exceptions to legal lending limits on obligations when secured by shipping documents, warehouse receipts, and other documents of title covering certain commodities.

Perfecting Security Interest

Perfecting a security interest in inventory within the framework of the Code is relatively simple. First, it is always advisable before entering into the financing arrangement to initiate a search of the appropriate records to determine whether there is already on file one or more financing statements covering the anticipated collateral. If so, these items should be canceled or cleared up to the lender's satisfaction. Next, a security agreement should be obtained, followed by the filing of an appropriate financing statement, followed by another check to make certain that no intervening liens have been entered into the records, and, as a last step, funds should be advanced. The appropriate location for filing a financing statement on inventory is sometimes a confusing issue among lenders and a point which needs to be considered. Articles 9–102, 9–103, 9–104, and particularly 9–401 of the Code set forth the various rules and considerations on this subject. Usually the proper place for filing on inventory will be in the state or states where the inventory is physically located. One noteworthy exception occurs in the event goods are classified as inventory by reason of their being leased by the debtor to others and their being mobile. Under these circumstances, a financing statement should be filed in the state in which the debtor's chief place of business is located. Mobile goods are generally defined as a type normally used in more than one jurisdiction such as automotive equipment, rolling stock, and road building equipment. Multiple filing and/or legal advice is recommended if the lender has any doubts in a given situation.

The wording and content of the bank's notes, security agreement, and financing statement are a matter best left to the bank's counsel, and these forms should be reviewed periodically regarding their adequacy in light of changing circumstances. Particular care should be exercised in ensuring that all inventory of the debtor, if that is the intent, is covered whether it is now existing or hereafter acquired and that the proceeds of the inventory are also covered.

Loans to farmers deserve special attention since it is doubtful under the Code whether a farmer can have inventory or not. Section 9–109(3) states "If goods are farm products they are neither equipment nor inventory." This section also defines farm products. Goods are farm products "if they are crops or livestock or supplies used or produced in farming operations or if they are products of crops or livestock in their unmanufactured states . . . , and if they are in the possession of a debtor engaged in raising, fattening, grazing or other farming operations." Loans secured by farm products require different treatment and the applicable provisions of the Code should be adhered to when a loan is secured by farm products.

It should also be remembered that a purchase money security interest in a debtor's inventory can take priority over an after-acquired property clause. Purchasers of chattel paper or conditional sales contracts generated by the sale of the debtor's inventory can also obtain a prior position with respect to the proceeds of inventory.

If an inventory loan is to be handled under a warehouse receipt arrangement, it is well to bear in mind Section 7–503(1) of the Code which states in part, "a document of title confers no right in goods against a person who before issuance of the document had a legal or a perfected security interest in them. . . ." Whenever a situation arises where one creditor has a security interest in inventory and another creditor might be lending against warehouse receipts some conflicting points of law can be involved. This, from both a practical and legal standpoint, is not a desirable situation, but in the event the lender encounters this situation legal advice is recommended. In addition, a holder of a negotiable document of title which has been duly negotiated can take priority over an earlier security interest which has been temporarily perfected or perfected by filing a financing statement.

Perfecting a security interest in a *negotiable* document can be accomplished in three ways.

1. Filing a financing statement.
2. Taking possession of the document.
3. May be temporarily perfected without filing or taking possession for 21 days from the time it attaches if it is created for new value pursuant to a written security agreement.

A security interest in goods in the possession of a bailee (warehouseman) who has issued a *nonnegotiable* document of title may be perfected in one of three ways:

1. By issuance of the document in the name of the secured party (the lender).
2. By taking possession of an assigned nonnegotiable document issued in someone else's name and notifying the warehouseman of the secured party's interest.
3. By filing a financing statement on the goods themselves.

In light of the provisions of the Code mentioned above and others, the safest course of action is to file financing statements and also maintain possession of warehouse receipts. One should also search the appropriate records to ascertain that no other party has perfected a security interest in the goods covered by warehouse receipts. Care should be exercised to make certain a borrower has paid storage charges on goods warehoused since Section 7–209 gives the warehouseman a prior lien against the merchandise for storage costs.

The most important of the points covered is a critical review of a loan on a regular basis. A thorough review of the borrower's annual audit, particularly a close examination of figures relating to the inventory and the ratio of cost of sales to inventory can give some good clues regarding the overall condition of a loan.

LOANS SECURED BY ACCOUNTS RECEIVABLE

Section 9–106 of the Code defines accounts as "any right to payment for goods sold or leased or for services rendered which is not evidenced by an instrument or chattel paper." General intangibles are normally included when financing receivables, and this term covers miscellaneous types of contractual rights such as goodwill, literary rights, rights to performance, trademarks, patents, and so forth.

Accounts receivable lending is especially applicable for new and growing businesses in which working capital or capital is relatively modest, or in which other factors dictate a secured loan. Receivables financing can be a very beneficial medium for both the borrower and lender. It can provide the borrower with cash needed to take discounts and othewise assist a growing borrower to become a mature, strong, and desirable customer. Receivable financing is also appropriate for the borrower with seasonal characteristics, such as a retail merchant during the Christmas period. Of course, accounts receivable lending can go hand in hand with inventory financing. However, the normal situation is to look first to the accounts receivable and secondly to the inventory. As a general rule, accounts receivable financing presents less risk to the lender than does an inventory loan for several reasons. First, an account is one step closer to cash than inventory. Second, most lenders can determine the value of accounts by analyzing the credit standing of the account debtor, a process they are thoroughly familiar with, in contrast to trying to establish the value of a given inventory. In addition, control over the collateral is somewhat simpler. Finally, the overall creditworthiness of a receivables borrower is usually superior to that of a borrower seeking inventory financing.

Accounts receivable, like inventory, must bear certain relationship to sales or cost of sales in a going concern. Except in cases where repayment will come from cash generated by the reduction of an asset, many receivable loans will in fact be term loans, even though handled on a short-term basis. Accordingly receivable lines or loans should be structured only after good cash flow projections have been completed.

Establishing Value

Basically, the two elements which establish the value of accounts are the validity and the collectability of the accounts. After the lender has received from the prospective borrower a complete listing and

aging of all accounts receivable outstanding as of a given date, judgment on the validity and collectability of the accounts must be made.
Perhaps the first thing to look at in this connection is the industry
within which the prospective borrower is operating and the line of
business of the account debtors. Some industries have a history of high-
credit losses and slow-paying record. Certain loans might be excluded
on this basis. Other questions which aid in determining validity and
collectibility are:

1. *Partial Shipments.* Do any of the accounts represent monies
   owed your borrower for a shipment under a larger order? If they
   do and in the event of liquidation, the collectibility of the accounts
   in question might be doubtful.
2. *Validity of Order.* Has the merchandise covered by the accounts
   receivable actually been ordered by your borrower's customers?
3. *Sale and Delivery.* Do all accounts represent unqualified sales
   and has delivery been made?
4. *Product Quality.* Does your customer sell a good quality product,
   and what is the record of rejection and allowances?
5. *Reciprocity.* Does a borrower purchase from any account debtors? If so, the possibility of offsets exists.
6. *Advance Deposits.* Does the borrower hold deposits from customers for merchandise on future delivery? If so, these deposits
   might be offset against future receivables.
7. *Account Turnover and Aging.* Has the turnover and aging of
   the accounts been analyzed, and how does the turnover of the
   receivables compare with industry figures, prior years, and with
   your borrower's selling terms?
8. *Account Concentration.* What is the spread of the accounts? Do
   one or two accounts represent a disproportionate dollar volume
   of the total accounts receivable?
9. *Loss Experience.* What is your borrower's loss experience?
10. *Collectibility.* Have we satisfied ourselves as to the collectibility
    of the significant dollar value of the total accounts receivable?
11. *Audit.* Have we verified and confirmed the validity of the out-
    standing accounts directly with the account debtors?

After these and other factors have been considered, it should be
possible to arrive at a dollar figure which the lender should be able
to collect from liquidating the receivables. If, for example, a borrower
has $100,000 in valid outstanding accounts, and the lender estimates
that collections in a liquidation would amount to $95,000 he would
automatically set at least a 5 percent margin for uncollectible accounts.
More than likely the lender would set the margin at a higher percentage in recognition of the fact that the composition of the accounts
will change, and a factor of 5 percent for doubtful accounts may not

be adequate. For purposes of discussion, let us assume that the lender decides on a 15 percent margin of doubtful accounts. In addition to this, it is estimated that attorney's fees and collection expenses will be $15,000. So, in this particular example, a 30 percent margin or a $70,000 loan might be appropriate.

Methods Used

The particular method of handling a receivables loan will depend to a large extent upon the circumstances involved in each particular case. Some of the more prevalent types of arrangements range from a blanket assignment to nonnotification to direct notification to factoring. Under a blanket assignment the lender simply obtains a perfected security interest in whatever accounts might be existent and generally has little, if any, control over the collateral. When a loan is structured in this way the lender first admits that the loan will not stand as an unsecured transaction and furthermore suffers from the delusion that one has a secured loan, when, in most cases, just the opposite is true. In the author's opinion, there is no justification for handling a loan on this basis.

Nonnotification is the terminology used to indicate that the borrower's account debtors are not notified that monies due the borrower have been assigned to the lender. There are many variations of nonnotification financing, and they differ principally in the extent to which the lender goes in trying to continuously analyze those previously mentioned factors influencing validity and collectibility. The principal safeguards utilized by lenders are:

1. Audits of the borrower's records.
2. Independent verification of outstanding accounts.
3. Control over proceeds of accounts.

Under a strict type arrangement, the lender audits the books of the borrower and verifies the existence of receivables directly with account debtors on a continuous basis. In addition, the lender places strict controls over record-keeping procedures so that one is reasonably sure that any new accounts are valid ones. Collections are usually segregated and controlled. In this way the lender can take a beginning balance of accounts receivables, add new accounts, deduct payments and therefore determine what accounts are outstanding, their validity as well as their quality. It is impossible to recommend any set procedure concerning the proper method of handling a nonnotification loan without first knowing all the circumstances surrounding the credit and considering a number of other factors. As a minimum, one would think that if reliance is to be placed on the collateral values, the lender should receive as a minimum a complete listing and aging of receivables

on a periodic basis. Additionally, some independent verification with
account debtors is necessary. This, coupled with good financial information and a regular review process, should give some credence to collateral values and the overall status of a given credit.

In some cases, it is quite simple to set up an accounts receivable
loan on a direct notification basis in which the account debtor acknowledges the existence of an account prior to disbursement of loan proceeds and agrees to remit payments directly to the lender. This can
be accomplished in a number of ways. One of the simplest ways of
doing this is to have a separate note tied to each invoice with coinciding
maturity dates. The advantages of this particular type of arrangement
are that the account is verified before funds are advanced and that
the lender has control over the proceeds and immediately knows when
an account becomes slow or uncollectible. Of course, the disadvantage
is that this system is cumbersome if one is dealing with a borrower
who has many accounts. This particular system can be simplified somewhat by eliminating the feature of having one note for each invoice
and by setting up the accounts receivable line based on the total of
the invoices outstanding under direct notification. The major disadvantage of direct-notification financing is borrower resistance to the direct-
notification aspect.

Regardless of the method used to control and evaluate the collateral,
the overall loan or line should be covered by a written loan agreement
detailing exactly how the line or loan will be handled. Since factoring
involves the outright sale of accounts as opposed to lending against
accounts this subject will not be covered.

Perfecting the Security Interest

The procedure to perfect a security interest in accounts receivable
is very similar to that used in an inventory loan. It should entail a
search of the records to determine if there are existing any prior liens
on the accounts receivable. It is extremely important to make certain
that no other lender is financing the borrower's inventory. In this case,
as a result of claiming the proceeds of inventory, the other lender
could have a prior perfected security interest in the accounts receivable
resulting from the sale of the inventory. After this has been done, a
security agreement should be obtained and the appropriate financing
statement filed. Another check should be made of the records to be
certain that there have not been intervening liens before funds are
advanced. In general terms, financing statements are normally written
or worded so that they cover all accounts, contract rights, and general
intangibles now existing or hereafter arising and the rights of the debtor
in goods and the proceeds of the described collateral.

Generally, adherence to the steps mentioned above will protect the lender and will provide him with a perfected security interest in the collateral of the debtor. The appropriate place for perfecting a security interest in accounts receivable, contract rights, and general intangibles is governed by Sections 9–103 and 9–401 of the Code. Accounts or contract rights require filing where the assignor of accounts or contract rights keeps his records concerning them. General intangibles require filing in the state where the assignor's "chief place of business" is located. Official comment 3 to Section 9–103 clarifies "chief place of business" as meaning the place from which in fact the debtor manages the main part of the business operations and not the place of incorporation. If there is any doubt concerning where the assignor of accounts or contract rights maintains his records concerning them, multiple filing and/or legal advice is recommended. The same procedure should be followed if there is any doubt about the assignor's chief place of business when filing on general intangibles.

There are a couple of other topics which need special mention. Any loan based on the assignment of receivables or contracts from the federal government must comply with the Miller Act or the Assignment of Claims Act of 1940 and the lender should be thoroughly familiar with its provisions. The assignee should file written notice of the assignment with the government and should also send a copy to any surety who might be involved. The provisions of this act are beyond the scope of this chapter. Perhaps the best advice is to consult with the bank's counsel on contracts or receivables of this nature unless one is thoroughly familiar with this type of financing.

Another extremely complex area within the realm of receivables financing is the financing of contractors' receivables. This area is fraught with both practical and legal pitfalls too numerous to mention, and, if experience has not already illustrated this point, one need only talk with someone who has engaged in this form of financing. Contractors are a vital segment of the economy and are important customers to the banking community; any comments made are certainly not intended to discredit this particular industry. In the author's opinion, financing contractors is a perfectly legitimate and sound banking practice. Usually the major assets of a contractor are the accounts receivable, equipment, and often real estate. Normally equipment and real estate are much better collateral than accounts receivable.

LOANS SECURED BY STOCKS AND BONDS

Since most lenders are thoroughly familiar with loans secured by stocks and bonds, coverage of this subject will be rather brief. Compared with receivables and inventory lending, this is a relatively safe and clean-cut form of financing and can be handled in most cases without extensive experience or special staff. Complacency is probably the biggest enemy when problems which have arisen on loans secured by those types of collateral are considered. Failure to have or adhere to lending policy and/or failure to comply with the basics of credit is the connotation intended for the word complacency. Before making a loan secured by stocks and/or bonds, the lender should bear in mind this axiom: "A loan which has to be repaid by the liquidation of collateral is not a good loan."

Stocks and bonds may be traded on the major exchanges, over-the-counter or locally, while others may be closely held and have little or no marketability. Stocks generally take the form of either common stocks or preferred stocks with principal categories of bonds broken down into corporates, federal governments, and municipals. The most common federal government obligations are Treasury bills, Treasury notes, certificates of indebtedness and Treasury bonds.

Some of the elements which have an influence on value of stocks and bonds can be divided into quantitative and qualitative. The quantitative factors include such things as operating statistics, balance sheet position, capitalization, trends within the company, earnings, and dividends. Some of the more important qualitative factors are matters such as the nature of the business, its relative position within an industry, its physical, geographical and operating characteristics, the quality of management, its stability, and its trend of earnings. Based on these and other factors, the market mechanism forms its opinion of the security and expresses its opinion in terms of price, price stability, marketability, yield, and so forth.

There are a number of sources of information readily available to the lender for assistance in evaluating a particular security. In many cases a thorough analysis of an issue has already been done by such independent companies as Standard & Poor's, Moody's, various brokerage houses, and many of the larger banks. As a general rule, stocks and bonds traded on the major exchanges and government securities have a high degree of marketability. Many over-the-counter issues also have a broad and stable market. Some caution should be exercised in lending against some over-the-counter and locally traded issues since the prices quoted in some cases may be at an artificial level and the sale of a sizable block of stock could drastically reduce the market price of the particular issue under consideration. Additionally, some diversification of collateral is usually desirable, and a loan without diversified collateral deserves closer scrutiny.

Special care should be exercised before making any loan secured by stocks or bonds in a closely held corporation. These securities may or may not have value, and in most cases they cannot be readily converted to cash. Banks are also prohibited from making loans secured by their own stock. Lenders may encounter problems in lending against securities which are restricted and/or those which have not been registered under the Federal Securities Act. If one contemplates a transaction of this type, it is strongly suggested that he consult with his counsel.

The circumstances surrounding each loan dictate the proper margin and generalizations can often be dangerous. Therefore, none will be made. Consideration of these factors and others should enable the lender to estabish the value of the collateral and, at the same time, to get a pretty good idea of margin needed. Lending policy should establish broad guidelines within each lender's institution and should address the question of desirable and undesirable types of collateral and establish margin requirements for each form of collateral.

Control and Evaluation

Control and evaluation of securities is a relatively easy task since the lender will in most cases have possession of the securities themselves and therefore have control over them. The process of evaluation should entail regular and frequent review of the value of the collateral and whether proper margins are being maintained. Control over negotiable collateral should also entail systems to detect any stock splits or stock dividends which could erode the bank's margin. Establishing sound auditing procedures is essential to ensure that dual control over substitutions and releases is maintained.

Section 9–304(1) of the Code states that a security interest in money or instruments (other than instruments which constitute part of chattel paper) can be perfected only by the secured party's taking possession. This section goes on to mention several temporary exceptions to the above, but any method of perfection other than possession can present some serious problems. Maintaining possession of instruments is highly desirable, and before exceptions are made, the lender should carefully review the applicable provisions of the Code and seek legal advice if necessary. Some of the common items of documentation used in making loans against stocks and bonds are listed below:

1. *Note.*   The form and content of a secured note should be reviewed by bank's counsel.
2. *Possession of Stock or Bond.*   This is necessary to perfect security interest.
3. *Stock or Bond Power.*   This form assigns the owners interest and gives the lender the power of attorney to sell the collateral.
4. *Hypothecation Agreement.*   This form is necessary when the security is owned by a party other than the borrower.
5. *Special Resolutions.*   When corporations borrow or pledge assets, special resolutions authorizing them are called for.

6. *Form U-1.* The Federal Reserve requires a statement of purpose on loans directly or indirectly secured by stock regardless of the purpose of the loan. The term stock generally includes any security convertible into stock or which otherwise entitles the owner to share or participate in any profits of the issuing company. If the loan is for the purpose of purchasing or carrying securities, it is also subject to the credit limitations and restrictions of Regulation U-1.

7. *Collateral Agreement.* This is an optional agreement which the lender may consider. It can, among other things, provide that the lender will also have a lien on any assets in the lender's possession.

In summary, loans secured by stocks and bonds are highly desirable and a safe form of lending, provided that:

1. Bank policy is adhered to.
2. Credit fundamentals are followed.
3. A careful analysis is conducted to establish collateral values and proper margins.
4. The collateral is in the lender's possession.
5. The value of collateral and the overall loan is reviewed on a regular basis.

Some of the more difficult and prevalent forms of secured lending have been covered in preceding paragraphs. Space permits only a brief mention of some other areas of secured lending.

LOANS SECURED BY CASH VALUE OF LIFE INSURANCE POLICIES

Loans secured by life insurance policies are a relatively comprehensive subject and are covered thoroughly by an excellent book, *Manual on Life Insurance Loans* published by the American Bankers Association. In addition, the ABA has designed and distributes forms which will assist lenders in successfully handling loans secured by life insurance policies. These forms are:

1. Form No. 16. "Life Insurance Assignment Questionnaire."
2. Form No. 10. "Life Insurance Assignment."
3. Form No. 12. "Life Insurance Assignment Release."

Many aspects of a loan secured by life insurance policies will be covered by using these or similar forms. There are many different types of insurance policies in existence; some of the more common ones are referred to as term, whole life, limited payment, endorsement, annuity, industrial, and group. Normally, a lender takes an assignment of a life insurance policy as protection against the borrower's death and/or as collateral when the policy has cash value. Loans which have policies assigned without cash value should not be classified as secured loans. Consequently, this discussion is related principally to those loans secured by cash values of insurance policies. Some of the basic steps to be considered in making a loan secured by life insurance are:

1. Credit fundamentals should be determined.
2. A thorough and comprehensive review of the policy should be undertaken since every policy has different characteristics.
3. Credit standing of the insurance company should be checked.
4. Completed questionnaire (Form No. 16) should be signed by the insuring company. This form will verify the ownership of the policy, the terms of premium payment, premium lapse provisions, notification provisions in the event of premium nonpayment, cash values and encumbrances, liens on the insuring company's records, beneficiary, and many other pertinent features.
5. A completed assignment form should be signed by the owner, the beneficiary in some cases, and acknowledged by the insuring company.

There are many other points to be considered, but instead, a look at a few potential problem areas is more relevant:

1. *Incontestability.* Generally after two years a policy becomes incontestable in the event of suicide by the insured. Suicide before two years generally provides only for a return of premiums.
2. *Does the beneficiary have to sign the assignment?* It is *always safer* to have the owner and beneficiary sign. In certain states, it may be adequate for only the owner to sign if the beneficiary designation is revocable and rights of the beneficiary are clearly subordinated in the policy and community property is not involved.
3. *Assignability.* Policy must be assignable.
4. *Settlement options.* The lender should be satisfied with settlement options or have them amended.
5. *Community property.* In community property states, the husband and wife should both sign the assignment form, and furthermore, the lender would be well advised to seek legal aid in some cases.
6. *Special precautions and documentation.* These factors may be called for if the insured is not the owner of the policy or if the policy is owned by a corporation or if the policy is assigned to secure the debt of someone other than the owner.

LOANS SECURED BY PETROLEUM PRODUCTION, SHIP MORTGAGES, AND AIRCRAFT

Loans secured by a mortgage and assignment of production of oil and gas properties, ship mortgages, equipment, and aircraft generally fall within the realm of term lending, a subject covered elsewhere in this handbook. In a few instances, these forms of collateral are used in connection with short-term lending. Therefore, coverage will be limited to a few random comments.

A direct production petroleum loan may be defined as a self-liquidating loan with repayment coming from the oil and gas runs derived from the mortgaged properties. Geography will in part determine whether a lender is justified in entering into this field of lending, but, in general, this type of lending is a highly profitable endeavor for many banks engaged in it for several reasons. First, the oil and gas runs usually permit a relatively quick and regular payback varying from a few months to several years. Second, loans of this type command good rates and often generate excellent deposit relationships. Perhaps the greatest drawback from most lenders is the necessity of determining the value of the oil and gas reserves which constitute the lender's collateral. Lenders engaged in petroleum financing on a large-scale basis will normally employ a petroleum engineer or use the services of firms specializing in this field. In layman's terms, the engineer establishes the present value of the income stream to be derived from the oil and/or gas runs. As a rule of thumb many lenders then advance 50 percent of the estimated present value. Some of the other major considerations in this type of lending are:

1. There is an inverse relationship between risk and the number of wells securing a loan. Lenders will usually require a minimum of two wells before lending against production.
2. The lender must ascertain that the title to any mortgaged property is clear.
3. There must be a connection with a pipeline or a valid purchase for the production.
4. The operators of the well should be competent and the lender thoroughly satisfied with their ability.

Loans secured by boats, ships, and aircraft will be mentioned only for the purpose of pointing out their unique legal status. The Ship Mortgage Act of 1920 affords a lender much superior protection by granting the lender a preferred ship mortgage. Generally a lender may obtain a preferred ship mortgage of vessels of the United States exceeding five tons (as a rule of thumb 35 feet in length.) If the vessel is a towboat, scow, lighter, car float, canal boat, or tank vessel, a minimum displacement of 25 gross tons applies. The rights obtained under a preferred ship mortgage are far superior to those obtained by having a security interest in the vessel. A preferred ship mortgage can be primed or defeated only by:

1. Prior maritime liens which attach before the date of the mortgage.
2. Tort liens created when the vessel does something offensive to society such as running into another vessel.
3. Crews wages.
4. Salvor's liens which can be created if a qualified salvor saves the vessel.

The risk associated with these four situations which can prime a preferred ship mortgage can be virtually eliminated by the lender. First, the lender should know the borrower and require an affidavit that there are no prior liens. Under the Ship Mortgage Act, a false statement subjects the borrower to two years in a federal prison, and a $1,000 fine or both. This is usually sufficient protection against prior liens. The lender protects himself against Torts by having proper protection and indemnity insurance assigned, and hull insurance protects him from salvor's liens. Crews wages seldom present a major problem since a crew will promptly quit if they are not paid and the lender will soon be appraised of the circumstances. By utilizing the preferred ship mortgage and proper insurance, the lender can eliminate virtually all of the legal problems that can evolve if the lender simply relies on a security interest. In addition, the lender can charge whatever rate he deems appropriate, regardless of state usury laws, and he will be operating under this federal statute and within some well-defined legal grounds. While there are no insurmountable difficulties involved in properly documenting a preferred ship mortgage, there are a number of fine points to be considered and the lender will usually benefit by allowing counsel to prepare the documentation and by obtaining a legal opinion.

The financing of aircraft is covered by the Federal Aviation Registration Act within Section 503 of the Federal Aviation Act (49-U.S.C., Sec. 403). The Federal Aviation Registration Act makes provision for the recordation of conveyances affecting the title to, or interest in, civil aircraft of the United States and provides that no such conveyance thereafter made or given shall be valid against any person other than the maker or his or her heirs or devisee, and any person having actual notice thereof until so recorded. In essence, failure to follow the provisions of the act can place the lender in a precarious position with respect to third parties. The requirements for recording liens and conveyances are contained in Federal Aviation Regulations Volume II, Part 40 "Recording of Aircraft Titles and Security Documents." For recordation of liens and conveyances send to FAA Aircraft Registry, Department of Transportation, Oklahoma City, Oklahoma. In addition to complying with this act, it may be desirable to perfect a security interest under the Uniform Commercial Code.

CONCLUSION

Thus far, a positive approach to secured lending has been emphasized. However, every lender despite due diligence will be faced with the problems of a failing borrower, liquidating collateral, or worse yet a bankrupt borrower. This unfortunate situation can be caused by many factors, but usually they will fall within the three broad areas of adversity, mismanagement, or fraud. If the lender can first pinpoint exactly what the problem is, he will be in a much better position to determine what course of action to take. If fraud has been committed, the lender obviously can no longer consider working with the borrower. Under the other circumstances, the lender will often benefit by continuing to work with a borrower.

Probably the most difficult decision facing a lender is determining when it becomes necessary to call a loan and to begin the process of liquidating collateral. Experience and sound judgment are two critical intangible qualities the lender must possess or rely upon when making this decision, Therefore, it is highly desirable to utilize the collective experience and judgment of a senior loan committee or similar group when faced with this decision.

Once a decision has been made, immediate action and follow-up should ensue. Failures or delay in following-up will often prove to be costly and will result in a loss of control over the credit. A prudent lender should always seek legal advice when a problem loan is encountered and well before a decision to liquidate a borrower is made. Legal advice at an early stage is an invaluable aid in weighing the alternate courses or action, preventing or rectifying costly errors in documentation and avoiding the multitude of legal problems which a lender can encounter. Consideration of the following questions will often assist the lender:

1. What are the facts?
2. What is the problem or problems?
3. What is the lender's legal position?
4. What are the various alternatives for a solution to the problem?
5. What is the best solution?
6. Has proper emphasis been placed on immediate follow-up?
7. Has the lending institution taken full advantage of the experience and judgment possessed by its personnel in considering the above questions?

Secured lending offers opportunity, challenge, risk, and reward to the lender. Loans secured by some forms of collateral are inherently more difficult to manage and involve a higher degree of risk than others. The extent to which a particular institution engages in the various types of secured lending should be established by lending policy. Secured lending is an endeavor where shortcuts expose the lender to inordinate risk. On the other hand, a careful and deliberate approach to each loan will minimize risk and maximize the rewards for the lender.

Chapter 49 _____

Commodity and In-Transit Loans

Allen Good*

Jack Robison†

GENERAL

Commodity lending, while requiring a certain amount of specialization and acquired skills, is basically another form of inventory and accounts receivable financing. The commodities themselves and the credit of their purchasers provide the security for the loans. In essence there is little difference between securing a lien on the output of a small parts manufacturer than on hogsheads of tobacco or bales of cotton. When the product moves into the avenues of commerce, the proceeds of the sale serve to retire the loan.

There are numerous types of loans which can be classified as commodity loans. A New York banker sees a commodity loan as one financing the purchase and resale of such items as coffee, cocoa, sugar, or precious metals. A Chicago banker would deal with loans involving grain or cattle while a Memphis banker finances cotton and a West Coast loan officer works with cotton, fresh vegetables, and wine. Commodity loans, while similar to other categories of secured loans, have several unique characteristics. Usually, a commodity loan is:

1. Quite large in amount.
2. On a demand basis.
3. To a company which is highly leveraged.
4. Based on certain margin requirements.

_____

* Vice President, First Tennessee Bank N.A., Memphis, Tennessee.

† Assistant Treasurer, Cook Industries Inc., Memphis, Tennessee (formerly Vice President, First Tennessee Bank N.A., Memphis, Tennessee).

5. Financing a commodity which is very marketable.
6. Heavily reliant on the activities of a futures market.

Commodity loans also display two characteristics of the genre of loans involving inventory or accounts receivable; they usually are short term and are secured.

A commodity banker, therefore, must have a sound general background in lending. He or she must then acquire the special skills needed in commodity lending. These include understanding fully the rules of secured lending, filing under the Uniform Commercial Code, negotiable instruments, and warehousing; understanding the workings of the commodity futures markets, hedging, and the concept of basis; and being thoroughly familiar with the unique characteristics of commodity merchants, their leverage positions, high volume, and low margins. A commodity banker does *not* need to be involved in financing commodities before they are purchased by the merchant from the producer. Producer loans have distinctly different characteristics and are handled in a different manner. This chapter will deal with that period from the purchase of the commodity from the producer to the passing of title and collection of the proceeds of the sale to the ultimate user.

While banks may lend unsecured to commodity firms (which will be covered later), most commodity loans are secured either by warehouse receipts or by in-transit documents. These will be discussed separately below.

SECURED COMMODITY LOANS—WAREHOUSE RECEIPTS

When a commodity merchant purchases a quantity of some product, be it 100 bales of cotton or 100 bags of coffee, he or she generally requires financing in order to make the purchase. Most banks will provide the financing only if it is secured by warehouse receipts conveying title to the goods financed. In most cases, the product is stored in warehouses ranging from those licensed by the federal and state governments to private storehouses owned by the merchant. The warehouse receipts issued by these companies are diverse in style and quality.

Generally commodity bankers prefer third-party bonded negotiable warehouse receipts. In this instance, the warehouseman has no financial interest in the goods stored and his sole purpose is providing storage for hire.

Warehouses

The phrase "licensed bonded warehouse" does not imply absolute protection. The company which supplies the bond is providing financial protection of some kind, but it may be only a nominal value compared to the value of the stored goods. The rationale for a lower bond is that the bonding company and the warehouseman hope that most shortages will be discovered at an early stage and for only a nominal amount. Few bonds cover large discrepancies. Most commodity bankers put more emphasis on the agency under whose regulations the warehouse receipt is issued and its audit program than they do on the bonds which cover the warehouse.

Basically, warehouses are licensed under either federal or state regulatory agencies which have their own auditors charged with periodically inspecting the warehouses. Some feel that the federally licensed warehouses have an edge over those licensed by individual states because the federal inspectors are better paid and better trained. Some warehousemen would rather be regulated by state laws than federal laws. Overall, there appear to have been fewer losses in the past involving commodities stored in federally licensed warehouses than in those supervised by the states.

Another type of warehouse receipt which deserves mention is the field warehouse receipt. This document is issued by an independent field warehouse company which is hired to establish a facility on the premises of the merchant or borrower for the benefit of a third party such as the lender who wishes to be secured. This usually is required when a federal or state warehouse facility is not available or practical. In this case, a bond is established for a larger amount than for government warehouses and is of great importance to the lender.

Field warehousing is more flexible and lends itself to more situations, but it is more expensive than the alternate methods. Finally, care should be taken in accepting a field warehouse receipt with attention to the reputation and financial strength of the company plus the amount of the bond and by whom it is issued.

Negotiability

The negotiability of a warehouse receipt is its most important characteristic. Without the negotiable feature, a commodity lender has no control over the title of the product covered and would be unable to take possession of the goods in the event of default by the borrower. Many receipts are issued to order and must be endorsed to become negotiable. In recent times, many warehouses have been issuing receipts to the order of bearer, eliminating the need for endorsement. While this reduces the amount of paperwork involved, it places an extra burden on the holders since security must be provided to prevent loss or theft of the receipts. If bearer receipts are lost, an expensive bond must be posted with the warehouseman before he will issue duplicate receipts. The danger inherent in lost or stolen bearer receipts is in the reliance on the receipt by an innocent third party wishing to use the receipt as collateral or to reclaim the goods from the warehouse.

A commodity banker also may lend against nonnegotiable warehouse receipts issued to the bank's order. This complicates the bank's collateral procedures, though, by requiring the bank to agree to release of the goods before they may be removed from the warehouse and by requiring the signing or endorsing the receipts and tracking them through the movement of the goods. In addition different laws govern negotiable and nonnegotiable receipts. In many cases, the lender is in a better position by holding a negotiable receipt than a nonnegotiable one in his favor.

Insurance

The insurance coverage on financed goods while they are in storage also is of considerable importance to the lender. Most warehousing companies are required to carry insurance on the goods which they store. For added protection, many commodity firms are required by the lenders to carry additional, secondary insurance coverage on their own. In most cases, this is quite inexpensive. The commodity bankers must always ascertain that adequate insurance coverage exists on the goods financed and that this coverage runs to them either through the warehouse receipt or by assignment of the coverage by the insured financed party.

Storage Charges

Another factor which must be considered by the commodity banker when lending secured by warehouse receipts is the payment of storage charges. In some cases, the storage charges follow the receipt itself, and must be paid by the holder of the receipt before the goods can be released and shipped by the warehouseman. Should the warehouse receipt carry a storage date that is quite old, accrued storage charges could be considerable. Some warehouse receipts require regular payment of storage charges on a monthly or quarterly basis. In this case as well, the lender must ascertain that the accrued storage charges are paid to the warehouseman before the goods can be released.

As a rule when the goods are covered by negotiable receipts, the warehouseman can only charge storage against the particular goods which the particular receipts cover. This does not hold true in the case of nonnegotiable warehouse receipts. The warehouseman can accrue storage charges, sometimes for a long period of time, as long as there are any goods at all in the warehouse held for a particular borrower. He can hold any of these goods against payment of any charges owed him by the borrower even though some of the charges are for goods already released. These charges would accrue against any nonnegotiable receipts presented, so the banker presenting such receipts for release of the goods could be faced with making such payments. For this reason, the commodity banker must exercise care when accepting and handling nonnegotiable receipts.

Uniform Commercial Code

The Uniform Commercial Code (UCC) has been generally adopted throughout the United States. Commodity bankers must be acutely aware of the UCC and its applications to their unique form of lending. As a rule, the states applying the UCC do not require that a lender file to protect a security interest on loans secured by warehouse receipts. Mere possession of the receipts protects the lender's interest in the goods covered. If a loan was made secured by warehouse receipts and was repaid while the covered goods were still in the warehouse, filing under the UCC would not concern the commodity banker. This is seldom the case, however. Usually, the borrower must ship, invoice, and collect his receivable before he is able to retire the loan. In this instance, the lender must relinquish the warehouse receipts in order to obtain release and shipment from the warehouse where the goods are stored. The warehouse receipts are released to the borrower (or warehouseman) against a trust receipt which immediately brings the transaction within the jurisdiction of the Uniform Commercial Code. Therefore, the bank in almost all cases will be required to file to protect its interest under the UCC of the borrower's state as well as its own. Such filing pertains more to lending against in-transit documents and will be covered again at that point. It should be noted that filing under the UCC can be slightly different according to the state jurisdiction involved. For this reason, legal counsel should be contacted by commodity bankers to ensure that they are completely protected.

Demand Loans

A commodity loan generally is made in one of three forms, one of which is a variation of one of the others. The most common form of commodity loan is the demand note. This type of loan is the easiest form of loan to call should the banker consider the situation involving the borrower grave enough or degenerating to the point that calling the loan quickly will prevent a later loss or default. In such a case, the banker is not tempted to wait until a specific maturity date to make a decision. Procrastination in calling a commodity loan often has been one of the chief reasons for becoming involved in a loss or workout situation. When a commodity loan is made, a specified amount of margin over the amount of the loan should be available in the value of the commodity financed. By calling the demand loan quickly, the banker can use this margin as a buffer to avoid or minimize any losses.

The demand loan has other advantages. It is more readily adaptable to working on a pooled basis for a particular customer who is a large-volume merchant with constant buying, selling, borrowing, and repaying. If all loans are on demand and all collateral is pooled against the total loans, the borrower can obtain additional funds or repay as funds are needed or collected according to the volume of business during a particular period. Another advantage of the demand loan for bankers is the ability to tie the loan to the prime rate and keep it on a so-called floating basis moving with the prime rate as it moves. This avoids being tied to a fixed rate which could work to the bank's disadvantage during a period of rising costs of funds.

Discount Loans

The other major category of commodity loan is the one made on a discounted basis. Many borrowers prefer this type of loan for tax purposes as it allows them to deduct interest expense as it accrues during the period of the loan rather than when repayment is made. It also protects the borrower against rising interest rates since the discount is fixed at the time of borrowing. In addition, it is not unusual for a commodity banker to see large borrowers who use more than one bank finding the necessary funds to pay off discounted notes prior to maturity in a market with declining rates, but leaving such loans on the books until maturity during a period of rising interest rates.

Bankers' Acceptances

Related to discount loans are bankers' acceptance loans. This medium for financing has been available for several decades, but came into active use by commodity bankers during periods of extremely tight money. The bankers' acceptance as it is used in commodity financing is a draft drawn on the bank for a specific period of time, usually up to 180 days, and accepted by the bank which also attaches or endorses an eligibility statement to the draft. To be eligible for rediscount at the Federal Reserve Bank or in the bankers' acceptance money market, the draft must cover the storage of readily marketable commodities or the shipment of such commodities either abroad or within the United States. The draft is discounted and may either be held in the accepting bank's own loan portfolio, making it the same as a regular discount loan, or sold through a dealer into the bankers' acceptance market. These instruments compete in the money market with other short-term paper such as commercial paper and Treasury bills and are actively traded. By selling its acceptances in the market, the commodity bank can fund its commodity loans thereby giving it greater capacity to continue lending or increase loans even in periods of tight money. This is particularly important to commodity bankers, since they are constantly called upon to finance the movement of vitally needed commodities whether loanable funds are available or not.

Margins

One of the most important aspects of commodity financing is the maintenance of adequate margins by borrowers against their loans. As has been previously noted, most secured commodity lending is highly leveraged since the lender is looking primarily to the collateral. Nevertheless, particular attention should be paid to the amount of margin that is in an account at all times. According to *Webster's New Collegiate Dictionary*, 7th ed., margin can be both "cash or collateral that is deposited . . . to secure . . . from loss on a contract" or "a customer's equity if his account is terminated at prevailing market prices." The commodity banker must require that the borrower maintain sufficient margin against his loan by either (1) keeping on deposit enough cash that can be used by the banker to make up for any loss he might take by liquidating the collateral during a period of declining prices, or (2) always maintaining as collateral sufficient quantities of the commodity being financed to be able to retire the loan by liquidation of the collateral at any given price level in the market.

In order to ascertain the amount of margin in an account, the banker usually must obtain a position report from the customer which reflects both the market and "basis" position. In general, in commodity financing, "basis" refers to the difference between the spot or current price of the commodity and its price on the futures market. Should a merchant have outstanding any contracts to buy or sell a commodity in the future, the commodity banker needs to compare those to the current price of the commodity or to the price on any firm sales to determine any inherent losses or gains for the merchant's account. This helps to indicate the overall financial position at that given moment. Obviously, this position constantly is changing as both current and futures prices fluctuate. A merchant may have a large profit in a commodity currently if he purchased it at a price considerably lower than the current market price (i.e., he is maintaining a large margin), but if he has sold the commodity on the futures market at a price lower than the current one, his "basis" position will pull down his market position and affect his overall margin with the lender. By knowing the merchant's full market and basis position, the banker is able to estimate what effect future occurrences will have on the borrower. For instance, if a merchant has sold a commodity for a fixed price and has not hedged the sale in the futures market (or by some other means), it becomes apparent a built-in loss is present should prices rise before he covers his sale. By valuing the merchant's collateral position daily, the banker is in a position to call the loan and liquidate any collateral before its value falls below the amount of the loan.

Marketability

Almost as important as the maintenance of margins in commodity financing is the marketability of the commodity being financed. Even though a futures market exists for the commodity, the banker still may be in control of quantities that are not deliverable. The greater the marketability of a commodity, the less the risk that the banker must take in financing it. The length of time taken to liquidate an inventory, usually governed by market conditions, can determine whether or not a loss will be taken at liquidation.

Influence of the Government

The subjects of prices and margins in commodity financing cannot be totally covered without some reference to the role played by the U.S. government. For many years the government was a major factor to be considered in the financing of agricultural products. High support prices and large stocks maintained by the Commodity Credit Corporation had a decided effect on commodity prices by keeping them relatively stable. In the early 1970s, changes in government policies led to the sale of most of its surplus commodities and the lowering of support prices. This added some hazards to commodity financing. Formerly the government provided a floor at which a commodity would trade as manifested in the support price. Similarly, a ceiling was maintained because of the large surpluses which the government would sell when the price attained a certain level. The government's activities, therefore, kept large swings in commodity prices at a minimum and reduced the risk to the commodity banker. With the government on the sidelines, there were extremely large fluctuations in the prices of several commodities; namely, cotton, soybeans, and wheat. The amount of government involvement in the commodity field in the future will have a decided effect on the prices of these several commodities and perhaps others. Those who champion free enterprise object to this involvement. However, they admit that large price fluctuations are hazardous to the producers, merchants, bankers, and final users of the commodities involved.

SECURED COMMODITY LOANS—IN-TRANSIT DOCUMENTS

To better understand the differences between lending secured by warehouse receipts and lending secured by in-transit documents, it might be helpful to outline the various steps in a typical commodity transaction. (Some commodity bankers insist there are no "typical" commodity transactions.) If a merchant believes the price of a commodity is low enough whereby he can make a decent profit at resale, he will purchase a quantity of the commodity at the spot or current market price. The commodity will be stored in a warehouse of some kind and the merchant will receive warehouse receipts denoting title to the goods. In order to pay for the commodity, he will usually borrow about 85 percent of the value of the commodity from his bank, depositing the warehouse receipts as collateral for the loan.

At a later date, when the merchant sells the commodity to the final user, his price generally will also cover transportation and all charges up to the user's warehouse. Therefore, the merchant must obtain a release from the warehouse by presenting the warehouse receipts to the warehouseman and ship the commodity by truck, train, or barge to the final user. At this point, the bank must relinquish the warehouse receipts to the warehouseman. When shipment is made to the user, various shipping documents (namely, an invoice and a bill of lading which carries title to the goods) are drawn and forwarded to the user for payment against presentation of the documents.

During the period from relinquishing the warehouse receipt to receipt of payment from the final user, the commodity banker has much less control over the ownership of the goods. Any control is maintained through the control of the shipping or in-transit documents drawn covering the movement of the commodity to the user. At this stage, it is imperative that the commodity banker be filed with the relevant state authorities under the Uniform Commercial Code. The filing puts all creditors on notice that the commodity banker has a security interest in the inventory which is in transit and the resulting accounts receivable running from the user to the commodity merchant.

Trust Receipts

When the commodity banker relinquishes the warehouse receipts securing the loan, this is accomplished against a trust receipt prepared by the borrower. In essence, the trust receipt states that the bank has released in trust to the borrower the title documents to a specified quantity and type of goods, and that it still retains a security interest in that title. Some commodity bankers feel that the use of trust receipts constitutes a hazard to perfecting a security interest in a particular commodity. The trust receipt is necessary, however, for often it is the only instrument available to denote security interest in the goods.

The drawbacks to the use of a trust receipt include:

1. The bank must have had the original title document in its possession at the time of release.
2. The holder must be able to identify the collateral beyond the shadow of a doubt.
3. The UCC is unclear as to the period of validity of a trust receipt.

The last two conditions pose most of the problems. A trust receipt cannot merely state it covers "200 bales of cotton stored in XYZ Warehouse." It must state exactly which 200 bales and list the warehouse receipt numbers. Often the description on the receipt is incomplete or inaccurate and would not stand up against a claim against the collateral by a holder in due course of the warehouse receipts. The expiration date of a trust receipt generally cannot be more than 21 days from the date of issuance, but the individual codes often are unclear as to this point. The essential point is that the trust receipt is not a pure title document and is not a strong indication of the bank's security interest in the goods.

One of the ways to avoid the use of trust receipts and reduce the bank's exposure is for the bank to forward the warehouse receipts directly to the warehouseman. The bank must include instructions for the warehouseman to load and ship the commodity to a particular consignee, returning all bills of lading covering the shipment directly to the bank for the account of the borrower. By using this procedure, the bank avoids releasing title or collateral documents to the borrower and thereby avoids the risk inherent in so doing. Risk is further reduced by instructing the borrower to invoice the ultimate buyer through the bank. All documentation is given to the bank to attach to a draft and the bill of lading. These documents then are forwarded for collection to the buyer through normal banking channels. Some banks will give immediate credit against the borrower's loan account when the documents are deposited for collection. More recently there has been a movement among banks to credit the borrower only when collection has been made. The rationale for this is the fact that it is easier to keep track of loans outstanding than collections outstanding.

Bills of Lading

The most important in-transit document is the bill of lading. These documents are issued by the transportation company charged with moving the commodity from one place to another, generally from the borrower's selected warehouse to that of the final user. The bill of lading is issued in two ways: negotiable or to order and nonnegotiable or "straight." The difference between the two forms is considerable.

The carrier which issues a nonnegotiable or straight bill of lading normally has discharged its duty when the goods covered by the lading are delivered directly to the consignee. A holder of the bill of lading during the course of the movement of the goods had no claim to title of the goods and they may be delivered to the consignee without surrender of the bill of lading. In fact, he may not even have it in his possession at delivery. Obviously, if a commodity banker wishes to retain his security interest in the goods (which are still his collateral until the final user has paid for them) he will not accept a nonnegotiable bill of lading from the merchant.

The commodity banker still has title to the goods being shipped as long as the bill of lading is negotiable or issued to order. It can be issued to the order of the shipper/borrower or to the order of the bank. Occasionally the bill of lading will simply state "Issued to order." The carrier which issues a negotiable bill of lading is required to deliver the goods only to the holder of the bill of lading which covers their shipment. Because of this characteristic, the commodity banker has the ability to take title to the goods in the event of default by the buyer, and to apply the proceeds of the sale to the outstanding loans.

Freight Forwarders

Since many commodity merchants are exporters, the commodity banker needs to enlist the services of international freight forwarders in protecting the interest in the goods being shipped abroad and in assisting in the collection of the proceeds of the sale. When a commodity is destined for export, it is not released from the warehouse to the final user, but to a freight forwarder located in a port of exit from the United States. The forwarder must maintain control of the goods from the time the truck, railroad car or barge enters the port marshaling area until the time the commodity is loaded safely on board a steamship and a steamship company bill of lading is issued. Usually the forwarder has already booked cargo space for the commodity and is assuming the responsibility for delivering to the ocean carrier. Therefore, the inland transportation company bill of lading either shows the freight forwarder, acting as agent for the merchant (and his banker), as the consignee or must again be to order and surrendered to the carrier by the forwarder as a holder in due course. Banks prefer the negotiable bill of lading which they can send to the freight forwarder with instructions to load the commodity and return to the bank the negotiable steamship bills of lading which also are title documents.

As in the case with domestic shipments, the merchant combines the other needed shipping documents and drafts with the ocean bill of lading or title document still in the lending bank's possession. These documents are then either presented for payment against an export letter of credit or forwarded for collection to a correspondent bank abroad. The foreign bank is responsible for surrendering the shipping documents against either payment or acceptance of a time draft by the foreign buyer and ultimately remitting the proceeds to the merchant's U.S. bank. Here again the commodity bank may give immediate credit for the documents when deposited for collection or wait until the collection procedure is complete before crediting the merchant or his loan account. In case immediate credit is given, the exporter is usually charged interest for the period the collection is outstanding. Occasionally a bank makes prior arrangements to finance an export sale and discounts an exporter's draft without recourse. This procedure is more fully an international banking function and will not be covered here.

Suffice it to say, during the period that the commodity is in transit from the warehouse to storage on board an ocean vessel, the freight forwarder is an important agent for the commodity banker and must act to protect the bank's interest at all times.

COMMODITY LOANS TO GRAIN COMPANIES

Commodity loans covering the merchandising of grain usually are of some magnitude since grain usually is shipped in large quantities. A further complicating factor is that grain companies usually store grain in elevators where they have substantial ownership. Consequently, very few third-party warehouse receipts are issued to serve as collateral for the commodity banker. Therefore, the banker is usually compelled to apply one of three styles of lending to the situation depending upon the type of borrower.

If the loan is to one of the extremely large grain concerns, it usually is on an unsecured basis and is made completely on the strength of the company's financial statement. A second category of loan would be one where the credit does not quite justify that it be unsecured, but the borrower has a strong net worth and is considered to be completely trustworthy and competent in the industry. In such an instance, the loan is made on the basis of a filing against inventory and accounts receivable under the Uniform Commercial Code. The bank does not require that warehouse receipts be deposited as collateral, but looks solely to the Code filing for security.

A loan to a small grain concern with a small net worth will require full security by the bank and complete control of the collateral. This type of loan usually is secured by warehouse receipts issued by a field warehouse company which controls the flow of the inventory on the borrower's premises and guarantees to the lender that the inventory pledged to the bank is on hand at all times.

Unsecured Commodity Loans

Mention has been made previously about unsecured commodity loans. Generally these are made only to the largest, most prestigious grain companies. Lending to such firms must be made against the same criteria used for other unsecured loans; namely, the character and reputation of the firm, the capability of its financial condition to take on the extension of additional credit, and its capacity to repay the loan. A word of caution should be noted, however, in that many commodity firms are highly leveraged. Therefore, certain standard measurement ratios such as the proportions of inventory to total current assets or debt to worth become meaningless at certain periods of the firm's financial year. Usually the fiscal year-end will occur at the lowest point in the business cycle in order to avoid conditions which might lead to distortions in the financial statements.

With sufficient historical data available on the firm along with a strong financial condition and a good reputation in the industry, the commodity banker can generally lend on an unsecured basis to a major commodity firm with confidence.

HEDGING AND THE FUTURES MARKET

The operation of the futures markets for various commodities is another complete subject in itself. If such a market exists for a particular commodity, it is of utmost importance to commodity merchants and indirectly to their bankers. It has been said that it would be extremely difficult for the merchants to exist without a futures market. Accordingly banks would be precluded from much commodity financing in the absence of these markets as the risks resulting from unhedged positions would be prohibitive.

Hedging can probably best be defined as the vehicle used to shift unwanted market risks from one party to one more willing and/or able to assume these risks. By hedging on the futures markets, commodity companies usually have been able to accumulate with a lower risk factor large quantities of goods anticipating a sale at a later date and at a small margin of profit. Almost by definition, commodity merchants acting as brokers or middlemen between the producers and the users work on miniscule profit margins. Because the margins are small, the merchant must transact a large turnover in order to meet overhead and make a profit. Accordingly, he must protect his small margins as best he can by hedging his purchases and sales.

Besides providing a price hedge, the futures market gives the merchant some flexibility. In times of tight supply, as a last resort, the market is a source of physical delivery of the commodity purchased. For every forward purchase there is a sale which the seller must be prepared to deliver at the maturity of the contract. When the actual market is weak, the futures market also can become the buyer of a commodity which has been sold on a forward basis.

Another advantage to the futures market is that it provides an opportunity to carry large positions in a commodity at a fraction of normal industry costs. The interest cost for putting up original and maintenance margin on futures contracts to buy a commodity is far less than the interest cost on loans to buy and carry physical inventory plus storage costs. If storage of the commodity is in company-owned facilities, additional costs accrue for the space and personnel to handle the physical inventory. By contracting to buy certain quantities of a commodity at a certain price on a certain day in the future, the merchants avoid all of the expenses of physical handling until they need the commodity. Most commodity firms work in both the physical and futures markets depending upon their expectations, their customer base, and their ability to obtain financing.

In the discussion of margin in a previous section mention was made of the two inventory positions, market and "basis." The market position, or the difference between what the merchant has paid for a quantity of the product and what he has sold it for, is easily ascertained. The basis position is more complicated to learn but is essentially the difference between the current prices of the spot commodity and that of the same commodity at a future date.

The futures market affords protection to the merchants (and thereby their bankers) by giving them a place to sell any physical inventory which they have on hand which has not already been sold. In like manner, the merchants often contract to buy a quantity of a product in the future when they see the opportunity of making a profit on a definite sale based on the futures price. The merchants can move back and forth between the physical and futures markets and use many combinations or variations of purchases and sales. It is not unusual for a single specific quantity of a product to be bought and sold many times in the future by several companies. In fact, it is common for one company to buy and sell one particular contract more than once during a period of time running over several weeks or months. Hopefully, the company will make a small margin of profit each time it turns that particular contract but this is not always the case.

One other function that the futures market provides is a base for pricing. Merchandising risks are assumed with the knowledge that the actual price of a commodity and the futures price do not always move with a 100 percent correlation; there are fluctuating differences between these prices and the market. Therefore, many commodity prices are based on the futures market and expressed in "points," or increments of a dollar or a cent, on or off the futures price. When the actual commodity is traded at a price lower than the futures price it is said to be traded at a discount. If it is traded higher than the futures price it is at a premium.

The skillful use of the futures market by a commodity firm cannot only provide protection against losses from violent price fluctuations but also reduce the costs of carrying large physical inventories. The merchant must always keep his or her banker informed of both the market and basis positions in the futures market so that the banker can have an estimate of the merchant's volume of transactions as well as any profits or losses caused by the firm's market activities. Without this market, the merchant would be unable to deal in the large volumes necessary to be profitable and his commodity banker would not feel safe in extending financing for large open or unhedged positions.

CONCLUSION

Not every bank is called upon the make commodity loans. However, certain sections of the United States have certain types of commodities that are extremely important to the economy of that locale. It is the commodity banker's function to assist commodity customers by financing their operations in the same manner that the retail banker finances automobile loans, the mortgage banker finances construction and real estate loans, and the invesment banker finances activities in the debt and equity markets.

While commodity loans generally are for large amounts, the banker for the most part can rely completely on the value of his collateral given that he has perfected his lien on that collateral. In spite of the fact that most commodity financing is highly leveraged, the experience of commodity banks over the years has been excellent and the losses, especially when compared to the total volume of financing done, have been at a minimum. In fact, the largest losses have involved fraudulent actions on the part of the borrowers. With proper policing and auditing this type of loss can be avoided.

Because of the great reliance on collateral, commodity banking is specialized and requires specialized lending officers. Once they have acquired the unique skills and methods used in commodity banking, the bankers will find it is not all that complicated. Traditionally it has been a profitable segment of banking and well worth the special handling which it requires.

Chapter 50

Longer Term Lending to Business

*Claude H. Booker, Jr.**

W. C. Henry†

INTRODUCTION

One of the most significant changes that has occurred in commercial bank lending since the 1930s has been the development of term lending. By definition, a term loan is simply one that has a final maturity of more than one year from the date that it is made. The form and characteristics of such loans, however, may differ widely for a variety of reasons. The purpose of this chapter is to provide a general discussion of the major factors to be considered in the study of this important field of lending.

There is a sharp distinction between longer term lending to business and short-term lending. The source of repayment of short-term loans normally consists of the conversion of an asset, and in the case of secured short-term credit the lender relies on the protection afforded by collateral values. The classic example of a short-term loan would be one that is granted a retail merchant for seasonal inventory purchases, with repayment coming from the liquidation of that inventory in the normal course of business. Longer term loans, on the other hand, are primarily dependent upon the continuing profitable operation of the borrower for ultimate repayment. Thus, careful examination of the cash flow of a business is critical to the analysis of term loan requests. For purposes of this discussion, cash flow is defined as net after tax earnings plus other noncash charges to income, such as depreciation.

---

*President, First National Bank and Trust Company, Augusta, Georgia.

† Group Vice President, Trust Company Bank, Atlanta, Georgia.

In the typical term loan arrangement, an agreement is negotiated between lender and borrower dealing with the specifics of the manner in which the credit is to be handled. This agreement is in written form, and while in some instances it is incorporated in the note itself, most term loan agreements are separate documents. Since term loans vary so widely as to amount, purpose, maturity, rate, collateral, and covenant considerations, the loan agreement is a tailor-made instrument reflecting the needs and requirements of the parties. A detailed discussion of the elements comprising such an agreement follows later in this chapter.

HISTORY AND EVOLUTION OF TERM LENDING

As we know it today, term lending is a relatively new concept in the administration of commercial bank credit. It is probably accurate to state that modern term lending has its roots in the years of the Great Depression. During that very difficult period in our economic history, the relatively low level of business activity resulted in a substantial liquidation of bank credit and left the banking system with large excess reserves seeking profitable employment. Most commercial enterprises found their profit margins severely reduced, and managements were challenged with the task of finding ways to operate successfully in the extremely hostile economic climate. In all probability, the earliest term loans were negotiated for the purpose of restructuring debt and capital accounts by providing funds to retire bonds, debentures, and preferred stock which had been issued during a time when interest rates were much higher.

During the 1930s there also appeared to be a change in the attitude of supervisory authorities toward such credit arrangements and gradually term lending began to achieve a status of respectability among commercial bank lenders. As this country began to slowly emerge from the Great Depression and particularly as the tremendous pressures on our productive capacity caused by World War II made themselves felt, the uses to which term loans were put changed dramatically. The emphasis shifted to the need for expansion and modernization of plant and equipment, increased working capital requirements to support higher levels of sales, and, in some instances, to provide funds for mergers and acquisitions.

The volume of term loans handled by banks of all sizes has grown tremendously, and today term loans outstanding represent a major portion of total loans in the portfolios of many banks.

BANK POLICY CONSIDERATIONS

There are a number of policy considerations which a particular bank will want to take into account in determining its relative interest in aggressively seeking opportunities to make term loans in any volume. Clearly, one of the first major factors to consider is the nature and volatility of its deposits. There are some banking institutions which regularly and predictably experience a wide fluctuation in deposits, particularly demand deposits. It is a well-known fact that many banks located in agricultural communities are especially vulnerable to seasonal influences which will cause their deposits to shrink 50 percent or more. Those same seasonal influences which cause a runoff in deposits also create a heavy loan demand. Thus, banks which are confronted with this situation must maintain a relatively high degree of liquidity in order to be prepared to meet the needs of their customers. Obviously, then, a large commitment to term loans with their attendant less liquid features must be viewed with prudence and caution when planning the investment of bank funds in such institutions. On the other hand, banks located in communities with more diversified economies where deposit patterns are relatively stable may choose to allocate a larger share of lendable funds to term loans.

In addition to an analysis of its deposit structure, a bank should carefully consider its loan demand pattern when contemplating the degree of commitment to term lending. It is axiomatic that diversification of the loan portfolio is highly desirable. A close examination of the type of loan demand generated in its trade area is of great importance in reaching decisions as to the funds which can be allocated to longer-term commitments. Implicit in such an examination is the necessity for analyzing the present investment of bank funds along with a projection of future needs. Obviously, while the overall loan account represents the largest segment of the assets of most banks, the elements of the loan account should be structured in such a way that they reflect the general investment policy of the institution.

The adequacy of the capital account is another major consideration. If capital is limited relative to deposits and risk assets, the prudent bank will exercise caution in expanding its volume in such loans. Capital represents a cushion of safety for depositors, and any bank which pursues a loan policy of overtrading its capital account does so at its peril.

Another vital concern to management in the formulation of policy with regard to term loans involves an objective analysis of the qualifications of its lending personnel. As a general rule, term lending requires a more sophisticated approach to credit research and analysis, and should not be undertaken unless capable, experienced and well-trained people are available to provide the necessary expertise in the handling of such credits. While all loans carry varying degrees of risk, term loans, which are dependent upon continued profitable operations of business enterprises over a period of years for successful repayment, demand mature credit judgment if they are to be handled safely.

Finally, in any discussion of policy it must be recognized that altered circumstances may well change the emphasis a bank wishes to give to term lending. Changing economic conditions, significant shifts in the pattern of a particular industry, and changes in the character and trend of a bank's deposits and assets are but a few of the things which should be under constant review if bank policy is to keep in step with reality.

VARIOUS FORMS OF TERM LOANS

There are no steadfast rules for structuring the repayment schedule for term loans. Because each such loan is the result of a particular need, it makes sense to design a payment schedule which is tailored to conform to the anticipated cash flow of the borrower. The most simple form is the serial term loan, in which the proceeds are advanced at once and are repaid over a stated number of years. Payments may be called for monthly, quarterly, or even annually, though quarterly payments are most frequently used. It is not entirely uncommon for the repayment schedule to call for less than proportionate payments in the early years of a credit, with stepped-up payments in the final years. There are also cases involving a balloon payment; for example, a seven-year credit calling for payments at the rate of 10 percent per year but with the entire balance due at the end of the seventh year (such a case would commonly be described as "ten-year amortization with a seventh year balloon").

Revolving credits are usually short-term commitments, or are combined with term loan commitments as described below. Occasionally, however, it will suit the needs of a borrower to have a bank commitment for a revolving credit extending for up to three years (seldom more). In these cases the borrower will pay the bank a commitment, or standby, fee (typically 0.25 percent or 0.50 percent per annum) for that portion of the commitment which is not in use ("the daily unused balance"). The borrower is willing to pay the fee in order to have the assurance that credit will be available when needed, as the obligation to lend becomes a contractual obligation of the bank so long as the company remains in compliance with the requirements placed upon it by the loan agreement. There will be a discussion of term loan agreements later in this chapter.

Oftentimes a borrower will not need to draw down (borrow) the entire term loan proceeds at one time. In these situations, such as where construction of facilties is involved, or where equipment orders involve lead-time and staggered deliveries, a combination revolving credit/serial term loan will be used. An example would be an airline which has ordered several aircraft to be built for delivery at intervals several months apart so that each can be integrated into the airline's system before the next delivery date. The loan agreement in this case might provide for a $50 million revolving credit for, say, 18 months, with the amount owing at maturity to be converted to a term loan. This enables the airline to use the credit facility most efficiently, as it can, during the period of the "revolver," draw funds as needed and make temporary paybacks during periods when it has excess cash. If, at the end of the 18 months, it has accumulated more profit than had been anticipated, it may want to have the credit converted to term at something less than the amount committed by the bank, and the terms of such agreements usually permit this.

ANALYZING THE RISK

Not every borrower which is a reasonable risk for a seasonal line of credit is a candidate for term financing. Bank term loans, by definition and by custom, fall between the short-term seasonal borrowing needs and the truly long-term requirements (10–20 years or more) which are the province of insurance company lenders, public debt issues or equity capital. In seasonal borrowing, where loans accommodate a buildup in inventory and receivables, which in turn convert back to cash after the peak season, the leveraging of equity with debt is efficient in that it avoids the borrower having either too much equity in slow seasons or too little for peak seasons. In contrast, a term loan is usually predicated upon repayment out of future earnings (plus depreciation throw-off) rather than from liquidation of short-term assets.

The borrower is thus taking a greater risk with term credit, because if sufficient profits are not generated it will have to reduce the scope of its business by liquidating assets in the best way it can. In extreme cases this could mean complete liquidation or sale of the business. The bank loan officer, therefore, needs to satisfy himself that the borrower's industry has stable characteristics, that the borrowing entity has capable management and that its plans for future growth are well founded.

There are no specific analytical standards which are peculiar to term loans, and an attempt to establish firm guidelines might lead the lender to overlook some special characteristic of the borrower or its particular industry. Obviously, the first basis for attempting to judge the future earnings capability of a business is to be throughly familiar with its operating and balance sheet history. Changing conditions in the industry should be known and understood. Capability and depth of management should be evaluated.

A forecast of cash flow and balance sheet results should be examined critically. Every banker with more than just a few years experience can recall pie-in-the-sky forecasts presented in impressive format but based on the simple assumption of a growth rate of x percent per year. Because the purpose of term loans is nearly always to permit the acquisition of productive assets (there are exceptions, such as where the stock of a deceased shareholder is being bought in), it is axiomatic that earnings in the future should increase. Nevertheless, the lending officer should zero in on the forecasted results with questions designed to bring answers which reveal the extent of thought and planning which created them.

TERM LOAN AGREEMENTS

An attempt at a complete discussion of all the possible provisions of a term loan agreement would extend to an entire volume. In form, such an agreement can be as short and simple as a one- or two-page "letter agreement"; or it can be a formal, legalistic document of well over 100 pages. This discussion will cover the general format typical of term loan agreements and the common sense approach which should be used in setting the terms.

A term loan agreement is intended to be a legally binding contract. It may be in relatively simple letter form (a letter from bank to borrower, prepared in duplicate and executed by both parties, each of whom retains a copy) where the amount is modest in relation to the financial strength and stability of the borrower and where the term is not especiall long (three–four years). Such a letter agreement will simply describe the purpose and amount of the loan, its repayment terms, interest rate, collateral (if any), and state a requirement that the borrower furnish periodic financial statements.

More often, however, the loan agreement will be a formalized legal document. While a loan officer with appropriate experience might write the agreement himself, in which case he or she should have it reviewed by the bank's legal counsel, the drafting of the agreement is more often done by the attorney after full discussion with the officer and perhaps with the borrower and its attorney.

The typical formal agreement will begin with recitations of existing fact ("Whereas, Borrower is a corporation duly incorporated and validly existing under the laws of . . ."), covering such matters as the nature of the business, corporate authority to enter into the agreement, the existence or absence of litigation against the company or of liens against its assets, and such other things a fertile mind might deem appropriate.

Next will be a description of the credit terms. This will cover provisions relating to mandatory or voluntary prepayment as well as stating the amount of the credit, repayment schedule and interest (365-day basis, 360-day basis, changing when prime rate changes, and so on).

Usually, voluntary prepayment will be allowed without penalty except where the prepayment funds were borrowed from another bank. Mandatory prepayment might be required to the extent of a portion of earnings in excess of a specified level ("capture of profits" clause), or in the event of any substantial liquidation of assets (e.g., sale of a plant or of a subsidiary).

Next will generally follow lists of covenants, both affirmative and negative. Typically affirmative covenants (things the borrower will do) require the furnishing of annual audits and interim statements, the continuance of corporate existence, maintenance of adequate insurance, the keeping of properties in good repair and the like. Negative covenants might place limitations on the amount of any other indebtedness, put a limitation on annual capital expenditures, require a minimum current ratio, prohibit mergers, and limit dividends, among other things.

Finally, the agreement will specify those happenings which would constitute events of default. These will include failure to make principal and interest payments when due, voluntary or involuntary bankruptcy, and violation of any loan covenant (sometimes granting a grace period of 30 days to correct certain violations). The existence of a condition of default gives the bank the option, subject to any period of grace allowed for the borrower to cure the condition, to accelerate the debt maturity and demand payment. This option would be exercised and the loan called in the event of bankruptcy, but in most cases where lesser events of default occur and where the borrower's ability to pay has not been severely diminished, the bank will negotiate strengthened terms, perhaps taking collateral or additional collateral, and will in return waive its present right (but not any future right) to accelerate maturity.

As indicated earlier, the designing of a term loan agreement demands a common sense approach. The number of possible restraints is limitless. A good loan agreement is one which sets boundaries which give the bank effective protection without putting undue restrictions on management discretion.

AFTER THE LOAN IS MADE

It is only prudent to monitor compliance with the restrictive provisions (the covenants) for the life of the term loan. In most banks a loan committee will review the loan annually upon receipt of fiscal year-end financial statements. The account officer should review interim statements, quarterly or monthly, so as to stay continually abreast of compliance and of changing conditions which could lead to a breach of compliance.

Many term loan agreements require the submission, with each interim financial statement, of a certificate of the borrower's chief financial officer to the effect that no condition exists which constitutes default or would through passage of time lead to a default. Independent accountants cannot be required to submit such a certification, but the loan agreement can require that they issue a statement to the effect that during the course of their examination nothing which would constitute or lead to an event of default came to their attention.

Careful monitoring often results in heading off trouble before it arises. At the very least, it precludes the embarrassment of surprise. The prudent investor doesn't put his or her stock away and forget it; likewise, the prudent lender doesn't rest on an assumption that the last dollar of the term loan will be returned on schedule.

CONCLUSION

There is no question but that the term loan has a place in the inventory of bank services. The foregoing paragraphs emphasize the fact that such a loan requires more than ordinary skill and experience on the part of the lending institution and that constant review should be maintained. For the average bank, long-term credits encompassing 10 to 20 years should be minimized, and in some cases avoided completely.

The lending bank should always be careful to determine if a proposed term loan is to the advantage of the prospective borrower, or if added funds should be more wisely acquired through increased equity capital. Both the lender and the borrower should be in complete accord with the need for the loan and the ability to repay it on schedule, and the borrower should not be unmindful that the very future of the business could be at stake.

Chapter 51

Equipment Leasing

*Milton M. Harris**

The total amount of all of the equipment leasing written to date, or in any one year is unknown. There are many types of leases, and many types of lessors. It is estimated that the total original cost of equipment leased is over $10 billion, and that close to a billion dollars of new equipment is leased annually. Bank participation in leasing probably exceeds $2 billion.

Proposed changes in accounting treatment of leases in financial statements of lessees, and the tightening of requirements by the Internal Revenue Service for lessors wishing to make use of the tax benefits of ownership, raise some questions as to the future of leasing. However, corporations will continue to require the financing of equipment, and though the types of equipment leases may change, equipment leasing in some form will continue to flourish.

DEFINITION

An equipment lease is a contract which enables an equipment user (the lessee) to secure the use of equipment by making specified payments (rentals) to the owner (the lessor).

Such leases may include a variety of terms relating to maintenance, insurance, payment of personal property taxes, early termination, end use of the equipment, use of depreciation, and treatment of the investment tax credit.

---

* President, Maryland National Leasing Corporation, Baltimore, Maryland.

TYPES OF EQUIPMENT LEASES

In general, equipment leases fall into two broad categories, nonpayout and full payout. In a nonpayout lease the lessor receives a guarantee of rentals in the initial lease insufficient to pay for the entire cost of the equipment. The lessor must secure a series of new lessees to obtain full return. Often such a lessor will provide various services as part of the lease, thus the name "service lease" or "full service lease" is often applied to such an arrangement. Usually the lessor pays for maintenance, insurance, and personal property taxes.

The Federal Reserve Board does not allow national banks to participate in such leases except that such banks are allowed to consider a residual value of the equipment up to 20 percent of the original cost in computing return. As a practical matter, most banks are not in a position to readily perform the services that are usually offered by a manufacturer, nor are they so knowledgeable about equipment that they might want to speculate in future equipment values. Most independent lessors who have had financial problems, have been nonpayout lessors who estimated incorrectly their ability to re-lease or sell equipment. A notable example is the group of equipment leasing companies who wrote short-term (often as little as one year) leases on IBM-360 computers. Every company so engaged had serious problems when the residual value of the equipment did not meet expectations.

The focus of this chapter will, therefore, be the *full payout* equipment lease. This is the type of lease most written by all financial institutions. These leases are categorized by their structures and accounting treatment.

The *finance* lease, now called the "capital lease" by the Financial Accounting Standards Board (FASB), is an equipment lease in which the user of the equipment (the lessee) enjoys the advantages of ownership of the leased equipment. This means that the lessee obtains the benefits of accelerated depreciation and the investment tax credit (ITC), and has the right to acquire the equipment at a predetermined price when the original lease term ends. Such a lease will probably be treated by the lessee and lessor as a loan for accounting and income tax purposes.

Such a *capital* lease usually meets one or more of the following criteria: (1) Transfers title to the equipment to the lessee at the end of the lease term for a predetermined price. (2) Contains a bargain purchase option. (3) Has a lease term equal to 75 percent or more of the equipment's useful life. (4) Has an estimated residual value at the end of the lease term of less than 25 percent of the equipment's original cost. (5) The equipment is special purpose to the lessee, and so will have little economic value at the lease's termination to anyone other than the original lessee.

The *true* lease is now called the *operating* lease by the FASB. The term *operating* has led to some confusion since operating lease has been used to refer to a lease in which the lessor provided services, such as a manufacturer leasing his own product, usually a *nonpayout* transaction. In this type of lease, the lessor enjoys the advantages of ownership, in that he looks to the residual value for part of his return.

The FASB Exposure Draft of August 26, 1975 was modified by the Revision Exposure Draft of July 22, 1976. A final "Statement of Financial Accounting Standards No. 13," dated November 1976 was issued. Under the terms of this statement, a lessee must classify all leases as either capital or operating. A capital lease is one which meets one or more of the following conditions:

1. The lease transfers ownership of the property to the lessee by the end of the lease term.
2. The lease contains a bargain purchase option.
3. The lease term is equal to 75 percent or more of the estimated economic life of the leased property.
4. The present value of the minimum lease payments less certain costs of lessor equals or exceeds 90 percent of the original equipment cost (less any investment tax credit retained by lessor).

All other leases are classified as operating leases.

From the standpoint of the lessor, if a lease meets any one of the preceding criteria and both of the following criteria, it shall be classified as a sales type lease (by a vendor) or a direct financing lease (by a financial institution):

1. Collectibility is reasonably predictable.
2. There are not important unknown unreimbursable costs.

Any lease which does not meet the above standards is classified as an operating lease.

The percentages of residual value and lease term duration do not equal FASB definitions. They do meet the guidelines set forth in the Internal Revenue's Revenue Procedure 75–21 dated April 11, 1975. The tax implications are of greater import to most lessors than FASB proposed accounting treatment. If the proposed FASB exposure draft is accepted, most lessors will treat leases as operating for tax purposes, to obtain maximum tax benefits, but capital for accounting purposes to enable them to obtain maximum reported earnings by using the *finance method* of accounting rather than the *operating method*. If a lessor were forced to report lease income for *book* on the same basis as *tax*, his book would show the losses taken for tax purposes. Most lessors would not find this acceptable since continued leasing would continue to show increasing losses.

Under the FASB Statement No. 13, even though a lease is accounted for by the lessee as an operating lease, the lessor may account for it as a capital lease, and the reverse as well. In addition, the accounting and tax treatments need not be the same by lessor or lessee.

The Leveraged Lease. This type of lease is a true or operating lease with something added. In a leveraged lease, the lessor, instead of supplying all of the funds necessary to purchase the equipment to be leased, forms a trust and supplies only a part of the purchase price. The remaining funds necessary are borrowed by the trust from an institutional lender. It is this borrowing or *leverage* that causes the lease to be called "leveraged," or "with debt." This debt is secured by the equipment being leased, and the underlying credit of the lessee. Neither the lessee nor the equity participant, however, guarantees the debt, which is solely the obligation of the borrowing trust.

Although the lessee has the sole obligation of paying rentals to the trust, and the trust is obligated to the equity participant and to the lenders, the equity participant and lenders look beyond the trust, to the credit of the lessee in making their credit decision.

For tax purposes, a minimum of 20 percent *equity* is necessary in such a leveraged lease, but 30 percent to 40 percent equity is not uncommon. The equity participant, since he obtains 100 percent of the tax benefits of accelerated depreciation and often the investment tax credit, as well as 100 percent of the equipment's residual value, is able to provide the lessee with a lease rate often substantially below the debt rate of the trust.

For example:

Total equipment cost	$1,000,000
Equity provided by bank	300,000
Debt provided by insurance company	700,000
Term	15 years
Depreciation	10 years to 10% salvage
Residual	20% of original cost
Lease rate	6.5%
Debt rate	10.0%
Investment tax credit	$ 100,000
Estimated residual	200,000
Total rentals.	1,595,295
Total principal repaid	700,000
Total interest paid	680,474
Total debt service	1,380,474
Rentals less debt service	214,821
Yield to lessor	26.97%
Tax rate	50.0%

In addition, the lessor gains the value of accelerated depreciation in the beginning of the lease (see Exhibit 51–1 for the analysis of this transaction) and receives the benefits of funds earned by the *pool* set up for payment of future taxes. This pool or fund for future taxes is considered to earn a *return on investment* (ROI), or *pool rate*. In this analysis the ROI is a 3.5 percent annual after-tax rate.

Exhibit 51–1
Leveraged Lease

Year	Rents	Principal Amortization	Interest	Depreciation
1................	$ 106,353	$ 22,032	$ 70,000	$100,000
2................	106,353	24,235	67,797	180,000
3................	106,353	26,658	65,373	155,294
4................	106,353	29,324	62,708	136,471
5................	106,353	32,257	59,775	117,647
6................	106,353	35,482	56,549	98,824
7................	106,353	39,030	53,001	80,000
8................	106,353	42,934	49,098	31,764
9................	106,353	47,227	44,805	
10...............	106,353	51,950	40,082	
11...............	106,353	57,145	34,887	
12...............	106,353	62,859	29,173	
13...............	106,353	69,145	22,887	
14...............	106,353	76,059	15,972	
15...............	106,353	83,665	8,366	
Total	$1,595,295	$700,002	$680,473	$900,000

	Taxes Saved/Paid	Cash Flow	Tax Fund	After-Tax Cash Flow
1...........	$ 31,824	$146,145	0	$146,145
2...........	70,722	85,043	0	85,043
3...........	57,157	71,478	0	71,478
4...........	46,413	60,734	0	60,734
5...........	35,535	49,856	$45,392	4,463
6...........	24,510	38,831	38,831	0
7...........	13,324	27,645	27,645	0
8...........	−12,745	1,576	1,576	0
9...........	−30,774	−16,453		0
10...........	−33,135	−18,814		0
11...........	−35,733	−21,412		0
12...........	−38,590	−24,269		0
13...........	−41,733	−27,412		0
14...........	−45,190	−30,869		0
15...........	−48,993	115,328		115,328
Total..........	$− 7,408	$457,407		$483,191

The following takes place for income tax purposes in year 1:

+ Rentals...............................	$106,353
− Depreciation	100,000
− Interest.............................	70,000
Net loss for taxes.....................	−63,647
Taxes saved	$ 31,824

The cash flow is as follows:

+ Rentals...............................	$106,353
+ ITC (investment tax credit)	100,000
+ Taxes saved..........................	31,834
Total in	238,177
− Interest.............................	70,000
− Principal...........................	22,032
Net in	$146,145

Exhibit 51–1 (*continued*)

In year 15 for taxes the printout shows:

+ Rentals..............................	$106,353
— Depreciation	0
— Interest.............................	8,366
Net profit for taxes....................	97,987
Taxes paid...........................	$ 48,993

(This is exclusive of the residual value.)

The cash flow is as follows:

+ Rentals..............................	$106,353	
+ ITC.................................	0	
+ Taxes saved..........................	0	
+ Residual............................	200,000	
Total in.............................	306,353	
— Interest.............................	8,366	
— Principal............................	83,665	
— Taxes paid	48,993	(Exclusive of residual)
— Taxes paid	50,000	(On net residual value)
	$115,329	

In the cash flow figure, the residual of $200,000 less an offset of $100,000 salvage, results in a $50,000 net tax due.

In evaluating leveraged leases, it is necessary not only to see a printout, but to know how the computer program is structured, what it indicates, and what it combines or eliminates.

Under the present and proposed methods of accounting for leveraged leases, the full economic benefits to the lessor are not usually translated directly into book earnings. One reason is that the treatment of the investment tax credit may be such that it is spread over the lease term rather than "flowed through" directly to first-year earnings, which would reflect the economic benefits actually received.

In addition, the funds earned by the pool for future taxes is not usually reflected in book earnings, although the lessor receives the economic benefit of such funds.

In the past, however, generally accepted accounting principles *allowed* lessors to bring into book income the "pool" earnings, plus otherwise "front-loading" earnings, although *not recommending* such treatment. Consequently, some lessors derived substantially higher book earnings from leveraged leasing than other lessors participating in the same transactions. Now, under FASB Statement No. 13, all lessors will put less emphasis on "pool earnings" and will seek transactions less tax motivated. Book earnings are increased by added equity and reducing debt, since interest costs reduce book earnings. Book earnings are increased by tax savings, but not by earnings on funds put aside for future taxes; therefore, transactions utilizing excess funds to speed up debt repayment are preferable to merely allowing excess funds to accumulate for future tax payment.

The result of this conservative accounting treatment has been the increase of the equity portion in leveraged leases, with the lessening of borrowed funds. Thus, the transaction gives the lessor more benefits from rentals, less debt repayment, less emphasis on the tax savings (and the tax pool) and a resulting increase in book earnings, often at the expense of economic yields.

All of the above leases, capital, operating, and leveraged are usually net leases, with the lessee responsible for maintenance, personal property taxes, and insurance, as well as all other expenses connected with operation of the equipment, except the lessor's state and federal income taxes.

ATTRACTIONS TO LESSORS AND LESSEES

Why banks find it attractive to act as equipment lessors:

1. The return or yields on equipment leasing will generally exceed the yields obtained from loans to the same company.
2. When a bank writes true leases, and obtains the equipment's value at the lease termination, it gradually builds up a considerable hedge against inflation by its ownership of varied types of equipment, at least some of which should appreciate beyond original estimates.
3. Equipment leases can be written for short payback periods when so desired, or written for long "lock-in" periods when rates are attractive. Rentals may be fixed rate or fluctuating. Thus a bank can create a portfolio suitable to its particular requirements.
4. Many banks feel that if their present customers want to lease, they must be able to provide such service or lose prestige and perhaps the account relationship as well.
5. Equipment leasing may be used as a competitive tool to enlarge the banks list of customers and prestige, both locally and nationally.

Why corporations lease equipment instead of borrowing:

1. Avoids the use of cash, conserving working capital, usually not even a down payment is required.
2. Avoids the use of short-term bank lines, conserving borrowing capacity for financing inventory, accounts receivable, and other short-term assets.
3. Provides intermediate term financing, longer than most bank lines, but shorter than most insurance loans.

4. Provides a new source of funds, enlarging the pool of capital available to the lessee. During periods of expansion, or tight money, this added source of funds may be invaluable.
5. Allows the delay of permanent financing when long-term rates are unattractive.
6. Allows the delay of equity financing when the terms would be unacceptable due to market conditions.
7. Provides flexible financing, structured to specific circumstances, available in odd amounts, and on short notice.
8. Avoids the restrictions common to loan agreements.
9. Allows the lessee to trade the value of the investment tax credit and depreciation, which cannot be used in a timely manner, for lower rentals.
10. Provides a lower cost for intermediate term financing than for short-term borrowing when all factors are considered. For example: assuming a 10 percent prime rate, a borrower maintaining 10 percent balances when the line is not in use, incurs a true cost of 12.90 percent assuming 100 percent usage. If the line is only 90 percent used, the true cost is 13.05 percent. A 30-day period "out of the banks" raises the cost to 13.19 percent. Equipment leasing at 12.5 percent would be lower as well as longer term.
11. May be used to obtain equipment not foreseen in capital budget planning.
12. Frees funds for ownership of such appreciating assets as land.
13. Allows the equipment to pay for itself out of earnings rather than capital investment.
14. Allows repayment in depreciated dollars, lowering true cost compared to purchase for cash.

Any or all of these reasons may be valid in a particular situation. The specific reasons are many and varied. In general, large corporations lease because of leasing's ease and convenience. Smaller corporations lease not only because of ease and convenience, but because equipment leasing is often more available than alternative methods of finance, particularly in times of "tight money" when debt money may be virtually impossible to obtain.

ALTERNATIVES OPEN TO A BANK WHICH WISHES TO PARTICIPATE IN THE EQUIPMENT LEASING

Financing equipment leasing companies is the easiest, perhaps the riskiest, and certainly the least profitable method for a bank wishing to participate in equipment leasing. It is the easiest method because there are many lessors, from national to local in scope, all requiring as much money as they can obtain. It is the riskiest, because the bank is usually unable to evaluate the true worth of the borrower, or his receivables. Generally accepted accounting practices allow such latitude in book accounting that a company on the verge of receivership may appear to be quite profitable. Earnings are front-loaded and residuals are booked in year one, although actual cash may be obtained only after the lease's termination, if ever. Often the underlying portfolio is composed of substandard credit risks, borrowing at high rates, with minimum credit evaluation, documentation and collateral. These are often credits the bank would not accept at any rate.

This is often the least profitable business since the banks usually lend at low rates, competing (at the same time) with their own commercial loan department and thus really add nothing to net loans.

If a bank does lend to a leasing company, the following minimum safeguards should be taken:

1. Earnings statements should be developed indicating profit net of any estimated residuals.
2. Cash flow statements, excluding estimated residuals, should be developed.
3. The equipment leasing companies documentation package, credit evaluation procedure, UCC filing procedures and insurance coverage (of leased assets) should be analyzed for quality and accuracy.

Another way for a bank to participate in equipment leasing is to appoint an individual in the bank to evaluate, structure, and complete various types of equipment leases for the bank's customers. This procedure has the advantage of low cost. Its disadvantages are that the person so designated may be poorly qualified, and since most leasing is sold rather than bought, the volume of business will probably be minimal. This method is most common to smaller banks.

The next step for a bank is to set up a group of individuals to handle equipment leasing in the bank. Many large banks use such a group to meet the needs of bank customers, or potential bank customers, rather than mount a large-scale solicitation program to develop equipment leasing activity. Establishing a group may permit a greater degree of expertise to be developed, and allows the handling of a larger volume. This method is being used by a number of medium to large banks.

The same format as above, only changing the equipment leasing group from a bank operation to a bank subsidiary, has been used by some banks. This allows a different compensation plan, some insulation from liability and makes out of state operations easier from a taxation viewpoint.

In most larger bank holding companies, the equipment leasing group is a subsidiary of the holding company.

A negative aspect of this structure is that the subsidiary may not borrow from its associated bank. Thus the low cost of funds enjoyed by other structures is forbidden. The benefits include financing outside of the bank structure, some bank insulation from liability, a more autonomous organization, improved state income tax position, and the potential for a national identity.

In evaluating which of the above methods of participating in equipment leasing is best for a particular bank, the following questions should be asked:

1. How much money does the institution wish to invest in equipment leasing?
2. What type of lease will be most beneficial?
3. What are the bank's objectives?
   a. Cash income?
   b. Tax shelter? What is the bank's taxable income for this year? The next five years?
   c. A hedge against inflation?
   d. Obtain new bank business? Local? National?
   e. Satisfy present customers?

   Perhaps all of these, or perhaps none of these, may be a given bank's objective.
4. What is the bank's present level of experience? Is it enough to gain its objectives? If not, how much assistance is required? Where will it come from? What will it cost?
5. How long will it take to show profits? What is the ultimate goal?
6. Is the bank willing and able to make the necessary long-term commitment?

Many of these questions are complex. However, failure to answer them has caused many banks to enter the equipment leasing business for the wrong reasons. Often the banks have given up leasing based upon equally poor planning.

CREDIT EVALUATION

In general, the same credit evaluation used for granting term loans of equal duration should be used for granting equipment leases. In addition, the following should be considered:

1. When doing 100 percent financing, the lessor will often find that the equipment's value in a distress situation will be insufficient to meet the lessee's obligation. The secured nature of the lease must not obscure this important fact.

2. A lease does not allow the lessor to demand payment in full except when in default, or when the lessee is in receivership or bankruptcy. This control is considerably less than in the usual loan arrangement.
3. Because of the above, the lessee's credit should be better than required for a comparable term loan, not poorer. Many leasing novices lose sight of this, and lease equipment to marginal credits based upon the value of the equipment.
4. It is possible to obtain down payments, security deposits, advance payments, additional collateral, and personal guaranties, depending on the individual situation. Thus a borderline lease may be developed into a secure one.
5. When lesser credits are being considered, the maximum term should be five years unless there is a substantial front end deposit of some nature. For better credits, terms to ten years and beyond are customary.
6. In the case of an operating or leveraged lease, an early default can cause a loss of all of the tax benefits through sale of the equipment. In such a case, tax credits previously taken may be lost, increasing your exposure. Most lessors restrict such leases to better credits.

YIELD EVALUATION

"Capital" or "Finance" Lease.   Since such a lease has the economic impact of a loan, with no tax implications, its evaluation is very similar to a term loan. Economic benefits derive from:

a. The difference between funds disbursed and rentals received, synonymous with interest for a loan.
b. Any rentals received in advance (will increase yield).
c. Any security deposits received at the leases origination (will increase yield).
d. Any termination fees, charges paid at the end of the lease (will increase yield). Lessors writing this type of lease usually use a standard reference book of tables, showing yields for various combinations of rentals and fees.

"Operating" or "True" Lease.   Analysis becomes more complex, since the value of accelerated depreciation, the estimated residual value of the leased equipment, and perhaps the investment tax credit, must all be added to the value of the rentals received. Economic benefits derive from:

a. The difference between the funds disbursed and rental received, comparable with interest for a loan or the rentals from a capital lease.

b. The value of accelerated depreciation, the use of funds which would have been used to pay federal and/or state income taxes. Since money has a "time" value, the funds obtained from delaying taxes can be quite valuable.

c. If the lessor elects to use the investment tax credit, this results in an immediate tax savings, which unlike the value of accelerated depreciation, is not offset by future liability.

d. At the end of the lease, the equipment may be leased at "fair market rental" or sold for "fair market value" either to the present lessee or a third party. In either case the lessor may obtain substantial economic advantage.

Lessors writing this type of lease usually compute their yield with the aid of a computer program.

The most difficult part of the yield analysis is the estimation of residual values.

a. The lessee and lessor represent to the Internal Revenue Service that such residuals are at least 20 percent of the original cost of the equipment.

b. The impacts of inflation, technological change, changes in law or customs, and wear, are all unknown.

c. Equipment of little value in an open sale, may be of considerable value to an existing lessee who will wish to continue rentals almost indefinitely if a reduction from the original rentals is offered.

Probably the best approach is to evaluate each transaction three ways; with no residual, with your best estimate, and with 20 percent of original cost. If the yield meets your minimum yield standards without any residual, it is obviously a sound transaction. It is also well to consider *all* of the residuals in your portfolio as a "pool." Thus, if your average residual ranges between nothing (very unlikely) and 50 percent, it is quite easy to substantiate a 20 percent figure for IRS and your own accountants.

The leveraged lease yield evaluation becomes even more complex. Since in addition to the factors affecting yield for an operating lease, repayment of debt, interest, and the establishment of a "pool" for further taxes, with ROI on the "pool," all affect yield. Also, the tax benefits and residual benefits are magnified by the borrowing. The economic benefits are as follows:

a. The difference between funds disbursed, and rentals received, comparable to other types of leases. This difference may be quite small due to the increased benefits from other sources.

b. The value of accelerated depreciation. This value is an increased benefit (as compared to an unleveraged lease) since it is greater in proportion to funds invested.

c. The investment tax credit, if taken by lessor, also has a greater value than in an unleveraged lease, since it is greater in relation to funds invested.

d. The equipment's residual value at the end of the lease is also magnified.

A simplified comparison is shown in Exhibit 51–2.

Note that the effect of receiving a $100,000 investment tax credit for the operating lease is equal to 10 percent of funds invested, and a $100,000 investment tax credit is 40 percent of funds invested in the leveraged lease.

Exhibit 51–2
Yield Evaluation of Leveraged Lease

	Capital Lease	*Operating Lease*	*Leveraged Lease*
Amount......................	$1,000,000	$1,000,000	$1,000,000
Funds invested..............	All	All	250,000
Term	10 years	10 years	10 years
Annual rental................	$ 159,345	$ 159,345	$ 159,345
Total rental.................	$1,593,450	$1,593,450	$1,593,450
Residual....................	0	$ 50,000	$ 50,000
Termination fee..............	$ 50,000	0	0
Total received	$1,643,450	$1,643,450	$1,643,450
Nonrecourse interest	0	0	$ 450,000
Net profit exclusive of tax benefits..............	$ 643,450	$ 643,450	$ 193,450
As a percentage of investment	64.345%	64.345%	77.380%
Additional benefits:			
Accelerated depreciation......	No	Yes	Yes
Investment tax credit.........	No	$ 100,000	$ 100,000

Obviously the return on investment for the operating lease is higher than for the financial lease, and higher for the leveraged lease than either.

BOOK EARNINGS, CASH EARNINGS, AND TAXABLE EARNINGS

In dealing with a capital lease, the book earnings from rentals equal the cash earnings and taxable earnings. Any termination fees or bargain purchase options cause book to exceed cash or taxable earnings.

For example:

Lease amount............................ $1,000,000
Lease rate 10%
Tax rate 51.64%
Term..................................... 10 years
Annual rentals $159,345
Termination fee......................... $ 50,000
Total receivable......................... $159,345 × 10 = $1,593,450   Rentals
                                                            50,000   Residual
                         Total benefits $1,643,450

Year One

	Book Earnings	*Cash Earnings*	*Tax Earnings*
From rental	$159,345.00	$159,345.00	$159,345.00
From residual....................	9,090.91	—	—
Total income	168,435.91	159,345.00	159,345.00
Less amortization	61,000.00	—	61,000.00
Net:			
Before taxes	107,435.91	159,345.00	98,345.00
After taxes.....................	55,866.67	112,139.40	51,139.40

In the following years, book earnings decline as the residual adds less and less to income. Cash earnings continue level until the last year when the residual is realized. Taxable earnings decline as the amortization factor increases, but increases in the last year as the residual is realized.

Year Ten

	Book Earnings	*Cash Earnings*	*Tax Earnings*
From rental	$159,345.00	$159,345.00	$159,345.00
From residual....................	909.91	50,000.00	50,000.00
Total income	160,254.91	209,345.00	209,345.00
Less amortization	150,000.00	—	150,000.00
Net:			
Before taxes	10,254.91	209,345.00	59,345.00
After taxes.....................	5,332.55	180,859.40	30,859.40

In an operating lease the differences are even greater.
For example:

		Terms of Lease
Lease amount......................	$1,000,000	10% salvage
Rate	10%	5% residual
Term	10 years	48% income tax rate
Depreciation	8 years	
Annual rentals....................	159,345	
Investment tax credit..............	None (to lessee)	

Year One

	Book Earnings	Cash Earnings	Tax Earnings
From rental...............	$159,345.00	$159,345.00	$159,345.00
From residual..............	9,090.91	—	—
Total income..............	168,435.91	159,345.00	159,345.00
Less amortization depreciation	61,000.00		125,000.00 (½ year depreciation)
Net:			
Before taxes..............	107,435.91	159,345.00	34,345.00
After taxes...............	55,866.67	142,859.40	17,859.40

Book earnings show $107,435.91 B/T, A/T $55,866.67, but cash earnings are $159,345 B/T of which only $34,348 is taxable. After tax is paid $142,859.40 is after-tax cash earnings.

Year Two

	Book Earnings	Cash Earnings	Tax Earnings
From rental.........	$159,345.00	$159,345.00	$159,345.00
From residual	8,181.82	—	—
Total income	167,526.82	159,345.00	159,345.00
Less amortization....	68,000.00	—	218,750.00
Net:			
Before taxes.......	99,526.82	159,345.00	Before tax (59,405.00) (loss)
After taxes	51,753.95	187,859.40	28,514.40 (tax saved)

As the lease progresses, tax shelter turns into tax liabilities.

Year Ten

	Book Earnings	Cash Earnings	Tax Earnings
From rentals	$159,345.00	$159,345.00	$159,345.00
From residual	909.41	50,000.00	50,000.00
Total income..............	160,254.91	209,345.00	209,345.00
Less amortization..........	150,000.00	—	100,000.00 (salvage)
Net:			
Before taxes..............	10,254.91	209,345.00	109,345.00
After taxes	5,332.55	156,859.40	56,859.40

If the investment tax credit is taken by the lessor, the difference between book, cash and tax incomes during the first year is further accentuated.

For leveraged leasing the picture is complicated by the introduction of debt, with its principal repayment a cash outlay but not a tax deduction, and interest, with its cash outlay and tax deduction. Often book earnings are small, since the economic justification is primarily cash flows realized from tax avoidance (ITC) and tax deferral (accelerated depreciation).

A simplified example using the same situation as used above in the operating lease example, with the addition of a ten-year loan of $700,000 bearing interest at 8 percent and annual repayments of $101,976 to cover principal and interest is shown in Exhibit 51-3.

There is considerable discussion about recording the book earnings. Being considered are a number of ways designed to record earnings more in tune with the actual cash flows, which are high during the first years of the lease, decline, and then increase with the realization of a residual. In general, conservative opinion indicates spreading income over the entire lease period. Some banks have been spreading income over the shorter payback period.

The treatment of residuals has also been open to considerable discussion. Generally accepted accounting principles allow residuals to be

Exhibit 51-3
Use of 10-Year Debt

Year One	Book Earnings	Cash Earnings	Tax Earnings
From rentals	$159,345.00	$159,345.00	$159,345.00
From residuals	9,090.91	—	—
Total income	168,435.91	159,345.00	159,345.00
Less amortization depreciation.	61,000.00	47,600.00	125,000.00
Interest	54,376.00	54,376.00	54,376.00
Net:			
Before taxes	53,059.91	47,369.00	(20,031.00) (before taxes loss)
After taxes	27,591.15	56,983.88 (Including tax saved)	9,614.88 (taxes saved)

Year Ten			
From rentals	$159,345.00	$159,345.00	$159,345.00
From residuals	909.41	50,000.00	50,000.00
Total income	160,254.91	209,345.00	209,345.00
Less amortization depreciation.	150,000.00	97,300.00	100,000.00 (salvage)
Less interest	4,676.00	4,676.00	4,676.00
Net:			
Before taxes	5,578.41	107,369.00	104,669.00
After taxes	2,900.77	57,127.88	54,427.88

booked on the basis of "sum-of-the-years'-digits," starting with the first year, even though the equipment may not be sold for many years. In the meanwhile the residual is an estimate, optimistic, or pessimistic, as only time will tell.

A further consideration is the effect of the tax savings generated by the equipment leasing group upon the parent's tax picture. Since an equipment leasing effort which is writing tax-motivated equipment leases will usually not only shelter its own income, but develop excess tax deductions, the parent's tax picture is quite important in gauging how much of such excess shelter should be developed. The parent's income tax bill and potential income tax bills are the final limiting factor upon the amount of operating and leveraged leases which can be written by its leasing group.

There are several ways by which the parent corporation may compensate the equipment leasing group for the tax benefits obtained. (*a*) The parent may make a cash payment to the leasing group, equal to the tax payments permanently avoided through the ITC. (*b*) The parent may make a cash payment to the leasing group equal to the tax payment permanently avoided through the ITC, and for taxes deferred by accelerating depreciation, on the grounds that as a practical matter, sure tax-deferral benefits will continue indefinitely. (*c*) The parent may set up a reserve on the books of the leasing group to reduce borrowings, thus giving the effect of a cash payment, without going through the profit and loss statement. The reserve will equal the total amount of taxes avoided and deferred, and has the effect of a loan of equity, or perhaps subordinated debt.

There are two methods of showing the effect of the investment tax credit, as in ownership, flow-through, and spreading.

OBTAINING BUSINESS

There are numerous ways in which a bank equipment leasing company may obtain business. Each has its own advantages and disadvantages.

1. A bank may obtain equipment leasing prospects through its own Commercial and Retail Loan Division. Advantage—no added cost. Disadvantage—competing with your own company, only a little added business.

2. Local vendors of various types of equipment are constantly seeking financing. Such dealers are a good source of leads. Disadvantages—constant pressure for undue speed in credit approval and compromise of credit standards. Failure of vendor to provide service may be a problem. Advantage—a constant stream of varied credits.

3. Prospecting requires a trained sales force. Its main advantage

is a steady stream of varied business. Its disadvantage is the cost of maintaining the sales force.

4. Brokers vary from prestigious investment bankers to local free-lancers working out of a phone booth. Advantage—a wide variety of types of credits and equipment. Disadvantages—the broker has a conflict of interest in trying to sell the lease at its lowest rate and trying to obtain the highest return to the lessor. Sometimes the broker does not give the lessor all of the pertinent facts. The lessor has little direct contact with the lessee and must continue to pay fees if any added business is written.

Some banks are participating their leases with other banks and are probably better sources than most brokers, since they, unlike the brokers, are investing their own funds.

COMPETITION

A bank equipment leasing company faces competition from many sources. Among these are the bank's Commercial Department, other local banks and their leasing companies, the equipment leasing operations of many major money center banks, the major finance companies, numerous investment bankers, many large brokers, and a multitude of small brokers and equipment leasing companies.

Facing all of this competition, it is only because of the constant demand for financing that so many equipment lessors have been successful. Most of the top 1,000 companies are contacted on a routine basis by 20 or more lessors. It is among the smaller companies below the top 1,000 in size, that the best opportunities abound for the bank lessor.

Since rates are quite competitive, on all levels, and competitive almost to the point of profitlessness for some larger transactions, the bank-lessor will also find better profit margins available from smaller companies.

SUMMARY

Although the rewards can be substantial, a potential bank lessor should research leasing, and its desirability, in depth before making a commitment. A realistic assessment of the possible benefits, costs, and the bank's chances of accomplishing its objectives, can be most useful in preventing a premature entry into, and even more hasty exit from, uncharted waters.

Chapter 52

Agricultural Loans

Leslie W. Peterson*

Richard O. Hawkins†

INTRODUCTION

Commercial banks, the nations largest lenders to production agriculture, are being challenged to meet the growing credit needs of a rapidly changing agricultural industry. Agriculture has evolved from the labor intensive way of life of a few decades ago into a mechanized, high technology, capital intensive industry operated by an increasingly sophisticated group of farm businessmen. These farm businessmen used over $90 billion in credit in 1975. It is estimated that this figure will double by 1985.

Banks are only one of several sources of credit to agriculture. The Farm Credit Administration, insurance companies, captive finance companies, and government agencies also extend direct credit to farmers. This offers the farmer several alternative sources for part or all of his or her credit needs. Banks, however, have the advantages in being the only lenders that offer checking accounts and other financial services. These financial services, together with a sound agricultural loan program, administered by trained and experienced personnel, give banks an attractive package to offer their farm customers.

A modern farm operation requires skilled financial and cash flow management. Borrowed funds are an important part of cash flow management because internally generated cash flows from marketing of production are seldom adequate to provide all necessary cash require-

---

* President, Farmers State Bank, Trimont, Minnesota.

† Extension Economist, Farm Management, University of Minnesota, St. Paul, Minnesota.

ments throughout the year. These borrowed funds can best be provided by a prearranged "line of credit" with a qualified agricultural banker or lender. This line of credit should be adequate to cover peak cash needs provided sufficient cash flow is generated in the farm operation to satisfactorily service the debt incurred.

Establishing a satisfactory line of credit requires a close working relationship between the farmer and a qualified loan officer.

More and more the success of agricultural lending in banks is dependent upon loan officers who are astute in banking practices but even more important, understand the technology of production agriculture and are able to make sound judgments about the "human factors" in farming. These judgments must be made in the knowledge of the individual farmer's goals and ambitions, his selection and application of technology, his ability to successfully plan and carry out a potentially profitable farm operation on a day-to-day basis.

To do this the loan officer must be well grounded in farm management principles and be willing to spend the necessary time with each borrower to thoroughly review his plans and counsel with him in the profitable use of capital, both internally generated and borrowed.

The loan officer must also be able to analyze a credit request to determine a line of credit to be advanced. He or she must assess risk exposure, repayment capacity and determine the security interest required to adequately protect the bank. This "credit analysis" process using the skills of a competent loan officer, is the key to successful and profitable agricultural lending.

The remainder of this chapter will deal with the credit request, the credit analysis, and the administration of the agricultural loan.

THE AGRICULTURAL CREDIT REQUEST

Credit applications should originate with an interview with the bank customer or potential borrower. With new customer applications, this interview should first surface any existing bank-customer relationships or family relationships which may influence a decision. The interview should then be directed to the human factors as well as the nature of the farm business and reasons for the credit request. From this interview the loan officer can generally evaluate the request and the risks involved. Without spending the time necessary for a complete credit analysis, the loan officer can determine the desirability of pursuing the request further. If, during the interview, it becomes obvious that the loan cannot be made, the interview should be terminated with a tactful explanation of the reasons why. However, if it appears that the loan can be made, the loan officer should proceed with a loan application.

The loan application is the basic document to begin a credit file for a new borrower and it can also be used as a basis for updating the file of an existing borrower. The application should include:

1. Date, name, and address.
2. A brief personal and family history including marital status, number of dependents, and their ages.
3. Education and farm experience.
4. Amount and purpose of the loan desired.
5. Term of the loan and repayment source, including alternative sources of repayment if intended sources do not materialize.
6. Brief description of the size and type of farm operation: land owned, land leased and terms of lease, crops raised, livestock raised, special facilities available, and location of facilities.

The loan officer should next discuss the bank's loan procedures and the responsibilities of both the borrower and the bank, including the borrower's responsibilities in providing satisfactory information and farm records for loan documentation.

This meeting can also effectively be used as a training session by a skilled loan officer. He or she should explain the credit analysis forms in such a way that the borrower will be able to complete part or all of the forms unaided in the future and recognize the importance of this information in making useful business management decisions.

The size of the loan request, the character of the borrower, the apparent risk involved and bank policy should determine the extent of the loan documentation and security necessary for each line of credit. The objective of the credit analysis procedure is to establish a satisfactory "line of credit" that will assure the farmer adequate funds when needed to supplement internally generated cash flow, and to assure adequate and orderly repayment capacity from the earnings of the farm operation.

ANALYSIS OF THE CREDIT

In analyzing an application for a line of credit for today's agriculture, prime importance must be given to assessing the applicant as a person and as a farm manager as well as assessing the nature of the farm business itself. The assessment of both can perhaps best be handled in a framework that permits the analysis of the farm business's past, current, and future profitability, repayment capacity and financial soundness under the management of the applicant. The tools necessary to make such an analysis include: (1) financial statements; (2) income and expense statements; (3) profit and loss statements; (4) comparative trend statements; and (5) partial and complete enterprise and total farm budgets including annual and long-term plans from which cash flow statements can be derived.

While using these tools the competent loan officers will keep a log of pertinent comments, and make the necessary farm visits and inspection reports.

It is commonly held that the analysis of the credit for a new applicant or for a very large line must be more thorough than that of the ordinary, regular farm customer. To be sure, such applications must be thoroughly analyzed, but the importance of providing a detailed analysis of the regular customer's application cannot be overlooked both in terms of identifying troubled lines early enough to make necessary adjustments and in identifying lines that have good potential for increasing bank profits in the future. In all cases, the analysis should focus on the financial strength, the profitability and the repayment capacity of the applicant both now and in the future.

Analyzing Financial Soundness

The financial statement is the basic tool for this analysis. It provides a summary of how funds have been invested in the business (assets) and the financing methods used (liabilities and net worth) as of a given point in time. For most farm businesses, the analysis of financial soundness will be better served if the financial statement is divided into meaningful categories of assets and liabilities. Common practice divides assets and liabilities into at least two and preferably three categories. A two category division would separate nonreal estate assets and liabilities from those pertaining to real estate. A three category division would further separate the nonreal estate assets and liabilities into current and intermediate categories. The basic components of this type of financial statement are shown below.

ASSETS

A. Current .... _____
B. Intermediate .... _____
C. Total current and intermediate
    $(A + B)$ .... ========

D. Long term .... _____
E. Total assets $(C + D)$ .... ========

LIABILITIES AND NET WORTH

F. Current .... _____
G. Intermediate .... _____
H. Total current and intermediate
    $(F + G)$ .... ========

I. Long term .... _____
J. Total liabilities $(H + I)$ .... ========
K. Owner's net worth $(E - J)$ .... ========

Under this division, current assets would be defined as cash or other assets that will or can become cash within the business year and current liabilities are those payable during the same business year. Intermediate assets would be those resources used to support production rather than go for sale and having a useful life from one to ten years. Intermediate liabilities would be notes and contracts written for one to ten years for meeting other than seasonal needs and usually in support of intermediate assets. Long-term assets include the real estate and those assets attached to the real estate such as drainage tile and certain structures and having a life of more than ten years. Assets having a life of more than ten years, but financed with intermediate type debt, should be listed in the intermediate asset category to provide for realistic analysis of the financial statement. Long-term liabilities are those directly associated with the long-term assets and any other debt that is deferred over a longer than ten-year period.

How assets are valued depends on the emphasis being given to financial statement analysis in a particular bank. If bank policy is mainly interested in the applicant's and its own liquidity position in case of default, all assets should be valued at conservative market values that could be attained on the basis of a short notice sellout. When bank policy suggests the analysis be framed in determining financial progress of the borrower—conservative market values should be used on current assets, depreciated values on intermediate assets and cost plus improvements minus depreciation on real estate with periodic adjustments for inflation duly noted on the statement. When the focus of analysis is more on profitability in the future and the applicant's ability under the stress of inflation as well as the best investment opportunities, market values on all categories should be considered.

Actual analysis of the financial statement hinges on bank policy in regards to purpose of the analysis and, therefore, asset valuation methods. Once the statement is complete, a visit to the business to verify the quantity and quality of the assets is strongly recommended.

The applicant's net worth can now be calculated and selected ratios used to determine degrees of financial soundness. Four ratios are suggested as key indicators of financial soundness given today's agricultural situation.

1. *Total Asset—Liability Ratio.* Showing how much the business is in debt. A normal standard is a 2:1 situation where the applicant has as much equity capital in the business as the lender has debt capital. This minimum standard can be violated where management capacity, profitability, and debt service capacity warrant.
2. *Current and Intermediate Asset—Liability Ratio.* Showing the financial solvency of the nonreal estate portion of the business.

This is an especially important measure in times of inflation when land values used may make the whole business look good when, in fact, it may be tending toward insolvency.

3. *Current Asset—Liability Ratio.* Showing current assets available to meet current indebtedness especially as a protection factor if the following year's cash flow should be disrupted for some reason.

4. *Long-Term Asset—Liability Ratio.* Showing land financial base strength and indicating the refinancing possibilities for shorter term debt.

When possible, the applicant's financial statement ratios should be compared to those from previous years. Care must be taken in putting too much emphasis on the results of any of the aforementioned ratios until they are related to profitability and repayment capacity trends and future prospects.

Analyzing Profitability

The financial statements, together with the income and expense statement, give the basic information necessary to calculate the current profitability situation. A brief outline of a profit and loss statement follows.

Gross farm receipts..................................	$_____
Less total cash operating expenses	_____
Net cash (farm) income................................	_____
Adjustments for inventory	_____
Net operating profit.....................................	_____
Adjustment for capital items	_____
Farm profit or loss	_____

Net cash income adjusted for inventory change of the farm assets normally listed in the current asset category equals net operating profit. This figure, in turn, adjusted for change in value of the inventory of capital assets such as breeding livestock, machinery and equipment, building and improvements, gives the profit or loss figure for the year.

The profit figure (defined as returns to labor, management and equity capital) in itself provides little insight into assessing the business until it is related to the resources used in producing that level of returns. The loan officer can add several dimensions to the analysis of the applicant's current situation by calculating labor and management earnings, percent return to investment and percent return to net worth from the profit figures as follows:

Returns to labor and management = Profit
— (Net worth X Percent return on net worth if invested elsewhere).

Percent returns to total investment =
$$\frac{\text{Profit} + \text{Interest paid} - \text{Charge for labor and management}}{\text{Average total farm assets over the year}}$$

Percent returns to net worth =
$$\frac{\text{Profit} - \text{Charge for labor and management}}{\text{Average net worth over the year}}$$

These measures permit the loan officer and the client to compare the business with other similar businesses, and to compare rates of return against the going rates for other investments and for debt capital.

Two additional ratios allow for further definition of the current situation. They are the asset turnover ratio and the capital profit margin.

$$\text{Asset turnover} = \frac{\text{Gross receipts}}{\text{Total farm assets}}$$

Net profit margin =
$$\frac{\text{Profit} + \text{Interest paid} - \text{Charge for labor and management}}{\text{Gross receipts}}$$

The asset turnover ratio is a measure of how efficiently the applicant has used capital resources to generate output (sales per dollar invested). The higher the ratio the more effectively assets are being used. The net profit margin measures the return to capital per unit of sales; thus, the higher the ratio the more favorable the situation.

These two measures help explain why return to farm investment may be high or low. A low-asset turnover ratio and poor net profit margin suggests the business might be suffering from inefficient production, high overhead expenses, or poor prices per unit sold. Such conditions might lead to consideration of financing recommended crop and livestock practices before further significant investment in capital goods.

These measures should also be compared to those of similar businesses and can be used as bench marks to observe the trend on any particular farm.

All of the profitability measures and, to some extent the financial measures, should be viewed in terms of general conditions such as good or bad weather, price breaks, and so on. that occurred during the year being analyzed. Finally, these measures should be compared to those of previous years, when available, to determine trends, and to note the applicant's ability to make progress under existing conditions.

Analyzing Repayment Capacity

Repayment capacity is determined through the use of budgets which allow the projection of cash flows for the loan period. When this analysis is complete, the results can be used with the financial and profitability measures already discussed to project their direction and standing at the end of the loan period. An example of the basics of a cash flow statement follows:

	Months, Quarters or Year	
Cash Inflows:		
Total cash farm income	———	———
Total nonfarm income	———	———
Beginning cash balance	———	———
New loans from other sources	———	———
Total cash available (1)	═══	═══
Cash Outflows:		
Total cash operating expenses	———	———
Total net capital purchases	———	———
Family living expense	———	———
Income tax and social security due	———	———
Total cash required (2)	═══	═══
Projected surplus or deficit (1 − 2)	———	———
Bank loan balance existing	———	———
Bank loan balance end of period	———	———

Cash flow budgeting requires the projection of the physical side of the business; that is, type and volume of production and the kind and volume of inputs to be used. Cash available to the business is determined by adding any beginning cash balances to the value of all projected sales, other farm income, nonfarm income, and borrowings from other sources. Valuation of projected sales must be done carefully using realistic but conservative market prices and realistic production goals. Care must also be taken in livestock operations to provide for feed needs out of production to the next harvesting period.

Cash that will flow out of the business is identified by budgeting out and adding up all farm expenses as they will likely occur, planned capital purchases, scheduled debt payments, and family living needs. This cash flow plan should be by periods of time reasonable for the type of the applicant's business. A minimum would be an annual projection but a monthly or quarterly projection is strongly recommended to better determine the likely amount the line of credit will need to be. When projections for each time period have been made, deficits or surpluses of cash are calculated by subtracting cash outflows from cash available. The line of credit can then be calculated in terms of the bank financing all deficits and receiving repayment out of all surpluses. When this is done monthly, the likely peak of the loan can be determined as well as the likely "pay down" on the line for the year. The "pay down" compared to the beginning bank loan identifies the projected bank loan balance at year's end.

Using income and expense figures from the cash flow along with projected inventory changes and projected loan repayment, the likely financial and profitability measures at the end of the period can be calculated.

It should be recommended if not required that the applicant keep an actual cash flow record during the period. If this is done, deviations from the plan can be identified early and necessary adjustments made. This type of control procedure should be considered essential on new lines, very large lines, and borderline cases.

Adding up the Score

When the analysis of the credit is complete and recorded in the credit file, the loan officer is in a position to make a judgment on proceeding with the loan. The measures calculated allow a study of the applicant's financial strength, particularly in terms of the bank's risk and exposure, the volume and profitability of the business in terms of future viability of the operations, and the cash flow characteristics in terms of repayment capacity and ending loan balance. The competent loan officer will also be able to make judgments in terms of the applicant's use of sound production and marketing practices based on the considerations that have gone into the cash flow projection.

When the situation appears to be weak, the loan officer might suggest the applicant budget out a longer term look at the operation of perhaps three to five years. From this he or she might determine possible reorganization of resource use and/or acquisition, or a more controlled or rapid expansion that could lead to a more profitable business and a situation the bank could work with.

Finally, it should be emphasized that while the loan officer may decide to "short cut" the credit analysis on any particular request, thorough loan analysis stands a better chance of reaching a loan decision in the best interests of the applicant and the bank.

LOAN ADMINISTRATION

After completing the loan analysis, the loan officer can assess the risk exposure and determine the type and amount of collateral available and necessary to adequately secure the loan.

Almost without exception, it is essential that an agricultural line of credit be secured. The legal aspects of securing a loan vary from state to state so it is necessary to use sound legal counsel in establishing procedures within each bank. However, it is the loan officer's responsibility to see that these procedures are followed on each loan. The security taken will depend upon the type of loan and the financial position of the borrower. A security interest should always include the source of the anticipated repayment and then additional security as deemed necessary.

With line of credit financing, use of a blanket security interest including all of the property and inventories disclosed in the credit analysis documents is sound banking procedure. All overlapping debt or outside debt should have been disclosed in these documents. Verification of the bank's security position should be made with the filing authorities having jurisdiction.

Maintenance of a credit file containing the application, analysis documents, and security instruments on each borrower is essential. Good banking practice also dictates use of a section in each file for administrative purposes. This section should include:

1. Comparative analysis sheet (spread sheet) with key items from the financial statement and profit and loss statement for three and preferably five years for comparison purposes.
2. Comment sheet and inspection report on which the loan officer can maintain factual information on advances and repayment, but more important, record confidential observations concerning management and collateral position from discussions with the borrower and from on-farm visits.
3. Verification of security interest from proper filing authority.

It is desirable to establish procedures within the bank for content and organization of credit files to provide all loan officers with quick access to information on a particular borrower. Use of a checklist in each file for documentation and required information may be useful. This checklist might include:

1. A list of the credit analysis documents required.
2. Renewal or review date.
3. List of security instruments required and expiration dates.
4. Insurance requirements.
5. Documents properly signed.
6. Government regulations complied with.
7. Corporation or partnership authorizations on file.
8. Financial data verified.
   a. From records.
   b. By inspection.

A line of credit should be reviewed at least annually to update the credit analysis documents, check solvency and financial progress, and budget the credit needs for the next year. With multiple crop and livestock operations where there is more than one turnover each year, the review may have to be more often to adequately monitor the line of credit. Annual on-farm visits will permit the loan officer to appraise management, inspect collateral, and establish a closer working relationship with the borrower. These visits are an important part of an effective agricultural loan program.

Line of credit financing with one lender provides advantages to both the borrower and the bank. With proper budgeting and cash flow planning, credit needs can be determined in advance and commitments made for both disbursement and repayment of loans.

The loan commitment can be based upon the cash flow projections with only notations of the time and amount on a comment sheet in the credit file. In large, more complex lines of credit, the bank may wish to use a formal loan agreement. Use of a loan agreement spelling out the obligations of both borrower and lender can prevent misunderstandings and disagreements. A well-drafted loan agreement may also facilitate liquidation in the event of insolvency. Use of legal counsel in drafting loan agreements is desirable.

"Split lines of credit" outside of the control of the primary lender should be avoided. Any loan applicant with a large number of scattered debts or old accounts payable should be carefully scrutinized. This is an indication of poor management and it makes it almost impossible to structure total debt in line with the borrower's ability to repay.

There are, however, situations where the use of other lenders may be an advantage to the bank. These are:

1. Participations on large lines of credit that exceed the bank's legal lending limit.
2. Long-term credit such as real estate mortgages for land purchase or major capital improvements.
3. Dealer credit on large equipment or to purchase production inputs that may be interest free or where special warranties may be provided for a period of time.

With outside debt, it is essential that the lender extending the operating line of credit remain in control so that solvency and financial progress are continually monitored and repayment schedules can be structured in line with the borrower's ability to service all of his or her debt. It is the lender's responsibility to detect adverse trends in a credit line and to either suggest corrective measures or to initiate liquidation before a borrower reaches insolvency.

A competent agricultural loan officer can also assist in formulating effective marketing strategies and assist in the use of such marketing tools as forward contracting, hedging in the futures market and basis contracting. Orderly farm marketing practices can favorably affect cash flow, reduce the need for borrowed funds and, with volatile prices, enhance profitability.

The first step in any marketing plan is to determine the cost of unit production, something that can be done as part of the credit analysis procedures. Use of the marketing tools mentioned requires special expertise on the part of both the lender and borrower and a good working relationship with a competent commodity broker.

CONCLUSION

Production agriculture is a segmented industry composed of thousands of individually owned and operated farm units, with over half of their operating credit coming from small rural banks. Thus, an infinite number and variety of custom loan requests must be evaluated. Though the type and complexity of the loans may differ greatly, the fundamental objective in agricultural lending is the extension of credit that is safe and profitable to the borrower and the lender as well. Use of the credit analysis tools discussed by a qualified loan officer can make this possible.

Chapter 53

Construction Mortgage and Real Estate Warehousing Loans

John R. Gallaudet*

Construction mortgage lending differs from regular mortgage lending in that the former involves short-term lending with disbursement of funds made as construction progresses. Regular mortgage lending is normally done with full disbursement being made on the land and a completed structure with the term being for a number of years and the interest rate at a fixed figure. In construction lending the term may vary from as short as four months up to five years, the term depending on the construction time required. Disbursements, mostly termed "advances," are made after inspections either on predetermined schedule of construction items completed or on a percentage of work completed, usually presented in requisition form with the elements of construction each being itemized and shown as a percentage of work completed. The interest rate can either be fixed or tied to a movable prime rate.

Construction lending presents the highest degree of risk in the mortgage lending operation. There are safeguards however, that, properly used, can reduce the risk to an acceptable level.

The advantages of having a construction lending program are: The higher return; the shorter term; and the ability to offer a complete service as part of a general mortgage lending activity.

MARKETING

The marketing of construction loans presents no special problem to the lender. Time-honored sources are builders, attorneys, mortgage

---

* Vice President, The National State Bank, Elizabeth, New Jersey.

brokers, real estate brokers, and in some cases, other lenders who do not make construction loans but are willing to take the long-term loan. Cultivation of these sources to develop a steady flow of loans is desirable. Many lenders have developed a group of builders well known to them from past performance. This cultivation requires time and a very careful credit and performance review of each new builder. Credit reviews can be carried out in the normal way. Performance reviews are best done by interviewing the builders' customers and trade supply sources. It should be remembered that no one using the current building methods builds a completely perfect structure, and a customer's complaint, if any, should be analyzed with this fact in mind. An important factor is whether or not the builder is willing to stand behind the construction and make necessary adjustments and repairs.

Trade suppliers tend to extend credit beyond good credit practice since they wish to retain the builder's business in a highly competitive field. Any analyses of interviews with them should take cognizance of this fact.

Careful construction lenders constantly review their builder's group. Losses by builders are not uncommon and their ability to withstand losses is of paramount consideration. Excellent sources of information for analysis and discussions are the builder himself, other builders, and subcontractors. These subcontractors depend on the builders for new work and are sometimes chary with their information but are the first people to be affected if a builder is having financial problems. Membership and attendance at trade association meetings are excellent methods of keeping abreast of a builder's financial condition.

The watchword in all loan marketing is "Know Your Builder."

UNDERWRITING THE LOAN

Underwriting includes a feasibility study, loan amounts, rates, fees, term, method of advances, documentation, and takeouts.

The feasibility study appears to be an extra effort to put the loan on the books, but is simply a determination as to whether or not one should go further with the underwriting.

In some cases, particularly with large loans, a professional feasibility study will be presented. Such a study should be carefully analyzed. The analysis of the finished study constitutes the lender's own feasibility study. If a feasibility study is not offered, it should be required or the lender should make the study.

All feasibility studies, written or oral, should make a determination as to whether: this building is needed; the market can absorb this new project; the location is proper; the design is acceptable and compatible with the location; all governmental regulations can be complied with; it is possible to build within the construction budget; if an income property, the income and expense projection are proper; the construction time is reasonable; the marketing is proper; and the builder is known to you and has previously done this type of construction (if not, is it reasonable to expect he can accomplish it?). As an example, a builder of single-family houses who suddenly proposes a high-rise apartment structure should raise some questions as to his technical ability. If the same builder proposed a two-story garden apartment, it is not unreasonable to expect he would competently accomplish the building since the construction differs only slightly from single-family home construction.

If the lender's own experience does not allow him or her to answer to these questions, there are numerous experts available who can be hired on a fee basis to assist in the evaluation of the situation. In all cases the questions should be answered if one wishes to avoid a problem loan. It is considerably easier to take any existing property with a history of success and underwrite a loan than it is to envision a new structure and analyze its potential for success.

If the feasibility study shows the proposed loan as a successful project the next consideration is the loan amount. Loan amounts for the long-term loan are calculated as a percentage of the appraisal. The percentage varies in accordance with lenders' policies and the maximums established by the regulatory authorities.

The construction loan, as a general rule, should be less than the amount of the long-term loan. The actual amount will vary, based on the conditions in the long-term loan commitment. An allowance, historically figured at 10 percent, should be deducted from the original calculation to allow for override costs should the builder fail to finish the structure. Much experience has shown that, if a builder abandons a job, the undisbursed amount will not be enough to finish the project. There are no available statistics that indicate how much more might be needed to finish. For a new builder, brought into finish the work, to charge an additional amount is not unreasonable. The new builder must correct errors if any, and in effect guarantee another builder's work.

The long-term commitment or "takeout," as it is commonly called for an income property may require a rental achievement or a construction achievement or both. All takeouts must be carefully examined to make certain that the bank is willing to comply with stated terms and that the feasibility study indicates that it is feasible to comply without undue risk.

An example might be a takeout from a long-term lender for a two-story garden apartment upon which the bank is contemplating a construction loan. The takeout will disburse upon full completion of the project, but also will require a rental achievement of 75 percent of the projected rent roll. This provision means there must be leases signed for at least the 75 percent required before the long-term lender will disburse, thus paying off the bank's construction loan. A completed building or buildings, with no tenants, would not permit disbursement by the "takeout." If the feasibility study shows a demand for apartments in the price class and in the area, the risk is reasonable.

To further explain the example, most apartment builders will complete buildings and keep subcontractors moving to completion of additional buildings. This procedure allows actual occupancy of the earliest constructed buildings, accelerating the rental momentum, and minimizing the construction loan risk.

An example of poor underwriting occurred recently when a lender permitted a builder to erect a garden apartment complex of 400 units (40 buildings, 10 apartments each) and each trade finished all 40 buildings as a group. This schedule meant that no units could be occupied until all were complete. Occupancy dates were too far in the future to attract tenants; thus, very few leases were signed before the complex was completed. During the construction period competing builders had met a large part of the market and the delays caused the takeout to expire. The lender is now in the rental business and will be until he can successfully fill up the complex and sell it.

In residential building, primarily in the single-family house, construction lending percentages seem to range from 65 percent to 75 percent of appraisal of land and the proposed dwelling. While this segment is the simplest form of construction lending, particular emphasis in the feasibility study should be placed on the questions of location and market absorption. Custom construction is not a problem, except as to completion, but in the financing of developments the bank can expect a request to loan on various models, plus an inventory of unsold houses. Builders prefer to have an inventory so they can make almost immediate delivery to a customer and also keep the subcontractors busy. How many units should be permitted ahead of sales is a matter of judgment based on an opinion of market absorption.

The two predominant methods of making loans on developments are:

a. Make construction mortgage loans on individual units with repayment coming as the units are sold and the long-term mortgages placed.
b. Enter into a blanket construction loan on the tract, or a section thereof, and grant releases as the houses are sold and the long-term mortgages placed.

Advances as the construction progresses will be the same in both methods. With method (*a*) the term of each loan would be about six months under normal construction conditions. Under method (*b*) the loan term would extend to the time necessary to construct and sell the houses. This is usually a negotiated term.

Under method (*b*) the documentation is much easier and less costly since there is only one set of mortgage documents, plus the releases. The dollar amount of the releases is a negotiated figure usually ranging from 110 percent to 150 percent of the dollar amount allocated to each dwelling. The purpose of the excess is to have the loan pay out prior to the last units being constructed and, therefore, eliminating any need for a loan extension to allow for the sale of some last units.

To place a construction loan in the portfolio costs more in time, appraisal, legal fees, and the management of the loan than a regular mortgage loan. For instance, the time and cost involved in making three or more advances, depending on the type of property, are an immediate and known type of expense. For these additional costs the lender is normally compensated by charging fees over and above the interest received.

Fees and the method of collection do not differ greatly in residential and nonresidential lending except that they must be tailored to fit within a state's usury laws, if any. Fees are expressed as a percentage of the loan, or a flat dollar amount as agreed upon. The amounts are calculated, based upon whether or not the lender is absorbing legal fees, appraisal costs, inspection fees, and so on. Fees are a negotiable item based on competition and costs. It is poor underwriting to allow competition to force fees so low that the lender is not compensated for out-of-pocket costs and personnel time.

The collection of fees is also negotiable. The optimum is to collect in full upon acceptance by the borrower of the commitment. However, this is often compromised. Many fee schedules call for payment of a portion of the fee at acceptance of the commitment and the balance at the first advance. Some fee schedules call for a portion to be paid at acceptance of the commitment and the balance proportionally at each advance. The latter schedule should be avoided since the use of these funds during the life of the loan is a part of the gross return.

Fees vary with market levels and the availability of money. In the past few years the normal seems to range from one half of 1 percent up to 3 percent, or flat dollar amounts approximating the percentage figure. Care should be exercised in the charging of fees so that the loan is not lost or so overcharged as to weaken the ability of the builder to complete within the construction budget.

Interest on construction loans is figured upon the amount of money actually disbursed for the time period used. Construction loans interest charges are often offered as a percentage over the moving prime rate, with interest payments being charged monthly and figured on the prime rate as of the date of billing. Other arrangements, such as quarterly interest payments or deducting the interest from advances, are also used. In many loans, made as a percentage over the moving prime rate, the loan provisions call for a ceiling and a floor. This establishes a maximum and minimum rate regardless of this prime rate's movement. The same collection arrangements can be made when the interest rate is a flat rate. For orderly bookkeeping and the early use of the funds, the monthly collection is the preferred method.

ADVANCES

Advances (sometimes termed disbursements or interim payments) are funds paid over to the borrower as the construction progresses.

Legal requirements for making an advance vary with the title laws of the 50 states. As a minimum requirement, the lender must assure himself that he continues to have a good and marketable first lien as each advance is made. The two most used methods differ, depending upon whether the loan is on residential or nonresidential property.

On residential property, a preestablished schedule of construction items as they are built into the structure is used. This allows the builder a fixed amount of money determined as a percentage of the loan after the completion of certain items of construction. Good practice is to require a completed enclosure with the roughing installed before the first advance is made.

Included as Exhibit 53–1 is a typical advance schedule which allows for three advances for a pre-sold home or four advances for speculative building. This schedule has been used for a number of years with constant updating as building techniques improve. For instance, the heating system some years ago was an item in the first advance. Modern technology has improved house heaters to the point that they are now much smaller and installed as a unit instead of as boiler sections. They are easily handled by two people and are therefore subject to theft from the job. Simple logic required a change to allow the installation of the heater as a completion item when the structure could be secured. Similar changes will be necessary if solar heating ever becomes a factor in home building. This type of construction inspection schedule requires only minimum training for its use by the lender's own personnel, thus avoiding outside inspectors and their cost.

Advances on nonresidential loans, including all high-rise units, commercial, industrial, and special-purpose structures are implemented by the use of construction items schedules. These schedules are usually prepared by the project architect or the builder. They are far more detailed than a residential schedule, and some lenders have adopted their own forms. These schedules are presented for an advance based on the percentage of completed work in each construction category—

Exhibit 53–1

CONSTRUCTION CHECKLIST—FOUR ADVANCE SCHEDULE

Property: _____

First Advance 40%

Date

_____ __ 1. Foundations completed.
_____ __ 2. Dwelling framed and entirely sheathed.
_____ __ 3. All roof areas completely shingled.
_____ __ 4. All window sash (except picture window, if any) and partition studding in place.
_____ __ 5. Chimneys and fireplaces (except fireplace facings) erected.
_____ __ 6. Rough flooring laid.
_____ __ 7. Rough plumbing and electric complete.
_____ __ 8. Heating risers in walls of one-and-a-half- and two-story dwellings.

Second Advance 30%

_____ __ 9. Insulation installed.
_____ __ 10. Exterior surface complete, including prime coat of paint.
_____ __ 11. Cellar bottom cemented.
_____ __ 12. Interior staircases installed.
_____ __ 13. All exterior porches and steps in place.
_____ __ 14. Plastering complete (if dry wall, taped and spackled) ready for trim. Wood paneling not required at this stage.

Third Advance 15%

A completely finished unit is required with the following *exceptions:*

_____ __ 15. Scraping and finishing floors.
_____ __ 16. Leaders and gutters installed.
_____ __ 17. Interior decorating (trim must be painted—two coats).
_____ __ 18. Electric fixtures installed.
_____ __ 19. Linoleum and/or floor tile installed; kitchen, halls, family room only.
_____ __ 20. Finish grade, seed and shrub.
_____ __ 21. Service walks and driveways installed.
_____ __ 22. Plumbing fixtures except bathtub and shower stalls.
_____ __ 23. Ovens and ranges installed.

Fourth Advance 15% (Final)

A completely finished dwelling, ready for immediate occupancy. Offsite construction must be finished or proof of proper bonds furnished.

If interior decorating and electric fixtures are left to an owner's choice then escrows of one and one half times the cost are to be withheld. The same escrow procedure is to be followed if floors are left unfinished. Escrow $____

Note:
1. For 3-Advance schedule eliminate no. 3 Advance from the 4-Advance schedule.
2. If other than normal building materials are to be used (i.e., carpeting over subfloors, complete wood panel walls) or construction procedures not in accordance with the above list are contemplated these changes must be approved prior to the granting of a commitment.
3. Minimum acceptable specifications are those approved by the Federal Housing Administration, local building codes, and this bank.

steel erection, carpentry, masonry, and so on. The schedules will also include what is known as software—architects' fees, legal fees, and items other than actual construction. Since these are part of the costs, they can be used as a percentage of an advance, but it is not recommended that any advance be made on a percentage of software alone.

The project architect will usually certify as to the requisitions presented in accordance with the schedule. In addition to this certification, prudent lending requires that the structure be inspected and the advance certified by a qualified person employed by the lender. If none is available a qualified person or firm should be hired by the lender on a fee basis. Many architectural and/or engineering firms offer this service. It is recommended that the lender pay the fee inspector directly and this cost be included in the overall construction fee for the loan.

Depending on the circumstances of the loan, and particularly in large loans and loans for government construction, a portion of the advance should be retained. This retention is usually established as 10 percent of each advance and is deducted from the agreed-upon amount of the disbursement at each advance. The purpose of the withholding is to have funds available, upon completion, to correct any construction errors. It is, in effect a monetary guarantee of proper construction. A place for the deduction of the retention is found in most construction schedules. Most retention agreements call for the release of the funds 30 days after completion, if all errors are corrected. In practice, many of them run far longer in time. If a retention is not required in the builder's contract, whether it is required or not is a matter of the lender's judgment.

Despite the safeguards already covered, there are three more cautions that prudent lending requires as a part of each construction loan.

1. Advances should not be made on material or supplies delivered to the job, but not yet incorporated into the structure. Remember the loan is on the structure. For example, 100,000 bricks in pallets lying on the job site are not security for an advance.
2. At each advance someone from the bank staff should inspect the structure prior to the disbursement. There is no substitute for this inspection. While it might appear that no one on the staff is technically qualified to make a proper inspection, the bricks may be used as an example. If the staff inspector visits the job and the construction requisition says that half of the brickwork is in place, but only a quarter of it is actually "laid up," something is obviously wrong with the inspection practice. This is the time to correct it, not at completion, when a discovery of an overadvance means that a problem loan may have been created.

3. Staff personnel should be scheduled to inspect each construction loan at least each 30 days, even if an advance has not been requested. This inspection schedule will give early warning of an abandoned job and provide information on jobs that are slowing down in time to make possible corrections.

If the bank is doing a large volume of construction loans, it is good practice to rotate the inspectors so that one inspector does not always inspect the same builder's work.

In the original negotiations with the borrower the work volume can be reduced, and with it costs, if the agreement is to make advances not more than one each 30 days. This arrangement is not always possible in residential construction but is not unusual in the nonresidential field.

TAKEOUTS (LONG-TERM LOANS)

In every construction loan there must be a provision for the long-term loan to pay off the construction loan. The lender may make both the construction and the long-term loan. In this case the documentation should be in one package to avoid unnecessary cost.

The borrower may already possess a takeout commitment from another lender or the lender may make a tentative commitment for the construction loan subject to the borrower producing a satisfactory takeout. In some cases a construction lender may have knowledge of a long-term loan source and will assist the borrower in providing the takeout. A fee is normally charged for this service.

Takeout letters of commitment vary widely from a simple one-page letter to complicated documents. A construction lender must carefully examine the commitment to determine whether the terms of the commitment can be complied with. Compliance must be based both on the ability of the lender and the borrower. Some of the questions that will arise from an examination of the commitment are:

1. Can the structure be completed within the allotted time?
2. If there is a rental achievement required, does your feasibility study show that this can be accomplished?
3. If speculative sales are a part of the loan, can the market absorb these sales and can the units be constructed within the allotted time?
4. Are there any items in the commitment which permit a cancellation, other than failure to perform the major requirements?
5. If there is a slowdown in projected sales or rentals can the borrower carry the extra interest and overhead burden?

6. Is the takeout lender of sufficient financial strength to pay out when required?
7. Can a time extension be had, if necessary, from the takeout, and, if not, is the bank prepared to take the long-term loan into its own portfolio for disposal later?

Paramount sources of long-term mortgage lending are insurance companies, savings banks, and savings and loan associations. These institutions constantly seek good mortgage investments as a large part of their investment portfolio. If the borrower is to be assisted in obtaining the long-term loan, it is necessary to maintain current knowledge of the types of construction and the terms these lenders are using to place mortgages.

Some long-term lenders will insist on a tripartite agreement between the construction lender, the borrower, and themselves. In a tripartite agreement the lenders agree to lend and the borrower agrees to borrow. The agreement strengthens the takeout commitment by making a contract and assures the long-term lender that he or she will receive the loan. Most long-term lenders need to forecast investments a year or two in advance and the tripartite agreement assures delivery of the loan, even if interest rates are more favorable from other sources at delivery date. To the construction lender the agreement is helpful, since anything that strengthens the takeout commitment is an advantage.

A basic form of tripartite agreement is included as Exhibit 53–2.

Exhibit 53–2
Tripartite Buy and Sell Agreement

This Agreement entered into by and between   hereinafter referred to as Holder and THE SOLID INSURANCE COMPANY, hereinafter referred to as Purchaser.

WHEREAS, the Purchaser has entered into a commitment dated   with   to extend a mortgage loan in the amount of   dollars on a   story building to be erected at   , and the Holder has entered into an agreement with   to extend a mortgage loan for the construction of said   story building to be erected prior to the permanent financing of Purchaser, and it is the desire of the Holder to assure itself that, upon completion of the building according to the terms and conditions of said letter of commitment, the Purchaser will purchase the note and mortgage securing it from the Holder for the principal amount advanced by Holder, up to a maximum of   dollars subject to the terms and conditions set forth in its letter of commitment, and it is the desire of Purchaser to assure itself that said note and mortgage securing the construction loan for the erection of said   story building will be assigned to it by Holder upon the completion of said building according to the terms and conditions of its letter of commitment.

NOW, THEREFORE, in consideration of the mutual promises herein contained the Holder hereby agrees to sell and the Purchaser hereby agrees to buy the note and mortgage executed by   , for the erection of said   story building   , in the face amount of   dollars, said note and mortgage bearing date of   , 19   , but not exceeding the amount specified in said commitment for which the Borrower is then entitled, upon completion of the improvements according to the terms and conditions of the letter of commitment of Purchaser dated   , provided however, that said construction shall have been completed and said purchase effectuated on or before   , and subject to compliance by said   with the terms and conditions of said letter of commitment.

IN WITNESS WHEREOF, the said   and THE SOLID INSURANCE COMPANY have hereunto caused their hands to be set this-
day of   19

Signed in the presence of:

BY: _____

_____

_____

_____

_____ THE SOLID INSURANCE COMPANY

_____ BY: _____

The undersigned agree to carry out the tenor of the above agreement and agree not to participate in or induce any breach of the foregoing agreement by either party.

_____

_____

Dated: _____

DOCUMENTATION

In addition to a regular mortgage document and the evidence of debt (i.e., bond, note, etc.) one should include a Construction Rider or what is becoming more popular, a Construction Loan Agreement. The Construction Loan Agreement supplements the commitment letter and delineates the terms and arrangements of the loan so that there is no misunderstanding.

Both the rider (Exhibit 53–3) and the agreement should comply

EXHIBIT 53–3

Rider Attached To
Mortgage From:

To:

Dated:

Encumbering Lands and Premises
Known as:

It is further agreed by the mortgagors, that in the event that they shall not complete the construction of the building or buildings now being erected, or to be erected on the premise hereby mortgaged, in accordance with plans and specifications submitted to the mortgagee, on or before   , or if work on said construction should cease before completion, and the said work should remain abandoned for a period of 15 days, then and in either event, the entire principal sum of the bond secured by this mortgage and interest thereon, shall at once become due and payable, at the option of the mortgagee, and in the event of abandonment of work upon the construction of the said building or buildings for the period of 15 days as aforesaid, the mortgagee may, at its option, also enter into and upon the mortgaged premises and complete the construction of the said building or buildings hereby giving to the mortgagee full power and authority to make such entry and to enter into such contracts or arrangements as may be necessary to complete the said building or buildings, and monies expended by the mortgagee in connection with such completion of construction shall be added to the principal amount of said bond and secured by these presents, and shall be payable by the mortgagors on demand, with interest at the rate

The right and privilege are hereby given and granted to the mortgagee to enter upon the premises covered by this mortgage and to fully inspect the same at all times during construction of said building or buildings, and until completion thereof and until the monies secured thereby shall have been fully disbursed.

In addition to the agreements, covenants, and conditions contained in the mortgage to which this rider is attached, and of which it forms a part, it is further agreed by and between the parties hereto:

Upon request of the mortgagors, the mortgagee may hereafter, at its option, at any time before full payment of this mortgage, make further advances to the mortgagors, and any such further advance, with interest, shall be secured by this mortgage and accompanying bond; provided, however, that the amount of principal secured by this mortgage and remaining unpaid, shall not at the time of and including any such advance, exceed the original principal sum thereby secured.

The mortgagors do covenant and agree to and with the mortgagee to repay all such further advances made as aforesaid, with interest; that such further advances shall be secured by this mortgage and accompanying bond; and that all of the covenants and agreements in this mortgage contained shall apply to such further advances as well as to the original principal sum herein recited.

The word "mortgagee" as used in this rider shall be construed to mean the owner and holder of the security instrument to which this rider is attached, or any assignee or transferee thereof. The word "mortgagors" as used in this rider shall be construed to mean the maker or makers of said security instrument and also the vendees, dovisees, successors, heirs, and assigns of such mortgagor; and the word "mortgage" as used in this rider shall be construed to mean the security instrument to which this rider is attached. The rider attached to and forming a part of the mortgage for $ dated   is identified therewith by the following signatures. The rider attached hereto and executed by the mortgagors is hereby made a part of the within mortgage.

Attest: By:_____

_____

with state statutes. The agreement may be a lengthy document if all of the important details are covered.

To make certain that the documentation is acceptable to the institution providing the takeout, the title work and the proposed mortgage, and other papers should be submitted to the long-term lender prior to the bank's advancing any funds to its borrower. This practice prevents disputes as to documentation and title at the time the loan is delivered.

Many institutions require that the construction lender use the takeout documentation forms. If these are required, they should also be prepared and submitted with the title work.

Construction lending, if properly underwritten, managed, and documented makes for profitable lending with an acceptable level of risk.

MORTGAGE LOAN WAREHOUSING

This type of real estate-related loan is usually in the form of a line of credit perhaps better described as a type of "secured time loan."

Customers are primarily mortgage banking firms but savings and loan association, savings banks, and occasionally other commercial banks may wish to use this type of borrowing.

Basically a commitment is made to loan up to fixed maximum, with disbursements being made upon delivery of closed mortgage loans, mostly federal government-insured or guaranteed loans, but conventional mortgage loans are sometimes utilized. Terms of these loans vary somewhat and will be described later. Repayments are made when loans are delivered to investors.

The advantages of a bank's entering into this type of lending program are: (1) the interest return, (2) secured loans, (3) securing compensating balances and fees, and (4) the opportunity to make construction loans.

Interest rates are always subject to negotiation, depending on the borrower, the security offered, and the compensating balances. Two popular methods are to fix the rate at some percentage above a moving prime or charge the same rate as the coupon rate on the loans offered as security. In some unusual cases the rate is fixed *at* the moving prime.

Compensating balances usually run from 10 to 20 percent of the line in use, but are also subject to negotiation.

Construction loan opportunities may range from making nonresidential construction loans brokered through the mortgage banker or doing all the construction lending for the tract that the residential loans emanate from. Types of lines are as follows:

Revolving Lines. This credit is usually for a substantial sum that continuously revolves for an indefinite period with a cancellation possible by a specific advance notice. It may be used for presold or non-presold loans.

Nonrevolving Lines. This is a credit for a fixed sum and a specific number of loans. It is a line of credit in that more than one disbursement can be made as loans are delivered. The agreement can have a fixed expiration or several expiration dates depending on loan deliveries. Expiration dates are usually keyed to investor delivery dates. This type of line is primarily used for presold loans.

Deferred Lines. This type of credit may run for periods of up to 18 months or longer. It is secured by loans that are presold and waiting to be delivered at some future date. Quite often the agreement will call for the documentation to be approved and the mortgage recorded in the name of the investor. This type of line is generally extended to savings banks, savings and loan associations, and other commercial banks.

Repurchase Lines. These lines are generally used by mortgage companies who are not federally approved lenders. The warehousing bank closes the loans in its own name against a commitment obtained by the mortgage company issued by the investor in the name of the warehousing bank.

Under the first three lines, the mortgages are assigned to and the documents held by the warehousing bank as security for the loan. There are some variations of this practice but they are not important.

Presold loans are those which an investor has committed to purchase, and are the most desirable and comparatively free of risk. In warehousing non-presold loans, strict attention should be given to the capital and capability of the mortgage company customer. The customer's capital ability to repurchase the loans and its sales aggressiveness and past performance should be scrutinized.

Particular attention must be given to writing in safeguards to prevent the buildup of loans and the time allowed for the customer to move loans out of the line. If the agreement allows, say, 180 days for a presold loan to be moved out of the line, it is advisable to reduce that term to, perhaps 90 days for non-presold loans. If the customer produces a commitment from an investor, to purchase these non-presold loans, the term can be adjusted to meet the delivery date.

Any individual loan is only worth what the investor will pay for it. In the case of presold loans, this value is established by the investor's commitment to purchase. In the case of non-presold loans the value is determined by the general market.

A continuous knowledge of the purchase market for these loans is an essential part of operations. Loans should not be taken into the line at more than their current market or presold value. The current value can change either up or down and this is one of the risks in warehouse lending. Interest rates on government-insured or guaranteed loans are established by the controlling agencies. An increase in the rate can lower the value of the loans in the line or a decrease in rate can increase the value. Market decreases in value can be overcome by arrangements to hold the loans until the market improves or requiring the customer to repurchase.

When mortgage warehousing lines first came into being, most banks charged a service fee to handle each loan. As competition for these lines increased and compensating balances have been evaluated, fees have been adjusted by negotiation. Since warehousing lines require more than average detail, some fee should be arranged to cover the extra personnel costs.

The detail, other than bookkeeping which the computer can do, is concentrated in reviewing the loans when they are received and in preparing them for delivery to the investor. The loan review is the most important portion of loan management in these lines. Each loan must be reviewed to make certain that the proper documentation is present and that the documents are currently prepared.

Personnel can be trained to do the review. A part of that training should be a briefing by legal counsel. Counsel should prepare a checklist for day-to-day use. After a reasonable amount of training, most person-nel should be able effectively to review the loans.

Delivery requires a substantial amount of detail work in preparing lists, assembling documents, and typing of transmittal letters.

The key to profitable mortgage warehousing lines is underwriting negotiation and loan management. Properly underwritten and man-aged, this type of credit is profitable and has an acceptable level of risk.

Chapter 54

Residential Mortgage Loans

*James M. Walsh**

Residential mortgage lending is that type of financing provided to persons who will occupy the real estate for their homes. The real estate they own, through the vehicle of a mortgage or deed of trust, becomes security for the loan.

FORMS OF HOME OWNERSHIP

Home ownership is divided into three important classifications which should be seen as legal entities and not as physical structures. It is unimportant at this time that we have a mental image of a building; we are simply talking about ownership form. These three ownership forms are the single-family house, the condominium, and the cooperative.

The single-family house is a dwelling that is separate and apart in ownership from others and is placed so that it has an access of its own to all the necessary things that permit it to exist without support, in a legal sense, from other structures. Legally, its ownership is not dependent on other structures for existence.

The condominium is a form of residence that depends on other structures for its existence. It may be a part of a large structure or a freestanding building dependent on other such buildings for the group which owns certain areas common to all the structures. Essentially, it is described as a dwelling which, although legally independent, has ownership of certain areas which are used and owned by all members of the group which form the condominium. These common areas are

* Vice President, Equibank N.A., Pittsburgh, Pennsylvania.

walks, green areas, playgrounds, elevators, and such other necessary elements to the efficient use of the dwelling. Necessary to the condominium is a legal entity called a condominium association in which all dwelling owners have an ownership interest.

The cooperative is a form of ownership in which the occupier of a dwelling unit has a share in a corporation which owns a structure or structures. The user-occupier of the dwelling, by his or her ownership of a share in the corporation, has an undisputed right to occupy and to use the facilities common to all owners.

The condominium and cooperative can be seen to be very comparable in type of structure, but quite unlike in legal ownership.

FINANCING FOR INDIVIDUAL OWNERSHIP

All three forms of dwelling units can be, and are, capable of being financed for individual ownership. It is this financing of ownership that is our concern. Few people today can own their dwellings without financial assistance from the commercial bank, mutual savings bank, savings and loan association, insurance company, or private lender. The approach to financing is essentially the same in all cases for the lender who must evaluate the risks which attend the lending.

The financial institution which seeks mortgage loans for its portfolio should first have examined its position in the financial community with regard to the needs it must serve. It has planned the extent of its assets to be placed in various forms of short- and long-term obligations and where mortgage lending fits in the allocation of these assets. This financial service to the community is determined then by bank size, diversity of interest, and community needs. This is a part of the management of the bank's assets.

Essential is the definition of risk. The risk is defined by underwriting the lending request; that is, by estimating the value of the security for the loan, and the potential borrower's ability to repay the loan over a period of time consistent with the anticipated future economic life of the security. Of the two elements to the underwriting task, the more important with respect to preservation of principal is the appraisal of the real estate.

Appraisal Methods

Real estate appraisal in a general sense uses techniques which have been carefully defined, but productive only when used by the experienced practitioner. The techniques which bring a value decision; i.e., the appraisal, are referred to as the "cost," "market," and "income" approaches. The real estate appraisers who perform their tasks with thoughtful appreciation of the problems and who explore the valuation problem from its various aspects give due consideration to all techniques and arrive at their conclusions in a logical manner.

The cost approach to value has for its basic premise that nothing is worth more than it would cost to reproduce. In other words, the cost of building a house on a lot will limit the price to be paid for a similar house already in existence in a similar location. The concept is the "principle of substitution," and is not difficult to understand. The achievement of the result, the cost of reproduction, is not so easily obtained without a careful market study.

Where does the information come from? Builders of similar structures can be a valuable source, but they are limited by their own experience. Subcontractors look at only a small part of the building problem. The answer is in careful study of a broad, local market. The appraiser, using the cost approach to value, must have full knowledge of the components of the building and the ability to assimilate information from various sources into a form that will provide an intelligible conclusion. These sources, whose study precedes a conclusion, are the study on a continual basis of the prices housing has as it reaches the market; price is decided not just by cost, but by a multitude of factors which reflect demand. Appraisers, in an effort to carefully monitor demand, use services (Boeckh, Marshall & Swift and others) which keep current with prices of housing production and permit the appraisers to reinforce their own studies with information obtained from these highly objective sources which make a business out of continuous study and provide conclusions which are the basis for a vital element in real estate valuation.

The cost approach to real estate value is then summarized by an examination of available data collected by the appraiser or extracted from information supplied by a cost service for the purpose of arriving at a supportable conclusion which will, when examined by the appraiser, assist in the final estimate of value.

Essential to the cost approach to value is the depreciation the existing property has suffered during its life. Depreciation is divided into three categories: physical, functional, and economic. Physical depreciation is that which has occurred through use. Functional depreciation is that which results from those factors that are inherent to the property and are usually those found in its design. Economic depreciation, or obsolescence, are those that result from factors outside the property, such as a location which adversely affects desirability. These forms of depreciation are not necessarily found in all appraisal problems, but, when found, result in limitations of value which are deducted from the cost of reproducing the property.

The market approach to value has no "cost service" or similar source of information. The appraiser looks at recent sales of similar properties which can be characterized as "comparables." These sales, to be used for comparison with the property under appraisal, become the appraiser's base for moving to the conclusion which is independent of the "cost approach."

The careful real estate appraiser provides a description of each "comparable" property which is used to support the conclusion. The real estate appraiser usually, but not necessarily, prepares a chart of comparison which sets forth those matters for consideration which are vital to the conclusion and by which the comparable properties differ from the property under appraisal.

The chart or grid of comparable properties, prepared by the appraiser, shows the considerations which are of particular importance. They are "sale date," location, number of rooms, baths, condition, quality of construction, parking, and sales price per square foot. All these considerations, as they compare to the subject property, are given a price which becomes an adjustment to bring the comparable property to the subject property. That is, the comparables are either better or worse than the subject with the comparison expressed in dollars.

The third source, independent from the others, is the income approach to value. Although useful in theory, it has little or no contribution to the ultimate appraisal of a dwelling. However, it must be considered as a technique so that the entire range of information sources will have been used to produce a good end product.

This "income approach" selects from the market those properties which have been rented and later sold. A multiple, either monthly or annually, is determined from available information and this multiple applied to the estimated rent per period for the property under appraisal. For example, if three comparable properties are found to have sold for $30,000, $32,000, and $33,000 and rented on a monthly basis for $400, $450, and $475, respectively, the "multiplier" for each is the sale price divided by the monthly rent. In this example, the multipliers will be 75, 71, and 71, respectively. The appraiser then selects, based on experience, a multiplier from this information, somewhere between 71 and 75. He or she estimates the monthly rental of the property under appraisal and multiplies monthly rent by the monthly factor to arrive at a value conclusion.

As previously mentioned, this is not an ordinarily valid source of appraisal information, so that its use is very limited and is seldom effective unless there is a substantial and dependable body of information from which to extract a valid conclusion.

The appraiser next moves to the correlation of information and here prepares the final estimate, the money expressed in dollars he or she believes the property to be worth.

The appraiser makes a very important contribution to the loan decision and in many cases "makes" the loan decision through his work. No real estate loan should be made without the appraisal since it provides to the loan officer an opinion of value of the security for the loan. Because of the appraiser's importance, bank management must carefully consider whether to employ staff appraisers, use outside professionals or use both in arriving at loan decisions.

TYPES OF LOANS

As the loan officer reviews the loan to be granted to the applicant, he has four types to consider: conventional, private mortgage insurance, insured by the Federal Housing Administration, or guaranteed by the Veterans Administration. All four loans types are used by lenders and do not, in the ordinary case, present difficulties because of diversity of procedure.

Conventional Loans

The conventional loan places the entire loan decision with the lender; he is not required to obtain approval from other sources. The procedure is relatively simple: application, verification of information, appraisal, decision, and closing.

The private mortgage insurance company, through its work, provides a check on the lender and assists him in his decision as the amount of the loan, as a percentage of value, exceeds the limits that the lender considers to be appropriately conservative. There are a number of such companies in existence at this time that are providing a necessary service to mortgage lenders; the lenders are brought the benefits of expert analysis by underwriters who are exposed to many lending problems. The lender which uses private insurance of mortgage loans should first determine the acceptability through credit analysis of the insurance company. The insurance company must demonstrate through its balance sheet its ability to pay its losses and that it has underwriting capability to minimize them.

FHA Insured Loans

The Federal Housing Administration (FHA), which had its beginning in the early 30s, more than any other government or private body, made substantial contributions to the wide distribution of home ownership in the country. These contributions related particularly to real estate appraisal, architectural assistance, credit analysis, and land development; the Federal Housing Administration took practically the entire burden of risk from the lender by providing insurance of loans secured by single family residences.

The FHA insured loan has added to marketability of mortgage loans since, through the insurance of the loan, the risk became standardized. With the risk known and limited through insurance by a governmental body, mortgage loans became marketable throughout the United States. Eastern banks and insurance companies became able to make investments in other parts of the country, providing investment opportunities to capital surplus areas and funds to areas of capital shortage.

The FHA works in an uncomplicated way by reviewing the details of an application and agreeing through a commitment to insure a loan when made. The review by the FHA is essentially underwriting of the loan; the property is appraised and the credit of the borrower is considered in order to determine the probability of repayment. Down payments are set at minimums from time to time and interest rates are changed to reflect money market conditions. Charges to the borrower are controlled through regulation. Loan maturities are related to the economic life of the real estate, as in the case of conventional mortgage lending. These loans are a valuable part of any well-balanced mortgage loan portfolio.

VA Loans

The Veterans Administration, toward the end of World War II, in an effort to assist homecoming veterans to obtain housing they seriously needed, provided a mortgage guarantee program which placed limits on risk for mortgage lenders in consideration for the lender being willing to advance all or a large part of the cost of the veteran's dwelling. This guarantee program continues to exist today.

The Veterans Administration program provides that the lender, after foreclosure, receive a payment up to $17,500, but not more than 60 percent of the loan balance at the time of foreclosure. The Veterans Administration reserves to itself the option of purchasing the foreclosed real estate from the mortgage lender at the mortgage balance and thereby providing to the lender a total reimbursement for the principal amount of the loan plus the delinquent interest.

Like the Federal Housing Administration, the Veterans Administration sets maximum interest rates for the loans it guarantees as well as limiting the term of the loan in relationship to the future economic life of the real estate.

COMPETITIVE FORCES

In the field of mortgage lending, the competitive forces of down payment, interest rate and loan term must be considered by the lender.

The mortgage lender is required, if he desires to lend effectively, to respond to competition with periodic changes which will meet the market. The business of mortgage lending is never static and the effective lender must be willing to carefully evaluate his requirements in order to meet ever changing competitive forces.

Interest rates are determined by the marketplace with careful attention to usury laws of the various states. These usury laws set interest rate limits and at times, because markets decree higher rates, result in a limitation on the amount of money available for mortgage loans; lendable funds will, within limits, seek the highest rate when risks are relatively similar.

As mentioned earlier, in the case of both FHA insured and VA guaranteed loans, interest rate maximums are set by the Department of Housing and Urban Development and the Veterans Administration. When market forces require higher yields to mortgage lenders, these lenders charge to the seller of the real estate a fee called "discount" or "points" for the purpose of raising the yield. Through experience, it has become practice to charge a 1 percent fee at loan closing to the seller in order to increase the yield by 0.125 percent.

For example, the legal maximum interest rate is determined by the FHA and VA to be 8 percent at a time when the market for such funds is 8.5 percent. Since it is not legally permissible for the lender to charge the 8.5 percent market rate, he charges a discount to produce a higher yield. In order to raise the yield to 8.5 percent on a loan carrying an 8 percent coupon rate, the lender charges to the seller (charging the buyer is illegal) a discount or points of 4 percent of the loan amount. If 0.125 percent in yield is achieved by charging 1 percent, the lender charges 4 percent to the seller at the loan closing.

Determining Size of Payment

Effective and conservative mortgage lending requires that the lender, through length of repayment, permit amortization to be scheduled so that the buyer-mortgagor may be able to repay the debt within the limits of his anticipated income. To preserve a conservative approach, real estate appraisers are asked to give an opinion of "future economic life"; i.e., the time expressed in years during which the dwelling may be expected to retain marketability. This future economic life, less five years, is the pattern usually followed by lenders in setting the maximum loan term.

While the property value is under study, the credit side of the problem is being evaluated in order to decide the purchaser's capability of meeting the monthly payments during the life of the loan.

The applicant has provided to the lender a full statement of his assets, liabilities and income from all sources. These are studied to decide whether the information is completely true in all respects. The procedure for checking the validity of the information is through verifying with asset sources the existence of the bank accounts or other liquid assets, through a verification of employment with the applicant's employer, and through a credit reporting agency the applicant's paying habits.

When a completely documented file is constructed by the lender, he is in a position to decide the capability of the applicant for debt repayment. It would be folly to permit a borrower to receive funds which he could not repay from his income; for this reason the lender develops certain income requirements to provide that the debt be serviced. It is generally accepted in the national market for mortgage loans that the interest, principal, taxes and insurance should not exceed 25 percent of the applicant's income. When all debt payments, which extend beyond seven months, are added to mortgage debt service, the total should not exceed 33 percent.[1]

The use of these bench marks (that is, 25 percent and 33 percent) are by no means complete assurance of debt repayment, but can be considered as reasonable and will permit the mortgage lender to operate effectively within his market. Further considerations in making the loan decision are the amount of down payment, the stability of the applicant's employment, and the anticipated future increase of his or her income.

Value of Single Family Mortgage Lending

Single-family mortgage lending, given the absence of severe economic depression or community reliance on an industry that may discontinue operations causing widespread unemployment, can be a valuable tool for the banker. The loans generated by this activity will form a solid base for other banking services to the mortgagors. Providing funds for home ownership opens the door to checking accounts, savings accounts, installment loans, automobile financing, and other services provided by the bank. A unique and long-lasting relationship is begun by this type of lending and the loan itself is an excellent source of dependable interest income.

Single-family mortgage lending, as it contributes to home ownership, serves the community in a very important way. It makes possible a measure of independence for the homeowner who will generally exhibit pride in the care of his property. In neighborhoods where properties are owned by the occupants, there will be evidence of good condi-

---

[1] *Home Mortgages Underwriting Guidelines*, Federal Home Loan Mortgage Corporation, Publication No. 19, March 1976.

tion, neat appearance, and family stability. Where neighborhoods have declined, individual home ownership will have been scarce and absentee landlords have been only interested in providing a minimum of upkeep to the properties to preserve income from the rent.

SECONDARY MORTGAGE MARKET

Lending institutions should be particularly interested in residential lending and aware of the means available to expand service to their communities through use of the secondary mortgage market. Use of secondary market facilities provides funds for loans on a constant basis when the lending institution has a lessened interest in such lending for its own portfolio.

This secondary market also provides an excellent source of lending discipline which will guide and assist underwriters in producing loans of high quality. The lender is not bound by his or her own internal approach to lending, but has the benefit of the experience, thinking, and new ideas of those who are involved in a large volume of such lending.

Secondary market sources available to a lender are the Federal Home Loan Mortgage Corporation (Freddie Mac), the Federal National Mortgage Association (Fannie Mae), and the Government National Mortgage Corporation. These government-sponsored secondary market lenders exist for the purpose of providing mortgage funds, especially during times when money is in short supply. The knowledgeable mortgage lenders will make themselves aware of the lending programs available to expand their lending ability.

OTHER OWNERSHIP FORMS

In addition to the single-family dwelling and the condominium, there are two other forms of ownership that are closely related, though not in wide use at this time: The planned unit development (PUD) and the deminimis planned unit development. Although these forms are limited in use, they should be understood as to form.

The planned unit development is very similar to a condominium. The owners of the dwelling units have an ownership share in certain common property, owned and maintained by a homeowner's association. The common property requires automatic, nonseverable membership in the homeowner's association with mandatory assessments.[2] The common property is an important contributor to the value of each unit which is the security for the loan.

---

[2] Ibid.

A deminimis PUD has legal construction similar to the PUD. However, the value of the dwelling unit is not substantially affected by the rights to use of common areas.

The third form of home ownership is the cooperative. Cooperatives may be defined as "a form of multiple ownership of real estate in which a corporation or business trust entity holds title to a property and grants the occupancy rights to particular apartments or units to shareholders by means of proprietary leases or similar arrangements."[3]

Though they have been used for many years, this form is not so common as the single-family residence or the condominium, and the reason is simply financing. In the case of the more common forms, ownership is severed so that a specific mortgage lien may exist; the cooperative does not enjoy severability.

Cooperative ownership has a form very similar to that of a corporation or partnership with shares of ownership in the whole and the right to occupy a unit or units. The body which owns the real estate borrows with the entire structure or structures as security, not individual units. Because of such legal form of ownership, an owner who sells must seek out a purchaser financially capable of a substantial investment if the selling ownership is of long duration, and has formed a substantial equity.

CONCLUSION

Residential mortgage lending is an important part of each commercial bank loan portfolio. It provides a service to the community, loans of high quality, and a customer base for further services. Procedures should be set forth by the lending institution which will permit an evaluation of all the risks relating to the loan. The risks can be limited by appraisal of the security and careful underwriting.

Effective mortgage lending is best achieved through balancing the portfolio among the various types of mortgage loans which have been described.

---

[3] Gavin A. Brown, comp., *Mortgage Banking Terms: A Working Glossary* (New York: Mortgage Bankers Association, May 1975).

Chapter 55

Mortgage Lending: Income-Producing Properties

James M. Walsh*

Mortgage lending has three separate and distinct divisions which are unlike in risk and require different methods of analysis prior to the decision to make the loan. The first, residential mortgage lending, has been treated in Chapter 54 of this book. The second division is that which is the subject of this chapter. The third division, construction lending, is covered in Chapter 53.

An income-producing property is that which is anticipated to have a reasonably assured income stream over a period of time for repayment of debt and return to the owner. It is a property which is expected to produce rents which will, after payment of necessary expenses, leave more than sufficient income to pay periodically the interest on the loan and to amortize the debt; i.e., debt service.

Before we discuss the methods used in underwriting such loans, it is important that we distinguish between loans for which repayment depends on the income received from the real estate itself and those which depend on the success of a business venture. It is vital that we make such a distinction since we are looking forward to liquidation of the security to preserve the principal that has been invested and the interest that has been accrued.

The best example of the latter instance is the industrial building which may be of a certain size and configuration to accommodate a particular type of manufacturing facility. If the owner-user should experience financial difficulty resulting in the lender's acquisition through

* Vice President, Equibank N.A., Pittsburgh, Pennsylvania.

foreclosure, the market for the building, because of its structural peculiarities, may be limited. This limitation would then result in a lower
price and possible loss to the lender if cost were the guide in appraising
the real estate.

LIMITING RISK—LOANS ON RESIDENTIAL PROPERTY

When underwriting the risk prior to lending secured by real estate,
risks are limited through appraisal. The goal in appraisal is to arrive
at a value estimate which properly justifies the investment of the owner
and the loan from the lender. From the lender's viewpoint, the attempt
is to arrive at a value which the lender believes will be obtained when
the property is sold after foreclosure; the lender must anticipate
ownership.

Techniques of Appraisal

In the valuation of residential real estate, the reliance is most heavily
weighted in favor of the market approach; the greatest weight in the
case of income-producing properties is the income approach. The income approach is most heavily weighted because the value is found
in the certainty and amount of the income stream.

The task of valuation is similar in the case of each income-producing
property, though the specific application and considerations vary according to the problem and sources of information. The effort is toward
estimating net income after the receipt of rents and payment of the
expenses incident to maintaining the property.

The first and most common type of income-producing property is
the rental apartment building or buildings. We do not distinguish for
these considerations whether the property is a high-rise elevator building or garden apartments. The problem of finding the answer to value
is approached in the same way: gross income less expenses equals net
income; net income is capitalized into value.

Since apartment buildings are groups of living units which are rented
to tenants for specific periods at certain amounts, we must first look
to the competing market for the stability of the rental income. How
can we be assured that the gross income (i.e., the annual rent) will
be available for a long period in sufficient amounts? When this question
is answered, the first step has been taken toward finding the value
of the security.

Gross income is estimated through a research of the availability of
similar units which are providing, or will provide, competition to the
existing or proposed building. The appraiser studies the rents being
paid by the tenants in comparable existing buildings and the rate of

occupancy enjoyed by them. If apartments are showing a significant vacancy rate, the appraiser will be expected to find the reason for the vacancy. If, on the other hand, there is no vacancy, he or she should explain the reason for this condition. This latter situation is indicative of insufficient units or rents which are below the market.

When forecasting income, it is necessary to forecast a vacancy rate since rents contracted for are not always received. Some apartments rent immediately upon the tenant moving out; the normal situation is that there is some time before an acceptable replacement tenant can be found. Not all tenants pay the contract rent on time and some leave the premises without having paid all the rent due. The realistic appraisal of an apartment building considers some loss of rent by the owner.

The expenses which are paid by the owner in order to maintain the property are next considered in an effort to arrive at the net income prior to servicing the debt. All these expenses again are compared to those experienced by other properties to assure the appraiser that he or she has studied those that are necessary for consideration and that the final expense estimates are within reason as dictated by the experience of other similar properties. Of particular interest is the expense to a project through utilities which recently have been such to place burdens on income-producing real estate which seriously reduce net income potential.

The final result is net income. With the capitalization of net income, the appraiser achieves the valuation through the income approach. Net income divided by rate of capitalization equals value.

It is obvious that the rate of capitalization is an important function of an appraisal which is the foundation for a loan decision. Therefore, the selection of the rate of capitalization considers the lender's rate for the loan and the return desired by the owner of the equity. Through blending these rates of return, the appraiser arrives at the rate of capitalization. There are a number of methods of acquiring a rate of capitalization and those form, in themselves, an interesting study of a necessary and important factor in the valuation of real estate. If the rate selection considers the lending and equity rates, it is usually adequate in the hands of an experienced appraiser.

Further Underwriting Considerations

Appraisal of real estate is not the last consideration prior to the loan decision. There still remains consideration of the term over which the money may be loaned. That decision is important, obviously, because of the need to match the return of the loan funds with the period during which the security will be productive. Financial tables have been developed which will show the loan officer the rate of payment for various interest rates and terms. These tables will show the percentage of outstanding loan balance at the end of each year of amortization. The tables are contained in a very comprehensive publication by the Financial Publishing Company of Boston, Massachusetts.

Although the underwriting of a loan secured by an income-producing property relies most heavily on the "income" approach to value, the cost approach can be found to be very enlightening as a further source of information. As in the case of the single-family residence, service companies have developed a method of computing the probable cost of certain types of building structures. Boeckh's, Marshall & Swift, and others describe the structures so that the problem at hand may be compared closely to the example. When the comparison is made, it is only necessary to follow through with the established procedure to arrive at an opinion of cost and the conclusion for the cost approach. The services do not, of course, relieve the appraisers of the necessity for study of the local market through their own sources to reinforce the use of the cost services.

The appraisers are never permitted to simply apply arithmetic formulas to perform their work; they must be perceptive and studious as they approach each task. They must bring the force of their experience with many appraisals of differing types of real estate into the problem.

The third approach to value is that of the study of sales of similar properties; i.e., the market approach. Through experience, the appraiser has been able to view properties in locations near the subject property and which are like the subject in many ways, such as type of construction, size, age, and services offered. When a body of such information is available and has been compared with the property under appraisal, the appraiser should logically support this conclusion. This conclusion, like the income and cost approaches, is arrived at from sources and through methods much different from the prior methods of evaluation.

The appraisers, who perform their tasks with care, use all three methods to formulate a final value conclusion. From the independent conclusions of cost, market and income, and their correlation, they arrive at the value estimate. The appraisers are required, in this last step in the appraisal process, to pursue a logical course and discuss the pertinent factors which led to the value conclusion.

An appraisal of an apartment building does not place total reliance on the proper investigation of the income stream. It also considers the stability afforded the income stream by the location of the structure and the suitability of the physical layout. The appraiser is expected to make adequate comparisons with competing properties in order to suitably support the conclusions that are reached concerning this part of the appraisal problem.

The income stream may be compared to a pyramid, the apex of which is net income and the supporting blocks the elements of appraisal and underwriting.

Exhibit 55–1

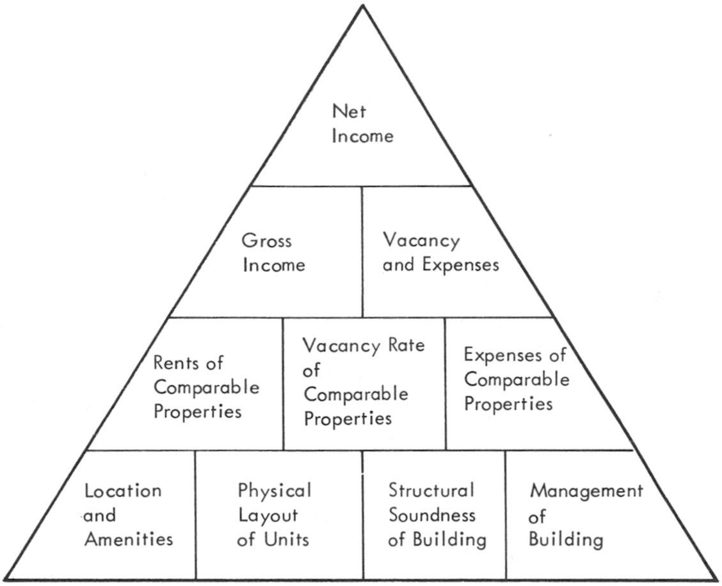

Debt Service Coverage

When the net income of an income-producing property has been estimated and capitalized to produce an estimate of value, it is placed in the hands of the underwriter; i.e., the bank loan officer, for the loan decision. If he accepts the appraiser's conclusion, his major concern is the income support that will be provided to the loan he is asked to make. The problem is essentially the adequacy of debt service coverage.

Obviously, the loan officer does not desire to lend funds secured by real estate which will not be repaid from its income. To match debt service to net income would not provide assurance of sufficient income to the owner and protection against miscalculations of expense items. Therefore, debt service coverage must be the first consideration of the lending officer after he has accepted the appraiser's conclusions.

Debt service coverage will vary according to type of income-producing property with the strength of support of net income being the critical consideration. If debt service coverage for an apartment project is suitable at 1.25, then the mortgage loan supported by a net lease of a credit tenant would require something less, probably 1.15. As the quality of the income stream increases, debt service coverage decreases and, conversely, as this quality diminishes the lender should require greater coverage of debt service by the net income which the real estate produces.

Other Residential Producing Properties

The example of an apartment building has been used to demonstrate the considerations that are primary to the loan decision because of the relative lack of complexity of appraising an apartment building. The other types of income-producing properties require similar considerations, but the types of information and the information sources vary according to the problem.

THE SHOPPING CENTER

The appraisal of a shopping center requires the same basic approach as that of the apartment development; that is, the forecast of gross income and debt service coverage. However, the source of gross income (i.e., rent) is composed of companies of varying creditworthiness. The expense side of the problem involves different considerations because the expenses of a shopping center are obviously different from those of an apartment. Vacancy allowance takes on an entirely different perspective. Lease terms are such that it is necessary to look forward to increasing expenses during the term of the lease with necessary rental adjustments. The loan officer, who considers a loan secured by a lien on a shopping center or other property which has a similar income source, must look carefully at the problem through the leases and credit standing of the tenants which support the valuation.

The strength of the income stream is found in the creditworthiness of the tenants and the quality of the lease obligations. The most creditworthy tenants are usually those which are nationally rated by Dun and Bradstreet or those which have had debt obligations rated by Moody's or Standard & Poor's. If the tenant does not possess a rating from these or similar sources, the underwriter must then analyze the financial statements and decide on the quality of the tenant. The most creditworthy of tenants which occupy larger sections of the center are properly described as "anchor" tenants. They are the tenants which are the major attractions for customers. Following these are the strong local tenants which, although not nationally rated, possess good balance sheets with an ability to function successfully in the local market. The third group are those that may be described as local, weak, and yet able to function with some success because they provide a necessary service to the customers of the center.

Of the three types of tenants, the greater the degree of creditworthiness, the lower the rent obligation per square foot and the longer the length of the lease with options on the part of the tenant to renew. The tenant possessing a strong balance sheet and national credit rating is very much aware of his or her necessity to the shopping center and will negotiate the lease from a position of strength. This tenant will attempt to acquire the greatest flexibility with respect to renewal options so that at the end of the lease term, he will renew the lease at terms favorable to him or will not renew if he is not satisfied with the return on his investment in the center. The most creditworthy tenant will attempt to fix his basic obligation (rent per square foot) for a long period with escalation only tied to increases in certain expenses.

Lease terms are shorter in the agreement between the strong local tenant and the owner, because the owner-lessor wants some flexibility for lease renewal and ability to choose a replacement tenant, or to increase rent. The strong local tenant will pay a rent per square foot greater than the nationally rated tenant and will be of substantial value to the center.

The weak local tenant is also of great importance to the center's success; this is usually a local merchant who occupies a minimal amount of space and provides a very necessary retail service. He or she is considered replaceable with greater ease than either the nationally rated or strong local tenant. This tenant characteristically pays the highest rent per square foot and has the shortest lease term and limited option rights for renewal of the lease.

Escalation

The shopping center developer must provide for increases in expenses, particularly taxes. This protection of the income stream is called "escalation." A base year (usually the year of full tax assessment) is selected and increases in taxes and other expenses that occur after the base year are assumed as increased rental obligations, according to an agreed-upon formula. The formula generally considers the area occupied by the tenant as it relates to the total area assessed by the taxing body. It is obvious that increases in expenses can serously erode the income stream if the owner-developer-lessor does not protect the income against expense increases which cannot be planned with mathematical accuracy.

Protection of the income stream can also be obtained by passing on to the tenant increases in expenses for maintenance of the shopping center and particularly in the area of parking lot maintenance.

Vacancy

Vacancy of a portion of the center must be considered. There always is a concern that a tenant may leave voluntarily or suffer financial reverses which force the elimination of his or her contribution to the income stream. The most creditworthy tenant is generally not accorded a vacancy rate; his default and consequent lack of contribution to the income stream is deemed to be a remote possibility. Furthermore, a vacancy allowance against such income would require consideration of loss of income to a substantial section of the development with serious impairment of the economic viability of the project. In other words, the impact of vacancy would be so substantial that if any allowance were made for it, net income would be adversely affected and seriously limit the ability of the lender to lend.

The other tenants, who are not owners of nationally acknowledged balance sheets, should be accorded some vacancy allowance. The amount of such allowance (i.e., the restriction of the income stream) becomes a matter of judgment by the appraiser and the loan officer. In this matter, as in so many other problems relating to the appraisal of real estate, there is no rule that can be given for guidance. The question can only be answered through consideration of the problem by experienced appraisers and underwriters who have knowledge of comparable problems.

The Developer

The shopping center is a world composed of many forces of varying strengths guided by the developer. The developer will be an expert planner, part builder, part manager, and the rest a careful and expert negotiator. He will also be very knowledgeable regarding financing. Negotiation, however, is at the heart of any successful real estate venture, but in a shopping center of size it is probably more important than in any other type of development.

Careful knowledge and evaluation of a prospective developer's attributes is required as part of the loan underwriting process. It is necessary for the loan officer to look carefully into the developer's background. The best argument in favor of a developer is his or her association with past successful ventures which compare to that which is the subject of the loan application. The risks are high and the careful choice of a borrower will limit the risk.

Construction of the Legal Entity

It is not unusual to find the ownership of a shopping center divided into more than one entity. This is the case when the most creditworthy occupants are not tenants, but owners of the land on which the buildings are located. The developer owns the land adjacent to that owned by the occupants and provides the legal right of the owner-occupant to use the parking lots and other amenities provided by the development.

The legal construction of a large shopping center is, in itself, a task of great importance because of the variety of entities which contribute to the whole. These entities may be landowners, owners of leaseholds, tenants, equity owners, and owners of rights to access to mall corridors, parking, or other amenities. The formulation of these legal documents is of extreme importance to the lender whose security is found in the real estate. Owners of legal rights must have their ownership carefully defined since this ownership affects the value of the lender's lien; the lender obtains security through the value of the borrower's ownership.

OFFICE BUILDINGS

The financing of an office building presents a problem for the loan officer not unlike the problems of the apartment building and the shopping center; the income approach to value is the loan's support.

However, the problem of valuation of an office building has its own peculiarities. Expenses are usually the complete concern of the owner in the usual case with protection provided by escalation provisions in the leases. Expense categories are different from the other two types of properties. The principle of valuation is the same and the loan officer should have little difficulty in applying the principle to the problem.

Of particular concern to the loan officer as he examines the appraisal of an office building is the method of computing the area to be occupied by the various tenants, and the inclusion or exclusion in the rent base of elevators, stairwells, rest rooms, and hallways. Whether these latter are included or excluded in computations of area is less important than proper comparison with other such properties, since these comparable properties are the competition which must be met by the owner-developer.

GENERAL CONSIDERATIONS

Lending money with income-producing real estate as security requires that the value of the security be carefully estimated through adequate appraisal. As mentioned earlier in this chapter, it is necessary for the lender to distinguish between the loan supported by real estate and that which has for its support the net worth of the borrower.

For the permanent lender, that is, the lender who commits to a fixed interest rate over a long period, it is necessary to protect against those forces which will cause failure of the project. Some of these considerations are quality of construction, restriction on amount of the loan, shortening of maturity with longer amortization, and the weight of a debt burden which produces an unsatisfactory return to the developer.

Construction quality is first considered with an examination of the plans and specifications by a person particularly qualified; i.e., an architect, an engineer, or persons from both these disciplines. Assured that the construction is properly planned, the next step is to examine the construction as it progresses. The examination of construction should be performed by those who are technically qualified and have examined the plans and specifications prior to the beginning of construction.

Extremely important in providing assurance of construction adequacy is the ability of the soil to carry the load of the structure. Throughout the world, there exist varying soils problems (i.e., ability of the ground to support the proposed structure), which must be considered before starting the building that has been planned. This might seem a very basic consideration, but any lender active in this type of lending can assure us that it is not unusual to find that prospective borrowers have inadequately planned in this area. There are engineers who are specialists in soils problems and their study should be required by the lender.

LIMITING THE AMOUNT OF THE LOAN

The loan amount is usually 75 percent of the indicated value, however, the permanent lender often protects his institution from excessive lending by providing that the loan be made in two stages. The first stage of the loan (about 85 percent of the permanent loan) is called the "floor" loan. The difference between the "floor" and "ceiling"; i.e., full disbursement, is called the "gap" or "gap loan."

When a lender issues a permanent commitment that is divided into two disbursement stages, he is taking a conservative course for protection against a high vacancy rate which ultimately adversely affects economic value. Even the most careful and expert appraiser will not always have been able to predict absolutely the success of a project, therefore, the permanent lender will follow his business judgment in the matter of disbursement of the loan.

The first advance after the completion of construction (i.e., the floor loan) occurs immediately upon completion and issuance of the certificate of occupancy. The loan is funded by the permanent lender whether the structure, usually an apartment development, is rented or vacant. If the apartment does not achieve a certain gross income level from tenants within a specific period, the balance of the loan, the "gap," is not funded and the principal of the loan does not exceed the "floor" amount.

LIMITATION OF TERM

Another method used by a lender to protect against an unsuccessful project or increases in interest rates is the shortened maturity with a long-term amortization rate. Even though payments are calculated on an amortization that befits the probable economic life of the real estate, the repayment of the loan balance is called for when there is still a substantial balance remaining. The permanent lender assumes that he will be able to ask for complete repayment of the loan balance or become the owner of the real estate through foreclosure of the matured loan. To repay the loan, the borrower must refinance; it is unreasonable to assume that the borrower would have access to funds without the support of either the original permanent lender or another lender of equal financial ability.

Therefore, in theory at least, the lender is protected by a maturity which is shorter than full amortization. In the most practical aspect, the borrower will simply reopen negotiations with the lender who will find himself forced to decide on ownership through legally opposed foreclosure or a refinancing of the debt over the balance of the amortization period.

THE PURCHASE AND SALE AGREEMENT

The issuance of a permanent commitment by a lender who desires the loan is by no means an assurance of his acquisition of the loan when it is scheduled to become a part of his loan portfolio. To protect the issuer of the permanent commitment, the construction lender and the borrower, there has been devised a three-party agreement, called a "purchase and sale" or "buy-sell" agreement.

The three parties to the transaction (the borrower, the permanent lender, and the construction lender) agree among themselves that they will each perform according to the terms of the contract. The construction lender will sell the loan to the permanent lender upon completion of the project. The permanent lender will purchase the loan from the construction lender and affirms that the loan documents prepared by the construction lender are in proper form. The developer-borrower acknowledges the existence of these obligations and is himself obligated to cooperate in the matter of loan sale and purchase.

CONCLUSION

Real estate lending with an income-producing property as security places heavy reliance on the appraisers and their ability to forecast the success of the project. The appraisers must ably show that their studies have included all the facets of the problems at hand and that their valuations, though recognized to be estimates, have been logically developed.

Essential to any successful project is a resourceful, experienced developer who has access to funds which will permit him to overcome the adversities of cost overrun which are all too common in real estate development. There are many real estate developers of minimal competence who will attempt to borrow funds for ill-conceived projects. It is the duty of the bank loan officer to sort out and reject those that are not properly planned since the unsuccessful developer shifts his burden to the bank when he decides that there is little or no hope of success.

There are also many successful, well-financed and experienced developers whose work is the source of well-structured loans which are necessary to the business of banking. Often these people start with small projects and move ahead into those of larger size; they must be identified early by the loan officer and careful attempts made to assist them by financing these ventures.

The usual source of long-term commitments for mortgage loans of $1 million or greater is the insurance company or mutual savings bank. These financial institutions function with great effectiveness in this market because of their ability to lend in all parts of the United States and Canada on projects having similarities of legal and financial construction. The commercial banker, therefore, is well advised to seek for the client this type of funding rather than finance the project requiring expenditure of very large sums.

Large money center banks maintain appraisal and underwriting staffs which have a level of competence equal to those of the life insurance companies and mutual savings banks. Those commercial banks that do not lend frequently to developers of large projects are well advised to function as correspondents of another long-term lender possessing greater experience.

There are excellent lending opportunities available to commercial bankers in this area of mortgage financing, but it is vital to successful lending that proper appraisal and underwriting practices be used to reasonably assure success.

Chapter 56

Consumer Credit—Role and Concepts

*James L. Smith**

In the last 40 years the status of consumer credit in commercial banking has grown markedly and has changed from a financial service in which few banks were involved to one of the most widespread and profitable services offered by retail banks. Consumer credit has expanded not only to share the general prosperity of the nation, but to contribute substantially to high levels of consumer expenditures which are the basis for that prosperity. Financing these higher levels of consumption and providing a consumer with automobiles and the many household items that they demanded have helped provide the strong demand for consumer credit.

The first identifiable phase in the development of consumer credit in commercial banking was a period of slow growth and general skepticism about the proper role of commercial banks in the field, plus apprehension about the consumer committing future income for conveniences and current pleasures. Roughly, that period covered from the 1930s through the close of World War II. The second development or era was the very aggressive postwar period characterized by the general expansion of banking services. Consumer demand that was built up during the war years, coupled with the emerging new mobility of our population, resulted in the rapid growth of completely new cities, and a strong demand for automobile and personal loans. The banking industry responded by allocating increased resources to consumer credit and by adjusting the conditions under which consumer

---

* Senior Vice President, Security Pacific National Bank, Los Angeles, California.

credit was extended. "Add-on," or discounted rates, were the universal practice of lenders, and the consumer credit business was considered very profitable by banks. Even during economic downturns, consumer credit held up well.

That growth period resulted in an increase in total consumer credit held by all lenders to approximately $200 billion by 1976. A major part of that growth was financed by commercial banks which were willing to reduce their liquidity as reflected by a substantial expansion in average loan deposit ratios. However, it has become obvious to bank management that the opportunities for such rapid growth are not infinite. In the recent periods of extremely heavy total loan demand, it became necessary to have accurate profit performance information on each component of the asset structure.

Those pressures led to the third and current phase in the development of consumer credit. Consumer credit managers now have the responsibility to support their requests for funding new programs and expansion of existing plans, and to do so competitively with other resource needs in the bank. To provide adequate information in support of consumer credit departments, managers rely heavily upon functional cost analysis which focuses attention on the areas that need operational improvement. Consumer credit has a relatively fixed-income potential, normally restricted by legal or competitive limitations, or both. This added attention to profit potential has caused significant changes in the methods by which the product is priced and the way the product is offered. Bank charge cards, revolving credit, and consumer leasing all became popular during this most recent period in development of consumer credit.

TRENDS IN CONSUMER CREDIT

The shift to asset ownership continues even in our "disposable" society. Just as the purchase of an automobile substitutes for the payment for public transportation, and acquiring a home washing machine and dryer substitutes for a trip to the laundromat, the television set has become a substantial substitute for going to the movies. This trend toward the acquisition of larger volumes and ranges of personal goods by much of our society has been made possible by an increasing affluence, aided in great part by consumer credit. In addition, women have joined the work force at an increasing rate and expanded the income levels upon which consumer finance could be based.

Over the longer term, this growth will continue and may even accelerate. In the years immediately ahead, the largest age group will be in the family formation age group. With rising incomes, these families will be able to use credit heavily to obtain the things their families need and want and to do so before they are able to accumulate the resources to acquire them out of current income. There will be a reordering of priorities in spending which will provide additional opportunities for bank lenders. And, as in the past, consumer credit will continue to serve not only as a catalyst in maintaining a dynamic economy but as a generator of growth and stability.

Quite a variety of financial institutions participate in the consumer credit market. The share of market of these institutions has changed over the years and will continue to be modified by competitive conditions, as well as by laws and regulation. Exhibit 56–1 shows the percentage of installment credit held by financial institutions and other grantors of consumer credit for the period 1943–76. Financial institutions in total, have increased their share of that credit from 71.1 percent in 1940 to 87.1 percent in 1976. Credit granted by retail stores and automobile dealers has declined correspondingly. The proportion of the market accounted for by commercial banks has grown from 26.3 percent in 1940 to 47.8 percent in 1976, slightly under the all-time high. In recent years credit unions have grown rapidly in market share and now account for 17.1 percent of the total, as compared with 3.1 percent in 1940. Expected changes in the future in the structure of financial institutions will modify the market share still further and continue to influence the conditions under which such credit is extended.

Types of Installment Credit by Commercial Banks

Exhibit 56–2 shows the changing relative importance of several principal types of consumer credit extended by commercial banks. Purchased automobile paper, or consumer credit originated through dealer financed plans, increased from 23.3 percent of the total consumer loans in 1940 to 35.2 percent in 1965–66. Since that time the relative importance of this type of consumer credit has declined; that portion was only 23.3 percent in 1975. A partial explanation of that decline is, of course, the increase in other categories of credit such as bank charge cards and revolving credit, which are shown under "other consumer goods." In addition, more careful functional cost analysis programs which have been developed and used more intensively in the industry in recent years have indicated lower profit potential for this type of lending. This segment of the consumer loan portfolio is very labor intensive and has been affected sharply by rising compensation costs as salaries have risen faster than other types of bank costs. In addition to the more restricted profit margins, the negative influence of restrictive legislation has contributed to decline in the indirect loan totals in commercial banks. Many banks across the country have made the

Exhibit 56–1

Percentage Holdings of Installment Credit by Financial Institutions and Retail Outlets: 1940–1976

Year End	Total Install- ment Credit	Total Finan- cial Insti- tutions	Commer- cial Banks	Sales Finance Com- panies	Credit Union	Con- sumer Finance Com- panies	Other	Total Retail	Auto Deal- ers	Depart- ment Stores	Furni- ture Stores	Appli- ance Stores	Other
1940	100.0	71.1	26.3	28.6	3.1	13.1		28.9	3.0	7.1	8.6	3.6	6.6
1945	100.0	72.1	30.2	12.2	4.1	25.6		28.9	1.1	5.3	9.7	0.7	11.0
1950	100.0	81.6	40.0	26.1	4.1	11.4		18.4	2.0	5.1	5.5	1.6	4.2
1955	100.0	84.4	36.5	29.2	5.8	9.2	3.7	15.6	1.7	5.2	3.6	1.3	3.8
1960	100.0	85.3	38.8	25.0	9.1	8.8	3.6	14.7	0.8	7.2	2.6	0.8	3.3
1965	100.0	86.3	40.6	21.4	10.3	10.3	3.7	13.6	0.4	7.4			5.8
1970	100.1	87.4	42.0	21.1	12.4	10.4	1.5	13.6	0.3				13.3
1975	100.0	88.9	48.5	22.6	15.6		2.2	11.3					
1976	100.0	87.1	47.8	22.2	17.1		2.2	10.7					

Note: Data under Sales Finance Companies cover all finance companies after 1970. Data for certain institutions not available for all years.
Source: Federal Reserve Statistical Release G 19; Board of Governors of the Federal Reserve System.

Exhibit 56-2
Types of Installment Credit Held by Commercial Banks Expressed as Percentages: 1940–1975

| Year End | Total | Auto Paper | | Other Consumer Goods | Repair and Moderni- zation | Personal Loans |
		Purchased	Direct			
1940	100.0	23.2	19.0	16.0	11.4	30.3
1945	100.0	8.9	19.2	15.3	14.8	41.8
1950	100.0	20.3	22.3	25.1	14.4	17.9
1955	100.0	30.5	19.5	19.3	12.6	18.1
1960	100.0	31.9	16.9	16.5	13.2	21.5
1965	100.0	35.3	19.5	14.4	8.9	21.9
1970	100.0	28.5	17.4	24.0	6.8	23.3
1975	100.0	23.3	16.7	35.2	6.2	18.6

Source: Federal Reserve Statistical Release G18; Board of Governors of the Federal Reserve System.

decision to discontinue their dealer financing plans in favor of only making automobile loans to their own customers. An added advantage of this change is that, making automobile loans in this manner, strengthens the customer ties to the banks. However, the volume of dealer generated paper has been very difficult to replace, and this switch has contributed to the decline of total outstandings in the automobile loan category.

Another complication in the move from indirect dealer financing to direct financing is the establishment by many banks of leasing plans. These lease programs are directly generated by the bank or by dealers and sold to the bank's leasing section. These plans provide a higher profit level to the bank but require a level of expertise which many banks do not have.

Home repair and modernization loans have declined in relative importance in bank consumer credit portfolios. In the postwar era from 1946 through 1960, this category of loans accounted for 12.6 percent to 14.8 percent of bank consumer lending. That proportion has dropped in recent years to a range of 5 percent to 7 percent. Added competition from other financial institutions in the consumer credit field and natural ties that some of these institutions have to the building industry account for part of that decline. In the last ten years the category of loans labeled "other consumer goods" has doubled in relative importance from 14 percent to 15 percent of total consumer loans to 35.2 percent in 1975. The 1975 level represented a substantial increase from the 1974 figure. This category of loans included bank card charge credits and revolving credits, both of which have had substantial growth in the last few years and represent a major change in the broad consumer credit field.

THE CHANGING LEGAL ENVIRONMENT

The role of government in all phases of business life continues to expand. Over the years that role has changed from a posture of providing the basic rules within which business could operate to a more active role establishing specific requirements for many areas of business practice.

The consumer credit industry has been the target of special-purpose legislation that is affecting the industry to a substantial degree. National legislation in the form of the Truth in Lending Law, the Fair Credit Billing Act, and the Unfair Collections Practices Act must be a concern to every bank consumer credit department. In addition, many states have passed similar legislation. Most of these laws are interpreted and administered by a specific regulatory agency. The volume of laws, along with the ever-changing interpretations by the regulatory bodies, places a substantial burden upon those who grant consumer credit.

Because of the complexity of these laws, no attempt will be made here to cover the substance of this legislation. However, each bank consumer credit department must have the benefit of legal counsel to interpret these laws and regulations and ensure that the bank is complying with the requirements. While many people believe that total burden of regulation in the consumer credit field is much greater than necessary, banks have no choice but to provide the personnel and the systems of control necessary to comply with the rules, even though in doing so, consumers may find credit more difficult to secure and more expensive. The direct and indirect expenses of regulation are borne by the consumer as the higher costs work up through to the price of the service.

There is no evidence that the role of government in the consumer field will not continue to expand, both in the form of additional legislation, as well as through expanded interpretations by regulatory agencies. But a far more ominous aspect of the legal environment in the consumer credit field is in the area of judicial decisions. Recent decisions by courts have greatly altered collection procedures and reduced creditor remedies. Judicial activism promises greater inroads into this field. The immediate retroactive effect, and the almost certain ambiguity of interpretations among the various courts, cause these decisions to have major impact on the consumer banker.

CONSUMERISM

The consumer credit field has been affected directly by the modern consumerism movement. It is necessary to understand that movement to be able to interpret the rationales for the extensive legislation protecting consumers from those who extend credit to them.

The present consumerism movement, while it is unique in many ways, is not new. There have been previous periods of strong consumer movements in our history. Understandably, these were associated with periods of great social change and economic dislocations. The 1900s and the 1930s are notable examples. Each of these periods was a time of economic upheaval and involved journalistic exposés revealing danger to health and safety. In those previous movements, the basic issue of safety and sanitation that affected both rich and poor were raised.

The modern consumer movement is more sophisticated. An affluent and more highly educated society has raised the issues of reliability, quality, and the fullness of information in the uses of credit. These are key targets in the present consumerism movement. In that movement there is a perception that business is unresponsive to consumer needs. That perception originated in the rapid growth of the 1960s with unparalleled economic expansion. Rapid technological advances, mass marketing of services, and the development of new banking products and services have combined with changing values in the market and society to create an environment in which bankers are viewed as part of the faceless society. This phenomenon will be further complicated by a movement toward a cashless society.

Bankers must work diligently to preserve personal contact with customers. Bankers have responsibility to participate in consumer education at every level and at every opportunity. That responsibility includes providing information to legislators, both at the state and federal levels, as to the impact of existing legislation and the need for proposed new laws.

Banks must join with the public in providing the four basic rights to the consumer, as first defined by Betty Furness when she was Adviser on Consumer Affairs to the White House:

1. The right to be informed.
2. The right to choose between products.
3. The right to be protected.
4. The right to be heard.

In summary, the real reasons for consumer dissatisfaction are lack of personal service, indifferent attitudes, and inconvenience. Bankers view the consumer as an individual who must be dealt with in an honest and straightforward manner. Further, banks should not have the attitude that consumerism is entirely negative but should seek positive opportunities in the consumer movement.

COMPETITION

Competition is always keen in the consumer credit area. The volume of such credit held by various financial institutions has changed when there were basic changes in the types of credit consumers wanted. Examples are the realignment of automobile financing as private finance companies withdrew and the expanded role of credit unions in this field. Banks have introduced the charge cards to provide the consumer credit on a different basis from the past. The banks have enjoyed an obvious competitive advantage since banks had the structural format necessary to offer credit in this manner. Levels of competition have been enhanced through imagination and ingenuity of consumer loan officers within banks and in other financial institutions.

Currently there is much discussion of a restructuring of the nation's financial system. The recommendations by the Hunt Commission on the role of the various financial institutions have not been implemented, but many of those recommended changes will take place in the years immediately ahead.

The consumer credit segment of the banking industry is always affected by such broad changes as they have occurred on overall commercial banking. The industry's lack of product differentiation and high-cost product decisions and promotion have led to four main trends:

1. Pronounced expansion of services and markets.
2. The shift from the employment of surplus capital to one of securing adequate capital, now a primary concern of bank management.
3. Rapid movement to electronic banking.
4. The blurring of distinctions among various kinds of financial institutions.

The consumer credit department of the bank shares in all of those trends and is influenced by each of them. Added to these changes has been the expansion of bank holding companies into the ownership of consumer finance companies and consumer credit-related insurance activities. There have been established nationwide finance company structures selling an expanded range of financial services. These finance companies, though owned by bank holding companies, offer direct competition to the consumer credit departments of banks.

The many changes that have taken place in the competitive structure of the industry in the past promise that there will be continuous changes in the future. The forthcoming changes will be influenced by regulations, along with basic competitive forces. Banks should not expect any more stability in the consumer credit industry in the future than has existed in the recent past.

CONCLUSIONS

In all the studies of the future of banking, there are two principal areas of agreement. The first is that banks are going to be under increasing pressure to sustain acceptable levels of profit. The second conclusion is that the field of consumer credit services will continue to grow both in absolute terms and relative to the total bank services market. If these two conclusions prove to be true, there will be continued pressure on the role of the consumer banker.

No longer will the mystique of the "add-on" rate be sufficient to camouflage the consumer lending department's performance. This type of credit has the disadvantage in the bank today in being a fixed-rate loan. The rapid turnover, or high liquidity of consumer loans, when maturities were shorter was cited as an advantage in being able to "roll-out" low rate loans in favor of newer high rate loans. As maturities have expanded to 4-year financing on automobiles, 10 years on property improvement loans, and up to 15 years on mobile home contracts, this advantage has been lost. The banking industry should expect consumer finance programs of the future to use some form of variable rate structures which will help keep these loans competitive for funds within the broad financial planning by bank management. Such programs will involve a simple interest loan agreement on a monthly billing basis, coupled with improved credit scoring to improve the acceptability of new applications. More effective credit monitoring will be utilized to maintain current information on each borrower. Consumer credit will be extended under intense competitive conditions in which consumers will have many choices and sources for that credit. From the bank's point of view, more accurate cost information and more effective financial analysis within the bank will place increased emphasis on the relative profitability of the various types of consumer credit.

What about the consumer of the future? Consumers will have more leisure time and more recreation and will expect to finance these activities through consumer credit institutions. American consumers are well informed and they will be involved and skeptical. They will react more and more as a group through consumer activists, as these groups attempt to organize official representation through the government and through business groups, including banking.

Chapter 57

Primary Areas of Consumer Credit

*William B. McNeill**

INTRODUCTION

For several years consumer credit in commercial banking has experienced accelerated expansion and diversification. Banks placing increased emphasis on retail banking will have concentrated more attention on diversification of consumer services. The scope of consumer services provided varies depending on the bank's objectives, facilities, and availability of trained personnel.

Yields on well-managed consumer loan portfolios have created considerable support for expanding the scope and funding of the consumer credit program. Stability of revenue from consumer loans is of special interest during periods when there is a continuing decline in the prime rate. The consumer business, by virtue of the longer maturity, is not as sensitive to fluctuations in the prime rate as business and other short-term loans. Consequently, the consumer portfolio contributes to stabilizing revenue without reflecting the peaks and valleys experienced on short-term loan classifications.

An increasing number of commercial banks are providing a broad retail consumer credit service in promoting the one-stop banking concept. The major consumer services that are provided are discussed briefly in the following paragraphs.

Forms of consumer credit most generally available in commercial banks will include direct lending, open-end revolving credit, and, available in fewer banks, indirect dealer originated business. This chapter will deal briefly with all three types, their sources of origin and promotion-development.

---

* Senior Vice President, Branch Banking and Trust Company, Wilson, North Carolina.

DIRECT LENDING

There are many inherent benefits derived from a direct lending program since the program can be operated in conjunction with other assignments, or separated, depending on facilities and personnel. Special requirements may vary from a freestanding desk located on the loan officer's platform and occupied by a loan officer engaged in the dual role of commercial and consumer lending to a separate departmentalized operation staffed exclusively by consumer loan personnel.

The customer-bank relationship in direct lending is established when the applicant visits the bank for a direct loan service. For a prospective new customer, this involves an interview to determine purpose of the loan and amount of funds required. Subject to the purpose and amount falling within the criteria and perimeters established for the bank's direct lending program, a loan credit statement will be developed from the interview to provide personal data and a disclosure of income, assets, and liabilities.

The Credit Statement

The credit statement provides the same purpose to the consumer credit manager as the foundation of a structure to a builder. Without knowledge of loan purpose, amount of loan, how secured, antecedents of the applicant, profession, employment, income, assets, and liabilities, there would be limited opportunity for developing the information necessary to evaluate character, capacity, creditworthiness, or collateral benefits. Any attempt to service loan applications on face value subordinates the operation to a clerical capacity of filling orders.

The Credit Interview

Without a credit statement on a majority of the applicants, the investigator would be unable to pass along any factual information to the credit analyst. Applications frequently lead to information on undisclosed obligations. The applicant through convenience or short memory frequently fails to provide the interviewer with a complete listing of all fixed and open accounts or revolving credit obligations. The experienced interviewer will, in many instances, detect a hesitancy on the part of the applicant to be forthright in identifying creditors along with the amount of obligation and terms.

The Credit Investigation

It is extremely difficult to judge the paying habits or status of applicant's obligations on the basis of personal appearance. Most credit managers prefer to use factual information which includes an examination of the applicant's credit statement and information on antecedents, residence, employment, income by source and type, prospects of future income, amount of debt, amount of fixed monthly obligations, and performance on fixed obligations. Finally, creditworthiness must be evaluated after taking into account the amount of additional debt that will be added by approval of the loan application, along with the effect on the applicant's monthly debt commitment to disposable income.

The percentage of applicants that fall into the gray area that require a comprehensive credit investigation will vary by region and geographical location. The rural applicant may enjoy less expensive housing and the advantages of producing a portion of the family's food for consumption, and thus conserving resources and increasing the number of disposable dollars for commitment to debt repayment obligations.

There is a second group of applicants whose credit application will reflect sufficient evidence of responsibility to merit extension of credit with a minimum credit investigation. Normally the applicant's lenders will consist of two or more major creditors such as commercial banks, mortgage loan company, or sales finance companies, with the balance of debt represented by open charge accounts.

The third group, representing a lesser percentage of applicants, will reflect sufficient substance and amount of information already available in bank to require minimum investigation. Usually two telephone calls, one to the applicant's banking connection and one to a major supplier, will verify profession-employment information represented on the credit application.

Credit Evaluation

After completing the credit investigation, factual information developed will be passed along to the credit analyst for evaluation. Evaluation will include: character of the applicant, evidence of stability of residence, employment, prospects of future advancement and increased earnings, extent of obligations, performance on fixed and open account obligations, and the relation of applicant's obligations to uncommitted disposable income.

Amount of Credit

The experienced credit examiner can recognize and eliminate substandard applicants on the basis of the credit application. Where it is obvious that the applicant is not eligible for the loan service requested, the experienced credit examiner will evaluate the feasibility of approaching the applicant's needs on the basis of a larger loan for the purpose of retiring a sufficient number of existing secured obligations to establish a balance between fixed monthly obligations and uncommitted disposable income. This approach is to the mutual benefit of applicant and lender by providing a monthly payment that can be met out of income and, in many instances, freeing up collateral which can secure the lender's loan.

Frequency of Disclosure Statements and Credit Investigations

Lenders who do not use the safeguards of new or updated credit statements or investigations at predetermined intervals must be prepared to absorb defaults. To guard against customer's becoming overloaded with debt obligations, frequent disclosures, and credit updates are desirable. When dealing with consumers who use multisources of credit, most credit personnel consider it prudent to require an update of disclosure and credit investigation at intervals of 12 months on unsecured lending and 24 months on secured loans. This precaution protects both the customer and lender.

The ratio of default on loans structured from a current disclosure statement and credit investigation are low.

Loan Closing

Loan closing is the final step in the lending process for successful applicants. The staff member possessing the authority will approve the loan request and will most probably supervise, if not actively engage in, the loan closing. At this point, the applicant has been informed of the approval and should be introduced to other banking services. The convenience of depositing the proceeds will be explained, providing customer with the option of a monthly payment draft service to facilitate monthly payments on due date, and eliminate inconvenience and cost of monthly check, postage, or transportation to the office where payment will be made. The loan officer providing the loan closing service has the customer's personal and financial statement with all data developed. That officer is in the best position to anticipate retail banking services that the customer needs and are not currently being used.

Loan Classifications and Terms

While the scope of loan services are planned to accommodate the broader needs of creditworthy consumers, the majority of the total receivables will be made up of loans on automobiles, household furnishings, musical instruments, property improvement, recreational vehicles, and unsecured in the form of installment or open-end revolving credit. Over 40 percent of most direct loan portfolios consist of passenger car receivables. Some banks provide mobile home loans to finance the purchase of a new or used mobile home either to be occupied as a residence or as a vacation facility.

A broad, general guideline should be established governing the maturities eligible on each loan classification. A key factor affecting loan maturity that must be taken into account is depreciation on collateral pledged as security so as to prevent depreciation exceeding the loan amortization. A second factor is the bank's policy requirements on cash flow and liquidity.

Profitability

Direct lending is expensive for the lender. The components that must be taken into account in analyzing the cost of providing this credit includes: facilities to accommodate the person-to-person interview; credit investigation and loan closing; staff to support a volume direct loan operation; and the time element required for the disclosure, the credit investigation, and the update and file maintenance.

The added cost of regulatory compliance has become a major consideration in consumer lending. A continued trend of increased consumer regulatory requirements will result in a more restricted loan policy at higher costs to the consumer.

With continued inflation in operating costs, it is reasonable to assume that more emphasis will be directed to the profitability of the consumer loan program. The absence of accurate cost accounting systems result in poor pricing decisions and possibly accounts for much of the discount pricing associated with direct lending. The loan made to finance the purchase of a new automobile or other major ticket items continues at a fixed return for the term of the loan which may be 48 months or longer. The impact of this type lending may have an adverse effect on the consumer department's contribution to the profitability of the bank.

Benefits to Customer and Bank

Numerous benefits accrue to both the applicant and bank from a direct lending program. The applicant gains the protection of a loan service that is structured to his or her ability and is less likely to become the victim of an overextension of credit. A commercial bank with qualified loan personnel to provide consumer budgetary and counseling services will have the opportunity to establish a continuing relationship with customers served and developing a "booster's club" of satisfied customers. The experienced credit person who takes the time to analyze applicant's disposable income in relation to obligations will provide a much needed service to an increasing number of families who have not learned money management. Failure to examine and take into account debts versus disposable income creates a pyramiding debt future for many borrowing families. New loans are contracted to make payments on existing debt obligations with the process continuing until the family either receives help through some form of counseling-debt consolidation service, or they become candidates for a relocation or bankruptcy to escape from the pressures of creditors. The final loan may have been made for the purpose of defraying the cost of the move or petitioning for bankruptcy. The interviewer who fails to establish the purpose of the loan may pass up the opportunity of providing the real service needed to the applicant-customer and protect lender's investment.

Loan personnel engaged in direct lending receive satisfaction from the expressions of appreciation and tangible results observed from helping people to help themselves. It is satisfying to assist any deserving applicant with a loan service which makes possible ownership of major ticket items ranging from appliances or furnishings for the apartment-home to transportation for the family, leisure time recreational equipment, or for refurbishing or expanding an old residence purchased or new residence made larger to accommodate the family needs. With households being formed at a high rate the need for consumer credit is expected to continue increasing during the years ahead, creating the market and need for a continued expansion of the retail consumer lending program.

Marketing Direct Consumer Loan Services

The marketing effort for consumer loan services will most generally be coordinated through the bank's marketing department with featured programs or promotionals highlighting various services throughout the year. Varying approaches are used to communicate with present and former customers. Added exposure to both active and former customers can be achieved through the use of inserts and direct mail. With the cost of making a new loan continuing to rise, it becomes more important to utilize fully in-bank promotions to market consumer loan service to customers using other banking services. This marketing approach has been presented in various forms with possibly the most popular being the "club concept" of packaging services with a preferred consumer loan rate offered to club members.

Banks which have introduced simple interest loans are reported to be receiving excellent reception from present active customers as well as favorable publicity for prospective new customers who actively evaluate sources and cost of consumer credit. The concept of paying for funds used for the exact length of time used holds very strong appeal for the creditworthy individual. The privilege of early payment without penalty, or of lump payments to principal resulting into shortening the term of the loan obligation, provides additional attraction for the knowledgeable individual seeking consumer credit. Consumer education will continue creating an awareness of the advantages gained from more precise credit arrangements. The aggressive marketing department will capitalize on this interest and promote these advantages.

Direct Lending to Small Business

Certain precautions are involved in lending to self-employed consumers or small, individually owned businesses of the "country store" variety. By and large, this type of borrower does not have adequate financial or operating information for the bank to make a satisfactory loan evaluation. Loan applications are generally for operating capital or assistance to finance the purchase of equipment, which may or may not be so specialized as to have a limited market for disposal. When loans of this type are to be placed in the consumer department for servicing, particular care should be directed to the designation of loan personnel with training in qualifying and structuring small business loans. Most consumer personnel at the loan unit level will not be equipped by training or experience to engage in this type lending.

Loan applications received from individuals where the purpose is for financing used heavy duty tractor-trailers, bulldozers, front-end loaders, and all such other specialized equipment should be subject to a very rigid test to establish that the credit decision can be based on the financial responsibility and creditworthiness of the applicant. The safest formula to be utilized for this type of lending is to affix a collateral value not to exceed 25 percent of the purchase price in the event the customer's business venture is unsuccessful and it becomes necessary for him or her to dispose of the equipment.

Source of Appraisals

Methods for developing appraisals will depend, in large measure, on the type of collateral involved. This can cover a very broad spectrum, depending on the scope of the bank's eligible loan classifications. The emphasis placed on inspections and appraisals will be influenced by type of collateral financed or pledged to secure the loan obligation.

Where equipment is new, as in the case of titled vehicles, the bank can devise its own appraisals for purposes of determining the maximum advance. In order to relate sticker price to dealer-merchant's factory cost, the bank may subscribe to an invoice guide service which provides the basic dealer cost of the vehicle and optional equipment. Any attempt to utilize the guide in pricing out dealer's cost on each individual vehicle involves a time-consuming operation. It is desirable to use an alternate approach of establishing the percentage of markup contained in the manufacturer's advertised sticker price. The percentage of markup factor can be applied to the basic cost and optional equipment. When transportation is added to base cost with accessories, the result will be the dealer's laid down cost. This approach enables the lender to establish advances up to a maximum allowable percentage of the advertised delivered price on each manufactured product by model and size. Full-size vehicles carry a different markup from the intermediates, compacts, or subcompacts. Accessories carry a different percentage profit from the basic vehicle and makes it necessary to separate the basic vehicle cost from the equipment options and accessories, or engage in averaging with an allowance for the percentage of cost represented by options and accessories to the total. While this system will not produce 100 percent accurate cost data, it will be close and may be the most desirable approach in the absence of access to the dealer's factory invoice.

On other types of new equipment financed which do not have the wide range of options, the lender can establish the percentage of dealer-merchant profit markup and operate on the basis of advancing up to x percentage of the customer's purchase price. This will provide knowledge of the advance to the relation of dealer-merchant's factory cost.

The more difficult appraisals involve used equipment owned by the applicant and being offered as security to collateralize the loan. There is no substitute for personal inspection and examination of the equipment as a supplement to the appraiser's knowledge of the value. Personal inspection can establish general appearance, opinion of maintenance received, and general condition. When appraisals are needed on unfamiliar equipment or real estate, the safest policy is to engage the services of an appraiser who is qualified to furnish the bank with an objective appraisal of the quick market value at the time of appraisal, and also an opinion as to the demand in the case of specialized equipment.

General Precautions in Direct Lending

Credit risks can be reduced by taking the necessary precautions to establish standards and guidelines for each loan classification. Failure to provide loan personnel with policies covering advances and maturities creates a void for the inexperienced staff member in the direct lending program. Each staff member should not be allowed to use his or her own personal evaluation.

Safeguards should include the preparation of personnel for the direct lending assignment through an educational and training program. This type investment will make a major contribution toward avoiding unnecessary losses and creating an excessive number of problem accounts.

Most credit people agree that a loan properly closed is half collected. Steps which should precede the loan closing are:

1. A completed disclosure statement to identify applicant's employment, profession, income, assets, and liabilities.
2. An investigation to determine character, capacity, creditworthiness, and stability of the applicant.
3. Examination of disposable income in relationship to debt obligations, including cost of living allowances so as to determine the applicant's ability to perform on additional debt obligation.
4. With a favorable reading, the loan closing follows with the contractual obligation reviewed with the applicant. A firm loan closing provides the applicant-customer with the amount, time, place, and manner in which each payment is to be received.

Lien Perfection

Liens on tangible collateral are perfected by one of the following means:

1. Vehicle liens are perfected by a filing with the Motor Vehicle Department in the state in which the vehicle is registered. The lender's lien will be entered on the certificate of title issued.
2. Liens on nontitled property are perfected by a Uniform Commercial Code filing in the county of residence and, in the case of a multilocated business, dual filing with the secretary of state's office may be required.
3. Nonfiling insurance may be substituted to insure lender's investment in loans secured by personal property where the balances do not exceed the dollar limit provided by the policy.
4. Aircraft liens filing is provided by Federal Aviation Authority with a centralized service provided in Oklahoma City.
5. Security interest in real property is perfected by deed of trust recorded in the county in which the property is located.

Since the period of time required for gaining a preferred lien varies by class of business, each lender is governed by the laws of the state of operation.

UNSECURED OPEN-END REVOLVING CREDIT

Unsecured, open-end revolving credit is one of the fast-growing forms of consumer credit. With the growth in automation, demand deposit account overdraft of credit forms are expected to continue gaining in popularity, increasing the amount of unsecured revolving credit. With the overdraft line of credit, only one visit to the bank is necessary to establish credit which can be used as needed wherever a personal check is honored. The initial concept of overdraft credit was that it would be used to guard against overdrafts, or for emergencies and shortages until the next pay period. However, the convenience of open-end revolving credit is a contributing factor in expanding the use of this form of credit to include purchases of $1,000 or greater. This form of credit is generally available in increments up to a maximum of $5,000. With proper structuring of the credit at the time of inception, this can be a trouble-free form of credit to service. Consequently, it can become the most profitable.

INDIRECT DEALER ORIGINATED FINANCING

The indirect dealer originated business involves the time payment sale generated by a selling dealer-merchant with the receivable discounted to the bank. At time of purchase, the consumer chooses the dealer-merchant's time payment plan from choice or necessity. In many instances, identity of the financial institution, or holder of the security instrument, will not be made known to the consumer until after the sale has been concluded and the purchase money security agreement prepared.

Classes of Dealer Originated Business

Numerous articles of merchandise are sold on time payment terms and discounted with a lender. The following types of business make up most of the total volume.

Motor dealer business is originated by dealers selling passenger cars or commercial vehicles. Business potential varies from metropolitan high-volume operators marketing 200 to 500 new vehicles monthly to the small-town dealer whose annual new car sales may be less than 100.

The plan of purchase varies between region and lender. The metropolitan dealer will normally have three or more active finance outlets, including at least one commercial bank, while the small operator's account may be serviced by one financial institution.

Farm machinery dealers' time payment sales are generally shared with a captive company, operated as a finance subsidiary of the dealer's manufacturer, and with credit production associations or commercial banks. Many of the captive companies operate on a plan with a limited liability to the selling dealer, while credit production associations discount purchases at a preferred money cost to the merchant. The variances in plan and pricing have created a very competitive condition for farm equipment time payment sales business.

Mobile home merchants have supplied commercial banks with a substantial dollar volume of "large ticket" account balances in recent years. The primary attraction of this class of business has been the favorable yields on large account balances. The glamour which had attracted this business on an increasing scale during the roaring 60s began to disappear by 1973. Bank management began a reevaluation of the negative factors, including maturities up to 180 months, the adverse effect on cash flow, limited collateral benefits, and high repossession ratios. By 1976, many commercial banks had substantially curtailed volume and commitments. Others have discontinued mobile home financing as a class of business. The future outlook is one of caution.

Recreational vehicles and equipment merchants provide an additional source for "large ticket" balance accounts with maturities of 60 months or longer. Sales were on a rising scale until interrupted by the energy crisis in 1973 and 1974. Three years later, sales again gained momentum. Banks equipped to service this class of business can build sizable receivables at an accelerated rate.

There are numerous additional business classifications serviced by commercial banks including appliances, home furnishings, TVs, musical instruments, commercial refrigeration, fixtures, small equipment, and property improvement. These groupings are not the most attractive due to the small, average account balance financed, and their relationship to the total aggregate time payment sales business. Large ticket sales capture the attention of lenders who want to employ additional funds with minimum increases in operating costs.

Bank Plans of Retail Financing

Plans vary by locality and by lender within a given region. Many banks operate very successfully on a repurchase plan for the dealer-merchant. Under this plan of operation, the time payment receivable is discounted with dealer assuming contingent liability for repurchase of the receivable in the event of a default that requires foreclosure on collateral. The lender normally accepts responsibility for servicing the account to include effecting repossession of merchandise on a defaulted instrument and redelivering to the selling dealer-merchant.

When redelivery has been made, the merchant becomes liable for the repurchase of the instrument for the net cancellation balance outstanding. Expenses incurred in servicing the account and effecting repossession and/or redelivery becomes an expense to be defrayed by the lender. Many dealers operate on a repurchase plan by preference to gain the more favorable money costs on the sale of the receivable.

Optional repurchase or limited recourse is a popular plan with dealer-merchants who are concerned with limiting their contingent liability on business discounted. Under this plan of operation, the dealer is normally extended the option of repurchasing the account for the estimated wholesale market value of the merchandise with any deficiency charged to the dealer reserve account (see below). Under this plan of operation, the dealer will receive up to 50 percent of the net reserves generated monthly.

No Liability

No liability discounts carry repurchase requirements beyond the warranties or representations made on the assignment of the purchase money security agreement as to the validity of the sale, and representations made to include good title and perfecting lien in the name of the lender. Dollar amount of reserves realized from the discount become payable with the sale or at the close of business at the end of the month in which business is sold.

Dealer Reserve Accounts

Dealer reserves are created on time payment sales where the retail finance charge is greater than the cost of funds paid to the lender on the discount. The differential is credited to a dealer reserve account. Another method of establishing a reserve is through the discount arrangement where the amount of the cash advanced to the dealer is less than 100 percent of the unpaid balance financed, and the difference is placed in a separate account identified as a "holdback" reserve account. Both types of reserves usually become payable as earned depending on the class of business, maturity, and the bank's plan of operation.

Dealer Services Provided by Bank Plan

A bank may limit its services to discounting acceptable time payment receivables acquired from the selling dealer-merchant. Many banks consider this to be the most desirable relationship to establish with their dealer-merchants in the trading area served. This relationship extends the bank's retail services into dealer-merchant organizations for the convenience of present, as well as prospective new customers, desiring the services of local bank financing.

Wholesale Floor Planning

Wholesale floor planning services provided by many banks expand the scope of commitment extended to the dealer-merchant. Floor planning generally involves a credit commitment to the manufacturer or distributor guaranteeing payment of merchandise shipped for the account of the dealer-merchant. The commitment to provide a wholesale flooring service creates added responsibilities to develop controls for servicing this specialized class of business.

Floor plan financing is a loss leader in terms of yield. The rate charged is generally within one point of the bank's prime interest rate, therefore profitability is dependent on the amount, spread, and quality of the retail business acquired. Profitability is directly affected by the proportion of wholesale floor plan dollars provided to retail financing by the bank.

The bank contemplating the extension of its services to include wholesale floor planning should be prepared to make a continuing commitment. Entry in the wholesale market and then withdrawal creates a loss of confidence from the interruption which can be costly in terms of business loss. Reentry opportunities at a later date would be reduced.

Other Loan Services

Capital loan service may be provided by banks which offer the total dealer service program. Term loans are made to provide operating capital for expansion or to purchase the interest of a partner or a stockholder. Capital loans are most generally secured by the assets of the business and amortized in monthly payments to be paid out of earnings over periods up to 60 months.

Mortgage loan service is often provided by commercial banks for the purposes of expanding an existing plant facility or financing the cost of a new facility. Loan is secured by the real property and/or other assets with the repayment schedule amortized monthly over a term up to 120 months.

Pricing of a capital loan or mortgage service may be on a fixed term rate, however, more often the rate will fluctuate and be prime plus x number of points, estimated in most instances to be up to two points above the dealer's wholesale floor plan rate.

Pricing Indirect Dealer Services

Pricing bank's services to maintain a profitable position may prove to be difficult, particularly to the lender extending a combination of wholesale floor plan and a capital loan service, and attempting to maintain a competitive pricing posture on retail business acquired. Dealer business is highly competitive and unless bank is in a position to control operating costs, competition may force rate concessions to the point of diminishing returns. Unsatisfactory yields was a major factor which prompted the independent sales finance companies to exit from the automobile business during the 60s. The economics of the decision dictated that their funds could be more profitably employed in other business classifications.

Precautions in Indirect Dealer Financing

Pitfalls which a lender must be aware of when operating in a dealer originated business environment are:

1. Undertaking to engage in indirect dealer originated business without a competent staff. This is not a numbers business; therefore the enthusiasm of eager, unprepared staff members can create major problems.
2. Attempting to adapt to a dealer's plan in order to meet a competitive proposal can be disastrous. The bank staff responsible for the acquisition, processing, and servicing of the dealer business should not be expected to change from a repurchase to a no liability plan of operation without adequate preparation. While a degree of flexibility is desirable to cope with day-to-day operation, there should be no implied commitment to change operating plans to meet new competition.
3. Extending a flooring accommodation to the dealer, along with a term loan service without close controls to assist the dealer in fulfilling the commitment contained in the loan agreement can prove troublesome. The absence of an effective control program will most likely create an imbalance of receivables, resulting in an erosion of yield from the account. Lenders have the responsibility of maintaining records to keep the dealer informed of the account performance.

Benefits to Bank

Benefits anticipated from the extension of a full dealer service should be predetermined and consistent with the bank's objectives. The extension of a full dealer service program to protect the bank's commercial relationship with the dealer account may be sufficient reason for a bank in a given locality for the decision to make the commitment to provide a dealer program. In other circumstances, the bank's incentive may be to accelerate the expansion of its customer base for marketing other banking services. The dealer whose clientele are currently using multibanking services and residing within the area serviced by the bank offers potential collateral benefits and will increase the value of the dealer's account. The bank that wants to increase the number of dollars employed in retail receivables over a short period of time may consider this route to its objective. Most banks will consider the profit potential in the dealer program and that consideration will rarely be subordinated to a secondary objective. The business can be conducted on a profitable basis by refusing to compromise the plan of operation and pricing of services extended.

Marketing the Indirect Dealer Plan

1. Plan to invest the time required for the research and fact finding to identify the game plan. It helps to know something about plans that competitors are currently offering to the dealer-merchants in the area to be solicited.
2. After developing information on the most popular plan in use, the newcomer should take inventory of the services it has to offer and rate of return needed to create a profit.
3. If all factors are found to be favorable, the program will probably get the signal to move ahead. The bank must be in a position to mount the business development effort required to penetrate the marketplace and gain an entree into dealer organizations. After securing a commitment from the management of the dealer business and completing operating agreements, the undertaking has just begun. It is then necessary to train the dealer's sales and department managers in the bank's plan and create a preference for the new bank plan. The activation of the new account may prove to be more difficult than acquiring the signed agreement which only services as a license for installation of the plan and the opportunity for the cultivation process to gain allies within the sales organization. Whenever the new bank is forced to compete head on with the same plan and type operation, the process of gaining support to develop any worthwhile volume is normally slow.

Banks that have introduced simple interest financing on dealer originated business have provided the dealer sales organization with an effective tool in making a new and different approach in attracting the creditworthy purchaser who can command credit from a bank or credit union to finance the purchase. Customer preference for simple interest financing, added to the advantages accruing to the selling dealer, creates the most attractive development introduced by the finance industry to date.

The bank offering simple interest financing may elect to solicit the dealer on the basis of gaining a share of the retail business. In this way the simple interest plan will complement the dealer's add-on interest plan of financing from the factory finance connection. The simple interest plan will most generally attract the creditworthy customer with a strong preference to pay finance charges on the declining account balance only. Many of the simple interest plans provide credit insurance coverage with the monthly premium cost predicated on the declining unpaid balance.

Advantages accruing to the selling dealer from such a plan are numerous, including increased time payment penetration through flexibility in tailoring the obligation to the customer's individual requirements. Participation from finance charges and credit insurance commissions on a monthly earned basis is beneficial to dealer and eliminates accrued unearned taxable reserves associated with add-on interest plan. Cancellations involving prepayment of accounts and substitution of vehicles are made easy with the transaction paid out and removed from file without penalty to dealer or customer. The resistance to early prepayments is eliminated with the customer's cost predicated on a daily cost factor on the amount financed for length of time outstanding. More important to the dealer is providing a plan of financing which all business and professional buyers will endorse. All of these features accrue to the dealer's benefit when he makes a comparison of the simple interest versus add-on plan of financing.

Dealer Service Company Plan

The commercial bank that is not staffed to provide a dealer service may elect to utilize the services of an outside professional organization to provide for the acquisition of dealer originated receivables on classes of business such as automobiles, farm machinery, and mobile homes. The dealer service company's plan may provide both retail and wholesale flooring services with the lender furnishing the capital.

Mechanics of the dealer service company plan basically provides the lender with the opportunity of protecting its commercial relationship with local dealers on given business classifications, thereby eliminating the possible loss of business to a competitor. The bank provides the capital and makes the credit decision on business accepted. The dealer service company furnishes the dealer acquisition know-how, services the wholesale business, and makes the outside contacts required to service retail business. The bank is protected against loss by credit indemnity insurance purchased by the dealer service company and paid for out of service fee received from the bank.

Any evaluation as to profitability of the dealer service company plan must take into account the collateral benefits realized from protecting the uninterrupted business relationship with business customers. An additional "plus" is the value of developing a base of customers eligible for other banking services. All of these advantages may very well provide adequate compensation for the low yield returned on the funds employed.

Future Trends in Dealer Financing

Beginning in 1974, the trend of commercial banks was to curtail their commitment to dealer originated financing. Many of the large banks have curtailed, if not suspended, their business in dealer wholesale floor planning and curtailed substantially the solicitation of dealer originated business. Withdrawal from the dealer program has been caused, in part, by the erosion of yield and failure to maintain acceptable control over losses. Even with the curtailed emphasis placed on the dealer auto originated business, the banking's share of the time payment receivables increased by approximately $1 billion during the 36-month period ending November 30, 1976 (as reported by the Federal Reserve Board). When one takes into account that a substantial portion of the indirect dealer originated business, formerly serviced by commercial banks, moved to the captive finance companies, the continued increase in auto receivables generated by commercial banks is significant. The continued trend by banks of curtailing dealer originated business points in the direction of increased emphasis on the value of establishing direct customer relationship with the bank.

SUMMARY

In recent years most commercial banks have expanded the scope of consumer credit services offered. More banks are providing a larger variety of loan services, both secured and unsecured, than previously offered. The expansion of consumer services has reflected the awareness by commercial banking to provide full customer service as part of the convenience of one-stop banking and eliminate the necessity for split banking. Profit derived from consumer loan activities becomes increasingly significant in providing a satisfactory yield on a bank's portfolio.

Many commercial banks have elected to curtail, or completely withdraw, from the indirect dealer originated business. Reasons for curtailment are varied; however, in many instances, the contributing factors include attempting to change operating plans without adequate preparation, with resulting loss of control. In other instances, the erosion of revenue in cases where the bank elected to buy its way into the dealer account which permitted the erosion of rates in meeting competition removed the margin of operating profit necessary to the business. Other banks have continued to expand their dealer programs by operating under a controlled concept with rates structured to provide an adequate profit on bank investment.

SECTION IX

INTERNATIONAL BANKING

Chapter 58

International Relationships
of U.S. Banks

Constant M. Van Vlierden*

William Hurst†

Multinational banks have attracted a great deal of publicity as a result of the international economic problems of recent years. The problems related to the international monetary system established at Bretton Woods in 1944, the rise in oil prices in 1973, and the global industrial recession of 1974–75 all drew attention to the vital role which banks play in facilitating both investment and other financial transfers as well as flows of real goods and services among nations. Since World War II, U.S. commercial banks have assumed a major role in providing these international financial services.

This chapter attempts to explain why U.S. banks rose to such a prominent position in the postwar world economy. The first section outlines a brief history of the international expansion of U.S. banks, their place in the structure of the international monetary system, and the geographical and organizational aspects of this expansion. The second section is directed more specifically to the conditions which promoted the rapid international growth of U.S. banks in the postwar period. The final section discusses some of the results of this growth in terms of the development of new sets of relationships among banks, governments, and international organizations.

---
* Executive Vice President, Bank of America, San Francisco, California.
† Vice President, Bank of America, San Francisco, California.

THE HISTORICAL DEVELOPMENT OF INTERNATIONAL BANKING
IN THE UNITED STATES

Background

Prior to World War I little international banking was done in the United States. Foreign trade financing was handled by special foreign trade firms which performed letter-of-credit functions. It was not until 1917 that New York banks began, in any significant way, to develop foreign trade departments, largely in response to the increased demand for U.S. goods arising out of the material shortages caused by the war. The growth period of 1917 to 1920 was not sustained during the inter-war (between World War I and World War II) period. The U.S. banks were not ready to assume a large international role in a world of great political and economic uncertainty.

All of this changed as a result of the Bretton Woods agreement of 1944, which established a system based on a gold exchange standard. Britain and the United States disagreed over the structure of the new system. Britain wanted a system biased toward liquidity creation; the United States wanted the emphasis to be on domestic adjustment. In other words, the British wanted the emphasis placed on the creation of sufficient liquidity to support a growth in world trade and invest-ment, but which would also be sufficient in times of uncertainty. The United States wanted the emphasis placed on adjustment of balance of payments disequilibrium (deficits or surpluses) through domestic monetary and fiscal policy. They compromised, and the new system provided neither enough liquidity to accommodate deficit-troubled nations, nor any agreed norms to guide the alternative of domestic adjustment.

This situation made it even more important for the United States to provide long-term capital to much of the rest of the world in the postwar years. This is the natural function of the reserve center in a gold exchange standard: the center country performs international financial intermediation. During the 1950s, this role was of great impor-tance, since capital inflows and the provision of trade financing services were vital to the economic recovery in Europe and elsewhere.

In the early post-World War II period, U.S. banks largely restricted themselves to trade financing. As the world economy began to revive, they not only directly financed the expansion of world trade, but pro-vided credit to U.S. corporations for overseas operations, to foreign corporations, and to foreign governments. The U.S. banks began to realize the global benefits of operating as dollar-based banks, taking advantage of the role of the dollar as a reserve and settlement currency.

U.S. banks now hold a key position in international banking. Among the top 15 banks in the world (ranked by total assets), the 3 largest are American. The other 12 consist of 6 from Japan, 3 from France, 2 from Great Britain, and 1 from West Germany. U.S. banks have more than 700 foreign branches and more than 1,600 foreign subsidiaries and affiliates. At the end of July 1976, these branches had claims on foreigners (less claims on other branches of the parent bank) totalling $158.3 billion. When foreign branch claims on foreigners booked in the domestic offices of U.S. banks are added, the total is $238.8 billion. This represents 25.0 percent of the total assets of U.S. commercial banks.

The Geographical Spread of U.S. Banks

At the beginning of 1975, 125 member banks of the Federal Reserve System had 732 overseas branches. Postwar growth centered in Western Europe, particularly London, and to a lesser extent, Latin America and Asia, particularly Japan. The largest number of branches are now in Latin America (363), followed by Europe (167), the Caribbean (166), Asia (138), and Africa (5). These figures are not, however, an accurate indication of the sources and uses of funds at overseas branches since the customers are not necessarily residents of the country in which the branch with which they do business is located. Host country laws may prohibit foreign branches, even though overseas branch assets or liabilities may originate in that country. Exhibit 58–1 gives a better indication of actual sources and uses of funds.

Even though Latin America has the largest number of branches, Europe is the largest source of business for overseas branches. Latin America, a capital deficit area, remains the largest net user of funds

Exhibit 58–1
Geographical Distribution of Assets and Liabilities of Major Foreign Branches* of U.S. Banks, December 31, 1976
(in $ billions)

Country of Customer	Assets	Liabilities
Europe	86.4	73.8
Latin America and Caribbean	38.4	24.9
Asia and the Middle East	27.9	29.7
Africa	5.9	2.5
Canada	2.4	4.4

* Includes branches with U.S. dollar liabilities of $10 million or more in various countries in Europe, and in the Bahamas and Cayman Islands; $30 million or more in Panama, Japan, Hong Kong, and Singapore; and $100 million or more in other countries.

General note: Figures have been adjusted to exclude accounts between branches of the same parent bank.

Source: Federal Reserve Statistical Releases.

($13.5 billion). Asia, including the Middle East, and Canada are net suppliers of funds to overseas branches of U.S. banks. In relative terms, the largest net user of funds is Africa, whose liabilities to U.S. overseas branches are more than twice its claims.

London is the major overseas center for U.S. banks. It has long been a global center not only for metals and other commodity trading, but also for commercial banking and many other financial activities, such as merchant banking, insurance, and foreign exchange. In addition, London is the primary center for the financial infrastructure associated with the Eurodollar market. At the end of February 1977, 43.7 percent of the gross assets of European branches of U.S. banks were in branches located in the United Kingdom. These U.K. branches held assets worth $78.3 billion, 77.0 percent of which were payable in U.S. dollars. Even though the continued decline in the value of Sterling has adversely affected the capitalization of banks in the United Kingdom, London remains the focal point of international banking, but there have been important shifts of offshore money operations to the Caribbean and Panama.

The next most important growth area after the United Kingdom has been continental Europe where, subject to national regulations on foreign banking, U.S. banks have been able to engage in a wide variety of wholesale and retail commercial banking activities, as well as related financial functions. Most of this growth came during the 1960s, since prior to 1958 the major Western European currencies were not convertible freely into other currencies, thus restricting any banking activities that required active use of foreign exchange markets. The establishment of the European Economic Community (EEC) provided a powerful incentive for U.S. banks to move into this larger market to serve the needs of both indigenous business and U.S. corporations investing in Europe.

Japan closely followed Europe as a growth area; the first branches were established in the early days of the occupation. Following the recovery phase, Japan consistently maintained the highest economic growth rate of any of the industrialized countries. The postwar recovery of Japan offered opportunities for trade financing in U.S. dollars in which most trade was denominated (over 80 percent of Japan's trade is still invoiced in U.S. dollars).

The next major growth area for U.S. international banks was in the developing areas of the world. These areas offered higher gains—and higher risks—to U.S. banks, while at the same time providing much needed economic benefits to the host countries themselves. The strengthening of a banking structure in a country promotes a more efficient allocation of resources through financial intermediation, provides incentives for capital holders to save and invest, and promotes capital inflows necessary for growth. Latin America has been the traditional area of expansion for U.S. banks in less developed countries. Here, U.S. banks perform some retail banking functions in addition to trade financing and providing services for corporations and governments. Asia has also provided an important source of business for U.S. banks, particularly in Japan as previously mentioned. The rise of new money centers in Singapore and Hong Kong facilitated the extension of the offshore dollar market to Asia. Expansion in Africa has been more limited. In Africa, economic, political, and social conditions often do not favor the establishment of branches or wholly owned subsidiaries of U.S. banks. Banking services in this area of the world have been largely provided by the French and British banks established there during the colonial period. Their position has steadily eroded, however, in the face of anticolonialism and nationalism, as it has elsewhere. In Africa, the development was toward consortia banks in which the United States, and banks of other nationalities, joined as shareholders to become international banks without a particular national label.

The period of rapid branch expansion is probably over. The largest U.S. banks are already in most of the geographical and functional areas where they wish to be involved, and newcomers to the international scene will have great difficulty in obtaining licenses to operate in these markets unless they can offer some unique special service. The major growth area of the 1960s, Western Europe, is a highly competitive market with indigenous banks actively expanding their foreign operations. The future growth areas will be in the less developed countries where a higher risk factor will encourage caution on the part of U.S. banks.[1] Up to 1976, loan loss ratios were smaller in international than in domestic U.S. lending.[2]

Organizational and Functional Expansion

Diversification into financial activities other than commercial banking has encouraged banks to develop new organizational forms for asset and liability management. A large international bank will have a complicated international structure, which, when simplified, resembles that illustrated in Exhibit 58–2.

There are five major organizational aspects to international banking: the correspondent bank relationships, the foreign department within

---

[1] On the current growth prospects for U.S. international banking, see Thomas H. Hanley, *United States Multinational Banking: Current and Prospective Strategies* (n.p.: Salomon Brothers, June 1976), pp. 32–36.

[2] See F. B. Ruckdeschel, "Risk in Foreign and Domestic Lending Activities of U.S. Banks," *Columbia Journal of World Business*, Winter 1975, pp. 50–57.

EXHIBIT 58–2
U.S. Bank Holding Company Organization

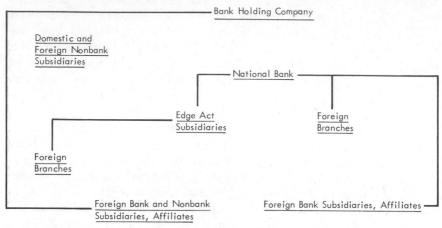

the domestic bank, the overseas representative offices and branches,
the Edge Act subsidiaries and foreign subsidiaries or affiliates.

The foreign department is the oldest of these organizational innovations. Beginning with traditional trade financing functions, such as providing letters of credit, the foreign department became more active
in both foreign deposit and lending operations. Banks which do not
have a large enough volume of business to justify the existence of a
foreign department may rely on larger U.S. correspondent banks to
handle their foreign business. Banks with foreign departments, but
without an international division with overseas branches must rely
on foreign correspondent banks to carry on their overseas business.

The next level of evolution involves the establishment of foreign
branches. The major advantage of a branch is that it allows the bank
to tap a wider market by being physically located within that market,
while at the same time providing better services directly to its customers rather than relying on another bank. There are also multinational
advantages to a network of overseas branches whereby the establishment of a branch not only results in the development of business for
that branch, but all other branches in different countries as the number
of countries in which customers can be accommodated expands. The
period of most rapid growth in foreign branches was during the 1960s.
In 1950 only seven Federal Reserve member banks had a total of 95
foreign branches; by 1960 there were still only eight banks with 124
branches. In 1972 the number of banks had risen to 107 and branches
to 627. The major reason for this growth was the development of
the Eurocurrency markets and the controls on foreign lending under

the Voluntary Foreign Credit Restraint program, and other controls on foreign investment, begun in 1965 and ending in January 1974.

Perhaps the most interesting innovation in the international relationships of U.S. banks has been the so-called Edge Act subsidiaries. They achieved some popularity during the same period that foreign branch networks expanded rapidly, the number rising from 10 in 1960 to 87 in 1972. The term originated in 1919 with the passage of the Edge Act, supplementing the Federal Reserve Act to provide for federal chartering of international banking corporations. These subsidiaries can offer a full range of international banking services, but cannot engage in domestic banking. This provision, however, was not actively used to establish a full-scale international banking operation until Bank of America established its first Edge Act bank in New York in 1950. The usefulness of the act, from the banker's perspective, is that it allows a bank to establish an international banking operation in another state. For example, many of these corporations were established by banks located outside New York in order to obtain access to the international banking market in that city. Edge Act corporations can also be used as vehicles for establishing wholly or partially owned foreign banking operations. As a result of amendments of the Banking Holding Company Act, holding companies can also be used for this purpose. This enables a commercial bank to engage in a wider range of financial activities than is permitted in the United States. In a few instances, smaller banks have collaborated to establish a jointly owned Edge Act corporation. The widespread use of these corporations in recent years has stimulated the growth of regional international banking centers in the United States, notably in Chicago, Miami, Houston, San Francisco, and Los Angeles.

A number of U.S. banks have also followed a strategy of expanding the types of financial services offered overseas by investing directly in financial corporations in foreign countries engaged in merchant banking, leasing, factoring, and investment advisory services as well as consumer and commercial finance companies. A recent development in this area has been the consortia banks which are formed by a group of U.S. and foreign banks primarily for the purpose of making large-, medium- and long-term loans, and to engage in offshore underwriting of securities. Consortia banks enable the shareholders to participate in the international capital markets by sharing the fixed costs usually associated with such an operation and to provide a wider access to such markets than would be possible for a single bank. In addition, these links to other foreign shareholder banks provide greater placing powers for private placements, syndications, and underwriting.

The geographical and functional expansion described above has occurred at a rapid rate and it has been difficult for certain banks to provide adequate control procedures and to maintain necessary liquidity through stable sources of funding. These problems have also been intensified by rapid changes in the operating environment in many parts of the world. In this connection, the central problem has been the development of sufficient skilled personnel to perform effectively in overseas line and staff positions. Taxation and general economic considerations have made it costly to send U.S. employees to overseas locations, with the result that most banks develop host country citizens where suitably qualified individuals are available. Such hiring practices have the added advantage of reducing the bank's vulnerability in certain countries with strong nationalistic tendencies. These problems have been somewhat less difficult for the large banks operating on a multinational scale with larger staffs which can be shifted from country to country and from positions of lesser to greater responsibility.

A related problem has been that of devising an appropriate organizational pattern for controlling a global financial institution. The dominant strategy to date appears to be the traditional one of centralized control of overseas operations from the U.S. head office and many of the large banks tend to follow this pattern. There has also been a trend, however toward decentralization with banks shifting the bulk of their administrative and credit responsibility from their U.S. headquarters to regional centers overseas.

A final major problem relates to organizing for research and policy making in a global environment. International banking involves a higher degree of uncertainty simply because of the number of different markets in which operations are carried out. For this reason, banks have preferred to extend short-term, trade-related credit rather than medium-term credit. They have also been reluctant to extend credit where the source of foreign exchange necessary to service and repay the loan is not known. Banks must and are developing systematic ways of assessing and dealing with the more complex problems of global exposure. The most salient problems here are those of country risk evaluation, as banks move more into the less developed areas of the world, and the management of international flow of funds in a world of floating exchange rates and unpredictable controls on foreign exchange activities by individual countries. All of these problems focus on the necessity of providing the necessary liquidity in a changing environment through the effective management of assets and liabilities on a global basis.

THE EXPANSION OF U.S. INTERNATIONAL BANKING SINCE WORLD WAR II

The reasons for the postwar spread of international banking may be classified under four headings: the global economy, the international banking market, the policies of the U.S. government, and the policies of foreign governments.

The Global Economy

Economists, political scientists, and sociologists are increasingly prone to describe the world economy as growing more and more interdependent. While there may be differences in opinion as to whether rising interdependence is either inevitable or desirable, there does seem to be general agreement that both the volume and the elasticities relating to international trade and finance are increasing. The value of world exports has risen from less than $100 billion in 1950 to $876 billion in 1975. Although the growth slowed in 1975 as a result of the global recession, it is estimated that the growth of 10 percent to 12 percent was resumed in 1976. This growth was due in part to the nature of the demand for traded goods, such that incremental economic changes in a country caused larger changes in the flow of goods and services than had previously been experienced. At the same time, both direct and portfolio investment became more mobile in response to not only monetary, but also general economic and political conditions.[3] These developments have provided ample opportunity for the expansion of international banking, both in its more traditional functions of trade financing and direct foreign lendings, and in its newer functions in international investment banking outside the United States and nonbank financial activities.

At the macroeconomic level, the apparent tendency for business cycles in major industrial countries to coincide in timing has produced exaggerated balance of payments effects which require temporary financing. This relatively recent convergence of cyclical trends, which reflects increasing interdependence, has also been accompanied by an apparent willingness of U.S. banks to lend to the rest of the world in recessionary times. During the interwar period capital outflows from the United States were supply determined: when the United States boomed it exported capital to the rest of the world, and vice versa during a recession. This situation resulted in capital flows which were globally procyclical. During the postwar period, the United States became a mature financial center; capital outflows are now more determined by demand. Hence, when the United States is in a recession it exports capital, helping the rest of the world economy to expand. The result is a countercyclical pattern of capital flows.[4] More recently,

---

[3] On the rising mobility of trade and capital, see R. M. Cooper, *The Economics of Interdependence* (New York: McGraw Hill Book Co., 1968), passim.

[4] C. P. Kindleberger, *The World in Depression, 1929–1939* (Berkeley and Los Angeles: University of California Press, 1974).

the addition of recycling of petrodollars from the Organization of Petroleum Countries (OPEC) has added to these flows.

The International Banking Market

The major motive behind the international growth of U.S. banks has been the desire to maintain or enhance the rate of growth of earnings by acquiring foreign assets and liabilities, and to reduce risk through diversification. Posed as an optimization problem, a bank may try to maximize earnings at a given level of risk, or to minimize risk for a given earnings target. The wisdom of "going international" is confirmed by the impressive rates of growth in international earnings shown by U.S. banks. In 1975, the 13 largest U.S. banks derived 47.7 percent of their total earnings from international business. Between 1970 and 1975, these earnings had grown at a compound annual rate of 36.5 percent.[5]

It would be unrealistic to assume that such growth rates can be sustained in the future. As competition has increased U.S. banks are already losing market shares in world deposits to French, German, and Japanese banks.[6] However, the U.S. banks will continue to have a substantial competitive advantage as long as the U.S. dollar continues to play a central role in the world economy, despite the fact that European and Japanese banks have become increasingly active in U.S. dollar markets.

An additional reason for the rapid rise of U.S. banks to a predominant position has been the development of banking technology in the United States which they have been able to export to overseas branches, subsidiaries, and affiliates. This technology includes new or improved banking services such as installment finance, equipment leasing, credit cards, and various computer-based services. Also included would be the ability to link major financial markets on a global basis using advanced data processing and management information systems.

Overseas expansion has probably been a self-reinforcing process, adding to the total resources of the bank and providing more capability for further global expansion. Overseas growth reinforces the bank's domestic competitive position, widening the gap between the large international banks and their less-internationalized domestic competitors. In an effort to reduce this gap, some banks without an international capability have attempted piecemeal international expansion programs

---

[5] For earnings data on individual banks, see Hanley, *United States Multinational Banking,* p. 13.

[6] For statistical evidence of this trend, see R. Z. Aliber, "International Banking: Growth and Regulation," *Columbia Journal of World Business,* Winter 1975, pp. 11–13.

whereby they sought to gain access to one or two overseas markets. Such operations were not cost efficient in terms of prospective earnings and certain of those banks also lacked adequate risk management skills. The result was that some of these banks were not successful in their ventures.

Policies of the U.S. Government

One of the incentives for U.S. banks to expand overseas has been the generally less restrictive nature of banking laws and regulations overseas as compared to the United States. Particularly important have been restrictions limiting growth in the United States, such as restrictions on branch banking. In many foreign countries the types of banking services that can be offered are broader than in the domestic market. Banks have also transferred offshore funding operations to foreign countries because of monetary restraints in the United States, such as reserve requirements and ceilings on the interest rates paid on deposits, which have the effect of making U.S. banks not competitive in attracting overseas deposits.

Another major incentive was the capital outflow controls implemented by the U.S. government between 1963 and 1974 in order to reduce the large capital outflows which had become a major factor in the persisting deficits in the U.S. balance of payments. In July 1963, President Kennedy announced the Interest Equalization Tax (IET) to penalize U.S. purchasers of foreign securities at a rate of 15 percent of foreign stock and 2.75 to 15 percent on debt securities, depending on the maturity. In 1965, the Gore Amendment broadened the IET to cover bank loans of one year or more. In that same year, President Johnson announced the Voluntary Foreign Credit Restraint (VFCR) program, restricting outstanding bank credit to nonresidents of the United States to 105 percent of the amount outstanding at the end of 1964; exceptions were allowed on certain types of transactions, such as prior loan commitments and export credits.[7] Similar restrictions were placed at the same time on the direct foreign investments of U.S. corporations under the Office of Foreign Direct Investment administered by the Department of Commerce.

These controls forced U.S. banks to shift foreign lending activity to overseas bases, so as to operate outside the jurisdiction of the controls, and at the same time caused U.S. corporations to shift their foreign financing needs to offshore sources. Unfortunately smaller banks, lacking access to offshore markets, also lacked a volume of business which

---

[7] "Guidelines for Banks and Nonbank Financial Institutions," *Federal Reserve Bulletin,* March 1965.

could justify the establishment of an offshore operation. Hence, an indirect effect of the controls was to reinforce the dominant position of the large banks. Andrew Brimmer, formerly a Federal Reserve Board member responsible for the VFCR, has noted this effect on the pattern of international expansion by U.S. banks:

We have recognized all along that this program, as well as other programs, has involved some problems. The Board has been increasingly concerned about the incidental impact of this program upon the competitive position of the banks. Basing the program upon a situation prevailing at a particular date tended to "freeze" the competitive situation. While this was not desirable, it was not easily avoidable and was acceptable for a temporary program. However, as the program has been carried forward, possible distortions in competitive positions and, more basically, in the allocation of resources become more and more important.[8]

The termination of the controls in January 1974 was, at the time widely predicted to have the effect of discouraging further overseas expansion of U.S. banks and to encourage them to conduct their international business from a U.S. base. This does not seem to have been the case, and for good reasons. Foreign locations obviously have advantages which continued after the abolition of U.S. capital controls. The Eurodollar market, for example, is still attractive to U.S. banks and provides an important source of funding for offshore lending.[9]

Policies of Foreign Governments

Interdependence between national economies may be rising, but what is often forgotten is that the technical capacity and willingness of governments to control trade and payments is also increasing. This is especially evident in banking, which is heavily regulated. Consequently, the rate and direction of growth of U.S. international banks has been strongly influenced by government and passivity. The type of reaction which occurs depends largely on the efficiency of the local capital market and on attitudes to foreign direct investment.[10] At the same time, all overseas expansion through new branches or investments

---

[8] Statement of Governor Brimmer, U.S. Congress, Joint Economic Committee, *A Review of Balance of Payments Policies* (Hearings before the Subcommittee on International Exchange and Payments. 91st cong., 2d sess. [Washington, D.C.: U.S. Government Printing Office, 1969]), pp. 162–163.

[9] On the nondeath of the Euromarkets following the removal of the U.S. controls, see V. van Dine, "The U.S. Market after Controls," *Euromoney*, March 1974; and H. Evers, "New York's International Revival," *The Banker*, September 1975.

[10] A country by country survey of restrictions on U.S. banks may be found in U.S. Congress, House Committee on Banking, Currency and Housing, *International Banking: A Supplement to a Compendium of Papers Prepared for the Fine Study*, 94th cong., 2d sess. (Washington, D.C.: U.S. Government Printing Office, 1976), App. C.

by U.S. banks must be approved by the Federal Reserve and subject to the criteria it applies. This requirement does not apply to nonbanking U.S. corporations.

Several potentially interesting markets have been denied to U.S. banks. Australia has not allowed foreign banks to establish commercial banking operations since World War II, although merchant and nonbank financial operations with Australian equity participation have been permitted. Canada is another country that effectively prohibits foreign branch banking.

At the other extreme are countries which have actively encouraged the entry of U.S. banks, usually to help the balance of payments. The British government has been deliberately liberal in allowing foreign banks into England, making London the center of Eurocurrency market. Foreign exchange earnings from such financial services are important to Britain's balance of payments. More recently, other countries in the Caribbean, Middle East, and Far East, as well as Panama, have made concerted efforts to attract international financial institutions. Singapore, for example, is the focus of the growing Asian-dollar market largely because the government eliminated the taxation of interest payments to foreigners in 1968. In 1976, the government of the Philippines announced its intent to implement banking laws designed to establish an offshore banking center in Manila.

Finally, there are those countries which are attractive locations for U.S. banks and neither encourage nor discourage their entry. West Germany, France, Belgium, Italy, and the Netherlands are all generally open to U.S. banks.

NEW INTERNATIONAL RELATIONSHIPS OF U.S. BANKS

The expanding global operations of U.S. banks have put them into new and complex relationships with sovereign governments, and has significantly altered interbank relationships. Furthermore, because of the scope and magnitude of their role as global intermediaries, the U.S. banks have become a major determinant of the efficiency and effectiveness of the currently evolving international financial system.

Banks and Governments

Because of the international monetary system within which they operated, international banks appeared to have made some aspects of government policy more complex, especially in the areas of monetary and exchange rate policy. During the 1960s, for example, countries often found their domestic monetary policies being thwarted by international capital flows. In 1966 and again in 1969, the Federal Reserve

Board's deflationary domestic credit policy was offset to some extent by an inflow of funds from the foreign branches of U.S. banks.[11] West Germany had similar problems in attempting to maintain a consistently lower rate of inflation than its trading partners because of an inflow of funds attracted by strong currency. Yet this problem was more the fault of the exchange rate system than of the banks. Under fixed exchange rates, it is difficult for countries to maintain independent monetary policies, and the higher mobility of capital has enhanced the speed with which offsetting capital flows occur. Governments are not, of course, totally helpless in the face of such developments. They can control bothersome capital flows, at least until transfer and substitution effects offset the initial impact of controls. A more effective solution to regain higher monetary autonomy is to allow the exchange rate to fluctuate permitting a part of the adjustment to be made in the exchange rate and reducing the magnitude of capital flows.

However, flexible exchange rates can also pose problems for governments to the extent that the exchange rate is determined by speculative forces, rather than the relative rates of inflation in different countries. Such problems properly fall within the responsibility of central banks to intervene in foreign exchange markets to preserve orderly conditions with respect to their own currency. Nevertheless, international banks are frequently cited improperly as aiding and abetting speculative activities. For example, a recent study for the House Banking Committee noted that claims of U.S. banks on nonbank foreigners, and claims on liabilities to foreign banks, show a high degree of correlation with currency crises.[12] In defense of the banks, however, a study presented to the Senate Foreign Relations Committee pointed out that these correlations may only indicate the extent to which banks were the vehicles through which funds moved, rather than speculating for their own accounts.[13] While banks do constitute the market in which foreign exchange transactions for customers are consumated, a major source of speculation against exchange rate changes has no direct relationship to this market. It is common practice to apply "leads and lags" to the settlement of transactions in a currency where a change in exchange rates is anticipated. This is simply done by accelerating receipts of a currency and by delaying payments where a depreciation

[11] See R. C. Marston, "American Monetary Policy and the Structure of the Eurodollar Market," *Princeton Studies in International Finance No. 34* (Princeton, N.J.: Princeton University Press, 1974).

[12] U.S. Congress, House Committee on Banking, Currency and Housing, *International Banking*, pp. 206–07.

[13] U.S. Senate, Committee on Foreign Relations, *Multinational Corporations in the Dollar Devaluation Crisis, A Staff Report Prepared for the Subcommittee on Multinational Corporations* (Committee Print, 94th cong., 1st sess. [Washington, D.C.: U.S. Government Printing Office, June 1975]), p. 89.

is expected and doing the opposite in the case of an appreciate for a currency.

On the other hand, it should be recognized that international banks can be helpful to governments in solving problems and carrying out financial policies. For example, the rise in oil prices in 1973 posed a massive financial intermediation problem which U.S. banks met quite effectively. Short-term capital inflows into U.S. banks in 1974 rose 37 percent to $95 billion; during the same period, short-term outflows rose 88 percent to $39 billion. This would suggest that the U.S. short-term capital account was the vehicle for a considerable amount of recycling of OPEC oil revenues back to oil-consuming nations. U.S. banks are continuing to perform this function. At the end of 1976, foreign branches of U.S. banks had liabilities to OPEC members totaling $13.6 billion, and assets of $2.7 billion, the difference representing funding which had been recycled to non-OPEC users.

Governments have also become more interested in international banking from a regulatory standpoint. In the United States, the Comptroller of the Currency monitors geographical concentration of bank loans as a part of its examination of national banks and in 1974, extended its examination procedures to include foreign subsidiaries and affiliates. The Federal Reserve, through its approval authority for overseas branches and investments of U.S. banks, monitors the rate of expansion of foreign activities through additional investments. Finally, the internal controls established by banks on country and currency exposure are audited.

More recently, the question has arisen as to whether banks should be subject to some kind of supranational regulations, particularly in the Eurocurrency markets. The governors of the central banks of the Group of Ten have been meeting as the Blunden Committee, examining national regulatory conditions and possible cooperative regulations among central banks. One of the key issues here is the "lender of last resort" question. Central banks have the responsibility of maintaining the liquidity of banks operating in their own currencies. This means, for example, that in times of crisis the central bank must be a lender to banks in instances where the banks are solvent, but the liquidity of the banking system is threatened. However, in the case of offshore markets dealing in currencies other than that of the country in which the market is located, there is no single "lender of last resort." The largest, and therefore, the most visible, example of this is the London Eurocurrency market and it is the absence of a lender of last resort that has caused many to refer to this market as "unregulated." In the meetings of the Blunden Committee there was general agreement that this responsibility should be on the basis of the nationality of the bank's charter, rather than that of the country in which the market is located. Of particular concern to the committee were consortium banks where the shareholders are major banks of several different nationalities. Here it was agreed that the shareholder banks should be responsible for their share of the consortium liabilities. The Federal Reserve already acts as lender of last resort to U.S. banks, and for this reason claims an interest in further regulatory powers over the foreign activities of U.S. banks. The banks are naturally inclined to argue that they should not be prevented from doing that which is authorized by local banking authorities, in order to remain competitive overseas.

Finally, in dealing with governments, banks are now being called upon to assume more sovereign risk credit than in the past. This has been primarily the result of the large balance of payments deficits which have resulted from the increased cost of petroleum and the global recession of 1974–75. Consequently, banks must refine their systems of evaluating the nature of sovereign risk in a manner which is realistic in the light of a changing economic and political environment. Although certainly not limited to them, the problem has been most acute in the developing countries. A number of these countries now have large debt servicing requirements to U.S. banks. Exhibit 58–3 cites data on the largest of these.

The claims of U.S. banks on nonoil-producing less developed countries, at the end of 1976 have been estimated to be $45–50 billion. The comparable estimate for all commercial banks (U.S. and foreign) is $70–75 billion. U.S. banks, therefore, hold about 65 percent of the external bank claims on these countries. It is frequently asserted that these figures are not a cause for alarm because no countries have deliberately repudiated external debt since the Castro takeover in Cuba. This is true, but somewhat misleading, since there have been a number of debt renegotiations because of the inability of debtor governments

Exhibit 58–3
Claims of U.S. Banks on Selected Less Developed Countries, March 31, 1977 ($ millions)

Latin America:	
Argentina	1,298
Brazil	13,856
Mexico	13,001
Asia	
Indonesia	2,222
Philippines	2,294
South Korea	3,234
Taiwan	2,566

Source: *Treasury Bulletin*; Federal Reserve *Statistical Releases on Assets and Liabilities of Foreign Branches of U.S. Banks.*

to meet original maturity schedules. While there is nothing new about such debt restructuring, in instances in which adverse balance of payments developments have occurred, the present situation does differ with respect to the number of countries simultaneously involved and the aggregate amounts which might be subject to debt servicing problems.

There are ways in which banks can reduce this risk by encouraging the correction of deficits by internal adjustment, rather than additional external borrowing. A private bank cannot impose such discipline of a sovereign government, but it can lend in conjunction with an international organization, such as the International Monetary Fund, which has the capacity to apply discipline in servicing debt and in the adoption of appropriate economic policies. They can seek legal safeguards, such as a waiver of sovereign immunity in the courts of a third country. They can also change the nature of their lending practices and, for example, make more project loans producing measurable foreign exchange earnings, rather than making general-purpose loans for which the source of repayment is not specified.

Interbank Relationships

Relationships between banks have become more complex, both because of the changing nature of the economic environment, and because banking techniques are becoming more sophisticated. This has been particularly apparent in the case of consortia banks where several major banks are co-shareholders. After the collapse of the Herstatt Bank in 1974 there was a severe tiering of banks. This tiering resulted from depositor preference for larger, financially stronger banks. With such a tiering, several levels of interest rates evolved with the largest paying the lowest rate, the next largest a slightly higher rate and so on down to the smaller, more vulnerable banks which could only obtain funds at very high rates of interest. Lesser known banks and some consortia banks, therefore, found it very difficult to obtain funds in the Eurocurrency market. It was no longer taken for granted that because a consortium had shareholders of unquestioned credit standing, it would qualify for a preferential market position. In an effort to cope with this kind of problem, the Bank of England requested from shareholders in consortia banks "acknowledgements of moral responsibility for their investments in London."[14] This has led to a more direct involvement by shareholder banks in the operations of their affiliates and the development of better management reporting systems than previously existed.

---

[14] See "Banking on the Book," *The Economist*, February 14, 1976, pp. 56–57.

There are several types of activities that are salient sources of difficulty. One is the increasingly widespread use of syndicated loans, and the responsibility of syndicate managers to provide full and accurate information to other members of the syndicate. Failure to do so can lead to legal disputes. Disputes may also involve government agencies as well as banks.

These kinds of disputes tend to occur in the high-risk areas of banks' asset portfolios.

The result of such interbank disputes, however, has, in one sense been positive. Banks participating in syndicated loans now generally recognize that they must have their own skills with which to analyze risk rather than to depend on the analysis and information supplied by the syndicate leader. Similarly, it is recognized that each bank must provide its own follow-up after a credit has been committed or an investment made in a subsidiary or affiliate. This has meant that unless a bank has available, or can develop the necessary management information system and other necessary skills as well as adequate control mechanisms, it probably will be unwilling to undertake additional overseas commitments.

CONCLUSIONS

Between 1960 and 1976, U.S. banks went through a period of extraordinarily rapid global expansion, after which they entered a period of consolidation and reevaluation. The strategy of sustainable international expansion is forcing banks to face the question of the appropriate international exposure in terms of their desired trade-off of risk and gain, as well as the proper degree of diversification required in their loan portfolio. In addition to such a review of management policies, there should be a reexamination and strengthening of their control mechanisms and more stringent rules instituted to safeguard their integrity. Current technology should be fully applied to the development of management information systems which supply the accounting data necessary for effective asset and liability management on a current and continuing basis. Organizational change is also required; each bank must find the mix of centralization and decentralization appropriate to its global goals. Finally, the large U.S. multinational banks must recognize that as a major factor in the international financial system they will not lack governments claiming jurisdiction over their activities, and the problem they face of defining and efficiently pursuing their global goals is indeed a formidable one.

Chapter 59

Meeting the Banking Needs of Multinational Companies

*John A. Waage**

WHAT IS A MULTINATIONAL COMPANY?

There is no agreed definition of what constitutes a multinational company. Different analysts and authorities look at the concept in different ways for different purposes. The tendency is to devise a definition, either narrow or broad, for a particular study or for the largest umbrella. Indeed, as world economic growth continues and more companies of all nationalities "go abroad," the observer who commented that although he might not be able to define a multinational company precisely he could recognize one when he saw it, has to be less sure of himself.

Fortunately, international bankers have little need for a tidy theoretical definition. For them, and inherent in any definition of a multinational company, it is only necessary that the company be operationally positioned in more than one country. The nationality or nationalities of ownership of the parent, the manner in which the company's total activities are organized, the form or degree of ownership of country units, the scale and relative importance of total or foreign production or sales are not directly relevant. These factors do have a bearing on the nature of credit judgments reached by bankers and on prospects for doing profitable banking business with some or all of the company but they do not affect an international bank's willingness to consider working with it.

---

* Vice Chairman of the Board, Manufacturers Hanover Trust Company, New York, N.Y.

789

THE RAPID GROWTH OF MULTINATIONAL COMPANIES AND INTERNATIONAL BANKS

Historically, a few U.S. and foreign banks were international before the growth of multinational companies began to accelerate after World War I. In the post World War II era the multinational companies, large and small, did precede the banks in rapid expansion internationally. They were under pressures of exchange, trade, and other controls to re-establish, preserve or expand their foreign markets and competitive positions. They were also stimulated to rationalize production and distribution, and to grow under the impetus of national investment promotion programs or regional efforts at economic integration such as the European Economic Community.

Meeting increasingly sophisticated, changing and expanding financial needs of the multinationals and their cost-conscious treasurers has been an important factor in the process of almost explosive bank growth internationally that has taken place during the past 10 to 15 years. To an important degree also, however, banks expanded rapidly abroad from their own national base in response to their own individual perceptions of their growth needs and opportunities, competitive bank pressures, the international financial and monetary environment, and sometimes, it seems, essentially only to garner prestige. Primary targets for the banks were important money market or trade centers. To meet the complex needs of multinationals, and other customers, bankers increasingly have become unable to simply rush around the world selling head office loans or looking for correspondent business. They must be on site and operating in their chosen overseas markets.

WHAT ARE THE BANKING NEEDS OF THE MULTINATIONALS

The banking needs of multinational companies are as unsusceptible of precise definition as is the multinational itself. The banking needs vary with the company's size and financial strength, with the form of organization of the company and its overseas entities, with the sophistication and philosophy of management. They also depend upon the financial state of the world, the state of major money centers and upon politically based national monetary, credit, and exchange conditions in the countries in which the companies operate. Banking needs to be fulfilled by international banks vary in different parts of the world depending upon the adequacy of the banking industry and the state of the art in that part of the world. Succinctly, if not highly illuminating, the banking needs of multinational companies are whatever management, including the treasurer, say they are and whatever services banks can convince them are useful or more economically efficient to obtain from banks.

Bankers' Views

International banks feel the responsibility to respond to the financial needs, domestic and foreign, of all their customers: business, governmental, banking, and private. For major banks this has implied a full service, or department store, approach although not all the products in all banks are of equally high quality, and not all offered services are utilized by all customers. Most banks operating internationally have confined this full service objective to a head office or corporate family capability. Some others, which had tended to think in the same terms for their overseas operations as well, by 1974 had learned the error of their ways. The challenge to banks, recognized more widely in recent years, is to develop and sell those financial and closely related services they can perform efficiently, economically, and at a profit.

Multinational Views

The large, well-developed multinational, at one end of the multinational spectrum, views many of its banking needs as essentially a *buy* or *make* type of decision. Factors affecting this decision include organizational structure, size and nature of funds flows and demands, and financial and monetary characteristics implicit in the geographic position of the enterprise. The larger and more worldly-wise it is, the more it seeks to maximize in-company settlements and credit. The multinational, where possible, seeks to direct to the international commercial banks the residual or special characteristic business which it cannot handle, can handle only with difficulty, at relatively greater cost, or finds otherwise inconvenient.

The multinational company is acutely conscious of the relative creditworthiness of the parent and subsidiary elements of the complex, and trades on it. With business growth and inflation, the scale of the various financial service requirements of multinational enterprise is continually growing. However, while international banking opportunities grow, companies also may arrive at new *make* decisions which have the opposite impact. Moreover, commercial banks, even when they may possess, for example, a Euromoney center merchant bank or factoring subsidiary within the corporate family, are not the only source of credit to the company. Not only is a particularly wide range of nonbank financing institutions available when one looks internationally, but companies may have interests in foreign banks, make their own direct arrangements with, say, insurance companies, directly issue their own equities, or issue their own short-term commercial paper. Corporate treasurers are very cost conscious; international banks are also becoming very much so.

A Catalog of Services and Needs

The gamut of services offered by a major international commercial bank family constitutes a veritable catalog. Although the catalog offers some perennial stock items such as letters of credit, exchange transfers, acceptance financing, foreign collections, and so on, as the multinationals, the banks, and the world economy grow in size and complexity, the existing products in the catalog are improved and new ones developed.

The range of the needs of multinational companies and the services provided by international banks is broad and technical. It includes macroeconomic and marketing data; information on tax, exchange control, investment and labor regulations; information and recommendations about local bank connections in some instances; performance of traditional letter of credit and exchange operations, including hedging and swaps; international funds concentration and money management; working capital and medium-term loans; long-term loan placements and bond underwritings, including both private and public placements; leasing of all kinds of physical assets; factoring of receivables; merger and acquisition assistance; and pension and profit-sharing management. If a multinational company encounters need for a new financial service, banks will seek to devise a way to provide it. Under the competitive pressure of other financial institutions and in response to the innovative creations of multinational treasurers, the modern aggressive international bank seeks to anticipate or discover business needs that can be fulfilled rather than react to them.

NEEDS AND RESPONSES ARE DYNAMIC

More important than any catalog of the services that multinational companies need at a given point in time and that international banks organize themselves to perform, is constant recognition of the dynamic character of both sides of the equation. The past 15 years have been a period of profound and rapid change—for international business, for the international banks, and for the international economy, especially its immediately relevant monetary aspects.

In the foreign sphere, except for the several banks from a few countries that had established local funding bases in their overseas branches, until the explosive growth of the 1960s most banks with foreign departments engaged primarily in letter of credit international trade financing and foreign exchange transactions through selected correspondent banks in the principal trading countries.

Since then, banks aiming to become "international" have flowered with imaginative institution building, lending techniques, and credit instruments. They have allocated some of their most capable, aggressive executive talent to these efforts. Not unnaturally, in the process there has been much trial and error, with accompanying inefficiency, ineffectiveness, and high costs, especially in the forming of national or multinational joint venture institutions, branch positioning, and market and lending strategies. There were also unhappy experiences with management spread too thinly to be effective and questions sometimes were raised about capital adequacy.

In the past several years since what some have called the confidence crisis of 1974 there have been many second thoughts and much self-examination by banks operating internationally: reassessments of strategy, reviews of procedures to evaluate the credit risks of customers and transactions, and, above all, close attention has been given to cost/benefit relationships. These are reflections of the maturing of international banking.

With floating exchange rates, changing accounting standards and regulatory requirements in many countries, and often apparently widening differences in economic and political conditions or goals in important markets as part of their work environment, treasurers indeed are finding many of their decisions becoming ever more complex. The achievement by banks of widespread geographic positioning, impressive financing capability, and a high order of technical skills has provided corporate treasurers with more options. It has not reduced their responsibilities; nor can it—but when the decisions are reached, international banks also make the implementation easier.

Worldwide positioning and structures of affiliated financial institutions enable banks to lend in local currencies, dollars, third currencies or currency baskets. They can offer multiple currency drawing and repayment options. They can draw upon national or international markets to provide treasurers with financing for trade movements, for working capital, or for the purchase of capital assets. Banks extend credit to the multinational's head office, international group, regional, or national company. Banks and their affiliates can provide an advantageous leasing alternative to capital goods purchases in many parts of the world. They can provide national or international money market instruments for short-term treasury investment.

EXTERNAL FACTORS AFFECT THE FINANCING NEEDS OF MULTINATIONALS

The financial services multinationals need and international banks can provide are obviously influenced by more than simply the structure and facilities of the two forms of institution. Those features, which may reflect technological, historical, and philosophical influences, as well as current product and marketing aims, do not reckon with external factors which reinforce the multinational's need for continuous close banking relationships. External environmental factors both influence the course of business transactions between banks and their multinational customers and also may lead to the development of new financial market techniques or instruments. Perhaps the most striking example of this is the banks' development of the Eurocurrency market, and in that market the development of a number of new instruments and techniques.

Illustrative of some of these external factors that can make international life difficult for company treasurers, and sometimes for bankers too, are disharmonies in fiscal and monetary policies among countries as they take differing approaches to persistent inflation, recession, an overvalued currency, and balance of payments difficulties. Thus, there may be a sudden credit crunch in a major country as the authorities seek abruptly to restrain monetary growth. The company may find its international expansion plans adversely affected by foreign investment controls and "voluntary" credit restraint programs in the principal financial capital export source. To defend their balance of payments and foreign exchange reserve positions, countries which are important in the operations of multinational companies may adopt credit policies designed to encourage borrowing abroad. A country with long-established facilities for international financing may decide that it can no longer do so, as in the case of the prohibition of sterling financing of third country trade transactions.

Fixed or flexible exchange rates, prior local currency deposits against future imports, credit restrictions, capital flow, or other exchange restrictions all form part of the external working environment of the multinational company. Major international banks are not usually capable of changing this environment, although in some instances even in this respect their support of corrective programs by their foreign government customers may facilitate less disruptive adjustment. They do have the adaptibility and flexibility to help multinational companies work within this external climate where at all possible. Their response may not always be instantaneous, particularly if the response is to basic change in the international economic system. An effective, sophisticated major international merchant bank is not created overnight.

BANK PRICING AND UNBUNDLING

The years 1973–75, with previously unknown rates of general inflation, the worst widespread depression since the 1930s, the culmination of a decade or so of extremely rapid bank expansion abroad—all in the context of a prolonged period of ever-increasing international loan demand—mark a watershed. From the beginning of the great expansion of commercial banking abroad, first the U.S. banks and in more recent years those of other countries, in efforts to meet the needs of the multinationals and other customers, concentrated on geographic positioning and market services.

They expected to make a profit and overall they made impressive profits, not only in absolute terms and compound annual growth rates but as an increasing share of bank total profits. The quality of earning assets in their overseas portfolios has been generally high. The most common problems in international lending have had their roots in broad economic difficulties that result in renegotiation and rescheduling or refinancing, but loan losses have been remarkably low, representing only a small fraction of those in domestic experience.

Bank Costing and Pricing

The establishment of overseas branches, subsidiaries, and affiliates has been expensive in terms of money, time, and managerial talent. The approximately ten-fold increase in the number of U.S. banks with overseas branches and the quadrupling of the number of overseas branches during the decade ending 1975 brought on costs that continue. For a number of banks with overseas operations, they would be happier to be without these activities. For others these changes developed a higher cost structure than before the expansion. Inflation, even where it may be coming under better control, leaves its long-term legacy in salaries and equipment expense. Over the past decade, noninterest expense, including provision for loan losses, rose by more than 40 percent from 2.55 percent to 3.68 percent of earning assets for all insured banks in the United States. Over the same period, net interest income, as a percent of earning assets, went up by only 25 percent.

In their efforts to grow, confront the competition, and increase profits, the larger and more aggressive banks leveraged their capital with long-term debt and funded their hefty growth in assets with rising amounts of purchased money. There are limits to the use of either of these sources of funds. Over the years ahead leverage and liability management will give banks less "lift" than they did in the 1960s and early 1970s. New large increases in bank assets and liabilities will require increases in the equity capital base.

The imperative to increase equity and to better contain high noninterest expense overhead has led banks to greater concentration on productivity, customer profitability, and return on invested assets. On the income side, by far the largest single source of banking earnings is net interest income. In consequence, not only is increased attention being given to loan pricing but also to practicing the maxim that it is not only a matter of knowing what you *can* sell but what you *want* to sell. Other existing and new bank service products are receiving similar attention. Considering the assets employed, the capital tied up, and the people allocated, the services must yield their absolute and relative fair share, or potential fair share, toward earnings. At least that is the objective.

On the other side of the ledger, since most banks have to look to retained earnings as the major source of additional equity, and expense is the other factor determining pretax operating earnings, interest and noninterest expense are receiving similar management focus. Indeed, the multinational companies in recent years have also been seeking to generate internally a larger share of the funds they need.

By judicious selection of the funds purchased, including interest rate arbitrage among major international money market centers, a significant improvement in the cost of banking's raw material can be, and has been, achieved. Control of noninterest expense, except in times of emergency, can be managed only with perseverence over an extended period of time. In most international banks, however, systems and procedures toward this end have been in being for a number of years and have become a permanent part of management.

Since control of noninterest expense in its narrowest sense is primarily a matter of marginal changes or cutbacks to slow the increase of costs, primary attention has to be focussed on cost effectiveness, or productivity. Banking was slower than most industries in developing effective cost accounting. Banks have been seeking to make up for lost time. Serious efforts are being made to allocate rationally the costs of computer services, credit analysis, loan work-out units, marketing, and other staff function or back office overhead.

The major forward-looking effort, extensively employing the profit-center technique, is continuous improvement in managing and allocating resources so as to improve return on assets and, for example, to maximize earnings per employee, one measure of productivity, or to be conscious of where in the organization, and why, earnings per employee are low or declining. This returns the focus to product pricing. Frequently the pricing of loans and other bank services to multinational companies and other bank customers has been unduly low when margins were set with insufficient regard to up-to-date and accurate costing.

Multinational Desires For "Unbundling"

In recent years many banks that serve multinational companies have moved in the direction of unbundling their service product charges. Some of those customers of the bank department store also have indicated a preference for a greater unbundling of bank services so that the customer can purchase only those desired after cost and effectiveness analysis, rather than being induced to select them on the basis of the membership card of compensating balances. Banks and companies are moving in the same direction in this regard, albeit for different reasons and with the end of the road unclear in terms of the feasible degree of unbundling and whether resulting bank service costs to the customer company will be more or less expensive.

Treasurers of customer companies have argued that, since they are being asked to pay, essentially by maintaining compensating balances, for having available service they may not need, they are encouraged to use services, not really required, just because they are available. Such usage they contend, may have the effect of misleading banks as to the real demand for what are actually unnecessary services. With appropriate pricing and the customer bearing the full cost of production for the services, it is suggested, perhaps the consumption of many bank-offered services might be considerably reduced. Corporate treasurers have been encouraged by traditional pricing structures to do all of their banking where they borrow their money, it is asserted. As a consequence, any individual company borrower is caused to carry the overhead for services not being utilized. In effect, corporate treasurers are also precluded from purchasing the best product in whichever bank store that product is to be found.

It is also sometimes asserted that the "membership card" approach tends to encourage development of a broad but perhaps shallow range of services because of limits on allocable bank resources, thus acting as a constraint on specialization and the more efficient production of financial services. On the other hand, it is pointed out, progressive innovative banks may develop superior services at considerable expense but find difficulty in successfully marketing them because company treasurers already are getting perhaps inferior services elsewhere by paying for them with "double counted" compensating balances.

Many of these company observations are simply a recognition of the reality that in its first phase bank expansion around the world concentrated on positioning, staffing, and creating a base of business activity. As we have noted, the basic trend in the direction of unbundling has been in process for a number of years. Bank departments that were entirely "service" have developed "products" sold for a fee. Economic information and consultation are examples. In some instances when a bank has had difficulty in "putting it together" profitably, such as the stock transfer function for a multinational company, it has terminated the operation. Other banks have devoted special energies to that problem, modernized their systems and created an efficient, profitable operation, economic to the company and fulfilling its rigorous needs. Others, for example payroll handling, have been converted from a free to a fee operation.

It is possible to overemphasize the degree of dependence for any single service that a multinational company has upon one international bank. In general, the larger company employs several banks, frequently including international banks of non-U.S. nationality. In the process of allocating its business, the company can take account of special strengths or weaknesses of its banks. This in itself provides incentive to banks to maintain or achieve quality services. Especially with regard to lending, most banks would prefer not to be a company's sole financial partner and carry "all the eggs."

Perceptive progressive management in both banks and companies can easily become impatient with the pace of structural change. Most of today's international bank managers are aware of the point they have reached; they have a reasonably accurate awareness of the strengths and weaknesses of their institutions. They believe they know where they want to be five or perhaps ten years from now. All they need is money, lead-time, and the right people with requisite training.

It will continue to be true that a large international bank will offer more service products than perhaps any given multinational company may need or wish to utilize. International banking, however, has reached a level of maturity that promises an increasingly high order of technical operational efficiency in the provision of its service products around the world, wherever it is permissible and advantageous to do so.

OUTLOOK

The very rapid physical expansion of banks outside their own borders is probably over. International expansion will continue, particularly as new parts of the world, economically and financially speaking, become interesting. Some banks will draw back further than they have from particular types of activity or geographic locations. Where permitted by host countries to operate, banks probably will concentrate on intensive rather than extensive development of markets that appear promising. More carefully conceived marketing strategies will underlie these efforts. Experience has shown that it is not necessary to have a branch on every foreign corner to do business with important multinational companies and other major customers. New positioning will be decided by management only after much more rigorous scrutiny of the congruence between the local situation and its realistic potential and the bank's calculated market strategy than sometimes was applied in the past.

International loan demand during the next decade will be contained only by the extent to which banks will allow their overseas credit portfolios to grow. For U.S. international banks overseas, loan demand by multinational and other customers will continue to outpace the growth of domestic loan demand for the foreseeable future, especially considering the legal barriers to interstate banking that exist. For international banks, growth in earning assets, of necessity, will be more closely related to equity growth, and much of that will be achieved through retained earnings. Repetition of the rise in bank leverage experienced during the decade or so of most rapid growth is not possible.

More discriminating selectivity in credit standards and yield will be exercised in responding to the demand for loans. When banks are able, they may not always be willing. They are much less likely to "reach" for loans as they often did in the late 60s early 70s. Pricing policies will continue to become more sophisticated, and very much cost oriented. Cost analysis will become further refined and productivity improvement will continue to have high internal management priority.

Intense competition by international banks of various nationalities and the expansion of unbundled bank services with separate fees, may lead to further reduction in requirement of compensating balances. In the past few years in the United States such balances kept in noninterest bearing demand accounts have declined from an average of 15–20 percent to 10–15 percent. In other countries, particularly where inflation is substantial and official ceilings on maximum lending interest rates exist, requirements are often higher. Compensating balances enrich the effective rate of return on nominal bank lending rates. This can be a relevant factor if legal or public relations ceilings are in effect. Negotiating fees, commitment fees, participation fees, and so on, may well become more routine but there probably will not be a significant movement away from the requirement of compensating balances. Much more the trend is that such balances will no longer be double-counted as compensation for free nonloan services.

International banks and multinational company treasurers both are being pressed by the exigencies of the economic environment, advancing technology, and perceived business opportunity to recognize the essentiality of rational, highly sophisticated costing and pricing abilities and policies. The twin-pronged long-term aims of international banks will be to provide efficiently performed services that are in fact necessary to their multinational customers, and to insure that their marginal or unnecessary activities are reduced to the minimum. The prospects are for increasing use of bank pricing mechanisms that permit multinational companies to select the particular financial services they are willing to pay for and for banks to sell those services at remunerative prices.

Chapter 60 _____

Commercial Banks in the Eurocurrency Markets

Lawrence N. DeLeers, Jr.*

ORIGIN AND GROWTH

Dealing in foreign currency deposit balances undoubtedly can be traced back as far as the development of the concept of foreign exchange. Not until regular dealing in dollar deposits began in the London foreign exchange market in 1957, however, was the practice either sufficiently repetitive or formalized to warrant the designation of a new form of international money market.

Happily, the lack of descriptive material on this market existing at its inception has been remedied. The serious reader can today refer to several authoritative sources on subjects ranging from theoretical implications of the market to its practical operation. A wealth of statistical information is also available for those with the courage to delve into same.

This chapter attempts to survey the operation of the Eurocurrency market using the perspective of a participating bank. Given that perspective, the source and use of funds in the market are surveyed as are the risks attendant and the appropriate controls typically employed. Finally, Eurocurrency loan provisions are examined. Unfortunately, the scope of this chapter precludes in-depth treatment of any of these major areas of interest. Its purpose will be served, however, if the reader obtains an understanding of the basics of the marketplace as well as the desire to learn more about it.

_____

* First Vice President, First Wisconsin National Bank of Milwaukee, Milwaukee, Wisconsin.

During its nearly 20 years of formal existence, the Eurocurrency market has gone through several phases of development. The early 1960s saw the growth in the formalization of approaches to the taking and placing of Eurocurrency deposits between banks and for the funding of loans denominated in Eurocurrencies. While the operational formalities were being set and mechanical conventions established, the aggregate size of the market grew roughly in proportion to the banks entering the marketplace. Starting in the mid-1960s, the expansion of the marketplace occurred from several points of view: more banks entered the marketplace; different instruments were introduced (for example, the Eurodollar certificate of deposit); U.S. balance of payment restrictive measures made offshore dollar borrowing attractive for many and vital for some; and, generally, familiarity with the market grew, itself producing new financing capacity and options at a time when they were eagerly accepted by the international financial community. The growth of the late 1960s carried over to the 1970s until the effect of the collapse of the Bretton Woods system followed by certain celebrated banking failures exerted a welcomed sobering influence. The latter events served to curb the unwise practices (cursory credit judgments, dual standards, final maturity extensions beyond reason, rate trimming and the like) that had developed. Both the volume of dealing and the aggregate size of the market suffered somewhat as well during this period of readjustment and reappraisal. While making the adjustment called for, the Eurocurrency market played its part in the recycling of currencies brought into focus by the so-called 1973 oil crises.

In 1977, it is fair to say that the Eurocurrency market has not reached maturity in the strictest sense because of its inherent dynamism; that is, its capability to cope with change in a responsive manner. It is a market which, Dr. Paul Einzig has said on several occasions, "is here to stay for better or for worse." That its permanence is for the "better" is the concern and task of every responsible international banker. Reckless practices and abuses will lead to poorly conceived, and likely unilateral attempts at restrictive regulation which could well lead to a regrettable and unnatural demise.

NATURE OF THE MARKET

Definition of the Term "Eurocurrency"

The word "Eurocurrency" has been used heavily over the past several years and has doubtlessly been confusing to many. Perhaps the simplest way to define "Eurocurrency" is to say that it means deposit balances in a given currency owned by a nonresident of the country of said currency and/or which is freely and actively traded in the Eurocurrency market. Some have attempted to simplify the definition of the word even further by saying that a Eurocurrency deposit is an offshore deposit. An American company, for example, could take domestic dollar balances and place them on deposit in the Eurocurrency market with the same bank and in the process convert the deposit from a domestic deposit to a Eurocurrency deposit.

The number of currencies traded in the Eurocurrency market has grown over the years to include all freely convertible currencies of which the following are most frequently found in rate quotations:

Dollar (U.S.)	Guilder
Dollar (Canadian)	French Franc
Sterling	Swiss Franc
Deutsche Mark	Yen

Of the foregoing, the U.S. dollar remains, however, the most actively traded and dominant element of the market. U.S. banks, moreover, in the aggregate are extremely active dealers in Eurocurrencies through their offshore branches.

The Supply of Funds

The overall extent of the Eurocurrency market is difficult to determine in a precise fashion. Current estimates range from $250 billion to $450 billion. The size of the market, however, is only important as one of the elements used in judging its viability. While the market has had both periods of expansion and contraction, it has clearly proven to be viable.

The origin of funds is an important element to examine as well when considering market viability. Where do the Eurocurrency deposits originate which provide the funding for Eurocurrency loans? Simply put, from the excess balances of banks on one hand and of companies and individuals on the other hand. Of these two major sources, the banks are clearly the major suppliers to the market. The type of bank can range from a country's central bank, through the commercial and merchant banking sector to the specialized and/or secondary type of bank. Banks firmly established in the Eurocurrency market, morcover, have tended to be constant suppliers (at admittedly differing levels depending upon circumstances) while the nonbanking supply segment has tended to be much more rate conscious and generally more sporadically liquid. On a national source basis, those countries with large international reserves, for example, certain middle eastern nations, contribute heavily to market sourcing.

Market Uses and Users

The Interbank Market. As stated, banks are the principal suppliers to the market (placers) but they are takers as well. They take Eurocurrencies to fund Eurocurrency loans and to fund their own time deposit placements in the interbank market, as well as to fund arbitrage transactions. The term "interbank market" is largely self-explanatory. It refers to the aggregation of banks taking and/or placing Eurocurrency deposits either directly with one another or through an established broker network. Whichever approach is used, direct or broker, the funds settlement involved is done directly on a bank-to-bank basis.

Interbank market dealings of banks are not subject to any centrally coordinated set of controls and/or regulations. Prices are set quite largely on the basis of the laws of supply and demand. With this apparent lack of control or regulation, many have said, over the years, that participation in the interbank market is fraught with danger. While the need to operate prudently and knowledgeably is undeniable, it is hard to refute the opposite school of thought which maintains that the lack of centralized control is a definite plus factor. This school holds that such control would strangle the otherwise flexible and vital responsiveness produced by a free market environment.

What these two extreme schools of thought sometimes fail to realize is that controls do exist. They are not controls imposed by some single central authority, but rather by the banks themselves as well as by the regulatory agencies of the banks' home countries. Necessarily, such controls are primarily related to the current situation in a given bank or of the banking system or economy within a given country.

Taking U.S. banks and the U.S. banking system as a case in point, the following kinds of controls exist or have existed at some point in time:

A. Controls Imposed by the Individual Bank
1. Credit standards covering Eurocurrency time deposit placements and/or certificates of deposit purchased as well as loans.
2. Absolute limits, by currency, for the aggregate of Eurocurrency assets by type.
3. Pricing policies.
4. Limits with respect to the matching of the maturities between assets and liabilities as well as to the matching of currency types.
5. Limits as to the nature and aggregate size of various categories of risk to be assumed in the earning asset portfolio such as country risk, government sector versus private sector, and types of industry.
6. Standards and policies with respect to collateralization as well

       as to terms and conditions, such as maximum maturities and amortization requirements.

B. Controls Imposed by Regulatory Agencies
1. Reserve requirements on Eurocurrency loans granted to U.S. residents for use in the United States.
2. Regulation against soliciting domestic source deposit switching to the Eurocurrency market.
3. Intensive on-sight and head office examination of Eurocurrency branches of U.S. banks.
4. Restrictions on domestic funding of foreign branch operations.
5. Full asset and liability, and foreign exchange, reporting on a regular basis to the various controlling authorities.

Given these types of controls, and the foregoing lists are by no means all inclusive, it is clear that regulation of the market does, in fact, exist. It is not a centralized nor fully coordinated control. Pragmatically, however, it can doubtlessly be demonstrated that, given intelligent performance, it is the best form of control. A centralized form of control over a group of internationally diverse participants could easily be either too restrictive to serve all national economic interests or too loose to be of any real value.

As stated earlier, rates in this free market environment are almost solely determined by the operation of the laws of supply and demand. Potentially, each of the tens of thousands of Eurocurrency transactions consummated daily will have different rates notwithstanding similarities in maturities. From this point of view, there are strong similarities between the Eurocurrency interbank and the foreign exchange markets. A given bank placing two $1 million deposits, each for one month, an hour apart in the trading day is likely to receive two different rates for same. In addition to the operation of the basic laws of supply and demand, of course, the market sets rates on the basis of creditworthiness. The credit standing of a given bank may in turn be based on the financial characteristics and reputation of the specific bank and/ or on the basis of its belonging to a group of banks (say, within a given country) having similar characteristics in the eyes of the creditor side of the market. Whatever the judgmental and tangible elements comprising the rate determination for each transaction, the significant point is that the process is a market process not hindered by artificial controls or determinants. As a side note, it is interesting to watch both the interaction between short (overnight) Eurodollar rates and the U.S. federal funds rate on one hand and Eurocurrency rates, in general, against the combination of foreign exchange and internal interest rates of all currencies on the other hand. That they generally move together, leaving little room for pure arbitrage on a fully hedged basis, notwithstanding the unregulated rate setting mechanism speaks favorably for both the sophistication of the market, as well as for the quality of worldwide communications existent today.

The center of the Eurocurrency market has been and continues to be the financial center of London, commonly referred to as the City. Here one finds the aggregation of direct participants in the Eurocurrency market. British banks, subsidiaries of the clearing banks, merchant banks, branches of foreign banks from countries all over the world, large and small multinational banks, and others form the bulk of direct banking participants in the Eurocurrency interbank marketplace. They are assisted by a highly sophisticated brokerage system which puts "placer" and "taker" together. The brokers are indirect participants and do not place or take deposits in the interbank market for their own accounts. Nor, as stated earlier, do they handle the funds transfers resulting from consummated transactions. There are banks, corporations and others who either place or take Eurocurrency funds who are not considered direct market participants as they do not operate with a presence directly in the "City." Additionally, there are banks with offices in Nassau, the Caymans, Luxembourg, and other centers which deal regularly in the interbank market, but which are considered something less than direct participants due to their lack of a physical presence in the center of the market. Indirect market participation on the "taking" side can lead to the taking bank paying a slight margin above the interbank rate. This added margin has less to do with the credit standing of the bank than with the fact that the bank is not a "direct participant."

Other forms of rate differentials do exist, however, which relate directly to the market's (placing banks) appraisal of the standing of the taking bank. For many years, in fact until the 1973 to 1974 period which saw the San Diego, Herstatt, and Franklin related failures, banks did not differentiate by rate in the credit standing of banks with whom they were willing to deal in the Eurocurrency market. While perhaps an oversimplification, it is generally fair to say that a bank was either on a placing bank's approved dealing list (at some limit or set of limits) or it was not. If it was on the approved list, it got the deposit at the rate then existing. If not, the deal did not materialize. There were no rate differentials.

With the above-mentioned failures came the realization by banks in general to the need for the use of the same kind of informed credit judgment when dealing with other banks that is generally used in granting credit to commercial firms and/or individuals. This awakening and the use of a variety of standards and analytical methods led to the informal, but nonetheless real, development of a tier system in the interbank market. The largest and most undoubted banks, in the first tier, were able to obtain Eurocurrency deposits at the interbank market rate for all available periods. The second tier, just under the undoubted level, would typically pay a slight margin over interbank on some and perhaps all deposit maturities taken. The third tier of banks, while still considered acceptable risks, would generally pay a higher margin over "interbank" and might, in fact, have found some of the longer deposit maturities unavailable to them.

The tier system, in this relatively free market has continued, but is not applied uniformaly bank by bank. Each bank makes its own credit judgment. Naturally, therefore, a given bank may be viewed as a first tier risk by one bank and as a second or third tier risk by another bank. This lack of uniformity in ratings could be viewed as a shortcoming in the system. Whatever the uniformity or lack of same in bank-to-bank credit ratings, however, the important point is that more analytical and informed judgments are now being made than was previously the case.

Commercial Borrowers and Depositors. Commercial borrowers in the Eurocurrency market tend to be large multinational companies utilizing loan proceeds in the conduct of their international business. This is particularly true of the typical U.S. firm, however, a wide range of special-purpose functions does exist. In some cases, for example, a largely domestic U.S. firm may arrange for a Eurodollar standby line of credit to guard against the possibility of lack of funds availability domestically to meet some known future requirements. Such facility could, in certain circumstances, provide a temporary interest rate hedge for the potential borrower as well. On the other side of the market, many of the larger commercial firms will use the Eurocurrency market as a temporary investment medium. This, of course, is only attractive when a positive yield differential occurs and is only possible when regulations permit. Such deposits will usually be in one of two forms. The first, and by far the most common, is on the basis of a simple confirmation from the bank stating acceptance of the deposit, date of same, the currency denomination, principal amount and rate, and the maturity date.

This, of course, is a nonnegotiable instrument with fixed maturity ranging from overnight placement out to six months and less frequently for longer periods. For those depositors wishing more flexibility in their temporary investment media negotiable certificates of deposit, usually limited to either dollars or Sterling, are available which offer liquidity through a well-developed secondary market.

Included as users of this large and responsive marketplace as either borrowers or depositors include government entities and central banks of both developed and developing countries alike. The scope of this work precludes a detailed examination of the range of vehicles and purposes involved for this class of market participant. Suffice it to say that they generally relate to either balance of payment or developmental projects. In this context, as well, the Eurocurrency market has proven an extremely useful vehicle in fulfilling international financial needs.

Relationship to Foreign Exchange Market

It would be misleading to suggest that the Eurocurrency market functions in a vacuum without interaction with the world's other major financial markets. As suggested earlier, there is generally a strong relationship between movement in the U.S. Federal Reserve funds rates and the overnight and short-term (under one month) Eurodollar rates. Similarly, general movements in the U.S. prime lending rate are usually either followed or anticipated by changes in the Eurodollar rates. These relationships are not exact, nor do movements between rates in the various markets occur on a strictly proportional basis, but the direction and timing are usually close to being parallel.

The relationship existing between the foreign exchange, Eurocurrency, and internal money markets, however, are quite exact and aberrations allowing opportunities for fully hedged rate arbitrage are generally very short lived. An example would seem to be in order to clarify this concept:

Let us assume that the interbank deposit rate for one-month dollars is 6 percent while one month Sterling deposits can be placed at 12 percent.

On the surface it would appear that it would be a good move to take one-month dollar deposits at 6 percent, sell the dollars for Sterling at spot, and place the Sterling on deposit for the same one-month period at 12 percent. On further consideration, the 6 percent clear profit would only be assured if the Sterling deposit were sold forward one month to yield the same amount of dollars originally obtained. If this were not done, a decline in the dollar/ Sterling exchange rate over the month in question could more than offset the favorable 6 percent interest rate margin. Calculating the foreign exchange market discount on forward sales of Sterling against dollars and converting same to a per annum interest rate basis, it would be found that the discount probably would offset the apparent interest rate advantage.

In the past, a fully hedged swap transaction such as that described above (that is, a transaction where one currency is taken, sold spot for a second currency which in turn is placed out and a forward sale— all with matched dates—is executed to produce the precise principal amount of currency originally taken) could have produced a profit. With today's sophisticated communications networks, widespread and in-depth market knowledge and the resulting responsiveness in the world's markets, however, such opportunities are few and far between. For a commercial bank to engage in unhedged rate arbitrage transactions in any scale outside of normal operations and/or approved limits, moreover, is unwise, particularly with the extreme volatility existing in the foreign exchange markets.

A parallel exists between the bank which engages in unhedged rate arbitrage transactions and commercial firms who borrow in a Eurocurrency other than that which will provide the source of repayment. Clearly, from the example given previously, if a commercial firm borrows Eurodeutsche Marks in order to minimize the interest rate (when dollars will, in fact, be the source of repayment rather than DM) that firm is taking a foreign exchange risk. If it hedges such risk through the foreign exchange market, the apparent interest rate advantage disappears. While this reasoning is quite fundamental, many firms over the past several years have not followed the rule of borrowing only in the currency from which the repayment will be forthcoming. Of these companies, some have been lucky but many have had to report much higher than anticipated borrowing costs to their boards and stockholders which in some cases must have been more than just a minor embarrassment. Commercial banks making such loans, undoubtedly in certain instances, shared in the embarrassment having failed to knowledgeably advise their client of the full range of risks being undertaken.

BANK MANAGEMENT OF A EUROCURRENCY BOOK

The foregoing description of the Eurocurrency marketplace, its range of participants, and some of the operations occurring therein leads naturally to an examination of how commercial banks manage their Eurocurrency portfolios or "books." When speaking of a Eurocurrency book, the specific reference is to two general categories of earning assets and various subdivisions thereof. They are the temporary investment (deposit placements and CDs purchased) and loan books. Consideration of the earning assets alone, however, without viewing the deposit liabilities supporting same would be an even more serious violation of the principles of asset/liability management for a Eurocurrency bank than for a solely domestic banking operation. The two sides of the balance sheet are directly related not only from the source and use of funds viewpoint, but also from the flow of funds and maturity matching viewpoints with their resulting impact on the profit and loss statement; an impact even greater than would normally be assumed because of the nature of the market and its pricing mechanism.

What risks does a commercial bank face in managing a Eurocurrency book? What controls are typically employed to minimize these risks? What conditions should exist before a bank begins operating in the Eurocurrency market? The following answers to these and related questions will be viewed chiefly from the perspective of an American bank dealing, or contemplating dealing, in the Eurocurrency market on a direct basis as previously described.

Risks Involved

Of the risks involved, the credit risk is the most obvious. Prior to the start of the 1970s many American banks dealing in the Eurocurrency market could have been correctly criticized for employing a dual standard. One standard, that is, for appraising Eurocurrency market credit risks and a different, more rigorous standard utilized in viewing domestic credit risks. As mentioned earlier, the shock of a series of bank failures forced banks to more seriously evaluate the standing of other banks to which credit was extended in the interbank market. A similar tightening of analytical and policy standards was employed generally by banks in their approach to viewing credit risks associated with potential Eurocurrency loans to commercial firms, as well as to governmental entities. While some exceptions undoubtedly still exist, it is fair to say that U.S. banks have now reached the point where the dual standard referred to has been substantially reduced. This welcome development has its roots in not only the self-realization by the banks of the need for proper and complete credit analysis of Eurocurrency loan risks, but also due to a tightening of the examination standards of the various U.S. regulatory agencies. The delivery risk can be related to both a bank's credit standing and its operating efficiency. Return of a maturing deposit or placement of funds covering a new deposit after the agreed-upon date is referred to as "late delivery." Repetitive instances of late delivery on the part of a given bank can be symptomatic of a larger problem and deserve to be investigated thoroughly.

Another risk, perhaps not so apparent but nonetheless important, faced by banks in managing their Eurocurrency books is the rate risk. In no other market is it more important to pay close attention to the matching of maturities on the liability and asset sides of the balance sheet. Unrestrained borrowing short and lending long can produce disastrous results given the rapid rate curve inversions that can and do occur in this marketplace. While short-term rates can appear attractively low, it is unwise to rely too heavily on short-term deposits taken to fund longer term deposits placed and loans. Not only can a rate inversion occur, but also, and more commonly, the general rate structure moves upward. What looked like a good rate margin today between short and long maturities can rapidly disappear or even turn negative. The longer term placements and loans, in other words, are locked in and the bank is faced with paying higher and higher rates for the short-term funding deposits or, if possible, taking longer term matching deposits producing a substantially lower net interest margin than originally anticipated. At best, this produces high volatility and a lack of reasonable predictability in profits and at worst losses that are extremely hard to justify.

The currency risk is another category of risk which must be first understood and then guarded against. It takes two forms: First, the risk encountered when one currency is taken to fund an earning asset in another currency; and second, when a term commitment (loan or placement) is made in a currency other than that of the bank's home country without assurance of the supply of such currency during the term of the commitment. The second form, currency availability, is generally well understood. Appropriate safeguards ranging from currency standby lines during the life of the commitment through bank currency option clauses within loan agreements are normally taken.

Controls Employed

Once the range of risks in Eurocurrency portfolio management is well understood, banks are in a position to provide adequate policies, procedures and accounting/reporting systems necessary to control same. The controls flow from policy decisions taken. No matter how appropriate the policies and the controls or limits flowing therefrom, however, "effective control" will not be achieved unless accounting and reporting systems provide timely, accurate and complete details on the earning asset books, the supporting liabilities, and profits or losses generated by the various segments of the operation.

Having set policies relating to a given bank's specific situation and needs, controls which typically fall within the following three major categories, are established:

Major Eurocurrency Book Control Categories

1. Currency limits.
2. Credit limits.
3. Time gap limits.

Currency limits are generally employed as an overall control on the absolute size of the earning asset book in each currency in which the bank has decided to deal. The limit set per currency will depend on a variety of factors including:

1. Whether or not it is the home currency of the bank.
2. The needs of the bank's natural customers.
3. The bank's evaluation of the depth and strength of the market.
4. The bank's evaluation of its own capacity to deal both prudently and competitively in such currency.

This basic form of aggregate control, it can safely be said, is employed in one or another form by virtually all banks operating in the Eurocurrency market. Like most controls, this kind of limit should be capable of change if after a thorough analysis of underlying conditions such change is warranted. In a broad sense, moreover, U.S. banks have absolute book size constraints imposed upon them, albeit indirectly, by regulatory agency examination of capital adequacy factors.

Credit limits discussed earlier in another context form another category of control. In the Eurocurrency market limits established by banks tend to be rather complex. This is due to the fact that when viewing a given customer, be it a bank or a commercial firm, when doing a thorough job in establishing the credit limits, each of the risks involved having an impact on or relationship to the extension of credit should be included. Hence, credit limits established by the most thorough banks will include, for example, limits on foreign exchange dealings as well as for straight extensions of credit through the lending function. The complexity of credit limits is not only due to the need to incorporate all elements in a given relationship having a true impact on credit, but also due to the need to aggregate all defined credit extensions to a given name by all branches of a given bank. In the latter case, the problem of accurate and timely credit exposure reporting is exemplified best by the situation which occurs when several branches of a multibranch bank extend various types of credit to various divisions of a large multinational corporation doing business in several countries. The need for not only a rationally developed set of credit limits but also a communications and record-keeping system that provides accurate and very timely information on outstandings and remaining availability against such limits is obvious. That this need is obvious does not mean that all banks have such timely systems. The supporting evidence for such contention would undoubtedly be found in internal and/or agency reports of examination containing citations of cases of line excesses.

Time gap limits are, of course, necessary unless a bank fully matches, date by date, the maturities of deposits taken with those of the assets funded thereby. If a bank does not do so (and it would be safe to say that no major bank dealing in the Eurocurrency market consistently achieves a complete matching) then limits establishing the maximum permissible degree of mismatch should be established. Adherence to such limits not only establishes the maximum negative earnings impact a severe and prolonged reversal of rates could produce, but also establishes a discipline for the dealing desk. The continual review of the Eurocurrency book by the dealers in relationship to these limits and current market conditions enhances the ability to make adjustments when necessary as well as the willingness to do so.

The time gap limits referred to in practice vary considerably from bank to bank. The following example, however, will serve to clarify the approach taken.

The bank's cumulative long or short position in Eurodollars (within any two-week time period) will not exceed $10 million. Let us then apply this limit to the following hypothetical Eurodollar book position:

Eurodollar Book Time Gap Limit (millions of dollars)

Two-Week Period Ending	Placements or Loans Maturing	Deposits Taken Maturing	Two-Week Position	Cumulative Position
3–7	$10.0	$ 5.0	$+5.0	$+ 5.0
3–21	5.0	10.0	−5.0	0
4–4	5.0	10.0	−5.0	− 5.0
4–18	5.0	10.0	−5.0	−10.0
5–2	5.0	10.0	−5.0	−15.0

In this example, the Eurodollar book is within the cumulative time gap limit for all periods except the last. Unfortunately, the scope of this chapter precludes a more complete examination of the more sophisticated concepts underlying and uses of the time gap limit. Suffice it to say that this form of limit finds its parallel in the foreign exchange operation and that to operate a Eurocurrency book without one would be as unwise as relying in the foreign exchange field solely on net forward positions without regard to the spread of maturities between forward purchases and forward sales.

Conditions Precedent

Given the foregoing summary comments on risks encountered and controls employed in management of a Eurocurrency book, certain conditions precedent can be set forth the absence of which should preclude any bank's entry into Eurocurrency market operations. It is clear that effective controls must be established. Good accounting and reporting systems must exist so that adherence to the controls can be continually monitored. The necessary technical market dealing skills and corresponding knowledge must exist or be acquired before the fact.

These factors, it could be argued, are self-evident. In fact, most, but not all, of the banks now dealing in the market undoubtedly would score fairly high marks. An extremely important condition precedent on which a smaller number of banks would score highly is the commercial rationale underlying their original entry to the marketplace. Why a bank decides to enter a marketplace as technically complex as the Eurodollar market will, at least in the short run, dictate the manner in which it deals. If an entering bank has clearly defined, qualified customer needs it is seeking to fill (that is, if it has an existent commercial base) its chances of responsible and profitable dealing have to be greater than the bank which enters the market motivated largely by the herd instinct. The latter bank could easily spin its wheels for a considerable period while seeking its niche in the market while at the same time be tempted to take unwise market and/or credit risks in an attempt to cover its overhead. This represents an unhappy situation which more than one bank has come to regret.

THE EUROCURRENCY LOAN

Given a sound commercial reason to enter the market, the skills, and know-how required, the controls and limits and all the other factors, a bank dealing in the Eurocurrency market will obtain its largest interest margins and, correspondingly, encounter its highest credit risk in the loan portion of its earning asset portfolio. As covered previously, Eurocurrency loans are to a variety of borrower types and for a diversity of purposes upon which each bank will make its own decisions. Typically, however, loan agreements in the Euromarket have certain common elements of importance. Similar to domestic term or revolving loan agreements, certain covenants will be included as required by the bank covering initial and continuing conditions on which it agrees to lend. Because of the nature of the marketplace, however, nearly every Eurocurrency loan agreement will be very specific about the following factors:

1. *Rate Definition.* Because of the volatile nature of rates in the market as described earlier, the definition of the rate in a Euro-agreement tends to be very explicit. It is, moreover, described as some margin above the London Interbank Offer Rate. The following typical definition illustrates the point:

 "The rate applicable will be 1.5 percent above the London Interbank Offered Rate available to the lending bank at 11:00 A.M.

London time two days prior to the drawdown or rollover for deposits of like amount, maturity and currency." In some cases, the arithmetic average of the rate available to two or more reference banks, rounded upward to the nearest 0.125 percent is employed. In recent years, with unsettled conditions in the market existent, additions to the rate definition have been added to provide alternate rates in case the bank is not able to fund its commitment to the borrower from the Eurocurrency market. This approach becomes extremely important when the agreement provides multicurrency options to the borrower.

2. *Regulatory Protection Clauses.* With the decentralized regulation of the market mentioned earlier, banks generally seek protection in the loan agreement from the impact of both existing and new regulations. As a case in point, most agreements contain a clause which contains words to the effect that if any regulation comes into force which by the creation of reserves or by other means increases the cost to the bank of funding the specific loan, then such cost will be for the account of the borrower. Of course, the borrowers are generally given the option of prepayment without penalty if they consider the added cost too burdensome.

3. *Operational Specifications.* These specifications are generally more complex in Eurocurrency loan agreements to both avoid misunderstandings and to conform to the nature of the marketplace. Drawdowns must generally be pre-advised from 5 to 15 business days in advance and are specified typically in Clearing House Funds (if dollars) as are corresponding repayments. If prepayments are permitted, they are generally allowed only at interest payment (rollover/resetting) dates unless complicated provisions for interest loss coverage are incorporated. The evidence of debt ranging from individual notes through a master note to a simple "loan account" is very clearly described. The mathematical method used to calculate interest is clearly set forth: For Eurodollars, for example, it is actual days over 360.

4. *Maturity and Amortization.* These provisions are similar to those in domestic agreements. Differences of importance, however, do exist. For example, in a multicurrency agreement amortization/maturity dates must be clearly defined to be business days in the principal financial center of the home country of the currency to be repaid. Theoretically, for example, under a DM borrowing, U.S. banks could be closed on a specified day, but as long as the banks in Frankfurt were open that day, settlement would be expected.

5. *Borrower Covenants.* As stated earlier, bank covenants are now not dissimilar to those found in the typical domestic loan agree-

ment. They will incorporate those terms and conditions the lending bank feels are appropriate to the credit extended. This state of affairs, however, did not always exist. Not too many years ago, banks employed a dual standard in the extension of credit which carried over into instances of remarkably lax loan agreements notwithstanding employment of the full range of terms singularly appropriate to the Eurocurrency market as cited above. Currently, however, Eurocurrency loan agreements have become stronger, not only with respect to market mechanics, but also with respect to underlying credit aspects.

On the mechanical or operational side of the Eurocurrency loan agreement, it should be noted that market conditions change and, therefore, so must the operational agreement conditions. Imprecise definitions, moreover, of the rate setting mechanism, the acceptable conditions for prepayment and the way in which multicurrency options may be exercised, to name but a few, can lead to difficult and costly misunderstandings with customers. Given the disappearance of the dual credit standard, there should be no greater risk in granting an offshore loan than a domestic loan to the same borrower, except for the mechanical market differences. These differences, in short, must be understood and must be incorporated into the loan agreement. Consider the bank that grants a multicurrency option loan to its good client who draws down Eurodeutsche Mark and, thus, finds at first renewal Eurodeutsche Mark are no longer available to it and that it has no provision for an alternate solution and has no choice (if it is to honor its continuing commitment to its client) but to obtain spot DM in the foreign exchange market. In the example, the bank could have lost a considerable amount of money without any form of default on the part of its customer. A properly drawn loan agreement, simply covering mechanics, would have avoided the problem entirely.

SUMMARY

This chapter has described the environment in which U.S. banks and others operate when dealing in the Eurocurrency market. Over the years, this marketplace has proven itself to be both resilient and flexible.

On one hand, it has survived both minor and severe recessions, as well as the passing of the Bretton Woods system and the failure of several small and large market participants. In the past, merchants of doom have predicted that any one of these events or certainly a combination of them would spell the collapse of the marketplace. The market has not disintegrated. Thus far, it has proven itself resilient and has given evidence that the form of decentralized control which does exist has been workable.

That the market is flexible is undeniable. It has met many forms of borrowing needs from many types of borrowers. It has developed new tools and new channels of communication and it has, for the major bank participants, fostered the concept of worldwide asset and liability management benefiting both the banks themselves and their customers.

This market, however, is highly complex and carries with it risks that must be well understood and protected against. It is not a market that should be entered without the proper underlying commercial rationale. It is a market requiring a high level of technical expertise, timely and appropriate controls, and reporting systems.

Chapter 61

Special Aspects of International Credits

*Donald R. Mandich**

Essentially, the basic business processes throughout the world are pursued by mankind in similar ways, such as rendering services, extracting raw materials, converting materials to another form, or buying and selling goods. A lender might assist any of these processes if the likelihood of repayment seems reasonable and the risk of involvement does not appear to be excessive.

Within his or her own country a lender operates with a feeling of comfort in regard to the legal framework, the business customs, the accounting conventions, and the many pressures that bear on a business by the country's economic trends and political manifestations.

Once a lender ventures across national borders, he is well advised to exercise extreme caution in assuming that any of the environmental elements of the business process are similar. However, these differences should *not* be extrapolated to arrive at the conclusion that *everything is different.* The basic business processes are much the same and the *fundamentals* of credit analysis remain unchanged, and if the lender can maintain his focus on these, he may avoid losing track of the essential risk-repayment analyses and in turn avoid problems.

Sections VII and VIII of this book cover the fundamental concepts of all credit extension. They should be considered the basic building blocks for any material contained in this chapter, and most of that material will not be repeated. This chapter will dwell primarily on special, additional aspects of international lending. Throughout, the

---

* President, Detroit Bank and Trust Company, Detroit, Michigan.

focus will be directed toward the aspects of lending across national borders, such as from the United States to any foreign country, or from London (or Nassau) to other foreign countries. Local loans in foreign countries made by the local branches of U.S. banks in local currency are primarily "domestic" type loans and will not be covered in this chapter.

Prior to World War II, the activity of U.S. banks in international lending was minimal and was mainly for the purpose of financing imports and exports. The war left the dollar as *the* major world currency and emphasis naturally shifted to it as the unit of account for international transactions. Over the same period, the demand arose for dollar loans. The initial involvement of U.S. banks in international lending on a large scale can be traced back to the mid-1950s. Two decades is not a long period of time, but from a modest beginning the lending by U.S. banks has reached gigantic totals, financing not only U.S. imports and exports, but all types of needs around the world and has proportionately far exceeded the involvement of any country in international lending in recent history. During these two decades considerable sophistication has developed in lending practices; however, the industry still has some distance to travel before international lending techniques achieve the more solid framework underpinning the domestic lending techniques of many U.S. banks. In addition, because international lending has been considered so foreign by many banks, analyses have often not been challenged strongly enough by bank management. As a result, a few practices have evolved based more on myth than logic, and it will probably be a decade or more before experience and good logic will fully unseat these traditions.[1]

TYPES OF INTERNATIONAL LOANS

International lending can be basically divided into two types—government loans or loans to the private sector.

Government loans have a variety of purposes—general borrowings for the Treasury, loans to finance imports or projects in the private sector, loans to develop roads, ports, or irrigations systems, and loans for the many other reasons that governments need funds. Actually, the purpose of a government loan is primarily one of interest to the extent that it will provide more insight to that country's future balance of payments; i.e., does the loan produce foreign exchange or will it save foreign exchange for the country in the future? In the simplest terms *all foreign government loans are undertaken to fill or replenish that country's holdings of foreign exchange,* regardless of the project

---

[1] See "Fallacies in International Banking," *The Bankers Magazine,* Spring 1974.

purpose that is attached to it. Foreign currencies (e.g., dollars) are not needed for local projects except to that extent that such projects include foreign goods or services.

Loans to the private sector generally fall into two classes—loans to finance the movement of goods (i.e., imports or exports) or loans to finance the multitude of other projects in which businesses get involved. Loans for imports provide the importer (and the country) with the foreign exchange to pay for the import. Loans to finance exports give the exporter (and his or her country) the foreign exchange proceeds a little faster than they would receive them in the normal course. Loans to finance other projects such as the construction of a new plant or the expansion of inventory are simply loans to increase the foreign country's holdings of hard currencies, except to the extent that the proceeds are used to purchase foreign goods or services for the project. The borrower is unconcerned with this truism, and simply knows that if he can borrow dollars he can exchange them for local currency (indirectly released by the central bank) which he can use for any business purpose.

Loans to the private sector may be to purely local companies or to subsidiaries of U.S. companies—with or without support of the parent. Occasionally, loans are made to individuals for personal or investment purposes. Private sector loans also include loans directly to foreign commercial banks for a variety of purposes. Depending upon the country, these might appear either as a loan to the bank or as a deposit.

In recent years leasing has become more popular as a financing device. This is probably one of the more complex types of international transactions, as it takes careful legal and tax planning to build a good transaction wherein the domicile of the lessor may be in a different tax environment than its parent, in a different country than the source of funds, in a different country than the lessee, and possibly the leased item may be in a fifth country.

Loans for the movement of goods comprise a substantial amount of total international lending. Such loans have developed complex practices and terminology and include devices such as letters of credit and banker's acceptances. The subject of letters of credit itself would fill a book. However, a short explanation may be useful.

An export from the United States could arise from a purchase order in dollars from a company in, say, Italy. If the exporter is comfortable with the credit standing of the buyer and the likelihood that the buyer can obtain dollars in Italy to pay on the due date, he will ship the goods and await payment. On the other hand, he may be unsure of the credit standing of the buyer and ask that the buyer have his bank write the exporter a letter saying that the bank will guarantee payment.

Hence, a *letter of credit* arises which in usage has become very formalized and is surrounded with an extensive list of traditional practices and an extensive legal framework. The cost of the guarantee of payment is paid by the importer, but is part of the total transaction cost and is allocated between buyer and seller somewhere in the transaction negotiation. A further variation is a case where the exporter might not feel comfortable even with a letter from the Italian bank and insist that the letter be sent to his local American bank which in turn will add its confirmation (guarantee) at a fee to be paid by the importer.

Usually, the American exporter will want his money when the goods are shipped and will draft upon his American bank (in the case immediately above). However, the importer may desire time to receive the goods before paying and ask for a delay of 90 days, or more. If a 90-day delay is agreeable to all parties, a 90-day time draft will be presented by the exporter to his American bank after the goods are shipped. The American bank will affix its guarantee to the draft by marking it "accepted" with the bank's name and an authorized signature. The bank has now created a *banker's acceptance,* which in essence is an IOU of the bank. The exporter can either hold the draft until the maturity date, can sell it in the market through a broker anytime before the maturity date, or sell it to the accepting bank at the market rate of discount; the bank can then either hold it as an investment or sell it in the market. The interest cost of discounting the acceptance is usually borne by the exporter, but if the term of the acceptance is longer than his usual practice for domestic sales, he may adjust the price of the goods to compensate.

In handling the above transactions the American bank will probably establish lines of credit (or at least internal limits) for the foreign banks for which it confirms letters of credit or creates acceptances. Obviously, the U.S. bank will have to perform the usual credit analyses on the banks, as well as analyses of the risks of the countries in which the banks are domiciled.

In the case of an import by a U.S. company, a U.S. bank may be asked to present a letter of credit to a foreign exporter (directly or through a foreign bank) and the entire process is reversed. However, if acceptance financing is desired to finance the goods while enroute and the transaction is denominated in dollars, the U.S. bank will provide it. In that event, as far as the American bank is concerned, all of the credit risk in the case of an import lies with the local importer.

The foregoing is a thumbnail sketch of handling transactions involving the movement of goods. If a bank should undertake this business, it is well advised to have on its staff a person competent in letters of credit. The need to analyze foreign banks and countries cannot be overemphasized. Some familiarity with the import practices in foreign countries is also necessary for exporters, as some countries require letters of credit to be issued by a local bank before *any* import can legally be undertaken, or else the necessary foreign exchange will not be made available to pay for the import. However, such a letter of credit is not an ironclad guarantee that the exchange will be available; it is more an expression of intent. Analysis of the country must also be performed in advance to determine the likelihood of exchange being available.

TRANSLATION AND ANALYSIS OF FOREIGN STATEMENTS

The basic objectives in analyzing foreign financial statements are the same as in domestic lending. The lender wishes to understand the nature of the customer's business activity so that he or she can determine that future cash flows will likely provide the funds to repay either short- or long-term loans. In addition, the lender wishes to understand the figures well enough to appraise the trends of the borrower, the character of the assets, and the actual or potential claims on the assets, so that a judgment as to risks can be made.

Statement translations involve both the selection of appropriate English words to describe the account captions, as well as the conversion of the foreign currency to dollars. Differences in practice exist in converting foreign currency values to dollars. Some banks feel that the figures should simply be left in the foreign currency. Others spread both the foreign currency and the equivalent dollar value at the date of the statement. Still others (especially those using a computer facility) convert all the figures to dollars at the rate existing on the date of the latest statement, including a recasting of historical information at the latest rate. Each lender will have to select an approach that suits his or her tastes.

The process of translating account captions from foreign statements is an area in which much work and study remain to be done by U.S. banks. Many commercial terms translate easily from one language to another, but the accounting conventions, legal significances, and underlying business practices vary substantially from one country to another, and no assumptions should be made. In all cases, comprehensive analyses of the anticipated cash flow must be performed to be satisfied that repayments of any loans will be forthcoming.

The global expansion of the large American accounting firms (the so-called Big Eight) is having a good influence on accounting conventions and practices in many countries. Several of the Big Eight firms publish worthwhile material explaining the translation of business financial statements in various foreign countries together with information on the local taxation and unusual business practices. However, there remains much to be done on translation of foreign bank state-

ments. It is not sufficient to assume that a foreign country cannot permit
one of its large banks to fail and therefore all analysis is superfluous.

The translation and analysis of foreign central bank statements is
probably a useful exercise. However, since the central bank of a country
is a government entity and its obligations are thereby directly or indirectly government obligations, the real analysis that must be pursued
is the country's holdings of gold and foreign exchange and the trends
of such holdings. Most central bank statements can be manipulated
with "mirrors"—capital can be raised at will with the infusion of local
government bonds, and bad assets can be switched to budget appropriations for other government entities, leaving the central bank in an
apparently strong condition. Thorough understanding of a central
bank's figures may provide some interesting information on the bank,
the government, and the monetary process, but, as indicated above,
repayment of foreign loans comes only from hard currencies.

In many foreign countries it is common for companies to have numerous subsidiaries which are not consolidated on the published financial statements. Too many bankers have been too timid in insisting
on all of the details of such statements. Such timidity seems to vary
directly with the size of the company or the strength of the country.
International lenders should insist on the same details from foreign
borrowers as expected from U.S. borrowers.

A problem can arise when a foreign bank asks an American bank
to lend to a foreign company with the guarantee of the foreign bank.
Frequently, the information supplied about the borrower is meager,
and the American bank is reluctant to insist on more detail. If the
foreign bank is large and apparently sophisticated in its lending, the
lack of detail might be excused. On the other hand, if the guarantor
is less sophisticated, the American bank probably should study the
credit fully and not hand the guarantor a bad piece of paper if the
American bank ultimately has to look to the guarantee.

As a summary comment, it should be noted that while the analysis
of the financial data of foreign borrowers requires special techniques
and efforts, this exercise is not an end in itself. The financial information
is also to be used to give the lender greater insight in appraising the
people with whom he or she is dealing and their managerial abilities.

COUNTRY RISK

Loans to a government or one of its official entities are essentially
a country risk.[2] Loans to the private sector also contain varying ele-

---

[2] Loans to a government or one of its official entities involve a differing legal risk,
sometimes referred to as "sovereign risk." Invariably, it is difficult or impossible to
sue a government without its permission, if at all. Therefore, analyses of country risks
are equally important for public and private sector loans.

ments of country risk. Few companies can operate completely independently of their environment, unless the borrower is a multinational concern with the ability to repay from external sources.

Analysis of country risk is usually classified as a combination of analysis of (*a*) economic risk, and (*b*) political risk. However, because of its unique importance, the analysis of the country's international liquidity should be given the status of a separate category.

Caution should be exercised in analyzing individual countries and arriving at final judgements on the acceptability of the composite of economic and political risk. Economic averages can be misleading as indicators of ability to repay. Norms for individual economic indicators cannot be applied to all countries. Each country analysis is a somewhat unique exercise to determine whether the economy seems to be functioning reasonably well, that the political mechanism seems to be in control, and that the trends suggest a continuance of reasonable performance and stability at least throughout the life of any proposed loans.[3]

Economic Risk

Any approach to analyzing a foreign country should be done with the warning firmly in mind that the statistical raw material is of varying quality and reliability. The development of statistics can be costly and budget priorities vary from country to country. Furthermore, definitions and statistical techniques are subject to varying opinions, and it cannot be assumed that an economic indicator used in one country is comparable to those in others. Perhaps the best source of information for that which it publishes is the International Monetary Fund (IMF). Regular visits by calling officers to borrowing countries should be used to corroborate the analysis of the country and to obtain additional data, if necessary, from government and (possibly) private sources.

Aside from the reliability of the statistical data, another concern of the country analyst is the fact that one country cannot be compared directly to others. For example, the economy of a developing country cannot be compared directly to the United States. In the United States most of the residents participate in the economy in varying ways, whereas perhaps one third of the population of a developing country does not participate at all in its measured economy, and the gradual absorption of that one third into some sector of the economy over a period of years will present a continually changing picture which can be a challenge to any analyst.

While retaining the caveats mentioned above in the forefront of

---

[3] See "Some Observations on Country Risk Analysis and Setting Country Limits," *The Bankers Magazine*, Fall 1977.

all analytical thought, it would seem that the following economic indicators would be the minimum to be observed for a period of at least five years:

1. Gross National Product
    a. Annual total of GNP.
    b. Annual percent change of actual GNP.
    c. Annual percent change of real GNP; i.e., adjusted for inflation.
    d. Real GNP per capital.
2. Industrial Production
    a. Index of level of industrial production.
    b. Annual percent change of industrial production index.
3. Population
    a. Total population,
    b. Rate of growth.
4. Employment
    a. Unemployment percentage.
    b. A comparison of agricultural and industrial employment to total population.
5. Wages
    a. Index of wage level.
    b. Annual percent change of wage index.
6. Money Supply
    a. Actual money supply.
    b. Rate of growth each year.
7. Inflation Indices
    a. Consumer price index.
    b. Annual percent change in consumer price index.
    c. Wholesale price index.
    d. Annual percent change in wholesale price index.
8. In addition to the above indicators, other that are special to a given economy should be monitored closely; for example, tourism, or mining production and world prices of the commodities mined, or production of agricultural items such as cocoa and its world price.

All of the above statistics give a basic indication of economic trends and potential pressures that might develop, particularly from excessive inflation. Economic trends can strongly affect political developments in a country. Poor economic performance might lead to substantial political change.

International Liquidity

The analysis of international liquidity is undoubtedly part of the economic analysis of any country, but as mentioned above, it is of such importance that special emphasis is warranted. Indeed a country might be quite stagnant in its economic growth, or have severe inflation, and yet manage its international liquidity so as to meet all external obligations quite readily.

Essentially, a country's international liquidity is its holdings of gold and hard foreign currencies. This can be augmented by its holdings of Special Drawing Rights of the International Monetary Fund and its Reserve Position in the Fund. Changes in the total holdings are created by (*a*) surpluses or deficits in the country's balance on current account (i.e., the difference between its imports and exports of goods and services), and (*b*) the net of all capital flows.

Considerable attention to all components of the balance of payments is warranted. Are imports increasing faster than exports? Is the country vulnerable to losing an important part of its exports in the world markets? Is tourism increasing or decreasing? Is the local political posture encouraging or discouraging tourism? Is the official rate of exchange for the country's currency encouraging imports and discouraging tourism or vice versa?

A country might suffer a continuing deficit in its balance of trade and make up the difference in capital flows; i.e., borrowings abroad and investments within the country by foreigners. This pattern might persist over some period of time. However, it is worth considering as a philosophical concept that *over a long period of time a country's balance of trade will be its balance of payments;* i.e., borrowings must be repaid or stabilized and investments must eventually create a reverse cash flow of repatriated earnings.

In viewing a country's international liquidity the primary question is: How much is enough? Unfortunately, countries do not publish balance sheets with a scheduling of all external debt maturities (public and private). Therefore, this analysis must be approached by viewing past history coupled with any fragmentary knowledge of the debt structure that the analyst can accumulate from various published sources, such as statistics in the *U.S. Treasury Bulletin,* announcements of large borrowings, data on inward capital flows (if given in adequate detail to be useful), and from information in occasional prospectuses for borrowings. To eliminate this effort, which can be much of a guessing game, it would be worthwhile if one of the organized professional groups of American bankers or the government undertook an annual survey of debt maturities by country for the mutual benefit of all lenders.

In viewing the historical data two ratios are usually used: (*a*) the number of months of reserves of gold and hard currencies in relation to annual imports, and (*b*) the debt service ratio; i.e., the annual requirements for debt amortization (principal and interest) of the public sector in relation to earnings from exports of goods and services. In viewing either ratio the trend is perhaps as important as the absolute level.

In the case of the number of months of reserves versus imports, a period of at least three to four months is desirable. However, individual countries seem to operate satisfactorily on lesser amounts. Some study of the actual nature of a country's reserves is useful in viewing this ratio, as its gold may be the backing for its currency, or there may be other restrictions on the allocation of foreign reserves.

The debt service ratio has no absolute level that is safe or bad for all countries. As a rule of thumb, 20 percent to 25 percent or more can be considered serious. However, each country must be analyzed as to its trends and its capacity for adjustment: Does it have access to temporary outside borrowings and can it control imports if necessary? Unfortunately, the details of the indebtedness of the private sector may be unknown, and any conclusions should be tempered by this lack of information.

Political Risk

While serious efforts are made by most international lenders to analyze the available economic data for a country, the analysis of political risk is more difficult as fewer quantitative indicators are available. Presumably, if a lender places funds in a country, he or she is satisfied with the government, its attitude toward debt, and its likely future administration of the country, whether it be a dictatorship or a government elected by the people. If it is a country with an elected government, trends in elections may point to a forthcoming change in leadership, such as occurred in 1970 when the Communists won the national elections in Chile. However, most election trends are difficult to analyze, if a trend should exist at all, and usually the information for lesser offices and off-year elections takes considerable effort to develop from outside the country. Additionally, the exact temperaments and goals of individual political parties and their leaders are often difficult for an outsider to appraise; the analysis of cultural and religious influences in politics can also be challenging.

In countries where dictatorships prevail and control is dependent on the army or police force, the question of succession is apt to be quite uncertain. Direct questioning about future control in such countries usually elicits the comment that the military is in firm control and undoubtedly will remain so—suggesting that little if any change can be expected. Despite such assurances for many years in Portugal, the death of Salazar in 1970 brought swift and unexpected changes.

The biggest danger of political change for a lender is the fear of mismanagement of the economic affairs of a country with the subsequent inability to pay its external indebtedness, or worse yet, the fear that a new government might be militant and unfriendly to the free world and expropriate externally owned assets and repudiate external indebtedness, such as did Russia in 1917 and Cuba in 1960.

As indicated above, close information on the political situations in foreign countries is difficult to develop. The news media, furthermore, tend to be shallow and sensational in their reporting, if they choose to report certain events at all. The only recourse that a lender has is to make serious efforts to obtain information within the country itself and to hope that unexpected internal and external pressures do not develop to cause an unpredictable and undesirable series of events.

LEGAL PROBLEMS

Domestic lenders operate within a framework of laws that are a part of their daily routine, and with which they usually feel fairly comfortable. When loans are made across national borders, none of the legal framework of the foreign country can be taken for granted. Each foreign country has its own system of laws with its own roots, such as the English law or the Napoleonic Code, or whatever. In translating any lending documents from one language to another it might be difficult or impossible to give exact translations. Words, commercial terms, and phrases may have unique and different legal significances in each country. At times it can seem nearly impossible to achieve a clear understanding of the legal circumstances surrounding an international loan. A lawsuit against a foreign company in an American court may produce nothing if the borrower's assets are in the foreign country.

Part of the solution to these legal impediments is to obtain competent legal counsel in both countries and to satisfy both with all documents and to have borrower and lender be aware of their rights and any potential problems. A second part of the solution is to deal only with borrowers of satisfactory reputation and credit standing. Like casualty insurance, it is desirable to have good legal counsel, but it is better not to have to rely on it.

Having accepted the underlying problem of the confusion of alien laws, a foreign lender is further confronted with two specific categories of legal problems: (*a*) laws imposed on American lenders by foreign countries, and (*b*) laws imposed on American lenders by their own country.

Foreign laws affecting American lenders are best identified with the assistance of local legal counsel. They may include the need to register to determine tax status (such as in Mexico), the need for borrowers to record the indebtedness with the government to ensure that the dollars will be made available for repayment, and very commonly the withholding of taxes on the interest paid on the loan (which *may* be recoverable from the lender's U.S. tax bill).

American laws affecting lending to foreign customers include primarily a formula limiting recovery on U.S. taxes of taxes withheld on interest abroad. There are also the usual percentage restrictions for legal limit loans and loans to the bank's own affiliates. At the present time, the U.S. government imposes reserve requirements on funds lent to a U.S. resident by the branch of a U.S. bank. The Interest Equalization Tax Act (P.L. 88–563) imposes no tax on foreign loans at the moment, but it did from 1963 to 1974 at varying rates, and tax rates may again be established on this standby authority if the government wishes to discourage foreign lending by Americans. From March 1965 to January 1974, the Voluntary Foreign Credit Restraint Program imposed quantitative limits on foreign loans made by U.S. banks with funds derived within the United States.

FOREIGN CURRENCY LOANS

At times U.S. banks might make a loan in a currency different from the currency used to fund the loan; for example, a Deutsche Mark loan made from funds secured as U.S. dollars or a Mexican peso loan funded with U.S. dollars. If a bank should exchange dollars for a foreign currency and use the foreign currency to make a loan, it has the option of selling in the foreign exchange future market the proceeds it expects to receive from collection of the loan. In the case of a Deutsche Mark loan funded with dollars the interest rate for Deutsche Marks would be lower (than the U.S. interest rate) in today's markets, and the bank would probably try to increase its yield from the spread between the current market/dollar exchange rate and that rate in the forward market. In the case of a Mexican peso loan funded with dollars, it would cost the bank x percent to sell the pesos forward. The bank may choose to cover the exchange risk or carry the exposure until the due date of the note.

In both of the cases described above there is an element of interest earned as well as a foreign exchange earning or cost. It is strongly suggested that all loan operations run a balanced position with the loans and the funding being in the same currency. If they are not, it is suggested that the loan department obtain an internal foreign exchange contract with its own foreign exchange desk at arm's length rates. This will sort out the true interest earned on the loan from the foreign exchange income or expense. It will also put the foreign currency exposure on the records of the exchange trading department where it can be carried without a cover, or hedged, depending on its trading authorities. Of importance is the consideration that the foreign exchange dealers will monitor any open positions constantly and be in a better position to take protective action than if the exposure is filed away somewhere in the loan records.[4]

At times foreign currency loans are offered at rates that are unattractive if the foreign exchange aspects are properly evaluated. The system of internal contracts, suggested above, should help to avoid improper pricing on this type of loan.

SYNDICATED LOANS AND BROKER PAPER

As international lending business expanded significantly in the late 1960s, credits tended to get larger, and borrowers sought to obtain larger individual loans rather than a number of small accommodations. Banks were also looking for more fee income. Syndication of loans provided that vehicle.

The best prospects for participating in large transactions would seem to be smaller banks that wish to be involved in international lending but do not have sufficient staff to cover all markets. In practice, however, the very large banks have routinely joined each other in large deals, and it may not yet be decided as to who was helping whom.

Syndicated loans have the characteristics and aspects of any other loan. However, an added feature is that the bank leading the syndicate has to form a group; i.e., sell participations. The technique of selling participations has not always been ideal, as it typically involves a phone call seeking an expression of interest—within a day or two, unless others should fully subscribe the offering. A brief sketch is usually offered over the phone with the promise of full details later if interest is indicated. On occasion the "full details" are not always so full, and pressure is exerted if the tentative participant wishes to withdraw. A basic implication is that the offering bank is well acquainted with the borrower and that this should add considerably to the feeling of comfort of all participants. However, banks that buy participations should fully satisfy themselves on all aspects of any credit before they buy. Furthermore, full disclosures and abundant information are for the mutual protection of buyer and seller, as there have been sizable lawsuits against leaders of syndicates on credits that were not paid, charging that inadequate disclosures were made on the initial offerings.

The compensation for participants in many syndicates has at times been too thin. If participants do not waver from the minimum interest rates required, the problem will correct itself—rates will rise to the proper level.

---

[4] See D. R. Mandich, ed., *Foreign Exchange Trading Techniques and Controls,* Washington, D.C., American Bankers Association, (1977), Chapter VII for a discussion of loans funded in a different currency.

Closely aligned to the banks that syndicate loans are the nonbank brokers which may be large, established underwriting firms or tiny one-person operations. As banks have become more and more active internationally, the list of nonbank brokers has diminished, but a number of active ones remain on the scene and seem to fill a needed role.

A caveat in dealing with brokers is that the buyer of any notes must know in advance the payee to whom the notes have been originally issued and who the endorsers were or will be. In the United States even a nonrecourse endorsement carries the guarantee that the note is genuine and that the parties executing it have the capacity to do so. If a broker should appear as the last endorser, the buyer of the paper would be well advised to check the credit standing and the amount of capital of the broker. If the capital is not sizable, it would be better to have the notes reissued and delivered directly to the buying bank. This may make it difficult for the broker to obtain the desired commission, if he or she expects to obtain a profit from the lowering of the effective interest rate at the time of resale. Therefore, the verification of the signatures on the note by a commercial bank may be offered. If an error should be made in such verifications, however, the responsibility of the verifying bank is questionable.

MATURITIES OF LOANS

Until the mid-1960s international lending was primarily short term, up to six months or a year, and primarily for the movement of goods. Occasionally, a lender might grant an outright loan for as long as five years, but only as an exception and for good compensation. Grace periods were typically a year or 18 months at the most. The term of financing was tied to traditional reasoning; e.g., if the borrower was importing trucks, the loan would not be for more than three or four years, the useful life of the equipment on the foreign roads. Competition, and possibly a reach for earnings, caused maturities to lengthen during the early 1970s to 12 years with grace periods as long as 6 years. (Certainly this reflected a departure from domestic lending standards where term loans of eight to ten years were the outside limit.) The lengthening of terms tended to ignore the underlying use of the funds and to look more at the country's overall balance of payments data, the merits of which can be supported by some good arguments when loans are to government entities.

The recession year of 1975 was accompanied by generally more conservative attitudes, and international loan maturities contracted to a maximum of five years. Since mid-1976 maturities have begun to lengthen.

The principal justification for long-term loans seemed to be because interest rates were typically adjusted every six months, and therefore there was no rate risk. Obviously, this ignores the question of credit risk and the question of the role of a commercial bank and the need for liquidity in its assets. The long-term bond market for international borrowings is not large or well structured. Consequently, borrowers seeking longer maturities have found themselves dealing mainly with their banks and often inviting them to bid against each other for transactions. Bidding arrangements may not develop the close relationships that are of mutual interest to the lender and the borrower. The experiences of the early 1970s have shown that customer loyalty cannot be purchased with the longest loan maturities, nor can the loyalty of lenders be gained by paying the lowest tolerable interest rates.

FUNDING

The funding of international loans can come from domestic or foreign sources, such as Eurodollars. Until 1965, when the United States placed restrictions on lending abroad, most foreign loans were financed with domestic funds. Since 1965, the proportion of offshore financing (mainly Eurodollars) increased rapidly and now provides a substantial majority of the funding.

In the 1960s, particularly the early part of the decade, there was concern that the Eurodollar market was too new and uncertain to guarantee funding for longer term loans. It was then used as a source for shorter loans mainly, and foreign banks obtained standby commitments from American banks to insure availability of dollars over longer periods to back the funding for their longer term loans. Today it appears as if the Eurodollar market is "here to stay." It has great size, efficiency, and apparent stability.

At times the relative costs of funds in the U.S. market and the Eurodollar market is almost identical; at other times there can be a wide variance. Certain borrowers will tend to swing from one market to the other to save borrowing costs, which can be inconvenient to U.S. lenders, but it can also provide opportunities to the same lenders for cheaper funding at times.

INTEREST RATES

During the two decades (1955 to the present) of the growth of international lending among U.S. banks, the industry changed from fixed interest rates with wide spreads to floating rates (tied to the U.S. prime rate or the cost of Eurodollars with changes no less often than each six months) with narrow spreads. As recently as the mid-1960s, spreads over the cost of money were typically a minimum of 2 percent for short- or long-term loans, and spreads of even 4 percent were very common.

In the late 1960s spreads moved down to as low as 0.625 percent to 0.75 percent, and more than a few term loans were booked as low as 0.375 percent and even 0.125 percent. The rationale for the lower rates was the pressure of competition. However, during the same period many banks increased their loans and deposits by increasing their ratios of deposits to capital and also introducing capital notes on their balance sheets. It would seem that stockholders should have benefited from the increased leverage rather than borrowers, as stockholders assume all of the risk of loss if any of the assets introduced by higher leverage should be charged off.

If the reader would create a theoretical bank with only international loans, purchased deposits, stockholders' equity, and *no operating expenses except interest,* a trial and error computation would reflect that a spread of 1.5 percent over the cost of money (and over the costs of any required cash reserves) is the absolute minimum needed to produce a 12.5 percent return on capital after taxes.[5] However, every bank has some operating expenses, and the minimum spread should be approximately 1.75 percent. (This should reflect total compensation, including the effect of any free deposit balances).

COUNTRY LIMITS

With the emergence of concern for bank capital adequacy since 1974, the related question of concentrations of international loans and country limits has become topical. The questions basically are: Should there be a portfolio limit for a given country related to a percentage of a bank's capital (including or excluding capital notes)? Should there be sublimits within the country limit for loans to the public and private sector? and should there be limits on the amount of term lending? Although it theoretically might be desirable, an American bank ordinarily does not concern itself with a country limit for the United States, since a majority of its assets *and* liabilities are domestic.

The optimum size of any country limit is a matter of judgment and is difficult to quantify. Decisions of management of one bank might leave another totally uncomfortable. Despite the difficulties, however, it would seem that every bank should have *written* country limits approved by a designated member of management, or better yet by an executive committee or an asset—liability management committee.

---

[5] See "International Loans: Profit Center or Loss Leader," *Journal of Commercial Bank Lending,* September 1972.

A bank management really cannot claim that limits are too complex to be set in exact terms; in such a case the policy is obviously one of having no limits.

Thus far no rule of thumb exists as to whether a bank should commit an amount equal to 10 percent, 50 percent, or 100 percent or more of its capital in a single foreign country. A practical consideration is whether, after tax considerations, a bank would care to lose as much as a year's earnings, or more, if unexpected developments should occur too quickly in a foreign country to reduce the total exposure significantly. Even in a highly developed country which appears to be quite stable, it is often very difficult to detect gradual changes in the economic or political structure that would prompt a reduction in country exposure. For example, in the 1950s the strength of the U.S. dollar was undoubted—"paper gold" it was called. Yet by the end of the next decade it was under severe pressure and would soon devalue. In retrospect the signs of deterioration were quite obvious.

The good is often the familiar, and as we do business in countries over a period of time we are apt to gain confidence and possibly cease to probe deeply enough for weaknesses; and if indeed weaknesses are detected and diagnosed as severe, when is the time to have the courage of one's convictions and begin the withdrawal process? Experience has shown that, if a lender waits until the moment of crisis to seek a reduction in loans, it is usually impossible to achieve reductions in significant amounts. On the other hand, there is the risk that the problems are apt to be temporary with substantial correction forthcoming, and suspension of business in that country might later be regretted.

Each bank management should meet the problem of establishing specific country guidelines in dollars and should do so in writing; this exercise is probably the real value of having guidelines, even though universal, quantitative formulas cannot be developed. Guidelines should be reviewed at least annually for the more stable countries and perhaps more often for problem areas or for areas where the bank has a sizable commitment. As to the size of guidelines, the only answer appears to be the size that makes a bank's management feel comfortable, and the size that seems prudent for that bank. The total guideline for each country should include amounts for short- and long-term accommodations and specific strategies, such as perhaps letting term loans run off in a country that seems headed for problems.

CONCLUSION

At the outset it was stated that the fundamentals of credit analysis should be applied just as vigorously to international credits as to domestic credits. The material covered in the chapter summarizes the special aspects of international lending[6] which might suggest that the international lending must be approached differently from domestic credits. However, international credit analyses need not be approached differently, but should receive more care, and the analysis should be more thorough to cover the special *additional* aspects of international lending.

---

[6] See F. John Mathis, ed., *Offshore Lending by U.S. Commercial Banks,* New York and Philadelphia: Bankers Association for Foreign Trade and Robert Morris Associates, 1975).

SECTION X

RETAIL BANKING

Chapter 62

The Function of Retail Banking

*A. Gordon Oliver**

This chapter's primary purpose will be to examine the areas of organization and management in banks to ensure profitable delivery of consumer banking services. First, however, a crucial question: Is serving the retail customer desirable and essential for every bank, and if so, what is required to do the job well? These questions should be answered before even thinking about the organization and management requirements of retail banking—serving the consumer.

Many banks have chosen not to compete for the retail business. Because of the complexities of the function, the increased costs associated with staffing and equipment, and increasingly cumbersome regulations and legislation affecting retail banking, many banks today are limiting their retail activity and, in fact, some have indicated almost complete withdrawal from consumer banking. This step does not mean that such banks will not prosper.

On the other hand, studies such as Booz, Allen and Hamilton's "The Challenge Ahead for Banking" (1975) indicate that through this decade and into the next, commercial banks can expect the greatest growth in both the source of funds (deposits) and the use of funds (loans) to be from consumers. Therefore, a bank must carefully weigh the positive and negative aspects of competing for consumer business. If, after doing so, a bank believes that it wants to participate in the retail arena for deposit growth, then the next step is to take a close look at the environment in which it will be competing.

* Executive Vice President, The Citizens and Southern National Bank, Augusta, Georgia.

THE ENVIRONMENT

The environment of retail banking is changing. Competition for the retail customer is much keener today than it was even five years ago and is increasing daily. Particularly as nonbank financial institutions obtain broader powers, it is more difficult to attract and hold the consumer to one institution. Savings and loan associations, other thrift institutions, credit unions, and retail merchants are gaining opportunities to offer near checking accounts, consumer loans, charge cards, and debit cards.

At the same time, costs for delivering retail services in the traditional manner through full-service offices are increasing at a rapid rate. Often the new competition brings with it pressures on prices for the service bearing no relationship to the costs of delivering those services. Legislation and regulation pushed by "consumer representatives" make the legal environment much more difficult to deal with and help push the costs of serving the consumer even higher.

In addition, consumer attitudes change quickly as a result of economic events such as swings in unemployment and inflation. Also, basic attitudes change over the long term. An example of the latter is that, in the past, Americans as a whole have historically been very optimistic about the future. That is, a very large part of the people believed that, with passage of time, their economic and social position would improve. Studies today show a dramatic decrease in the percentage of people who have this optimism about the future and a corresponding increase in those who are pessimistic. Another example is the declining level of confidence in business generally. The significant point is, immediate decisions must be made against this background of changing general attitudes. An understanding of the shifts in consumer attitudes, both over the long term as well as reactions to current phenomenon, is important to attracting and holding retail customers.

Technological developments and the acceptance of those technological changes also must be plugged into the total equation of evaluating consumer banking. All bankers are familiar with the developments of electronic funds transfer such as automatic teller machines and point of sale terminals, as well as the arguments for and against implementing such new techniques and technology. Unquestionably, however, these developments are having a big impact on banking today, particularly on the retail sector. An understanding of these developments—permitting knowledgeable decisions based on cost, acceptance by the consumer and demand by the customer—is absolutely necessary to compete for the attention of the retail customer, and at the same time maintain delivery of services with a price/cost spread that will allow profitable growth.

ORGANIZATIONAL CONSIDERATIONS

Organization for successful retail banking depends on many varied factors. Among those factors are experience, commitment and market penetration in the retail area. If the bank has had a significant share of its retail market for a long time, its opportunities, limitations, and even profitability requirements are different from those affecting a bank making a new decision to enter the retail market. For example, the bank with a significant branch system serving the retail public has problems and opportunities much different from those of a whole-sale bank desiring to enter the retail field. The local environment (bank and nonbank competition), state and federal laws, and regulations have great bearing on opportunities as well as on the marketing methods that can be successfully employed.

There are obviously different opportunities and problems which require vastly different organizational structures for branch systems, holding company banks, and unit banks. Each structure has unique advantages and disadvantages in the retail banking area, but certainly the legal structure has great bearing on the organizational structure of retail banking within the institution. Branch banking permits the establishment of service delivery units convenient to customers but requires a more extensive management structure than unit banking. On the other hand, unit banking on the retail side can probably be more easily controlled in delivering service in a more standard and uniform manner. The unit bank, in penetrating a larger market that extends beyond its immediate trading area has to rely more on mass-marketing techniques.

There is no one system that works best for all institutions, but in larger organizations, the likelihood is greater that certain functions within the retail organization will be considered "staff" to support the "direct line" functions of serving the customer. For example, large branching or holding company bank organizations usually have central-ized staff marketing, personnel and planning functions that may or may not directly report through the line management chain.

The purpose here is not to develop an ideal organizational chart that will work for all institutions—which is impossible—but rather to discuss the broad functions that must be managed in any retail banking organization regardless of size and structure. These functions include: (1) planning, (2) knowing what it costs, (3) knowing the market, (4) selecting and delivering services, (5) marketing, (6) personnel adminis-tration, (7) monitoring, (8) keeping abreast of legal requirements, and (9) interacting with other departments and functions of the bank.

PLANNING FOR PROFITABILITY

Planning in the retail sector includes determining the long-term objectives of retail banking, how these fit in with the total objectives of the bank, and establishing short-term objectives with a plan for accomplishing them. For example, a projection of the environment in which a bank operates for three to five years permits a more direct and successful approach, immediately and over time. With the complicated, competitive environment which exists today, it is increasingly difficult to remain profitable if a bank simply "wants" to do more business with more customers next year than it did last; or if it "wants" to sell more checking accounts next quarter than in the last quarter. A simple objective to increase deposits each year by 10 percent (or some other number) without an analysis of projected growth in employment for the area, economic forecasts, and competition, may give a goal to shoot for, but it will not provide the knowledge necessary to design a plan for achieving those goals.

KNOWING WHAT IT COSTS

Much too little is known about costs in retail banking. Even though both large and small banks deal in transactions of small denominations on the deposit and lending sides of the bank, methods have not been developed for accurately determining the processing costs associated with the delivery of most service. However, as competition grows, an understanding of the fundamental costs for determining whether to offer or continue a particular service is essential.

Few banks know how much it costs to prepare a checking account statement, pay a check, or process a loan payment—all of which are basic banking functions. On the other hand, expenses are increasing and competitive factors and/or legal restrictions inhibit the ability to increase prices. Consequently there is an obvious cost/price squeeze. And, of course, having an accounting staff to determine costs in itself adds to cost.

Closely associated with the analysis of costs of processing is the analysis of total costs of service delivery and profitability. Traditionally retail banking services have been offered through "full-service" offices whether the bank is a unit bank, holding company affiliate, or branch bank. The cost of bricks and mortar, equipment and staffing for "full-service" banking, together with the changing desires of the customer, raise doubt as to the need for that type facility to serve the public now or in the future. Limited service facilities should be considered. For example, free standing automatic teller machines, mini-branches with automated equipment and limited staff, money shops, or personal loan offices from storefront operations may be a part of the answer, particularly for delivering services in new markets. The important question is not necessarily, where is a new complete "full-service" bank or branch office needed, but how can desirable and needed retail banking services be taken to a particular group of customers in the most convenient, inexpensive, and acceptable way?

Costs are obviously an important factor in selecting a method of serving the customers. Perhaps even more important, however, are the attitudes of the people in the local community. Markets are vastly different. What is acceptable—perhaps even demanded—in a large city may be entirely unacceptable in a rural community. One market may put a tremendous premium on time and efficiency, permitting the rapid development and use of automatic teller machines, while another market may put a greater premium on personal service, making electronic funds transfer (EFT) services unacceptable.

To compete successfully in the retail environment, long-term objectives should be clearly outlined so that short-term planning, generally on the basis of one year at a time, can be fit to those long-term objectives. Knowledge of costs—both processing costs as well as costs of service delivery facilities—provides the background for intelligent decisions in reaching those objectives. Such planning also gives a frame of reference for making immediate decisions in reacting to competition in price, offering new services, or discontinuing services that are not profitable.

KNOWING THE MARKET

As already noted, attitudes of consumers change over time. To make matters more complicated, the desires, aspirations, and needs of the various groups within a market are not all the same nor do they remain static. The financial needs of young married people are vastly different from those of a retired couple. The needs and desires of an executive in a high-income bracket are not the same as those of a blue-collar worker. Some understanding of the various factors within the market the bank is trying to serve is imperative. Certainly in the planning process, this understanding is required even to determine which segments of the community can produce the kind of retail business that is desirable and that can be attracted on a profitable basis, and the services that are required in order to attract that business.

Banking has been slow to utilize sophisticated market research techniques when compared to other industry groups. But, today the more aggressive banks recognize market research as a critical function to successful competition in the modern environment. Larger financial institutions conduct extensive market research in an attempt to answer questions about customers and prospects. Market research can be elaborate and expensive, but meaningful information can also be obtained simply and inexpensively. There are numerous firms today specializing in bank research and larger banking units have developed very sophisticated market research staffs. Consequently, smaller banks can look to correspondent banks for systems and assistance in making decisions within their marketing environment.

Knowledge of the desires, demands, and attitudes of the various segments of consumer groups is not sufficient. In addition, knowledge of the competition—commercial banks, thrift institutions, credit unions, and other financial institutions, their structures, long-term goals and objectives, and methods of competition—are also important ingredients for successful decision making. A well-thought-out plan for measuring these various elements of the market, presently and over time, is essential.

WHAT RETAIL SERVICES SHOULD BE OFFERED

Traditionally banks offered deposit and loan services to customers; but today, a vast array of new services such as direct deposit of payroll, electronic funds transfer, and individual retirement accounts are coming on the scene. What services are attractive to the retail customer? Can a commercial bank, if its major objective is to attract consumer deposits, do so without offering consumer loans, real estate mortgages, and charge cards? The list of retail banking services that are available in various commercial banks today would be extremely long.

Can any one bank expect to offer every conceivable service that would be attractive to at least some segment of the market? Perhaps the very large banks on the West Coast or in New York can, but most banks will have to be selective if they expect to remain profitable. The other side of that proposition is: What basic services are absolutely necessary to attract a depositing customer? Then, what additional services can be offered which will get sufficient acceptance to justify the additional services as profit producers for the bank? Other than the very basic consumer banking services such as checking accounts, savings accounts, and consumer loans, the answer to the question of what services to offer varies with each bank.

Banking is replete with examples of the "domino" theory. That is, when one bank offers a particular service, a competitor automatically feels that it must offer that service without considering whether it can do so profitably. For example, with the introduction of the "service package," the idea immediately swept the banking industry—without good projections by individual banks of what the combination of services would do in penetrating the market, increasing income, increasing costs, or if, in fact, it would even be favorably received by the customers and prospects.

With the introduction of electronic funds transfer and the various services related to it such as automatic teller machines and point of sale terminals, a very thorough analysis is even more important than would be the case in just adding another type of savings instrument. The front-end investment as well as the ongoing costs for such services are great. Consequently, the risk of the wrong decision has much greater impact on the success of the bank.

MARKETING ACTIVITIES

Although many banks, large and small, have a specific marketing staff or marketing director, everything done in banking is marketing. Product development, pricing, projecting profitability, selling depository services, selling loans, advertising and promotion, public relations efforts, all are related to marketing. Whether the formal function is performed by a staff or by the president of the bank, the important thing is to recognize that marketing goes on all the time in almost every function performed in a bank—even collecting past dues and handling complaints.

Public relations is such an important part of retail banking that this responsibility should also be considered in the organization structure. Every employee and officer is involved in public relations in everything that he or she does; the image of the bank to its various publics is too important to leave to chance. Research can be a vital tool in measuring public attitudes and the needs to be addressed. Without specific responsibility assigned for the public relations effort, the messages to the various publics will lack consistency and will not project the best impression of the bank to the public.

PERSONNEL FUNCTION

In the complex competitive environment of today, professionals with sound training and experience are essential. Selecting the right people for retail banking is just the beginning.

Because of turnover, as well as the constant need for increased knowledge, there are continuing training and educational needs. Many banks have specialized departments for working with all areas of the bank in designing and conducting training programs to improve and update the effectiveness of the staff. There are also a great number of educational opportunities through the various banking organizations as well as correspondent banks to supplement a small bank's training effort. The individual bank should assess the level of knowledge of its consumer banking personnel, determine its training requirements, and seek specific solutions to specific needs.

In their retail organizations, many banks have gone to "personal banker programs," assigning responsibility and accountability to specific "personal bankers" for handling all the banking needs for specific customers or groups of customers. Planning for personal performance (i.e., setting and assigning goals, motivating, measuring results, and in short, managing performance) are just as important in the retail banking sector as in any other area of the bank.

Communication is an important ingredient of the personnel administration function. Larger banks develop policy manuals, operating guides, and newsletters for making sure that organizational policies and procedures are understood. Some system for communicating policies, procedures, and changes in regulations through the various levels in management is vital. The people dealing with the public day-to-day have a "need to know."

MONITORING EFFORTS

To effectively manage consumer banking efforts, management must have feedback. It needs feedback on: (1) how services are received by the consumer, (2) whether management policies are being carried out, (3) whether the attitudes outlined in policy are being conveyed to the consumer, (4) how its programs contrast with the competition, (5) whether credits are properly administered and documented, and (6) how its customers perceive that they are being treated. This list could be extended on and on, but the point is that management must have sources for knowing what is really going on between its customer contact people and the public.

Perhaps the most effective method is still that of being available, on the banking floor, interacting with customers and bank personnel. That's not always possible so other methods may be needed. Various tools of market research can be used to gain vital feedback, such as shopping or attitudinal surveys. Through such methods, valuable insight can be gained into how the bank and its staff are perceived from the customer's viewpoint in simple day-to-day transactions. In addition, operational and credit audits furnish an immense amount of information about how business is being conducted.

Effective methods for knowing how management policies are being carried out and how service delivery compares to the competition are absolutely necessary in competing in the consumer market.

THE LEGAL ENVIRONMENT

The complexity of the laws and regulations affecting consumer banking has already been mentioned. Increasingly, the need to keep abreast of changes in laws and regulations, the task of interpreting the changes, and effectively implementing the necessary requirements are essential to consumer banking. The penalties for not doing so are great, both competitively and legally.

This is not to suggest that every bank needs a legal staff but it does suggest that the organization, through its attorneys, its correspondent banks, its trade associations, and regulators must provide the facility for knowing the legal and regulatory requirements and implementing change.

Until the last few years, this was a relatively simple task. With the advent of such things as Regulation Z, the Fair Credit Billing Act, and Equal Credit Opportunity Act, the regulation of consumer banking is becoming progressively more costly and complicated. Certainly it is an area that cannot be ignored by the organization competing in the consumer market.

CONCEPTS IN RETAIL MANAGEMENT

In determining what management organization will work best for any individual institution, many factors must be taken into consideration. The historical involvement in retail banking and the legal structure permitted, such as statewide branching versus unit banks or holding company banks, have been mentioned. Based on the individual set of circumstances, different management concepts have been applied successfully by different organizations. It would be well to discuss just a few of the more recent concepts of organization for managing and motivating toward desired performance in retail banking.

Profit Center Concept. The profit center concept is usually applied to a line unit within the organization such as a branch bank or a personal banking unit. Generally the unit will have its own profit and loss statement and the performance of the unit is measured to a great extent on profit performance. The concept has the advantage of being profit oriented in the delivery of services to the customer. Carried to the extreme, it can have the disadvantage of detracting from good customer service, particularly in the delivery of individual services that, while important to the total mix of retail banking services, may not be big profit producers. The accounting system necessary for providing profit center income and expense information may also be very expensive except for large banks which can spread the costs over larger systems. Even then, profitability of a branch or unit may be difficult to define because of factors such as the availability of loan demand, or internal transfer rates or pricing which may be beyond the control of the profit center manager.

Production Center Concept.   This concept recognizes that many elements affecting profitability of a retail banking unit are outside the control of the unit manager and puts the emphasis more on sales production. The concept gives more weight to the numbers and amounts of loans produced, the numbers and balances of checking and savings accounts generated, and the number of customers attracted to the bank for any service as opposed to the overall profitability of the unit.

Product or Service Manager Concept.   The concept of product or service management has been developed for many years in commercial banking but is gaining more acceptance in the retail area. Product managers in the retail area are generally managers for a group of related retail banking services or managers for a particularly large single service. For example, a product manager may have responsibility for consumer lending, electronic funds transfer, time deposits, or depository services, including time and demand deposits and related services such as travelers checks, safe deposit services, and money orders. Generally, the responsibility of the retail product manager is very broad and may include: (1) product development, (2) updating services, (3) costing and setting prices, (4) marketing, (5) establishing and monitoring credit policies, (6) keeping abreast of and interpreting regulatory and legal requirements, and (7) training the staff to deliver the particular service or group of services. Such product specialists are generally organized into staff functions. They can provide an effective method of focusing attention on the specific services and keeping up with the necessary changes in services to make them competitive and successful.

INTERACTION WITH THE BANK AS A WHOLE

The policies and practices of the retail banking area, to be most effective, must be consistent with the policies of the corporate area, the operations and data processing functions, as well as other areas such as the trust department. There is an opportunity to trade on the goodwill of one area to the benefit of the other, but in order to make the most use of that goodwill, there is a need for good communications and coordination of policies and practices for dealing with customers day to day.

CONCLUSION

The retail banking environment—the consumer market, the competition, the services, the regulations—are increasingly complex and present challenging opportunities for the future. To attract successfully and profitably service consumer business will require more knowledgeable management in the future than in the past.

Each bank has particular circumstances that affect its opportunities and organizational needs such as its market penetration, size, corporate structure, competition, and local regulations. Regardless of the peculiarities of the specific environment, knowing the market, knowing the costs, planning what services to offer at what price and to whom, will be even more important in the future to compete for profitable retail business.

If bank management believes that consumer deposits are important to the bank's future, then management must have a strong commitment to finding ways of serving efficiently the financial needs of the consumer. Keeping up with these changes in the next few years will keep even the most imaginative bankers on their toes.

Chapter 63 _____

Development, Pricing, and Merchandising—Retail Banking Services

*Robert M. Freeman**
Alexander B. Berry III†

INTRODUCTION

This chapter assesses pricing and merchandising strategies for new retail products and services at both the evaluation and implementation stages.[1] It also suggests criteria for evaluating the effectiveness of existing product lines. The need for these strategies and a disciplined method of applying them are mandated by these considerations.

The emergence and expansion of an electronic banking mode probably will standardize and make routine the character and delivery of many existing consumer services.

It also is evident that commercial banking will lose its virtual monopoly with respect to funds transfers—checking accounts—and probably will pay customers' interest on these funds. Implicit in this development will be the surrendering of our claim as the only *full-service* institutions for individuals and families.

Facing the banking industry, we believe, will be an operating environment in the retail field characterized by:

_____

* Senior Executive Vice President, Bank of Virginia, Richmond, Virginia.

† Senior Vice President, Bank of Virginia, Richmond, Virginia.

[1] The authors are especially grateful to Philip W. Hughes, Assistant Vice President of Bank of Virginia Company, for his assistance in preparing this chapter.

1. *More competition.*
2. *From more competitors,* including ones such as the large retail stores that traditionally have not been considered competitors.
3. *Armed with more banklike powers.*

In this emerging new environment, the ability to compete successfully will necessitate ever-increasing concern for:

1. Realistic and competitive cost-price structures.
2. Evaluation procedures that link product lines and service techniques to understood organizational objectives.
3. Implementation techniques that effectively merchandise retail product lines in a manner that stresses institutional distinctiveness.
4. Product and service compatability with existing and projected manned and machine-based distribution systems.

THE CUSTOMER AND IDEAS: WHERE IT ALL STARTS

The subject of this chapter, properly enough, is *the customer.* It is the marketplace. It is the consumer's perceived wants and needs and a commercial bank's ability to design, implement, and monitor product lines that satisfy them at a profit. Profitability is the result of serving customers well—efficiently, at their convenience, and fairly.

Performance, however, does not begin when a product is sold. Rather, the starting point is the idea, that inspiration to create new programs or improve old methods.

A primary source of ideas is a bank's own people, officers, and staff alike. Indeed, in the retail area an idea expressed by a teller often proves more valuable than one suggested by a ranking executive, if only because the teller or new account clerk deals most closely with customers.

While obvious, this source too frequently is overlooked. The same is true of the customer in his or her contact with bank staff members.

Our point is that the first step in new product development must be both an awareness of where ideas come from, the many sources of innovation and fresh thought, *and* a working method for directing ideas to where they can be acted on. In this sense, product development should be an integral part of an organization's management philosophy. It follows that the administration of product development must be given a high priority in a bank's managerial scheme, with specific responsibility for accomplishing this task assigned to a senior staff officer.

Another major source of ideas is the competition, whether it is the bank or thrift institution down the street or an organization completely outside of banking. Clearly implied is that the essence of product development is an awareness of what is happening today, even what most reasonably may happen tomorrow. It is being alert to change.

Finally, it should be emphasized that not all ideas are good ones, and not all good ideas are good for one's organization. Some can create more problems than profits and disturb rather than satisfy customers. For this reason, product development involves the *equally* difficult discipline of saying, "no." This honest discipline, moreover, needs to be built into each stage of product development; it must be visible as the idea moves from notion to fleshed-out concept and then to the two distinct stages with which this chapter chiefly is concerned: the *evaluation stage* and the *implementation stage.*

PRODUCT EVALUATION

Evaluation means just that. It involves raising questions and obtaining satisfactory answers. Its conclusion is the yes or no decision to proceed with implementation. The most vital questions are these:

Is the product consistent with the bank's objectives, with where it is now, and where it wants to be at some point in the future?

Consistency requires the comparison of product concept and corporate objectives. For example, if a bank is committed to an expansion of automated delivery systems for its retail product lines, product concepts requiring extensive manual processing could be out of step with understood priorities, perhaps even in conflict with them.

Similarly, a product concept should be evaluated for its effect on an organization's current product mix. To be determined is whether the product will prove complementary or will weaken the product mix, and whether it will replace not one but several current lines. Then, too, it should be determined whether the product inherently can be a device for cross-selling, or for laying a groundwork for products *likely* to evolve given predictable changes in tomorrow's operating environment. A word of caution. A bank can make its product mix too broad; it can create so many products that it minimizes the effective selling of any one product.

Is the product consistent with customer attitudes and expectations?

Over a period of years, customers tend to form well-defined attitudes toward *their* bank. For example, a bank that traditionally has pioneered in the consumer services area is expected to remain at the leading edge of change and to maintain a highly visible retail orientation. To be considered, therefore, is whether a product enhances this image or reputation as well as whether maintaining this image is consistent with longer term corporate objectives. Said differently, product concepts should have an understood present and future that fits both corporate and customer expectations.

Extensive external and internal research will be required to develop satisfactory answers to this question. Most important, the targeted sales (volume) potential indicates promotional strategy, and suggests acceptable price ranges. It immediately installs a bottom-line orientation.

External research can be conducted either by an outside firm or by a bank's own research department. Internal research need not be as extensive, nor even conducted in a scientific manner using a statistically valid market sample. But it should not be overlooked; too often, unfortunately, it is. Opinions of bank employees in line capacities who have continuing contact with customer groups likely to use a new product are essential to the framing of valid decisions regarding customer acceptance and distribution methodology. External and internal research results need to be compared to identify areas of agreement *and* disagreement.

Adequate research in the evaluation stage also yields information that later may be utilized to define or refine a new product's distinctive features.

Will the product meet internal tests such as legality, operations and systems feasibility, and profitability requirements?
Legality tests apply not only to the product concept, but also to projected means for promoting and delivering it. Legality recognizes compliance with existing law and regulation as well as *reasonable* consumer expectations concerning disclosure and fair treatment.

Early in the evaluation stage, operations and systems personnel should develop a flowchart identifying and integrating the various procedures linked to product introduction. This is a basic step, of course. But it must be complete, comprehensive, and should embrace people and equipment. A bank usually will develop a master flowchart and then additional subordinate flowcharts reflecting departmental responsibilities and areas of integration. Accordingly, operations and systems and marketing each would develop a flowchart depicting their respective activities in minute detail. Key decision points in turn would be integrated into the master chart. A decision point, and there need not be too many of them, occurs when a major and usually a costly step is taken; for example, committing to computer programming or involving the advertising agency.

Cost analysis should be assigned to each element; for example, computer time and programming, customer contact staff education and training, supervisory training, procedural and customer forms, and so on. Additional labor force and machine needs, tentative though they may be, should be identified and subjected to cost estimation. Potential duplication or conflict with other products or processes should be perceived and costed; particularly, all applications involving computer technology should be surveyed to determine whether a new product can be integrated easily or whether expensive modifications will be required. Equally, does the product concept blend with *anticipated* future systems and processing changes.

For all intents and purposes, the flowchart is a checklist. Cited are all the areas of day-to-day operational activity that the product concept will affect in the developmental stages and when it becomes a part of the bank's normal range of services. This cost of the activity is determined; costs are translated into dollars, including dollars that might be expensed immediately or amortized (automatic teller machines, for example) over a period of time. Bear in mind that these are estimates only. However, experience suggests that more than one *unsuccessful* product would have failed the evaluation stage testing if the *total* accounting for people, machine, and procedures were handled systematically and at an early period.

Finally, profitability projections are required. What a product will cost must be evaluated against what it might produce, chiefly in dollar terms but also with respect to such intangibles as corporate image, cross-sell inducement, and so on. Image, in part at least, refers to how a bank and its product line are perceived in the marketplace and reflects such characteristics as quality. True, this characteristic is difficult to define and measure but it is important in creating that vital distinctive difference.

Initial market research, as noted, should indicate acceptable price levels for the product and reasonable projections regarding sales volume. Income estimates, what it earns less what it costs, should cover a defined inception period and possibly the first several years of a product's life. The concern is not only with how much income a successful product ultimately will produce, but the point in time at which it will have paid for itself and recovered start-up expenditures. As a general rule, the longer that *time* is stretched out, the less likely it will be that profits can be maximized; as well, the more likely it is that new external forces (competition, technological advances, just simply change) will intervene to minimize product performance and profitability.

Profitability projections also should include the cost of not doing business. It is possible that the failure to offer a product that can't be cost justified in its own right will lead customers to another competitor, thereby causing a bank to surrender profits from other existing products and services. Free checking commonly is cited as a "loss leader." So are safe deposit facilities. Nonetheless, the "loss leader" must be carefully evaluated if the best possible decision is to be made, and "giving away the bank" avoided. There is a subtle yet critical difference between just responding to competition and remaining competitive.

Interrelated is the cost of being too successful with a new product, especially in the early weeks and months following its introduction. Euphoria can lead to program expansion at the expense of other activities. Looked on differently, too much of a good thing can distort portfolio balance. For example, a too successful residential mortgage lending program could lock up too many dollars for an unnecessarily lengthy period of time. In the case of a product aimed specifically at a market *segment,* quick and unexpected success can lead to market enlargement along lines best characterized as uncoordinated and undisciplined, and possibly with adverse consequences. Simply said, it is not always true that what works for ten customers will work for a hundred or a thousand. Accordingly, marketing goals should be defined clearly and well understood; then, adhere to them.

The final set of questions raised in the evaluation stage focuses on the external environment:

> *What effect, if any, will the product have on your bank and non-bank competitors? How are they likely to respond?*
>
> *In the case of a holding company, will the product compete with the activities of bank-related units, and to what effect?*
>
> *Do product sales and income projections correlate with economic forecasts and trends?*
>
> *Does the product satisfy or conflict with consumerist perceptions regarding quality or fairness; interrelated, could it be victimized by regulatory constraints or, for the same reason, become more costly to administer?*

The evaluation stage generally closes with a report to management synthesizing the foregoing considerations and containing a precise recommendation that the product concept is poor, fair, or excellent. This seems a simple step, but too often it is not. Personalities, politics, and competition have to be reckoned with in the decision-making process. This realization should not weaken nor detract from a disciplined approach to new product evaluation. Neither can it be ignored.

PRODUCT IMPLEMENTATION

Assuming that senior management acts favorably on the recommendations evolving from the product evaluation stage, implementation should begin with the assembling of a task force headed by the product development officer or another *senior* staff officer. It should consist of representatives from at least the following areas:

Marketing and advertising.

Operations and systems.

Retail service (customer contact).

Staff training and education.

Legal.

The nature of a specific product might require the inclusion of one or more additional task force members (i.e., trust; credit administration, or the finance division with respect to marketing debt and equity instruments, and so on). The task force leader or product manager assures close coordination by preparing an implementation schedule which assigns responsibilities, establishes completion dates for various phases of the program, and defines critical decision points. It is an extension of the flowchart developed in the evaluation stage, except that its orientation stresses *when* rather than *if.* This schedule is monitored continually and updated as needed. Understandably, different products will require implementation schedules that vary in duration and complexity. There even may be more than one schedule. For example, the implementation of an on-line automatic teller machine (ATM) system supported by a CIS (central information system) capability might require three years to establish; within this framework, however, a bank might schedule—and desire to treat distinctively—the introduction of a number of off-line ATMs at a few selected locations.

All cost data assembled by task force members in fulfilling individual assignments should be passed on to the product manager. Too often this is not done, resulting in duplication, inaccuracies, and possibly pricing problems.

Marketing and Advertising

Research performed at the evaluation stage is reviewed to reassess the market for the product; commonly, additional research will be required to "fine tune" both a product's specific features and appropriate merchandising techniques, including distribution channels.

Where applicable, a promotional campaign is laid out, then reviewed and adjusted as other phases of the product implementation stage are completed. This campaign plan should distinguish between *external* (advertising, chiefly) and *internal* promotion. Bank staff members can't sell what they don't understand. Internal promotion is designed to inform, train, instruct, and motivate personnel who will sell and administer selling. This process should begin early in the implementation stage, possibly with branch administrators first, and then filtering down through management layers to tellers and customer service representatives.

The importance of external and internal promotion understandably increases with the complexity of the product to be introduced and its relationship to existing product lines, especially if they are to be replaced by or cross-sold with the new product. Complexity refers to such factors as a product's technical features, how narrow or broad a market segment is served, geographic considerations, and even similarities to competitor products.

Media advertising, direct mail brochures, in-house training manuals, and other explanatory materials should be developed with two objectives in mind: first, to introduce the new product and *sustain* sales, and second, to coordinate with other promotional activities and overall corporate objectives, including such intangibles as image.

Operations and Systems

The assignment of operations and systems is simple enough: line personnel selling and servicing the new product must be supported efficiently or costs will escalate, morale and motivation will deteriorate, and sales projections probably will not materialize. Support includes procedures and manuals, customer and administrative forms, equipment, systems compatibility, access to computer time, and so on. This responsibility, moreover, embraces all phases of produce implementation: testing and experimentation; the introduction of the product; the possible phaseout of existing product lines, and the continuing service requirements identified with the new product. In this respect, product selling can only be as good as its back-room support. Investigate thoroughly, and then allow for the unknown, the unexpected, and the unforeseen.

Retail Service

Our Golden Rule is: Your people can't sell what they don't understand. Developing this awareness comes through training and education. And the first and ever-continuing step in this process is *listening* to the customer contact staff and its managers. If a new product must be tailored to customer needs and wants, it also must fit the perceptions and capabilities of a bank's sales force. A key element in this assignment is an appraisal of work force needs. Will more people need to be hired? Will the training time required adversely affect current operations? Will special schooling be needed to cope with new equipment? These are just a few questions from the top of a long list.

Staff Training and Education

This requirement already has been touched on. It is the general assignment of each task force member. But it must be coordinated and structured. A unified and comprehensive training program should be someone's *specific* responsibility; otherwise this critical job won't be done. *Too often, it is not,* and this tendency appears to increase geometrically with product complexity and its application to the electronic mode.

Product *training* essentially involves "nuts and bolts." It deals with what a bank is selling, how to sell, and even monitor sales. Product *education,* on the other hand, focuses on *why.* Why bother? How does it fit into the overall scheme of things? How does it help our customers? How does it affect my job today and for the long run? In the past, banks seldom bothered with the *why* of a new product and the many related questions, especially as it involved nonmanagerial personnel. They just performed as instructed. Change, product complexity, technology, life-style alterations, consumerism, government regulations— all of these forces have combined to compel a growing need for product education. Joining with them is the consumer as bank customer. Increasingly, he or she feels a need to know more about a given product and its specific features. Individual retirement accounts or debit cards are a case in point.

Looked at somewhat differently, customers may need to be *trained* in the use of a new product. Debit cards and the automated machines they access are products that can't easily be explained; they must be *demonstrated.* Transaction volume, moreover, may necessitate large-scale initial and continuing community education programs to deal with consumer fears, both real and perceived. In all likelihood, this assignment should intensify as the transition to an electronic banking environment further alters the very nature of the banking business.

Legal

Counsel reviews forms and procedures and promotional materials as they are developed throughout the implementation stage. Traditionally, counsel has focused on existing law and regulation; today, more so in the future, counsel will need to take a somewhat longer view and consider whether a new product *possibly* or *probably* will be threatened by change, especially with respect to a widening range of consumerist legislation. This applies to product features, distribution procedures, and marketing techniques, including the use of sales tools such as premiums. Involved, moreover, could be actions taken during the implementation stage to bring about changes in existing law and regulation. For example, banks in a number of states worked to enact changes in the law that *exempted* ATMs from branching restrictions *prior* to introducing electronic machines.

The Monitoring Mechanism

The implementation stage does not end when the new product is introduced to the public. Nor does cost analysis end at this time. The final step is monitoring; its duration—*at the very least*—is until the new product's profitability has recovered its developmental costs.

Accurate statistics must be maintained to measure progress toward stated objectives and, more important, to determine the need for:

Alterations in the product's features.

Additional staff (or consumer) training.

Additional work force.

Distribution system changes.

Additional advertising and promotional activities.

Alterations in the marketing of a bank's complementary or competitive product lines.

PRICING

Effective pricing strategies presuppose a realistic determination of *total* costs, including *indirect* expenditures such as customer education programs or expenses related to the replacement of an outdated product. After all, there is a cost in taking something off the shelf. It also assumes that sales volume projections are reasonable as the product implementation stage passes into product introduction.

Total costs should be divided into two categories: first, research and development expenditures—what it costs to enter the marketplace; and second, the maintenance expenses during the projected life of the product—what it costs to make the product successful in terms of understood corporate objectives, be they income, image, market share, or market positioning.

A basic formula can be utilized in an approach to pricing. These essential costs are assessed as follows:

Processing and systems operations.

Systems maintenance, including product processing equipment.

Cost of funds, where applicable; this includes deposits and other purchased liabilities.

Promotion and merchandising expenses, including related public relations activities.

Customer contact personnel expenditures, including training.

Administrative overhead.

Taxes, licenses, insurance, etc.

To this *total cost,* a bank adds research and development expenditures amortized over a predetermined period of time. Then add in profit expectations. What should result is a price range that correlates with careful market research and its sales projections.

It is important to note that research and development costs should include not only tangibles such as equipment, advertising expenses, operations forms, computer time, training manuals, additional labor force, statement "stuffers" and other mailing solicitations, but also *people-time.* How many work force hours will be required to learn all that is needed about a new product? And how much of this expenditure is at the expense of merchandising existing products effectively? Another intangible cost may be expenses associated with possible legal ramifications. And still another intangible cost becomes the extent to which a bank's new product excites a competitive response, especially one that necessitates additional marketing expenditures to assure the achievement of a new product's sales goals. There is one cost for innovating a distinctive product; there is an add-on cost related to a possible competitive response. You don't price in a vacuum.

The competitive factor also comes into play with respect to income projections for both existing products and the new product. It may cross-sell effectively; it may entice new customers and, implicitly, their use of other products and services. Flipping this coin, it may satisfy some of a bank's customers, but drive others away, especially if it appears contrary to the image a bank has created over time. Finally, there is the cost—or loss of income or market share—that is attributable to not offering a product. In this respect, overall corporate profitability may suffer from not offering "free checking," not introducing automated teller machines, or not providing both Master Charge and BankAmericard (now VISA).

All of these considerations influence pricing strategies. They add to or subtract from research efforts (and legal or regulatory constraints, if applicable) determining customer interest within prescribed price ranges.

At this point, the product development coordinator will have at his or her disposal all of the information needed to perform the final critical tests to determine price. First, rate sensitivity analyses must be performed. Various price ranges should be surveyed to determine to what extent a change in price results in a change in the size and scope of the market. Such tests will, in short, determine the quantity as well as the quality to be anticipated at various price levels. The next step is to add previously determined costs at each level to determine marginal profitability, or "spread." It is important to remember that volume may not be the only consideration in setting a price. Customers must be of a sufficient quality that a total banking relationship can reasonably be anticipated. Otherwise, their marginal profitability may not be worth it to the bank in the long run.

In the future, it is possible that the total customer relationship with the bank should be assessed in estimating retail profitability levels and establishing price structures. A customer with several long-standing profitable relationships can and probably should be offered a lower price due to the fact that his or her overall relationship is producing an acceptable level of profitability to the bank which can be expected to continue for a long period of time. Banks follow this practice in the commercial area. Such considerations may result in various unit prices for packages of retail services, not each of which may be profitable yet will contribute to the overall profitability of a customer relationship.

Finally, the sensitivity of a variety of volume projections with regard to effects on cost levels should be assessed.

Having gone through this procedure, bank management is faced with this essential question: considering costs and desired profits, will this product sell at the necessary price in light of customer preferences and competitive products—both yours and your competitor's?

CONCLUSION

Skillful product management results in effective service from a customer's standpoint and a profitable service from the bank's. This duality should never be overlooked; poor products most often emerge when it is: when, too frequently, customer needs are subordinated.

As we have seen in this chapter, a variety of elements combine to determine customer satisfaction and bank profitability. Further, each of these elements interfaces at every step in the path from idea to concept to product evaluation, implementation, introduction, and maintenance. How a bank deals with each element, individually and in combination with others, ultimately contributes to a product's success or failure in the marketplace.

We also have learned that success is measured equally in terms of the net income a product generates, the customers it satisfies, the new customers it brings to the bank, and the extent to which it furthers acknowledged corporate objectives. Commonly, success tends to be viewed as increased share of market—*your additional portion* of core deposits, credit card outstandings, personal loans, capital, whatever. Just watch the numbers. The real trick is making sure that a bank increases *profitable* market share, or one that potentially will be. It also involves holding onto gains.

The principal characteristics of skillful product management are:

1. Structured, disciplined, and accountable coordination among the many areas of a bank that become involved in product development—in devising, promoting, distributing, supporting, selling, and monitoring a new product or retail service.
2. An understanding of *total* costs, including the cost of not providing a product.
3. Actions designed to make sure that bank sales personnel understand what they are selling, how to do the job, and perhaps *why* this product is important to the bank and their career. Keep in mind our Golden Rule: people won't buy what they don't understand; bank people likewise can't sell what they don't understand, nor believe in. Accordingly, training and education always must be a maximum effort.
4. Comprehension of the linkage, whether complementary or conflicting, to existing product lines.
5. The performance of systematic and valid research that indicates, evaluates, and monitors:

    a. Reasonable sales projections.
    b. Customer (market) interest at prescribed price levels.
    c. Staff capacity and motivation.
    d. Operations and systems compatibility.
    e. Product cross-sell potential.
    f. Distribution patterns.
    g. Product improvement or modification needs.

Product management is not conducted in isolation. It must interface with an array of external or environmental considerations: competition, technological advances; legislative and regulatory change, and the socioeconomic dimension. These externals particularly influence product lifetime, the moment of its birth, maturity, and death.

Finally, skillful product management recognizes that products serve customers. They satisfy needs and wants to be sure. No less, however, they satisfy his or her distinctive relationship with our bank. They keep the customer *our* customer. This view is critical as retail banking confronts a future characterized by more competition from more competitors armed with more banklike powers.

One other view also is critical. *Money is a product.* Banks buy and sell money and related financial services at a price. The spread covers expenses, taxes, and profits.

This simplification is important in emphasizing the idea that money in the customer's mind is as much a product as cars, appliances, toothpaste, clothes, and whatever. Accordingly, it must be marketed, and this process involves all bank employees, from chief executive officer to the teller on his or her first working day. Marketing is a philosophy of doing business that must permeate the entire organization.

In the past, customers came to a bank to borrow, save or invest. Money—the product—was rationed, on both sides of the ledger for that matter. Over the past decade or two, a marked change in approach has occurred. Increasingly, banks have reached out to customers. We went into the business of selling, and wherever possible, selling in a distinctive manner. Image, convenience, quality, efficiency, accuracy, and price became the hallmarks of successful selling. The point of this chapter is that they don't just happen. They must be achieved through the discipline of marketing, of understanding customers and of serving them well.

Chapter 64

The Organization and Operation of a Consumer Loan Department

Robert B. Shanahan*

THE ORGANIZATION

Integral Part of the Total Bank

Installment credit has become a sophisticated product. Installment lending today encompasses not only traditional lending such as loans for automobiles, white goods, home improvements, and the like, but also a wide variety of closed-end installment loans and open-end consumer loans. Depending on the size and makeup of the bank, it may have within the installment loan division or department, sections dealing with personal loans; automobile loans; recreational vehicle loans; boat, airplane, or swimming pool financing; home modernization and mobile home financing; indirect financing, both at the retail level and floor plan accommodations; revolving credit and bank card loans; automated forms of line of credit loans triggered by overdrafting through off-premises banking machines at a merchant's place of business, and many other types.

Many installment loan departments even have small-term business loans handled on an installment basis. Given this wide variety of product lines, it becomes apparent that organization and staffing of an installment loan department will vary greatly from bank to bank. Difference in product lines, organizational structure, state laws and in-bank makeup, will affect choice of structure. The size of the bank, whether

* Executive Vice President, Liberty National Bank and Trust Company, Buffalo, New York.

or not it is a unit bank or has branches, its location and status within a corporate structure will all influence the type of structure needed.

However, certain obvious needs have developed in the past decade that help guide us in organizing and staffing an installment loan department. Through the introduction of lines of credit, single statement banking, personal banking marketing, total customer cross-selling techniques, and the like, it becomes very apparent that installment lending has become an integral part of the total bank. It can, no longer, in any size bank, sit on the side and be looked on as a department to invest a given number of dollars on behalf of the bank. It is now a part of the total image of the bank and, depending on size, becomes a major factor in profitability accounting.

Partially as a result of this expansion into so many areas and as a part of the total consumer movement, installment lending has become regulated by many agencies at both the federal and state level. Much of this legislation is complicated legislation and requires keen analysis on the part of banks' installment loan managers.

Also in the past decade electronic data processing has become a part of the installment lending departments of almost all banks and again adds to the requirements of the organization and affects staffing. Whereas formerly a person with excellent credit judgment and some ability to manage people could manage the installment loan department, today's organization must be headed by a person who has a myriad of talents, including a keen knowledge of the product line, legislative restrictions and guidelines, electronic data processing (EDP) implications, and money management techniques.

Choosing a Department Head

The first basic decision in staffing and organizing an installment loan department is to choose its head. Bank size will be important in this decision. In a small bank[1] an officer of proven credit ability should be chosen. That officer should have a keen awareness and understanding of today's legislative framework and a working knowledge of the total bank. Ideally, this person will also have some proven ability in the area of managing people.

In days past in small banks the consumer loan manager could also manage other functions. In today's needs for tracking legislation, developing product lines, controlling credit quality, protecting profitability, automating loan input on to bank EDP systems, and so on, this is no

---

[1] For purposes of this discussion, a small bank will be one deemed to have installment loan outstandings of $0–$10 million; a medium-sized bank that of $10 million–$50 million; and a large bank that of more than $50 million.

longer advisable. The installment loan manager should be dedicated to the proper administration and control of that service and to being a part of the top management team of the bank. In small- and medium-sized banks, where consumer credit may have a substantial impact on total earnings, this person should be part of the senior management team of the bank. In larger banks, he or she should be a senior officer who either sits on the Senior Management Committee of the bank, or, in the case of very large banks, reports to a member of the Management Committee.

Chain of Command

In establishing or supervising the consumer loan department, the department head should draw a very clear organizational chart showing the line of authority and the functions to be managed. This, along with a work flow chart will help in establishing the total organization. Again, bank size will influence that organization and work flow chart.

Functional or Service Offering

In drawing the organizational chart, two basic types seem to have evolved. Under the first one, organizational responsibility flows from product line control. For example, there may be a direct loan department, and indirect loan department, a bank card department, a business term loan department, and so on. These departments normally will all make use of another department in the division, usually called an operations department.

The second method is to organize on a functional reporting basis. This type of organization may have a credit department, an adjustment department, a business development department, and operations department, and an administration department, and so on.

Most banks started out with the product line organizational style but more and more banks, especially large banks, are switching to organizations based on functions. Product line organizations cause banks to have a myriad of small departments with one or two credit people, collection people, and so on in each department. This is cause for constant problems due to vacations, sickness, and so on, and also may have shortcomings in regard to proper backup, training, and flexibility.

By organizing on a functional basis bankwide, depth of personnel is provided in each department (such as credit, and adjustment) and gives greater flexibility, backup, training, and provides for more advancement opportunities to the personnel.

Choosing Personnel

In choosing personnel, size continues to have a bearing. In the smaller banks and consumer loan departments, there will probably be a chief clerk and operations person to supervise all of the internal operations of the department. The department head probably will directly supervise the loan operation. Someone directly under the department head and at a high level in the department will keep abreast of all legislative and regulatory needs. The fourth person will probably supervise collection and adjustment areas.

In the medium-sized banks there would definitely be an operations officer, a person in charge of credit area, administrative assistant to the department head who would concentrate on legislative matters, a department head for adjustment, and others as that particular bank's product line dictates. In both small- and medium-sized banks, the operations officer will correlate all activities with the bank's EDP department.

In the larger banks with outstandings of $50 million or more, it is necessary to have a chain of command that can exercise full and proper control while it functions economically. The head of the division will probably have one or two administrative officers directly under him or her to whom the department heads report. The department heads may well include managers for credit, new business, adjustments, recoveries, operations, and a specialist in legislative matters. In large branch networks, depending on the total bank setup, it may also be necessary to have a loan unit that is used by the branch system to assist or control the decision-making process. This would be staffed by experienced credit persons in the total loan area.

Where to Locate

The installment loan department should always exist as a separate department. In a small unit bank it, of course, would be located as part of the bank itself just as the commercial or other departments. In larger unit banks, customer contact personnel may be integrated into the banking floor while the rest of the department may be in another part of the bank.

With the advent of modern techniques such as isolated terminal input to computers, telephone communications, and the like, the larger banks no longer have a need for their installment loan departments to be in the bank's headquarters building. This may still be desirable and, if the bank's headquarters building has good space at reasonable rental it can be a plus. But in banks where main office space requirements are at a premium, or priced extremely high, a consumer loan division can be placed out in a low rental facility in a suburban location. This is based on the assumption that loan personnel are located in each branch.

Today very few people physically visit the consumer loan department, but instead use phone contact. Those that do visit the consumer loan department normally have automobile transportation. By moving the entire department or division to suburban locations, with a single-floor facility, laid out by consultants with the knowledge of modern-day consumer lending needs and work flows, many large banks can achieve efficiencies that cannot be had in high rent, downtown, oftentimes separated and multifloored layouts.

POLICY CONSIDERATIONS

Service Offerings

Many policy considerations enter into the organization and operation of the consumer loan department. Some decisions must be made prior to the establishment of the department and others may be made after entering into this area.

The first consideration will have to do with what service offerings will be made by the bank. Traditionally, automobile loans have accounted for the major portion of installment loans. Automobile loans attract a wide variety of consumers for a fairly sizable installment loan at unusually attractive rates and provides a security interest in a product that is easily sold. In general, income levels and loss ratios in automobile financing have been attractive to banks who enter this field with properly trained employees.

In addition to automobile loans there are a number of product lines (see Chapter 57) that should be considered by the bank and what policies to purchase and what not to purchase should be established.

Direct or Indirect

A major consideration from a policy level will be whether or not to loan both directly and indirectly. A direct loan is a two-party loan entered into between the customer and the bank. An indirect loan is a three-party loan in which the bank purchases or acquires the loan from a third party, such as an automobile dealer or a home improvement contractor.

Normally, a bank will find that the amount of direct installment loans outstanding will be limited by the percentage of penetration in other product lines that that bank has achieved. For instance, if a bank has about 15 percent of the commercial bank deposits in its service area, it can probably hope to achieve a level of about 15 percent of the direct consumer loan bank volume in that area if the bank aggressively markets its product. To achieve a higher percentage usually will require the bank to enter the indirect loan business where they can achieve installment loan outstandings in excess of the percentage of the market they control in other product lines in their service area.

Many banks form dealer departments in their installment divisions and do complete dealer financing including, but not limited to, purchase of retail contracts, capital loans, and commercial loans to the dealer, floor plan arrangements for inventory requirements, and working capital loans on proper occasions.

Dealer loans and floor plan loans are highly specialized types of financing and require control by people with sophistication in those particular lines. It is not advisable to enter the dealer business unless it is possible to provide the level of control that only an experienced person can bring to the function. If a bank is starting a new dealer department, it is advisable to secure a fully experienced department head from some other bank or finance company. Once a bank is in the business it normally can train its own successors.

Closed End or Open-End

Another policy consideration is whether or not to offer both closed end (or traditional installment loans) or open-end lines of credit and bank card loans. Most line of credit services can be handled on a fairly low overhead basis, whereas bank card operations are normally associated with a high overhead. The important point is to analyze alternatives carefully, and have projections and knowledge available before the policy decision is made.

Degree of Centralization

A final policy consideration for medium- and large-sized banks in branch units concerns itself with the degree of centralization or decentralization. Will branch personnel have high- or low-lending authority? Will they adjust or follow delinquent loans, have autonomy, or be controlled in the installment lending division, and approve indirect loans? These decisions will largely depend on the bank's policy in regard to its branches. If sophisticated loan personnel are placed at the branches and given liberal authority in the commercial area, it normally follows that they can be trained to make most installment loans with proper controls from a centralized consumer loan division.

Depending on the structure of the bank, collection activities are normally shared by the central office responsible for consumer credit. In the area of indirect or dealer loans, many banks have experienced difficulty in decentralizing operations. In many instances, floor plan and dealer loans can be more effectively controlled by the central consumer loan department. Also in most instances, the purchase of indirect paper is best accomplished on a centralized basis, although in some specific situations there may be exceptions to this general rule.

THE IMPORTANCE OF SPECIFIC POLICIES

Loan Policy

A strong consumer loan department will have established credit policies in its consumer loan area. As a bank grows in size and number of outlets, this becomes more and more imperative. The policy statement for consumer lending should include what types of loans the bank will make, what minimum dollar amount each type of loan is required for the offering to be considered, what security will be deemed acceptable and what loan instruments will be used. In some banks, there will even be a definite point-system criteria used in determining an applicant's eligibility for a loan.

In setting policy the management will, of necessity, incorporate all that is necessary to ensure that legal and regulatory restrictions and needs are met. Policy should be stated in written form that can be updated as policy changes are made. If the bank has an operating manual, this policy should be a part of that manual.

Lending Authorities

Lending authorities will be controlled and must be clearly defined in order to ensure the proper responsibility and control the quality of the loan portfolio.

In a unit bank, authority will be concentrated in the consumer contact personnel and the consumer loan departments administrative officers. Indirect loaning authority will normally be given only to specialists in the consumer credit division's credit department. In large banks and most branch systems, a pyramid type of loan authority administration will be in effect. Branch loan officers and interviewers will be authorized to approve loans within certain limits. This authority will vary depending upon whether the loan is secured or unsecured and whether it is close end or open end.

The branch manager normally will be responsible for recommending all loan authorities in the branch. In turn, the branch manager will have a higher loan authority than junior officers. Loan authority will be determined by recommendations submitted to the loan administration committee by an officer in the administrative section of the consumer loan division or branch division, depending on the approach of the bank involved.

The lending authority will be higher for the central loan platform, if one exists, and the credit officers in the consumer loan division. The top consumer loan authority will be reserved for the division head of the consumer loan division, and indirect loan authority will usually be reserved for specialists in the consumer loan division.

In large banks, with large dealer departments, there may be a separate loan committee in the consumer loan division to handle dealer loans up to certain limits. Above those limits, larger loans would go to the senior loan committee in the bank. In all cases where the bank has dealer loans, the officer in charge of the consumer loan division should be a member of the senior loan committee. This will allow the bank to have a unified loan policy in both the commercial and consumer areas and to have a highly integrated loan portfolio through the constant interchange afforded among the commercial, mortgage, and installment areas at senior levels.

Usually loan authorities are reviewed every six months and recommended changes are made to the officer in charge of the installment lending division, who in turn endorses them and presents them to the bank's senior loan committee for approval.

Credit Policy

Basic credit policy should be set up in written form to guide the department and ensure uniformity of policy in the consumer loan department. Credit policy must be carefully worded to ensure compliance with all federal and state legislation and regulation. Credit policy must ensure that there will be no discriminatory practices. Procedures for rejecting loans also should be part of credit policy.

Rate Policies

In setting rates the fair market price for the product line should be determined. In addition, those prices should conform to all existing legislation in regard to maximum rates. Management should know what competitors are doing but the product line must be priced to produce the profit needs predetermined by policy guidelines. A price should be established on each product and a determination made as to who may make exceptions to that price, and under what circumstances. All of this information should be clearly disseminated to all appropriate personnel. Each lending officer must be advised that variances from policy should be carefully considered for legal implications especially in the area of discrimination.

The need for central control of rate and credit policies must be emphasized. Individual lending officers cannot be expected to have a full and complete working knowledge of all of the laws and regulations that are frequently changed.

However, it can be expected that these officers will follow clear-cut policy statements which are formed to help them carry out their lending functions while adhering to all legislative and social restrictions. All rates should be fair, produce a reasonable profit to the bank, and reflect the overall economic considerations that the bank may face during the terms of the loans involved.

LEGAL CONSIDERATION

Organize for Control

In organizing and operating a consumer credit department, it is imperative that the head of the department be completely satisfied that the staff is aware of all of the legislative and regulatory activities that affect the consumer lending area. He or she must be able to assure the bank's management that the bank is operating within the law and within the scope of all state and federal regulations.

This has become a major area of concern for all banks. Most regulations in regard to consumer credit are extremely complicated and some require years of court action before they are fully clarified. In the smaller banks it behooves the head of the consumer credit department to have a personal, working knowledge of all of these laws and regulations. In turn, the bank must support the department head by providing free and full access to counsel.

In medium and large banks, the head of the consumer division should have an assistant or officer in the administrative section that reports directly to the department head and is specialized in the legislative area. He or she must make constant use of legislative counsel. In most large banks the consumer lending division will have a specialized counsel assigned to it. In many instances this counsel is not from general counsel but is picked for his or her specialty in the consumer area.

No form or contract should be used that does not have the specific approval of counsel. If the bank uses outside services and outside service organizations, it behooves the head of the consumer loan department to assure either in a personal interview or through the use of counsel, that these outside service organizations are complying with all necessary regulations and laws.

This area of consumer loan organization and operation has changed in the last few years. The cost of constantly monitoring the legislative area has increased several hundredfold. However, no bank should attempt shortcuts in this area.

The head of the department, through his or her counsel or specialist, should have a working knowledge of the Truth-in-Lending law. The most fundamental section of this regulation is Title I which is commonly referred to as Regulation Z. Equally important is a full working knowledge of Title IV of the Fair Credit Billing Act and Title VII of the Equal Credit Opportunity Act. The department head must also be concerned with the Federal Trade Commission's regulations concerned with the preservation of consumers' claims and defenses. Knowledge of the Real Estate Settlement Procedures Act and the Home Mortgage Disclosure Act is also necessary if mortgages and real estate loans are accepted in the department.

For national banks, regulations by the Comptroller of the Currency covering lending practices at national banks must be adhered to closely. In each state a myriad of laws and regulations affect the consumer loan area. And, most recently, both the comptroller for national banks and state banking department for state banks are instituting practices in bank examinations regarding consumer protection compliance.

Methods for Monitoring

It is suggested that the officer or person who monitors these legal considerations be specifically designated so that others in the organization will know where information may be obtained. All banks should name a consumer compliance officer.

Departmental management should also communicate with the auditor, since, besides other audit functions, the auditor must accept the responsibility of auditing consumer compliance areas.

Communicating

It is preferable that resolutions of the board of directors outline the responsibilities of the officer in charge of the consumer division, the consumer compliance officer, and the auditor in these important legal areas.

THE OPERATION OF THE DEPARTMENT

Variables to Consider

Banks that make consumer loans should establish an "operations department." In small banks this may be an operations clerk. In large banks this will be a highly specialized, fully mechanized work force which is specialized in many areas. Part of the bank's ability to achieve proper profitability will be how efficiently the operations department of the consumer division will function. The operations sections will be responsible for all of the housekeeping of the department. This department will enter new loans to the system, handle the preparation and mailing of coupon books and billings, keep all of the necessary record information and files, control all forms and procedures keeping them as simple as possible, take care of all documentation, post all payments, and cause all exception and control reports to be printed for the use of the departments in the consumer division.

In small banks these operating procedures will be done manually, but in operating the installment loan department it must be remembered that profitability, to a large extent, depends on efficient operations.

In days long past, consumer departments could produce gross yields in the area of 9–12 percent while incurring money costs of 1 percent or 2 percent. Regulations and losses were minimal and operating needs simple. In those times operating efficiencies were not often considered. When consumer areas could provide yields sometimes more than double that in other areas of the bank, with almost nonexistent money costs, profit levels were so high that inefficiencies often were permitted.

However, now consumer loan departments must compete with other areas of the bank for funds that often are priced extremely high. They must loan these funds out in a competitive market that includes not only other banks, but also is constantly expanding from freer entry from both financial and retail organizations.

In the meantime, legal and regulatory restrictions have added tremendous needs to the system and increased prices of operating dramatically. All of this leads to a continuing trend toward a narrow profit margin in the consumer lending banks. Unless bank's consumer lending departments can become extremely efficient, many banks will find themselves priced out of business in this competitive market.

Small banks may not be able to bring aboard sophisticated automation but they can, through proper management techniques, develop a high proficiency and individual production levels that will allow them to become competitive. Smaller banks must examine their product lines and avoid those which require so much manual activity that proper profit levels will not be able to be achieved.

In operating and establishing a consumer loan division, most banks should not attempt to become all things to all people but should specialize in the area where they feel they can deliver needed and wanted services at a reasonable profit.

Medium- and large-sized banks should automate their operations department in every area so that lower costs can be achieved through this method. Large banks' consumer departments will only prove profitable if highly automated, low-priced operations become commonplace.

The head of the operations department of the installment section should be completely conversant with EDP and must be able to transmit to the software department of their banks in a meaningful way all of the needs of the department.

Checks and Balances

In organizing and operating this department, constant correlation with the auditor is necessary. Each time automation moves forward conferences with the auditor to provide for proper audit trails should be held at a very early stage.

COLLECTIONS, ADJUSTMENTS, RECOVERIES

Organization of Collection Department

In organizing and operating the consumer division, great importance must be given to the collection, adjustment, and recovery area. In all but the smallest banks, some form of collection effort will be necessary. Some medium- and large-sized banks allow a certain amount of collection efforts at individual branch levels but after accounts reach a certain level of delinquency, they are normally referred to a central collection department. In many others, all collections and adjustments are the responsibility of this collection and adjustment department. In some small- and medium-unit banks, collections may well be handled by those persons who originally instituted the loan. A few large banks also refer collections back to the person or branch who originally made the loan and have a centralized unit only for control of the activities of the individuals to whom the loans are sent.

Formerly the collection officer was chosen for his or her ability to inspire a work force and install proper collection techniques to minimize loss ratios. The bank still must look for these qualities but it must become increasingly sensitive to choosing an individual who can properly control the total collection effort to see that all legal and regulatory restraints are adhered to in the collection area.

Collection Procedures, Notices, and Calls

In organizing the collection department the head of the consumer division will expect the department head for collections, adjustments, and recoveries to institute collection procedures that will most effectively allow the bank to collect its receivables and continue its credit policies.

Additionally, the department head in collections will be responsible to provide management reports and establish recovery procedures for loans that reach the charge-off stage. In medium- and large-sized banks most collection departments will have a department head, and one or more inside (telephone) and outside adjusters. Depending on size, it may also have a specialist on recoveries or a separate subdepartment for that function. They also will have clerical staffs to support the activities.

It is suggested and still seems to hold credence that a bank operates its collection and adjustment department on the premise that most debt problems arise through circumstances beyond the control of the borrower and that creditors are willing to discuss and work out problems with their customers.

To organize the collection efforts decisions will have to be made as to what methods will be used. Most banks send out late notices, preferably computer produced, when the accounts become a certain number of days delinquent. Banks vary from one to three notices. Following these written notices, if the delinquency continues, normally the account is assigned to an inside telephone adjuster.

It is the duty of this adjuster to contact the customer and to determine what the cause of the delinquency is and to attempt to work out an acceptable repayment procedure for both the bank and the customer.

Adjusters must be trained to have a fair knowledge of the regulations regarding collection procedures and should be also educated in the ethics of the particular bank. Consumer credit collection practices should be based on the presumption that every debtor expects to repay and delinquencies arise through circumstances beyond the debtor's control. All communications with the customer should be based on this presumption.

Telephone adjusters should be taught to determine the cause of delinquency and indicate their willingness to arrange a mutually satisfactory repayment schedule. Personal abuse, harassment, threats and other unconscionable tactics should be forbidden. Collectors should understand that they are dealing with individuals about highly personal matters and must maintain integrity when dealing with the individuals.

Attorneys, process servers, and other agents representing the bank should be advised of the standards of service that the bank expects of them.

When the telephone adjuster can no longer obtain action on the account, in most banks the account will go to an outside adjuster for a personal call. In other banks it will be returned to the collection manager for the decision in regard to further action.

Normally, the collection department in small- and medium-sized banks will also have the responsibility to repossess the security on loans which go bad and dispose of the security on behalf of the bank. This same department will normally be responsible for recovery of both internal and external charge-offs. In large banks separate departments may be organized to recover the assets charged off in the collection department.

The head of the consumer division should see that there is close correlation between the collection department and the credit department so that those establishing credit policies will be fully advised of the bank's ability to collect the consumer paper produced. It is an old axiom that a bank's basic credit policies are determined by its ability to collect the loans. For this reason the collection department and the credit department must work closely together.

THE BRANCH FUNCTION

Manager's Participation

In organizing and operating a consumer credit department the branch manager and his or her platform people play an important role. The role of the branch manager and the amount of authority and the autonomy that they may or may not have, will usually be determined by overall bank philosophy. That is to say, if the bank is a small bank where the installment loan department head, in effect, can personally be involved in most of the loans, then the department head and the branch manager will work closely together. In very small banks this is usually done on an informal basis without the necessity for clear-cut definitions of autonomy.

However, in medium-sized branch systems and in large-sized unit and branch banks where controls become imperative, it is important that the role of the branch manager be clearly defined. In medium and large banks where the branch manager is charged with the responsibility and profitability for the branch, it is usually necessary to provide him with reasonable loan authority so that he can function without unnecessary constraints. The branch produces the direct loans in a branch system and the installment division services and controls. If the branch manager is discouraged from producing loans, the system is inhibited severely. In a bank where the branch manager is given full authority to run his branch within well-organized policy lines, and is given liberal commercial lending authority, and is responsible for profitability, he should be given liberal consumer loan authority. The branch manager should also know clearly whom to go to for authority in excess of his own.

The question of where the branch manager gets authority is usually resolved by the structure of a particular bank. If, in a particular bank, there is a branch administration division that has complete control of all areas of branching, then normally the head of this branch division would grant or recommend the lending authority for a branch manager within previously approved guidelines and with the consent and review of the consumer lending head. However, in most banks the branch division has control of operating procedures but not lending authorities. It usually follows that the branch manager will receive consumer lending authority by action of, or recommendation of, the head of the consumer lending division. In most cases, the branch manager should be given permission to recommend preestablished limits of authority for those in the branch that report to them and are responsible for the loan function. These recommendations by the branch manager would be approved by branch administration or the consumer lending division, whichever is appropriate.

If a bank has a well-seasoned branch group with a low turnover rate that has been trained properly in the use of consumer credit, then the bank should encourage a decentralization of loan authorities and a high degree of autonomy for the managers. In these situations, the consumer loan department must constantly be communicating both written and orally all policy changes and guidelines.

Branch Dealer Relations

As previously stated, it is often advisable to have dealer loans handled by specialists in the consumer division. However, geographical considerations and bank's general policy may dictate some branch handling of dealer loans.

Collections in Branches

The same philosophy applies to branch collections. If the branch is autonomous in most regards, and profitability accounting is in practice whereby the branch is charged for all loan losses, then the manager should probably have some voice in the collection efforts expended on the delinquent accounts that originate in the branch. However, since the adjustment and collection area is one that requires more and more training in regard to legal constraints, and since the cost of collection efforts constantly rises and must be controlled, most banks are centralizing control of collections.

Where profitability accounting is in place and centralized collections are in use, computer printouts of delinquencies that have reached the charge-off stage are often provided to the branch managers so that the managers may call with suggestions if they have some knowledge of the account.

In organizing the installment loan department, the principal need is to clarify the branch manager's role in regards to credit and collection so that he or she may be clearly advised of what is expected. Many different systems can succeed if the system is well communicated to both the consumer department and the individual branch managers.

COST CONTROL AND AUDITING

Problems of Cost Control

In establishing and organizing a consumer loan department, it is imperative that adequate cost control procedures be adopted. The installment loan department head should work closely with the controller's department to secure good cost control. The department head must see to it as he or she organizes the department that they will receive the proper management input to allow them to make effective decisions that leads to the correct bottom-line profitability. The department head must have full knowledge of the product lines and the gross and net yields that these product lines will produce. He or she must have full knowledge of delinquency and loss ratios and operating costs, and must be fully informed of what competitors are charging for their product lines. The manager should be constantly judging from money market conditions what areas of the portfolio should receive additional impetus and what areas should be constrained.

Auditing

In organizing an installment department and its operational procedures, constant communications with the bank's auditor must be maintained. It is imperative that the auditor agree that the method of operation that the department head is developing is proper.

In the operation of this department year in and year out, each time operating procedures are to be changed, the auditor should be consulted. This is especially important as the installment manager automates various procedures.

MISCELLANEOUS CONSIDERATIONS

Insurance

In organizing an installment loan department, insurance needs must be considered. In a small bank the installment loan manager should consult with whomever the bank uses for its insurance to outline what coverage should be provided for in the consumer department. Consideration should be given to offering credit life insurance and health and accident insurance to the borrower. Just as important, insurance coverage to protect the bank itself should be considered. Such coverage as single-interest insurance and insurance on floor plan vehicles, and repossessed merchandise should be evaluated. Policy lines regarding casualty insurance on security must also be established.

In large banks one of the officers in the installment division usually will be given the responsibility for follow up on insurance needs. In small banks the head of the department will probably assume this responsibility.

MANAGEMENT REPORTING

Sufficiency of Reports

The final consideration in operating and establishing a consumer loan division is that of providing the senior management of the bank with the proper management reports. Monthly reports covering the major aspects of the division should be forwarded to senior management. These reports should contain volume figures on purchases, outstandings, and other pertinent items regarding the portfolio of the department. A separate section should detail delinquency percentages and dollar amount delinquent and charge-offs by major categories. All of the information in these reports should be presented with comparisons to some historical base either a month ago or a year ago, whichever is the preference of senior management.

Beside management reports, in organizing the consumer department, the department head should work with the accounting department to develop financial information that will be reported on a monthly basis. In general, financial information will follow the same pattern for the consumer division as for the other income-producing divisions.

Chapter 65

Bank Cards

*D. Dale Browning**

Bank cards have had a meteoric rise in retail banking in the past two decades. The use of these charge cards has revolutionized consumer credit, both in terms of credit concepts and in procedures. These rapid developments have coincided with the expanded use of systems capable of servicing the complex networks that have developed. Bank card programs evolved from local offerings to nationwide systems. That development has been characterized by intense competition at all levels.

BANK CARD OPERATIONS

Organizational Structure

While it is obviously not possible to typify with any brevity all bank card operations, it is possible to outline the main organizational areas that constitute the heart of most bank card operations.

Simply stated, most bank card operations can be viewed as six organizational units: (1) administration, (2) credit, (3) collections, (4) operations, (5) account servicing, and (6) security. In many banks, the job responsibilities of the various areas overlap, and the distinction between two or more areas (credit and collections, for example) may not be readily discernible.

Administration

"Administration" tends to be a cliché in banking circles, including job functions performed by personnel ranging from the chief executive

---

* Senior Vice President, Colorado National Bank, Denver, Colorado.

officer (CEO) to the head teller. In the typical bank card operation, the administration area usually consists of the senior officer responsible for the bank card program and supporting staff.

Credit and Collections

Credit and collections are two areas that may be distinguishable, or may be treated as a single organizational entity. The functions of these two areas consist of conducting new account analysis and adjunct credit investigation, establishment and control of credit lines, collection of delinquent and overline accounts, and possibly performing merchant authorizations, (i.e., the function of granting the authority to merchants to consummate a cardholder sale when the amount of the sale exceeds a predetermined dollar amount—floor limit).

Operations

Operations typically includes functions pertaining to data capture (from sales drafts), data processing (and possibly transmission), accounting, card production, mail handling, and general supplies. The names by which these functions are known may vary from bank to bank, but in essence the duties are generally the same.

Service Departments

Most card operations have personnel whose job consists of providing service to cardholders, merchants and/or agent banks. These functions are usually separate, although personnel in these areas may report to the same manager.

Service to Merchants

Merchant service areas may be subdivided into a sales staff who actually calls on existing or prospective member merchants, and an accounting staff with responsibility for compiling and disseminating merchant-related accounting data. Typically, merchants are assessed a "discount" (charge) of between 2 percent and 5 percent of each bank card sale for participating in one of the two national programs. For this fee, bank cards provide to the merchant improved liquidity, guaranteed sales, and minimal risk.

In both major national bank card programs, the principal, or issuing bank, is responsible for contracting with local merchants for acceptance of the bank card. Although many of the contractual arrangements are standardized to comply with either Interbank Card Association

(ICA) or VISA U.S.A., Inc. (VISA) operating procedures, the issuing bank does have the latitude to determine the discount, or participation fee, that will be assessed to the merchant.

Customer Service

The customer service department of a bank card operation performs a myriad of functions related to the task of providing the cardholder with information and service. Although it is impossible to list all of the services performed by this area, customer service representatives spend a great deal of their time researching customer questions or inquiries related to account balances, requests for draft copies, merchandise disputes, finance charges, and billing questions. Most operations now expedite cardholder servicing through on-line cathode-ray tube (CRT) access to cardholder files.

Agent Bank Service

Many of the larger bank card issuers, both Master Charge and VISA (formerly BankAmericard) have relationships with smaller financial institutions which act in an agent capacity. Agent institutions are those that have elected not to issue cards, and at most carry only a portion of the receivables attributable to any cards issued by their principal. The advantage of this relationship is that it enables smaller banks to offer bank card programs to their customers without incurring the expense or risk that is associated with issuing cards. Typically, the principal bank will reimburse its agent banks for services performed. Larger issuers may have an internal department whose sole function is agent bank servicing. This department may be known as the correspondent bank department or agent bank relations. The role of this area differs from that of the traditional commercial bank or correspondent bank department, in that typically bank card departments of this type are concerned primarily with providing in-house service to existing agent institutions.

Fraud Control

Every principal bank in VISA U.S.A., Inc. and principal banks working in conjunction with associations in Interbank Card Association are responsible for security and fraud investigation activities. Each individual issuing institution must take precautions to ensure that the assets of the organization (primarily in the form of plastics) are secured. This involves a variety of procedures ranging from simple audit controls in smaller operations to full-time security guards and complex electronic detection equipment employed by large issuers. Larger organizations may employ full-time security officers who will typically have a background in law enforcement or industrial security. In the VISA (Blue, White, and Gold—BWG) system, each principal bank is responsible for administrating its own fraud control procedures. ICA members rely heavily on their associations for fraud control and investigation, although some larger issuers also maintain their own investigations staff. In the area of fraud control, VISA and ICA members work closely together.

One of the primary methods utilized by the two national bank card organizations in controlling fraud (and collection problems) is the national authorization systems (see below, Base I and "Interbank National Authorizations System"). A merchant is required to call for an authorization, or approval, prior to completing a sale above a predetermined amount to a VISA (BWG) or Master Charge cardholder. The predetermined amount, which is known as the merchant "floor limit," may be changed from time to time by card issuers in an attempt to apprehend users of stolen cards. Because merchants must call in for approval on sales exceeding floor limits, bank card investigators code accounts that are reported to be lost or stolen. This coding of accounts serves to alert investigators and merchants of the attempted unauthorized use of a bank card and is a very useful deterrent in preventing fraud losses.

In both the Master Charge and VISA (BWG) systems, merchants are periodically warned of cards that are no longer valid. Master Charge banks distribute at regular intervals a "hot card list" that gives all of the cards for a particular issuer that should not be honored by a merchant.

VISA issuers distribute "hot cards" which identify only a small number of accounts that may not be accepted by the merchant. In the VISA (BWG) system, merchants are categorized by type and location and receive a hot card only if they are the type of merchant in a specific location that is likely to receive a stolen card. The hot cards are usually valid for only a short period of time.

EVOLUTION OF BANK CARD ASSOCIATIONS

BankAmericard (now VISA)

BankAmericard, which was the first domestic bank card that evolved beyond a local program, was developed by Bank of America in 1958 for introduction in California. At the time of its introduction BankAmericard was designed to provide for consumers a method of purchasing goods or services that was easy, widely recognized and accepted, carried the prestigious name of the bank, and offered a prenegotiated line of credit.

Through their nationwide network of correspondent banks, officials of Bank of America recognized that the BankAmericard program could be marketed on a nationwide basis. To select and administrate Bank-Americard franchisees (banks who paid a fee to use the BankAmericard name and packaged program), Bank of America in 1966 created the subsidiary Bank of America Service Corporation. This service-oriented subsidiary had two primary functions: (1) to license banks for the BankAmericard program, and (2) to establish uniform operating procedures so that all banks participating in the BankAmericard program could interchange, or cooperatively process items (sales drafts) for each other. The latter function, by far the more important of the two, expanded for the first time the scope of bank card programs beyond a strictly regional base. The BankAmericard name was changed to VISA in 1977.

Master Charge

In 1966, a group of New York banks banded together to form Inter-bank Card Inc., which subsequently became the Interbank Card Association (ICA). Initially the purpose of ICA was to administer a regional bank card program for 14 New York banks. The same year (1966) four large California banks joined together to form the Western States Bankcard Association, (WSBA), using "Master Charge" for their card name. The commonality of goals of these two associations, and the desire of the principal members to establish a program which would be competitive with BankAmericard nationally, led the two groups to a 1967 merger. ICA remained as the national governing body, and WSBA became a processing member association. The name Master Charge survived the merger to appear on the majority of cards issued by ICA members.

ORGANIZATION OF BANK CARD ASSOCIATIONS

VISA U.S.A., Inc.

While the Bank of America Service Corp. more than surpassed its initial goals for marketing BankAmericard to licensees, the system that resulted grew at such a rate that problems of administration and coordination resulted, particularly in the period 1968–70. To address problems in the areas of draft interchange, authorizations, and fraud control, various committees were formed by the licensee banks to develop solutions to these problems.

In an attempt to resolve these problems, and to serve various needs of the growing BankAmericard system, National BankAmericard, Inc. (NBI) was established in July 1970, as the governing body for the licensee banks which had previously operated their BankAmericard programs under the jurisdiction of the Bank of America Service Corporation. In essence, the member banks purchased from the Bank of America the right to coordinate the domestic BankAmericard program.

At that time, Bank of America relinquished its dominant position in the BankAmericard system and became a member of NBI. The bank did, however, retain ownership of the name BankAmericard and the Blue, White, and Gold Bands design service mark. In an attempt to achieve international uniformity, all BWG programs adopted the name of "VISA" during a transition period beginning in 1977, and in concert with the introduction of VISA, NBI changed its name to VISA U.S.A., Inc.

VISA is structured as an independent, nonstock membership corporation, whose membership consists of the licensee banks of the BankAmericard program. The purpose of VISA is to administer, promote, and further develop the VISA system throughout the United States. Historically, VISA U.S.A., Inc. has exerted a strong centralized role in the determination of policies and procedures governing the VISA program.

Organization.   VISA U.S.A., Inc. is organized according to the following four subgroups:

Proprietary members.
Board of Directors.
VISA U.S.A., Inc. staff.
Member advisory groups.

Proprietary Members.   When VISA U.S.A., Inc. was first formed, membership was limited to domestic, commercial banks. Since 1970, however, an evolutionary process has resulted in restructured membership requirements. In 1977, membership eligibility has been expanded to include mutual savings banks, industrial banks, savings and loan associations, and credit unions.

To insure consistency in the administration of the VISA program, VISA U.S.A., Inc. dictates that members adhere to rules and regulations that have been developed over a period of time by VISA U.S.A., Inc. with the assistance of the membership. Any changes in this body of rules and regulations must be approved by the board prior to promulgation to the membership.

Board of Directors.   The board of directors consists of an appointed director, several at-large directors and regional directors, and a VISA president. All directors are selected by vote of the membership. As with other corporations, the board of directors meets at regular intervals to evaluate issues critical to the continuing viability of the VISA system. For example, the directors review every new application for admission to the Blue, White, and Gold program. Additionally, all changes to the corporation Bylaws must be approved by a vote of the directors.

VISA U.S.A., Inc. Staff. The VISA staff, headquartered in San Francisco, provides assistance to VISA members in matters related to operations, marketing, law, and research. Staff members also play an important role in representing the membership in a lobbying capacity before federal and state legislative bodies.

In addition to serving in an advisory capacity, VISA staff members operate BASE I and BASE II, which are systems designed to enable the membership to obtain authorizations for cardholder purchases (BASE I) and electronically exchange information captured from VISA sales drafts (BASE II).

Advisory Groups. Member advisory groups are selected from the membership to provide input to the VISA staff on matters perceived to be of importance to the VISA system. The advisory groups have no decision-making powers, but rather assist VISA in determining what recommendations the membership wishes the corporation to make to the board.

BASE I. BASE I is the BWG authorization network. BASE I is owned by VISA and operated by VISA staff members for the purpose of providing authorizations for Blue, White, and Gold merchant transactions.

The membership can elect to use BASE I in one of several fashions. Depending upon the sophistication of the member, BASE I can grant authorizations from a "negative file" (a list of cardholders to whom the member does not want to grant an authorization), an authorization inquiry can be "switched" by BASE from an inquiring merchant bank to the issuing bank, whose personnel can make the authorization decision, or the member can "interface," or link its own computers with the computer of BASE I. In the latter instance, a program based on predetermined criteria, housed in the issuing bank's computer, responds to authorization requests. Many members have elected to use a combination of these authorization methods. In addition, issuing members may elect to have their merchants call BASE I directly, rather than calling the member for authorizations. The member then is responsible only for providing to BASE I the appropriate negative file information.

BASE II. BASE II facilitates, using the BASE I network, the electronic transmission of draft data for interchange. In the BWG system, all sales drafts are "truncated" or stopped at the first processing bank receiving the merchant deposit. Information contained on sales drafts is captured by the processor and subsequently transmitted to the card-issuing institution (over the same dedicated telephone lines used in the BASE I network) where the information is captured and posted to the cardholder's account.

Funding. The operations of VISA U.S.A., Inc. and its staff are funded by the membership of the BWG system. Every financial organization joining the Blue, White, and Gold program is assessed a membership fee. Proprietary, or card-issuing organizations, also support VISA and the system through payment of service fees which are determined by sales volume, and fees associated with the usage of BASE I and BASE II. In addition, members reimburse each other through interchange fees. Interchange is defined as the process of member banks exchanging electronically information pertinent to a sale made at a merchant signed through one member bank by a cardholder whose card was issued by a different member bank.

In the BWG system, when an interchange transaction occurs, the member with whom the cardholder is associated is entitled to a percent of the dollars involved in the sales transaction from the merchant bank.

Organizational Characteristics. The evolution of the BWG system has been characterized by the strength of solely owned processing entities (as opposed to processing associations which are characteristic of ICA). Solely owned processing entities have some operational and conceptual advantages to processing associations, but disadvantages also exist. Normally, a solely owned processing entity issues VISA to customers residing in a geographic area that is contiguous to the institution itself. Generally, such an institution must rely upon its own retail consumers residing in the immediate area for its cardholder base. This restriction naturally limits the growth potential for any one single institution.

Start-up costs associated with a bank card program are significant, and can tend to put undue strain on the capital structure of any single institution attempting to enter the market. Unfortunately, these costs are duplicated, often unnecessarily, as financial organizations situated in close proximity to each other develop their bank card programs independently. Where such duplication exists, the counter efforts of the competing institutions often have the effect of minimizing the market impact of either program.

There are, however, some significant advantages to the "solely owned" concept. Perhaps most importantly, such programs benefit from the consistency of policy making and goal setting that results when one management group is responsible for establishing and administering these disciplines. As an adjunct to this, the decision process is generally much more expedient and consistent when a single group of decision makers is involved, than when a group holds this responsibility. One of the most significant barriers to entry in a bank card program is the cost of necessary computer hardware. In a single institution, however, this hardware is usually already in place and being used for variety of other purposes. The bank card program, once developed, often makes existing hardware even more productive.

VISA International Service Association

Following the formation of NBI to administer the domestic Bank-Americard program, Bank of America Service Corporation continued for some time to oversee the international operations of BankAmericard. In 1972, the international members of BankAmericard began exploring the possibility of forming a multinational membership corporation to administer the Blue, White, and Gold Bands bank card program worldwide. These deliberations culminated in 1974 with the incorporation of IBANCO, a multinational, nonstock corporation. IBANCO, Ltd., administers and promotes on behalf of its members, a worldwide system of bank cards using the Blue, White, and Gold Bands design. In 1977 the name IBANCO was changed to VISA International Service Association to reflect the international conversion of BWG programs to VISA.

Interbank Card Association (ICA)

ICA was created to assist groups and associations of Master Charge banks to compete with the emerging BankAmericard system, interchange Master Charge transactions nationally and internationally, and cooperatively address national bank card issues and problems. Initially, ICA intended to allow members to retain their local identity through unique card design. The majority of members, however, elected to operate with the Master Charge trademark. The Interbank marks design, however, not "Master Charge," is the common identifier for interchange purposes.

The membership of ICA is made up of financial institutions, albeit primarily commercial banks, located throughout the world. Unlike VISA U.S.A., Inc., the membership of ICA consists largely of groups and associations. These groups and associations play a dominant role in the Master Charge system in determining local operating policies and procedures.

ICA Organization. The organization of ICA is similar in many respects to VISA, but differs in that international members are represented on the board of directors. ICA domestic membership consists of associations, principal members, affiliated principal members, and affiliated associated members. These titles primarily indicate varying degrees of participation in the Master Charge program by member financial institutions. The essential difference in the levels of participation center around whether the member is a processor, an issuer, an issuer's agent, or some combination of the three.

Interbank is managed by a board of directors who are elected annually from the membership. The board, in turn, appoints the president of ICA. Directors are elected from banks and associations representing various geographical regions. The board rules on applications for membership in ICA, establishes operating rules and regulations, and determines the structure of fees assessed to the membership. In addition to domestic representation, directors representing Europe, the Far East, and Mexico, or Canada, also sit on the board. The international interbank system, however, is very loosely organized with associations and groups retaining a great deal of local autonomy.

Committees.   The Interbank board and staff are assisted in matters of policy and procedure by standing committees and ad hoc committees. These committees, which roughly correspond to the advisory committees of VISA U.S.A., Inc., are selected from the membership, and provide input to the board on operational procedures, security, marketing, and advertising. Through the activities of these committees, the board and ICA staff receive direct input from the membership.

ICA Staff.   From the standpoint of determining policy and procedures, the staff of Interbank plays a less important role in the functioning of the Master Charge network than the staff of VISA does for BWG. The Interbank staff, which is comparatively small, is limited in the main to providing support and guidance to the membership. Functions of the staff include overseeing research, gathering statistics, operations, member communications, international operations, public relations, advertising, marketing, security, and processing new member applications.

Funding.   Financial institutions wishing to become a member of ICA are assessed an initial membership fee. Thereafter, members are assessed annual dues which are based on the number of active accounts (Master Charge and VISA) in their portfolio. International Communications Systems, Inc. (ICS), a service bureau that administers the Master Charge authorization system, charges members (or their associations) for authorization services. In addition to fees paid to ICA and ICS, members also reimburse each other through their processors for interchange transactions. Unlike VISA, ICA Interchange fees are predicated on a per item charge plus a small percentage of each transaction. Finally, members who belong to groups or associations are charged by the association for processing and other services conducted by the association for the mutual benefit of its members.

Interbank National Authorization System (INAS). The authorizations and electronic interchange networks of Interbank are operated by quasi-independent service bureaus and not ICA staff. INAS, like BASE I, switches authorization messages between processing centers. Unlike BASE I, however, INAS is not staffed by authorizations personnel per se, and cannot, therefore, provide operator-assisted negative file authorizations for members. (INAS does have on-line negative file capability available for member usage.) Interbank operating regulations dictate that merchant authorizations originate with a processing member ("Merchant Direct" authorization service as offered by VISA is not available to Master Charge merchants). Although VISA introduced BASE I somewhat before Interbank completed INAS, INAS is rapidly approaching parity in sophistication.

Interbank Network for Electronic Transfers (INET). ICA also utilizes their authorization network as the foundation for the electronic exchange of draft information between processors. Like VISA, ICA has chosen to truncate sales drafts at the first processor who receives them. Information from the sales drafts is captured by the processor and subsequently transmitted to the issuing member. During periods of low authorization volume, International Credit System (ICS), a subsidiary of a St. Louis based processing member of ICA which contracts to run the INET system, transmits electronic draft information to ICA members through the INAS switch.

Interbank Associations. A great many of the functions and responsibilities that are handled by VISA in the BWG system, are accomplished by the associations that form the backbone of the Master Charge program. Associations, as the name implies, are groups of financial institutions (primarily commercial banks) that have banded together to achieve a common goal, which in this case is processing Master Charge sales. The associations typically do much more than just processing, however. Although as independent organizations the functions each association performs vary, an association will normally assume responsibility for marketing, investigations, security, authorizations, reporting, national interchange, research and development, data capture and retrieval, and merchant accounting for the member banks of the association.

Principal Bank Responsibilities. It would be misleading to imply that because they cooperatively process Master Charge, the principal banks comprising an association do not compete among themselves for cardholders and merchants—the very reverse is the rule. Each association principal member is responsible for establishing and administering credit policy, servicing cardholders, setting merchant discount rates, determining service charges, establishing agent bank relationships, providing account support to the association, and aiding in investigation activities. The foregoing list of duties and responsibilities of association and principal banks is not intended to be all inclusive, and may vary from association to association, and from bank to bank.

INTERBANK ASSOCIATIONS

Advantages

In the discussion of VISA, the advantages of the single-processing entity concept, which permeates the BWG system, were outlined. Many advantages are also inherent in the association concept. The capital requirements for starting a bank card program, which are formidable, are spread among a group of institutions and are therefore within the reach of many organizations that could not solely bear the costs. Second, associations avoid the duplication of facilities and staff that is characteristic of the BWG system. One centralized staff, located in a single facility, can do the processing work for many banks.

Operating jointly, several banks can have a much greater impact on a given market than could any of the banks acting alone. Many small banks have a limited number of dollars available for marketing bank cards; but when their marketing dollars and support are combined with a number of other banks, the impact can be significant.

Whereas the bank card market of a single bank is often limited to its immediate geographical area and existing customer base, the association broadens, through cooperative marketing efforts, the marketing horizons of the smaller banks. Naturally, the individual banks conduct their own marketing campaigns in addition to the joint association program, in an attempt to establish product differentiation, singling out the benefits (perceived or real) of their own Master Charge program.

Disadvantages

Policy decisions can be difficult to achieve expediently in associations. Conceivably it could be quite difficult to get a bank card policy consensus from a number of banks which are highly competitive in every area except the processing of Master Charge drafts. If this conflict occurred among association members, the decision-making process, which is essential to the success of any business venture, could come to a virtual standstill. Operational and servicing procedures can also be cumbersome under the association concept, as in many cases both the principal banks and the association are involved in customer servicing and accounting.

COMPARISON OF ICA AND VISA

It is significant that two systems which differ in many ways, have over the years yielded results that are remarkably similar. Exhibit 65–1 delineates pertinent statistics for the two national card programs for the calendar years 1970 and 1976. Although the "outstandings" statistics for 1976, viewed alone, are impressive, the two card programs together accounted for slightly less than 5 percent of total retail credit extended in the United States during the year 1976.

Exhibit 65–1
Comparison of Interbank and VISA Domestic Statistics*

	1970	1976
Gross Volume:		
(year, in thousands)		
VISA....................................	$ 2,773,500	$11,100,000
Interbank...............................	4,143,500	13,700,000
Outstandings:		
(end of year, in thousands)		
VISA....................................	n.a.	5,200,000
Interbank...............................	n.a.	6,500,000
Cardholders:		
VISA....................................	25,958,000	33,900,000
Interbank...............................	35,938,000	40,700,000
Accounts:		
VISA....................................	15,270,000	20,600,000
Interbank...............................	21,632,000	25,000,000
Active Accounts:		
VISA....................................	6,670,000	13,700,000
Interbank...............................	8,604,000	16,700,000
Merchant Outlets:		
VISA....................................	679,518	1,321,000
Interbank...............................	869,549	1,368,000
Participating Banks:		
VISA....................................	3,751	7,879
Interbank...............................	5,360	8,594

n.a. = not available.
* Some figures have been rounded to simplify comparisons.
Sources: Kneeland Moore, Interbank Card Association, and Ronald Schmidt, VISA U.S.A., Inc.

DUALITY

Duality (the participation by a financial institution in both national bank card programs) has been a significant issue since the formation of the two national bank card associations in the late 60s. VISA has taken a leadership role in formulating policies governing dual card participation, while ICA has elected to remain tacit.

Summarizing the important events that have affected duality, VISA initially ruled that its members could not participate as card issuing members of ICA. Following a suit by the Worthen Bank and Trust of Little Rock, Arkansas, VISA compromised and allowed for "limited participation" on the part of its members in both national card programs. A business ruling by the Justice Department in 1975, failed to provide NBI with the necessary support to maintain that constrictive posture, and subsequently in 1976, NBI issued a fiat that allowed its members to participate to any degree desired in the Interbank program.

This decision on the part of VISA U.S.A., Inc. remains highly controversial. Many bankers feel that the ultimate result of dual card participation will be a de facto merger of ICA and VISA, resulting in a quasi-utility and hence increased government regulation. Others look with favor on the decision, as they feel it will allow them to provide more complete banking services to their customers.

DEBIT CARDS

While debit cards are still very much in their infancy and are undergoing a dynamic evolutionary process, it is important to recognize that debit cards have added a new dimension to bank cards. Bank cards traditionally have been credit cards; that is, use of a bank card created a debt by the cardholder to the issuer. True debit cards allow cardholders to access funds on deposit as they would if they were writing a check. Other types of so-called debit cards are actually check guarantee cards and are used in conjunction with normal bank checks. Both national associations have made tentative steps into the debit card market, but currently no program exists on a national level that is at all comparable in size with either Master Charge or VISA credit.

Entree

A great deal of disagreement still exists among bankers on the proper evolutionary process for debit cards. NBI initially elected to utilize existing BWG systems with its "Entree" card, which is a draft-oriented debit card.

"Entree" is similar in many respects to VISA. The card itself utilizes the familiar Blue, White, and Gold Bands design, enabling merchants and agent banks to follow identical processing procedures for Entree and VISA sales drafts. The difference between Entree and VISA becomes apparent only when Blue, White, and Gold sales drafts reach a processing or card-issuing bank. At that point, Entree sales are posted to the cardholder's checking account while VISA sales are treated as a credit transaction and posted to a VISA account.

Signet

ICA meanwhile has announced their intent to offer "Signet," which is designed to be a national check guarantee program operating totally independently of Master Charge. Unlike Entree, Signet will be a check-oriented system. Merchants and banks participating in the program will sign separate agreements which are unrelated to the Master Charge program. A totally new and independent authorization system is being developed by ICA to enable merchants to obtain guarantees for Signet transactions. Once a guarantee has been recorded on a check, however, the merchant and participating banks will utilize normal check-clearing channels for processing the guaranteed check.

Many debit card and check guarantee programs also exist at the local and regional level. These programs range in sophistication from manual check guarantee procedures to on-line real time EFTS (electronic funds transfer systems).

EFTS DEVELOPMENT

A discussion of EFTS, per se, is beyond the scope of this chapter. It is important, and relevant, however, to briefly delineate the contributions bank cards have made to the development of EFTS. Both VISA and ICA have developed and implemented vast sophisticated networks (BASE I and II, and INAS and INET) for the electronic exchange of data. These networks have opened entire new vistas and opportunities which were unknown ten years ago. The previously described functions of authorizations, interchange, paper truncation, and draft capture and transmission, have been the result of recent dramatic changes in computer hardware and software and the development of accompanying personnel expertise.

The sheer size of the two national bank card systems and the volume of transactions processed through these systems, have forced banks to develop volume-processing expertise. Certainly the manual equipment that was characteristic of bank proof operations only a short time ago, was not conducive to processing the transaction volumes that resulted from the development of bank cards. Paper truncation, which eliminates the flow of paper through the bank card systems, is a crucial prerequisite to EFTS. Both VISA and ICA now have the capability of exchanging electronically, information captured from paper sales drafts. As previously described, actual sales drafts are no longer exchanged by licensee members in either system.

While the above-mentioned electronic gains are deservedly impressive, other EFT-related benefits have accrued from the evolution of bank cards. Relationships have been established between banks and their merchant customers and cardholder customers that will facilitate any future EFT developments. Cardholders have become accustomed to receiving computer-printed "facsimile drafts" or, in many cases, a computer-generated descriptive bill in lieu of any drafts.

Merchants, on the other hand, have learned to accept nationwide authorizations, computer-printed statements, and plastic cards with embossing and encoding, all integral parts of EFTS. These procedures are all important in establishing a proper foundation for future EFTS developments.

While the bank card industry cannot lay claim to the success (or failure) of future EFTS, historians will certainly view EFTS as the natural evolutionary product of a process that had its real beginnings with bank cards.

SUMMARY

In a period of slightly more than one decade, the two major bank card organizations have evolved from relatively significant regional programs to international programs of considerable consequence. As Exhibit 65–1 illustrated, gross sales volume in 1976 for VISA and Interbank together totaled more than $24 billion, an increase of approximately 300 percent in six years. While growth of the two systems has slowed somewhat in recent years, prognosticators suggest that sales volumes for the two programs will continue to increase significantly in the foreseeable future.

The future of bank cards, as a medium of exchange, is unknown. By almost any standard, however, bank card programs now contribute significantly to the profit picture of many banks. Certainly the convenience offered by the two national bank card programs has filled a real void in consumer financing.

There can be no question that bank card programs have been extremely important in establishing a base for future EFT developments. Many view bank cards, including debit cards, as vehicles which will enable banks to gradually and logically develop a viable cost-justified system of EFT. To be successful, the cost of EFTS must be shared by merchants, consumers, and banks. Bank cards pioneered this cost-sharing approach, which marks a dramatic departure from some other areas of commercial banking where competition has outweighed prudence in establishing price structures.

The success of the recent past and the opportunities on the horizon suggest the future of bank cards is indeed bright.

Chapter 66

Safekeeping Services

*James A. Cassin**

INTRODUCTION

Over the years retail banking has evolved from a routine, rather basic operation to a very sophisticated, highly regulated, technically involved, and, therefore, demanding part of the full-service bank. This evolution has been the result of many forces and factors which have combined to produce rapid changes in the banking industry. Whereas it used to be that only a few customers were seeking a few retail banking products, the situation is now such that virtually every consumer is invited to shop the financial marketplace for a wide range of asset and liability products as well as improved services and ingenious marketing gimmicks.

In the midst of these changes in the role of retail banking, it is important to remember that perception of an institution's security remains an essential ingredient in the mixture of reasons for consumer selection of a banking relationship.

For purposes of this chapter, it is important to contrast and highlight two types of safekeeping services frequently offered by commercial banks—safe deposit services and custody services. *Safe deposit services* are defined as those services which offer the customer the opportunity to store his valuables in a vault protected with all due diligence by the operating institution. Safe deposit services enable the customers to benefit from the security offered by a bank while retaining sole control over their valuables. *Custody services* are defined as those services which are offered for purposes of securing, handling, or collecting a customer's assets and their periodic proceeds. In practice, different

---

*Senior Vice President, First National Bank, Chicago, Illinois.

895

institutions offer a wide range of custody services under various labels and for slightly different purposes. The term custody services refers to the entire breadth of bank services for the handling of the retail customer's securities. This distinction is important from both a legal and bank management standpoint. Custody services, given this working definition, clearly exclude safe deposit services since the latter operation can never "handle" valuables. The simplest statement to distinguish the two services is the following: safe deposit operations are concerned only with the customer's access to his or her valuables, custody operations are concerned with the handling of the customer's assets themselves.

The major focus of this chapter is on safe deposit services. Safe deposit services are typically included in the retail banking organization while custody services more frequently are integrated into other commercial bank activities.

SAFE DEPOSIT SERVICES

The safe deposit department has traditionally been thought of as a service area whose purpose is to meet the desire of commercial bank customers for personal safekeeping services. While this is in fact an important role for the safe deposit department, the operation is much more than a service area—it is a source of revenue, a generator of additional business for other bank departments (rather than just a recipient of other department's business), and a means of developing positive customer relations. The safe deposit operation is unique since it is the one place in which the dollar value of a customer's assets is unknown. It is one place that always requires personal interface with customers as a part of routine business.

Legal rules may vary from state to state and all procedures, operations, and agreements should be reviewed for conformance with the legal rules which apply to the bank's geographic area.

OPERATIONAL PROCEDURES

The Contract

Safe deposit operations are controlled by a contract which contains the rules and conditions which govern the vault operation. The contract is *the* basic document in that it sets forth the relationship between the renter and the safe deposit department. To confirm that it limits the vault's (and the bank's) liability to acceptable levels, the contract should be reviewed at regular intervals by management and legal counsel.

The following are routine provisions which should normally be included in the contract. Since state laws vary in terms of the legal obligations of safe deposit operations, only general guidelines are presented. However, the following list suggests those provisions that every bank should consider for inclusion in the contract subject to the constraints of the governing state laws.

1. The vault's *name* should appear in a prominent place.
2. A *liability clause* should state that the vault is obligated to exercise ordinary care and diligence to prevent the opening of a safe by any person not having access to it. The contract should specify that the vault is *not* to be considered an insurer of the contents. The mere fact that a customer believes that something is missing does not imply that an improper access has been made.
3. The relationship between the renter and his or her deputy is one of principal and agent. As such, the contract should consider the role of *deputies* and might include the following types of specifications.
    a. The authority of the deputy continues until revoked by his or her principal or until death of the principal.
    b. The vault is not liable for permitting access to a deputy until it receives written notice that his or her authority has been canceled.
    c. The vault may refuse to honor authorization and powers not executed in its office and in the presence of a member of its staff.
4. The contract should specify that *co-renters* have equal rights of access and that any one of them has the authority to exchange, surrender, or transfer a safe.
5. In the event of impending *litigations,* or unresolved *claims,* the contract should specify that if by any process against a person having access to a safe the vault is forbidden from allowing the safe to be opened by such persons, this safe may be closed to all persons until the process is resolved. In the case of conflicting claims, the vault may suspend all right of access until advised by counsel of its rights arising out of such claims. Such suspension may continue until a release in favor of the vault is received or until the vault is advised by its counsel that the claim is without merit.
6. *Rental* and expiration dates should be specified in the contract.
7. *Termination* procedures should also be included. The renter who wishes to terminate ordinarily need only remove the contents from his or her safe, surrender the keys, and sign a receipt and discharge. The contract might also specify that the renter gets

no refund of the unused rent at termination. The contract may also be terminated by the vault. Notice should be given to the customer (at least ten days in advance) in writing via registered mail to safeguard the vault's interests. If rent has been paid in advance, the vault must send a check to the renter for the unused part of the rent. The contract should specify that the vault may drill open the safe, remove the contents, and store them at the owner's risk, subject to usual storage charges if the customer fails to comply with certain specified procedures.

8. The contract should specify the inheritance *tax examination* procedures that the vault is required to follow. Where applicable, the vault should outline its legal requirements regarding examination of safes and waivers from inheritance tax authorities.

9. The contract should affirm the safe deposit company's authority to fix business *days* and business *hours.* The contract should also include a provision which absolves the vault from liability if the doors or locks fail to operate properly.

10. The company should reserve the right in the contract to make such *amendments and additions* to the rules and conditions as in its judgment may from time to time be prudent, desirable, or proper in the conduct of its business.

This is not meant to be an exhaustive list of contract provisions. Each vault manager, in consort with counsel, should carefully evaluate contract provisions to assure that they adhere to state laws while limiting the liability of the vault.

TYPES OF RENTALS

Safe deposit boxes may be rented to individuals, to two or more persons as co-renters, to a corporation, to an unincorporated organization, to a partnership, to a fiduciary, or to a government agency.

Individual Rentals

In accepting an individual rental account, it is important to have assurance that the name given by the renter is the legal name and that the address given is the actual place of residence.

Co-Renters

Each co-renter must sign the contract. In the typical contract, each co-renter may have full access to the box, even to remove the contents and surrender the box, without the knowledge or physical presence of the other co-renter.

Although co-renters have equal rights of access to the box, this alone does not give them survivorship rights to the contents of the box. A safe deposit box is not a method of transferring title to property. Vault management is never in a position to advise as to the ownership of the contents of a box and can only specify the contacted rights of access to the box.

A co-renter can neither add to nor remove from the contract another co-renter's name unless the other co-renter consents to the change. Any renter, however, has the option of removing his or her own name from the contract.

Corporations

When renting to a corporation, the contract is signed in the name of the corporation. The contract should be signed by an authorized officer of the corporation in his or her official capacity.

When renting the box, the vault should ask for a certified copy of a resolution of the board of directors authorizing rental of the box and specifying the persons, either by name or title, who are to have access. The resolution should be attested to by the secretary of the corporation and it should bear the corporate seal if there is one.

If individuals are authorized access by name, a new resolution will be required whenever a change is made in authorization. If authorization is designated by title only, a certified signature of the new officer is required for a change in authorization.

Unincorporated Organizations

The procedure for renting to associations or unincorporated organizations is similar to that used in corporate rentals.

Partnerships

When renting to a partnership, a copy of the partnership agreement should be secured from the renters. If possible, all partners should sign the contract. If this is not possible, the signatures of one or more general partners is normally acceptable. The signature of any partner who is to have right to access to the box must be secured. A partnership authorization form should be completed, indicating who shall have access to the box. A new authorization form should accompany any change in authorization for access.

Fiduciaries

As a group, fiduciaries are taken to include executors, administrators, guardians, conservators, and trustees. Trustees may be named under will, under agreement, or in bankruptcy. Receivers in bankruptcy are also included in this group.

All rentals to fiduciaries should clearly state the nature of the rental and should be supported by documentary evidence of the authority of the renter.

Government Agencies

Boxes may be rented to a municipality or a public corporation. Proper authority can be verified by public officials, for example: the corporation counsel for city officials; the state's attorney for county officials; and the attorney general for state officials.

Minors

It is never advisable to rent a box to a minor since a minor can typically repudiate a contract at any time. If an exception is made, the minor should not be permitted to appoint a deputy.

DEPUTIES

A renter may wish to authorize a deputy, or agent, access to his or her box. The renter may appoint a deputy simply by signing a proper appointment of deputy form.

There is no contract between the deputy and the vault company. The renter should be informed of the following facts when considering a deputy appointment.

1. The renter—not the vault—is responsible for the conduct of the deputy.
2. The deputy has unrestricted access to the safe deposit box and the vault management cannot implement any special instructions governing this access.
3. In case of the death of a deputy, an inheritance tax examination may be necessary (depending upon individual state laws).
4. The renter may cancel the access authority of his or her deputy, in writing, at any time; the renter's death or incapacity will cancel such authority.

General powers of attorney are generally considered to be too broad and not specific enough to be recognized for access to a safe deposit box. For instance, the signer may not have considered that the "broad powers" given in such an instrument may cause the attorney in fact to try to gain access to his or her safe deposit box. Courts have held, too that where access authority was not specifically given in a power, such authority was specifically excluded.

There may come a set of circumstances that make it desirable to consider accepting a general power. At that time, the power and the circumstances should be discussed with counsel and together decide what is to be done.

ACCESS PROCEDURES

Much of the vault's liability—in both a legal sense and a practical sense—is a result of some form of improper access. Access procedures which will protect the safe deposit company and all its customers are of primary importance.

Most safe deposit companies use a signature system when granting access to the vault. This simply means that each time a customer requests access to his box, he signs an access ticket in the presence of the vault attendant. This procedure has a twofold purpose. First, it provides a means of identification; second, it provides proof that the access was made, in case it is disputed at a later date. *Proper identification of each person requesting access is extremely important.* Mere possession of the key is not evidence of the right of access.

Increasingly, safe deposit operations are finding it helpful to require the customer to provide some type of identification. Additionally, modern technology is being used particularly in high traffic operations. For example, small automated cameras can be located at the signature counters to photograph the customers when the access ticket is received.

The following rules help guide in granting, or denying access:

Require that a customer with more than one safe deposit box sign a separate access ticket for each box to which access is requested.

When a contract requires joint access by two or more renters, never deviate from its terms under any circumstances. The customers have jointly stipulated the access requirements and only they can jointly change them.

Never act on telephone, telegraph, or cable communications requesting access.

Never allow access (even to a deputy) on notice of death, mental incapacity, or bankruptcy of a renter or one of several renters, until legal requirements have been properly fulfilled.

Never allow access if served with a garnishment, injunction, or other restraining order without first consulting counsel.

Never grant access to an agent of an agent, because a deputy may not appoint a deputy.

The customer's key should never be in the vault's possession, even when granting access, unless the attendant is in full view of the customer. Boxes should not be opened or examined in the vault, but only in special private rooms provided for that purpose. Insist that the customer use one (most contracts require this).

These procedures may seem tedious, but they serve to protect the vault from potential liability and unfair accusations while assuring the customer of the vault's concern for security and confidentiality of his or her valuables.

AUDIT PROCEDURES

In developing proper audit procedures, the vault manager should keep in mind the need to maximize control of operations while adhering to the prescriptions of the bank's general audit procedures. The size of the operation will, in part, dictate the frequency of reporting.

VAULT EQUIPMENT

The quality of the safe deposit vault equipment is important for two reasons. First, such equipment represents a substantial capital investment for the company and proper regular maintenance can reduce expenses in the long run which might result from the need for complete overhauls or major repairs. Second, the promise of the safe deposit operation is one of security and to meet this pledge management must be assured that vault equipment is functioning flawlessly. The safe deposit company can be held liable for ignoring flaws in vault equipment which lead to loss of box contents. The vault equipment should be maintained and serviced by an accredited safe or lock company on a regular contract basis.

CUSTOMER RELATIONS

As a service area, the primary responsibility of the safe deposit department is to establish and maintain positive relations with all customers. The safe deposit operation is people intensive and the generation of additional business is directly related to the quality of the vault's personal service. In most banks, the safe deposit department is regarded as a place which operates so as to meet the needs of customers with other account relationships and customers who might be inclined to establish other account relationships. This expectation, then, places a responsibility on the operation to always provide quality service.

When selecting staff, the manager should look for personal attitudes and attributes which will reflect the objective of customer service. In training of the staff, the vault manager should seek to accomplish a dual goal of having employees who are knowledgeable about the vault's overall operation and sensitive to customer concerns.

Confidentiality should be a strict guideline for all staff. A customer's business affairs should never be discussed with anyone else.

The safe deposit staff should also be prepared to handle the disturbed customer with a polite objectivity. Customers can become emotionally upset for many reasons. In all cases involving such customers it is essential to deal with the customer's feelings before trying to reason with him. Once the customer is more comfortable one can begin to explore the problems in greater detail. Approaching problems in this way serves to retain goodwill while protecting the operation from unfair accusations.

Safe deposit staff often are not given sufficient recognition and rewards to reflect their importance in the organization. Vault management and bank management should realize the importance of this first line of service staff and assure that monetary and nonmonetary rewards are allocated in accordance with appropriate organizational recognition.

LEGAL COUNSEL

Throughout this chapter it has been suggested that all operational procedures which might in any way affect the vault's liability should be carefully reviewed with legal counsel. At the same time, it is equally important that the vault manager have a working knowledge of the fundamental legal principles governing the safe deposit business. As in any operation, decisions must sometimes be made rapidly and legal counsel may not be available. An irritated customer may suddenly produce an attorney who although not knowledgeable of the law governing safe deposit operations, may attempt to intimidate the vault staff with nimble, legal footwork. The vault manager with some knowledge of the legal principles governing his or her business can handle such situations well and make it easier to work with the bank's own legal counsel. Remember that legal counsel should be used to assist the vault management in limiting liability and that the most competent counsel cannot anticipate and prepare for all potential problems.

PRICING

The safe deposit operation should be viewed as a profit-generating business. Although the operation is important in providing services which will encourage multiple product customer relationships, and therefore indirectly generate profitable business, safe deposit services should always be viewed as a potential source of revenue in and of themselves. Pricing strategy should be determined on the basis of costs and the price the market will bear given competitive factors.

All too often, rental fees are held firm for long periods of time while increasing costs erode the operation's profits. Vault managers are often held responsible for profit gains or losses while the pricing structure is ignored. Customers realize that business expenses increase over time and are unlikely to consider a reasonable price increase to be sufficient reason to seek safe deposit services at another institution. Naturally, flexible pricing in order to compete effectively is essential, particularly in generating new business.

There are other sources of revenue available to the safe deposit operation aside from the obvious rental fee income. For example, past-due rent charges, increased key deposits, and drilling charges are all potential sources of revenue. While the market might be unwilling to bear increased rental charges, there may be little objection to increasing such other fees as those listed. Furthermore, these other charges serve to recoup expenses which may be rising dramatically and which in fact affect a very small part of the customer base.

SECURITY

Implicit in the operation of the safe deposit department is a promise of "security." What this promise means and how it can or should be interpreted are complicated and unresolved issues. A pledge of security—explicit or implicit—raises many legal questions which must be carefully reviewed with counsel when drafting the contract and any marketing literature. Although the safe deposit operation's liability is of major concern, management should carefully consider the implications of a breakdown in security (whether the vault's fault or not) in customer confidence.

The issue of security of the vault itself has increased in importance in the last decade as a result of sophisticated burglary attempts and radical political movements. The vault represents a "challenge" to many burglars and it represents a bastian of capitalism to radical groups. Both of these elements have understandably caused vault managers a great deal of concern, but each for different reasons.

The vault manager must take every precaution to prevent the disastrous results that would be produced from an explosive device being placed in the vault. In a small operation, the safe deposit staff can become familiar enough with the customers to quickly determine any abnormal activity or requests. However, the targets of potential disaster are typically the larger banks whose volume of customers make it nearly impossible to identify with certainty all customer transactions. The vault manager should then be concerned with two things—access procedures and initial rental processing.

The most important ingredient in vault security is to verify the identity of all safe deposit box customers before rental of a box. Some banks require that the applicant have an existing account relationship. Contacts may include a clause which permits the bank to enter the box under circumstances giving grounds for suspicions of the commission of a crime in or around the safe deposit vault. Whatever, the method, adequate precautions must be a part of the routine operational procedures.

The so-called disaster concerns of vault security are important, but the vast majority of claims for losses are based on alleged negligence of the vault and/or its employees. While procedures should be designed so as to prevent the "worst" from occurring, security procedures should be standard and routine so as to prevent any potential losses.

CUSTODY SERVICES

Safe deposit services fulfill the needs of customers who want the security offered by a bank, yet wish to retain complete control of their own valuables. However, the safe deposit operation is concerned only with access, never with assets. This distinction is important to remember in a discussion of the second major type of safekeeping service offered by banks—custody services.

Custody services have been referred to as those services which a bank offers for purposes of securing, handling, or collecting of assets and their periodic proceeds. A wide array of services are available and they differ in functional composition as well as in organizational format. Some institutions deal with all types of securities under one safekeeping department. Other institutions offer slightly different services depending upon the type of security (equity or fixed income, bearer or registered form) through multiple department involvement. The major purposes of this section will be to point out certain operational considerations, discuss issues of limiting liability, and review some of the current developments in the offering of custodial services. To avoid any confusion, it should be emphasized that the term "custody services" is used descriptively and no serious distinctions are being made between the terms "safekeeping services" and "custody services" as they apply to the handling of securities.

Operational Considerations

Since there exists such a wide array of custody services provided by banks, it is important to specify exactly what services are being rendered in any given relationship. If an institution segments its services organizationally in such a way that a given relationship with a given department means the provision of specific services, then an "agreement" has been implicitly stated. In this situation the absence of a formal written agreement does not significantly alter the bank's responsibilities.

Although relationships with corporations and correspondent banks frequently do not necessitate that a formal written agreement be executed for each custody arrangement, written agreements continue to be used in custody relationships with individuals. In any case, the bank and customer typically agree to arrangements such as the following to consummate the agreement.

1. Designation of the individual(s) who, either in his or her own right, or as agent for an organization, has been authorized to enter into the agreement and to act in accordance with the terms of the agreement.
2. Designation of the desired form of registration for the securities held in custody and the name and address of the person to whom information is to be sent.
3. Delineation of the specific responsibilities of the bank, such as:
    a. Responsibility for the storage of specific securities.
    b. Preparation of periodic and regular informational documentation.
    c. Handling of exchanges of securities under instructions from the customer.
    d. Disposition of security proceeds as requested by the customer.
    e. Preparation of reports upon the customer's request describing securities held and indicating the par value of bonds and the number of shares held of stock in custody.
    f. Prescription of the method for collection of fees and expenses.

Liability

The relationship between a bank and its customers resulting from the deposit of securities with it for safekeeping is considered that of bailor and bailee. This relation means that the very thing deposited must be returned to the depositor, and to carry out this obligation the bank must use ordinary care and diligence in safekeeping the securities. As with safe deposit services, a bank does not assume liability as an insurer and, therefore, is liable only for loss resulting from its failure to exercise such care as required by law. The exercise of "ordinary care" is demonstrated by such things as the provision of modern vaults, adequate police protection, and the use of protective devices. This responsibility is imposed upon the bank whether or not it is stated in the typical agreement form governing the operation of a custody relationship. Other types of risks assumed by the bank performing custody services are insurable and policies covering loss by employee dishonesty, burglary, robbery, holdup, theft, damage, destruction, or mysterious disappearance are ordinarily covered by a "bankers blanket bond" plus excess policies for burglary and robbery.

Well-documented practices are also desirable to govern the care given to the protection of securities and the records maintained to control the servicing of securities and to process customer requests. In order to discharge this responsibility it is necessary to maintain records to assure the timely crediting of income and payments resulting from called, redeemed, and matured bonds to a customer's account. In addition, procedures to be followed in exchanging securities, processing stock dividends, and other types of security transactions are required. There is always the risk that, despite tight controls, a bank may fail to process a security, thereby subjecting the account to the loss of a stock dividend, exchange rights, or other damages. In such cases, subject to the limitations stated in the custody agreement, the bank will normally assume responsibility for the oversight. The possibility of such losses can be minimized by regular reference to available security services which report changes affecting customer holdings.

Current Developments

Improved technology has greatly facilitated the ease with which a bank can provide custody services. Regular reports as simple as an advice of credit or as complex as an analysis of all of a corporation's security holdings can be generated rapidly and accurately.

While custody services continue to be important products for security features, they are increasingly marketable as information-oriented systems. The more sophisticated consumer seeks more than a safe place for securities—he seeks a safe place that will meet his needs for timely and accurate information. Clearly, custody services offered by banks will become more and more information oriented as technological advances continue to evolve to meet the customer's detailed desires.

SUMMARY

This chapter has attempted to cover some of the key issues involved in retail safekeeping services. The subject is a complicated subject and a complete treatment of all issues is beyond the scope of this chapter.

Safekeeping services will continue to play an important role in the retail banking environment. Improved technology will continue to have its impact on safekeeping services, especially in terms of informational flows. At the same time, safe deposit services will always remain a people intensive service. Safe deposit services may in the future be the one operation which requires that the customer come to the bank to conduct business. As retail banking continues to evolve, safekeeping services may prove to be the lead product in generating multiple relationships. Clearly, then, all forms of retail safekeeping services require the attention and concern of the management of growth-oriented banks.

Chapter 67 _____

Electronic Delivery Systems for Retail Services

Robert M. Klingler*

THE NEED FOR NEW RETAIL DELIVERY SYSTEMS

A new delivery system for retail banking services is rapidly emerging. It is a system based on automation and electronic messages versus the manned brick and mortar, paper-based system of today. The changes are occurring rapidly, but in an evolutionary manner rather than revolutionary. New systems are being installed to complement the existing delivery system rather than to replace it.

The consumer acceptance of this new system, the proper legal or regulatory treatment of it, the potential security and privacy risks in its evolution, and the economic justification for its implementation are all areas that are rapidly changing and where there are far more questions and controversy than answers. Consequently, a chapter of this nature has two major inherent risks. First, the information presented may be somewhat outdated due to the necessary time lag between writing and your reading. Second, the information presented must be considered somewhat biased, as the author is admittedly biased because his direct experience in automated banking.

The new delivery system could include, but would certainly not be limited to the much discussed electronic funds transfer (EFT). True electronic funds transfer may be the end result of these efforts and may someday actually replace the paper-based system. But many of the new developments in automated banking have been designed to

---

* Vice President, The Central Trust Company, N.A., Cincinnati, Ohio.

enhance the check system, to make the check an improved payment vehicle.

There seem to be two principal forces behind this movement toward automated banking. The first is simply the competitive requirement to meet the customer's demand for greater convenience. Of the factors affecting a customer's choice of a financial institutions, location, and hours typically rank right at the top of the list. Automated banking facilities allow the bank to take products and services to the customer at a time and place convenient to the customer rather than the financial institution. Time and place convenience for the customer is the key. Technological advances now allow banks to deliver services around the clock and in far more locations than previously possible. Is it necessary? Are not numerous brick and mortar branches open as much as 25 percent of the hours of a week sufficient to serve the public? Possibly, but in the author's opinion, we need only to look at the trend in hours throughout the retailing industry for the answer.

The second force is pure economics. Banking is a labor-intensive industry and if it is to progress, banking must, like any industry, improve productivity. Bankers must hold down personnel costs in the delivery of products and services. This does not mean a less personal approach to banking. But rather it means taking advantage of technological advances and letting machines do what machines do best, and people do what people do best. It means reducing the heavily routine transaction-oriented type of business now handled in manned banking facilities by diverting that activity to machines and allowing for greater personal service for the more complex transactions and problems.

ESTABLISHING OBJECTIVES AND JUSTIFICATIONS

It is unfortunate but probably true that much of the activity in automated banking to date has been predicated on keeping up with the Jones, or in this case, the bank down the street. Economically justifying a specific venture in automated banking is difficult in that it usually is based on controversial assumptions. Further, factors differ so widely between banks and their marketplaces that anything other than broad generalizations on economic justification would be inappropriate.

What can be more easily discussed are the broad goals or objectives of some of the initial attempts in automated banking. The objectives seem to fall in three major categories.

The first objective and probably the most common is to increase or, at least retain, a share of the retail market. There are success stories indicating that well-designed and marketed automated programs can impact a share of the maket. Customers' choice of a financial institution is based largely on time and place convenience. Whether major long-term shifts in market share are possible probably depends upon the ability of the competition to respond and the timeliness of that response. As large automated machine networks are complicated and expensive, competition response times may be quite long.

A second objective may be to develop new sources of fee revenue. What the retail customer will pay, or even whether he or she will pay at all, for the added convenience in this new delivery system remains to be seen. Many studies have been made on this subject with conflicting results and now there is little experience in either direction. Few banks are charging customers directly for the use of automated services or facilities. However, many are charging indirectly by making the "access device," usually a plastic debit card, part of an account relationship requiring a larger fee or balance than the competitive market would justify without the debit card.

A second source of fee revenue is the retail merchant. The acceptance of checks by a merchant may be necessary as a customer service, but involves a number of definable costs. The bad check write-off itself and the collection effort to minimize that write-off are obvious expenses well known to almost all merchants who accept checks. But the large volume check-cashing retail stores, such as the supermarkets, are also aware of the labor expense involved in authorizing checks, the cost of maintaining their own check-cashing systems, and the loss of available cash balances due to float. To the extent that automated systems can reduce these expenses, transaction fees can be available from this source. These services will be discussed later in the chapter.

The third objective of developing a new delivery system is cost reduction. The theory behind electronic funds transfer is that electronic impulses are cheaper than paper messages. There can probably be little argument as to the validity of this theory but the problem occurs in getting there. If the bank must maintain both delivery systems, electronics and paper, during a period of evolutionary change, then the cost of both systems will surely be greater than the present paper-based system. There are those who also would argue that it is not a matter of alternatives, that the present paper-based system will simply be unable to handle the volume of transactions in the future. It would seem to the author that this particular theory ignores advances which might be made in the paper-based system such as check truncation at the original bank of deposit. Even if valid, these changes are undoubtedly very long-term and would seem to have little impact on the thinking of most banks in their current planning.

Most banks appear to be looking at automated facilities as cost alternatives to other means of providing time and place convenience. For many, the installation of automated teller machines is seen as an alternative to extended weekday or Saturday banking hours. Off-premise automated teller machines or clerk-activated terminals providing deposit and withdrawal service can be an attractive cost alternative to expensive brick and mortar facilities. Routine transactions handled through electronic terminals may postpone the need to add to a teller staff. The mathematics involved is relatively easy, however, the basic assumptions are arguable. Can you compare a withdrawal from an automated teller machine at 10:00 P.M. on a Saturday evening to a withdrawal over a teller window at 2:00 P.M. Thursday? Will sufficient people be satisfied with an automated facility inside a supermarket or is a full-service traditional branch a requirement to attract new customers?

The important point, of course, is that whichever objective or combination of objectives is chosen, that choice will dictate what type of approach is made to automated banking. And the investment in these facilities can then only be justified in terms of reaching those objectives.

Let us now review very briefly the various possible components of a new electronic retail delivery system.

AUTOMATED TELLER MACHINES

The automated teller machine (ATM), has most often been the initial step in automated banking. Installed through-the-wall at branch sites, it offers customers for the first time true time convenience. This facility provides the customer with a reason to carry a plastic access card and remember a four-digit personal identification number (PIN). Initial usage is typically a cash withdrawal from either a checking or savings account, but as the customer gains confidence in the reliability of the equipment, deposit transactions grow in number. In a mature program withdrawals outnumber deposits on almost a 4:1 ratio, however, in dollars, deposits typically run almost 2:1 over withdrawals. Transfers between accounts and payment of utility bills and loan accounts grow with customer confidence. On ATMs operated on-line, the bank usually has an option of offering balance inquiry. Where available this function often accounts for approximately 20 percent of the transactions.

The most commonly used measure for the consumer acceptance of ATMs has been the number of transactions per month per machine. This measure has a major weakness in that it may not correspond to the principal objective in the installation of the equipment. However, it is a statistic typically kept by banks and consequently one that is easily compared. In 1977, a number of automated programs are reporting average monthly transactions of 5,000 to 8,000 with a few programs averaging 10,000 transactions a month and higher.

For those banks deciding to install ATMs, the major questions are location and mode of operation, on-line versus off-line.

Off-premise locations are becoming more popular as the legal and regulatory picture begins to clear. By going off-premise, a bank begins to offer place as well as time convenience. The most popular off-premise location appears to be the supermarket to take advantage of the customer's very similar grocery shopping and banking patterns. For years, a popular branch location strategy has been to locate close to major supermarkets. The advent of the ATM allows one to take that strategy one step further, to locate facilities not just close to but actually inside the supermarket. Other off-premise locations showing promise are major plant and office buildings, hospitals, airports, university campuses, and shopping centers.

Experience to date indicates that the off-premise ATM cannot be used to attack a brand new market, but is most effectively used as a satellite facility for a full-service branch located reasonably nearby.

The question of on-line versus off-line operation usually revolves around two principal areas, marketing and security. On-line operation theoretically allows a bank to issue access cards to all of their customers thereby greatly reducing a potential marketing problem. In addition, balance inquiry can be offered as a function on the machine. Larger cash-back limits may be granted to the customer, theoretically, although not practically, up to the full available balance in his or her account. The importance of these advantages is really dependent upon the off-line alternatives. A well-designed and complete automated customer information file, if available, can be used to establish card issue criteria and reasonable cash-back limits for the vast majority of the bank's customers. In the area of security, the question is principally one of economics. Off-line operation will allow customers to overdraw their accounts and undoubtedly result in some losses. This risk of loss must then be measured against the added cost of on-line operation.

For many banks the question of putting ATMs on-line is a question of when rather than whether. As more and more functions are performed on-line, the cost of placing ATMs on-line is relatively reduced and made more practical.

Whatever mode of operation, the most important factor in the success or failure of an ATM program is the reliability of the equipment. In short, the ATMs must work. They must be available when the customer chooses to use them. Experience has shown that most customers will tolerate a single occasion of machine unavailability, but the second occasion will result in a total loss of confidence and the customer will not rely on the ATM in the future. While ATMs are a product of new electronic technology, they are still highly mechanical devices and most downtime problems are the result of simple mechanical breakdowns.

POINT OF SALE TERMINALS

If the wisdom of installing ATMs is debatable, the investment in point of sale terminals (POS) is down right arguable. The state of the art of POS terminals is in its infancy. The rewards, however, for early entry in the field may be substantial. ATM systems can be duplicated, and experience has shown that the second, third, and even the fourth bank in a specific market can launch highly successful ATM programs. This seems much less likely with POS terminal networks. It may be debatable whether even the largest cities in the country could support more than two systems and it seems highly likely that most metropolitan areas will be dominated by a single terminal network. Access to these terminal networks by competing financial institutions is therefore an extremely controversial and political argument. In 1977, there do not seem to be any clear solutions to this controversy coming from either within the financial industry or the federal government. Quite obviously, the answer to this access question will have a major impact on the economics of establishing a POS network.

Because of the potential rewards, and in spite of the legal unknowns, a number of banks and other financial institutions have been very active in establishing POS terminal programs. These programs typically involve three categories of service provided through POS terminals.

Often the initial venture and certainly the most common within the banking industry has been check authorization or guarantee. Deposit taking utilizing POS terminals has been pioneered principally by the thrift industry. Finally, true electronic funds transfer, while rare at this time is the expressed goal of many institutions.

Check Authorization Systems

Check authorization differs from check guarantee simply in where the ultimate risk of loss lies with returned checks. Check guarantee is really a check-factoring service whereby the bank buys back from the retailer any returned item that has been properly validated via a POS terminal. In return for either of these services, the retailer normally pays a transaction fee to the bank. However, some financial institutions have elected to be compensated by an exchange of service with the retailer, usually the acceptance of deposits.

Since the fixed costs of a POS network are huge when compared to variable costs, the bank must seek out merchants that will have high transaction volumes. Supermarkets fit this category. As a result, supermarkets have been the necessary initial subscribers to regional POS programs.

Although each bank can decide which types of checks it wishes to guarantee, merchants, in general, will object to any program that does not cover all types of checks that they have been regularly accepting. For the supermarket, this means payroll, social security, and welfare checks as well as personal checks.

Merchants desire a check cashing system that is applicable to all of their customers, not just a portion who happen to have an account with bank X. This can be accomplished by a joint venture involving all of the financial institutions in the area, or it can be provided by a single financial institution who is willing to guarantee checks drawn on other banks. Whichever the case, the merchant is highly unlikely to allow more than one terminal or one system in the store.

All POS terminals can be divided into two major categories; customer activated and clerk activated. Clerk-activated terminals are POS devices which are operated by store personnel to process inquiries. Normally the imputed message contains as a minimum, the customer's card account number, dollar amount of the transaction, if known, and the customer's personal identification number (PIN), if required. In some cases information such as check sequence number, social security number, driver's license number, and expiration date is used. The card number is either manually indexed into the terminal's keyboard or the device may be equipped with a magnetic stripe reader. For security purposes the customer's personal identification number is almost always entered by the customer. Response to inquiries can be audio response, visual display, or printed message.

The advantage of a clerk-activated terminal over a customer-activated terminal is principally price. The terminal can be far less complicated and hence, less costly. In addition, training efforts are greatly reduced since only store personnel will be required to know how to operate the device instead of the store's customers. Errors are reduced, and customer confusion and reluctance to use a new device are for the most part overcome.

The most common application for clerk-activated terminals is in retail stores where the amount of the check is usually known at the time of validation, and where only personal checks are typically involved. Time and labor costs involved in the authorization procedure are important but probably secondary to simply avoiding bad checks. Therefore, the cheaper clerk-activated terminal is sufficient.

An attractive side feature to any retail POS service is the ability to receive on-line credit card authorizations. A common source of irritation to merchants is the length of time required to receive a verbal authorization for purchases that exceed the established floor limit. In contrast, on-line authorization via a POS terminal can be accomplished in a matter of seconds.

Customer-activated terminals are devices that will not only accept a transaction but will print some type of message on the check or document which will be easily recognizable by store personnel as an authorized item. Normally, the data necessary to conduct a transaction is exactly the same as with clerk-activated terminals with the lone addition being the insertion of the document.

The major advantage of a customer-activated terminal lies in the ability of the merchant to reduce labor costs associated with the verification of checks. Customer-activated terminals have found the widest application in supermarkets and other high-volume outlets such as discount stores with multiple checkout lanes.

Whether check authorization or guarantee proves to be a step toward or away from true electronic funds transfer is probably dependent upon the choice made in file access. Is a positive file check of actual account balances necessary or is a negative file approach sufficient or even preferable? A negative file approach checks only for negative experience on a specific account. Has a check been returned for insufficient funds and is the item still outstanding? If this or no other negative information is available, such as a stolen or lost access card, or unusual activity in the account, the authorization is given. No check on account balance is made.

While this negative file approach may appear to be extremely risky, it may come closer to fitting the customer's and, consequently, the retailer's current needs. A study by Arthur Andersen & Co. in Memphis, Tennessee, estimated that 6 percent of all checks presented are not covered by available funds at the time of presentation. However, only about 1 percent of the checks are actually returned NSF. The use of a positive file would require a change in the shopping habits or banking habits of about 5 percent of the market. This may be unacceptable to customer, retailer, and bank alike. Further a positive file check authorization system may requrire a complex and expensive message switching facility in order to satisfy the merchant's requirement that the system include virtually all of his or her customers. Without this positive file access, true funds transfer is not possible. Consequently, the choice of positive versus negative file approach hinges on costs, customer and merchant preferences, and long-range objectives of the bank.

Deposit Taking

Deposit taking through POS terminals principally in supermarkets has been pioneered by the thrift industry.

The philosophy behind this approach is identical to that discussed earlier with off-premise ATMs. The degree of attractiveness of this alternative for banks is a matter of opinion and controversy. At first glance it appears to be a financial coup for the bank by vastly increasing its number of "branches" with relatively small capital expenditures and the use of someone else's personnel.

Upon closer inspection, however, this potential windfall is tempered by the following factors. First, the use of supermarket personnel places a third party in the position of middleman between the customer and his or her bank. And representing the bank in a warm, helpful, polite manner may not be the highest priority item in that individual's job description. Further, and this may be the author's biased opinion again, most customers would prefer to deal directly with their financial institution either through machines or directly with bank personnel as opposed to a third-party middleman.

Second, retailers are likely to eventually insist on some form of compensation if they are required to provide this labor-intensive service. While the capital requirement for this type of delivery system is relatively small, the cost per transaction may compare unfavorably with more automated systems. In spite of these factors, merchant-manned POS terminals providing routine deposit and withdrawal services are likely to be used as satellite facilities in the new delivery system.

Evaluation of EFTS

Electronic funds transfer has been discussed repeatedly throughout the chapter. A complete review of the many potential obstacles confronting the financial industry in implementing EFT goes far beyond the scope of this chapter. But the legal, consumer, and technical problems are the subjects of a great deal of examination by almost all financial journals. For this chapter, let's review the rather uncomplicated evolution of check authorization to funds transfer.

As described earlier, a positive file check authorization system includes all the necessary information to, not just authorize, but complete the transaction in its entirety. We are identifying the customer, at least to the bank's satisfaction, with a plastic card and PIN. We are locating the customer's account and current balance. The location of the terminal can tell us the merchant and the account to which the funds are to be transferred. The amount of the transaction can be entered by the merchant and verified by the customer. The merchant's receipt can serve also as a description of the payment method. This, of course, is a gross oversimplification. But all the components are there. Will the customer accept it?

Starting with check authorization, the banks are slowly educating the customers that the addition of plastic cards and personal identification numbers increase the negotiability of their checks. From an enhancement to the checking account, the next step is to make the card and PIN an integral part of the account, and finally to demonstrate that the check itself is no longer necessary.

DIRECT DEPOSIT AND PREAUTHORIZED PAYMENTS

Two forms of automated banking have been around for years, direct deposit and preauthorized payments.

Many people within the banking industry have received pay in the form of a direct deposit to the bank's accounts rather than a paycheck or cash. Outside the banking industry, however, relatively few employees have authorized their employers to deposit their pay directly to their individual accounts. For this service to be efficient all of the employees of a single concern must accept direct deposit. And for this situation to be possible all financial institutions must be in a position to accept these deposits so as to give each employee a choice in picking his or her depository. Automated clearinghouses have been organized across the country in the last three years to provide this clearinghouse function electronically. Acceptance, however, has been slow. Whether it is the cooperation required from competing banks, the loss of float on the paychecks, or simply a lack of interest by the employee, the volume of direct deposit activity to date has been extremely low.

The federal government has been the biggest proponent of direct deposit through the social security system. As other arms of the government, such as the military, begin to push direct deposit, consumer awareness will be heightened and the movement may pick up some momentum. Direct deposit is essential if we are ever going to get to a less-check electronic delivery system.

Preauthorized payments have also been with the banks for years, but in a very limited manner. Most banks are allowing their customers to preauthorize a charge to their checking account for recurring payments such as installment loan and real estate mortgage payments. The most common instance involving third parties is probably preauthorized payments of insurance premiums. While the service has also been offered in connection with utility payments and other monthly bills, it appears practical only on payments which are predetermined in both time and amount.

AUTOMATIC TELEPHONE PAYMENTS

This service, which is in its early developmental stage, allows customers to initiate payments or transfer funds between accounts usually through a touch tone telephone. Some institutions provide clerk assistance for customers who have conventional rotary dial phones. Through a touch tone phone the customer enters his or her identification number and a transaction code to identify the company to be paid or the account to be credited. The dollar amount is entered by depressing the buttons on the telephone and the computer system routes the transaction to the user's account.

Thrift institutions probably receive the greatest benefits from pay-by-phone services since this permits them to offer demand deposit services. In the long run commercial banks may benefit from lower handling and operating costs by reducing the number of checks that need to be processed. At the present time, most programs are being offered on a fee basis, either a set monthly rate or a per bill charge.

The greatest benefit of automated telephone payment systems to the consumer is ease and convenience. Under this system the user does not have to prepare checks and address envelopes to pay bills, does not have to leave his or her home or office to use the service, and is not limited by banking hours. In addition, the user will save postage, may draw funds in an interest-bearing account in some cases and, unlike the case of preauthorized payments, will always control the amount and timing of disbursement.

The major disadvantage is the high development, promotion, equipment, and operating costs of establishing an automated telephone payment system for financial institutions, particularly, in its early stages when usage is low.

BALANCE INQUIRY

Customer-activated, on-line balance inquiry has been provided primarily through automated teller machines. The advantages of this feature is that it enables customers to determine their current balances before conducting their transactions.

Another method used by banks in offering balance inquiry service is through an on-line terminal located inside the bank lobby. This alternative expands the market of customers beyond just automated teller users. On the other hand it limits the number of hours that the service is available to existing banking hours.

Perhaps the major shortcoming of any balance inquiry service is the questionable value of informing customers of their current checking account balance. Seldom will this balance correspond to the customer's checkbook balance due to outstanding checks and unposted deposits. This may confuse customers more than it helps them. It may also cause customers to withdraw funds which they believe are available only to have checks returned on their account a few days later.

On the other hand, the balance inquiry service should result in reducing the number of instances a teller must satisfy a customer's request for his or her balance. More importantly the service has the potential of being expanded to include other types of inquiries, such as savings account balance, as well as interest paid and interest earned for the year for tax purposes.

Finally, a possible fringe benefit may occur with the bank lobby balance inquiry terminal. For those customers who are reluctant to conduct an "electronic transaction" the balance inquiry terminal offers an ideal opportunity to introduce customers to using an automated banking device without having to overcome their fear of *disturbing* their accounts. They may learn that for some routine transactions, automated equipment is fast, efficient, and confidential.

SUMMARY

The many components of this new electronic delivery system for retail services are obviously quite varied and controversial. The state of the art in electronic banking is at an initial highly complex stage. Each financial institution must evaluate these options with respect to its own goals and objectives. It must take into consideration its financial and personnel limitations and its competitive environment. Most importantly, no bank can afford to ignore the impact of this electronic delivery system.

MANAGING NONDEPOSIT ASSETS FOR THE PUBLIC

Chapter 68 _____

The Function and Organization of Fiduciary Services

David E. Ellison*

CHARACTERISTICS OF FIDUCIARY SERVICES

Traditionally Section XI of this book would have been entitled "Trust Services of Banks." Times change, however, and while the long-used organizational name, trust department, is still the most commonly used designation for the banking unit providing such services, it is increasingly common to hear of asset management services, or some other like term, calling attention to the broader fiduciary purposes now being undertaken by banks.

Over the last few decades the increasing complexity of laws and regulations and the dramatic growth of fiduciary assets have caused many changes in traditional trust services. As a result, it is increasingly difficult to convey a clear definition of "trust services." Indeed, the very complexity of trust services has created the need for persons knowledgeable enough to identify the specific trust services that will meet the needs of individual customers. This skill is basic to "estate planning."

Regardless of the name used to describe and refer to such services, they all involve fiduciary relationships. The latter is defined in Black's *Law Dictionary*, Fourth Edition, as:

Fiduciary Relationship. A relationship subsisting between two persons in regard to a business, contract, or a piece of property . . . of such a character that each must repose trust and confidence in the other and must exercise a corresponding degree of fairness and good faith.

---

* Senior Vice President, Seattle-First National Bank, Seattle, Washington.

Fiduciary relationships fall within two broad categories, trust and agencies. They can be defined as:

Trust. A fiduciary relationship with respect to property, subjecting the person by whom the title to the property is held to equitable duties to deal with the property for the benefit of another person, which arises as a result of a manifestation to create it.[1]

Essentials of the Trust

1. *It is a relationship.* More than just a duty or obligation, the trust is the entire relationship between trustee and beneficiary with respect to the property which is the subject of the trust.
2. *Fiduciary character of the relationship.* Trustee is a fiduciary with respect to the beneficiary.
3. *Trust must involve a property interest.* Unless a property interest is involved, a relationship cannot be a trust.
4. *Equitable duties are imposed upon the trustee.* Equitable, not legal, with differences in creation, enforcement, and termination.
5. *Manifestation of intention.* There must be intent to create a trust, and the intent must be manifested in some manner. The test is objective, not subjective.

Agency. The fiduciary relation which results from the manifestation of consent by one person to another that the other shall act on his behalf and subject to his control, and consent by the other so to act. The one for whom action is to be taken is the Principal. The one who is to act is the Agent.[2]

Essentials of Agency

1. *An agent has power to bind his principal to a legal relationship.* Such power usually includes the power to subject the principal to personal liability.
2. *An agent is a fiduciary.* The agent has agreed to act on behalf of the principal (within the scope of the employment) in the manner as defined above.
3. *An agent is subject to the control of his principal.* The principal's right to control is continuous during the relationship, and exists even though not exercised.

The complexity of trust services clouds the essential nature of the services provided. Most services (see Chapter 69) are designed to meet broad public needs and each trust is subject to modification to meet its specific requirements. However, in general trusts and agencies can be dissected and identified by major service objectives.

---

[1] *Restatement, Second, Trusts,* Section 2. For further information on the nature of a trust, see *Scott on Trusts,* 3d ed., vol. I, sec. 2.

[2] *Restatement, Second, Agency,* Section 1.

The service objectives of trust and agency relationships can be broadly separated into five categories. The number of service objectives included in an individual account will, of course, vary by business line and account, but the analysis of any fiduciary service will soon identify the mix of the service objectives selected to accomplish the particular task. The five service objectives are:

1. Record Keeping. Banks have traditionally rendered record-keeping services through their trust activities. Among the earliest services were those of transfer agent and registrar. Among the newest application is record keeping for investment counselors and mutual funds.

Nearly all personal trusts and agencies and the majority of employee benefit relationships involve record keeping of transactions and the reporting of results.

In this day of increasing sophistication of record keeping—and higher costs—there is more delegation by individual trustees of the record-keeping function. Indeed, record-keeping companies other than banks are increasingly competitive in serving trustees with administrative and computer programs. Often a bank may be the purchasing trustee.

2. Safekeeping. Another early service of trust departments and still an important one is safekeeping. Securities or other assets are held for safety. In simple safekeeping accounts record keeping is normally minimal, with only a receipt and delivery ticket involved.

However, safekeeping is present as a service objective of most fiduciary services. But, it is not necessarily included—as in the case where a bank as agent is given investment direction of a portfolio without possession of the assets.

3. Personal and Financial Counseling. From its earliest inceptions, the trust relationship was used to convey property to those persons as trustee who could be expected to provide effective personal and financial counseling to the beneficiaries. The family friend, lawyer, accountant, or banker were often selected as trustee because they knew the family and could be relied upon to counsel them wisely. While such appointments were most often combined with authority for management of the assets, the service objectives included counseling. Often the objective can be attained by naming a qualified individual as co-fiduciary with a bank. In most trusts, however, it is expected that the trust officer will fill such a role, whether specifically detailed in the establishing document or not. Obviously, the trust officer's role will vary from account to account, from one set of circumstances to another, but the most common trademark of the trust relationship is the personal and financial counseling of beneficiaries.

4. Investing. The service objective "investing" has become increasingly and relatively more important as the trust business has developed and grown and as our society has become more complex. In the earliest use of trusts in an agricultural society, the principal asset of most accounts was land. The purpose of the trust was to ensure retention of the land. Other assets were similarly husbanded and investment expertise was directed to preservation and utilization of existing assets, not the sale and purchase of securities. Chapter 70 reviews the present state of the investment art.

The investment authority of the bank may be exclusive or shared with others. Co-fiduciaries may share authority equally or each may have special authority separate from the other.

5. Control.   The trust relationship was born from the need to control assets during one's absence. Similarly, it appealed to those who needed or wished to control assets or situations after death. Today, this remains a significant component of many trusts. Obviously, retention of such controls by the person setting up the relationship will have tax consequences determined by the extent and direction of such retained or granted authority, but the desire or need to assure desired results after transfer of property can still be recognized in many trust accounts.

ORGANIZATIONAL FORM

Fiduciary activities of national banks are regulated by the federal government and are supervised by the Comptroller of Currency. State banks are supervised by state banking supervisory organizations and, if members, the Federal Reserve. Also, there is an increasing amount of the reporting of investment activities to the Securities and Exchange Commission.

Regulation 9 of the Comptroller of Currency provides that all trust activities must be separate from those of the bank and that the responsibility for such activities rests with the board of directors. Specific prohibitions are placed on self-dealing, both between the bank and trust accounts and bank officers and trust accounts. Any trust moneys placed with the bank while awaiting investment or distribution must be secured by bank collateral.

The board of directors may delegate to officers(s) and committee(s) as they deem best but cannot escape final accountability.

Regulation 9 of the Comptroller of the Currency provides for internal supervision of trust activities by bank auditors reporting directly to a directors' trust examination committee. In addition national examiners from the Comptroller's Office or the Federal Reserve make regular and detailed examinations of trust activities to determine compliance with practices and procedures established by law and regulation.

Traditionally, all trust activities were placed in one organizational unit. In the majority of banks this format is still followed. However, the high degree of specialization required in diverse trust activities has caused many banks to segregate in separate organizational units either their investment or pension activities or both.[3]

PROFITABILITY

In the early development of the trust business in the United States fees of the trustee were generally computed as a percentage of the income earned from trust assets. However, when economic conditions caused wide swings in income, fluctuations in earnings of the trustee resulted that had little relationship to expenses. Gradually it evolved that fee income was more often based on principal value or partly on principal value and partly on income. This change seemed to relate trust department earnings more nearly to expenses as long as principal values increased at approximately the same rate that inflation increased operating expenses. The new approach, however, could not accommodate acceleration of inflation to double digits, especially when that same exceedingly high inflation caused principal values to significantly decrease. As a result the trust business is now undergoing a reappraisal of how fee income should be measured.

The trust department is often the largest depositor in the bank and in most banks there is recognition that such deposits are a profitable source of noninterest-bearing funds for the bank. These deposits represent funds, usually of small size in each trust, that collectively aggregate a sizable amount. Individually, these funds are too small to effectively invest, are held for a short time during the investment process, or represent moneys for distribution. The trend is to allocate any earnings and credits for such deposits to the customer's trust account as earnings. There is, of course, a size and time limitation on how small a sum can be invested without administrative and computer costs exceeding benefits to the customer. However, the increasing ability of trustees to invest small sums through common trust funds made up of short-term money instruments or pooled savings accounts have made credit for such uninvested funds a smaller percentage contribution to trust profitability.

COMPETITION

Traditionally, the major competitors of the bank as executor and trustee were the surviving spouse, adult children, the family lawyer,

---

[3] Donald S. Green and Mary Schuelke, *The Trust Activities of the Banking Industry* (New York: Association of Reserve City Bankers, 1975).

or a close relative or friend. In traditional trust services that is still the situation.

However, as trust services have increasingly emphasized their investment expertise and the pension field has provided the major growth opportunity, new competition has included investment counselors, brokerage firms, and insurance companies. Thrift institutions are also gradually attaining limited trust powers and moving toward full equality with commercial banks in providing trust services.

Chapter 69

Fiduciary Services by Business Line

David E. Ellison*

There is little uniformity in the definition of fiduciary business lines. The complexity of such services has in most banks dictated an organizational structure divided into broad service categories, rather than by function or customer. Definition of business lines has thus been secondary to the definition of the specific services to be provided by each organizational unit. The business lines segmentation that follows should therefore be accepted only as that of the author and as an aid in understanding the scope of fiduciary services.

Since fiduciary services can be broadly categorized as trusts or agencies, it is helpful to first review briefly how each may be established and terminated.

THE BANK AS TRUSTEE

A trust can be established either during the lifetime of an individual or upon the death of an individual. A corporation may establish a trust. A trust can be as restrictive or as liberal as the party establishing the trust (the trustor) desires. The trust does not have to terminate on the death of the party establishing the trust. The law does provide limitations on how long a trust can exist and within that time it will terminate only by its own terms. The bank may act as sole trustee or jointly with another or with another having authority to make final decisions.

---

* Senior Vice President, Seattle—First National Bank, Seattle, Washington.

THE BANK AS AGENT

An agency agreement can be established only during the lifetime of an individual, the principal, and terminates upon death. A corporation may also establish an agency. Within these limitations the agreement can be as restrictive or as liberal as the party establishing it desires, with the exception that the power of the principal to direct must be preserved.

BUSINESS LINE I, PERSONAL TRUST SERVICES

Personal trust services can be divided broadly between accounts established by an individual for himself or herself, and those established for others.

Accounts for the Trustor

Living Trusts. Living trusts are generally established for one or more of the following purposes:

a. To provide investment management and record keeping and safekeeping assistance for the individual establishing the trust. Frequently, an individual, or a busy professional or business executive will use this device to assure proper attention for his or her assets.

b. To provide a vehicle for management of an individual's assets during his or her lifetime and, further, to provide an uninterrupted vehicle for the management of such assets after death.

c. Generally speaking, the purposes listed below for the establishment of a testamentary trust are also applicable to a living trust.

Self-Employed Retirement Plans. Trusts created during life are the chosen instruments of the federal government for encouraging individual retirement plans. Deposits made to a trust meeting required specifications will be allowed as a deduction against current income.

Agencies. Most agencies provide for the safekeeping of securities and record keeping. Many also provide that the agent will regularly review the assets in the account and recommend investment action.

A growing use of agencies provides for investment direction by the bank, at times with an after-the-fact review. Such accounts are usually referred to as managing agencies or investment counseling accounts.

Probate and Administration. A major service to individuals is the settlement of estates. While the average person often views estate matters as simple and uncomplicated, it is seldom the case. The bank as executor (if appointed by the will) or as administrator (if the appointment is by the court in the absence of a will) performs tasks that may be readily understood but can be most difficult and demanding in execution. They include:

a. Ascertaining the nature and location of all assets and benefits in which the decedent had, or the estate had, an interest.
b. Marshaling the assets and interests of the estate.
c. Conserving the assets and interests of the estate.
d. Paying legitimate claims against the estate, and rejecting those that are not proper.
e. Determining and paying, or arranging for the payment of, all taxes (income, estate, inheritance, personal property, real property, and so on) of the decedent or the estate.
f. Providing funds for the family of the decedent during probate.
g. Distributing the estate in accordance with the directions of the decedent (expressed in his or her will), or in accordance with the laws of descent and distribution of the state or domicile (if the decedent died without a will).

Guardianships and Conservatorships. When a person is not of age or no longer capable of handling and managing his own affairs, the bank may be appointed by the court as guardian or conservator of his property.

Because of the stigma in the mind of many persons about guardianships and incompetency, several states have provided for the appointment of a conservator for those persons who are not incompetent but because of age or infliction cannot take care of their affairs. The duties of guardians and conservators are quite alike.

The duties and responsibilities of the guardian or conservator are to manage the estate and undertake the following tasks:

a. Ascertaining the nature and location of all assets and benefits in which the ward has an interest.
b. Marshaling the assets and interests of the ward.
c. Paying legitimate claims against the ward.
d. Conserving and managing the assets and interests of the ward.
e. Determining and paying all taxes (income, personal property, real property, and so on) of the ward.
f. Paying to, or for the benefit of, the ward sufficient funds for his or her reasonable care, support, maintenance, health and education consistent with his or her accustomed standard of living, the estate available, and the orders of the court.
g. Preparing and submitting periodic accountings to the court.
h. Upon the ward reaching the age of majority or regaining his mental

competency, distributing to him the remaining assets of the guardianship estate.

i. Upon the death of the ward distributing the remaining assets of the guardianship estate to the ward's personal representative.

Financial Planning.   The rapidly increasing complexity of business and investing has created a demand for financial planning services to individuals. Because it is a natural extension of other trust activities, several larger banks have formally entered the field and others provide such services on a less structured and complete basis.

Accounts Established for Benefit of Other Than the Trustor

Testamentary Trusts.   A trust established by the provisions of a decedent's will is the usual means of placing property in trust for another person. The trust takes effect only at death and prior to that time can be altered or canceled unilaterally by changing the terms of the will. The bank, as prospective trustee, is not a party to the trust until death occurs.

A testamentary trust is usually established for one or more of the following purposes:

a. To provide management of the estate for a family member—spouse, child, or parent.
b. To assure conservation of the estate for the benefit of an improvident family member.
c. To provide unity of management of property not readily susceptible to division.
d. To minimize taxes (income, estate, and inheritance).

Life Insurance Trusts.   A life insurance trust is somewhat of a cross between a living trust and a testamentary trust. Like the living trust, it is an operative trust agreement when it is executed. However, if the only asset of the trust is the designation of the trustee as beneficiary of life insurance, as is usually the case, then like the testamentary trust the active asset management by the trustee commences only on the trustor's (policyholder's) death.

Gifts in Trust.   Gifts of property are placed in trust rather than given outright in many cases. The terms of the trust as to distribution of income and principal and as to control by trustor to direct, modify, or revoke, will of course affect the gift, income, and estate tax treatment of the trust. Some of the most common gift trusts are designed:

a. For the benefit of minor children.
b. For the protection of a family member or to provide the beneficiary with a source of income.

c. To begin the process of asset accumulation for a child not skilled in asset management.

Charitable Trusts. Trusts are also commonly used as the vehicle for holding assets for charitable purposes. By either a living or testamentary trust, a vehicle comparable to a private or public foundation may be created without the need for incorporation of the foundation.

BUSINESS LINE II. SERVICES FOR CORPORATIONS

Employee Benefit Accounts

These accounts are generally categorized as follows:

Pension Accounts (Defined Benefits). The company contribution is determined by actuarial studies designed to fund the cost of benefits promised to employees under the plan.

Profit Sharing Accounts (Defined Contribution Plans). Contributions are provided out of the profits of the business as determined by the plan terms. The benefit that will ultimately flow to employees is not defined.

Money Purchase Pension and Thrift (Savings) Accounts. These accounts are based on company contributions to a fund for each participant. Money purchase pension plans customarily establish company contributions as a fixed percentage of compensation of the employee. Thrift or savings plans customarily use a formula whereby the company contributes a predetermined percentage of authorized employee contributions. Benefits to the employee under either type of plan depend upon investment results.

Employee Stock Ownership Trusts (ESOTs). These accounts have become a significant alternative to other employee benefit plans. An ESOT establishes an individual account for each employee and contributions to the trust may be invested fully in stock of the employer corporation. Contributions by the employer are based on a formula but are not necessarily dependent on profitability. Benefits to the employee are defined in terms of securities of the employer corporation.

Bank as Agent in Employee Benefit Plans. The bank may also participate in employee benefit plans as an agent and its duties and responsibilities will, of course, depend completely upon the terms of the agency agreement. However, such responsibilities will usually be defined in terms of record keeping, safekeeping, and investments.

Investment Management for Charitable Foundations

Charitable foundations are major customers for trust investment services. The sizable pools of capital held by foundations requires skilled investment management. The experience of banks in advising on the investment of tax-free pension funds has made them particularly well equipped and experienced to provide investment management for tax-free charitable funds.

Business Advisory Accounts

Business advisory services by bank trust departments are of fairly recent origin and are not yet universally available. They have their beginnings in the expertise developed in trust departments through the management of closely held corporations or proprietorships held in trust accounts as assets, usually upon the death of the owner or proprietor. Such services will usually encompass business appraisals and financial consulting. Classes and seminars on business management may be included.

Trustee for Bond Issues

Acting as trustee for bond issues is a well-recognized trust service. The appointment as trustee is made by the bond indenture, with the duties of the trustee usually encompassing:

a. Representation of the bondholders.
b. Payment of interest and principal when due.
c. Ascertainment that required insurance is maintained and that real estate taxes are paid.
d. Seeing that sinking-fund deposits are made punctually and that funds are invested promptly as instructed.
e. Acting for bondholders in the event of default by the company in their covenants, or in settlement of insurance claims.

Paying Agent for Bond Issues

The bank may also act as paying agent for bond issues with principal obligations to pay only valid coupons and bonds and to cremate or return to the obligor all paid items.

Transfer Agent

A long-time corporate service of banks is that of transfer agent for stock of corporations. Principal duties are spelled out in the agency agreement but usually include:

a. Maintaining records of stock ownership.
b. Issuing stock certificates.

c. Replacing lost stock certificates.
d. Disbursing dividends.
e. Filing reports of dividends paid to federal government and states.
f. Furnishing shareholder lists to the corporation.
g. Issuing, mailing, and reconciling proxies for shareholder meetings.
h. Mailing annual and quarterly reports and miscellaneous items.

Bank trust departments offer a variety of services for corporate customers. How these services are organized will vary among banks and the needs of each bank's customers.

Chapter 70

Investment Management of Securities as Fiduciary Assets

*David E. Ellison**

John R. Boyd, C.F.A.†

Constraints on trust investing have always been provided by the law. In the early history of the trust business in the United States trustees generally could invest only in a list of securities approved by state statutes. Permissible investments were most often limited to fixed-income securities, principally government and corporate bonds. Investment selection was limited. This restriction turned out to be a denial to trustees of sufficient flexibility to meet changing needs and resulted in a state-by-state move to the so-called prudent man rule.

Originally conceived by the Massachusetts court, it spread to all other states over time, either by court degree or legislation.

While its terms may vary between states, broadly the prudent man rule provides: "Trust funds will be invested as (1) a prudent man would invest; (2) under the circumstances of the account."

Under the prudent man rule, the policies and practices of the industry in investment decision making have been gradually evolving. Flexibility to meet changing requirements was provided by the rule, although at greatly increased risk of surcharge to the trustee.

Most bank trust departments have investment units which are responsible for the management of assets placed in its care. Over $300 billion in assets are currently managed by bank trust departments in

* Senior Vice President, Seattle-First National Bank, Seattle, Washington.
† Vice President, Seattle-First National Bank, Seattle, Washington.

the United States and while these assets include real estate, the most common are cash equivalents, fixed-income securities, and equities.

As a general rule, the larger the assets under management, the larger the investment staff required. Small trust departments unable to afford several investment persons often subscribe to services offered by larger bank trust departments and rely upon them for specialized types of investment information and assistance, thus increasing their competitive posture.

The activities of the investment function can best be described in terms of the decision-making process; i.e., the manner and methods by which investment decisions are made. Its format will, of course, vary but there are significant elements common to the activities of most trust investment departments. These are:

1. The use of investment committees.
2. Investment research and forecasting.
3. Portfolio management.
4. Establishment of investment objectives.
5. Securities trading.

INVESTMENT COMMITTEES

Most trust investment departments use a committee system in their investment decision making. The size of the assets under management, investment philosophy, and the types and number of accounts under management will to a large extent determine the membership and use of committees. Many banks use investment committees on two levels. The first level involves a senior investment committee, which establishes investment philosophy and determines broad investment policy. Guidelines for the allocation of assets among capital markets may be made and reviewed by this group. Often the membership of this committee includes outside directors of the bank, senior officers of the bank, senior personnel of the trust investment department, and the bank's senior economist.

A second level committee may consider tactics to be employed in investing. Concerns may include the levels of fixed income and stock markets, guidelines for portfolio allocation, and review of performance.

In general terms, trust investment committees attempt to deal with broad policy and strategy on a longer term horizon and with tactics in the short-term deployment of assets. Banks will vary greatly in the delegation of specific authority to act between individuals and committees. However, committees are generally used to address those areas of the investment process which need input of several different disciplines (economics and financial analysis) to arrive at a course of action or series of broadly applicable investment decisions. It is difficult to precisely define the individual bank application of the committee system.

INVESTMENT RESEARCH AND FORECASTING

All trust departments utilize a wide variety of investment information in arriving at investment decisions. This information is generally categorized in three basic types: (*a*) economic data and forecasts, (*b*) industry/company data and forecasts, (*c*) securities market data and forecasts.

Economic Data and Forecasts

Forecasts of economic developments provide a broad framework within which to initiate the investment process. Forecasts are most often made for the near-term (the next 12 months) and for the longer term (three to five years). Economists, in conjunction with trust department officers, attempt to determine future changes in the basic economy, such as expected growth rates in gross national product, unemployment, government spending, and inflation. When the changes and magnitude of the changes for the economy have been identified and quantified, general statements are prepared, reflecting the effect of these anticipated changes upon future interest rates and stock prices. The value of economic analysis is that it provides the parameters within which market forecasts can be developed and indicates to the trust investment department future changes which could impact the level of securities prices.

One tool which is often employed by the economist is the econometric model. In its simplest form, the model is a set of mathematical equations and variables which represent all aspects of the economy. The output from such a model is used by the economist to make general judgments about the structure and changes which could occur under a given set of circumstances. Models provide substantial detail and can be used to isolate changes in trend, thereby providing the economist with an orderly means of evaluating the basic economic interrelationships.

The economist and the investment officer must take into consideration developments that are social and political in nature, both domestically and internationally. As an example it is now evident that changes in price levels and currency values can come about suddenly and have a significant impact on the U.S. economy and capital markets. Therefore, the thorough researchers will attempt to foresee the likelihood and effect of such events.

Economic forecasts are only as accurate as the experience and judgment of the forecasters in analyzing and projecting historical data. To be useful to the trust investment department, this data must be correlated with capital market and industry analysis.

Industry/Company Data and Forecasts

Based upon its judgment of the future of the economy, the trust investment department examines specific industries and individual companies to determine their relative investment attractiveness. It is important that the security analyst compare the economist's broad conclusions with his or her appraisal of specific industries and specific companies within industries. The purpose of industry analysis is to determine what the prospects are for a particular industry and to compare this with the outlook for other industries so that a rating of relative attractiveness can be made. The security analyst is trained to examine balance sheets and income statements of corporations and to gather other information from numerous sources, including industry trade publications, research material produced by brokerage houses, and interviews with company management. This work is conducted to evaluate the financial future of a company. In some banks the securities analysts are assigned industries (such as steel, autos, and computers) or they may be assigned individual companies. Some trust investment departments divide the analysts' work by market groups (such as high-growth companies or cyclicals). Regardless of the basis used to assign industries or companies, the security analyst's basic job is to quantify the financial future and prospects for a group of companies. In addition, he or she may be asked to assign a probable rate of return and identify the corresponding level of risk which is being assumed by investment in such companies. The methods by which this is done vary greatly between trust investment departments.

Securities Market Data and Forecasts

A third major input to investment decision making is information concerning the relationship between economic and securities research and market levels. Both interest rates and stock prices are affected by the level of economic activity over the long run. However, the direction and magnitude of movement in the short run may have little to do with either economic or political events. Historically, stock prices have moved downward in advance of recessions and upward during recessions. The timing and extent of such movements varies greatly and there appears to be no precise method of forecasting the extent or the direction in which security prices will move.

There is much historical data on the movement of stock prices and interest rates. Some forecasters believe that a careful and thorough analysis of past security market movements will reveal certain patterns or relationships which will be useful in forecasting future price movement. Others suggest that the structure of the marketplace and the economy have changed so greatly over the past decade that historical occurrences have little value in projecting future security prices.

In recent years a considerable body of evidence has been assembled which suggests that, over the short run at least, the level of securities prices is impossible to project continuously or accurately.

In spite of the difficulty, virtually all trust investment departments attempt to forecast the future level of stock prices and interest rates, at least over the short term. The methods which are employed vary considerably but the goal remains the same—to accurately translate economic forecasts into forecasts for stock prices and interest rates.

There are those trust investment departments who rely on timing the securities markets. They move a portion of the portfolio from cash equivalents to common stocks or long bonds based upon anticipated relative movements in those markets.

Some trust investment departments attempt to forecast the level of securities markets over an intermediate period (one to three years). They invest a certain portion of their portfolios in common stocks and maintain that percentage through time. They do not attempt to "time" the market, but rather they stay invested at an established level of equity investment. Over the past 40 years the equity market has had an upward bias and as long as the economy continues to grow the upward trend in stock prices should remain intact. Some trust investment departments do not attempt to time the market but rather seek to identify attractive individual investment opportunities for the long term.

Another technique used to make future investment decisions is the identification of relationships between the level of interest rates for high-quality, fixed-income obligations and current earnings of and dividend yields on common stocks. The forecaster appraises this relationship and becomes more or less invested on the appraisal of whether or not yield spread is large enough to warrant an increased investment in common stocks.

Most large trust investment departments rely on several of the above techniques to forecast future market movements. They analyze historical data, review economic forecasts, both internally and externally generated, and they then establish a conditional forecast which is further detailed in investment strategy and portfolio tactics. Sophisticated forecasting techniques assisted by computer models make the task of accurately forecasting the future price levels of security markets more precise; however, the problem of correctly forecasting the level of securities markets is far from resolved.

PORTFOLIO MANAGEMENT

Economists and security analysts collect and evaluate investment information for use in the decisions among investment choices. The portfolio manager is the person charged with the responsibility of utilizing such information in selecting the proper assets to meet the investment objectives of a particular portfolio. Broadly, he or she utilizes the guidance and opinion produced by committees and economic and security research to implement an investment policy designed to meet the client's needs. One of the most important assignments of the portfolio manager is the analysis of individual account requirements, and in the light of investment policy their interpretation into a meaningful account objective.

ESTABLISHMENT OF INVESTMENT OBJECTIVES

The setting of investment objectives for accounts is a subjective but necessary part of successful investing. For individual investors, the portfolio manager must be aware of basic information, such as age, health, tax bracket, and total net worth. He must have a clear understanding of what the individual wishes to accomplish with his assets. The establishment of investment objectives in retirement accounts is particularly specialized and in larger banks is generally handled by the separate organizational unit assigned such accounts.

Setting realistic and workable investment objectives requires that the portfolio manager have at his disposal not only account information but also necessary investment information and organizational guidance. The level of interest rates and the prices of individual stocks change substantially each year; so do the needs of individual and corporate trust customers, although in most cases more slowly than the movements in markets. The portfolio manager must review and routinely adjust the asset mix and individual securities to meet the changing needs of the customer.

The major considerations in setting investment objectives are: (*a*) variability in the rate of return (*b*) liquidity, and (*c*) time horizon.

Variability in the Rate of Return

Probably the biggest problem portfolio managers face is determining the amount of fluctuation in principal value that is appropriate for a specific account. By investing in obligations of the U.S. government, the risk of principal loss is negligible. However, depending upon term, even this security may fluctuate in value. With stocks, there is no certainty of principal repayment. The portfolio manager must properly evaluate the potential loss of principal as well as the potential return on assets, relating this to the circumstances and needs of the account. The principal portfolio method used to control this risk and to reduce it is diversification. Since the movement of individual investments and markets can be predicted with less exactness than the total market, risk is reduced by spreading investments over many securities and markets.

Only communication with the customer can provide the information necessary to establish the foundation on which a portfolio is built.

Targets of portfolio return can be stated in dollars (such as produces income of $500 per month) or relative to an index (S&P 500) or in percentage terms (a growth rate of 5 percent in principal per year). Whatever method is adopted, the portfolio manager must be aware of the customer's ability to absorb and live with potential loss of principal. The investment objective enables the portfolio manager to become clearly aware of the customer's needs.

Liquidity

Any discussion of investment allocation should address the question of how much of a specific account should be immediately available for conversion into cash. For individual accounts, cash equivalents are necessary for emergencies, illness, or death. For retirement accounts they are necessary for benefit payments. A liquidity reserve may also allow the portfolio manager to take advantage of future investment opportunities. The proper amount of liquidity for a specific account depends upon the circumstances of the customer and to a lesser degree the investment policy of the trust investment manager.

Generally there is a cost associated with holding cash equivalents since short-term obligations return a lower rate of return to the investor than the same quality instrument of longer maturity. The reserve can be expressed in absolute terms ($100,000 will be invested in 90-day Treasury bills) or in percentage terms (5 percent of the account will be held in 90-day prime-rated commercial paper). The liquidity level must be adjusted as the account needs and price levels of the securities markets change.

Time Horizon

Accounts have time horizons which vary from several months to several decades. A probate account may be liquidated in 30 days, while a pension account may be invested with a 40-year outlook.

The portfolio manager should establish a method and action plan to properly balance the longer term needs (several years) with the short-term or immediate goals (a year or less). The portfolio manager must be careful not to meet short-term goals at the expense of missing longer range objectives.

Depending upon the policy of the bank, the investment officer will meet with the customer on an established cycle to review and analyze investment results and the account objectives.

Ideally the customer should be the sole determinant of the account objective. Realistically of course, many are not sufficiently informed and trained to do so. Thus the portfolio manager or other assigned trust officer must be prepared to assist and guide the inquiry and process. Care must be taken however not to substitute the opinion and judgment of the bank for the proper goals and desires of the customer.

SECURITIES TRADING

Most larger trust investment departments have at least one securities trader. After the portfolio manager has made a selection of securities for purchase or sale, he or she prepares a buy order which is given to the securities trader. The trader has a brokerage house execute the order. A number of brokerage houses have specialized or separate departments to work exclusively with institutions. The trader, after executing an order, reports back to the portfolio manager the details of the transactions and the settlement date. The trader then sends the trading ticket to the operations department with precise delivery instructions.

In most instances the securities trader is interested in the price movements of stocks and bonds over the very near term (two to five days). He informs the portfolio manager on the general condition of the markets and makes him aware of price movements and the ability of the market to accept the transaction. In large trust investment departments, traders, like portfolio managers, may specialize in fixed-income securities or equities. In smaller institutions the portfolio manager may also act as the trader, calling the brokerage house directly, placing the order, and completing the appropriate paperwork.

The brokerage industry has changed from fixed rates to negotiated rates for executing security transactions. Until 1975 the New York Stock Exchange had a pricing schedule under which all member firms charged the same rates. This schedule was modified and by 1976 the price which brokerage houses charged for specific transactions was determined by the brokerage house representative and the trust investment department trader—hence the term "negotiated rates." As a result the trader now has not only the responsibility of getting the best price for a purchase or sale of securities but must determine and negotiate an appropriate and reasonable commission.

PERFORMANCE MEASUREMENT

Measurement of performance should depend upon the identification of the specific objectives to be measured and an agreement upon the results that will constitute performance or lack of it. It should encompass both measurement of risk and reward. Unfortunately performance measurement often disregards such matters and merely compares results with those of one or more market indexes. The time period of such comparison is also often too short to be meaningful.

Fortunately, the perceived trend is the comparison of investment results with stated goals. Performance is also being measured for risk by attempts to diagnose the level of risk which the trustee has assumed in producing the return. Much development remains to be done before current methods of risk-reward analysis are fully accepted.

There are many performance services offered by consultants, brokerage houses and banks which can be used to measure portfolio performance. They can be helpful in carrying out the primary purpose of performance measurement, the establishment of more effective communication between the bank and the customer.

EMPLOYEE RETIREMENT INCOME SECURITY ACT OF 1974

ERISA (Employee Retirement Income Security Act) is a sweeping piece of legislation that affects the management of virtually all private retirement plans. The act is designed to protect the retirement benefits of employees. Broad guidelines are established pertaining to portfolio diversification, liquidity requirements, and the quality of investments. The act contains a federal prudent man standard which requires in part that the investment manager will act with the care, skill, prudence, and diligence of a prudent man under the circumstances.

Bank trust departments have historically operated under the prudent man rule. The new federal standard may impose no greater degree of care than does its historic counterpart. However, the trend is to hold corporate fiduciaries to a standard based upon the prudence of the expert and likewise the ERISA requirement may require a standard higher than that of the individual investor. It is generally agreed that regardless of the federal standard, bank trust departments may expect greater concern from asset owners with respect to investment results. This increased concern on the part of trust clients will require trust investment departments to record in greater detail their investment policies and portfolio decisions. Overall it is too early to determine the full effect ERISA will have on the management of retirement funds.

TRENDS AND DEVELOPMENTS

The building of ever more sophisticated econometric models which attempt to quantify the future of capital markets will continue, but with increasing emphasis upon political and social changes. The investment objective setting process will become more quantified as asset owners become more involved in the investment decision-making process. Large, sophisticated pools of capital such as retirement funds, will develop their own capabilities to measure investment performance and to determine if the asset manager is meeting the agreed investment objectives. More effective communication between asset managers and the owner of assets will result in better long-term investment performance.

The United States is affected significantly by developments in foreign economies. The level of economic activity varies from country to country, but there is an increasing interdependence between the U.S. economy and those of foreign countries. As a result there is a trend toward diversification of large portfolios through direct investment in foreign stocks and bonds. Trust investment departments commonly have purchased equities in American multinational companies which operate in virtually every country of the world, thereby providing the investor with participation in the growth of world economies. This indirect participation is now being augmented by limited purchases of foreign securities.

Additional risks may be taken by owning foreign securities. There is political risk that a foreign country will change its government. There is also the risk that currency may be revalued. When dollars are traded for a foreign security, the investor may not be able to transfer the principal back into the same U.S. dollar equivalent. A third problem may arise when a foreign economy goes through unfavorable changes such as rapid inflation or depletion of natural resources. Yet despite these risks, large bank trust investment departments appear to be moving in the direction of direct investment in foreign securities in order to gain the advantage of diversification.

In universities as well as in the industry much work is being done on portfolio theory, risk definition, performance measurement, and the techniques of forecasting. New approaches and theories will gradually be accepted and used by professional investment advisors. Bank trust departments, are expected to further develop their expertise in investing the assets placed in their care. They have the organizations and resources to continue their dominance of the market.

SUMMARY

The trust investment department collects, analyzes, evaluates, and summarizes economic, market, industry, and company data, sets investment policy, strategy and tactics, and provides portfolio managers with the guidance and tools to select investments and to make an appropriate allocation of assets in individual accounts. Of special importance to such tasks are the organization structure of the department and its investment philosophy and guidelines. Various disciplines are involved in the effective management of assets, and investment committees often provide a framework in which policy and guidelines can be best established. The development of investment objectives ensures that the customer's assets will be managed in accordance with his or her desires and needs and that the risk of principal loss and the forecasted rates of return to be earned are appropriate for his or her circumstances. The coordination of the investment officer's activities—securities analysts, portfolio managers, securities traders—requires an organizational structure which is disciplined, facilitates consistency, and has the flexibility to accommodate the ever-changing investment environment.

_____ SECTION XII

MARKETING
THE BANK'S SERVICES

Chapter 71

Developing the Marketing Plan and Strategies

Richard M. Rosenberg*

There is, perhaps, no more misunderstood direction given by bank senior management than is contained in the order, "Develop a marketing plan!" This order or direction is misunderstood because neither the senior management nor the marketing department usually has previously defined the ultimate purpose of the marketing plan. Is it to penetrate or increase share of a new market such as young adults, senior citizens, or small business? Is the purpose of the marketing plan to increase share of a service such as accounts receivable loans or is the purpose of the marketing plan to improve penetration of a specific geographical area?

Thus, before developing the marketing plan strategy, it is critical to determine what is the purpose of the finished product. Once this is determined, the marketing plan, which is a flexible document, depending on the data available, the circumstances, and its purpose, can be tailored to meet a specific need. Too often, without defining the purpose, marketing plans are developed solely for the purpose of developing marketing plans.

With this caveat and introduction, the author believes it should be obvious that there is no one method of developing a marketing plan, but there are certain aspects common to most.

MARKET ANALYSIS AND CURRENT MARKET POSITIONS

Regardless of whether the purpose of the plan is to increase geographic penetration, market share among a particular customer seg-

---

* Executive Vice President, Wells Fargo Bank, San Francisco, California.

ment, or increase service usage, the first step usually is to determine the characteristics of the customers whom the bank wishes to serve in a particular market or with a particular service. Although the characteristics of customers are almost infinite, data gathering and analysis is expensive, and consequently, attention should be given only to those characteristics that are most important and that will help to formulate effective marketing strategies.

For example, in developing a marketing plan for a credit card program, it is usually important to know the age characteristics of the potential market since young households have a much greater propensity to use revolving credit than do older households. However, in developing a marketing plan for the penetration of small businesses through accounts receivable financing, the working capital characteristic of the business is a much more important factor than the age of the individuals who will make the decision to use accounts receivable financing in the operation of the business.

Thus, the first step in the marketing plan is to determine the important characteristics of the market. Some of the factors that should be considered include:

1. Who are your customers and prospects (name, type, size)?
2. Who makes the decision to buy (male, female, financial vice president, or president)?
3. What is the location of your customers and prospects?
4. How price sensitive is the target group of customers and prospects?
5. What are their banking characteristic (average deposit size, average loan size, seasonal credit requirements)?
6. What is the attitude of the target market toward your institution?
7. What are the characteristics of the "best" customers depending on the marketing plan objectives (households that are fund suppliers or households that are fund users)?

Banking Market Penetration or Share of Market

The classic cliché, "if you don't know where you want to go, any road will take you there," can be adapted to the market share section of a marketing plan, "If you don't know your market share when you begin, you won't know it after you have developed and implemented the plan."

Therefore, you will not know the effectiveness of a marketing plan or strategy and whether it has been worth the time, effort, and funds that have been expended. Without market share measurements, incorrect decisions may follow since there is no objective means of evaluating the strategies. For that reason, it is important to incorporate an analysis of the bank's market position into the marketing plan as a bench mark from which to measure progress.

But, just as the phrase, "marketing plan," is often misunderstood and misused, market share is another misunderstood and, therefore, often misused concept.

Market share can be measured in an infinite number of ways, and thus it is important to determine the relevance of a particular market share to the marketing strategy. The classic example of a market share statistic that at one time had meaning, but today has very little relevance in determining market share for many major regional and money center banks is their share of *total* deposits.

Prior to the widespread use of negotiable certificates of deposit, *total* deposit growth was the result of the successful market effort of any bank involved. But the total deposits figure today, when negotiable certificates of deposit over $100,000 are included in the base, makes the data relatively meaningless for measuring marketing achievement. This came about because the price that a bank is willing to pay for negotiable certificates of deposit has an impact on its market share of total deposits but tells nothing about its marketing effectiveness. As a result, it may be much more useful to measure demand deposit share, passbook savings share, or time deposits under $100,000, but *not* to measure share of total deposits. Other useful market share data that may be incorporated into a marketing plan include share of accounts by size range (obtained from appropriate Federal Reserve district statistics), and, of course, deposit and loan data obtained by reading annual and quarterly reports and 10–K reports of appropriate competitors and then calculating market share from these sources.

Competitive Factors

The final procedure necessary in determining current market position when developing the marketing plan is delineating the competitive factors involved. This section can, of course, be very elaborate or very simple depending on the purpose of the plan and the amount of competitive intelligence that is available.

Typically, this section should include a discussion of all the competitors that are involved in a particular market and/or a service. In today's current financial environment, it is critical that banks be aware of and develop plans not only to meet competition from bank competitors, but from nonbank competitors as well. As the thrift industry gains greater powers, it is becoming more obvious that in developing a marketing plan, a competitive analysis must be made of not only the banks with which the institution competes, but all other competitors in the market, such as savings and loan associations, credit unions, mutual savings banks, insurance companies, and finance companies.

In developing the competitive analysis, it is often useful to set forth in tabular form the strengths and weaknesses of all competitors relative to the bank's own position in these categories. These tables would include such factors as pricing policies, convenience of locations, reputation, quality of staff, customer base, promotional techniques of competitors, and quality of products and services.

A sound, competitive analysis is often a key to the success of the entire marketing plan and ultimately the marketing results achieved. A sound analysis allows an institution to capitalize on its strengths, shore up its critical weaknesses, and prevents wasting of resources in areas where there is little or no likelihood of success because of the competitive position.

EXTERNAL ENVIRONMENT FACTORS AFFECTING THE MARKETING PLAN

Every well-conceived marketing plan should be developed in the context of the external environment that has a bearing on its execution. It is, of course, extremely difficult to project with any degree of accuracy and even more difficult, if not impossible, to control those external factors that are so critical to success, but the plan should address those external factors that are most relevant to the plan. The degree of sensitivity of the plan to these external factors and details of the magnitude of the risks inherent in the plan because of these external factors should be discussed in this section of the plan.

Four of the most common external factors that are usually considered in developing a market plan include: (1) the economic environment, (2) anticipated technological changes, (3) the sociological environment, and (4) regulatory and legislative positions.

The economic environment that has been forecast is usually basic to any marketing plan being developed. For example, if the plan is designed to increase an institution's share of passbook savings under a particular rate scenario, but the actual rate scenario under which the plan operates is different by 300 basis points, an entire strategy may require revision. Thus the external economic assumptions on which the plan is based should always be incorporated into the formal document. Although this sounds elementary and basic, it cannot be overemphasized since the strategies as well as the actual value of meeting the marketing objectives outlined cannot be determined without taking into consideration the economic environment under which the plan is assumed operating.

For example, the value of acquiring $10 million in 6 percent consumer certificates of deposit may justify a certain amount of promotional expense with a 6.5 percent prime rate, but an entirely different strategy and an entirely different promotional expense may be justified in a 8.5 percent prime rate. For that reason, no marketing plan is complete without detailing the economic environment and especially the interest rate scenario under which it will be implemented.

To a lesser extent, it is also important to make certain key assumptions concerning the technological, sociological, and regulatory environment under which the plan will be operating. Here, again, key assumptions must be made that are not always certain and not always quantifiable. For example, a plan may assume that banking machines will be installed at certain number of off-site locations, at a specific cost (including machine costs, real estate, and operational costs) as a result of favorable legislative and regulatory changes. The evaluator of such a marketing plan should be made aware of all of the critical, external variables necessary for the success of the plan. In this hypothetical case cited of banking machines, some of the critical external variables include (a) favorable legislation, (b) favorable regulation, and (c) ability to acquire desirable real estate.

The listing of critical variables throughout the plan is obviously useful because it focuses the attention of all parties on those areas that can make or break a plan, but the critical variables section in the external environment section is especially important because there may be no alternative but canceling a marketing plan if, for example, an unfavorable ruling on a regulation is received.

ESTABLISHMENT OF STRATEGIC MARKETING OBJECTIVES

It is only after the current market position has been determined and only after external environmental factors have been evaluated that the author of a marketing plan is in a position to directly develop the plan and the marketing strategies necessary to implement such a plan.

The first and most critical step at this stage of the process is in the key positioning questions which include: What kind of bank are we? What kind of bank do we want to be? What markets do we want to serve? What products and services do we wish to offer?

In an earlier and less complex time, most banks believed they could profitably serve all segments of the financial market, but it is becoming increasingly apparent that as a result of the more complex financial needs of both individuals and business, that the banking industry is entering a new era. This new era will require increased specialization and the most important decision for the survival of a banking institution may be its decision in determining the position of the institution.

Should we be a retail bank? Should we be a wholesale bank? Can we serve some elements of the wholesale market while primarily being a retail bank? Can we expand our service area? Can we expand our services to include long-term mortgages? Can we ignore the international market? All of these are positioning questions, and until they are answered, the other elements of a marketing plan are not very useful because they may be inconsistent with the basic position the institution wishes to occupy. Therefore, positioning is a prerequisite because well-conceived strategic and tactical marketing plans should be designed to be of assistance in taking an institution to a predetermined objective or position.

ESTABLISHMENT OF TACTICAL MARKETING OBJECTIVES

The establishment of marketing objectives is the final step before developing the marketing strategies to be employed. Objectives can be set in a variety of ways, but the more precise the objective, usually the more effective are the strategies that can be developed to reach the objectives.

Bank marketing objectives are usually established in terms of volume, such as total automobile loans outstanding or total demand deposits; or expressed in terms of share of market, such as an increase in passbook savings share of 25 points. Since measuring share of market in many categories is often very difficult in the short run because of the lack of competitive data, volume goal is a more common method of establishing a marketing objective.

There are, of course, variations and refinements that can be made in setting these broad objectives. For example, in setting a deposit volume objective, a subobjective may be to require the average deposit account to increase by x amount of dollars in order to ensure that the volume objective is not achieved by attracting a large number of small balance accounts. A loan volume objective may not only call for an increase of a certain amount of loan outstandings, but may also require that the increase is at a designated spread over a projected cost of funds. It may also include a subgoal that the loss ratio is not to exceed a specified level. These subgoals may thus ensure that the marketing objective is achieved in a manner consistent with the overall objectives of the bank.

There are usually three considerations that must be addressed in establishing both the primary marketing objective as well as any objectives that are prerequisites or conditions imposed on the primary objective. These three conditions are profitability, share of market, and economies of scale.

Profitability is, of course, a critical condition that is usually imposed on any volume objective. Marketing plans that are developed solely to generate volume without consideration for profitability have long been criticized and rightly so. This situation takes on even more meaning in a banking environment in which considerably greater attention is being paid to leverage factors and return on asset ratios. Marketing plans, consequently, must be prepared with much greater attention being paid than heretofore to the margin or return on the marketing investment.

For this reason, marketing objectives must be formulated that an achievement of the objective for a particular segment of the market or for a particular service will result in satisfactory profitability, either in a short run or in a long run, or both, for the bank. In establishing an objective that calls for an increase share of market, this should only be considered if the increase in share will lead to increased profitability within a reasonable time period.

Too often, market share considerations are given preference in establishing an objective over profitability considerations. This clearly can be avoided if marketing objectives are required in the marketing plan to be expressed in terms of profitability over specific time periods.

Because many costs in a bank are fixed costs, such as the physical structure of a branch office, computer installations, and certain personnel costs, an increase in share of market can be a very worthwhile objective if the increase lowers the unit cost of existing transactions and thus makes an existing market or service more profitable in an overall sense. Thus, it can be seen that, increasingly, such financial factors as economies of scale, fixed and variable costs, and return on investment are necessary ingredients in any marketing plan.

MARKETING IMPLEMENTATION PLAN

Although all of the foregoing, to some degree, are necessary to the creation of an effective marketing plan, the quality and creativity of the actual strategies to be employed are what will ultimately determine success in the competitive marketplace.

In developing the implementation procedure to reach a marketing objective, it may be necessary to create four or five subplans, such as a marketing research plan, a product development plan, a sales plan, and promotional plan.

Not all of these plans are necessary for every product or service, nor does the developer of the plan often have the time or resources to complete all phases of these subplans, but the more comprehensive they can be, the greater the chances of success.

Limitations of space do not allow detailed discussion of each of these subplans, but some of the key factors of each of these plans may be helpful to the individual producing a marketing plan for his or her institution.

Marketing Research Plan

The marketing research plan may incorporate such factors as:

1. Potential market for the service or institution.
2. Estimate of achievable market share over a specified time period.
3. Identification of primary customers.
4. Characteristics of the primary and secondary markets (financial habits, age, size, location, attitudes relative to competing institutions).
5. Measurement of the effectiveness of the institution's own and competitive advertising.
6. Measurement of the effectiveness of the sales calling effort.
7. Requirements for new products or services desired by the primary and secondary markets.
8. Identifiable trends among potential customers.
9. Feasibility of changing the financial habits of potential customers.
10. Feasibility and probability levels of customers switching financial institutions to adopt a service.
11. Levels of acceptance of a new service.

Product Development Plan

Although not every marketing plan will include a product development plan, an increasing number of market analyses are indicating that the method to achieve strategic objectives is to develop new products or services to meet the needs of a target market segment. These new products may range from a high-limit revolving credit line in the consumer market to the development of a new cash management techniques to reach the corporate market with noncredit services.

Regardless of the product or service, most product development plans will incorporate the following features: (1) a description of the key elements of the new product or service; (2) the return on investment to be achieved at certain specified demand levels; (3) degree of exclusivity of product to be developed; (4) effect on existing products or services, and whether alternatives are available by upgrading or improving existing products; (5) packaging techniques that may be incorporated in the new service or product in order to increase sales of existing services; and (6) pricing policy for the new product or new service. This may include the fee structure, balances, balances and/ or fees or fees in lieu of balances.

Communications Plan

Virtually every marketing plan will include a communications plan. Since communications, be it in the form of advertising or public relations, is an integral part of almost all marketing strategies and often is the most costly element in the entire marketing plan.

The communications plan to be most effective is usually divided into two parts—the external communications plan and the internal communications plan.

External Communications Plan. Any advertising to be utilized in the marketing plan should be detailed in the external communications plan and should be consistent with specified advertising objectives. Advertising objectives should be defined, both in terms of the creative message to be used as well as the target audience on which the communications plan will primarily focus. Obviously, the target audience in the advertising plan should be consistent with the target market for the service.

By requiring the communications plan to specifically address its objectives in terms of message and audience, there is less likelihood of an inconsistency—such as the communications message promoting loans during a restricted money period when the bank is seeking deposits. In addition, requiring a strict definition of the target audience in the communications plan ensures greater discipline in media selection. As a result, the cost of the advertising can be measured against the target audience rather than against the total audience that will receive the communications message.

The advertising plan will include such factors as budget, advertising, media to be employed, including TV, radio, newspaper, outdoor, magazine, direct mail, and point of purchase. Most importantly, the communications plan will include a timetable in order to ensure coordination with other elements of the marketing plan.

Internal Communications Plan. The internal communications plan is as vital as the external communications plan although, too often, it is given minimal attention because the media employed are less costly and less glamorous. Nevertheless, an informed, motivated, and enthusiastic staff is critical to the success of the marketing plan and to achieve these levels of involvement among the staff requires a well-conceived, internal communications plan.

Elements that may be incorporated into an internal communications plan include: (1) staff meeting (content and format should be detailed); (2) visual aids; (3) mailings to staff members at home and their job location; (4) advance reprints of external communications; and (5) operations manuals developed from a customer's viewpoint.

Sales Plan

The internal communications plan is also usually an integral part of the sales plan. The sales plan may be divided into two sections— the sales training plan, and the sales action plan.

The comprehensiveness of the sales action plan will depend on the degree of complexity on the services to be offered and the scope of the selling efforts required by the individual bank officers and staff members. The sales training plan should include training both in product knowledge and selling techniques for the particular service involved or the market segment that will be addressed.

Sales Training Plan. The sales training plan should help the individuals involved in the training to answer such questions as the following:

1. How do I sell most effectively?
2. What are the benefits of the service to customers?
3. How are other officers and departments in the bank capable of helping me in my sales of this product or service?
4. How do I most effectively use the sales aids that I have available for explaining the product or service?

Of course, prior to accomplishing any training, it is important to determine exactly which employees should receive the training as training expense is another cost element that must be considered in the development of the marketing plan.

Sales Action Plan. The identification of the individuals in the bank who should receive sales training will be helpful in developing the sales action plan as it gives some indication as to the sales resources that will be available in implementing the marketing plan.

The sales action plan may include the following elements: (1) an assignment plan for prospects; (2) sales probability and profitability versus expense of the calling effort; (3) number of calls to be made by each officer or staff member; (4) desirability of using industry's specialists against certain target markets; (5) sales support necessary—for example, a cash management specialist accompanying a loan-oriented calling officer or a credit card specialist accompanying an officer calling on a retail merchant; (6) any incentive compensation that may be used, such as commissions or merchandise awards for achieving certain sales or sales referrals; (7) sales meetings and distribution of sales intelligence gathered by the sales staff; (8) assignment of the responsibility for conversion and servicing of prospects who become customers; (9) research support available to the sales team, such as Dun & Bradstreet reports, or profiles of key prospects; (10) sales analysis format and frequency; (11) establishment of sales goals in terms of number of calls, sales, size of customers, and multiplicity of services sold.

All of the above are elements that may be incorporated into a sales action plan, but the list is by no means exclusive. It will be obvious to the developer of a marketing plan that there are other elements that sometimes may be useful in a sales plan. A marketing plan is not complete, however, without a sales plan because ultimately all other elements of the marketing plan are dependent on the sale being made or the market penetrated to the degree necessary to achieve the strategic objective.

MARKETING EVALUATION PROCESS

The final section of the marketing plan is usually devoted to the methods and processes by which the strategies and the results obtained from those strategies will be monitored and evaluated. A control monitoring and evaluation process is necessary in many aspects of banking operations, but it is especially necessary in the marketing area because of the dynamic nature of the marketing process.

The actual monitoring process can be comprehensive or simple depending upon the nature of the plan, the service involved, and the size and characteristics of the market being served. However, at a minimum, there are at least two areas that should be included in the monitoring and evaluation strategy. These are market response and competitive response.

Market Response

Evaluation of the market response should include an analysis of whether the forecasted market penetration is being achieved. Deviations or variations from the plan should be highlighted with some evaluation as to the cause of any variation. Detailed analysis of variations from the plan may require further research. Variations may also require revisions to the plan or, in an extreme case, cancellation of the plan because of the failure to achieve satisfactory results either in the terms of market penetration or profitability.

Competitive Response

A second factor that should almost always be incorporated in the monitoring process of a marketing plan is the method by which an evaluation will be made of the competitive response. Even an apparent nonresponse to a particular strategy by the competition may be an important element in this evaluation.

Finally, the marketing plan should, if possible, contain certain contingency factors, anticipating that changes in the marketplace will occur as a result of the actions that have been instituted and the competitive response to those strategies.

CONCLUSION

In summary, there is no unique format for a marketing plan, but the features of a typical marketing plan as described in this chapter and as listed in the outline below are necessary for most bank marketing plans:

A. Market analysis and current market positions.
    1. Banking market penetration or share of market.
    2. Competitive factors.
B. External environmental factors affecting the marketing plan.
C. Establishment of strategic marketing objectives.
D. Establishment of tactical marketing objective.
E. Marketing implementation plan.
    1. Marketing research plan.
    2. Product development plan.
    3. Communications plan.
        a. External communications plan.
        b. Internal communications plan.
    4. Sales plan.
        a. Sales training plan.
        b. Sales action plan.
    5. Promotion plan.
F. Marketing evaluation process.

Chapter 72

Developing Corporate Services

Robert R. Robertson[*]

DEFINITION OF CORPORATE SERVICES

Corporate services are those directly or indirectly profitable services which are provided to companies by a bank for the purpose of establishing and expanding the companies' financial dependency on the bank.

The term "corporate services" technically is a misnomer since such services are offered to any business entity, whether it is a corporation, a partnership, or a proprietorship. Over time, the term "corporate services" simply has been accepted for brevity.

The profitability of a corporate service occasionally is quite direct and identifiable, but more often it is indirect and perhaps difficult to measure. In keeping with the definition of corporate services, one corporate service of questionable profitability might be offered to a company in order to increase the financial dependency of the company on the bank and thus cause the company to accept additional corporate services which result in an overall relationship that does meet the profitability standards of the bank while simultaneously providing acceptable benefits to the company.

EXAMPLES OF CORPORATE SERVICES

Corporate services, according to the previous definition, includes any banking service used by a business entity, whether such a service is a traditional one offered by all banks or an innovative one offered only by imaginative banks. Of course, there are many corporate services which fall in the middle of the spectrum.

---

[*] Senior Vice President, First City National Bank, Houston, Texas.

Examples of traditional corporate services are commercial loans, standard demand deposit accounts, certificates of deposit, cashier's checks, and any other common banking services which are associated with any bank. The purpose in discussing corporate services, however, implies that attention is not to be placed on the traditional services, but on the services that truly are innovative or that at least have allowed the offering banks to be thought of as above average, if not outstanding.

Examples of the more imaginative corporate services are:

A. Planning Services.
   1. Cash forecasting.
   2. Cash budgeting.
B. Money Management Services
   1. Lockbox processing.
   2. Depository check processing.
   3. Preauthorized check processing.
   4. Zero-balance account processing.
   5. Payable-through draft processing.
   6. Remote disbursing.
   7. Wire transfer of funds.
   8. International check clearing.
C. Consulting and Analysis Services
   1. Lockbox location analysis.
   2. Disbursement analysis.
   3. Mergers and acquisitions counseling.
   4. Lease versus purchase counseling.
   5. Source of funds analysis.
   6. Title XI ship financing assistance.
   7. Float analysis.
   8. Investment services.
   9. Employee retail banking package.
  10. Real estate appraisal.
  11. Plant site location assistance.
  12. Credit information and investigation.
D. Accounting and Bookkeeping Services
   1. Data transmission.
   2. Account reconciliation.
   3. Balance reporting.
   4. Automated payroll processing.

Banks which successfully offer a range of imaginative corporate services, in addition to the traditional ones, have certain characteristics which are all or partly lacking in banks which limit their corporate services to the traditional ones. These characteristics include:

a. The desire to expand commercial relationships.
b. Aggressive management.
c. Motivated officers and employees.
d. Effective interdepartmental communication and cooperation.
e. Sound intermediate- and long-range planning.
f. Costing and pricing capabilities which allow determination of the planned and actual profitability of a new service.
g. An established approval process covering the conception, development, and implementation of new service ideas.
h. Proper new service training for pertinent officers and employees.
i. Officer and employee recognition and reward for accepted new service ideas.
j. Effective marketing of new services.
k. An image of retaining services once they are started.

THE NEED FOR CORPORATE SERVICES

Two vital areas which speak to the need for corporate services are identified by the basic desire of a bank first simply to survive and second to excel among its competitors so as to meet or exceed stockholder expectations and so as to attract capital, if needed, at a reasonable price.

Survival

The banking industry today is more dynamic than it was in the relatively recent past. It likely will become even more dynamic in the future.

One cause of the increase in the rate of change in the industry is the higher value of money. In recent years, the secular trend of interest rates has been upward; companies in general can no longer afford to leave surplus funds on deposit with banks or to have inadequate control over the funds which necessarily flow through banks.

Another cause is the ever-increasing computerization of banks. This computerization offers far more new service opportunities for banks than have been conceived.

Another cause is the staggering volume of paper that now flows through banking channels. As is implied by the planning for electronic funds transfer systems, the paper volume eventually would become economically unmanageable.

Another cause is the increasing sophistication of the commercial customer. This increasing sophistication leads directly to increased demands on banking capabilities.

These several causes which are producing major changes in the banking industry are by no means all inclusive. The examples do serve, however, to underscore the fact that the industry is dynamic, and it then becomes obvious that individual banks must be dynamic also if they are to improve their chances of survival. One principal ingredient is the forward looking creation of new and improved corporate services.

Competition

Since banks are service organizations, a principal way one bank can distinguish itself is through the implementation of innovative and profitable corporate services for which there is an existing or created need by the commercial customers and prospects of the bank.

The benefit of distinguishing itself in this manner reaches not only to the bank itself, but also to the banking industry and to the commercial customers of the banking industry.

Obviously, a bank which leads in the creation of innovative corporate services will excel among its banking competitors; however, its need to compete does not stop with other banks.

The banking industry is but part of a larger financial industry which includes finance companies, leasing companies, investment banks, savings and loan associations, insurance companies, foreign financing, and the commercial paper market. The banking industry must compete with all of these other segments of the financial industry, and to the extent that one bank can lead other banks in offering new and improved corporate services, then that one bank has helped its entire industry to excel.

Finally, a bank can and should compete productively in several ways with its own commercial customers. First, as the sophistication of a bank's commercial customers increases, the demands on its banking capabilities by its commercial customers will increase. If these demands are not met, the commercial customers will find other solutions. The commercial paper market is perhaps an imperfect example. In any event, a bank not only should meet reasonable demands, but should anticipate these demands with the introduction of feasible corporate services.

Second, a bank can profitably perform certain functions for commercial customers more economically than each customer can perform the function for itself. In general, this is true for financial type functions which are common to most companies and which a bank can perform for many companies, thereby offering economies of volume. Examples are account reconciliation, lockbox location analysis, and disbursement point location analysis.

CREATION OF INNOVATIVE CORPORATE SERVICES

It is fundamental in accomplishing most undertakings efficiently that the first action required is the establishment of the ultimate goal. The goal is then broken into the steps which will lead to its accomplishment. These steps serve the purpose of converting a general desire into the specific work that can be assigned to individuals. Having assigned the work steps to individuals in the proper priority, completion dates can be determined and the first work step can be commenced. The process of accomplishing the goal is then under way.

So it is with new and improved corporate services. Accomplishing the goal of creating a successfully operating new corporate service is preceeded by weeks, or months, or perhaps years of performing the work steps that lead to that satisfactory conclusion.

The following basic work steps are suggested in order to accomplish the goal of creating a successfully operating new corporate service:

a. Conception of innovative corporate service ideas.
b. Tentative approval of a particular corporate service conceptual idea.
c. Development of the corporate service conceptual idea.
d. Final approval of the new corporate service.
e. Implementation of the new corporate service.

The following five sections will focus on each of the above five basic work steps.

CONCEPTION OF INNOVATIVE CORPORATE SERVICE IDEAS

The first step in accomplishing the goal of creating a successfully operating new corporate service is the conception of innovative corporate service ideas.

To accomplish this first step, the following requirements perhaps are critical:

Ongoing Consideration

By the very nature of the term *conception,* it is a process which must be ongoing. The conceiver does not know where his or her thoughts may lead. There is, therefore, no way to know when to start or stop the conception process. Awareness of the need to conceive is a frame of mind which should be encouraged continuously in order to have a constant flow of ideas because only a small percentage of ideas ultimately will satisfy the many criteria for an accepted new corporate service.

Specific Assignment of Authority, Responsibility, and Accountability

Specific authority, responsibility, and accountability must be assigned for the conception of innovative corporate service ideas if this crucial area truly is to receive ongoing consideration such that an acceptable flow of quality ideas is generated. Further, such an assignment identifies the individual who should receive the ideas of others. Others whose ideas should be sought are employees, customers, other banks, professional groups, and consulting firms.

Too few banks assign such authority, responsibility, and accountability.

TENTATIVE APPROVAL OF A PARTICULAR CORPORATE SERVICE CONCEPTUAL IDEA

When a corporate service idea is still in the conceptual stage, it should receive tentative approval before any development work is done. Executive management should at least agree that the particular service falls in a direction that the bank wishes to go, or the time spent on development might be wasted. Tentative approval also adds executive management support to the development phase, and validly conditions executive management for the final recommendation.

DEVELOPMENT OF THE CORPORATE SERVICE CONCEPTUAL IDEA

Development of a corporate service conceptual idea is the phase that determines the feasibility of converting a conceptual idea into an actual service. Responsibility might be placed with an individual or a committee to determine the feasibility. If a committee is appointed, it should include people who have special knowledge of the proposed new service and people who will be affected by the proposed new service. Further, these individuals should be as senior as possible so as to benefit from their seasoning and so as to obtain their understanding and agreement, and that of their subordinates.

The report of the Development Committee, depending on the service studied, should include such topics as introduction, new service description, potential benefits, cost, profitability, market, implementation, and recommendation.

The section "Hypothetical New Corporate Service Case," below, includes an outline of a development study for a registered bank holding company.

FINAL APPROVAL OF THE NEW CORPORATE SERVICE

The Development Committee report should be presented to executive management for final approval. Executive management awareness already exists due to having previously obtained tentative approval. Final approval, or rejection, should, therefore, be swift. A further expedient is to distribute the report to executive management several days before the meeting is held to act on the report.

IMPLEMENTATION OF THE NEW CORPORATE SERVICE

The new corporate service implementation steps will vary in complexity depending on the service involved. For quality implementation of a new corporate service, however, the implementation process should include such steps as:

a. Assignment of authority, responsibility, and accountability for planning, organizing, leading, and controlling the implementation and ongoing operation of the new service.
b. Internal communication of a description of the new corporate service and the authority which has approved it.
c. Training of all persons involved.
d. Possible execution of a pilot project to gain actual experience on a limited scale.
e. Evaluation of the pilot project results.
f. Designation of full implementation date.
g. Internal communication of the implementation date.
h. External marketing of the new corporate service and the implementation date.
i. Executive management motivation of all involved.
j. Implementation.

PLANNING, ORGANIZING, LEADING, AND CONTROLLING NEW CORPORATE SERVICES

Assignment of authority, responsibility, and accountability for planning, organizing, leading, and controlling the new corporate service was mentioned in Section "Implementation of the New Corporate Service," and the assignment chronologically should occur then, or earlier.

A description of the classical management functions of planning, organizing, leading, and controlling is a topic in itself, and is not within the scope of this chapter. Suffice it to say that the professional application of these management principles is critical for the successful implementation of a new corporate service as well as for the ongoing success of the new service.

HYPOTHETICAL NEW CORPORATE SERVICE CASE

Registered bank holding companies have increased significantly in number during the past few years, so a hypothetical new corporate service case will be presented which deals with a registered bank holding company.

The new corporate service to be considered in the hypothetical case is the creation of a "regional services package."

In the Section "Creation of Innovative Corporate Services," five basic work steps were recommended for the creation of a corporate service. This case will follow those five steps.

Conception of Innovative Corporate Service Ideas

An individual in the hypothetical registered bank holding company conceives the idea of a "regional services package" and believes that such a corporate service must be one reason why a bank holding company exists.

As part of the conception process, this individual defines his idea in writing so that others understand it as he does and the chance of misunderstanding is reduced.

His definition is: The "regional services package" is the marketing, within the region served by the holding company member banks, of various corporate services available at any member bank to corporate customers of any member bank. This approach will be effective in two ways: First, companies with operations in several cities in the region can have their total banking needs in the region handled by one account officer at one member bank. Second, services available at one member bank can be offered to companies in other cities in the region through other member banks.

The conception phase ends with this definition. No further work is done until the idea receives tentative approval.

Tentative Approval of a Particular Idea

The individual informally presents his conceptual idea to the president of the holding company. The president is impressed by the idea and places the proposal on the agenda of the next meeting of the member bank chief executive officers. At this meeting, tentative approval of the proposal is received and a development study is requested.

Development of the Corporate Service Conceptual Idea

A Development Committee is created, and is composed of senior officers from several of the member banks in order to gain interbank input. Further, the individual committee members are persons who will be directly affected if the new service is implemented.

The committee members each take responsibility for a portion of the development work. Numerous meetings, each with an agenda, are held over a period of several months.

The committee completes its development task by producing a study report which has the following table of contents:

TABLE OF CONTENTS

1. Introduction
   a. Regional Services Package Definition
   b. Development Committee Assignment
   c. Approach
   d. Conclusion in Summary
2. Potential Benefits
3. Services to Be Included
4. Profitability System for Bank Compensation
   a. Pricing of Services to Customers
   b. Billing of Customers
   c. Distribution of Fees and Balances to Participating Banks
5. Marketing and Advertising
   a. Definition of Market
   b. Marketing Objective
   c. Marketing Strategy
   d. Advertising
6. Assignment of Responsibilities
   a. Coordination
   b. Reporting and Controlling
   c. Training
   d. Implementation
7. Conclusion
   a. Recommendation
   b. Commitment Required
   c. Cost
8. Appendix

Final Approval of the New Corporate Service

The Development Committee presents its report to the next meeting of the member bank chief executive officers. At this meeting, final approval is given to implement the new service. Also at this meeting, a specific individual is given authority, responsibility, and accountability to organize, plan, lead, and control the implementation and ongoing operation of the new service. In addition, each chief executive officer commits to assign a senior officer at the bank to be the regional services package liason officer, thus providing for effective communication concerning this service throughout the member bank network.

Implementation of the new service is now ready to proceed. The individual who received this assignment should clearly understand his responsibility and the source of his authority.

Implementation of the New Corporate Service

The individual responsible for this new service first prepares in writing the implementation steps he or she proposes to take. These steps are in far more detail than the portion of the Development Committee report which discussed implementation. Since overall approval of the new service has been obtained, the individual may simply receive approval of his proposed implementation steps from the persons to whom he is accountable.

The detailed implementation proposal which is submitted has the following table of contents:

TABLE OF CONTENTS

1. Plan
   a. Key Objective of the Regional Services Package
   b. Critical Objectives
   c. Specific Objectives
2. Organization
   a. Organization Chart
   b. Job Descriptions
   c. Personnel Assignments
3. Leadership
   a. Communication
   b. Training
4. Control
   a. Standards
   b. Budget
   c. Reports Required
5. Marketing
   a. Internal Publicity
   b. External Publicity

The above five parts of the Table of Contents are copiously explained in the text of the implementation proposal. While all five parts are important, a great deal of attention is placed on part 1, the plan, which is defined as determining the key objective, the critical objectives, and the specific objectives of the regional services package.

Widespread communication and understanding of the key, critical, and specific objectives help to gain vertical and horizontal agreement concerning all that follows in the implementation and ongoing operation of the regional services package.

The key objective is determined to be: Marketing, within the region served by the holding company member banks, specified corporate services available at any member bank to corporate customers of any member bank so that companies with operations in several cities in the region can have their total banking needs in the region handled by one account officer at one member bank; and so that services available at one member bank can be offered to companies in other cities in the region through other member banks.

Several critical objectives are determined. A representative critical objective is: Planned and actual costs of the regional services package are to be monitored as well as planned and actual benefits in order to insure that the service is profitable.

Another representative critical objective is: Customer usage of the regional services package is to increase annually by an amount equal to 10 percent of the number of customers for which the service was designed until at least 70 percent of such customers are using the service.

Another representative critical objective is: Customers participating in the regional services package are to be surveyed annually and the quality of the service is to be ranked in the "excellent" category by at least 85 percent of the respondents.

A number of specific objectives also are determined which are to be acted upon immediately in order to allow the critical objectives to be accomplished, which in turn allow the key objective to be accomplished.

One such specific objective, which corresponds to one of the critical objectives mentioned, is: Create within 30 days a procedure for measuring and reporting the planned and actual costs and benefits of the regional services package.

Another such specific objective, which corresponds to another of the critical objectives mentioned, is: Create within 90 days a procedure for determining the number of potential customers for the regional services package, and for measuring the number of such customers using the service.

Still another such specific objective, which corresponds to another of the critical objectives mentioned, is: Develop by year-end a regional services package customer survey which provides for ranking of quality of the service by the users.

These examples of objectives simply show the nature of the work contained in the implementation proposal. This proposal is the last step in converting a conceptual idea into specific tasks.

The detailed implementation proposal is approved, and action begins. If successful, the holding company will have taken another step to enhance its professional reputation, to excel among its banking competitors, to aid its industry in better competing with other industries, and to provide improved service to its commercial customers through a more simplified approach.

Chapter 73

Correspondent Bank Services

John W. H. Gushée*

The term correspondent banking has traditionally been used to describe that relationship which exists when one commercial bank maintains a demand account with another, generally in return for some services received.

The bank providing the service is referred to as the correspondent or city bank. The one utilizing the service is known as the respondent, country, or more recently, community bank. It is not uncommon for larger banks to actually maintain demand accounts with each other for which each receives certain services. These are referred to as reciprocal relationships.

HISTORY AND SCOPE

The roots of correspondent banking go back to the early 1800s when interbank deposits were established to provide a means of redeeming bank notes outside of one's own geographic area. Correspondent relationships as we think of them today, however, gained real importance in the 1830s and have been a permanent part of the banking structure ever since. Commercial banks originally viewed themselves as regional monopolies, so cooperation and not competition between one city and another was considered normal. The history of early banking includes such modern-day elements as several banks participating in a joint loan and banks joining together to provide liquidity facilities for each other.

The very function of the commercial banking system as a financial

---

* Senior Vice President, The Arizona Bank, Phoenix, Arizona.

intermediary and clearinghouse for checks and drafts created the need for flexibility and compatibility and led to a large and sophisticated correspondent network.

Today there are approximately 14,600 independent commercial banks operating in the United States. It is safe to say that nearly every one of these banks has at least one correspondent relationship. Actually, studies have indicated the average number of correspondent accounts to be slightly in excess of six, with between two and three such relationships pinpointed as particularly important or primary. At the end of March 1977, according to an American Bankers Association survey, there were 371 banks in 41 states, the District of Columbia, and Puerto Rico, having deposits in the aggregate of $5 million or more from other domestic commercial banks. These are referred to as "due to" accounts and the total of these demand deposits was $33.7 billion. This figure does contain some double counting; however, it is still impressive and would represent an estimated annual compensation for services received considerably in excess of $1 billion. If interbank time deposits and accounts of foreign banks were added, total correspondent balances for U.S. banks would have been in excess of $45 billion.

New York City banks held almost 55 percent of these domestic demand correspondent balances and have traditionally been a dominant factor in the business. However, large regional banks are also important in correspondent banking. Their share of the market has been increasing in recent years. In addition, there are a number of smaller banks located principally in states which restrict branch banking which have long had well-organized and sophisticated correspondent banking operations. These departments have provided a significant portion of the demand deposits and often the net profit of those banks. This, of course, is due to the numerous small unit banks in their marketing areas.

INTERBANK SERVICES

Correspondent banking developed from its early beginnings as merely a vehicle for settlement of items between banks to an industry in which a long list of services are available. The traditional services are outlined below under the broad categories of general banking, credit services, investment services, international services, trust services, and management assistance and special services. Some correspondents enjoy an expertise in particular areas, and it would be rare for a respondent to obtain all services from one bank. Some country banks have found that access to at least one major money center bank and one regional correspondent possibly in its own state, provide a good blend of the services required. Four specific services are reported by respondents to be most important: loan participations, check clearing, securities safekeeping, and Federal Reserve funds transactions.

GENERAL BANKING

Many of the general banking services provided by correspondents are services which are available through a Federal Reserve Bank. However, there are approximately 9,000 banks which are not members of the Federal Reserve System and look to other commercial banks for help with these functions. In addition, geography often dictates to a member bank the use of a regional correspondent instead of a Federal Reserve Bank, and in certain fields these banks have been able to offer services on a more competitive basis.

Another consideration is that nonmember banks generally use correspondent balances to help meet reserve requirements under state laws. These balances do double duty when they are used to support services obtained from a correspondent as well.

Check Clearing

The clearing of checks is one of the most basic services traditionally provided by correspondent banks. In the past, this service was particularly important to those who were not members of the Federal Reserve System, as they had no other practical way to collect deposited items drawn outside the bank's immediate geographic area or outside the limits of a local clearinghouse. Efficient collection of these items is an important feature to be able to offer one's customers. A customer must know when funds represented by these checks are collected and must know approximately when it can be assumed that an item will not be returned or dishonored by a drawee bank. Banks must offer their customers competitive clearing times, particularly if they have large national firms located in their marketing area. In addition, the sending bank itself benefits from fast collection of items, as this cuts down the amount of float it might have to absorb.

Many large correspondent banks have developed sophisticated programs for handling transit items. These include the innovative use of transportation and development of sophisticated sending patterns to provide respondents with fast check clearing service. Country bankers have found that in check collection, the quickest distance between two points is not always a straight line, and often a regional correspondent can offer faster collection of checks in other cities than banks actually operating there.

It is not uncommon for a correspondent today to be able to provide a sending bank with computerized studies of his or her outgoing cash letters to assure that the most efficient collection avenues are being utilized. Some banks will provide ledger and estimated collected positions on a daily basis, either by wire, telephone, or through a computer terminal, so that the sending bank can more accurately forecast the amount of excess funds available for investment.

It was thought that with the formation of the Regional Check Processing Centers, clearing activity outside the Federal Reserve System would be reduced. This may prove to be true, particularly if the Federal Reserve becomes more competitive in this whole process; however, check clearing is still a major function of the correspondent network.

Many banks utilize a clearinghouse to exchange local items. A correspondent account can be used as a means of settlement for this exchange. A nonmember bank can also use its account with a correspondent for entries originated by a Federal Reserve Bank such as debits covering incoming cash letters.

Funds Transfer

A correspondent can offer a smaller bank access to virtually the entire banking system for same day transfer of funds, through either the larger bank's own correspondent network or that bank's account with a Federal Reserve Bank. The number of wire transfers nationwide has increased dramatically. Efficient handling of these transfers is important, as is prompt notification to the respondent bank of credits to its account. This information must be received in time for the respondent to invest these funds if they are considered excess for reserve purposes.

Coin and Currency

One benefit of membership in the Federal Reserve System is inexpensive access to a supply of coin and currency. This is a service almost all nonmember banks receive from a correspondent. Although some of the Federal Reserve Banks will supply nonmembers with coin and currency, transportation charges could be quite heavy, and geographic considerations would dictate the use of a relatively close correspondent bank instead. A flexible shipment schedule can help the community bank minimize the amount of cash on hand and thus the risk of theft or loss and also reduce the loss of investment income which may occur when there is excess cash in the vault.

Collections

The collection department of a large bank handles numerous items for correspondents. Although it is not absolutely necessary, it makes more sense to send collection items direct to a correspondent, as remittance can be received quicker by credit to an account than by dispatch of a draft or cashier's check through the mail. In addition, some correspondents will waive collection fees or put them in an account analysis instead of deducting the fee from the remittance itself.

Noncash collections include many items such as bonds, coupons, and acceptances. Cash collections would include checks sent outside of the normal cash letter route for special handling and specific notification of payment. It is, of course, better to send these directly to the drawee bank, whether or not it is a correspondent.

CREDIT SERVICES

A correspondent can offer a bank a number of credit-related services, some long standing and some of recent origin.

Loan Participations

According to surveys among banks, one of the most important services a correspondent can provide is overline credit facilities. A small bank can easily run into legal limit problems in financing an important local customer. The bank may not wish to share this relationship with another local financial institution and accordingly overline; that is, participate, the excess borrowings to a correspondent. Some smaller banks might not have loan officers who are familiar with specialized types of financing, such as loans to natural resource companies, interim construction financing, and even some agricultural and cattle credits. Therefore, another reason for overlining loans or at least consulting with a correspondent, is to take advantage of a correspondent's specific knowledge in certain types of credits and/or documentation and make use of the particular expertise a larger bank might have.

Smaller banks are likely to have wide swings in seasonal loan demand. A correspondent can assist in meeting these peaks with overline accommodations. This type of facility would be particularly important in agricultural areas. Another reason for a small bank overlining particular credits would be to reduce its concentration in certain types of loans.

It is important for the smaller bank to recognize the need to provide detailed credit information to its correspondent when requesting any overline. A correspondent should be able to make an independent and intelligent loan decision. In the long run this is of equal benefit to the smaller bank in assuring that its loan portfolio maintains adequate quality. Conversely, it is important for the correspondent to honor the relationship which the local bank enjoys with its customer. The city bank should not attempt to replace the local bank either in the credit or in offering other services, except with the full understanding of the respondent bank.

Smaller banks often look to their correspondents for downstream loan participations. These can be in connection with a mutual customer where the correspondent may act as an agent bank or could be loans which the country bank wishes to purchase for a short period when it is experiencing particularly slack loan demand. The correspondent should be cognizant of its responsibility to downstream only high-quality credits, even if this requires some rate concession, unless the smaller bank is fully equipped to carefully analyze each credit offered. Conversely, the respondent should be fully cognizant that his or her bank is assuming the credit risk involved in any such loan participation. These loans can be covered by a repurchase agreement from the correspondent provided that bank is not so prohibited by a legal limit problem. There are several complicated legal questions being raised concerning interbank credit participations, including questions relating to the Securities Acts of 1933–34, and prudence would dictate careful review by attorneys for both banks in complicated situations.

Direct Lending

During the past decade a whole new field of interbank lending has appeared in which correspondents play an important role. This would be in direct loans between banks and bank holding companies.

The growth of bank assets was rapid in the 1960s and this, of course, created the need for additional capital. Some of this capital has been supplied in the form of subordinated loans from correspondent banks. These loans were generally of an intermediate term nature and were either to be paid out of future sale of equity securities or amortized from bank earnings. There is a point of view that this type of loan does not increase the capital of the banking system as a whole. In addition, bank regulatory authorities are not enthusiastic about interbank capital lending; however, for some small banks this may be one of the few viable sources of capital needed for growth.

Lines of credit to bank holding companies also became common during this period of time. These lines are used by the holding companies for general corporate purposes but principally to fund finance oriented subsidiaries such as leasing, mortgage banking, and consumer or commercial finance operations. In some instances the lines provided by correspondents are used as a backup to commercial paper sold by the holding company.

The sale of Federal Reserve funds represents an interbank credit exposure, and under the Federal Deposit Insurance Corporation (FDIC) guidelines, term funds actually must be shown in the bank's loan account. This market has become very significant with industry outstandings reaching as high as $30 billion. With the slowdown in the economy and difficulties encountered by some banks in the mid 1970's, direct lending between banking entities diminished somewhat; however, it is still considered an important part of interbank relationships.

Credit Information

Another traditional service provided by correspondent banks is the availability of credit information and investigation services. A smaller bank may have requests from local customers for normal trade credit checkings or may need the information for its own account. These inquiries would generally be handled through the larger bank's credit department. Most large banks belong to the Robert Morris Associates, a national association of bank loan and credit officers, which has established guidelines for the exchange of credit information. Even though a smaller bank may not be a member, it would be helpful to be familiar with these guidelines in requesting and exchanging credit information with other banks, due to recent restrictive legislation in this area.

Other Credit Services

With the growth of holding companies, correspondents have been able to offer specialized types of financing to their respondents' customers through affiliated companies. Examples would be in the field of direct leasing, factoring, or account receivable financing, specialized real estate transactions, and intermediate- and even long-term credits. Use of a correspondent's affiliates for these generally nonbankable transactions assists a local bank in meeting its customers' total financing needs.

A correspondent can offer another credit service by providing loans secured by bank stock or other assets to assist individuals either in the formation of a new bank or acquisition of the ownership of an existing one. This is a service which would be more prevalent in unit banking states. A correspondent also can offer loans to smaller bank's officers and directors which the bank itself might not be able to make, due to limiting laws or regulations. Both normal prudence and legislation in this area indicate that it is important that these particular types of loans be structured and priced carefully to avoid any possible hint of conflict of interest on the part of either bank, the officers involved, or various stockholder groups.

PORTFOLIO AND INVESTMENT SERVICES

A correspondent can be of particular service to a respondent in managing its investment portfolio and meeting liquidity requirements.

These services would fall into three categories: purchase, sale and trading of securities, and liquidity instruments; safekeeping and custodial services; and investment advice.

Securities Trading

Most major banks maintain active trading operations and can assist respondents in the purchase or sale of the full range of government and agency obligations, municipal securities and negotiable time certificates of deposit. A correspondent can also be a source of commercial paper and participations in broker loans when the yields on these types of investments become attractive.

Of particular importance during the past ten years has been the market for liquidity instruments, particularly Federal Reserve funds and repurchase agreements. In recent years many large- and medium-sized member banks have employed the practice of liability management and have found the private banking system a source of day-to-day liquidity for which they previously turned to Federal Reserve Banks. Nonmember banks usually do not enjoy the privilege of borrowing from the Federal Reserve and must obtain short-term funds from their correspondents. During periods of tight money, smaller banks often enjoy excess liquidity and find a convenient outlet for these funds selling them in the Federal Reserve funds market. Large correspondent banks generally maintain positions on both sides of this market and are able to provide temporary liquidity to respondents, even when they are in net purchased positions themselves. The whole Federal Reserve funds market has grown so extensively that many banks have formalized their approval process for this type of activity.

Safekeeping Services

It is often impractical for a bank to physically hold the securities which it has purchased for its investment account. The mailing charges can be expensive and maintaining adequate vault procedures a problem. In the case of trading accounts, it is also important to have the securities available for quick delivery. A correspondent bank, particularly those in active money centers such as New York City, can provide a valuable service acting as custodian for these instruments. This is particularly true of nonmembers which do not utilize the custodial services available at a Federal Reserve Bank.

The securities departments will, upon either wire or telephonic instructions, receive and deliver securities from the safekeeping account, making the appropriate entries for payment to the correspondent account. As part of this service, the correspondent will provide periodic reports of securities being held which are available for review by the bank's management. In addition, the securities department will make whatever arrangements are necessary for pledging of its securities to cover public funds which a respondent bank may have in its deposit base. During the past ten years the amount of activity in trading of securities has increased significantly and the value of a relationship with a correspondent offering an efficient and well-run securities department has become apparent.

Investment Advice

Many small banks look to a correspondent for investment advice in maintaining a properly balanced securities portfolio. Interest rates, securities prices, and even bond quality have fluctuated widely in recent years, and a knowledgeable city correspondent can be of real assistance in suggesting a blend of types and maturities of instruments. In some cases this service is quite comprehensive and includes regular consultations with the smaller bank's management and periodic analyses of its portfolio.

INTERNATIONAL SERVICES

The field of international banking has expanded significantly during the past decade. The number of banks maintaining overseas offices has increased and now includes numerous regionals, in addition to the traditional money center banks which have long had important international commitments. Many larger domestic banks who do not have extensive overseas offices of their own do maintain a large network of correspondent relationships with foreign banks. It can rely on these contacts in assisting respondents. A country bank, then, through its city correspondent, can secure access to almost any financial center throughout the world.

International services available through a correspondent fall broadly into three major areas: operational services, financial services, and marketing services.

Operating Services

The principal operating service would be the clearing of foreign checks and cash items. The collection of foreign drafts and processing of foreign currency are also important services. In addition, a correspondent can handle the mechanics of transferring funds to and from foreign countries either for the bank's own account or for its customers.

A correspondent can also be a source for the purchase and sale of foreign exchange.

Financial Services

It is not practical for a relatively small bank to have on its own staff someone with all the specialized knowledge which may be necessary to service its customers with their international banking needs. Accordingly, a correspondent can help by providing financial services to a smaller bank's customers. The city bank can issue letters of credit in its own name and can assist the country bank in processing documentary collections, as well as providing counsel in completing complicated international transactions. The correspondent can also assist its respondent in providing pre-export credit facilities to its local customers. Many larger banks can also be particularly helpful in arranging financing where an Export-Import Bank guarantee or insurance from the Federal Credit Insurance Association is desirable. The arrangements with either organization can be somewhat complex; however, the services they provide are applicable to even small companies, and a local bank which has access through a correspondent to this type of financing may find itself with a competitive advantage.

Marketing Services

In the area of marketing and business development, some of the larger correspondent banks can provide overall information on the international scene, including such things as in-depth country studies and current economic and political information on world markets. Introductions to government officials and business executives in other countries can easily be made by a correspondent who maintains a worldwide network of branches. In recent years participations in syndications of foreign loans have also been offered to respondent banks who might be able to take advantage of some of the special tax considerations and have excess funds to invest.

TRUST SERVICES

The major trust department services usually offered by correspondent banks involve investment counseling and acting as a securities custodian. In some instances where a community bank has no trust operation of its own, it may look to a correspondent to provide its major customers with trust services. That way, it is in a position to offer a total banking package. This service would also include counseling with the principal officers and directors of the smaller bank's major corporate clients.

Correspondents also offer stockholder services such as acting as registrar and transfer agent, and more recently, some banks have been able to offer their respondents a dividend reinvestment package.

Investment Counseling

Investment advice offered by correspondent banks is usually available on three levels, depending on the amount the respondent wishes to pay in fees or balances. The basic service would essentially be information received through the mail. This could include a list of equities currently being recommended, technical analysis of the stock market, and/or individual issues and portfolio strategy. The second level of service would include personal access to research departments and individuals in the correspondent bank's trust investment area. Generally, the correspondent would have an account administrator who would handle such communications. The complete service would include individual portfolio analysis of trust customers and almost daily counseling, including periodic visits by investment analysts and account executives to the respondent's place of business.

Custodial Services

A correspondent can offer safekeeping facilities for trust assets. As with the bank's investment portfolio, it is often not practical for a smaller bank to house its own securities, and thus it is simpler to domicile them with a correspondent. Access to central securities depositories is also possible by utilizing a correspondent's membership in such organizations. This service will become more important as the trend toward security certificate automation and book entry programs increases. The correspondent with the custodial account can provide a detailed analysis of the securities held and, of course, process coupons, dividends, and so on. Some banks offer a total automated individual trust accounting package either with or without the custodial service.

MANAGEMENT ASSISTANCE AND SPECIAL SERVICES

In addition to specific operating and credit-oriented services, there are a number of other areas in which a correspondent can be of assistance to a country bank.

Management Consulting

One of the most important services which a smaller bank can obtain from its city correspondent is access to the larger bank's specialized departments and the opportunity to take advantage of the experience and management expertise which the larger bank has developed. A correspondent can be of assistance in developing personnel programs and organizational structure and marketing plans. Some banks specialize in assisting their respondents in branch location studies. Some will actually assist in performing a director's audit for a respondent bank. Visits with department heads at the larger bank can be very helpful to the management of a smaller bank in organizing its own plan for growth and change. As the tools of asset and liability management and profit planning become more sophisticated, a smaller bank can benefit from the time, effort, and expertise which its larger correspondent has expended along these lines. It is not uncommon for a smaller bank to send employees to a larger bank for on-the-job training for a period of weeks or sometimes even months. This would be in specialized areas such as international, trust, or credit department operations.

Consulting has become even more important with the increased complexity of operating small businesses, including banks. A correspondent can provide a vital service by helping a country bank keep current on the numerous legislative and regulatory changes being layered on the banking industry. Truth in Lending, OSHA, ERISA, and ECOA are but a few new terms an already overworked bank president must learn to deal with.

A rather specialized extension of the management consulting activity would be seminars which are held by some of the larger banks for their respondents. The program would usually include information on the state of the economy, discussion of current topics of interest, or controversy in the field of banking itself, and perhaps lectures on new or unique services or trends which would be of interest to smaller banks.

Automated Data Processing

The computerization of many of the bookkeeping functions of banking created the need for another important service which some correspondents have been able to offer smaller banks. It is generally not practical for a small bank to incur the considerable expense involved in acquiring the computer hardware necessary to automate its operations. However, it is important they be able to take advantage of the efficiencies and cost savings available with automation. By utilizing a correspondent's computer center, a smaller bank can get access to all types of programs such as accounting for demand and savings accounts, automation of all three loan classifications, commercial, consumer and real estate, and even general ledger entries.

In the future the availability of smaller and less costly computers may encourage some banks to do their own processing instead of relying on a correspondent's computer center. On the other hand, a smaller bank may use such equipment merely to gather information which is transmitted in a paperless form for processing by the correspondent, thus still depending heavily on the larger bank's operating capabilities.

This introduces the whole new area of electronic funds transfer systems (EFTS) and how these systems will affect correspondent relationships. This question is presently in a state of flux, due to regulatory uncertainties; however, there is little doubt that it will have an effect on the business of correspondent banking. There is the chance that electronic funds transfer systems will introduce new competition to smaller banks, sometimes from their own correspondents. On the other hand, it is quite conceivable that smaller banks in the future will be looking to correspondents to help them take advantage of such devices as automated teller machines, point-of-sale terminals, and an automated clearinghouse with its paperless debits and credits.

Business Development

A traditional and important service usually offered by a correspondent is assistance in new business development. It would be customary for a correspondent to refer to its respondent any customers who are moving to that bank's marketing area. This would include introductions and recommendations to corporate customers who are building a new facility or opening a regional office in the respondent's city. These types of introductions would include trust customers who might be relocating as well as those looking for commercial services. During the past ten years there has been a tendency for correspondent banks to enlarge their customer base and, accordingly, a city bank might have relationships with more than one bank in a particular area. In this instance, the referral of new business becomes more complicated. The city bank will try to apportion it fairly; however, often it will give priority to the respondent bank who first contacts it and requests a recommendation. This means it has thus become important for a banker to be aware of what is happening in the community and not just assume that good corporate business will be referred to him without some action on his part as well.

Credit Card

Use of bank issued credit cards have become almost as common as the writing of checks. It is often not practical for a small bank to join one of the major national card chains on its own, although it may wish to offer this service to its customers. In that case, a correspondent can be of assistance. It can set up a program whereby the card is issued in the respondent bank name, thereby preserving its identity, but the larger bank would take care of all the recordkeeping and funding requirements.

Other Management Services

Correspondents can offer a number of services to a country bank's employees such as stock purchase plans, pension and profit sharing and group insurance plans. A few of the larger city banks publish and distribute to their correspondents periodic brochures and pamphlets covering the economy, both domestic and international, statistical information on the specific geographic areas, and special topics of interest to bankers in general.

Corporate cash management has become much more sophisticated in the last few years and a correspondent can assist a smaller bank in providing these services to its customer. This would include both specialized disbursing plans and assistance in concentration or lockbox banking.

CORRESPONDENT BANKING'S CHANGING ENVIRONMENT

The whole field of commercial banking has changed dramatically in recent years and the area of correspondent banking is no exception. Partially in recognition of this, the American Banker's Association established a separate Correspondent Banking Division as recently as 1971. Some specific changes have been commented on in a review of services offered by correspondent banks; however, there are other areas which should be noted in any discussion of the subject.

Compensation

As the investment value of overnight funds increased dramatically in the 1960s and 1970s, respondents became much more sensitive to the level of their due from accounts and were not as likely to leave excess funds uninvested. At the same time, the relationship between a correspondent and respondent bank has become much more quantified. The use of an account analysis form on a periodic basis has become customary for almost all accounts where there is any appreciable activity. This has had the dual effect of requiring the correspondent to place a value on the services which it is performing and also specifically indicates the minimum level of balances which a respondent should maintain to properly compensate the servicing bank.

The form of analysis varies with some banks reporting unit prices and others using average dollar of balances required for each service.

There seems to be no uniformity in computing the earnings credit allowed by various banks, although generally they are tied to money market rates. Prices on individual items vary significantly, as much as 200 percent to 300 percent from bank to bank. This variance appears to be geographic and the prices posted by competing banks in any one area are generally comparable. It is necessary to weigh the unit price, reserve requirement, and earnings credit all together before the real cost to the respondent bank is known.

There are several major problems for the city correspondent in using a standard account analysis. First, some banks admit they do not have accurate and reliable cost figures and therefore the prices quoted may or may not cover the cost of providing the service. In addition, there are numerous nonanalyzed services such as consulting and new business referrals which are difficult to quantify and so are generally not included in an analysis. The community bank should keep in mind that compensation is not only for services received today but to assure that its correspondents are on hand to help in the future should special assistance be necessary. This is particularly true of non-member banks who do not have easy access to the Federal Reserve. Therefore, the decision as to the level of compensation agreed upon between the correspondent and respondent banks is still quite subjective.

Quantification of the correspondent-respondent relationship could eventually lead to more services being sold on a fee basis. The present consensus is that deposits are the lifeblood of the commercial banking industry and accordingly most bankers would prefer to be compensated with balances instead of fees.

The entire area of costs, compensation, and true profitability will be a topic of much discussion and analysis in the years ahead. Meanwhile, just as the correspondent needs to recognize the importance of offering good service, the respondent must recognize the need of maintaining a relationship which is profitable to the city bank.

Credit Exposure

Another area in which there has been considerable change of late is the recognition of significant interbank credit exposure. With the failure of several major banks in the early 1970s came the realization that at any one time the amount of credit exposure one bank might have with another was not insignificant. Four specific areas of risk are generally recognized. First is the transaction risk arising from the large sums that are transferred from bank to bank on daily verbal instructions, basically on faith that each bank will complete its end of the transaction as pledged. The second would be deposit exposure, both in "due from" accounts and time certificates of deposits which might be purchased to satisfy reserve requirements by nonmember banks or as part of the investment portfolio. Interbank lending itself is an obvious area of additional credit exposure including such accomodations as capital loans, holding company lines of credit and Federal Reserve funds transactions. The last area of interbank exposure uncovered in recent years is in the field of foreign exchange trading.

Bankers began to realize that at any one time the individual exposure one institution might have with another could be very significant. Accordingly, it is no longer unusual for a bank to perform some credit analysis of other banks it may be doing business with and to establish internal guidelines for specific transactions and overall exposure. There are now a number of reporting services available which provide detailed statistical information on a large number of banks. The figures are taken from Call Reports and include summary statements of condition as well as various ratios relating to liquidity, loan loss reserve coverage, and capital adequacy. Use of these services can simplify the analysts role when faced with the necessity of reviewing literally dozens of banks.

Future Challenges

During the past few years the future of correspondent banking has been the topic of much discussion, with some feeling that its future is in jeopardy. There are a number of factors which affect these discussions. The holding company movement is a prime one. There is the feeling that as more and more unit banks become part of banking chains, there will be a smaller market for correspondent services. Also, the banks which are becoming large holding company operations are developing an in-house capability of providing essentially the same services which were traditionally provided by major city banks in the past, creating more competition for what could be a shrinking market.

There is a definite move toward nationwide banking. Most major money center banks have opened Edge Act and Loan Production Offices in cities far removed from their headquarters. Depending on the legislative process, nationwide point-of-sale and other EFTS networks would further this move. Some large bank holding companies have small loan and mortgage banking subsidiaries operating in the markets of some of their best correspondents. There is no question but that the breakdown of geographic barriers will impact correspondent relationships. However, as long as there continues to be the need for the services provided through this system, it would appear that the move to nationwide banking would create change in correspondent banking but certainly not eliminate it.

Another factor that could impact the correspondent banking industry in the future is the role of the Federal Reserve System. There has been discussion about requiring all commercial banks to maintain their reserves with the Federal Reserve. The Board of Governors claims this would increase the effectiveness of monetary policy, but it would also have a significant impact on correspondent relationships. There is also some indication that Federal Reserve Banks are interested in providing more and more services to nonmember banks, perhaps on a fee basis. The pricing structure arrived at by the Federal Reserve would seriously affect correspondent relationships unless the commercial banking system is able to compete profitably.

Although some factors would seem to be a possible depressant on future growth of correspondent banking, other markets are opening which some banks have been quick to take advantage of. Specifically this would be in the sale of services to nonbank financial institutions such as the savings and loan and credit union industries.

CONCLUSION

There has always been a premium on cordial relationships in correspondent banking. This rapport is essential as personal contact will continue to be very important in interbank dealings. However, there is also a growing need for sophistication on the part of the correspondent banker, due to the wide range of complicated services he offers and the wide range of respondents he services. Respondents vary both as to size and as to type of geographic area and market they themselves service. Some are retail banks, others wholesale. Some are commercially oriented, others agricultural. Some operate as units, others as branch banks. It is important for the correspondent officer to understand these distinctions in order to be able to satisfy each bank's quite individual needs.

It is also essential today for the correspondent officer to know and spend time with operating people in the respondent bank as well as the president and chairman. The people on the line are, after all, the ones who must be satisfied on a daily basis with the services received.

The competent correspondent officer of the future will have to be an all-around knowledgeable banker and the most successful will be the one who can best use his own personal resources and his bank's products and services to help his customer cope with change and meet his own management responsibilities.

Chapter 74

Bank Advertising—Principles and Guidelines

M. Carl Sneeden*

For many years most people in banking did not understand advertising—nor did they try. Too often, advertising was considered a luxury, and not a necessity. If advertising had been termed "sales calls" or "officer calls," it would have been understood immediately, simply because there is no other way to make such a mass of calls at an affordable price stating one's message accurately and concisely in an organized way. [1] In other words, something had to be done to reduce the cost of sales/calls and at the same time increase the penetration of the marketplace. Advertising was, and is, that way.

As the marketplace grows increasingly complex and the relationship of the consumer and banker becomes increasingly more remote and impersonal, it seems only natural that advertising must play an ever more important role in banking.[2]

As advertising has progressed from the luxury status to the status of an essential element in banking, management has said that the function must be held accountable in terms of measurable achievement just as any other department or function is held accountable in the

---

* Vice President, Third National Bank, Nashville, Tennessee.

[1] Richard H. Stansfield, *How to Sell Advertising to Management* (Chicago: The Dartnell Corporation, 1969), p. 2.

[2] *Corporate Policies and Procedures on Advertising and Promotion* (Washington, D.C.: Sub-Council on Advertising and Promotion of the National Business Council for Consumer Affairs, 1972), p. 5.

organization. It must grow out of and be adjusted to the total marketing plan.[3]

We have witnessed several changes in attitude in advertising over the past few years. In the 50s, it seemed that the only thing needed was a better mousetrap and money to promote it. However, in the late 50s technology started to make itself heard. It seemed somewhat more difficult to establish that unique selling proposition. Toward the end of the "product" era, there was an avalanche of "me too" products that descended on the marketplace. Whenever anyone completed or introduced their better mousetrap, two or more just like it quickly followed and all claimed to be better than the first one.

In the 60s, most companies found that their reputation or their image was more important in selling a product than any specific product feature. But again, just as the "me too" products killed the product era in the 50s, the "me too" companies killed the image era. However, today most companies feel more than anything the need to create a position in the prospect's mind. Most writers have called this era the "positioning" era. Today, positioning is used in a broader sense to mean what the advertising does for the product in the prospect's mind.[4] In other words, some advertisers are using advertising to position a product, and not to communicate its advantages or any features. When you have positioned the product, you then have placed it in a certain way in the consumer's mind. After making that all-important decision of consumer mind positioning, you must then have a strategy to get you there. The marketing strategy would be the master plan.

A creative strategy must also be determined and it should cover at least five points. A creative strategy must (1) have an objective and state what the advertising should do, (2) have a target audience determining who the consumer will be, (3) have key consumer benefits determining why the consumer would want to purchase your product or service, (4) have support—a real reason for the consumer to believe in the benefit that he will receive from your service, and (5) have personality—a statement of the product's tone and manner.

PLANNING

It is very important to plan in advance to stretch the advertising budget. Setting an appropriate budget is the preliminary step but there are other steps that will help stretch the budget. Plan ads that can be repeated. This will save money on production and leave more

---

[3] Roger Barton, *Advertising Handbook* (Englewood Cliffs, N.J. Prentice-Hall, Inc., 1950), p. 110.

[4] Kenneth Roman and Jane Maas, *How to Advertise* (New York: St. Martin's Press, 1976).

money to pay for space insertions. Plan the campaign as a unit and not piecemeal. This enables an individual to utilize the same art, photography, headlines, and so on for such things as ads, direct mail pieces, and in-bank displays. It will also provide an excellent opportunity to set a style and avoid wandering off the track—going off in all directions and not getting anywhere.

Plan printing so several pieces can be run at one time. This will give several colors at the price of one. It will save money on presswork by printing several mailers simultaneously on a large sheet and will help save money on paper through quantity purchasing. Plan space advertising to take full advantage of frequency discounts by discriminate use of rate holders which can cut drastically the cost of some larger insertions. The same principle applies to the broadcast media, but it takes a smart buyer to buy TV and radio time properly.

Plan the timing of news releases to coordinate with and hopefully reenforce advertising mileage. There are hundreds of good media for advertising and no single bank can, nor would it want to, use them all. It is up to the advertising manager to determine which media can best reach the target audience and then allocate the resources accordingly. Generally, a medium should be chosen with three things in mind:

1. The character of the market—how many people do you want to reach? What kind? Where do they live?
2. The nature of the product—and its appeal.
3. The selling approach—a slogan identification, long copy story, or a short spot.

Have the right story for the right medium (don't particularly advertise "we're a woman's bank" on television during the World Series), and stay in the medium in which you can compete and look strong (don't let your advertisement become a spot filler on the last page of the newspaper more than once).[5] Always consider the reputation and appearance of the medium selected. Remember your image is very important during the positioning era.

The pros and cons of the various media and how each should be used most effectively should be considered:

1. Press Media. The press is the first of the media to be considered. The business press is the most efficient and economical means devised to reach the tens of thousands of hidden buying influences throughout the market.[6] The word "press" covers newspapers and

[5] Burton R. Durkerr, *How to Make Advertising Work* (New York: McGraw-Hill Book Company, 1964), p. 132.

[6] Richard H. Stansfield, *Advertising Manager's Handbook* (Chicago: The Dartnell Corporation, 1969), p. 1068.

magazines. Although this medium is very powerful and comparatively low in cost, the ad must appear in the right publication in order to reach the prime prospects.

Magazines are the most selective of all media. They have the advantages of good graphic quality and selectivity of audience. Magazines have long lives. They are circulated over an extended period of time. They also have the confidence of their audience. (Remember to tailor the ad to the particular consumer of the magazine selected.)

A disadvantage of magazines is that their circulation may cover too large a territory. The bank may not wish to advertise to an entire region of the country. Also, magazine copy is sometimes long in preparation time.

The newspaper is probably one of the favorite media for bankers. Newspapers can completely saturate the local market area. Newspapers also have the advantage of a broad and diversified appeal. The bank can reach all kinds of people. Scheduling is satisfactory and the rates are usually good.

A disadvantage is that a small-space advertisement can get lost in the paper. It may wind up as inconspicuous filler. Also, color quality is generally poor. There are some pointers for using the newspaper. Use enough space to be seen; don't be subtle, the reader is in a hurry; and remember to use specific sections of the paper, depending on which market the bank wants to attract.

There are several ways to be effective in print advertising. It is very important that the message be in the headline and that headline is used to flag the prospect. Always offer a benefit in the headline and very definitely inject news in the headline. Sometimes long headlines can be more effective than short ones, but always avoid a negative within the headline. Be sure to look for story appeal in the illustration. Photographs are almost always better than drawings. Be sure to use simple layouts and put a caption under the photograph. Do not print body copy in reverse type. It looks good but it generally reduces the readership of the ad.

2. Broadcast Media—Radio and Television. Both of these media have network, regional and local advertising time available. Banks are usually concerned with local advertising.

There are several things to consider in deciding whether to use a broadcast medium. Costs can be quite high and the advertisement is at the mercy of the show's rating. Commitments, particularly with TV, can be long indeed, from 13 to 52 weeks. Generally, a simple message is better for the broadcast medium. Think in terms of saying all that should be said in 10 or 30 seconds. TV has the advantage of being able to attract visually. A demonstration of one's product or service is effective. The picture should do most of the work. It is also important that the format of the program be considered in where an advertising spot is placed. A program format can be totally unfavorable to an ad.

Radio has the disadvantage in product advertising simply for lack of visuals. However, it has been suggested that since radio is in fact the theatre of the mind, be creative!

In both broadcast media make sure the advertisements are done professionally or they will suffer in comparison to the network ads. It is well to ask for responses from the audience to judge just how effectively the ad is reaching the market.

There are more radios than people in the United States today, more than 400 million sets in homes, cars, boats, or on the beaches. Since almost everyone has a radio, people tend to listen alone and they choose exactly the kind of programing they want to hear. Because they do, that audience segmentation is a great advantage for bank advertisers. Radio permits one to select the audience. There are several points to remember in trying to achieve a better radio commercial. First, be sure to stretch the listener's imagination. What will make the ad memorable? Always present one idea. Be sure to mention the bank's name and its promise early. Don't overlook the use of music because it can help. However, it must be kept simple. Have enough commercials for the bank's campaigns. You need more radio commercials than television commercials. Humorous commercials fare the worst with repetition.

It is important to remember that prime time for radio is 6 A.M. to 10 A.M. Sometimes, it is a good idea to hear your radio commercials spliced into a tape of several minutes of actual program content. Select your audience by station, time of day, and season of the year. Rely on the flexibility of radio to keep your message current and again, above all—be *sure* to stretch the listener's imagination.

In producing a television commercial, be sure that the advertisement is effective and that the best dramatic technique was used for the product and the strategy. In producing television commercial, look at a story board of your commercial. There is only one simple rule for looking at a story board—look at the pictures first. Ask yourself if they are telling the story of your commercial—then look at the words. From this point, you are able to decide if the story board will make an effective commercial. The pictures must tell the story. Look for key visual and grab the viewer's attention within the first few seconds. Be direct—a good commercial is always uncomplicated. Be sure to register the name of the bank's service visually. Always have a payoff by showing the advantages of the service. The tone of the advertising must also reflect your product's personality. Avoid too many words in the commercial and keep in the back of your mind that you are building a campaign and not just individual commercials.

It is sometimes important that the commercial be entertaining as well as hard sell. However, if you can remove the sales message from the commercial and still have a commercial, the entertainment portion of your message is getting in the way. Use humor when it can contribute to the sale, music when it can reenforce the message of your service, emotion to involve the viewer, and any unusual film techniques to drive home the message to the consumer.

3. Direct Mail Media. Direct mail is also a selective media. It is possible to choose people for the mailing list that you already know a great deal about. There are also definite disadvantages to direct mailing. Rising postage cost is a major one. Mailing lists can be very expensive, and they are very difficult and time consuming to keep up to date.

If direct mail is used, it should be worthwhile and interesting. People receive a great deal of "junk" mail and your ad must stand out. Have the advertisment fit the job to be done. If you wish to reach small loan prospects, a brightly colored folder might do the trick. A more subdued ad might be necessary for the person who would use your trust department.

Personalize the mail. By all means, use a name and *spell it correctly.* Hand-addressed mail will catch the attention quickly, but it is not practical in most cases. Make it easy for the prospect to act. Give the bank's address and phone number. You may wish to include the name of a person (i.e., personal banker) who could give special help. Most of all, direct mail is an accountable medium. It is very easy to figure its costs and your results.

4. In-bank Displays. In-bank displays are effective if you wish to have your present customers expand their use of the bank's services. The ad should be located at the point of heaviest traffic. The ad should be uncomplicated. It is best to feature one service at a time. Change the display often or the customers will stop noticing it. Keep the display in good condition or it will be to your disadvantage if the customers do notice it. In this day of the drive-in window, consider displays there. Many customers use only the drive-in window.

5. Transit and Outdoor Advertising. Car cards, bus posters, station ads and billboards are overlooked much of the time. There are advantages to using such media. People see the ads under good reading conditions. People riding the bus or passengers in cars may have little to do other than read ads. There is also little competition in some of these media. Short messages and strong artwork are necessary for this type of ad. A disadvantage is that the same people are exposed to the ad. The signs also deteriorate rapidly and must constantly be maintained.

Another advantage of outdoor is the ability to zero in on your target. It is usually the most localized of all the media and you can select an audience with precision, and reach the consumer outside of his or her home, often on the way to buy. Look for a big idea. Keep it simple—always use bold lettering; use art for impact, and color for readability. Use the locations to your advantage. Look for something that is memorable. Announce new products with an extra bang. Remind people about the bank's television campaign by tying in your outdoor boards. And always be sure to ride the boards. You cannot always tell by sitting in your office or even by looking at one board which has been posted for your approval, what works and what is not working until you get out and drive around to personally view your boards.

In transit advertising, there are four points to consider in dealing with copy. Think about your audience, buy special routes, and use transit to deliver a coupon. "Take-ones" are sometimes useful; be imaginative.

6.   Novelty Items.   Finally, novelty items are used often to advertise. Calendars, personal diaries, or other often-used items are appreciated and repeat your message many times. The cost of the item must always be weighted against the results.

HOW TO CREATE MEDIA PLANS

The average consumer is bombarded with over 1,500 different advertisements per day. As an extension of the total marketing strategy, simply put your money where your business is—or where you want it to be. By specifying your objectives, you then build around the answers to the questions—Who? When? Where? How often? and In what way?

First, you must decide whom you would like to reach. Your target audience must be defined by their demographics including age, sex, income, education, occupation, buying habits, or family status. And if you know their life-styles or attitudes, you should describe those to your media planner.

You must then decide when you would want to reach your target audience. For instance, if you were selling Individual Retirement Accounts (IRAs), it would make a lot more sense to concentrate your efforts toward the latter part of the year showing the benefits of the tax shelter factor with an IRA.

Then, where is your consumer? Most commercial bankers would know where their consumers live; however, on a national scope such as corporate headquarters in one state and city and an affiliate company in another, utmost importance must be given in determining effective means of targeting in on specific areas. Also, market segments within your own localized area must be considered in finding where and how dollars are spent.

Next, you must decide how often you want to reach them. This involves the concepts of reach and frequency and impact. For instance, if you were trying to reach 60 percent of the homes to make them aware of your new service or product, then it cannot be done if your reach is less than 60 percent, and as the reach goes up, the frequency would come down. It has been said that people forget 60 percent of what they learn within a half day, so the more repetition, the better the retention.

Finally, you must consider in what way you would want to reach your target audience. You must consider the best environment for the copy. For example, it would be totally useless to advertise in a local newspaper for correspondent banking relationships.

In obtaining better media plans, always be sure to establish marketing objectives and strategies. Allow the right timetable for developing that plan and be sure to include your media planner in meetings with your copy people concerning the overall campaign.

RESEARCH: PRETESTING AND POSTTESTING

Research for advertising differs from market and product research in that it concentrates mainly on testing copy and other advertising elements in terms of readership and results. Most current pretesting concentrates on the bank's promotional strategy and with the analysis of whether the intended messages via specific advertisements are communicable to the target audience. Within the overall framework of pretesting, the elements most often under evaluation are the following: (1) message recall, (2) narrative playback, (3) sponsor identification, (4) presence of any deleterious elements, and (5) presence of any confusing elements. The purpose for research of this type is to correct problem areas so the bank can maximize the probability of communicating the intended message to its target audience and maximizing the probability that the target audience will realize just *which bank* is communicating the message.

If ads are pretested one against the other, or if several slogans, themes, headlines, copy approaches, product features, and user benefits are pretested, the most effective one may be used. Specific objectives make development of survey questions and interpretations of results both easier and considerably more valid. And by having specific objectives, it is then possible for the advertising manager to measure accurately and precisely the effectiveness of an advertising campaign.

Some marketers have felt that posttesting is unnecessary because it is asked to tell you what you already know. To make things even more confusing, the market environment may change drastically since the spot was first placed. There are critical factors adversely affecting the validity of information to be derived from a follow-up. It is difficult to rely on a respondent's memory on the television spot alone, since it was supported by other media. If testing is to be done, it should focus on those particular areas which can assist you in determining what to do next.

Posttesting should concentrate on the impact of the bank's overall strategies, as well as an assessment of the current and/or projected state of the marketplace environment. Within this framework, posttesting should concentrate on the following factors for both your bank and your competitors: (1) consumer awareness of the marketing effort, (2) consumer attitudinal shifts which relate to image and intended use of product, and (3) consumer behavioral shifts—for example—"Did they change banks or buy your services?"

In short, pretesting should focus on will it communicate, while posttesting research should focus on did it sell.

ADVERTISING AGENCIES

Of all marketing expenditures, advertising is usually the largest single expenditure. In most instances, these expenditures are channeled through an advertising agency. There are three ways of utilizing an agency: (1) for specific, one-time needs with the bank's own advertising department doing most of the work, (2) in conjunction with the advertising manager (here the manager may be the only person directly employed by the bank in the advertising field and he may direct the agency's efforts), and (3) complete utilization of the agency for the agency's full services.

There are definite advantages in using an agency. Advertising is not a business to be conducted on the basis of guesswork. If it is worth doing, it is worth doing well. It should be handled by those who have made it their full-time business. They know the pitfalls, problems, and opportunities associated with advertising.

An agency will devote its time to preparing, producing, placing, and checking advertisements, as well as supervising the entire operation. The bank that uses an agency must be involved in the overall planning strategies of the total marketing plan. Agencies also do research in market areas, and can be of great assistance to those banks that lack research departments.

Few banks use a "half and half" plan anymore. The staggering cost of photography and art equipment, plus specialty personnel, make the cost of this approach prohibitive. Banks should not be in the art and photography business. Another reason for using an agency is that new ideas are secured. Agencies must produce or they lose accounts. Agency personnel are also in a position to keep up with marketing trends. Many media representatives actually prefer working with agency personnel because of their trained skills and their experience with the media.

A good recommendation for an agency is membership in AAAA— American Association of Advertising Agencies. Requirements for membership are high. Other considerations are (1) output for other clients, (2) length of time in business, (3) growth record, (4) physical appearance of office and employees, (5) persons who would work on your account and how many other accounts they would handle, (6) experience in the banking field, and (7) size—Is the agency large enough to handle the bank's needs—or are they too large?

The client and agency relationship should be a partnership. A strong bond of trust should develop between the two partners. By keeping secrets from each other, the advertising will most certainly suffer. The bank can get the most out of an agency by always being very explicit in its instructions—letting them know exactly what it wants them to do and how it will check on them to be sure the goal is accomplished. By giving the agency specific, realistic, attainable objectives, you accomplish your number one priority in being a productive advertising manager.

The cost of an agency depends on how much and what kind of services it renders. However, the cost should be considered in terms of return on investment.

It has been said that all people, especially men, have a feeling of expertise in the following areas: (1) building fires, (2) making the world's greatest martini, and (3) writing advertising copy. And an advertising director can receive more advice and opinions in one day than the average person receives in a year.

Help from within the bank is most vital. Specialists in various phases of banking services must be called upon in planning and executing ads pertaining to their particular field of expertise. Also, a complete review of final copy is a must to ensure accuracy. They should not, however, expect to inject creative approach in either copy or art work.

CONCLUSION

An advertising manager must deal with many difficult problems, but he should remain firm in his convictions. An advertising manager's greatest responsibility is to keep his bank "on target" and to justify his existence by providing contributions to the bottom line. He must constantly be aware of new products affecting his area, and competitor's advertising, both locally and regionally.

There are too many banks these days that do not know specifically where they are or where they are going—but they are getting there very fast. The reason for this is that they are not willing to take time, energy, patience, and provide funds to create a realistic marketing plan. Without that written plan, many a bank becomes an "unguided missile."

A written plan is one of the greatest benefits ever devised for the advertising director. It provides him with guidelines for daily, weekly, and monthly activities. It also helps in providing for monitoring results.

Chapter 75 _____

Bank Advertising—The Budgeting Process

*M. Carl Sneeden**

As each bank approaches the overall advertising effort, it must consider how resources will be allocated to advertising. A budget is a plan for allocating resources for expected expenditures. Most structured companies of any size or stability operate from a rather precise budget and this companywide budget is broken down into individual departmental budgets. Two areas are of concern: (1) how the bank determines the portion of the resources that will be allocated to advertising (the department and/or function), and (2) how the manager of the advertising department decides to break down the allocated resources—by media, process, and so on.

Many of the corporate budgeting methods were derived from attitudes toward the function of advertising, and just as attitudes have changed considerably, so have the budgeting methods.

BUDGETING METHODS

There are two basic approaches to budgeting for advertising. The first approach is a passive one. Some of the formulas used in this approach are (1) percentage of sales, (2) competitive parity, (3) "what's left over," and (4) arbitrary allocation. The second approach is active. Typically, in this approach marketing objectives are stated and needs are analyzed. Then funds are appropriated on a "need" or task basis.[1]

---

* Vice President, Third National Bank, Nashville, Tennessee.

[1] David L. Hurwood and James K. Brown, *Some Guidelines for Advertising Budgeting* (New York: The Conference Board, Inc., 1972), p. 5.

Percentage of Sales

The first method examined is the percentage of sales method. The advertising-sales ratio (A/S) can be either a determinant or an analytical tool. In terms of analysis, it is used like other ratios—a convenient summary figure enabling executives and analysts to compare advertising expenditures and sales associated with them. These ratios may have to do with advertising in different markets, advertising in successive time periods, advertising under varying expenditure strategies, and advertising by the company versus its competitors.

The entire basis for this method hinges on an expected market response from a given expenditure. A tool for predicting what the allocation should be is the "demand schedule" or "response curve." This is merely a graphic representation of the A/S ratio experienced in the past with applications of varying amounts of advertising.[2] (See Exhibit 75-1.)

Budgeting by this method is in the form of "what's needed to obtain the desired revenue volume." Experience may indicate that a particular percentage of gross sales or income spent on advertising will maintain a certain positive volume of sales. The basis for the ratio may be either past revenues, or projected future revenues. At any rate, the total amount allocated on the percentage basis is then divided among all sales expenses. One can eventually show that on each unit of sale (dollar of revenue) has done a satisfactory job of advertising.[3]

The limitations of the A/S method (or any other ratio method) are numerous. If the ratio is used year after year without newfound basis, the cause and effect relationship between advertising and market response is reversed. The advertising budget should be controlled for the purpose of accomplishing something—a sales objective. The sales should not control the advertising allocation.

Also, the A/S method may fail to recognize changed conditions. Using the same percentage year after year implies that (1) there was a logical basis for it to begin with, and (2) nothing has happened since to alter the amount of advertising needed. Even if the percentage were logical at the outset, the fluidity of the market and new management objectives could render the percentage obsolete.

The same percentage needed year after year also implies that no change has occurred in the rate of market response to the level of advertising investment. This rarely occurs except over a limited range of expenditure. Additional expenditures for advertising usually yield change in relative productivity in terms of market response.[4]

---

[2] Ibid., p. 6.

[3] Roger Barton, *Advertising Handbook* (Englewood Cliffs, N.J.: Prentice-Hall, Inc., 1950), p. 112.

[4] Hurwood and Brown, *Some Guidelines for Advertising Budgeting*, p. 7.

Exhibit 75-1

The Marketing Response Curve: Revenue as a Function of Advertising (thousands of dollars)

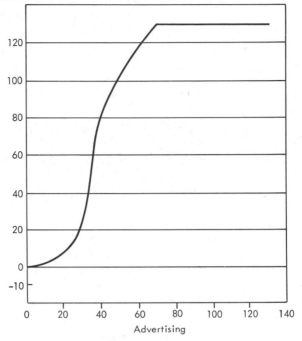

Three factors define the shape of the response curve:

1. An exponential sales decay constant—the rate at which sales fall off in the absence of advertising (because of product obsolescence, competing advertising, and so on).
2. The saturation level, which can be defined as the practical limit of sales that can be generated, depending on the product of service being promoted and also on the advertising medium being used.
3. The response constant—the sales generated per advertising dollar when sales—zero. For example, if a company had no sales and decided to spend $5,000 per month on advertising, and sales went from $0 per month to $10,000 per month as a result of the advertising, the sales response constant would be $10,000/$5,000 or 2. These factors are parameters that remain constant from one calculation to another until new assumptions are made or new values are discovered.

Three variables also affect the curve:

1. The rate of sales/revenue at a given time.
2. The increase in rate of sales at a given time.
3. The rate of advertising expenditure.

Adapted from: David L. Hurwood and James K. Brown, *Some Guidelines For Advertising Budgeting* (New York: The Conference Board, Inc., 1972), p. 61.

Lastly the A/S method gives the advertising department unique treatment as compared with other departments. Other departments tend to determine budgets more logically. It implies that advertising is a luxury and, therefore, expendable. The ratio method can be used, but if it is used it should be treated as a starting point to be adjusted with needs.

Competitive Analysis

Competitive analysis is the next budgeting method to be considered. Tracking competitive advertising strategies is considered normal and essential. Also, comparing your bank to the industry norm can be revealing. The information thus derived can be available in (1) enabling a comparison of the company's expenditures and results with those of important competitors or the industry norm, and (2) permitting the marking of various computations involving share of the market, share of industry advertising, or both.

In comparing company similarities in expenditures, it is well to compare with selected competitors. If sharp differences are found, it would be wise to look for reasons. It has been shown that overall marketers selling comparable services or goods to similar markets under similar conditions, tend to have similar marketing-cost ratios. This is because a fixed market responds the same way to the same approaches from each seller. As responses are the same, sellers become more alike in their appeals.[5] Studying competitors does not mean that you will, or even that you would want to, duplicate them. It only means that you wish to know where your organization is outperforming others and, likewise, where your organization does not perform as well.

The objection to using the company parity budgeting method is that it is not wise to match competitors in spending without weighing all the facts and consequences. It may well be that the data available on a competitor is insufficient for comparison with your company. The data may cover more than one service when you only need data on one service. Suppliers of services are not as fortunate as product producers in that there is not as much data available. Even if you could determine the exact amount a competitor allocated for advertising one service, you would also have to match his or her campaign medium for medium, market approach for market approach, to get the same results. The sheer magnitude of resources is not as important as the effectiveness of programs. Long-range plans of the competitor could make a vital difference in advertising allocations and should be considered. Finally, a strong competitor may be financially so powerful that

---

[5] Ibid., p. 8.

it would be folly to try and match his or her spending. Your company cannot benefit from overspending. There are shrewder ways to outdo competitors than by matching their expenditures—sharp, original advertising and improved services.[6] (See Exhibits 75–2 and 75–3.)

Available Funds

The third method that we shall consider is that of available funds. The financing of any marketing element with available funds (money left over) can hardly be termed "budgeting." This automatically treats advertising as a managerial activity that should be financed with little regard for needs, objectives, or opportunities. Even if media requirements of resources were modest as compared with sales force requirements, budgeting by this method might be too small to do even a modestly effective job.

Budgeting by funds available might not support other marketing functions.

It has been pointed out that a certain level of promotional intensity is required before the promotion's presence can be felt in the market.[7]

This method benefits the company in that it assures that the company will make a satisfactory profit or break even in the short run. The need for profits cannot be questioned, but there must be a provision for long-term profits. It is shortsighted to achieve a good current profit picture by withholding funds from advertising on which many future sales and profits depend.

Use of this method can result in one of two possible ends, neither of which is satisfactory:

1. Spend what the company can afford—the budget will be too small.
2. Spend all that the company can afford—the budget will be larger than necessary.

Need Determination

Heretofore, the budgeting methods that have been discussed have been passive. Not much research or real analysis is necessary in the passive methods. In fact, one might say the passive methods allow external factors to set the budget. The active approach on the other hand, allows the department to submit a budget recommendation based on need. The method involved is commonly referred to as the task method or the objective method.

---

[6] Ibid., p. 12.
[7] Ibid., p. 12.

Exhibit 75–2

Average Marketing Expenditures By Service Type and Deposit Size: All Reporting Banks—1976

Service Type	Deposits (in $millions)								
	Under $5	$5–10	$10–25	$25–50	$50–100	$100–250	$250–500	$500–1 billion	$Over $1 billion
Retail									
Savings (regular, special, CDs, bonds)	$ 7.4	$2.1	$ 4.6	$ 7.3	$13.7	$ 29.8	$ 51.8	$ 84.6	$ 351.8
Checking (regular and/or special)	2.5	2.4	3.8	6.5	9.0	16.6	33.4	43.0	317.8
Bank service packages (with checking)	6.1	1.6	3.1	4.5	19.3	23.2	41.2	56.7	307.8
Personal loans (exclude mortgage)	3.0	1.3	2.7	5.9	9.8	24.5	57.6	105.7	346.2
Mortgage loans	0.9	0.4	1.7	2.1	3.8	5.3	8.9	7.5	51.7
Credit cards	0.1	0.5	0.6	1.9	5.7	7.2	15.2	34.7	172.0
Consumer EFTS services	—	0.3	2.2	5.0	9.7	19.1	47.8	86.3	122.4
Commercial									
Commercial banking services (include loans)	2.9	1.2	2.3	3.9	7.4	9.2	19.9	45.0	197.8
Automated services for business (include commercial EFTS)	—	—	0.5	2.3	4.4	4.6	5.6	32.4	51.8
Institutional									
Corporate advertising	4.1	2.3	3.2	6.2	32.5	26.1	59.5	100.2	405.8
Corporate public relations	4.1	1.0	2.6	5.2	8.8	17.0	33.0	53.7	165.8
Trust									
Trust services	2.4	1.3	12.4	2.4	3.7	5.9	10.1	25.2	77.6
Other	1.6	1.7	5.1	7.3	11.2	17.4	34.2	51.1	223.4
Total	$16.8	$7.7	$18.0	$33.8	$78.8	$132.5	$288.2	$521.6	$2,077.2

Source: Bank Marketing Association, *Analysis of 1976 Bank Marketing Expenditures*. (Reproduced with the permission of the Bank Marketing Association.)

Exhibit 75–3
Percentage of Reporting Bank Budgets Spent on Each Service in 1976 by Deposit Size

Service Type	Deposits (in $millions)								
	Under $5	$5–10	$10–25	$25–50	$50–100	$100–250	$250–500	$500–$1 billion	Over $1 billion
Retail									
Savings (regular, special, CDs bonds)	38%	24%	23%	20%	16%	21%	17%	15%	15%
Checking (regular and/or special)	13	26	19	17	10	10	10	7	11
Bank service packages (with checking)	16	10	8	6	10	8	6	7	8
Personal loans (exclude mortgage)	11	12	11	14	11	16	17	19	15
Mortgage loans	2	2	4	3	2	1	1	—	1
Credit cards	—	1	1	2	3	3	3	4	6
Consumer EFTS services	—	—	1	3	3	4	7	7	4
Commercial									
Commercial banking services (include loans)	8	9	6	7	6	4	5	7	7
Automated services for business (include commercial EFTS)	—	—	—	1	1	1	—	2	1
Institutional									
Corporate advertising	6	9	9	12	27	15	16	15	17
Corporate public relations	3	5	6	9	7	9	8	8	6
Trust									
Trust services	3	2	7	3	3	3	3	5	3
Other	1	2	4	3	3	4	4	5	5
Total	100%	100%	100%	100%	100%	100%	100%	100%	100%

Note: Figures do not total due to rounding.
Source: Bank Marketing Association, *Analysis of 1976 Bank Marketing Expenditures*. (Reproduced with the permission of the Bank Marketing Association.)

The object of the task method is to build a budget based on concrete estimates of the various jobs to be done. The A/S method, the expenditure patterns of the industry, the amount of resources available, past experience, and many other factors must necessarily be considered in the process of working out the advertising budget; but none of these factors can be allowed to dominate the decision on various segments of the budget if an economically valid budget is to be achieved under the task method.[8]

In using the task method one must approach budgeting systematically. The governing considerations should be the marketplace objectives. The first step is to look at the marketing program as a whole. It may be that the advertising functions make up the marketing department to a large extent. On the other hand, it may be that advertising plays a smaller role in the context of the entire marketing program. No matter what the case, the objectives of the entire marketing program should be set forth in writing. The objectives may be stated in terms of the company, in terms of service, campaigns, and/or markets.

After the objectives of the marketing program are defined, it is necessary to determine what part advertising will play in helping to achieve the total program. After advertising objectives are known, it is necessary to determine the cost of producing the advertisments and the cost of disseminating the material through the various media. This, in effect, becomes the provisional advertising budget. At this point it might also be well to stress that it is recommended that a contingency fund be added to the budget after the known and expected costs are set forth. This fund should be about 2.5 percent of the total amount budgeted.[9]

The budget thus far described is called provisional at this point because the approval must come from top management, who probably have had little to do with its determination to this point. It is well to have management look not only at the figures of the budget, but also at the objectives that the figures represent. Have management assign priorities to the objectives so that if budget trimming is necessary, management will have already decided what objectives do not necessarily have to be accomplished.

One criticism of the task method is that it is pointless to set objectives since the company has no way of knowing for sure how much or what kind of advertising will be required to achieve the objectives. There is no doubt that this method requires much probing and research, and that experience can play an important part.

---

[8] Barton, *Advertising Handbook*, p. 114.

[9] Richard H. Stansfield, *How to Sell Advertising to Management* (Chicago: The Dartnell Corporation, 1969.), p. 2.

The broad applicability of the task method (to new and existing products and services, to large and small campaigns) allows the company to expend resources for research. The same research can be widely helpful in areas other than budgeting. The task method rests on data collected from both experience and research. The data then must be sifted and projected to the marketing problem (objective) under consideration. Inherent in this method are two requirements: (1) the systematic working out of objectives, and (2) the continuous gathering and analysis of marketing-response data.

An important step in this method is to measure the value of the objective and to determine whether each objective is worth the probable cost of obtaining it. In other words, what intensity of demand (what position and shape of the demand schedule) is an economically sound target? From another angle, this simply means that objectives should be framed in the light of probable contribution to profits.

The neglect of this element in budget planning has contributed largely to the skepticism about the usefulness of advertising. Many senior bank managers say that in looking at advertising budgets they cannot see sound, analytical reasoning. They desire to have proposals closely related to profits—return on investment. This is where the advantages of the task method rest.[10]

To draw some conclusions about budgeting methods, it has to be said that all the methods mentioned have advantages and drawbacks. All methods might be used, but used critically in light of their strong points. It seems best to approach budgeting from the active side, using research and experience and then temper the results of this method with knowledge derived from the more passive methods.

MARGINAL ANALYSIS

It has already been noted that managers want to have proposals closely related to profits. They want to know what they will receive after resources have been put into advertising. It is also well to know what the boundaries should be on advertising expenditures—what are the minimum and maximum amounts that should be spent. Marginal analysis is the link between advertising expenditures and profits. It provides a framework for establishing advertising goals and budgeting funds necessary to accomplish them.

Marginal analysis says that, in order to maximize profitability, money should be spent on advertising (or on any productive resource), once the break-even point is passed, until the last dollar spent brings in one additional net dollar of revenue; or in economic terminology, until

---

[10] Hurwood and Brown, *Some Guidelines for Advertising Budgeting*, p. 14.

the marginal cost (MC) of advertising equals the marginal net revenue (MR) it produces.

An advertising budget of a smaller amount is not optimal, because before the point of equilibrium of marginal revenue and marginal cost, an additional dollar spent on advertising will yield more than an additional dollar of net revenue. And an advertising budget of greater amount is not optimal, because the last dollar spent on advertising will result in less than an extra dollar of net revenue. (See Exhibit 75–4.)

The closer the company gets to drawing its "market response to advertising curve" the closer it can pattern its advertising budget in accordance with the principles of marginal analysis. In applying this economic principle, one must also be constantly aware of the ever-changing marketplace.

The principle is also subject to modification if there is a significant time lag between expenditure and revenue as a result of that expenditure. Generally, revenue produced by advertising is not generated immediately or in one sum, but is a stream of income over a period of time. This income should be discounted to its present value by a suitable rate of interest, usually, the company's opportunity cost or cost of capital. The same should be done with successive advertising expenditures in a campaign.

This approach has wide appeal to managers. It is mathematically demonstrable; also, it imposes discipline on those responsible for devising advertising campaigns, in that they must be able to justify their recommendations in terms of expenditure.

It may seem that this approach would not be workable if one would not directly relate revenue to particular advertising campaigns; however, some firms have found that the model can be applied successfully even in the absence of information about how revenues vary with advertising and sales promotion. The advertising achievements to look for are improvements in consumer knowledge, attitude, preference

Exhibit 75–4
Schedule of Expenditure Levels, with Associated Sales Revenues and Profits

In the sample that will follow, three simplifying assumptions are made:

1. Advertising is the only element of the marketing mix under consideration.
2. Sales revenue is defined as sales revenue net of nonadvertising costs. (Revenue left after deducting all costs except the advertising.)
3. Advertising must be purchased in increments of $10,000.

How much should be spent on advertising? Inspection of the schedule tells the answer— $60,000. With this input, total profit is greatest—$62,000. If another $10,000 were spent on advertising, bringing the total to $70,000, the marginal revenue would be only $8,000, and hence total profits would drop to $60,000.

Exhibit 75–4 (*continued*)
A. Schedule of Expenditure Levels

Total Advertising Expenditure	(1) Marginal Advertising Expenditure	(2) Total Sales Revenue	(3) Marginal Sales Revenue	(4) Total Profit (Col. 3 − Col. 1	(5) Marginal Profit (Col. 4 − Col. 2)
0...............	—	0	—	0	0
10...............	10	0	0	(10)	(10)
20...............	10	5	5	(15)	(5)
30...............	10	30	25	0	15
40...............	10	80	50	40	40
50...............	10	110	30	60	20
60...............	10	122	12	62	2
70...............	10	130	8	60	(2)
80...............	10	130	0	50	(10)

B. Total Revenue and Total Profit as Functions of Advertising Expenditures ($ thousands)

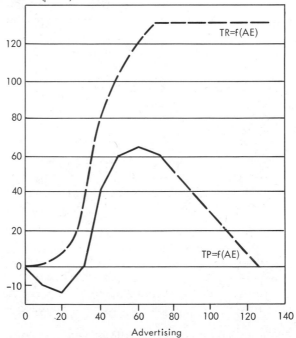

Sales/Revenue (profit)

Source: David L. Hurwood and James K. Brown, *Some Guidelines for Advertising Budgeting* (New York: The Conference Board, Inc., 1972), pp. 16–17.

and intention to use the service of the company. The market response related to advertising can be determined by analyzing the changes recorded in the respondent's attitudes in successive interviews or by a sampling of new customers (why did you decide to try our bank?). Results of these kinds of programs do indicate that advertising can be made accountable.

This is not to say that applying marginal analysis is easy. Those who can apply it rather well are retailers and mail-order houses. They generally enjoy uncomplicated marketing programs, and the impact their advertising has is quickly reflected in revenues.

Another problem with marginal analysis is that it is difficult to predict what the impact of advertising will be. It is also hard to know what the lingering effect, during the period of a present advertising campaign, of previous company advertising has been. For how long will the new campaign have an effect? When will it begin to register an effect? The activities of competitors can also influence market response considerably. There are many variables from one time period to the next.

Some of these problems can be overcome or at least estimated from an analysis of past advertising campaigns and also through market tests of new campaigns. Few advocates of marginal analysis contend that it provides easy answers, but it is very necessary in establishing the optimal advertising budget and useful in budget justification.

FRAMEWORK FOR BUDGETING DECISIONS AND RESEARCH

Now that budgeting methods and the importance of analytical budgeting have been covered we must discuss when—in what time frame—budgeting decisions should take place.

The requirements for matching advertising budget to advertising need have been alluded to generally in preceding discussions, but the requirements do constitute a sturdy framework for budgeting decisions on a cyclical basis.

They are as follows:

1. Formulate the marketing objectives for the budget period—marketing objectives that are compatible with the long- and short-term objectives of the company.
2. Agree on the tasks that advertising (along with other components of the marketing mix) is to accomplish if these marketing objectives are to be reached.
3. Assemble and analyze data necessary for developing the scale and specifications of an advertising campaign likely to carry out these tasks. These data include indications or sound estimates of past advertising results in efforts comparable to those now proposed.[11]

---

[11] Ibid., p. 37.

The first two requirements have to do with goal setting. It is important to note that these goals should be related in two ways to the entire company (not just the marketing program). The first way for these goals to relate to the company is that they should tie in and support both the long-range and the short-range plans of the company. Each department/function within the company must be aware of the plans of the company in order to give the best support possible. The second relationship that the goals should have to the company is in maximizing overall profit. This is where marginal analysis can be of great value.

The goal-setting steps are somewhat contingent on the third step

EXHIBIT 75–5
Flowchart for Planning and Evaluating the Advertising Budget

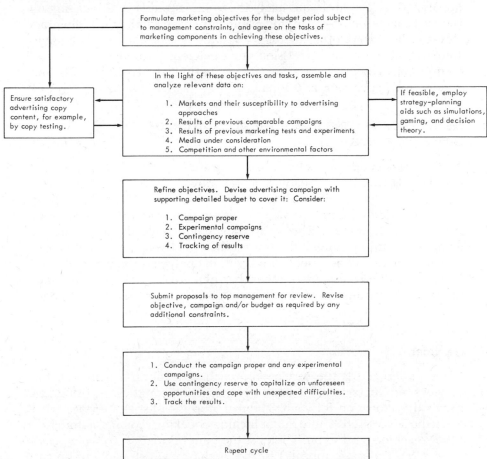

Source: David L. Hurwood and James K. Brown, *Some Guidelines for Advertising Budgeting* (New York: The Conference Board, Inc., 1972), p. 38.

if a valid budget is to be made. If assembly and analysis of data on markets and market response to advertising is bypassed, budgeting by task or objectives is only good in theory. It is worth little in actual practice. Undoubtably, this research and analysis is the most difficult part of the entire budgeting process.

Some companies find it helpful to develop diagrams or flowcharts for showing how various budgeting activities are related and to show how they fit into a time sequence. (See Exhibit 75–5.) Such a chart provides a visual framework for planning and analysis, and helps to ensure that all essential factors are accounted for. At any one time, a company may be involved in several of these cycles, each cycle representing separate services or campaigns; and the company may be at a different stage in each cycle.

In looking more closely at the advertising cycle, it becomes readily apparent that research and analysis are like strands interweaving all the cyclical elements—planning, campaign, execution, and evaluation. Research is vital in other elements besides that of planning a budget. Research helps make advertising more efficient in media analysis and testing, copy research, tracking, and evaluating advertising results, and conducting experimental campaigns.

METHODS OF SETTING FORTH THE ALLOCATION OF BUDGETED FUNDS

If the task method has been used in the determinations of the allocated funds, there will already be a breakdown of the budget according to objectives. It is quite possible that this will be detailed in nature. If the task method is not used up to this point, the advertising manager must decide how he will show his departments allotment of funds in a detailed manner. Even if the task method has been used, it is conceivable that there will be a need or interest in analyzing the departmental budget in a different manner other than objective. There are a number of ways to show allocations for the advertising department in a budget format.

Services

One approach is the service approach. This approach lists all the services (products) that the bank wants to sell through advertising and shows the allocation for each. The first step is to list the services that are to be advertised. These might include checking, savings, automated teller machine, and so on. Then list the general market to which each service has the most appeal. List the media by which each group can be reached most effectively. List the months when each service should ideally receive major emphasis. From the information gathered, draw up a tentative "control calendar" for the projected program.

Corporate Advertising

A more general way to break down allocated resources is between corporate advertising and services advertising. Corporate advertising sells an intangible idea—actually it sells a positive idea of the company. The company sells its own capabilities—quality of service, friendly staff, dominance of market. A favorable public opinion constitutes a valuable business asset. Human attitudes have a significant effect on business success. Not only can corporate advertising exert a great influence on future sales, it can also determine the company's ability to attract employees, particularly high-caliber executives.

There are two ways of communicating a corporate image to the public. One way is through publicity—news releases, newspaper, TV, radio. This is advertising for which no money need be expended. The second way is by the regular advertising method.[12] It seems that companies are leaning more heavily on corporate image than ever before. More advertising campaigns focus on the corporation as opposed to services. There is no doubt that it can be an important element.

Processes

Another plan for showing the allocation of resources is the process plan. There is a process for developing every ad that is used. The theme must be developed, the medium for delivery must be chosen, copy must be written, and the layout or format must be designed.

It is quite possible to break a budget down into costs for each of these items. This kind of budget generally allocates percentages of the money to each process, depending on which process is deemed the most important. For example, if theme development were considered highly critical to the effectiveness of the advertising program, a manager might allocate 25 percent of the resources available to theme development.

---

[12] Walter Kennedy, *Bank Management* (Boston: Bankers Publishing Company, 1969), p. 243.

Chapter 76 _____

Community Relations Programs

Willis Johnson, Jr.*

A. B. Padgett†

Banks and their communities are, in a very real sense, reflections of each other. It is almost impossible to identify a healthy community in this nation which does not have one or more progressive banks serving it. There is equal difficulty in conceiving a successful banking operation in a stagnant community environment.

Good banks and good communities grow hand in hand, nurturing each other. Every bank, no matter how large or small, has a definite stake in the economic and geographical areas in which it has a franchise to operate. General community well-being stems in significant measure from the involvement, initiative, and leadership of the banks and bankers who are a part of that community.

This fundamental interdependence between the bank and the community carries with it both responsibilities and opportunities which are the subject of this chapter.

THE ROLE OF COMMUNITY LEADERSHIP

By and large, banks and bankers hold a respected place in their communities. The ability to control money and credit does, indeed, represent a base of power that must be exercised fairly and judiciously. As a primary source of funds for private and public purposes, banks have come to symbolize strength and integrity. Although the results

---

* Vice President, Trust Company Bank, Atlanta, Georgia.

† Vice President, Trust Company Bank, Atlanta, Georgia.

are not all that might be desired, public opinion surveys indicate that bankers collectively are held in high esteem, ranking near the top of all business, professional, and industry groups in America. While high scores on such attitudinal studies are not, in themselves, the end results to be sought, it is imperative that bankers continually review the condition of their community relations programs to maintain and improve their effectiveness as good citizens.

Because of the qualities inherent in banking, the community usually expects a great deal from its banks and bankers. These expectations often take forms which cannot be converted into direct or measurable returns to the institution. The willingness and interest of bankers in making themselves available for community service is an important basis for a good community relations program. In most communities, it is almost impossible to identify any worthwhile activities and projects which do not have bankers fulfilling a leadership capacity.

A CORPORATE RESPONSIBILITY

Without intending to labor the point, it should be recognized that a bank enjoys innumerable direct and indirect benefit by virtue of the fact that it can operate in a community that has an educated, healthy, stable, and morally responsible population. It is from this community that the bank draws its primary source of customers and its employees. Maintaining a climate that is favorable to the bank's profitable and successful operation is not merely a matter of community concern but a question of enlightened self-interest serving the needs of the bank, its management and staff, and its stockholders.

In its role of corporate citizen, the bank has certain obligations and duties which are not dissimilar to those which must be shared by all concerned, individual citizens. The bank, as a corporate institution, shares in diverse benefits much as individuals who participate in civic, charitable, and other community endeavors designed for the benefit of the whole or significant segments.

The most fundamental element in any bank's community relations program is to render effective banking services which meet the needs of the community in a consistent and comprehensive manner. The bank whose service is slovenly and inadequately delivered can hardly built good community relations.

TERMINOLOGY

Often in seeking to describe or label the bank's areas of involvement and responsibility, a variety of terms is employed—such as corporate citizenship, social responsibility, public affairs, urban affairs, community affairs, and the old standby public relations.

No purpose would be served here by seeking to dissect the fine points of meaning in these differing shades of terminology. Although these terms do not necessarily mean precisely the same thing, they do encompass large areas of overlap. They also mean different things to different people, depending on how one chooses to define them.

Such terms are useful in helping to describe corporate and individual concerns within communities. The labels used to describe these activities are far less important than the underlying philosophy and the procedures employed in organizing and conducting the bank's relationships with its environment.

Much of the terminology now used in community relations, which has come increasingly in vogue during the past decade, conveys implications of relationships with minority groups, consumer groups, and poverty-oriented programs. Such specialized areas are, indeed, elements of the total community relations program for most banks. However, it is important that bank management maintains a proper balance and perspective of the total picture, based on the particular needs and conditions within any given community.

TWO BASIC INGREDIENTS

Banks can work with their communities in two primary ways. One of these is the intelligent and creative application of financial resources (including credit policies) and the other is the careful application of human resources in roles of leadership and support of those activities with which the bank wishes to identify. Management must constantly be concerned about the serious danger that either or both of these two aspects of community involvement can get out of hand without adequate planning, management, and control.

RESPONSIBILITY

The board of directors should consider the bank's community relations as part of its overall responsibility in the management of the institution. From time to time, it is entirely appropriate for the board to ask for an accounting and review of those programs of the bank which affect the community. Bank directors are generally in the forefront of community activities of all sorts and can be the source of constructive ideas and guidance in selecting areas that warrant special emphasis by the bank.

The chief executive officer of the bank must accept the primary responsibility for the institution's posture and performance in the area of community relations. In addition to exercising this basic management responsibility, the chief executive helps set the tone for the entire organization through examples of leadership and through encouragement of the officers and staff to participate in appropriate activities. The organization will sense the spirit of genuine commitment and enthusiasm that the chief executive applies to community affairs.

Because of his high visibility and position in the community, the chief executive often finds himself called upon by outside sources to give a great deal of personal time and involvement in key community undertakings. It takes considerable judgment and selectivity to avoid the problems that arise when the chief executive overcommits himself. This can become counterproductive in that he is unable to give the time and attention necessary to do well all of the jobs which he may have accepted, often under various pressures.

In a small bank, the senior officer may well find it necessary to assume virtually all of the bank's direct involvement since there may be no one else to whom these duties can be assigned. However, in medium-sized and larger banks, it is obvious that top management must delegate great portions of responsibility in the interests of getting the jobs done without impairing the operation of the bank. In such delegation, it must continue to be a responsibility of the chief executive to monitor the activities and commitments for the organization as a whole, both in terms of dollars and the work force.

ORGANIZATION

Larger banks will generally find it highly desirable to concentrate the administration and day-to-day responsibility for community relations in the hands of a designated officer who reports to the chief executive officer. The precise organizational structure will vary from bank to bank and will depend on the special needs of the institution and its development in relation to community affairs.

In the case of relatively modest community relations, this responsibility may well become an added function of the person assigned the job of managing the bank's public relations. The size and composition of the staff necessary to conduct a well-rounded community relations functions must be determined by each bank. It is important that the bank's approach to its community relations be communicated to and understood by as many members of the staff as possible. Every officer and employee should have a feel for management's philosophy and attitudes in the area of community involvement.

There should be either a written or clearly enunciated statement of policy establishing internal guidelines for the recruitment of staff members for various community projects. Middle managers and supervisors should have reasonable criteria for allowing those under their supervision to use bank time in community matters. This coordination of the work force is one of the major responsibilities of the community relations officer.

THE COMMUNITY RELATIONS OFFICER

An essential element in the profile of the community relations officer must be a strong, personal interest in the community and a commitment to work enthusiastically on activities whose purpose is to make the community a better place in which to live. There is no easily defined educational background which equips one for such responsibilities. Experience and post-performance are the ingredients which count the most.

Since this position is highly specialized, it is not necessary that this job be performed by one who has had previous line officer experience in the bank. However, the person selected to perform this job must have a general knowledge of banking and its processes. The person in this position can perform more effectively if he or she has been a resident of the community for several years. Well-established contacts throughout the community are an essential for effective coordination in relating the resources and interests of the bank to the problems of the community. A key concern of the community relations officer must be development and maintenance of good peer relationships with all facets of the community.

A TYPICAL JOB DESCRIPTION

The job description for a community affairs officer might read as follows:

> To coordinate the various activities of the bank as a corporate citizen and to encourage the involvement of officers and employees in meaningful civic activities and to project and make known to the community, when appropriate, the bank's contributions in the development of the community, its work toward the solution of current problems, and the determination of future goals.
>
> To develop and recommend plans, policies, and programs.
>
> To establish basic objectives for assigned functions consistent with overall bank policies.
>
> To stay abreast of and to evaluate processes and problems in attaining objectives, and to take timely and necessary actions as required.
>
> To keep the chief executive officer informed of the current state of all functions for which the community relations officer is responsible, including evaluations and recommendations.

To assist the chief executive officer as necessary in representing the bank, and to act as the spokesman for the bank in various community organizations.

MATTERS OF STYLE

Management styles and philosophies vary widely from bank to bank. Some institutions project a very aggressive and outgoing corporate personality while others tend to show a highly conservative approach. Between these extremes lie all shades of variation. There is no reason to feel that the bank's approach to community relations should evidence a significantly different style from the approach taken in all other matters. Perhaps the key point here is the need to establish absolute credibility and acceptability of the bank's programs within the community.

STATEMENT OF POLICY

In the interest of uniform and consistent actions, it would be highly desirable for the bank to establish a written statement of policy (Exhibit 76-1) as a guideline that is available to the entire organization in the conduct of community affairs. By having such a definition of policy in writing, it is much easier to determine those things which are appropriate and those things which are inappropriate for the institution. The statement of policy should delineate the broad parameters within which decisions for action can be made. While nobody likes to hide behind the statement, "This is not our policy," the fact that something is outside of the policy gives great support to a negative decision which should be explained in as specific manner as possible. A statement of policy should be a positive declaration of the bank's position; however, the community relations officer frequently needs ample backing when negative decisions must be made, often in the face of heavy pressure from outside sources.

DIRECT VERSUS INDIRECT

A bank's community relations activities generally follow one of two main thrusts. The first involves independent programs conceived and executed by the bank, itself, as the sole or leading participant. The other relates to ways by which the bank joins in as a participant in existing or proposed programs without necessarily exerting a dominant or leadership role. Although, the latter process may result in fewer immediate and direct public relations benefits to the institution, it may well provide a stronger avenue for long-range influence on community affairs.

Exhibit 76–1
Example of a Bank's Statement of Policy Concerning Involvement in Community Affairs

We believe that the role of (Bank Name) in Community Affairs lies somewhere between two extremes of thought; namely, that our only role is to maximize our profits and that all of society's ills can be solved by business.

It would be imprudent for this Bank to divert its resouces to the extent that we no longer are capable of fulfilling our responsibility of rendering good banking services. On the other hand, it would be fool-hardy to ignore the problems that exist which, if not tackled, could ulti-mately destroy the prosperity and well being of the community.

By our past actions we have demonstrated this Bank's unique role of being a leader in trying to meet some of the problems of our commu-nity. We do need to sustain a viable city because only in such an environ-ment can we serve the community; therefore, we do have a selfish desire to save the city where we live and work and on whose help and strength we are dependent.

We are committed to an active role of trying to ameliorate social and economic stagnation and to develop our most important resource—people. The present role of the Community Affairs Coordinator is to use the resources of this Bank and several Trust Funds in helping solve some of the problems of this community. Basically, the Bank has worked through existing organizations and sometimes, by working behind the scenes has accomplished more than if it had taken the lead role in all such endeavors.

Our success is attributed to the intelligent and energetic men and women who have been recruited by this Bank and who have a commit-ment to improve the quality of life which they see as consistent with their commitment to the world of finance and commerce. We will con-tinue to recruit the best minds because we have decided to accept the added mission of investing a portion of our human and material resources in trying to alleviate some of the problems of society.

We must continue to support our Minority Lending program, our Affirmative Action Program, and to assume a leadership role in getting new answers to old problems.

In addition, we have launched a Consumer Education Program, which will give this Bank the opportunity to project its concern for the consumer and to develop an image as the consumer bank.

The future role of the Coordinator of Community Affairs will be to continue to coordinate the various departments of the bank which have the continuing programs listed above; to serve as staff for our giving program; to be a community translator to management; and to serve as manpower coordinator in encouraging our people to be involved in community affairs.

In considering the public relations impact of good community programs, there is absolutely nothing wrong with the bank getting its full measure of credit for those things it does in the interests of the community. But this recognition should always be the secondary consideration where genuine community concerns are involved. The question before management should not be, "What can we do in the community that will get us a lot of good P.R.?", but "What can we do in the community that will help the community?"

A BANK FOUNDATION?

Many banks find it advantageous to create a private, nonprofit foundation as a vehicle for effectively coordinating and administering the funds which are made available for community and charitable purposes. Within the foundation framework, it is possible to maximize the dollars which are available, using appropriate tax advantages, and to minimize the pressure which are often exerted by nonqualified sources for support of one case or another. There appears to be no shortage of "good causes" clamoring for bank financial support. Through the foundation approach, the bank can significantly tighten the criteria used to determine where funds may properly be channeled.

Generally, a group of senior officers of the banks will be formally designated as a Donations Committee, meeting periodically to consider requests for funds received by the bank and its foundation, and to consider creative and constructive uses to which available funds may be applied. The community relations officer should certainly serve as a member of the Donations Committee, possibly as secretary, with the chief executive officer often in the role of chairman.

Through its foundation, the bank can take a more formal approach to processing applications and requests for support. Those making such requests can be required to provide detailed operational and financial data which the Donations Committee can review carefully to ensure that funds are being allocated only to appropriate and qualified recipients.

The foundation approach permits maximum objectivity and deliberation in making decisions about the distribution of funds. Through the foundation, it is also possible to concentrate this responsibility into the hands of selected representatives of senior management who are most concerned and involved with community considerations. Appropriate legal and tax counsel should be sought in establishing and operating a bank-sponsored foundation.

Through a judicious and full use of tax effects available for various categories of contributions and donations, the bank can get considerable extra mileage out of the dollars which it is willing to commit to worthwhile and qualified community programs. Banks should take advantage of all provisions of current tax regulations to maximize the impact of the funds allocated to community matters.

Organizations which seek financial support from the bank and/or its foundation should be required to provide maximum information about themselves, the amount they are requesting, the purposes for which grants would be used, and a list of other contributors. They should also be asked to provide budgets and a Determination Letter (as to the tax status) from the Internal Revenue Service whenever this is appropriate.

In the interests of maintaining this information in a concise and

Exhibit 76–2

**Fact Sheet
for Grant Consideration**

Name of organization_____

Address_____

      City   Zip   State

Amount Requested_____

Name of individual making application_____

Position in organization_____

Board of Directors or Trustees:

        Name   Business or Profession

_____   _____

_____   _____

_____   _____

_____   _____

Purpose for which grant will be used if made_____

_____

_____

_____

_____

_____

Other contributors_____

_____

_____

_____

Attached budget and IRS Determination Letter

consistent manner, the bank and/or foundation may wish to use a simple form (Exhibit 76–2).

BUDGETING COMMUNITY RELATIONS

Preparation of a budget for community relations and activities should be prepared on a tentative basis in the fall of each year, with the budget being place in final form as early as possible in the new year. If there is a bank-sponsored foundation, the Donations Committee should make a thorough review of the budget and give its approval. In the absence of a foundation, there nevertheless should be a management committee charged with the review of all requests for grants and significant donations, as well as to maintain the bank's policies about its monetary contributions.

According to recent surveys the level of corporate giving ranged downward from a high of 5.65 percent of net income before taxes, with the median being 1.38 percent The United Way, known by different names in different communities, received the largest percentage of giving, 36.4 percent. This was included in the 48.5 percent total representing corporate contributions directed to health and welfare giving. Education received 22.6 percent, cultural affairs 7.8 percent civic activities 13.8 percent, and all other, including religous activities, constituted 9.7 percent.

Generally speaking, the bank's giving policy should be divided into those contributions which recur each year, such as The United Way, and nonrecurring contributions such as capital fund drives which are for a limited number of years.

DEFINING SPECIFIC AREAS

Community relations can generally be divided into several major categories, which include the following:

1. Community Services. This involves the United Way, its member agencies, and all other community agencies which deal with human needs.

2. Educational. There are many ways in which banks can work with local elementary and high schools as well as institutions of higher learning which may be in the community. The bank may wish to place emphasis on privately endowed institutions since they do not have access to public funds. A Matching Gifts plan by which the bank or foundation matches employee educational gifts may be of interest.

In addition to providing grants, many banks find it worthwhile to offer informational and educational programs designed to help people of all ages know more about various aspects of economics, banking, and personal money management. Junior Achievement sponsorship fits this category.

Making members of the staff available to speak to civic groups and to teach school classes can be very rewarding. A bank tour program can also help strengthen the ties between the bank and its community.

3. Cultural.   There are virtually no limits on what a bank might want to do toward local cultural enrichment. This could involve bank-sponsored exhibitions, concerts, and other programs related to music and the arts. Most communities have many organizations with a cultural orientation which welcome bank support and involvement.

4. Health and Recreational.   Organizations which are dedicated to seeking cures and controls for diseases and the improvement of health provide a wide variety of opportunities for bank support.

Beyond financial contributions, banks can sponsor blood drives, health fairs, checkup drives, and the like.

An example of a meaningful and lasting recreational contribution would be purchase of a piece of property which the bank might make available to the community as a park or picnic area. Banks also purchase swings and other recreational equipment for distribution throughout the community.

5. Religious.   Interdenominational and joint religious councils provide an appropriate means for bank support of programs designed to help people in such matters as emergency assistance, food and clothing. In most cases, it is unwise for a bank to become heavily identified with any one religious denomination.

6. Special Situations.   In special situations, banks may justify community relations programs designed primarily to benefit minority groups (blacks, American Indians, other ethnic and cultural groups). An example would be assistance in the publication of a Spanish language newspaper in the community heavily populated by Cuban exiles or a Vietnamese newsletter for circulation among re-settled refugees from that country.

The only limitations on the potential scope of specific community relations programs are imagination and resources.

PUBLIC VERSUS PRIVATE

Federal, state, and local governments play increasing roles in every community through funding and regulations affecting areas which have historically and traditionally been considered to be in the private sector. Bank policies should take into account the present situation and future expectations for governmental involvement in those activities of particular interest to the bank.

Very often, it is entirely practical for a bank to give effective supplemental financial support and local leadership to programs which are predominantly public in nature.

OTHER AREAS OF SERVICE

Many bankers find satisfaction in holding public office, placing them in positions which can have major influence on local public policies in many fields.

There are many public and private efforts under way to restore or rebuild downtown areas and neighborhoods. Banks can cooperate in such projects through direct contributions, special credit considerations, and individual leadership.

Banks are frequently in the forefront of community industrial and economic development activities, producing not only broad benefits for the area in general but also opening up the possibilities of significant new banking relationships.

MINORITY LOAN PROGRAMS

One area that affect community relations is closely connected to the credit aspect of banking; namely, minority loan programs. There are a large number of individuals and businesses identified with minority groups which do not meet the qualifications for regular bank credit by normal standards. Many banks have elected to make a commitment of dollars and the work force to aid in the development of minority businesses which can qualify for assistance from the Small Business Administration. Participating banks provide educational and technical services to these marginal credits, and seek to help minority business entrepreneurs become better managers and financially self-sustaining. This can be a difficult area for a bank to engage in since the chances for failure are unusually high. However, banks which are concerned about the well-being of the total business environment must do all they can to upgrade the quality and ability of minority business leaders who have the potential of assuming more responsible positions within the community.

BANK PEOPLE-POWER

Determining who within the bank will do what, when, with whom, and how much in community relations is one of the major considerations that must be worked out by the community relations officer. Through personal knowledge, questionnaires, personnel records, and other information, the community relations officer needs a good handle

Exhibit 76–3
Record of Community Activities

Your Name: _____
Department Name: _____
Department Number: _____
Department Location: _____
COMMUNITY ACTIVITIES (Example: United Way, Civitan Club)

Organization	Position	Estimated Bank Hours for 1977	Estimated Personal Hours for 1977
_____	_____	_____	_____
_____	_____	_____	_____
_____	_____	_____	_____
_____	_____	_____	_____
_____	_____	_____	_____
_____	_____	_____	_____
_____	_____	_____	_____
_____	_____	_____	_____
_____	_____	_____	_____
_____	_____	_____	_____

BUSINESS AND PROFESSIONAL GROUPS (Example: American Management Association)

_____	_____	_____	_____
_____	_____	_____	_____
_____	_____	_____	_____
_____	_____	_____	_____
_____	_____	_____	_____

SOCIAL CLUBS AND SOCIETIES (Example: Capital City Club, social fraternities)

_____	_____	_____	_____
_____	_____	_____	_____
_____	_____	_____	_____
_____	_____	_____	_____
_____	_____	_____	_____

OTHER (Such as church involvement and office held)

_____	_____	_____	_____
_____	_____	_____	_____
_____	_____	_____	_____
_____	_____	_____	_____

on the types of talent and interests held by various individuals within the organization.

While there should be considerable freedom for individuals to become involved on their own in various aspects of community life, there can be a danger that too many individuals may become involved in a single project, such as The United Way or a particular fund-raising drive.

Central records should be maintained by the community relations officer showing what each individual has been doing in the way of community activities, both on bank time and personal time. A simple form (Exhibit 76–3) can be used to make an annual audit of such participation by members of the organization. This puts at the community relations officer's fingertips at a frequently updated record of the personal involvement of management, officers, and whatever other staff levels for which the bank wishes to maintain such records. Requiring officers to fill out this type form each year is a gentle reminder that the bank has ongoing concern for its people participating broadly in community affairs. These records can be used to evaluate individual activities as a part of a personnel evaluation program.

MEASURING EFFECTIVENESS

The effectiveness of a bank's community relations programs is, at best, difficult to measure.

To the degree that specific goals can be set for stated periods of time, such as a calendar year, it is possible for the community relations officer to evaluate how well the bank performs in meeting these goals. Through the budgeting process, it can be determined whether or not the bank is fulfilling its financial obligations in various areas of the community.

Through periodic surveys of bank personnel (see Exhibit 76–3), the bank can summarize the number of people-hours the staff is spending in work with all of the civic, cultural, educational, religious, social, and other agencies in the community—both on bank and personal time. This can be expressed as an estimated percentage of total work hours available to the institution. Many banks may find that this is a much greater amount of time than they realize.

Surveys of community awareness and attitudes can be structured to give insights into public reaction to community relations programs. In a large institution, this might be a highly sophisticated study probing into many fine points of awareness. For a small bank, it could be as simple as occasional conversations between bank management and community leaders in an informal setting.

Economic barometers available for the local chamber of commerce and other sources may provide continuous data reflecting the effects of certain types of bank community programs.

Assumptions by management are an inexact form of evaluation. However, most banks sense whether or not they are making adequate community contributions. The community relations officer should seek to devise as many ways as possible to determine whether or not various programs are accomplishing their purposes, whether such programs should be expanded or phased out, and whether or not the bank is doing at least its fair share in maintaining and building a favorable community environment.

DEVELOPING LEADERSHIP

In addition to the more obvious direct and indirect benefits which the bank realizes through a good community relations programs, there are important side benefits to the bank and its people. The area of community affairs offers an excellent vehicle for the development of leadership potential within the bank staff. This has significance not only for the community as a whole but for the further evolution of the bank's own management. By working as "loaned executives" during United Way campaigns and in other community-oriented efforts, younger men and women find an excellent opportunity to test their wings as they move up the ladder toward positions of greater responsibility within the organization. Senior management can observe and evaluate the up and coming members of the staff in situations that reflect the ability to work with people and to accomplish meaningful community contributions outside the banking environment.

SOME PUBLIC RELATIONS ASPECTS

If the community relations officer and the public relations officer are not the same person, there is an obvious need for these two officers to work together very closely. There should be a clear delineation of responsibilities and duties.

Banks are constantly called on for donations and participation in matters that may be more public relations than community relations and there is a very thin line between these two areas of concern.

Some of the more traditional public relations activities, which have a distinct bearing on community relations, are among the following:

Providing bank facilities for community meetings. Many banks and branch offices have special rooms set aside for such purposes.

Distribution of maps, brochures, and other community-oriented literature.

Maintenance of a public relations budget to handle small donations, purchase of tickets to community events, and the like.

Sponsorship of special events.

Programs to recognize outstanding young people in the community in various activities—scholarship, citizenship, accomplishments in 4-H work, and similar youth programs.

Bank-sponsored advertisements promoting specific community events, programs, and activities.

Giveaway items at community affairs.

The list is almost endless.

SUMMARY

No bank can afford to abdicate its responsibility for community involvement and leadership. The management of every bank needs to maintain some systematic, organized process to establish priorities and to ensure that the bank's priorities are consistent with the needs of the community. Many of the things banks do in the name of "community relations" are often the result of pressures from good customers and special groups. There is no reason to think there will be any diminution in these situations which place the bank in a reactionary position.

But there is a need today greater than ever before for banks to exercise creative and imaginative approaches to the problems of their communities. Through the application of enlightened self-interest, banks are peculiarly positioned through their resources of people-power and financial strength to effect changes that will make this a better world for everyone, starting at the level of the local community. It is incumbent on the senior management of every bank to make certain that the emphasis be place on constructive action rather than passive reaction.

Chapter 77

Marketing Research in Banking

Kenneth R. Dew*

Marketing research to a bank is similar to what an intelligence section is to the military. The primary responsibility is that of gathering, organizing, tabulating, and interpreting data vital to successful operation. It is employed basically to support management in the unrelenting task of making the best decisions—decisions which require careful analysis of all available information and alternatives.[1]

Research and information do not represent a substitute for judgment, but should be thought of as a tool for minimizing risks assumed by management. Marketing research serves as a tremendous aid in developing strategy and tactics for top management.

Included under the broader definition are such elements as market and economic analysis, attitudinal profiles, share of market trends, advertising effectiveness, location of facilities, product research and development, pricing, and a host of related activities.

Marketing research is not limited to academic exercise and stargazing. It is a very practical discipline designed to generate hard facts which can be reviewed and used in the task of providing better, more widely accepted services. To be productive, it has to be timely, factual, and flexible in style.

A marketing research program should not be undertaken as some short-lived experiment merely because it appears to be the fashionable thing to do. Above all, valid research has to be (1) conducted by capable

---

* Senior Vice President, Bankers Trust Company, Des Moines, Iowa.

[1] There are those who prefer to use "marketing information system" or other comparable terms as definitive titles for total marketing research and retrieval systems. For purposes of the following discussion, and in an effort to avoid semantic debate, marketing research will be considered as the appropriate label covering this entire function.

personnel, (2) on a continuing basis, (3) used as a tool, but not taken as the final answer, and (4) interpreted fairly and objectively.

MANAGEMENT SUPPORT

Like any other function, marketing research, to be successful, must be endorsed, and actively supported by management. Without this backing, the program is limited at best and more likely doomed to failure from the outset. Nor should too much be expected too soon. It may take time for research efforts to pay off.

The marketing researcher is obligated to use research dollars wisely and bank management is obligated to provide adequate resources for doing the job. Executives who hold deep reservation about the value of research in their banks and concomitant funds to underwrite the assignment might take a lesson from that classical observation of the railroad industry as cited by Ted Levitt, in "Marketing Myopia."[2] He persuasively holds that railroading's inability to identify changing views and needs of the American public almost destroyed the industry. Railroad executives felt they were in "Railroading" instead of the transportation business. They would see it no other way until it was almost too late.

There is an analogy here for today's highly competitive world of banking. Under continuous attack from nonbanking financial organizations, severely criticized by some legislators and oftentimes challenged by a suspicious public, banking cannot afford to make the same mistake. Anticipating ever-changing financial requirements of business, government and consumers is best accomplished through sound marketing research techniques. It is incumbent upon management that proper emphasis be placed on this capability and that adequate priority be given to assure banking's viability in the future. The consequences of not doing so are evident.

ECONOMIC JUSTIFICATION

Placing an exact value on the return from dollars invested in marketing research is difficult. Subsequently, budgeting funds for an activity which may defy measurement in precise terms can become an arduous task.

How much should be spent by a bank for its marketing research program?

There is no more clear-cut answer to this question than there is for advertising. Many variables must be considered in light of a bank's

---

[2] Theodore Levitt, "Marketing Myopia," *Harvard Business Review,* July–August 1960, pp. 45–56.

goals and objectives. Relative strengths and weaknesses have to be compared with those of the competition. Potential markets must be assessed and overall strategy has to be developed.

The answer also depends upon how much research has been conducted in the past. Starting up an entirely new program will obviously require heavier investment than a mature program which has systematically scheduled required tasks from year to year. Whether the responsibility is assumed by an internal staff, outside professionals or a combination of these has a very firm bearing on expenditures. Market size and available data are also cost considerations.

There is no rule of thumb suggesting what portion of the marketing budget should be devoted to research. Many marketing professionals do agree on one key fact, however. If marketing efforts are to be directed efficiently, marketing research must furnish necessary intelligence for performing the job.

Regardless of the size of the marketing budget, capable research can fine tune the program and keep it on target. It is largely a matter of employing marketing dollars in the optimum manner and using the best mix of research, promotion, and sales.

To illustrate, if no research had been done previously, redirecting a small portion of the advertising budget toward needed research should increase advertising effectiveness more than enough to compensate for the nominal time/space reduction. A knowledgeable banker should not consider spending substantial advertising dollars year after year without attempting to determine whether the bank's message was coming across and how it was being perceived. This same principle applies to the sales and other promotional areas, as well.

Major research projects can sometimes represent a burdensome expenditure during a single year in which the study is made. Should this become a serious obstacle, it is a generally accepted rule that the Internal Revenue Service will permit amortization of research costs over an extended period of time, perhaps three-to-five years, depending upon the span over which research findings are thought to be current and in process of implementation.

AVOIDING THE PITFALLS

Like any other banking activity, marketing research offers a number of possible traps. Perhaps the most treacherous lie in technical areas such as the statistical, questionnaire design, or interpretation of data. Others can be found deep in conceptual framework. Among those to avoid are:

Permitting the ill-equipped or indifferent to carry out assignments. High levels of sensitivity and awareness are vital to the competent researcher. Inquisitiveness and a strong desire to diagnose the "why" of behavior are valuable traits. Research requires considerable creative input and personal involvement. Anyone who does not genuinely like this type work should not be called upon to engage in it.

Thinking that marketing research represents most of the marketing effort. As stated earlier, research must be considered an integral part of a bank's total marketing program, but it cannot substitute for other factors, such as advertising, sales, and public relations. Certainly it is an aid in direction setting and measurement, but placing unwarranted pressure on the research function to produce miracles can only bring frustration and disappointment.

Expecting research findings to provide indisputable evidence and infallible recommendations. Significant trends, highly touted forecasts and confident claims backed by mountains of supporting data still cannot guarantee success. So long as that unpredictable human factor is present, potential error and misinterpretation exist. This fact should not discourage or undermine one's faith in marketing research practices, however, but is intended to serve as a flag of caution when judgments are based upon research efforts.

Letting an aura of mystery and highly technical terms surround the effort. If marketing research cannot be carried on in a manner which can be understood by management, then serious doubts about credibility will inevitably occur. While those skills and highly specialized techniques which serve as the base for professional research are necessary, they should not be flaunted before the layman as secret weapons. We become defensive about the unknown. Marketing research does not need that type resistance.

DEVELOPING THE RESEARCH PROGRAM

The first step in establishing a marketing research program is to place one person in charge of the job. Second, this person must report to a superior who has the ability to set research priorities intelligently and the authority to see that once completed they are implemented effectively. While these requisites may seem fundamental, it is surprising how often they are overlooked.

What personal attributes are desirable for the marketing research director? There are a number. Among the more important are a natural curiosity and an unwillingness to always accept the obvious. For example, the consistent response from interviewees when asked, "Why did you choose XYZ Bank?", is for reasons of convenience. The apparent implication suggests location convenience.

However, with a little probing, it is soon found that "convenience" means many things to many people. To some it means drive-in convenience. To others it means being recognized by a teller who will cash their checks without the usual time-consuming hassle of calling a remote account service department for verification.

Convenience to work. Convenience to home. Convenience while shopping. All these and dozens of other reasons for convenience have to be viewed analytically by an aroused marketing researcher who can knife through the layers of conditioned response and verbal camouflage to uncover the real forces propelling customers to their chosen banks.

The person responsible for a bank's marketing research program must be a team player. He should understand established corporate goals and understand his special role in attaining the bank's objectives.

Above-average knowledge of human behavior, a fundamental grasp of statistics, the faculty for defining a research assignment clearly, and the ability to communicate ideas are among the more vital attributes favoring the researcher's successful performance.

Internal Information Base

The initial step in building a solid research base calls for development of a customer information file—preferably within an electronic system. These files are obviously drawn from internal data relating to customer activity in the past or present tense. Since it is a generally accepted fact that the best market potential for new business rests with existing customers, it is not difficult to give this task top priority.

Other data to be carried in the base could include (1) customer profiles according to services used; (2) analysis of depositors and borrowers by age, income, education, sex, and residence; (3) trends experienced in opening and closing accounts; (4) opinions held by customers of the bank; and (5) ultimately a customer profitability schedule.

It is likely that a valuable by-product generated from this developmental effort would accrue in the form of newly discovered internal information sources. It is astonishing how often records and useful data are maintained within a bank, but many of those who could use the information are not aware of its existence.

External Research Efforts

Accumulation of external marketing data begins where internal research ends. The two areas receiving principal emphasis are those involving (1) prospective customer groups and (2) competitive forces.

Researching the Competition. While much can be learned through unplanned observation, systematic information gathering and analysis of other bank or nonbank financial activities should be conducted on a continuing basis. Without knowledge of what competitors are doing—successfully or unsuccessfully—a bank can find itself quite vulnerable to outside pressures and changing customer preferences.

Periodic Comparative Analysis. At quarterly or other desired intervals, a comparative analysis is a good way to size up relative progress among banks and other competing institutions within a given market. Deposit and loan growth are traditional measures. These can be broken into various classifications.

The acid test comes when shares of the market are calculated. (A secondary test of internal consequence can also be made simultaneously by comparing actual progress to established goals for the period.) Although some banks attempt to conceal these data, quarterly statements are available in local media or through regulatory authorities. The important point is that trends should be identified and assessed in light of strategic goals and objectives.

Probing for Potential Customers and Prospective New Services. Successful pursuit of new business requires knowledge of financial wants and needs prevailing in the market. A logical way of developing this information is through contact with prospective customers.

This may be accomplished through personal interviews and conversational input derived from sales calls or within structured "focus groups" which seem to have been a growing source of ideas and information in recent years. It is imperative that, once prospects and potential new services are targeted, information is disseminated to appropriate persons within the bank so that follow-up can be expedited.

The Quick 'n Dirty Venture

Marketing researchers are oftentimes called upon for certain "firefighting" tasks. A competitor may suddenly have announced free checking accounts. Regulation Q might have been revised, increasing maximum permissive rates, with some banks raising rates and others, for some unknown reason holding at the old levels. Perhaps a new branch office is not attracting the business it should. Management wonders why and wants answers immediately!

Under these circumstances, there is little time for procrastination. The marketing researcher has to come up with fast answers—answers that are on target. There is little time to dwell on research protocol and techniques. Experienced research specialists who have weathered their share of such crash projects, prefer to use the term "quick 'n dirty" to characterize the nature of the job.

Frequently, projects of this type offer valuable facts, despite pressures involved. It is possible that the short time allowed for vacillation and mind-changing lends an unsuspected degree of reliability to the effort. Whatever the case, these "short-order" assignments are an integral part of the research program. It may be a little discomforting, but results are frequently quite rewarding.

Professional Participation

Research support for banks of all sizes and description is usually available at nearby colleges and universities, from private research firms, specialized publications, banking associations, and other sources such as advertising agencies, regulatory bodies, and census data. Each, characterized by its own strengths, weaknesses and limitations, can make a substantial contribution to the bank's research program.

Among the most productive funds a bank can invest for research assistance are those spent with experienced professionals at college and university locations. Quite often, teams of upper level educators form their own private consulting firms or can arrange research projects for selected clients through the school's educational framework. Students may or may not engage in the fieldwork depending on school practices or policies. When supported by computer systems and well-grounded in practical experience, excellent research results can be expected from this source.

One key benefit can be that of lower cost. Any qualified research professional requires adequate compensation, but sometimes substantial dollars can be saved when academicians are permitted to handle the project. Lower overhead and less expensive student assistance may account for a portion of potential savings.

Private research firms operating at local, national, and international levels are available to banks. One major advantage they can offer is a broader view of the banking industry—or related industries. Consequently, when undertaking an assignment, these firms usually begin the task with at least some awareness of what is happening within the business. They can be expected to have a network of far-ranging contacts which provide opportunity for comparison with other similar banks and organizations.

Larger firms also are in a position to (1) call on skilled staff members with special talents, (2) utilize computer equipment, and (3) deploy trained field personnel who are capable of acting quickly and efficiently. Perhaps the greatest deterrent to employing professional research firms is cost. Their fees may appear to be somewhat high in relation to other research alternatives. However, numerous factors such as experience, speed, reliability, and objectivity must be weighed carefully before this becomes the deciding consideration.

EXECUTING THE MARKETING RESEARCH PROJECT

The first step to be taken with any research project is that of defining the problem. Among other questions to be answered are: What is the purpose of the research? Where are the answers most likely to be found? Which methods should be adopted to collect needed information? How much time and how many dollars will the job require? When will research findings and recommendations be implemented?

Once these questions have been answered, the project is ready to begin.

Marketing researchers tend to be very thorough. Moreover, the better ones are inclined to be quite curious and creative. These are among the long list of reasons for carefully defining the scope of a research assignment. If, for example, management wants to know how its physical facilities compare with competitors' in eyes of the consumer, then that's the project. Attempts to ascertain how employees, competitors, stockholders, or commercial customers feel about these offices is not relevant. It might be interesting information, but it would not be particularly helpful. Good researchers recognize practical limitations.

Responsibility for delineating parameters of a research project rests equally with management and the research specialist. It is essential that both are in communication so that what is ordered can be delivered.

Budgeting

The same considerations are required for research budgeting as for any other activity. Whether this is projected on an annual basis or one task at a time, the principles remain essentially the same.

Regardless of whether research is managed by bank personnel or outsiders, total costs will include directly or indirectly:

1. Salaries of supervisors, field interviewers, secretaries and clerical personnel.
2. Office space and utilities.
3. Transportation (if personal interviews are conducted) and out-of-pocket expense.
4. Computer time, if utilized.
5. Printing of questionnaires, reports, and other related documents.
6. Report preparation and presentation.
7. Other miscellaneous costs such as telephone, interviewer audit, testing of questionnaire, sample selection, and postage.

No mattter how efficient and cost-conscious researchers attempt to be, dollars are necessary if the job is done correctly. Even though costs may appear to be rather steep at first glance, once it is fully understood that several phases must be completed in order to accomplish the project, these dollars are relinquished less reluctantly. Professional standards must be maintained if findings are to be credible.

Needless to say, pennies saved at the expense of inadequate sampling, ill-equipped interviewers or inept reporting represent foolish frugality.

Questionnaire Design

Preparation and design of the questionnaire may be the single most important step of the research process, because this is the medium through which input is derived. There is a popular expression among computer operators, "Garbage in; garbage out." The same applies to marketing research studies.

Information gained is related directly to knowledge and intelligence which go into questionnaire makeup. Whether to be used for personal, telephone, or direct-mail interviews, attributes of a well-designed questionnaire include:

Simplicity for interviewer and interviewee. The interviewing technique dictates to some degree the format a questionnaire follows. For example, the direct-mail questionnaire should be easily read and understood, brief, conveniently returned, and carry with it some reason or incentive to urge quick response.

Questionnaires drawn for personal interviews should provide a give-and-take guideline for the interviewer, while still maintaining control of the dialogue. Telephone interviews usually call for a combination of mail and person-to-person techniques because they involve only verbal feedback and limited time for probing.

Client anonymity to interviewer and interviewee, if possible. This control encourages objective answers because it discourages bias developed through leading questions of a prejudiced interviewer. It also prevents an aggressive person who is subject of the interview from intimidating an interviewer into revealing the sponsor's name.

Naturalness in structure so that key questions blend unsuspiciously into the total questionnaire format. It is essential for the sake of reliability that answers sought through the questionnaire be as valid as humanly possible. This can be accomplished most effectively when questions blend smoothly into a sequence of items presented casually to the interviewee in a conversational manner.

Layout which is conducive to efficient tabulation. Since this can be a tedious, time-consuming task, it is desirable that responses be easily compiled. Of course, when information is fed directly into the computer from the questionnaires, established keypunch guidelines must be observed.

Designing questionnaires is an art drawn from training, experience, and a few mistakes! Knowledge in areas such as human behavior, communications, sociology, and graphics serves the designer well.

Interviewing Techniques

As indicated previously, there are three forms through which research materials can be generated from a respondent. These are (1) face-to-face or personal, (2) telephone, and (3) direct-mail techniques. Each has its own strengths and other not so good qualities.

Personal interviews enjoy some advantages over other types. It is possible to gather more data through two-way dialogue. Also, vague replies can be clarified more readily because of the personal contact.

On the other hand, these interviews are considerably more expensive than other forms. And when an interviewer is not skilled, he or she can bias the interviewee's response through inadequate phrasing of questions, with leading statements and by misinterpretation of responses.

Telephone interviews can be conducted quickly and economically. They are ideal in researching certain situations. For example, a study designed to determine the promotional value of telephone delivered time-and-temperature service would quite logically be conducted by telephone.

However, there may be a degree of built-in error when the telephone is used for random sample interviewing simply because not everyone has a telephone. Another potential problem stems from telephone abuse in recent years in which so-called interviewers have used "research" as the means to slip in an unwanted sales presentation.

Mail questionnaires offer several advantages which create appeal to the researcher. They are low-cost, yet restricted very little by geographical boundaries. Interviewer bias is nonexistent and valid random sampling is easily achieved.

Perhaps the chief shortcoming of mail questionnaires lies in their uncertainty of response and possible slow return. Neither do they provide means to clarify questionable points which frequently occur as a result of word connotation and unfamiliar terminology

The researcher's choice of interviewing techniques depends upon several factors including costs involved, depth of questions, time requirements and subject matter. The choice is not always easy.

Tabulation

Although it represents one of the less creative steps in the research process, tabulation is nonetheless important. It can be a simple matter of manually classifying and counting responses or can become a complex effort involving computer tabulating and cross-tabulating for finite comparison. Suffice it to say, this may not be the most glamorous job in the research field, but complete accuracy is essential to validity.

Interpretation

There is no magic formula for easy interpretation of tabulated findings. Open-mindedness coupled with the ability to recognize both good and bad news is requisite. What is important though, is the ability to sift out extraneous data and use remaining facts to formulate action plans.

When research objectives are clearly defined at the outset and pursued to completion, interpretation of findings should not be difficult, except when significant differences fail to appear in tabulation. When this is the case, data might need to be "massaged" or it may become necessary to conduct additional study in order to reach conclusions with any level of confidence.

This becomes the true test of the researcher's judgment.

Implementation

Once the research project has been finished and interpretation has suggested appropriate recommendations, the actual implementation must begin. Without this final payoff, the energy and expense of research merely amounts to academic exercise. No statement could be more fitting than the old adage, "The proof is in the eating."

Whether findings relate to a need for redirection of advertising, the opportunity to develop new products or a flaw in teller service, the overriding purpose of marketing research is to assist in coordinating the marketing mix so that synergistic qualities are permitted to flourish. In simplest terms, implementation of research must be service and profit oriented. It must directly or indirectly assist somehow in maximizing profit over the long run.

Consequently, the burden of justifying research expenditures eventually falls to a large extent on the shoulders of management. Researchers rarely have the position or power required to see that their recommendations are honored, because recommendations often prescribe basic changes in strategy or policy. This assignment then falls to management, which is obligated to respond.

This is not to suggest that the researcher be relieved of further responsibility once the specific research assignment has been completed. He is expected to offer continuing counsel and encouragement to those charged with implementation of his findings. Furthermore, since the job remains of measuring reliability and the degree of success experienced through the implementation process, he has reason to remain involved.

In other words, it seems to be in a bank's best interest to keep the researcher on the implementation team rather than freeing him from further activity in a given assignment. As a result, he continues to exert personal energy in efforts to make his recommendations pay off.

ROLE OF MARKETING RESEARCH IN THE FUTURE

Keener competition, the accelerating rate of change in business, more discriminating customers, narrowing profit margins—these and a number of related challenges are compelling the banking industry to become better informed and more responsive to its many publics. Marketing research provides much of the necessary framework for accomplishing this task.

It is generally conceded that marketing research and its supporting activities will assume a role of growing importance to banking in the future. To succeed and survive, management must continually strive to make more knowledgeable decisions. This will be done through better planning and improved access to information. Marketing research can be of enormous help to executives in both these categories.

Greater Sophistication

Greater sophistication and improved investigative techniques will lend credibility to the research function. Substantial progress has been enjoyed in recent years by banks, private research firms and educational institutions as concerted efforts have been made to refine and sharpen their research tools of the trade.

For example, a team of instructors on the faculty of a local university in this writer's community have developed a 15,000 word computerized dictionary and a program called Quester which enables the user to uncover submerged attitudes and hidden opinion through analysis of an individual's personal vocabulary and word usage.

Currently employed in a number of clinical tests ranging from copy writing effectiveness to mate selection, reliability of the program is proving exceptionally high.

A nationally known private research firm is using with notable success a technique titled multivariate analysis designed to ferret out the real reasons business leaders choose their banks—not necessarily why they say they do! The confidence level of this program continues to rise through experience and modification.

Some of the greatest challenges ever to face the industry are appearing daily in the electronic funds transfer race. How do bankers convince customers that an electronic impulse is better than a paper check? What will the consumer take most readily in place of the old, reliable checkbook? Is this new delivery system going to be accepted by corporate treasurers, consumers, and correspondents? If so, under what terms?

These are but a few of the fundamental questions marketing managers, chief executive officers, and marketing researchers must answer in the near future.

Computer Utilization

Computer availability for the researcher has taken some time in getting here, and even today actual capabilities of these powerful electronic "brains" have hardly been tested. In most cases, they traditionally have been utilized as oversize adding machines or high-speed account posting machines.

Capacity for ingesting, sorting, and analyzing research data is just now being exercised on a limited scale. Forecasting and model stimulation have been introduced by a few large, advanced banks, but the preponderant number of the 14,500 organizations have not really become acquainted with research potential offered through computer equipment. Benefits for users are tremendous.

To maintain competitive positions and in order to pursue increasing shares of market, management must urge the harnessing of computer power for greater use by marketing research specialists.

Managing Change and Product Development

It is evident that marketing research represents indispensable aid to banks and bankers in crucial areas of social change and new product development. The two go hand in hand.

Alvin Toffler, in his book titled, *Future Shock,* states:

> . . . A silent but rapid attrition kills off the old, and new products sweep in like a tide.
>
> "Products that used to sell for twenty-five years," writes economist Robert Theobald, "now often count on no more than five. In the volatile pharmaceutical and electronic fields the period is often as short as six months." As the pace of change accelerates further, corporations may create new products knowing full well that they will remain on the market for only a matter of a few weeks.[3]

While it is true that banking products can be expected to enjoy a longer shelf life than most consumer goods, principal facts cannot be denied. All banks are caught up in the transient, ever-changing world Toffler so vividly portrays.

---

[3] Alvin Toffler, *Future Shock* (New York: Bantam Books, Random House, Inc., 1971), pp. 71–72.

Because of its dynamic position in this country, the banking industry finds itself repeatedly on the leading edge of change. Properly conceived and intelligently applied marketing research techniques clearly offer an important means for smoothing out the rough road leading into the future.

Whether we like the prospects or not, the banking industry must meet the accelerating rate of change by anticipating and responding to the financial needs of our society. It is both a matter of surviving and thriving. Moreover, if our responses are too slow, the sharp edge of change may cut right into vital organs of the banking industry.

Under these pressures, bankers are beginning to realize that they cannot be all things to all people. In true marketing style, they are determining what capabilities and resources can most efficiently be dedicated to serving customer needs at a reasonable profit.

Those days of designing a financial product at the president's whim or because operations personnel want to demonstrate what can be done with new computer equipment are over. Today's competition and rising costs make wild gambling on new services too dangerous. Hunches oftentimes fail to pay off. Research may not offer guarantees either, but it certainly can be employed to improve odds for success.

Product research, development, and management require that a bank "get it together" if it wants to compete. This task is not relegated to a token staff directed by a handful of people engaging in weekly skull sessions and brainstorming for the sheer joy of mental gymnastics. Everyone within the bank is involved in one way or another.

It is time for bankers to (1) decide where each product stands in its life cycle, (2) evaluate the mix of its products, and (3) attempt to correlate future customer needs with present and anticipated capabilities for serving these requirements. Marketing research controls the switch that provides the means for illuminating the way. It can light the path to customer satisfaction and resulting bank progress or it can lead to a dead end if not implemented intelligently. There is a choice.

SECTION XIII

BANK REGULATION
AND SUPERVISION

Chapter 78

The Office of the Comptroller of the Currency and the Structure of American Banking

James E. Smith*

Robert R. Dince†

THE BACKGROUND

The American banking system is unique; nothing quite like it exists anywhere else in the world. The United States has approximately 15,000 commercial banks of all sizes and forms of organization. In addition, there are thousands of mutual savings banks, savings and loan associations, and credit unions that also act as financial intermediaries. American banks are increasingly involved in international banking. The diversity in the American banking system provides efficient and effective financial services to our complex economy. Most other countries with similarly complex social and economic systems have not developed the same diversity and flexibility in their banking systems.

The present diverse structure of the American banking system is rooted in the historical development of the system of federal and state government. The needs of the economy and the onset of the Civil War demonstrated that the old state bank system was inadequate.

---

* Executive Vice President, First Chicago Corporation, Chicago, Illinois. (Formerly, 23d Comptroller of the Currency.)

† Associate Deputy Comptroller of the Currency for Economic Research and Operational Analysis, Washington, D.C.

For that reason, Congress created, in 1863, a national currency and a system of nationally chartered banks. The Office of the Comptroller of the Currency (OCC) was established within the Treasury Department to supervise that currency and to charter and regulate national banks.

Repeated financial crises over the next 50 years led to the creation, in 1913, of the Federal Reserve System (Fed) which was to provide both a flexible money supply and lender of last resort. In 1933, the Federal Deposit Insurance Corporation (FDIC) was forced to help insure the safety of depositors' monies.

Before the creation of the OCC, commercial banks could be chartered only by the states. All national banks are required by statute to belong to the Federal Reserve System and to be insured under the Federal Deposit Insurance Act. The comptroller is one of three members of the board of the FDIC, and is a member of the interagency committee which coordinates federal banking supervisory policy.

The OCC is the only federal agency with authority to charter new banks or branches. The Fed and the FDIC only ratify or reject chartering decisions already made by a bank regulator. The FDIC has significant insurance and receivership functions not possessed by the other two agencies and the Fed has monetary responsibilities which overshadow its bank regulatory functions. The Fed is also the principal regulator of bank holding companies, the development of which has been significant in recent years. Approximately 68.2 percent of American banking resources today are controlled by holding companies.

BANKING AND REGULATION

Diversity in state and federal regulation provides the kind of creative response that is ideal in a capitalistic society. Innovations can originate in one segment of the banking system and variations on those innovations can be tested in other segments. A sharing of the experiences of all segments should lead to an adoption of the best innovations and a rejection of the worst. In many instances, a ruling by one agency has stimulated the industry and other regulators to permit rapid and beneficial technological change. A recent example of that was the Comptroller's 1974 ruling on electronic banking terminals. That action encouraged 26 states to pass enabling legislation for state banks and thus permitting the creation of an embryonic electronic funds transfer system. The economy holds many examples of industries that are regulated by a single, monolithic federal agency moribund and unresponsive to a changing environment (i.e., railroads, pipelines). Such agencies have sometimes been captured by their industries and then turned their attention toward protecting the members of that industry. Our society is based upon competition as the most efficient way of allocating resources, and such protection is inconsistent with competition and innovation.

The present dual banking system has permitted innovation in areas such as NOW (negotiable orders of withdrawal) accounts and anti-redlining legislation at the state level while, at the federal level, the Federal Reserve Board has developed expertise in writing consumer regulations and the OCC is experimenting with new techniques in enforcing consumer laws. The OCC also has recently installed new examination procedures and methods of using bank financial data for supervisory purposes that are expected to be models for the other agencies, both state and federal.

The present bank regulatory system works well. The entire system continues to improve steadily, contributing to the orderly functioning of an efficient banking system. During the sharp economic recession of 1974–75, a few, well-publicized, large bank failures did not result in a dollar of loss to depositors. A financial crisis did not develop. The system has survived major shocks with only minor damage and new methods are being developed to meet the identified problems in bank regulation.

CHARTERING POLICY AT THE OCC

The chartering policy of the OCC is the key to a viable dual banking system. Essentially the OCC's policy is to maintain a sound national banking system without placing undue restraints on new entry. The important relationship between banking and the monetary system precludes unlimited free entry. Although each new entrant to the market increases the competitive alternatives, the OCC believes it is not in the public interest to charter so many banks that none can grow to a size sufficient to offer a full range of needed services. In chartering banks the OCC admits only those qualified applicants that can be economically supported and profitably operated. Further, a new banking office will not be approved if its establishment threatens the viability of a newly chartered independent bank. Such protection of a newly chartered bank typically does not last more than one year.

Banking Factors

In evaluating a new bank application, the following factors are considered.

Income and Expenses. Projections of income and expenses of the proposed bank should be based on realistic, supportable estimates of deposit and loan volume.

Management.   Organizers, proposed directors, and officers should have reputations evidencing honesty and integrity. They should have successful employment and business histories, and should be responsible in financial affairs. A majority of the organizers and directors of a proposed independent bank should be from the community where the bank is to be located. Proposed officers should be able to demonstrate relevant experience and skills. Management, officers, and directors are subject to prior approval by the OCC. To encourage community support, wide distribution of stock is desirable. Maximum ownership, direct or indirect, by a single interest group is limited to 10 percent of the new capital stock. Subscribers are not expected to finance more than 50 percent of the issue price. Some of those restrictions will not apply if the new bank is to be legally affiliated with a bank holding company.

Capital.   Capital must be sufficient to support operations for at least three years. Capital should equal at least 10 percent of estimated deposits and 15 percent of estimated loans at the end of the third year. Capital should be adequate to enable the new bank to provide the necessary banking services, including loans of sufficient size to meet the needs of prospective customers. Capital should be sufficient to purchase, build, or lease a suitable permanent banking facility and equipment. Total fixed asset investment should not exceed 40 percent of initial capital. Capital should normally not be less than $1 million.

Market Factors

In evaluating a new bank application, the following factors will be considered:

Economic Condition and Growth Potential.   The current economic condition or the growth potential of the market in a new bank's proposed primary service area is important in determining the bank's probable success.

Market Share.   A determination of the portion of the avilable banking business a new bank could acquire and whether that business would be profitable is important.

Banking opportunity may be indicated in a number of ways, including trends of population, employment, residential and commercial construction, sales, company payrolls, and new businesses established. Geographic and environmental restrictions on further development should be fully explored. The growth and size of competing banks and other financial institutions are imporant indicators of a new bank's potential market.

An important change in the OCC's chartering policy has occurred recently; the OCC now offers rejected applicants the reasons their application was denied. That administrative change came about in response to critics who claimed a lack of "due process" by the agency.

IMPACT OF THE MCFADDEN ACT ON NATIONAL BANKS

The original purpose of the McFadden Act (44 Stat. 1223), enacted nearly 50 years ago was to grant authority to national banks to establish branch offices on a geographical basis equal to the state banks in their state of corporate residence. Thus as to geographic expansion a national bank is subject to the dictates of the statutes of the state in which its principal office is situated.

In the main the quality of banking services and the vitality of the system have benefited from the dual sources of charter state and national. The competitive interaction produced by the dual system has certainly been a force for innovation and improvement. By mandating the preeminence of state law, the McFadden Act has largely negated this beneficial effect in the important area of structure. The statute did not contemplate either the urbanization of certain markets or the structural efficiencies available through technology. Likewise, its authors did not foresee the entry and growth of other deposit institutions (credit unions, savings banks, and savings and loan associations) which have been free to expand their territory untouched by the constraining influence of the McFadden Act.

CUSTOMER ACCESS TO BANKING

The structural impact of the McFadden Act is not widely understood. State restrictions on branch banking have denied equal access to banking for many Americans. Some measure of these restrictions can be obtained from reviewing the 50 largest Standard Metropolitan Statistical Areas (SMSA), divided into three groups by type of branching. Approximately 16.4 million workers live in SMSAs where the most severe restrictions on branching exist. Of those, 5.4 million meet the Census Bureau's definition of commuters; that is, they cross a legal or municipal boundary of some sort in their trips to work. Thus, one worker in three of these restricted branching SMSAs is legally prohibited from banking in the same financial institution both where he works and where he lives.

The second group of SMSAs which allow limited area branching, typically into neighboring counties, house approximately 8.3 million workers of which 3.2 million fit the Census Bureau's definition of commuters. The remaining SMSAs, which have minimal prohibitions against wide-area branching contain 10.3 million workers, 2.5 million of whom are defined as commuters. This material is summarized in Exhibit 78–1. According to these figures, only one worker in four in those SMSAs is guaranteed the right to bank through one institution both where he works and where he lives. The McFadden Act may have reflected the socioeconomic pattern of the 1920s, but it places at a disadvantage the working American in the mid-1970s whose home to work trip was 9.4 miles every day (1973 estimate).

Extrapolation from these statistics reveals that almost half of all workers in the United States live in restricted or, at best, limited branching areas. In the 50 largest SMSAs, 48.4 percent of the commuting workers may choose a bank either where they live or where they work but cannot be served by the same institution in both locations. Even where branching is permitted statewide, interstate workers are at a disadvantage. In New York City, for example, recent figures show that approximately 318,000 workers daily cross a state line on their way to work. In the Washington D.C., market area, 336,000 workers cross a state or district line to get to work. There are, of course, other advantages of branching in addition to convenience to customers.

Many bankers have shown farsighted leadership in pushing for less restrictive branching laws, but others continue to support restrictive branching, fearing more competition. In their drive to protect themselves from competition of other banks, large and small, they are ignoring the expanding savings and loan industry and the even more rapidly expanding credit unions. Bankers who forget the growing powers of thrift institutions and the fact that they are not under the McFadden Act at the federal level may win the battle against other banks, only to lose the war against increasingly aggressive nonbank competitors.

Exhibit 78–1
Commuting Flows in the 50 Largest SMSAs* (1970 data)

		Resident Workers	Commuters	Percent Commuters
I.	Limited branching			
	a. Unit banking	8,351,565	2,390,708	28.6%
	b. Countywide branching	8,052,610	2,985,971	37.1
	Subtotal.	16,404,175	5,376,751	32.8
II.	Contiguous county branching.	8,259,632	3,229,394	39.1
III.	Statewide branching.	10,330,431	2,512,303	24.3
	Total	34,994,238	11,118,376	31.8

* Broken down by type of branching permitted.

In any event, the public has been the loser for some time, in terms of not having an optimum legal environment to encourage locational convenience for banking services.

RETAIL ELECTRONIC BANKING

The advent of sophisticated computers and electronic communications facilities has provided financial institutions with the potential for customer communication of account instructions through devices as simple as the telephone. Regulations adopted by the Federal Home Loan Bank Board, in 1974, permitted federally chartered savings and loan associations to establish such terminals at locations remote from existing main offices or branches. The National Credit Union Administration followed with similar regulatory authority for credit unions and a number of state authorities concluded that such devices were not branch banks and therefore could be established by banks without regard to locational and other restrictions under state branch banking statutes.

In December 1974, the Comptroller issued an interpretive ruling expressing the view that customer-bank communication terminals (CBCTs) were not branch banks and consequently could be established by national banks without reference to federal or state branch banking statutes. In October 1976, the Supreme Court refused to review several federal circuit court rulings which had disagreed with the Comptroller's interpretation. As a result, national banks desiring to establish electronic banking terminals are subject to the location and capital requirements imposed by state law on brick and mortar branches. Application of the McFadden Act to the developing electronic funds transfer environment significantly inhibits the ability of national banks to make that new technology available to the maximum number of retail banking customers.

Almost without exception, those studying the electronic transfer of funds issue have concluded that the terminals for public access must be excluded from the conventional legal definitions of branch banking. To place the development of these electronic systems under branching restrictions will certainly lessen the likelihood of such systems achieving their natural levels of operating efficiency.

OCC POSITION

The regulatory approach of the Office of the Comptroller of the Currency to bank market structure has been to encourage maximum competition among providers of financial services. In effect, the market should develop in a way which will offer the consumer the maximum number of choices. As representatives of the Department of Justice Antitrust Division have testified, CBCT development is uniquely suited to providing the consumer with such choices. Unlike brick and mortar branches, electronic terminals may be shared by numerous financial institutions, thereby multiplying the choices available to a consumer at any particular location. Moreover, available evidence suggests that electronic funds transfer facilitated by CBCTs may be more accurate and reliable and less subject to fraud than the transfers using a paper-based system. Subjecting such terminals to the branching restrictions of myriad state laws and to application procedures which invite dilatory protests is undesirable.

THE FUTURE

Change has been a dominant characteristic of commercial banking for the past 20 years. Such changes include new and more sophisticated financial services to handle the credit and cash management requirements of larger, more diverse and complex corporate organizations. New financial instruments of intermediation tapping new sources of funds and creating new responsibilities for sound liability management. Expansion into new markets and financial services through enlarged use of the holding company corporate structure, as well as expansion internationally around the globe with branches, wholly owned subsidiaries, and consortium investments. Greater call for foreign exchange services in a world increasingly interrelated economically and financially—an undertaking made more challenging by the shift away from fixed exchange rates. Increased use of the computer and other technology for internal management, as well as the external application to provide new and more convenient financial services. These are but a few (albeit very significant) manifestations of these currents of change.

The momentum of change seems unlikely to abate. The potential for new technologies to open the way for offering old services in new and more efficient ways will certainly be a continuing force. Another force maintaining (perhaps increasing) the momentum of change for banking will be the intensification of competition. New competitive challenges are already predictable from a variety of sources and it is reasonable to expect augmentation of these presures from wellheads not yet tapped. Among the presently identifiable ingredients for a more competitive marketplace for financial services are: new lending, investment, and deposit powers for savings banks, savings and loan associations, and credit unions; the possible evolution of nondeposit financial organizations into more banklike form; and the enlarging presence of foreign banks in our domestic markets tracking foreign marketing and investment expansion in the United States.

If it is assumed that the nation's public policy will continue to find that the maintenance of a stable and responsive banking system requires some type of governmental oversight, it is then essential that the instrumentalities of that oversight, the federal and state banking agencies, be continuously cognizant of and adaptable to this process of change.

The need for this capacity to comprehend and adapt to change has been harshly underlined by the failure of some larger banks— events not experienced since the Great Depression. It is not suggested that governmental oversight could have (or should have) prevented all of these failures, but there is basis for concluding that certain of the failures might have been avoided by the contribution of more modern supervisory practice. That process of change is now under way. Both the rationale and the operative details of this change are important and valid subjects for public debate. For that debate to produce results in terms of a banking and financial system that broadly and efficiently serves the needs of the American public, it is essential that bankers and banking experts contribute importantly to this debate.

While the OCC's engagement in early 1974 of a national accounting and management consulting firm (Haskins and Sells) to conduct a full-scale evaluation of that agency's objectives and operations may be the most overt reflection of a commitment to modernization, the fact is that both the FDIC and the Federal Reserve System have also been actively involved in a number of important efforts at self-evaluation and institutional modernization. Greater coordination and communication among the three banking agencies assures that proven reforms and modifications will be installed by all of the agencies.

In the past, governmental regulation and supervision of banking have tended to give its major emphasis to the regulatory component; namely, monitoring compliance with a code of law and regulation applied uniformly across all units in the regulated industry. This approach may have been appropriate in the simpler world of the past when there was less diversity, both of size and activity, within the banking community and when transactional activities for all units moved at a much slower pace. So long as banking is a "regulated industry," there may always be a need for the uniform application of some fundamental code of sound and ethical behavior. However, because of the variety, complexity, and sheer velocity of activities present in modern banking, it is unlikely that effective governmental oversight can be accomplished through principal reliance on the regulatory mode. Rather the emphasis must be on supervision, utilizing sophisticated methods of examination and financial analysis—and where indicated and necessary such flexible tools of enforcement as cease and desist orders.

The changes in the OCC are aimed, in the main, at updating and increasing the professional stature of the supervisory function. The objectives, as well as the methodology, of the periodic, on-site examination have undergone a total revision. Today's examination utilizes procedures designed to comprehend the modern bank as a process, giving particular emphasis to the formulation and execution of credit and investment policies, to the adequacy of internal and external control systems (including systems for periodic loan review), to earnings performance, and to the sufficiency of reserves for loan losses. Traditional methods, which devoted a preponderance of time and resources to detailed loan portfolio evaluation, demonstrate a declining effectiveness to identify weaknesses or gaps in operations at a sufficiently early stage to permit the prevention of serious problems.

All three federal agencies—the OCC with the National Bank Surveillance System (NBSS)—are seeking to develop computer-based early warning systems. The NBSS represents an ambitious effort at systematized financial analysis, using quarterly reports of condition and income as its primary data source. To date this system shows great promise. In addition to flagging deteriorating trends in specific areas, it produces excellent current analysis for use in customizing the on-site examination to the indicated weaknesses of a particular bank.

The changes that are occurring in OCC are fundamental and far-reaching. The "state of the art" of bank regulation and supervision is being advanced. The new systems and analytical techniques being used will demand new levels of professionalism for supervisory personnel. To achieve that goal, the OCC has adopted modern management practices to create a Division of Human Resources charged with the integrated responsibility for recruiting, continuously training, objectively promoting, and fairly compensating that indispensable resource of effective bank supervision—the professional bank examiner.

CONCLUSION

At the foundation of a healthy, growing U.S. economy there must be a sound, yet adaptive and innovative, private banking system. Because that banking system meets the economy's credit and investment needs from individual and corporate deposits, that system will probably always have to be the subject of some mode of governmental oversight. Such oversight is, of course, primarily concerned with assuring the continued soundness of the banking system. But the achievement of soundness must not needlessly inhibit innovation and managed risk taking in banking, which are absolutely essential to sustained economic vitality. To strike that delicate balance, government oversight must move away from rote regulation to modern, professional supervision. The day may yet come when we will with more comprehensive financial disclosure be willing to place primary reliance in the discipline of the market; but that will be the next round in advancing the "state of the art."

Chapter 79

Regulations on Bank Soundness, Competition, and Structure—State Banking Departments

Lawrence E. Kreider*

PURPOSE AND GOALS OF STATE BANKING DEPARTMENTS

Each State has a state banking department headed by a state bank commissioner or official of comparable title. State banking departments are the primary chartering, examining, and regulatory bodies for state-chartered commercial plus mutual savings banks.

Traditionally, the primary goal of state banking departments has been to assure soundness of state-chartered banks through authorized chartering, examination, and regulatory functions. State banking departments generally believe that the strength and soundness of banks are of singular socioeconomic importance to respective trade areas: if a bank fails it has much greater impact on a community than if a filling station fails.

In like manner, the Office of the Comptroller of the Currency has worked to assure the soundness of national banks. The Office of the Comptroller of the Currency and state banking departments generally have been successful in the past half century in their respective efforts. There were two exceptions to this good record—the early 1930s and mid-1970s. Both periods were in the aftermath of abnormal financial disruptions and other dislocations largely beyond the control of state banking departments and the Office of the Comptroller.

Although strong state-chartered banks capable of sustained service

* Executive Vice President, Conference of State Bank Supervisors, Washington, D.C.

to respective trade areas remain a primary goal of state banking departments, other goals have increased in importance. Competition between financial institutions, competitive equality between state and national banks, competitive equality between banks and other financial institutions, quality of financial services to individual bank customers and the cost of delivering financial services to consumers, business, and government have added new dimensions to the goals and roles of some state banking departments.

GOALS OF STATE BANK COMMISSIONERS AS A UNITED BODY

Although the primary goal of each state banking department is directed toward each respective state, state bank commissioners nationwide are organized into a Conference of State Bank Supervisors (CSBS).

CSBS has two primary goals. The first is to achieve and maintain strong and effective state banking departments nationwide. This goal is pursued by CSBS through formal educational and other support programs designed to train examiners, develop banking department management skills, achieve appropriate state statutes, obtain adequate departmental budgets, and assure acceptable working relationships with other state and federal officials.

The second major goal of CSBS is to achieve and maintain a banking and bank regulatory structure which has adequate state/federal checks and balances—a system which minimizes government monopoly in bank regulation. This goal is pursued through the companion goal of strong and effective state banking departments and through various state and federal legislative efforts.

CSBS and individual state banking departments also share certain goals with one or more federal regulatory agencies. These include effective working relationships with other state and federal groups; a banking and bank regulatory structure which will permit and encourage banks to serve most effectively each respective trade area; and a structure which protects against adverse consequences of monopolistic government control by a state or federal regulator.

Within the CSBS structure, state banking departments and state-chartered banks join ranks to pursue those goals which the two hold in common. Both groups want strong state banking departments and both want a dual system of state/federal checks and balances free of regulatory monopoly. These two goals are in the public interest , and the joint effort of the two groups in pursuit of these goals can be more successful than either or both working separately.

COMPOSITION OF STATE SYSTEM

The state bank regulatory system includes 53 banking departments—50 states plus Guam, Puerto Rico, and the Virgin Islands.

Banking department heads in 48 states are appointed by respective governors; in Colorado the head serves under a State Civil Service statute and in Florida plus each of the three territories banking heads are elected officials.

The lengths of commissioners' terms varies. The majority serve at the will of each respective governor. Although the average length of tenure of state bank commissioners is considered by some to be too short for optimum effectiveness, positions generally have become more professional in nature with continuance from one administration to another more frequently accepted by incoming governors. Increasingly it is recognized as good practical politics to retain qualified commissioners from one administration to another, even when the incoming governor is of a different political party than his or her predecessor. This has had a positive effect on the stability and capability of state banking departments. As of December 1, 1976, the average tenure of state bank commissioners was twice as long as that of federal bank regulatory appointees.

In addition to 53 state bank commissioners, there are approximately 2,000 professional state bank examiners and support personnel. Like comissioners, examiners and support personnel have become increasingly well qualified through training programs and experience. In the past decade, state banking departments have increased significantly their abilities to take their rightful places in the bank regulatory structure of the nation.

PLACE IN REGULATORY STRUCTURE

State banking departments collectively are one of several state and federal government groups which regulate banks in one way or another. State banking departments, however, are the primary chartering and regulatory authorities for state-chartered commercial and mutual savings banks.

Unlike national banks, most state-chartered banks are still subjected to a largely duplicatory chartering, examination and regulatory oversight be it either the Federal Deposit Insurance Corporation or Federal Reserve System (Fed). In one way or another, the FDIC still examines and regulates most of the approximately 8,500 state-chartered, nonmember commercial banks and some 500 mutual savings banks; and in various ways the Federal Reserve System examines and regulates most of the approximately 1,000 state-chartered member banks.

Notwithstanding this traditional pattern of duplicatory oversight of state-chartered banks, changes are evolving. In several states, unnecessary duplication has been reduced by diverse forms of sharing of responsibilities between state banking departments and the FDIC and/

or Fed. In three states, the FDIC withdrew from the examination of significant proportions of state-chartered banks for a period of several years. Quality of examination and supervision was maintained. A comparable formal program was successfully carried out between one state banking department and the Fed.

As the few remaining state banking departments become fully capable of discharging chartering, examination, and regulatory responsibilities on a parity with federal counterparts, state banking departments likely will have an opportunity to assume these responsibilities on a parity with the Office of the Comptroller of the Currency. The trend is slowly in the direction of state responsibilities consistent with capabilities. As is normal under such circumstances, however, there is a long time lag between the ability of state banking departments to assume full responsibilities and the withdrawal of federal regulators from unnecessary duplicatory oversight.

STATE LEADERSHIP IN NEW TECHNIQUES AND PROCEDURES

As state banking departments have become more capable, they have exercised more leadership in regulatory matters.

Beyond individual capabilities of job performance, the nationwide system of decentralized state banking departments inherently fosters sound experimentation. States have diverse economic environments and banking department structures. These encourage diverse types of experiments. State bank commissioners have diverse backgrounds. This infuses a flow of new concepts into the system. And individual states, being relatively small and representing only a fraction of the whole, can experiment in a more manageable fashion and with a minimum of risk if experiments fail.

The decentralized state system has yielded several successful experiments in recent years. About a decade ago, the California Banking Department initiated what is called "top down" examination. The primary focal point of this experiment—which was adopted as policy—was an evaluation of bank management, policies, and procedures prior to detailed examination of individual credits. As a consequence of the success of this experiment, the concept and techniques have been a part of the curriculum of the CSBS School for Senior Personnel for several years, and other state banking departments now place increased emphasis on each bank's management, policies, and procedures while continuing to examine adequately the individual asset and liability items. More recently, the Office of the Comptroller of the Currency announced that a comparable approach would be followed in the examination of national banks.

Other state experiments have included the selective "mini-exam" technique by the Indiana Department of Financial Institutions. Through controlled experimentation and change, the mini-exam has evolved as a selective tool which saves time and money yet maintains basic goals of the examination exercise.

State banking departments have also been leaders in early warning statistical techniques. The Illinois Banking Department was among the first in the nation to experiment with a statistical reporting early warning system. With improvements based on experience, the system continued in use.

Finally, much of the early off-premises electronic funds transfer (EFT) experimentation was at the state level, and was made possible by early EFT legislation by states.

INHERENT STRENGTHS OF STATE BANKING DEPARTMENTS

State banking departments have certain inherent strengths:

1. Their offices generally are closer geographically to communities and bank trade areas. They are in a good position to know each local environment, its economic problems, and its financial needs.
2. By virtue of relative proximity to the people of each community, the state regulatory system is inherently more responsive to the thinking of the citizens of each bank's trade area. State banking departments reflect more accurately the will of the public of each trade area and state with less formal procedures. Reflecting relative proximity to those served by banks, state banking commissioners can accurately evaluate consumer, business, and state or local government needs.
3. Reflecting the decentralized, less bureaucratic state structure, state banking departments have a higher proportion of their personnel in line functions.
4. On national as well as state and local issues the state banking and bank regulatory system has an inherent quality of thoughtful deliberation reflecting the consolidated views of a relatively large number of people. As a consequence, the collective judgments of the state system tend to be relatively free of major mistakes.
5. The state system, reflecting the proximity of banking departments to the public, has an inherent financial discipline. Although it is widely believed that some state banking departments are inadequately financed, the state regulatory system nationwide produces good service per dollar spent.
6. The state system can act with relative speed, responsiveness, and flexibility on matters affecting each community.

INHERENT WEAKNESSES OF STATE SYSTEM

Although the state banking department regulatory system has inherent strengths reflecting its decentralized and flexible structure, it has certain tendencies for weakness reflecting somewhat those same structural characteristics.

The decentralized state system has to work harder to coordinate a nationwide effort, whether it be in educational or banking structure matters. When a course of action appears appropriate, for example, it is inherently more difficult to coordinate 53 states plus independent territories than it is for one person to issue an order directing all within a system to pursue a given course of action. Further, a centralized authority can publicize a policy decision and course of action with more force of authority than can a decentralized system, in part because a minority from within a decentralized system may not agree with the consensus decision and may be disposed publicly to say so.

STATE AND NATIONAL SYSTEMS COMPLEMENT ONE ANOTHER

The dual banking system is most frequently praised for its reinforcement of state/federal checks and balances; and the system merits praise on this score. It is important to protect against monopoly power in bank regulation. But quite aside from this somewhat competitive quality, the two systems are highly complementary in many ways. Each spawns good, diverse ideas which are then frequently adopted by the other and each can motivate or implement some things better than the other.

As one example of this complementary quality of innovation and implementation, the earliest ideas, experimentation and workable statutes on off-premises EFT facilities came from states. States were inherently in a better position to perform those early experimental roles. Then, in a complementary fashion, the national bank regulatory system, reflecting its centralized structure, was inherently better postured to provide a stimulant which motivated study, further experimentation and a movement toward workable state and federal statutes. There are those would argue that the national stimulant was overly dramatic and imperfect in its approach, but it has been argued that in net it was mutually complementary with the state system. The national system did that which the states could not have done as expeditiously and vice versa.

Reflecting complementary factors and careful planning, primary regulators of state and national banks now enjoy a better working relationship than considered feasible a decade ago.

EVOLVING PATTERNS OF STATE BANKING DEPARTMENTS

The ability of the state banking department regulatory system to assure safety and soundness, protect the public interest, contribute to competition, and help mold the banking structure is being enhanced by several favorable patterns of events.

First, individual state banking departments have increased significantly their capabilities in the past decade. At least ten fall in this category. States have increased the number of banking department personnel, raised levels of training, reduced salary disparities vis-à-vis federal counterparts, selected commissioners of a more professional stature, assumed stronger positions as individual departments in national affairs, and achieved a more effective voice collectively through CSBS in national affairs.

Some deficiencies, however, are being corrected only slowly. A limited numer of state banking departments have not taken full advantage of educational efforts, even though education nationwide has increased sharply. Some must labor under inadequate statutes, even though a great amount of recodification nationwide has taken place in the past decade. A few still have frustrating political problems within their states, even though banking department policies nearly always, if not always, are consistent with policies of respective state administrations. Several states are handicapped by bank examiner pay scales below federal counterparts, even though in the past decade disparities generally have narrowed. And a few departments have concerns about handling trouble banks, even though state banking departments have had a record of bank closures at least as good as their federal counterparts in the past decade.

Notwithstanding only partial solutions to some problems, the overall pattern of state banking departments is one of an increasingly responsible role and more nearly one of parity with that of the primary regulator of national banks. In most states, banking departments are well qualified to charter, examine, and regulate banks.

Chapter 80 _____

Regulations on Competition and Structure—Federal Reserve System

*Philip E. Coldwell**

As the nation's central bank, the Federal Reserve System's primary mission is to formulate and conduct monetary policy. In addition, the Federal Reserve shares responsibility for supervision and regulation of the banking system. An important part of the regulatory process is concerned with the preservation of a competitive banking system. This chapter describes the concerns which led to adoption of banking structure legislation and the activities of the Federal Reserve System in implementing these laws.

BANK STRUCTURE LEGISLATION

The Federal Reserve's responsibilities for the regulation of bank structure are grounded upon three apparent congressional concerns. First, Congress has indicated its desire to preserve a competitive banking system within the constraint of maintaining the safety and soundness of financial institutions. A high degree of competition provides businesses and consumers with a full range of banking services at a reasonable cost. Competition encourages individual banks to produce banking services by the lowest cost method of production and creates incentives for the development of new and better banking services. However, unconstrained competition in banking would require free

---

* Member, Board of Governors, Federal Reserve System, Washington, D.C.

entry and exit from the industry. In order to minimize exit by failure, the degree of competition is restricted. For example, controls over entry into the industry are used to limit the number of firms in a given market so that overbanking does not weaken banks and lead to bank failures.

Second, regulation of the structure of the banking industry is designed to prevent an undue concentration of financial, economic, and political power. An excessive degree of concentration of the banking industry would give the banks oligopoly pricing powers, power over the allocation of credit, and excessive political power. The fear of an excessive concentration of financial power has had a long tradition in the United States. In large measure, the current structure of the American banking system reflects past decisions designed to prevent the accumulation of economic and political power by the banks. The battles over the First and Second Banks of the United States and the free banking era of the mid-1800s were expressions of the fear of concentrated economic power.

A third congressional concern, closely related to the first two, is the desire to maintain a separation between commercial banking and other lines of commerce. This desire was reflected in the Banking Act of 1933 which prohibited commercial banks from engaging in securities underwriting (except for certain governmental securities). The separation of commercial banking from other lines of commerce was intended both to prevent an undue concentration of economic power and to avoid situations in which the nonbanking activities of the institution would threaten the solvency of the bank or create conflicts of interest.

The three congressional concerns with the structure of the banking system are reflected in the legislation under which the Federal Reserve and the other banking agencies exercise their powers. The two major statutes under which the Federal Reserve makes structural decisions are the Bank Merger Act of 1960 (as amended) and the Bank Holding Company Act of 1956 (as amended). The following sections describe the responsibilities, policies, and procedures of the Federal Reserve System in implementing these laws.

BANK MERGERS

The merger of two or more banks requires the prior approval of one of the federal banking agencies. The Federal Reserve System has the responsibility for acting on the merger application if the bank resulting from the merger is to be a state member bank. If the resulting bank is to be a national bank, the Comptroller of the Currency has the responsibility, and if the resulting bank is to be an insured state nonmember bank, the Federal Deposit Insurance Corporation is the decision-making agency. In all cases, the responsible agency has a statutory obligation to seek reports on the competitive implications of the proposed merger from the other two agencies and from the Department of Justice. Since state member banks are a small proportion of the total banking industry, the Federal Reserve's decision-making role in mergers is somewhat limited, though it does provide the competitive factor advice to other agencies.

The Bank Merger Act of 1960 prohibits any merger which would create a monopoly or further any attempt or conspiracy to create a monopoly. While most proposed mergers would not create a monopoly, many involve some reduction of competition. In cases in which the proposed merger would substantially lessen competition or tend to create a monopoly, the banking agencies are prohibited from approving the merger unless there is a finding that the anticompetitive effects of the merger would be clearly outweighed by the positive effects of the merger on the public's needs and convenience. The statute requires the agencies to examine the present and future managerial and financial prospects of the banks to determine if the banking factors are consistent with approval of the merger.

Even if the banking agency determines that the merger would not substantially lessen competition or that the positive banking factors outweigh the negative competitive effects, the merger can be blocked by the Department of Justice pending a court determination of whether or not the merger would constitute a violation of the Sherman or Clayton Antitrust laws.

The procedure used by the Board in assessing the competitive impact of a proposed merger begins with the definition of the market or markets within which the applicant banks operate. Reflecting concern for those bank customers whose banking options are restricted geographically, the local banking market is the market considered. This market may be approximated by a Standard Metropolitan Statistical Area (SMSA), a county, or some other local market definition.

For a horizontal merger between two banks operating in the same market, the market share of each bank and the ranking of each bank in the market are calculated. The impact of the proposed merger on the concentration ratio for the market and the market rank of the surviving bank are then determined. There are no fixed rules relative to the maximum market shares which would be inconsistent with approval of the application. However, the Federal Reserve is constantly mindful of the possibilities of excessive concentration in such applications.

Cases in which merging banks operate in different banking markets within a state normally involve no elimination of existing competition.

However, the merger may result in the elimination of possible future competition, especially if state law permits the acquiring bank to branch de novo into the acquired bank's market or the acquiring bank could establish a de novo bank holding company subsidiary bank in the market.

The Board has examined with great care the competitive impact of emergency mergers of failing banks, and has attempted to minimize any adverse competitive effects resulting from the takeover of a failing bank. However, when a large bank is failing it is sometimes difficult to find a merger partner large enough to absorb the failing bank without resulting in some undesirable increase in market concentration or a substantial diminution of competition.

BANK HOLDING COMPANY ACQUISITIONS OF BANKS

In contrast to the divided regulatory authority over bank mergers, the Bank Holding Company Act of 1956 charged the Federal Reserve System with the regulation of bank holding companies. According to the legislation, a bank holding company is defined as a company owning (or otherwise controlling) 25 percent or more of any class of voting stock of a bank. The original holding company law and the major amendments in 1970 give the Federal Reserve power to regulate the formation of bank holding companies, the acquisition of banks by bank holding companies, and the activities of nonbank subsidiaries of bank holding companies.

The basic statutory criteria for the acquisition of a bank by a bank holding company and the analytical procedures used to evaluate the application are the same as those applied to bank merger applications. The Board analyzes the degree of anticompetitive impact against the public benefits expected to follow from approval of the acquisition.

Early in the establishment of bank holding company regulation, the Board determined that it would seek to foster increased competition. The Federal Reserve did not establish any percentage limitations on the market shares of individual banking organizations, but in each case looked at local and statewide concentration as well as examining the effects of its actions on the needs and convenience of the public.

In general, the Board has been willing to approve acquisitions in markets in which the holding company was not already represented. However, the Board has looked with some disfavor upon the acquisition of the largest banks in a major market by large bank holding companies headquartered elsewhere if these acquisitions would tend to diminish competition in the state, to raise the level of concentration to an excessive degree, or to eliminate an independent bank which could otherwise form a competing holding company. The Board has also been careful in approving acquisitions for large bank holding companies when the bank to be acquired could be the vehicle for market entrance by a small bank holding company especially in states dominated by a few large banking organizations.

The Board has established policies to permit expansion of bank holding companies, but to prevent any holding company from being dominant in a given state or market if the dominance was based on new bank acquisitions. Moreover, the Board has generally looked with favor on the establishment of de novo offices, especially in markets in which the lead bank was not represented or in peripheral areas of the same market if the lead bank is a wholesale bank and the de novo bank is a suburban retail bank.

The Board has been mindful that a decline of independent organizations in a state would tend to concentrate power and has gone out of its way to limit the wholesale takeover of those independent banks which can provide meaningful competition for the bank holding company affiliates. In this regard, the Board has denied some significant acquisitions of banks located in the same market as the lead bank of the holding company, and has denied acquisitions when the independent bank could provide the best competitive framework within a particular banking market. Naturally, the Board's policies have not met with the total favor of either the independent banks or the holding companies. The independents have claimed that the Board's policy is threatening the dual banking system and reducing the ability of independent banks to compete in various markets. The holding companies have viewed Board policy as limiting their ability to expand. The Federal Reserve believes that its policies have been procompetitive, have been reasonably balanced between the positions of the independents and the holding companies, and most importantly, have been guided by the public interest.

Another dimension of the Board's policy concerning holding company acquisitions has been its insistence that some degree of strength be imparted by the holding company to its banking subsidiaries. In a number of instances, this policy has caused the Board to deny acquisitions because the burdensome debt position of the holding company would require excessive dividends or upstream payments to service the debt. In situations where the holding company is already overextended, new acquisitions have been denied because the strength of the entire organization must come from the subsidiary banks to the holding company rather than any contribution of the holding company to the banks.

Similarly, the Board has denied acquisitions where the lead bank or a significant unit within the organization has been in financial difficulty or under particular financial stress at the time of the proposed acquisition. The well-publicized "go-slow" policy that the Board adopted in 1974 reflected its concern that the health of the basic financial organization should come first and that expansion of the bank holding company should not be permitted to divert the management or financial resources of the holding company away from correcting existing problems.

The Board has been particularly mindful of situations where a bank holding company or a major bank under financial stress has sought to merge with other financial organizations under emergency conditions. In these situations, the Board has looked with great care at the competitive impact of the emergency acquisitions or mergers with a view toward limiting any anticompetitive impact wherever possible. In furtherance of this attitude, the Board has asked Congress to permit interstate acquisitions of holding companies or major banking units where competitive situations within the state are such that a strong anticompetitive flavor would develop from a within-the-state takeover. While the Board has been accused of attempting to foster an interstate banking system which would permit holding companies or commercial banks to operate nationwide, this has certainly not been the basic thrust nor predetermined policy of the Board. Instead, the Board's very limited request, and one which it would apply in very few instances, has been aimed more at maintaining competition within a state and within a particular banking market.

Another concern of the Federal Reserve has been the development of commonly owned chains of one bank holding companies. Since early 1976, it has been the policy of the Board regarding new acquisitions or formations to treat such chains of one bank holding companies as if they were multibank holding companies. If a single one bank holding company in a chain is in difficulty this will reflect unfavorably upon the creation of a new one bank holding company by the same principals. The substitution of a chain of one bank holding companies for a single multibank holding company has the same potential anticompetitive effect found in the acquisition of single banks by the multibank companies. Similarly, the Board has become concerned about the basically unrestrained acquisition of banks and their subsequent formation into one bank holding companies by individuals who already own banks in the same banking market. The establishment of a series of one bank holding companies owned by the same people could dominate a particular banking market.

In summary, the Federal Reserve System has attempted to regulate the growth of bank holding companies in a flexible manner designed to increase the resources available to subsidiary banks, promote competition and prevent the elimination of strong independent banks, and prevent the excessive concentration of economic resources. Given the recent declines in concentration ratios in the majority of banking markets, the Board believes that its policies are achieving the objectives.

HOLDING COMPANY NONBANKING ACTIVITIES

As discussed earlier, Congress for many years has favored a separation of banking and commerce. This policy was reaffirmed when Congress enacted the Banking Holding Company Act which, among other things, prevents holding companies, with certain exceptions, from engaging in nonbanking activities. However, Congress has recognized that a complete prohibition of bank holding company involvement in nonbanking activities probably would not be in the public interest. Over the years, many banking organizations had acquired considerable skill in various bank-related areas, and permitting bank holding companies to enter certain of these activities would not only be procompetitive, but would improve the quality of services provided to the public. Moreover, it seemed illogical to prevent bank holding companies from engaging in some of the nonbank activities which their banks were allowed to conduct.

The most significant exception to the general prohibition on nonbank activities is contained in Section 4(c)(8) of the act, which allows holding companies to undertake those activities that are "so closely related to banking or managing or controlling banks as to be a proper incident thereto."

As of the beginning of 1977, the Board of Governors had designated by regulation the following 12 nonbanking activities to be permissible activities for bank holding companies, subject to certain qualifications:

1. Making or acquiring, for its own account or the account of others, loans and other extensions of credit, such as would be made by a mortgage, finance, credit card, or factoring company.
2. Operating as an industrial bank, a Morris Plan bank, or an industrial loan company.
3. Servicing loans and other extensions of credit.
4. Performing trust activities.
5. Acting as an investment or financial adviser.
6. Leasing real and personal property.
7. Making equity and debt investments in corporations or projects designed primarily to promote community welfare.
8. Providing bookkeeping and data-processing services.
9. Acting as an insurance agent or broker.
10. Acting as an underwriter for credit life insurance and credit accident and health insurance directly related to extensions of credit by the bank holding company system.

11. Providing courier services.
12. Providing management consulting advice to nonaffiliated banks.

Before a bank holding company can acquire more than 5 percent of the shares of a company engaging in a permissible nonbanking activity, it must obtain the approval of the Board of Governors. In making its decisions on individual applications, the Board is required by the statute to analyze the competitive effects of the proposal, as well as a number of other public interest considerations. Moreover, the Board is instructed to approve only those applications that would appear to result in net public benefits.

In evaluating the competitive impact of a proposed acquisition of a nonbank company, the Board determines in which product and geographic markets the nonbank company operates, and to what extent, if any, the proposed acquisition would eliminate any existing competition. Moreover, the Board assesses the effect of the acquisition on future competition. Finally, the Board is required to evaluate the impact of the proposal on the financial condition of the holding company and its banks, and whether the acquisition would result in efficiencies, greater convenience to the public, conflicts of interest, or an undue concentration of resources. As a matter of policy, the Board has given significant weight to the competitive effects of proposed nonbank acquisitions, and has typically denied those involving significant adverse effects. The Board typically has shown a preference for holding companies to enter nonbanking activities de novo.

As a result of the rapid movement of bank holding companies into nonbanking activities, particularly during the early 1970s, holding companies are now an important factor in such industries as mortgage banking, consumer finance, factoring, and leasing. However, because of the size of holding company banks, the total assets of nonbank affiliates are still less than 5 percent of consolidated total assets of bank holding companies.

In allowing bank holding companies to enter bank-related activities, the Board has been mindful of the need to protect bank affiliates from possible abuse in transactions with nonbank affiliates. Indeed, in the last several years, the sale of low-quality assets by several real estate-oriented nonbank affiliates to bank affiliates of the holding company did significant damage to these banks. In carrying out the objective of protecting banks from abuse, the Board has recently set up a reporting system for monitoring transactions between bank affiliates and the rest of the holding company organization. In addition, the Federal Reserve reviews such transactions during periodic examinations of state member banks, the holding company parent, and various nonbank affiliates of the holding company.

BRANCH BANKING

In addition to its major tasks under the Bank Merger Act and the Bank Holding Company Act, the Federal Reserve System has other responsibilities which directly or indirectly affect the structure of the banking system.

The oldest structural power of the Federal Reserve is the right to approve or deny branch offices of state member banks. This power derives from the Federal Reserve Act and is constrained by the branching limitations imposed by the McFadden Act of 1927 and the Banking Act of 1933.

Branch applications, most of which are considered by the Reserve Banks under delegated authority, are judged on the basis of the adequacy of the bank's capital and management, the convenience and needs of the community, the competitive situation, the prospects for profitable operation of the new branch, and the reasonableness of the bank's investment in bank premises.

The development of Electronic Funds Transfer System (EFTS) adds a new dimension to the regulation of branching. To the extent that customer-bank communication terminals (CBCTs) can perform many routine banking functions, banks in some of the branching states may find a reduced need for traditional bricks and mortar branches. In the unit banking states, the CBCT might limit the development of traditional branches if branching restrictions were eased.

MAXIMUM RATES ON DEPOSITS

The maximum rates that may be paid by member banks on time and savings deposits are set by the Board of Governors under provisions of Regulation Q. In addition, the Federal Deposit Insurance Corporation has similar authority to set ceiling rates on deposits of nonmember commercial banks and mutual savings banks, while the Federal Home Loan Bank Board sets such rates for insured savings and loan associations. Any change in rate ceilings is made only after consultation among these three regulatory authorities.

In recent years, the board has moved steadily away from a firm ceiling on all types of time and savings accounts. In particular, in the early 1970s the board suspended the maximum rate on time deposits in denominations of $100,000 or more, and it has raised ceiling rates on certain longer term time deposits in denominations of less than $100,000. However, in response to concerns of the housing industry, the board has not made frequent alterations of the maximum rate on savings accounts.

At present, thrift institutions are allowed to pay slightly higher maximum rates on certain types of deposits than commercial banks. Moreover, Congress has mandated that any future change in the present differential must be approved by Congress. Under certain circumstances, these rate differentials may give thrift institutions a competitive advantage over commercial banks in attracting deposits. Over time, this advantage could result in thrift institutions capturing a larger share, and commercial banks a smaller share, of the time and savings deposit market than would have occurred if there were no rate ceiling differentials.

It is widely recognized that the present system for setting maximum rates has certain undesirable features. First, ceiling rates and the existence of differentials among institutions tend to dampen competition between different types of financial institutions. Second, ceiling rates tend to encourage disintermediation during periods of rising and relatively high-interest rates. This disintermediation has had particularly harsh effects on thrift institutions and ultimately on the housing market. Third, rate ceilings have an adverse impact on savers, who often receive lower rates of interest on their deposits than would be the case if ceilings were not in effect.

The Board of Governors is generally interested in reducing the constraints of Regulation Q on banks, and as a general proposition favors the gradual elimination of Regulation Q. However, the successful elimination of Regulation Q seems closely tied to easing existing restrictions on the types of assets and liabilities of thrift institutions so that these organizations can obtain a better balance between the maturity structure of their assets and liabilities.

MONETARY POLICY EFFECTS

Indirectly the Federal Reserve is also involved in competitive effects through its primary field of monetary policy formulation. As the Open Market Committee desk seeks to fulfill the directive of the committee and move toward either increasing or reducing the availability of credit in the nation, there is an obvious tie to the degree of competition which is evident both in the handling of open-market purchases and in the handling of credit between elements of the banking system. The Federal Reserve makes no effort to insure that credit is channeled into a particular part of the banking industry but instead has adopted policies which have permitted the movement of funds in a much broader sense between all elements. For example, the Federal Reserve has permitted the creation of a federal funds market which enables the sale or purchase of excess reserves from one bank to another. Similarly it has permitted and indeed encouraged a more rapid movement of funds in the payments mechanism both by improving its handling of checks being processed or sorted at the Reserve Banks and by encouraging the development of an electronic funds transfer system. These actions have encouraged the more intensive use of funds and in effect have improved the competition for such funds among the financial institutions of the United States.

The Federal Reserve defends the competitive marketplace by making no attempt to allocate credit in its handling of open-market transactions. It has taken steps to ensure that competition can work among the banking units so that the funds available can be channeled in and out of the banking system in the most effective manner. The mere fact that the Federal Reserve in its handling of monetary policy has not chosen to adopt regulations or patterns of action which direct the allocation of credit is in itself strong competitive support. In contrast other central banks quite often direct credit to particular types of industries or services according to the social priorities of their nation. It has been the position of the Federal Reserve that such credit allocation can best be handled by the open market in a free enterprise system rather than a directed form of credit allocation with the central bank or other units of government directing the credit flows according to their particular determination of priority.

CONCLUSION

The responsibilities of the Federal Reserve System for bank structure continue to be an important part of the Board's work. These responsibilities continue to grow and evolve over time as the nature of the banking industry changes. However, the Board's basic objectives remain constant—to preserve and strengthen a sound and competitive banking system.

Chapter 81

The FDIC, Deposit Insurance, and Systemwide Risk

*Frank Wille**

The Federal Deposit Insurance Company was the last of the three federal banking agencies to be established. Created by the Banking Act of 1933, after a traumatic decade when thousands of banks failed, the FDIC has one overriding mission: to protect the banking *system* against a loss of public confidence. It accomplishes this mission through a deposit insurance program in which 98 percent of the nation's commercial banks and 69 percent of its mutual savings banks participate,[1] through its regulation and oversight of some 9,000 state-chartered insured banks which do not belong to the Federal Reserve System and through its participation with other bank supervisory agencies in cooperative efforts to promote safe and sound banking practices which are at the same time responsive to changing perceptions of public need.

JURISDICTION CHANGES SINCE THE MID-60s

The ten years since 1966 have brought dramatic changes in the breadth and relative importance of FDIC jurisdiction. The *number*

---

* Cadwalader, Wickersham and Taft, Attorneys, New York, N.Y. and Washington, D.C. (Formerly, Chairman, Federal Deposit Insurance Corporation, Washington, D.C.)

[1] Uninsured trust companies which do not accept deposits from the general public comprised 79 of the nation's 286 uninsured commercial banks as of December 31, 1976. Many of the other uninsured banks and trust companies cater only to specialized groups of depositors. All of the nation's 144 federally uninsured mutual savings banks were located in Massachusetts on that date and participated in a separate deposit insurance program maintained by that state.

of insured nonmember commercial banks over which FDIC has direct supervisory responsibility increased by 1,258 (from just under 55 percent of the nation's insured commercial banks to just under 60 percent), the *total assets of insured nonmember banks* increased by almost $235 billion (from about 26 percent of the total assets of all insured banks to well over 34 percent of such total), and the *number of full-service banking offices operated by insured nonmember banks* increased by approximately 8,800 (from roughly 39 percent of the total number of offices of all insured banks to about 43 percent of the total). Moreover, an increasing percentage of the nation's larger commercial banks are today within the state nonmember category. Thus, at year-end 1966, FDIC had general supervisory authority over only 40 of the 415 insured commercial banks in the country with domestic deposits of more than $100 million, the largest nonmember commercial bank then being about $715 million in deposit size. At year-end 1976, the FDIC was supervising 268 of the 985 insured commercial banks in the country with more than $100 million in domestic deposits, the largest nonmember commercial bank then being $2 billion in deposit size.[2] In addition, FDIC at year-end 1976 had exclusive federal jurisdiction over some 170 mutual savings banks in the same size category, the largest of which had $4.3 billion in deposits. This contrasts with 105 such mutual savings banks at year-end 1966, the largest of which had $2.4 billion in deposits. Finally, in its liquidation and receivership activities over the past ten years, FDIC has had to cope with almost twice as many bank failures as there were in the ten years prior to January 1, 1967. Not only were there more bank failures, on the average, during the most recent ten years, the average size of the banks that failed also increased dramatically, with the eight largest bank failures in FDIC history all taking place between October 1973 and year-end 1976. At the present time, FDIC is responsible for about 80 open liquidations, in which it is seeking to collect thousands of loans and other assets with an aggregate book value of more than $2.6 billion.

To carry out its responsibilities, the FDIC has more than 3,500 employees—only 15 percent of whom are engaged full-time in the receivership activities so well publicized when an insured bank fails. Most other FDIC employees, directly or indirectly, are engaged in the agency's supervisory activities over state nonmember banks. These employees carry out the FDIC's bank examination and investigatory activities in 14 regional offices throughout the country, with review activities and a variety of related staff functions centered in the FDIC's Washing-

---

[2] Then as now, about 60 percent of all insured commercial banks in this size category were national banks supervised by the Comptroller of the Currency. The percentage increase in large banks subject to FDIC jurisdiction was caused almost entirely by a diminishing percentage of state member banks among the total number.

ton headquarters. A three-member board of directors, consisting of the Chairman, the Comptroller of the Currency ex officio and a third presidential appointee, determines corporation policy, takes official action not delegated to others, and directs the activities of career personnel.

THE BUILDING BLOCKS OF PUBLIC CONFIDENCE

Maintaining public confidence in the banking system is not the same thing as maintaining public confidence in the individual banks that make up the total system. With the number of banks in this country as large as it is, aberrations in performance can be and are tolerated on an individual bank basis that could not possibly be tolerated in the banking system as a whole. A bank which consistently fails to provide its customers with efficient, courteous and up-to-date service or consistently fails to provide its customer base with credit suffers in time a visible erosion of public support, but this does not mean that the public loses confidence in the system, particularly if it can obtain better service and the credit desired with substantially equal convenience at some competing bank. Similarly, depositors, creditors and stockholders may lose confidence in a particular bank if its earnings performance is consistently below that of its competitors because of unwise investment decisions, excessive loan losses, uncontrolled expenses, inadequate capital or general inefficiency and incompetence, but this does not signal a corresponding loss of confidence in the entire system. Likewise, the public's adverse reaction to the limited number of banks whose officers tolerate illegal bank activity, favored treatment of "insiders," improper speculation with "other people's money," or even participate personally in criminal misconduct does not necessarily mean there has been a loss of confidence in the banking system as a whole.

The danger to confidence in the system comes when the public assumes that *far too many* of the nation's 15,000 banks are conducting themselves in ways which are unsafe, unsound, arbitrary, or illegal. In this climate, the damage to public confidence will be compounded if bank customers generally come to believe that they are being inadequately protected by those in public office; i.e., their elected representatives and the large number of bank supervisory personnel whose job it is to enforce the law and promote bank safety and soundness.

From that vantage point, the individual banker might be well advised to take in stride the large number of legislative and regulatory actions taken in recent years that are intended to promote public confidence in the banking system as a whole, even though they add to the burdens of an individual bank's management or performance. The

Bank Protection Act of 1968 is one obvious example of such legislation at the federal level. Less obvious examples include federal and state laws such as Truth in Lending Acts, Fair Credit Reporting Acts, and Equal Credit Opportunity Acts, all of which are designed to assure the fair treatment of borrowers who do not have the bargaining power of the banks with which they deal. Yet another area of regulatory activity where the ultimate goal may also be said to be public confidence in the entire system is that of more detailed and accurate disclosure of individual bank financial condition and performance, the assumption being that it will be easier, not harder, for most banks to raise the capital they need if all banks are subject to more meaningful disclosure requirements on a uniform basis.

Supervisory efforts to prevent a loss of confidence in "far too many" individual banks from endangering public confidence in the system as a whole is the real purpose of the traditional examination work and the more recent "early warning" work being conducted by the three federal bank agencies and various state banking departments. Bank supervisors no longer consider it their function to protect individual banks against the benefits to the public of increased competition or to protect stubborn managements against the folly of repeated mistakes. Indeed, general acceptance of a banking system with 15,000 units and a well-developed system of deposit insurance presupposes that some banks, despite supervisory efforts to encourage the correction of unsafe, unsound or illegal practices, will be forced out of business. What the agencies are all seeking is to minimize the damage to the system as a whole when that happens. FDIC in addition, as administrator of the nation's deposit insurance system, is charged with the special duty of minimizing the impact of such failures on individual depositors and the local communities in which such banks operate. That special function, if it is efficiently performed, also contributes significantly to the maintenance of public confidence in the system—despite the fact that there has been an obvious loss of confidence in the individual banks that have failed.

THE MEASUREMENT OF SYSTEMWIDE RISK

The FDIC's payment of deposit insurance claims comes only after the many other safeguards built into the nation's banking system have been used and exhausted. Bank managements have numerous incentives for improved performance, particularly in the earnings area; bank capital, composed largely of retained earnings, provides a significant cushion within which to absorb unusual losses; the supervisory agencies have extraordinary—although not unlimited—powers to force corrective action upon individual banks; the Federal Reserve System can provide liquidity assistance with stiff requirements for remedial action, when the correspondent bank network reaches the point where it considers future advances made independently of the central bank to be imprudent; and the FDIC itself has a number of options which, under appropriate circumstances, before or after failure, can be used to avoid the necessity for actually paying off deposit insurance claims.

No bank performs a useful public purpose without undertaking some significant risks in the extension of service and credit, and it is largely the accuracy with which the seriousness of those risks is measured that determines whether these other safeguards will be successful if, as and when their use becomes necessary. Every bank management has its own means of assessing the risks which may be found in the bank's assets and liabilities. In large banks, these systems can become quite elaborate and continuous with the use of internal and outside auditors supplementing the efforts of line managers. Obviously, the quality of these evaluations differs significantly among the nation's 15,000 banks, but the banks most likely to show consistently superior performance are those which appraise these risks the best and use the resulting information intelligently and in a timely fashion. Ideally, the sum total of these individual bank appraisals of internal risk should produce a fairly close approximation of the risks throughout the system.

Aggregations of individual bank data, however, tend to be more reassuring than they should be because the incidence and dispersion of greater than average risk tend to get lost in the statistics that report a hypothetical "all-bank" performance. This deficiency is partially overcome by reporting composite information by size of bank, thereby permitting a comparison to be made between the average performance of one size group and the average performance of another size group. A grasp of the incidence and dispersion of greater than average risk remains elusive, however, if the size group covers a wide range of banks with quite different characteristics (e.g., all banks over $500 million) and if there is no further indication of how many banks fall within or without a specified percentile of the composite performance.

Total net operating income for all insured banks before applicable income taxes and before securities gains and losses in the investment portfolio, for example, has always substantially exceeded both the provision for possible loan losses and the losses actually charged against reserves for all insured banks during the same period. Even during the peak year 1975 when loan losses exceeded $3.8 billion for all insured banks, this relationship held. Accumulated reserves for additional losses at the end of the same year were well over $6 billion. Similarly, the total capital accounts of insured commercial banks and the total surplus accounts of insured mutual savings banks aggregated almost $72 billion at the end of 1975 without regard to the additional cushion provided by subordinated notes and debentures then outstanding. In relation to the loan losses reported by bank managements and the aggregate loan classifications imposed by bank examiners, these figures were extremely reassuring to most observers attempting to assess systemwide risk during the nation's most serious recession since 1933.

The aggregate figures did not indicate, of course, that loan losses for many insured banks were excessive, that a substantial number of these banks were operating at a net loss and that their capital accounts were being correspondingly reduced rather than increased through retained earnings. Moreover, the insured banks with disproportionate risks tended, upon further analysis, to be (a) commercial banks with an unusually high percentage of their total loans committed to real estate development projects, or (b) rapidly growing commercial banks in the size categories above $50 million in deposits.

An accurate view of systemwide risk requires more, therefore, than aggregate figures for all insured banks or even for those within a given size category. The "early warning" systems presently being devised by the three federal bank agencies and several of the larger state banking departments will undoubtedly help this refinement process. So will the studies currently being produced by a number of independent banking analysts and services using the call-report data tapes produced by the three federal bank agencies and information from publicly available filings of the larger banks. But for the foreseeable future, the best available assessment of systemwide risk will continue to come from the examination process which is an integral part of the federal deposit insurance program.

BANK EXAMINATIONS AND THE DEVELOPMENT OF "PROBLEM BANK" LISTS

Recent laws at both the federal and state levels have added to the breadth of fact-finding expected of a bank examiner, but the examiner's most important function remains the evaluation of an individual bank's financial condition and the development of the facts necessary to support that evaluation. These evaluations, in the case of the federal bank agencies, are reviewed intensively at the examiner's regional office and frequently also at the agency's Washington headquarters. Such reviews are essential parts of the interpretive process because examiners-in-charge (and regional supervisors) differ in thoroughness, perspective, knowledge, and experience. The review process also adds the significant element of comparison—between the individual bank and other banks based on location, size, asset mix, deposit structure, and other factors. In addition, reports prepared by one agency may be provided to another agency to integrate the information available on affiliated banks or on all banks within the agency's jurisdiction. Thus, the Comptroller of the Currency and the FDIC both have access to reports prepared by the bank holding company staff of the Federal Reserve System, while the Federal Reserve System is entitled to receive all national bank reports of examination and in practice may also review the FDIC reports of examination of nonmember bank affiliates of a bank holding company system. The FDIC, as the nation's deposit insurer, regularly receives and reviews reports of examination prepared by the other two federal agencies with respect to banks over $100 million in size, a random sampling of reports on banks below that cutoff size, and such other reports of examination as it requires to assess its risks "for insurance purposes."

From all the information available to it, every bank agency prepares and revises periodically a list of those banks under its jurisdiction which show significant weaknesses relative to the vast majority of banks and which require especially close supervision. The FDIC's list of such banks, which is commonly but probably too broadly referred to as its list of "problem banks," is the only agency compilation that bears a rough relation to systemwide risk because it includes all insured banks regardless of the agency that regulates them at the federal level.

Although the list itself is not publicly available, the FDIC has released an increasing amount of information on its contents. The FDIC's 1976 *Annual Report*, for example, revealed that at the end of that year the list contained 379 banks with total deposits of more than $59 billion. However, only 115 of these banks were considered to be in either of the FDIC's two most serious categories, and their total deposits were only $7.1 billion. The estimated amount of deposits actually insured in these banks was $24 billion and $5.1 billion, respectively. Moreover, the banks whose names appear on these problem lists are constantly changing. During 1976, 188 banks were added to the FDIC's problem bank list, while 158 were removed (16 of them by actual failure). This reflects the overall experience of the FDIC in recent years that about 75 percent of the banks listed on a given date will still be operating and will no longer be considered in a problem status of any kind two years thereafter. Of the 115 serious problem banks at year-end 1976, 92 had deposits of less than $50 million. Nine of the remaining 23 banks fell between $50 million and $100 million in deposits, ten between $100 and $500 million, three between $500 million and $1 billion, and only one had deposits of $1 billion or more. No bank over $200 million in deposit size was considered to be in imminent danger of failure.

The 379 banks listed on the FDIC's problem bank list at year-end 1976 represented the highest number of banks on any such list in 28 years. Nonetheless, there were reasons in December 1976 to believe that the number of banks on the list would decline in the immediate future. Problem bank lists are primarily developed on the basis of reports of examination, which are normally received for review throughout the 12 months preceding the preparation of the list. The reports of examination, in turn, reflect dates of examination that precede receipt by as much as six months. Thus, even though periodic reports may be obtained from a bank once listed on a problem bank list, the listing itself tends to reflect information which is not completely current. The dramatic increase in problem banks on the FDIC's list between year-end 1974 (when they numbered 183) and year-end 1975 (when 349 banks were listed) and the further increase between year-end 1975 and year-end 1976 no doubt reflected the length and severity of the 1974–1975 recession in the economy as a whole. Moreover, since many of the loans criticized in 1976 reports of examination reflected real estate development loans, the problem bank totals also reflected the long workout periods needed by banks as they awaited a general recovery in many of the nation's real estate markets.

While "problem bank" lists accentuate the negative in the banking system at any one time, they are just as necessary as refined statistics for different size categories in assessing accurately the seriousness, breadth, and dispersion of the risks taken by the banking system.

FDIC'S OPTIONS FOR CONTAINING SYSTEMWIDE RISK

When an insured bank appears on the brink of failure, despite the strenuous efforts of its management and its normal supervisory authorities to revive the bank or merge it into a healthy bank without FDIC assistance, the FDIC must use one of four options under present law, some of which may not be available in any given case.

The first, which is always available under the law, is to let the bank close and proceed promptly to the payment of insured deposits. Currently, each depositor is protected to the extent of all deposits held in the same right and capacity up to $40,000, except that government units having time and savings deposits in an insured bank within their state are protected to a maximum of $100,000 held in the same right and capacity. When this option is used, payments of insured claims almost always begin within seven days of the date of failure. Since 1934, 303 of the nation's 535 bank failures have been handled by the payment of insured deposits in this way, but only 8 such "payoffs" in 40 bank failure cases have occurred in the last five years.

The direct payment of insured deposits is not today the FDIC's preferred method of handling a bank failure. Partly this reflects the rising incidence of larger banks with larger numbers of depositors among the banks that fail. Partly it reflects the fact that while losses to depositors have been very small since 1934 (an estimated $19.7 million), all of those losses have fallen on "excess" depositors in failed banks which the FDIC has "paid off" rather than transferred to another insured bank—the practical effect of the latter being 100 percent deposit insurance. Statutory payoffs can occur, nonetheless, when efforts to arrange a deposit assumption prove unsuccessful, when the deposits over the statutory ceilings are de minimis in number and amount, or when the statutory criteria required for a deposit assumption appear not be met.

When the FDIC determines that it can "reduce the risk or avert a threatened loss to the Corporation," 12 U.S.C. §1823(e), it can utilize the second of its options: the merger of a failing bank or the assumption of its deposit liabilities by another insured bank with FDIC financial assistance. This assistance may take various forms: the FDIC may purchase the assets or grant a loan secured by the assets of the failed bank (the result of which is to balance with FDIC cash the liabilities assumed less the assets found acceptable to the takeover bank), it may agree to idemnify the takeover bank against loss by reason of the transaction, or it may take a capital note from the assuming bank to provide it with the capital necessary to support its suddenly expanded deposit base. In several recent failures, particularly those of larger banks, all three forms of assistance were employed.

Without exception in recent years, the FDIC's willingness to use the "purchase and assumption" method of dealing with a failed bank has been encouraged by the agreement of the takeover bank to pay a healthy premium, or price, for the overall transaction—$89.5 million in the case of the Crocker National Bank takeover of the deposits and offices of the failed United States National Bank, San Diego; $125 million in the case of the takeover by European American Bank and Trust Company of the deposits and offices of the failed Franklin National Bank, New York; and lesser amounts in the case of smaller failed banks. This premium, of course, provides an additional cushion for loss in the liquidation of the failed bank's assets over and above the net capital of the bank on the day the bank closed. In that sense, the premium serves to minimize FDIC's net loss, but it also enhances the possibility of an eventual recovery by the failed bank's subordinated noteholders and shareholders.

The FDIC has also had authority since its early days to organize and operate for two years a special type of bank called a "deposit insurance national bank," when this appeared desirable in order to provide limited banking services in a community which would otherwise be deprived of banking services because of a bank failure. A deposit insurance national bank is organized as a nonstock company and managed by an executive officer appointed by the FDIC board of directors. The FDIC provides the funds necessary to begin operations (in an amount equal to the insured deposits of the failed bank, which are assumed by the new bank) and must cover its operating losses, if any. Normally, the new bank performs only limited banking functions although the Comptroller of the Currency may authorize it to offer an unlimited range of banking services. If a deposit insurance national bank is organized, the FDIC attempts to transfer its ownership to private hands within the two-year period authorized by law, offering the stock first to shareholders of the bank that failed in accordance with the terms of the Federal Deposit Insurance Act. If the stock offering is not successful, the law requires that the bank be closed and the FDIC then assumes its assets and obligations, liquidating both as in a normal receivership. Unlike a deposit assumption, the use of this third option does not result in 100 percent deposit insurance. Instead, it provides a breathing spell to regain community support for a local bank and avoids the possible congestion or anxiety sometimes caused by a statutory payoff. There have been only two recent instances of a deposit insurance national bank being created. One occurred when a small minority bank in Kansas City, Missouri, failed in 1974. The other occurred when the Peoples National Bank of the Virgin Islands failed in 1975.

In 1950, the Federal Deposit Insurance Act was amended to provide FDIC with its fourth option in dealing with distressed banks about to fail. Section 13(c) of the act, added at that time, authorizes the FDIC to provide specified forms of assistance to an open and operating insured bank if it finds (*a*) that but for the contemplated assistance, the bank "is in danger of closing" and (*b*) that the continuation of the bank as an independent entity is "essential to provide adequate banking service in the community." By year-end 1976, the FDIC had used this authority on only three occasions since 1950: the first being in 1971 when the Unity Bank and Trust Company, Boston, Massachusetts, a small minority bank, was in danger of closing, the second being in 1972 to avoid the failure of the $1 billion deposit Bank of the Commonwealth, Detroit's fourth largest bank, and the third being in 1974 to provide short-term liquidity to American Bank and Trust, Orangeburg, South Carolina, to prevent its failure before a satisfactory purchase and assumption transaction with a sound bank could be arranged.

FINANCIAL RESOURCES OF THE FDIC

With a significant increase since 1966 in the number of larger banks on the FDIC's "problem bank" list and with the failure or near failure in 1972, 1973, and 1974 of three banks in the $1 billion and up size category, public attention began to be directed to the financial resources available to the FDIC to honor the government's deposit insurance commitment. In fact, only a fraction of the resources available to the FDIC has been utilized in the 539 instances since 1933 when FDIC funds have been required. The resources available to FDIC include (1) insurance premiums paid each year by the nation's insured banks at the rate of one twelfth of 1 percent of domestic deposits (before computation of a legally mandated refund based on the current year's loss experience); (2) the investment income on the federal deposit insurance fund accumulated since 1933 out of the annual premiums not refunded to the nation's banks and the reinvestment of income from prior years; (3) the principal amount of the fund which stood at \$7.2 billion at the end of 1976; and (4) a \$3 billion call upon the U.S. Treasury anytime funds in that amount are needed for FDIC purposes—an authority the FDIC has never found it necessary to use in its 43-year history. For the calendar year 1976, the FDIC reported total incoming revenues of \$1.1 billion, almost exclusively the result of the premiums and investment income described in (1) and (2) above. This revenue, moreover, which is available annually for the FDIC's expenses and insurance losses, has been increasing in recent years at the rate of almost \$100 million per year, while the principal of the trust fund itself has been increasing more than \$500 million per year.

Compared to the resources available, the FDIC's total disbursement over 43 years of \$2.3 billion in connection with the failure of 535 insured banks and the near-failure of four others has been very low. Most of the funds initially disbursed are eventually recovered through the liquidation of failed bank assets for which FDIC is responsible. At year-end 1976, the FDIC estimated that its likely loss on these total disbursements would amount to no more than \$285 million— less than 5 percent of the total deposits in the 539 banks involved and slightly more than 10 percent of the FDIC's initial outlay.

The record shows that FDIC's initial outlays to prevent or minimize deposit loss to the American public have been much lower than the deposit totals of the banks involved and far below the resources available to it. In the case of the three largest banks to require FDIC financial assistance to date (Bank of the Commonwealth, United States National Bank, and Franklin National Bank), the FDIC's initial outlays aggregated \$350 million, including \$150 million of capital note support for the two takeover banks in the latter cases. This amount, which was about 10 percent of their aggregate deposits at the time the aid was granted, represents only one third of the FDIC's *annual* current income and less than one twentieth of the current principal of the FDIC trust fund. Moreover, despite increases in deposit insurance ceilings, the number of bank failures and the need for increased disbursements by FDIC, the trust fund continues to equal about 0.8 percent of total domestic deposits and about 1.2 percent of total insured deposits, percentages which have moved within only a very narrow range over the past 20 years.

CONCLUSION

Over the years since 1933, 99.8 percent of the depositors in all 535 insured banks that have failed have received or are assured payment of their deposits in full, such deposits amounting to 99.6 percent of the total deposits in those banks. Most observers believe that this unique deposit insurance program has been an unqualified success in containing systemwide risk. It has supplemented bank earnings, bank capital and the liquidity assistance available from the Federal Reserve System by providing the financial resources and statutory authority to deal with hundreds of individual bank breakdowns in the American banking system over the last 44 years. More importantly, despite economic recession and the magnitude of individual bank problems, the FDIC's ability to honor the government's deposit insurance commitments has been of incalculable value in maintaining public confidence in the banking system as a whole.

Chapter 82

The Nature and Purpose
of Supervisory Examinations[1]

Michael Doman*

Each bank manager, regardless of size and location, must as a matter of fact give careful attention to prevailing regulatory considerations and attitudes. Regulatory requirements and constraints rank equally with the other forces that affect bank management—operations, money supply, liquidity problems, and borrowing demands.

The need for bank supervision has been clearly established by over 100 years of banking history in this country. Politically, it is assumed that bank supervision is in the public interest.

STRUCTURE OF BANK SUPERVISION

Every national bank, as is true with every insured bank, is subject to regulation by a federal agency or a state agency. The authority for the federal agency with respect to national banks is contained in Title 12 of the United States Code. This code enumerates all of the operating powers and organizational structures of national bank associations in this country.

The structure of banking supervision in the United States is quite complex. National banks are chartered and supervised by the Comptroller of the Currency. State banks are chartered by the various state banking departments, which also claim examining responsibility.

---

[1] The views expressed in this chapter are those of the author and not necessarily of the Comptroller of the Currency.

* Regional Administrator of National Banks, Eleventh National Bank Region, Dallas, Texas.

In addition, two other nonchartering federal agencies exercise overview of state banks. All state banks which are members of the Federal Reserve System are subject to a review by the district Federal Reserve Bank in addition to a review by the state banking departments. All state banks which are not members of the Federal Reserve System but which are insured by the Federal Deposit Insurance Corporation are subject to examination supervision by the Federal Deposit Insurance Corporation examiners.

State banks are generally subject to two examining agencies. The method of operation of these examining forces will vary from state to state, but examinations are frequently conducted on a simultaneous basis.

The Federal Deposit Insurance Corporation and the Federal Reserve Bank both accept the examination reports as prepared by the representative of the Comptroller of the Currency. The Comptroller of the Currency is also a member of the board of the Federal Deposit Insurance Corporation, again lending to further overlap and coordination of this supervisory effort.

The Office of the Comptroller of the Currency is a bureau of the U.S. Department of the Treasury, charged with the statutory responsibility of examining each national bank four times during a two-year period. One of those examinations may be waived during the two-year cycle.

OBJECTIVES OF BANK SUPERVISION

In general, the structure of bank supervision is the result of bad banking experience. The three major developments to date are: (1) Wild-cat banking before the Civil War, which resulted in the national banking system and the Office of the Comptroller of the Currency. (2) Money panics 50 years later created the Federal Reserve System. (3) Collapse of two fifths of the banks in the depression of the early 1930s gave us the Federal Deposit Insurance Corporation.

Statutory

The Preamble of the Banking Act of 1935 states that the act was intended "to provide for the sound, effective and uninterrupted operation of the banking system and for other purposes."

Concepts

Regulation of banking is fundamentally different from regulation of public utilities and other industries. In most other industries, primary concern is with the abuse of monopoly or near-monopoly. In banking with over 14,000 independent units, regulation is less concerned with monopoly or pricing than with soundness in operations.

The key which unlocks the entire structure of effective bank supervision is a rather short and simply stated philosophy—regulation involves influencing bank behavior. This philosophy does not place a responsibility to assure bank behavior or to be responsible for bank behavior as is suggested from time to time during periods of above-average banking problems. The standards of operations which would evolve if the bank regulator would be required to assure or to be responsible for bank behavior would be inconsistent with the free enterprise system.

Influence on bank behavior may be exercised through several means. It can be exercised through public disclosure and the resulting market-imposed disciplines, through market entries such as de novo chartering, branching, EFTS (electronic funds transfer system), and other technological breakthroughs, and through the direct examination activity.

Purpose of Supervision

Why single out banking for this stringent government overview? The answer, of course, is that Congress has determined that it is in the public interest to have a banking industry which is sound and operational within adequate measures of safety and in which the public may have implicit faith.

Commercial banks act as principal fiduciaries for the financial affairs of the community. It is essential that an optimum degree of confidence be maintained in the banking industry of the community in order that orderly and desired commerce can be conducted. The purpose of the supervisory effort is to establish and maintain this degree of confidence. The objective is achieved through procedures and inquiries during the examination process, which ascertains that the commercial bank is liquid and solvent.

The matter of solvency is important to permit the public to have confidence that all funds entrusted to the commercial bank will be available at full and timely redemption and that checks drawn upon the commercial bank will be negotiated in the normal course of business.

The matter of liquidity is important to give assurance to the public that funds entrusted to the commercial bank will be returned promptly and as needed and that commitments made by the commercial bank can be relied upon. The ongoing examination process will also make an appropriate determination that adequate performance takes place in an established form so that the bank can continue to operate in that manner.

Functions of Bank Regulation

The functions of bank regulation consist chiefly of three responsibilities; namely (1) supervision, (2) regulation, and (3) chartering. These functions are closely related and are often interwoven; however, they may also be found in juxtaposition with one another at various times.

The supervision function essentially assures performance and safety at the highest level desired in the public interest.

The regulation function chiefly assures responsiveness to meet the emerging needs and demands of the public interest.

The chartering function primarily assures an appropriate financial structure to meet the public financial needs.

The supervision function is fulfilled through periodic on-the-scene examinations of the records of the bank. The Comptroller of the Currency is required by statute to examine every national bank under the schedule described above. That statute conveys to the examiner the power to make a thorough examination of all affairs of the bank and includes the power to administer oaths and to examine all affiliates of the bank as shall be necessary to disclose the effects upon the affairs of the bank. This power to examine also includes examination of all trust departments of national banks.

These examinations, in the broad sense, are made to determine the conditions, conduct, and affairs, generally, of banks. The immediate and primary objectives are to determine whether the bank is solvent, whether the bank has sufficient liquid provisions to meet all demands placed upon it during the ordinary course of business, and whether the bank is operating within the framework of applicable banking laws. Every phase of banking activity found in the particular bank under examination in subject to scrutiny.

The rising complexities and sophistication, as well as mobility of modern-day banking, have resulted in some rearrangement of conceptual principles in the use of examination tools. Certain general underlying assumptions are made involving an ongoing outlook, as opposed to a liquidation outlook.

Each national bank is a self-determined business enterprise operated to earn a profit sufficient to satisfy ownership, creditor, and depositor interests. As business so motivated, an underlying assumption as to the "going-concern" value of the enterprise can be made. The realities of that approach, versus liquidation, contain the seeds of entirely differing viewpoints as a basis for operations, financial reporting, and supervisory examinations.

Because of the very nature of their objectives, supervisory agencies have in the past used the liquidation viewpoint rather than the ongoing theory as a basis for examination. A qualitative examination of any account; e.g., loans, effectively reflects the liquidation concept in practice as the intent is to allow to remain in the loan account only those loans judged to have liquidation value.

Accordingly, the carrying amounts of assets of commercial banks are reduced to current fair market values by write-downs, charge-offs, or allocated reserves, in whole or in part, in order to determine sufficiency of remaining capital. The question to be answered is whether the depositor will be able to redeem his or her deposit at full amount if the bank were placed in liquidation at a precise moment of time. Primarily, the liquidation concept says that a bank, to be considered solvent, must have capital remaining after all liabilities have been subtracted from current values of the assets.

The ongoing concept embodies the principle of recognition of the profit generation ability of the bank at levels necessary to absorb reasonable asset losses along with the costs of operations. In other words, the adequacy of capital funds of the bank, or the solvency of the bank, becomes a test of whether the operating results of the bank provide sufficient profits to meet all expenses and losses as well as provide for growth and a return to shareholders.

The acceptance of the ongoing concept by examiners requires a great deal more knowledge of the bank, including, in part the present profitability, the policies and procedures which will assure continued profit generation, anticipated liquidity demands arising from the bank's customers, and the general administration of the affairs of the bank.

With the increased capabilities of identifying operating trends through computer data base systems, such as the National Bank Surveillance System, the ongoing concept for financial accounting, record keeping, and reporting will be more a part of supervisory examining philosophy. Liquidation concepts and capabilities, however, must remain for appropriate use.

THE EXAMINATION PROCESS

The examination consists essentially of five basic procedures which are followed in all national banks regardless of size or location. They consist of (1) an evaluation of the nature, breadth, and effectiveness of the internal controls of the bank, including all audit, financial, and administrative controls; (2) proof of all assets and liability accounts against the bank's records; (3) verification of all assets; (4) partial verification of liabilities; and (5) most important of all, the appraisal of all assets to determine their current reasonable value in relation to their carrying value and their potential soundness as bank assets, if retained in the present status over future periods of time.

The evaluation of the internal controls consists of a careful analysis of operating policies and procedures through an inspection of appropriate manuals or through careful interview with bank personnel, determination of an internal program to monitor compliance with such policies and procedures, and substantiation of compliance.

The study of the internal guidelines of the bank, together with an in-depth review and appraisal of internal and external auditing, is used to establish the scope for examination of each function, asset, liability, income, or expense. Judgment is exercised as to whether to reexamine that which has been examined, based on the timing, quality, and independence of work previously done. From these preliminary tasks, it is possible to choose those subjective steps to be performed during the examination. To the extent that any object of examination has been acceptably audited, and is currently being operated within a sphere of sound internal controls, the examiner may spend correspondingly less time on that objective.

The evaluation of internal controls procedure consists of inspection of four principal administrative functions during a preexamination visit to the bank or during the initial stages of the examination. The internal audit program is reviewed for independence and reporting requirements to the board or designated committees, for completeness of application to all functional areas of the bank, for documentation of scope and quality of work performed, and for competence of the audit staff.

The external audit program is reviewed through an inspection of the contract, through a review and discussion of all rendered reports, recommendations and letter to the board, and through an inspection of the external auditor's working papers. The independence of the external auditor must be clearly established.

Policy and procedure manuals are reviewed, In the event formal manuals are not available, an attempt is made to identify the general operating guidelines of the bank from other sources in the bank.

The obvious cornerstone to the requirement for established policies and objectives is the need to communicate to management and operating personnel that which is expected of them as formulated by the board of directors. The passage of time may dictate the need to add to or delete from policy. Also, some policy instruments in one bank may not be necessarily applicable to another bank.

The importance of policy is of such magnitude as to need more than specific mechanics. Not only should the overall bank policy contain a preface stating goals and objectives, but ideally each subsection should have its own such introduction. The inclusion of broad and even philosophical goals is important as this gives rise to originality, hence the individuality factor which bank officers desire. Stated goals will also provide the basis for development of policy, i.e., if the board's goal are that the bank should serve its community, then the policy should define the community and what constitutes service. That which is stated in developed policy should likewise not be in stated goals and objectives philosophy.

The overall bank policy statement should define all of the needed, detailed functional policies such as loan policy, liquidity policy, liability management policy, earnings, and investments to name some of the more important ones.

Aside from the usual functional aspects, two administrative topics will add meaning to the policy statement. Having a policy neatly typed up and tucked away to show to the examiners is one thing, while keeping it up to date and using it as a working document is quite another. Since a board of directors has the legal responsibility for the sound operations of a bank, it should also know when its policies are not carried out. Accordingly, the policy itself should fix responsibility to monitor operational compliance and to report the results to the board. Without this administrative ingredient, all of the previous policy development is incomplete. The monitoring function may possibly be delegated to the auditor, whose independent reporting to the board should already exist as a matter of prudent internal controls.

The second important administrative policy ingredient is a necessary structure for effecting needed policy changes. A great deal of flexibility can be attained by keeping stated policies current which permit the bank to be continually responsive to the needs of its marketplace and economic developments.

The broad policies of the bank should be to provide the ground rules of operation in order to maintain a sound condition, while policy monitoring offers an insight of the overall internal assessment of the condition of the bank. Soundly conceived policies can be strongly influential in producing a sound and profitable bank.

Lastly, the bank's internal review program is evaluated as to scope or review, size of loans selected for audit in various departments, and the quality of the work performed. Based upon the results of this inquiry, the scope of loan examination procedures may be determined.

Proofs and verifications of assets and liabilities are basic audit procedures.

The appraisal of assets is based upon information taken from the books and records of the bank and upon statements made to the examiner by officers and employees of the bank. In the course of these examination procedures, the examiner gains sufficient insight into policies and practices, the ability of management and the effectiveness thereof, to make an appropriate evaluation.

Certain phases of the examination receive more emphasis than others. Inasmuch as loan accounts represent the major assets of most national banks, the principal thrust of the examination is to the appraisal of the loan account. The examiner evaluates the quality and liquidity of each loan in the bank. In the process he or she will ascertain whether supporting documents are bona fide, whether collateral when pledged is in possession or control and has been properly asigned, and whether the loan is collectible based upon collateral values and the sound worth of the maker. All loans determined to be of marginal quality are classified as substandard, doubtful, or loss, or judged as other loans for special mention. The rating of substandard is used to convey the existence of a positive weakness which will jeopardize the liquidity of the loan.

A doubtful rating is assigned where there is a high probability of loss, but where other factors may strengthen the loan. Loans rated "loss" are considered uncollectible or of such little value that continuation as a bank asset is not warranted. All assets of the bank classified "loss" must be charged off during the examination.

Other loans especially mentioned are considered currently protected but potentially weak financial credit risks are identified.

The quality evaluation of the loan account is conducted by inspection of individual loans selected as a percentile of the bank's capital funds by a numerical statistical sampling and a biased examiner selection. Evaluation of quality may also be established through acceptance of the work performed by the bank's internal review process to the extent that such internal functions meet selected standards. These standards require a review of all loans over an established amount at periodic intervals of not less than annually. Classifications must be assigned which are comparable to supervisory personnel. Summations must be available to substantiate the credit rating.

Having obtained and proven credence of the internal loan review summation of individual credits, and to the extent the same facts exist as of the time of the review, such credit conclusions may then be accepted for examination purposes, instead of performing the examination credit on each individual line.

An examiner appraisal of the investment account is conducted by not to the same depth as for loans since rating services and market quotations are readily available to indicate quality and soundness. All other assets are closely reviewed, such as fixed assets which are reviewed in terms of adequacy for operations. Cash and liquidity provisions are also reviewed. The examiner must consider and determine whether the bank's capital funds are reasonably adequate in relation to risk distribution, business volumes, and future growth. He or she will also analyze earnings, audit controls, insurance coverage, both fidelity and indemnity, and will also conduct an investigation for violations of banking laws. The examiner is required to review at length all conditions disclosed by the management of the bank.

Follow-up Procedures

A comprehensive report is then prepared and submitted to the regulatory agency. This report incorporates not only factual data gathered, but will also cite areas of unjustified risk and policies or practices which are regarded as unsound and unsafe. An appraisal of management and policies is also set forth.

The examiner and the examination report have been generally shielded from subpoena, and by this means an unusual rapport and frankness with bankers has evolved. It should also be noted that the examiner is prohibited under criminal statute from unauthorized disclosure of the affairs of the bank and its customers except to the regulatory agency and directors and officials of the bank.

A copy of the principal report is supplied to the board of directors of the bank for its use in the guidance of the affairs of the bank. A supplemental report, confidential in nature, is submitted for the agency's use and information only. The examination reports are used as the basis for determination by the regional and Washington offices of a need for further supervisory action. Each bank is rated according to the major components of the bank's operation: Capital adequacy, asset quality, and management.

The capital adequacy rating is predicated upon several factors, the chief among which are the volume of business enjoyed, the inherent risk in the asset structure, management record, and earnings records. Request for the injection of capital may be predicated upon one or several of these factors. Bank management is usually expected to be responsive to such request.

The asset quality rating consists of the determination of the ratio of capital funds to assets not considered to be of bankable quality. Ordinarily capital impairment of 0–30 percent will create no undue concern. Conditions over 30 percent will usually evoke a letter of attention to the board of directors. Conditions reflecting 40 percent or more are considered severe, and 80 percent levels are rated critical.

A meeting of the board of directors of the bank will be convened when the ratio is 40 percent or more to attempt to obtain assurances of corrective measures. The bank will also be scheduled for more frequent examinations as well as periodic visitations by an examiner. The directorate will also be requested to make formal periodic reports on corrective efforts.

The management rating is somewhat self-evident. It is largely based upon the examiner's evaluation of effectiveness and the results of operations to date.

The ultimate objective of the information contained in the report is to establish regulating of interest in the ongoing affairs of the bank.

When problem situations are identified, supervisors employ a number of tools available to them. Ordinarily, the supervisor will convene a meeting of the board of directors, seek direct face-to-face conferences with management and directors, and/or issue correspondence and other types of directives; the prevailing theme of all such activities is one of identifying the underlying corrosive factors and the elimination of these factors through recommended changes. Also discussed will be adjustments in lending policy and operating procedures, management capabilities, and capital adequacy.

In the event severe or critical conditions are encountered where there has been no response to previous requests and recommendations, several measures are available to the bank regulator. In addition to accelerated examinations and periodic visitations, the Comptroller may employ cease and desist powers, enter into an operating agreement with the board, or cause suspension, or removal of the officials responsible. Further, the Comptroller may revoke the charter, recommend withdrawal of deposit insurance, or place the bank into conservatorship or receivership, depending upon the severity of the condition and the potential for correction.

Early Warning Systems

A significant examination tool has been implemented through the inauguration of a system designed to monitor national bank operations, known as the national bank surveillance system. The system's component parts include: (1) A data collection network; (2) a computer-based monitoring system to detect unusual or significantly changed circumstances within a bank or the national banking system; and (3) an evaluation of the impact of these changes by experienced specialists.

The capability of the system makes it possible to identify banks with significantly changed circumstances. By using numerous key performance indicators, each bank is compared to a group of selected peer banks. The system also produces reports which rank the severity of changes being experienced by banks as measured by selected summary ratios, thus identifying those banks which require supervisory inquiry on a priority basis. Of equal significance is the fact that the system provides an examination of selected functions of a national bank without the requirement of traditional on-site inspections.

THE REGULATION PROCESS

The regulatory function of bank regulation is not so easily tracked nor does it have a definite form. Regulation in the broad sense involves the interpretation of banking statutes so as to blend legislative desires with contemporary public interests.

Title 12 of the United States Code is broad and in part states national banks may exercise "all such incidental powers as shall be necessary to carry on the business of banking." Debate has raged for years whether this should be construed as meaning that the bank should be permitted to carry on financially oriented business activities (such as computer services, credit life insurance) or be limited to financially related activities or services which are inherent in the business of banking, such as extension of credit.

It is through this interpretive function that each bank regulator imposes his or her particular uniqueness upon the industry. Interpretations will range over a broad array of subjects from a chapter when a national bank was not permitted to establish a hitching post simply because the statutes were silent in this respect, to the rulings during the 1960s permitting activities such as credit cards. Recent interpretation has been made that customer-bank communication terminals (known as point of sales, EFTS) may be operated by national banks.

The regulatory function is most critical in establishing a viable industry responsive to public needs and interest. Ideally, a regulator can seek to attain a banking structure consistent with best banking performance, from the public standpoint, only when he has at his disposal avenues for change. In banking, it should be remembered, vestiges exist, many of a provincial nature, which place restraints on maximum achievements. A federal regulator is required to observe certain state-imposed restrictions with respect to those banks officed in those states.

During the past decade the Office of the Comptroller of the Currency has expressed, by action, its belief that government regulation is not necessarily the best way to meet the needs of the banking public. Far more effective can be the simple injection of competition. This philosophy has resulted in newly organized banks or the establishment of de novo banking facilities.

THE CHARTER PROCESS

The chartering function is largely to balance public interests, needs, convenience, and choice. Any group of five natural persons may file an application with the comptroller of the currency seeking to organize and establish a national banking institution. The Comptroller, under published regulations, will view the proposal based upon five criteria. These criteria are: (1) the adequacy of capital, which is generally a subjective determination; (2) the capability of the proposed management; (3) the character and standing of the applicants themselves and their potential to guide the bank in a safe and sound manner; (4) the convenience and needs of the community;[2] (5) a judgment whether the degree of need and support will be sufficient to permit the bank to operate at profitable levels.

OTHER EXAMINATION RESPONSIBILITIES

In addition to the foregoing responsibilities, the bank supervisor has a number of other responsibilities, including enforcement of consumer laws, both state and federal, certain currency reporting requirements, and promulgation of regulations with respect to the securities of national banks.

The Comptroller's Office has established defined examination procedures in four areas.

Trust

The examination process, in broad terms, parallels the commercial department process including an evaluation of all administrative controls, a determination of proper audit measures and verifications, and confirmation of compliance with applicable statutes and regulations, both state and federal, ascertainment of adherence to controlling instruments and documents, and observation of prudent man policies and practice. Exposure to potential litigation is carefully noted for strengthening measures.

During the process the examiner will recognize the separation of activities of the trust and commercial departments, in particular with respect to potential conflict of interests and insider information. The examiner will ascertain profitability levels and determine capital allocation.

Consumer

The examintion process primarily is to establish the degree of compliance with applicable law and secondarily, the impact upon solvency and liquidity. The examiner employs an unbiased selection process to gain an insight into potential departures from statutory requirements. Administrative controls and monitoring efforts, internal and external, will be reviewed.

Bank officials are required to institute prompt corrective action

---

[2] This consideration consists of a balance of the existing, or potentially emerging, unfulfilled economic need of a described service area with the relative convenience of existing institutions, and the benefits to be received from the introduction of another competitive choice.

when required, including the advisability of restitutions in appropriate situations.

EDP

The examination process, ascertains that data-processing center operations are no less adequate than required in the national bank itself, if the bank were performing the service. Examination inquiry will encompass the total spectrum of internal and operating controls, physical security, and timeliness of data productions.

Examinations are also conducted of nonbank data service centers which provide data to national banks. Similar standards of operations are required. A report of examination is rendered.

International

The examination process is identical to the commercial banking department, including a review of controls and an evaluation of assets. Examinations are conducted at overseas branch office locations although the domestic office usually maintains full information of activities and risk.

SECTION XIV

THE U.S. BANKING SYSTEM

Chapter 83

The Evolving Banking Structure

Carter H. Golembe*

The American banking structure is in a state of transition. Of course the same statement could have been made at any time in the past, but not with the significance that must attach to it today. In 1950, for example, one could predict with reasonable certainty that the banking structure ten years hence would not have changed very much. This conclusion could not be reached today, for the next ten years, with any confidence.

This chapter is divided into two major sections. The first contains a broad overview of the banking structure as it existed in the middle 1970s. The second section discusses the various forces that are likely to bring about a significant change in that structure over the next decade or so. No predictions are offered; readers will have to evaluate for themselves the degrees of importance that attach to various of these forces of change, and the ways in which they are likely to work their effect on the banking structure.

A few definitions and subject constraints should be noted. The industry that will be described is essentially the commercial banking industry as defined today; i.e., depository institutions that, among other things, offer demand deposit facilities to the general public and provide financing to corporate business. Occasionally, for the sake of completeness more than anything else, mutual savings bank are mentioned in the analysis. However, other depository thrift institutions, such as savings and loan associations and credit unions, are not covered in the discussion of "banking" structure, although such an exclusion may not be justified much longer, if indeed it is justified today.

---

* Chairman, Golembe Associates Inc., Washington, D.C.

By "structure" we mean essentially the number, size, and organizational form of banks. We are not concerned with their assets and liabilities, except to the extent that important changes in the mix on either side of the balance sheet might have an effect on structure. Nor will we cover the regulatory structure—federal or state—although to the extent that changes in regulations will have an important bearing on the banking structure, appropriate references will be made.

THE AMERICAN BANKING STRUCTURE IN THE MIDDLE 1970s

As has been true for many decades, the American banking structure is characterized by a large number of independent banks, the majority of which are of quite small size. As of December 31, 1976, there were 14,698 commercial banks, with total deposits of $845 billion, yielding an average size per bank of $57.5 million, and a median size of about $17 million. Both the number of banks and their average and median sizes have been increasing slowly over recent decades. In 1965, for example, there were 13,818 commercial banks, and the average and median sizes were $24 million and $6 million, respectively.

Since 1963 the number of branches of commercial banks has exceeded the number of main offices. This disparity has widened with each succeeding year, so that at the end of 1976, there were 31,404 branches of commercial banks. Combined, main offices and branches totaled over 45,000, representing over a 50 percent increase over the same total ten years earlier. Obviously, the number of branches has grown at a much faster rate than the number of main offices, although both have moved upward rather consistently.

Organizational Form.   Commercial banks are, with a few exceptions, organized as corporations. Savings banks—aside from a few stock savings banks—are organized as mutual institutions. Other depository institutions, such as savings and loan associations, may be organized either as stock or mutual, although the latter predominates.

The organizational form that has, in some ways, revolutionized the commercial banking structure during the past decade is the bank holding company. Although not unique to banking, and not even new to banking, nonetheless bank holding companies were not of any significance as late as the time of passage of the Bank Holding Company Act of 1956, which still serves as the basic expression of federal government policy with respect to bank holding companies. In 1956, there were 56 multibank holding companies (two or more bank subsidiaries) registered with the Board of Governors of the Federal Reserve System. These companies accounted for only 7.5 percent of all commercial bank deposits and 5.7 percent of all offices. At the time, holding companies having only one bank subsidiary were not required to register with the Federal Reserve Board, and therefore there is no precise information on their number. However, it appears that these were almost all small institutions, usually joining together an insurance activity with a banking activity. Probably they did not number more than a few hundred. In any event they were of no importance in terms of the percentage of all commercial bank deposits or of commercial bank offices.

The bank holding company picture is far different today of course. For reasons that have been discussed in many other places, the commercial banking industry during the middle and late 1960s sought the freedom for product expansion and geographic expansion that was not possible through the bank itself (or at least was becoming increasingly difficult) and turned to the formation of one-bank holding companies. On December 31, 1970, Congress adopted the Bank Holding Company Act Amendments of 1970, placing all bank holding companies, regardless of the number of bank subsidiaries, under the regulation and supervision of the Federal Reserve Board. Substantial change—at the time considered a liberalizing change—was made in the nonbank activities in which bank holding companies might engage. This change took the form not of a list of activities authorized by the Congress but, rather, the laying down of broad guidelines in the Bank Holding Company Act, and the lodging of authority in the Federal Reserve Board to supervise this expansion.

By the end of 1976, there were 1,919 bank holding companies, with 3,791 commercial bank subsidiaries (about 25 percent of all commercial banks) and with almost 70 percent of total deposits in the commercial banking system. Over 80 percent of these companies were one-bank holding companies. Multibank companies, of course, are most likely to be found in states that severely restrict branching, and several multibank companies are "grandfathered" to operate across state lines, having done so prior to 1956.

Class of Bank.   A useful and important categorization of banks is by class; i.e., by nature of charter and membership in the Federal Reserve or FDIC. By law, all national banks must be members of the Federal Reserve System, while membership in that system is optional for state-chartered banks. Also provided by statute is automatic insurance of deposits by the Federal Deposit Insurance Corporation for all commercial banks that are members of the Federal Reserve System (FRS). State chartered banks that are not members of the Federal Reserve System may nevertheless receive FDIC insurance protection for their depositors, subject to FDIC approval.

As of December 31, 1976, the number and deposits of commercial banks by class are shown in Exhibit 83–1.

It will be noted that national banks comprise approximately 32.2

Exhibit 83–1
Number and Deposits of Commercial Banks, December 31, 1976

		Deposits	Percent	
Item	*Number*	*(Millions)*	*Number*	*Deposits*
All commercial banks...................	14,698	$845,057	100.0%	100.0%
National banks	4,737	472,124	32.2	55.9
State banks, FRS	1,023	149,482	7.1	17.7
Insured state banks, not				
members FRS.....................	8,651	209,318	58.8	24.8
State banks not insured				
by FDIC.........................	287	14,133	1.9	1.6

Source: FDIC, *Annual Report*, 1976.

percent of all commercial banks but hold about 55.9 percent of all commercial bank deposits. Such banks are supervised directly by the Office of the Comptroller of the Currency and are subject to the National Bank Act as well as certain other federal statutes. In terms of number, most commercial banks are state chartered, nonmembers of the Federal Reserve System, supervised at the federal level by the FDIC. These banks are of smaller size on average than either national banks or those state-chartered banks that have opted for membership in the Federal Reserve System. Banks in the latter group are supervised by the Federal Reserve.

State-chartered banks are also supervised by the various state agencies, resulting in dual supervision (i.e., federal and state) for those state banks that are insured, or that are insured and also members of the Federal Reserve System. The relatively small number of state-chartered banks whose deposits are not insured by FDIC are supervised only by state authorities.

The supervisory role of the FDIC is understated in Exhibit 83–1 to some extent because of the omission of mutual savings banks. These banks numbered 473 on December 31, 1976 and are located in only 17 states. Over 69 percent of the number, holding $98 billion in deposits, are also members of the FDIC and therefore subject, at the federal level, to supervision by that agency.

Changes in the distribution of commercial banks by class occur regularly, as a result of new bank charters, mergers, and various types of conversion by operating banks. The most noticeable trend in recent years has been the decline in the number of state member banks, resulting to some extent from conversions to national charter but, for the most part, from abandonment of membership in the Federal Reserve System. Whereas state member banks comprised 10.2 percent of all commercial banks and held 24.5 percent of all commercial bank deposits in 1965, data above shows noticeable declines in both categories.

The number of state-chartered, nonmember banks, by way of contrast, has increased rather significantly. The FDIC, it will be noted, supervises more commercial banks than the Office of the Comptroller of the Currency and the Federal Reserve combined. Moreover, the portion of deposits held in nonmember banks has been increasing, rising from 16.6 percent in 1965 to the 26.4 percent shown in the above distribution. This has resulted in part from the desire of banks, both national and statemember, to conserve expenses by utilizing the more favorable reserve requirement provisions applicable to state nonmember banks. Also it reflects the level of chartering activity by the states, where 923 out of 1,471 new banks beginning operation in a five-year period ending in 1975 were FDIC-insured state banks not choosing membership in the Federal Reserve System.

Multioffice Banking. As has been true during the entire history of banking in the United States, there are more banks that operate only a single office, with no branches, than there are banks operating branches. However the number of banks in the latter category has increased, totaling 5,739 at the end of 1976. As indicated earlier, these branching banks had 31,404 branch offices at that date.

Multioffice banking also takes other forms, the most notable of which is through bank subsidiaries of multibank holding companies. This form of multioffice banking is of course most likely to be found in states that prohibit or severely restrict branching, but nevertheless permit holding company banking. At the end of 1976, there were 316 multibank holding companies, with 2,422 bank subsidiaries. Generally speaking, where both branching and multioffice banking by bank holding companies is permitted, the bankers have opted for branching. Thus in states such as California and North Carolina, branching is extensive, and most of the holding companies are of the one-bank variety.

Various other forms of multioffice banking exist, but unfortunately reliable data are not available. In states that prohibit or severely restrict branching, chain banking is frequently found. That is, in a personal capacity an individual may own or control two or more banks. In some instances such ownership or control is simply reflective of investment decisions by the individual; in other instances the chains may be operated under some kind of common policy and resemble, to that extent at least, branching or holding company systems.

Except for chains, severe geographic limitations apply to multioffice banking by commercial banks. In the case of branching, national banks may operate branches only within the states in which they are located, and then only over the geographic area that is also permitted for state-chartered institutions in the same state. State laws vary widely, ranging from extreme restrictions on branching in about 15 states, to various kinds of limited area branching (county or multicounty, most commonly) in about 15 states, and statewide branching in another 20 states.

Precise classification is difficult, in large part because of the various types of branches permitted (ranging from so-called tellers' windows to full-service branches) and certain other restrictions that indirectly constrain the geographic areas over which branching may be conducted, such as so-called home-office protection statutes, that preclude branching into an area, at least on a de novo basis, where a bank is already situated.

Where permitted by the states, bank holding companies may only operate in the states in which they are located, in accordance with the Bank Holding Company Act of 1956. A small number of bank holding companies operating interstate prior to 1956 were permitted to continue to do so. Federal law does provide for interstate operation of bank holding companies when a state expressly permits out-of-state holding companies to enter, but there have only been a few instances of this.

Concentration. A structural characteristic of American banking that receives a large measure of attention—for reasons that are not altogether clear—is the concentration of banking resources. Concentration is the portion of banking deposits or assets held by one or several banks or banking organizations in a given geographic area. Clearly, some measures of concentration may be of importance in evaluating the competitive implications of a merger, while other concentration measures are only of general interest and of little economic significance.

In the latter category probably falls measures such as the proportion of all deposits held by the 100 largest commercial banks or banking organizations in the country. As of December 31, 1976, the 100 largest banking organizations (i.e., bank holding companies or banks) held 49.7 percent of all commercial bank deposits. This percentage was approximately the same as that of December 31, 1960, when it was 49.5 percent.

State concentration figures are of little more significance than national figures. For the most part, measures showing percentages of all commercial bank deposits held by one, three, or five largest banking organizations in the state indicate that states that permit relatively unrestricted branching (in terms of geographic area) are somewhat more highly concentrated than states that severely limit that form of multioffice banking. However, the correlation is not perfect. For example, both California and New Jersey permit branching throughout the entire state; the three largest banking organizations in California hold 62.1 percent of all deposits while the three largest banking organizations in New Jersey hold only 21.9 percent.

The trend of statewide concentration ratios is mixed, with some states showing increases in concentration and some showing decreases. To a considerable extent this may reflect the number of banks selected for measurement, and also the rapidity with which medium-size banks may be growing, as compared with smaller and larger size banks.

To the extent that they are meaningful at all, concentration measures can be constructed for relevant banking markets. However, the number of such markets is so great as to preclude any presentation of data here. Even generalization is difficult. However, one important observation should be made. For those states that severely restrict multioffice banking, particularly branching, statewide concentration ratios may be low relative to states that do not have such restrictions and yet concentration ratios in individual markets are likely to be much higher. That is, in a strong unit banking state, there may be many more banks in the state, relative to population say, than in a liberal branching state, but in any single market in the unit state customers are likely to have fewer banking alternatives available. A state with a liberal branching law may have in a given community, five branches of different banks, whereas if branching had been prohibited, all such business might well have been handled by only one or two banks.

Product Expansion. For the most part, the services provided by banks are not directly related to structure. However, since passage of the Bank Holding Company Act Amendments of 1970, many banking services are now provided through holding company affiliates that are separate from the banking affiliates of the same company. In addition, it is frequently the case that banks will offer services through a wholly owned subsidiary of the bank rather than through a department. A decision to provide banking services through bank-related facilities or subsidiaries will be dependent upon a number of factors. In the case of the holding companies, the most important factor is the ability of the holding company to provide services on an interstate basis whereas, if done directly by the bank, such services might be challenged (at least in some states) as a violation of a state's branching laws. The nature of the services that can be provided by bank holding companies is spelled out by regulations of the Federal Reserve Board, and applications to commence activity on a de novo basis, or through acquisition, must be approved by the Federal Reserve.

THE CHANGING BANKING STRUCTURE

The present banking structure is a result of legislation and attitudes that reflect the 1920s and, in particular, the early 1930s. The principal activity of the time was the erection of various types of boundaries for commercial banks and for other depository institutions. It is these boundaries that, to a considerable extent, have shaped banking structure over the succeeding 45 years.

An important boundary that was drawn or perpetuated in the 1930s was the distinction between types of institutions. Commercial banks were carefully distinguished from depository thrift institutions, particularly savings and loan associations and credit unions. The lending and depository powers of the two groups of institutions were quite separate and, in addition, separate regulatory systems, taxing procedures, and insurance provisions were provided.

Another most important set of boundaries had to do with geographic expansion by commercial banks. The Banking Act of 1933 amended the McFadden Act to provide, as already indicated, that national banks might branch in each state over those areas available for branching by state-chartered banks under state law. But this was a close decision; strong and nearly successful efforts had been made to free national banks from state limitations and provide, instead, areawide branching, regardless of state lines. That effort failed, and instead the state line was raised to a level of mystical significance for geographic expansion by commercial banks, with many states free to restrict branching areas even further, or prohibit branching altogether.

The Bank Holding Company Act was fitted into this framework, albeit by a last-minute amendment offered by Senator Paul Douglas of Illinois. That is, bank holding companies cannot expand across state lines, as we pointed out earlier, unless a state specifically permits an out-of-state holding company to acquire or organize a banking institution in its state.

Another set of boundaries or limitations related to types of business. For example the Banking Act of 1933 also provided that a wall should be created between investment banking and commercial banking, despite the fact that for more than a century the two had been intertwined. Commercial banks retain, therefore, only a limited investment banking capability, relating primarily to the obligations of governmental units.

Still another type of boundary that was erected had to do with the amounts that banks could pay for their basic raw material; i.e., deposits. Payment of interest on demand deposits was prohibited, and payment of interest on savings and time deposits was made subject to regulation by the Federal Reserve and the FDIC, depending upon whether or not the bank was a member of the Federal Reserve System. The barrier was strengthened in 1966 when Congress extended such interest regulation to the thrift institutions.

Without exception, each of these barriers is under attack at the present time. Indeed, there has been considerable erosion in several, and the prospect for the complete dismantling for the entire set of barriers over the next decade seems quite high. And since these constraints are, in many ways, the corset that holds the present structure together, it must follow that when the barriers go, so will the present structure. What will take its place is a question that only the most courageous might address.

In terms of the banking structure described earlier in this chapter, perhaps the most obvious impact will result from the expanded loan and deposit powers of the depository thrift institutions. In some parts of the country these institutions are already in the checking account business (or in a close substitute, the Negotiable Order of Withdrawal or NOW account business) and in other parts of the country various devices are being experimented with to provide full or virtually full entry into a business that for many years had been exclusively held by commercial banks. Similarly, loan and investment powers have been broadened or are in the process of being broadened, extending in some instances even to trust powers. In short, within a relatively short time the kinds of numbers discussed earlier in connection with commercial banks will be unrealistic or irrelevant. What we have, in effect, is the momentary entry into the commercial banking system of some 6,000 depository thrift institutions, and the probable entry shortly thereafter of an additional 20,000 credit unions.

The geographic boundaries are also under attack. Within the states there is a slow but persistent movement toward liberalizing state branching laws. If nothing else happens, one would be justified in assuming that over the next ten years rather substantial changes would have occurred in this direction. But something else is happening, namely the advent of the off-premise electronic facilities that can handle a variety of banking operations.

The legal snarl over these electronic devices in which commercial banks are now enmeshed as a result of the McFadden Act will, one must assume (if there is any logic to the world at all), be resolved. Projection of the number of branches therefore becomes completely impossible, for several reasons. First, if every device that communicates an instruction to a bank is to be denominated as a branch, the possible number becomes huge and irrelevant. Second, the present, traditional branch is likely to be replaced in part—though certainly not completely—by electronic devices. But no one can predict just what that rate of substitution will be. The point, of course, is the standard classification of offices into main offices and branches, and projections as to their future numbers, become virtually meaningless.

The elimination of barriers on interest payments, both on demand deposits and savings and time deposits, can also be rather confidently predicted. The former is likely to occur before the latter. The resulting cost pressures on banks and on depository thrift institutions will be great. There is no question that institutions will have to adapt, and indeed their entire price structure will be changed. But certainly the initial effect will be a downward pressure on earnings as the adjustment process proceeds.

Any scenario that foresees a large number of new competitors for the retail business of commercial banks, a relaxation of antibranching laws, and upward pressures on cost must lead to the conclusion that an increase in the trend of mergers will occur. On economic grounds alone, one should expect the number of mergers to rise, perhaps quite sharply by the early 1980s. In addition, many chain and multibank holding company systems are likely to consolidate their now "independent" banks.

By the same token, one would expect that the updrift in the number of new bank formations will slow or be reversed. It does not take much of a change in either the merger or charter trend to foresee a substantial decline in the number of banks now characterized as commercial—and perhaps a substantial decline in the number of depository thrift institutions as well.

How far this decline will go is again not susceptible to precise description. Still, the decline could be substantial enough—perhaps resulting after ten years or so in a reduction equal to about one third of the present number of operating institutions. If so, this would be the first time in the history of the United States that a substantial reduction in the number of banks was not accompanied by a severe regional or national recession.

Another boundary is that which divides federal regulation and supervision of banks among three agencies. The structure has been briefly described earlier in the chapter. Over the next ten years it is not unlikely that there will be some change in this structure. Some persons are advocating complete consolidation, while many others (the Hunt Commission, for example) have put forward various reorganization plans that would eliminate at least one of the agencies, and combine certain of the functions of the other two. Obviously, to the extent that a reorganization of the federal bank regulatory structure is consummated, the traditional distribution of banks by class might be seriously altered or possibly even obliterated.

Still another boundary, related to that described immediately above, is the distinction between banks that must retain their reserve balances with the Federal Reserve Banks, and banks that are not required to do so. The Federal Reserve is of course concerned about the cost of Federal Reserve membership, and has long been seeking uniform reserve requirements, applicable to all insured banks and established by the Federal Reserve Board. Should this occur, or should there be a substantial increase in the attractiveness of lodging reserves with Federal Reserve Banks, other structural changes will certainly occur. For example, once remaining outside of the Federal Reserve System no longer has any substantial cost benefit, many banks may be willing to join the system, and it is not unlikely that many of these, particularly the larger banks, would opt for national charters rather than state charters. The various possibilities resulting from uniform reserve requirements are intriguing, but not susceptible to precise definition. It is simply important to observe that the classical division of commercial banks by classes, and the distribution between national and state charters, might change drastically—indeed should be expected to change drastically—if there is any substantial reorganization of the federal bank regulatory structure and, more importantly, if any change occurs in the reserve requirements to which banks are now subject.

CONCLUDING OBSERVATIONS

The assignment in this chapter was to discuss the evolving banking structure. Fortunately, it did not request a description of how that structure might appear some 5, 10 or 15 years out. As is apparent from the foregoing, the author does not anticipate any substantial change over the next five years, in terms of a banking structure that would be unrecognizable compared with today's. But if asked what the structure might look like in 10 or 15 years, the only answer that can be given is that it is likely to be far different than that with which we are familiar in the middle 1970s.

Chapter 84 _____

Influence of Monetary Policy on Commercial Banking[1]

David P. Eastburn*

W. Lee Hoskins†

Commercial banks are the front-line troops when it comes to implementing monetary policy. Because of this connection, they as a group are influenced heavily by the actions of the nation's monetary policymakers. This influence is reflected not only in the volume of commercial bank activity but also in the composition of bank assets and liabilities.

Changes in monetary policy affect both sides of the banker's balance sheet, but commercial bankers must consider more than monetary policy as they pursue their goals of solvency and increased earnings. At times, bankers and policymakers may seem to be working at cross purposes. But in fact, over the long haul, their interests are compatible and even complementary, for a strong economy provides the kind of environment needed for commercial banking's growth.

MONETARY POLICY: WHAT, WHY, AND HOW?

Keeping an economy on track with respect to growth, employment, and price stability is a complicated business. Decisions of business leaders, labor leaders, and government officials, as well as the whims of

---

[1] The views expressed are those of the authors and do not necessarily reflect those of the Federal Reserve Bank of Philadelphia or the Federal Reserve Board.

* President, Federal Reserve Bank, Philadelphia, Pennsylvania.

† Vice President and Director of Research, Federal Reserve Bank, Philadelphia, Pennsylvania.

nature and chance, all impact on the stability and efficiency of U.S. economic activity. Monetary policy is only one of the planks in the structure that houses our economic system, but it's an important one. The job of any economy is to transform available resources into products that are in demand, and a well-managed money supply plays a key role in making sure that this job is done smoothly.

Policymaking. Responsibility for monetary policy lies primarily with the Federal Reserve System—the U.S. central bank. Policymakers at the Federal Reserve (Fed) are charged with managing the nation's money so as to produce stable prices, high employment, and stability in the external value of the dollar. Their objective is to foster a monetary environment that will further these economic goals.

The main tools available to the Fed for implementing policy are open-market operations (buying and selling government securities), raising or lowering the discount rate (the interest rate on loans to member banks), and altering reserve requirements (the assets member banks have to keep on hand). These tools don't achieve the Fed's policy goals directly. At first they affect just the financial markets, and only over time is their influence transmitted to the rest of the economy. So policymakers at the Fed must have a method of linking their policy tools to their economic goals. What the policymaker is looking for is a method that is not only effective but also relatively easy to control.

The most appropriate method has been a matter of much debate, both in academic circles and in the Federal Reserve System itself. Prior to the mid-1960s, the Fed emphasized money market conditions—principally movements in interest rates and in the levels of member bank reserves. Since then, the growth rate of the money stock[2] and related measures of economic health also have been employed by policymakers.

Growth in the money stock is believed to be related to overall economic activity. Over the past 60 years, trends in money growth have run almost parallel to trends in GNP (see Exhibit 84–1). But more important from the policymaker's view is the notion that *changes* in money growth influence changes in GNP. Two explanations of this process have been around for some time. One explanation, often associated with the Keynesian school of thought, is that if people find they are holding more money than they desire, they purchase *financial assets.* These purchases lead to declines in *interest rates* which tend to stimulate investment spending. And an increase in spending results in economic expansion. Money affects the economy *indirectly* through

---

[2] Money can be defined in several ways. Monetary policymakers are concerned mainly with M_1 and M_2 but also look at several other measures. M_1 is currency in the hands of the nonbank public plus demand deposits at commercial banks. M_2 consists of M_1 plus consumer time and savings accounts at commercial banks.

EXHIBIT 84–1
Gross National Product and Money Supply, 1915–1976

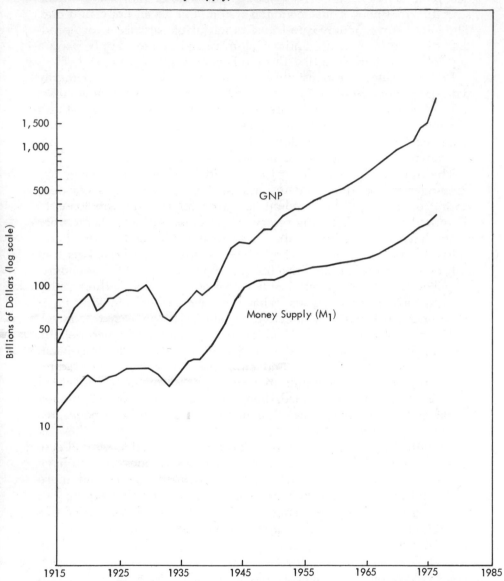

Sources: *Historical Statistics of the United States: Colonial Times to 1970*, U.S. Department of Commerce, Bureau of the Census; *Banking and Monetary Statistics*, Board of Governors of the Federal Reserve System; and *Federal Reserve Bulletin*.

interest rates, according to this view. The other view, which is more closely associated with the Monetarist school of thought (popularized by Nobel prize-winning economist Milton Friedman), does not rely so heavily on the interest rate link between money growth and spending. According to this explanation, both individual consumers and corporate businesses spend or lend money when they find they are holding more of it than they want. They purchase *real assets* (goods) as well as financial assets. Increased spending and lending stimulate production and thus the economy. In this view, money *directly* affects economic activity and interest rates play a less crucial role.

No matter which of these explanations, or which blend of the two, ultimately is accepted, both suggest that changes in money growth have a substantial impact on the economy. Thus policymakers can use money growth and associated interest rate changes as a means of nudging the economy into line with their employment, price, and output objectives. For example, if economic activity is straining capacity and putting upward pressures on prices, Fed policymakers can act to slow money growth and raise interest rates. And, if the economy is growing too slowly to employ all resources fully, policymakers may take actions to encourage more rapid money growth and lower interest rates.

Yet the policymaker's task is not as simple as it appears. It can take a long time before any change in money growth has its full impact on the economy (some estimates run as high as five years). And as world events unfold, yesterday's prescription for monetary growth may not fit today's economy. Moreover, concern over financial markets and interest rate movements often dominates the short-run picture in the policymaking process. During these periods the Fed may be shooting for a particular interest rate target, leaving its longer run target of money growth to play a secondary role. Finally, the impact of any given policy initiative on prices or employment may not conform to our expectations. Speeding up or slowing down monetary growth by a certain percentage at a particular point in the business cycle may not have the expected impact on employment. And the same is true for policy-induced interest rate changes. Deciding how much money to pump into the economy, and when, and whether to pay more attention to interest rates or to money growth, is a tricky business. Nevertheless, policymakers must select a stance, and considerations of money growth and interest rates are the key elements of this selection process.

Transmitting Policy through the Banking System. Commercial banks have the power to create and destroy money. That's why the Fed works through commercial banks to control the money stock. The largest component of the money stock is in demand deposits (checking accounts) at commercial banks (see Exhibit 84–2). Banks create demand deposits when they lend. A borrower is credited with a demand deposit for the amount of his or her loan, so the bank gains an asset (the loan) when it issues a liability (the deposit). The banking system as a whole is limited in this deposit expansion by the funds it must keep on hand to cover checks presented for payment and by the funds it is required to hold by law. Member banks of the Federal Reserve System must hold reserves equal to a prescribed percentage of deposits, and most state laws require nonmember banks to hold reserves.

Exhibit 84–2
Money Stock (M₁) as of August 31, 1977
(billions of dollars)

Demand deposits*	$244.6
Currency†	85.8
Total	$330.4

* Demand deposits are balances payable on demand at all commercial banks, except those due to domestic commercial banks and those due to the U.S. government. To avoid double counting, cash items in the process of collection and Federal Reserve float are also deducted.
† Currency includes all currency and coin outside the Treasury, Reserve Banks, and commercial banks.
Source: *Federal Reserve Bulletin.*

The Fed can induce the banking system to increase or decrease the nation's money stock by buying or selling government securities in the open market, thereby increasing or decreasing bank reserves. For example, if the Fed's goal is to stimulate a sluggish economy, it can inject reserves into the banking system simply by purchasing government securities in the open market. The Fed gives its check to the seller, and the seller deposits the check at a commercial bank. When the check is presented to the Fed for payment, the commercial bank's reserve account is credited. With increased reserve balances, the bank can make additional loans by issuing deposits to borrowers. And borrowers will want more loans if this money creation process leads to a drop in loan rates. Since commercial banks keep less than a dollar in reserve for every dollar of deposits issued, a $1 increase in reserves results in an even larger increase in deposits and hence in the money stock.[3] The Fed can speed money stock growth by accelerating the process and slow it by decelerating the process.

In short, monetary policy attempts to affect employment, prices, and economic growth by influencing money expansion and interest rates. And commercial bank reserves are the key to this control. By injecting or withdrawing reserves the Fed induces banks to make more or less money available. When the Fed goes about altering bank reserves, both the direct effects on financial markets and the indirect effects on the economy overall will influence the kinds of adjustments bankers make in their balance sheets.

MONETARY ACTION AND BANKER REACTION

The policymaker looks at the economy as a whole, but the banker must focus on his or her own corporation's profitability, liquidity, and solvency. Monetary policy is just one more item to cope with in addition to customer loan demand, deposit flows, and market interest rates.

In today's competitive financial world, the banker who is insensitive to profits attracts the wrath of the stockholders and faces the possibility of early retirement. So it is not surprising that commercial banks try to structure their asset and liability portfolios for the greatest possible returns consistent with continued solvency. Commercial banks cannot always accurately predict future loan demand, interest rates, and deposit flows. Consequently, they hold liquid assets as a buffer against the unexpected. Some of this buffer may be held in earning assets such as Treasury bills and some may be held in nonearning assets such as cash reserves. This liquidity gives them flexibility in taking advantage of new profit opportunities as they arise or in meeting unexpected cash or deposit drains.

When Federal Reserve initiatives alter the cost and revenue picture, banks change the makeup of their holdings to reflect the new or anticipated conditions. For example, if total reserves are increased by a Fed purchase of government securities, banks may find that they no longer hold the most profitable distribution of assets and liabilities.

---

[3] Member banks generally issue about $4.50 in demand deposits for each dollar of reserves. Total demand deposits are usually one-third higher than member bank demand deposits, so for each $4.50 in member bank deposits we can expect $6 in total demand deposits ($4.50 × 1^1/$_3$ = $6.00). The public mixes about 1 part demand deposits to .3 part currency. Thus, $6 of demand deposits translates into about $7.80 worth of money ($6.00 × 1.3 = $7.80). So if the Fed increases reserves by $1 billion, the money stock increases some $7.8 billion if all these links hold tight. Although the Fed most commonly uses open-market operations to influence bank reserves, it can get similar results by changing reserve requirements or by lending to member banks through the discount window.

With a higher ratio of nonearning to earning assets, there is an incentive to expand loans and investments. Fed actions can affect the liability side of the balance sheet too. A withdrawal of reserves from the banking system can lead to a change in the distribution of liabilities as bankers go to money market sources or the Fed for funds to satisfy customer loan demand.

Moreover, bankers watch carefully for signs of a change in the Fed's policy stance in order to take into account its consequent impact on market interest rates. Expected changes in interest rates can influence bank portfolio strategy for they can generate capital gains and losses. A capital gain on a bond portfolio occurs when bond rates fall and a loss occurs when rates rise. Thus bank investment managers try to anticipate changes in market rates in order to position their portfolio so as to reduce expected capital losses or to increase potential gains.

For example, suppose bank portfolio managers believe that several months down the road the Fed will tighten policy and market interest rates will shift upward. Such managers may begin to alter their portfolios by shortening maturity structures and keeping more liquid positions. By doing so, they hope to reduce capital losses when bond rates rise and take advantage of investing at higher rates later. If bond rates are expected to fall, portfolio managers would reverse the process in hopes of achieving capital gains and "locking in" investments at the higher rate.

Thus bankers, in attempting to peer into the future and plan their portfolio strategy, often take anticipated policy actions by the Fed into account. And by so doing, they may alter their investment holdings.

How the distribution of bank assets and liabilities finally turns out also will be influenced by restrictions in financial markets. The Fed can slow money growth by holding reserves back from the banking system and letting money market interest rates rise as banks bid for funds. When this happens, restrictions in financial markets put certain assets and liabilities at a disadvantage. Take the case of mortgage ceiling rates that exist in some states. As market interest rates rise and the gap between them and mortgage ceilings narrows, banks find that it pays them to shift their efforts to other kinds of lending, and mortgage money disappears. Moreover, the Fed uses Regulation Q to set ceilings on the interest rates that commercial banks can pay on time and savings deposits. When market interest rates rise significantly above the ceilings, some bank deposits will be attracted to higher yields available in the market. In situations of this kind, banks seek alternative sources of funds which can substantially alter the distribution of their liabilities.

Thus the actions that the Fed takes affect both costs and revenues at commercial banks. Initiatives that change money growth or interest rates can induce banks to alter their lending and investing activities. And restrictions on financial markets that close off traditional sources of funds and borrowers bring on further restructuring of bank balance sheets.

IMPACT OF MONETARY POLICY ON COMMERCIAL BANKING: THE RECORD

As the Fed swings into action, bankers make adjustments in their balance sheets in the interest of earning profits. But what kinds of changes do they make and what is the impact on profits? A look at past trends in bank assets and liabilities in comparison with tight and easy monetary policies gives a pretty good indication.

There are several ways to define tight money. Many people identify it with high interest rates. But interest rates can be a poor indicator of tight money. If interest rates sufficed to characterize monetary policy, then, in comparison with most of the 1950s, the last ten years might qualify as a tight money period. Yet much of the rise in interest rates over this period was caused by high inflation. Lenders have to build expected inflation into their loan charges if they are to recover the value of loans in terms of purchasing power. The result is high interest rates during periods of anticipated inflation.

A better indicator of Fed-induced tight or easy money is the monetary growth rate. From this point of view, tight money or restrictive policy can be defined as a condition in which the rate of money growth falls significantly below an established trend—a trend to which economic activity has become adjusted. A significant deceleration below this trend makes money tight in the sense that it makes planned expenditures more difficult to finance and boosts borrowing costs relative to expected money returns on investment. Using a procedure to define significant decelerations in money growth developed by William Poole, we can identify three periods of tight money or restrictive monetary policy in the years since 1960.[4] One problem with this procedure is

---

[4] These periods are May–February 1966, April–November 1969, and September 1973–September 1974. The procedure used to identify tight money is to define an established trend of money growth. The trend is based on two-year averages. A significant deceleration occurs when money growth drops below the projected established trends by an amount that normally would induce a recession. The tight money period is terminated at the point where the business expansion peaked. This is done because a recession itself can induce changes in bank portfolio behavior. Thus, by terminating tight money periods at the peak, the problem posed by trying to disentangle the effects of recession and slow monetary growth on bank portfolio behavior is avoided. In addition, monetary policy usually takes a less restrictive stance or turns "easy" during recessions. (The 1974 peak was chosen because two of the major indicators of business cycles—employment and the industrial production index—peaked in the fall of 1974.) For a full discussion of the development of this criterion, see William Poole, "The Relationship of Monetary Decelerations to Business Cycle Peaks: Another Look at the Evidence," *The Journal of Finance*, vol. 30 (1974), p. 697.

that it does not separate the impact on bank portfolio behavior of a general economic slowdown from the impact of restrictive monetary policy. However, to the extent that policy actions induce a decline in economic activity, the consequence on bank behavior can be attributed directly to monetary policy.

Liability Adjustments: Large Banks.   Monetary policy actions have brought about significant adjustments in the liability side of bank balance sheets. However, they affect the liability picture for large and small banks somewhat differently. Large banks (over $100 million in deposits) comprised only 6 percent of the 14,633 commercial banks in the United States in 1975, but they accounted for more than 85 percent of total bank deposits. A key innovation for large banks since 1960 was the issuing of liabilities at competitive interest rates to generate funds for investment or liquidity.[5] This practice, known as liability management, helped large banks raise funds outside the normal deposit channels by selling liabilities. While monetary policy actions cannot take sole credit for this development, they probably played some role in the expanded use of liability management.

Prior to the 1960s, bankers sold assets (usually Treasury securities), borrowed from the Fed, or tapped the federal funds market when they needed money to satisfy customer credit demand during tight money periods. But by the mid-1960s, many had begun to sell measurable amounts of liabilities in the form of large certificates of deposits. During the first tight money period of the decade, large CDs ($100,000 or more) were of little help to bankers in raising funds because money market interest rates exceeded the ceiling rates that the Fed permitted them to pay. Bankers were unable to roll over maturing CDs at a time of strong customer demand for credit (see Exhibit 84–3). Some bankers adjusted the liability side of their balance sheets by seeking dollars from abroad. Larger banks moved aggressively to draw in funds from the Eurodollar market. This source of funds appealed to bankers because they could use all the borrowings for lending without holding a portion in reserve at the Fed. Bankers also increased their borrowing from the Fed. These adjustments helped large banks weather the rigors of a tight money period in which the availability of funds in the CD market was curtailed.

In 1969, monetary policymakers again moved to slow monetary growth because of inflationary pressures building in the economy. Money market rates were already above the permissible rate on large CDs, and a substantial runoff of CD money was under way. Banks continued to tap the Eurodollar market along with increased borrow-

---

[5] For a detailed description of this practice, see Donald M. DePamphilis, "The Short-Term Commercial Bank Adjustment Process and Federal Reserve Regulations," *New England economic Review,* May/June 1974, pp. 14–23.

EXHIBIT 84-3
Selected Liabilities of Commercial Banks, 1961–1977

Billions of Dollars

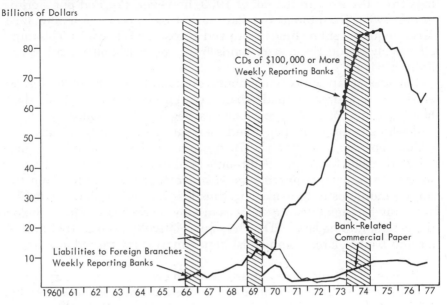

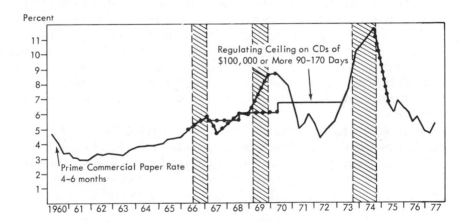

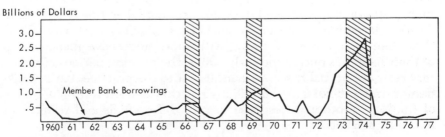

Note: Shaded areas indicate tight money periods; see footnote 4.
Source: *Federal Reserve Bulletin.*

ings from the Fed. In the fall of 1969, however, the Fed put a crimp in borrowing from the Eurodollar market by imposing a marginal reserve requirement on funds borrowed abroad by U.S. banks. This move effectively raised the cost of funds from the Eurodollar market (see Exhibit 84–3).

Bankers, in attempts to maintain profitability and liquidity, discovered a new source of funds—bank-related commercial paper. Bank holding companies and their affiliates began raising funds by issuing and selling commercial paper and then purchasing existing loans from affiliated banks. In the fall of 1970, however, the Fed altered its regulations to make funds raised through bank-related commercial paper subject to reserve requirements—a move that made funds from this source more costly to banks and thus less attractive. Bankers moved aggressively back into large CDs as money market rates dipped below the ceiling rate on large CDs. The now relatively more costly Eurodollar and bank-related commercial paper markets withered as a source of funds.

By late 1973, inflationary pressures again prompted monetary policymakers to slow the growth of money in the economy. From September 1973 to September 1974, the Fed retained a restrictive grip on bank reserves and monetary expansion. But this time the Fed removed the ceiling rate on large CDs as money market rates climbed above the ceiling rate. This action kept banks from being forced out of the CD market as they had been in past tight money periods, providing they were willing to pay the price for funds. The CD market flourished during this tight money period (see Exhibit 84–3). And banks whose customers were willing to pay the price could get the funds they wanted.

Responding to the removal of ceilings on large CDs, weekly reporting banks raised more than three times what they had raised through CDs in previous periods of monetary restraint. In addition, member banks relied to a much greater extent on borrowings from the Fed. Banks largely ignored nondeposit sources of funds and the Eurodollar market.

In sum, monetary policy action had a strong influence on the adjustments large banks made to the liability side of their portfolios. Tight money substantially reduced the volume of bank liabilities (see Exhibit 84–4) as large banks altered the makeup of liability portfolios. While these banks already were toying with more aggressive management of their liabilities during the early 1960s, the ensuing periods of monetary restraint probably served as a catalyst to the practice. Large banks demonstrated flexibility and initiative as they shifted from one source of funds to another in response to rate differentials and restrictions in credit markets.

EXHIBIT 84–4
Net Increase in Liabilities of Commercial Banks and Their Affiliates*

Billions of Dollars

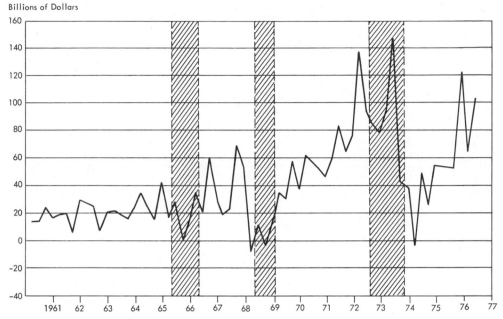

Note: Shaded areas indicate tight money periods. See footnote 4.
* Commercial banks, domestic affiliates, Edge Act corporations, agencies of foreign banks, and banks in U.S. possessions. Liabilities includes deposit and nondeposit sources of funds.
Source: *Flow of Funds Accounts.*

Liability Side Developments: Small Banks.

Small banks (less than $100 million in deposits) did not have the range of alternative sources of funds available to their larger counterparts. When monetary policy turned restrictive, small banks had to rely on their primary source of funds—deposits.

A major development on the liability side of the balance sheet of all banks is the shift to time deposits as the largest source of funds. Exhibit 84–5 shows this trend for small banks. In 1960 demand deposits accounted for the lion's share of deposits in small banks. By 1966 time deposits had grown to equal the level of demand deposit balances. And by the end of 1975 time deposits clearly dominated the deposit picture of small banks.

The three periods of restrictive monetary policy appear to have had only a temporary impact on the changing distribution of deposits in small banks. And restrictions in credit markets played a role in these temporary changes. When market interest rates rose substantially above the rate banks were legally permitted to pay during tight money

EXHIBIT 84–5
Total Deposits of All Banks with Less than $100 Million in Deposits

Billions of Dollars

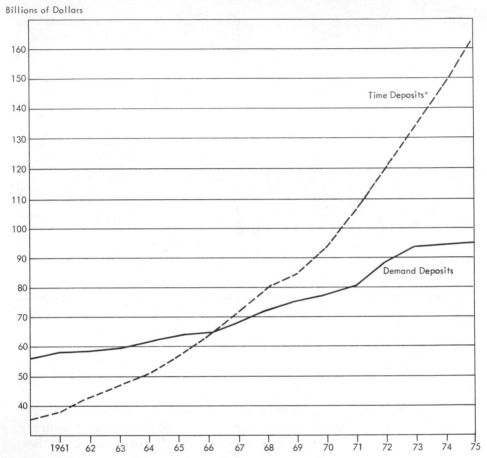

* Time and savings deposits and certificates of deposit.
Source: Federal Deposit Insurance Corporation.

periods, time deposit growth began to shrink as some small savers
shifted funds into higher yielding alternatives such as Treasury bills.
This process, known as disintermediation, occurred, at least briefly,
in each of the tight money periods since 1960 but had no lasting impact
on the long-term trends.

Some economists have argued that small banks in nonmetropolitan
markets feel less of an impact on their deposit liabilities during tight
money periods than do large money market banks. Most policy actions,
in their view, affect large banks first and then spread slowly throughout
the banking system. Thus, according to this argument, the more iso-

lated small banks are from their big city competitors, the less likely they are to feel the full impact of shifts in monetary policy. However, the existence of a widespread and sophisticated federal funds market does link small rural banks to major money markets. Thus if monetary policy turns restrictive and large banks find their reserves pinched, they may turn to the federal funds market. In doing so they bid up the price and induce small banks to continue to supply funds, and these funds are transferred immediately. In the past, small banks have been net sellers of such funds, and hence they have been linked directly to major money markets and changes in monetary policy.

In sum, small banks did not have the flexibility on the liability side of the balance sheet that large banks had. Nor did small banks appear to be as insulated from monetary policy actions as some believed. While temporary shifts in the composition of deposits at small banks occurred as monetary policy changed gears, these shifts were overshadowed by the long-term trend toward greater reliance on time deposits as a source of funds

Asset Adjustments: Large and Small Banks. The asset side of the balance sheet also changed as monetary policy shifted its stance during the last 15 years. But because commercial banking for the most part remains a business of borrowing short and lending long, the impact of monetary policy on the liability side of the balance sheet often receives more attention than its impact on the asset side. The fact that a hefty portion of bank liabilities shows up in the policymakers' money targets also increases emphasis on the liability side. The influence of monetary policy on the availability and cost of funds has a direct impact on bankers seeking funds to lend. But when lending and investing, bankers at both large and small banks have a host of things to take into account besides the current cost of funds if they are to earn a profit over the long haul. Creditworthiness of the borrower, long-term prospects for the customer's industry, and the establishment of a continuing bank-customer relationship are important considerations for bank profitability. And relative profitability of loans and securities has a strong influence on which assets bankers add to their portfolios. This is true for large banks as well as small ones.

Exhibit 84–6 shows a clear long-term trend in bank asset distribution toward loans and away from securities in the period since 1960. Yet three times during this period, a restrictive monetary policy and a faltering economy have disrupted this trend. During each of the tight money periods, the loan share of bank assets slowed its upward trend and then declined during the subsequent business slowdowns. Also, the trend in the share of bank assets invested in securities was reversed during or immediately following each of the restrictive policy periods. This asset adjustment occurred even though the spread between loan

EXHIBIT 84–6
Holdings of Loans and Securities as Share of Total Assets, Commercial Banks, 1961–1977

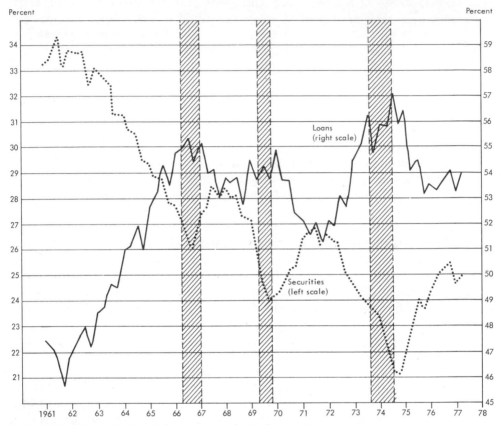

Note: Shaded areas indicate tight money periods. See footnote 4.
Source: *Federal Reserve Bulletin.*

rates and security yields tended to narrow up to the peaks of the
business expansions (which are the end points of the tight money periods). A closing of the spread should make securities more attractive
buys to bankers relative to loans. But bankers continue to make loans
even if securities must be sold at a capital loss. Why?

The answer is that bankers apparently have their eyes on long-term
profits rather than short-term gains. They do not shift into securities
because they want to retain their established customers. Satisfying
customer loan demand when funds are scarce means that customers
are more likely to stick around the rest of the time, supplying deposit
balances, and requesting loans. Thus bankers, because they look at
profitability over the long haul, try to meet the credit demand of cus-

tomers who have a continuing reltionship with them even if doing so might mean sacrificing some short-term gain.[6]

Some large banks have begun to tie changes in the prime rate to changes in money market rates, and this may keep the spread between loan rates and security yields from narrowing in the future. But the *effective* loan changes still may be held down by reducing compensatory balance requirements. If so, the same kind of asset adjustment will continue to take place.

Immediately after tight money periods, the share of bank assets in loans drops off sharply while the share in securities rises. This adjustment runs counter to the long-term trend and probably reflects a drop in loan demand that is part of an overall slump. It is difficult to separate the impact of a general economic slowdown from the impact of tight money. But to the extent that monetary policy induces a drop in GNP, the consequences on bank behavior can be attributed directly to the policy action.

In short, commercial asset distribution, while dominated by the long-term trend of loan growth and a declining role for securities, is affected by shifts in monetary policy. What these aggregated figures may mask is the differential impact of policy on banks of different sizes and business orientations—for example, wholesale and retail banks. Consequently, the schematic picture of asset distribution may not be applicable to the behavior of this or that individual bank.

The Bottom Line. It is hard to get a grip on just how monetary policy affects profitability and induces bankers to adjust their liability and asset holdings. Matching profit data with tight money periods poses a problem because profit data usually are generated on a calendar year basis while tight money periods often encompass only a part of a year or parts of two calendar years. Further, during one of the three recent tight money periods (1969), accounting changes were made that affected the calculation of profitability measures.

To get a more accurate appraisal of the impact, we have brought together in Exhibit 84–7 the return-on-capital figures for all six tight money periods since World War II. For large banks, the average rate of return on capital during tight money years (9.08 percent) was slightly lower than the average rate for all other years since 1946 (9.16 percent). Thus, despite the major asset and liability adjustment large banks made during both tight money periods, their average rate of return to capital remained relatively stable. Small banks generated about the same profit rate as large banks. However, they did suffer a larger drop in performance during tight money years. Unfortunately, these figures are not

---

[6] For a detailed analysis of this phenomenon, see J. H. Wood, *Commercial Bank Loan and Investment Behavior* (New York: John Wiley & Sons Inc., 1975), pp. 1–153.

Exhibit 84–7
Average Rate of Return to Capital, 1946–1977 (net profit per $100 of total capital accounts)

	Small Banks* (percent)	Large Banks* (percent)
During tight money years................	9.04%	9.08%
During other years	9.44	9.16

Note: Tight money years are those years in which conditions of tight money have existed for at least one month. There are 12 years in which this occurred. In 1969, changes in tax treatment and accounting definition resulted in an upward shift in subsequent net profit figures.

Above figures are arithmetic means of annual data for designated tight and easy money years. The annual data are weighted means of figures given for banks in various deposit size categories.

* Small banks are those with less than $100,000,000 in deposits, and large banks are those with more than $100,000,000 in deposits.

Source of Component Figures: Federal Deposit Insurance Corporation, *Annual Reports*.

able to show what rate of return banks might have earned if restrictive monetary policy and the following business slowdowns had not occurred. Finally, these judgments should be taken with a word of caution, since they are based on limited and unrefined data.[7]

POLICYMAKER AND BANKER: CROSS PURPOSES?

At first glance, it may appear that the adjustments bankers make often are at odds with monetary policy objectives. The Fed took action in 1973 to slow an inflation-prone economy at the same time bankers were trying to make loans that would stimulate economic growth. Nor was there any obvious appearance of harmony when the Fed tried to speed up economic recovery during the 1974–75 recession. It appeared that some bankers, concerned about solvency and liquidity after suffering large loan losses, were being extremely cautions in lending. Even as the Fed injected reserves to stimulate money growth, bankers seemed to be building liquidity rather than lending, thereby holding back the recovery. The best current evidence is that business leaders found nonbank sources of funds rather than that bankers gave up their goal of making profitable loans.[8]

As so often happens, first appearances are deceiving. There is no

---

[7] Economic literature offers surprisingly little empirical evidence on the relation of monetary policy to bank profitability. The available evidence is tentative and inconclusive. See, for example, Stuart I. Greenbaum, Mukhtor M. Ali, and Ronald C. Morris, "Monetary Policy and Banking Profits," *Journal of Finance*, vol. 31 (1976), pp. 89–101; and William J. Brown, *Tight Money and Bank Profits* (New York: American Bankers Association, 1967), pp. 1–19.

[8] See Alton Gilbert, "Bank Financing of the Recovery," *Review*, Federal Reserve Bank of St. Louis, July 1976, p. 2.

incompatibility of goals, for it is the banker's quest for profitability that ultimately permits the policymaker to pursue his or her goals for the economy. As the Fed tightens up on bank reserves, bankers continue to seek funds for lending to their customers. The price of funds rises and bankers pass much of the increase along to customers. Marginal borrowers, facing higher loan charges, drop out of the loan market. These borrowers may postpone planned spending—which can help slow the economy. If bankers decide not to pursue profitability and solvency, they can continue to lend temporarily by paying a high price for lendable funds and lending at lower rates. But such a practice can lead to a loss in profits and ultimately to insolvency.

The banker's quest for profits also aids the monetary policymaker in stimulating economic recovery. As the Fed injects reserves into the banking system during a recession, bankers find themselves holding added excess reserves that are earning no return. In the interest of profitability, they seek to invest and lend a portion of the excess reserves. Competition by bankers for loans and investments tends to lower market interest rates and attract borrowers. As borrowing and spending increase, they stimulate economic expansion. Because bankers are interested in profits, policymakers again are able to pursue their objectives in the economy.

The goals of bankers and policymakers are compatible also from a longer run perspective. If policymakers are successful at evening out jarring fluctuations in the economy, bankers and their customers gain. A boom-bust cycle for the economy creates uncertainty, can result in costly mistakes, and can result in an inefficient use of economic resources. In a smoothly growing economy, bankers spend their energies on evaluating loans and allocating credit to its most profitable uses. They spend less of their resources on guessing where the economy as a whole is going next.

Moreover, if monetary policy helps keep economic resources fully employed, then economic growth can be sustained. Sustained growth generates more lending opportunities for bankers and more output for society. Thus success for policymakers at smoothing out economic disturbances is compatible with bankers' desires for profitability and solvency.

THE FUTURE

During the past decade and a half, commercial banking and monetary policy have undergone substantial change. Bankers have established liability management firmly as a tool for adjusting the liability side of the balance sheet while shifting their assets more into loans and away from security investments. Moreover, the commercial banker has become more sophisticated with respect to monetary policy actions. He watches carefully for signs of a change in policy stance and attempts to take into account its consequent impact on economic activity when planning portfolio strategy.

Monetary policy has aided this growing sophistication by shedding much of its mystique during the period. While money market conditions are still an important ingredient in the formation of policy decisions, there has been a shift in emphasis toward the importance of money growth. Many observers feel this shift in emphasis makes it easier to interpret and identify changes in Federal Reserve policy. Moreover, the Fed now is announcing its money growth targets each quarter for the ensuing 12 months. The result is that money growth and its relation to the economy are discussed widely and are analyzed in a host of financial reports and publications. While these developments have not changed the basic link between policymaking and commercial banking, they have brought it into sharper focus.

In the future, the commercial banking environment will be shaped, in part, by developments in technology, governmental attitudes toward credit allocation, and increasing competition. The major development in technology is already with us—electronic fund transfer systems (EFTS). These systems range from point-of-sale terminals to automated clearinghouses, and they are likely to have a large impact on the day-to-day operations of commercial banks as well as on those of the Fed as they gain wider acceptance. It is likely that EFTS will permit individuals and corporations to get more mileage out of their existing money balances as the transfer of funds becomes faster. One implication of a faster transfer system is that the economy as a whole can get by with a smaller money stock. This development does not have to lessen the Fed's control over money, however, because the basic link of reserve growth to money growth will remain intact.

In addition to facing the challenge of adjusting to an automated payments mechanism, bankers also could face a host of new regulations aimed at allocating credit selectively. This is not a new issue, but it is one that is likely to receive its day in court as Congress seeks new methods for dealing with social and economic problems. The idea behind selective credit controls is to direct credit into particular sectors of the economy that Congress deems to be high on the list of social priorities. The small business and housing sectors often are cited as high-priority items deserving governmental aid. An expansion of credit policies in these areas could have an impact on both banking and monetary policy actions. Commercial banks could be influenced to alter their distribution of assets and liabilities substantially to reflect these social goals. The impact on bank growth and profitability would depend on the type of controls employed and on how efficiently bankers adjust to them. And the Fed, in conducting monetary policy, would have to be even more sensitive to the impact of its actions on particular credit markets. Unfortunately, attempts to assess the impact of credit controls are hampered because so little is known about the links between credit flows and their impact on the production of goods deemed to be socially desirable.

These changes are likely to occur at the same time bankers will be facing increasing competition from thrift institutions. Full demand-deposit powers and greater lending latitudes for thrift institutions are distinct possibilities in the coming decade. The problem for commercial banks is to develop or maintain the flexibility and initiative to meet the competitive challenge by improving the efficiency of their operations. The problem for monetary policy is one of retaining control over money growth while treating different classes of financial institutions equitably. One possible solution is to require all financial institutions issuing liabilities that become a means of payment to be members of the Federal Reserve System. An alternative is to impose uniform reserve requirements on all such institutions. Either of these alternatives would preserve Federal Reserve control over money growth and, ultimately, over employment and inflation.

In sum, the next decade, like the last one, will pose new challenges for the commercial banker and the monetary policymaker. While the financial and economic environment in which they operate will be different from today's, it will be subject to the same fundamental relationship that currently binds commercial banking to monetary policymaking. And if both bankers and policymakers have learned from past failures and successes, they will be well armed to cope with the coming change.

Chapter 85

Fiscal Policy, Debt Management, and Commercial Banking

*Tilford C. Gaines**

FISCAL POLICY

Fiscal policy is the government policy that attempts to influence economic development through taxing and spending decisions. A cut in taxes or an increase in federal government spending is believed to encourage economic expansion, while an increase in taxes or a cut in spending restrains the economy.

The difference between receipts and expenditures constitutes the federal government deficit or surplus. In recent years, the budget has almost invariably been in deficit. In fiscal 1976, for example, the deficit totaled more than $66 billion, and in fiscal 1977 (the fiscal year has been changed from July 1–June 30 to October 1–September 30) the deficit was $48 billion. Deficits of this magnitude clearly have a strong influence upon economic behavior, price inflation, and the conduct of monetary policy. While the Federal Reserve System has responsibility for managing the country's money and credit system, it encounters difficulties exercising this responsibility in periods when the federal budget is badly out of balance. The national debt at any point in time is the result of the cumulative deficit over the life of the country. As of the end of fiscal 1977, the national debt totaled $690 billion, more than double the $341 billion of debt at the end of fiscal 1967.

Prior to the 1930s, the objective of government fiscal policy was to achieve a balanced budget, year in and year out. The Great Depression of the 1930s, however, led to emphasis upon the use of the budget

* Senior Vice President and Economist, Manufacturers Hanover Trust Company, New York, New York.

for countercylical purposes. In other words, instead of aiming consistently for a balanced budget, policy became one of aiming at a surplus in periods of strong economic activity or inflation threats and of aiming for a deficit in periods of recession and underemployment in the economy. The concept of the "cyclically balanced" budget rather than the annually balanced budget was broadly accepted by both conservatives and liberals. The difficulty, however, was Congress and the administration in office found it politically easier to cut taxes or increase spending than to raise taxes or reduce spending. As a consequence, budget deficits have tended to prevail rather than a cyclically balanced budget.

In recent years, a new budgetary concept has been accepted in Washington, the so-called high (or full) employment budget. This concept is viewed by many as a form of rationalizing the tendency for the budget to be in deficit most of the time. It states that a federal budget is in balance when the economy is fully employed, with the definition of full employment usually being 4 percent unemployment in the labor force. Under this concept, even the huge budget deficits of recent years can be explained away in view of the fact that unemployment has tended to hold at unusually high levels.

There are a great many difficulties with the high-employment budget concept. For one, it does not allow for demographic shifts in the composition of the labor force. A large part of the high unemployment in recent years has been due to the unusually rapid flow of teenagers and women into the labor force. Often these new entrants to the labor force lack the necessary skills to obtain productive employment and, therefore, are put to work only under conditions of severe labor shortages. Another shortcoming of the high-employment budget concept is that it measures employment in terms of labor force employment and does not contemplate the extent of employment of capital and equipment. There have been times, such as in late 1973 and early 1974, when productive resources other than labor were seriously strained at the same time that the labor force unemployment rate was unusually high.

The principal reason for concern about the high-employment budget concept is that it tends to emphasize putting peple to work whatever the cost in terms of price inflation. A large budget deficit at times of pressure upon the country's productive capacity coupled with an accommodative monetary policy, can be a direct cause of price inflation. If the net spending injected into the economy by the federal government exceeds the ability of the economy to generate products, the result is a classic case of too many dollars chasing too few goods, leading to price inflation. In recent years, analysis of fiscal policy has become considerably more sophisticated than earlier. It is now generally recognized, both among liberals and conservatives, that fiscal policy aimed at generating inflation must be aimed partly at encouraging industry to invest in new plant and equipment. But the principal thrust of thinking of the budget remains concern about labor force unemployment rather than price inflation.

In comprehending fiscal policy, it is necessary to look behind and beyond the unified budget accounts. For example, the taxing and spending policies of state and local governments also have an impact upon economic well-being and price inflation. Also, spending and taxing for the federal government trust funds (the largest of which is the social security fund) while included in the budget numbers should be analyzed separately. For many years a surplus in the trust funds helped to finance deficits elsewhere in the budget, while currently the trust funds themselves are incurring disturbingly large deficits.

Finally, in analyzing fiscal policy it is necessary to look at the many government agencies that are not contained in the unified budget. These are the agencies that provide financing in agriculture, housing, and other fields. Just like the federal government debt, their debt continues to grow year by year in reflection of deficits in their own budgets. It perhaps is not fully accurate to describe their budgets as being in deficit, since the lending function they perform is analogous to the function performed by the private financial system. At the same time, to the extent that the cost of their programs outruns their receipts, so that they must rely upon borrowing to finance their outlays, they have a similar effect upon economic activity and upon price inflation as a deficit in the unified federal budget.

DEBT MANAGEMENT

In addition to the effect that the federal government has upon the economy through its taxing and spending policies, it has a quite separate effect through the measures it employs to manage the public debt. As noted earlier, the public debt at the end of fiscal 1977 came to $690 billion. This amount of federal debt obligations outstanding is a sizable proportion of total public and private debt. The Treasury's decisions in its frequent trips to the market as to the maturity of the instruments to be offered and other terms, can have an important impact upon credit markets in this country and, for that matter, upon world credit markets.

The most important objective of Treasury debt management, obviously, is to assure an availability of funds as bills come due. It is this cash flow concept that determines the timing of Treasury financing. But there are a great many other considerations all included under the umbrella of interference with the marketplace. For example, there has been rather considerable concern in recent years that financing huge government deficits might "crowd out" other borrowers. While "crowding out" has not occurred in any measurable way, the possibility was a very real risk, a risk that could become an observable fact at any time in the near future unless the size of the deficit to be financed is brought under control.

The sheer magnitude of the task of financing the federal government is the most important consideration in appraising the potential for market disruption. In fiscal 1976, when the budget deficit to be financed totaled $65.6 billion, the Treasury actually financed $87.2 billion, without allowing for the weekly roll-over of Treasury bills. In addition to the huge deficit that had to be financed, the Treasury had to refund maturing obligations. This combined job of cash financing and refunding caused the Treasury to be in the money market on 23 separate occasions during the fiscal year. On each of those occasions, there was the real possibility that the securities offered by the Treasury might not be acceptable to the market, leading to a financing failure that could be deeply disturbing to the rest of the market.

The techniques employed by the Treasury in financing U.S. government debt involve appraisal of the ownership of maturing debt to be refunded, maturities to be placed on new issues, the selection of debt instruments to employ, and a number of other considerations. With regard to ownership of maturing debt, as of the end of fiscal 1976, more than $150 billion of the outstanding $632 billion was ownd by federal agencies, particularly the government trust funds and the Federal Reserve System. To the extent that government institutions own a sizable part of maturing debt, the Treasury's concern about not achieving a successful financing is minimized. The government institutions will automatically roll over their maturing securities. At the other extreme, the share of the maturing debt held by individuals and households is an important consideration since reaching these investors with the Treasury offering can be a complicated venture. Also, as discussed later, ownership of maturing debt by commercial banks and thrift institutions may pose a refunding problem at times of unusually tight money.

Whether the particular financing is to borrow new money or to refund existing debt, or a mixture of both, selection of the maturities to use on the new issue is a matter of critical judgment. In the first place, the market for long-term debt obligations is much narrower than the market for short to intermediate obligations. Therefore, offerings of long-term bonds must be limited in size if they are not to have an adverse impact upon the market for corporate debentures, municipal bonds, and mortgages. While money is "fungible," the latitude for short-term investment funds to move into intermediate- or long-term investments is limited. Short-term investors invariably invest primarily at short term, while long-term investors almost invariably invest at long term. Another consideration in selecting the maturity of the new security issue is the desire to avoid concentrating too much debt in short maturities that might create financing problems as the burden of short-term debt matures. This consideration often is encompassed in a desire to prevent the average maturity of the public debt from becoming too short. But one cannot really comprehend this aspect of debt management solely in terms of average maturity. After all, selling only $1 of a perpetual obligation would theoretically make the average maturity of the debt infinitely long.

So, in the case of selecting a maturity, judgments are involved as to the type of security investors prefer and the amounts of investable funds available at that maturity. Because of this consideration, a typical Treasury financing, especially refundings, will offer investors two or more maturities. Each maturity offered will bear a different rate of interest that reflects the Treasury's judgment as to the interest rate necessary to attract the desired amount of money. If the Treasury underestimates this rate of interest the result could be a "financial failure" in which subscriptions for the securities offered fall short of the amount needed to complete the financing. On the other hand, if the rate of interest offered is too large, it could lead to harmful repercussions for the rest of the money market as investors interpret the high rate of interest offered by the Treasury as indicative of a bearish outlook for the money market.

Types of Securities Used

There are four types of securities that the Treasury may use in its financing. First are Treasury bills, which are securities of one year or shorter maturity sold at auction on a discount basis. As of the end of fiscal 1976, there was a total of $161.2 billion of Treasury bills outstanding. The second instrument is certificates of indebtedness which also are of one year or shorter maturity but are sold at a price related to par and carry interest coupons. At present there are no certificates of indebtedness outstanding, and it is possible that the Treasury will not again return to the use of such instruments. Third, Treasury notes are sold with initial maturities of one to ten years at a price related to par and carry interest coupons. At the end of fiscal 1976 there were $191.8 billion notes outstanding. In recent years the Treasury has relied most heavily upon notes in its effort to create a debt structure that will provide for orderly maturities in the years ahead. Finally, Treasury bonds are securities with an original maturity of more than ten years, sold at a price related to par, and bearing interest coupons.

At the end of fiscal 1976, there were $39.6 billion of Treasury bonds outstanding with maturities ranging from 3 years to 24 years.

In financing the public debt, the Treasury relies upon a variety of techniques ranging from the sales at auction of Treasury bills, at a discount, to sales of coupon securities at a fixed price. In any given financing, there might be and often is a variety of techniques used. In other words, the Treasury might offer 5-year notes at a fixed price, 9-month bills at auction, and a 25-year bond at competitive bidding. It should be reemphasized that the selection of the maturity, the interest rate (if any), and the offering technique is calculated to do the financing job with minimum disturbance to the rest of the market.

In addition to financing the direct Treasury debt, financing and refinancing the government agencies is a major part of total public debt management. As of the end of fiscal 1976, agency securities outstanding totaled $98.7 billion, including issues of the farm credit agencies, the housing agencies, the Export-Import Bank, and others. Generally, the same considerations that guide the financing of the direct public debt are applicable to financing the government agencies.

Interest Ceilings

In concluding the discussion of Treasury financing techniques, at least passing reference should be made to a legal stipulation that for many years impeded the ability of the Treasury to maintain an orderly debt structure. Under the Second Liberty Loan Act, as amended, the final financing of World War I stipulated a 4¼ percent rate of interest on the bonds included in the financing. In subsequent years, the rate of interest the Treasury had to pay to sell bonds remained consistently below 4¼ percent, so that the "ceiling" rate specified in the act was meaningless. But by the late 1950s interest rates had risen to the point where a 4¼ percent coupon on bonds was not salable—a rate established by the Congress for a single financing had become the permanent law of the land. In recent years, however, Congress has permitted limited bond sales at whatever rates of interest the market might demand, thus partially freeing the debt managers to control the average maturity of the debt and to maintain a more orderly debt structure.

PUBLIC FINANCE AND THE COMMERCIAL BANKING SYSTEM

Commercial banks play a central role in implementing government fiscal policy and Treasury debt management operations. In fiscal 1976, when the Treasury marketed $87.2 billion of U.S. government securities (excluding weekly sales of three-month and six-month bills), commercial banks accounted for $34.8 billion of the original allotments.

But banks were partly intermediaries since they added only $22.8 billion to their holdings of governments in that fiscal year, which indicates their role as underwriter and distributor to other investors in U.S. government securities. It is not an exaggeration to say that were it not for commercial banks the Treasury would not be able to finance itself or that, alternatively, another type of financial intermediary would have to be created.

While the banking system greatly assists orderly financing of the U.S. government, there are dangers inherent in this banking function. The ability of banks to underwrite the Treasury depends in significant degree upon the willingness of the Federal Reserve System to supply the reserves needed by the banks to support their investment portfolios. There can be times when supplying such reserves would be contrary to sound, noninflationary monetary policy.

The most striking illustration of such a situation occurred during World War II. Between the end of calendar 1941 and December 1946, the total of the U.S. government debt grew by 308 percent, from $56.3 billion to $229.5 billion. During this same interval banks added $53 billion to their holdings of government securities, and the Federal Reserve System added $21 billion. In total, the banking system financed 43 percent of the net wartime government deficits. Because of unwillingness to levy the taxes required to pay the unprecedented costs of the war, the Federal Reserve found itself in the position either of underwriting the U.S. Treasury or of seeing interest rates drive sharply higher. More important was the risk that the U.S. military capability might be impaired by financial constraints. The upshot was that in the five years of December 1941 to December 1946, the money supply (currency and demand deposits in banks) increased by 129 percent, and, "as the night follows the day," consumer prices rose by 33 percent. If a longer period were used, inflation would have shown approximately the same rise as the money supply.

It does not necessarily follow that in another period as critical as the early 1940s the same financing mistakes would be made. It should be remembered that the country in 1941 was just emerging from the worst depression in its history. The emphasis was upon putting the unemployed back to work rather than upon fighting inflation. The new "Keynesian Doctrine" had just appeared. As a result, Federal Reserve policy was aimed at keeping interest rates steady rather than at controlling either the money supply or price inflation. During the war years, the Federal Reserve intervened in the market to hold interest rates on U.S. government obligations in a range between 0.375 percent on 90-day Treasury bills to 2.5 percent on long-term Treasury bonds. This intervention took the form of buying all Government securities offered to the Fed at the pegged price. Since these purchases created reserves that commercial banks might use to support larger asset and liability positions, this policy effectively turned control of the monetary system over to private investors and the Treasury.

It might be hoped that this Treasury financing dilemma of World War II that led to inflationary bank financing of government deficits will not be repeated. But the danger of a recurrence of this situation arises whenever the government's deficit presses against the capacity of the private, nonbank financial market to provide the money. Such a situation has existed in recent years. The huge Treasury deficits in 1975 and 1976 were financed without undue pressure upon interest rates or undue reliance upon purchases by commercial banks only because the credit needs of business were minimal. There was room for the market to accommodate the Treasury. In early 1977, the question of possible inflationary financing of the big government deficit arose again, particularly if business credit needs had accelerated in pace with the improvement in the economy.

Beyond the functions of the banks as net buyers of government and agency securities in financing the U.S. government, their role as underwriters remains. The very largest banks fit this function largely by buying new Treasury issues for their own accounts, at their own risk, to resell to correspondent banks. Often a profitable speculation, but not always. More commonly, commercial banks of *all* sizes act as middlemen, submitting orders for new Treasury securities on the request of their nonbank customers. This is a valuable service for the nonbank customers (both businesses and households) and for the Treasury in placing its debt.

It may also be a marginally profitable operation for the bank involved. When orders for new government securities are placed through a bank, the original payment takes the form of a charge to the customer's account and a credit to the Treasury's tax and loan account. During the time that the money remains in the Treasury tax and loan account, the bank should earn a residual return on the balance over and above whatever interest payment it must make to the Treasury. Also, many banks charge a small fee for handling the subscription and the bank entries.

Much more important than the role of banks in financing and underwriting the Treasury is their ongoing role as financial middlemen for the federal government in all of its fiscal operations. Virtually all the cash payments in and out of government and agency accounts process through the tax and loan accounts at commercial banks. Banks receive daily the withheld income taxes, the payroll (social security) taxes, excise taxes and other federal tax revenues that flow into the Treasury tax and loan accounts. As the Treasury needs these funds to meet its payments, they are called upon, the size and timing of the call depending upon the size of the bank involved.

As remarked earlier, if we did not have a commercial banking system we would have to invent one. It is true that fiscal policy ultimately depends upon the balance between receipts and expenditures by the federal government. It is true that deficits and surpluses have important economic effects. But underlying the importance of commercial banks to the government is their role as the intermediaries through which taxes are collected and payments made. The federal government is the country's largest user of financial services, and its ability to operate depends literally upon the role of the banks in processing its transactions.

Chapter 86

The Rise of Minority Banking

Edward J. Gannon*

David B. Harper†

On August 12, 1963, the Riverside National Bank opened its doors for business in Houston, Texas. Although it was only 1 of 300 banks opened that year, and in spite of its size (initial capital was less than $500,000) the opening was significant because it marked the beginning of a new era of minority banking[1] in the United States.

Minority banking is not a new development; blacks opened several banks about the time of the Civil War, 100 years before Riverside. The number fluctuated with the ups and downs of the economy over the next 70 years; new ones opened and others closed. The last big shakeout occurred in the 1930s when the number of all banks was drastically reduced. Only seven minority banks that were in business in 1934 are still operating today. These seven were joined by three banks that were organized by blacks immediately after World War II.

So in 1963 when the Riverside National Bank opened there were only ten black-owned banks in the country. Their combined assets totaled $87 million at year-end 1962. During the 13 years after Riverside opened there was a dramatic growth in both the number and size of minority banks. As of June 30, 1976, there were 83 minority banks in operation with total assets of over $1.3 billion.

---

* Executive Vice President, Charls E. Walker Associates, Inc., Washington, D.C.

† President, Gateway National Bank, St. Louis, Missouri.

[1] Minority banks are banks owned or controlled by blacks, Hispanic-Americans, Asian-Americans, or American Indians. Recently the definition used by the Treasury Department has been expanded to include banks owned, controlled, and managed by women.

What provided the impetus for this rapid rise in minority banking? What problems have these banks encountered? What positive factors are at work for these banks? What are their prospects for success?

IMPETUS FOR GROWTH

There can be little doubt that the major impetus behind the rapid growth of minority banking was the massive Civil Rights Movement of the 1960s. Through legislation, regulations and court decisions, discriminatory practices in housing, employment, education, and many other aspects of society were gradually being dismantled. While these developments were attracting daily headlines in the press another approach was being advocated by some of the leaders of minority groups. These spokesmen concluded that changes in the political and social areas would be meaningless unless they were accompanied by similar gains in the economic area. As these ideas spread, talk about black capitalism and minority business enterprise increased. The objective of this movement, simply stated, was to encourage minority groups to get into the economic mainstream and this meant taking the necessary steps to increase ownership and control of some of the companies and institutions that make up the economic structure.

While efforts were made in many industries, banking appeared to be the most fertile. It was definitely a community-oriented service industry. It was an industry that was experiencing a fast rate of growth. Moreover, there were models of minority-owned banks that could be followed.

Although the goals of different groups organizing minority banks varied, they did have many common objectives. They sensed that the market for banking services was growing among minority households and businesses. Income for minority groups, while still below the national average was steadily increasing and more minority businesses were being established. Minority banks believed they were closer to this market and could do a better job of providing the needed banking services than other banks. They also felt they could slow or even reverse the flow of capital out of minority communities. Most importantly they believed they could provide these services at a profit.

PROBLEMS CROP UP EARLY

Every new business faces problems, but for some of the minority banks the list of obstacles seemed almost overwhelming. Moreover the problems for these banks started long before they even opened their offices. The two major ingredients of any new venture, raising adequate capital and finding qualified management, were particularly difficult for the minority banks.

Because of past discrimination, there was an acute shortage of experienced bank managers. Therefore some of the early managers of minority banks were recruited from nonbank areas, such as real estate, insurance, or other business fields.

Problems of Raising Capital

Most of the groups organizing new banks had difficulty in raising the capital to get started. In many cases it took two or three years to sell the initial stock. In a few cases the task of raising the capital was so severe that plans for those particular banks were simply dropped. One favorable result of this capital shortage was that it assured broad ownership of the stock in the minority community rather than being held by a few wealthy individuals.

Assembling a board of directors was also a problem for most minority banks. The bank regulatory agencies require the board to be representative of a broad range of the community with particular emphasis on experienced business leaders. The new banks were able to secure doctors, dentists, lawyers, ministers, and other professionals but found it difficult to attract established men and women from the business sector.

Once the banks opened they encountered a whole series of new problems. For the most part, the individuals in their service areas had low incomes. This meant that the average account balance was lower than for nonminority banks. At the same time account activity was high which pushed up the cost of bookkeeping. In short, minority banks found they had to hire more employees per million dollars of deposits than their major bank competitors.

Nor did the minority banks find a large backlog of creditworthy borrowers waiting to take out loans. Many existing businesses in the area served by the banks had spotty performance records. Potential entrepreneurs expected the fledgling banks to provide both the venture capital and the operating cash to get them started. While minority banks have provided credit for small businesses, either directly or with a Small Business Administration (SBA) guarantee, they soon discovered what other bankers have long known; that is, providing the necessary service and guidance to a new small business is both time-consuming and expensive.

Lending Problems

Many of the banks organized in the 1960s were too eager to put their deposits to work in the form of loans in the community. As a result many bad loans were made during the first few years of operation. These loans came back to haunt the banks in later years when they had to be written off. Writing off loans was an expensive experience for most of the bankers. For several it created serious problems, and in three cases the minority banks were closed.

Establishing the credit policies in the new minority banks was very difficult. They were under pressure to make business and personal loans in order to fulfill their commitments to the community. They were also anxious to make loans to earn the necessary profits. Some of the new banks were criticized for not making enough loans to the minority groups they served. Others were criticized for making socially desirable but economically unsound loans. Whichever approach the banks followed they were going to be criticized by the community or stockholders, or in some cases both.

In a study of "Performance Characteristics of High-Earning Minority Banks"[2] it was shown that a group of 11 minority banks with the highest earnings record over a four-year period had a smaller percentage of their loan funds in commercial, industrial, and consumer loans than did the other 33 banks selected for the study. On the other hand, the study showed the high-earning banks had a higher percentage of their loans in real estate than the control group banks.

Other Problem Areas

The combination of high operating expenses and high loan losses has reduced the profitability of some banks and has kept others in a loss position. Yet, in spite of these losses, many observers of minority banks have been surprised that there were not more failures particularly during the 1974–75 recession—the worst economic downturn since the 1930s. While unemployment for the population as a whole reached a peak of 8.9 percent, for minorities it was even higher. To make matters worse, much of the minority unemployment was concentrated in urban areas served by the minority banks.

This is not an exhaustive list of the difficulties faced by the new minority banks. Each of the banks could add its own list of problems that had to be surmounted. However, even this partial list should make it clear to anyone that a charter for a new minority bank is not an automatic passport to easy street.

---

[2] Bruce J. Summers and James F. Tucker, "Performance Characteristics of High-Earning Minority Banks," Federal Reserve Bank of Richmond, *Economic Review,* vol. 62, no. 6 (November/December 1976). There have been many studies of various aspects of minority banking over the past decade. Most of these studies had very limited use because the statistical base was too small and covered a very brief period. The Summers/Tucker study is useful because it compares various operating characteristics of banks that had been in operation for at least four years. This enabled the authors to analyze 44—over 50 percent—of the banks in operation at the end of 1976.

POSITIVE FACTORS AT WORK

In spite of all the obstacles there are a number of positive forces at work that provide the continuing momentum for the minority bank movement. Let's examine some of the more important ones.

Perhaps the most significant factor spurring the growth of minority banks is the slow but steady rise in family incomes among minority groups. As earnings rise so does the need for additional banking services. As this trend continues, given a rising economy, the average account size will grow as will the size of the average loan. Moreover, rising incomes will also tend to increase the prospects for many minority businesses, which are also customers of the banks.

Minority bankers were correct in their assessment that they were closer to the minority market for bank services than their competitors. One study of banking patterns in a midwestern city[3] shows that over 20 percent of the customers at a new minority bank had not had a previous banking relationship. The study also showed that customers who shifted to the minority bank used more services than they were using at their bank.

Convenience Factor

Primarily due to the convenience factor most new community-type banks attract new customers when they open. However, the minority banks injected an element of pride in the communities. Residents frequently referred to the banks as "our bank." The widespread stock ownership in the banks helped spread this close identification with the banks. At the same time the banks were viewed as symbols of the establishment which would be controlled by, and add some stability to, the minority community.

Although it is almost impossible to quantify, minority banks did create an element of competition in the banking markets they serve. These new institutions offered an alternative to individuals and businesses who previously had little choice in banking matters. As a result many banks, in areas served by minority institutions, were forced to take a harder look at the services they were providing their minority customers. (The competitive aspect is hard to isolate because there was a concerted effort to increase minority business lending by all banks as a result of government and private emphasis on development of more minority businesses.)

Another area that provides encouragement to the banks is the expanding labor force pool. Over the past decade the banking industry

---

[3] Samuel I. Doctors, Allan R. Drebin, and Edward D. Irons, "The Impact of Minority Banks on Communities," *The Bankers Magazine*, Spring 1975.

as a whole has made great progress in opening up employment opportunities for minorities. According to the Treasury Department minorities represented 16 percent of the total banking work force of 1,042,984 in 1976. More importantly, 6 percent of the officers and managers in banks were in the minority category.

Opportunities for Minority Students

These new opportunities in major banks, along with the developments in minority banking, have encouraged more minority students to seek careers in banking. One major New York bank regularly sent recruiters to the predominantly black colleges in the late 1950s and early 1960s. The bank did not receive one job application from all of its visits. The reason was simple: the students did not believe there were opportunities in banking and they prepared for and selected other careers. As the opportunities began to open there was a massive shift in study patterns at the black colleges, with accounting and business administration quickly becoming very popular majors.

The importance of these changes should not be minimized. As more and more minority students pursue courses in business and finance and then gain experience in these areas many additional opportunities will be available. They can stay with a large bank, or go to work for one of the minority banks. Or they can put their financial experience to use in another field of business, again with either a large firm or a minority business. The important point is that a pool of experienced financial talent is being slowly but surely developed.

The changing personnel makeup in the major banks can help the minority banks solve their management problems. Since the minority banks are small they cannot afford extensive on-the-job training programs. However, in recent years these banks have been able to attract managers who have gained experience with the big banks. It has been interesting to note that in almost every change of chief executive officers in minority banks in the past few years the new executive has had more banking experience than his or her predecessor.

To speed up the management development process, the American Bankers Association, in cooperation with the National Bankers Association (the trade association of the minority banks) established a middle-management training program for minority employees. During 1969—the first year of the program—21 blacks participated. In later years the program was expanded to include both men and women, and Hispanics and American Indians as well as blacks.

The National Bankers Association (NBA), which was founded in 1927 as the National Negro Bankers Association, established a Washington headquarters in 1968. With financial assistance from the Commerce

Department's Office of Minority Business Enterprise (OMBE), the NBA conducts regional workshops and seminars for senior management and the directors of minority banks. The attendance at these seminars, as well as the attendance and participation at the NBA annual convention, has increased significantly with the growth of minority banking.

Programs of Assistance

The Office of Minority Business Enterprise also played a key role in another government program designed to assist these banks. That program was the minority bank deposit program sponsored jointly by OMBE and the Treasury Department. The goal of the program, started in September 1970, was to increase deposits in minority banks by $100 million over a one-year period. Of the total, $65 million was to come from the private sector and $35 million from federal government agencies and departments that utilized various services of commercial banks.

The program proved to be one of the most successful and least expensive the government ever sponsored to stimulate minority business activity. At the end of the first year total deposits in the banks had grown by $155.5 million, and government deposits had increased by $33.7 million. Moreover, the government side of the program was continued and at year-end 1976 government deposits were close to $100 million. In the process, total government deposits in all banks did not increase; minority banks were simply awarded some of the business that was previously handled by other banks.

Major corporations have also continued to utilize minority banks in various ways. For example, many corporations pay part of their taxes through minority banks. Others maintain checking and savings accounts, while still others have established lines of credit with some of the banks. In recent years minority banks have been able to join together in small groups to handle large loans that no individual small bank could make. This practice of loan participation is expected to grow as minority banks become more experienced in putting the large loans together.

In discussing the positive factors at work for minority banks it is hard to overemphasize the role played by the major banks and the American Bankers Association (ABA). All of the minority banks have developed close working relationships with one or more major correspondent banks. The major banks have provided guidance, training, and many other helpful services. They have also arranged for the minority banks to participate in large loans.

The ABA has also assisted the new banks in a variety of ways. In addition to the management development program mentioned earlier the ABA has made scholarships available to minority bankers so they can attend ABA-sponsored specialized banking schools.

The ABA has also established "Minbanc"—a closed-end investment company—which invests in minority banks to bolster their capital positions. Since it was organized in 1972, Minbanc has raised $4.4 million through the sale of stock to major banks. To date it has invested $2,750,000 in eight banks. Minbanc is not a source of capital for new minority banks. It will not invest in a bank until it has been in operation for a minimum of three years. Once the Minbanc board decides to inject capital into a bank it can do so in a variety of ways. It can purchase stock in the bank, buy debentures, or even purchase the bank building and lease it back to the bank.

When students at the predominantly black colleges started to become more interested in banking, the ABA Urban Affairs Committee decided to encourage the colleges to offer more programs related to banking. The ABA invited the black colleges to submit proposals for establishing centers on banking education on their campuses. Over 40 colleges responded with proposals. Of these the ABA visited seven and in 1974 selected Howard University in Washington, D.C., and Texas Southern University in Houston for the program.

The two schools are receiving grants totaling $400,000 over a five-year period. There are four basic elements to the programs run by the colleges. First, the faculty is encouraged to undertake banking research projects. Second, scholarships for banking students are provided. Third, the schools run cooperative education programs with banks in their respective areas. And, fourth, the faculties are working on ways to improve the banking curriculum.

Since the inception of the program, the Urban Affairs Committee has monitored the activities at the two schools. The results show that there has been a steady rise in the number of scholarships, the number of interns in the cooperative education program and the number of research projects.

PROSPECTS FOR FUTURE

Have the minority banks lived up to the promises of their founders? What are the prospects for their success in the future?

As is the case with any fast-moving development, statistics lag behind the actual situation. Studies on minority banks are almost outdated before they are published. This process is further complicated in the case of minority banks because new ones are opening at a fast rate—approximately 20 new banks were in the organizing process in 1977—others have been closed and still a third variation, changing from non-minority to minority status, or vice versa, occurs with some frequency.

But given the evidence available to date it is fair to make some general comments about the minority bank movement.

First, on the negative side, many of the new banks were overanxious to put their deposits to work in the form of loans. As a result they were forced to make marginal, high-risk loans, which, given their size, these banks cannot afford to do.

Second, although there are several exceptions, the minority banks as a group have not generated the profits necessary to insure their growth and stability. This is by far the most serious shortcoming of the new banks. If they do not get costs under control and operate at a profit they will not be able to meet any of the other worthy objectives they have set.

On the positive side the minority banks have many factors working for them. The founders were correct in their assessment that minority individuals were willing to invest in the stock of these community-oriented banks. The stockholders see the merits of having a local banking institution controlled by members of the minority community.

The founders were also correct in their assumption that they could attract new entrants into the market for banking services and that they could also provide additional services for customers who have previously banked at other institutions. Moreover, with the assistance of government and business leaders these institutions have also been able to attract deposits from outside their immediate market area.

In attempting to appraise the outlook for minority banks two major developments appear to justify the optimistic view held by the banks.

First, the energy shortage, and the changing life-style that will evolve as a result, have forced government officials at all levels as well as businesses and individuals to focus on the need to revitalize urban centers. Massive housing rehabilitation and neighborhood revitalization programs are now under way in many of the nation's major cities.

Early in 1977, Secretary of Housing and Urban Development Patricia Harris stated that the department would direct more of its resources to the improvement of housing in the inner cities. The Commerce Department, through the Economic Development Administration, also plans to channel more of its development funds into cities.

The practice of redlining—lenders refusing to lend money in deteriorating neighborhoods—is being attacked at both the federal and local level. As a result financial institutions will be much more conscious of their investment policies in the cities they serve.

Early in his administration President Carter recognized the role minority banks play in serving their communities. He pledged his support to not only continue, but to expand the federal government's minority bank deposit program. With more funds expected to flow into urban areas from the federal government the minority banks can be expected to realize a continued growth in deposits from this source.

The second major development that gives rise to the optimistic outlook can be summed up in one word—"confidence." When many of the new minority banks were in the organization stage, the founders were not sure the banks would open. (Some didn't get past the first hurdle.) Even after the banks opened there were still many doubts about the viability of the institutions. These doubts were shared by the founders and potential customers within the community served by the banks.

But as the minority banks have grown in size and financial strength, confidence in the banks has also grown. It is evident in the officers and directors of the banks. It is evident in the view the customers have of the banks. And it is certainly evident in the government's approach to the banks.

Although confidence is such an intangible factor and almost impossible to measure it is one of the most important ingredients in the banking industry. As the bankers increase their own confidence through experience, their customers and the communities they serve will realize that these new minority banks are not a passing fad and that the banks can play an ever-increasing role in the economic development of minority communities.

SECTION XV

THE YEARS AHEAD

Chapter 87

The Next Ten Years in U.S. Banking

*Paul S. Nadler**

Any observers of the banking scene who wish to predict what will happen in the next decade must first humble themselves by looking backward and seeing how poor the forecasts were that were made ten years ago. For some of the dramatic changes predicted for American banking as we looked forward to the 1970s have just plain turned out to be incorrect, and others, while correct in trend, have been far more modest than forecasters had assumed they would be.

What were some of the major predictions of how banking would change in the 1970s?

Diversification. With the start of the congeneric trend in the 1960s, most observers felt that by the mid-1970s, the major banks would no longer be just banks. They would have become "full financial service" companies in which commercial banking would be only one of the many services offered the public.

Liability Management. It was felt that through the new process of buying time and savings deposits and Eurodollars, selling commercial paper, and other techniques of liability management, the more aggressive banks would be able to free themselves from the impact of credit restraint. They would then find that the willingness to pay the going rates for funds would be the only limit on their ability to obtain all the money they wanted to meet loan commitments and to fund investment opportunities.

Scientific Management. "The computer's great strength is logic, and its great weakness is paper handling, yet the banking industry

---

* Professor of Business Administration, Rutgers University, Newark, New Jersey.

uses its computers for paper handling and not for logic." This was the comment made by observers as they predicted that banks would become great users of the techniques of operations research and scientific management. Banking decisions would be far more based on facts and data and less on hunches and opinions. This was another forecast of the mid-1960s made by those looking ahead.

The Checkless Society. It was assumed that by the mid-1970s we would see far fewer checks, with payments made by telephonic transfer, pushing buttons at points of sale, and automatic preauthorization of payment. This was the most exciting of the forecasts that proved to be vastly exaggerated.

Selling Services Rather Than Money. Many, both inside banking and outside, had predicted that by the mid-1970s, banks would earn more of their income from the sale of services for fees than from the lending and investing of money.

Fewer and Larger Banks. Finally, most observers felt that we would see a decline in the number of banks, as larger banks swallowed up smaller ones and became more nationwide in scope, either directly or through the establishment of nonbanking affiliates and loan production offices. Most forecasts predicted a reduction from about 13,500 banks to between 5,000 and 7,000 by the end of the 1970s, as opposed to the modest expansion in the number of commercial banking organizations we have actually witnessed.

This background must be kept firmly in mind as one looks at the next ten years in commercial banking. For not only can today's forecasters learn from their failures of the past decade, but also an examination of why previous predictions went wrong can help make present forecasts somewhat more accurate. At least this is our hope.

In any event, certain trends are quite apparent today that should play a major role in shaping banking's changes over the next ten years.

And if one were to sum up the general tone of the conclusions reached, it would be that change in banking in the next decade will be more modest—more in keeping with what we really saw happen in the last decade rather than what we had predicted would happen.

With this background, here are some of the expected changes:

THE COMPETITIVE ENVIRONMENT

One point can be made with certainty as one looks ahead: the banking environment will be far more competitive than in the past.

We are truly witnessing the development of "scrambled finance," under which each type of financial institution wants to get into the business of the others.

Already we see savings banks and savings and loan associations diversifying into consumer credit, checking account services, credit cards, home improvement loans, and even trust services. The NOW account (negotiable order of withdrawal) is a means by which "thrifts" can offer interest on checking accounts and thus attain full parity with commercial banks in the meeting of the basic financial needs of the individual. Credit unions also offer full payments systems through share drafts, and consumer finance companies are expanding their payments operations too. In sum, the attitude of each institution is "what's mine is mine and what's yours is negotiable." But the end product is likely to be a structure; under which the public will have far more choices as to where to bank than was the case in the past. To all financial institutions, profits will be harder to come by in this more intense competitive environment.

REGULATORY ENVIRONMENT CHANGES

Along with greater competition among financial institutions will come a basic change in the regulatory environment to match this more intense environment of competition.

It is likely that restraints such as the Regulation Q interest rate ceiling that restricts competition for time and savings deposits will be relaxed or abandoned. Thrifts may have to face the same reserve requirements and controls as banks, since the differences among the institutions will gradually disappear. And restraints on geographical expansion are likely to be relaxed further, so that institutions can take advantage of the opportunities that electronic funds transfer offer for giving the public the convenience of banking from afar. Movement of money will thus involve a national network like the telephone system rather than remaining a process of being known personally at a bank window or checkout counter.

Regulatory changes may also include revisions of our credit control structure. As indicated above, banks tried to relieve Federal Reserve restraints on tight money through aggressive liability management. What they found, however, was that the public in general and the money market in particular limited this ability to gain funds no matter how tight money became. For when a bank practiced liability management to an extreme, investors would not place new funds into its deposits and certificates no matter the rate offered, out of fear of the inherent risk involved.

Thus the Federal Reserve found that aggressive banks could not buy their way out of credit restraint through liability management. But it further found that many banks tried to limit the impact of credit restraint on them through leaving the Federal Reserve System, so that they would not have required reserves locked up in nonearning assets at the Fed.

From the vantage point of the mid-1970s, it appears that the response to this slippage of Fed authority may well be through the use of the carrot of interest payment on reserve balances rather than the stick of mandatory reserve requirements at the Fed for any bank wanting FDIC insurance. And it also appears as if this should do the trick of winning more banks back into the Federal Reserve System to gain the advantage of interest on their required reserves. At the same time, thrift institutions that offer checking accounts are also likely to be required to maintain reserves at either the Federal Reserve or at the Federal Home Loan Banks of their districts.

This means that while the regulatory environment will be more benign from the standpoint of regulations, such as interest rate ceilings, it also means that the role of the central bank as a regulator of credit policy may be easier to handle and somewhat more efficient, because of the greater percentage of institutions directly subject to its policies.

Also on the regulatory scene, we should see other artificial restraints that limit bank and thrift institution activities relaxed. Notable among these should be the easing or elimination of state usury ceilings that now limit rates charged on mortgages and other credits to rates below those available on similar obligations in other states. With this should also come the freedom for far greater usage of the variable rate mortgage and variable rate deposit, so that banks and their borrowers alike can have income and charges that move up and down to reflect going rates in the market.

To the public, this means less worry about whether the taking out of a mortgage was well timed over the business and interest rate cycle, and to institutions, it means freedom from the dilemma of variable rate savings having to be placed into fixed-rate assets. The result should be a greater flow of money into mortgages over the entire business cycle and a lessening of the disintermediation that now develops when open-market interest rates exceed those banks and thrifts are allowed to pay or can afford to pay.

Eased regulation, then, should bring an eased flow of money to the areas that have been pinched for funds when credit was tight in past business cycle periods.

STRUCTURE

While the regulatory structure limiting the geographical expansion of bank operations should be relaxed in the decade ahead, from the present vantage point it appears that the most important factor bringing bank expansion geographically and thus structure change will be electronic funds transfer mechanisms.

In the same way that an airline can serve customers in a city through telephonic connections to a central reservations and information center, a bank will be able to serve people who live and work far from its offices through the use of EFTS. Already we see the following:

1. People can deposit social security checks and payroll checks in banks located far from where they live or work through automatic deposit programs that do not even involve the writing of a check. It merely involves the movement of electronic information from the payer to the payee's bank or thrift institution.
2. Credit cards and debit cards, with national acceptance, are becoming a basic means of payment for goods and services that were formerly paid for by check or cash. A bank or thrift can issue a card to a user who lives and works far from its banking offices.
3. The point of sale terminals at grocery stores and other retail locations are generally being offered on a nonexclusive basis. The retail outlets that allow their establishment on their premises want them open to all customers of the retailer. In addition, regulators and government officials are opposing monopoly installations.

Thus it is likely that as time passes, POS terminals and free-standing automatic teller machines for that matter may well become like public telephones—installations that can be used to hook into any bank or thrift in the nation, just as one pay phone can be hooked into any other telephone in the nation or the world, no matter who services it.

On top of this, the costs of remote banking are likely to be so great that few institutions will want to offer POS terminals and automatic teller machines off-premises without having their costs and use shared by other institutions.

Thus the customer of one bank will be able to move money in and out of his account from machines anywhere, just as he can call home from anywhere.

The result will be that routine banking can go on without the customer ever having to see the bank's office. And this will breed both better public service, with money becoming a nationwide utility, and also more banking competition. The latter will result because local geographic monopolies will disappear. And if a bank is not offering top-quality service and competitive rates, people will be able to bank with institutions located elsewhere just as conveniently as they can bank with the hometown people.

But here a warning must be issued. We had thought ten years ago that trends in geographic expansion would lead to the extinction of the community bank, and we were wrong. The local organization is a hardy breed. It can provide most customer services and, knowing its customers intimately, it can make quick decisions on credits. We are likely to see some decline in the number of individual banks and even in the number of banking offices, as automatic terminals provide the convenience the public wants and needs. But the number of banks will decline only slowly. For if one thing is sure, many Americans like their local community banks and will stick with them unless service and prices become so out of line that they are forced to switch. And this is not likely to happen to too many independent institutions.

Where banks exist simply because the law has not allowed branching, and where all that is needed is a small, lightly staffed branch, the efforts at more efficient banking should lead to merger and acquisition. And in all cases, we are likely to see fewer marble buildings and more modest-sized, movable bank facilities, with storefront branches becoming more popular when terminals cannot do the full job in serving a locality.

But the day when America is down to 5,000 banks or less still appears far in the future. People like the community bank, and where the banking business is adequate to support an independent organization, we are not likely to see the bank swallowed up by larger institutions, except in those cases where the banker is just not doing the job.

In sum, banking service will cross community, county, and state lines, and bank organizations may even gain permission to branch in neighboring states in a few instances, under reciprocal agreements between states. But the unusual combination of large and small banks and thrifts that has characterized America up to now should remain intact.

BANK SERVICE

If we have learned anything from the period of the early 1970s, it is that banking is not going to expand and take over the entire financial service area.

The heady environment of the late 1960s, as banks established one-bank holding companies, was a period in which many banks looked at the investor approval given faster growing nonbank organizations and felt that if banks entered these other fields, bank stocks too would be given the higher price to earnings multiples that these more glamorous fields had received.

Bankers thus diversified into finance company operations, mortgage banking, establishing and managing real estate investment trusts, and a host of other areas that were not part of traditional banking but rather were part of the so-called congeneric structure of bank-related activities.

History shows that in many instances these outside activities caused serious trouble for the bank holding companies that undertook them. First, they involved a type of aggressiveness and risk taking that was not indigenous to banking and bank people. And second, the banks did not have the proper talent to run these organizations as they needed to be run. The recession of the early 1970s later brought many of these nonbank operations into positions of serious difficulty, and many bankers concluded that taking deposits and making loans, without going into so many nonbank areas, is a pretty good business by itself.

Certainly banking will continue to operate to a degree in these nonbank areas, but the major attention will return to commercial banking.

Even in the securities area, an arena in which we see frequent stories of possible bank competition against securities firms, there is not likely to be too much bank expansion. For laws and regulations limit bank expansion, and in addition many bankers just do not see profits in these areas of heavy paperwork and high risk.

This is not to say that banking is likely to remain static on service provision. Rather it appears that instead of continuing to look more to distant areas as opportunities for growth, banking will try to develop services that will be offshoots of present banking operations.

Thus we are likely to see bankers offering more help to customers in bill paying, inventory control, tax preparation and the other areas of financial documentation and funds flow that can be tied to the handling of the payments function.

Bankers now know that electronic funds transfer will not become the major force for the less check society and the reduction of paper handling that bankers hope it will be unless and until the industry is able to offer the public something more than just the elimination of checks (and of the public's cherished float).

These financially related bookkeeping and payments services should become more important, both for individuals and business firms, as banks try to become full financial counselors on money management and flow rather than merely the movers of money through the nation.

PEOPLE

Another area of certainty is that banks will require more skilled people and personnel with more diverse training than in the past.

One lesson of the late 1960s and early 1970s is that machines will not replace judgment. We had thought that we would see operations research techniques and scientific management help banking do its job and help make decisions more accurate and impersonal on granting credit, pricing services, establishing branches, controlling investments, and the like. What we found was that the machines cannot replace good training and intuition and years of experience.

Certainly we are developing computerized programs, but the need for bank talent should be increased rather than curbed.

Where banking faces people problems is in middle management. For there simply will not be as much need for middle managers whose function is managing the staffs in entry and lower level positions.

If banking is to prosper, it must become a more capital intensive and less labor intensive industry. And this is happening. We are reducing the number of people needed to handle routine bank functions, and the developments of EFTS should reduce this need for people in routine functions even more. Thus the career path of moving up to be a supervisor of the hoards of workers is being eliminated as the hoards of workers are reduced. And what is needed instead is a type of individual who can help provide the personal financial service to the bank's customers mentioned above.

We are likely, then, to see a change in banking that will alter the traditional career paths markedly. More and more, outsiders who have talents needed for the more complex banking services will be hired, and fewer opportunities for people to move up from entry level positions into bank management will develop. The result will be a need for even greater pressure on banking to reduce the number of clerical and routine employees, because the aggressive ones among them will no longer have the opportunities they used to have, and their unrest in static positions may lead to efforts at union organization.

Banking then will try to be more and more like the telephone company, where routine operations handle themselves, and the people on the premises are utilized for the exception transactions.

Those who move up will have more exciting challenges, but there is likely to be a wider gap between routine jobs and officer jobs than in the past, with less opportunities for movement up through the ranks because of the more complex talents needed in higher banking positions.

PROFIT

With competition growing in the entire financial sector, and with diversified services not the boon to bank income they had been expected to be, bank profits will be under squeeze in the years ahead.

Banks formerly had three good sources of profit going for them:

1. Interest rates were rising and banks could earn more year after year.
2. Banks were becoming more aggressive and switching from low-yielding loans and investments to higher yielding ones.
3. The public was not too interest rate sensitive, and banks could get money fairly cheaply.

Now all three are gone. The period of the sharp rises in interest rates are over, banks are about as aggressive as they are allowed to be, and the depositor knows the value of his or her funds and wants adequate reward for their use.

Bankers also realize that it will be hard to widen the spread between costs of funds and returns on funds in the competitive environment we face today. So they are recognizing that profits will come to the banks that are more efficient and those that are best able to earn extra income from selling the use of the talent and techniques they have on board.

One result of the profit's squeeze is that the industry is becoming more earnings conscious and is less interested in size as the basic determinant of whether a bank is doing a good job.

More and more banks are pricing services so that they offer a profit, and if the customer refuses to pay this price because he can get a lower price across the street, the banker is more likely to help him across the street and into the lobby of the competitor and less likely to reduce his price to loss leader levels than in the past.

In addition, more and more banks are beginning to turn greater attention to the types of customers who truly are dependent upon the banks and who cannot go elsewhere to get cheaper money when the banks try to charge prices for services and credit that are fully compensatory. This means that bankers are concentrating more on serving the medium-sized company that cannot turn to the money market for funds and are downgrading the courting of the larger corporation that has fund sources elsewhere. It also means that if the thrifts are willing to provide checking account services below bank costs and otherwise undercut bank operations by charging rates below what banks can afford to charge, more bankers are becoming resigned to letting the business go elsewhere rather than accepting a loss simply to have larger numbers of accounts and volumes of funds on the books.

Bankers well recognize that they will need capital to back growth. They also know that with bank stocks frequently in public disfavor, they cannot count on tapping the capital market for new equity without seriously eroding the equity positions of present shareholders when bank shares sell below book value, as frequently is the case.

Leverage has been pushed about as far as it can go in many instances. And banks also realize that too much reliance on leveraged capital positions discourages many potential borrowers from using a bank. For they fear that the undercapitalized bank will not be able to give them the credit accommodation they may need at a later date. Thus many banks have decided that they need capital as a sign of strength and as a means of backing growth, but that the only feasible means of getting new capital will be through retained earnings.

This helps explain why bankers are finally switching their emphasis from footings and growth over to profits and the "bottom line."

It is a healthy change, and it makes banking more businesslike than in the past in determining which services to provide, how to price them, and what to do if the competition is giving away the bank.

This emphasis on profit is also eliminating the old image of the bank as a comfortable place to work in which no one ever gets fired.

For the emphasis on profit has forced bankers to be hard nosed in employment policies as in everything else. And this includes eliminating employees if the jobs they do no longer are needed or if they are not able to handle the more complex activities that banking now involves.

The conflict involved here is a difficult one. For banking, like other industries, has taken upon itself the obligation of meeting social goals of aiding the community, under the principal of long-range self-interest. The basic attitude of the forward thinking banker is that if the community deteriorates, the bank's prospects will deteriorate too. Thus bankers have been leaders in urban renewal, rural redevelopment, and other programs of social betterment.

Bankers have also taken upon themselves the obligation of helping the disadvantaged to gain bank training and banking opportunities, and banks are working on meeting the spirit and not just the letter of every affirmative action program.

This brings a decided conflict between the social goals of banking and the profit goals. And the effort to meet both conflicting goals helps explain why bankers have been among the leaders in trying to develop new techniques that can make the industry more efficient and generate more income from the greater use of the talent now on board.

To say that banking will solve all its problems of profits squeezes in the next decade, however, would involve too optimistic an evaluation of the competitive environment and of the jobs that banking has taken upon itself as good public citizens. The Golden Days when banking profits were assured and all banks had earnings growth year after year are far behind us.

CONCLUSION

This, then, is the banking industry we are likely to see in the decade ahead. It is an industry whose competitors will be far more diverse than in the past, because of the widened powers of formerly specialized competitors such as credit unions and thrift institutions.

It is an industry in which banking will become more impersonal and automatic, to save costs of paper handling. Yet it is still trying to carry water on the other shoulder through management information systems, control files, and other automatic devices that can help maintain an available picture of the individual and his wants and needs even as his routine banking becomes more automatic.

It is an industry in which the types of financial services offered will be far greater than in the past, and people will find that their banks will be able to take many routine financial tasks off their hands. But the people will also find that they will be paying for these services in hard dollars and cents.

It also appears likely that our fixation with cheap money will end, and that banks will be allowed to pay more for time and savings deposits than in the past. But the place this money will have to come from is from higher charges on borrowing customers. If we are truly in a capital short nation, this is only as it should be; for the providers of the capital should be amply rewarded for their thrift while those who wish to use other people's money should pay what the funds are worth.

Finally, it is an industry that will continue to operate with a crazy patchwork structure; for banks will range in size from giant multinational organizations with thousands of branches and remote terminals in thousands of other locations, down to the unit bank that may or may not decide to connect to the electronic devices for remote deposit and withdrawal of funds that will be made available to it on a shared cost and usage basis.

Yet this is the strength of American banking—the choice between types of banks and other financial servicers that keeps each institution on its toes and leads to innovations such as the NOW account and the point of sale terminal as a means of gaining an edge—albeit a temporary one—on one's competitors.

The only development that could truly harm this industry would be if its leaders were so paranoid against change that they asked the legislators in Congress and the state houses to pass legislation prohibiting the type of dynamic change that we have seen. And even then, it is likely that some innovators, either inside the establishment or outside, would find ways around some of these new laws, just as thrifts got around controls on demand deposits through telephonic transfer of savings funds and the use of point of sale terminals and the public got around interest rate ceilings through disintermediation.

To those who fear change, it should be heartening to remember that the changes ahead will be about as moderate in their development as have been the changes in the decade just ended, and that the worst fears of what change would do to traditional banking have just not materialized.

But to those bankers and others who oppose change altogether and hold the opinion that banking should always have been just what it is today, there are enough alterations in the environment and function of banking around the corner to make complacency a dangerous stance indeed.

The public truly wants more efficient and more convenient banking. And institutions that alter their policies and programs to provide what the public wants will be the ones that survive and prosper in the next ten years.

INDEX

INDEX

Index

A

Accounting statements of banks
conventional, 295
management-oriented, 295–96
Accounting system of banks
accrual basis, 327
"call report," 327
cash basis, 327
conformity to general principles, 326
expense accounts, 333–37
general ledger, 327
income accounts, 333–34
income statement, 333–37
federal funds purchased, 335
federal funds sold, 334
fiduciary activity, 334
furniture and equipment, 335
interest
on borrowed money, 335
on deposits, 335
and fees on loans, 333
on securities, 334
loan loss provision, 335
occupancy expense, 335
salaries and employee benefits, 334–35
service charges, commissions, and
fees, 334
as management tool, 337
report of condition, 327
statement of condition, 327–33
capital reserves, 332–33
cash and due from banks, 327–28
common stock, 332
demand deposits, 330
equity capital, 332–33
federal funds
purchased, 330
sold, 329
interest receivable, 329
investments, 328–29
liabilities for borrowed money, 330
loans, 329
reserve for loan losses, 329
savings deposits, 330

Accounting system of banks—Cont.
statement of condition—Cont.
subordinated notes and debentures,
331
surplus, 332
time deposits, 330
users, 326
Advertising by banks; see also Budgeting
of bank advertising
accountability, 990–91
agencies, 998–99
advantages, 998–99
cost, 999
relationship with, 999
selecting, 999
utilizing, 998
changes in approach, 991
image era, 991
positioning era, 991
product era, 991
creative strategy, 991
direct mail, 995
frequency discounts, 992
in-bank displays, 995
job openings, 114–15
media plans, 996–97
defining target audience, 996
locating target audience, 996
reaching target audience, 997
timing messages, 996–97
media
pros and cons, 992–96
selection, 992–96
novelty items, 996
outdoor advertising, 995–96
posttesting, 997–98
press media, 992–93
business press, 992
magazines, 993
newspapers, 993
pretesting, 997
radio and television, 993–95
repeat ads, 991
research, 997–98
simultaneous printing, 992
transit advertising, 995–96

Affiliate banking, 28, 47
Affirmative Action Programs in banks; *see also* Equal employment opportunity
  administered by Office of Federal Contract Compliance, 192
  Compliance Review of Treasury Department, 198–99
  components, 194–98
  contents, 193
  development, 197
  Executive Orders requiring, 192
  goal setting, 197
  implementation, 195, 198
  personnel practices audit, 196–97
  policy
    dissemination, 195
    statement, 194
  preliminary research, 193–94
  training managers and supervisors on, 193, 195, 197–98
  work force analyses, 196
Age Discrimination in Employment Act, 206–7
Agency securities; *see* Government agency securities
Agricultural loans
  administration, 699–702
    blanket security interest, 700
    credit file, 700
    marketing assistance, 702
    one-lender line of credit, 701
    security loan, 699–700
    "split lines of credit," 701
  analyzing line of credit application, 693–99
    analytical tools, 693–94
    applicant and business, 693
    financial soundness, 694–96
      asset and liability categories, 694–95
      financial statement, 694–96
      indicators, 695–96
    judgment of loan officer, 699
    profitability, 696–97
      asset turnover ratio, 697
      net profit margin, 697
      percent returns to net worth, 697
      percent returns to total investment, 697
      profit and loss statement, 696
    repayment capacity, 697–98
      cash flow budgeting, 698–99
  credit request, 692–93
    interview, 692
    loan
      application, 692–93
      documentation and security, 693
  lines of credit, 691–701
  loan officer, role of, 692, 699

Agricultural loans—*Cont.*
  sources, 691
  volume, 691
American Bankers Association
  "Bank Exposure Analysis Flowchart," 376
  Bank Protection Manual, 379
  Bank Resource and Exposure Checklists, 376
  Correspondent Banking Division, 986
  correspondent banking survey, 974
  Digest of Bank Insurance, 381, 384
  Disaster Planning Guide, 379
  Insurance and Protection Division, 377, 386
  Manual on Life Insurance Loans, 644
  Minbanc, 1152
  minority banks, assistance to, 1151–52
  minority employee training, 1150
  Monetary and Payments System Planning Committee, 248–49
  Occupational Safety and Health of Bank Employees, 379
  Salary Administration for Community Banks, 170
  Urban Affairs Committee, 1152
American Institute of Banking, 185, 197
American Institute of Certified Public Accountants, 350–52, 580
Asset/liability management of banks; *see also* Liquidity requirement planning of banks
  actual and perceived risks, 440–41
  asset creation and funding, 433–34
  balance sheets, changing composition of, 434–36, 443
  evolution of, 434–36
    asset/liability management in mid-1970s, 436
    liability management in 1960s, 435–36
    open market in 1940s and 1950s, 434
  focus on overall position, 440–42
  as integrated funds management philosophy, 433
  portfolio management, 433–34
    customer-negotiated, 434
  principles of, 436–43
  risk differentiation, 437–40
    credit risk, 437
    interest-rate risk, 437–40
      balance sheet structure, 437
      changes in external spreads, 438
      changes in internal spreads, 437–38
    liquidity risk, 437
  risk substitution, 441–42
  trading management, 433–34
  trends, 443–44

Asset/liability management of banks—
Cont.
  uncertainty, consideration of, 442–43
    alternative strategies, 442–43
    economic scenarios, 442–43
    forecasting, 442
Asset management services of banks; *see*
  Fiduciary services of banks
Assignment of Claims Act, 641
Association of Primary Dealers in Government Securities, 490
Auditor; *see* Audits, external, of banks; Audits, internal, of banks; *and* Internal
  control of banks
Audits, external, of banks; *see also* Audits,
  internal, of banks
  attitude of capital funds suppliers, 350
  auditor, external, 351–54
    functions, 351, 354–63
    selection, 352–54
    standards, 354
    qualifications, 353–54
  board of directors, responsibilities of,
    348–50
  legal annual report requirements, 349
  need for, 348–53, 363
  problems of, 357–60
    control
      of asset and liability records, 357–
        58, 360
      of cash and negotiable assets, 357–
        58, 360
    maintaining surprise element, 358–59
    planning, 360
    staffing, 359
    timing, 359–60
  relationship to internal audit and con-
    trol, 350–52
  reports, 360–63
    adverse opinion, 361–62
    deviations from standard form, 361–
      62
    without financial statements, 362
    on internal auditing and control, 362–
      63
    long-form, 361
    qualified opinion, 361–62
    short-form, 361
  scope, 354–57
    confirmation with third parties, 356
    counting negotiable items, 355
    evaluating assets, 356–57
    evaluating internal audit and control,
      354–55
    inspecting documents, 355
    reviewing specialized departments or
      activities, 355
    separate auditing of departments,
      functions, or accounts, 355

Audits—*Cont.*
  scope—*Cont.*
    simultaneous accounting, 355
    tasting transactions and entries, 355
  test nature of, 351
Audits, internal, of banks; *see also* Audits,
  external, of banks
  audit committee, 338–39
  auditor, internal, 338–47
    authority, 339
    educational programs, 340
    electronic data processing knowledge,
      343–45
    professional designation, 340
    qualifications, 339–40
    responsibilities, 338–41, 344, 347
    role in internal control, 345–47
    staff, 339
    status, 338
    and systems development, 344
  board of directors, responsibilities of,
    338–40
  budget, 341
  defalcations, 341
  documentation, 342
  electronic data processing audit pro-
    gram, 344
  electronic data processing audit special-
    ists, 343–44
  findings, 342–43
  follow-up, 343
  objectives, 341
  "operational auditing," 346–47
  procedures, extent of, 341–42
  purposes, 338
  scope, 338
  software programs, 344–45
  recommendations, 341
  relationship to external audits, 350–52,
    354–55
  report, 343
  timetable, 341
  work papers, 342
Automated banking; *see* Retail services of
  banks, electronic delivery systems for

B

Balance sheet management, 59–91
BankAmericard; *see* Bank cards
Bank Administration Institute, 180–84,
  339–40
Bank of America, 68–69
Bank of America Service Corporation; *see*
  Bank Cards
Bank cards
  contributions to electronic fund transfer
    systems, 893–94

Bank cards—*Cont.*
  debit cards, 892–93
    check guarantee cards, 892–93
    defined, 892
    Entree, 892
    Signet, 893
  duality, 891–92
  evolution of bank card associations, 882–83
    BankAmericard, 882–83
    Master Charge, 883
  fraud control, 881–82
    audit controls, 881
    electronic detection equipment, 881–82
    hot card lists, 882
    national authorization systems, 882
    security guards, 881
    security officers, 882
  growth in use, 879, 894
  IBANCO, 887
  ICA and VISA compared, 891
  interbank associations, 890–91
    advantages, 891
    disadvantages, 891
  Interbank Card Association (ICA), 887–90
    funding, 888
    Interbank National Authorization System, 889
    Interbank Network for Electronic Transfers, 889
    International Communications Systems, Inc., 888
    membership, 887
    organization, 887–88
    origins, 887
    responsibilities of principal banks, 889–90
  organization of bank card associations, 883–90
  organization of bank card operations, 879–82
    administration, 879–80
    credit and collections, 880
    service departments, 880–81
  VISA International Service Association, 887
  VISA U.S.A., Inc., 883–87
    BASE I, 885
    BASE II, 885–86
    Blue, White, and Gold program, 882, 884–87
    funding, 886
    National BankAmericard, Inc., 884
    origins in BankAmericard, 883–84
    "solely owned" concept, 886–87
    structure, 884
    subgroups, 884–85

Bank holding companies; *see* Federal Reserve System
Bank Holding Company Act, 5, 777, 1107; *see also* Federal Reserve System
Bank Merger Act; *see* Federal Reserve System
Bankers Blanket Bond, 382
Banking structure of United States
  expected changes, 1112–15
    in distribution
      of banks by class, 1114
      of national and state banks, 1114–15
    increased mergers, 1114
    in interest payment barriers, 1114
    in legislative barriers, 1112–13
    liberalized state branching laws, 1113
    in loan and deposit powers of thrift institutions, 1113
    off-premise facilities, 1113
  in middle 1970s, 1106–11
    barriers, 1111–12
      on geographic expansion, 1112
      on interest, 1112
      on types of business, 1112
      on types of institutions, 1112
    branches, 1106
    classes of banks, 1107–9
      membership in Federal Reserve or FDIC, 1107–9
      nature of charter, 1107–9
      state-chartered nonmember banks, 1109
      state member banks, 1108
    concentration, 1110–11
    multioffice banking, 1109–10
    number, 1106
    organizational forms, 1106–7
    product expansion, 1111
    size, 1106
Big Eight accounting firms, 821
Blunden Committee, 785–86
Bond Buyer Index, 517; *see also* Municipal bonds
Branch banking, state restrictions on, 1053–55
Bretton Woods agreement, 772
Budgeting of bank advertising; *see also* Advertising by banks
  allocating budgeted funds, 1014–15
    corporate advertising, 1015
    process plan, 1015
    services approach, 1014–15
  available funds method, 1005
  competitive analysis method, 1004–5, 1006–7
  marginal analysis, 1009–12
  methods, 1001–9

Budgeting of bank advertising—*Cont.*
  need determination method, 1005,
    1008–9
  objective method, 1005, 1008–9
  percentage of sales method, 1002–4
  task method, 1005, 1008–9
  timing budget research and decisions,
    1012–14
Business loans, longer term; *see* Longer
  term loans to business

C

Capital in banks; *see also* Capital planning
  in banks
  adequacy, 457–61, 466
    decline in capital ratios, 458
    earnings as determinant, 459
    regulatory standards of, 458–59
    relativity of, 460–61
  bank capital and bank holding company
    capital, 455–56
  defined, 454–55
  functions of, 455–60
  sources, 463–64
    debt instruments, 463
    retained earnings, 463–64
    sale of equity, 463
Capital planning in banks; *see also* Capital
  in banks
  balanced growth, increased emphasis
    on, 465–66
  "building block" approach, 462
  consolidated basis, 462
  difficulties in, 465
  earnings objectives, 464
    earnings per share, 464
    return
      on assets, 464
      on equity, 464
  external constraints, 461–62, 465
  internal constraints, 462
  purposes, 461, 465
  small versus large banks, 462–63
Cash Management Bills, 485
Central banks, 784–85
Certificates of deposit, 404, 437–38, 471–
  72
Checks
  clearing, 243
  computer processing of, 243–44
  cost
    to banking system, 242–43
    to society, 242–43
  number used, 241–42
  productivity gains in processing, 244
Chief executive office of bank, 54–55

Chief executive officer of bank
  community relations responsibilities, 53,
    1018–19
  corporate planning functions, 285–87
  delegation of authority by, 52
  determination of reserved authority, 52
  policymaking functions, 62–63
  relations
    with board of directors, 53
    with government, 53
    with key customers, 53
Citicorp, 105–9
Civil Rights Act of 1964, 189, 191–92
Commodity Credit Corporation, 657
Commodity loans
  bankers' acceptance loans, 655–56
  characteristics, 650–51
  commodity banker, qualifications of, 651
  demand loans, 654–55
  discount loans, 655
  government influence on commodity
    prices and financing, 657–58
  to grain companies, 661–62
    filing against inventory and accounts
      receivable, 661
    full security and complete control of
      collateral, 661–62
    unsecured, 661–62
  hedging and futures market, 662–64
    advantages of futures market, 662–64
    discount and premium prices, 664
  margins, 656–57
  marketability, 657
  secured by in-transit documents, 658–61
    bills of lading, 659–60
      negotiable or to order, 660
      nonnegotiable or straight, 660
    functions of international freight for-
      warder, 660
    handling of exported shipments, 661
    trust receipts, 658–59
  types, 650
  warehouse receipts, 651–54
    bearer receipts, 652–53
    field warehousing, 652
    insurance coverage, 653
    licensed bonded warehouses, 651–52
    negotiability, 652–53
    nonnegotiable, 653–54
    storage charges, 653–54
    and Uniform Commercial Code, 654
Communication of bank policies and
  objectives
  advertising, 93
  aid in solving community problems, 96
  changes in environment for, 87–88
    bigness, 87
    improved communications technol-
      ogy, 87

Communication of bank policies and
    objectives—*Cont.*
  increased influence of public opinion,
      87
  urbanization, 87
  "communications audit," 90–91
  evaluation of current programs, 90
  market study, 90–91
  opinion research, 90
  communications staff, 89
  continuing programs, 92–93
  criteria for programs, 93–94
  evaluation, 94
  implementation, 94
  lip service syndrome, 96–97
  planning, 88–94
  public affairs programs, 95–96
  public dissatisfaction with, 86–87
  public relations, 89–90
  secrecy detrimental, 88–89
  senior management involvement, 89
  special projects, 93
  style of, 94–95
  tools for, 93
Community relations programs of banks
  application of financial and human re-
      sources, 1018
  board of directors and chief executive
      officer, 1018–19
  budgeting, 1025
  categories, 1025–26
    community, 1025
    cultural, 1026
    educational, 1025–26
    health and recreational, 1026
    religious, 1026
    special situations, 1026
  community leadership of banks and
      bankers, 1016–17
  community relations officer, 1020–21
  corporate responsibility of banks, 1017
  creation of bank-sponsored foundation,
      1023–25
  enlightened self-interest of banks, 1017
  independent bank programs, 1021
  industrial and economic development,
      1027
  interdependence between bank and
      community, 1016
  measuring effectiveness, 1029–30
  minority loan programs, 1027
  organization, 1019–20
  participation by bank in programs, 1021,
      1026–27
  policy statement, 1021–22
  public relations aspects, 1030–31
  records on community activities of bank
      personnel, 1027–29

Community relations programs of banks—
    Cont.
  restoration efforts, 1027
  use in developing bank leadership, 1030
Comptroller of the Currency; *see* Office of
    the Comptroller of the Currency
Computers
  effect on interest computations, 71
  in routine bank decision making, 57–58
  skills inventories, 105
Conference of State Bank Supervisors; *see*
    State banking departments
Construction mortgage loans
  advances, 708–11
    defined, 708
    legal requirements, 708
    on nonresidential property, 708, 710
      certification of project architect, 710
      construction items schedule, 708,
          710
      inspection by or for lender, 710
      retention agreement, 710
    precautions, 710–11
      inspect construction site regularly,
          711
      inspect prior to disbursement, 710
      make advances only on additions to
          structure, 710
      rotate inspectors, 711
    on residential property, 708–9
  advantages, 703
  differences from regular mortgage loans,
      703
  disbursements, 708–11
  documentation, 713–15
    Construction Loan Agreement, 713,
        715
    Construction Rider, 713–15
    submission to long-term lender, 715
  interim payments, 708–11
  marketing of, 703–4
    performance reviews, 704
    sources, 703–4
  takeouts, 711–13
    sources of, 712
    takeout letters of commitment, 711–
        12
    tripartite agreements, 712–13
  underwriting
    calculation of loan amount, 705
      for developments, 706–7
      examination of takeout, 705–6
      override costs allowance, 705
      for residential buildings, 706
    feasibility study, 704–5
    fees and fee schedules, 707
    interest and interest payment, 707–8
    term, 706–7
Consumer banking; *see* Retail banking

Consumer credit, primary areas of
dealer-originated financing, 759–66
  bank plans, 760–61
    obligatory dealer repurchase, 760–61
    optional dealer repurchase, 761
  benefits to bank of full dealer service, 763–64
  capital loan service, 762
  classes, 759–60
    farm equipment time payment sales, 759–60
    mobile home account balances, 760
    motor dealer business, 759
    recreational vehicles and equipment balances, 760
  dealer reserve accounts, 761
  dealer service company plan, 765–66
  discounting time payment receivables, 761–62
  marketing indirect dealer plan, 764–65
  mortgage loan service, 762
  no liability discounts, 761
  pitfalls of indirect dealer financing, 763
  trends in, 766–67
  wholesale floor planning services, 762
direct lending, 751–58
  amount of credit, 752–53
  appraisal methods, 756–57
    equipment owned by applicant, 757
    new equipment, 756–57
  benefits to customer and bank, 754–55
  classification and terms, 753–54
  closing, 753, 758
  credit
    evaluation, 752
    interview, 751
    investigation, 751–53
    statement, 751, 753
  educational and training program, 758
  lien perfection, 758
    aircraft, 758
    nontitled property, 758
    real property, 758
    vehicle, 758
  marketing services, 755–56
    "club concept," 755
    early payments without penalty, 756
    programs and promotions, 755
    simple interest loans, 756
  profitability, 754
  to small business, 756

Consumer credit—*Cont.*
 direct lending—*Cont.*
  special requirements, 751
  standards and guidelines, 757–58
 expansion of consumer credit in commercial banking, 750
 overdraft credit, 759
 unsecured open-end revolving credit, 759
Consumer credit, role and concepts
 "add-on" rate, 742, 749
 changing legal environment, 746
  Fair Credit Billing Act, 746
  judicial decisions, 746
  regulatory agencies, 746
  special-purpose legislation, 746
  Truth in Lending Law, 746
  Unfair Collections Practices Act, 746
 competition, 747–48
 consumerism, 746–47
  historical antecedents, 746
  issues posed by, 746
  response of bankers, 746
 effect of overall trends in banking, 748
 phases in financing by commercial banks, 741–42
 prospects, 749
  cost information, 749
  credit monitoring, 749
  financial analysis, 749
  growth, 749
  variable rate structures, 749
 trends in consumer credit, 742–45
  market share of financial institutions, 743–44
  shift to asset ownership, 742–43
  types extended by commercial banks, 743, 745
    automobile paper, 743, 745
    credit cards, 745
    home repair and modernization, 745
    leasing plans, 745
    revolving credits, 745
Consumer Credit Protection Act, 214
Consumer loan department
 auditing, 877
 automobile loans, 866
 bank card loans, 867
 branch function, 875–77
  branch manager's loan authority, 875–76
  collections, 876–77
  dealer relations, 876
 centralization, degree of, 867–68
  collection activities, 867–68
  lending authority, 867
 closed-end loans, 867

Consumer loan department—*Cont.*
  collections, adjustments, and recoveries,
      873–75
    attorneys, 874
    collection officer, 873
    collection procedures, 873–75
    coordination with credit department,
        875
    ethics of, 874
    late notices, 874
    process servers, 874
    recovery procedures, 874
    telephone adjusters, 874–75
  consumer loan manager, 863–64
  cost control, 877
  installment credit, types of, 862
  insurance needs, 877–78
    bank insurance, 878
    borrower credit life and health and ac-
        cident insurance, 878
  legal considerations, 870–71
    communicating, 871
    Equal Credit Opportunity Act, 871
    Fair Credit Billing Act, 871
    Home Mortgage Disclosure Act, 871
    monitoring, 871
    Real Estate Settlement Procedures
        Act, 871
    staff familiarity with, 870
    Truth in Lending law, 871
    use of counsel, 870
  operations, 871–73
    correlation with auditor, 873
    efficiency, 872–73
    housekeeping responsibilities, 872
    narrowing profit margins, 872
  organization, 862–66
    choosing personnel, 865
    effects of electronic data processing,
        863
    functional basis, 864
    integral part of total bank, 863
    location, 865–66
    product line control, 864
    selecting head, 863–64
    structural determinants, 862–63
    work flow chart, 864
  policy considerations, 866–70
    credit policy, 869
    direct loans versus indirect loans, 866–
        67
      dealer departments, 867
      dealer loans, 867
      floor plan loans, 867
      market potential, 866–67
    lending authorities, 868–69
      in branch systems, 868–69
      in large banks, 868–69
      in unit banks, 868

Consumer loan department—*Cont.*
  policy considerations—*Cont.*
    loan policy statement, 868
    rate policies, 869–70
    service offerings, 866
Consumerism
  effect on consumer credit, 746–47
  impact on bank social policies, 67–68
  institutionalization, 68
Control and measurement of bank finan-
    cial performance; *see also* Costs in
    banks *and* Profitability in banks
  accounting and financial information,
      313
  accurate reporting, 316–17
  average cost of funds, 320–21
  average investment portfolio earnings,
      320–21
  common language, need for, 314–15
  educating managers, 316
  goal congruence, 317
  marginal evaluation of funds, 321, 324
  performance indicators, 317–19, 322–23
    corporate level, 317–18
    lower level, 318–19
  pool rate of funds between profit cen-
      ters, 320–21, 324
  purposes, 313–14
  recognition of performance, 315
  report responsibility, 317
  reporting system, 319–20
  review process, 324–25
  standards of performance, 315
  tailoring system to organization, 317
  timely reporting, 316–17
  valuation rate of funds between profit
      centers, 320–21, 324
Corporate planning for banks; *see also*
    Profit planning and budgeting of
    banks
  action plans, 281–82
  annual cycle of, 283–85
  annual planning program, 275, 283–85
  budget plan, 282, 284–85
  business or operational plan, 283
  chief executive officer, role of, 285–87
  comparative data base, 279
  core problems, 280
  corporate plan, 283, 285
  current objectives and strategies state-
      ment, 279–81
  current position statement, 279
  developing unique philosophy and tech-
      niques, 273
  environmental analysis, 277–79
  establishing objectives, 279–81
  evolution of, 274–75
  expectations from, 275–76
  financial objectives, 280

Corporate planning for banks—*Cont.*
future objectives statement, 281
intermediate or operational planning
program, 275
management
objectives, 281
values, 280
managers, role of, 286–87
market position objectives, 280–81
performance controls, 282
plan to plan document, 277, 283
planning coordinator, 286
planning manual, 277, 283
planning process, 276–85
public responsibility objectives, 281
relationship to bank size, 286–87
situation appraisal, 277–79
statement of purpose, 281
strategic management, 279–81
strategic planning process, 275
Corporate responsibility; *see* Social policies
of banks
Corporate services of banks
characteristics of innovative banks, 962–
63
defined, 961
innovation process, 965–72
conception, 965–66, 968
development, 966, 969
final approval, 967, 970
hypothetical case, 968–72
implementation, 967, 970–72
planning, organizing, leading, and
controlling, 967–68
tentative approval, 966, 968–69
innovative, 962
profitability, 961
traditional, 962
why offered, 963–64
Correspondent bank services
automated data processing, 984–85
changes in correspondent banking, 986–
89
compensation, 986–87
potential challenges, 988–89
holding company movement, 989
move toward nationwide banking,
989
possible changes in Federal Reserve
System, 989
correspondent banking defined, 973
credit services, 977–79
credit information, 979
direct lending, 978–79
loan participations, 977–78
downstream, 978
overline accommodations, 977
loans to officers and directors, 979

Correspondent bank services—*Cont.*
credit services—*Cont.*
sale of Federal Reserve funds, 978–79
specialized financing, 979
extent of correspondent banking, 974
general banking services, 975–77
check clearing, 975–76
coin and currency, 976
collections, 976–77
funds transfer, 976
history of correspondent banking, 28,
973–74
international services, 981–82
financial, 982
marketing, 982
operating, 981–82
management consulting, 983–84
director's audit, 984
information on legislative and regulatory changes, 984
marketing plans, 984
on-the-job training, 984
personnel programs, 984
seminars, 984
portfolio and investment services, 979–
81
investment advice, 981
safekeeping, 980–81
securities trading, 980
trust services, 982–83
custodial services, 983
investment counseling, 983
Costs in banks; *see also* Pricing of services
and Profitability in banks
allocation of, 298–99
allocation-handling methods, 299
direct, 299
reciprocal, 299
step, 299
allocation procedures, 298–99
fixed dollars, 298
fixed percentage, 299
percentage of activity, 298–99
standards, 298
transfer price, 299
breakdown of, 296
direct production, 296
direct support, 297
fixed, 297
general and administrative, 297
indirect support, 297
interest, allocation of, 297–98
overhead, 297
responsibility centers, 298
selling, 297
transfer basis for allocating, 298–99
variable, 297

Credit arrangements, seasonal and
     revolving
  financing needs of business concerns,
     613
  lines of credit, 614–16
     backup, 615–16
     and commercial paper market, 616
     legal status, 615
     secondary and tertiary, 615–16
     terms, 614–15
     uses, 615
     pricing, 618–21
        balance requirements, changes in,
           619–21
        bases for new techniques, 618–20
        charges for credit services, 619–21
        deficient balance fee, 620–21
        and higher interest rates, 619
        and reduction in "excess" balances,
           619
        total yield concept, 619–21
     revolving, 616–18
        analysis by loan officer, 617
        defined, 616
        loan agreement, 617–18
        origins, 616–17
        uses, 616–17
     working capital cycle, 614
Credit decisions, financial analysis for
  common-size industry comparison
     method, 593–94
  comparison method, 583–87
     analysis of data, 586–87
     classification of items, 586
     comparison forms, 583–86
  elements of credit decision, 579
  evaluation of borrower, 598–99
     economic influences, 598–99
     financial information, 598
        going concern concept, 598
        liquidation concept, 598
     management, 599
  financial statements, 580–83
     company staff, 583
     CPA, 580–83
        disclaimer or denial of opinion, 582–
           83
        qualified opinion, 581–82
        unaudited, 583
        unqualified opinion, 580–81
  forecasting financial statement data,
     595–98
  making the decision, 599–601
     determining repayment sources, 600
     selecting solutions, 600
     social and ethical considerations, 600–
        601
     weighing creditworthiness, 599–600
     weighing solutions, 599–600

Credit decisions—*Cont.*
  pro forma statements, 595
  ratio method, 588–93
     capital strength ratios, 589–90
     considerations in using ratios, 588
     coverage ratios, 591
     efficiency ratios, 590–91
     liquidity ratios, 588–89
     profitability ratios, 591–92
  statement of financial position, 594–95
  trend percentage method, 587
Credit and loan administration by banks
  commercial loan accounting, 564–66
     loan officer performance, 565
     policy compliance, 564
     portfolio information, 565
     quality control, 564
  credit department, 558–59
     credit analysis, 559
     record keeping, 558–59
  functions of, 556–57
  line loan officer, 556–57
  loan authority, 557–58
  loan review, 561–64
     classification of loans, 563
     necessitated by bank growth, 561–62
     reporting, 563
     special reviews, 562
     staff qualifications, 563–64, 566
     timing, 562
  relationship to credit policy, 556–57
  training of lending staff, 559–61
Credit policy for banks
  adaptation to bank's specific needs, 543–
     44
  administration, 554–55
  areas covered by, 542–43
     delegation of authority, 542–43, 546–
        48
     granting procedures, 543, 554–55
     legal considerations, 542
     market area, 543–44
     pricing, 543, 548–49
     standards, 543–44, 549–54
     types, 543–46
  distribution of types of loans, 544–46
  house limits for individuals, 544
  justifications for written policy, 541–
     42
  lending standards, 549–54
     commercial loans, 549–50
     construction loans, 553
     consumer loans, 553–54
     general and specific principles, 550–
        53
     mortgage loans, 553
  loan authority, 546–48
     categories, 546–47

Credit policy for banks—*Cont.*
  loan authority—*Cont.*
    differing views on, 547–48
    loan approval function, 547
  loan and credit procedures, 554
  pricing guidelines, 548–49
  reasons for having, 541, 556
Credit systems and procedures of banks
  integrating, 569–70
  loan administration procedures, 571–75
    approval, 571–72
    closing, 572–73
      exception processing, 573
      use of counsel, 573
    collection, 573–74
      compromising full repayment, 574
      problem loans, 573–74
      reporting, 574
      use of collection specialists, 573–74
      use of officer of account, 573–74
    pricing, 572
    review, 574–75
      of borrower characteristics, 574
      of loan documents, 574
      of loan procedures, 574–75
      of loan quality, 574–75
  loan auditing, 569
  loan procedure defined, 568
  loan reports, 576–77
    to bank regulatory agencies, 577
    daily loan activity, 576
    daily transaction journal, 576
    delinquency, 576
    loan maturing, 576
    loan status, 576
    routine reports to management, 576–77
    special reports to management, 576–77
      forward commitment, 577
      portfolio liquidity, 577
      risk concentration, 577
  portfolio
    control and planning, 569
    organization, 575–76
Custodial services of banks
  current developments, 907
    improved technology, 907
    information-oriented services, 907
  defined, 895–96, 905
  implicit agreements, 906
  liability of banks, 906–7
    insurable risks, 907
    "ordinary care," 907
    responsibility for processing oversights, 907
  variations among banks, 905
  written agreements, 906

D

Data processing systems; *see* Managing bank data processing systems
Defense Civil Preparedness Agency, 379
Depository Bonds, 484
Directors, board of
  attributes, 20
  audit committee, 338–39
  and bank community relations, 1018
  and bank management, 20–21, 24, 53
  and bank trust activities, 926
  Business Development Committee, 24
  composition, 21
  data to stockholders on, 15–16
  duties, 17–18
  election, 16
  Examining Committee, 22–23
  Executive Committee, 22
  and external auditing program, 348–50, 354–57
  fees, 21
  indemnification, 19
  interlocking membership, 21
  and internal auditing program, 338–40, 353
  length of service, 16
  liabilities, 18–19
  management evaluation committee, 24
  management participation on, 21
  nomination, 15–16
  number, 16
  oath, 17
  policymaking functions, 62–63
  powers, 18
  qualifications, 16–17
  removal, 16
  and resource allocation, 398
  responsibilities, 17, 19–20
  retainers, 21–22
  retirement, 25
  risk and insurance management policy, 384–85
  Salary Committee, 23
  standing committees, 22–25
  and supervisory authorities, 352–53
  Trust Committee, 23
Disclosures by banks, 14

E

Edge Act subsidiaries, 777
Electronic delivery systems of banks; *see* Retail services of banks, electronic delivery systems for
Electronic funds transfer systems (EFTS) in banks
  advantages to consumer, 247, 253–54

Electronic funds transfer systems (EFTS)
  in banks—*Cont.*
  automated clearing houses, 248–51
    consumer control, 250–51
    delivery systems, 250
    functions, 250–51
    operations, 249
    organizational structure, 250
    origins, 248–49
    services, 248
    transactions, 248–49
  automated teller machines, 251–52
  Bank Wire System, 245–46
  BankAmericard System, 246
  bases for introducing, 243–45
  Clearing House Interbank Payments
    System, 246
  consumer issues, 254
  current status, 241, 245–47
  Federal Reserve Wire System, 245
  Interbank Network Authorization Sys-
    tem, 246
  National Commission on Electronic
    Funds Transfer, 245
  point-of-sale services, 252–53
  Society of Worldwide Interbank Finan-
    cial Telecommunications, 246
  telephone bill-paying system, 253
Employee development in banks; *see* Personnel development in banks
Employee incentives and benefit programs
  of banks
  accidental death and dismemberment
    insurance, 183
  administrative services contract, 184–85
  benefit categories, 180
  benefit characteristics, 180
  components, 178
  cost, 178
  dental expense insurance, 184
  disability insurance, 183
  education, 185
  effectiveness, and cost analysis, 179–80,
    186–87
  and employee motivation, 179
  evaluation of, 178–79
  food service facilities, 186
  free services, 186
  growth of, 178
  incentive compensation, 180
  legally required payments, 178, 181
  legislation affecting, 177
  life insurance, group, 183
  medical expense plans, 184–85
    basic medical and hospital, 184
    major medical, 184
    self-administered, 184–85
  old age and survivors insurance, 181
  pension plans, 181–82

Employee incentives and benefit programs
  of banks—*Cont.*
  profit-sharing plans, 181–82
  salary and wages for time not worked,
    180–81
  sick pay, 184
  social security, 181
  stock purchase plans, 185–86
  thrift/savings plans, 182–83
  training, 185
  trends, 179
  vacations, 180–81
  voluntary payments, 181–85
  worker's compensation insurance, 181
Employee Retirement Income Security
  Act of 1974, 182, 944–45
Employee selection by banks; *see also* Manpower planning and management of
  banks
  assessment of candidates, 130–31
  determination of job, 111–12
  employment application, 118–20
    discriminatory questions, 118–19
    information categories, 120
    job relatedness of questions, 119
    use in interview, 120
  human resource staffing system, compo-
    nents of, 110–11
  integration with company goals, 110
  interview, 123–30
    discriminatory questions, 124–29
    preliminary, 118
    primary questions answered by, 124–
      30
    rejecting applicant, 130
    selling applicant, 130
  job
    analysis, 111
    descriptions, 111
    specifications, 111–13
  medical examinations, 130
  personnel needs, estimation of, 110–11
  recruitment, 112–17
    advertising, 114–15
    affected by community relationships,
      117
    campuses, 115–16
    community colleges, 115–16
    condition of labor market, 113
    cooperative education, 116
    differentiating successful employees,
      113–14
    employee referrals, 114
    employment agencies, 116–17
    market for, 113–14
    monitoring methods and results, 112
    nontraditional sources, 113–14
    prospect file, 117
    referral sources, 113

Employee selection by banks—*Cont.*
  recruitment—*Cont.*
    statutory restrictions, 114–15, 117
    traditional sources, 113–14
    walk-in applicants, 114
  reference checks, 130
  standardized process for, 118–31
  tests, 120–23
    administration, 123
    rejecting minorities at higher rate, 120–23
    validation, 120–23
  uniform treatment of applicants, 118
Employee training by banks
  assignment of training function, 133–34
  characteristics of training managers, 135–36
  cost-benefit relationships, 135
  decentralization of, 134
  effectiveness, determinants of, 134
  facilities, 137–39
  funds for, 133
  line managers and supervisors, role of, 134
  performance objectives, 133
  personnel department, role of, 134
  recruitment of training staff, 137
  senior management, role of, 133
  size of training staff, 136–37
  terminology, 132
  time for, 133
  timetable, 133
  training manager, functions of, 134–35
  training programs, 139–41
    components, 141
    obstacles to success, 142
    obtaining management approval, 140
    own program, 139–40
    pilot programs, 140
    purchased programs, 139–40
    tracking results, 141
Environment of bank management
  and chief executive officer, 53–54
  Communist countries, 49
  creates demand for leadership, 49
  economic downturn in 1970s, 51
  Free World, 49
  impact on policies, 60–61, 67
  pressures for more managed economies, 49–50
  response of top management, 54–55
  sociolegal, 53–54
Equal Credit Opportunity Act, 871
Equal employment opportunity; *see also*
    Affirmative Action Programs in banks
  complaint resolution, 190–91
  Contract Compliance Programs, 192–93
  federal, state, and local legislation, 189–90

Equal employment opportunity—*Cont.*
  leadership expected from banks, 188
  reporting requirements, 191
  response to discrimination charge, 191
Equal Employment Opportunity
    Commission
  guidelines, interpretations, and decisions, 189
  powers under Civil Rights Act of 1964, 189
  restricts employee referrals, 114
Equal Pay Act, 205
Equipment leasing
  alternatives for bank participation in, 680–82
    appoint individual or group to handle, 681
    establish subsidiary to handle, 681–82
    evaluation of, 682
    finance equipment leasing companies, 680–81
  attractions
    to lessees, 679–80
    to lessors, 679
  competitive sources, 690
  credit evaluation, 682–83
  defined, 673
  earnings, 685–89
    book, 685–89
    cash, 685–89
    taxable, 685–89
  obtaining bank business, 689–90
  types of equipment leases, 674–79
    full payment, 674–76
      capital lease, 674–75
      direct financing lease, 675
      finance lease, 674–75
      operating lease, 675–76
      sales type lease, 675
      tax considerations, 675
      true lease, 675–76
    leveraged lease, 676–79
    net leases, 679
    nonpayment ("service lease" or "full service lease"), 674
    restrictions on bank participation, 674
  volume, 673
  yield evaluation, 683–85
    capital or finance lease, 683
    leveraged lease, 684–85
    operating or true lease, 683–84
Eurocurrency markets of commercial
    banks
  bank management of Eurocurrency
    books, 808–12
    controls employed, 810–12
      accounting and reporting requirements, 810

Eurocurrency markets of commercial
    banks—*Cont.*
  bank management of Eurocurrency
      books—*Cont.*
    controls employed—*Cont.*
      credit limits, 811
      currency limits, 810–11
      time gap limits, 811–12
    risks involved, 809–10
      credit risk, 809
      currency risk, 810
      delivery risk, 809
      rate risk, 809–10
    temporary investment and loan books,
        808
  commercial borrowers and depositors,
      806–7
    central banks, 806
    government entities, 806
    multinational companies, 806
    nonnegotiable deposits, 806
    secondary market, 806
  conditions of entry into Eurocurrency
      operations, 812–13
    customer needs, 813
    effective controls, 812
    good accounting and reporting sys-
        tems, 812–13
    technical skills, 813
  currencies traded, 802
Eurocurrency defined, 801–2
Eurocurrency loan agreement, 813–15
  borrower covenants, 813–14
    operational specifications, 813
    rate definition, 813
    regulatory protection clauses, 813
  extent of, 802
  hedged and unhedged rate arbitrage,
      807–8
  interbank market, 803–6
    bank controls, 803
    brokerage system, 805
    centered in London, 804
    indirect participation, 805
    price determination, 803–4
    rate differentials, 804–6
    regulatory agency controls, 803–4
    tier system, 805–6
  market uses and users, 472–73, 803–7
  offshore deposit and Eurocurrency de-
      posit, 802
  origin, 800
  phases, 801, 815–16
  relationship to foreign exchange and in-
      ternal money markets, 807–8
  supply of funds, 802
Eurodollars, 472–73, 831; *see also* Euro-
    currency markets of commercial banks
Export-Import Bank, 508

F

Fair Credit Billing Act, 746, 871
Fair Labor Standards Act, 201–6
Farm Credit System, 495–501; *see also*
    Government agency securities
Farmers Home Administration, 508
Federal Aviation Authority, 758
Federal Aviation Registration Act, 647
Federal Contract Compliance, Office of,
    192
Federal Deposit Insurance Corporation
  achievements, 1089
  assessing risks of individual banks, 1082
  bank examinations, 1083–84
  bank failures, 1079
  and bank mergers, 1069
  among bases of public confidence in
      banking system, 1080–81
  extent of coverage, 457
  financial resources, 1087–89
    bank insurance premiums, 1088
    call on U.S. Treasury, 1088
    disbursements compared to, 1088
    investment income, 1088
    principle of FDIC fund, 1088
  insured nonmember commercial banks,
      1079
  jurisdictional changes, 1078–79
  measuring systemwide risk, 1082–83
    pitfalls of aggregate figures, 1082–83
  mission, 1078
  and Office of the Comptroller of the Cur-
      rency, 1050
  open liquidations, 1079
  options for containing systemwide risk,
      1085–87
    assistance to "essential" bank in dan-
        ger of closing, 1087
    establishment of deposit insurance na-
        tional bank, 1086–87
    let bank close and pay insured depos-
        its, 1085–86
    purchase and assumption of deposit li-
        abilities by other bank, 1086
  problem bank lists, 1084–85
  safeguards in banking system, 1081–82
  staff functions, 1079
Federal Home Loan Bank Board, 1055
Federal Home Loan Banks, 495–98, 502–
    4; *see also* Government agency
    securities
Federal Home Loan Mortgage Corpora-
    tion, 503–4; *see also* Government
    agency securities
Federal Insurance Contributions Act, 212
Federal National Mortgage Association,
    495–98, 501–2; *see also* Government
    agency securities

Federal regulations governing bank employees; *see also* Affirmative Action Programs in banks *and* Equal employment opportunity
Age Discrimination in Employment Act, 206–9
Comptroller of the Currency, regulations of, 215
Consumer Credit Protection Act, 214
Executive Order 11701, 215
Fair Labor Standards Act (Wage-Hour Law), 201–6
child labor restrictions, 205–6
enforcement, 207
equal pay, 205
exempt employees, 204–5
hours worked, definition of, 202
minimum wage requirements, 202
overtime requirements, 202
record retention requirements, 207–9
regular rate of pay, definition of, 203
workweek, definition of, 203
workweek, fluctuating, 203–4
Federal Reserve System Board of Governors, rules and regulations of, 216
National Labor Relations Act, 207–11
collective bargaining, 211
employee rights, 207, 210
enforcement, 211
unfair labor practices, 210–11
Occupational Safety and Health Act, 213–14
Social Security Act, 211–13
coverage, 211–12
determination of social security taxes, 212
financing, 211–12
programs, 212–13
Universal Military Training and Service Act, 214
U.S. Code, Title 12, 216–17
Federal Reserve Act, 402–3
Federal Reserve System
bank holding companies regulated by, 409–10, 1070
and bank holding company bank acquisitions, 1070–73
bases
for approval, 1070–73
for denial, 1070–73
mergers under financial stress, 1072
one-bank holding companies, 1072
and bank holding company nonbanking activities, 1073–74
acquiring shares in nonbanking company, 1074
growth, 1074

Federal Reserve System—*Cont.*
and bank holding company nonbanking activities—*Cont.*
monitoring transactions between bank and nonbank affiliates, 1074
permitted by Bank Holding Company Act, 1073
specified by Board of Governors, 1073–74
and bank mergers, 1068–70
anticompetitive effects versus positive effects, 1069
of failing banks, 1070
monopoly prohibited, 1069
prior federal banking agency approval required, 1068–69
and branch banking, 1075
effects of customer-bank communication terminals, 1075
review of branch applications, 1075
clearinghouse mechanism, 447–48
and federal funds trading, 452
float in, 450–51
functions, 1067
and maximum deposit rates, 1075–76
alterations in, 1075
consultation with Federal Deposit Insurance Corporation and Federal Home Loan Bank Board, 1075
differential between thrift institutions and commercial banks, 1075–76
Regulation Q, 1075–76
monetary policy effects, 1076–77
credit allocation left to open market, 1077
funds movement throughout banking industry permitted, 1076–77
more intensive funds use encouraged, 1076–77
and Office of the Comptroller of the Currency, 1050
open-market operations, 470–72, 492–93
reasons for creation, 1050
reserve requirements, 402, 446–47, 470–71, 492–93
and Treasury balances, 450
Fiduciary services of banks; *see also* Investment management of securities by banks
agencies, 924–26, 930
characteristics, 923–26
competition, 927–28
control, 926
fee income from, 927
fiduciary relationships, 923–26
government regulations, 926
investing, 925–26
organizational forms, 926–27, 929
personal and financial counseling, 925

Fiduciary services of banks—*Cont.*
  personal trust services, 930–33
    accounts benefiting others than
        trustor, 932–33
      charitable trusts, 933
      gifts in trust, 932–33
      life insurance trusts, 932
      testamentary trusts, 932
    accounts for trustor, 930–32
      agencies, 930
      financial planning, 931–32
      guardianships and conservatorships,
          931–32
      probate and administration, 931–32
      self-employed retirement plans, 930
    profitability, 927
    record keeping, 925
    safekeeping, 925
    services for corporations, 933–35
      business advisory accounts, 934
      employee benefit accounts, 933
        bank as agent, 933
        employee stock ownership trusts,
            933
        money purchase pension and thrift
            accounts, 933
        pension accounts, 933
        profit-sharing accounts, 933
      investment management for charita-
          ble foundations, 933–34
      paying agent for bond issues, 934
      transfer agent for corporation stock,
          934–35
      trustees for bond issues, 934
    trusts, 924–26, 929
Financial Accounting Standards Board, 5,
    674–76, 678
Financial information on banks, demand
    for, 4–5
Financial intermediation by banks, 401
Fiscal policy and commercial banking
    balanced budget, 1136
    banks as government's financial middle-
        men, 1143–44
    countercyclical budget, 1136–37
    federal deficit and surplus, 1136–37
    fiscal policy defined, 1136
    high employment budget, 1137–38
    implementation of fiscal policy by com-
        mercial banks, 1141–44
    limitations of unified budget accounts,
        1138
    national debt, 1136
"Float" eliminated by automated clearing
    houses, 251
Fringe benefits; *see* Employee incentives
    and benefit programs
Future trading, 477–78

G

Government agency securities; *see also*
    Government securities
  agency debt expansion, 495–96
  "Big-Five" issues, 495–98
    agency names, 495
    bid and asked spread, 497
    bonds and debentures, 496
    bond-issuing process, 497–98
    compared with direct governments,
        496–97
    Farm Credit System, 495–501
    Federal Home Loan Banks, 495–98,
        502–4
    Federal Intermediate Credit Banks,
        495–98
    Federal Land Banks, 495–98
    Federal National Mortgage Associa-
        tion, 495–98, 501–2
    secondary market, 496
  defined, 495
  District of Columbia Armory Board, 508,
      510
  Export-Import Bank, 508
  Farm Credit System, 498–501
    Banks for Cooperatives, 498–99
    bonds and discount rates, 499
    Farm Credit Act, 498
    Farm Credit Administration, 498
    Farm Credit Bank discount rates, 500–
        501
    Federal Intermediate Credit Banks,
        499–500
    Federal Land Banks, 500
    functions, 498
  Farmers Home Administration, 508
  Federal Home Loan Banks, 502–4
    consolidated bonds, 503
    consolidated discount rates, 503
    Federal Home Loan Bank Board, 502
    Federal Home Loan Bank System, 502
    operations, 502–3
  Federal Home Loan Mortgage Corpora-
      tion, 503–4
    guaranteed mortgage certificates, 504
    participation certificates, 504
  Federal National Mortgage Association,
      501–2
    debentures, 501–2
    operations, 501
    short-term discount notes, 502
  Government National Mortgage Associ-
      ation, 505–7
    functions, 505–6
    mortgage-backed securities program,
        507

Government agency securities—*Cont.*
Government National Mortgage
Association—*Cont.*
participation certificates, 506
pass-through certificates, 507
Tennessee Valley Authority, 505
total outstanding, 509
U.S. Postal Service, 504–5
Government securities; *see also* Government agency securities
marketable issues of U.S. Treasury, 484
nonmarketable issues of U.S. Treasury, 484
open-market operations of Federal Reserve System, 492–93
public debt, 484–90
reasons for increase in federal debt, 482–84
Treasury bills, 484–88
auction sale of, 484–86
Cash Management Bills, 485
discount computations, 486
Tax Anticipation Bills, 485
trading in, 486
yield computations, 487–88
Treasury notes and bonds, 488–90
average-price option, 489
characteristics, 488
discretionary amount and allotment amendments, 490
dollar-basis cash auction, 489
Dutch-auction technique, 489
issuance, 488–90
"rights offering," 488–89
"rights value," 488–89
volume, 488
yield-basis cash auction, 489
yield-spread subscription technique, 489–90
yields, 488
Treasury securities, 480–82
impact on interest rates, 482
reasons for acceptance, 480
volume, 481
Treasury securities markets, 490–92
book-entry safekeeping system, 492
dealer profit margins, 491
delivery, 490, 492
determinants of prices, 490–91
payment, 490
primary market, 490
risks and rewards, 493–94
safekeeping banks, 490
Treasury bill quotations, 491
Treasury note and bond quotations, 491–92
volume of federal debt, 481
Group banking; *see* Holding company banking

H

Holding company banking
advantages, 43–44
bank holding company, 27
disadvantages, 44–45
multibank holding company, 27
reasons for growth, 42–43
structural alternatives, 45–46
trends, 46–47
Home Mortgage Disclosure Act, 871
House Banking Committee, 784

I

"Image" of banking, 95
In-transit loans; *see* Commodity loans
Information systems for banks
ambiguity of language, 255
communicating through, 258–59
"computerese" problem, 255
confusion concerning, 255
as corporate resources, 267
data and information compared, 256–57
data processing and information systems compared, 257–58
gains of corporate philosophy on, 268–70
generalizations covering, 267–68
integrating production and management information systems, 262–64
integrating required skills, 265–67
interrelationships between operations, data processing, and information systems, 259–62
investment, not expense, 267
parochial views of, 265–66
require sharing, 267
using data processing to support management process, 264–65
Installment credit; *see* Consumer loan department
Installment loan department; *see* Consumer loan department
Institute of Internal Auditors, 340–41
Insurance in banks; *see* Risk management in banks
Interest Equalization Tax, 781, 828
Interest rate sensitivity, 394
Interest rate trends, 430–32
Internal control of banks
"conflict of interest policy," 346
defined, 350–51
dual control, 345–46
dual custody, 345–46
fraud, prevention and detection of, 346
functions, 345
job rotation, 345

Internal control of banks—*Cont.*
  joint custody, 345–46
  relationship to external audits, 350–52,
    354–55
  reviewed by auditor, 345
  separation of duties, 345
  vacation requirement, 345
International banking; *see* Eurocurrency
    markets of commercial banks; Interna-
    tional credits; International relation-
    ships of U.S. banks; *and* Multinational
    companies, meeting banking needs of
International credits
  broker paper, 830
    endorsement verification, 830
  country limits, 832–33
  country risk, 822–27
    cautions, 823
    economic risk, 823–24
      indicators of, 824
      noncomparability of national econo-
        mies, 823
      varying reliability of statistics, 823
    international liquidity, 824–26
      balance of payments components,
        825
      capital flows, 825
      debt service ratio, 825–26
      defined, 825
      ratio of gold and hard currency re-
        serves to imports, 825–26
    political risk, 826–27
  evolution of international lending of U.S.
    banks, 818
  foreign currency loans, 828–29
  foreign financial statements, translation
    and analysis of, 821–22
    central bank statements, 822
    differences in practices, 821
    purposes, 821–22
  funding, 831
    domestic sources, 831
    Eurodollars, 831
    foreign sources, 831
    offshore financing, 831
    relative cost in U.S. and Eurodollar
      markets, 831
  interest rates, 831–32
    fixed, 831
    floating, 831
    spreads, 831–32
  legal problems, 827–28
    different significances of legal terms,
      827
    laws imposed on U.S. lenders by for-
      eign countries, 827–28
    laws imposed on U.S. lenders by
      Unites States, 827–28
    legal differences, 827

International credits—*Cont.*
  loan maturities, 830–31
    shifts in length, 830
    short-term versus long-term, 830–31
  relations to credit fundamentals, 817
  sovereign risk, 822–27
  syndicated loans, 829
  types of, 818–21
    government loans, 818–19
      effect on foreign exchange, 818–19
      purposes, 818–19
    loans to private sector, 819–21
      to banks, 819
      banker's acceptances, 820
      to companies, 819
      to finance movement of goods, 819–
        21
      to finance projects, 819
      to individuals, 819
      leasing, 819
      letters of credit, 819–21
International Monetary Fund, 787, 823,
    825
International relationships of U.S. banks
  changes in, 783–88
    assumption of sovereign risk credit,
      786–87
    growth in government regulation, 785
    impact on government monetary and
      exchange rate policy, 783–85
    implementing government financial
      policy, 785
    new interbank relationships, 787–88
      bank tiering, 787
      disputes, 788
      syndicated loans, 788
    consortium banks, 786–87
    current tasks, 788
  development of international banking in
    United States, 772–78
    current position, 772–73
    functional expansion, 777
    geographic spread, 773–75
      developing areas, 775
      foreign assets and liabilities, 773
      major growth areas, 774–75
      net suppliers and users of funds,
        773–74
      overseas branches, 773–74
      prospects, 775
    organizational expansion, 775–78
      consortia banks, 777
      correspondent banks, 776
      Edge Act subsidiaries, 777
      foreign branches, 776
      foreign department, 776
      regional international banking cen-
        ters, 777

International relationships of U.S. banks—
Cont.
development of international banking in
United States—*Cont.*
problems, 777–78
developing personnel, 778
devising organizational patterns,
778
maintaining liquidity, 778
organizing for research and policy
making, 778
providing control procedures, 778
Eurocurrency market, 785
"lender of last resort" question, 785
reasons for expansion of U.S. international banking, 779–83
growth in international banking market, 780–81
increasingly interdependent world
economy, 779–80
capital flows, 779
coinciding business cycles, 779
export growth, 779
policies of foreign governments, 782–
83
U.S. policies, 781–82
Investment management of securities by
banks
bases for account investment objectives,
941–43
liquidity needs, 942
time horizon, 942–43
variability in rate of return, 941–42
effect of Employment Retirement Income Security Act of 1974, 944–
45
investment committees, 937–38
functions, 937–38
second level committees, 937
senior investment committees, 937
investment research and forecasting,
938–41, 945
economic data and forecasts, 938–39
industry-company data and forecasts,
939
securities market data and forecasts,
939–41
identifying fixed-income/common
stock yield relationships, 940
maintaining percentages in common stocks, 940
timing securities markets, 940
legal constraints on trust investing, 936,
944
performance measurement, 944
portfolio management, 941–45
prudent man rule, 936, 944
purchases of foreign securities, 945

Investment management of securities by
banks—*Cont.*
securities trading, 943–44
negotiated rates, 943–44
role of bank securities trading, 943
size of bank investment staff, 937
Investors in bank; *see* Stockholders of bank

L

Legal and regulatory constraints on banks
bank holding companies, 409–10
activities permitted by Federal Reserve Board, 409
Bank Holding Company Act of 1956,
403
flexibility as compared with banks, 409
restraints imposed by Federal Reserve
Board, 409–10
dual nature of chartering and regulation,
402
federal funds loans, 405
Federal Reserve Act of 1913, 402–3
interest rate ceilings on deposits, 403–5
purposes, 401–3
on raising funds, 403–5
reserve requirements, 402, 404
retained earnings, 405
sales of capital stock, 405
sales of subordinated debt, 405
on uses of funds, 405–9
discretionary, 408
cease and desist orders, 408
officer removal proceedings, 408
equity investments, 406–7
foreign activities, 408
investments, 408
loans, 407–8
to affiliates, 407
maximum to one borrower, 407
mortgage, 407
to officers, 407
stock market, 407–8
ownership of tangible property, 406
purposes, 405–6
trust activities, 408–9
Liability management, 412–13, 429–30
Limited area branching, 1053–54
Liquidity requirement planning of banks;
see also Asset/liability management of
banks
analyzing loans and deposits, 422–23
assets to meet liquidity needs, 427–30
keeping cash at minimum, 427–28
liability management, 429–30
liquidity account, 428–29
balance sheet components useful in,
415–16

Liquidity requirement planning of
  banks—*Cont.*
  cyclical fluctuations affect, 418–19
  cyclical interest rate trends, adaptations
    to, 430–32
  decisions imprecise, 414–15
    arguable answers, 414
    "how much" and "when" judgmental,
      414–15, 432
    well-informed guesses, 414
  deposits with correspondents, 428
  discipline in, 413
  estimating liquidity needs, 423–28
    "baseline" procedure, 423
    exceptions to floor-ceiling estimates,
      426
    "hard-core" deposits, 423
    loan ceiling, 425–26
    lowest deposit level (floor) forecast,
      424
  evaluation of overall risks, 416–17
  Federal Reserve deposits, 428
  framework for analysis, 415–16
  government security purchases, 417
  informed judgment in, 413–18
  investment account, function of, 418
  investments a residual, 417
  liquidity account, function of, 418
  liquidity needs, bases for, 418
  loan runoff, 428
  long-term liabilities, 431–32
  obligations to customers, 417
  political vulnerability, 417
  shifts in, 411–13
    asset allocation in 1930s and 1940s,
      411–12
    asset management after World War II,
      412
    funds management in mid-1970s, 412–
      13
    liability management from early 1960s
      to mid-1970s, 412–13
  short-term liabilities, 431–32
  trend charts, use of, 419–22
    categories covered, 421–22
    layered, 420
    recession-recovery, 421
    semilogarithmic, 419–20
Loans
  agricultural; *see* Agricultural loans
  to business, longer terms; *see* Longer
    term lending to business
  commodity; *see* Commodity loans
  in-transit; *see* Commodity loans
  secured; *see* Secured lending
London Interbank Offer Rate, 473, 813–
  14

Longer term lending to business
  analyzing risk, 669–70
  bank policy considerations, 666–68
    adequacy of capital account, 667
    altered circumstances, 667–68
    loan demand pattern, 667
    nature and volatility of deposits, 667
    qualifications of lending personnel,
      667
  term lending, 665–66
    defined, 665
    distinguished from short-term lend-
      ing, 665
    evolution of, 666
    growth in volume, 666
    typical arrangement, 666
  term loan agreements, 670–72
    formal agreements, typical provisions
      of, 670–71
      covenants, 671
      credit terms, 670–71
      events of default, 671
      "letter agreement," 670
      monitoring, 671–72
  term loan forms, 668–69
    balloon payment, 668
    revolving credit, 668
    revolving credit/serial, 668–69
    serial, 668
    stepped-up payments, 668

                          M

McFadden Act, 1053–54, 1075
Management of bank; *see also* Management process in banking
  accommodation to worker's viewpoint,
    154
  environment of; *see* Environment of
    bank management
  functions of chief executive officer, 51–
    54; *see also* Chief executive officer
    of bank
  relations with board of directors, 20–21;
    see also Directors, board of
Management process in banking
  banker as manager, 74–75
  control, 83–85
    balancing of objectives required, 84
    cost considerations, 84
    exercise of, 83–84
    human relations aspects, 84–85
    legal requirements, 85
    monitoring system needed, 83
    role of internal auditor, 85
    use of norms, 84

Management process in banking—*Cont.*
coordination, 79–82
communication requirements, 80–81
conferences and meetings, 81
negotiation, 81
organizational complexity necessitates, 79–80
role of manager, 80
sensitivity to human dimension demanded, 80
environmental impact on, 75
magnitude of decisions, 75–76
motivation, 82–83
compensation review, 82
development review, 82
evaluation techniques, 82
incentives, 82–83
job satisfaction, 82
rewards, 82–83
organization, 77–79
delegation of authority, 79
functional, 78
geographic, 78
human resource development, 79
job description, 78–79
relationship to planning, 77–78
stress on team accomplishment, 78
planning, 76–77
bases for, 76
long- and short-range objectives, 77
responsibility for, 77
techniques, 74, 76–77
time span of decisions, 75–76
Managing bank data processing systems
computer operations department, 233–35
controls, 233–37
cooperative computer centers, 239–40
correspondent bank, 231–32
data processing management, 233
data processing section, 233–34
executive management involvement, 232–33
facilities planning, 238
growing importance of, 240
in-house, 232–39
performance reports, 235, 237
policy standards and procedures, 238
project development department, 233–38
scheduling, 235, 237
security measures, 235, 237
service bureau, 231–32
software development, 235–36
software purchase, 235–36
technical support, 238–39

Manpower planning and management of banks; *see also* Employee selection by banks
functions, 102–4
closing gap between available and needed human resources, 103–4
evaluating existing human resources, 103
forecasting needed number and kinds of people, 103
measuring gap between available and needed human resources, 103
methods used by Citicorp, 105–9
Career Development Program, 108–9
decentralization, 106
group reviews, 106
placement and transfer service, 108
reviews by chairman and president, 106–7
of affirmative action possibilities, 108
of high-potential individuals, 107–8
of key positions, 107
principles, 109
integration with strategic planning, 109
top-management commitment, 109
reasons for, 101–2
demand for new and higher skills, 102
"ripple effect" of bank decision making, 102
tools, 104–5
computerized skills inventories, 105
firsthand knowledge of people, 104
prime indicator method, 104
replacement chart, 105
succession plan, 105
Marketing plan and strategies of banks
establishing strategic marketing objectives, 953–54
establishing tactical marketing objectives, 954–55
profitability, market share, and economy of scale considerations, 954–55
subobjectives, 954
volume, 954
external factors affecting, 952–53
implementation, 955–59
communications plan, 956–57
external, 957
internal, 957
evaluation process, 959
competitive response, 959
market response, 959
marketing research plan, 956
product development plan, 956

Marketing plan and strategies of banks—
    Cont.
  implementation—*Cont.*
    sales plan, 957–59
      action, 958–59
      training, 958
    market analysis and market share, 949–
      52
      important customer characteristics,
        950
      position of bank and nonbank com-
        petitors, 951–52
      relevant market share criteria, 951
    positioning objectives, 953–54
Marketing research in banking
  amortization of costs, 1034
  application, 1032
  budgeting considerations, 1033–34,
    1039–40
  defined, 1032
  developing research program, 1035–38
    building internal information base,
      1036
    customer information file, 1036
    external research, 1036–37
      comparative analysis, 1036–37
      potential customers, 1037
      prospective services, 1037
      quick 'n dirty venture, 1037–38
    professional participation, 1038
      colleges and universities, 1038
      research firms, 1038
    selecting market research director,
      1035–36
  economic justification, 1033–34
  elements of, 1032
  executing projects, 1038–43
    budgeting, 1039–40
    defining problem, 1038–39
    implementation, 1042–43
    interpretation of tabulated findings,
      1042
    interviewing techniques, 1041
    questionnaire design, 1040
    resolving initial questions, 1038–39
    tabulation, 1041
  future role of, 1043–45
    aiding management of social change
      and product development, 1044–
      45
    applying improved investigative tech-
      niques, 1043
    providing answers to fundamental
      questions, 1043–44
    utilizing computer capabilities, 1044
  management support required, 1033
  pitfalls, 1034–35
  purposes, 1032–33
Master Charge; *see* Bank cards

Minbanc, 1152
Minority banking
  growth in 1960s and 1970s, 1145
    historical antecedents, 1145
    impetus for growth, 1146
  positive factors, 1149–52
    aid
      from American Bankers Association,
        1151–52
      from major banks, 1151
    convenience, 1149
    government deposit assistance pro-
      gram, 1151
    Minbanc, 1152
    minority banking students, 1150–51
    minority labor force pool, 1149–50
    rising minority incomes, 1149
    utilization by major corporations, 1151
  problems, 1146–48
    assembling board of directors, 1147
    credit policies, 1148
    finding creditworthy borrowers, 1147
    high costs, 1147
    loan write-offs, 1147–48, 1153
    low account balances, 1147
    low profits, 1153
    raising capital, 1147
  prospects, 1150–52
    aided by urban redevelopment, 1151
    difficulties, 1151
    expansion of government deposits,
      1151
    growth in confidence, 1152
Monetary policy and commercial banking
  banker reaction to monetary policy,
    1121–23
    asset/liability redistribution, 1121–23
    portfolio strategy shifts, 1122
  compatibility of policymakers' and bank-
    ers' goals, 1132–33
  growing banker sophistication on mone-
    tary policy, 1134
  impact of monetary policy on commer-
    cial banking, 1123–32
    asset adjustments, 1129–31
    liability adjustments of large banks,
      1124–26
      bank-related commercial paper,
        1126
      Eurodollar funds, 1124–26
      expanded use of liability manage-
        ment, 1124–26
      large CDs, 1124, 1126
    liability developments in small banks,
      1127–29
      disintermediation in tight money
        periods, 1127–29
      long-term shift to time deposits,
        1127

Monetary policy and commercial banking—*Cont.*
impact of monetary policy on commercial banking—*Cont.*
policy measured by monetary growth rate, 1123–24
rate of return on bank capital, 1131–32
monetary policymaking, 1117–19
money growth
and interest rate changes, 1117–19
targets of Federal Reserve System, 1134
objectives, 1117
tools of Federal Reserve System, 1117
discount rate, 1117
open-market operations, 1117
reserve requirements, 1117
possible requirements for selective credit allocation, 1134–35
transmitting monetary policy through banking system, 1119–21
Money position management of banks; *see also* Asset/liability management of banks *and* Liquidity requirement planning of banks
accounting mechanism for reserve requirements, 446–47
analyzing reserve availability, 449–53
currency in circulation, 450
float of Federal Reserve System, 450–51
fluctuation in required reserves, 449–50
foreign exchange holdings, 451–52
foreign official deposits, 451–52
impact of Treasury balances, 450
purchase and sale of U.S. securities, 452
check clearinghouse mechanism of Federal Reserve System, 447–48
correspondent bank demand balances, 448
Federal Reserve Regulation D, 446
forecasting reserve availability, 453
historically necessary, 445–46
interbank money transfers, 445
money position manager, 448–49, 452–53
reserve requirements, 446–47
vault cash, 447
Money position manager; *see* Money position management of banks
Moody's Investors Service, 515
Morris, Robert, Associates, 979
Mortgage loan warehousing; *see* Real estate warehousing loans

Mortgage loans
construction; *see* Construction mortgage loans
on income-producing property
residential; *see* Residential mortgage loans
appraisers, role of, 740
commercial banks, insurance companies, and mutual savings banks, role of, 740
considerations of permanent lender, 738–39
amount of loan, 738–39
ceiling, 738
floor loan, 738–39
"gap" or "gap loan," 738–39
construction quality, 738
limitation of term, 739
shortened maturity with longer amortization, 739
developer, role of, 740
income-producing property defined, 729
office buildings, 737
purchase and sale agreement of permanent lender, construction lender, and developer-borrower, 739–40
residential property, 730–34
appraisal of rental apartment buildings, 730–31
estimate of gross income, 730–31
expense estimates, 731
forecast of vacancy rates, 731
income, cost, and market approaches to value, 730–32
rate of capitalization, 731
value estimate, 732–33
debt service coverage, 733–34
shopping center, 734–37
appraisal approach, 734–35
creditworthiness of tenants, 734–35
quality of lease obligations, 734–35
attributes of developer, 736
escalation, 735–36
legal rights in, 737
vacancy allowance, 736
Multinational companies, banking needs of
bank costing and pricing, 795–96
control of noninterest expense, 796
increase in purchased money, 795
increased attention to loan pricing, 795–96
increased long-term debt, 795
rising costs, 795
buy or make approach of multinationals, 791, 793
dynamic needs and responses, 793
external factors affecting, 793–94
capital flow restrictions, 794

Multinational companies, banking needs
   of—*Cont.*
   external factors affecting—*Cont.*
      credit rate restrictions, 794
      exchange rate policies, 794
   full service approach of international
      banks, 791–93, 795
   geographic positioning approach of
      banks, 795
   growth of multinationals, 790
   multinational companies defined, 789
   outlook of U.S. international banks, 798–
      800
      intensive development of markets,
         798
      reduced compensating balance re-
         quirements, 799
      selectivity in credit standards and
         yield, 799
      separate fees, 799
      slower expansion, 798
      unbundled services, 799
   unbundling bank service product
      charges, 796–99
      desired by multinational treasurers,
         796–97
      drawbacks of "membership card" ap-
         proach, 797
      introduction of fee operations, 797–99
   variations in, 790
Municipal bonds
   bonds designated as, 511, 520
   categories, 511–12
      general obligation, 511–12, 519
      revenue, 511–12, 519
   dealer banks, 513, 520–21
   defined, 512
   degree of risk, determinants of, 519
      ability to pay, 519
      revised capitalization possibilities, 519
      willingness to pay, 519
   diversification opportunities, 516–17
   market structure, 517–18
      dealers, 517
      index, 517–18
      volume, 517
   markets for, 512–13
      operations, 512–13
      primary, 512–13
      regulation of, 513
      secondary, 513
   maturity schedules of banks, 514–15
   portfolio management by banks, 518
      income, 518
      liquidity, 518
      safety, 518
   proposed optional taxable, 519–20
   quality, 519

Municipal bonds—*Cont.*
   ratings, 515–16, 519
      controversy over, 515
      disclosure issue, 515–16
      independent analyses by banks, 516
      local services, 516
      Moody's Investors Service, 515
      nonrated, 515
      Standard & Poor's, 515
   serial maturities, 512
   term bonds, 512
   use in bank portfolios, 513–15, 518, 520
Municipal Rulemaking Board, 513, 515–
   16, 521

                            N

National Bank Surveillance System, 1058
National Bankers Association, 1150–51
National Commission on Electronic Funds
   Transfer, 245
National Credit Union Administration,
   1055
National Labor Relations Act, 207–11
National Labor Relations Board, 207
Negotiable order of withdrawal (NOW),
   405, 1113, 1158

                            O

Office of the Comptroller of the Currency
   and bank mergers, 1068
   and changes in commercial banking,
      1056–57
   chartering policy, 1051–53
      criteria, 1100–1101
      evaluation of new bank application,
         1051–53
         capital, 1052
         economic condition and growth po-
            tential of market, 1052
         income and expenses, 1051
         management, 1052
         market share, 1052
         stock distribution, 1052
      rejected applicants given reasons,
         1053
      soundness without undue restraints,
         1051
   creation of Division of Human Re-
      sources, 1058
   development of computer-based bank
      early warning system, 1058
   encourages maximum competition in
      providing financial services, 1055–
      56

Office of the Comptroller of the Currency—*Cont.*
establishment, 1049–50
examination procedures in trust, consumer, electronic data processing, and international areas, 1101–2
innovations encouraged by, 1050–51
objectives and operations evaluated, 1057
on-site examinations, 1058, 1063
original functions, 1050
requires bank annual report, 349
requires bank trust department audits, 349
ruling on customer-bank communication terminals, 1055–56
ruling on electronic banking terminals, 1050
shift from regulation to supervision, 1057–59
Office of Foreign Direct Investment, 781
Offshore financing; *see* International credits
Organization of commercial banks; *see* Structure of commercial banks
Organization of Petroleum Exporting Countries, 780, 785

P

Personal identification number (PIN), 912, 915, 917–18
Personnel development in banks
evaluation of programs, 162–63
goal of, 154
individually tailored programs, 160–62
analysis of employee, 161
assessment of bank's needs, 161
development program, 161
evidence of absence, 160–61
matchup of skills to needs, 155, 161–62
performance appraisal, 161–62
timetable of training, 161
management by objectives (MBO), 155–60
advantages, 160
applicability, 156
connotations of, 155–56
disadvantages, 160
discussion/acceptance of goals, 158
evaluation, 159–60
goals in, 156
listing duties, 157
measurements in, 156
objectives in, 156
results, 160

Personnel development in banks—*Cont.*
management by objectives (MBO)—*Cont.*
reviews, frequency of, 159
setting goals, 157
steps, 156–60
target dates, 159
timetables, 158–59
types of goals, 157–58
matchup of employees to jobs, 155
on-the-job training, 162
performance, measurement of, 154–55
accommodation to employee individualism, 155
clerical jobs, 154–55
"development jobs," 155
employee participation in appraisal, 155
entry-level jobs, 154–55
performance-oriented programs, 162–63
Peter Principle, 104 n.
Policies of banks
adaptability of, 61–63
basic, 61
consistency of, 61–63
designed to achieve goals, 57
environmental influences on, 60–61
evolution, 58–59
feedback for modification of, 58
fine tuning, 60
hierarchy of, 59–61
implementation, 58, 60–61
made within framework of established policies and procedures, 56–57
makers of; *see* Policy makers of banks
origination, 58–59
proposals of, 59
routine decision making delegated to computers, 57–58
self-imposed laws, 57
subject to statutes, 56, 59
subordinate, 61
Policy makers of banks
chief executive officer, 61–62; *see also* Chief executive officer of bank
directors, board of, 61–62; *see also* Directors, board of
responsibilities, 61
Portfolio management of banks
authority and control procedures, 536–38
portfolio manager, 537
review, 537
senior investment committee, 537
separation from trading function, 537–38
written policy, 536

Portfolio management of banks—*Cont.*
  improving government security returns,
    535–36
    lending government securities, 535
    liability management, 536
    repurchase agreements ("Repos"), 535
    resale agreements, 535
  investment objectives and constraints,
    522–25
    income needs, 524
    investment effort, 524
    investment personnel, 524
    liquidity requirements, 524
    pledging requirements for public
      funds, 524
    risk position, 523–24
      capital position, 523–24
      deposits, 523
      guidelines, 523
      loan portfolios, 523
      ratios, 523
    tax position, 524–25
  portfolio strategies, 525–28
    diversification, 526
    maturity structure, 527–28
      "cyclical," 528
      "dumbbell" or "hourglass," 527–
        28
      ladder, 527
      "modified ladder," 528
    quality, 526
    "swing" account, 525
  swapping, 528–35
    arbitrage, 530
    defined, 528–29
    gain trading, 534
    intermarket swap, 531–32
    open-ending, 534–35
    substitution or replacement swap,
      530–31
    tax-loss trading, 533–34
    yield anticipation swap, 532
    yield pick-up swap, 529–30
  "three-part" strategy, 525–26
    income account, 525
    liquidity, 525
    liquidity account, 525
    marketability, 525
    safety, 525–26
Press relations of banks, 13–14; *see also*
  Community relations programs of
  banks
Pricing of bank services; *see also* Costs in
  banks *and* Profitability in banks
  controls on, 310
  cost as basis for, 311–12
  reasons for reductions, 310

Pricing of bank services—*Cont.*
  and required profit margin, 311
  sales volume as function of, 311–12
Problem loans
  bankruptcy, 609–10
  continuation of problem business,
    606–8
    interim continuation, 606–7
    steps to improve situation, 607–8
  costs to bank, 602
  defined, 602
  early warning signs, 604–5
    conditions at place of business, 604
    credit reports, 604–5
    delay in furnishing financial informa-
      tion, 604
    level of balances, 604
    relations with trade suppliers, 604
  events to watch for, 603–4
    industry trends, 604
    management
      change, 604
      habits, 604
    overall economic deterioration, 604
    rapid expansion, 604
  fact finding and reevaluation, 605–6
  liquidation of problem business, 608–9
Professionalization of banking, 50–51
Profit planning and budgeting of banks; *see
  also* Corporate planning for banks
  budgeting
    defined, 288
    process, 289–90
      comparison of performance with
        budget, 290
      controls, 290
      expense projections, 289–90
      external factors considered, 289
      income projections, 289
      personnel involved, 289
    and profit planning contrasted, 289
  capital uses in profit planning, 292
  computer facilities decisions in profit
    planning, 292
  origins of profit planning, 288–89
  people factor in profit planning, 292–93
  profit centers in profit planning, 293–94
  profit planning process, 290–94
    business judgments rendered, 292–93
    corporate profit goal established, 290–
      91
    environmental conditions assessed,
      291
    monitoring and control, 293–94
    product mix determined, 291–92
  responsibility center units in profit plan-
    ning, 292–93
  zero-based budgeting, 288

Profitability in banks; *see also* Control and management of bank financial performance; Costs in banks; *and* Pricing of bank services
applications of profitability analysis, 295
customer, 300–303
correspondent bank customers, 303–5
items included, 304
large corporate customers, 303–5
profit contribution, 304–6
profit goal, 305
source and use statement, 304
organizational, 300–303
direct production centers, 301
direct profit centers, 301
overhead centers, 301–2
direct support centers, 302
indirect support centers, 302
profit center report, 302–3
pyramiding of income and expenses, 300
reporting system, 300
responsibility centers, 300–302
product, 306–11
assessment of, 306
responsibility centers, 306
support centers, 306
Prospects of U.S. banking
bank service, 1161–62, 1166
bookkeeping and payments, 1162
experience of early 1970s, 1161–62
nonbank operations, 1161–62
securities area, 1162
changes in regulatory environment, 1158–59
credit control structure, 1158–59
reserve balances of Federal Reserve, 1159
restraints on geographic expansion, 1158
restrictions on time and savings deposits competition, 1158, 1166
state usury ceilings, 1159
community banks, 1161, 1166
effects of profit squeeze, 1163–65
elimination of unnecessary employees, 1165
selectivity in attracting customers, 1164
service pricing for profit, 1164, 1166
electronic funds transfer mechanisms, 1159–60, 1166
potential uses, 1160
present uses, 1160
errors in predictions for 1970s, 1156–57
mergers and acquisitions, 1161, 1166
more competitive banking environment, 1157–58, 1165–66

Prospects of U.S. banking—*Cont.*
need for more skilled personnel, 1162–63
reduction of routine functions, 1163
variable rate mortgages and deposits, 1159
Public accountants, independent; *see* Audits, external, of banks *and* Credit decisions, financial analysis for
Public debt management and commercial banking
criteria for selection of maturities, 1139–40
implementation of public debt management by commercial banks, 1141–44
dangers in, 1142–43
distributors, 1142
underwriters, 1142–43
interest ceilings on Treasury financing, 1141
Treasury financing of deficits and maturing obligations, 1138–39
types of Treasury securities, 1140–41
certificates of indebtedness, 1140
Treasury bills, 1140
Treasury bonds, 1140–41
Treasury notes, 1140
Public franchise, banks as, 65–66
Public opinion, growth in influence of, 87

R

Real Estate Settlement Procedures Act, 871
Real estate warehousing loans
advantages for lending bank, 716
customers for, 715
defined, 715–16
fees, 717
interest rates, 717
non-presold loans, 717
presold loans, 717
review, 717–18
risks, 717
types, 716–17
deferred lines, 716
nonrevolving lines, 716
repurchase lines, 716
revolving lines, 716
Repurchase agreements (Repos or RP), 472, 493
Residential mortgage loans
appraisal methods, 720–23
cost approach, 721
defined, 721
depreciation—physical, functional, economic, 721

Residential mortgage loans—*Cont.*
  appraisal methods—*Cont.*
    cost approach—*Cont.*
      information services, 721
      information sources, 721
      "principle of substitution," 721
    income approach, 722
      based on sales of rented properties,
        722
    market approach, 721–22
      based on sales of similar properties,
        722
      considerations, 722
    role of appraiser in loan decisions, 723
  competitive forces, 724–26
    and interest rates, 725
      discount fee or points, 725
      maximums set by FHA and VA, 725
      rates determined by marketplace,
        725
      usury laws, 725
    and size of payment, 725–26
      estimate of "future economic life,"
        725
      evaluation of purchaser's capability,
        725–26
  cooperative ownership, 728
  defined, 719
  deminimis planned unit development,
    728
  financing for individual ownership, 720–
    27
  home ownership classifications, 719–20
    condominium, 719–20
    cooperative, 720, 728
    single-family home, 719
  planned unit development, 727
  secondary mortgage market, 726
    Federal Home Loan Mortgage Corpo-
      ration (Freddie Mac), 727
    Federal National Mortgage Corpora-
      tion (Fannie Mae), 727
    Government National Mortgage Cor-
      poration (Ginnie Mae), 727
  types, 723–24
    conventional, 723
      decision by lender, 723
      use of private mortgage insurance
        company, 723
    FHA insured, 723–24
      contributions of FHA, 723–24
      FHA review, 724
    VA, 724
  value of single-family mortgage lending,
    725–26
Resource allocation in banks
  asset-liability relationships, 392–95
    elements of analysis, 394

Resource allocation in banks—*Cont.*
  asset-liability relationships—*Cont.*
    savings deposits, 393–94
    understanding deposit base, 392–94
    capital structure, 392
      comparison with industry averages,
        392
      projection
        of capital needs, 392
        of internal capital generation, 392
  definition of bank resources, 390
  factors necessitating realignment of,
    389, 399
  personnel resources, 390–91
    indicators of quality, 390
    relationship
      to goals, 390–91
      to programs, 391
    survey of management team and po-
      tential replacements, 390
  technological capacity, 391
  utilization of resources, 395–99
    adequate utilization, 395
    aggressive allocation, 397
    board of directors in, 398
    committee structure in, 398
    computer models as basis for strate-
      gies, 397–98
    defensive allocation, 397
    econometric models, 397
    immediately allocable resources, 395–
      96
    investment portfolio, 396–97
    linear programming models, 397
    long-range plan, 396
    mechanical models, 397
    monitoring results, 399
    overutilization, 395
    planning system in, 398
    shorter term tactical requirements,
      396
    underutilization, 395
Retail banking
  communication, 844
  concepts in retail management, 845–46
    product or service manager concept,
      846
    production center concept, 846
    profit center concept, 845–46
  concerns of, 849
  costs of, 840–41
    processing costs of service delivery,
      840
    total costs of service delivery, 840
  customer attitudes to methods used, 841
  drawbacks, 837
  environment of, 838
    competition of nonbank financial insti-
      tutions, 838, 848–49

Retail banking—*Cont.*
  environment of—*Cont.*
    new legislation and regulation, 838
    rising costs, 838
    shifts in consumer attitudes, 838
    technological developments, 838,
      848–49
  feedback to management, 844
  full-service offices, 840
  keeping abreast of laws and regulations,
    845
  limited service facilities, 840–41
  market research, 841–42
    on competition, 842
    on customers and prospects, 841–42
  marketing, 843
  monitoring, 844
  organizational considerations, 839
    branch systems, 839
    experience, 839
    holding companies, 839
    laws and regulations, 839
    local competition, 839
    market penetration, 839
    unit banks, 839
  "personal banker programs," 844
  personnel function, 843–44
  potential, 837
  profitability planning, 840
  public relations, 843
  selection of services offered, 842–43
Retail banking services
  money as a product, 860–61
  pricing, 857–59
    competitive factor, 858
    determination of costs, 857–58
      maintenance expenses, 857–58
      research and development costs,
        858
    intangible costs, 858
    marginal profitability determinations,
      859
    profit expectations, 858
    rate sensitivity analyses, 858
    retail service packages, 859
  product evaluation, 850–53
    internal tests, 851–53
      cost analyses, 851–52
      flowchart as checklist, 851–52
      legality tests, 851
      operational feasibility, 851
      profitability projections, 852–53
        acceptable price levels, 852
        cost of not offering product, 852–
          53
        marketing goals, 853
        sales volume, 852
      in relation to anticipated external ef-
        fects, 853

Retail banking services—*Cont.*
  product evaluation—*Cont.*
    in relation to bank objectives, 850
    in relation to customer expectations,
      850–51
    report to management, 853
  product implementation, 853–57
    assembling task force, 853–54
    customer education, 856
    internal promotion, 854–55
    legal review, 856–57
    marketing and advertising, 854–55
    meeting work force needs, 855
    monitoring
      to assess need for changes, 857
      progress, 857
    operations and systems support, 855
    scheduling, 854
    staff training, 856
  skillful product management, 859–60
    characteristics, 860
    external considerations, 860
    results, 859–60
  source of ideas, 849–50
Retail services of banks, electronic delivery
  systems for
  automated teller machines, 912–14
    customer acceptance measures, 912
    deposit-withdrawal ratios, 912
    off-premise location, 913
    on-line versus off-line operations, 913
    reliability, 913–14
  automatic telephone payment systems,
    918–19
  balance inquiry service, 919–20
    advantages, 920
    methods, 919
    shortcomings, 919
  direct deposit, 918
    of pay, 918
    by social security system, 918
  forces behind new retail delivery sys-
    tems, 910
    customer convenience, 910
    need to improve banking productiv-
      ity, 910
  nature of new retail delivery systems,
    909–10
    based on automated electronic mes-
      sages, 909
    include electronic funds transfer, 909
    include improvements in check sys-
      tem, 909–10
  objectives of previous automated bank-
    ing efforts, 910–12
    cost reduction, 911–12
    fee revenue, 911
    retail market share, 910–11
  pay-by-phone services, 918–19

Retail services of banks, electronic delivery
    systems for—*Cont.*
  point of sale terminals, 914–18
    check authorization systems, 914–16
      check guarantee distinguished
        from, 914–15
      merchant's demand for inclusion of
        all customers, 915–16
      negative file approach, 916
      positive file approach, 916
    clerk-activated, 915
    customer-activated, 915–16
    deposit taking, 916–17
    electronic funds transfer, 917–18
    on-line credit card authorization, 915–
      16
    uncertainties connected with, 914
  preauthorized payments, 918
Retirement Plan Bonds, 484
Reverse repurchase agreements (Repos or
    RP), 472, 493
Revolving credit; *see* Credit arrangements,
    seasonal and revolving
Risk and Insurance Management Society,
    377, 380
Risk management in banks
  accidental loss possibilities, 373
  actuarial forecasts, 378
  administration, 384–86
    communications, 385
    organization, 385
    outside assistance, 385–86
    responsibilities, 385
    written policy statement, 384–85
  elements, 374
  exposure identification, 374–77
    accidental loss exposures, 375–76
      direct, 375
      human, 375–76
      indirect, 375
      natural, 375
      third-party liabilities, 376
    identification of bank resources, 374–
      75
      financial, 375
      human, 374–75
      intangible, 375
      natural, 375
      physical, 374
    methods of, 376–77
  indirect exposure, 377–78
  indirect losses, 377–78
  purposes, 373–74
  relation to insurance, 373–74
  risk control, 379–80
    coordinated approach to, 379
    emergency preparedness, 379
    fragmentation of, 379–80
    personnel and safety, 379

Risk management in banks—*Cont.*
  risk control—*Cont.*
    property conservation, 379
    protection and security, 379
  risk evaluation, 377–79
    definition, 377
    of human or intangible resources, 377
    loss records, 378
    maximum possible loss, 378
    maximum probable loss, 378
    potential frequency of exposure, 378
    potential severity of exposure, 378
    of real or personal property, 377
  risk financing and insurance, 380–84
    categories, 382–83
      bank liability coverages, 382–83
      bank property coverages, 382–83
      departmental coverages, 383
      employee benefits coverages, 383
      financial coverages, 382
    funding alternatives to insurance,
      380–81
    general insurance standards, 383–84
      expiration dates, 384
      limits, 383–84
      loss adjustment, 384
      named insured, 383
      notice of cancellation, 384
      participation in risk, 384
      premium payments, 384
    objective of, 380
    risk retention, 380–81
    selection of insurance agent or
      broker, 381–82
      open bidding, 382
      presentation, 382
      selective bidding, 382
  simulation models, 378
  value of resources, 377
Risk management officer; *see* Risk manage-
    ment in banks

                              S

Safe deposit services of banks
  access procedures, 901–2
    access tickets, 901
    private rooms, 902
    proper identification, 901
    rules on access, 901–2
    signature system, 901
  advantages for bank, 896
  audit procedures, 902
  contractual guidelines, 896–98
    access in event of litigation or unre-
      solved claims, 897
    inheritance tax examination proce-
      dures, 898

Safe deposit services of banks—*Cont.*
    contractual guidelines—*Cont.*
        liability clause, 897
        rights of co-renters, 897
        role of deputies, 897
        termination procedures, 897–98
        vault manager's familiarity with, 903
    customer relations, 902–3
        and generation of other business,
            902–3
        handling disturbed customers, 903
        staff selection, training, rewards, 903
    defined, 895
    deputies, 900–901
    general powers of attorney, 900–901
    legal counsel, use of, 903
    legal rules, 896
    pricing, 904
        based on costs and competition, 904
        nonfee income, 904
    security, 904–5
        legal issues, 904
        means for maintaining, 905
        reasons for increased importance,
            904–5
    types of rentals, 898–900
        co-renters, 898–99
        corporations, 899
        fiduciaries, 900
        government agencies, 900
        individuals, 898
        minors, 900
        partnerships, 899
        unincorporated organizations, 899
    vault equipment, 902
Safekeeping services of banks; *see* Custody
    services of banks *and* Safe deposit
    services of banks
Salary administration in banks
    applicants, analysis of, 176
    bench mark jobs, 167–68
    equal employment opportunity compli-
        ance, 175
    establishing program of, 166–71
    evaluating salary program, 176
    increases
        amount of, 168–69
        frequency of, 168–69
    informing employees on program of, 171
    job
        comparability, analysis of, 167
        descriptions, 196
        evaluation systems, 169–70
        questionnaires, 166
        ranking, 169
        slotting, 169
    keys to success in, 164–65
        individual's pay based on perform-
            ance, 165

Salary administration in banks—*Cont.*
    keys to success in—*Cont.*
        pay structure based on competitive
            levels, 165
        performance standards and goals, 165
    labor market, defining, 166–67
    merit increase budgets, 174–75
    objectives, 164
    pay levels, determining, 167
    pay planning, 174–75
    performance evaluation, 172–74
        appraisal, 173–74
        categorization, 173
        ranking, 174
        separating from increases, 174
    performance
        ratings, analysis of, 176
        standards, 174
    productivity planning, 171–72
        employee accountabilities, 171
        reviewing objectives, 172
        setting objectives, 172
    salary ranges, 168
    salary surveys, 168
    turnover analysis, 176
    updating program of, 170–71
*Salary Administration for Community
    Banks,* 170
Satellite banking, 27, 47
Seasonal credit; *see* Credit arrangements,
    seasonal and revolving
Second Liberty Bond Act, 484, 1141
Secured lending
    accounts receivable loans, 637–41
        accounts defined, 637
        advantages over inventory loans, 637
        applications, 637
        compliance with Assignment of
            Claims Act, 641
        contractors' receivables, 641
        establishing value, 637–39
            judging collectibility, 637–39
            judging validity, 637–38
        methods, 639–40
            blanket assignment, 639
            direct notification, 640
            nonnotification, 639–40
        perfecting security interest, 640–
            41
    aircraft, 647
        compliance with Federal Aviation
            Registration Act, 647
    boats and ships, 646–47
        lender protection of Ship Mortgage
            Act, 646–47
        provision for risks, 647
    collateral defined, 622
    elements of policy, 623

Secured lending—*Cont.*
  inventory loans, 626–37
    control systems, 630–34
      blanket assignment, 630
      collateral control service, use of, 632
      commercial finance companies, use
        of, 632
      correspondent banks, use of, 632
      items to be considered, 631–32
      reports of inventory on hand, 630–
        31
      steps in supervising loans, 631
      warehouse receipts, use of, 633–34
    determining proper margin, 626–30
      difficulties of, 626
      establishing value, 626–30
      inventory defined, 626
    perfecting security interest, 635–37
      in inventory, 635–37
      in negotiable document, 636
      in nonnegotiable document of title,
        636
  life insurance policies, cash value of,
    644–45
    potential problem areas, 645
    steps in making loans, 645
  petroleum production, 645–46
    advantages, 646
    characteristics, 646
    considerations, 646
    drawbacks, 646
  phases in, 624–26
    controlling and evaluating collateral,
      624–25
    determining proper margin of collat-
      eral, 624
    establishing value of collateral, 624
    obtaining perfected security interest
      in collateral, 625–26
    regularly reviewing overall credit,
      626
  problems, 648
    failing or bankrupt borrower, 648
    liquidity collateral, 648
      considerations, 648
      procedures, 648
  reasons for using, 623–24
  security agreement, 625, 635
  security interest, 625–26
  stocks and bonds, 641–44
    control and evaluation, 643–44
    documentation for loans against, 643–
      44
    influences on value, 642–43
    marketability, 642
    types, 642
  Uniform Commercial Code, 625–27,
    633–37

Securities Acts Amendments of 1964, 358–
  59
Security dealers and banks, 13
Self-Employed Contributions Act, 212
Services of banks
  automatic funds transfers, 228
  automatic overdraft coverage, 228
  charge card systems, 228
  combined statements, 228
  delivering, 223–26
    audio response units, 223
    automatic teller machines, 223
    batch processing by computer sys-
      tems, 223
    check handling, 223
    communications networks, 223–25
    complex systems management, 225–
      26
    information distribution to corporate
      customers, 225
    on-line terminal systems, 223
    remote job entry systems, 223
  descriptive statements, 228
  electronic funds transfer systems, 228–
    29
  identifying market for, 222–23
    data bases, 222–23
    information accessing, 222–23
  point of sale systems, 228–29
  possible changes in, 221
  posting and statements for customer ac-
    counts, 228
  processing data, 226–28
    check clearing and posting, 226–27
    reader/sorter equipment, 227–28
Ship Mortgage Act of 1920, 646–47
Short-term money market
  arbitrage markets, 477
  bankers acceptances, 475–76
    applications, 476
    defined, 475
    described, 476
    "ineligible" acceptances, 476
  certificates of deposit (CDs), 471–72
  characteristics of instruments, 469
  commercial paper, 474–75
    bank, 475
    prime finance, 474–75
    prime industrial, 475
  definition of, 469
  Eurocurrency, 472–73
  Eurodollars, 472–73
  federal funds, 470–71
    defined, 470
    trading in, 470–71
  foreign money market securities, 473–
    74
  functions, 469

Short-term money market—*Cont.*
hedging in interest-rate future contracts, 477–78
Government National Mortgage Association Pass-through Certificates, 477
long hedge, 478
short hedge, 478
U.S. Treasury bills, 477
historical antecedents, 470
investment considerations, 478–79
liquidity, 479
quality, 478–79
liquidity defined, 469–70
marketable securities, 470
"near money," 470
origins of, 470
relationship to demand accounts, 470
repurchase agreements (Repos or RP), 472
secondary reserves, 470
transfers from demand accounts to savings accounts, 472
Social policies of banks
Bank of America principles and methodologies, 68–72
community service, 66–67
consumerism, impact of, 67–68
expectations of public, 67–68
general principles, statement of, 68–69
historical precedent, 64–65
identifying problems and issues, 70
imlllmentation, 70–71
monitoring, 69–70
practices encompassed by, 71–72
precepts for dealing with, 72–73
questioning of, 64–65
reasons for current importance, 65–67
relationship to regulation, 66
specific issues, statements on, 69
Social Security Act, 211–13
Standard & Poor's municipal security ratings, 515
State banking departments
Conference of State Bank Supervisors, 1061
and federal regulatory agencies, 1061
goals, 1061
programs, 1061, 1063
and state-chartered banks, 1061
duplicatory oversight of state-chartered banks, 1062–63
functions, 1060, 1062, 1066
increased capabilities, 1066
inherent strengths, 1064
inherent weaknesses, 1065

State banking departments—*Cont.*
leadership in new techniques and procedures, 1063
early warning statistical techniques, 1064
electronic funds transfer experiments, 1064
mini-exam, 1063–64
"top-down" examination, 1063
new goals and roles, 1060–61
organization of state bank regulatory system, 1061–62
place in regulatory structure, 1062–63, 1065
problems, 1066
record, 1066
state bank commissioner, 1060, 1062
State-chartered banks; *see* State banking departments
Stockholders of bank
annual meetings, 10–11
annual reports to, 12
contacts with, 9–13
correspondence with, 12
demand for information by, 6
developing profile of, 6
disclosures to, 14
need to acquire, 3
programs for, 8–9
report meetings, 11–12
sales of stock, 13
surveys of, 6–8
Stocks of banks, 3–4
Structure of commercial banks
affiliate banking, 28, 47
branch banking, 27, 30–35, 39–42
centralization versus decentralization, 30–35
advantages of decentralization, 32–34
authority of branch or subsidiary banks, 30–35
disadvantages of decentralization, 32, 34–35
chain banking, 27–28, 47
correspondent banking, 28–29, 47
end result, grouping by, 29–30
factors determining, 26
group banking, 27–28, 47
grouping of functions, 29–30
holding company banking, 27, 43–47
line functions, 30
profit center approach, 29–30
regionalization, 35–37
advantages and disadvantages, 35–36
characteristics, 35
region/head office relationships, 36–37
types, 35–36
satellite banking, 28, 47

Structure of commercial banks—*Cont.*
  specialization, grouping by, 29
  staff functions, 30
  unit banking, 27, 37–39
Supervisors of bank employees
  adjustment to role, 149–50
  authority, 152
  buffer between employees and manage-
      ment, 143–44, 151–52
  consequences of failure, 149
  dual responsibilities, 144
  effect on profitability, 152–53
  improving supervisory performance,
      145–49
  neglect of, 145
  "playing God," 150
  psychological needs, 152
  selection, 146–49
    Assessment Centers, 146–48
      advantages, 147
      disadvantages, 147
      evaluators, 147–48
      techniques, 147
    performance record, 148–49
    test project, 149
  styles of supervision, 150–51
    autocratic, 150
    democratic, 151
    free-reign, 150–51
  training, 145–46
Supervisory examinations of banks
  charter process, 1100–1101
  examination process, 1094–99
    appraisal of assets, 1096–97
      capital funds, 1097
      fixed assets, 1097
      investments, 1097
      loans, 1096–97
    early warning systems, 1099
    evaluation of internal controls, 1094–
        95
      policy statement, 1095–96
      review of external audit program,
          1095
    follow-up procedures, 1098–99
      action in problem situations, 1099
      rating by regional and Washington
          offices, 1098
      report to regulatory agency and
          board of directors, 1098
    proofs and verifications of assets and
        liabilities, 1096–97
  functions of bank regulation, 1093
    chartering, 1093, 1100–1101
    regulation, 1093, 1099–1100
    supervision, 1093–99
  objectives of bank supervision, 1091–93
    concepts, 1091–92

Supervisory examinations of banks—*Cont.*
  objectives of bank supervision—*Cont.*
    establish and maintain public confi-
        dence in banks, 1092
    influence bank behavior, 1092
    statutory, 1091
  regulation process, 1099–1100
    interpretation by regulation, 1100
    observance of state-imposed restric-
        tions, 1100
  special examination procedures, 1101–2
    consumer area, 1101–2
    electronic data processing area, 1102
    international area, 1102
    trust area, 1101
  structure of bank supervision, 1090–91
    Federal Deposit Insurance Corpora-
        tion, 1091
    Federal Reserve System, 1091
    Office of Comptroller of Currency,
        1090–91
    result of bad banking experience, 1091
    state banking departments, 1090–91
  supervision function, 1093–94
    liquidation outlook versus ongoing
        outlook, 1093–94
    periodic examination of bank records,
        1093

T

Tax Anticipation Bills, 485
Tax planning of banks
  accelerated depreciation, 367–68
  accretion of discount of investment
      securities, 366
  amortization of premium on taxable
      bonds, 366
  bad debt reserve, 367–69
  budget presupposed by, 364
  budgeting of tax-exempt income, 365
  capital gains, 367–68
  coordination with financial plans and
      projections, 364, 371–72
  foreign taxes, 367
  and future tax legislation, 371
  implementation, 371–72
  investment tax credit, 366–67
  municipal securities, 365
  net operating loss carry-back, 369–70
  philosophy for, 370–71
  preplanning tax liability, 371
  purpose, 364, 372
  reserve for loan losses, 367–69
  responsibility for, 364
  state and local franchise taxes, 367
  state and local income taxes, 367

Tax planning of banks—*Cont.*
  tax-exempt securities, 365
  tax preference items, 367–69
Tax Reform Act of 1969, 367–68
Tax Reform Act of 1976, 368–70
Term lending; *see* Longer term lending to
  business
Treasury Bonds, 484
Treasury securities, 480–94
Trust investing by banks; *see* Investment
  management of securities by banks
Trust services of banks; *see* Fiduciary ser-
  vices of banks
Truth in Lending Law, 746, 871

U

Unfair Collections Practices Act, 746
Uniform Commercial Code
  definition of inventory, 626
  on farm products, 635
  perfecting security interest
    in accounts receivable, 641
    in inventory, 635–37
  and secured transactions, 625–26
  security interest in money or instru-
    ments, 643
  on warehouse receipts, 633–34, 654

Unit banks
  advantages, 38
  characteristics, 37–38
  definition, 27
  disadvantages, 38
  extent, 37
  ownership, 38
  prospects, 38–39
Universal Military Training and Service
  Act, 214
U.S. banking, prospects of; *see* Prospects
  of U.S. banking
U.S. Chamber of Commerce fringe benefits studies, 178
U.S. Savings Bonds, 484

V

VISA U.S.A., Inc.; *see* Bank cards
Voluntary Foreign Credit Restraint Program, 777, 781–82, 828

W

Wage-Hour Law, 201–6
Warehouses, types of, 633–34
Weil's Law, 104 n.
Wide-area branching, 1054

*This book has been set in 10 and 9 point Gael,
leaded 2 points. Section numbers and titles and
chapter numbers and titles have been set in
18 point Compano. The size of the type page
is 27 by 45½ picas.*